Due Return	Due Return
Date Date	Date Date

Frank M. Lassman, Ph.D.

Robert O. Fisch, M.D.

Dolores K. Vetter, Ph.D.

Elaine S. La Benz, M.A.

EARLY CORRELATES OF SPEECH, LANGUAGE, AND HEARING

The Collaborative Perinatal Project of the National Institute of Neurological and Communicative Disorders and Stroke

with

James R. Boen, Ph.D.
Frederic L. Darley, Ph.D.
Warren H. Fay, Ph.D.
Elaine N. Frankowski, M.S.
Katherine Hirst, M.A.
Paul J. La Benz, Sc.D.
Richard R. Monson, M.D., Sc.D.
Earl D. Schubert, Ph.D.
Allen R. Sullivan, Ph.D.
Kenneth F. Swaiman, M.D.
Harris Winitz, Ph.D.

Paul J. La Benz, Sc.D., Co-Editor
Elaine S. La Benz, M.A., Co-Editor

PSG Publishing Company
Littleton, Massachusetts

Library of Congress Cataloging in Publication Data

Main entry under title:
Early correlates of speech, language, and hearing.

   Includes bibliographies and index.
   1.   Communicative disorders in children—Etiology.
2.   Developmental neurology—Longitudinal studies.
3.   Communicative disorders in children—Longitudinal
studies.   4.   Collaborative Perinatal Project.
I.   Lassman, Frank M.   II.   LaBenz, Paul J.
III.   LaBenz, Elaine S. [DNLM: 1.   Hearing disorders—
In infancy and childhood.   2.   Hearing disorders—
Etiology.   3.   Language disorders—In infancy and childhood.
4.   Language disorders—Etiology.   5.   Speech
disorders—In infancy and childhood.
6.   Perinatology.   WL340.3 E12]
RJ496.C67E37   618.9′28′55071   79-11098
ISBN 0-88416-214-1

© 1980 PSG Publishing Company, Inc.

Printed in U.S.A.

ISBN 0-88416-214-1

Library of Congress Catalog Card Number 79-11098

   This study was supported by the National Institute of Neurological and Communicative Disorders and Stroke of the National Institutes of Health (Contract No. NIH NO1-NS-4-2326), Paul J. La Benz, Sc.D., Project Officer, Frank M. Lassman, Ph.D., and Robert O. Fisch, M.D., Principal Investigators.

   This work was supported in part by a grant of computer time from the Health Science Computer Center, a University of Minnesota computer service facility. The Minnesota Child Development Study was also supported in part by a grant No. 16-P-56810/5-18 from the Rehabilitation Services Administration, Office of Human Development, Department of Health, Education and Welfare, Washington, D.C., for the University of Minnesota Medical Rehabilitation Research and Training Center.

CONTENTS

Contributors

James R. Boen, Ph.D.
Professor, Biometry, School of Public Health, University of Minnesota

Frederic L. Darley, Ph.D.
Professor, Communication Disorders, Mayo Clinic, University of Minnesota

Warren H. Fay, Ph.D.
Professor of Speech Pathology, Crippled Children's Division, University of Oregon Health Sciences Center

Robert O. Fisch, M.D.
Professor, Pediatrics, University of Minnesota

Elaine N. Frankowski, M.S.
Instructor, Computer Sciences Department
former Research Fellow, Pediatrics, University of Minnesota

Katherine Hirst, M.A.
Department of Emergency Medicine, University of Colorado Medical Center

Elaine S. La Benz, M.A.
former Assistant Professor, Otolaryngology and Pediatric Neurology, University of Minnesota

Paul J. La Benz, Sc.D.
former Staff Consultant, Developmental Neurology Branch, Neurological Disorders Program, National Institute of Neurological and Communicative Disorders and Stroke

Frank M. Lassman, Ph.D.
Professor, Otolaryngology, Communication Disorders, Physical Medicine and Rehabilitation, University of Minnesota

Richard R. Monson, M.D., Sc.D.
Associate Professor Drug Epidemiology Unit, Boston University School of Medicine and Department of Epidemiology, Harvard School of Public Health

Earl D. Schubert, Ph.D.
Professor, Hearing and Speech Science, Stanford University

Allen R. Sullivan, Ph.D.
Deputy Associate Superintendent, Special Education, Dallas Independent School District and former Associate Professor of Urban Education, University of Minnesota

Kenneth F. Swaiman, M.D.
Professor and Director, Pediatric Neurology, University of Minnesota

Dolores K. Vetter, Ph.D.
Professor, Communicative Disorders, University of Wisconsin-Madison and former Visiting Associate Professor, Otolaryngology, University of Minnesota (1974–76)

Harris Winitz, Ph.D.
Professor, Psychology, Speech and Hearing Science, University of Missouri-Kansas City

Scientific Management Panel

Frank M. Lassman, Ph.D.
Co-Principal Investigator, Chairperson
Robert O. Fisch, M.D.
Co-Principal Investigator, Co-Chairperson

Mary K. Bilek, M.S.
Statistician
James R. Boen, Ph.D.
Consultant, Biometry
Frederic L. Darley, Ph.D.
Consultant, Speech and Language
Warren H. Fay, Ph.D.
Consultant, Speech and Language
Elaine S. La Benz, M.A.
Co-Investigator
Earl D. Schubert, Ph.D.
Consultant, Hearing
Allen R. Sullivan, Ph.D.
Consultant, Cultural and Ethnic Matters
Kenneth F. Swaiman, M.D.
Consultant, Pediatric Neurology
John M. Taborn, Ph.D.
Consultant, Cultural and Ethnic Matters
Dolores K. Vetter, Ph.D.
Co-Investigator
Harris Winitz, Ph.D.
Consultant, Speech and Language

Special Consultants

Sarah H. Broman, Ph.D.
Research Psychologist, Developmental Neurology Branch, Neurological Disorders Program, NINCDS

Pi-Nian Chang, Ph.D.
Assistant Professor and former Research Associate, Departments of Pediatrics and Psychiatry and Program in Health Care Psychology, University of Minnesota

Joseph S. Drage, M.D.
Chief, Developmental Neurology Branch, Neurological Disorders Program, NINCDS

Paul J. La Benz, Sc.D.
Staff Consultant and Project Officer, Developmental Neurology Branch, Neurological Disorders Program, NINCDS

Jean G. Oliver, M.A.
Speech Pathologist, Developmental Neurology Branch, Neurological Disorders Program, NINCDS

David Rubinstein, M.A.
Associate Chief, Office of Biometry and Epidemiology, NINCDS

The Collaborating Institutions

Boston, Massachusetts
Harvard Medical School
Boston Lying-in Hospital and
Children's Hospital Medical Center

Richmond, Virginia
Virginia Commonwealth University
Medical College of Virginia

Philadelphia, Pennsylvania
University of Pennsylvania
Pennsylvania Hospital and
The Children's Hospital of Philadelphia

Baltimore, Maryland
The Johns Hopkins University School
  of Medicine
The Johns Hopkins Hospital

New York, New York
Columbia University College of
  Physicians and Surgeons
Columbia-Presbyterian Medical Center

Minneapolis, Minnesota
University of Minnesota Hospitals
Health Sciences Center

New York, New York
New York Medical College
Metropolitan Hospital

Portland, Oregon
University of Oregon Medical School

Memphis, Tennessee
University of Tennessee College
  of Medicine
Gailor Hospital

Providence, Rhode Island
Brown University
Child Study Center

New Orleans, Louisiana
Charity Hospital
Tulane University School of Medicine
  Medical Center
Louisiana State University

Buffalo, New York
University of Buffalo
Children's Hospital

Foreword

This volume, *Early Correlates of Speech, Language and Hearing,* is the major report from the Collaborative Perinatal Project of the National Institute of Neurological and Communicative Disorders and Stroke (NINCDS) focusing on speech, language and hearing disorders. The primary objective of the NINCDS Collaborative Perinatal Project is to develop associations between the conditions and events of pregnancy, labor, and delivery, and the outcome of the pregnancies. This volume reports on analyses which study the conditions and events of pregnancy, labor, and delivery as they relate to the child's speech, language and hearing development.

Data collection in the NINCDS Collaborative Perinatal Project began in 1959 and the last follow-up examinations on the children were completed in 1974. The data collection period covered some sixteen years. A Comprehensive Plan for Analysis and Interpretation of NINCDS Collaborative Perinatal Project Data was developed and approved by the NINCDS in 1973. The Comprehensive Plan identified ten primary data analysis efforts which were responsive to the original NINCDS Collaborative Perinatal Project objectives, developed in the mid-1950s, which were suitable for the data collected, and which were of importance to the mission of the NINCDS. Communicative disorders are a major component of the NINCDS research mission, and this volume contributes to fulfilling that mission and specifically fulfills one of the primary objectives of the NINCDS Collaborative Perinatal Project.

This report represents the product of Research Contract NO1-NS-4-2326. The Request for Proposals (RFP-NIH-NINDS-74-06) was issued by the NINCDS in December 1973, and fourteen proposals were received and reviewed by a Technical Merit Review Committee composed of outside experts. The contract was awarded to the University of Minnesota in June 1974. Frank M. Lassman, PhD., and Robert O. Fisch, M.D., of the University of Minnesota were Co-Principal Investigators and Paul J. La Benz, Sc.D., of NINCDS was Project Officer.

The NINCDS Collaborative Perinatal Project has presented challenges to the many individuals involved in the project. The willingness of the mothers and the children to participate in this longitudinal research effort, with repeated trips for follow-up examinations over many years, is in itself remarkable. The challenges in developing and maintaining the data collection phase of the project were monumental. There were twelve geographically-separated medical centers participating, and at each of them a multidisciplinary staff. Through the dedicated efforts and collaboration of all those involved in the project, the data were successfully collected and readied for the various analyses called for in the Comprehensive Plan. The magnitude of the data analysis effort as reported in this volume will be self-evident to the reader.

This volume represents an important contribution to the literature regarding speech, language and hearing disorders in children and will serve as a stimulus for new research efforts on their communicative disorders.

Joseph S. Drage, M.D.
Chief, Developmental Neurology Branch
Neurological Disorders Program
National Institute of Neurological and
Communicative Disorders and Stroke

Acknowledgments

This report resulted from a collaboration from its beginnings to its final moments of publication: collaboration among scientists, disciplines, institutions, departments, and the staff of the National Institute of Neurological and Communicative Disorders and Stroke, National Institutes of Health, sponsors of the project.

Much of the project's strength and many of its problems resulted from factors intrinsic to collaborative research and not necessarily unique to this project. Yet there were qualities parochial to this particular joint endeavor which the authors have attempted to elucidate. The longitudinal nature of the study involved children and their families in a continual association with the project's professional staff. For many families this was a nine-year relationship.

The planning, development, and execution of speech, language and hearing tests required the diverse yet conjoined talents of scientists, consultants, professional staffs, and the technical personnel who took the data into the initial refinement process. And the final data analyses and report of findings that comprise the bulk of this report demanded a positive group process of collaboration among substantive investigators, statisticians, systems analysts, programmers and computer specialists, statistical clerks, graphic artists and the typists who produced reams of copy in the many stages of production. Consistent with this collaborative design, chapters of the report were accomplished with multiple authorship although the major writing and composition was by the first author listed.

The principal investigators were Dr. Frank Lassman and Dr. Robert Fisch, and the co-investigators were Mrs. Elaine La Benz and Dr. Dolores Vetter. Dr. Vetter (University of Wisconsin) assumed a major responsibility for operations and the data analysis which contributed significantly to the timely and successful completion of the study. She was closely and most ably assisted by Ms. Elaine Frankowski, who was responsible for programming and for nursing the data through the computer centers. Dr. James Boen (University of Minnesota) was the source of wisdom and guidance on statistical decisions and interpretations throughout the project, and Mrs. Mary Bilek (University of Minnesota) provided statistical support in the early stages. Ms. Katherine Hirst led a team of statistical assistants and assistant programmers that included Gene Brundell, Jack Cahn, Melissa Croes, Tom Kovarik, Jean Marquardt, Bruce McClure, Kurt Riitters and Lester Strouse. A small grant of computer time was made by Mr. Jay Hamann, Associate Director of Health Computer Sciences at the University of Minnesota.

The consultants, familiar figures in modern research systems, accepted unusually active and responsible roles. They participated in periodic critical review of the progress of data analysis. In addition, a number of the consultants authored chapters of the final report. Included were Dr. Frederic Darley (Mayo Clinic), Dr. Warren Fay (University of Oregon, Health Sciences Center), Dr. Earl Schubert (Stanford University), and Dr. Harris Winitz (University of Missouri-Kansas City). They were joined by Dr. Kenneth Swaiman and Dr. Allen Sullivan of the University of Minnesota. Dr. Frederic Darley edited most of the first drafts for clarity, structural consistency, and grammatical usage.

The assistance and cooperation of the NINCDS staff was essential throughout the project. Dr. Joseph Drage, Chief of the Developmental Neurology Branch, provided advice, support, and encouragement during all phases of the project. Especially integral to the process were Dr. Paul La Benz and Mrs. Jean Oliver of the Developmental Neurology Branch, Neurological Disorders Program of NINCDS. Dr. La Benz supervised the collection of SLH data over the years, and was a critical yet beneficent helmsman throughout the data analysis as project officer. Mrs. Oliver worked closely with the SLH examiners and monitored the collection of data to ensure high standards of accuracy and completeness. In addition, Mrs. Oliver performed a wide variety of tasks invaluable to final preparation of the manuscript. Mrs. Frances Canning undertook a significant role in the preparation of tables and figures for publication. Mr. David Rubinstein, formerly Associate Chief of the Office of Biometry and Epidemiology, NINCDS, contributed importantly in the early stages of statistical planning and data reduction. Valuable data processing contributions were made by Mrs. Laverne Edmondson, Mrs. Stephana Ney, Mrs. Irene Ross, and the late Mrs. Barbara Katz, all of the Developmental Neurology Branch.

We thank the Directors of the National Institute of Neurological and Communicative Disorders and Stroke for their development and support of the Collaborative Perinatal Project: Dr. Pearce Bailey, Director from 1951 to 1959; Dr. Richard Masland, Director from 1959 to 1968; Dr. Edward MacNichol, Jr., Director from 1968 to 1972; and Dr. Donald Tower, Director from 1972 to present. We are grateful to Dr. Eldon Eagles, Deputy Director of NINCDS, for his support; to Dr. Heinz Berendes who directed the Project from 1960 to 1971 as Chief of the Perinatal Research Branch, NINCDS; and to Mr. William Weiss, Chief of the Office of Biometry and Epidemiology, NINCDS, for his valuable contributions to the handling of the data.

Without the active participation and cooperation of the project directors and staff at the twelve collaborating institutions this project could not have been carried forward. Special thanks must be given the 182 examiners who conducted the SLH examinations when the children were three and eight years of age. Their names are listed in Appendix 11.

Of particular note was the collaboration with the Drug Epidemiology Unit of the Boston University School of Medicine, Cambridge, Massachusetts. Under the leadership of Dr. Dennis Slone, an edited tape record of drug usage during pregnancy had been developed. With the advice and assistance of Dr. Slone and Dr. Syd Shapiro, the relative risk of individual drugs for hearing loss was studied and reported by Dr. Richard Monson.

We thank Ms. Ann Crowell, who did all the figures; Mrs. Mary Grothjan, who checked all the data for accuracy; Ms. Monica Bielinski, who, with Mrs. Grothjan, typed and proofread many early drafts and revisions of the manuscript; and Mrs. Edith Joseph, who typed the final edited manuscript.

We also thank Dr. John L. Peterson (University of Wisconsin-Madison), Dr. Sylvia O. Richardson (University of Cincinnati College of Medicine), and Dr. Bruce M. Siegenthaler (Pennsylvania State University) for reviewing the manuscript and providing many helpful suggestions to the authors and editors.

Special acknowledgment is owed Dr. Paul La Benz, Mrs. Elaine La Benz and Mrs. Jean Oliver for editing the manuscript and bringing it to publication.

To all who participated, we are deeply grateful.

F.M. Lassman

R.O. Fisch

Principal Investigators

## CHAPTER 1

History

Part A
The NINCDS Collaborative Perinatal Research Project

Robert O. Fisch, M.D.

The Collaborative Study on cerebral palsy, mental retardation, and other neurological and sensory disorders of infants and children represents the joint endeavor of 12 medical centers and the National Institute of Neurological and Communicative Disorders and Stroke (NINCDS).* The objective of the study was to determine the relationships among factors affecting women during pregnancy and the neurological and sensory defects of their offspring (Chipman et al., 1966).

The investigation was directed toward: (1) in-depth examination of the effect of factors already suspected, (2) identification of factors which were not presently suspected, and (3) elucidation of the mechanism by which these factors operated.

Historical Background of the Project

The causes of certain disorders affecting children, that is, cerebral palsy, epilepsy, defects of speech, language, and hearing, behavior syndromes, and reading or learning disabilities are, for the most part, unknown. The possibility that the origins of these conditions lie in the

---

* NINCDS was formerly the National Institute of Neurological Diseases and Stroke (NINDS) and before that was the National Institute of Neurological Diseases and Blindness (NINDB).

1

events that occur between conception and the early months of life initiated the development of perinatal research in NINCDS. For example, early experiments on guinea pigs showed that mental retardation could be caused by prenatal asphyxia. In 1953 the idea of organizing a multi-institutional collaborative project for perinatal studies where NINCDS would serve as a central laboratory and coordination center received encouragement. In 1954 the preliminary plans for the organization of the NINCDS Collaborative Perinatal Project were presented to the Appropriations Subcommittee of the House and Senate. In May of 1955 the purpose of the project was publicly announced. In 1957 detailed work was carried forward on the development of methods and examinations for the study. Increased appropriations in 1957 permitted enlarging the number of collaborating institutions. The pretest phase was launched in January 1958. The participating institutions at that time were Boston Lying-In Hospital, Boston; Brown University, Providence; Charity Hospital, New Orleans; Children's Hospital, Philadelphia; Children's Hospital, San Francisco (study incomplete); Columbia University Medical Center, New York; Johns Hopkins University Hospital, Baltimore; Medical College of Virginia, Richmond; New York Medical College, New York; University of Minnesota, Minneapolis; University of Oregon Medical School, Portland; Pennsylvania Hospital, Philadelphia; Yale University, New Haven (study incomplete); Children's Medical Center, Boston; the University of Tennessee, Memphis; and the University of Buffalo, Buffalo. These centers together provided a heterogeneous population not only racially but also socioeconomically.

Methodology of the Collaborative Project

The Collaborative Project on Cerebral Palsy and Mental Retardation was a pro-

spective study eventually involving the collaboration of 12 separate institutions in the United States. The study data were collected and recorded in a uniform fashion.* Children were followed from their mother's registration during pregnancy until they were eight years of age. A unique feature of this study was that the data recorded at any given time were not biased by reference to antecedent events. Data were recorded at the earliest possible time after events pertinent to the aims of the study had taken place. Records of these events in the form of standardized examinations or observation protocols were submitted, then coded and processed at the Perinatal Research Branch (PRB) of NINCDS.

The study design called for the systematic collection of data on a maximum of 60,000 pregnancies and eight years of follow-up of the children. Women were selected in accordance with a sampling technique approved for a given institution and were registered from January 1, 1959, until December 31, 1965. Upon admission into the collaborative project, a participant was interviewed, and complete information was recorded concerning past and present medical, obstetrical, menstrual, and gynecological history, including history of x-ray exposure, hospitalization, visits to physicians, and episodes of hospitalization which might have occurred. During one of the early visits to the prenatal clinic, socioeconomic information and the genetic history of the gravida (registered mother) and her family and of the father of the baby (FOB) and his family were obtained. A detailed physical examination of the gravida took place at subsequent visits during her pregnancy. Laboratory tests routinely performed included hemoglobin, complete urinalyses, serological tests

---

* Copies of all forms and their accompanying manuals are available upon request from the Developmental Neurology Branch, Neurological Disorders Program, NINCDS-NIH, Bethesda, Maryland 20014.

2

for syphilis, blood typing, Rh titer, and, if the patient was found to be Rh negative, the Coombs' Test. The patient returned to the prenatal clinic for reexamination at intervals of four weeks during the first seven months and at two-week intervals from the eighth month of pregnancy until delivery. At each visit interviews were conducted to elicit information on illness which had occurred since her last visit to the prenatal clinic. In addition, the presence or absence of certain events such as bleeding, meconium staining of amniotic fluid, and the presence or absence of fetal heart activity were noted. If the patient was examined during the prenatal period by a nonstudy physician or in a special clinic or was hospitalized for an intercurrent illness either in the study hospital facility or in an outside hospital, verification of this information was sought.

Blood samples of 20 ml were collected in a vacutainer at the first visit to the perinatal clinic. Samples of blood were drawn also at bi-monthly intervals throughout pregnancy, at delivery and, finally, at six weeks postpartum. The serum from the blood samples, after proper separation, was frozen and shipped to the Section on Infectious Diseases of the Perinatal Research Branch. Specimens of 5 ml of blood from abnormal children were obtained at four months of age whenever possible. Blood samples were obtained from all children at one year of age.

When the gravida was admitted to the hospital for delivery her physical status was determined and the delivery records were completed. A specially trained nurse was present at each delivery to record significant observations regarding the progress of labor and of delivery; these included one-, two-, and five-minute Apgar scores; meconium staining of amniotic fluid, and resuscitative measures. The obstetrician, after termination of delivery, completed the summary form of labor and delivery. The placenta was placed in a plastic bag; the bag was sealed to avoid evaporation and sent to the study's pathologist for examination.

Pediatric-neurologic examinations were conducted on neonates within the first 24 hours after birth, and again between 36 and 60 hours. If an infant remained in the hospital more than 24 hours after the second examination, a third examination was done prior to discharge. Infants who remained in the hospital longer than one week, such as premature infants, were examined at weekly intervals after the first week until discharged. Observations pertaining to body temperature, feeding, and intercurrent events were made and recorded together with other information such as drug administration and radiological and laboratory findings. Determination of bilirubin level was made on every child at 36 to 60 hours of age and repeated every 24 hours as long as the most recent value was above 10 mg%. Bilirubin determination on premature infants was done daily until five days of age and was continued if the most recent value was above 10 mg%. Hemoglobin and hematocrit determinations were obtained on every child at 48 hours of age. The A-B-O and Rh blood typings were performed at birth, followed by the Coombs' Test. Following the infant's discharge from the newborn nursery, precoded diagnostic summaries were completed by the responsible study physician.

Pediatric-neurologic examinations were administered also at four months, one year, and seven years of age.

The eight-month psychological evaluation consisted of the mental and motor scale of the research form of the Bayley Scales of Infant Development (Bayley, 1958).

The four-year psychological evaluation consisted of: (1) the Stanford-Binet Intelligence Scale, LM, Short Form (Terman and Merrill, 1960); (2) gross motor assessment, including line walking, hopping, and ball catching; (3) fine motor assessment, including the Wallin Pegboard, copying forms, stringing beads, and the Vineland revision of Porteus Maze III and IV; and (4) an adaptation of the Graham-Ernhart Block Sort Test (see PRB manuals). Maternal IQ scores were measured by the Science Research Associates Non-Verbal Form A-H at the children's four-year examination (SRA, 1947).

The seven-year psychological evaluation consisted of: (1) the Bender Gestalt Test for Young Children (Koppitz, 1964); (2) Wechsler Intelligence Scale for Children, Short Form (Wechsler, 1949); (3) Auditory-Vocal Association subtest from the Illinois Test of Psycholinguistic Abilities, Experimental Edition (McCarthy and Kirk, 1963); (4) Goodenough-Harris Draw-A-Person Test (Harris, 1963); and (5) the Jastak Wide Range Achievement Test of reading, spelling, and arithmetic (Jastak and Jastak, 1965). Visual screening was done also at seven years of age (Titmus, 1963).

Speech, language, and hearing examinations were conducted at three and eight years of age. These examinations will be discussed in other sections of the book.

Growth measurements (height, weight, and occipito-frontal head circumference) were uniformly taken at each examination by a trained nurse from the neonatal period to eight years.

Interval medical histories were obtained each time the child was seen for any of the examinations and also at two years and five years of age. The interval histories were used to establish particular information concerning possible visits to physicians or hospitals. If this information revealed that the child was hospitalized or was seen by a physician for anything other than routine care, a copy of the physician's or hospital's records was obtained and entered into the child's records.

During the seventh year of the child's life, the genetic and socioeconomic information collected prenatally was brought up to date. Subsequent to these examinations, a diagnostic summary was again completed for each child covering all conditions and events which had been recognized or which had been reported since the completion of the diagnostic summary at the age of one year.

All examinations had to be carried out within specified age limits according to protocol. All information was collected and recorded by trained interviewers and examiners who used standardized manuals containing instructions for filling out each form and giving definitions of specific items. To ensure accuracy, workshops, training seminars, and inter/intrainstitutional quality control seminars were conducted.

All records of examinations, interviews, and so forth, were reviewed by both a clerical and a professional person in the study to check for legibility and completeness and for compliance with the terms of the study's requirements and definitions. Corrections were made as required.

Upon completion of each editing procedure, forms were sent to the Perinatal Research Branch, where these records underwent review by highly trained professional and nonprofessional personnel. Any clarification or change on a form was made only after consultation with the institution submitting the data. The processing of these forms proceeded to a central coding facility where trained personnel followed precise coding manuals for conversion of data to punch cards and subsequent transfer to magnetic tape.

Problems Related to the Data Collection

Arrangements had to be made to assure a random selection of pregnant women registering for perinatal care, and 24-hour coverage of the labor and delivery rooms had to be assured. Collected information, prior to submission to the Perinatal Research Branch, had to be reviewed at the local level to detect incompleteness or inconsistency. Such problems had to be resolved locally as soon after the data collection as possible.

One of the major problems in this study, as in all longitudinal research, was sample maintenance. In a country with a highly mobile population it is difficult to maintain a study sample for a number of years. This problem is discussed further in Chapter 4.

Summary

In summary, this prospective study was carried out to obtain longitudinal information and to find relationships between perinatal, social, genetic, and postnatal events, and certain outcomes. The data were collected uniformly on a study sample drawn from a heterogeneous population in several geographic regions.

History

Part B
The Examinations of Speech, Language, and Hearing in the NINCDS Collaborative Perinatal Project

Frank M. Lassman, Ph.D.

The NINCDS Collaborative Perinatal Project investigators recognized early that a complete assessment of the neurological status of children would have to include the communicative skills: speech, language, and hearing. Communication was viewed as a complex involvement of all levels of the nervous system, so delicately balanced that compromise of any physical component by inheritance, disease, or trauma was likely to alter the normal development or maintenance of communicative behavior. This appreciation increased as the study matured and the focus of public interest and of medical specialists moved to the more subtle expressions of nervous system disorder.

The concern for speech and hearing manifestations of neurological disorder was formalized in a Bethesda, Maryland, meeting on March 3, 1958, called by Dr. Richard Masland, then Assistant Director of the National Institute of Neurological Diseases and Blindness (NINDB). The participants were a combination of intramural staff, speech, language, and hearing specialists from collaborating institutions, and selected consultants. From the outset, communicative behaviors were viewed as longitudinal and developmental. A number of proposals were considered with respect to the optimal times for evaluation: the neonatal period, eight months, 30 months, and 72 months of age.

The experimental version of the Bayley Scales of Infant Development* (Bayley, 1958) was already in use as the eight-month examination. These were viewed with favor since the Mental Development scale contained a number of items which sampled developing communicative skills. An item analysis of the Bayley Mental Development Scale (experimental version) reveals 32 items which are concerned with communication development. These subdivide into 22 hearing items, such as Responds to Sound of Bell and Adjusts to Words, and 14 speech and language items such as Vocalizes Attitudes Selectively and Vocalizes Four Different Syllables.†

The participants were invited to consider the development of a 30-month speech, language, and hearing examination. The first outcome of their deliberations was a proposal to change to 36 months for better examiner-subject relationships, reduced variability, and greater precision of measurement.

3YR Speech, Language, and Hearing (SLH) Examination

The responsibility for developing what came to be called the 3YR Examination of Speech, Language, and Hearing was shared by institute staff and an SLH committee of selected representatives from participating institutions. Martin Mendelson, Acting Head, Section on Behavioral Sciences, Perinatal Research Branch, NINDB, provided leadership and coordination with the support of Perinatal Research Branch administrative resources.

Speech, Language, and Hearing Committee

Institutional representation, variously known as the SLH Committee, SLH Subcommittee, and the SLH Subgroup, included:

Warren Fay	University of Oregon Medical School	Portland, Oregon
Shulamith Kastein	Columbia-Presbyterian Medical Center	New York, New York
Frank Lassman	University of Minnesota	Minneapolis, Minnesota
Doris Leberfeld	New York Medical College and Hunter College	New York, New York
Donald Nelson	University of Oregon Medical School	Portland, Oregon
Miriam Pauls-Hardy	Johns Hopkins Hospital	Baltimore, Maryland
Mary Wootton-Masland	Johns Hopkins Hospital	Baltimore, Maryland

Each of these individuals would contribute to the further development of the 3YR exam and be responsible for its implementation at the particular institution. Fay joined the committee when Nelson was unable to continue beyond the initial development of the exam.

The SLH Committee was augmented by consultants, usually for *ad hoc* purposes, in its work. Consultants included:

---

* Names of specific tests, variables, and indexes are capitalized throughout the text.
† Four of the Bayley items were of the language comprehension type which are placed in both hearing and language categories; for example, Adjusts to Words.

Miriam Fiedler   Harvard University   Cambridge, Massachusetts
William Hardy   Johns Hopkins Hospital   Baltimore, Maryland
Herold Lilywhite   University of Oregon   Portland, Oregon
Dorothea McCarthy   Fordham University   New York, New York
Mildred Templin   University of Minnesota   Minneapolis, Minnesota

At various times, there was communication with other members of the professional and scientific community about specific questions. For example, Wendell Johnson and Dean Williams were consulted regarding the fluency items to be described in the following section.

Development of the 3YR Examination

The objectives of the 3YR examination, as delineated for the Committee by Dr. Heinz Berendes, Chief of the Perinatal Research Branch, NINDB, were to *identify* nervous system disturbance not already recognized, to *affirm* cases considered suspect in the earlier exams, and to *describe* further communicative manifestations of underlying neurologic disorder.

Over a two-to-three-year period from 1960 to almost 1963, the Speech, Language, and Hearing Committee constructed and pretested a screening examination based on what was roughly an input-output model of communication. Examinations were found or developed to sample current performance in subdivisions of communication including hearing, language comprehension, auditory memory, language expression, speech mechanism, and speech production.

The examination was developed at a time when the study of speech, language, and hearing of children was based on imaginative and individualistic clinical procedures with high content validity. But although similar approaches and procedures were broadly employed, they were largely unstandardized and normative data on large samples were unavailable.

The SLH Committee set out to devise an instrument that could assess speech, language, and hearing in a short period of examination time, preferably within 60 to 90 minutes, to avoid fatigue and attention problems and to accommodate to local budgetary restrictions. It accepted a logistic limitation of one visit per child. The test had to be one that could be administered by Master's Degree speech pathologists or by graduate students under close supervision. With these temporal, scheduling, and personnel constraints in mind, a screening examination was constructed. With the possible exception of speech articulation, which was explored in some detail, the resultant examination used a sampling, screening approach which attempted to cover the breadth of the communicative areas.

An examination was devised that made liberal use of familiar but unstandardized clinical procedures. One test, the pure-tone sweep check of hearing, approximated standardization. Another, a word-repetition test of articulation, was similar to those used by Templin (1957) and others in developmental studies of articulation. The examination as a whole, however, represented the "state of the art" in 1963 as far as screening instruments were concerned.

The examination is described in detail in Chapter 3 and Appendix 1. Some of the considerations and rationale for several specific decisions of the subcommittee are explained in the next section.

Special Considerations and Rationale

General Because of the diversity intrinsic to the nature of collaborative research among 12 institutions, it was considered essential to specify in detail the requirements of environment, per-

8

sonnel, test methods and procedures, and data recording and retrieval. These requirements were set down in a test manual and further elaborated on a standard scoring form, both presented in Appendix 1. Responsibility for standard procedures was invested in supervisory personnel who were required, in addition, to review all protocols for completeness and for scoring accuracy.

Hearing A test of sensitivity for hearing and discriminating speech stimuli was considered to have high validity. It was also recognized that many tests of young children's hearing are inadequate because the child refuses to accept earphones on the head. These considerations led to the development of a recorded speech-hearing test which did not require earphones. A loudspeaker at a fixed distance from the child was the source of the speech.

The speech stimuli were lists of words of two syllables equally stressed, the so-called spondee words. Thresholds for spondee words have been shown to relate well to thresholds for understanding simple sentences, and were routinely used for testing the hearing of adults. To avoid penalizing the child who would not or could not repeat words, the child was permitted to point at pictures. Although hearing is more likely to be testable with this strategy, the picture identification paradigm did introduce a closed language set possibly resulting in a less difficult test.

The spondee screening test of hearing was very similar to the Verbal Auditory Screening for Children (VASC) reported later by Griffing, Simonton, and Hedgecock (1967). Spondees had, of course, been routinely employed for threshold testing, and spondee screening had been accomplished with adults in large-sample inventories, that is, the screening of college students. But reports on systematic study of spondee words as a screening device with children were not readily available.

The use of spondee words as the screening test of hearing was subject to the criticism that performance would be influenced by verbal ability despite the assistance of pictures and the closed set. There was also the possibility that a child could pass the screen despite a partial loss in hearing. This has been known to occur in the testing of adults. In order to obtain a more complete description of the child's hearing, a pure-tone screening "sweep check" of hearing was added to the test battery. Tests were conducted for each ear separately, under phones.

The use of two hearing tests introduced the possibility that one of them would succeed. Spondee screening could be accomplished without phones; pure-tone screening could be accomplished with "play audiometry" (instrumental conditioning) techniques, if the examiner desired.

Auditory Memory The screening of language reception, language expression, speech production, and a spondee hearing test must depend on remembered verbal material. In addition, the classical dyad of stimulus-response between examiner and examinee involves short-term memory and latency considerations. An attempt was made to separate short-term auditory memory from cognitive and other influences. Digit span was judged to be potentially least influenced by verbal abilities. A nonsense-syllable memory span test was added to reduce the effect of environmental factors.

At the time, digit repetition rates of one-per-second were standardized for the Wechsler Intelligence Scale for Children (Wechsler, 1949) and of two-per-second for the Illinois Test of Psycholinguistic Abilities (McCarthy and Kirk, 1963). The one-per-second rate was selected as a standard repetition rate for both digit and nonsense-syllable stimuli.

Speech Production Initially, the presence of stuttering was reported with clonic and tonic subdivisions available for descriptive scoring. After pretesting and discussion with selected consultants, the examination item was modified to separate measures of fluency and struggle behavior. This strategy would accept the presence of some nonfluent speech behaviors, such as repetitions and hesitations, as essentially normal and permit the recognition of struggle behaviors as exceptional.

Intelligibility was regarded as a potential global measure of speech production. Whether the child could be understood by a stranger in a test situation was considered of primary importance. Intelligibility was rated on a five-point scale. Scoring criteria were modified after pretesting suggested that initial scoring criteria were overly severe.

Pretesting the 3YR Exam

Pretesting of the proposed 3YR SLH examination was begun successively at the University of Oregon, Johns Hopkins University, Columbia University, New York Medical College, and the University of Minnesota in the fall of 1961 and into the winter of 1962. The pretest was organized to: (1) identify operational problems in its administration; (2) shorten and streamline the instrument; (3) standardize instructions, procedures, and scoring forms; (4) train examiners in the administration of the exam; (5) develop scoring criteria for the separate subtests; and (6) demonstrate the validity and reliability of the examination.

Pretest Sample The pretest sample was divided into normal and abnormal subjects. The criterion for abnormal was either one of the following: referral to or treatment by a speech, language, and hearing clinic *or* two or more abnormal findings on any of the four-month, eight-month, or 12-month examinations and consequent assignment to the abnormal category by a pediatrician. The latter criterion was used at Johns Hopkins only when the referral-treatment

criterion was found difficult to meet. An abnormal group of 111 subjects met either of these criteria.

A random sample of another 111 subjects, matched for age, race, sex, and institution, was designated as a normal criterion group when they did not meet either category of abnormal criteria.

Pretest Reliability and Validity Mendelson and the SLH Committee (1965) studied the reliability of scoring decisions made by pairs of examiners and observers during the examinations. Table 1B-1 from Mendelson's report shows the number and percent of agreements and disagreements for each of five (Auditory Memory was not included) SLH areas tested, for the total group and for the normal and abnormal subgroups. Although concordance is less than perfect, especially in language expression and speech mechanism, the relationship was considered acceptable in view of the preliminary and relatively unpracticed stage of the examination. These data contributed to a decision to have the test administrator also score the results.

The ability of the examination to differentiate between normal and abnormal groups was also studied by Mendelson et al. (1965). Table 1B-2 shows significant tetrachoric correlations for each SLH area.

It should be noted that the selection criteria used at Johns Hopkins could introduce children without actual speech, language, or hearing deficits into the abnormal group. Also, this method of analysis permits a child in the abnormal category to fail one SLH area while passing the others. This child would be congruent in one area and incongruent in the others.

Test Sequence Subtest sequence was informally studied during the pretest. If a subtest were rejected early in the total examination, the accomplishment of the remainder of the examination might be put at risk. Generally, language subtests

Table **1B-1**

Speech, Language and Hearing Pretest Examination tester-observer reliabilities.*

		Total				Normal				Abnormal			
		Number		Percent		Number		Percent		Number		Percent	
	N	Agree	Disagree	Agree	Disagree	Agree	Disagree	Agree	Disagree	Agree	Disagree	Agree	Disagree
Language Reception	100	95	5	95.0	5.0	49	1	98.0	2.0	46	4	92.0	8.0
Language Expression	100	89	11	89.0	11.0	46	4	92.0	8.0	43	7	86.0	14.0
Hearing†	96	90	6	93.8	6.2	48	2	96.0	4.0	42	4	91.3	8.7
Speech Mechanism†	96	86	10	89.6	10.4	47	3	94.0	6.0	39	7	84.8	15.2
Speech Production†	97	91	6	93.8	6.2	47	3	94.0	6.0	44	3	93.6	6.4

*From Mendelson et al., (1965).

†Remaining cases—examiner could not evaluate.

were easier to administer and contained intrinsic reward in the manipulation of toys. The pure-tone hearing screening test, which required wearing earphones, and the examination of the oral speech mechanism made more severe demands on the cooperation of the three-year-old child and the clinical skills of the examiner. It was decided that wherever possible the examination would be administered in the following sequence:

1. Language Reception
2. Language Expression
3. Hearing
4. Speech Mechanism
5. Speech Production
6. Auditory Memory

The sequence roughly followed the input-output functional model. Although the manual and scoring forms dictated this sequence, it was recognized that changes in sequence might be dictated by individual circumstances. The examiner was permitted to present the hearing test first if a hearing loss was suspected from early examination behavior. The examiner could defer the pure-tone hearing screen until last if the child rejected the first attempt to place the earphones.

Standardization and Quality Control

Considerable attention was given to developing instructions that could be understood easily and procedures that were likely to be accomplished in a uniform manner. The SLH representatives from the collaborating institutions convened seven times from May 1960 to October 1962 to construct and modify the instrument and report back on pretest results.

Each of the SLH representatives was also responsible for the supervision of the examiners in the institution represented. They were responsible for establishing

Table **1B-2**

Speech, Language and Hearing Pretest Examination tetrachoric r's by individual test areas for previously diagnosed normal vs. previously diagnosed abnormal groups.*

Criterion: Previous Diagnosis	N	Test Normal		Test Not Normal		$r_{tet.}$†	$\delta r_{tet.}$
		N	%	N	%		
Language Reception							
Normal	111	76	68.5	35	31.5	.60	.10
Abnormal	111	31	27.9	80	72.1		
Language Expression							
Normal	110	91	82.7	19	17.3	.72	.11
Abnormal	111	37	33.3	74	66.7		
Hearing							
Normal	107	85	79.4	22	20.6	.54	.11
Abnormal	98	45	45.9	53	54.1		
Speech Mechanism							
Normal	106	86	81.1	20	18.9	.52	.11
Abnormal	96	48	50.0	48	50.0		
Speech Production							
Normal	107	95	88.8	12	11.2	.79	.11
Abnormal	102	36	35.3	66	64.7		

*From Mendelson et al., (1965).

†A tetrachoric correlation coefficient may be regarded as significant if it is at least twice the size of its standard error.

uniform test procedures and for selecting and training new examiners.

Three standardization and training workshops were held for the examiners in April 1963, April 1964, and in September 1967. Uniformity in test administration and objectivity in scoring were emphasized. Instructions to the children had to be memorized. In the first meeting, the test manual was reviewed item by item and standard procedures were demonstrated and discussed, using three-year-old teaching subjects. The 1964 standardization conference examined appropriateness of facilities and equipment, logistics and operational problems. "Adequacy of the examination" was further defined and scoring criteria were reviewed for less than fully cooperative children. The 1967 standardization conference was addressed to newer examiners, many of whom had not attended the previous conferences. Test administration was again demonstrated and considerable attention was given to scoring standards.

The importance of maintaining standard procedures was emphasized at all the conferences. On the other hand, certain flexibilities were already a part of standardized procedures. For example, play audiometry or instrumental conditioning could be used in the pure-tone hearing screen, but it was not required.

Finally, both intramural and extramural quality control procedures were instituted. An extramural quality control program was instituted in 1967 which required representatives of each institutional team to visit other institutions. The SLH exam was administered by a visiting examiner and the results were compared with those obtained one to two months previously by a local examiner. Testing techniques were discussed and standard procedures were emphasized. From November 1969 to March 1970 examiner reliability was checked within institutions by retesting 5% of the children, chosen randomly, within a month of the first examination. Results were so similar that this program was terminated after three months.

The monitoring of data collection and scoring was implemented both at institutions and at the NINCDS Collaborative Perinatal Project central office. The SLH supervisor at each institution reviewed all forms for adherence to scoring criteria and for completeness. This procedure was repeated at the central data processing office. All discrepancies found were reported back to the institutions for comment and resolution.

8YR Speech, Language, and Hearing Examination

The end-point of the Collaborative Project was the 8YR Speech, Language, and Hearing (SLH) examination. Initially, a speech, language, and hearing examination at the time of the 7YR pediatric-neurological and psychological examinations seemed the most efficient and practical plan. But the argument prevailed that the 7YR examinations were too taxing to permit yet another examination on the same day. A test at six years was considered as one alternative. Age eight was favored because by this age children without deficits can use most grammatical forms of a language, can articulate most speech sounds correctly, can respond to standard audiometric procedures, and have developed elementary reading, writing, and spelling skills. A decision for an 8YR examination of speech, language, and hearing was made by principal investigators in late 1964 and construction of the examination was begun immediately.

Development of the 8YR SLH Exam: SLH Committee and Consultants

The 8YR examination was also referred to as the Final Speech, Language, and Hearing Examination. It was the product of the combined efforts of the Perinatal

Research Branch administrative and professional resources, of the Speech, Language, and Hearing Committee, comprised of selected professionals from collaborative institutions, and of consultants. Martin Mendelson initiated the process for the Perinatal Research Branch (PRB) followed shortly by Paul LaBenz who, in 1966, assumed full responsibility for the 8YR examination. The Speech, Language, and Hearing Committee included most of those involved with the 3YR exam: Fay, Kastein, Lassman, Leberfeld, Pauls-Hardy, and Wootton-Masland.

A draft of the 8YR SLH examination was prepared by the committee as early as January 1965 and pretesting began later that year. A modified 8YR SLH exam was presented to a panel of outside consultants in February 1966. The panel which gave general approval to the draft included representatives from the fields of speech pathology, audiology, linguistics, child development, and psychology. The consultants were:

designated Hearing (including Auditory Memory), Language Comprehension, Language Expression, Speech Mechanism, and Speech Production.

Direct incorporation of tests from the 3YR exam into the 8YR exam was considered desirable for purposes of developmental comparisons. As will be seen in Chapter 3, this was possible in only a few instances, for example, intelligibility and fluency ratings. Thus, although comparisons could be made between 3YR and 8YR exams within basic areas, direct numerical comparisons of scores were not possible. Wherever possible, appropriate existing instruments with standardized procedures, materials, and norms were included in the 8YR battery.

The time available for the 8YR examination imposed a limitation on its structure. A maximum of 90 minutes and a 75 minute average test time were considered desirable by the subcommittee. This time frame was found to be feasible during a pretesting period.

The fact that this was an examination

Katrina deHirsch	Columbia-Presbyterian	New York, New York
Leo Doerfler	University of Pittsburgh	Pittsburgh, Pennsylvania
Lloyd Dunn	George Peabody College for Teachers	Nashville, Tennessee
Jon Eisenson	Stanford University School of Medicine	Palo Alto, California
Earl Harford	Northwestern University	Evanston, Illinois
Frank Kleffner	Central Institute for the Deaf	St. Louis, Missouri
Paula Menyuk	Massachusetts Institute of Technology	Cambridge, Massachusetts
Seymour Rosenberg	Columbia University	New York, New York
Sol Saporta	University of Washington	Seattle, Washington
Joseph Spradlin	University of Kansas	Parsons, Kansas
Dean Williams	University of Iowa	Iowa City, Iowa

Special Considerations and Rationale

An effort was made to maintain the same structural categories of an input-output model seen in the 3YR exam. Hence, tests were organized into areas

for an eight-year-old child made possible the construction of a test instrument more intensive than at the 3YR level. It was possible at this age to construct a hearing test resembling the routine adult test battery of the day, including thresh-

14

old rather than screening tests, air-bone comparisons, auditory discrimination of speech, and a measure of auditory adaptation.

Language comprehension was reviewed in some detail using components of existing standardized instruments. The early development of reading was explored with tests of both oral and silent reading. Language expression was analysed for linguistic features, such as concepts and grammar, and differed from the 3YR exam by the inclusion of an evaluation of written communication.

The assessment of speech production and speech mechanism most closely duplicated the 3YR exam procedures with ratings of voice, of fluency, and of intelligibility unchanged. Speech mechanism ratings were simplified, but articulation was analysed in greater depth with a 50-item screening version of the Templin-Darley Test of Articulation (Templin and Darley, 1960).

Auditory memory was measured with digits and nonsense syllables as it had been at three years. But an 8YR digit span of ten forward was included to provide an adequate test range.

The 8YR Speech, Language, and Hearing Examination is presented in detail in Chapter 3 and Appendix 1. It contains components of nine standardized examinations of speech and language, including reading. The hearing test battery was routine and standard except for the inclusion of a special diagnostic test of auditory adaptation. Effort was directed in the remainder of the tests to extend the range of difficulty so as to be appropriate to this age level.

Pretesting the 8YR Exam

Although the first proposed version of the 8YR exam contained many standard subtests, pretesting was carried out to familiarize examiners with some of the items and to standardize procedures. Pretesting was considered necessary also to study the length of time needed to complete the test, to evaluate the adequacy of manual instructions and scoring forms, and other problems in test administration.

Test Sequence The subareas were examined in the following sequence:

1. Hearing and Auditory Memory
2. Language Comprehension
3. Language Expression
4. Speech Mechanism
5. Speech Production

Identifying hearing impairment at the outset was deemed important so that behaviors on other tests could be interpreted and adjustments could be made in test administration, for example, lighting for lipreading, talking louder, and so forth.

Standardization

The 8YR examination was expected to be more reliable than the 3YR exam because of the age difference itself as well as the use of standard measuring instruments. Examiners were required to memorize all instructions. The manual for test administration was written in great detail and was revised to reflect observations and experiences of the pretest. Examiner supervision was especially direct during the pretest.

A standardization and training conference for all examiners and supervisors was held in Memphis, Tennessee, in September 1967. It included an item-by-item review of the 8YR exam covering the rationale, the specific intent of the test items, proper administration, and uniform test procedures and scoring. The test was demonstrated with eight-year-old subjects, and scoring criteria were evaluated by means of group scoring of the demonstration tests. Proper hearing test administration occupied considerable attention and included equipment management, the use of masking, and the validity-dependence of the tests, especially the adaptation test, on procedural factors.

Between one and a half and two hours were needed to accomplish the test at that point. While greater proficiency in test administration could be expected to shorten the examination, it was clear that the test should be shortened further. An analysis of 35 pretest exams from Memphis and 44 from Minnesota was performed at PRB by Paul LaBenz. The analysis revealed that the naming subtest from the Minnesota Test for Differential Diagnosis of Aphasia (Schuell, 1965) was passed by every child examined. This test was clearly not sufficiently discriminative at the 8YR level and therefore was deleted, with a consequent reduction in total test time.

On-site visits were made by Paul La-Benz to review audiometer calibration, background noise, and sound-conditioned rooms, and to assist in the standardization of procedures. Regular calibration checks were required of all institutions.

Interexaminer and Interinstitutional Variability LaBenz (1967) studied the results obtained by 12 examiners (six pairs) at six institutions. The subjects were selected randomly (30 per examiner) from a pool of 1148 children. Performance on auditory discrimination, vocabulary, reading, and articulation tests were included in an analysis of variance because these were the most quantitatively scored in the test battery. On all four subtests, the variance contributed by examiners was not significant but significant differences did exist between institutions.

Quality control studies between institutions were conducted for the 8YR SLH exam in the same manner described earlier for the 3YR exam. Children were retested by visiting examiners within one to two months of initial testing by a local examiner. These quality control visits between institutional teams were organized and supervised by Jean Oliver of the Perinatal Research Branch and served an important standardization purpose. Interexaminer and interinstitutional agreement were important to the variable selection process described in Chapter 5.

Organization for Data Retrieval and Analysis

As examination records were received at the Perinatal Research Branch of NINDB, they were checked for completeness and for adherence to protocol. The information was coded and the data were put on cards and eventually on magnetic tape.

Task Force on 3YR and 8YR Speech, Language, and Hearing

A task force was formed in 1971 to begin the work of identifying and describing relationships between the outcomes at ages three and eight and their associations with antecedent events, that is, between the SLH performance at these ages and also their association with medical, social, and behavioral data. The task force consisted of the following individuals:

Leo Doerfler (Chairperson)	University of Pittsburgh Medical School	Pittsburgh, Pennsylvania
Harry Bierne	University of Buffalo Medical School	Buffalo, New York
Luke Gillespie	Boston Lying-In Hospital	Boston, Massachusetts
John V. Irwin	Memphis State University	Memphis, Tennessee
Frank Lassman	University of Minnesota Medical Center	Minneapolis, Minnesota
Earl Schubert	Stanford University	Palo Alto, California

Warren Torgerson	Johns Hopkins University	Baltimore, Maryland
Peter Workman	City University of New York	New York, New York
Eldon Eagles	Office of the Director NINCDS	Bethesda, Maryland
Bernard Fox	Perinatal Research Branch NINCDS	Bethesda, Maryland
Paul LaBenz	Perinatal Research Branch NINCDS	Bethesda, Maryland
Jean Oliver	Perinatal Research Branch NINCDS	Bethesda, Maryland
David Rubinstein	Office of Biometry and Epidemiology, NINCDS	Bethesda, Maryland

Strategy of Analysis and the Indexes

The Task Force developed an analysis strategy which called for the construction of a composite index of speech, language, and hearing. Test measures would be intercorrelated and factor-analyzed to derive the component variables of the index and any special weighting of the variables. The index could then be correlated with antecedent and, in the case of the 3YR measures, subsequent events.

John Irwin continued the process of index construction with the assistance of Paul LaBenz, Frank Lassman, and Earl Schubert. Three indexes were identified: (1) Neurological Involvement, (2) Communicative Effectiveness, and (3) Auditory Processing. The component measures for each index are presented in detail in Appendix 4.

All component measures were derived from the 8YR SLH exam. The Index of Neurological Involvement included sensory and motor expressions of neurological involvement. With the exception of the orientation items, language measures were notably absent from this index. The language variables were represented in a separate index designated Communicative Effectiveness. Visual and auditory comprehension, expressive language, and speech variables were included. The Index of Auditory Processing contained not only the auditory measures but also included others deemed by the Task Force to be dependent upon an intact auditory system.

Data Analysis Organization

The analysis of the speech, language, and hearing measures had proceeded to this stage by late 1973. A University of Minnesota team was awarded a contract to conduct the data analysis to begin in the summer of 1974. The team was under the leadership of Frank Lassman and Robert Fisch as coprincipal investigators, and Dolores Vetter and Elaine LaBenz, coinvestigators. A Scientific Management Panel, including the investigators and James Boen (Biostatistics), Elaine Frankowski (Systems Analysis), and SLH consultants Frederic Darley (Mayo Clinic), Warren Fay (Oregon), Earl Schubert (Stanford), and Harris Winitz (Missouri) would monitor the analysis as it proceeded and further refine the analysis as results began to unfold. Allen Sullivan and John Taborn would offer expertise on cultural variables and Kenneth Swaiman would provide additional strength in Pediatric Neurology. Paul LaBenz was appointed Project Officer and David Rubinstein Assistant Project Officer, to ensure close communication with the Perinatal Research Branch and to monitor and lend continuity to the analytic process.

The analysis was begun in the fall of 1974 and was completed, including final reports, in June 1977. The methods of

17

analysis are described in detail in Chapter 5 and the findings of that analysis comprise the bulk of this report.

References

1. Bayley, N. *COLR Research Form of the Bayley Scales of Mental and Motor Development.* Bethesda, Maryland: Perinatal Research Branch, NINCDS-NIH, 1958.

2. Chipman, S.C., Lilienfeld, A.M., Greenberg, B.G., and Donnelly, J.F. *Research Methodology and Needs in Perinatal Studies.* Springfield, Ill.: Charles C Thomas, 1966.

3. *Examiner Manual for the SRA Verbal and Non-Verbal Forms.* Chicago: Science Research Associates, 1947.

4. Griffing, T.S., Simonton, K.M., and Hedgecock, L.D. Verbal auditory screening for children. *Trans. Am. Acad. Ophthalmol. Otolaryngol.* Jan–Feb: 105–111, 1967.

5. Harris, D.B. *Children's Drawings as Measures of Intellectual Maturity.* New York: Harcourt, Brace and World, 1963.

6. Jastak, J.F., and Jastak, S.R. *The Wide Range Achievement Test (WRAT).* Wilmington, Delaware: Guidance Associates, 1965.

7. Koppitz, E.M. *The Bender Gestalt Test for Young Children.* New York: Grune and Stratton, 1964.

8. LaBenz, P. Personal Communication, 1967.

9. McCarthy, J.J., and Kirk, S.A. *The Construction, Standardization, and Statistical Characteristics of the Illinois Test of Psycholinguistic Abilities. Experimental Edition.* Urbana, Illinois: University of Illinois Press, 1963.

10. Mendelson, M.A., Lassman, F.M., Kastein, S., Leberfeld, D., Pauls-Hardy, M., Wootton-Masland, M., Nelson, D., and Templin, M.C. The development and analysis of a speech, language and hearing examination for the Collaborative Study of Cerebral Palsy. Unpublished, NINCDS, NIH, 1965.

11. *Reference Manual for the School Vision Tester.* Petersburg, Virginia: Titmus Optical Co., 1963.

12. Schuell, H. *Minnesota Test for Differential Diagnosis of Aphasia.* Minneapolis: University of Minnesota Press, 1965.

13. Templin, M.C. *Certain Language Skills in Children.* Minneapolis: University of Minnesota Press, 1957.

14. Templin, M.C., and Darley, F.L. *The Templin-Darley Test of Articulation.* Iowa City, Iowa: University of Iowa Press, 1960.

15. Terman, L.M., and Merrill, M.A. *Stanford-Binet Intelligence Scale.* Boston: Houghton Mifflin, 1960.

16. Wechsler, D. *The Wechsler Intelligence Scale for Children.* New York: The Psychological Corp., 1949.

## CHAPTER 2

Literature Review

Dolores K. Vetter, Ph.D.
Frank M. Lassman, Ph.D.

Relatively few large-sample studies of speech, language, and hearing are found in the literature. Those that are reported have surveyed the behavior using a cross-sectional sample (Templin, 1957; Hull et al., 1971), or have followed a sample longitudinally gathering vast quantities of data in the areas of health, physical, and sociocultural characteristics (French et al., 1968; Davie, Butler, and Goldstein, 1972; Broman, Nichols, and Kennedy, 1975). Since the present research contained aspects of both cross-sectional and longitudinal investigations, it seemed necessary to review the literature utilizing both methodologies.

Longitudinal Research

Three major research undertakings utilizing a longitudinal approach have presented data relevant to the prediction of speech, language, and hearing behavior. They are the Kauai Pregnancy Study, the British Perinatal Mortality and National Child Development Study, and earlier analyses of data from the NINCDS Collaborative Perinatal Project.

Kauai Pregnancy Study

The Kauai Pregnancy Study was a prospective effort to follow the mothers

19

and the products of their pregnancies on the Island of Kauai in the Hawaiian Islands in the mid-1950s (Yerushalmy et al., 1956; French and Bierman, 1962; Bierman et al., 1963; Bierman et al., 1965; Werner et al., 1967; French et al., 1968). Extensive information was gathered during the pregnancy and the first two years of life, and follow-up on acquired and congenital handicaps was also obtained at ten years of age. In general it was ". . . a broad epidemiologic approach to the investigation of many conditions that may be associated with the qualitative as well as the quantitative outcome of pregnancy" (French and Bierman, 1962, p. 835).

Specific analyses were concerned with fetal mortality since an attempt had been made to register the mothers as early in the pregnancy as possible, preferably from four weeks gestation. They found that 24% of pregnancies reaching four weeks gestation ended in fetal loss. No live birth occurred prior to 20 weeks gestation, and no fetal deaths occurred after 43 weeks gestation (French and Bierman, 1962; Bierman et al., 1965). Further findings indicated that 11.7 per 1000 single and twin live births died within the first week, 13.8 per 1000 died under 28 days, and four per 1000 died from 28 days to two years. These deaths were directly attributable to prenatal and natal causes.

Follow-up of 1963 liveborn infants during the first two years of life provided information on physical and mental handicaps of the children. The handicapping conditions included congenital defects, prematurity, birth injuries, cerebral palsy, convulsive disorders, and mental retardation. An estimated 17% of the liveborn study group showed some kind of deficit of prenatal or natal origin. Six percent of these required special care of relatively short term, and 4% required much more extensive diagnostic medical or education service and treatment, special education, or custodial care (Bierman et al., 1963; Bierman et al., 1965).

At the same time, Werner et al. (1967) investigated 670 of these children more intensively. These children had received a complete pediatric and psychological examination at about age two, and ratings were made of the severity of perinatal complications and of the quality of the child's environment at the same age. It was found that 88% of the children had no perinatal complications judged to be more than mild, 10% had moderate complications, and 2% had severe complications. The judged severity of perinatal complications was not affected by age of the mother, socioeconomic status, family stability, mother's intelligence, or ethnic origin. The pediatric and psychological evaluations showed 14% to be below average in health or physical status, 16% to be below average in intellectual development, and 12% to be below average in social development with higher percentages of these problems found in the moderate and severe classifications of perinatal complications. Judged quality of environment had a significant effect on both mental and social development at age two, and environmental effects became even more significant with increasing severity of perinatal complications.

French et al. (1968) reported a follow-up on acquired and congenital handicaps of 750 children in a time sample from the Kauai Pregnancy Study after ten years. At age ten, 6.6% of the children were moderately or severely handicapped as a result of physical defects, mental retardation, or both. The diagnosis which had been made at two years was occasionally not confirmed and there were changes in some of the children as a result of intervention and treatment. Still other children demonstrated handicaps which had not been apparent at age two or which were acquired as a result of accident or disease.

At age ten, mental retardation (IQ < 70) affected 1.5% of the children, and borderline intelligence (IQ 70 to 84) was present in 8.5%. Sensory defects of congenital or acquired origin were distributed as follows: hearing loss was present in 1.1% of the children, with half the cases attributed to congenital factors and the remainder to otitis media; visual problems varying in severity from blindness to uncorrected muscle imbalance or a refractive error 20/40 or more after corrections were found in 1.6% of the children.

These studies indicate the need for identification of factors contributing to handicapping conditions in young children. They also highlight the need for early recognition of such conditions and appropriate medical and educational intervention to maximize the potential for positive change in the child.

British Perinatal Mortality and National Child Development Study

The British Perinatal Mortality Survey originated from a comprehensive survey of the mothers and the products of the pregnancies which terminated during a single week of March 1958. Later the children became the population for the National Child Development Study (1958 Cohort). Several books (Butler and Bonham, 1963; Butler and Alberman, 1969; Pringle, Butler, and Davie, 1966; Davie et al., 1972) have reported the findings of the original survey and the follow-up of the children until seven years of age. It appears that a future publication will report the results of the follow-up at age 11 years.

Questionnaires were prepared by midwives and medical staff in attendance for 17,205 mothers (approximately 98% of the estimated national figure) during a week in March 1958. They found that 3.77% of these mothers delivered stillborn infants or liveborn infants who died within a week of delivery. Further, they collected information on all stillborn and neonatal deaths for March, April, and May 1958, and based the analyses published in *Perinatal Mortality* (1963) on this total population. They reported that deaths were related to parity, social class, age of the mother, and the mother's marital status. Deaths were also complexly related to length of gestation and birthweight as well as to a variety of primary necropsy findings, including congenital malformation, respiratory distress syndrome, and intrapartum anoxia.

Butler and Alberman (1969) presented a more complex analysis of the data from the British Perinatal Mortality Survey with an emphasis on high-risk pregnancies. They explored the association of the factors noted previously with perinatal mortality as well as with additional variables including smoking by the mother, height of the mother, and pre-eclampsia. More detailed analyses were performed of so-called "obstetrical causes of death" (for example, toxemia, Rh incompatibility) and so-called "environmental causes" (for example, malformation, antepartum hemorrhage). Extensive recommendations on obstetrical care were made with the goal of reducing perinatal mortality.

An initial analysis of the National Child Development Study (1958 Cohort) was published shortly after the seven-year follow-up of the children was completed (Pringle et al., 1966). The final report (Davie et al., 1972) presented a summary of the initial analysis and the results of the full analysis of the data gathered on 14,495 children born during the week in March 1958.

Follow-up information was obtained from three general sources: an educational assessment, a parental interview, and a medical examination. The educational assessment consisted of ratings of the child's behaviors, abilities, and attainments, using a social adjustment guide, a reading test, a copying designs test, a draw-a-man test, and a problem arithmetic test. The parental interview gathered information about the family and the home, father's education and occupation, mother's work, type of

21

housing, and household facilities. The medical examination required detailed observation and responses by the doctor of systemic abnormality or dysfunction. Specific laboratory tests were performed. Measurements were made of height, weight, and head circumference; hearing, speech, and vision were tested; and assessments of motor coordination and laterality were conducted.

The descriptive results were presented graphically with grouping on potentially confounding variables such as family size, social class, mother's working, and household facilities. They found that reading attainment was highly dependent on social class and, to a lesser degree, on family size even when allowance was made for social class. Sex difference favored girls. The arithmetic attainment showed smaller but similar effects for social class and family size, but the boys performed better than the girls. Parental education had an important positive effect on both reading and arithmetic even when allowance was made for the strong effects of social class, family size, and sex of the child.

The results of the speech evaluation indicated that only 1.1% of the seven-year-old children were reported to have a stammer or stutter when seen by the examining medical officer. However, over 6% of the children were reported by their mothers to have had such dysfluencies at some time during their seven years.

The children were asked to repeat short sentences in order that articulation could be evaluated. Girls made fewer errors than boys and there was a trend related to social class, with fewer errors being made by children of "higher profession" fathers.

The intelligibility of the seven-year-old children was judged by the medical officer on a four-point scale. Fourteen percent of the children were judged not to have fully intelligible speech. However, in 90% "almost all words were intelligible." Teachers made similar judgments as to whether a child was "difficult to understand because of poor speech;" 11% of the children were rated as meeting this standard "somewhat" and for 2.6% it "certainly" applied. Girls were more intelligible than boys according to ratings of both doctors and teachers. The social class trends which were found were questioned because of concern of the use of "middle class" speech as the standard. Some form of speech therapy was being given to 2.5% of all the children (3.3% of the boys and 1.6% of the girls).

An otological evaluation was also conducted as part of the medical examination. Of the children examined, 8.3% showed "signs of past or present otitis media;" for 10% of the children the doctors offered "no opinion." Almost 9% of the children had a purulent discharge from the ears at the time of examination; this incidence was highly related to social class. A clinical hearing test in which the children were asked to repeat a series of words designed to assess auditory acuity over the speech frequencies was administered to each child. Seventy-five percent of the children were able to repeat all the words perfectly; girls performed slightly better than boys.

Audiograms were obtained on 73% of the children on frequencies from 250 Hz to 8000 Hz. Of these children approximately 80% had normal hearing (no loss greater than 20 dB), 11% had no loss greater than 30 dB, and 4.5% had a loss of 35 dB or worse at one frequency; 5.7% showed a loss of 35 dB or worse at two or more frequencies, 4.2% of these being monaural losses. Of the binaural losses, 1.3% showed a moderate loss (35 to 50 dB), 0.2% showed a serious loss (55 to 70 dB), and 0.1% showed a severe loss (75 dB or worse). The authors suggested that an audiometric screening at 250 Hz, 1000 Hz, and 4000 Hz would have identified every hearing-impaired child but one in their sample.

The incidence of various congenital malformations and serious defects was reported by the National Child Development Study (1958 Cohort). Among conditions reported were cleft palate (1.5 per 1000), mongolism (0.8 per 1000), other "severe subabnormality" (1.5 per 1000), spina bifida and/or hydrocephalus (1.1 per 1000), and cerebral palsy (2.3 per 1000). These figures compared reasonably well with the prevalence of these conditions reported in other studies.

Various perinatal factors were evaluated for their relationship to later handicapping conditions. Children born more than three weeks before or three weeks after the expected delivery date demonstrated "educational handicaps" and "clumsiness" more often than children born between 37 and 42 weeks gestation. These findings were present even after the effects of social class and family size were taken into account. Birthweight, weighted for length of gestation, also was related to "educational handicaps" when the birthweight was low for length of gestation. Social class interacted significantly with birthweight (at gestational age) and prevalence of "educational backwardness."

The report concluded with a discussion of risk registers and the use of a mathematical model for optimizing the usefulness of such registers. It also pointed out the need for continued survey and evaluation of the performance abilities of children and the observation of the perinatal and environmental variables related to such abilities.

NINCDS Collaborative Perinatal Project

The data from the NINCDS Collaborative Perinatal Project have been analyzed and reported in two books to date, *The Women and Their Pregnancies* (Niswander and Gordon, 1972) and *Preschool IQ: Prenatal and Early Developmental Correlates* (Broman et al., 1975), and in numerous research publications. Niswander and Gordon presented an extremely detailed description of a specific cohort of mothers

enrolled in the Project. This cohort included those White and Black mothers chosen by the sampling frame of an institution for the first pregnancy observed by the study which resulted in a single birth (N = 39,215). Thus, a mother could appear only once in their sample regardless of the number of siblings in the study, and mothers producing multiple births were excluded.

They found that 48.6% of the mothers in this cohort were White, the remainder Black. The White mothers had a generally lower income and the Black mothers a generally higher income than that reported for Whites and Blacks in the U.S. Census. The distribution for age of the gravida peaked at the age interval 20 to 24 years for both White and Black mothers. Although there was large variability among the various institutions regarding education of the gravida, the median number of years of schooling for White mothers was almost 12 years, while the median for Black mothers lay in the interval of 9 to 11 years.

Niswander and Gordon then reported the relationships between numerous characteristics of the gravida (physical, health, and sociocultural variables) and fetal outcomes (perinatal deaths, stillbirths, neonatal deaths, and neurological abnormalities at one year of age). The complexity of the interrelationships makes it impossible to summarize the findings in any succinct fashion.

Broman et al. (1975) analyzed the data from the sample of children who took the four-year Stanford-Binet Intelligence Test, and whose mothers formed the same cohort as that used by Niswander and Gordon. They reported IQ scores for four race-sex groups: White-Male, mean = 102.8, SD = 16.5; White-Female, mean = 106.5, SD = 16.7; Black-Male, mean = 90.2, SD = 13.9; Black-Female, mean = 91.3, SD = 14.0; they presented their analyses within these groupings. Sixty-five prenatal, neonatal, infant, and early childhood variables were used in multiple regression analyses against IQ. The prenatal variables accounted for 20% of the IQ variance in each of the White groups, but only 11% of the variance among Black Females and 8% among Black Males. Variables which made the largest contributions were Education of Gravida, Socioeconomic Index, Number of Prenatal Visits and Maternal Age. When the neonatal variables were added, they increased the explained variance by only 1% to 2%. Some physical measurements of the children made small independent contributions. The infant and early childhood variables increased the accountable variance by 4 to 6%. In all, only 28% of the variance in IQ was accounted for among White Females, 25% among White Males, 17% among Black Females and 15% among Black Males. Maternal Education and the Socioeconomic Index contributed most of the explained variance throughout the analyses. Broman, Nichols, and Kennedy (1975) concluded that many variables were antecedents of preschool mental development, but few of them were effective predictors.

An ancillary study of the NINCDS Collaborative Perinatal Project was conducted by Bordley and Hardy (1972). They assessed the hearing of 1182 children born of high-risk mothers enrolled at Johns Hopkins Hospital as part of the Project. In addition to the standard hearing evaluations at ages three and eight years, these authors also observed the children's responses to a broad-spectrum acoustic stimulus (65 to 75 dB) when the infants were 48 hours old, and an acoustic response test employing a modified Ewing test technique at four months and at 12 months. The study reported essentially none of their findings at 48 hours, four months, 12 months, and three years, but concluded that the neonatal auditory screening had no relationship to hearing loss identified subsequently. In their discussion they stated that 98% of the children failing the eight-year test had given normal responses to the neonatal testing. In addition, they found that 5% of their sample had sensorineural losses, 11.6% had conductive losses, and 3.6% had mixed losses on the eight-year examination. They suggested that these high percentages may be a function of their high-risk inner city sample.

Cross-Sectional Research

Most research studies of the speech, language, and hearing of children have had, as study samples, groups identified at a single point in time. This body of literature would be impossible to review in its entirety since numerous volumes are published yearly. Therefore, only studies with large samples having specific relevance to the measurements made in the NINCDS Collaborative Perinatal Project will be reviewed.

A classic normative study of articulation, speech sound discrimination, sentence development, and vocabulary was conducted by Templin (1957). Her subjects were 480 white children from three to eight years of age. There were equal numbers of girls and boys (30) in each of eight age subgroups. The children were selected according to their fathers' occupations to be representative of the U.S. urban population: 30% were in the upper socioeconomic group; 70% were in the lower socioeconomic group.

On articulation measures Templin found that three-year-olds had approximately 50% of the accuracy of eight-year-olds over all items tested. Their accuracy of articulation of vowels and diphthongs was about 90%, consonant elements 60%, double-consonant clusters 40%, and triple-consonant clusters 30% of the eight-year-old performance. The children had essentially mature articulation by age eight; that is, 95% correct articulation of the 176 test items. While girls tended to achieve higher scores than boys, there was some inconsistency and

24

the differences were not often statistically significant. Templin found consistent differences in performance favoring the upper over the lower socioeconomic group. She pointed out that differences in IQ found between these two groups should be taken into account when interpreting these data.

Speech sound discrimination by the children also increased with age. Growth was more rapid at the younger ages and approached a ceiling near age eight. Inconsistent sex differences and a few significant differences favoring higher socioeconomic groups were also reported.

Differing rates of growth were found for the various measures of sentence development. Length of utterance for three-year-olds was 55% and grammatical accuracy was about 67% of that of the eight-year-olds, but at age eight both length of utterance and grammatical accuracy were still increasing. Recognition vocabulary showed a more substantial increment with age than did usage vocabulary. Sex differences were quite inconsistent, but there were consistent differences favoring subjects in the upper socioeconomic level on measures of sentence development and vocabulary.

The Peabody Picture Vocabulary Test (PPVT), Form B (Dunn, 1965), which was part of the 8YR speech, language, and hearing test battery of the NINCDS Collaborative Perinatal Project, was standardized on 4012 White children from two years six months to 18 years of age. The manual presents mean raw scores from 20.23, SD = 8.54, at the youngest age, to 110.57, SD = 14.77, for the oldest. At the age level seven years six months to eight years five months (the interval closest to the age range in the present study) the mean raw score was 65.92 and the standard deviation was 8.69. A large number of studies investigating the reliability and validity of the PPVT have found relatively high correlations between forms, between test and retest scores, and with various measures of intelligence. Although research studies have used the PPVT with Black children, there are, unfortunately, no standardization norms for them.

The Illinois Test of Psycholinguistic Abilities: Experimental Edition (ITPA) (McCarthy and Kirk, 1963) was standardized on 700 White children from Decatur, Illinois. Children had IQs between 80 and 120 and were distributed by age into 14 groups ranging from 2.5 to nine years. A broad spectrum of socioeconomic groups was represented. The split-half reliability for the total ITPA was .99. The Auditory-Vocal Automatic subtest, which was administered as a part of the 8YR speech, language, and hearing examination of the NINCDS Collaborative Perinatal Project, produced a split-half reliability coefficient of .95. It yielded a mean of 16.44 (SD = 3.45) for Males and a mean of 16.60 (SD = 3.66) for Females in the eight-year-old subgroup. A test of significance demonstrated no substantial differences between Males and Females. The correlation between social class, as measured by the breadwinner's occupation, and the Auditory-Vocal Automatic subtest was .02.

Eagles et al. (1963, 1967) reported on hearing sensitivity and related factors, including ear disease, in a representative group of 4078 children between the ages of five and 14 years selected from public and private schools in Pittsburgh, Pennsylvania. The sex distribution was approximately equal and there were 68.2% White and 31.8% non-White children in the study population. Examinations of the ears, nose, and throat were accomplished by three otolaryngologists who used standardized methods and forms. Four trained audiometric technicians determined the pure-tone threshold for each child at 250 Hz, 500 Hz, 1000 Hz, 2000 Hz, 4000 Hz, 6000 Hz, and 8000 Hz using the American Standard Reference Zero (ASA 1951). Additional information on each child was obtained from the parents and recorded on a medical history form.

They found that mean and median hearing levels were more sensitive than audiometric zero and that variations in hearing levels increased with each increase in frequency. In fact, 75% of the children had hearing levels more sensitive than audiometric zero and over 5% more sensitive than −5 dB. There was less than 1 dB difference on the average between ears. Girls had more sensitive hearing than boys except at 250 Hz, but the differences were quite small and there were no consistent differences between White and non-White children. There appeared to be an increase in sensitivity from age five to 12 to 13 years of age, followed by a slight drop in sensitivity at 14 to 15 years of age. The most important factors associated with hearing sensitivity were earaches and ear discharge.

Weber, McGovern, and Zink (1967) reported on 1000 children with hearing loss identified by the Colorado Hearing Conservation Program during the years 1960 through 1965. Their population was composed of 62% Males and 38% Females identified between the ages of three and 16+ years as having a loss. Almost 40% of the cases had conductive losses, 52.5% had sensorineural losses (of which 31% had only a 4000 Hz drop-off), 5.6% had mixed losses, and 1.9% had functional losses. While incidence remained at 3% of the whole study population over the five-year period, the severity of the losses was reduced.

Because past research involved various methodologies and restricted samples, data on speech and hearing have not been consistent. Consequently, the validity of these data has been questioned and they have been of limited usefulness in planning services. Therefore, a National Speech and Hearing Survey (Hull et al., 1971) was designed and data were collected in 1968 and 1969. A sampling

procedure using three stratifications was developed which provided for the random selection of 38,884 public school children in grades one through 12 to be tested for speech and hearing. The speech evaluation consisted of ratings of performance by the children on two types of responses: single words and contextual speech samples. The adult general American dialect pattern was used as the standard for a three-point scale. Bilateral pure-tone air conduction thresholds (ISO 1964) were determined for each child at 500 Hz, 1000 Hz, 2000 Hz, 3000 Hz, and 4000 Hz. When hearing levels differed by more than 40 dB between the child's two ears at any frequency, masking was used and thresholds were reestablished for the poorer ear at all frequencies. Only 0.81% of the hearing evaluations and 0.21% of the speech evaluations were considered unreliable; thus, the data analyses were based on 38,802 speech evaluations and 38,568 hearing evaluations.

The preliminary analyses indicated that articulation performance improved with increasing grade level of the child. Only 2% of the total population was rated as demonstrating "extreme deviation" from the adult general American dialect. Girls were rated higher than boys in each of the 12 grades. Further analyses were proposed for investigating the apparent grade and sex differences.

Analysis of the hearing data indicated a trend toward better hearing as grade level increased. No differences were apparent between ears or sexes at the various grades, except that Males showed a higher percentage of left ear "abnormalities" at 3000 Hz and 4000 Hz.

Previously it was pointed out that there is a paucity of large-sample research in speech, language, and hearing. The NINCDS Collaborative Perinatal Project provided unique opportunities to gather information on children's communicative abilities at two different times in their lives, and to relate these data to a host of physical, social, and behavioral variables. The associations between these antecedents and the SLH characteristics will be the substance of chapters to follow.

References

1. Bierman, J.M., Siegal, E., French, F.E., and Connor, A. The community impact of handicaps of perinatal or natal origin. *Publ. Health Rep.* 78:839–855, 1963.
2. Bierman, J.M., Siegal, E., French, F.E., and Simonian, K. Analyses of the outcome of all pregnancies in a community. *Am. J. Obst. Gynecol.* 91:37–45, 1965.
3. Bordley, J.E., and Hardy, J.B. A hearing survey on preschool children. *Trans. Am. Acad. Opthalmol. Otolaryngol.* 76:349–354, 1972.
4. Broman, S.H., Nichols, P.L., and Kennedy, W.A. *Preschool IQ: Prenatal and Early Developmental Correlates.* Hillsdale, New Jersey: Lawrence Erlbaum Associates, 1975.
5. Butler, N.R., and Alberman, E., Eds. *Perinatal Problems.* London: Livingstone, 1969.
6. Butler, N.R., and Bonham, D.G. *Perinatal Mortality.* London: Livingstone, 1963.
7. Davie, R., Butler, N.R., and Goldstein, H. *From Birth to Seven.* London: Livingstone, 1972.
8. Dunn, L.M. *Peabody Picture Vocabulary Test Manual.* Circle Pines, Minnesota: American Guidance Service, 1965.
9. Eagles, E.L., Wishik, S.M., Doerfler, L.G., Melnick, W., and Levine, H.S. Hearing sensitivity and hearing factors in children. *Laryngoscope* Monograph Suppl., 1963.
10. Eagles, E.L., Wishik, S.M. and Doerfler, L.G. Hearing sensitivity and ear disease in children. *Laryngoscope* Monograph Suppl., 1967.
11. French, F.E., and Bierman, J.M. Probabilities of fetal mortality. *Publ. Health Rep.* 77:835–847, 1962.
12. French, F.E., Connor, A., Bierman, J.M., Simonian, K.R., and Smith, R.S. Congenital and acquired handicaps of ten-year-olds—Report of a follow-up study, Kauai, Hawaii. *Am. J. Public Health* 58:1388–1395, 1968.
13. Hull, F.M., Mielke, P.W., Timmons, R.J., and Willeford, J.A. The national speech and hearing survey: Preliminary results. *ASHA* 13:501–509, 1971.
14. McCarthy, J.J., and Kirk, S.A. *The Construction, Standardization and Statistical Characteristics of the Illinois Test of Psycholinguistic Abilities. Experimental Edition.* Urbana, Illinois: University of Illinois Press, 1963.
15. Niswander, K.R., and Gordon, M. *The Women and Their Pregnancies.* Philadelphia: W.B. Saunders, 1972.
16. Pringle, M.L.K., Butler, N.R., and Davie, R. *11,000 Seven-Year-Olds.* London: Longmans, 1966.
17. Templin, M.C. *Certain Language Skills in Children.* Minneapolis: University of Minnesota Press, 1957.
18. Weber, H.J., McGovern, F.J., and Zink, D. An evaluation of 1000 children with hearing loss. *J. Speech Hear. Disord.* 32:343–354, 1967.
19. Werner, E., Simonian, K., Bierman, J.M., and French, F.E. Cumulative effect of perinatal complications and deprived environment on physical intellectual, and social development of preschool children. *Pediatrics* 39:490–505, 1967.
20. Yerushalmy, J., Bierman, J.M., Kemp, D., Connor, A., and French, F.E. Longitudinal studies of pregnancy on the Island of Kauai, Hawaii—analysis of previous reproductive history. *Am. J. Obst. Gynecol.* 71:80–96, 1956.

## CHAPTER 3

The Examinations of Speech, Language, and Hearing

Part A
Description of the Three Year Examination

Warren H. Fay, Ph.D.

The 3YR Speech, Language, and Hearing Examination was composed of a series of subtests, each designed to test a specific area: Language Reception, Language Expression, Hearing, Speech Mechanism, Speech Production, and Auditory Memory. The following is a brief description of the examination. A sample of the test forms (PS 10 to 17) and the manual for its administration are included in Appendix 1.

The Language Reception subtest was designed to determine whether the child had the ability to comprehend spoken commands and spoken questions as indicated through nonoral responses. An alternative group of items, described in the manual, was provided for further testing of the child who failed the subtest. For the first part of the subtest, Identification of Familiar Objects, the examiner requested the child to identify four toys: car, box, flag, and man. The second part, Understanding Action Words, involved five requested actions with these toys (for example, "Pick up the man," or "Shake the box"). The final part was Understanding Words Indicating Space Relationships and Direction; here the requests involved a different set of toys (table, box, truck, cat, and cup) and more complex imperatives (for example, "Put the cat in the box," "Turn the cup upside down/over"). In order to achieve a pass score on the first subitem, three of the four objects must have been identified correctly; on the other subitems, three of the five commands had to be executed correctly to be considered a pass.

The Language Expression subtest was composed of two parts plus an alternative section administered to children failing both sections of the main subtest. The first portion required verbal identification of five familiar objects: chair, scissors, dog, key, button. Four correct identifications were required for a pass. The second part, Use of Phrases or Sentences, was the examiner's (somewhat subjective) evaluation of the child's utterances which were collected and recorded through the use of the objects, pictures, and other dialogue throughout the examination. The checklist (pass or fail) covered sentence length, sentence structure, relevance, word order, and use of pronouns. To pass, a child needed to obtain a positive rating on four of the five items.

The Hearing subtest also had two sections. The Spondaic Word Test involved the child's repetition or identification of tape-recorded lists of spondees delivered sound field at two loudness levels (high and low)* using a specially designed loudspeaker and Wollensak tape-recorder system. After passing a high list, the child was given one or more ten-word lists at the low level. Any five consecutive or any seven of the ten words in a low list correctly repeated or identified by point-ing to pictures rated a pass. A pure-tone audiometric screening at 20 dB hearing level (ASA 1951) was used for the second part of the hearing subtest. Each ear was tested at 500, 1000, and 2000 Hz. To pass, either ear required adequate responses at all three frequencies.

For the Speech Mechanism subtest, the examiner demonstrated a series of lip and tongue postures with instruction to the child to imitate. Lip retraction and protrusion and tongue protrusion, lateralization, and elevation were tested in this manner. These items were scored pass or other, with an additional checklist for indicating specific deficiencies or abnormalities. Pass was defined as the ability of the child to perform the desired movement. This subtest also included an examination of the soft palate performed by examining structure and function during an elicited "ah" sound. Scoring was essentially the same as for lip and tongue movements. The last item of the speech mechanism examination was a test of oral diadochokinesis. Following the examiner's model, the child was to produce at least three repetitions per second of "buh" (lips) and "tuh" (tongue). Scoring for diadochokinesis consisted of ratings of pass, unsustained, or other.

The area of Speech Production was comprised of assessments of voice, articulation, intelligibility, and fluency. Clinical judgment was exercised in the evaluation of pitch, loudness, and quality of voice.

Articulation was assessed through imitation following the examiner's instructions: "I am going to say some words, and I want you to say them right after me." Sixty phonemes embedded in a list of 34 single-syllable test words were judged either correct, incorrect, or no response. The word list was compiled by Dr. Mildred Templin specifically for this examination. Scoring was as follows:

1. Vowels and diphthongs
   Normal   : 14 or more correct
   Suspect : 10–13

---

* Meter setting HI was equivalent to 72 dB over one Microbar at a distance of three feet as measured with a sound pressure level meter. This was equivalent to a moderate conversational voice (approximately 58 dB re normal speech-hearing threshold). The LO setting reduced output by 30 dB to the level of a very quiet voice (approximately 28 dB re normal speech-hearing threshold).

Abnormal: 9 or less
2. Initial consonants
   Normal   : 15 or more correct
   Suspect : 11–14
   Abnormal: 10 or less
3. Final consonants
   Normal   : 11 or more correct
   Suspect : 6–10
   Abnormal: 5 or less

The stated purpose of the intelligibility judgment was to assess the child's contextual speech as observed throughout the examination as well as in general conversation with a youngster. The performance was ranked on a five-point scale: (1) no difficulty in understanding, (2) some difficulty, (3) considerable difficulty, (4) unintelligible verbalization, and (5) no speech, plus an option for other. This procedure included also an unscored checklist of contributions to the impairment of intelligibility (for example, articulation, voice, rhythm, and so forth).

Fluency of speech production also involved a checklist based upon total performance. Dysfluent events and struggle behavior were each assessed quantitatively as none, some observed, and many observed.

Auditory memory for digits and nonsense syllables was the final subtest of the examination. For each portion (digits and syllables) four series were presented at the two-unit level and four at the three-unit level. First, the child was to repeat "4-2" following the examiner's model presentation at one digit per second (spoken with the aid of a stopwatch). Following this, the second pair ("8-5") was given. After the pairs were completed, the four triplets (for example, "3-6-2") were given in like manner. These, in turn, were followed by the pairs of nonsense syllables (for example,

"poo-bah"). Finally, the three-syllable series was presented. Correct repetition of one set from each series of four was required for passing the series. Thus, four scores of either pass or fail were obtained; one each for two digits, three digits, two syllables, and three syllables.

The concluding section of the examination was an unscored checklist of physical and behavioral observations. Included was a statement of health on the day of the examination and a series of observable physical anomalies of the head, face, ears, eyes, mouth, hands, arms, and legs. Both structural and functional anomalies were listed for each area. The list for the presence of unusual behavior included purposeless hand motions, unusual posturing, excessive crying or laughing, hyperactivity, hypoactivity, withdrawn behavior, perseveration, echolalia, and a lack or limitation of spontaneous communication.

The original instrument was designed to include individual and global summaries in each major area according to a three-point scale: normal, suspect, abnormal (see Appendix 1). These summaries and the rules governing them were designed primarily for clinical assessment and were not used in the analytic treatment of the data. Also, it became clear after the test was put into use that the standard pass or fail approach employed was not entirely appropriate for three-year-olds. A third option, inadequate, proved necessary for children who would not or could not perform sufficiently to allow a qualitative judgment of their performance. While the test as a whole had a classification for inadequacy, subsequent instructions allowed for designating some subtests as inadequate while preserving the bulk of the examination as adequate.

The Examinations of Speech Language, and Hearing

Part B

Description of the Eight Year Examination

Paul J. LaBenz, Sc.D.

Communicative proficiency was evaluated at the age of eight years by means of a battery of tests called the Final Speech, Language, and Hearing Examination. The examination covered five major aspects of communication designated as areas: Hearing, Language Comprehension, Language Expression, Speech Mechanism, and Speech Production. Each area included one or more subareas and these, in turn, were explored with one or more tests or items. For example, the area of Language Comprehension was composed of tests of auditory verbal comprehension, reading, and morphology. The subarea of auditory verbal comprehension was explored with three tests: Word Identification (vocabulary), Orientation (temporal and spatial), and Understanding a Story. Efforts were made to use existing standardized measures whenever possible. In a number of instances performance was evaluated by using unstandardized techniques and the examiner's judgment as necessary. The methods used at the 8YR level are described briefly in this section in the usual order of administering them. Copies of the examination manual and the record forms (PS 40 to 45) are included in Appendix 1.

The level of hearing was determined for each ear separately by means of a calibrated audiometer in a sound-treated room. Ears having hearing levels of 20 dB or poorer, measured by air conduction, were checked also by bone conduction audiometry. Discrimination for monosyllabic word lists also was tested for each ear. In addition, a monaural screening check was made for Abnormal Auditory Adaptation. Finally, although it is not considered a test of hearing in the usual sense, lists of digits and syllables were used to test auditory memory.

Pure-tone air conduction audiometry was performed monaurally to determine the hearing level of each ear. Tones were presented by earphones in the order 1000, 2000, 4000, 8000, 1000, 500, 250 Hz. Initial tonal presentations were given at 30 dB and increased in 10 dB increments if necessary to reach audibility, then reduced by 10 dB decrements to the point of inaudibility. Thereafter, tones were increased by 5 dB and then decreased by 10 dB until a threshold was determined. Response to at least two of three ascending presentations was accepted as a measurement of threshold. If one ear was reported by the child or his parent to be poorer than the other, the better ear was tested first. Otherwise, the right ear was tested first if the child's birthdate fell on an even-numbered date, and the left ear first if the birthdate was an odd number. Whenever a disparity of 40 dB or more was found between ears at any frequency, the hearing at that frequency was measured while masking the better ear with white noise. Masking levels usually were limited to the range 60 to 80 dB SPL. Audiometers were periodically checked to assure that they were within calibration specifications re ISO 1964. Numerical values for hearing levels at each of the prescribed frequencies were marked on a specially prepared form (PS 40, Appendix 1) together with

masking levels used and the examiner's judgment regarding the adequacy (reliability) of the test.

Bone conduction tests were administered whenever the air conduction hearing level was 20 dB or poorer at any frequency in the range 500 to 4000 Hz. The purpose of the test was to establish the presence of a sensorineural component. Bone conduction testing was done at all frequencies (500, 1000, 2000, 4000 Hz) even though the 20 dB criterion level might have been reached at only one of these frequencies. However, the other ear was not tested by bone conduction unless the 20 dB air conduction level was reached or exceeded in that ear also. The vibrator was applied to the mastoid region of the side to be tested and held there by means of a spring headband. The nontest ear was covered by an earphone through which white noise masking was delivered. The same method of ascending tone presentations was used as for air conduction testing. Masking was introduced at 60 dB SPL and was increased to 70 dB (and to 80 dB when considered necessary) to check for shifts in the threshold responses. Results and comments were entered on the record form as with air conduction testing.

Abnormal Auditory Adaptation, as an indicator of sensory dysfunction, was checked in each ear separately by using a tone of 4000 Hz presented 20 dB higher than the threshold previously measured by air conduction. For convenience, this check was made immediately after pure-tone air conduction testing and before the earphones were moved. The child was instructed to hold up his hand as long as he could hear the sustained tone. If he continued to hear 4000 Hz for 60 seconds (timed), he passed the test. If he failed to hear 4000 Hz for 60 seconds, he was presumed to be exhibiting at least 20 dB of adaptation and failed the test. He was then tested in the same ear with 500 Hz at 20 dB above the measured threshold for that frequency. The criterion for passing at 500 Hz was, similarly, the ability to hear the tone for 60 seconds. Whenever a child lowered his hand before 60 seconds had elapsed, he was asked whether or not he was sure, so as to rule out lapses of attention as a performance factor. Whenever a child continued to hold up his hand after cessation of either of the tones, 4000 Hz or 500 Hz, the test was considered inadequate because of probable inattention. He was then given a second opportunity to perform before a judgment of pass, fail, or inadequate was made.

Speech discrimination was tested by means of lists of 25 PBK monosyllabic words recorded on tape and presented monaurally by earphones. Five sample words, for demonstration purposes, preceded the test lists. Lists were presented at a level 30 dB above the previously measured air conduction threshold at 1000 Hz. Adjustment in the level of presentation was permitted, if required, for easy audibility. A calibration tone of 1000 Hz was recorded at the beginning of the word lists. The words were spoken by an experienced male speaker with a general American accent and had been recorded with the use of a VU monitor. One of four available lists was presented to each ear. A value of 4% was assigned to each word repeated correctly by the child. The level of presentation, the discrimination score, and the list numbers were entered on the form provided (PS 40, Appendix 1).

The ability to repeat sequences of spoken digits and nonsense syllables was tested under the designation of Auditory Memory. The digit series ranged in length from pairs to groups of ten; nonsense syllable series ranged from two to six in length. Two different test items were presented at each series length. The child was instructed to repeat the sequences which had been spoken by the examiner at the rate of one digit or one syllable per second. The score earned was the numerical length of the longest series repeated correctly. Correct repetition of both items at the child's highest level of recall (longest series repeated) earned an extra half-point bonus. For example, both items repeated correctly at the eight-digit level was scored 8.5 rather than 8.0. Verbatim responses as well as the numerical score were recorded on special forms (PS 40, Appendix 1).

Language Comprehension Area

The Language Comprehension portion of the test battery was composed of three subareas which dealt with Auditory Verbal Comprehension, Reading, and Linguistic Morphology. The first subarea, Auditory Verbal Comprehension, was assessed with respect to vocabulary development, the ability to understand verbally expressed concepts about time and space, and the ability to understand a simple story. Vocabulary development was evaluated by the use of the Peabody Picture Vocabulary Test (PPVT), Form B, (Dunn, 1965). The child responded to each word spoken by the examiner by pointing to the drawing which correctly represented the word in a set of four drawings. Basal and ceiling scores were determined in a standardized manner. The examiner entered on a special form (PS 41) the number of errors made, the raw score, and the vocabulary age taken from tables provided in the manual. As with each of the tests in the total battery, the examiner rated the test as adequate or not adequate by checking the appropriate box on the form.

The child's verbal concepts of time, spatial direction, and laterality were checked by means of twelve sentences requiring short verbal answers. This unstandardized set of items was termed Orientation. Three sentences were taken from the Detroit Test of Learning Aptitude (Baker and Leland, 1959), three from the Hawthorn Center Concepts Test (unpublished), and four from the Benton Laterality Test (Benton, 1959); the remaining two were devised by a consultant group. The child's answers were recorded verbatim (PS 41). His score was simply the number of correct answers given.

Auditory Verbal Comprehension was further examined by reading to the child a short story consisting of a single paragraph, then questioning him regarding its content. Story number II of the Durrell-Sullivan Reading Capacity and Achievement Tests (Durrell and Sullivan, 1945) was used for this purpose. The score achieved was the number of correct answers given to five questions about the story. Grade and age equivalents were derived from the raw score and recorded on the test form (PS 41).

Reading skill was assessed with the Gray Oral Reading Test, Form A (Gray, 1967). Six graded paragraphs were used to measure the ease and accuracy of reading performance at levels ranging from the first grade to the seventh. Comprehension of paragraph content was not measured. The examiner timed the child's reading and noted the number and types of errors made in each paragraph. Scores for each paragraph were obtained from a table entered with the time and error score. The total score for reading was the sum of the paragraph scores. By means of separate tables for boys and girls, the total score was converted to a grade score. All of this information, including a tabulation of errors by types, was set down on record forms (PS 41).

Reading comprehension was screened by asking the child to read, silently, the first paragraph of the Durrell-Sullivan Reading Capacity and Achievement Tests (Durrell and Sullivan, 1945). A sample paragraph was used for instruction before the test paragraph was read. Response was made by the child's marking the correct answer in five multiple choice statements about the paragraph. Age and grade equivalents were obtained from a conversion table. A score of five indicated

achievement at the ceiling level of grade 2.5 (age 7.4 years).

Knowledge of grammatical rules governing some plurals and common tenses was tested by the Auditory-Vocal Automatic subtest of the Illinois Test of Psycholinguistic Abilities, Experimental Edition (ITPA) (McCarthy and Kirk, 1963). This subtest consists of 22 test items of the sentence completion type. The number of correct responses was summed to obtain a raw score. This score was recorded on the test form (PS 41) together with an equivalent age level, ranging from 2 years 4 months through 9 years 6 months, derived from a table provided in the manual.

Language Expression Area

Expressive Language capability was evaluated by two means. The first was a rating by the examiner of the child's ability to discourse within a structured situation. The child was told that he would hear a short story which he would be asked to relate to the examiner afterward. A set of three sequential line drawings, illustrating the story, was placed before the child for his inspection; it was left in his sight while the examiner read a brief narrative about a boy and his dog, requiring less than a minute to present. The child's recounting of the story was rated on three-point scales for sequence, elaboration, relevance, and grammar. The total number of concepts mentioned was recorded also. In addition, an overall rating of Connected Discourse was made by the examiner. This was based on the clinical impression as to whether the performance was normal, suspect, or abnormal. The child's language expression throughout the entire testing period was taken into account when making this rating. The results were noted on the special form provided (PS 42).

Another aspect of expressive language was checked by obtaining a sample of the child's ability to Write to Dictation. A nonstandard set of four numerals, four letters of the alphabet, four short words, and two phrases of three words each was used. These simple test items were spoken slowly by the examiner and were written on a special form (PS 42) by the child. All items written legibly without error were marked as passes. Any item was scored as a fail if illegible or if it contained an error such as a reversal, substitution, addition, omission, or a transposition in sequence. Passes were summed by sets and in total to obtain a numerical score.

Speech Mechanism Area

Examination was made of the oral mechanism for speech in order to detect structural and functional deviations of the lips, tongue, and soft palate. The child was asked to imitate the examiner in performing retraction and protrusion of the lips, midline and lateral protrusion of the tongue, and elevation of the tongue to the alveolar ridge. The soft palate was observed for vigorous and symmetrical movement while the child repeated the sound "ah." Each of the movements performed was rated pass or fail. Structural abnormalities also were noted and recorded by the examiner on the test form (PS 43). Notation was made as to whether or not concomitant movements occurred during the child's attempts at imitating any of the required lip and tongue motions. A concomitant movement was any lateral or backward movement of the head or any facial grimace which occurred while attempting to imitate the examiner. Ratings of pass or fail were made independently of concomitant movements.

Speech Production Area

Speech Production was evaluated with respect to the rate and fluency of connected speech, the characteristics of voice, the intelligibility of speech, and articulation. The first three of these subareas were rated by the examiner; the last, Articulation, was scored (PS 44, Appendix 1).

Examiners were asked to judge the rate of the child's speech observed throughout the entire examination battery. No specific tasks were imposed and no specific procedures were prescribed. The rate at which the child habitually produced speech sounds while talking was rated either as adequate, too fast, too slow, or irregular. If none of these ratings could be given, it was marked "other" with explanatory comments by the examiner.

Dysfluencies such as hesitations, repetitions, and prolongations were noted if they occurred. Unusual effort in speaking was noted and recorded as struggle behavior. Both dysfluency and struggle behavior were rated independently and, depending upon the frequency of their occurrence, were recorded as none, some, or many.

Voice characteristics likewise were observed during the course of the entire examination. Ratings were given for pitch (adequate, too high, too low, monotonous, or other as described) and for loudness (adequate, too soft, too loud, or other as described). Also noted were the quality of phonation (adequate, breathy, hoarse, or other as described) and the quality of resonance (adequate, hypernasal, hyponasal, or other as described). No overall rating was made.

Intelligibility ratings also were based on the examiner's impression of the child's speech observed throughout the examination, rather than on the use of specific procedures. As in the 3YR examination, speech intelligibility was ranked on a five-point scale: (1) no difficulty in understanding, (2) some difficulty, (3) considerable difficulty, (4) unintelligible verbalizations, and (5) no speech, as well as "other." A checklist of speech deviations which contribute to impairment of intelligibility was provided (PS 44) for use by the examiner as a descriptive aid not intended for scoring.

Articulatory skills were tested by means of the Screening Test of the Templin-Darley Test of Articulation (Templin and Darley, 1960). This instrument consists of 50 pictures on 16 plates which the child was directed to identify verbally. Correct responses and errors were entered on the scoring sheet (PS 44) according to the phoneme or blend being tested and its position in the test word. The number of correctly articulated phonemes and consonant clusters constituted the score for the test. The performance was rated also on the basis of tentative norms as normal (score of 45 to 50), suspect (score of 40 to 44), or abnormal (score of 39 or less).

The final form (PS 45) in the examination battery was a checklist which the examiner used to note physical anomalies and behavioral peculiarities observed at test. Both functional and structural deviations were indicated. Observations pertained to the head, face, ears, eyes, mouth, and extremities. Unusual conditions of health on the day of the examination and the presence of prostheses (glasses, hearing aids, and so forth) were noted. Behavioral aberrations were indicated on a separate checklist (PS 45). The checklists were solely for descriptive purposes and were not scored.

Tests within the various areas and subareas of the examination were rated individually as to adequacy (reliability) and were scored separately. No overall score was calculated for the total battery of tests. Test findings were combined in a number of ways, however, in the analytic treatment of the data.

References

1. Baker, H.J., and Leland, B. *Detroit Tests of Learning Aptitude. Examiner's Manual.* Indianapolis, Indiana: Bobbs-Merrill, 1959.

2. Benton, A.L. *Right-Left Discrimination and Finger Localization.* New York: Paul B. Hoeber, 1959.

3. Dunn, L.M. *Peabody Picture Vocabulary Test Manual.* Circle Pines, Minnesota: American Guidance Service, 1965.

4. Durrell, D.D., and Sullivan, H.B. *Durrell-Sullivan Reading Capacity and Achievement Tests.* New York: Harcourt Brace & World, 1945.

5. Gray, W.S. *Gray Oral Reading Tests.* Indianapolis, Indiana: Bobbs-Merrill, 1967.

6. McCarthy, J.J., and Kirk, S.A. *The Construction, Standardization and Statistical Characteristics of the Illinois Test of Psycholinguistic Abilities. Experimental Edition.* Urbana: University of Illinois Press, 1963.

7. Templin, M.C., and Darley, F.L. *The Templin-Darley Test of Articulation.* Iowa City: University of Iowa Press, 1960.

8. The Hawthorn Center Concepts Test. Unpublished. The Hawthorn Center, Northville, Michigan.

## CHAPTER 4

The Sample

Paul J. LaBenz, Sc.D.

The NINCDS Collaborative Perinatal Project Population

The population sample from which the Speech, Language, and Hearing (SLH) study subsamples ultimately were drawn consisted of 55,908 pregnancies (Niswander and Gordon, 1972). Medical centers in 12 geographical locations cooperated in providing this sample. These collaborating units were located in urban areas. Six were in the northeastern states, four in the south, one in the north-central area, and one in the west. All but one (Buffalo) drew from a pool of clinic patients. It is not surprising, considering the sources, that the NINCDS Collaborative Perinatal Project (NCPP) sample had heavy representation at the lower end of the socioeconomic ladder and disproportionately large numbers of Blacks and Puerto Ricans as compared with the U.S. population at large. However, a sample having these characteristics provided a wide spectrum of obstetrical problems and was considered highly suitable to the aims of the NCPP study, although, clearly, not useful for determining prevalence figures which would be applicable to the general population.

Selection Procedures

Systematic procedures were used to select patients for the study. Several institutions selected all eligible patients, others selected every nth case. Minor adjustments in sampling ratios were made in several instances to bring the sample selected into line with numerical expectations and study capabilities. Eligibility for registration was fairly uniform from institution to institution and, in general, was based upon considerations such as admittance to the hospital clinic, geographical constraints, and the likelihood of availability for follow-up studies. Registration for inclusion in the NCPP study began in January through March of 1959 at eight locations, the following October in another (Tennessee), in March of 1960 at two others (New Orleans and Providence), and at the last (Buffalo) in October 1960. Registration was completed at all institutions at the end of December 1965 except for Columbia-Presbyterian Hospital (New York), which terminated registration on April 30, 1963, and Johns Hopkins Hospital (Baltimore), which terminated December 31, 1964. The last child was born in the NCPP study in September 1966.

The sizes of the sampling frames and of the samples selected by each institution are shown in Table 4-1. The sampling ratios used are given as averages to take into account certain small changes over time at several institutions. Ethnic groups are given in percentages. Institutions are listed in the order of initial registration. Monthly checks were made to assure that sampling was systematic and representative of the planned sampling frame characteristics.

Boston Lying-In Hospital contributed the largest number of cases to the NCPP sample, most of them White. All eligible clinic patients were registered in the study. The Children's Hospital Medical Center (Boston) performed follow-up studies on the children of registrants. Exclusions from the study included unwed mothers planning to relinquish their infants for adoption, as well as so-called "walk-ins" who presented for delivery without adequate prenatal data.

Walk-ins were also excluded by all of the other collaborating institutions.

Eligible registrants at the Medical College of Virginia (Richmond) comprised all White patients and, at various times, from one-fourth to two-thirds of Black patients who lived within certain geographical limits. The initial limits extended to a 50-mile radius of the city of Richmond but later were reduced to the city and two adjacent counties, then eventually to the city itself. White welfare cases, intended adoptions, and institutionalized wards of the state were excluded from the sample. Three-fourths of the registrants were Black and the rest, almost without exception, were White.

The Pennsylvania Hospital (Philadelphia) provided the second largest group of study cases, predominantly Black patients. Virtually all eligible patients were registered in the study. Only unregistered emergency deliveries and those intending to deliver elsewhere were excluded, in addition to the usual walk-in exclusion. Children were followed at the Children's Hospital of Philadelphia.

The sampling frame of Johns Hopkins Hospital (Baltimore) consisted of all clinic patients living within metropolitan limits. Sampling ranged from 20% to 40% except for the last year of registration, during which 100% of patients were registered for study. Transients and patients referred for care to county clinics were excluded. Three-fourths of the cases were Black, about one-fourth White.

Columbia-Presbyterian Medical Center (New York) registered one of every fifth and, for a time, every sixth of all clinic patients but later limited registrants to those who resided in Manhattan or the Bronx. Problems developed in following registrants because of housing dislocations related to urban renewal. Registration was terminated in April 1963. The relatively small sample contained a large proportion of Puerto Rican patients, about 30%. There was about the same

Table 4-1

Sample size by institution* and ethnic group in the NINCDS Collaborative Perinatal Project (NCPP) population.

Institution	Number of Cases		Ethnic Group of Selected Sample (%)				Average Sampling
	Eligible	Selected	White	Black	Puerto Rican	Other	Ratio
Boston Lying-In Hospital	13,137	13,137	89.0	9.6	0.1	1.3	1:1.0
Medical College of Virginia, Richmond	4,660	3,250	26.1	73.7	†	0.2	1:1.4
Pennsylvania Hospital, Philadelphia	10,457	10,315	9.4	87.3	3.2	0.1	1:1.0
Johns Hopkins Hospital, Baltimore	8,573	3,774	23.4	76.4	†	0.2	1:2.3
Columbia-Presbyterian Medical Center, New York	9,852	2,235	28.8	40.6	27.8	2.8	1:4.4
University of Minnesota Hospital, Minneapolis	3,468	3,275	94.1	0.7	0.1	5.1	1:1.1
New York Medical College, New York	27,380	4,709	6.3	34.1	59.2	0.4	1:5.8
University of Oregon Medical School, Portland	6,327	3,255	71.1	26.7	†	2.2	1:1.9
University of Tennessee College of Medicine, Memphis	20,552	3,553	0.7	99.3	—	—	1:5.8
Providence Lying-In Hospital	6,300	2,851	74.4	21.9	0.2	3.5	1:2.2
Charity Hospital, New Orleans	18,890	2,590	—	100.0	—	—	1:7.3
Children's Hospital, Buffalo	2,964	2,964	96.4	2.5	0.5	0.6	1:1.0
Total	**132,560**	**55,908**	**25,703**	**25,837**	**3,795**	**573**	
%			(46.0)	(46.2)	(6.8)	(1.0)	

*Listed in the order of initial registration.
†Less than 0.1%.

proportion of Whites and about 40% were Black.

The University of Minnesota Hospital (Minneapolis) registered virtually all clinic patients for study. When registration began, only those women currently married and less than 246 days advanced in pregnancy were eligible. These constraints were dropped within the first year and, other than walk-ins, the only exclusions were those few patients with linguistic difficulties. The study sample was over 90% White.

The sample collected at New York Medical College (New York) contained the highest proportion as well as the largest group of Puerto Ricans. About 60% of the study sample was Puerto Rican, as compared with some 34% Black and 6% White. The sampling frame included all clinic patients except for walk-ins and patients presenting for delivery only. Initial sampling of ten cases per week was increased in the second year to every ninth case and gradually reached a ratio of one in six.

The University of Oregon Medical School (Portland) gradually imposed ge-

39

ographic constraints upon its sampling frame and adjusted its sampling ratios accordingly. The earliest sampling frame included all clinic patients. Later these were restricted to Portland mailing addresses, then limited to a defined boundary within the county. Sampling ranged from every third case to every other case. Referrals from adoption agencies, wives of medical students, and walk-ins were excluded. The study sample was about 71% White and 27% Black.

The sampling frame at the University of Tennessee College of Medicine (Memphis) included all clinic patients and excluded only walk-ins. Sampling was done on a 10% basis for the first half year but was increased to every seventh case thereafter. The sample was almost entirely Black; less than 1% was White.

At the Providence Lying-In Hospital the sampling frame included all clinic patients except walk-ins. Sampling during the first few months was adjusted to yield a fixed number of cases, based on admission figures from previous weeks. The method was changed to a straight 50% of clinic cases. About three-fourths of the cases were White. The Children's Study Center of Brown University (Providence) followed the children.

Charity Hospital in New Orleans defined its sampling frame as all Black patients living in Orleans Parish and referred to the hospital by either Tulane or Louisiana State Medical Schools. Only walk-ins were excluded. Sampling began on a systematic 10% selection based on hospital record numbers but was increased later to one in eight, then one in six patients. The sample was 100% Black.

The sample collected at the Children's Hospital of Buffalo was unusual in that it consisted entirely of private patients referred by a group of cooperating obstetricians. The group numbered from four to 13 individuals at various times. The sample is almost entirely White. While limitations were placed at the outset on the number of referrals to be registered,

eventually the sample included all eligible cases. In addition to the general exclusion of walk-in patients, exclusions included those women who planned to move away and those who did not intend to deliver at Children's Hospital.

In summary, the NCPP study sample consisted of 55,908 cases systematically selected from a total of 132,560 pregnant women at institutions in 12 geographical locations, mainly in northeastern and southern states. All but about 5% were clinic patients and all lived in urban areas. Approximately 46% of the patients were White, 46% Black, 7% Puerto Rican, and 1% Oriental or other races.

The Speech, Language, and Hearing Study Subsamples

Children registered in the NCPP study were given SLH examinations at two ages. The first battery of tests was administered at the age of three years, the second at eight years. For various reasons, to be mentioned, not all of the NCPP children were tested. Further, the factors which contributed to losses of SLH data did not operate consistently at both ages. As a result, there are three subsamples of children with SLH data. The subsamples consist of those children who were examined only at age three years (3YR), those examined only at eight years (8YR), and those tested at both ages (3YR/8YR). The children who survived to age eight years but were not tested form a fourth group of cases (Non-SLH). It is of interest to examine and compare these groups with respect to certain demographic characteristics. Marked dissimilarities in the composition of the study subsamples and the untested group would, of course, suggest the operation of bias in the selection process. Comparing the SLH groups with the untested group is a more telling exercise than the comparison with the total NCPP population which includes the SLH groups within it.

Selection Procedures

All children registered in the NCPP study were routinely scheduled for SLH tests when they approached the prescribed ages. They were rescheduled for testing as necessary whenever they failed to keep appointments. In spite of systematic efforts to maintain the study sample (by pre-appointment reminders, home visits, and providing transport when needed), some children were not brought to test; others could not be tested within the set age limits. The time limits for testing were fixed at three years plus or minus two months and eight years plus or minus three months. Some tests were done outside these limits when it appeared that parental interest in continued participation in the NCPP study would be jeopardized by foregoing the test. The results of out-of-limits tests were not included in the study data.

Most of the collaborating institutions began to perform the 3YR SLH tests as the children in their respective samples became of age. Some losses of study data resulted from failures to keep appointments and from uncooperative behavior by the children. The greatest loss of 3YR data was caused by difficulties in providing space and staff at Boston and Philadelphia, where the largest numbers of NCPP cases were registered. These two institutions found it necessary to screen their three-year-old children for possible SLH problems and to test only the smaller number who were considered to have SLH deficits. Screening was performed by nonspecialists during home visits. As a result, only 1059 children who were given SLH tests at Boston and 460 who were tested at Philadelphia were available for inclusion in the 3YR group after culling for correctness of age and NCPP registration and completeness of data. Data from these two subsamples were analyzed by the study staff and were examined by a special group of consultants as part of an inquiry into the quality of the total NCPP data base (NINCDS Final Report, 1968). These data were judged suitable for inclusion within the larger SLH study subsamples because the prevalence and types of SLH problems in these subsamples did not differ significantly from those at other NCPP institutions.

The 8YR SLH examination likewise was routinely scheduled for all children upon reaching the prescribed age range. Boston, however, was delayed by problems of space and staff until two years after the first children registered there came of age. At midyear in 1970 the 8YR examination was discontinued for administrative reasons at six of the 12 participating centers. Examinations continued at Children's Medical Center in Boston, Children's Hospital at Buffalo, Johns Hopkins Hospital in Baltimore, and the Universities of Tennessee, Minnesota, and Oregon. The reduction in the size of the 8YR SLH subsample, as compared with the NCPP population, is mainly a reflection of these events.

In addition to the foregoing factors and events which decreased sample sizes and which operated largely beyond control, certain exclusions were applied which worked to reduce further the size of the SLH subsamples. The Puerto Rican, Oriental, and other small ethnic groups were deleted from the SLH study because of probable linguistic biases. Cases registered for special studies and those in unidentified cohorts also were excluded because of the potential presence of unspecifiable conditions. The method used for dealing with inadequate data is described in Chapter 5.

As a result of all these exclusionary effects, the SLH subsample sizes are 19,885 children in the 3YR group and 20,137 children in the 8YR group. A total of 12,464 children received both tests and were designated the 3YR/8YR group. At first glance these groups appear to form an inordinately small proportion of the NCPP population. However, a proper comparison should use, as a base, the number of NCPP children actually available for SLH tests, rather than the total number of pregnancies registered in the NCPP study.

For a variety of reasons, significant numbers of cases were excluded or lost to follow-up. There were 2106 women lost to the study because of moving away, refusing to participate after registration, or for other reasons which resulted in a lack of information on labor, delivery, or pediatric follow-up. An additional 562 pregnancies terminated in fetal deaths, 872 were stillbirths, and 912 children died within the first year of life. Another 147 died before the age of three years and 54 died between three and eight years. The outcome is unknown in 51 cases. Taking only the Whites and Blacks as eligible for SLH study excludes an additional 4368 cases from the other ethnic groups. These exclusions together number 9072 and reduce the NCPP population of children to 46,836 candidates for the SLH study. The proportion of NCPP children in the SLH groups calculated on this residual basis, therefore, changes from 35.6% to 42.5% at 3YR and from 36.0% to 43.07% at 8YR.

Demographic Characteristics

Race and Sex

A child's race was taken to be the same as the mother's race. This was determined by questioning during interview at registration. The numbers of children in the SLH study from each of the collaborating institutions is given in Table 4-2 by type of SLH examination and race. The percentages of Whites and Blacks are also shown.

Striking differences are apparent in the numbers of children contributed to the study by one and another institution, in the numbers included at each age level, and in the racial composition of the institutional subsamples. Racial composition at the institutional level was determined

largely by the characteristics of the populations they served rather than by the selection procedures used by the institutions. Similarly, the numbers of study cases contributed by each were based upon staff and facilities available and, to a lesser extent, resulted from unavoidable delays in starting. These interinstitutional differences in group size and racial proportions, then, are not the likely results of intentional bias in the selection of cases. The statement receives support from the finding that the proportions of Whites and Blacks appear fairly stable when the 3YR subsample is compared with the 8YR and with the 3YR/8YR group, despite dissimilarities in the sizes of these groups at certain of the institutions. There are unexplained discrepancies in the Non-SLH group, particularly at Virginia and Baltimore, where the ratios reverse; but these involve relatively small numbers of cases.

In total, the number of children who attempted the 3YR exam is nearly the same as the number who attempted only the 8YR exam. That these are not the same children, however, is clearly indicated by the finding that the group which attempted both exams, the 3YR/8YR subsample, is only about 60% of the size of the other groups. The proportions of Whites and Blacks show some sharp disparities in the totals for the subsamples. There are, for example, substantially more Blacks (57%) in the 3YR than in the 8YR (50%) subsample. The difference carries into the 3YR/8YR subsample as well (53%), since this group is composed of children who appear in both of the other SLH subsamples. In weighing these disparities, it should be remembered that the proportion of Whites and Blacks in the total NCPP population (Table 4-1) is approximately equal. The most striking racial disproportion occurs in the Non-SLH group, where two-thirds of the children are White. This fact is attributable mainly to subsample losses at Boston which contributed the largest

Table *4-2*

Subsample sizes by institution and race in the speech, language and hearing (SLH) study.

Subsample:	ALL 3YR		ALL 8YR		3YR/8YR		Non-SLH	
Race:	White	Black	White	Black	White	Black	White	Black
Institution	N %	N %	N %	N %	N %	N %	N %	N %
Boston Lying-In Hospital	940 / 89	119 / 11	3,661 / 89	440 / 11	527 / 89	64 / 11	5,297 / 91	528 / 9
Medical College of Virginia, Richmond	330 / 17	1,654 / 83	206 / 23	675 / 77	119 / 19	523 / 81	180 / 67	89 / 33
Pennsylvania Hospital, Philadelphia	37 / 8	423 / 92	196 / 9	2,004 / 91	17 / 6	248 / 94	363 / 16	1,976 / 84
Johns Hopkins Hospital, Baltimore	440 / 18	1,991 / 82	446 / 18	2,097 / 82	339 / 16	1,815 / 84	141 / 60	94 / 40
Columbia-Presbyterian Medical Center, New York	401 / 41	574 / 59	247 / 41	360 / 59	182 / 41	262 / 59	85 / 48	91 / 52
University of Minnesota Hospital, Minneapolis	2,022 / 99	14 / 1	1,987 / 99	10 / 1	1,679 / 99	10 / 1	432 / 99	4 / 1
New York Medical College, New York	126 / 12	903 / 88	18 / 7	224 / 93	16 / 7	199 / 93	110 / 20	427 / 80
University of Oregon Medical School, Portland	1,431 / 69	654 / 31	1,327 / 68	633 / 32	1,125 / 66	576 / 34	367 / 85	63 / 15
University of Tennessee College of Medicine, Memphis	9 / 0	2,619 / 100	9 / 0	2,775 / 100	6 / 0	2,336 / 100	11 / 4	238 / 96
Providence Lying-In Hospital	860 / 72	332 / 28	303 / 73	114 / 27	167 / 74	58 / 26	333 / 85	60 / 15
Charity Hospital, New Orleans	0 / 0	1,972 / 100	0 / 0	613 / 100	0 / 0	493 / 100	0 / 0	243 / 100
Children's Hospital, Buffalo	1,987 / 98	47 / 2	1,748 / 98	44 / 2	1,662 / 98	41 / 2	92 / 99	1 / 1
Totals	8,583 / 43	11,302 / 57	10,148 / 50	9,989 / 50	5,839 / 47	6,625 / 53	7,411 / 66	3,814 / 34
	19,885		20,137		12,464		11,225	

group (23.5%) to the NCPP study, most of whom were White (89%). Of the 7411 Whites in the Non-SLH group (Table 4-2), 5297 were contributed by Boston. This fact can be expected to influence the socioeconomic level and the mean IQ of the Non-SLH group, tending to raise both.

The proportions of Males and Females within SLH subsamples are close to normal expectation. Table 4-3 indicates nearly even splits between sexes, with a slight preponderance of Males, in the totals for each SLH subsample. The sex ratios hold fairly stable within racial groups as well. The Non-SLH group is slightly more disparate than the other groups, but this disparity in sex ratio is not remarkable.

Socioeconomic Status

The socioeconomic status of women registered in the study was indicated by means of an index (Myrianthopoulos and French, 1968) constructed from data obtained at interview. Education, occupation, and family income were used. The index was almost identical with the one devised by the U.S. Bureau of the Census (U.S. Bureau of the Census, 1963).

Table 4-3
Composition of SLH study subsamples by sex and race (%).

	3YR		8YR		3YR/8YR		Non-SLH	
	Male	Female	Male	Female	Male	Female	Male	Female
White	22.3	20.9	25.7	24.7	24.3	22.5	34.5	31.5
Black	28.3	28.5	24.6	25.0	26.6	26.6	17.1	16.9
Total	50.6	49.4	50.3	49.7	50.9	49.1	51.6	48.4
N	19,885		20,137		12,464		11,225	

In the NCPP Socioeconomic Index (SEI), the education of the head of the household was considered. Usually this was the husband unless no husband was present or unless the woman was the main recipient of income, earned or allotted; in this event her education was considered. Scores were derived by using the midpoints of percentile intervals for each educational level obtained from a cumulative distribution of educational levels achieved by heads of households. The scores were rounded and divided by ten to give single digits ranging from zero to nine in five categories.

Family income included all sources of income, even earnings by children. Income scores were derived the same way that education was scored, by rounded midpoints of percentile intervals on a cumulative curve. Scores ranged from zero to ten.

Occupation was that of the head of household or chief wage earner. The occupational classification of the U.S. Bureau of the Census was used. The average levels of income and education were combined for each occupation to yield a score. As with education and income, a cumulative distribution was drawn and midpoints of the percentile intervals were taken as the score of each occupation. Scores ranged from zero to nine.

The SEI was the average of the scores assigned for education, occupation, and income. In some instances of missing data, two scores were averaged. The range of SEI scores extends from zero to 9.5.

The socioeconomic characteristics of the NCPP population were described in some detail by Myrianthopoulos and French (1968) and Broman, Nichols, and Kennedy (1975). These characteristics may be summed briefly as follows:

1. The NCPP population was distributed with a skewness toward the lower side of the SEI scale as compared with the U.S. census population. The NCPP mean lay within the 4 to 4.9 range; the U.S. census mean was within 5 to 5.9.
2. The White NCPP population showed less skewness and was more nearly comparable to the U.S. population, but with less representation in the lowest two deciles. The NCPP Black population, while below the U.S. total population, was above the U.S. Black population; less than 30% lay within the lowest three deciles, as against over half the U.S. population.
3. Unmarried women in the NCPP sample were skewed toward the low end of the SEI scale, as compared with those who were married at any time. The group containing single, divorced, widowed, and separated women had the lowest scores and were skewed toward the low end of the scale, as compared with the married group which com-

prised about three-fourths of the NCPP population.

The median income of the NCPP population increased from about $4000, at the time of the prenatal computation, to about $8500 in 1973. Changes in the income levels resulting from inflationary and other economic factors have been entered into a recalculation of the SEI scores at seven years (Nichols, 1976). However, the earlier SEI scores appear to provide a satisfactory and adequate description of the SLH subsamples for the present purpose. The distributions of the SLH subsamples and the Non-SLH population by SEI are shown in Figure 4-1.

It is evident that the distribution of Blacks in all subsamples is markedly skewed toward the lower end of the SEI scale, with little more than 10% of cases in the upper two categories. The Whites, on the other hand, are distributed more evenly; only 3% lie within the lowest category (compared to about 15% of Blacks), whereas 20% to 30% are found in each of the upper categories. Distributions are similar for all age groups within races. The Non-SLH group closely resembles the SLH age groups for the respective races. Inspection of the SEI data tabulated by sex (not shown), irrespective of race, discloses that the frequencies are identical for both sexes in half the cells and within one percent in the other half.

None of the subsamples, including the Non-SLH group, shows any remarkable SEI disparity by sex.

Viewed from another perspective, the proportion of Whites and Blacks varies markedly within SEI score categories from one interval to another (Table 4-4). In the lowest category (SEI 0.0 to 1.9), the Blacks outnumber Whites by about six to one. The ratios change fairly uniformly within each SLH subsample as SEI scores increase. The ratios approach equality at the central category (SEI 4.0 to 5.9) and reverse to show about a twelvefold preponderance of Whites in the highest (SEI 8.0 to 9.5) category of scores. The Non-SLH group deviates somewhat from this pattern. There is a larger proportion of Whites in all categories, even at the lower levels of SEI. Possible bias in selection of cases is suggested by this deviation, although the reason for it is not clear. Termination of 8YR SLH testing at six of the collaborating institutions stands out as the single most striking factor likely to have biased sampling. However, the institutions which continued to test at eight years contributed together about 80% of the White children in the NCPP population and only about one-third of the Blacks; and SEI scores tend to be higher among Whites than among Blacks (Figure 4-1 and Table 4-3). Further, it is improbable that this event is responsible for the deviation noted in the Non-SLH

Table **4-4**

Socioeconomic Index at birth showing proportions of Whites and Blacks by subsample.

SEI	3YR		8YR		3YR/8YR		Non-SLH	
	White	Black	White	Black	White	Black	White	Black
0.0-1.9	14	86	15	85	16	84	34	66
2.0-3.9	27	73	28	72	30	70	47	53
4.0-5.9	42	58	44	56	48	52	63	37
6.0-7.9	65	35	70	30	73	27	81	19
8.0-9.5	92	8	93	7	92	8	90	10
Mean	5.7	3.6	5.8	3.7	5.8	3.6	5.8	4.1
SD	.23	.17	.22	.18	.23	.17	.21	.19

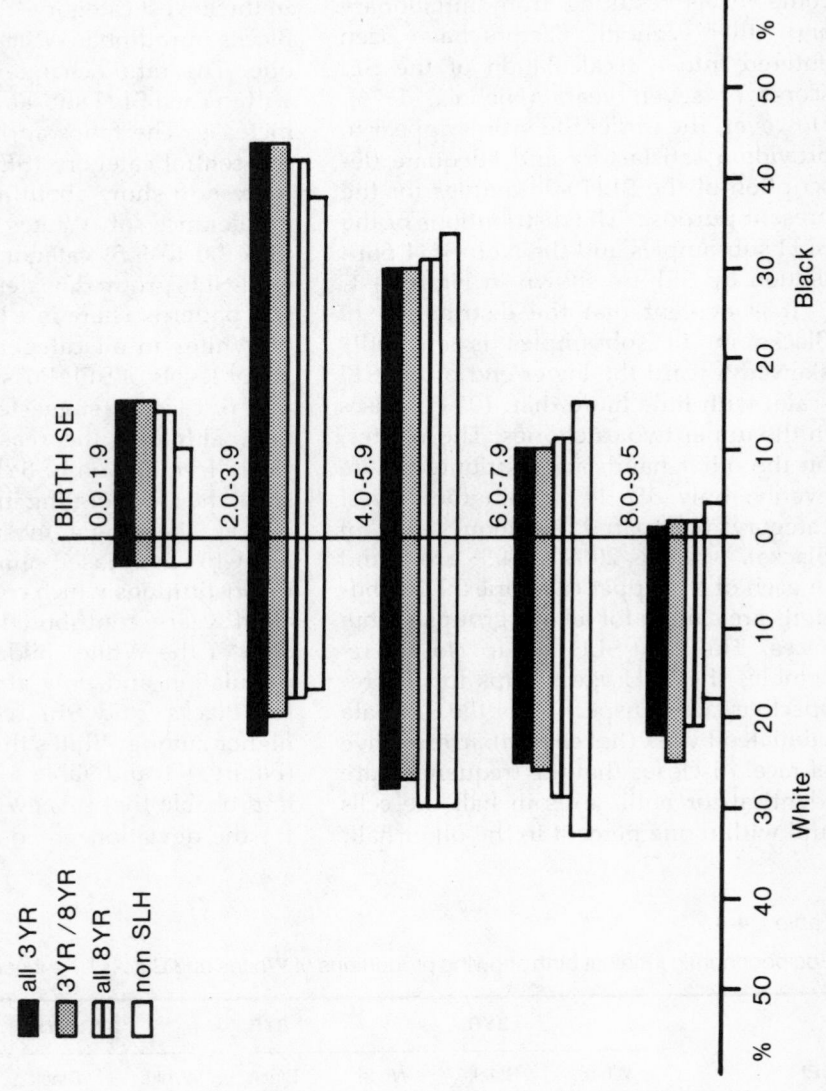

Figure 4-1

Distribution (%) of grouped Socioeconomic Index at birth by subsamples and race

46

group because any selection bias in the untested group (Non-SLH) would show some counterpart distortion in the tested (8YR) group. That this is not the case can be seen in the close resemblance between the SEI proportions at eight years to those at three years where altogether different factors operated. Possibly an element of self-selection was at play, such that Whites in the lower SEI levels may have attached less importance to SLH competence and therefore failed to appear for examination. Certainly an orderly relationship can be perceived in the change of racial proportions of the Non-SLH subsample with the change in SEI levels. It seems likely that the same biasing agent influenced both the 3YR and the 8YR sampling in a similar manner, whatever it may have been.

Age of Parents

The mean ages of the mothers range from 24.1 years for children in the 3YR subsample to 24.4 years for those in the 8YR subsample. The mean age for mothers of the 3YR/8YR group lies between these values at 24.2 years. Mothers of children who had neither exam (Non-SLH) are similar to those in the other groups, with a mean age of 24.2 years. Variability is identical for all subsamples except for the Non-SLH group, for which the standard deviation is fractionally smaller. These data appear in Figure 4-2. Black mothers in the study tend to be younger than White mothers. Within the combined groups 6% of Black mothers are 15 years old and younger, compared with 1% of Whites. Similarly, 31% of Blacks are under 20 years of age compared with 18% of Whites. The 20 to 29 years category includes 52% of Blacks and 63% of Whites, and only 17% and 19% respectively are over 30 years old. The distribution by sex of the children shows no notable disparities; the age groups of the mothers are similar within one or two percent. Distribution of the samples by socioeconomic index reveals

an orderly though small increase in mean age as SEI values increase.

Fathers of the study children are about three years older than mothers on the average (Figure 4-2). Means and standard deviations are virtually identical for all subsamples. No remarkable disparities are seen in the distribution of ages of fathers by race and sex of the children. Data on the father's race are less complete than for race of the mother; hence, the means and standard deviations are shown for composite totals rather than by race in each subsample (Figure 4-2). The mean ages are lower for the middle SEI scores and higher for the extremes. However, the differences are slight.

Education of Parents

White mothers averaged 11.4 years of schooling compared with 10.1 years for Black mothers. This advantage of slightly more than one year persists for all of the samples. The variability is virtually the same in all groups; standard deviations are on the order of 2.2 years. These data are displayed in Figure 4-3. Not surprisingly, there is a monotonic relationship between SEI and years of education, and between age and years of education. The distribution by years of schooling shows 12 years as modal and a tendency for proportionally more Whites to be found at the upper levels. Virtually no differences in means and variability could be seen relative to the sex of the children.

The education of the fathers (Figure 4-3) also averaged slightly more than 11 years in the composite. Race of fathers was poorly reported, as mentioned previously; hence, the mean is based on the total of Whites and Blacks combined, and it falls close to the means for White and Black mothers.

Marital Status of the Mothers

The percentages of women reportedly married at the time of registration differ only slightly from one subsample to an-

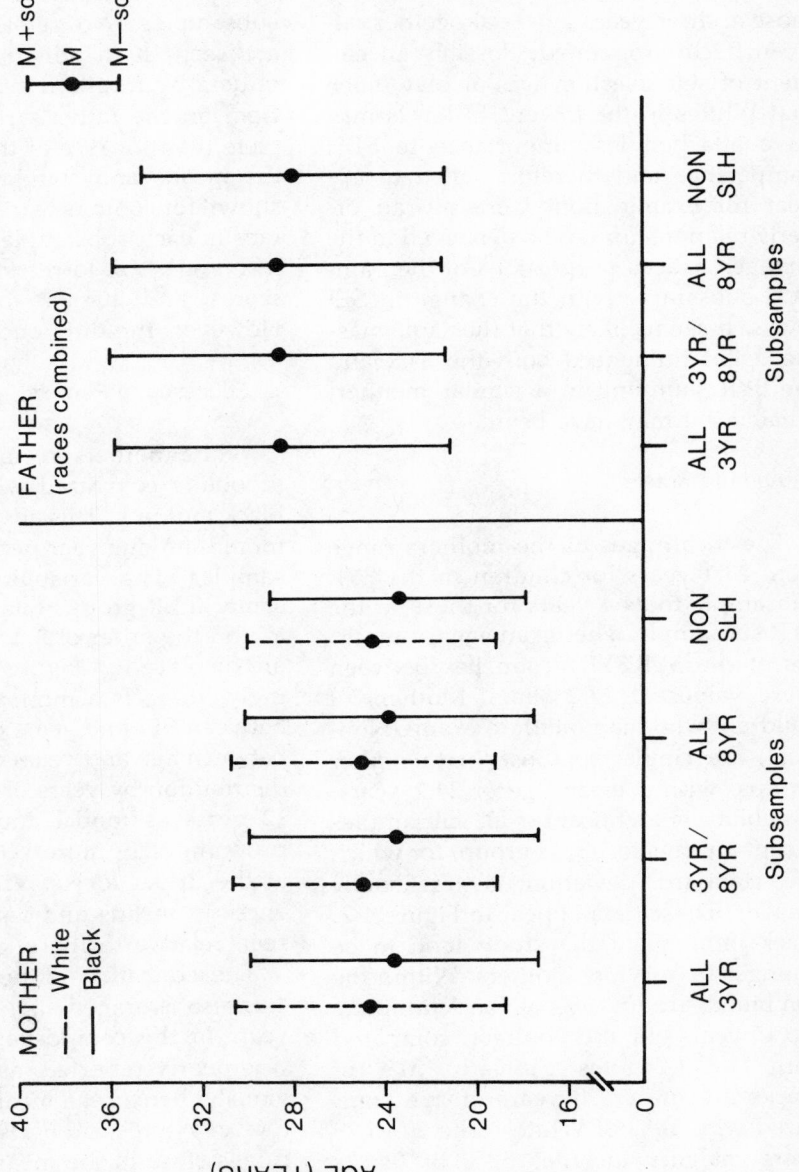

Figure 4-2

Average age of parents at birth of study child

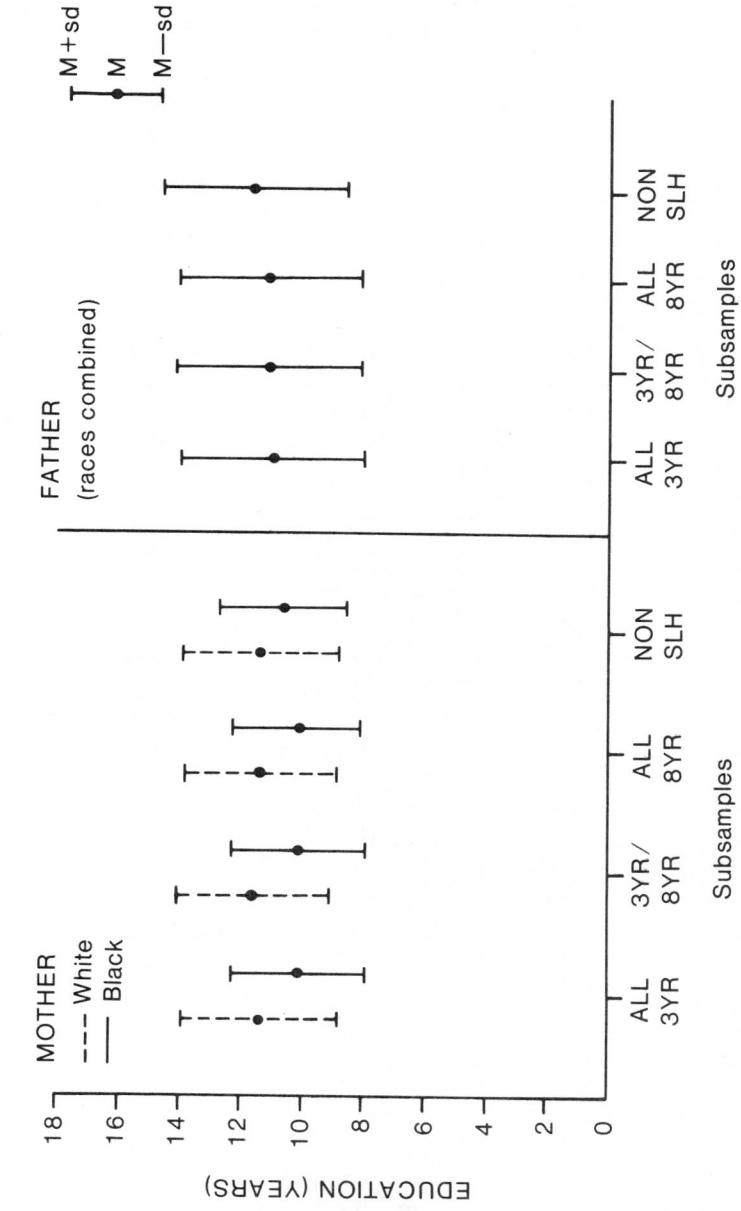

Figure 4-3

Average education of parents at birth of study child

49

Table **4-5**

Marital status of the mothers (%).

Status	3YR		8YR		3YR/8YR		Non-SLH	
	White*	Black	White	Black*	White*	Black	White*	Black
Single	5	25	4	25	5	26	6	26
Married	87	62	90	65	88	63	88	62
Common-law	0	2	0	1	0	1	0	1
Widowed	0	1	0	1	0	1	0	1
Divorced	3	1	2	1	3	1	2	1
Separated	6	9	4	8	5	8	4	9
Unknown	0	0	0	0	0	0	.01	0

*Not 100%, due to rounding.

other (Table 4-5). There are striking racial differences, however, within every sub-sample. Nearly 90% of Whites were married compared with 62% to 65% of Blacks. The same kind of disparity holds for the proportions registered as never married (single); 4% to 6% of Whites were single in contrast to about 25% of Blacks. Whites varied more than Blacks between subsamples as to those who formerly had been, but were not then, married (widowed, divorced, separated) but a larger percentage of Blacks were in that category. No remarkable differences could be seen with regard to the sex of the child (not shown), but there appears to be an effect associated with SEI (Figure 4-4). The percentage of married women increases strikingly as SEI increases. Conversely, the percentages of single and formerly married women decreases markedly as SEI rises.

The mean SEI was highest for presently married White women. They scored at 6.0 as compared with 4.0 for the presently married Black women. Those who were never married had mean SEI scores of approximately 4.1 in the White groups and 3.0 in the Black, varying slightly among subsamples. These scores were similar to those in the formerly married groups, where the mean SEI was about 3.9 for Whites and 3.1 for Blacks. Means for the several marital categories were virtually the same (±0.2) across all SLH subsamples and for the Non-SLH group as well, with exceptions for the never-married Whites and the presently-married Blacks, where means were higher at 4.7 and 4.6 respectively. Standard deviations ranged from 1.6 to 2.3 among Whites and from 1.4 to 1.8 among Blacks over all marital categories. However, within categories, the standard deviations did not vary more than ±0.2 for either race across subsamples. Variability was greatest within the presently married groups, both White and Black.

Birthweight

Mean birthweights are reasonably similar in all study samples. Table 4-6 shows the means and standard deviations of birthweight in grams by sex, race, and SEI for each subsample. Males outweigh Females by more than a hundred grams and Whites outweigh Blacks by more than two hundred grams, on the average, as was observed by Niswander and Gordon (1972). These differences are consistent within each subsample. Consistent differences can be noted also in weights relative to SEI; mean birthweights increase steadily as the SEI rises. Differences between successive SEI categories are of the order of 40 to 80 grams. The strong association between birth-

50

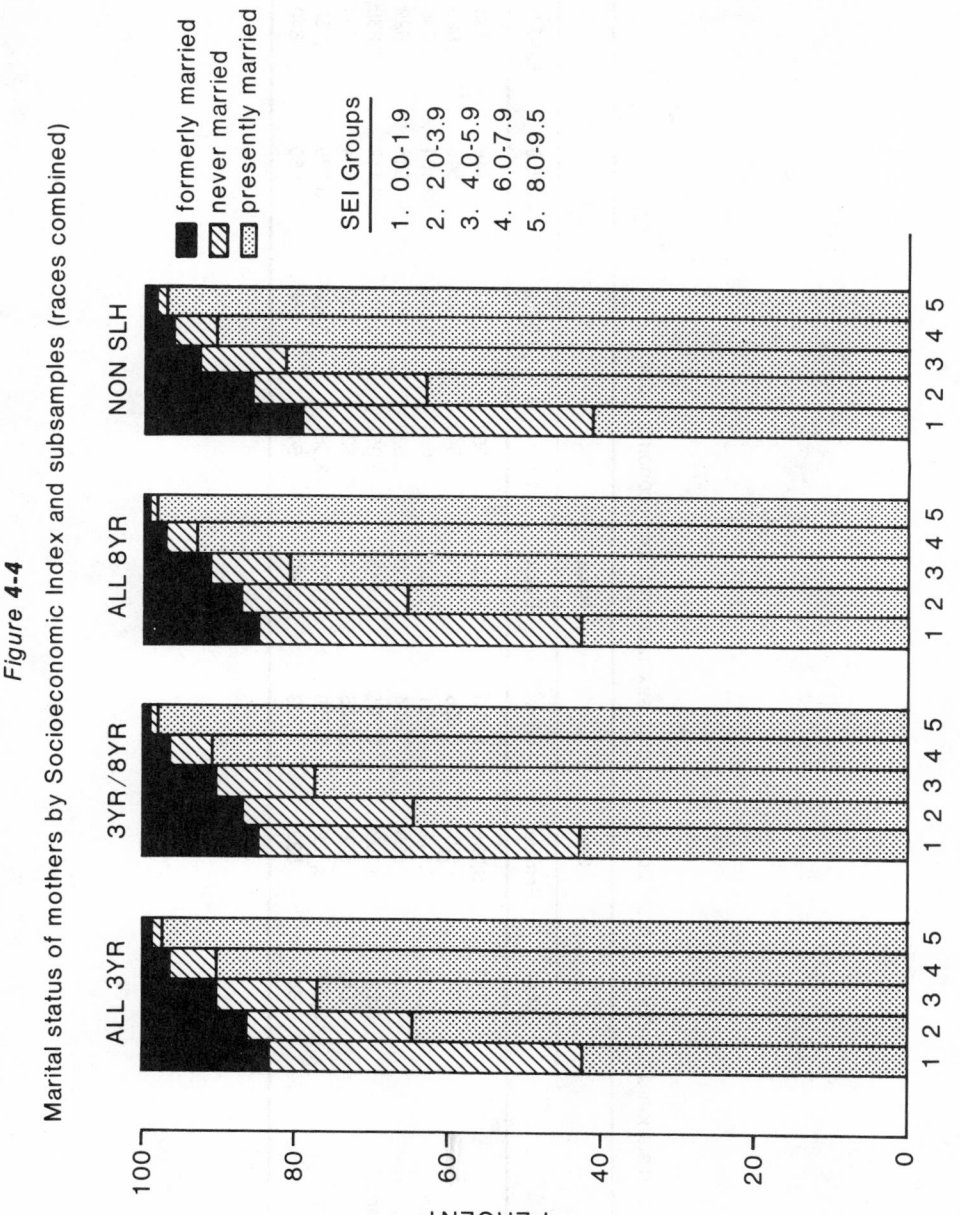

Figure 4-4

Marital status of mothers by Socioeconomic Index and subsamples (races combined)

51

Table **4-6**

Mean birthweight and standard deviations in grams by subsamples, sex, race and Socioeconomic Index.

Subsample		Sex		Race		SEI				
		Male	Female	White	Black	0.0-1.9	2.0-3.9	4.0-5.9	6.0-7.9	8.0-9.5
3YR	Mean	3,213	3,096	3,290	3,053	3,056	3,109	3,146	3,233	3,304
	SD	543	527	526	525	540	536	546	528	496
8YR	Mean	3,233	3,112	3,291	3,053	3,054	3,108	3,164	3,246	3,317
	SD	546	528	524	530	538	543	546	529	493
3YR/8YR	Mean	3,224	3,102	3,295	3,048	3,057	3,109	3,152	3,238	3,312
	SD	542	528	525	524	537	537	544	534	495
Non-SLH	Mean	3,279	3,122	3,279	3,055	3,067	3,133	3,179	3,265	3,319
	SD	547	533	533	540	547	550	550	540	498

weight and SEI is emphasized by the increase of about 250 grams in the highest category, as compared with the lowest. This difference is consistent within each study group.

Gestational Age

The gestational age of the child is the same estimate as the duration of maternal pregnancy. This statistic is considered here because it bears upon birthweight and is an important determinant of maturity at birth. The relationships between gestational age and birthweight are given in Table G of Appendix 9.

It is evident that the study subsamples do not differ substantially in gestational age, based on the data displayed in Table 4-7. Means and dispersion are virtually identical for Males and Females in all groups. Gestational ages for Whites tend to be slightly greater than for Blacks and the variance slightly smaller. This finding is in agreement with Niswander and Gordon (1972). There is also a trend toward higher gestational ages and lower variability as the SEI increases.

IQ at Age Four

Children in the NCPP study were tested with the abbreviated scale of the 1960 Revision of the Stanford-Binet Intelligence Scale (Form L-M) (Terman and Merrill, 1960) as close to age four years as was possible. Mean IQ scores are presented in Table 4-8 by race, sex, and SEI for the children in each group. The subsamples appear to be similar with respect to mean IQ. There are, however, small sex differences of about three points in favor of Females. Larger differences of the order of a standard deviation are

found between races; Whites score higher than Blacks. Variability is slightly lower for Blacks in the subsamples. The data are in good agreement with the results of Broman et al. (1975). Pronounced changes of mean IQ are evident relative to socioeconomic levels. Fairly orderly increases in IQ are associated with rises in SEI levels.

Appendix 9 provides additional physical, medical, and behavioral characteristics of the subsamples.

Summary

The speech, language, and hearing study subsamples consisted of 19,885 NCPP children given SLH tests at age three years, 20,137 tested at eight years and 12,464 tested at both ages. Several characteristics of these groups were compared with those of 11,225 NCPP children not given SLH tests. The four groups included only Whites and Blacks. Excluded from the three SLH study subsamples were children of other ethnic origins, those enrolled for special studies, and those tested out of age limits.

The 8YR group had approximately equal proportions of Whites and Blacks, but the 3YR and 3YR/8YR groups had somewhat more Blacks than Whites and the Non-SLH group was two-thirds White. Sex ratios were approximately equal in all groups. Socioeconomic characteristics were similar for all SLH subsamples and the Non-SLH group, although there was pronounced skewing toward lower SEI levels by Blacks within all groups. All SLH subsamples showed close similarity in age and education of parents, marital status of mothers, birthweight and gestational age, and IQ of the children at age four years.

Table **4-7**

Mean gestational age and standard deviations in weeks by subsamples, sex, race and Socioeconomic Index.

Subsample		Sex		Race		SEI				
		Male	Female	White	Black	0.0-1.9	2.0-3.9	4.0-5.9	6.0-7.9	8.0-9.5
3YR	Mean	39.3	39.4	40.0	38.9	38.8	39.2	39.2	39.7	40.0
	SD	3.1	3.2	2.6	3.4	3.8	3.3	3.1	2.7	2.1
8YR	Mean	39.4	39.4	40.0	38.8	38.7	39.2	39.4	39.7	40.0
	SD	3.1	3.1	2.5	3.5	3.8	3.5	3.1	2.6	2.1
3YR/8YR	Mean	39.4	39.4	40.0	38.9	38.8	39.2	39.4	39.7	40.0
	SD	3.1	3.2	2.5	3.5	3.8	3.4	3.1	2.7	2.1
Non-SLH	Mean	39.5	39.5	39.9	38.6	38.9	39.1	39.4	39.8	40.0
	SD	3.1	3.2	2.7	3.7	3.8	3.6	3.2	2.7	2.2

Table **4-8**

Mean IQ and standard deviations at 4YR by subsamples, race, sex and Socioeconomic Index.

Subsample		Race		Sex		SEI					Total
		White	Black	Male	Female	0.0-1.9	2.0-3.9	4.0-5.9	6.0-7.9	8.0-9.5	
3YR	Mean	102.8	90.4	94.4	97.1	87.2	90.9	95.1	101.6	112.4	95.7
	SD	16.4	13.6	15.9	16.2	13.5	13.8	14.4	15.4	16.0	16.1
8YR	Mean	104.9	90.9	96.6	99.3	87.7	91.6	97.0	104.0	113.2	98.0
	SD	16.3	13.8	16.4	16.8	13.6	14.2	15.1	15.5	16.3	16.7
3YR/8YR	Mean	103.5	90.5	95.3	98.0	87.6	91.2	95.5	102.0	112.5	96.7
	SD	16.4	13.4	16.0	16.4	13.2	13.9	14.3	15.4	15.9	16.2
Non-SLH	Mean	107.0	93.6	101.6	103.9	87.9	95.4	101.3	107.5	115.1	102.7
	SD	16.5	15.6	17.2	17.4	16.8	15.0	16.0	16.1	18.3	17.4

References

1. Broman, S.H., Nichols, P.L., and Kennedy, W.A. *Preschool IQ: Prenatal and Early Developmental Correlates.* Hillsdale, New Jersey: Lawrence Erlbaum Associates, 1975.

2. Myrianthopoulos, N.C., and French, K.S. An application of the U.S. Bureau of the Census Socioeconomic Index to a large diversified patient population. *Soc. Sci. Med.* 2:283–299, 1968.

3. Nichols, P. Personal communication, 1976.

4. NINCDS Perinatal Statistical *Ad Hoc* Committee Final Report. December, 1968.

5. Niswander, K.R., and Gordon, M. *The Women and Their Pregnancies.* Philadelphia: W.B. Saunders, 1972.

6. Terman, L.M., and Merrill, M.A. *Stanford-Binet Intelligence Scale.* Boston: Houghton Mifflin, 1960.

7. U.S. Bureau of the Census. *Methodology and Scores of Socioeconomic Status.* Working Paper No. 15. Washington, D.C.: Government Printing Office, 1963.

## CHAPTER 5

Procedures of Analysis

James R. Boen, Ph.D.
Dolores K. Vetter, Ph.D.
Elaine N. Frankowski, M.S.
Katherine Hirst, M.S.

Introduction and Overview of the Plan of Analysis, its Motivation and its Implementation

The NINCDS Collaborative Perinatal Project (NCPP) attempted to record about 5500 medical, physical, psychological, and social measures for each of the 55,908 pregnancies registered in the study. Of these, 306 directly reported measurements of speech, language, and hearing (SLH) performance on examinations given at ages three years and eight years or necessary ancillary information, such as child's school grade at the time of the examination. These measures are called SLH variables; all others are called NCPP variables. Both SLH and NCPP variables, as well as composite variables called indexes, are capitalized.

This study analyzed these SLH and NCPP data for the purpose of furthering understanding of etiological factors and to facilitate prevention, diagnosis, and treatment of speech, language, and hearing deficits. The statistical analysis used the techniques of correlation* and multi-

---

* When a bivariate (two variable) distribution is Gaussian, an optimal measure of association is the Pearson correlation coefficient. The great majority of bivariate distributions in this study are far from Gaussian, however. Though there is no optimal measure of bivariate association for non-Gaussian distributions, the Pearson correlation coefficient is one of the reasonable choices for a bivariate association and it is the measure chosen for this study.

ple linear regression, similar to the one used in the study of four-year IQ as described in Broman, Nichols, and Kennedy (1975). In addition, conditional probabilities were calculated to predict failure on SLH outcomes given success or failure on antecedent variables.

Because there would never be sufficient resources to examine all the possible relationships among SLH and NCPP variables, and because even a population of almost 60,000 is not large enough to prevent the appearance of an enormous number of spurious relationships among 5500 variables, systematic reduction of the number of variables preceded statistical analysis.

Every phase of this study was carried out under the guidance of members of a Scientific Management Panel (SMP). The SMP was composed of all investigators on the study staff and consulting experts in speech, language, hearing, pediatric neurology, sociology, education, and statistics. The panel met in plenum five times during the first year of the study to discuss the course and progress of the project and to plan future work. Between meetings, the SMP participated in each major step in the study by telephone, mail, and in small work groups. The SMP comprised a wide base of knowledge, experience, and expertise and provided the project with a periodic critical evaluation by people not involved in the day-to-day work process.

Before data analysis began, a study cohort and three study samples were chosen. Between 39,000 and 40,000 children in the NCPP sample of 55,908 took part in one of the SLH examinations. The major reduction of the sample to 27,558 resulted from restricting the sample to White and Black core study children who were tested in the proper age intervals and whose Socioeconomic Index at birth was recorded. This cohort includes siblings and multiple births but excludes children born to mothers in special studies (for example, diabetic mothers not in

the core sample) and children of "walk-in" mothers; that is, those about whom no prenatal data are available. Three SLH samples were chosen for final study: (1) the ALL 3YR sample: those children attempting a 3YR SLH examination between the ages of two years, 10 months, 16 days, and three years, one month, 15 days (N = 19,885); (2) the ALL 8YR sample: those children attempting an 8YR SLH examination between the ages of seven years, 10 months, and eight years, two months (N = 20,137); and (3) the 3YR/8YR sample: all children attempting both examinations within the legitimate age limits (N = 12,464). Certain demographic characteristics of these three samples were analyzed in depth and compared to the sample of children who had never attempted an SLH examination. These analyses are reported in Chapter 4.

Data analysis was preceded also by systematic reduction of both SLH and NCPP data. This began with an evaluation of the quality of the SLH data. Only those variables judged to be of sufficient quality and importance, or which were unique measures, were retained for further analysis. Concurrent with the detailed quality analysis and clinical evaluation of each SLH variable, some NCPP variables were eliminated from further consideration. For the basic study, NCPP variables served as predictors of SLH performance. Ideally every NCPP variable should be tested for its predictive potential. This would have entailed examining approximately 10^{1658} ($306 \times 2^{5500-1}$) possible pairs of NCPP and SLH variables. However, given limitations in resources and the inevitability of spurious relationships occurring in a data set of such size, NCPP variable reduction was deemed necessary and began with the SMP selecting only 1000 variables for first consideration. These latter were examined for redundancy and lack of reliability. About 400 were selected for further consideration as potential predictors and were screened both for proportion of missing data and correlation with SLH outcomes.

After final selection of the SLH variables and the three study samples, descriptive statistics (frequencies of scores, means, standard deviations, and standard errors) for each SLH variable were generated for each sample. To facilitate the explication of these frequencies, they were tabulated by the child's race, sex, and Socioeconomic Index, as well as by the total for the sample, and by the total for each of the 12 institutions.

Working in subgroups according to area of expertise, the SMP specified rules for combining several variables in one area of SLH performance into one composite measurement, called an index (Appendix 4). Each rule both selects the component variables of a particular index and describes how these variables will be combined to yield a numerical index score. In subsequent discussion, the word "index" is used to refer either to the rule (that is, the list of component variables and the method of combining their scores) or to the index score itself. The particular meaning of "index" should be clear from its context. If a single variable was judged to be a valuable indicator of performance, then the index consisted only of that variable, called a key variable. Thirty-five indexes, six of them containing only a key variable, were formulated by the SMP. The SMP constructed indexes as useful alternatives to numerous separate but related SLH variables. These indexes were used in this study as outcomes to be predicted and may be useful to clinicians as measures of performance. The SLH indexes were named to indicate the characteristic which the combined SLH variables attempted to measure (for example, 3YR Fluency included the SLH variables Dysfluent Events and Struggle Behavior).

For most indexes, if a child had a valid, interpretable score for each of the component measurements of the index, he received a score for that index unless the component scores were judged highly improbable and invalid by the clinical experts. For example, 3YR Fluency has two components: Dysfluent Events and Struggle Behavior; a combination of "no" Dysfluent Events and "much" Struggle Behavior was considered an improbable combination, so that no index score was given to a child having that combination of component scores. In one instance, 3YR Hearing Screen, a child received an index score despite missing data in one of the component measures. Most of the indexes were ordered in the clinically positive direction; that is, the higher the score of a particular index, the more desirable the SLH status. However, for the 3YR Hearing Screen, 8YR Hearing Severity, and 8YR Hearing Acuity the traditional clinical ordering (lower numbers indicating better performance) was maintained. A full definition of each index, including component variables, coding of the variables, rules for combining variables into outcomes, and ordering of outcomes, is given in Appendix 4.

After indexes were constructed and index scores were computed for each study child, descriptive statistics of the indexes were tabulated for each SLH sample by race, sex, Socioeconomic Index, and total for the samples. The index scores for each sample were also tabulated for each institution.

Analyses involving NCPP variables required some recoding of these variables. Some of them had been coded dichotomously at the NINCDS, some had been ordered in the clinically positive direction, and some in the clinically negative direction. Many NCPP variables had not been ordered at all but were categorical with more than two categories. To allow the use of the Pearson correlation coefficient, each categorical variable was dichotomized. To accomplish this, the categories were treated separately on the basis of the presence or absence of each coded trait, resulting in as many dichotomies as there were traits coded for that variable. Consequently, all naturally ordered NCPP variables and all dichotomous ones were appropriate for calculation of a Pearson correlation coefficient with the SLH indexes. The correlations of the adjusted set of NCPP variables with the SLH indexes were then calculated.

Data Reduction

Motivation

It is difficult to imagine another study of this magnitude on this topic being undertaken in the foreseeable future. The effort, time, and funds devoted to collecting the data were so enormous that these data might be considered priceless. In this regard, it seems negligent to set aside even one of the variables without a thorough investigation of its possible relation, both alone and in combination, to the rest of the study variables. It is natural to want to calculate all possible univariate multiple regressions of the 306 SLH variables on the 5500 NCPP variables. Those even more ambitious might want to perform all possible multivariate multiple regressions of the SLH variables on the NCPP variables.

For several reasons, not even all the possible univariate multiple regressions could be computed in this study. The first was the necessity of using computers efficiently. Multiple regression requires inversion of matrices and, while it is possible to invert a 5500 × 5500 matrix on the CDC CYBER 74 configuration available, it is extremely costly, time consuming, and wasteful of programmer effort.* The output from the regressions would have been massive, even with computer prescreening of that output. Reading the final computer output would have been too large a task, to say nothing of the effort involved in interpreting it.

Another limitation to analyzing 5500 potential predictors was the sample size of the study. Even if each of the 55,908

study children had complete data (which is unfortunately not the case), there were not enough children in the study to make exploration of 5500 potential predictors meaningful. Dividing the original data by race and sex would give an average of 15,000 [60,000 ÷ (2 × 2)] children in each category. With 5500 potential predictor variables, a sample size of 15,000 is too small to prevent spurious results. In fact, a slight majority of the children had data too incomplete to allow them to be included in our analysis; only 27,558 children (of 55,908) had some SLH examination results recorded at the proper age.

The number of different regression equations needed to perform all possible regressions of 5500 potential predictor variables on only one predictand is approximately 10^{1656} ($2^{5500} - 1$). Even a complete step-down algorithm would involve $(1 + 5500 + 5499 + \ldots + 2 + 1) = 15$ million regressions. A step-up algorithm could involve only a few regressions, depending upon how many upward steps are allowed. A step-up algorithm, however, is known by statisticians to be likely entirely to miss meaningful combinations of predictors (Mantel, 1970). For this reason, and because the project could afford to perform only the first few stages of a step-up algorithm, the step-up algorithm

---

* Since core memory cannot accommodate more than 120,000 matrix elements at one time, a 5500 × 5500 matrix must be brought into core storage from some mass storage device in segments, manipulated in segments, and returned to the mass storage device. No packaged subroutine available would handle this type of procedure; that is, no packaged subroutine would invert a matrix larger than 300 × 300. If the 5500 × 5500 matrix inversion were to be programmed for this project in single precision arithmetic, the computer cost would have been close to $100,000 (compared with a cost of 8¢ for inverting a 50 × 50 matrix). Considering the number of manipulations on each element of the matrix, there would have been no way to guarantee numerical accuracy using single precision arithmetic (14 significant decimal digits). N-precision arithmetic would have given better accuracy, but at a much greater computer cost.

was not chosen as a method of procedure. Hence, reduction of both SLH and NCPP variables was considered necessary.

SLH Variable Reduction

Evaluation of the data for quality was a prerequisite to variable reduction and further analysis. Quality was defined in terms of availability of data, distribution of values, and stability of data from 3YR to 8YR. Reduction of the number of SLH variables and identification of the most important SLH variables was accomplished through the process of quality analysis. Those variables judged unacceptable in quality were eliminated from further consideration. The SLH variables judged to be important and of acceptable quality were combined into indexes. Procedures used in the analysis of quality are described in the following sections.

Interinstitutional Quality Control

In addition to computer tapes of all available 3YR and 8YR SLH examinations, the Perinatal Research Branch (PRB) of NINCDS provided the study staff with the results of an interinstitutional quality control study. These results were incorporated into our own quality tables. Three times each year throughout the course of the Collaborative Perinatal Project, a small sample of children was randomly selected for reexamination. These reexaminations were performed by examiners from another institution participating in the study within one to two months of the original examination. Each of the children recalled was examined and scored by the visiting examiner with the original examiner scoring a new protocol as an observer. All retesting and observing was done without reference to the original test. The PRB then analyzed the data from a 3YR sample of 110 and an 8YR sample of 325 and compiled the results in three tables:

1. Test/retest—comparison of the score of the original examiner with the score of the visiting examiner.
2. Retest/observer—comparison of the score of the visiting examiner with the second score of the original examiner.
3. Test/observer—comparison of the first score of the original examiner with his second score.

Categorical test items (where n is the number of possible categories of response) were presented in $n \times n$ tables with agreement between examiners occurring on the diagonal. In the case of continuously-scored test items, the difference (magnitude and direction) between the two examiners' scores was determined and percents given for each possible difference or interval of differences.

For a time an intrainstitutional quality control study was conducted at each institution. It was similar to the interinstitutional program except that the original examiner and second examiner came from the same institution. It was terminated when analysis of the data showed little difference among examiners within the same institution.

Examiner differences were thought to be a source of variability in the testing situation and, therefore, a source of variability in the scores. This issue was reviewed by the SMP, some members of which had themselves been examiners in the study. The SMP recognized that examiner variability is an inherent part of the variability of the measuring instrument and cannot be reduced. There is no reason to believe that, if the study were to be conducted again with the same protocol, the examiners chosen would differ appreciably in abilities or knowledge from those in the present study. With a large group of examiners, any differences would be averaged out in the subsequent data analysis. For this reason, the SMP decided not to discard data from any of the examiners.

$$\phi = \sqrt{\frac{\chi^2}{N}}$$

The statistics and tapes provided by the PRB were used in the first stage of the quality study. Using an edited version of those tapes, the local staff conducted an analysis of the stability, or consistency, of scores from the 3YR test battery to the 8YR test battery. The analysis included only those children who had attempted both test batteries, were Black or White, and had sex coded Male or Female (N = 14,959). Comparisons were made between (1) variables which were directly comparable at three and eight years (for example, Speech Mechanism: Lips, Tongue, Soft Palate) and (2) variables which, while not identical, should be consistent (for example, Hearing), or should change in a predicted direction between three years and eight years (for example, Articulation).

Therefore, consistency means no change or change in an expected direction. For a few of the variables, no comparisons were possible because they occurred in only one of the examinations (for example, 3YR Diadochokinesis).

Except for Intelligibility, Dysfluent Events, and Struggle Behavior, the codes of all variables in the stability analysis were manipulated to yield dichotomous scores (pass/fail). Two-by-two tables indicating pass/fail agreement were calculated by race, sex, and total population. These tables were of the following format:

	Pass 3YR	Fail 3YR	Row totals
Pass 8YR	n, %	n, %	n, %
Fail 8YR	n, %	n, %	n, %
Column totals	n, %	n, %	N

The Chi squares (χ^2) were calculated and contingency coefficients (C) and phi coefficients (ϕ) were computed for each table according to the following formulas:

$$C = \sqrt{\frac{\chi^2}{N + \chi^2}}$$

For the three nondichotomous variables, similar tables were constructed according to the original scoring protocol (yielding 5 × 5 or 3 × 3 tables) and the chi-squares and contingency coefficients were computed. (The phi coefficient is not applicable to tables larger than 2 × 2).

In preparation for variable reduction, the local staff prepared two sets of tables: availability/missing-data tables which indicated what portion of the total cases had usable data; and reasonableness of value tables which showed the distribution of scores for those cases having usable data. These tables were compiled by major test area rather than by separate test item. For example, a single table was prepared for Auditory Memory, rather than separate tables for the test items two digits, three digits, two syllables, and so forth. Tables were compiled for each institution and for the total population.

The legitimate codes for each variable were provided to the local staff by the PRB. These included codes for "unknown response," "test not administered," "no response," and "other." Missing data were defined as blanks in the data file (called "not in the data file" or NIDF), the codes for "unknown response," "test not administered," or any code not in the list of legitimate codes for a particular variable. For any variable, if more than 10% of the cases fell into any of the categories defined as missing data, that variable was flagged in the availability/missing-data tables. There were many instances where several categories were flagged. For example, a variable could have 10%+ of its cases coded "no response," another 10%+ coded "test not administered," and still another

10%+ coded "other." In that case, all three categories were flagged. This flagging was done for the total sample, and for any subsample (White, Black, Male, or Female) which met the criterion of 10%+ of its cases coded with a missing-data category type. These tables were of the format shown on page 64. The distribution of missing data across institutions and across subsamples would be considered a factor in determining the randomness, or independence, of "missingness."

Reasonableness of values was measured in most cases by a pass/fail rate. For some continuously-scored tests, pass/fail criteria were not specified; a value of the mean minus one standard deviation (as determined from the frequency distribution of scores for the total population) and lower was considered fail, and all scores higher were considered pass. There were some tests where pass and marginal passes (for example, retraction with concomitant movement in the case of Lips: Retraction), and fail and marginal fails were combined to yield pass/fail scoring. In some instances, dichotomizing of scores was neither necessary nor appropriate and the original codes were kept intact (for example, none/some/many). Reasonableness of values tables gave percents of pass/fail for all the institutions and for the total population by race and sex.

An exception to this format was the summary table showing reasonableness of values for the 8YR Hearing tests (Air Conduction, Bone Conduction, Discrimination, Abnormal Auditory Adaptation). In this case, institutions were ranked from lowest (best) to highest for Air Conduction and Bone Conduction, and from highest (best score) to lowest (poorest score) for the discrimination and adaptation tests. Only the right ear was tabulated for Air Conduction, Bone Conduction, and Discrimination, as there were no appreciable ear differences. On the adaptation test there appeared to be ear differences possibly due to a learning ef-

fect, since the right ear was tested first. For this reason both right and left ears were presented.

The SMP members used the above information, in conjunction with their knowledge of difficulties in scoring and test administration, cultural bias of the variables tested, and other conditions inherent in the testing situation, to evaluate the quality of the individual SLH variables. By this process the 306 SLH variables (89 3YR and 217 8YR) were reduced to 77 (34 3YR and 43 8YR).

Acceptability Rating

Although no further reduction of SLH variables was intended, the 77 remaining SLH variables were correlated with each other to determine their value either as key variables or as components of an index. To facilitate determination of each variable's usefulness, the study staff constructed quality tables. From the stability analysis, phi and contingency coefficients were presented for paired 3YR and 8YR variables. For all variables the following information was presented:

1. Percent missing—based on the same criteria described in the previous section.
2. Percent pass—based on the same criteria described in the previous section.
3. Percent institutional variability— these figures were meant to reflect the spread of the distribution of proportion pass among the 12 institutions. They were based on the valid scores for each variable; codes comprising missing data were excluded. The valid codes were dichotomously categorized as pass/ fail, adequate/inadequate, normal/ abnormal, adequate/deviant, absent/ present, or none/some, depending on the original coding. From the distribution of frequencies between these two groupings, percents pass, adequate, and so forth were calcu-

Institutions	White				Black				Male				Female				All			
	NIDF	NR	NA	Other	NIDF	NR	NA	Other	NIDF	NR	NA	Other	NIDF	NR	NA	Other	NIDF	NR	NA	Other
Bost		•								•										
Buff																				
Char																				
Colum		•				•				•				•				•		
J Hop		•																		
Virg		•								•										
Minn		•								•				•				•		
NY Med																		•		
Oreg		•	•				•			•	•			•	•			•	•	
Penn		•	•							•	•			•				•	•	
Prov		•	•				•			•	•			•	•			•	•	
Tenn		•				•				•								•		
Total		•								•								•		

NIDF = Not in data file.
NR = No response.
NA = Not administered.

lated. For each variable, the minimum, median, and maximum percents found across the 12 institutions were presented.

4. Percent agreement test/retest—the percent of those instances where the examiners in the test/retest situation agreed (as previously described).

With the exception of (4), all figures were calculated from the same tape used to obtain the stability measures (N = 14,960 children who attempted both the 3YR and the 8YR SLH examinations regardless of the specified age limits, since stability measures were calculated before the final 3YR/8YR sample was selected).

Members of the SMP were then asked to rate the variables based on the statistics furnished in the quality tables, using their expert judgment and knowledge of the SLH examinations. The SMP used the following rating scale:

A = The variable is a good one; it looks promising for future use.
B = The variable is acceptable but not outstanding.
C = The variable has limited usefulness.

Letting A = 4, B = 3, and C = 2, mean rating scores were calculated and presented along with the original distribution of A's, B's, and C's. The SMP, meeting in plenum, discussed the results of this procedure. Those variables with too low an average rating were rejected, except where they measured performance for which there was no available substitute SLH variable. For example, 3YR Diadochokinesis received an acceptability mean score of 2.89 and 8YR adequacy of Word Identification (PPVT) was never subjected to analysis, yet each of these variables eventually became a component variable in an index.

Problems: Boston/Philadelphia 3YR Pre-Screen; 7YR Hearing Test

In the process of deciding which data to retain and which to omit, two special problems were encountered which required separate analysis.

The first dealt with a screening procedure adopted by the Boston and Philadelphia institutions. These two institutions felt that, because of limited time and space and the expense involved, they could not adhere to the sample selection procedures outlined by the NINCDS Collaborative Perinatal Project for the 3YR SLH test battery. They chose, instead, to use a screening procedure which involved an interview by a nonspecialist in the home. There was some variation in the two interviews. However, for the most part, information on the child's ability was obtained by questioning the mother; the child was observed throughout the entire interview but was asked only a few questions directly. Only those children who failed this screening, that is, were reported to have or exhibited speech, language, or hearing difficulties, were brought to the hospital for examination by specialists (Fiedler et al., 1971). In subsequent analysis involving a breakdown by institution, no real discrepancies among institutions were noted that could not be accounted for by the racial and socioeconomic composition of the population and, therefore, Boston and Philadelphia continued to be included in the study.

A second major problem was the early termination of the study at institutions in six locations: New Orleans, Philadelphia, Providence, Richmond, New York Medical, and New York Columbia. Some institutions collected larger samples during their participation, thus accounting for the appearance of uniformity in the sample sizes. Of significance to the SLH analysis was the discovery that four of the six institutions (New Orleans, Philadelphia, Providence, Richmond) had administered the pure-tone hearing section of the 8YR test battery to seven-year-olds (N = 8,949) who were not expected to return for test at age eight, and that these data had been included on the 8YR tape provided by the PRB. Therefore, these 7YR tests appeared as legitimate 8YR pure-tone tests with all other test items missing. The seven-year-old subjects were omitted from further analysis because of the missing data and because the hearing tests were given outside acceptable age limits for this study.

NCPP Variable Reduction

The process of reducing the number of NCPP variables was qualitatively and quantitatively different from the process of reducing the number of SLH variables. A quality analysis was not performed, but a retained variable was required to have few missing data. Each SMP member received psychological, pediatric, prenatal, obstetrical, family health history, socioeconomic, genetic and general-administrative manuals and protocols for the purpose of selecting all variables he considered in any way useful to the study. Only 898 of the 5500 NCPP variables were chosen by at least one SMP member. Many of those 898 were chosen by all SMP members, indicating considerable agreement regarding the importance of some NCPP variables. The study staff eliminated many duplicate measures and measures known to have many missing data. A variable such as the race of the father of the baby (FOB), while possibly a good predictor, was not accepted for use in the final analysis due to the extent of missing data; for 57% of the SLH children, the race of the father of the baby was unknown or not in the data file because the question was not on the early forms. As a result of further consultation with the SMP and consultants, measures from examinations which were judged unreliable were also eliminated.

After this screening, 363 NCPP variables remained.

Any categorical (unordered) variable with more than two valid codes was partitioned into dichotomous variables, one dichotomous variable for each valid code. Dichotomous variables have two possible response codes; namely, Yes or No. A dichotomous variable may be considered to be ordered; hence, this procedure corrected for the lack of ordering which invalidates use of the Pearson coefficient. For example, all of the variables recording blood type have responses of type A, type B, type AB or type O. Since there is no natural ordering of blood types, four dichotomous variables were formed with responses of A or not-A, B or not-B, AB or not-AB, and O or not-O. By this means the number of NCPP variables expanded from 363 to 901. A list of these 901 variables, with their sources, appears in Appendix 2.

The frequencies of missing data for the NCPP variables were tabulated over the union (27,558 children) of the three SLH samples. Any variable, ordinal or dichotomous, with more than 20% missing data was removed from further consideration. All NCPP variables (including the artificially created dichotomies) were then examined for balance. A variable with 99.9% or more of its responses on one code was judged to be too imbalanced to be suitable for calculation of the Pearson correlation with the SLH outcomes. Variables not suitable for Pearson correlation remained available for other analyses.

Missing Data

The term "missing data" includes several ways in which a numerical score for a variable or index for a particular child is either unavailable, or available but unusable. SLH and NCPP variables could be (a) not in data file, (b) coded erroneously, or, (c) coded unknown. Most 8YR SLH subtests contain an item Adequacy of Test, coded adequate, not adequate, or

66

unknown. Adequacy unknown occurs only when the subtest was not administered. Many children have variables with proper codes in a subtest coded inadequate.

Frequency tables of each SLH variable contain all codes, including unknown and miscode, as well as a count of the scores not in data file; frequency of Adequacy of Test is tabulated as a separate item. In the construction of indexes, any properly coded SLH variable from an inadequate subtest was not used; that is, it was treated as if it were unknown or not in data file. Except for special circumstances explained in Appendix 4, construction of indexes, no unknown SLH variable score was used to generate an index score.

NCPP variables have no adequacy ratings, but do have unknown codes as well as items coded not in the data file. For each child, only known NCPP variable scores were used.

Since indexes were constructed by the study staff following the above rules for excluding SLH variable scores, missing data for an index means only scores not in data file.

Index Construction

An index is a rule for combining more than one measurement into a single numerical score, the index score. By using indexes to measure a child's SLH performance in some areas, this study was able to focus on relatively few index scores instead of many separate SLH variable scores. 8YR Language Production, for example, replaces nine variable scores with one index score. Clinically, it is useful to know that a selection of items, when considered together, constitutes a single description of performance.

The SLH variables are measures of 3YR and 8YR SLH performance. In some instances (for example, 3YR Hypernasality, 8YR Articulation) a single SLH variable fully describes a child's perform-ance in an important area; such a variable is called a key variable. Key variables may be thought of as one-dimensional indexes of SLH performance. In other instances, for example, 8YR Hearing Severity, scores of several closely associated variables (in this case pure-tone hearing at different frequencies) were combined to define a measure of the child's performance. Yet another kind of index was intended to measure SLH performance in a broad area, such as Language Production, by combining scores from several parts of the SLH battery. Such an index gives both the research worker and the clinician a single scoring scale for performance that is multi-dimensional.

The SMP used the list of 77 SLH variables to construct indexes. The SMP was divided into subcommittees according to areas of expertise for the purpose of choosing index subsets of SLH variables. Thirty-five (not mutually exclusive) subsets were chosen, 12 indexes of 3YR SLH performance and 23 indexes of 8YR performance. Next, these subcommittees decided upon rules for combining the scores of the components of a subset into a single score.

The components of three other indexes of 8YR SLH performance had been chosen in 1972 by another SLH Task Force assembled by the PRB. These indexes were designated 8YR Neurological Involvement, 8YR Auditory Processing, and 8YR Communicative Effectiveness. This work group had not completely described the rules for combining the component variables for scoring; therefore, the SMP formulated these rules also.

Index scores were then computed for each study child. Some of the indexes are simple sums of the scores of their component variables; for example, 3YR Sentence Complexity is an index whose components are Sentence Structure, Word Order, Sentence Length, Relevance, and Use of Pronouns. A child who passes one of these components receives a 1 for that component; failure is scored as 0. The index sums the five component scores, which is equivalent to counting the number of components passed. The possible scores for this index are 0, 1, . . ., 5. A child who did not receive a 0 or 1 for all of the components did not receive any score for the index; that is, missing data on any of the components for a particular child resulted in no score for that index.

Other indexes are more complicated combinations of their component scores. 3YR Speech Mechanism is an index that combines the performances of Lip Retraction, Lip Diadochokinesis, and Tongue Diadochokinesis. A child who failed all three was given a score of 0 for that index and one who passed all three was given a 7. Passing Lip Retraction and failing the other two component measures yielded a score of 1. Passing Lip Diadochokinesis and failing the other two yielded a score of 2. Passing only Lip Diadochokinesis was judged by the subcommittee to indicate clinical performance superior to passing only Lip Retraction, so it was given a higher score. On this index also a missing or unknown score on any of the component variables resulted in a missing index score. Only pass/fail combinations of all three components yielded an index score.

The index 3YR Auditory Memory is even more complex since not all combinations of its five components yield a score. The details of the rule for this index, as well as for all the others, are found in Appendix 4. Except for Written Communication, which contains two measures from the 7YR Wide Range Achievement Test, all component variables of SLH indexes are from the two SLH test batteries.

A principal component analysis was performed for those indexes that are linear combinations of the scores of their component variables. Thus, for the selected components, the principal component technique selected linear combinations that are orthogonal to each other, and have maximum variance among all

linear combinations whose sum of squared coefficients is unity. The principal components, which can be viewed as computer-selected indexes, were found to have correlations greater than 0.85 with corresponding expert-formulated indexes.

Each index has a corresponding missingness profile. Missing index scores are due to missing data in one or more of the component variables. For indexes with five or fewer component variables, the missingness profile comprised all possible absent/present combinations of the variables. For indexes with more than five component variables, the number of combinations of missing components is at least $(2^6 - 1) = 63$, too many for comprehension in profile form; therefore, the missingness profile is given as the number of absent variables. Each missingness profile had its own set of possible outcomes which are presented in Appendix 4 along with the description of the indexes. Missingness profiles were not generated for the three indexes created by the 1972 NIH work group (8YR Neurological Involvement, 8YR Communicative Effectiveness, and 8YR Auditory Processing).

Frequencies of index scores and missingness profiles were tabulated. The SMP used these in reviewing each index to make changes and deletions where necessary. Some indexes were dropped or reconstructed due to redundancy (that is, they supplied no information not already provided by other indexes) or high degrees of missingness. Eight indexes (3YR No Speech, 8YR Hearing Acuity, and the six 8YR Monaural/Binaural Hearing Loss indexes) were intended for use in ancillary studies. The study retained 35 indexes in all: ten 3YR and 25 8YR. Descriptive statistics and frequency distributions of the indexes appear in Appendix 5.

The following 27 indexes remained as outcomes for correlation with NCPP potential predictors and for use as predictands in multiple regression:

3YR Speech Mechanism	8YR Speech Mechanism	8YR Written Communication
3YR Hypernasality	8YR Palatal Function and Hypernasality	8YR Language Production
3YR Fluency	8YR Fluency	8YR Concept Development
3YR Articulation	8YR Articulation	8YR Hearing Severity
3YR Intelligibility	8YR Intelligibility	8YR Total Conductive Loss
3YR Language Comprehension	8YR Language Comprehension	8YR Total Sensorineural Loss
3YR Sentence Complexity	8YR Auditory Memory	8YR Neurological Involvement
3YR Auditory Memory	8YR Digits	8YR Auditory Processing
3YR Hearing Screen	8YR Word Identification	8YR Communicative Effectiveness

Statistical Analyses

Descriptive Statistics and Frequency Distributions

It has already been indicated that the calculation of certain statistics was standard procedure in the analysis of the SLH variables and indexes. Frequencies of coded outcomes of the 77 SLH variables of acceptable quality were calculated by race (White, Black), sex, Socioeconomic Index,* and total sample size for each of the three SLH samples. Frequencies of scores for the 35* SLH indexes were calculated by race, sex, SEI, institution, and total for each of the SLH three samples. Means, standard deviations, and standard errors were calculated and presented where appropriate.

Appendices 3 and 5 present the descriptive statistics and frequency distributions of the SLH variables and indexes, respectively, for the SLH sample of 27,558 children; that is, the ALL 3YR sample was used to generate 3YR statistics and the ALL 8YR sample was used to generate the 8YR statistics.

---

* A child's Socioeconomic Index (SEI) was determined at birth with codes ranging from 0.0 through 9.5. The scores are grouped as follows: group 1 = 0.0 through 1.9; group 2 = 2.0 through 3.9; group 3 = 4.0 through 5.9; group 4 = 6.0 through 7.9; group 5 = 8.0 through 9.5. Tabulation by SEI means by these five SEI groups. (See Chapter 4).
* The 35 indexes comprise: nine 3YR indexes for basic study, one for ancillary study; 18 8YR indexes for basic study, seven for ancillary study. Of the 18 basic 8YR indexes, three were partially designed by the 1972 SLH work group.

Correlation Screen

Of the 901 NCPP variables (either those naturally ordered or those formed by dichotomization as described earlier in this chapter), 225 were excluded from the screening for any of three reasons.

First, if the missing data for an ordered variable or for an unordered one, before it was categorized, amounted to 20% or greater, that variable was excluded. An exception to this rule was made in a few instances where absence of data was caused by a code such as "not applicable." For example, for the parity variable, although there was a high percentage of missing data, most of it was derived from the code "no prior pregnancies." The subset of cases which had a prior pregnancy was considered of possible value for further analysis; therefore, the variable was included in the correlation analysis.

Second, if the frequency of occurrence in some category of an unordered variable was 27 or fewer (that is, less than 0.1% of the total sample of 27,558 had that characteristic), that category was excluded.

Third, an ordered variable with ten or fewer codes was eliminated if its distribution was so skewed that all codes but one had 27 or fewer responses.

The 18,252 (676 × 27) Pearson product moment correlations of the remaining 676 variables with each of the 27 basic SLH indexes were then calculated. The average absolute correlation of each NCPP variable with the 27 indexes was also computed by summing the absolute values of the 27 correlations of one NCPP variable with the indexes and dividing by 27. The great majority of the 676 average absolute correlations were <0.10: 63 NCPP variables had an average absolute correlation ≥0.10 and <0.15; 34 had an average absolute correlation ≥0.15. Of these 97 NCPP variables with average absolute correlations ≥0.10, most were measurements taken at four or seven years.

Multiple Regression

It is well known that multiple linear regression can give misleading results if one or more of the true underlying regression functions is seriously nonlinear. Regression results are particularly misleading when one of the underlying regression functions is not even monotonic. Although we did not examine all of the underlying regression functions for monotonicity, we did examine some; our collective belief about the relationships among the remaining variables used is that all of the relationships are monotonic. If that belief in monotonicity is correct, the true strength of relationship between any two variables could be underestimated by assuming linearity, but the estimated direction of relationship would be correct.

It was decided to use early antecedent variables (measured at birth to 1YR) wherever possible to predict SLH outcomes, and to use the same antecedent variables to predict both 3YR and 8YR outcomes. Twelve early antecedent NCPP variables were chosen for prediction. Eight of them have an average absolute

correlation with the SLH indexes greater than 0.10. Three of the eight are variables constructed to describe race and sex, and are called Race-Sex Markers in this study.* The other five are Education of Father, Education of Mother, Per Capita Income, Occupation of Father, and Four-Year IQ. Four additional variables (Birthweight, Gestational Age, Eight-Month Bayley Motor Score, and Eight-Month Bayley Mental Score) do not have an average absolute correlation greater than 0.10 with the indexes, but they were chosen to supplement the other eight because they appear frequently in the literature as indicators of pathology. These formed a set of 12 independent variables on which to regress the 27 SLH indexes.

Various combinations of independent measures (both NCPP variables and SLH indexes) were used to attempt to predict 3YR and 8YR outcomes. In all, five sets of independent predictor variables were chosen on which to regress the 18 8YR SLH indexes. They are:

a. At-Birth and Eight-Month (Bayley) variables and 4YR IQ.
b. At-Birth and Eight-Month (Bayley) variables.
c. At-Birth variables only.
d. 3YR SLH indexes and At-Birth variables.
e. 3YR SLH indexes only.

Two sets of independent variables were chosen on which to regress the nine 3YR SLH indexes. They are:

a. At-Birth and Eight-Month (Bayley) variables.
b. At-Birth variables.

The motivations for these choices are varied. The five sets of variables used with the 8YR indexes were chosen for the following reasons:

a. Regression with At-Birth and Eight-Month variables and 4YR IQ shows how well 8YR outcomes can

---

* Race and sex are described by only three *linearly independent* variables, since knowing the answers to the three questions: "Is the child a White Male?", "Is the child a White Female?", and "Is the child a Black Male?" is sufficient to determine all Race-Sex combinations. A "no" to all three questions is equivalent to saying that the child is a Black Female. Linear independence is necessary for the matrix inversion which is a part of the regression computation.

70

be predicted with all the information available to the study.

b. Regression without 4YR IQ was another check of its apparent dominance as a predictor of 8YR SLH behavior.

c. Regression without the Bayley scores and 4YR IQ demonstrates to what extent 8YR outcomes are predicted entirely by easily-measured at-birth events alone.

d. Adding the 3YR indexes to the At-Birth variables shows the extent to which the indexes created by the study group improve prediction of 8YR behavior.

e. Regression with the 3YR SLH indexes alone shows to what extent the study has succeeded in creating indexes of performance that are useful in predicting 8YR behavior.

The two sets of variables on which the 3YR indexes were regressed were chosen as follows:

a. Regressing the 3YR indexes on the At-Birth and Eight-Month variables uses all the information available to the study about the three-year-old.

b. Using only the At-Birth measures demonstrates again how much of a child's SLH behavior can be predicted by these readily available At-Birth events only.

The multiple regression equation computations were carried out in part with original computer programs and in part with the SPSS (Statistical Package for the Social Sciences) subprogram REGRESSION (Nie, Bent, and Hull, 1975) (Version 6.0 as implemented on the CDC CYBER 74 computer configuration by the University of Minnesota Computer Center). The multiple regression statistics, which are presented in Appendix 8, are (1) the multple correlation coefficient R and R^2, (2) the set of regression coefficients, β-coefficients, for the standardized independent variables, and (3) the constant term and set of regression coefficients, B-coefficients, for unstandardized independent variables. A standardized variable is calculated by the following formula:

$$\frac{x - \overline{x}}{s}$$

where $\overline{x}$ is the sample mean of the original variable x and s is the corresponding sample standard deviation. The relative absolute magnitudes of the β-coefficients measure the relative importance of the independent variables in the regression equation. The B-coefficients are used in computing individual prediction equations with unstandardized data.

Three of the variables in some of the regression equations are Race-Sex Markers. They arose as a compromise between (1) doing the regression analysis four times, once for each race-sex combination, and (2) not considering the interaction between race and sex at all. In order to do the regression analysis only once, but also consider race-sex interactions, three Race-Sex Markers were artificially created. To make the matrix involved in the regression amenable to mathematical manipulation, only three indicators could be used. Their values were set in the following way in order to solve a purely computational problem.

The β-coefficients of the Race-Sex Markers do not have the same interpre-

	Race-Sex Marker one	Race-Sex Marker two	Race-Sex Marker three
White Male	1	0	0
White Female	0	1	0
Black Male	0	0	1
Black Female	−1	−1	−1

71

tation as the β-coefficients associated with the other independent variables. For the other independent variables, the absolute magnitudes of the β-coefficients reflect the relative importance of their associated variables; larger β-coefficients, in *absolute* magnitude, are associated with more important predictors. This is not true of the β-coefficients of the Race-Sex Markers, so trying to use the β-coefficients to describe the relative importance of being a particular race and sex is unwieldy. But the B-coefficients of the Race-Sex Markers are useful as follows:

Let B_1, B_2, and B_3 denote the B's associated with Race-Sex Markers one, two, and three respectively. To obtain the predicted score of any index for a hypothetical or real child, multiply the B's by their corresponding hypothetical, or real, values for each of the predictor variables; that is, Birthweight, Gestational Age, and so forth. If the child is a White Male, his race-sex contribution to the predicted score is B_1. A White Female's race-sex contribution is B_2; a Black Male's contribution is B_3; and a Black Female's contribution is $(-B_1-B_2-B_3)$. It follows that two children who are exactly alike in their Birthweights, Gestational Ages, and so forth, but are not the same race and/or sex as each other will have different predicted scores determined solely by their race-sex B's. For example, a White Male who has the same birthweight as a Black Male has a predicted score B_1-B_3 higher. Similarly, a White Female has a predicted score $B_2-(-B_1-B_2-B_3) = 2B_2+B_1+B_3$ higher than a Black Female who is like her in every other respect.

To compare the effect of sex for the two races, note that a White Male has a predicted score B_1-B_2 higher than his twin White Female; a Black Male has a predicted score $B_3-(-B_1-B_2-B_3) = 2B_3+B_1+B_2$ higher than his twin Black

Female. It is thus seen that the comparison between races is sex-specific, and the comparison between sexes is race-specific.

Some of the regression output for 8YR Word Identification, as it is presented in Appendix 8, will illustrate the use and interpretation of the B- and β-coefficients and the multiple correlation coefficient. From Table 5-1 it is seen that, for 8YR Word Identification, the size of the β-coefficients is highly dependent on the presence of the standardized independent variable, 4YR IQ. The β-coefficient of 4YR IQ is 0.44; the next highest is the β-coefficient of Race-Sex Marker one, 0.31. No other β-coefficient in the regression has an absolute magnitude nearly as great; all the rest are less than 0.10. For the regression equation without 4YR IQ, however, Race-Sex Marker one has a coefficient of 0.37 and five other β-coefficients (those associated with Per Capita Income, Education of Mother, Education of Father, Race-Sex Marker two, and Race-Sex Marker three) are all greater than 0.10. That is, if 4YR IQ is included as a predictor, it and Race-Sex Marker one have almost all of the predictive importance. If 4YR IQ is excluded, Race-Sex Marker one has the greatest predictive power and five other independent variables now make a moderate, instead of negligible, contribution to the prediction.

The β-coefficients are the measures of predictive importance; but to compute a predicted index for an individual, it is much more convenient to use the B-coefficient since use of the latter does not require standardization of the input variables. For example, to predict 8YR Word Identification performance for a child using the regression equation without 4YR IQ, the child's birthweight in grams is multiplied by the coefficient 0.00067, his gestational age in weeks is multiplied by -0.018, etc. These products are then added to the constant term to yield the predicted score. Thus: predicted 8YR

72

Table 5-1

Excerpt of regression output for 8YR Word Identification predicted by At-Birth variables, Eight-Month (Bayley) variables and 4YR IQ.

Response Variable 8YR Word Identification	Coefficients of Independent Predictors			
	β	B	β	B
	At-Birth NCPP's Eight-Month NCPP's		At-Birth NCPP's Eight-Month NCPP's 4YR IQ	
Multiple R	.662		.753	
R Square	.438		.567	
Constant		33.23		23.68
Birthweight	.0368	.000676	.0134	.00246
Gestation Age	−.00568	−.0183	−.00115	−.00369
Education of Gravida	.152	.627	.0878	.363
Per Capita Income	.117	.00107	.0790	.000720
Education of F.O.B.	.132	.446	.0812	.275
Occupation of F.O.B.	.0724	1.602	.0414	.916
8-month Mental Score	.0679	.122	.0209	.0374
8-month Motor Score	.0637	.137	.0206	.0443
4YR IQ			.438	.260
Race-Sex Marker I	.367	5.121	.315	4.388
Race-Sex Marker II	.162	2.287	.0429	.604
Race-Sex Marker III	−.181	−2.552	−.075	−1.062

$$\text{Word Identification} = 33.23 + \sum_{i=1}^{11} x_i B_i$$

where the x_i's are the values of the 11 NCPP variables.

The multiple correlation coefficient, R, is a measure of the predictive ability of an entire set of predictors. It is the correlation between the linear combination of predictor variables, chosen by least squares, and the predictand, in this instance an index score. In the case of 8YR Word Identification, R is 0.75 using At-Birth and Eight-Month variables and 4YR IQ as predictors; using At-Birth and Eight-Month variables only, the R = 0.66. Squaring R yields the amount of variability in the outcome accounted for by the linear combination of predictor variables. Thus, the linear combination of the 12 predictors accounts for .56 (= $0.75^2 \times 100$) of the variance of 8YR Word Identification, whereas the linear combination without 4YR IQ accounts for .44 (= $0.66^2 \times 100$) of the variance.

The reader who wishes to compare the relative effects of using one set of predictors over another, applying the same type of analysis described above, is referred to Appendix 8.

Second Correlation Screen

Following the regression analysis, residuals were computed. A residual is the difference between a child's actual SLH index score and his predicted one. For 3YR indexes the residuals were computed with the equation derived from the regression design using At-Birth and Eight-Month variables; for the 8YR indexes, the At-Birth/Eight-Month/4YR IQ equation was used. Correlations between the 676 NCPP variables and the residuals were calculated. A high correlation would indicate that the original regression design would be substantially improved by inclusion of that NCPP variable in the list of predictor variables.

The correlations of the 676 NCPP

variables with the residuals were all extremely low, almost never more than 0.10 in absolute value. Exceptions were the correlations between the SLH indexes and items on both the Wechsler Intelligence Scale for Children and the Wide Range Achievement Test. These tests were administered at age seven. Such 7YR variables are obviously useless for predicting 3YR SLH outcomes because they occur four years too late. They are also too close in time to the actual 8YR outcomes to be considered useful predictors. As a result, the original regression equations remained unchanged.

Cross-Tabulations of Predictors with Index Outcomes

As previously stated, the Pearson product moment correlation was chosen as the measure of association between two ordered variables. This measure is considered optimal when the two variables have a bivariate Gaussian distribution. There is no optimal measure of association for most other bivariate distributions. In particular, if both variables are dichotomous, there are many reasonable candidates for measures of association.

no appreciable correlation existed where one was expected, or because a large correlation appeared that could not be explained without further examination of the two variables in association. As a result, another technique of analysis, the cross-tabulation, was used to allow examination of the frequencies of joint occurrences between NCPP variables and SLH indexes. A cross-tabulation may be viewed as an r × c contingency table. All indexes were dichotomized into pass/fail for the purposes of cross-tabulation analysis. Pass and fail criteria for the SLH indexes were set by using the frequencies of SLH index outcomes presented in Appendix 5. The bottom 10% (or the percentile closest to the tenth) was taken as the cut-off for failure, the other 90% as pass.

Two conditional probabilities were also provided with the cross-tabulation analysis: probability that a child failed B given that he failed A, and probability that a child failed B given he passed A; where A and B are two dichotomized measurements, and B occurs chronologically after A.

For example, using Birthweight as A and 3YR Speech Mechanism as B, the joint occurrences for the ALL 3YR sample (N = 19,885) are as follows:

3YR Speech Mechanism	Birthweight	
	Pass (2,501 through 4,000 gms)	Fail (2,500 gms and below)
Pass (score = 7)	12,663	1,451
Fail (score = 0 through 6)	4,179	603

Number of invalid scores: 989.
The two conditional probabilities are:
    Prob (fail 3YR Speech Mechanism given failed Birthweight) = 0.29,
    Prob (fail 3YR Speech Mechanism given passed Birthweight) = 0.25.

Some members of the SMP found that their expectations about the pair-wise associations between certain NCPP predictors and SLH indexes were not confirmed by the Pearson correlation; either because

There were some almost continuous NCPP variables which did not lend themselves easily to being dichotomized. These variables were processed through the use of SPSS (Statistical Package for the Social Sciences) subprogram CROSS-TABS, INTEGER MODE (1) (Version 6.0 as implemented on the CDC CYBER 74 computer configuration at the University of Minnesota Computer Center). This subprogram produced cross-tabulations for r × c tables, where r = 2 (Pass and Fail in the Index) and c = the number of levels of the NCPP variable; as an example, the following display shows the cross-tabulation for Education of the Gravida against 8YR Language Production:

Statistical Significance and Clinical Meaningfulness

The large sample sizes used in this study usually caused measurements of differences from hypothesized values to be statistically significant even though they may be clinically irrelevant. Some examples will demonstrate this phenomenon.

An observed correlation of .025 with a sample size of 10,000 is statistically significant at the .05 level. Substitution into

8YR Language Production		Education of Gravida		
		0-8 years	9-12 years	13 or more years
Fail	Count	n = 576	n = 1,386	n = 63
	Row pct	28.4%	68.4%	3.1%
	Col pct	19.0%	10.0%	2.5%
Pass	Count	n = 2,461	n = 12,440	n = 2,440
	Row pct	14.2%	71.7%	14.1%
	Col pct	81.0%	90.0%	97.5%

Number of missing observations: 771.

It can be seen that Education of Gravida was categorized by the number of years school was attended. Those mothers with eight years or less of school were in one group, those with nine to 12 years were in the second group, and those with 13 or more years of school were in the third group. The Pass or Fail on 8YR Language Production form the two rows with the bottom 10% of the distribution producing the Fail group. Within each cell is the frequency count, the row percent and the column percent. Comparison of the column percents for Fail across the three categories shows that as the amount of education increases, the percentages of children who fail decreases from 19.0% to 2.5%. Probability figures for these tables do not permit the same interpretation as for those calculated for the fourfold tables. The percent Fail on the index is the appropriate value to compare across categories of the NCPP variable.

a large sample formula for a 95% confidence interval, $\hat{\rho} \pm 2\sqrt{1/n}$, yields

$$.025 \pm 2\sqrt{1/10,000}$$
$$= .025 \pm 2(.01)$$
$$= .025 \pm .02$$

This does not contain zero. Therefore, the estimate of ρ is statistically significantly different from zero. However, a correlation of .025 accounts for only .0625% [$(.025)^2 = .000625$] of the variance, and would be difficult to defend as clinically meaningful. The confidence interval interpretation, which states that the true correlation is between .005 and .045 with 95% confidence, does not mislead the reader into believing that an observed correlation of .025 is important.

Similarly, the following comparison of the effects of two independent factors results in statistical significance due to the large sample sizes of this study. A common null hypothesis is that the difference between the two population

75

means, $\mu_1 - \mu_2$, is zero. A 95% confidence interval for differences of independent means can be calculated for large sample sizes using the following formula:

$$\overline{x}_1 - \overline{x}_2 \pm 2\sqrt{\frac{s_1^2}{n_1} + \frac{s_2^2}{n_2}}$$

The large sample sizes make the quantity $2\sqrt{s_1^2/n_1 + s_2^2/n_2}$ small so that $\overline{x}_1 - \overline{x}_2$ accurately estimates $\mu_1 - \mu_2$. For example, if factor 1 is being Female and factor 2 is being Male, the statistics for estimating Male and Female performances on 8YR Concept Development are:

factors	$\overline{x}_i$	s_i^2	n_i
1. Female	42.812	109.307	9744
2. Male	41.965	110.565	9864

A 95% confidence interval for the true difference between Male and Female performance is given by:

$$42.812 - 41.965 \pm 2\sqrt{\frac{109.307}{9744} + \frac{110.565}{9864}}$$
$$= .847 \pm 2\sqrt{.022}$$
$$= .847 \pm .297.$$

Hence, $.550 \leqslant \mu_1 - \mu_2 \leqslant 1.144$. This interval does not contain zero; therefore, the null hypothesis is rejected at the .05 level. The language clinician, however, may consider the effect of sex on 8YR Concept Development to be clinically negligible.

References

1. Broman, S.H., Nichols, P.L., and Kennedy, W.A. *Preschool IQ: Prenatal and Early Developmental Correlates.* Hillsdale, New Jersey: Lawrence Erlbaum Associates, 1975.

2. Fiedler, M.F., Lenneberg, E.H., Rolfe, U.T., and Drorbaugh, J.E. A speech screening procedure with three-year-old children. *Pediatrics* 48:268–276, 1971.

3. Mantel, N. Why stepdown procedures in variable selection. *Technometrics* 12:621, 1970.

4. Nie, N.H., Bent, D.H., and Hull, C.H. *SPSS.* 2nd Ed. New York: McGraw Hill, 1975.

## CHAPTER 6

Hearing

Earl D. Schubert, Ph.D.
Frank M. Lassman, Ph.D.
Paul J. LaBenz, Sc.D.

Introduction

Whether the hearing capabilities of a child vary from the norm to a degree that may measurably hamper speech and language development is a question not easily answered at an early age. Over a period of years, considerable ingenuity in devising tests for children has edged the point of successful measurement gradually earlier in the child's life. Still, it would be advantageous to detect, even at birth or before, any signs that auditory capabilities will not develop normally.

The well-known associations between speech and language development and hearing have been formulated from observations of the more severely hearing impaired. Associations between communicative competency and hearing levels varying within the range close to normal threshold are less well known and more difficult to measure. Data in the NCPP study of a large sample of children enable the investigation of possible associations between communicative abilities and hearing at marginally impaired levels. Conditions and events observed early in the child's history also are available for exploration of relationships with speech and language, as well as with hearing assessed at the age of three years and eight years. These associations with hearing, together with normative data, are reported in this chapter.

3YR Tests

For the three-year-old children, two of the tests given are quite appropriately considered tests of hearing. These are the Pure-Tone Screening Test and the Spondaic Word Test.

The Spondaic Word Test was given first as a screening test of speech discrimination. The test was administered as a sound field test, with the child seated so that his ears were about three feet from the loudspeaker. The words were reproduced by a Wollensak tape recorder, with two levels of reproduction available. Words produced at a moderate conversational level were used for orientation and instruction; those used for actual testing were estimated to be at a quiet conversa-

tional level. The calibration tone registered 72 dB SPL and 52 dB SPL, respectively.

It may be worth remarking that the lower testing level (52 dB SPL) is further above threshold than the pure-tone screening tones used. At the 20 dB HL screening level, the average SPL of the three conventional speech frequencies (.5K, 1K, 2K) would be 43 dB.

Changes between the orientation and the testing levels were achieved with a single 20 dB pad, so that there was no need to change the volume control of the tape recorder during the testing of the child. As is apparent from the lists shown in Table 6-1, there were four ten-word lists available at the test level. If the child responded readily to the three orientation

Table 6-1
Spondee words for the 3YR test.

Audible-Response Series			
List I (Hi)	List II (Hi)	List III (Lo)	List IV (Lo)
cowboy	doorbell	mailman	popcorn
baseball	flashlight	seesaw	icebox
hot dog	goldfish	ice cream	pancake
	lipstick	lipstick	pork chop
	football	haircut	ashtray
	sidewalk	toothbrush	ice cream
	toothpaste	outside	toothbrush
	oatmeal	sailboat	birthday
	cupcake	airplane	hairbrush
	bathtub	birthday	airport

Pointing-Response Series			
List V (Hi)	List VI (Hi)	List VII (Lo)	List VIII (Lo)
cowboy	bathtub	mailman	popgun
baseball	ice cream	bluebird	goldfish
hot dog	seesaw	toothbrush	necktie
	redbird	sailboat	flashlight
	hairbrush	airplane	teaspoon
	ice cream	sailboat	teaspoon
	redbird	airplane	goldfish
	hairbrush	mailman	popgun
	seesaw	toothbrush	flashlight
	bathtub	bluebird	necktie

words of List I, the tester moved immediately to List III. If the child repeated correctly the first five words of this low-level list (List III) or repeated correctly any seven of the ten words of that list, the child was considered to pass the spondee test. If there was any uncertainty of response to the three-word orientation list, the examiner would use part or all of the longer orientation list (List II) for further pretest instruction. Eventually, according to instructions, the child had to repeat five consecutive words at the low level, or repeat any seven of ten words of a low-level list (List III, IV, VII, or VIII) to be recorded as passing the spondee test.

Two of these low-level lists (List III and List IV) were used for testing the child who could give the required verbal response to these spondee words, and two (List VII and List VIII) were furnished with picture cards for the children who could be tested more readily through a pointing response. Six pictures were furnished with each of the lists of the spondee test.

3YR Pure-Tone Screen

The Pure-Tone Screening Test was a three-frequency test presented in the sequence: 2000, 1000, and 500 Hz in the right ear; and 500, 1000, and 2000 Hz in the left ear. The level employed was 20 dB above the ASA 1951 audiometric zero or approximately 30 dB re ISO 1964. Examiners were instructed to take special pains to put the child at ease and to encourage attentive listening. They were also cautioned about avoiding brief periods of high ambient noise at the test moment, even though the test rooms measured within sound level limits specified in the manual (Appendix 1).

Play audiometry techniques were considered permissible. Primarily, the examiner was advised to be satisfied that a child had given a reliable response to each frequency that was recorded as passed. If the child failed to respond to any one of the frequencies in a given ear, he had failed the Pure-Tone Screening Test for that ear. Thus, for the screening test at three years, we have no record of the number of children who failed to respond at a particular frequency. Data were analyzed separately by ears.

Pure-Tone Results

As can be seen from Table 6-2, of more than 16,000 children successfully screened, the number of children who fail the screening test by the criterion described above varies around 4% to 5%, depending somewhat on the race and sex of the sample and on the ear tested. The percent of the total sample and the subsamples of each race, sex, and SEI classification that passed these 3YR tests is shown in Figure 6-1.

In the Pittsburgh study of children age five to 14 (Eagles et al., 1963) the 95th percentile lay at 10 dB HL (same audiometric zero as the present study), and the 99th percentile at 28 dB HL for 500 Hz, 35 dB HL for 1K Hz, and 38 dB for 2K Hz. Thus, for between four and five percent of our 3YR sample to fail to hear a 20 dB HL tone at one of these frequencies amounts to reasonable agreement between the two studies.

It is admittedly difficult to interpret statistical checks when many tests have been performed on the same sample. In this instance, χ^2s have been computed but should be taken to be no more than rough indexes of the area where chance variation gives way to repeatable differences. Actually, the difference in the number of Male and Female children who failed the pure-tone screen seems to be a matter of chance, according to these data. In the Pittsburgh study of pure-tone thresholds of children ages five to 14, the mean of all Females for pure-tone measurement at these three frequencies indicates better hearing than, and is statistically different from, that for the Males

Table **6-2**

Number of children who passed or failed the 3YR Pure-Tone Screen Test.
Italic entries are percentages.

	Right Ear							
	Male		Female		White		Black	
Pass	8,244		8,169		6,964		9,449	
Fail	357	*4.2*	310	*3.7*	320	*4.4*	347	*3.5*
		$\chi^2 = 2.78$				$\chi^2 = 8.06^*$		

	Socioeconomic Index											
	0.0-1.9		2.0-3.9		4.0-5.9		6.0-7.9		8.0-9.5		Total†	
Pass	1,595		5,536		4,730		2,801		1,751		16,413	
Fail	71	*4.3*	236	*4.1*	193	*3.9*	102	*3.5*	65	*3.6*	667	*3.9*

	Left Ear							
	Male		Female		White		Black	
Pass	8,202		8,109		6,921		9,390	
Fail	386	*4.5*	342	*4.0*	344	*4.7*	384	*3.9*
		$\chi^2 = 2.09$				$\chi^2 = 6.62^{**}$		

	Socioeconomic Index											
	0.0-1.9		2.0-3.9		4.0-5.9		6.0-7.9		8.0-9.5		Total†	
Pass	1,589		5,501		4,702		2,793		1,726		16,311	
Fail	71	*4.3*	257	*4.5*	209	*4.3*	111	*3.8*	80	*4.4*	728	*4.3*

*p<.01
**p<.02
†14% not tested.

(t = 2.241; see Table 4 of Appendix 14, p. 198, Eagles et al., 1963).

The median also shows slightly better hearing for girls than for boys in that study; but the frequency distribution is not shown for boys and girls separately, so we cannot judge whether more boys than girls had thresholds worse than the 10 dB HL screening level.

But in the present study, the only one of these variables that seems to make a difference, if one consults the chi-square values, is race. Greater numbers of White children than Black failed the pure-tone screen. This is in agreement with Tenney and Edwards (1970) who screened 855 school children at 25 dB ISO at the same frequencies as reported here. Using de-tection of the screen-level tone at three of the four frequencies as a pass criterion, they report that only 2.7% of their Black children failed the test, whereas 7.4% of the White children failed. They suggested that some anatomical or structural difference may make Black children less vulnerable to otitis media. A check within our own data on 307 cases reveals lower incidence among Black children of anomalies associated with conductive loss problems; but whether this indicates less frequent occurrence or less frequent reporting is open to question. The reported instances are shown in Table 6-3. A more detailed report on these and other ear anomalies is presented later in this chapter.

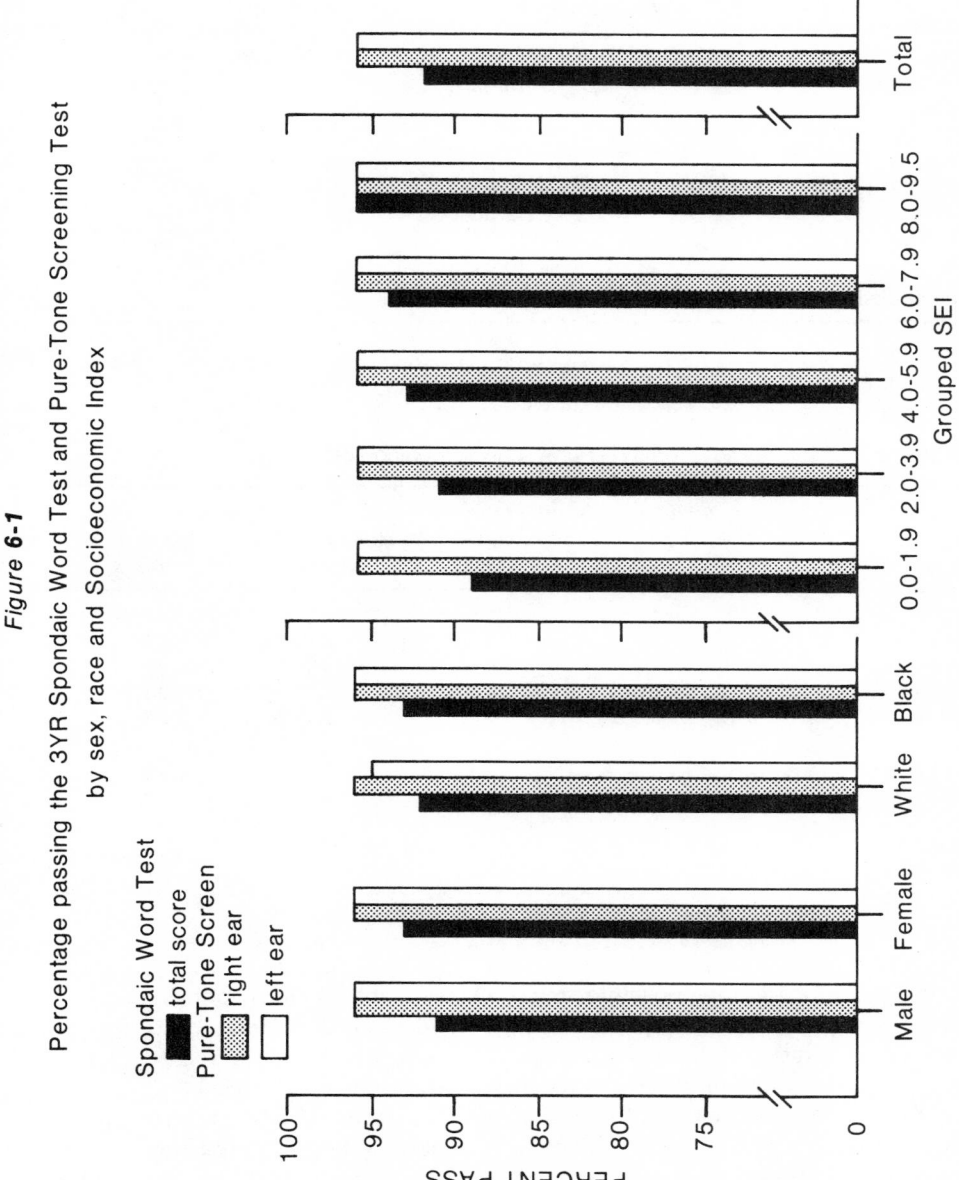

Figure **6-1**

Percentage passing the 3YR Spondaic Word Test and Pure-Tone Screening Test
by sex, race and Socioeconomic Index

81

Table **6-3**

Reported incidence of some anomalies associated with conductive losses in 307 children. For each ratio given, the denominator is the number of children in that race, sex or Socioeconomic Index group.

	Myringotomy with ventilating tubes	Scarred tympanic membrane	Infected pre-auricular sinus
White Male	23/122	14/122	1/122
White Female	15/52	15/52	0/52
Black Male	3/83	2/83	10/83
Black Female	3/50	1/50	19/50
SEI 0.0-1.9	1/21	2/21	2/21
SEI 2.0-3.9	9/95	5/95	16/95
SEI 4.0-5.9	12/86	11/86	7/86
SEI 6.0-7.9	12/74	10/74	4/74
SEI 8.0-9.5	10/31	4/31	1/31
Total Population	**44/307**	**32/307**	**30/307**

Table **6-4**

Percentage of children who failed 3YR Pure-Tone Screening Test.

	Right Ear Only (1)	Left Ear Only (2)	Monaural (1+2)	Binaural (3)	Total (1+2+3)
Total Sample	1.1	1.8	2.9	2.8	5.7
White Male	1.7	2.1	3.8	2.8	6.6
White Female	1.5	2.6	4.1	2.7	6.8
Black Male	0.6	1.5	2.1	3.2	5.3
Black Female	0.8	1.3	2.1	2.4	4.5
SEI 0.0-1.9	1.0	1.4	2.3	3.3	5.6
SEI 2.0-3.9	0.9	1.6	2.6	3.2	5.8
SEI 4.0-5.9	1.1	1.7	2.8	2.8	5.6
SEI 6.0-7.9	1.4	1.9	3.3	2.1	5.4
SEI 8.0-9.5	1.4	2.8	4.2	2.2	6.4

More is said of the possible race-related difference in hearing sensitivity in discussing the more detailed threshold measures taken at age eight. A comparison with the differences in White and Black children from the Pittsburgh study is complicated. Some of the Pittsburgh differences are of the right size to be above chance variation (of the order of twice the standard error), but they differ from one frequency to another within the frequencies tested in the present study (see Table 6 of Appendix 14, p. 200 of Eagles et al., 1963), and for our 3YR screen we have no record of failures at individual frequencies.

A particularly interesting pattern emerges from comparing the performance on right and left ears for the pure-tone screen. The percentage of children who failed the screen for the right ear only, the left ear only, and both ears is shown in Table 6-4.

In the total 3YR population there are

about equal numbers of monaural losses (497) and binaural losses (478), but the number of left ear monaural losses exceeds the recorded right ear losses by 308 to 189. A plausible explanation is that the apparent poorer left ear performance could be an order effect resulting from the systematic testing of the right ear first such that attention faltered by the time the left ear was reached.

In all *subgroups* of the sample, there is a greater percentage of left ear losses than right ear, seemingly more pronounced among Black children. At the same time, there is a smaller proportion of monaural losses than binaural losses in the Black children, somewhat the reverse of the situation among White children at this age. As seen in the lower part of Table 6-4, there is also a tendency for the percentage of monaural losses to increase with rising Socioeconomic Index. This is especially interesting when viewed together with the fact that percentage of binaural losses decreases with rise in socioeconomic status.

If one postulates a binaural loss as representing the worst condition, and the monaural loss as an intermediate stage, then the relatively higher proportion of binaural loss among Blacks and low socioeconomic categories would support a cultural and economic explanation of these findings. Another related possibility remains that children in higher SEI categories have less likelihood of severe ear disease and greater likelihood of detection and treatment when it occurs.

Results of the Spondaic Word Test

What can we discern in retrospect about the function of the Spondaic Word Test as it was given to these three-year-old children? Perhaps a look at the results is some help in understanding what the test, as given, might have been measuring. First of all, as can be seen in Table 6-5, more Males than Females failed the Spondaic Word Test. The χ^2 for this Male-Female difference in response to the Spondaic Word Test is large for a difference that would occur by chance alone. The difference does not occur for the Pure-Tone Screening Test, from which one must conclude that at this age the results of the Spondaic Word Test are not closely parallel to pure-tone hearing sensitivity. From the rather well-established fact that vocabulary grows

Table **6-5**

Number of children who passed or failed the Spondaic Word Test.
Italic entries are percentages.

	Sex and Race							
	Male		**Female**		**White**		**Black**	
Pass	7,941		8,189		7,037		9,093	
Fail	763	*8.8*	578	*6.6*	612	*8.0*	729	*7.4*
		$\chi^2 = 29.10^*$				$\chi^2 = 2.03$		

	Socioeconomic Index										
	0.0-1.9		**2.0-3.9**		**4.0-5.9**		**6.0-7.9**		**8.0-9.5**	**Total†**	
Pass	1,487		5,289		4,695		2,835		1,824	16,130	
Fail	178	*10.7*	536	*9.2*	368	*7.8*	175	*6.2*	84	*4.6*	1,341	*7.7*

*p <.001
†12% not tested

more rapidly for girls than for boys in this age range, this difference might have been predicted, but this would be on the assumption that the test was at least in part a test of vocabulary.

An interesting corollary is the indication in the lower part of Table 6-5 that the percentage of children failing the Spondaic Word Test grows progressively with decreasing SEI classification of the family. There is no comparable progression for failure of the Pure-Tone Screen. On the other hand, no reliable difference (again by our rough χ^2 index) in Spondaic Word Test results appears between White and Black children at this age.

If we look for a numerical index of the degree of concordance between sensitivity as measured by the Pure-Tone Screen and as measured by the spondees, the tetrachoric coefficients (an estimate of the product moment) between Pure-Tone Screen and spondees are .35 for the right ear and .33 for the left ear. When the Spondaic Word Test is given as a threshold test and is given monaurally, it functions in many cases as a reliable check on pure-tone results. For clinical (adult) patients with flat audiograms, Carhart and Porter (1971) found a correlation of 0.975 (n = 693), and even for patients with atypical audiogram configuration the correlation between pure-tone threshold and spondee threshold was 0.882. Of course, no direct comparison with the results shown here is possible, since the Spondaic Word Test was given using a loudspeaker in our sample, and both tests were administered as screening tests rather than as threshold tests.

There are, in fact, other indications of the lack of concordance between the Pure-Tone Screen and the Spondaic Word Test. One might suppose that with greater likelihood of middle-ear problems in children of low income families, a reliably greater proportion of three-year-old children in the lower socioeconomic brackets would fail the Pure-Tone Screen.

As seen in Table 6-2, this is apparently not the case. Actually, the small departures from equal proportions at each value of the SEI could easily have occurred through chance variation ($\chi^2 = 2.24$, df = 4). On the other hand, the different proportions failing the Spondaic Word Test are too large to occur by chance; the proportion obviously decreases as the SEI rises.

A closer look at the effect on the Spondaic Word Test of not having good enough hearing to pass the Pure-Tone Screen in both ears is afforded by Table 6-6, which compares the probability that a child who had at least one good ear (by the Pure-Tone Screen Test) passed the spondees with the probability that any child in the whole sample passed the spondees.

This is an interesting statistic because the group which passed the pure-tone screen in at least one ear should contain none of the binaural losses. If a child had at least one ear with hearing good enough to pass the pure-tone screen, then he should not have failed the spondee test because of not hearing the words. However, the percentage of this selected group which failed the Spondaic Word Test is only slightly higher than the percentage of the overall sample that failed the test. Again, children failed the Spondaic Word Test for reasons other than loss of hearing sensitivity as measured by the Pure-Tone Screen.

Even more persuasive on this same point is the fact that only 2.8% of the sample of three-year-olds failed the pure-tone screen in both ears, and therefore had binaural losses by that criterion (see Table 6-4); but 13% of the sample that took both of these tests failed the spondee test. Obviously something not sensitive to the pure-tone test was operating in a notable percentage of children who failed the spondees.

Further indication of the lack of concordance between the spondee and pure-tone tests in this population of

Table **6-6**

Probability that a child with at least one ear good enough to pass the Pure-Tone Screening Test failed the Spondaic Word Test.
The actual numbers involved are given in parentheses.*

	Probability that a child who passed the Pure-Tone Screening Test failed the Spondaic Word Test in at least one ear		Probability of failure on Spondaic Word Test. (Independent of pure-tone performance)
	Right Ear	Left Ear	
White Male	.11 (403/3,588)	.11 (403/3,581)	.14
White Female	.10 (329/3,376)	.10 (321/3,340)	.11
Black Male	.14 (630/4,656)	.13 (612/4,621)	.15
Black Female	.10 (470/4,793)	.10 (460/4,769)	.11
SEI 0.0-1.9	.15 (246/1,595)	.15 (244/1,589)	.17
SEI 2.0-3.9	.14 (749/5,536)	.13 (722/5,501)	.15
SEI 4.0-5.9	.10 (492/4,730)	.10 (485/4,702)	.12
SEI 6.0-7.9	.09 (243/2,801)	.09 (245/2,793)	.10
SEI 8.0-9.5	.06 (102/1,751)	.06 (100/1,726)	.07
Total Sample	**.11 (1,832/16,413)**	**.11 (1,796/16,311)**	**.13**

*Note that whether the child passed the Pure-Tone Screen in the right or the left ear has little effect on the probability of failing the spondees. However, the probability of failure is somewhat less among those who passed the screen in at least one ear than it is in the total sample.

Table **6-7**

Percentage of children failing spondee, pure-tone or both tests.

	Right Ear			Left Ear		
	Spondee Only	Pure-tone Only	Spondee and PT	Spondee Only	Pure-tone Only	Spondee and PT
White Male	11	2	3	11	2	3
White Female	9	2	2	9	3	2
Black Male	13	2	2	13	2	2
Black Female	9	2	1	9	2	1
SEI 0.0-1.9	15	2	2	15	2	2
SEI 2.0-3.9	13	2	2	13	2	3
SEI 4.0-5.9	10	2	2	10	2	2
SEI 6.0-7.9	8	2	2	8	2	2
SEI 8.0-9.5	6	2	2	6	3	2
Total Sample	**11**	**2**	**2**	**11**	**2**	**2**

three-year-olds can be seen in Table 6-7. Of those children who completed both a spondee and a right-ear-pure-tone test, 13% (11 + 2) failed the spondee test; but, of those who failed it, only 2% also failed the Pure-Tone Screen in the right ear. This proportion is approximately the same for the other ear, and is characteristic of all the subgroups. A considerably greater number of children failed the spondee test than failed the Pure-Tone Screen even though, as noted earlier, the spondee level at 52 dB SPL is further above normal threshold than the 20 dB hearing level of the Pure-Tone Screen.

We may still explore the notion that the spondee test was functioning as an additional measure of hearing capability which is sensitive to level, but relatively independent of the factors influencing the Pure-Tone Screen. However, the difference between the Male and Female percentage of failure seems to suggest something other than a pure hearing factor; and the decreasing percentage of failure as SEI rises is much more easily explained on grounds other than hearing ability. Is it really, at least in part, a test of another facet of hearing, or does it have to do mostly with testing factors or learning considerations independent of the hearing characteristics we wish to measure? Variation in vocabulary and language ability is one possible answer. A look at its relation to the other SLH vari-

ables at age three can help to clarify what it may have been measuring by showing what measures it co-varies with. Shown in Table 6-8 are the correlations of spondee results with other SLH variables taken at three years, arranged in order of decreasing size of coefficient. These coefficients are taken on thousands of pairs of measures, and therefore can be taken as stable estimates of the amount of co-variance between the measures.

Correlations between spondee results and Intelligibility and Articulation might be taken to indicate that some aspect of the child's ability to hear his own speech is related to his passing or failing the spondee test; but quite a number of other variables more apt to be considered linguistic, or at least only indirectly related to hearing, show correlation about as strong and stronger.

We must conclude, therefore, that for this large sample of three-year-olds, the

Table   6-8

Relation between the spondee test and 3YR variables.

Variable	Correlation Coefficient
Intelligibility	.24
Naming Objects	.20
Relevance	.20
Understanding Action Words	.19
Sentence Structure	.18
Use of Pronouns	.18
Identifying Familiar Objects	.17
Sentence Length	.17
Word Order	.17
Understanding Space Relations	.16
Vowel and Diphthong Articulation	.15
Three-syllable Memory	.14
Final Articulation	.14
Initial Articulation	.13
Three-digit Memory	.13
Two-syllable Memory	.13
Two-digit Memory	.13
Tongue Diadochokinesis	.12
Lip Diadochokinesis	.10
Voice Loudness	.08
Voice Quality	.07
Lip Protrusion	.07
Voice Pitch	.06

spondee test was not functioning as a corroborative test for hearing sensitivity, as it does for older patients. We may also quite safely conclude that whatever it was measuring co-varies with socioeconomic status. Because of the possible importance of an additional test of hearing at this early age, spondee results are inspected later in connection with the 8YR measures.

3YR Index and Earlier Measures

The three measures of hearing that were part of the 3YR battery of tests were a Pure-Tone Screen for the right ear, Pure-Tone Screen for the left ear, and a spondee test. These were combined into an index called the 3YR Hearing Screen, for which scores were assigned in the following manner: if the child failed all of these three tests, he was given a score of "0" for the 3YR Hearing Screen; if he passed only one of the three, he was assigned a score of "1"; and if he passed the Pure-Tone Screen in both ears, he was assigned a score of "2" irrespective of his performance on the spondee test. The latter decision was an arbitrary one. It tends to give the spondee score much less weight in the index and, in effect, is a pronouncement that the spondee test as used in this study was not measuring some factor closely related to hearing sensitivity.

Means of the various subgroups on the 3YR Hearing Screen are shown in Figure 6-2. It is evident from this figure that Blacks perform slightly better than Whites and that sex and SEI differences are negligible.

If we use 3YR screen scores to find indications from earlier examinations that might forecast difficulties in hearing at age three, there are measures that we might expect to be related. Other data that were taken represent measures that are not so directly related, but still might at least suggest a heightened probability of difficulty with hearing at age three.

These are variables such as the number of infectious diseases of the mother, the Apgar score of the child, the stage of gestation at which the mother registered (possibly related to the amount of prenatal medical care). Finally, there are other measures not usually considered to be related to hearing which, in a sample this large, might show at least a slight relation to the child's hearing. Examples of such measures are age of the mother, SEI preceding birth, amount of smoking by the mother, chronic hypertensive disease, and the like.

Correlations between a number of such selected NCPP variables and the 3YR Hearing Screen score were calculated, but in no case does the correlation appear strong enough to be useful. Curiously, the only coefficient as high as .10 is between 3YR Hearing Screen and Occupation of the Mother.

One must conclude that factors which are associated with the kind of hearing losses causing children to fail a 3YR screening test either are not present at an earlier age, or are present but not closely enough related to the measurements made on these children to be useful for prediction.

3YR Index and other 3YR SLH Measures

If we accept this failure to reveal predictive relevance to other characteristics of the child and look instead for parallels with indexes of his present behavior at three years of age, we do not fare much better. By inspecting a matrix of correlations between the 3YR Hearing Screen and other speech, language, and hearing variables measured (see Appendix 6), we find very few correlation coefficients that reach .10 or better. Screen scores do correlate (.11) with a judgment of the adequacy of the intelligibility of the child's speech, and more weakly with some more conceptually oriented measures; namely, Understanding Action Words, Sentence Structure, and the Relevance of

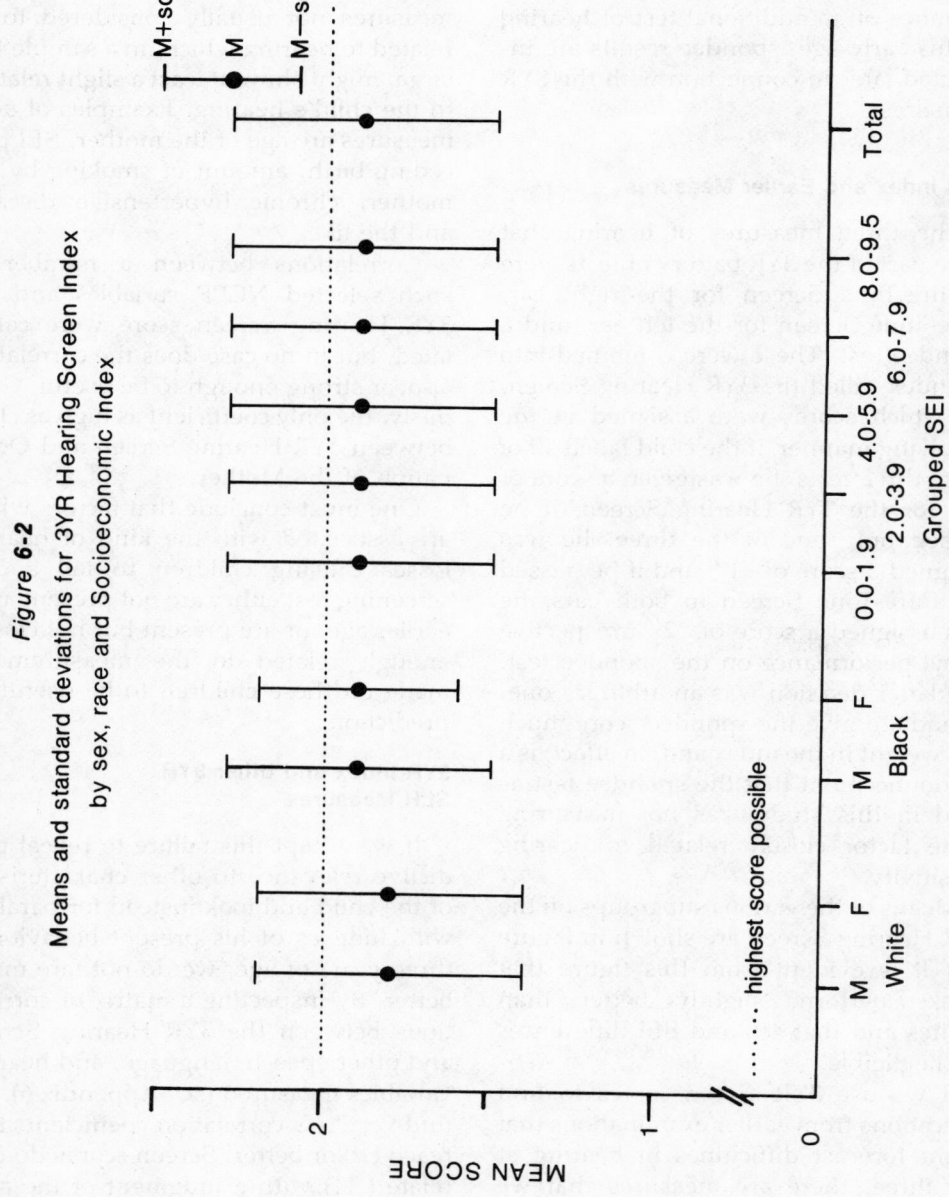

Figure 6-2

Means and standard deviations for 3YR Hearing Screen Index by sex, race and Socioeconomic Index

Utterances. These latter associations, though weak, possibly indicate that children with some early hearing deficit experience at least some communication deprivation at this stage of development. No relation worth remarking on appears with the measures of articulation or voice or with syllable or digit memory tests.

A further conceivable usefulness of these tests at three years, of course, could be the foreshadowing of the results of the examinations at eight years. These possible interrelations are explored later in this chapter.

8YR Hearing Battery

As part of the Final Speech, Language, and Hearing Examination, children of eight years of age were given several tests aimed at assessing their hearing capabilities. These consisted of: (1) a pure-tone air conduction examination with a follow-up bone conduction exam if threshold departed from 0 dB HL (ISO 1964) by at least 20 dB; (2) a test for abnormal decay of a sustained pure-tone of 4000 Hz, with a follow-up test at 500 Hz if the child did not continue to hear the tone for 60 seconds; and (3) a word discrimination test consisting of one of the standard Phonetically Balanced Kindergarten (PBK) lists of 25 words, presented at 30 dB above the child's measured pure-tone threshold at 1000 Hz. As a first step in evaluating the results, the tests are discussed here individually.

Pure-Tone Air Conduction Test

Standard procedures were used in testing the children for pure-tone air conduction sensitivity. An ascending method was recommended, consisting of identifying the sound of the tone for the child by starting well above his suspected threshold, then descending in 10 dB steps until the child no longer heard the tone. The level was then increased in 5 dB steps and the sequence repeated several times as necessary to establish the child's threshold. The lowest level at which a child responded to at least two of three presentations was considered his threshold. The frequencies were tested in this order: 1000, 2000, 4000, 8000, 1000, 500, 250 Hz. In testing the second ear, the measurement at 1000 Hz was made only one time. In those few instances for which it was known, the better ear was tested first. In the absence of any information about which ear might be better, the ear to be tested first was decided by the even or odd number of the date of the child's birthday.

Pure-Tone Results

The distribution of threshold measures for those of the 19,885 eight-year-old children who showed losses of less than 20 dB is shown in Figure 6-3 and the means in Figure 6-4 and Table 6-9. Figure 6-3, at first glance, appears to indicate less sensitivity (poorer hearing) at 500 Hz in this group than for the sample used to establish audiometric norms; that is, the modal value at that frequency for this sample is 10 dB HL rather than 0 dB HL. However, accurate comparison is not quite that simple. First of all, few large-sample distributions have been available to standard-setting groups. As nearly as can be discerned from reported discussions, such groups have not resolved satisfactorily the problem of which statistic should be used to anchor the value for the 0 dB hearing level. Davis and Usher (1957) have reviewed the important considerations and the varied population samples which have influenced the selection of audiometric zero. They raise, but do not attempt to answer, the question of how heavily the statistical distribution of hearing sensitivity rather than the performance of selected sensitive listeners should influence the fixing of audiometric zero. Harris, in his early discussion of the rationale for setting threshold norms, opts for the median

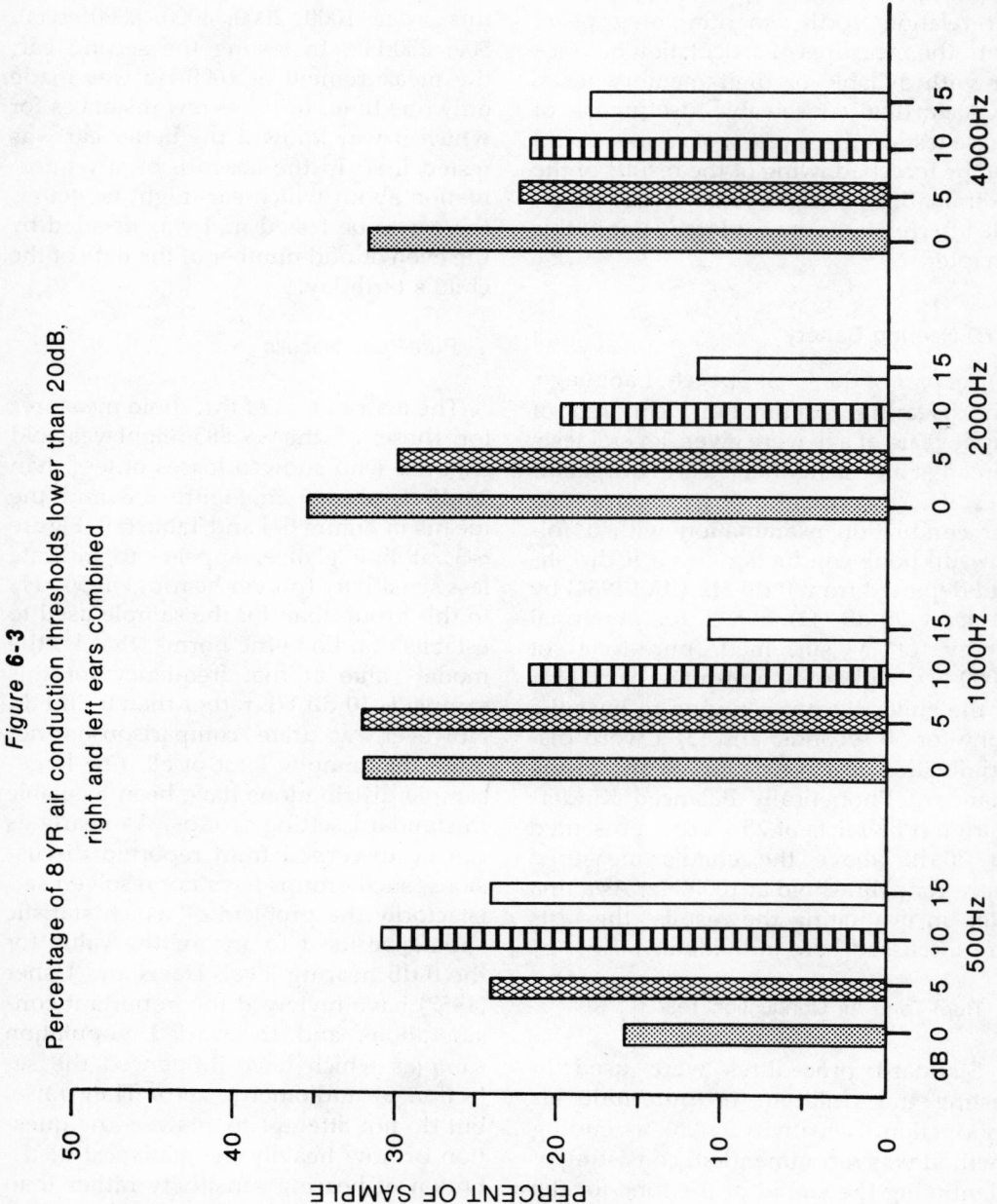

Figure 6-3

Percentage of 8 YR air conduction thresholds lower than 20dB.
right and left ears combined

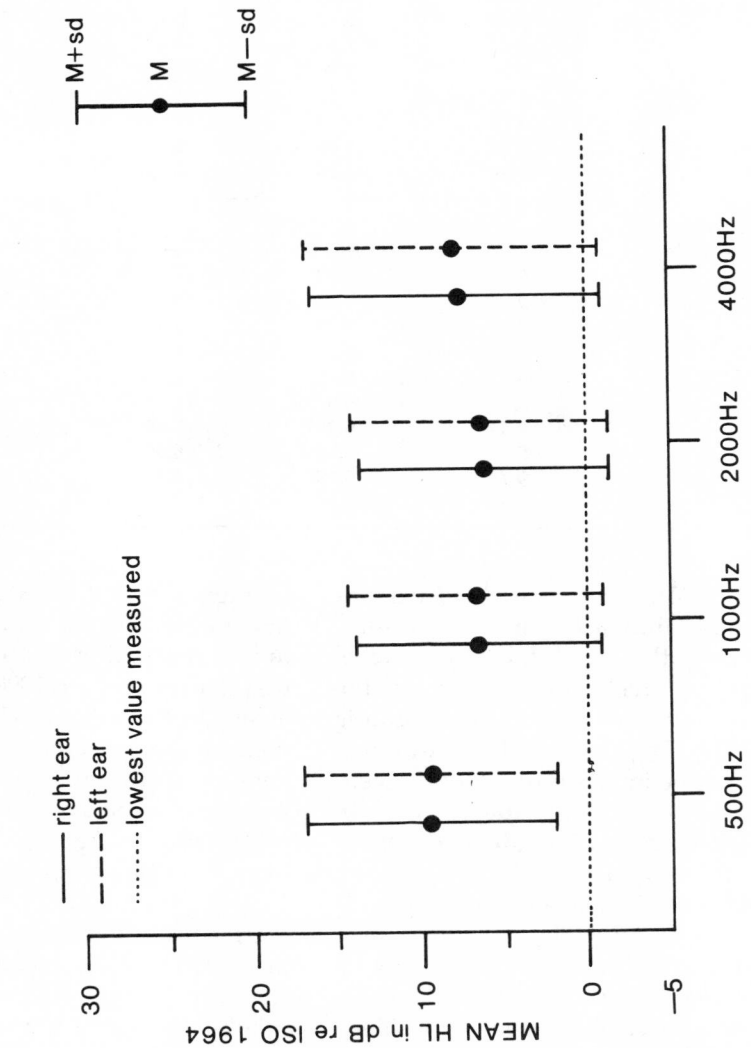

Figure **6-4**

Means and standard deviations for 8YR air conduction thresholds
for right and left ears

91

Table 6-9

Means for 8YR pure-tone air conduction hearing levels in dB re ISO 1964 by race, sex and Socioeconomic Index. Heavy type numbers are means for the right ear; italic numbers for the left.

	500	1K	2K	4K	8K
Total Sample	**9.58**	**6.85**	**6.46**	**8.07**	**10.1**
	9.59	*6.89*	*6.79*	*8.33*	*10.3*
White	**9.55**	**6.24**	**5.46**	**6.98**	**10.7**
	9.66	*6.41*	*5.76*	*7.48*	*11.0*
Black	**9.61**	**7.48**	**7.47**	**9.17**	**9.42**
	9.53	*7.38*	*7.83*	*9.18*	*9.54*
Male	**9.66**	**7.02**	**6.58**	**8.26**	**10.5**
	9.70	*7.12*	*7.04*	*8.68*	*10.7*
Female	**9.49**	**6.69**	**6.34**	**7.87**	**9.59**
	9.48	*6.66*	*6.53*	*7.96*	*9.85*

Socioeconomic Index

	500	1K	2K	4K	8K
0.0-1.9	**9.92**	**7.63**	**7.74**	**9.48**	**9.96**
	9.88	*7.57*	*8.15*	*9.49*	*10.1*
2.0-3.9	**9.71**	**7.36**	**7.17**	**8.86**	**10.3**
	9.65	*7.26*	*7.45*	*8.93*	*10.3*
4.0-5.9	**9.51**	**6.75**	**6.43**	**8.06**	**9.91**
	9.51	*6.87*	*6.81*	*8.33*	*10.1*
6.0-7.9	**9.44**	**6.34**	**5.59**	**7.33**	**9.99**
	9.52	*6.49*	*6.00*	*7.74*	*10.3*
8.0-9.5	**9.40**	**6.19**	**5.33**	**6.33**	**10.1**
	9.58	*6.19*	*5.47*	*6.97*	*10.5*

(Harris, 1954). Wisconsin State Fair investigators emphasize median values, recognizing the need for a normative measure relatively unaffected by the skewness of the distribution (Glorig et al., 1957). The shape of the distribution should not be ignored in any use of central-tendency measures for comparison purposes, since not only does the distribution contain cases with large losses, but it has been truncated by recording all values of 0 dB HL or less as zero.

Furthermore, in comparing results on these children with established standards, it is conceivable—even probable—that the child's increasing familiarity with the test procedure and continued practice in listening to threshold-level tones contributes to slightly better performance at those frequencies tested later. Planners of similar testing at the Wisconsin State Fair were concerned about possible rapid learning effects, so they retested the first frequency tested (1000 Hz) in both the first and second ear tested. For the adults in that study, there were five intervening frequencies before 1000 Hz was tested again. In the first ear tested, the second measures at 1000 Hz were significantly better than the first (p < .01). However, the same maneuver on the second ear tested showed no significant difference between measures at the same frequency. In the present study, the lower value (better hearing) obtained when retesting at 1000 Hz was accepted as the threshold measure at that frequency. Although the results presented for each ear contain some first-ear and some second-ear measures, the standard deviation might be enlarged by differences in first-ear and second-ear results, but the means should remain unbiased by the effect.

With these considerations in mind, probably the most relevant comparison which can be made is with the careful measurements on the 257 eight-year-olds of the Pittsburgh study of hearing in children (Eagles et al., 1963). The results turn out to be gratifyingly similar. A synopsis of the comparison appears in Table 6-10.

Transfer of the mean threshold value for the 257 eight-year-olds tested in the Pittsburgh study to equivalent hearing levels for the present study (ASA 1951 to ISO 1964) indicates that the mean threshold of the Pittsburgh sample at 500 Hz would be 9.3 dB HL. Considering the differences in method, care of equipment, selection of testers, and particularly the truncation of the distribution at 0 dB HL in the present study, the mean of 9.6 dB HL at 500 Hz for the present study is comfortably close, and might well be taken as assurance that ambient noise probably was not the dominant factor in shaping the distribution of measures at 500 Hz. The Pittsburgh test environments were such that 32 of the children tested showed a threshold of nearly 0 dB SPL at 500 Hz (see Table 1b, p. 184, Eagles et al., 1963). However, to make exact SPL comparisons, corrections should be made for transferring estimated SPL from W.E. 705A to TDH-39. At 1K Hz, where the distribution of the NCPP study shows about equal numbers of eight-year-olds with threshold at 0 dB

HL and +5 dB HL, a similar comparison with the Pittsburgh study shows a mean threshold level at 1K Hz for the current study of 6.9 dB HL against 8.2 dB HL for the Pittsburgh eight-year-old children. At 2K Hz the results are similar, with mean threshold levels of 6.6 dB HL and 6.7 dB HL for the current and the Pittsburgh studies, respectively.

If one were inclined to argue for the average hearing sensitivity of young children as the basis for setting audiometric zero, it might seem from the shape of the distribution of measures within the range of normal hearing that audiometric zero at 500 Hz is set slightly low. One other finding of the Pittsburgh study, however, is that from age five to age 13, children require progressively lower sound pressure level for threshold, especially at lower frequencies. Thus, at the most sensitive age conceivably all distributions would at least come closer to showing a modal value at the current 0 dB HL.

The comparisons of the various subgroups are made easier by scanning Figures 6-5, 6-6, and 6-7. From Table 6-9, it is clear that mean differences between Male and Female eight-year-olds are small. In Figure 6-5, the distribution of these measures also appears highly similar. A comparison of the means (Table 6-9) and

Table **6-10**

Comparison of air conduction hearing level means of the present study (NCPP) with means of eight-year-old children in the Pittsburgh study.*†

| | Pittsburgh | | | Pittsburgh | |
Freq.	Reported HL	Dial Rdg.* Ave.	ASA-ISO	Corrected HL	NCPP HL
500	−6.2	−4.7	14	9.3	9.6
1K	−4.3	−1.8	10	8.2	6.9
2K	−3.8	−1.3	8	6.7	6.6
4K	−2.3	0.2	6	6.2	8.2
8K	−2.1	0.4	11.5	11.9	10.1

*Data from Eagles et al., 1963, pp. 205 ff. (Tables 11b-d).
†The Pittsburgh study employed the rationale that measures taken with a 5dB step on the attenuator should be corrected by subtracting 2.5dB from the dial reading. For making comparisons with the present study, where such a correction has not been made, 2.5dB has been added to the reported Pittsburgh means.

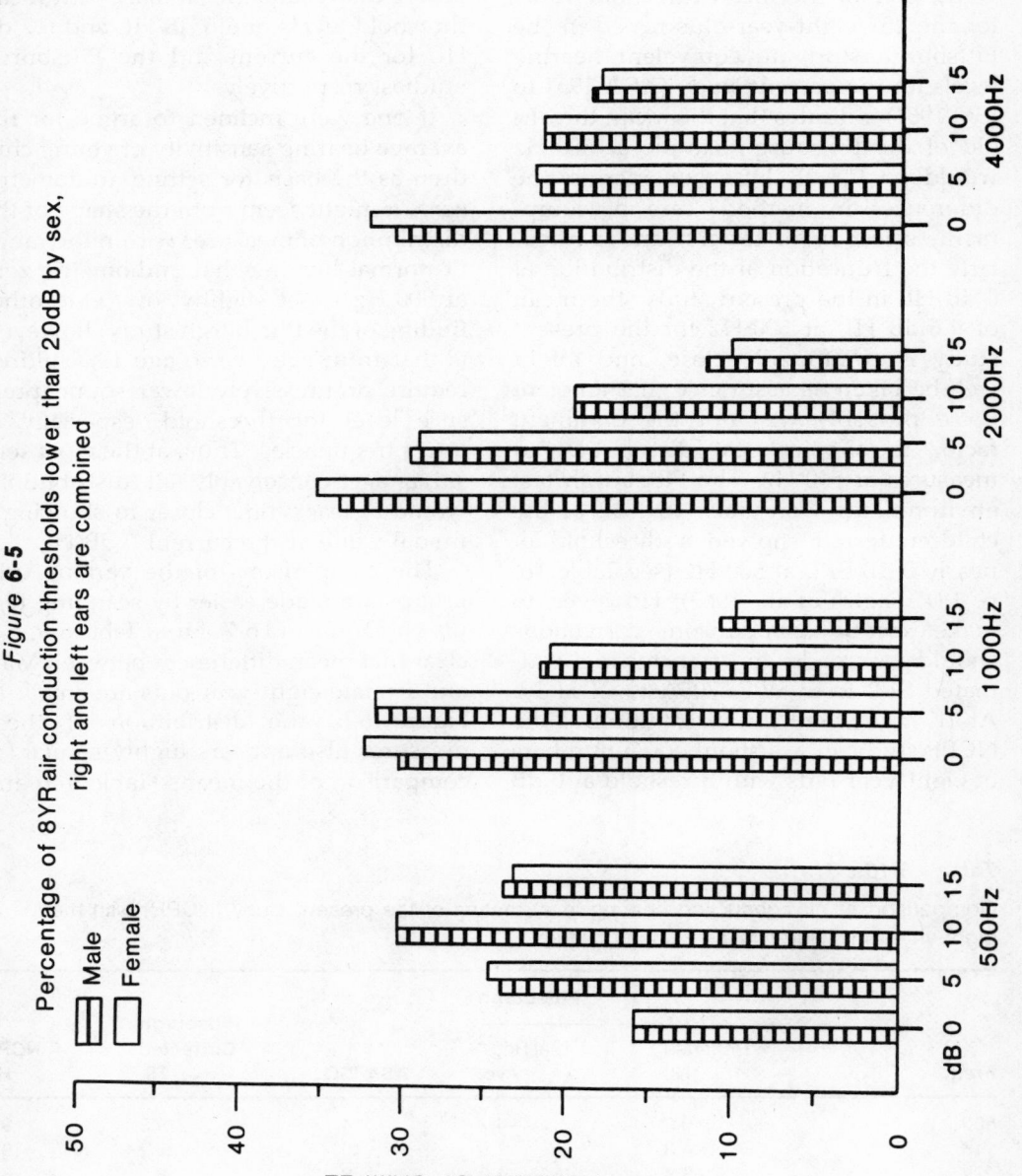

Figure 6-5

Percentage of 8YR air conduction thresholds lower than 20dB by sex,
right and left ears are combined

94

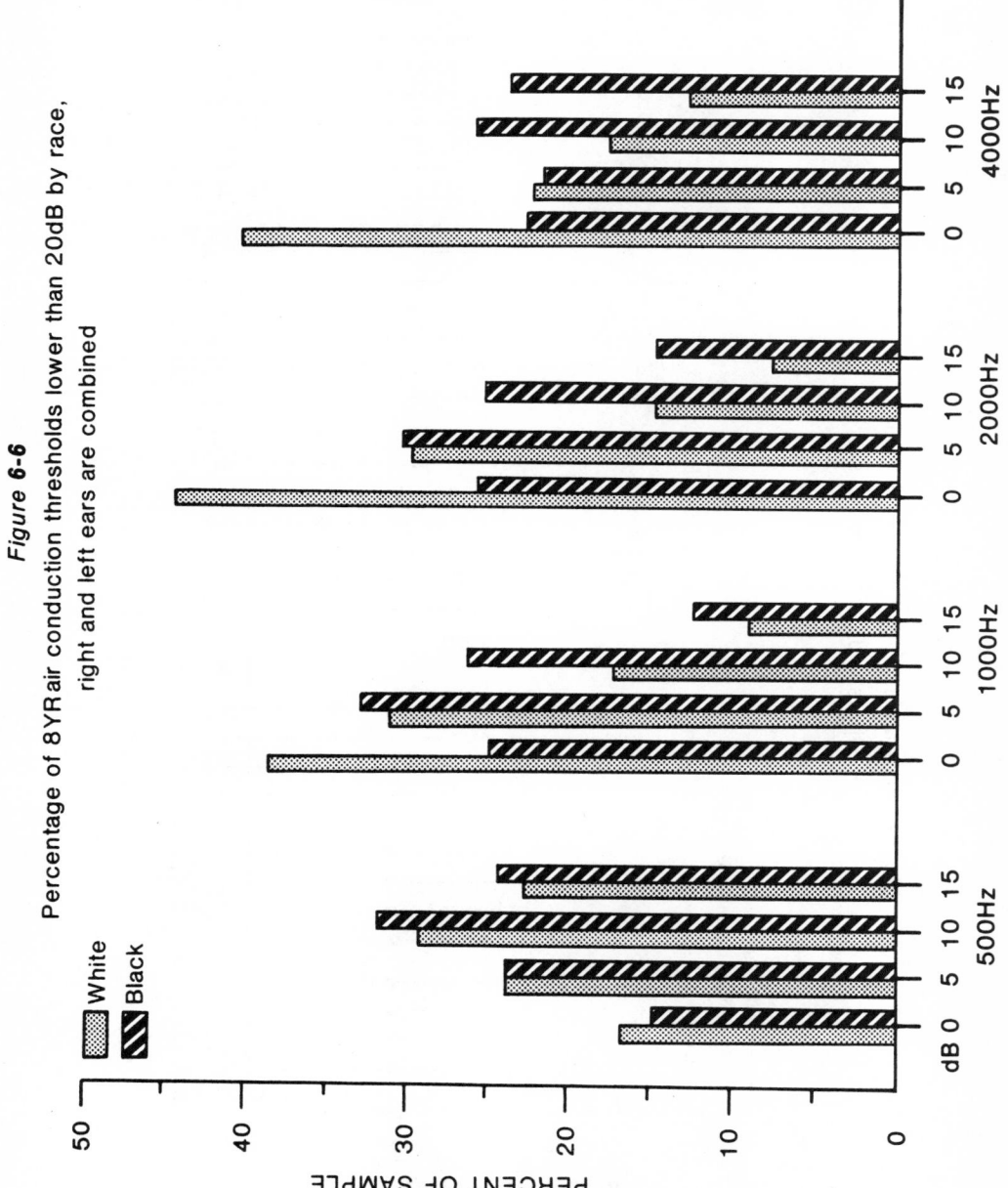

Figure 6-6

Percentage of 8YRair conduction thresholds lower than 20dB by race, right and left ears are combined

95

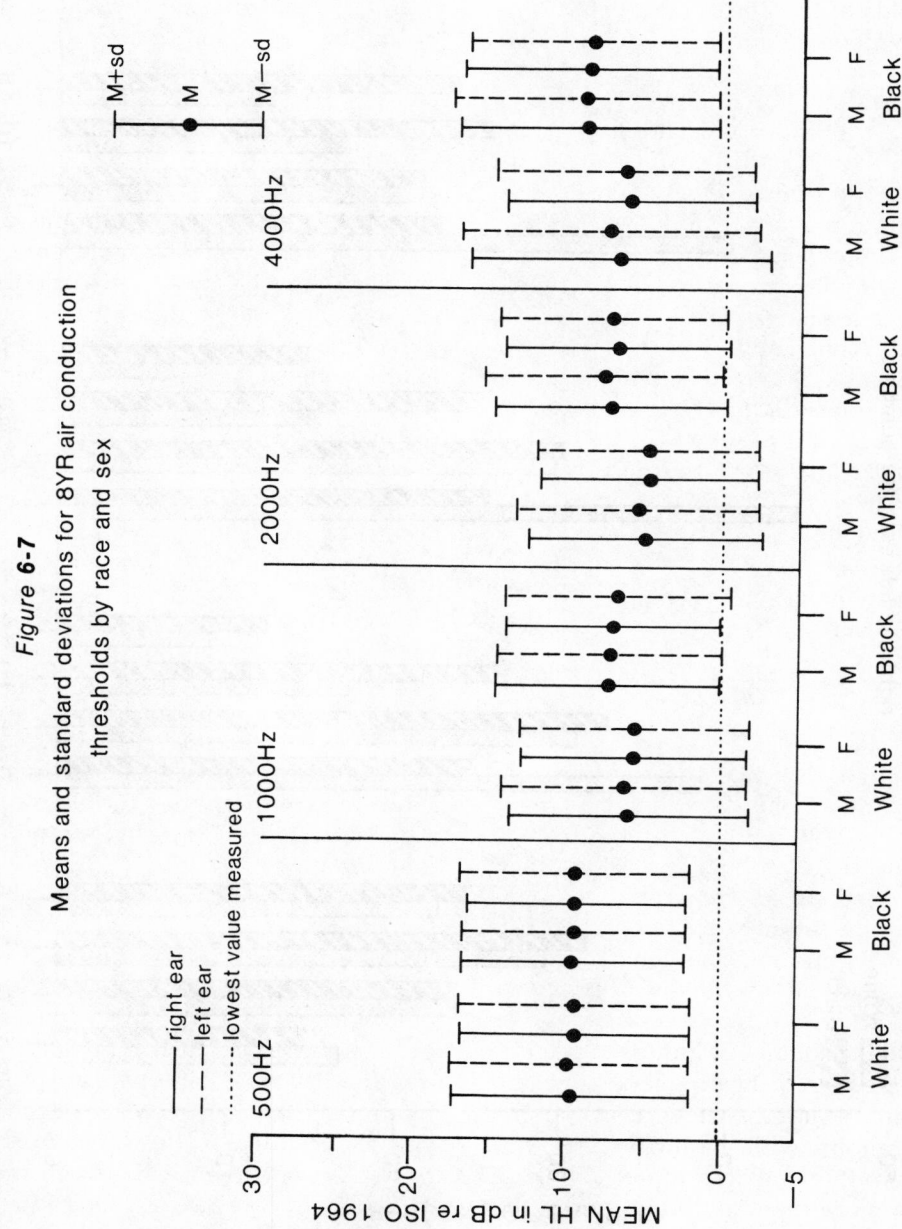

Figure 6-7

Means and standard deviations for 8YR air conduction thresholds by race and sex

96

the distribution (Figure 6-6) of Black and White children raises again the problem of the differing numbers of Black and White children who failed the 3YR Pure-Tone Screen. At eight years, the mean thresholds of the Black children are consistently poorer than those of the White children for test frequencies 1K Hz, 2K Hz, and 4K Hz. This seems to be at variance with the fact that more White children than Black failed the Pure-Tone Screen at three years. Since we have only screening results at 30 dB HL (ISO 1964) for the three-year-old children, we cannot tell whether thresholds for Black children have shifted from being more sensitive than White children at three years of age to being less sensitive at eight years. The question is of considerable interest to the general purposes of this study, but the answer must await further data. All in all, however, differences in pure-tone sensitivity among the various subgroups are too small to be useful in predicting hearing difficulty (see Tables 6-19, 6-20, and 6-21).

8YR Air Conduction vs. Socioeconomic Index

Although the differences in air conduction thresholds are not great, as shown in Table 6-9 and in Figures 6-8a and 6-8b, the distribution of air conduction measures as influenced by SEI shows some noteworthy trends, as indicated in Figure 6-9. The general shift of the distribution to a modal point above audiometric zero (poorer hearing) is characteristic of all SEI groups at 500 Hz. At this frequency, hearing levels of 5 and 10 dB are the largest categories for all SEI classifications, with the highest SEI classification showing this modal tendency slightly more than any other group. But at 1K Hz begins a definite tendency for the higher brackets of SEI to show progressively greater pure-tone sensitivity (better hearing), the differences in proportion being sufficiently larger than

their standard errors that there can be little doubt that these are reliable shifts. Again, however, unless it can be shown that SEI classification is not confounded with tester and test environment, it would be imprudent to generalize from this finding.

Whatever the underlying cause, the tendency is even more pronounced at 2K Hz, where the shape of distribution changes systematically from low SEI rating to high. Since audiometric zero is presumed to be set well within the range of normal variation, one must entertain the possibility that this systematic trend has no identifiable auditory basis, but is primarily an indication of increased testability of the children in the higher SEI brackets. Adopting that explanation, however, would require some other hypothesis for the absence of the pattern of 500 Hz.

Bone Conduction

When the air conduction threshold was poorer than audiometric zero by 20 dB or more at any frequency from 500 to 4000 Hz, the bone conduction thresholds were measured at 500, 1000, 2000, and 4000 Hz in that ear. The testing procedure was the same as for air conduction. Masking was used routinely in the nontest ear.

Results of the bone conduction test on approximately 3000 ears are shown in Figure 6-10 to Figure 6-16 and Table 6-11. The distribution of threshold measures for this group differs appreciably from the distribution of air conduction measures for the total sample. The primary difference is in the percentage of children who show 0 dB HL threshold for bone conduction. Differences between means are quite small, however. One interpretation is that whatever loss did contribute to their lowered sensitivity was conductive in most instances. Roughly 20 of each sex, out of this sample of some 700 Females and 800 Males, show a bone con-

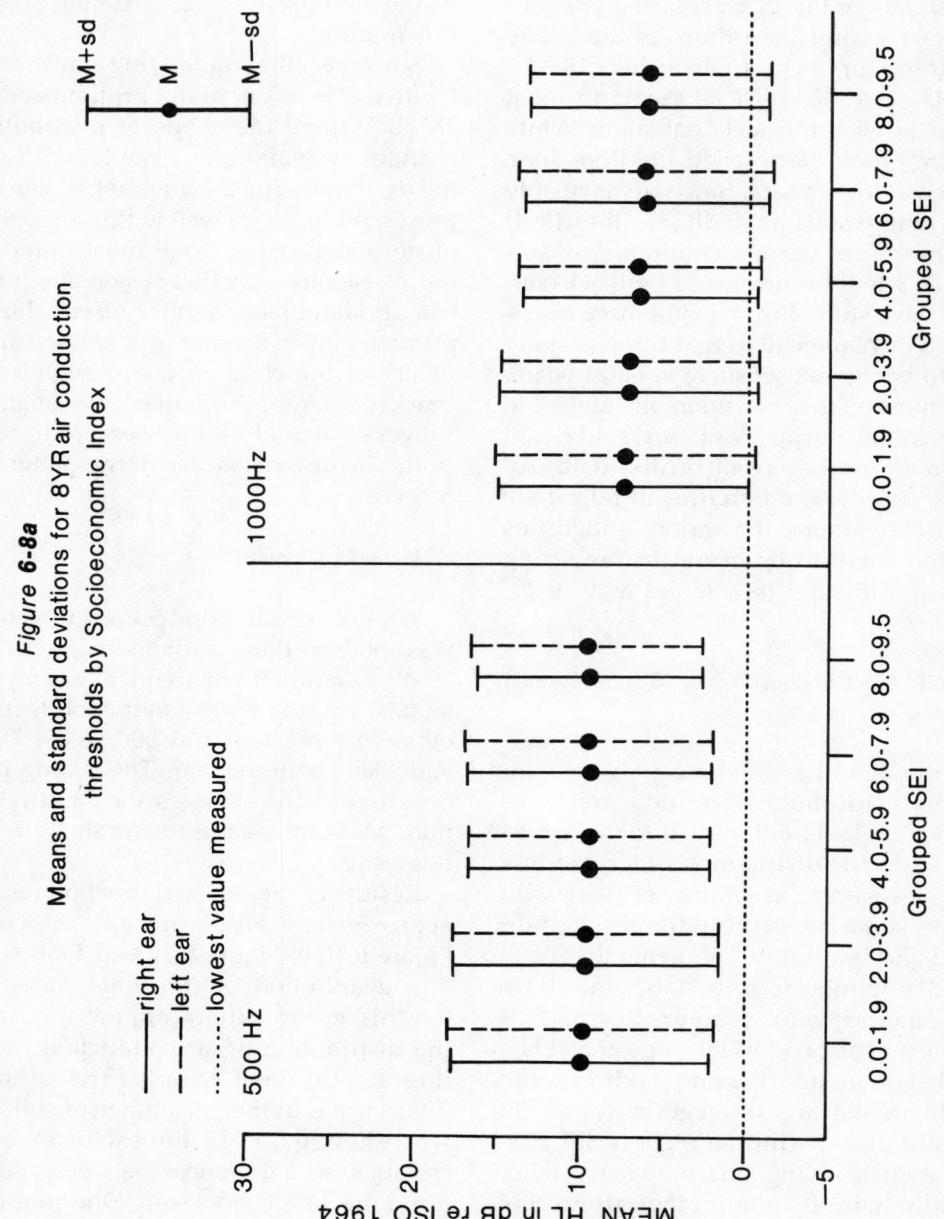

Figure 6-8a

Means and standard deviations for 8YR air conduction thresholds by Socioeconomic Index

M+sd

M

M—sd

right ear
left ear
lowest value measured

500 Hz

1000Hz

0.0-1.9 2.0-3.9 4.0-5.9 6.0-7.9 8.0-9.5
Grouped SEI

0.0-1.9 2.0-3.9 4.0-5.9 6.0-7.9 8.0-9.5
Grouped SEI

MEAN HL in dB re ISO 1964

30
20
10
0
—5

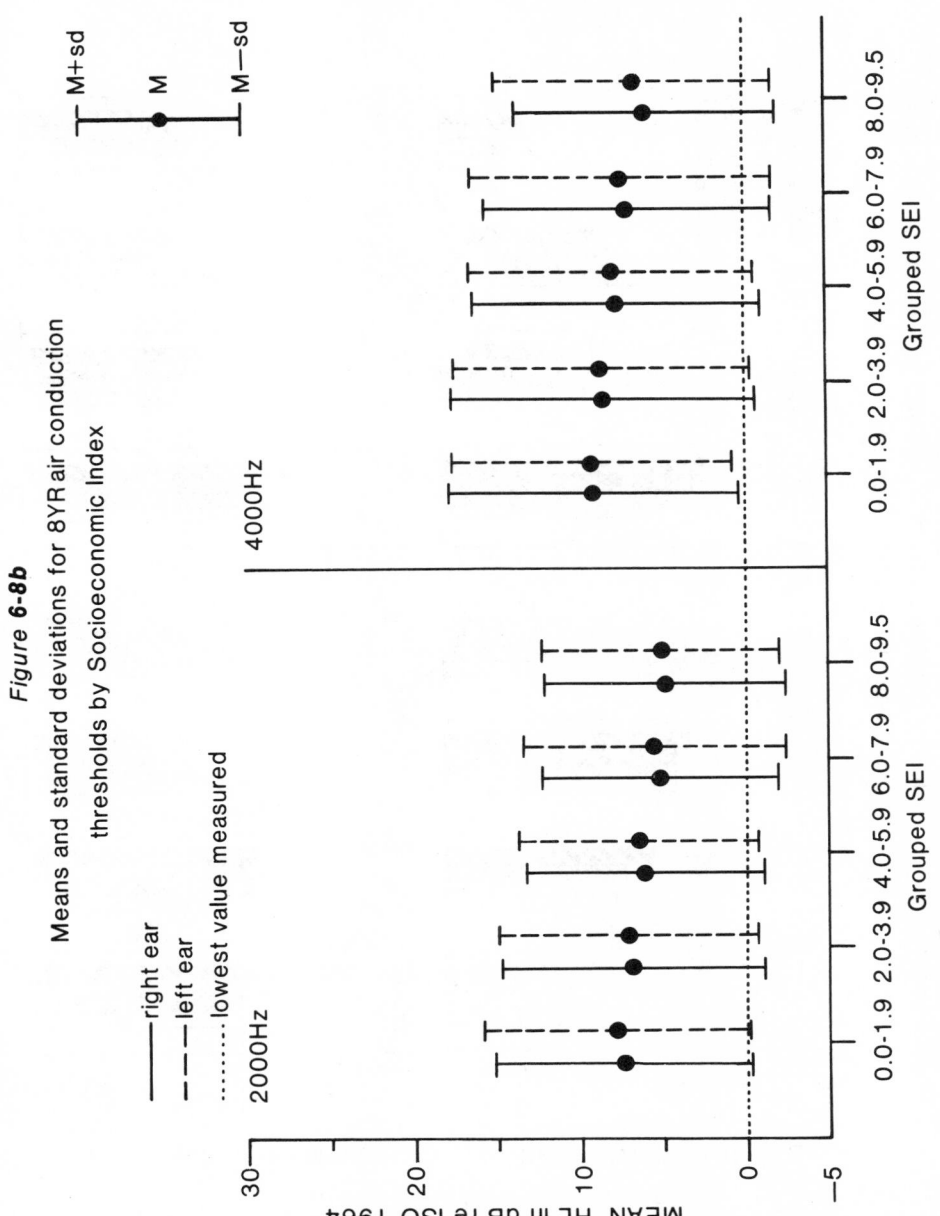

Figure *6-8b*

Means and standard deviations for 8YR air conduction thresholds by Socioeconomic Index

99

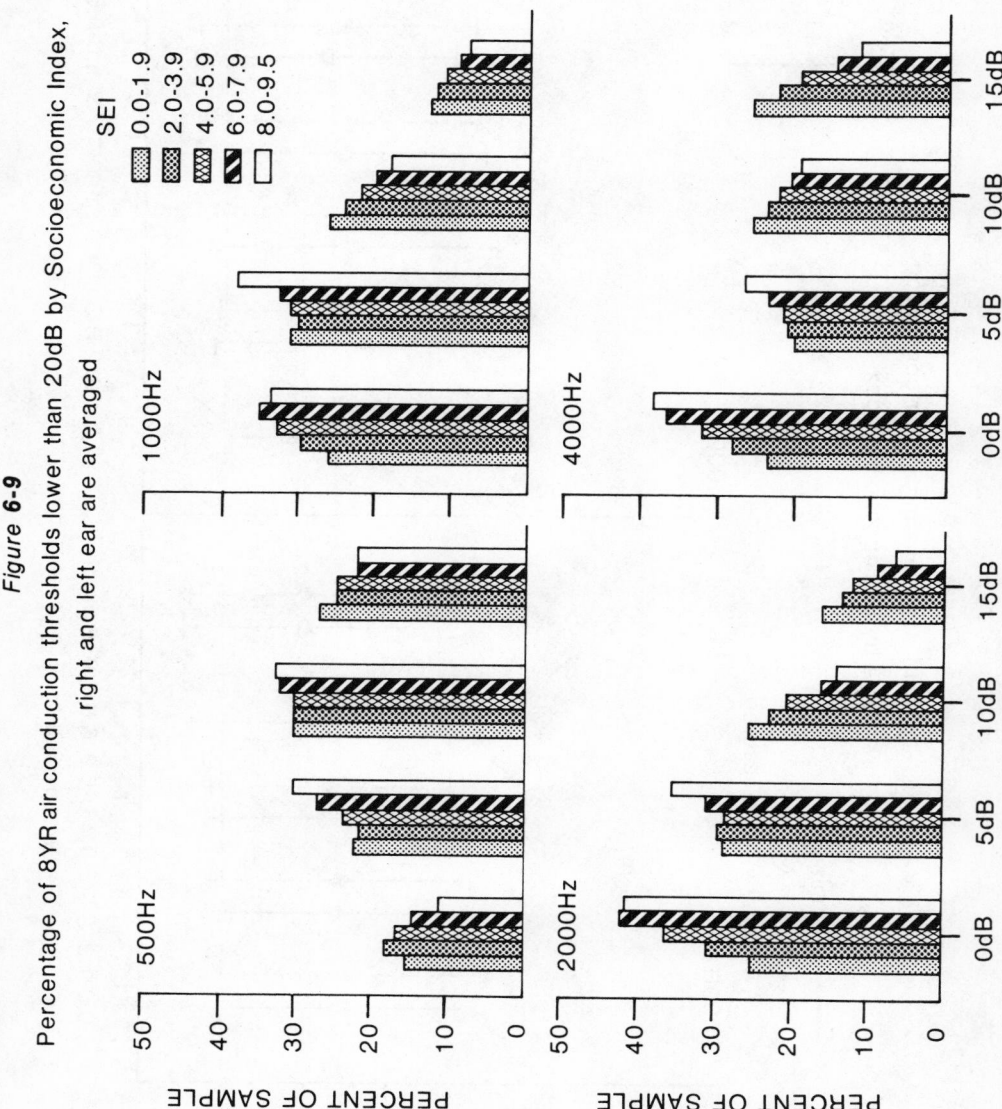

Figure **6-9**

Percentage of 8YR air conduction thresholds lower than 20dB by Socioeconomic Index, right and left ear are averaged

100

duction loss of 40 dB or greater. As might be expected, the distributions for Males and Females differ little. The distribution of measures on Black children does appear to differ from that of White children showing, in general, slightly poorer hearing by bone conduction at all four frequencies. Since the sample consisted of over 800 White children and nearly 700 Black children, this finding may be generalizable with the reservation that testers, equipment, and test environment were not precisely matched for the two samples.

The systematic change in shape of the distribution of scores with increasing socioeconomic status found with air conduction is not apparent in the distribution of bone conduction scores; a further indication that most eight-year-olds selected for bone conduction testing because they failed to hear by air conduction within 15 dB of normal threshold had conductive losses. The comparatively low correlation between bone conduction and air conduction measures (see Table 6-12) for the eight-year sample bears this out.

The correlation between pure-tone measures for both air and bone are shown in Table 6-12. These coefficients are attenuated somewhat by the truncation of the lower end of the distribution (all scores below 0 dB HL were recorded as 0 dB) but their relative sizes vary predictably. Correlations between adjacent frequencies in each ear are moderately high for both air and bone; correlations between air and bone at the same frequency are lower, but still higher than for different frequencies; correlations between air and bone at the same frequency are the highest of all; and those between air and bone at different frequencies are the lowest.

Eagles et al. (1963, p. 177) report correlations between different frequencies in the same ear. Their coefficients are higher than those shown here for air conduction pairs in the same ear; but the same pattern is apparent, with higher correlations between adjacent frequencies and gradually lower coefficients for frequencies increasingly further apart.

Test for Abnormal Auditory Adaptation (Tone Decay)

All eight-year-old children were given a test intended as a screening test for tone decay. After giving instructions, the examiner turned on a 4000 Hz tone at a level of 20 dB above the child's measured threshold at that frequency. The child was told to keep his hand raised as long as he could hear the tone. If he kept the hand raised for 60 seconds, he was considered to pass the test; that is, he showed no abnormal tone decay. If he dropped his hand before the 60 seconds passed, the examiner left the tone on but asked the child if the tone had gone away. This was an effort to make certain the child's attention had not wandered. At the end of 60 seconds, the tone was turned off. The child failed the test if the examiner judged that the tone became inaudible during the 60-second period. If a child failed this 4000 Hz screening test in either ear, the same test was given at 500 Hz in that ear.

The test is admittedly a screening test. It should identify those children who show abnormal tone decay of at least 20 dB, but only further testing could locate the magnitude and site of the problem.

This is a rather unusual test for eight-year-old children. A tone decay test of somewhat different form has been used in audiology clinics for nearly 20 years. In 1963, Green suggested that a screening test for tone decay might be a useful addition to the clinic battery. It has the advantage of requiring no more than a standard audiometer. The particular method used in this study has the disadvantage of permitting little comparison with other data since it differs from other methods.

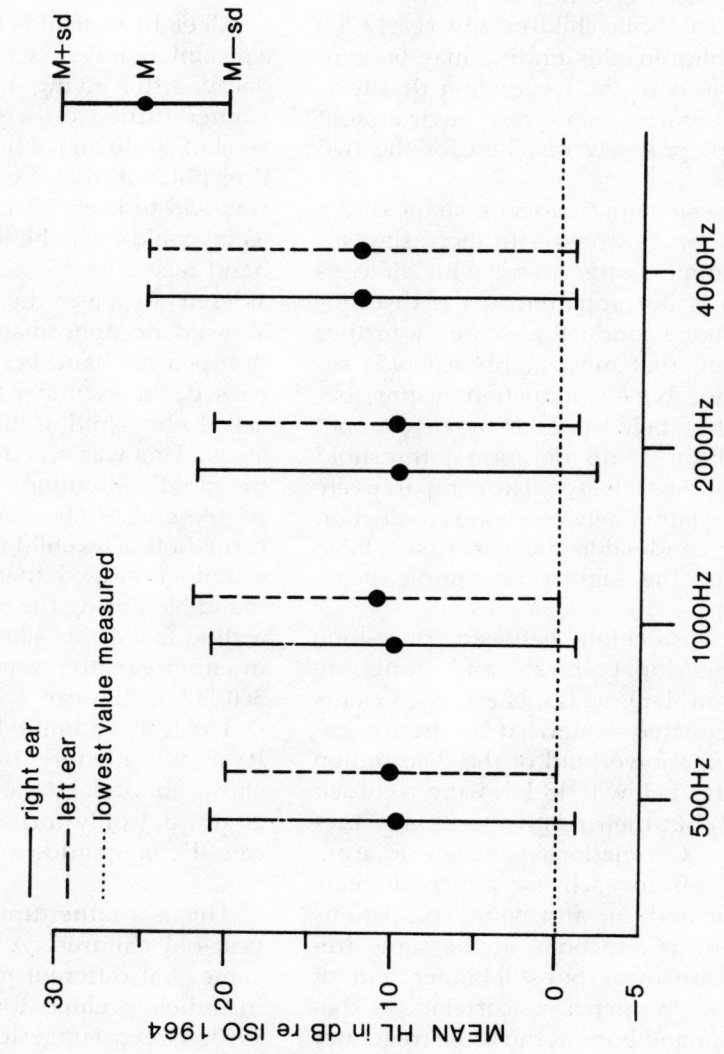

Figure 6-10
Means and standard deviations for 8YR bone conduction thresholds

right ear
left ear
lowest value measured

M+sd
M
M−sd

MEAN HL in dB re ISO 1964

30

20

10

0

−5

500Hz   1000Hz   2000Hz   4000Hz

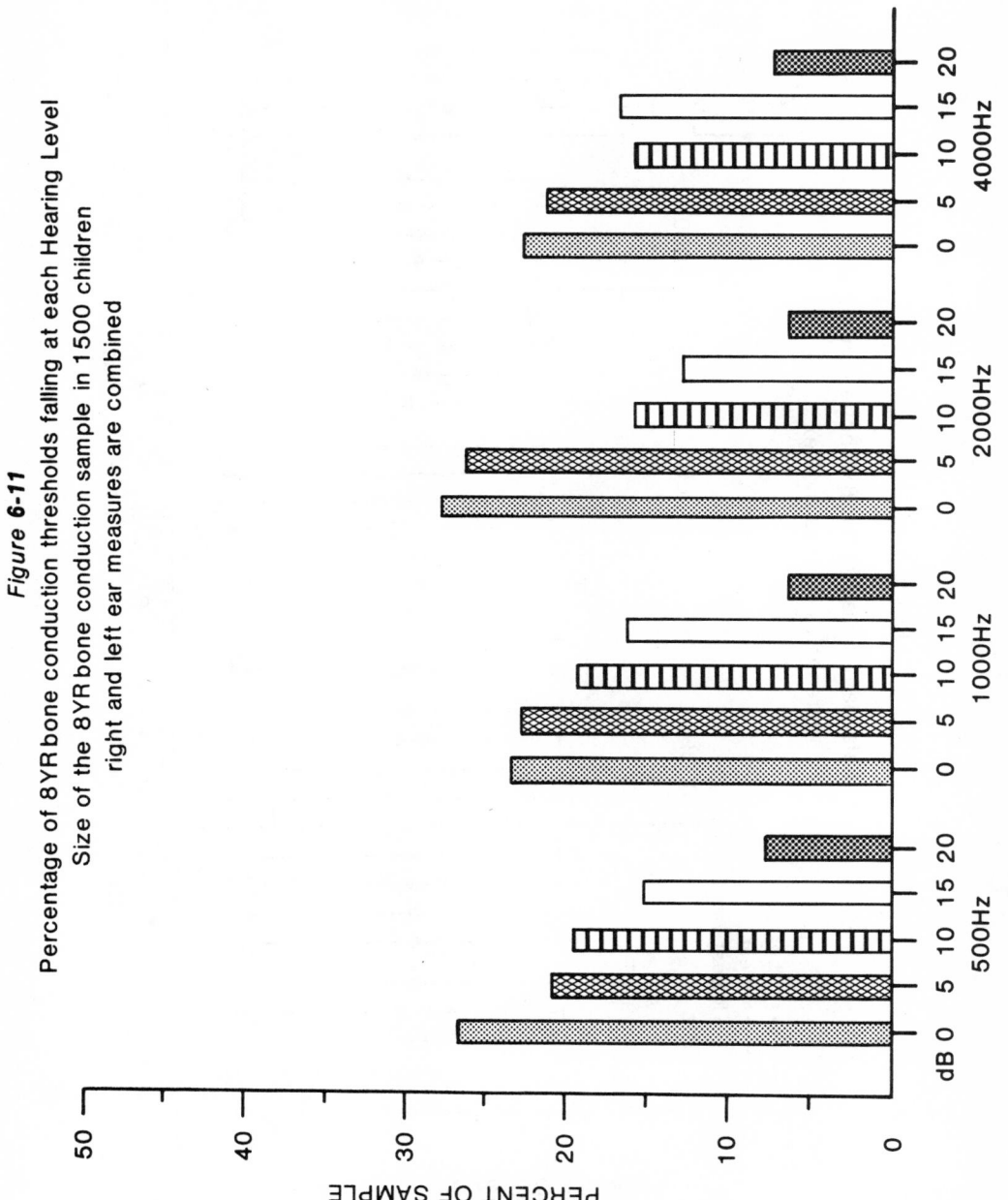

Figure **6-11**

Percentage of 8YR bone conduction thresholds falling at each Hearing Level
Size of the 8YR bone conduction sample in 1500 children
right and left ear measures are combined

Figure 6-12

Means and standard deviations for 8YR bone conduction
thresholds by race and sex

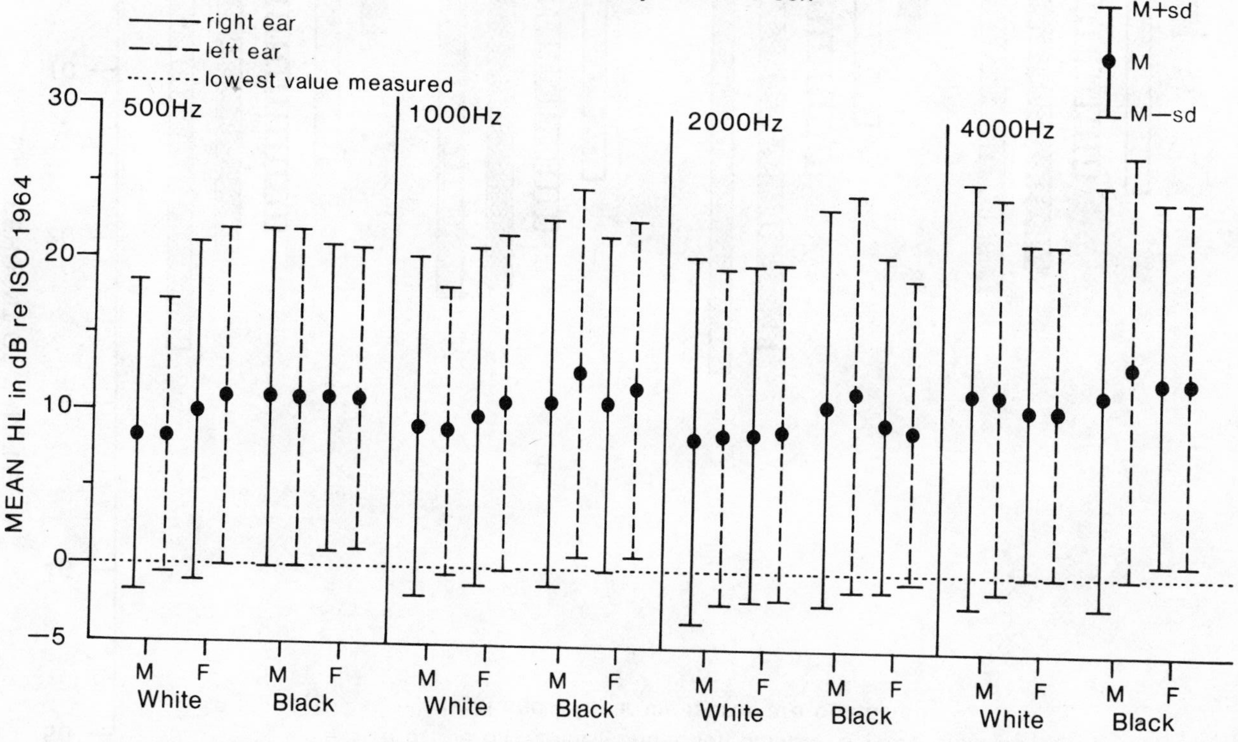

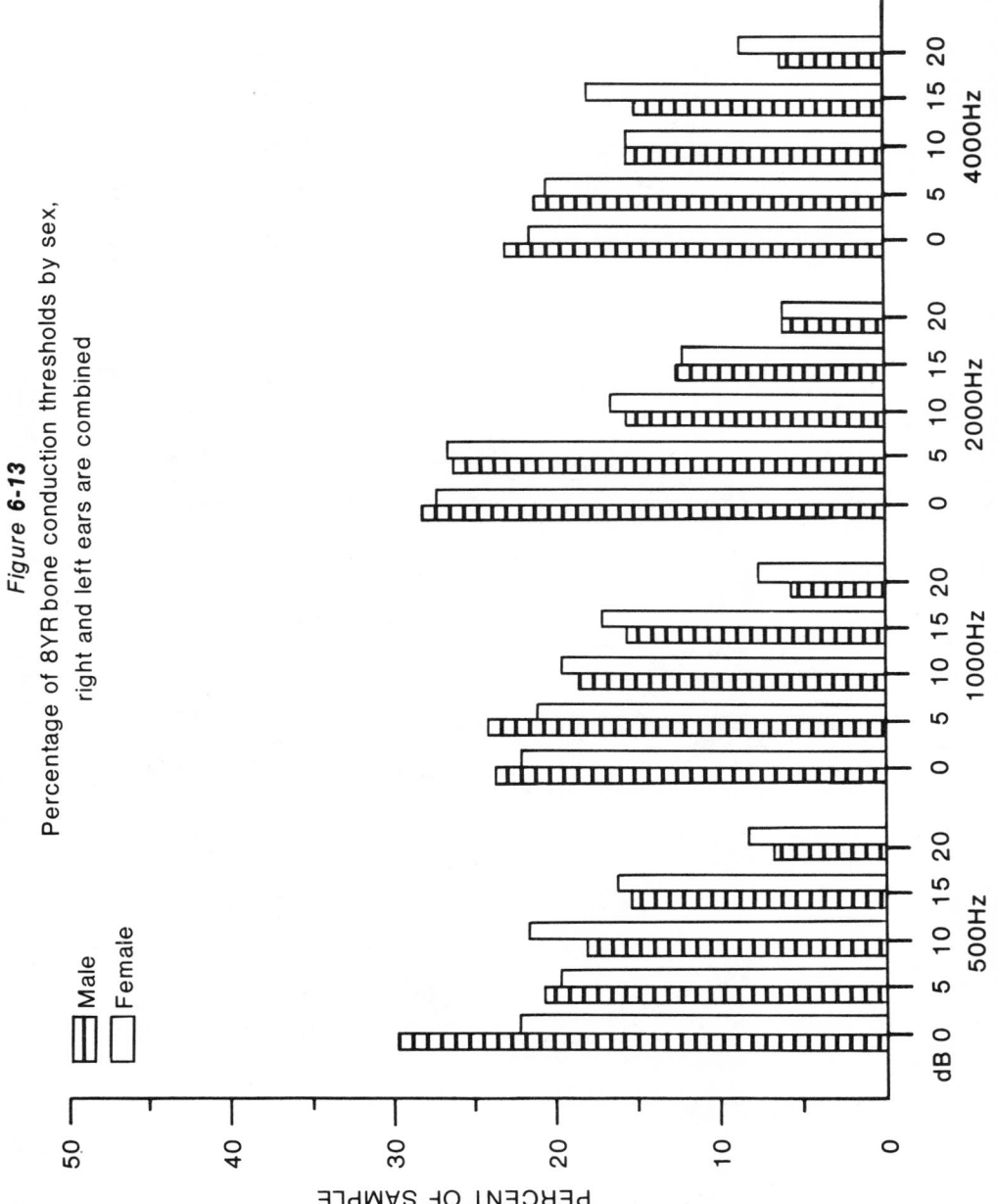

Figure **6-13**

Percentage of 8YR bone conduction thresholds by sex,
right and left ears are combined

105

Figure 6-14
Percentage of 8YR bone conduction thresholds by race, right and left ears combined

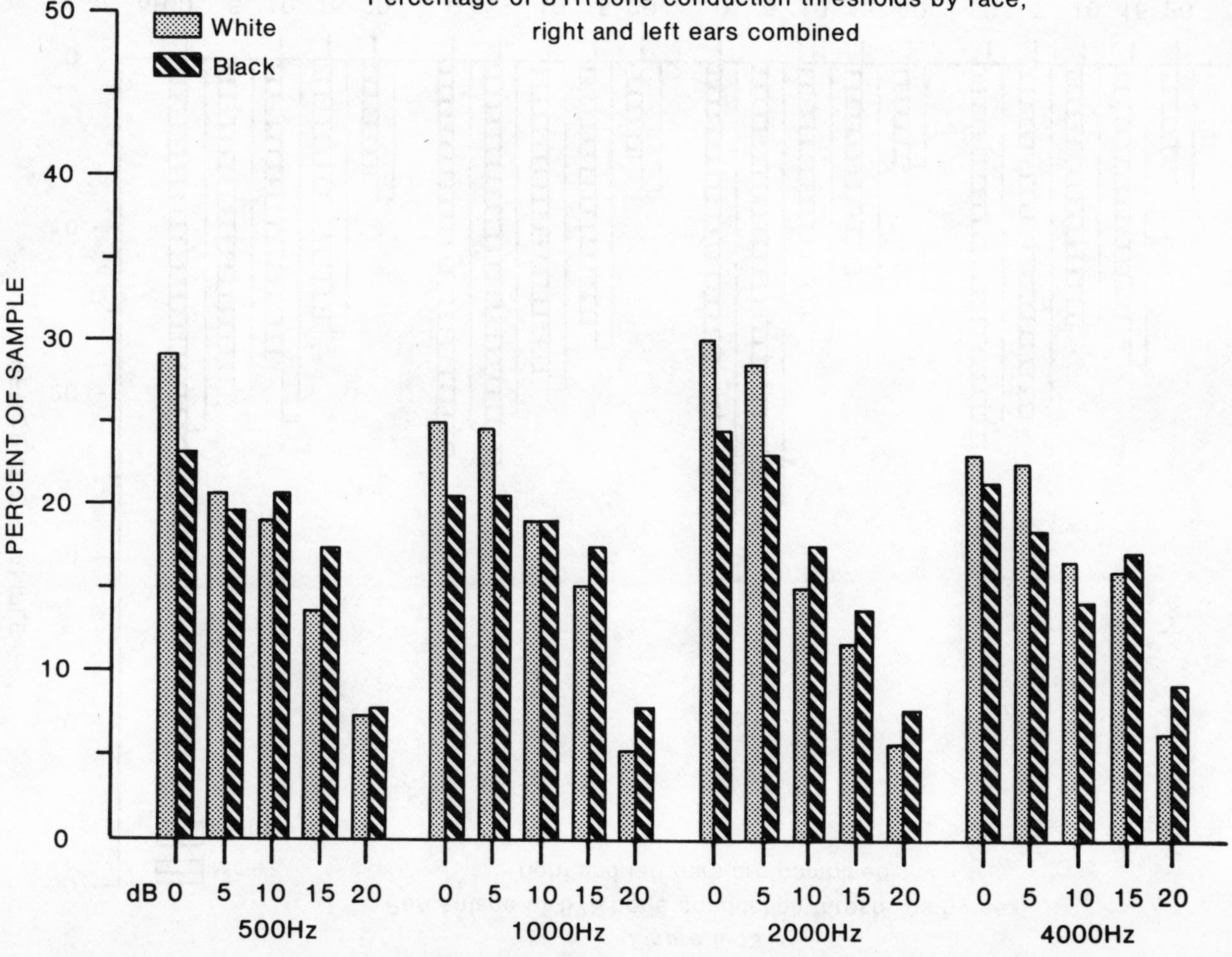

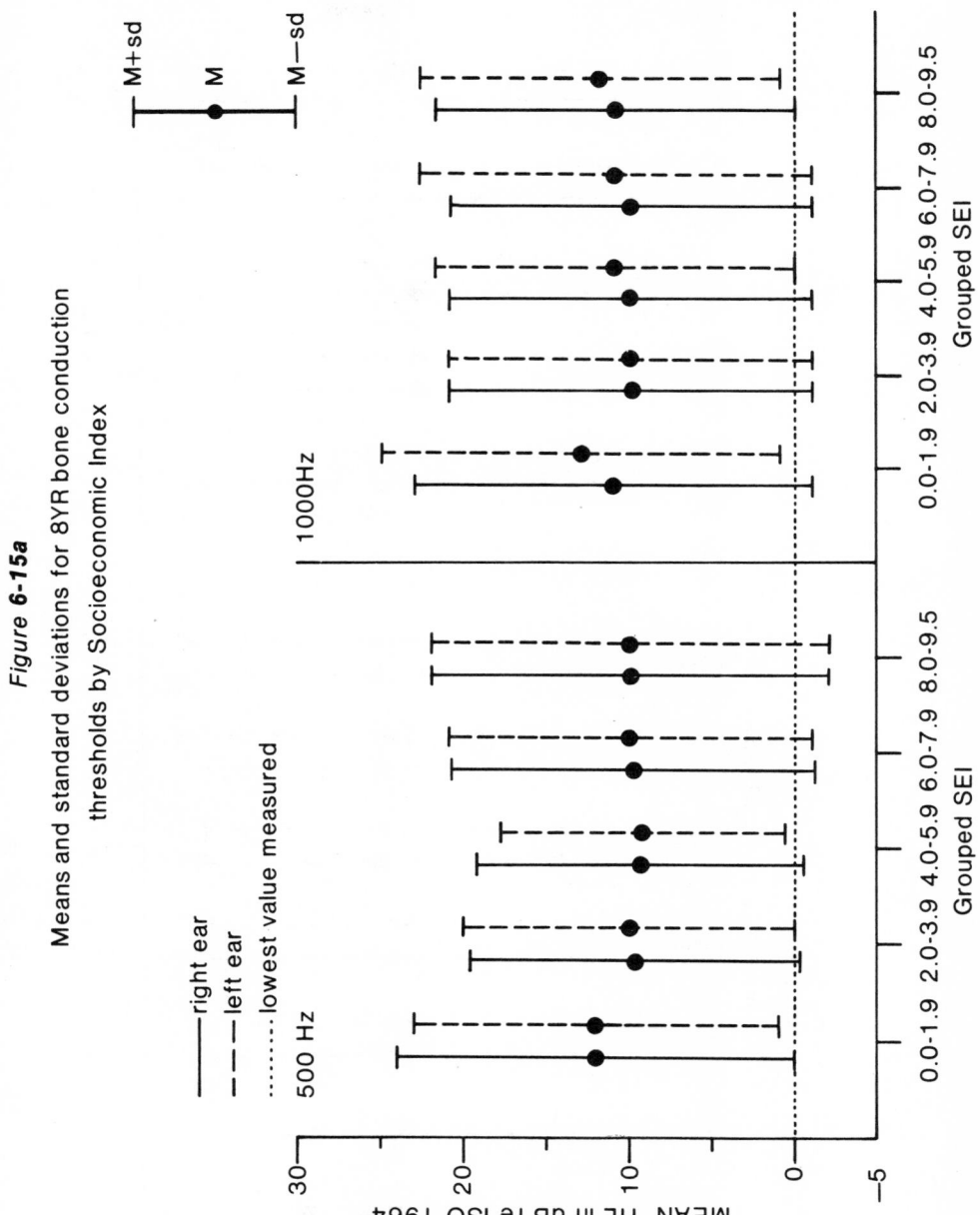

Figure **6-15a**

Means and standard deviations for 8YR bone conduction thresholds by Socioeconomic Index

107

Figure 6-15b

Means and standard deviations for 8YR bone conduction
thresholds by Socioeconomic Index

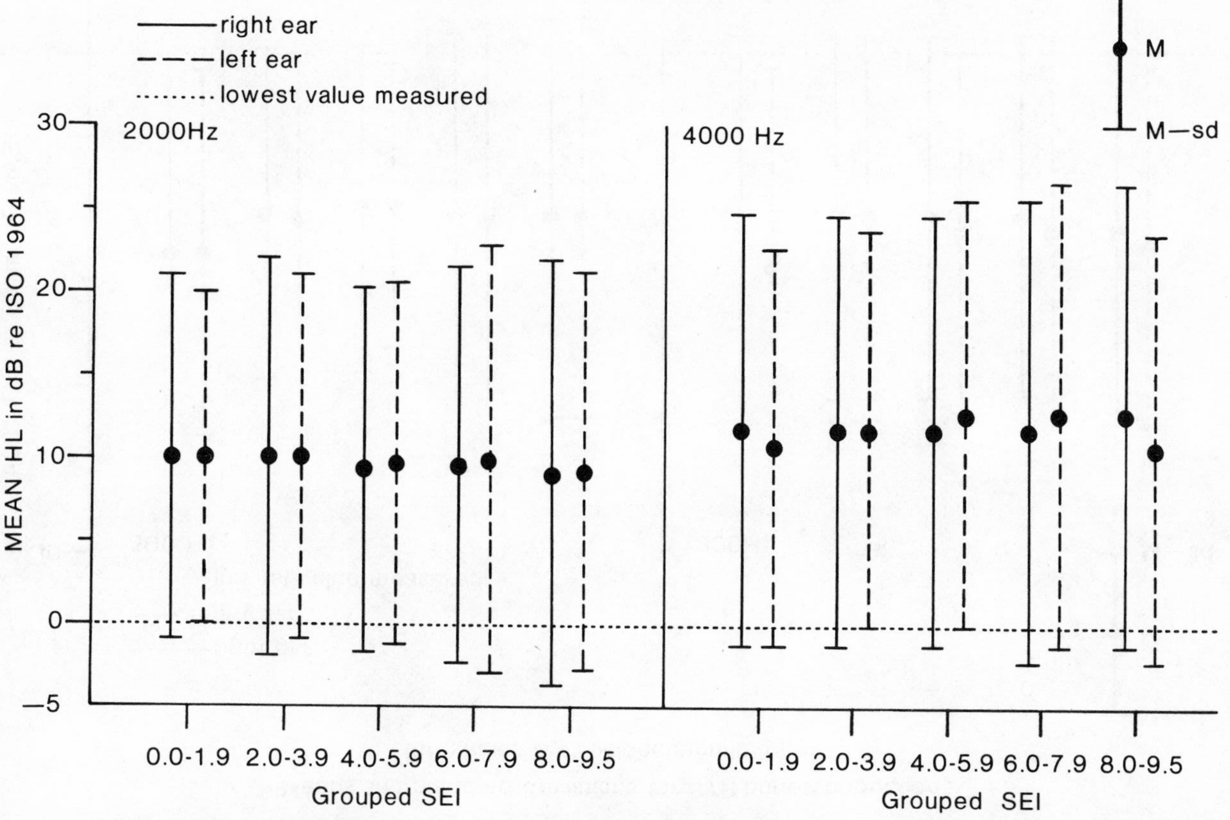

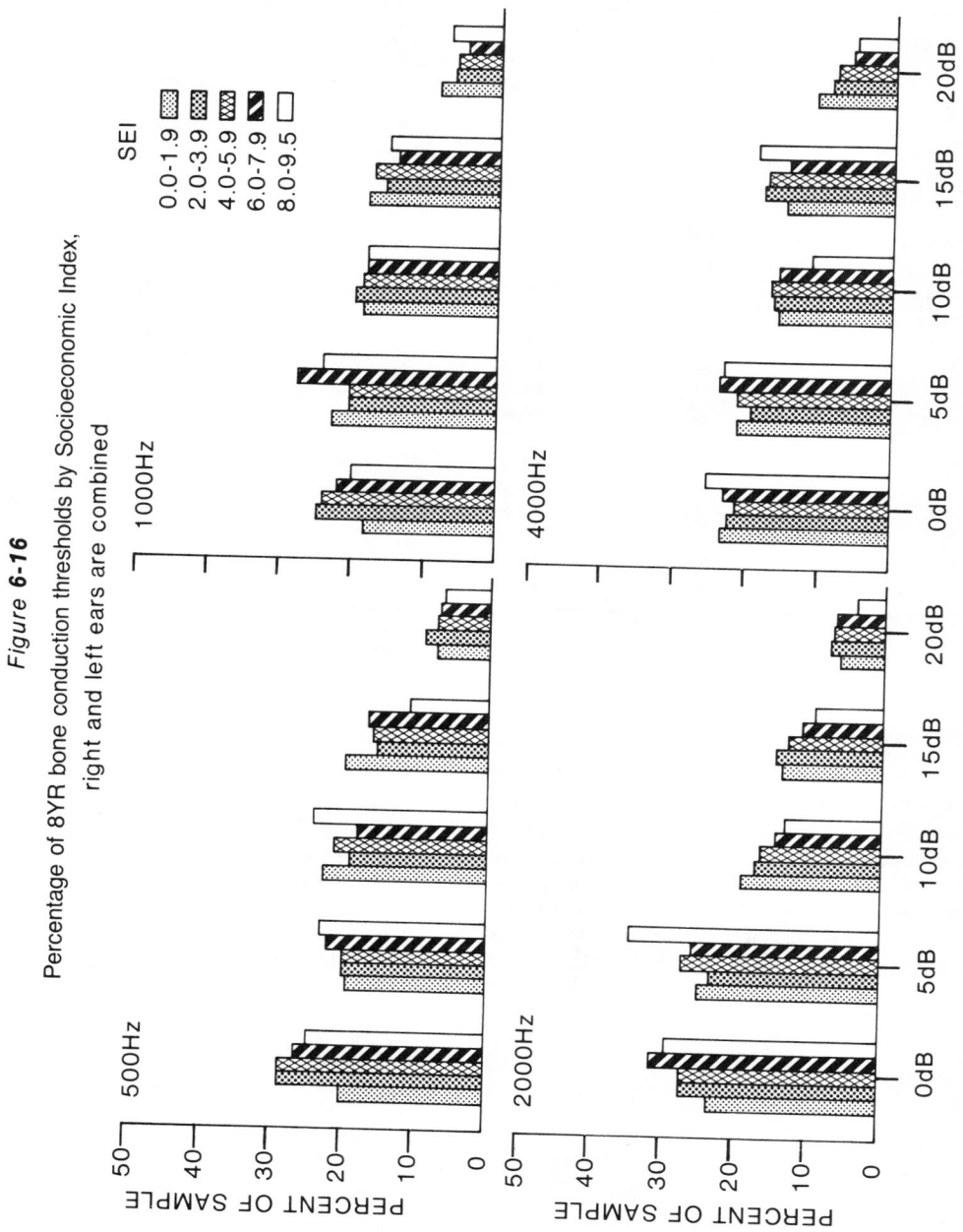

Figure **6-16**

Percentage of 8YR bone conduction thresholds by Socioeconomic Index, right and left ears are combined

SEI

0.0-1.9
2.0-3.9
4.0-5.9
6.0-7.9
8.0-9.5

500Hz

1000Hz

2000Hz

4000Hz

PERCENT OF SAMPLE

PERCENT OF SAMPLE

Table **6-11**

Means for 8YR pure-tone bone conduction hearing levels in dB re ISO 1964 by race, sex and Socioeconomic Index. Heavy type numbers are means for the right ear; italic numbers for the left.

	500	1K	2K	4K	N(Range)
Total sample	**10.08**	**10.63**	**9.97**	**12.51**	**1,490-1,503**
	10.34	*11.13*	*10.20*	*12.50*	*1,541-1,556*
White	**9.43**	**9.90**	**9.20**	**12.02**	**827-834**
	9.89	*10.27*	*9.42*	*11.72*	*898-908*
Black	**10.90**	**11.54**	**10.92**	**13.10**	**663-669**
	10.97	*12.33*	*11.28*	*13.61*	*643-649*
Male	**9.67**	**10.41**	**9.93**	**12.54**	**808-812**
	9.67	*10.67*	*10.60*	*12.95*	*851-864*
Female	**10.57**	**10.89**	**10.01**	**12.46**	**682-691**
	11.17	*11.70*	*9.70*	*11.94*	*690-695*
Socioeconomic Index					
0.0-1.9	**12.12**	**11.50**	**10.65**	**12.34**	**120-122**
	11.82	*12.77*	*10.32*	*11.59*	*131-136*
2.0-3.9	**9.88**	**10.64**	**10.34**	**12.49**	**480-485**
	10.38	*10.66*	*10.28*	*12.37*	*500-504*
4.0-5.9	**9.58**	**10.40**	**9.61**	**12.58**	**453-460**
	9.47	*11.02*	*9.97*	*12.73*	*439-444*
6.0-7.9	**10.07**	**10.41**	**9.90**	**12.25**	**297-299**
	10.70	*10.98*	*10.57*	*13.19*	*309-313*
8.0-9.5	**10.69**	**11.07**	**9.38**	**12.99**	**138-138**
	10.71	*11.83*	*9.70*	*11.67*	*160-162*

Table **6-12**

Correlations between pairs of 8YR pure-tone measures. Numbers in the triangular configurations are air-air or bone-bone pairs for the same ear; those in the small rectangles are between air or bone for different ears; and those in the large rectangle between air measures and bone measures.

Air Cond. Right			**Air Cond. Left**			**Bone Cond. Right**			**Bone Cond. Left**		
500	1K	2K	500	1K	2K	500	1K	2K	500	1K	2K
(500)	.75	.60	.62	.53	.42	.46	.46	.39	.42	.40	.30
	(1K)	.69	.53	.59	.46	.39	.53	.46	.38	.43	.34
		(2K)	.40	.45	.55	.37	.48	.63	.36	.41	.47
			(500)	.76	.60	.38	.40	.28	.47	.43	.32
				(1K)	.70	.37	.44	.35	.39	.52	.41
					(2K)	.36	.42	.48	.34	.44	.59
						(500)	.74	.58	.83	.70	.55
							(1K)	.71	.70	.82	.62
								(2K)	.56	.66	.76
									(500)	.71	.55
										(1K)	.70
											(2K)

110

Recently Olsen and Noffsinger (1974) proposed a nearly identical procedure as the preferred pattern for testing abnormal tone decay, pointing out that it is an easy procedure for the patient—certainly an important consideration in testing young children. Unfortunately, there is also a convincing argument that in practice the test was not successfully administered to all children. A contingency coefficient based on 300 children in this study who were retested by a second examiner shows almost no correspondence between first and second testing (C = .06). However, test-retest agreement was high; 94% for the right ear, and 97% for the left ear at 4000 Hz.

A summary of the results by sex, race, and socioeconomic rating is given in Table 6-13. More Black children than White fail to hear the 20 dB sensation level tone for 60 seconds, and more girls than boys fail the test. Perhaps the examiners more often failed to establish the game-playing atmosphere necessary for completion of the task for the Black children; and, in the same somewhat contrived vein, one might assert that eight-year-old girls are not so likely to play this sort of endurance game as boys are. Since the contingency coefficient was low and the correlation matrix (See Appendix 6) shows little relation of this test to other measurements, the abnormal adaptation measurements seem of doubtful value in this study.

Speech Discrimination Test

The Phonetically Balanced Kindergarten (PBK) lists were used to determine the child's ability to identify words at a soft conversational level, analogous to speech discrimination testing in the standard audiologic battery. The lists used are shown in Appendix 1. These lists were recorded on a tape by a male speaker. They were presented at a level 30 dB above the child's threshold for 1000 Hz, which predicts SRT closely (Carhart and Porter, 1971 p. 8), unless he considered this level too loud. In that relatively rare event, the level was reduced in 5 dB steps until he found it tolerable. If the words were considered too faint by the child, the tester was instructed to urge the child to respond and to increase the level only as necessary to elicit response. The test was given to each ear separately. The instructions given to the child included the admonition, "Even if you're not sure about it sometimes, tell me what the word sounds like to you."

As readily seen in Figure 6-17, the test was an easy one for eight-year-old children. The majority of the children did not miss more than one word, and only about five percent of the entire sample missed four words or more. Boys and girls scored virtually the same, indicating that the words did not tax the child's vocabulary (Brooks and Goetzinger, 1966).

The difference between the distribution of scores for the Black children and the White appears striking, but in reality the difference is based on three or four words out of the 25, and is likely either a culturally-determined difference in vocabulary or is attributable to differences in dialect between the child and the recorded speaker.

Discrimination scores show a dramatic change, however, with change in the Socioeconomic Index. As seen in Figure 6-18, the number of children who missed none of the words is definitely larger for each successively higher SEI rating. For those children who missed only one word, the percentage of children grows as SEI increases, but more slowly; and with higher values of SEI, the number of children who made more than two errors is smaller for each higher value of SEI. A similar pattern, though less striking, occurred for pure-tone air conduction results, yet discrimination shows negligible correlation with the 8YR pure-tone measures. Whatever causes discrimination and SEI scores to co-vary must be

Table **6-13**

Number of children who passed or failed the Abnormal Auditory Adaptation Test by race, sex and Socioeconomic Index. Italic entries are percentages.

4K Hz — Right Ear

	Male		Female		White		Black	
Pass	9,595		9,340		9,759		9,176	
Fail	221	*2.3*	283	*2.9*	195	*2.0*	309	*3.3*
		$\chi^2 = 8.91^*$				$\chi^2 = 69.1^*$		

Socioeconomic Index†

	1		2		3		4		5		Total Sample		
Pass	1,484		5,598		5,687		3,924		2,242		Pass	18,935	
Fail	59	*3.8*	167	*2.9*	166	*2.8*	85	*2.1*	26	*1.1*	Fail	504	*2.6*

4K Hz — Left Ear

	Male		Female		White		Black	
Pass	9,651		9,452		9,809		9,294	
Fail	163	*1.7*	217	*2.2*	148	*1.5*	232	*2.4*
		$\chi^2 = 8.66^*$				$\chi^2 = 22.93^*$		

Socioeconomic Index†

	1		2		3		4		5		Total Sample		
Pass	1,513		5,643		5,753		3,951		2,243		Pass	19,103	
Fail	39	*2.5*	131	*2.3*	125	*2.1*	61	*1.5*	24	*1.1*	Fail	380	*2.0*

500 Hz — Both Ears

	Male		Female		White		Black	
Pass	422		506		335		593	
Fail	26	*5.8*	49	*8.8*	33	*9.0*	42	*6.6*

Socioeconomic Index†

	1		2		3		4		5	
Pass	108		313		305		152		50	
Fail	6	*5.3*	33	*9.5*	23	*7.0*	12	*7.3*	1	*2.0*

*Significant at p<.01 level.
†Socioeconomic Index
   1 = 0.0-1.9
   2 = 2.0-3.9
   3 = 4.0-5.9
   4 = 6.0-7.9
   5 = 8.0-9.5

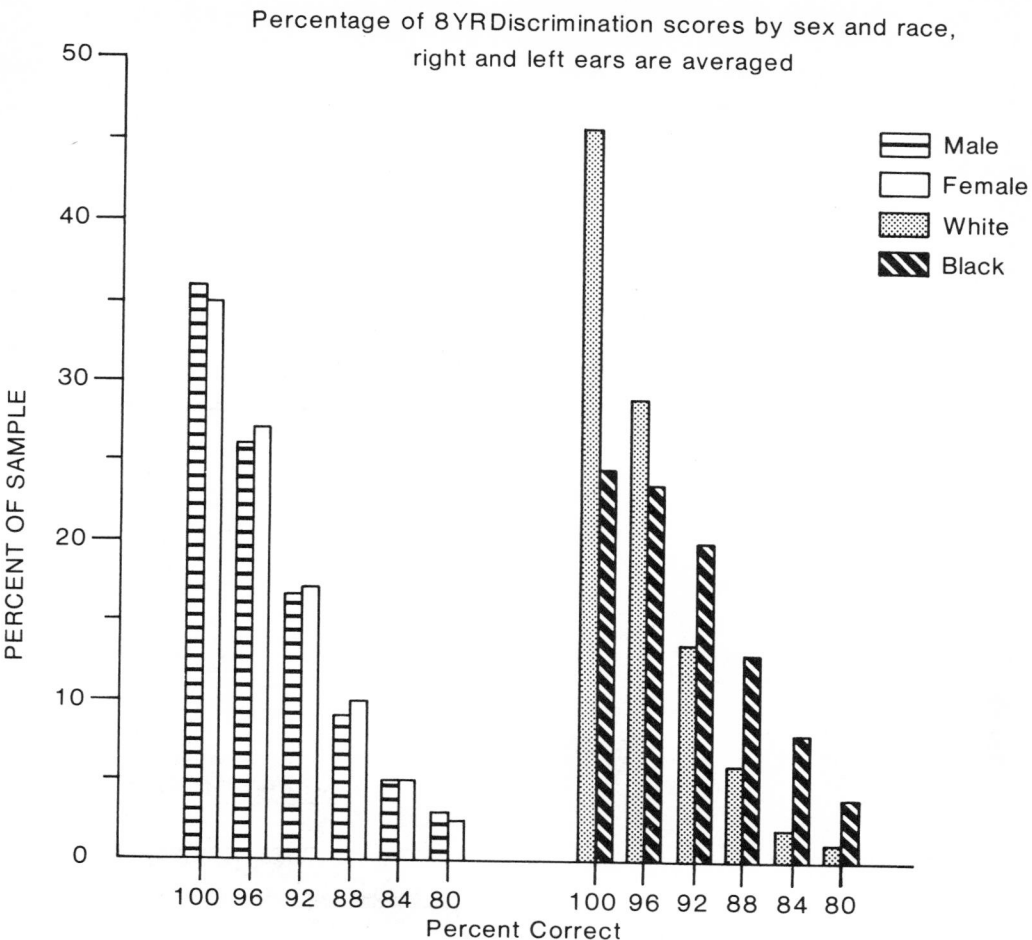

Figure *6-17*

Percentage of 8YR Discrimination scores by sex and race, right and left ears are averaged

Male
Female
White
Black

PERCENT OF SAMPLE

Percent Correct

relatively independent of the factor that contributes to the common variance of hearing sensitivity and SEI. Within this normal-hearing population, variation in discrimination scores may be attributable in part to such factors as word familiarity, aptitude for taking the test, likelihood of being misunderstood when responding, and other nonauditory variables. As in our earlier discussion of the results of the 3YR Spondaic Word Test, we can decide there is little variance in common between hearing sensitivity and discrimination scores, but we do not know whether the 8YR Discrimination Test also measures—or co-varies with—some

other factor that is inherently part of auditory ability.

This raises again, then, the very difficult question of whether or not word tests, as they were used here, can be shown to be testing anything properly considered hearing ability. The spondee test showed little common variance with pure-tone tests of sensitivitiy though it was given at a level close to threshold. It correlated even lower with measures of language performance at three years. It is difficult to make a judgment about the 8YR Discrimination Test, since it was given above threshold and not intended as a sensitivity test. Furthermore, even in

113

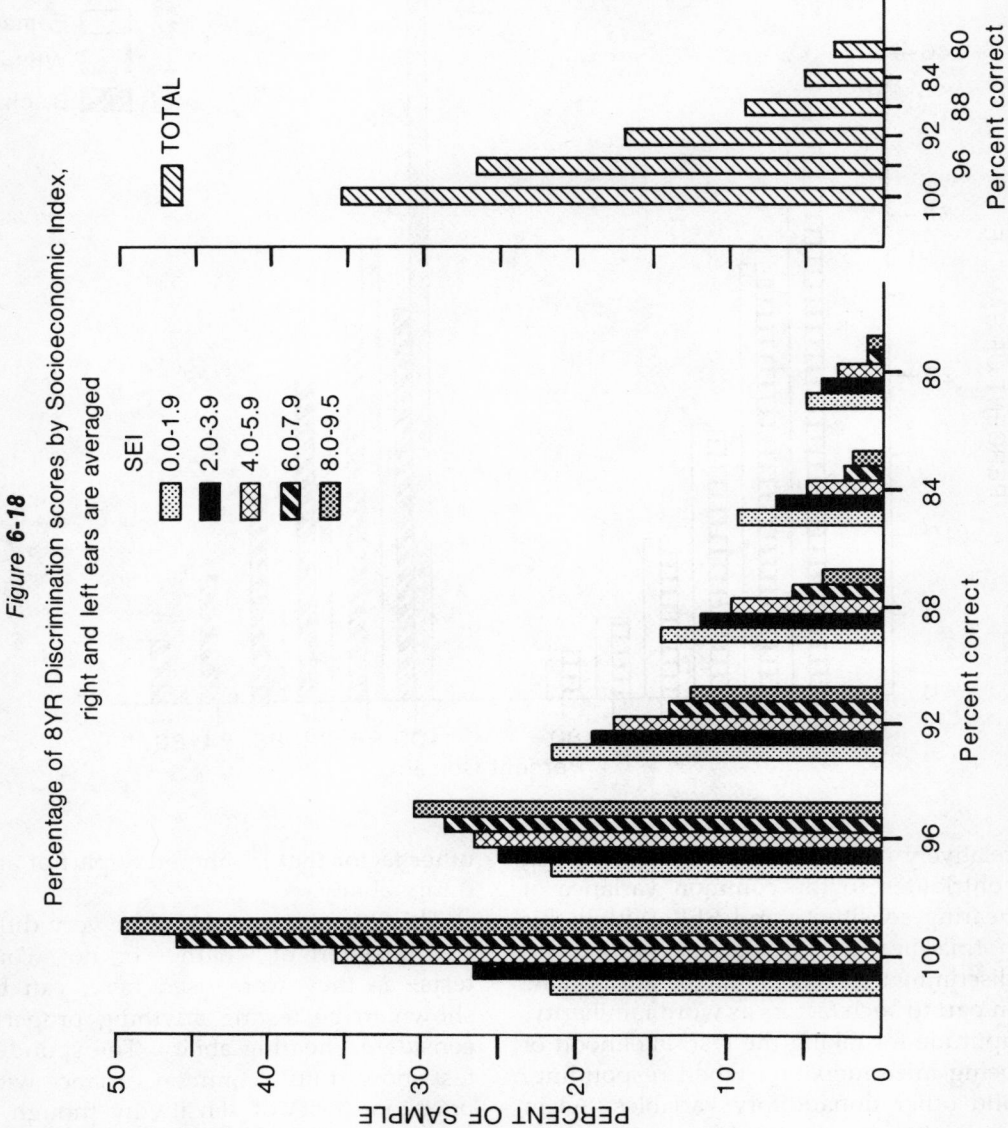

Figure 6-18

Percentage of 8YR Discrimination scores by Socioeconomic Index, right and left ears are averaged

114

adult patients on whom we have other audiologic tests, we do not have firm measures of the relationships between discrimination tests and other measures of hearing performance. At least part of the rationale underlying the use of the PBK test at this age is that it consists of words sufficiently familiar that it should not be a test of vocabulary or word familiarity. Is there evidence that it does measure some factor that should be called speech discrimination ability and which should be classified as an auditory attribute?

The fact that scores on 8YR Discrimination vary systematically with the SEI classification of the child's family does raise suspicion that word familiarity may be operating; and the difference in scores between Black and White children raises the question of whether or not dialect variation between the recorded speaker and the child being tested had an effect. The higher proportion of Black children in the lower SEI categories suggests that some interaction between race and SEI may be involved in this relationship. On the other hand, the fact that discrimination scores for right and left ears correlate only .53 indicates that, to at least some degree, some characteristic of the individual ear is being tested, not some characteristic of the child which is consistent from one test to the next. Unfortunately, this argument is weakened by the finding on a sample of about 300 children on whom test/retest procedures were done, that the estimated reliability was only .44.

Viewed with these reservations in mind, the results of the discrimination test provide a large mass of data on discrimination testing of eight-year-old children. First of all, if one looks to see which of the 3YR measures might foreshadow trouble with speech discrimination, as tested by the PBK lists, no close relations stand out. Correlations with these 3YR measures are shown in Table 6-14. Of course, the years between three and eight have been years of tremendous change in any child.

However, if one enters the list of variables in search of support for the hypothesis that discrimination scores ought to correlate most closely with hearing variables, some evidence for predictability is encountered. Although all correlations are low, the highest ones have to do, at least indirectly, with the child's hearing of his own speech (Articulation). Possibly this can also be claimed for Intelligibility and for those aspects of tongue movement that show a higher correlation than the average of the entire table. There is, of course, a possibility that the correlation with Intelligibility is at least partly ascribable to the inability of the examiner to understand the spoken responses of the child taking the PBK test. This we have no means of checking.

Scrutiny of a similar array for the 8YR variables shown in Table 6-15 leads to about the same conclusion. Discrimination scores are slightly more related to language-oriented variables, such as Morphology and Word Identification, than to more obviously speech-oriented measures like Articulation and Intelligibility. Only further investigation could determine whether the relation to language-oriented variables occurs because of a history of hearing difficulty during the developmental stage.

A different facet of the relation between discrimination and hearing is furnished by the correlations between discrimination and 8YR pure-tone tests at different frequencies (Table 6-15, upper portion). For 500 Hz and 1K Hz air conduction results the coefficients are very low; predictably, they are a little higher for 2K Hz air conduction. This latter has frequently been cited as evidence that identification of the consonants in consonant-vowel-consonant (CVC) words depends on energy in the higher frequencies. That the effect is so weak in these results speaks against their interpretation as a discrimination test for this essentially normal-hearing population.

The higher, but weak, coefficients for bone conduction scores indicate that

Table *6-14*

Correlations between 8YR Discrimination and 3YR variables.

Variables	Correlation Coefficients	
	R	L
Final Consonant Articulation	.29	.29
Initial Consonant Articulation	.20	.19
Understanding Space Relations	.17	.18
Lateral Tongue Movement	.16	.16
Tongue Elevation	.10	.11
Relevance	.11	.10
Intelligibility	.10	.10
Sentence Length	.10	.10
Understanding Action Words	.10	.10
Object Identification	.11	.09
Naming Objects	.09	.09
Spondee test	.09	.08
Voice Quality	.07	.09
Vowel and Diphthong Articulation	.08	.06
Word Order	.07	.07
Sentence Structure	.06	.05
Voice Loudness	.06	.05
Use of Pronouns	.06	.04
Two-digit Memory	.05	.04
Lip Diadochokinesis	.05	.04
Midline Tongue Protrusion	.04	.04
Tongue Diadochokinesis	.04	.03
Three-digit Memory	.04	.03
Lip Protrusion	.03	.03
Three-syllable Memory	.03	.03
Pure-tone Left	.02	.03
Pure-tone Right	.03	.02
Lip Retraction	.02	.03
Voice Pitch	.03	.02
Soft Palate Elevation	.01	-.01
Struggle Behavior	.00	-.01
Dysfluent Events	-.02	-.02

there is some dependence between hearing sensitivity and discrimination performance in a population with hearing loss.

The spondee test given to these children at three years, even though it was administered at a low level, was also an above-threshold word test; and it could be useful, since measures on thousands of children of homogeneous age are seldom available to us, to ask the questions of even incipient predictive value. If we analyze, in Table 6-16, the correlations between the 8YR measures and the spondee results at three years, we are essentially asking whether the children who failed the Spondaic Word Test differ in any discernible way, on the measures taken at eight years, from those children who passed the spondee test. Again, no strong associations were found; but for the highest of the weak correlations, the same mixture appeared between language variables and speech variables.

Table 6-15

Correlations between 8YR Discrimination Test and other 8YR measures.

Correlation with pure-tone thresholds

		Air Conduction						Bone Conduction				
		500		1K		2K		500		1K		2K
		R	L	R	L	R	L	R	L	R	L	R	L
Discrimination	R	.07	.03	.06	.05	.16	.10	.10	.17	.16	.15	.27	.17
	L	.05	.06	.06	.03	.11	.14	.12	.15	.13	.11	.15	.22

Correlations with other 8YR variables

	Correlation Coefficients	
Variables	R	L
Morphology	.34	.35
Word Identification	.34	.33
Articulation	.28	.27
Orientation	.26	.25
Writing from Dictation	.21	.22
Oral Reading	.22	.21
Silent Reading	.20	.20
Understanding a Story	.17	.18
Connected Discourse	.17	.18
Intelligibility	.18	.17
Soft Palate Function	.07	.09
Lateral Tongue Protrusion	.06	.07
Dysfluent Events	.06	.06
Speech Rate	.06	.06
Tongue Elevation	.05	.06
Voice Phonation	.06	.05
Lip Protrusion	.05	.05
Lip Retraction	.04	.03
Voice Loudness	.02	.03
Voice Pitch	.02	.01
Struggle Behavior	.01	.02
Midline Tongue Protrusion	.01	.01
Voice Resonance	.01	.00

8YR Hearing Measures and Selected 8YR Variables

As with the measures taken at age three, hearing sensitivity scores at age eight showed little relation to other measures of speech and language performance. Inspection of a correlation matrix of all eight-year variables reveals almost no coefficients that reach or exceed .30 (See Appendix 6). We must conclude that other measures of speech and language performance will be of little help in establishing or corroborating judgments about hearing deficiency, and that the reverse is also true. Within the restricted range of hearing sensitivity represented in this sample, the child apparently performs very nearly the same in spite of any apparent departure from "normal" sensitivity.

Table 6-16

Correlations between the 3YR Spondaic Word Test and 8YR variables.

Variables	Correlation Coefficients
8YR Writing from Dictation	.14
8YR Articulation	.13
8YR Intelligibility	.13
8YR Memory for Digits	.11
8YR Word Identification	.11
8YR Orientation	.11
8YR Oral Reading	.11
8YR Morphology	.11
8YR Connected Discourse	.10
8YR Silent Reading	.10
8YR Memory for Syllables	.07
8YR Understanding a Story	.06
8YR Voice Resonance	.06

If we interest ourselves in weaker relationships in a search for hints of predictive combinations, it is instructive to look at a smaller matrix of correlations between hearing measures and those variables that seem most likely to be at least weakly influenced by variation in hearing acuity. The list of measures selected for this kind of inspection can be seen at the left of Table 6-17. Clusters of correlations that rise above the average of the matrix, even though they are low and indicate only a weak relation, show some associations that are predictable but also some that are surprising. As can be seen, memory for digits and syllables is scarcely related to variation in auditory acuity in the range represented here even though a few cases of sensorineural loss, as measured by bone conduction scores, may have contributed a barely discernible effect.

The Word Identification and Morphology coefficients across the rows of hearing measures probably reflects some language deprivation in those children with larger losses and losses of several years duration. The consistently higher coefficients for Bone Conduction and Word Identification is a likely indication that in more severe losses language deprivation has been greater.

Performance on Connected Discourse is nearly unrelated to hearing acuity, though there is some indication that children who had trouble with discrimination also had trouble with this measure of language.

It might not have been predicted that a judgment of deviation in Voice Pitch tends to be associated, in at least some children, with nonconductive components of hearing loss. This is indicated by the rise in the coefficients between bone conduction measures and the judgments of both Rate of Speech and Voice Pitch. In fact, in the complete correlation matrix for all 8YR variables, the only variables that show a correlation with Voice Pitch above the .10 figure are the six measures of bone conduction.

Oddly, Voice Loudness, Phonation, and Resonance show no such increase. However, Voice Resonance appears to show a relation to air conduction measures which is slightly stronger for lower frequencies than it is for 2K Hz. Speech precision seems affected to some degree by hearing acuity, as indicated by the higher than average correlations associated with Intelligibility and Articulation.

118

Table **6-17**

Correlations between 8YR hearing variables, 3YR spondees and selected 8YR measures.

Variables	Air Cond. Right			Air Cond. Left			Bone Cond. Right			Bone Cond. Left			Disc. Right	Disc. Left	Spondee (3YR)
	500	1K	2K	500	1K	2K	500	1K	2K	500	1K	2K			
8YR Digits	.04	.04	.05	.03	.05	.06	.05	.10	.10	.04	.06	.10	.11	.11	.11
8YR Syllables	.04	.05	.06	.03	.04	.05	.03	.09	.11	.03	.07	.09	.09	.09	.07
8YR Word Identification	.11	.15	.16	.09	.13	.18	.20	.23	.22	.24	.23	.21	.34	.33	.11
8YR Oral Reading	.03	.07	.09	.04	.08	.11	.04	.10	.07	.07	.10	.14	.22	.21	.11
8YR Morphology	.10	.15	.16	.08	.13	.18	.15	.16	.14	.17	.17	.16	.34	.35	.11
8YR Connected Discourse	.08	.09	.07	.07	.11	.09	.06	.07	.05	.09	.12	.11	.17	.18	.10
8YR Rate of Speech	.05	.05	.05	.06	.06	.06	.14	.12	.11	.11	.12	.08	.06	.06	.04
8YR Voice Pitch	.07	.07	.07	.08	.07	.07	.15	.20	.18	.20	.15	.15	.02	.01	.02
8YR Voice Loudness	.03	.02	.04	.04	.03	.05	.07	.03	.09	.07	.03	.07	.02	.03	.00
8YR Voice Phonation	.06	.05	.05	.06	.04	.05	.08	.07	.07	.02	.01	.01	.06	.05	.03
8YR Voice Resonance	.12	.10	.07	.10	.10	.06	-.06	-.02	.02	-.04	-.01	.00	.01	.00	.06
8YR Intelligibility	.14	.15	.15	.13	.14	.15	.20	.22	.22	.18	.20	.17	.18	.17	.13
8YR Articulation	.14	.16	.17	.13	.16	.17	.14	.22	.20	.18	.19	.16	.28	.27	.13

119

8YR Hearing Indexes

The battery of hearing tests, as described earlier, included pure-tone air conduction measures at six different frequencies and a word discrimination test for each ear. The task of constructing descriptive indexes from combinations of these tests is made difficult by two factors. First of all, it is not reasonable to place any great weight on measures within 10 dB of audiometric zero. Not only is most of the variability in that range likely to be contributed by test conditions, but it is doubtful that even real variation among individuals in that range of hearing levels correlates with the other variables of interest. We cannot tell from the data which of these factors contributed to the consistently low correlation coefficients between the hearing measures and other variables. Second, the discrimination test given is probably more closely related to vocabulary differences than to hearing.

What evolved, then, from an attempt to devise indexes of hearing was what the audiologist usually extracts from a set of pure-tone measurements; namely, conventional indexes of the kinds of losses exhibited by patients. This is to say that we will deal essentially with hearing loss rather than with the variation of hearing ability within the normal range. A descriptive listing of these indexes is presented below. Additional details are given in Appendix 4. No child was assigned to one of these categories unless his air conduction loss was greater than 15 dB at any of the test frequencies used. For all children who met this condition, two determinations were made: (1) is the loss monaural or binaural? and (2) is the loss conductive or sensorineural?

Binaural Conductive

If the air conduction threshold at 500 or 1000 Hz was greater than 15 dB and the air-bone gap at 500 and 1000 Hz averaged greater than 10 dB in each of the two ears, the child was considered to have a binaural conductive loss. It should be borne in mind that any child given a bone conduction test had an air conduction loss greater than 20 dB at some frequency.

Monaural Conductive

If the above conditions held in one ear, but not both, then the child had a monaural conductive loss.

Binaural Sensorineural

If the pure-tone air conduction loss was equal to or greater than 30 dB at two or more of the test frequencies (500 Hz, 1000 Hz, 2000 Hz, 4000 Hz), *and* the average air-bone gap across the same frequencies was 10 dB or less, and these conditions held in both ears, the loss was considered to be binaural sensorineural.

Monaural Sensorineural

If the above conditions held in one ear, but not in both, then the child had a monaural sensorineural loss.

Mixed Loss

A loss was classed as a mixed loss if the maximum air conduction loss at two of the test frequencies was $\geq$ 30 dB and the measured bone conduction loss was $\geq$ 20 dB at two or more of the test frequencies. In addition, the loss was labeled mixed only if the air-bone gap was 10 dB or greater at two of these frequencies.

Furthermore, when using these indexes of hearing, sometimes the measure of interest is the amount of loss in the better ear, that is, essentially the functional hearing *acuity* of the child; whereas, for other purposes, the important measure is the degree of loss in the poorer ear—the *severity* of his loss. The means and the distribution of better-ear (acuity) thresholds for the total sample and the various subgroups are shown in Figures 6-19 to 6-21. For the poorer ear (severity), of course, such statistics differ. These are shown in Figures 6-22 to 6-24. These additional considerations, in effect, double the number of categories with designations such as Binaural Conductive Loss: Better Ear; Binaural Conductive Loss: Poorer Ear; and so on.

Finally, there are certain types of analyses for which the degree of the loss is not so important as the fact of its presence. In these instances, the sample is dichotomized and the terms used for the presence of hearing loss are Total Conductive Loss or Total Sensorineural Loss. Children with both types of loss were counted as members of both Total Conductive and Total Sensorineural categories. Except where these two labels are used for the 8YR indexes, the scores used in the analysis were the actual amount of measured hearing loss in dB.

3YR Hearing Screen and 8YR Hearing Indexes

Quite apart from the relations of hearing measures to other variables, one of the central questions in a study that measured hearing at different ages is how well hearing performance at the early age predicted hearing status at the later age. How do the hearing measures taken at three years of age relate to the more extensive measures taken at eight years? For the purpose of exploring these relations, the 3YR Hearing Screen was considered a pass/fail test. The children who passed pure-tones for only one ear, failed for both ears, or passed only spondees were considered to have failed. Only children who passed pure-tones in both ears were considered passed.

First of all, it should be noted that this method provides a high-yield screen. As seen in Table 6-18, the proportion of failures in the total sample is 12% and runs to 15% for White Female children. Somewhat more White children than Black children fail but the yield is high in all categories. To what extent are these the children who had a hearing loss at age eight by our definitions? A partial answer is furnished by Table 6-19, where it is possible to compare the probability that a child who failed the screen shows a loss at eight years with the probability that a child who passed the screen has a hearing loss. If the 3YR screen is a good test, ignoring the likelihood that remedial measures will have been taken on children who fail the test, the probabilities for the fail group should be higher than those for the pass group. Losses not detectable at three years should presumably affect both sets of probabilities equally. Obviously, the 3YR Hearing Screen was of some use in predicting the presence of hearing loss at age eight. In all subcategories of the sample, the evidence shows a greater likelihood of 8YR loss in the group that failed the 3YR screen than in the group that passed; least so, however, in the highest SEI bracket. Perhaps this last group is more likely to have received remedial attention for early losses.

A comparison of probabilities for the conductive and sensorineural losses is interesting because one might expect the conductive loss sample to be more changeable during this age span. Weber, McGovern, and Zink (1967), for example, have shown that this is true. Curiously the ratio of the pass and fail proportions for these two kinds of loss is about the same for the total sample; but the situation is slightly different for Black children and White children. In the group who failed the 3YR Hearing Screen, probability of a conductive loss at eight for White children is at least twice that for a sensorineural loss, whereas for the Black children the probability is about the same for either type of loss. It should also be noted, in making these comparisons, that the criterion for conductive loss is less

121

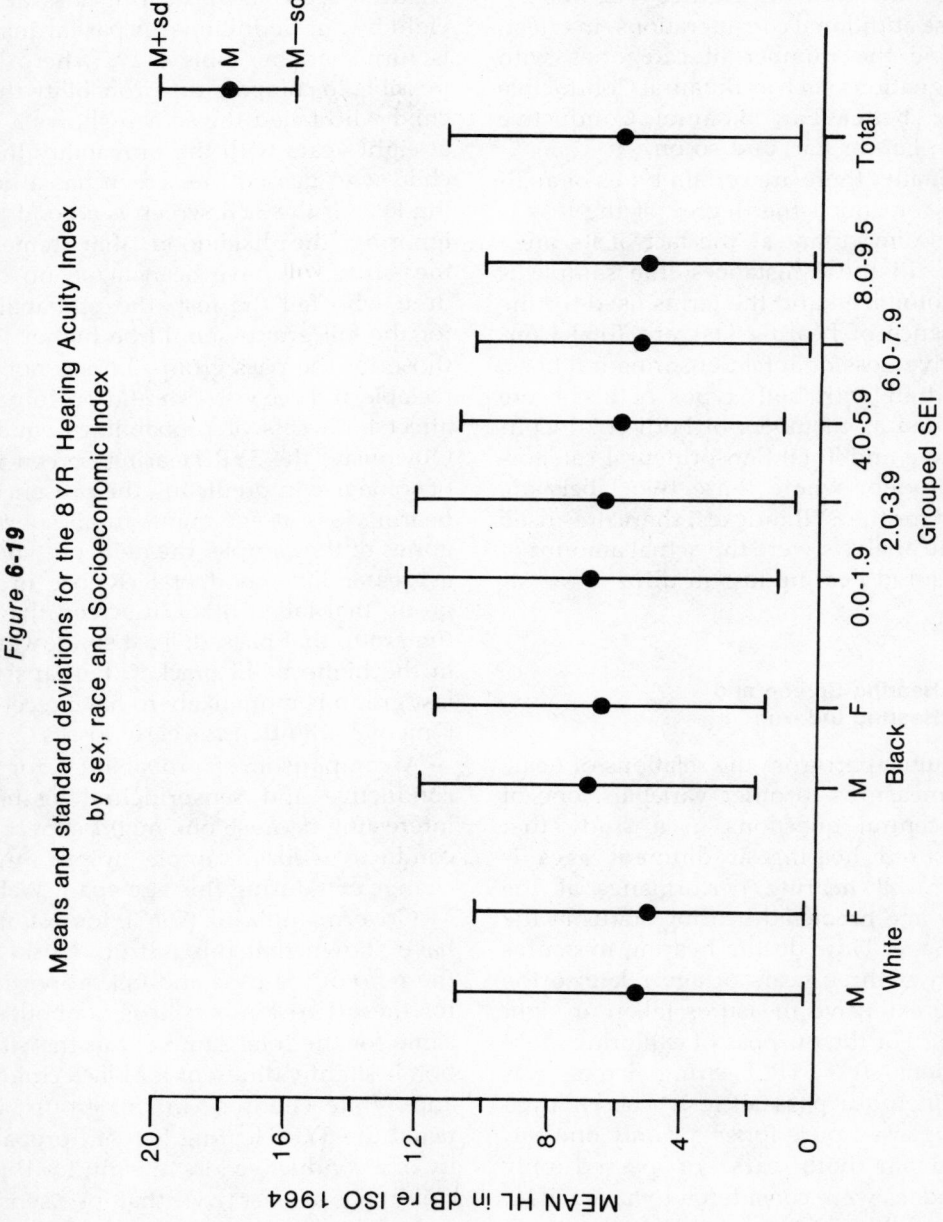

Figure 6-19

Means and standard deviations for the 8YR Hearing Acuity Index by sex, race and Socioeconomic Index

122

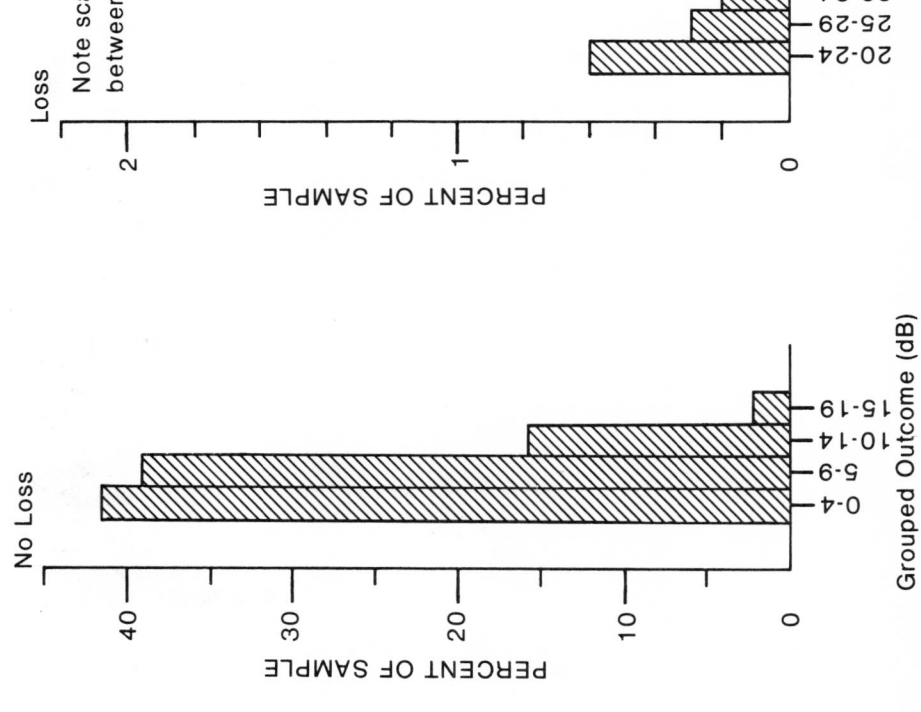

Figure 6-20

Distribution (%) of the 8YR Hearing Acuity Index outcomes (dB)

123

Figure **6-21**

Distribution (%) of the 8YR Hearing Acuity Index outcomes (dB)
by Socioeconomic Index

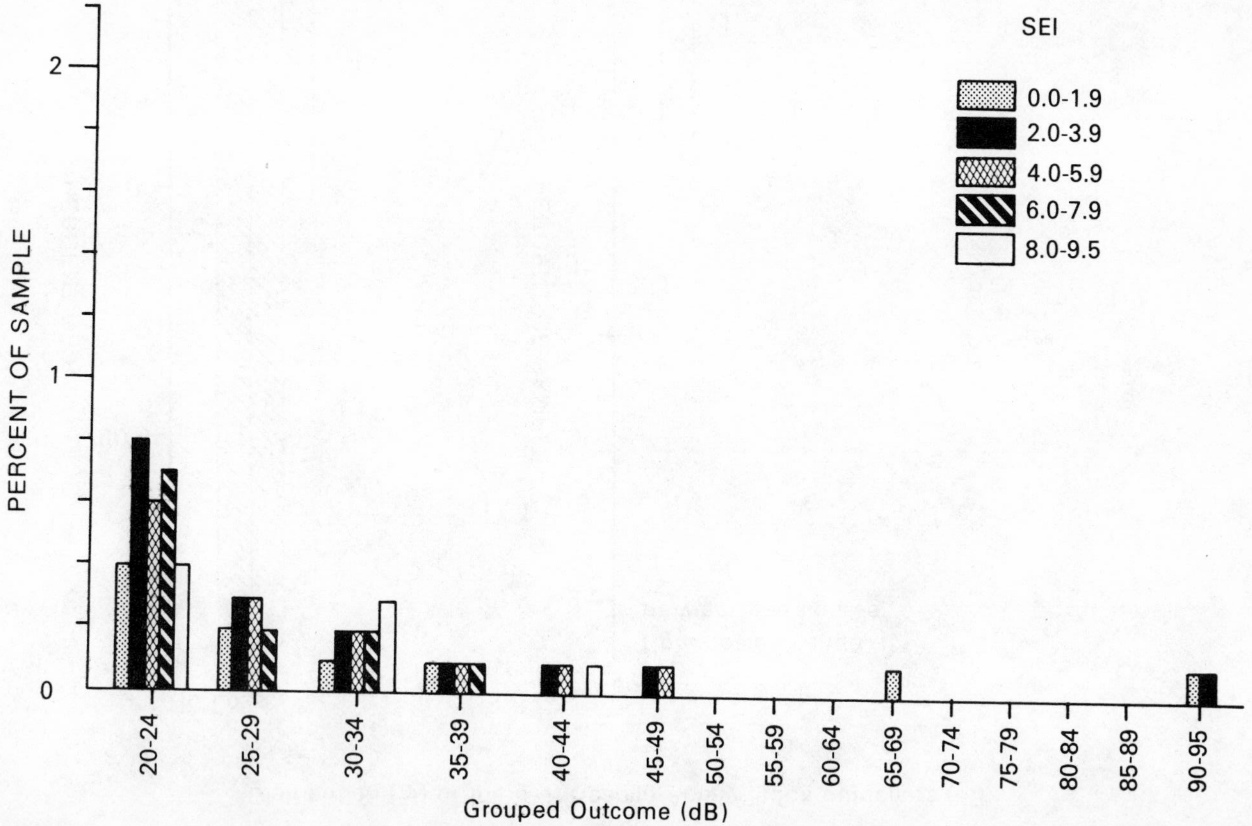

124

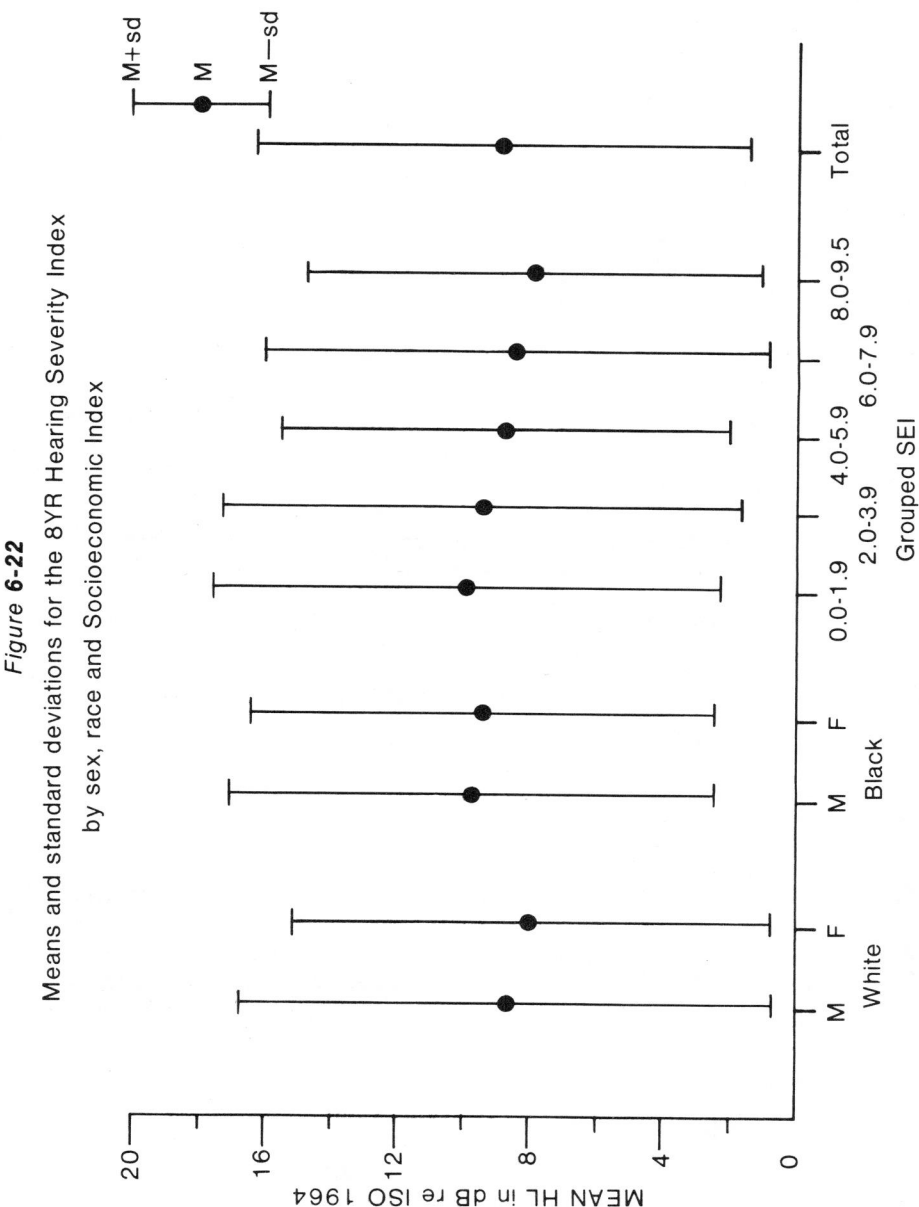

Figure **6-22**

Means and standard deviations for the 8YR Hearing Severity Index by sex, race and Socioeconomic Index

Figure **6-23**

Distribution (%) of the 8YR Hearing Severity Index outcomes (dB)

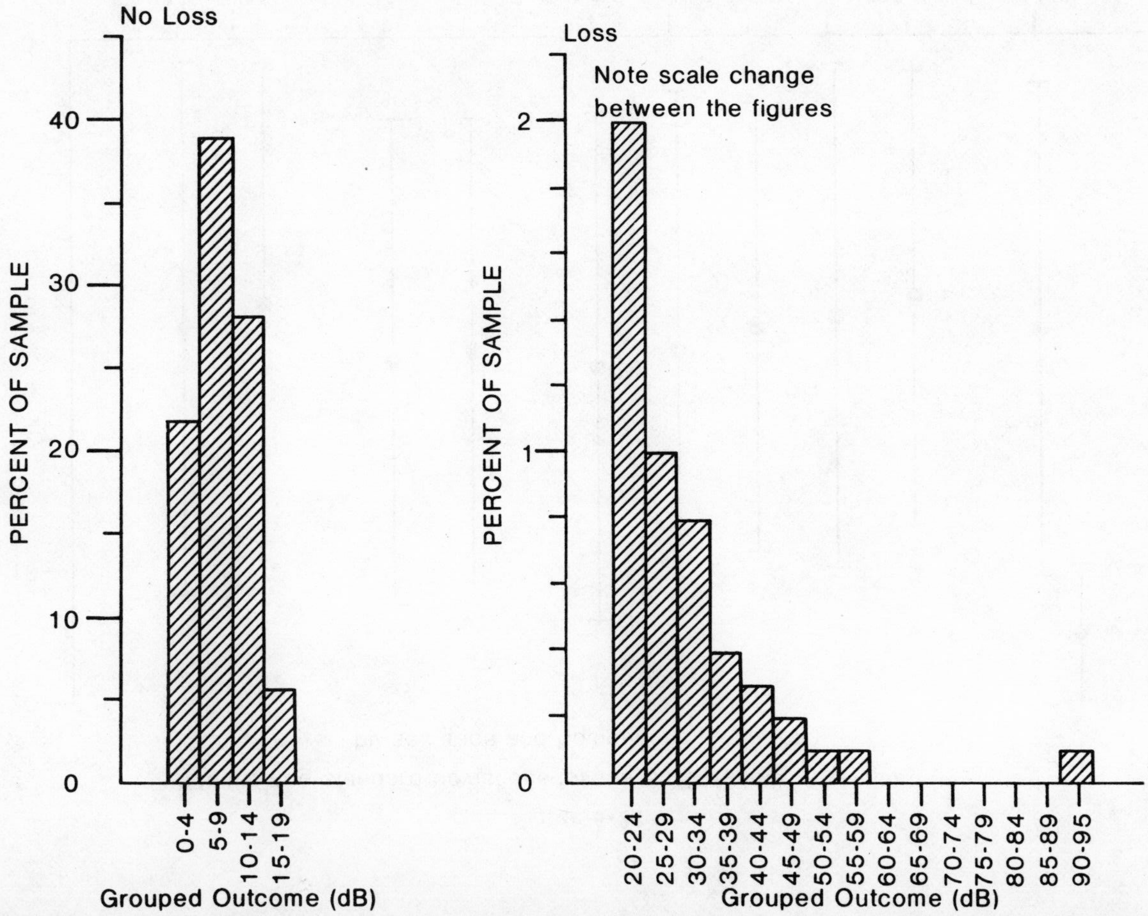

126

Figure **6-24**

Distribution (%) of the 8YR Hearing Severity Index outcomes (dB)
by Socioeconomic Index

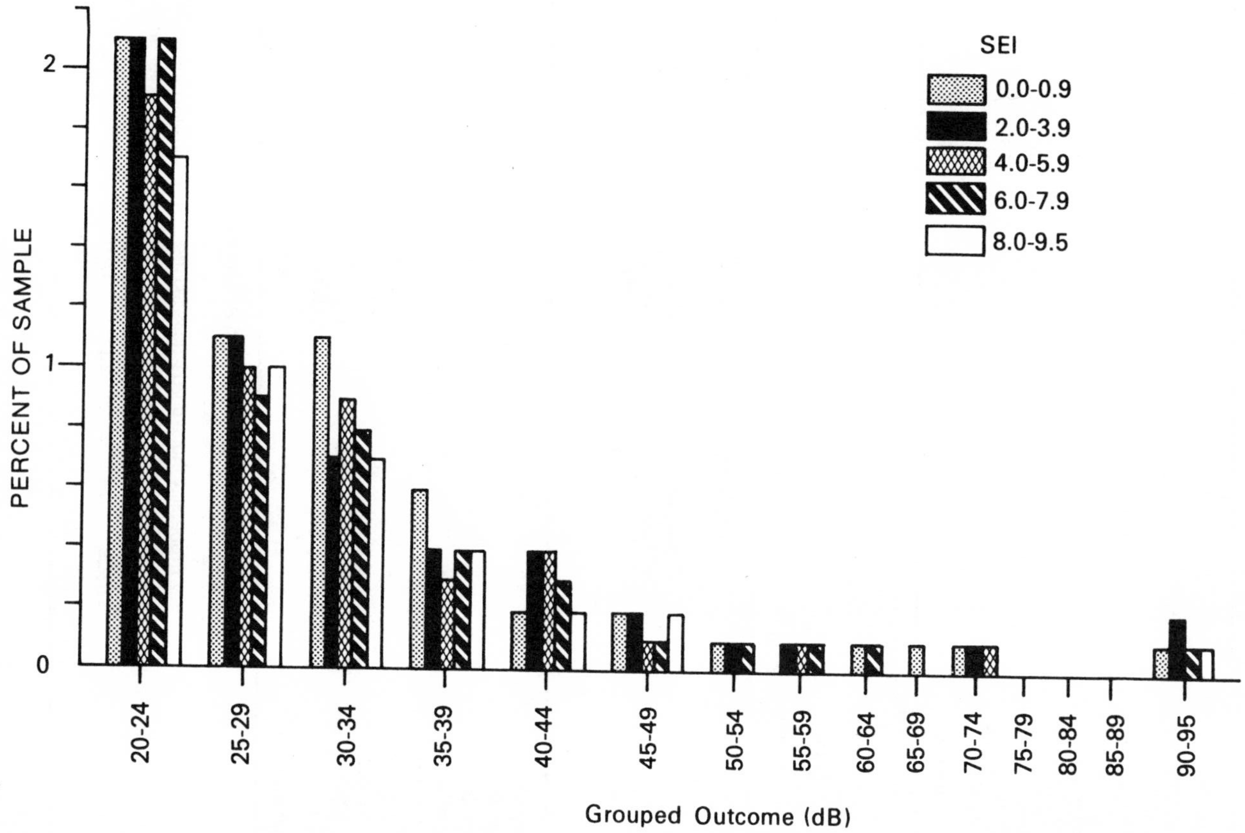

SEI

0.0-0.9
2.0-3.9
4.0-5.9
6.0-7.9
8.0-9.5

PERCENT OF SAMPLE

Grouped Outcome (dB)

Table 6-18

Proportions of the children completing both the 3YR and the 8YR tests who failed the 3YR Hearing Screen.*

	P	N
White Male	.13	(375/2,807)
White Female	.15	(392/2,622)
Black Male	.11	(319/2,966)
Black Female	.11	(322/3,052)
SEI 0.0-1.9	.11	(113/1,033)
SEI 2.0-3.9	.12	(436/3,633)
SEI 4.0-5.9	.12	(393/3,252)
SEI 6.0-7.9	.13	(268/2,036)
SEI 8.0-9.5	.13	(198/1,493)
Total Sample	**.12**	**(1,408/11,447)**

*Failure means failing pure-tones in one or both ears and/or passing only spondees.

Table 6-19

Relation between 3YR Hearing Screen and Hearing loss at eight years.

	3YR Hearing Screen and Conductive Loss			
	Probability that a child who failed the 3YR screen will have conductive loss at eight years.		Probability that a child who passed the 3YR screen will have conductive loss at eight years.	
	P	N	P	N
White Male	.14	(51/375)	.07	(160/2,432)
White Female	.10	(39/392)	.06	(133/2,230)
Black Male	.09	(30/319)	.05	(142/2,647)
Black Female	.09	(30/322)	.05	(125/2,730)
SEI 0.0-1.9	.09	(10/113)	.07	(60/920)
SEI 2.0-3.9	.12	(54/436)	.06	(190/3,197)
SEI 4.0-5.9	.11	(43/393)	.05	(148/2,859)
SEI 6.0-7.9	.12	(32/268)	.06	(106/1,768)
SEI 8.0-9.5	.06	(11/198)	.04	(56/1,295)
Total Sample	**.11**	**(150/1,408)**	**.06**	**(560/10,039)**

	3YR Hearing Screen and Sensorineural Loss			
	Probability that a child who failed the 3YR screen will have sensorineural loss at eight years.		Probability that a child who passed the 3YR screen will have sensorineural loss at eight years.	
	P	N	P	N
White Male	.06	(21/375)	.03	(70/2,432)
White Female	.04	(17/392)	.03	(58/2,230)
Black Male	.09	(28/319)	.03	(82/2,647)
Black Female	.07	(24/322)	.03	(89/2,730)
SEI 0.0-1.9	.07	(8/113)	.03	(28/920)
SEI 2.0-3.9	.07	(32/436)	.03	(105/3,197)
SEI 4.0-5.9	.07	(29/393)	.03	(81/2,859)
SEI 6.0-7.9	.07	(18/268)	.03	(57/1,768)
SEI 8.0-9.5	.02	(28/1,295)	.02	(3/198)
Total Sample	**.06**	**(90/1,408)**	**.03**	**(299/10,039)**

stringent here than the usual clinical criterion.

Basically, then, some estimate of the predictive value of the 3YR Hearing Screen was afforded by comparing the hearing at age eight of those children who passed or failed at three years. A more detailed look at the same information is available in Table 6-20. Here we retain the three categories of the 3YR Hearing Screen and show the actual numbers of children from each 8YR hearing-loss sample who might still be expected from each category if the 3YR tests had no predictive value. Suppose that instead of the 204 children who had a monaural conductive loss, a sample of 204 eight-year-olds was taken at random. If there were no predictability at all from those 3YR measures to the likelihood of hearing loss at eight years, then, on the average, only two of these 204 should be children who failed both ears for the pure-tone screen and also failed the Spondaic Word Test (got a 3YR Hearing Screen score of "0"); 22 of the 204 should be children who at age three passed for only one ear or passed only the spondee test (got a score of "1"); and the remaining 180 of the sample of 204 should be children who passed the pure-tone screen for both ears (a score of "2"). To the extent that the numbers observed in these categories, as shown in Table 6-20, do not agree with the numbers expected, there is some relation between the results of the 3YR Hearing Screen and hearing loss at eight years.

Other indexes of loss can be compared in the same way. It is clear that, in each case, some of the children who showed hearing loss at the age of eight are the ones who failed the hearing screen at the age of three; but the relation could hardly

be said to be close. The suggestion is, in fact, that for most categories the hearing losses measured at age eight were not present at age three in sufficient degree to lead to failure on a hearing screen. A possible exception is the Binaural Sensorineural category, where a high proportion of the children with hearing loss at eight years showed evidence of hearing trouble at three years.

The correlation coefficients shown are those computed between the actual scores on both measures; that is, the numerical score for the 3YR Hearing Screen and the computed loss in decibels.

8YR Hearing Loss Categories and Conventional Signs

Several of the observations of the child made in the course of his participation in the study seem rather directly related to the adequacy of his hearing. For example, as part of the pediatric examination at 12 months, the physician was instructed to note any abnormal ear conditions. The form lists these as Low-Set Ears, Deformed Pinna, Branchial Cleft Anomaly, Perforated Ear Drum, or other noninfectious ear conditions. An otoscopic examination by the physician was performed again as part of the neurological examination at seven years.

Shown as the denominators in Table 6-21 are the numbers of children in each of the 8YR hearing-loss categories whose record contained an entry for these observations. The numerator of each fraction is the number of children in that sample who were recorded as other than normal on the observation indicated. The proportion of the total 8YR sample re-

Table 6-20

The 3YR Hearing Screen as a predictor of poorer-ear and better-ear hearing at 8YR, comparing observed and expected frequencies and showing 3YR/8YR correlations.

8YR Index		3YR Hearing Screen Score*		Classified by 8YR Poorer-Ear Score		Classified by 8YR Better-Ear Score	
		Score	Cases (%)	Number Observed	Number Expected	Number Observed	Number Expected
Monaural		0	1	7	2.04	3	.85
Conductive		1	11	31	22.4	15	9.35
		2	88	166	179.5	67	74.8
				204		85	
	(r)†				(−.06)		(−.02)
Binaural		0	1	6	.89	7	.95
Conductive		1	11	11	9.79	11	10.5
		2	88	72	78.3	77	83.6
				89		95	
	(r)†				(−.10)		(−.05)
Monaural		0	1	4	1.28	4	.76
Sensorineural		1	11	20	14.1	8	8.36
		2	88	104	112.6	64	66.9
				128		76	
	(r)†				(−.21)		(−.14)
Binaural		0	1	10	.56	11	.61
Sensorineural		1	11	10	6.16	10	6.71
		2	88	36	49.3	40	53.7
				56		61	
	(r)†				(−.55)		(−.47)

*0: Fail pure-tones both ears, fail spondees.
 1: Pass pure-tones either ear, or pass spondees.
 2: Pass pure-tones both ears, disregard spondees.
†Correlation between 3YR Hearing Screen score and 8YR hearing level in decibels.

ceiving other than a normal judgment is shown in the second row from the bottom. The bottom row shows the total number of children who received that judgment. The proportions given agree with expectations from other data on hearing anomalies in children.

Note that in each sample shown in the cells of the table the number observed is at least a little higher than expected. In the Otoscopic Abnormality column, the Binaural Conductive sample shows a higher proportion than the others.

A total of 128 children were classified as having a Monaural Conductive loss at eight years and were assigned a better ear score. Of these 128, only one child was judged as showing evidence of deafness during the 12-month pediatric examination. Of the 333 children in the Monaural Conductive category who were assigned a poorer-ear score, three of them were judged to be showing signs of deafness at 12 months. If we take the larger number of children who were so judged from each of the four hearing-loss categories, a total of 35 children who had hearing loss by our definition at age eight were judged to show signs of deafness at the age of 12 months. The other of the 95 children who were judged deaf at 12 months either turned out to have a negli-

Table 6-21

8YR Hearing Indexes and conventional signs of hearing difficulty.

Loss Classification	Deafness	Observation reported on child during examination		
		Trouble Speaking	Unusual Ear Conditions	Otoscopic Abnormality
Monaural Conductive				
Better Ear	1/128*	4/126	4/136	16/123
Poorer Ear	3/333	6/333	16/359	52/305
Monaural Sensorineural				
Better Ear	6/118	3/116	5/134	21/132
Poorer Ear	11/186	4/186	5/211	28/190
Binaural Conductive				
Better Ear	3/167	4/169	11/180	41/163
Poorer Ear	3/155	3/157	10/168	38/151
Binaural Sensorineural				
Better Ear	18/93	10/95	8/105	13/101
Poorer Ear	18/87	10/89	8/100	13/95
Proportion in Total Sample	4/1,000	1/100	3/100	5/100
Number in Total Sample	95	245	845	1,186

*Numerator gives number of children judged not normal on observation.
Denominator gives number of children in hearing loss categories with observations.

gible hearing loss by the 8YR tests, may have dropped out of the study before age eight, or did not test satisfactorily for some reason.

A similar situation holds for the 1186 children who were singled out during the 7YR otoscopic examination, only about 100 of whom appear in the Monaural Conductive and Binaural Conductive samples, and of course far fewer in the sensorineural categories.

Overall, on this large sample of children, the table emphasizes that neither the presence nor the probability of eventual hearing loss is signaled with any certainty by these conventional early indications.

8YR Hearing Loss Categories and other NCPP Variables

It is already apparent to the reader of this report that a great deal of information was available on the children of the sample, from their prenatal history on through neonatal and pediatric examinations. The central question here is whether any of these measures, singly or in combination, will facilitate the prediction of hearing difficulty for the child in later years, or will increase the likelihood of detecting losses already present.

When faced with a mass of data, one way to reduce the number of variables for study is to select those which are judged by expert opinion to bear possible relation to the developing hearing process, and to follow this selection with a statistical search for suspected dependencies.

The following antecedent measures seemed to show the greatest likelihood of being related to existence of a hearing loss. The variables marked with an asterisk are those which showed a correlation coefficient of at least .20, an arbitrary cut-off.

* Gestation at Registration
  Parity
  Number of Cigarettes Per Day (Gravida)
* Weight Gain of Gravida

131

Number of Metabolic and Endocrine
  Conditions (Gravida)
* Number of Infectious Diseases During
  Pregnancy (Gravida)
  Education of Gravida
  Age of Father
* Five-minute Apgar Score
* Direct Coombs' Test
* Maximum Total Bilirubin
* Abnormal Ear Conditions (12 months)
  Syndromes (12 months)
  Birthweight
  Gestation at Delivery
* Acute Toxemia (Pre-eclampsia)
* Chronic Hypertensive Disease (Gravida)
  Rash or Skin Trouble (Gravida)
* Evidence of Deafness (1YR)
* Trouble Speaking (through 7YR)
* Ear Abnormalities (Otoscopic)
* Age of the Mother (Gravida)
  Education of the Mother
  Housing Density (Overcrowding)
  SEI at Birth
  Family Per Capita Income
  Education of Husband or Father of Baby
  Husband or Father Present in Home
* Eight-month Mental Score
  Eight-month Motor Score
  Four-year IQ
  Turns Head to Sound of Bell (Bayley)
* Turns Head to Sound of Rattle (Bayley)
* Enjoys Sound Production (Bayley)
* Social-Emotional Development (8 months)
* Brief Attention Span (4YR)
* Responds to Directions (4YR)
* Communication is Non-verbal (4YR)
* Wechsler Vocabulary Score (7YR)
* Wechsler Performance IQ (7YR)
* Wechsler Full-Scale IQ (7YR)
* Auditory-Vocal Association (ITPA) (7YR)

8YR Intelligibility
8YR Language Comprehension
8YR Auditory Memory
8YR Word Identification
8YR Written Communication
8YR Concept Development
8YR Neurological Involvement
8YR Communicative Effectiveness
8YR Auditory Processing

Finally, the measures of the hearing-loss samples were cross-tabulated with those SLH indexes which seemed most likely to show a relation with hearing difficulty. Indexes selected for such comparison were:

3YR Articulation
8YR Articulation

In general, the method for surveying for possible relations was first to correlate the variable scores with the hearing-loss scores for each category of hearing loss, and to scan the correlation matrix for coefficients that reached a magnitude of at least the arbitrarily chosen .20; then, for those pairs for which the correlation reached or exceeded that criterion, to compare the distribution of scores of the hearing-loss sample on the variable in question with the distribution expected on the basis of the performance of the entire sample on that variable. These comparisons are shown in Appendix 10. It should be noted, in inspecting these tables, that the discrepancies between distributions for the hearing-loss sample and for the total sample may not be reflected consistently in the size of the correlation coefficient. The correlation was run on the actual hearing-loss scores, whereas the "observed" entries in the table reflect simply presence or absence of hearing loss.

None of the measures selected shows any notable relation to monaural indexes, with the possible exception of shortness of attention span. From the performance of the entire sample, the number of children expected to have this characteristic would be only two out of the 71 children who have a monaural sensorineural loss, but four are observed instead.

The Direct Coombs' (Rh) test shows a

132

relation only with binaural conductive loss. There does seem to be also, for conductive losses, a somewhat greater number of children with low bilirubin, but the relation is not strong enough (r = .21) to have predictive value.

As might be expected, ear conditions visible to an examiner are more associated with binaural conductive loss conditions; the monaural conductive sample shows only negligible correlation. These directly observable indications have already been explored elsewhere in this report (Table 6-21).

In fact, this finding of weak relations seems to be the rule. The correlations that exceeded .20 and the comparison of observed and expected distributions are shown in Appendix 10, sections K through Q, for any reader who wishes to pursue a given measure. Only for the binaural sensorineural sample do the correlations occasionally reach a magnitude that might be useful for prediction. Here the comparatively strong correlation with the Articulation Index and with 8YR Intelligibility are already quite well established. The evidence of some language deprivation among children with binaural sensorineural losses is fairly well documented, and here it shows up in their performance on Language Comprehension, Word Identification, and Concept Development.

Testing Speech Discrimination in 8YR-Old Children

A sample of this size enables a closer look at the question of the functioning of PBK lists as a test of speech discrimination. The rationale for any proposed test of the adequacy of hearing for speech begins with face validity; that is, the lists consist of words sufficiently familiar to avoid testing vocabulary, and appropriately representative of speech sounds to be generalizable to the hearing of everyday speech. The test is administered at a level sufficiently above threshold to prevent its acting primarily as a test of sensitivity for speech sounds. Beyond these common-sense considerations, the data from a large sample of children permit us to discern whether, within the normal hearing population, the test co-varies with other measures that presumably are correlated with the ability to hear and understand above-threshold speech.

The measures chosen from the 8YR SLH battery for closer scrutiny of their relation to PBK test scores were: Morphology, Word Identification, Syllables, Digits, Oral Reading, Articulation, and Written Communication. Estimates of their co-variation with discrimination scores have been obtained in two related ways. First, coefficients of correlation were run between the scores on each selected variable and the better-ear score on the PBK lists. Coefficients of correlation between discrimination and other variables are shown in Table 6-22, and the joint distributions for most of these pairs are found in Appendix 10. Second, a comparison was made of the number of children who actually scored in a given interval on the "related" measure with the number *expected* to make that score assuming that the two measures are independent.

For this analysis, 8YR Discrimination scores were divided into three categories: more than five errors, four or five errors, and fewer than four errors. From a joint (bivariate) distribution of discrimination and the other variable of interest, the number of children expected in each of these three categories of discrimination scores was computed from the marginal totals of the distribution. This, then, is the number expected in that cell on the hypothesis that the two variables are not related. Any departure from the expected number in each score category of the discrimination range can be calculated for each category of the related variable. The value used is the difference between observed and expected values in number per thousand.

Table **6-22**

Correlations between 8YR Discrimination scores and selected 8YR language-related variables.
R_1 is the conventional coefficient.
R_2 includes also the possible contribution of a quadratic relation.

| | Correlation Coefficients | | | |
| | Better Ear | | Poorer Ear | |
Sample	R_1	R_2	R_1	R_2
Morphology				
Black	.311	.333	.253	.275
White	.214	.234	.181	.196
SEI 0.0-1.9	.320	.342	.255	.265
SEI 2.0-3.9	.293	.343	.261	.286
SEI 4.0-5.9	.327	.362	.284	.295
SEI 6.0-7.9	.328	.336	.246	.266
SEI 8.0-9.5	.136	.137	.107	.137
Word Identification				
Black	.298	.317	.244	.261
White	.179	.195	.169	.178
SEI 0.0-1.9	.337	.356	.268	.275
SEI 2.0-3.9	.285	.334	.258	.289
SEI 4.0-5.9	.303	.334	.270	.281
SEI 6.0-7.9	.264	.279	.214	.224
SEI 8.0-9.5	.083	.083	.101	.106
Syllables				
Black	.101	.108	.095	.097
White	.102	.116	.105	.120
SEI 0.0-1.9	.078	.083	.093	.093
SEI 2.0-3.9	.100	.108	.093	.094
SEI 4.0-5.9	.089	.105	.088	.100
SEI 6.0-7.9	.078	.085	.093	.098
SEI 8.0-9.5	.044	.053	.050	.071
Digits				
Black	.131	.136	.113	.118
White	.105	.123	.105	.120
SEI 0.0-1.9	.056	.057	.074	.077
SEI 2.0-3.9	.106	.116	.089	.096
SEI 4.0-5.9	.135	.147	.124	.131
SEI 6.0-7.9	.072	.083	.087	.095
SEI 8.0-9.5	.034	.041	.051	.055

Table **6-22** *(continued)*

Correlations between 8YR Discrimination scores and selected 8YR language-related variables.
R_1 is the conventional coefficient.
R_2 includes also the possible contribution of a quadratic relation.

| | Correlation Coefficients | | | |
| | Better Ear | | Poorer Ear | |
Sample	R_1	R_2	R_1	R_2
Oral Reading				
Black	.165	.169	.150	.155
White	.157	.179	.153	.168
SEI 0.0-1.9	.131	.133	.125	.127
SEI 2.0-3.9	.140	.153	.137	.150
SEI 4.0-5.9	.187	.213	.172	.189
SEI 6.0-7.9	.183	.190	.187	.193
SEI 8.0-9.5	.088	.093	.097	.101
Articulation				
Black	.282	.290	.251	.259
White	.123	.123	.097	.105
SEI 0.0-1.9	.313	.315	.289	.289
SEI 2.0-3.9	.263	.284	.256	.261
SEI 4.0-5.9	.245	.254	.201	.209
SEI 6.0-7.9	.180	.180	.141	.154
SEI 8.0-9.5	.032	.033	.025	.043
Written Communication				
Black	.189	.195	.166	.173
White	.178	.203	.165	.183
SEI 0.0-1.9	.151	.152	.154	.154
SEI 2.0-3.9	.154	.168	.132	.145
SEI 4.0-5.9	.200	.231	.189	.206
SEI 6.0-7.9	.209	.216	.205	.213
SEI 8.0-9.5	.095	.109	.090	.096

The tables (Appendix 10) give a summary of the relation between discrimination and the other variable in question and show the *pattern* of association better than the single coefficient. If the child who scores low on a language-related variable is also unusually poor on 8YR Discrimination, there appears in the chart a greater number than expected in the low-score category of discrimination scores. If the surmise is correct that the PBK list, as a speech discrimination test, is essentially free of vocabulary differences, the effect should tend to disappear toward the upper end of the more language-related dimension; that is, at that end the differences between the number of children observed and the number expected should tend toward zero. If this occurs, we may conclude that only those children who rank well below average in vocabulary show a discrimination score dependent on vocabulary.

Inspection of the tables indicates, however, that the prevalent pattern differs somewhat from that outcome. The sample of children who scored high on the related dimensions contains, in general, a greater than predicted number of children who scored high on the discrimination test. These data do not support the contention that performance above a certain level on language-related variables and discrimination scores on the PBK lists are unrelated.

Interestingly, a variable that does conform to the postulated pattern is Word Identification. It is not evident for White children, for whom the chance differences denoting independence of discrimination and Word Identification persist throughout the range. For both the Male and Female Black children, however, the apparent association of the two variables leads to more low discrimination scores than predicted in the lowest score category of Word Identification. This effect decreases gradually, though not always monotonically, with improving performance on Word Identification. Roughly, this pattern holds also for the two lowest SEI classifications. As SEI rating increases, independence between discrimination score and Word Identification is more evident, and they are almost totally independent for the highest SEI classification, as for White Male children. Of course, for these latter groups, the fact that dependence between the two measures is far weaker is evidenced also by the smaller correlation coefficients.

In almost all instances, the pattern of differences between the observed and expected number of children, and presumably the relation between discrimination score and language-related skills, differs systematically between Black and White children and between some SEI groups.

In Oral Reading, although the dependence is not strong, Black Male children who do most poorly on Oral Reading show 20 more children per thousand in the lower two discrimination categories than would be expected if Oral Reading and discrimination scores were independent. For Black Females, discre-

pancies are as great for the good oral readers as the poor ones.

The change in pattern from some association between the two variables to almost no effect of one variable on the other is readily apparent in the tables of articulation and discrimination scores for the five SEI classifications. For the highest SEI group the numbers of children observed in the three scoring categories agree with the number expected if the two variables were independent. This pattern holds also for Oral Reading scores and SEI groupings, but in a more complex manner; mid-range Oral Reading scores show little deviation from expected values throughout the five SEI groups.

Thus, the question of whether these PBK lists represent a test of speech discrimination sufficiently independent of language-related skills can be answered only in part from the data at hand. Similar testing and analysis on a wider age range of children would certainly be helpful in seeking a more comprehensive answer to this question.

Seasonal and Geographic Effects

The 8YR pure-tone data were inspected for possible seasonal and geographic peculiarities. Mean pure-tone threshold for the worse ear (severity) and the better ear (acuity) are shown in Table 6-23 by month of test for each institution. Some clustering of high mean thresholds could be observed in November and December, indicating that hearing tended to be poorer in the worse ear when tests were done in those months. However, the six institutions which showed this effect were widely dispersed geographically and unlikely to experience similar climatic conditions. No clustering could be observed for the opposite effect; that is, the months when hearing in the poorer ear was at its best showed scatter throughout the entire year. In the study of children ages five to 14 in Pittsburgh (Eagles et al., 1963), comparison of hearing levels for different months revealed

Table **6-23**

Variation in mean thresholds of 8YR-old children listed according to month of measurement and institution.
Numbers in ***italics*** represent the high and low means for each row.

	Jan.	Feb.	Mar.	Apr.	May	June	July	Aug.	Sep.	Oct.	Nov.	Dec.
Hearing Severity (Poorer ear)												
Boston	*7.6*	*7.6*	8.6	8.1	*8.8*	8.4	8.3	*7.6*	8.4	8.0	8.3	8.2
Buffalo	*9.3*	8.5	9.2	7.9	8.2	7.8	7.6	7.8	6.8	9.2	8.6	8.8
Charity	12.3	12.3	11.6	11.7	11.4	*9.3*	12.0	12.4	11.6	10.1	*12.7*	10.1
Columbia	8.7	8.2	8.6	8.0	8.2	7.6	*7.3*	7.5	8.0	8.5	*10.4*	9.5
Hopkins	9.0	9.9	9.3	*8.1*	9.0	9.0	9.7	10.0	10.5	9.7	9.4	*10.7*
Virginia	8.4	7.8	9.3	*6.7*	7.2	7.7	6.8	8.0	10.8	9.6	9.4	9.1
Minnesota	8.6	11.0	10.4	8.4	9.0	8.9	8.6	*8.1*	9.7	9.6	9.8	*11.6*
New York	10.3	*7.8*	*13.0*	10.5	9.8	11.8	9.3	10.0	8.5	9.3	10.5	9.7
Oregon	6.3	6.0	6.6	6.9	5.4	5.1	5.6	*4.5*	6.7	6.4	7.2	*9.0*
Pennsylvania	10.1	10.7	10.5	10.2	*9.9*	10.3	*11.5*	11.3	11.0	10.7	10.7	10.6
Providence	6.4	5.6	2.9	*2.8*	5.6	9.1	5.6	*10.3*	5.8	6.5	4.6	3.0
Tennessee	*9.4*	10.2	*11.9*	11.0	10.7	*11.9*	11.1	10.6	10.4	*9.4*	10.2	*9.4*
Hearing Acuity (Better ear)												
Boston	*4.3*	4.6	4.8	4.9	*5.2*	*5.2*	*5.2*	4.9	*5.2*	5.1	4.8	4.9
Buffalo	*6.6*	5.7	6.5	5.5	5.3	5.2	5.2	5.3	*4.7*	6.2	5.6	5.9
Charity	*9.2*	7.7	8.3	7.3	7.3	*6.2*	8.0	8.8	8.8	7.0	8.9	7.4
Columbia	6.2	5.5	6.1	5.2	5.8	5.9	*4.9*	5.3	6.0	5.7	*8.1*	6.6
Hopkins	6.0	6.6	5.7	*5.5*	6.1	5.9	6.7	6.8	*6.9*	5.9	6.2	6.8
Virginia	6.0	5.5	5.2	*4.2*	4.6	5.4	4.5	5.6	*7.7*	7.0	7.0	6.3
Minnesota	5.3	6.7	6.8	5.4	5.8	*5.0*	5.5	5.2	6.6	6.2	6.4	*7.6*
New York	7.3	6.0	*5.3*	6.7	5.6	*9.2*	7.2	7.2	6.4	5.5	6.6	6.6
Oregon	3.5	3.1	3.5	3.4	2.9	2.9	2.8	*2.2*	4.3	3.6	3.5	*5.1*
Pennsylvania	*8.1*	8.4	8.5	8.2	*8.1*	8.6	*9.1*	8.9	8.2	*8.1*	8.5	8.8
Providence	2.1	2.8	1.5	*1.1*	3.5	6.3	3.1	*8.8*	3.6	3.9	*1.1*	1.2
Tennessee	*6.2*	6.8	8.5	7.8	7.4	*8.7*	7.9	7.7	7.0	6.7	7.1	6.6

similar findings. Those investigators arbitrarily chose the right ear for month-to-month comparison. They report:

> The periods [of less sensitive hearing levels] during winter months occurred during epidemics of acute respiratory infection in the study population and those in May and July occurred when allergic manifestations were more common (Ibid., p. 94).

Oddly, however, their portrayal of the data (see their Figure 10.10, p. 93) does not support the statement. Although January and February of 1960 yielded levels of poorer-than-average sensitivity, the values for January and February of 1959 lie almost at the values of the overall mean levels for the entire period of the study. The children measured in July of 1958 exhibited poorer sensitivity than the overall mean at only two of the seven frequencies measured.

Thus, the children of the Pittsburgh study furnished no clear evidence that threshold levels differ measurably during the seasons when upper respiratory infection and allergic reactions are prevalent. A similar statement holds for the data reported here.

Differences between the highest and lowest mean thresholds for the poorer ear were generally of the order of 2 or 3 dB with a maximum as high as 7.5 dB at one institution (Providence). Data for the better ear show smaller differences, generally 1 or 2 dB, but with a maximum of 7.7 dB at that same institution. Seasonal clustering was weaker also for the better ear.

In brief, hearing of the poorer ear seems to be slightly worse in the colder months. But the effect is less pronounced in the better ear, as might be expected.

Abnormal Conditions of the Ear

On the assumption that abnormal ear conditions could have some bearing on the comprehension and expression of language and the precision of speech, their relationships were studied. These relationships could be dependent, such as Word Identification and hearing, or parallel, as in syndromes, or more general and not restricted to the ear mechanism.

A sample of children with abnormal conditions of the ear was obtained by report and by observation at *any* of the visits. Usually, the data were collected during pediatric examinations. A number of cases were included on the basis of reports from physicians, hospitals, and other sources external to the core study.

The abnormal conditions of the ear and the different numbers (mode and range) available depending upon the index studied* were:

*For a given abnormal condition of the ear, the component measure of an index may not have been available on all children.

		Modal N	*Range*
a.	Tympanic Membrane Anomaly	53	52–53
b.	Pre-auricular Sinus, Infected	30	29–30
c.	Peculiar Shaped Pinna	34	31–35
d.	Large Pinna	24	22–24
e.	Auricular Appendages	22	21–23
f.	Small External Auditory Canal	4	4-4
g.	Auricular Asymmetry	25	24–26
h.	Microtia	32	28–32
i.	Myringotomy with Ventilating Tubes	44	43–44
j.	Protruding Pinna	57	53–57
k.	Draining Ears	2067	2036–2098

The category labeled Tympanic Membrane Anomaly included calcification, scarring, perforation or thickening of the tympanic membrane, tympanosclerosis, and cholesteatoma.

The data presented here must not be construed as representing the incidence of these problems. This tabulation cannot be considered a complete roster of cases because unreported observations were possible within this selection procedure. Nevertheless, it is an available sample showing abnormal ear conditions compared to the total 8YR sample.

Hearing loss severity, conductive loss, and sensorineural loss were examined for each abnormal ear condition. Selected speech and language indexes and variables were reviewed relative to the particular ear conditions.

Results

Table 6-24 shows the means and standard deviations of hearing loss severity measures, and the percentage with conductive and sensorineural losses for each abnormal ear condition, as well as for the ALL 8YR population. The conditions are listed in order, least serious to most serious, for mean hearing loss severity.

The ordering of hearing loss severity seems to follow roughly a middle ear-external ear separation. The groups with poorest hearing included Myringotomy with Ventilating Tubes and Tympanic Membrane Anomaly, both evidence of middle ear compromise. The best hearing was found for Protruding Pinna, Auricular Appendages, and Auricular Asymmetry. Microtia and Peculiar Shaped Pinna were between these extremes. Although the Small External Canal group had the poorest hearing, it was a very small sample with a large standard deviation, which limits interpretation. The relatively good hearing in the Draining Ear category (10.7 dB) might be explained by the transitory nature of some conductive hearing impairments and the fact that these cases were collected partly by report.

A higher percentage of abnormal ear conditions in almost all categories showed conductive hearing losses rather than sensorineural. The only exceptions were Auricular Appendages, which

Table 6-24

Means and standard deviations for hearing loss severity and percent with hearing loss for abnormal ear conditions and the ALL 8YR sample.

Sample	8YR Hearing Loss Severity		8YR Conductive Loss	8YR Sensori-neural Loss
	$\overline{X}$	SD	%	%
Total ALL 8YR Population	8.6	7.3	5	2
Protruding Pinna	8.7	6.0	4	2
Auricular Appendages	9.6	6.9	4	4
Auricular Asymmetry	9.8	8.1	12	4
Draining Ears	10.7	9.8	12	4
Pre-auricular Sinus, Infected	11.3	6.3	3	7
Large Pinna	11.3	8.5	9	4
Microtia	12.5	16.1	11	7
Peculiar Shaped Pinna	13.3	16.7	12	6
Tympanic Membrane Anomaly	16.3	15.9	28	13
Myringotomy with Ventilating Tubes	16.6	12.2	30	2
Small External Auditory Canal	19.7	26.3	25	25

showed an equal likelihood of conductive and sensorineural, and Pre-auricular Sinus, Infected, which showed a 3% : 7% reversal. However, this is a difference of only one case. Further analysis disclosed that the pre-auricular sinus category was largely generated in one institution (Memphis), suggesting an institutional bias.

The relationship between abnormal ear conditions and selected language and speech indexes and variables is shown in Table 6-25. The possible contribution of abnormal ear conditions to the variance in certain 8YR language and speech indexes (specifically, Speech Mechanism, Palatal Function and Hypernasality, Fluency, and Intelligibility) appears small when the means and standard deviations are compared. Some trends seem noteworthy, however, and these are indicated in the table by underlined values. It can be seen that Microtia has the lowest mean value in nine of twelve selected speech and language indexes and is tied as lowest in two more subcategories. Its relatively large standard deviations suggest caution in interpretation. The frequent syndromal nature of Microtia may underlie the generally poor performance found.

A similar but less strong trend is seen for Peculiar Shaped Pinna, which is ranked second in six of the indexes. The others are scattered more randomly. A weak trend toward high mean scores is seen for Protruding Pinna, where some of the values exceed the means for the total 8YR population.

The possibility was considered that these trends are confounded by race and socioeconomic status since the selection of instances of abnormal ear conditions was not stringently controlled. Table 6-26 shows the composition of the categories by race, sex, and SEI for the Word Identification outcome. A heavy dependence of Word Identification performance on cultural and socioeconomic factors might safely be conjectured. Microtia shows a

two to one greater incidence for Blacks, no Females, and a trend toward lower SEI. Peculiar Shaped Pinna has a four to one ratio of Blacks to Whites, a majority of Males, and a trend toward lower SEI. This type of analysis lends additional need for caution against a simple interpretation of the relationships evidenced by the means and standard deviations.

It may also be noticed that, at least in this small sample, the use of ventilating tubes is greater in the higher socioeconomic categories. However, when these findings are interpreted, an explanation for the similar trend for Large Pinna and Protruding Pinna should be considered.

Hearing Sensitivity and Incidence of Hearing Loss in Various Subsamples

Several provocative comparisons emerge by separating from the total sample children with particular characteristics, with a view toward ascertaining whether those characteristics show some relation to hearing. Only children (singletons), siblings, twins, stutterers, retarded, cleft palate, cerebral palsied, and children with hearing loss were studied. In addition, children with low Apgar scores, prematures, and those in foster and adoptive homes were considered in this analysis.

Singletons were those who had no siblings at the time SEI data were collected, at birth and at seven years. Siblings were defined as the two oldest children in the study who were not the result of a multiple birth. Thus, there may have been older and younger children in the family or an intervening birth. The singleton group, 879 children, showed a mean pure-tone threshold for the poorer ear of 8.3 dB; slightly better hearing, on the average, than the 8.6 dB of the 8YR total sample.

A smaller percentage of this group showed conductive loss by our criterion than the total 8YR group—4% as op-

Table **6-25**

Means and standard deviations for 8YR indexes by abnormal ear conditions and the ALL 8YR sample.

Sample	N	8YR Speech Mechanism		8YR Palatal Function and Hyper-nasality		8YR Fluency		8YR Articulation		8YR Intelli-gibility		8YR Language Compre-hension	
		X̄	SD	X̄	SD	X̄	SD	X̄	SD	X̄	SD	X̄	SD
Total ALL 8YR Pop.	20,137	7.9	.68	3.0	.25	6.9	.55	46	6.4	2.9	.29	153	45
Tympanic Membrane Anomaly	51	8.0	.19	2.9	.41	6.9	.56	44.0	9.88	2.9	.38	155.4	37.64
Pre-auricular Sinus-Infected	30	7.9	.73	2.9	.37	6.7	.69	42.3	9.29	2.9	.25	136.7	37.41
Peculiar Shaped Pinna	35	7.7	1.09	3.0	.17	6.9	.37	42.2	12.10	2.9	.48	139.5	61.18
Large Pinna	24	7.7	1.00	2.9	.41	7.0	.00	45.5	6.04	2.8	.41	161.4	42.11
Auricular Appendages	23	8.0	.00	3.0	.21	6.9	.44	45.1	8.23	2.9	.29	158.2	46.27
Small External Auditory Canal	4	8.0	.00	3.0	.00	7.0	.00	45.3	4.65	3.0	.00	141.3	15.78
Auricular Asymmetry	26	7.4	1.33	3.0	.00	6.8	.56	43.8	8.87	2.9	.33	146.5	46.46
Microtia	31	7.7	1.01	2.8	.63	6.7	.79	40.6	11.62	2.8	.54	129.5	54.55
Myringotomy with Ventilating Tubes	44	7.8	.78	3.0	.30	6.9	.60	43.9	7.46	3.0	.21	165.9	38.27
Protruding Pinna	56	7.8	.75	3.0	.00	6.9	.39	45.3	8.38	2.9	.38	170.3	40.38
Draining Ears	2,659	7.9	.70	2.9	.32	6.9	.50	45.7	7.19	2.9	.33	159.7	43.97

Sample	N	8YR Auditory Memory		8YR Digits		8YR Word Identifi-cation		8YR Written Communi-cation		8YR Language Production		8YR Concept Develop-ment	
Total ALL 8YR Pop.	20,137	170	41	34	10	62	9.9	203	57	728	102	42	10
Tympanic Membrane Anomaly	51	168.6	38.99	31.1	9.89	64.8	7.45	197.8	60.53	726.4	115.94	43.4	10.84
Pre-auricular Sinus-Infected	30	164.1	27.05	31.7	10.03	56.7	9.89	196.4	59.97	723.4	111.84	40.1	9.10
Peculiar Shaped Pinna	35	154.9	59.42	28.2	12.67	56.1	14.17	168.9	72.32	678.3	172.05	36.3	11.51
Large Pinna	24	167.2	39.04	34.2	10.60	66.4	9.99	201.3	57.82	724.3	109.43	43.1	9.08
Auricular Appendages	23	166.4	45.37	31.1	8.99	62.7	10.56	183.1	48.62	714.2	125.78	41.0	9.17
Small External Auditory Canal	4	174.5	12.26	32.5	8.66	58.8	8.30	182.8	54.08	726.3	43.29	43.5	7.94
Auricular Asymmetry	26	172.5	49.60	35.6	12.94	61.3	9.18	180.6	58.82	729.5	96.26	42.0	11.75
Microtia	31	142.1	57.53	27.0	11.70	55.0	12.02	163.5	65.22	644.5	174.22	34.5	12.03
Myringotomy with Ventilating Tubes	44	170.1	39.33	30.3	8.10	66.4	7.80	208.7	64.22	733.5	79.82	44.4	8.94
Protruding Pinna	56	179.5	37.15	34.3	9.61	66.9	7.09	200.9	51.31	730.1	93.17	45.0	7.70
Draining Ears	2,659	172.1	40.98	33.4	10.20	64.6	9.49	204.6	59.16	735.9	101.12	43.9	10.10

Note: Underlined values indicate trends characterized by consistently low or high scores for certain abnormal ear conditions.

Table 6-26

Distribution of abnormal conditions of the ear by race, sex and SEI for the Word Identification outcome.

Category	White	Black	Invalid*	SEI 0.0-3.9	SEI 4.0-5.9	SEI 6.0-9.5
Tympanic Membrane Anomaly	44 (19F)	7 (2F)	1	15	15	21
Pre-auricular Sinus, Infected	1 (0F)	29 (19F)	0	18	7	5
Peculiar Shaped Pinna	7 (1F)	28 (11F)	0	20	10	5
Large Pinna	22 (1F)	2 (0F)	0	5	9	10
Auricular Appendages	11 (2F)	10 (3F)	1	11	4	6
Small External Auditory Canal	2 (2F)	2 (1F)	0	3	0	1
Auricular Asymmetry	10 (4F)	14 (4F)	1	11	7	7
Microtia	10 (0F)	20 (6F)	1	15	9	7
Myringotomy with Ventilating Tubes	38 (15F)	6 (3F)	0	10	12	22
Protruding Pinna	43(10F)	12 (1F)	2	16	14	25
Draining Ears	1,511 (684F)	569 (267F)	579	618	607	855

*Word Identification score not available.

posed to 5%. It may be that single children have better health care. Whether this accounts for the difference, or whether some more obscure factor also contributes to slightly better hearing in the singleton group, is not discernible from the data given. The sibling group of 3880 children had a mean threshold for the poorer ear differing only nominally from the 8YR total sample average (8.8 dB compared to 8.6 dB).

But, surprisingly, the 370 twins (185 pairs) in the sample differed from the total sample in having a mean pure-tone threshold of 9.8 dB in the poorer ear, roughly two standard errors poorer than the mean of all eight-year-olds. This indication that the hearing of twins differs from the unselected population is even more persuasive on inspection of the percentages of conductive and sensorineural loss in the twin sample. In this sample of twins, 7% of the members exceeded our conductive loss criterion and 4% were labeled as having sensorineural loss. It is pertinent that these percentages exceed the percentage of conductive and

sensorineural losses in the total sample by at least twice the standard error of proportion.* It would appear, then, that the probability of occurrence of both kinds of hearing loss in the twin sample is greater than in the unselected sample. Viewed together, the evidence of better hearing in the singleton sample and the greater likelihood of hearing loss in twins suggests that susceptibility to hearing loss in twins should be investigated further.

A partial explanation may lie in the relation between birthweight and the incidence of hearing loss as attested strongly by the number of babies with birthweight less than 1500 grams who later show conductive loss. Of this sample of 100 babies, 12% showed conductive loss (by our subclinical criterion) at the age of eight years. Since this is about five standard errors below the 5% representative of the total 8YR sample, there must have been some real contributing factor in this group, possibly a susceptibility to upper respiratory infections. Actually, both the pure-tone threshold scores and the percentage of conductive losses showed a consistent progression indicating less trouble with conductive

* For conductive loss $(PQ/N)^{1/2} = 0.0116$; for sensorineural loss $(PQ/N)^{1/2} = 0.0074$.

loss with increasing birthweight, as shown in Table 6-27. There is also some evidence, though less convincing, of greater sensorineural loss incidence in the lowest birthweights.

The hearing measures on a number of other groups that differ from the rest of the 8YR sample in ways that might conceivably affect hearing are listed in Table 6-28. For most of the groups listed, the findings of poorer hearing than for the unselected population are predictable from measurements already reported in the literature. This is not true for the sample of stutterers; but the sample of stutterers is small, and the numbers of losses shown, three conductive (9%) and one sensorineural (3%), could have occurred by chance.

The fact that the premature group differs so slightly from the total 8YR sample might plausibly be attributed to their early identification as children who need special medical monitoring. The low Apgar score group differs more than the premature sample, and it would be of considerable interest to know the etiology of both the conductive and sensorineural losses in these children. This deserves further attention.

Of additional relevance here is the group of children with WISC scores in the mentally retarded range, without accompanying syndromes. The grouped scores for the 7YR WISC IQ are shown in Table 6-29, where it is apparent that the sample of 553 children who score 70 and below on the WISC also shows poorer

Table **6-27**

Mean hearing level and percent with hearing loss at 8YR for five categories of birthweight (in gm).

Birthweight (gm)	N	Poorer Ear Hearing Level (dB)	Conductive Hearing Loss (%)	Sensorineural Hearing Loss (%)
<1,500	97	11.4	12	3
1,501-2,500	1,868	9.6	6	3
2,501-3,500	12,798	9.1	5	2
3,501-4,500	4,926	8.5	5	2
>4,500	163	8.2	4	2

Table **6-28**

Mean hearing level and percent with hearing loss at 8YR in subsamples with certain characteristics.

	N	Poorer Ear Hearing Level (dB)	Conductive Hearing Loss (%)	Sensorineural Hearing Loss (%)
Prematures	917	9.4	6	3
Low Apgar Score	617	9.9	7	5
Stutterers	35	11.4	9	3
Mentally Retarded	53	14.3	14	5
Cerebral Palsy	83	11.3	15	5
Cleft Palate	24	14.7	32	9
Total ALL 8YR Sample	**20,137**	**8.6**	**5**	**2**

143

Table **6-29**

Mean hearing level at 8YR by WISC IQ scores.

WISC IQ	N	Poorer Ear Hearing Level (dB)	Conductive Hearing Loss (%)	Sensorineural Hearing Loss (%)
≤50	48	11.3	0	4
51-60	92	12.4	10	9
61-70	413	11.1	8	4
71-80	1,670	10.5	6	3
81-90	3,467	9.7	4	3
91-100	5,268	8.9	5	2
101-110	4,540	8.3	5	2
111-120	2,374	7.9	5	2
>120	919	7.2	4	1

hearing than the total group. Since the correlation between pure-tone hearing and WISC IQ is low, it is likely that the difference in mean is attributable to greater incidence of hearing loss. However, children with lower IQs are difficult to test reliably.

There are interesting differences in the results of the hearing measurement of children who are adopted as compared to those in foster homes (not shown in table). The adopted sample had a mean pure-tone threshold for the poorer ear of 7.7 dB (compared to 8.6 dB for the total 8YR sample), whereas the sample of children living with foster parents had a mean threshold of 10.7 dB. The chance that either of these values occurred through random sampling of a population with a mean threshold of 8.6 dB is less than one in 100. The slightly better hearing of the adopted sample probably indicates that children with hearing loss tend to be excluded from the adopted group. This is supported somewhat by the fact that only 4% of this sample show loss by our 8YR total conductive loss criterion. The percentage for sensorineural losses does not deviate from that for the entire 8YR population. However, for the sample living in foster homes, the difference in the mean poor ear threshold is attributable to the presence in the sample of a greater proportion of children with losses. Ten percent of this sample show a conductive loss and five percent a sensorineural loss, both higher than the 5% and 2%, respectively, of the total 8YR samples.

Among these comparisons, the differences noted for only children and the seemingly poorer hearing for twins merit further comment. In neither instance was there a change in *average* hearing loss of the sample without a concomitant change in the percentage of losses in that sample; thus, the effect in each instance is to heighten the likelihood of loss occurring rather than to reflect a change in sensitivity in all members of the sample.

Summary
3YR Hearing Screen

Two screening tests of hearing at 3YR yielded dichotomous data. The hearing of each ear was assessed separately with a pure-tone sweep check at 500, 1000, and 2000 Hz. Failure at any one frequency was regarded as hearing failure for that ear.

The second hearing screen was a binaural sound field presentation of spondee words at 52 dB SPL. Repeating or picture-pointing five consecutive words or any seven out of ten passed the screen.

144

3YR Pure-Tone Screen

Between 4% and 5% of more than 16,000 children successfully screened failed one or more frequencies in at least one ear. There were no sex differences and about equal numbers of monaural (497) and binaural (478) pure-tone losses.

More White than Black children failed the pure-tone screen. The percentages of failures were: White Female, 6.8%; White Male, 6.6%; Black Male, 5.3%; Black Female, 4.5%. Left ear losses were more numerous than right ear, 308 to 189, and an order effect was considered probable since the right ear test was presented first and children of three years are likely to have lags in attention.

Although demonstrating less total failure, Black children showed more binaural failure than monaural. For all children, monaural losses increased and binaural losses decreased with rising SEI.

3YR Spondee Screen

There were 1341 (7.7%) failures on the spondee screen out of 16,130 successful tests (12% not administered). Thus, more children failed the spondee screen than the pure-tone, despite a less stringent spondee pass criterion. More Males than Females failed, 8.8% as opposed to 6.6%, but no race differences were observed. The percent failing decreased with SEI.

Spondee Screen and 3YR SLH Variables

The co-variance of spondee screen performance with other speech and language variables was studied by correlation. Generally, correlations were not high. The highest coefficient (.24) was with Intelligibility. The next nine correlations in order of magnitude (.20 to .16) were with language variables such as Naming Objects, Understanding Action Words, and Sentence Structure. Weaker correlations were found with Vowel and Diphthong Articulation (.15), Final Consonant Articulation (.14), and Initial Consonant Articulation (.13).

3YR Hearing Index and Medical and Nonmedical Antecedents

An index of 3YR Hearing was constructed by expert opinion. It included the spondee screen but gave greater weight to the pure-tone screen. No systematic relationship could be found between 3YR Hearing Index and any of a long list of selected NCPP variables. These included the number of infectious diseases of the mother, Apgar score, mother's age, smoking, chronic hypertension, history of hearing impairment in the family, SEI, and other variables that might be directly or remotely related. The highest coefficient (.10) was obtained with the mother's occupation (laborer, farmer) category.

3YR Hearing Index and Other 3YR SLH Measures

Similarly, the 3YR Hearing Index related only weakly with other speech and language measures. The highest correlations were only .12 with Intelligibility and with the verbal expression summary. The remaining coefficients of .10 and .11 were with other items of the language category: Understanding Action Words, Sentence Structure, Relevance, Word Order, and Use of Pronouns.

8YR Hearing Test Battery

Hearing was assessed at eight years in the following ways:

a. Pure-tone Air Condition, a threshold test, for 500, 1000, 2000, 4000, and 8000 Hz; each ear tested separately under phones. The better ear was tested first or, if unknown, order was determined by odd or even number of the child's birthday.

145

b. Pure-tone Bone Conduction, a threshold test, for 500, 1000, 2000, and 4000 Hz in any ear having an air conduction hearing level of 20 dB or more (ISO 1964) in one or more frequencies.
c. Abnormal Auditory Adaptation Test employing a tone decay procedure of 4000 Hz at 20 dB sensation level, 60 second criterion. If 4000 Hz was inaudible before 60 seconds had elapsed, the same procedure was repeated with 500 Hz.
d. Discrimination Test of hearing for speech, each ear tested separately using the phonetically-balanced kindergarten (PBK) lists of 25 words; presented under phones at 30 dB above AC threshold for 1000 Hz.

8YR Pure-Tone Air Conduction Test

Mean air conduction thresholds for the total 8YR sample of 20,137 children ranged from 6.46 dB to 10.27 dB HL, depending upon frequency and ear. Best hearing was found at 2000 Hz (right ear 6.46 dB, left ear 6.76 dB HL) and at 1000 Hz (right ear 6.85 dB, left ear 6.89 dB HL). Measures at 2000, 1000, and 500 Hz were shown to be close to measures derived in the Pittsburgh study of hearing sensitivity in children (Eagles et al, 1963).

Mean differences between Male and Female eight-year-olds were small but consistently favored Females. Blacks had higher (poorer) mean thresholds than Whites at 1000, 2000, and 4000 Hz; the differences were negligible at 500 Hz and 8000 Hz. With the exception of 500 Hz, threshold sensitivity was directly related to SEI. Correlations between mean AC thresholds were moderately high for adjacent frequencies and gradually lower as frequencies were farther apart.

8YR Pure-Tone Bone Conduction Test

The hearing of approximately 3000 ears was measured with bone conduction

(BC) pure-tones. White children had slightly lower (better) mean BC thresholds than Black children at all frequencies. There was no sex difference. There was no systematic change associated with SEI. Correlations between mean BC thresholds were moderate for adjacent frequencies, similar to the AC relationships, and lower for frequencies farther apart.

Abnormal Auditory Adaptation (Tone Decay)

There were 2.6% and 2.0% failures, right and left ear respectively, on a 4000 Hz stimulus tone decay test. More Blacks than Whites and more Females than Males failed; SEI showed some effect. An interexaminer (test-retest) contingency coefficient of .06 limited interpretation of the tone decay findings. A correlation matrix showed little or no relation to other measures.

Speech Discrimination

Over half of the eight-year-old children (63%) missed no more than one word of the PBK test. Indeed, over one-third of them (36%) had all 25 words correct. Eighty-eight percent of the children achieved a score of 88%. On the average, Whites scored higher than Blacks, a 12% to 16% difference. With each SEI increment, the number of children with more than two errors was smaller and the number with no errors increased.

Although correlations with 3YR speech, language, and hearing variables were generally low, the best correlations (.29 each ear) were with Final Consonant Articulation followed by Initial Consonant Articulation (.20 right, .19 left), Understanding Space Relations (.17 right, .18 left), and Lateral Tongue Movement (.16 each ear).

With 8YR variables, the best correlations were obtained with language and articulation measures: for example, Morphology, .34 and .35; Word Identification,

.34 and .33; Articulation, .28 and .27; and Intelligibility, .18 and .17. Correlations with speech mechanism and voice variables were very low, suggesting a generally normal performance by the marginally hearing impaired, as well as by the normal hearing, on these measures.

Discrimination correlated only weakly with 8YR pure-tone sensitivity, probably reflecting adjustments between list presentation levels and the children's hearing levels (30 dB re 1000 Hz HL), as well as the relatively good hearing of the sample. The best correlations were with 2000 Hz and these were generally better with bone conduction than air conduction. These findings suggest both auditory and verbal contributions to the discrimination measure.

8YR Hearing Measures and Selected SLH Variables

Hearing measures at age eight showed little relation to other 8YR speech and language measures. Memory for 8YR Digits and 8YR Syllables showed only low coefficients (.03 to .10) with single frequencies and only slightly stronger relationships (.11) with 8YR Discrimination. The highest correlations were with Morphology, Word Identification, Articulation, Oral Reading, and Intelligibility. Correlations were generally better with bone conduction than with air conduction. Articulation, similar to Intelligibility in correlations with pure-tone air and bone sensitivity, demonstrated higher correlations with 8YR Discrimination than did Intelligibility.

8YR Hearing Indexes

Statistical criteria and expert judgment were employed to construct hearing indexes at eight years. The indexes limited the importance of normal threshold hearing levels (less than 15 dB) and excluded discrimination scores because of their high verbal and cultural dependence. Auditory adaptation (tone decay)

was omitted because of the questionable reliability of the measure and lack of correlation with other variables. Reliance was placed entirely on the pure-tone sensitivity measures, air and bone, to construct six indexes: Monaural Conductive, Binaural Conductive, Monaural Sensorineural, Binaural Sensorineural, Monaural Mixed, and Binaural Mixed.

3YR Hearing Screen and 8YR Hearing Indexes

Of the 11,447 children who completed both 3YR and 8YR tests, 1408 or 12% failed the 3YR Hearing Screen. More Whites than Blacks failed and failure was comparably high in all subcategories of sex, race, and SEI. Regardless of sex, race, and SEI, failing the hearing screen at age three was a better predictor of failure at age eight than passing the hearing screen at age three. The prediction was least valid for the highest socioeconomic category, perhaps indicating better medical treatment.

Among those failing the 3YR Hearing Screen, White children were twice as likely to have a conductive as a sensorineural impairment at 8YR. For Black children, the likelihood was about equal for conductive or sensorineural losses and the prediction of the 3YR Hearing Screen was better. The greater the loss at eight, the more predictable it was at age three.

Abnormal Ear Conditions

Neither the presence nor the probability of hearing loss at eight years was signaled with any certainty by abnormal ear conditions observed at 12 months or as late as seven years. These included 854 children observed at 12 months to have low-set ears, deformed pinnae, branchial cleft anomalies, perforated drums, and other noninfectious ear conditions. Of 1186 children judged abnormal by otoscopic examination at seven years, about 100 appeared at eight years in the monaural and binaural conductive categories, and less than half that number in the sensorineural categories.

Judgment of Deafness at 12 Months

Only about 1% of the children who fall outside the normal hearing range and were included in either monaural or binaural conductive indexes at age eight received a judgment of deafness in the 12-month pediatric examination. The prediction capability improved with the sensorineural categories, where 19% to 21% had received deafness diagnoses at the 12-month examination.

8YR Hearing Indexes and Other Variables

The prediction of 8YR hearing indexes by antecedent medical or nonmedical factors was studied. A special list of variables thought to be related was drawn by expert opinion. A correlation screen was carried out. The hearing indexes were also correlated with a selected set of speech and language indexes, primarily from 8YR measures. Correlations of .20 or greater were identified and, for those variables, the distribution of scores of the hearing-loss sample was compared with the distribution expected on the basis of the performance of the entire sample.

In general, relationships were weak with the exception of the binaural sensorineural category. The Binaural Sensorineural Index showed correlation useful for prediction with 8YR Articulation (−.66), 8YR Intelligibility (−.66), and 8YR Word Identification (−.52). But even the Binaural Sensorineural Index correlated .20 or above with only one medical antecedent, Infectious Diseases During Pregnancy. Relationships with drug usage were studied separately and are described in Chapter 7.

With the possible exception of Short Attention Span, no variable seemed associated with monaural hearing loss indexes. The Direct Coombs' Test related weakly (−.23) to binaural losses, and then only to the conductive category. Likewise, bilirubin level correlated only .21 with binaural conductive losses; too low for prediction. The observable ear conditions and the ear syndromes showed positive correlations, .25 and .33, with binaural conductive loss, as expected.

Some of the 8-month Bayley items with face validity as hearing measures showed weak relationships with the binaural indexes at 8YR. For example, Enjoys Sound Production showed some association with a binaural conductive loss; and Turns Head to Sound of Rattle and 8-Month Mental Score with the Binaural Sensorineural Index. Turns Head to Sound of Bell did not attain the .20 correlation criterion with any of the indexes.

Special Studies

Several special studies were accomplished.

1. A sample of children with abnormal ear conditions was studied. Children with protruding pinnae, auricular appendages, or auricular asymmetry could hear about as well as the average of the total 8YR sample. Those with tympanic membrane anomalies and ventilating tubes showed the poorest hearing. Associated hearing impairments were predominantly conductive.

   Abnormal ear conditions seemed only weakly related to selected speech and language indexes. Children with microtia and peculiarly shaped pinnae showed lower average scores but these were confounded by race, sex, and socioeconomic status that could not be controlled in the selection procedures of this special study.

2. The effects of seasonal and geographic influences were reviewed. Hearing of the poorer ear seemed to worsen slightly in the colder

months, with less change in the better ear. No geographical differences could be identified.

3. A small advantage in hearing sensitivity of the poorer ear for singletons over siblings and twins was seen in the respective means and standard deviations. The mean difference between singletons and twins was 1.5 dB.

4. Adopted children showed a mean pure-tone threshold for the poorer ear of 7.7 dB compared to 8.6 dB for the total 8YR sample, whereas children living with foster parents had a mean threshold of 10.7 dB. The differences appear attributable to a greater incidence of hearing loss in the foster child sample and to fewer losses in the adopted child sample compared to the total 8YR sample.

5. Average hearing level of the poorer ear improved with birthweight. These relationships were also found for the conductive loss indexes but not for sensorineural indexes.

6. The trend of hearing level means suggests relationship with increasing 7YR IQ. An average threshold of 14.3 dB (ISO 1964) was found for the poorer ear of 53 children with 7YR IQ in the mentally retarded range. Most of the losses were of conductive type.

7. Children born with a cleft palate (N = 24) showed an average 8YR hearing level in the poorer ear of 14.7 dB (ISO 1964) compared to the 8.6 dB of the total sample. Conductive loss was found in 32%, sensorineural loss in 9%.

8. Premature children (N = 917) and those with a low 5-minute Apgar score (N = 617) were close in sensitivity of the poorer ear to the average of the total sample (9.4 dB and 9.9 dB, respectively).

9. Children with cerebral palsy (N = 83) had a small average loss (11.3 dB HL). The distribution suggested conductive problems in 15% of the sample, with 5% in the sensorineural category.

10. Children who showed both dysfluent and struggle behaviors (N = 35) had a small average loss (11.4 dB HL) in the poorer ear. Nine percent met conductive criteria and 3% were sensorineural, compared to 5% and 2%, respectively, for the total sample.

11. A special study of co-variance of speech discrimination with SLH indexes showed higher correlations with Morphology, Articulation, and Word Identification; less relationship was found with Oral Reading and the Written Communication Index, and only weak associations with the memory variables.

References

1. Brooks, R.S., and Goetzinger, C.P. Vocabulary variables and language skills in the PB discrimination of children. *J. Auditory Res.* 6:357–370, 1966.

2. Carhart, R., and Porter, L.S. Audiometric configuration and prediction of threshold for spondees. *J. Speech Hear. Res.* 14:486–495, 1971.

3. Davis, H., and Usher, J.R. What is zero hearing loss? *J. Speech Hear. Disord.* 22:662–690, 1957.

4. Eagles, E.L., Wishik, S.M., Doerfler, L.G., Melnick, W., and Levine, H.S. Hearing sensitivity and related factors in children. *Laryngoscope* Monograph Suppl., 1963.

5. Glorig, A., Wheeler, B., Quiggle, R., Grings, W., and Summerfield, A. 1954 Wisconsin State Fair Hearing Survey. *Subcommittee on Noise. Am. Acad. Ophthalmol. Otolaryngol.* 1957.

6. Green, D.S. The modified tone decay test (MTDT) as a screening proce-

dure for eighth nerve lesions. *J. Speech Hear. Disord.* 28:31–32, 1963.

7. Harris, J.D. Normal hearing and its relation to audiometry. *Laryngoscope* 64:928–957, 1954.

8. Olsen, W.O., and Noffsinger, D. Comparison of one new and three old tests of auditory adaptation. *Arch. Otolaryngol.* 99:94–99, 1974.

9. Tenney, H.K., III, and Edwards, C. Race as a variable in hearing screening. *Am. J. Dis. Child.* 120:547–550, 1970.

10. Weber, H.J., McGovern, F.J., and Zink, D. An evaluation of 1000 children with hearing loss. *J. Speech Hear. Disord.* 32:343–354, 1967.

## CHAPTER 7

Hearing Loss and Drug Exposure in Pregnancy

Richard R. Monson, M.D., Sc.D.

Since 1970, a group of investigators at Boston University School of Medicine have been analyzing the data from the NINCDS Collaborative Perinatal Project (NCPP) with respect to the association between physical birth defects and drugs used in pregnancy (Heinonen, Slone, and Shapiro, 1977). Details of the analysis of the relationship between birth defects and drug exposure in pregnancy have been presented (Heinonen et al., 1977; Slone et al., 1973). Of the 50,282 children included in this earlier analysis, it was found that 19,586 had adequate hearing measures at about eight years of age, and 424 (2%) of these children were found to have sensorineural hearing loss. In this chapter, we present an analysis of the relationship between sensorineural hearing loss and exposure to drugs at any time during pregnancy.

Methods

In brief, standard social and medical histories, including detailed medication histories, were taken for women at the time of entry into the NCPP study. Interviews on medicine usage were repeated at four week intervals. Hospital records and charts from private physicians were reviewed to complete the detailed drug and medical information.

Before the analysis of these data could proceed, an extensive reorganization of the data was necessary. The main reason was that the original coded drug infor-

151

mation was unsatisfactory. Many dissimilar drugs had been grouped together, so that it was necessary to review the original records in a number of instances in order to determine the actual drug exposure. A new drug dictionary was established and all data on drugs taken during pregnancy were recorded. Over 600 distinct pharmacological entities were taken by a sufficient number of mothers to permit analysis.

In evaluating the association between drugs and sensorineural hearing loss, the first step was to screen all drugs against hearing loss. Basically, the crude rate of hearing loss was computed for children who were exposed at any time during pregnancy to a drug and for those who were not exposed. The ratio of these two crude rates is the crude relative risk. Also, in this screening step, a relative risk standardized for hospital was computed using the Mantel-Haenszel procedure (Mantel and Haenszel, 1959). The results of this screening step are presented in Table 7-1.

Next, we considered the possibility that crude associations which were observed between a drug category and hearing loss were due to the presence of one or more confounding factors. By definition, in the data being evaluated, a confounding factor is some variable which is associated both with the drug and with hearing loss. Since the presence of one or more confounding factors may lead to a spurious association between a drug and hearing loss, it is necessary to control for such factors if they exist.

Several methods are available to control for potential confounding. In analyzing the data on birth defects and drugs in pregnancy, we elected to use the multiple logistic risk function, a multivariate technique (Heinonen et al., 1977; Slone et al., 1973). With this method, the possible confounding effects of 20 to 30 variables were controlled simultaneously. This was judged to be the most efficient strategy because of the large number of drugs and

birth defects compared. The computations needed were relatively complex and expensive.

In the current analysis we elected to use a traditional and simple approach to the control of potential confounding; that is, cross-classification. This was done for several reasons:

1. Only one outcome was being evaluated.
2. Crudely, there were relatively few associations found between drugs and hearing loss.
3. Crudely, there were relatively few factors of pregnancy which were found to be associated with hearing loss.
4. Since very little is currently known about drugs in pregnancy and hearing loss, any associations seen in these data will need independent confirmation on another sample.

The second step in our analysis was to evaluate the association between hearing loss and a number of characteristics in pregnancy which we felt could potentially be confounding (Table 7-2). In this table, information on drug exposure is not considered. The relative risk of 1.2 for the White group means that the rate of hearing loss in Whites was 1.2 times the rate in Blacks.

The third step in our analysis was to evaluate the association between drugs used in pregnancy and these characteristics in pregnancy. In this step, it was necessary to consider only characteristics which were associated with hearing loss. If some characteristic is not associated with hearing loss, it cannot affect any observed association between a drug and hearing loss. This step was repeated for a number of drug groups (Tables 7-3, 7-5, 7-7, 7-9, 7-11).

In the fourth step of our analysis we computed a standardized relative risk for hearing loss following drug exposure in pregnancy, controlling for factors which were associated with both drug exposure

Table 7-1

Association of drug categories with sensorineural hearing loss.

Drug		Total N exposed	n with hearing loss	Relative risk	
Group	Categories			Crude	Standardized*
Analgesics	All	13,510	296	1.0	1.1
	Non-addictives	13,170	287	1.0	1.1
	Narcotic	2,618	61	1.1	1.1
Antimicrobial and antibiotic agents	All	6,932	165	1.2	1.1
	Antibiotics	3,757	87	1.1	1.1
	Sulfonamides	2,075	68	1.6	1.5
	Miscellaneous Antimicrobials	1,193	22	0.8	0.8
		2,061	44	1.0	0.9
Immunizing agents	All	7,824	165	1.0	1.1
Antinauseants and antihistamines	All	6,083	127	1.0	0.9
	Antihistamines	5,389	108	0.9	0.9
	Phenothiazines	1,424	36	1.2	1.3
Sedatives and tranquilizers	All	6,167	153	1.2	1.2
	Barbiturates	5,455	135	1.2	1.1
	Non-barbiturates	1,444	34	1.1	1.2
	Antidepressants	66	3	2.1	2.2
Drugs affecting autonomic nervous system	All	5,276	123	1.1	1.1
	Sympathomimetic	4,224	97	1.1	1.1
	Parasympatholytic	2,274	51	1.0	1.1
Anesthetics	All	2,982	59	0.9	0.9
	Local	2,477	49	0.9	0.9
	General	178	5	1.3	1.4
Anticonvulsants	Non-barbiturate	161	5	1.4	1.3
Caffeine and other xanthines	All	5,435	132	1.2	1.2
Diuretics	All	6,109	128	1.0	1.0
Antihypertension agents	All	247	8	1.5	1.4
Cough medicine	All	2,836	61	1.0	1.0
Drugs taken for GI disturbances	All	648	14	1.0	1.0
Hormones	All	1,539	23	0.7	0.7
Inorganic compounds	All	4,080	86	1.0	1.0
Total population		**19,586**	**424**	—	—

*Standardized for hospital of birth.

153

Table **7-2**

Association of sensorineural hearing loss with selected characteristics of pregnancy.

Characteristic	Category	N	Children with hearing loss		Relative risk
			n	Rate/ 1,000	
Race	White	9,901	230	23.2	1.2
	Black	9,685	194	20.0	1.0*
Mother's age	<20	4,554	98	21.5	1.0
	20-34	13,430	288	21.4	1.0*
	≥35	1,602	38	23.7	1.1
Socioeconomic Index	≤3.9	7,409	163	22.0	1.3
	4.0-7.9	9,918	224	22.6	1.4
	≥8.0	2,259	37	16.4	1.0*
Sex	Male	9,875	220	22.3	1.1
	Female	9,711	204	21.0	1.0*
Birthweight (gm)	<2,500	1,744	44	25.2	1.2
	2,500-3,499	12,712	274	21.6	1.0*
	≥3,500	5,130	106	20.7	1.0
Prior stillbirth	Yes	1,094	29	26.5	1.2
	No	18,492	395	21.4	1.0*
Prior neonatal death	Yes	827	23	27.8	1.3
	No	18,759	401	21.4	1.0*
Length of pregnancy (lunar months)	5-7	229	7	30.6	1.4
	8+	19,357	417	21.5	1.0*
Hyperemesis gravidarum	Yes	233	13	55.8	2.6
	No	19,353	411	21.2	1.0*
Hypertension, acute or chronic	Yes	658	18	27.4	1.3
	No	18,928	406	21.5	1.0*
Bleeding during pregnancy (trimester)	3rd	2,871	62	21.6	1.0
	2nd	974	28	28.7	1.3
	1st	1,574	26	16.5	0.8
	None	14,167	308	21.7	1.0*
Weight change during pregnancy	None or loss	318	10	31.5	1.5
	Gain	19,268	414	21.5	1.0*
Diabetes mellitus	Yes	146	3	20.5	0.9
	No	19,440	421	21.7	1.0*
Hyperthyroidism	Yes	35	2	57.1	2.7
	No	19,551	422	21.6	1.0*
Urinary tract (infection)	Yes	241	6	23.9	1.1
	No	19,335	418	21.6	1.0*

*Reference category.

154

Table 7-2 (continued)

Association of sensorineural hearing loss with selected characteristics of pregnancy.

Characteristic	Category	N	Children with hearing loss		Relative risk
			n	Rate/ 1,000	
Hematuria	Yes	506	17	33.6	1.6
	No	19,080	407	21.3	1.0*
Bacterial infection	Yes	414	12	29.0	1.3
(after 4th LM)	No	19,172	412	21.5	1.0*
Cigarette smoking	≥30	648	32	49.4	2.2
(cig./day)	0-29	7,519	139	18.5	0.8
	None	11,419	253	22.2	1.0*
Prenatal x-ray	Yes	5,039	117	23.2	1.1
	No	14,547	307	21.2	1.0*

*Reference category.

and hearing loss (Tables 7-4, 7-6, 7-8, 7-10, 7-12). The decision as to whether or not to include a given factor was judgmental; if a factor was found to be weakly associated with both a drug and hearing loss (relative risk of 1.3 or so), it was elected not to control for this factor. Also, if a factor was quite uncommon, any confounding which it could introduce would be minimal.

In controlling by multiple cross-classification it is desirable to have as few factors present as necessary, so as to minimize the number of strata with only one or two persons in them. In deciding to control for relatively few potential confounding factors, our experience with respect to birth defects is relevant. In general, even after simultaneous control for 20 to 30 factors, the crude relative risk and the standardized relative risks tended to be similar for almost all drugs, indicating that in these data, associations due to confounding are uncommon.

Results

In Table 7-1 are presented the crude and hospital-standardized relative risks for sensorineural hearing loss following exposure in pregnancy to a variety of drugs. Two patterns are present: most relative risks are close to 1.0, and the crude and hospital-standardized relative risks are similar. Based on the grouping used in this table, standardized relative risks of 1.4 or greater were seen for sulfonamides, phenothiazines, antidepressants, general anesthetics, nonbarbiturate anticonvulsants and antihypertension agents. Because there were a relatively small number of children with hearing loss exposed to antidepressants, general anesthetics, nonbarbiturate anticonvulsants and antihypertension agents, no further analysis was performed for these drugs. These associations are based on small numbers and are clearly unstable. Control for confounding in the presence of such small numbers is not realistic. Further data are needed to evaluate the meaning of the association.

As seen in Table 7-2, most characteristics of pregnancy were found to be weakly or not associated with hearing loss. It was arbitrarily decided that any characteristic with a relative risk between 0.8 and 1.2 would not be considered further. Potentially confounding factors selected to be evaluated with respect to

Table 7-3

Association of the use of sulfonamides at any time during pregnancy with selected characteristics of pregnancy.

Characteristic	N Children with Factor	Percentage with Factor		
		Selected Sulfa Drugs*	Other Sulfa Drugs	No Sulfa Drugs
Socioeconomic Index ≥8.0†	2,259	7.5	7.9	12.0
Prior stillbirth or neonatal death	1,806	9.9	9.5	9.2
Pregnancy length less than 8 lunar months	229	1.4	1.1	1.2
Hyperemesis gravidarum†	233	1.9	1.5	1.1
Hypertension	658	1.9	3.8	3.3
Second trimester bleeding	974	10.3	9.0	7.9
No weight gain during pregnancy	318	2.8	1.9	1.6
Hyperthyroidism	35	0	0.2	0.2
Hematuria†	506	8.5	7.2	2.0
Bacterial infection after 4th lunar month†	414	1.9	3.3	2.0
More than 30 cigarettes/day	648	2.3	2.6	3.4
Number of children	**19,586**	**213**	**1,862**	**17,511**

*Sulfathiazole, sulfacetamide, sulfabenzamide, or sulfamethoxypyridazine.
†Potential confounding factors selected to be controlled.

Table 7-4

Crude and standardized* relative risk of sensorineural hearing loss associated with exposure to sulfa drugs during pregnancy.

Drug	N Children Exposed	Children with Hearing Loss		Relative Risk	
		n	Rate/1,000	Crude	Standardized*
All sulfa drugs	2,075	68	32.8	1.6	1.6
Selected†	213	12	56.3	2.9	2.8
Other	1,862	56	30.1	1.5	1.4
No sulfa drugs	17,511	356	20.3	1.0	1.0

*Standardized by Mantel-Haenszel method.
Factors controlled: Socioeconomic Index, hyperemesis gravidarum, hematuria, bacterial infection.
†Sulfathiazole, sulfacetamide, sulfabenzamide, or sulfamethoxypyridazine.

Table **7-5**

Association of the use of phenothiazines at any time during pregnancy with selected characteristics of pregnancy.

Characteristic	N Children with Factor	Percentage with Factor		
		Selected Phenothiazines*	Other Phenothiazines	No Phenothiazines
Socioeconomic Index ≥8.0	2,259	9.4	19.1	11.1
Prior stillbirth or neonatal death†	1,806	16.0	9.5	9.1
Pregnancy length less than 8 lunar months†	229	3.8	0.7	1.2
Hyperemesis gravidarum†	233	9.9	5.0	0.8
Hypertension	658	4.7	4.0	3.3
Second trimester bleeding	974	10.8	10.9	7.8
No weight gain during pregnancy†	318	4.7	2.6	0.2
Hyperthyroidism	35	0.5	0.5	0.2
Hematuria	506	2.4	4.3	2.5
Bacterial infection after 4th lunar month†	414	3.8	4.5	1.9
More than 30 cigarettes/day†	648	7.5	3.9	3.2
Number of children	**19,586**	**212**	**1,212**	**18,162**

*Promazine or buclizine.
†Potential confounding factors selected to be controlled.

Table **7-6**

Crude and standardized* relative risk of sensorineural hearing loss associated with exposure to phenothiazines during pregnancy.

Drug	N Children Exposed	Children with Hearing Loss		Relative Risk	
		n	Rate/1,000	Crude	Standardized*
All phenothiazines	1,424	36	25.7	1.2	1.1
Selected†	212	12	56.6	2.8	2.3
Other	1,212	24	19.8	0.9	0.9
No phenothiazines	18,162	388	21.4	1.0	1.0

*Standardized by Mantel-Haenszel method.
 Factors controlled: prior stillbirth or neonatal death, pregnancy length less than 8 lunar months, hyperemesis gravidarum, no weight gain during pregnancy, bacterial infection, more than 30 cigarettes/day.
†Promazine or buclizine.

Table 7-7

Association of the use of antibiotics at any time during pregnancy with selected characteristics of pregnancy.

Characteristic	N Children with Factor	Percentage with Factor		
		Streptomycin	Other Antibiotics	No Antibiotics
Socioeconomic Index ≥8.0	2,259	8.7	11.7	11.5
Prior stillbirth or neonatal death*	1,806	16.5	10.3	8.9
Pregnancy length less than 8 lunar months	229	2.4	1.0	1.2
Hyperemesis gravidarum	233	0.8	1.5	1.1
Hypertension	658	1.6	3.4	3.4
Second trimester bleeding*	974	13.4	8.8	7.8
No weight gain during pregnancy*	318	2.4	1.9	1.5
Hyperthyroidism	35	0.0	0.2	0.2
Hematuria	506	3.1	3.2	2.4
Bacterial infection after 4th* lunar month	414	10.2	5.8	1.2
More than 30 cigarettes/day	648	2.4	3.6	3.2
Number of children	**19,586**	**127**	**3,630**	**15,829**

*Potential confounding factors selected to be controlled.

Table 7-8

Crude and standardized* relative risk of sensorineural hearing loss associated with exposure to antibiotics during pregnancy.

Drug	N Children Exposed	Children With Hearing Loss		Relative Risk	
		n	Rate/1,000	Crude	Standardized*
All antibiotics	3,757	87	23.2	1.1	1.1
Streptomycin	127	6	47.2	2.3	2.2
Other	3,630	81	22.3	1.1	1.0
No antibiotics	15,829	337	21.3	1.0	1.0

*Standardized by Mantel-Haenszel method. Factors controlled: prior stillbirth or neonatal death, second trimester bleeding, no weight gain during pregnancy, bacterial infection.

Table 7-9

Association of the use of sympathomimetic at any time during pregnancy with selected characteristics of pregnancy.

| Characteristic | N Children with Factor | Percentage with Factor | | |
		Methamphetamine	Other Sympathomimetic	No Sympathomimetic
Socioeconomic Index ≥8.0	2,259	11.8	22.2	8.5
Prior stillbirth or neonatal death*	1,806	5.4	8.5	9.5
Pregnancy length less than 8 lunar months	229	0.9	0.6	1.3
Hyperemesis gravidarum	233	0.9	1.1	1.2
Hypertension	658	3.2	3.4	3.4
Second trimester bleeding	974	5.9	11.3	7.2
No weight gain during pregnancy*	318	2.3	1.3	1.7
Hyperthyroidism	35	0.5	0.1	0.2
Hematuria	506	3.6	2.4	2.6
Bacterial infection after 4th lunar month*	414	2.7	3.9	1.6
More than 30 cigarettes/day	648	2.3	3.8	3.2
Number of children	**19,586**	**221**	**4,003**	**15,362**

*Potential confounding factors selected to be controlled.

Table 7-10

Crude and standardized* relative risk of sensorineural hearing loss associated with exposure to sympathomimetic drugs during pregnancy.

| Drug | N Children Exposed | Children With Hearing Loss | | Relative Risk | |
		n	Rate/1,000	Crude	Standardized*
Sympathomimetic	4,224	97	23.0	1.1	1.1
Methamphetamine	221	13	58.8	2.9	2.9
Other	4,003	84	21.0	1.0	1.0
No Sympathomimetic	15,362	327	21.3	1.0	1.0

*Standardized by Mantel-Haenszel method. Factors controlled: Socioeconomic Index, no weight gain, bacterial infection.

Table 7-11

Association of the use of non-barbiturate tranquilizers at any time during pregnancy with selected characteristics of pregnancy.

Characteristic	N Children with Factor	Percentage with Factor		
		Selected Tranquilizers	Other Tranquilizers	No Tranquilizers
Socioeconomic Index ≥8.0†	2,259	23.8	25.7	10.4
Prior stillbirth or neonatal death*	1,806	10.5	11.0	9.1
Pregnancy length less than 8 lunar months	229	1.2	0.9	1.2
Hyperemesis gravidarum†	233	2.3	2.8	1.1
Hypertension†	658	8.1	4.0	3.3
Second trimester bleeding	974	9.3	13.1	7.7
No weight gain during pregnancy	318	1.2	1.5	1.6
Hyperthyroidism	35	0.6	0.4	0.2
Hematuria	506	2.4	4.3	2.5
Bacterial infection after 4th lunar month†	414	3.8	4.5	1.9
More than 30 cigarettes/ day†	648	8.1	7.2	3.0
Number of children	**19,586**	**172**	**1,272**	**18,142**

*17 separate drugs.
†Potential confounding factors selected to be controlled.

Table 7-12

Crude and standardized* relative risk of sensorineural hearing loss associated with exposure to non-barbiturate tranquilizers during pregnancy.

Drug	N Children Exposed	Children with Hearing Loss		Relative Risk	
		n	Rate/1,000	Crude	Standardized*
All tranquilizers	1,444	34	23.6	1.1	1.0
Selected†	172	10	58.1	2.8	2.4
Other	1,272	24	18.9	0.9	0.8
No tranquilizers	18,142	390	21.5	1.0	1.0

*Standardized by Mantel-Haenszel method.
Factors controlled: Socioeconomic Index, hyperemesis gravidarum, hypertension, bacterial infection, more than 30 cigarettes/day.
†17 separate drugs.

drugs taken in pregnancy included: Socioeconomic Index, prior stillbirth or neonatal death, length of pregnancy, hyperemesis gravidarum, hypertension, second trimester bleeding, no weight gain during pregnancy, hyperthyroidism, hematuria, bacterial infection after the fourth lunar month, and heavy cigarette smoking. Hyperthyroidism was not controlled because there were only two children with hearing loss born to hyperthyroid mothers.

In Tables 7-3 and 7-4, the associations between hearing loss and sulfa drugs are considered. Four factors (Socioeconomic Index, hyperemesis gravidarum, hematuria, and bacterial infection) were judged to be associated both with hearing loss and with sulfonamide exposure. These factors were controlled. Four sulfa drugs were separated from the other sulfa drugs because the crude association of hearing loss with each of these drugs was particularly high. As seen in Table 7-4, the crude and standardized relative risks differ only slightly, indicating that essentially no confounding was produced by the four factors which were controlled.

In Tables 7-5 and 7-6, the associations between hearing loss and phenothiazines are shown. Six factors were controlled: prior stillbirth or neonatal death, length of pregnancy, hyperemesis gravidarum, no weight gain, bacterial infection, and heavy cigarette smoking. As seen in Table 7-6, the crude association between phenothiazines and hearing loss was accounted for entirely by promazine or buclizine. A moderate amount of confounding was present, since the standardized relative risk of 2.3 is somewhat less than the crude relative risk of 2.8.

In Tables 7-7 and 7-8, the associations between antibiotics and hearing loss are considered. This analysis was performed in spite of the small number of exposed children with hearing loss because of the known association, in general, between streptomycin and hearing loss. Four factors were controlled: prior stillbirth or neonatal death, second trimester bleeding, no weight gain, and bacterial infection. No confounding was detected.

In Tables 7-9 and 7-10, the association between sympathomimetic drugs and hearing loss is presented. This association was evaluated because of the high crude relative risk of hearing loss following methamphetamine exposure. Three factors were controlled: Socioeconomic Index, no weight gain, and bacterial infection. No confounding was seen.

In Tables 7-11 and 7-12, the association between nonbarbiturate tranquilizers and hearing loss is shown. This association was evaluated because of the high relative risk of hearing loss following exposure to a group of 17 nonbarbiturate tranquilizers. This is a relatively heterogeneous group, and this association must be viewed with caution. Five factors were controlled: Socioeconomic Index, hyperemesis gravidarum, hypertension, bacterial infection, and heavy cigarette smoking. A moderate amount of confounding was present since the crude relative risk was 2.8 and the standardized relative risk was 2.4.

Discussion

The data presented in this chapter must be interpreted with caution. Little is known about sensorineural hearing loss following drug exposure in pregnancy. Until similar associations can be evaluated in independent data, these associations must be viewed as tentative.

None of the associations detected in these data could be totally accounted for by known confounding factors. It remains possible that unknown factors accounted for the associations between the drugs and hearing loss.

In summary, we have identified associations between sensorineural hearing loss and drug exposure during pregnancy to the following drugs: sulfonamide, promazine or buclizine, streptomycin, methamphetamine, and selected non-barbiturate tranquilizers. Also, based on small numbers, a positive association was seen with general anesthetics and with antihypertension agents. In order to assess whether any of these associations is causal, further independent data must be evaluated.

References

1. Heinonen, O.P., Slone, D., and Shapiro, S. *Birth Defects and Drugs in Pregnancy*. Acton, Massachusetts: Publishing Sciences Group, 1977.

2. Mantel, N., and Haenszel, W. Statistical aspects of the analysis of data from retrospective studies of disease. *J. Natl. Cancer Inst.* 22:719–748, 1959.

3. Slone, D., Heinonen, O.P., Monson, R.R., Shapiro, S., Hartz, S.C., and Rosenberg, L. Maternal drug exposures and fetal abnormalities. *Clin. Pharmacol. Ther.* 14:648–653, 1973.

## CHAPTER 8

Auditory
Memory

Elaine S. LaBenz, M.A.
Warren H. Fay, Ph.D.

Auditory memory span has been studied extensively both from the viewpoint that memory is an ability separate from other language abilities and that it is an integral part of general language competence. Tests using digits, syllables, or words have been most frequently used for its evaluation. They are usually quick and seemingly easy to administer and score. However, methodology is important (Lassman and Engelbart, 1967), and strict adherence to procedure was emphasized in the collection of data for this study. The analyses reported in this chapter are based on a sample which included all White and Black children who attempted either the 3YR or 8YR speech, language, and hearing (SLH) tests or both. There were 19,885 subjects in the ALL 3YR group and 20,137 in the ALL 8YR group.

At both the 3YR and 8YR levels, digit and syllable tests were administered live-voice at the rate of one unit per second. This procedure facilitated comparisons between the two age levels and also with the results of other studies since these are the most often used materials and methods of administration. In addition to digits and syllables, tests which seemed to involve memory but which did not penalize the subject for articulatory and grammatical differences or deficiencies were included in the auditory memory indexes. These included the Spondaic Word Test at age three and two 8YR variables, Understanding a Story

(Durrell and Sullivan, 1945) and Number of Concepts Recalled in Connected Discourse. The latter two tests tap longer term memory than the digit and syllable tests. While language comprehension is involved to some extent in these tests, the scoring did not penalize the child for misarticulations, sequence errors or other grammatical errors. Further description of these variables, most of which were specially constructed for the SLH batteries, and descriptive statistics follow. Scoring forms and manuals are found in Appendix 1.

The Auditory Memory Variables

3YR Digits

Four series of both two digits and three digits were provided. Once the child passed either of the Two-Digit Series, the Three-Digit Series were administered and discontinued when there was a pass. A Two-Digit Series was passed by 93% of the children with 7% failing; Three-Digit Series was passed by 74% of the subjects with 26% failing. These percentages, as well as those for the syllable tests, do not include the 7% to 10% of children who did not respond to the tests. Percentages of passes are graphed in Figure 8-1. It will be noted that only the two highest Socioeconomic Index (SEI) groups stood out as having clearly better performance on digits and syllables; the other groups did not show a consistent trend. This figure also illustrates that Blacks and Females performed better than Whites and Males.

3YR Syllables

The two-syllable test appeared to be the easiest of the short-term memory tests; 95% of the children passed this test and 5% failed. Three-Syllable Series had a slightly higher pass rate (78%, with 22% failing) than Three-Digit Series. The better performance on syllables is inter-esting in that the syllable test consisted of entirely novel material, whereas at least some three-year-olds would be expected to have some auditory familiarity with numbers. It is possible that this finding reflects a learning effect as digits were always presented first; better understanding of the test may have been achieved by the time syllables were presented.

Figure 8-1 shows the same trends for Three-Syllable Series as were observed in the Three-Digit Series distributions with Blacks performing best on Three-Syllable Series, followed by Females, Males, and Whites, in that order. The data do not follow the usual pattern of increasing performance with increasing SEI, with the exception of the two highest groups. Indeed, the lowest SEI group performed better than the next two higher groups, probably because of the large proportion of Black subjects in that group. It appears, then, that there is probably little SEI bias inherent in these tests.

3YR Spondaic Word Test

The two-syllable words used in this test should be largely familiar to three-year-olds. It is possible that familiarity increases with the advantages of better education associated with higher SEI, as a clear SEI trend was noted (Figure 8-2). It is also possible that familiarity facilitates repetition, although this did not appear to be true in a comparison of the digit and syllable tests. Interestingly, Black children and Females performed best, followed by Whites and Males as in the digit and syllable tests. Of the children who took this test, 92% passed.

8YR Digits

Eighteen series of digits ranging from two to ten in length, with two series of each length, were included in this test. One-half point credit was added if the subject could repeat the second series of

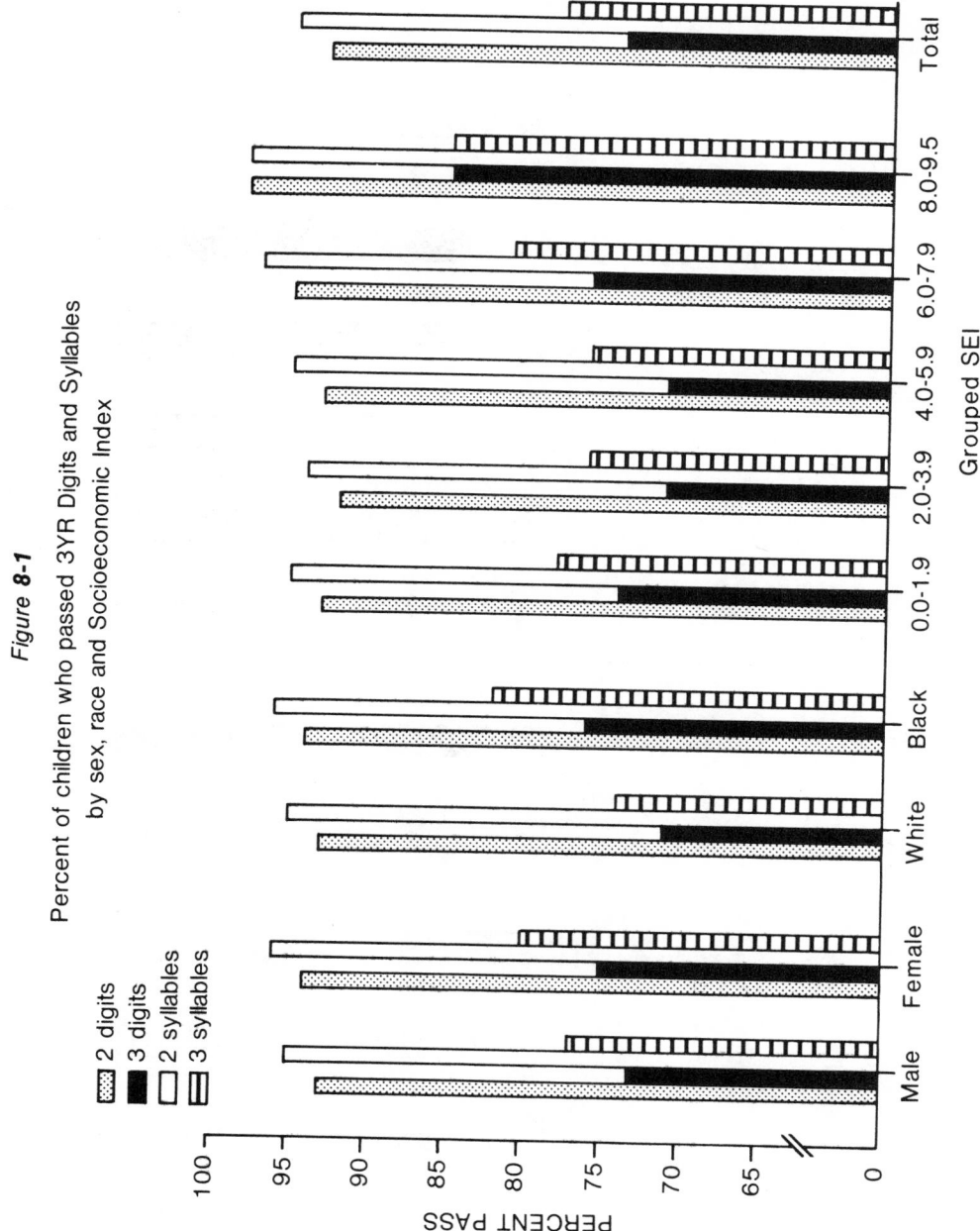

Figure *8-1*

Percent of children who passed 3YR Digits and Syllables
by sex, race and Socioeconomic Index

165

166

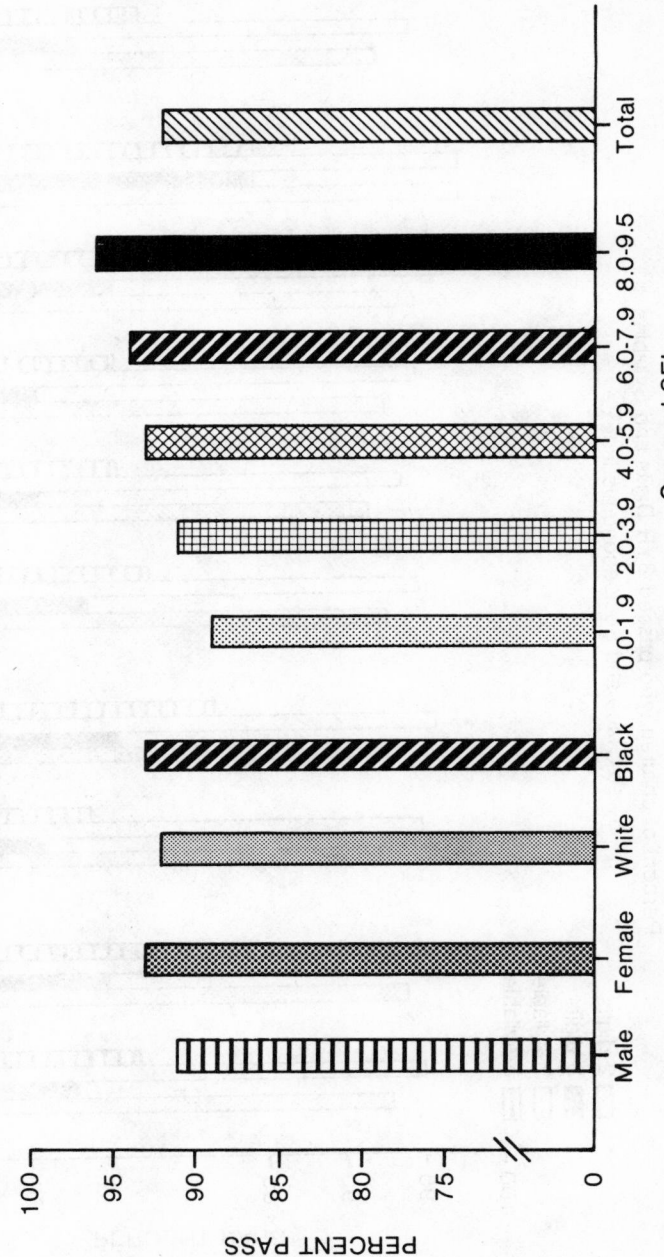

Figure **8-2**

Percent of children who passed the 3YR Spondaic Word Test by sex, race and Socioeconomic Index

the same length at the highest level achieved. The test began with a Two-Digit Series and was discontinued after failure of two series of the same length. Thus, the theoretical range was 0 to 10.5 (ten digits repeated twice). For these analyses scores of 2.0 and less were grouped, yielding an actual range of 2.0 to 10.5. The mean for the total group was 5.35 with a standard deviation of 1.0. As can be observed in Table 8-1 and Figure 8-3, means and standard deviations were similar for all subgroups, with differences in means of half a digit (actually .61) between the lowest and highest SEI groups. Missingness (unknown or invalid codes) was negligible, about 1%.

8YR Syllables

The syllable test was administered and scored in the same manner as the digit test, with two series each of syllable strings which ranged from two to six units in length. Again, scores of ≤ 2.0 were grouped; the actual range was 2.0 to 6.5 with a mean of 3.68 and a standard deviation of .71. Means and standard deviations were even closer for all subgroups than they were for 8YR Digits, as shown in Table 8-2 and Figure 8-4.

Connected Discourse: Concepts Recalled

One item, Number of Concepts Recalled by a subject after a five-sentence story was read to him, was extracted from the Connected Discourse Test for inclusion in the 8YR Auditory Memory Index. The actual and theoretical range was 0 to 18 concepts recalled. The mean for the total group was 11.33 with a standard deviation of 3.4. Differences between sex, race, and SEI groups were small, as may be observed in Table 8-3 and Figure 8-5. The trend, however, was toward better performance with rising socioeconomic status. Whites and Females performed slightly better than Males and Blacks.

Understanding A Story

This test required a child to answer five questions after listening to a ten-sentence story. Again, there were small differences between groups. Socioeconomic status had some effect, and Whites and Males performed slightly better than Females and Blacks. A mean of 3.01 questions answered correctly and a standard deviation of 1.32 was found for the total group, with a range of 0 to 5. Descriptive statistics are presented in Table 8-4 and Figure 8-6.

Intercorrelations of SLH Variables

At the 3YR level, the highest correlation found between any of the index variables was between three-digits and three-syllables ($r = .57$). Other correlations were .44 between two-digits and two-syllables and .36 between both two-digits and three-digits and two-syllables and three-syllables. Three-digits and two-syllables and two-digits and three-syllables correlated .33.

The Spondaic Word Test correlated .13 to .14 with the digit and syllable tests and, when correlated with the pure-tone hearing test, yielded r's of .35 and .33 for the right and left ears, respectively. The Spondaic Word Test had higher correlations with the language measures (.17 to .25) than the digit and syllable tests did (.09 to .23). All other r's for the 3YR Auditory Memory Index variables were $<.25$ with the majority $<.15$. Articulation and Intelligibility variables demonstrated relationships similar to the language variables with r's of .10 to .24. The other speech production and speech mechanism variables had low correlations with the auditory memory span measures, as did the pure-tone hearing test, with the exception of the spondaic word findings mentioned earlier.

The correlation between three-digits at 3YR and 8YR Digits was .25. An identical r was found between three-syllables at

Table 8-1

Means and standard deviations for 8YR Digits by sex, race, Socioeconomic Index and total.

	N	Mean	SD
Male	10,134	5.28	1.0
Female	10,003	5.42	1.0
White	10,148	5.42	1.0
Black	9,989	5.29	.95
SEI 0.0-1.9	1,631	5.10	.94
SEI 2.0-3.9	6,000	5.21	.97
SEI 4.0-5.9	6,073	5.32	.98
SEI 6.0-7.9	4,122	5.51	1.0
SEI 8.0-9.5	2,311	5.71	1.0
Total	**20,137**	**5.35**	**1.0**

Table 8-2

Means and standard deviations for 8YR Syllables by sex, race, Socioeconomic Index and total.

	N	Mean	SD
Male	9,988	3.65	.71
Female	9,853	3.71	.72
White	10,090	3.69	.72
Black	9,751	3.67	.71
SEI 0.0-1.9	1,596	3.60	.70
SEI 2.0-3.9	5,894	3.62	.71
SEI 4.0-5.9	5,970	3.68	.71
SEI 6.0-7.9	4,082	3.75	.71
SEI 8.0-9.5	2,299	3.78	.73
Total	**20,137**	**3.68**	**.71**

Table 8-3

Means and standard deviations for Number of Concepts Recalled by sex, race, Socioeconomic Index and total.

	N	Mean	SD
Male	9,947	11.22	3.40
Female	9,824	11.45	3.40
White	10,052	11.76	3.34
Black	9,719	10.88	3.41
SEI 0.0-1.9	1,588	10.42	3.65
SEI 2.0-3.9	5,869	10.72	3.47
SEI 4.0-5.9	5,947	11.28	3.30
SEI 6.0-7.9	4,070	11.92	3.24
SEI 8.0-9.5	2,297	12.60	3.04
Total	**20,137**	**11.33**	**3.40**

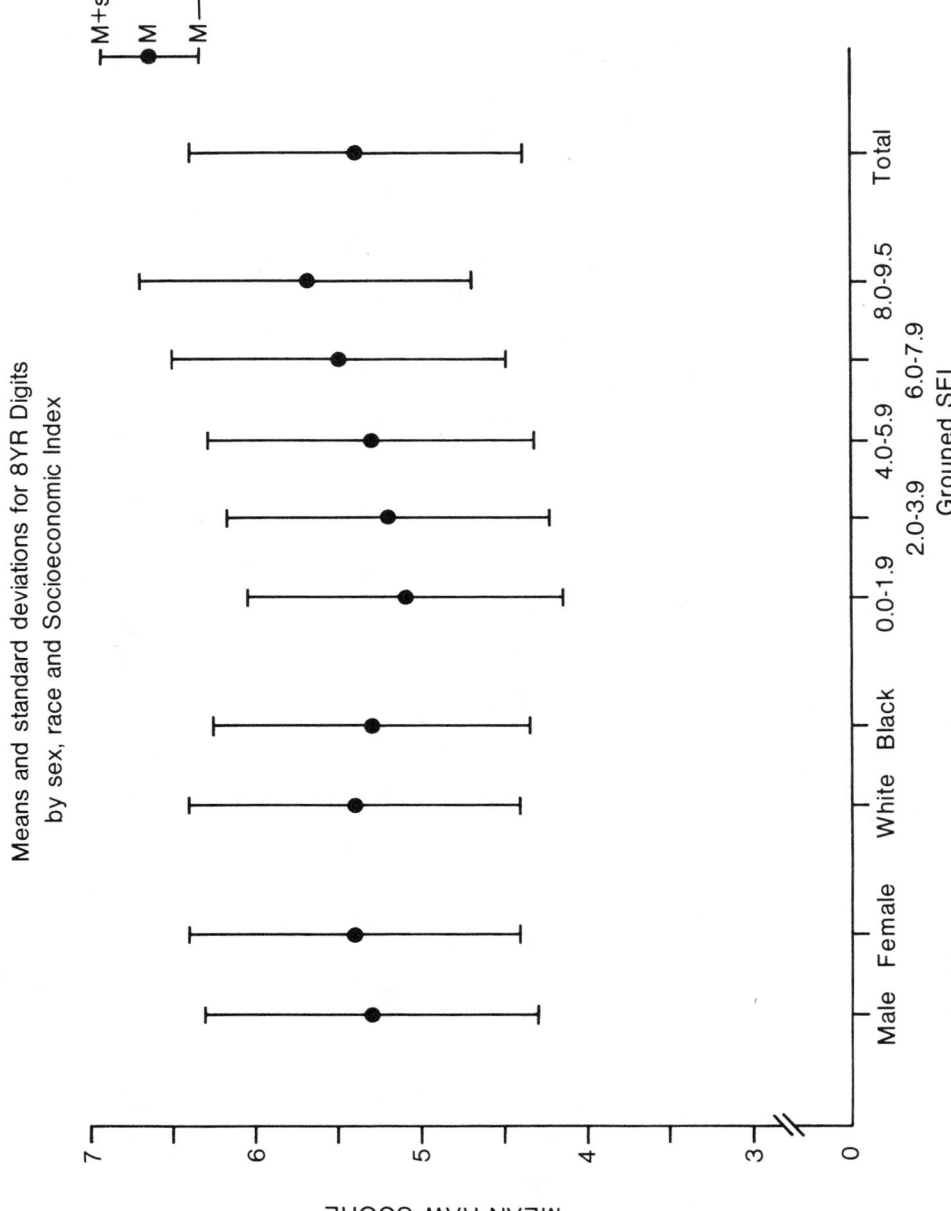

Figure **8-3**

Means and standard deviations for 8YR Digits
by sex, race and Socioeconomic Index

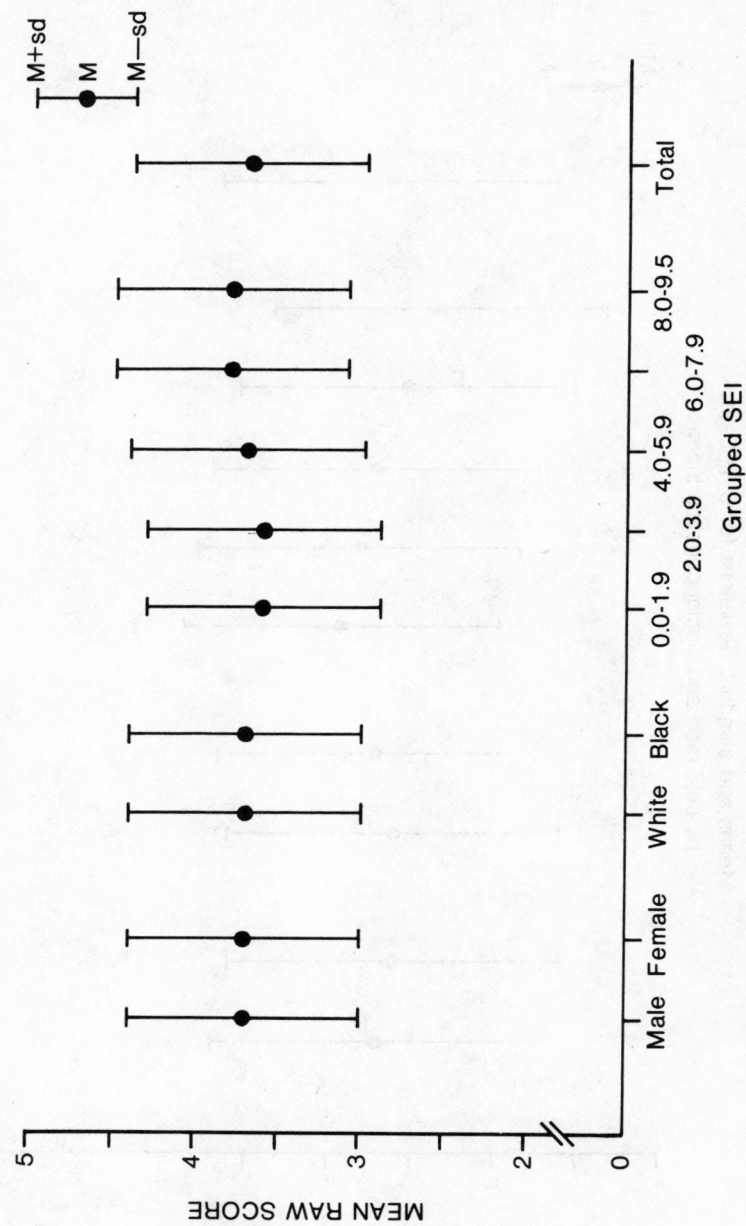

Figure **8-4**

Means and standard deviations for 8YR Syllables
by sex, race and Socioeconomic Index

170

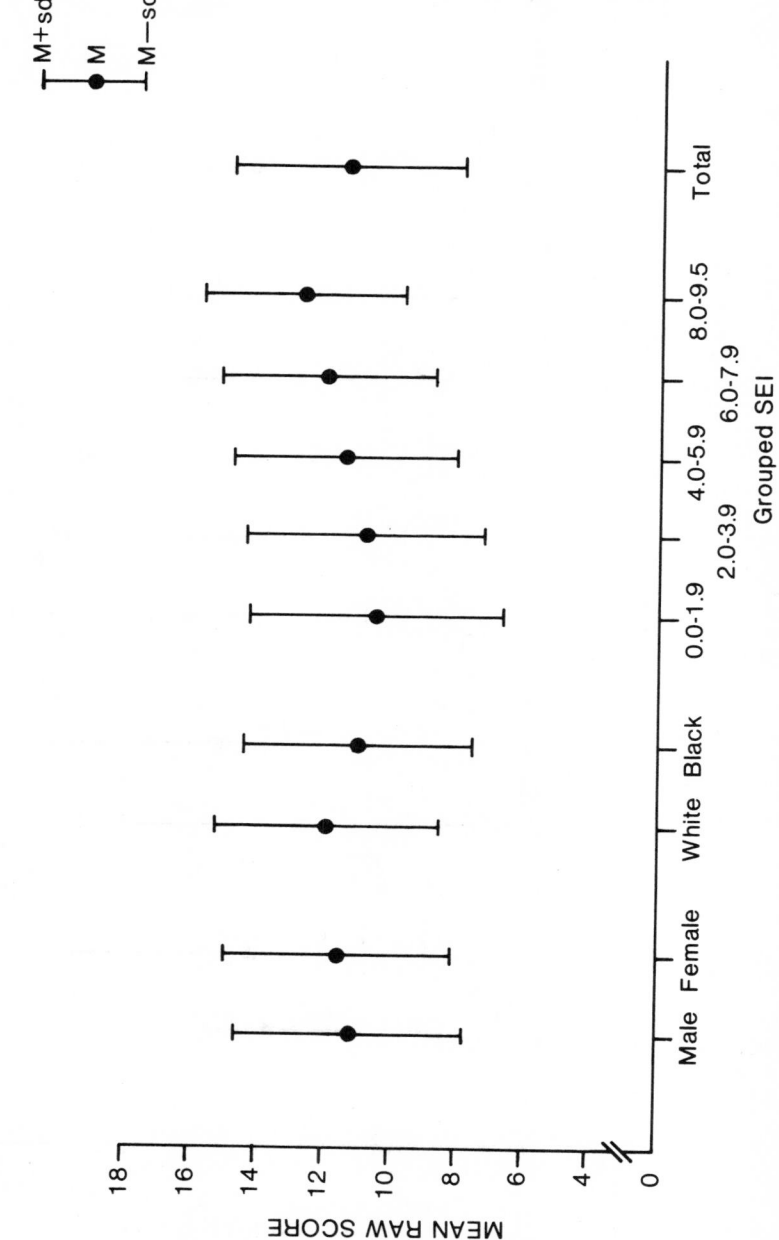

Figure 8-5

Means and standard deviations for Number of Concepts at 8YR by sex, race and Socioeconomic Index

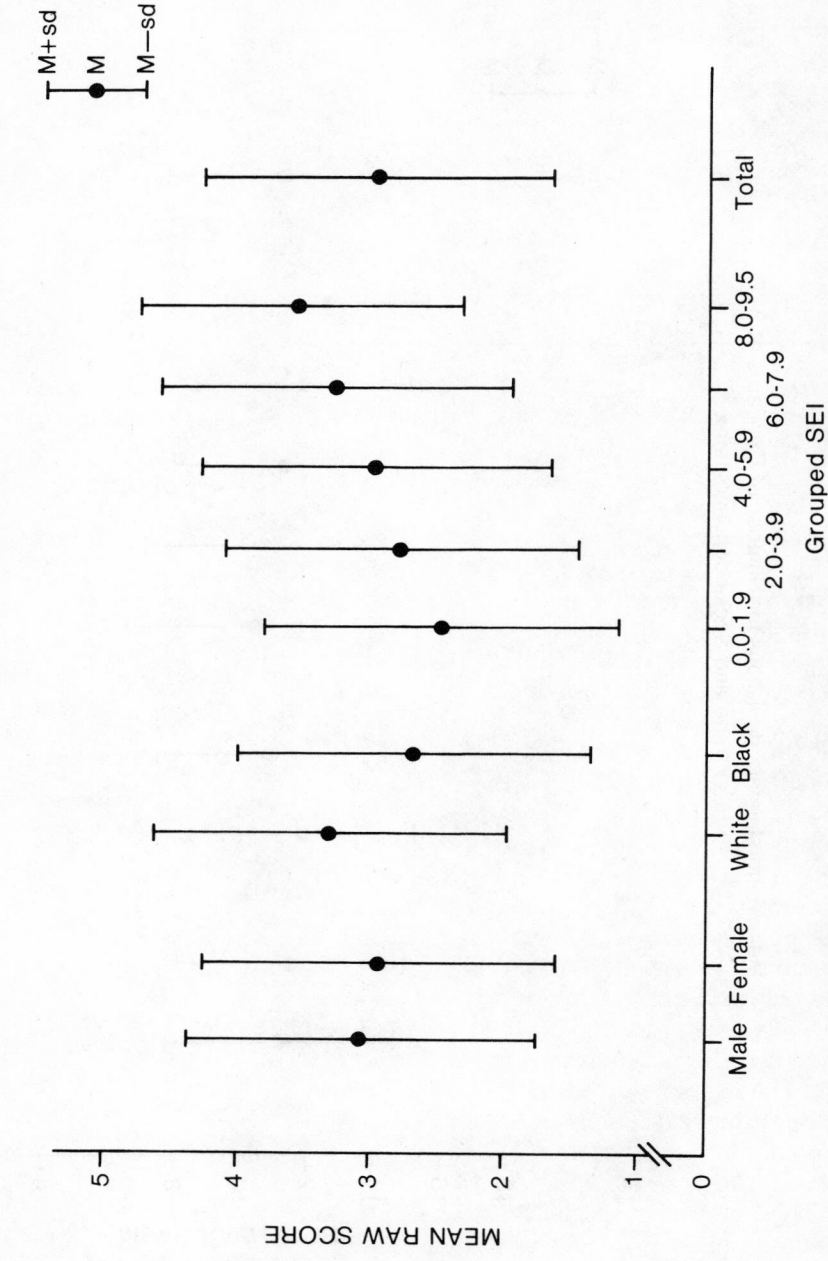

Figure **8-6**

Means and standard deviations for Understanding A Story at 8YR
by sex, race and Socioeconomic Index

172

Table **8-4**

Means and standard deviations for Understanding a Story by sex, race, Socioeconomic Index and total.

	N	Mean	SD
Male	9,991	3.11	1.32
Female	9,858	2.91	1.32
White	10,091	3.32	1.26
Black	9,758	2.69	1.30
SEI 0.0-1.9	1,599	2.52	1.31
SEI 2.0-3.9	5,895	2.75	1.31
SEI 4.0-5.9	5,977	2.97	1.30
SEI 6.0-7.9	4,080	3.28	1.26
SEI 8.0-9.5	2,298	3.62	1.18
Total	**20,137**	**3.01**	**1.32**

3YR and 8YR Syllables. Two-digits and two-syllables at 3YR yielded an r of .13 when correlated with digits and syllables at 8YR. The remainder of the 3YR/8YR correlations were low with the majority of them <.10.

Correlations between the 8YR SLH variables yielded somewhat higher values. Those above .30 included r = .44 for 8YR Digits with 8YR Syllables, .33 for 8YR Digits with Oral Reading (Gray, 1967), .31 for 8YR Digits with Silent Reading (Durrell and Sullivan, 1945) and .32 for 8YR Digits with Writing to Dictation. Understanding a Story correlated .41 with Morphology (McCarthy and Kirk, 1963) and .33 with the overall Connected Discourse rating. The individual elements of Connected Discourse were not entered into the correlation matrix, so the relationship of the Number of Concepts to other SLH variables is unavailable. The relationship of this subtest to the 8YR Auditory Memory Index will be reported in the following section on indexes.

The pattern of relationships observed between auditory memory variables and the 8YR SLH variables was similar to those described for the 3YR SLH variables. There were low r's with speech mechanism and hearing variables and somewhat stronger relationships with

language variables. Speech production measures had r's of <.10 with the exception of Articulation and Intelligibility, which had r's ranging from .12 to .19 when correlated with the index variables. All correlational material referred to throughout is found in Appendix 6.

The Auditory Memory Indexes*

Construction of the Indexes

Because motivation and attention are fleeting in the three-year-old, outcomes were ordered to give a score of three if the child passed either of the three-unit memory tests regardless of any failures on the two-unit and spondaic tests. Passing either Two-Syllable Series or Two-Digit Series yielded a score of two, and success on the Spondaic Word Test alone resulted in a score of one. Thus the range, theoretical and actual, for the 3YR Auditory Memory Index was 0 to 3. The similar correlational findings for two or three units, whether digits or syllables,

---

* In the following sections, 3YR Auditory Memory and 8YR Auditory Memory are used interchangeably with 3YR Auditory Memory Index and 8YR Auditory Memory Index. All other SLH indexes are defined in Appendix 4 and discussed in the appropriate substantive chapters.

with other SLH variables seemed to confirm the appropriateness of basing ordering on the number of units repeated.

Correlations of the component variables and the index yielded the following values: Two-Digit Series, r = .53; Three-Digit Series, r = .67; Two-Syllable Series, r = .57; Three-Syllable Series, r = .76; and Spondaic Word Test, r = .18. It follows that Three-Syllable Series, which had a higher pass rate than Three-Digit Series, contributed most heavily to the variance.

The missingness of data due to attentional or motivational problems was not considered a problem at the 8YR level; indeed, missingness amounted to less than 1% for any of the component variables. All components were given equal weighting. Scores of 0 to 340 were theoretically possible; the actual range was 0 to 335. The digit test at eight was retained as a key variable and the raw scores, ranging from 2.0 to 10.5, were recoded to yield values of 0 to 85. Rules for the construction of the indexes and key variables are listed in Appendix 4.

The 8YR Auditory Memory Index intercorrelations were .55 with 8YR Digits and .57 with 8YR Syllables. The r for Understanding a Story was .75, and for the Number of Concepts Recalled, .68. These intercorrelations indicate that each variable within the index contributed appreciably to the variance.

Descriptive Statistics

Descriptive statistics for the 3YR Auditory Memory Index are presented in Table 8-5 and Figure 8-7. The 8YR data are presented in Table 8-6 and Figure 8-8. At the 3YR level, there appeared not to be appreciable SEI bias in the index as there were only small socioeconomic differences, with the two highest groups performing only slightly better than the other three groups. Black Females stand out in Figure 8-7 as performing better than the other race and sex groups,

which showed little variation. In this figure, the dotted line marks the upper range, and the upper standard deviation is theoretical because the distribution is truncated. The mean for the total group was 2.82 with a standard deviation of .45.

The 8YR Auditory Memory Index distributions reveal a trend toward better performance with rising socioeconomic status. The performance of Whites was better than that of Blacks; sex differences did not emerge for either race. It is possible that the examiner variable played a role in the response elicited from the children, since almost all examiners were White. It seems unlikely that the test material itself was biased toward any one group because it was at a simple comprehension level except for the syllable test, which was novel for all groups. The mean score for 8YR Auditory Memory was 170.19; SD = 40.74.

The recoding of 8YR Digits resulted in a mean of 34 with a standard deviation of 10. The characteristics of the 8YR Digits distribution were discussed in the section dealing with single variables. As a key variable, 8YR Digits was subjected to the same basic analyses as the indexes and will be discussed in conjunction with them.

Intercorrelations and Cross-tabulations of the Indexes

Indexes at both age levels and 8YR Digits were correlated with all other SLH indexes and key variables. In addition, cross-tabulations were prepared showing the probabilities of failing the 8YR Auditory Memory Index given success or failure on selected indexes. Failure was defined as a score falling within or, in the case of a restricted range, closest to the lowest decile.

The 3YR Auditory Memory Index had low correlations with other 3YR indexes, only two being above .20: Sentence Complexity (.22) and Intelligibility (.21). When 3YR Auditory Memory was corre-

174

Table 8-5

Averages and standard deviations for ALL 3YR performance on the 3YR Auditory Memory Index by sex, race and Socioeconomic Index.

	Actual Range	Mean	SD	Median	Mode	Valid Codes	NIDF*
Male	0-3	2.81	0.46	3	3	7,761	2,298
Female	0-3	2.83	0.44	3	3	8,000	1,826
White	0-3	2.79	0.48	3	3	6,567	2,016
Black	0-3	2.85	0.43	3	3	9,194	2,108
SEI 0.0-1.9	0-3	2.81	0.48	3	3	1,518	443
SEI 2.0-3.9	0-3	2.79	0.49	3	3	5,250	1,575
SEI 4.0-5.9	0-3	2.81	0.46	3	3	4,502	1,260
SEI 6.0-7.9	0-3	2.85	0.40	3	3	2,736	582
SEI 8.0-9.5	0-3	2.92	0.30	3	3	1,755	264
Total	**0-3**	**2.82**	**0.45**	**3**	**3**	**15,761**	**4,124**

*NIDF = Not in data file.

Table 8-6

Averages and standard deviations for ALL 8YR performance on the 8YR Auditory Memory Index by sex, race and Socioeconomic Index.

	Actual Range	Mean	SD	Median	Mode	Valid Codes	NIDF*
Male	0-335	170.13	40.86	172.5	184.5	9,894	240
Female	8-315	170.25	40.62	170.5	170.5	9,758	245
White	0-335	178.26	39.99	180.5	204.5	9,894	254
Black	0-291	161.83	39.81	162.5	158.5	9,758	231
SEI 0.0-1.9	22-263	153.64	40.83	156.5	148.5	1,574	57
SEI 2.0-3.9	8-289	160.41	39.67	160.5	170.5	5,842	158
SEI 4.0-5.9	0-291	168.84	39.30	170.5	184.5	5,910	163
SEI 6.0-7.9	8-335	180.46	39.05	180.5	172.5	4,046	76
SEI 8.0-9.5	14-299	191.93	36.26	192.5	218.5	2,280	31
Total	**0-335**	**170.19**	**40.74**			**19,652**	**485**

*NIDF = Not in data file.

lated with 8YR indexes, r's were also low. The correlations with 8YR Digits and 8YR Auditory Memory were .23 and .17, respectively.

The 8YR Auditory Memory Index produced considerably higher values when correlated with other 8YR indexes with r's ranging from .02 (Hypernasality) to .77 (Language Comprehension). Correla-

tions with speech mechanism, voice, and hearing variables were <.10. Digits at 8YR demonstrated a similar pattern, but with r's ranging from .02 (Sensorineural Hearing Loss) to .55 (Auditory Memory).

Correlations and cross-tabulations of particular interest are presented in Table 8-7. All correlations are presented in Ap-

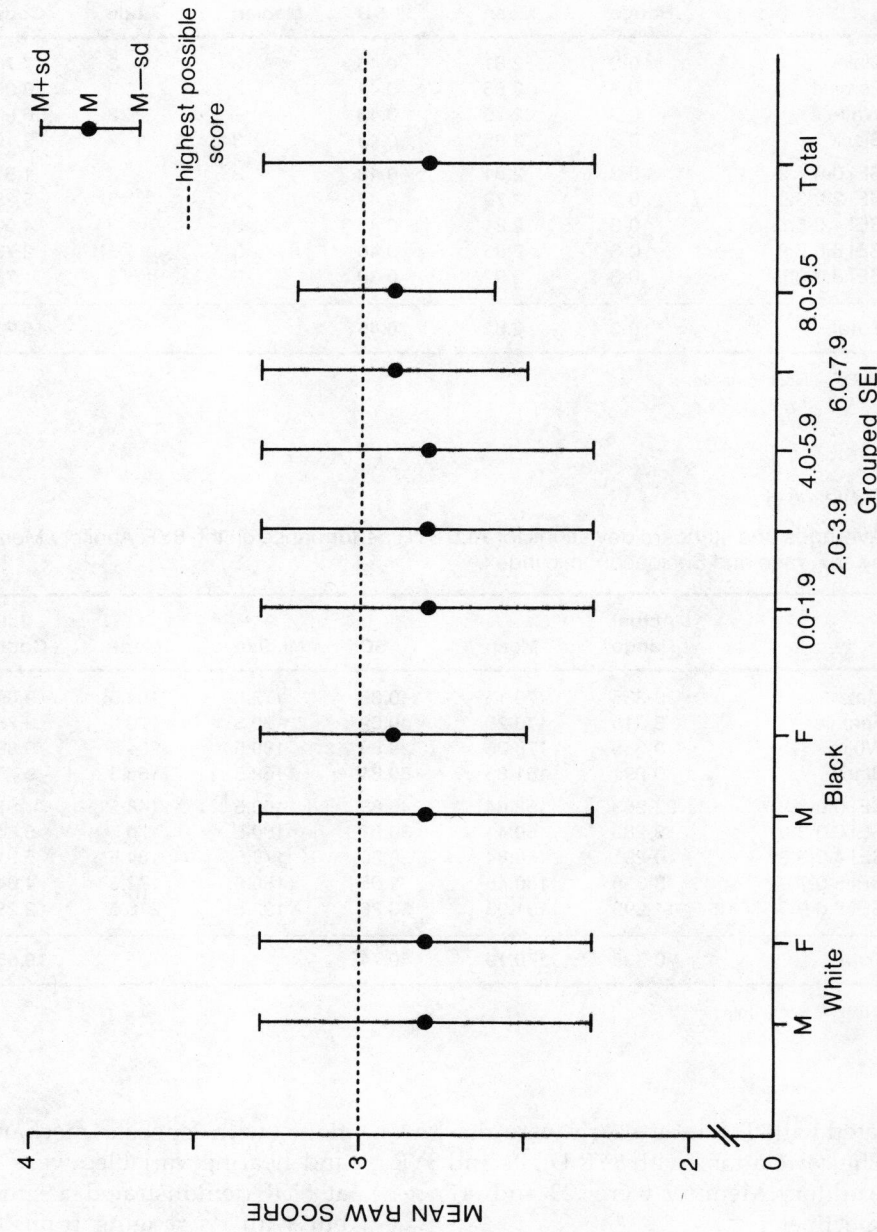

Figure 8-7

Means and standard deviations for the 3YR Auditory Memory Index by sex, race and Socioeconomic Index

176

Figure *8-8*

Means and standard deviations for the 8YR Auditory Memory Index by sex, race and Socioeconomic Index

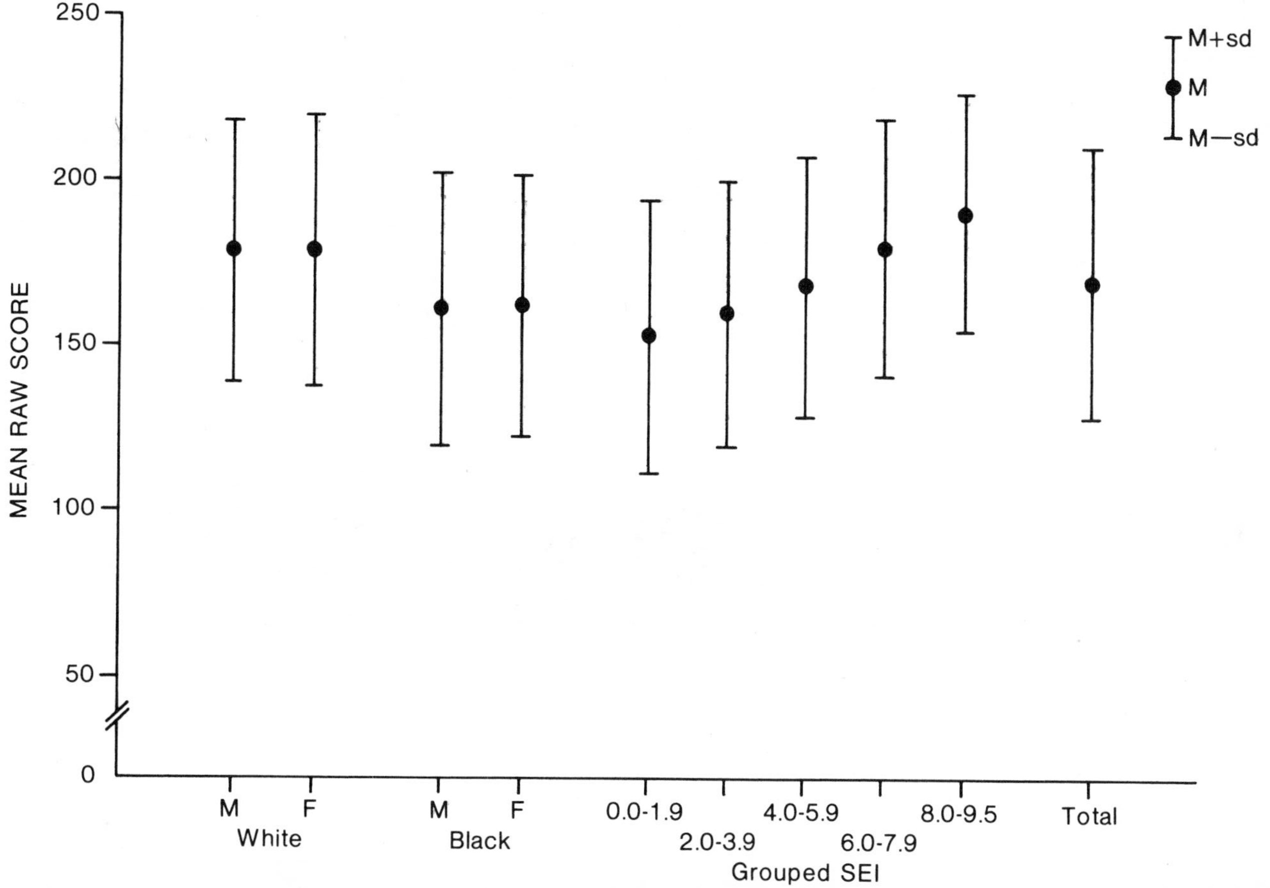

177

Table 8-7

Correlation coefficients and conditional probabilities for the 8YR Auditory Memory Index and selected SLH indexes.

Index	r	p(F2/F1)*	p(F2/P1)*
3YR Language Comprehension	.24	.26	.10
3YR Sentence Complexity	.20	.24	.10
3YR Auditory Memory	.17	.16	.08
8YR Language Comprehension	.77	.57	.06
8YR Written Communication	.45	.30	.09
8YR Concept Development	.69	†	†
8YR Auditory Processing	.69	†	†
8YR Communicative Effectiveness	.67	†	†
8YR Language Production	.54	†	†
8YR Digits	.55	†	†
8YR Word Identification	.50	†	†
8YR Articulation	.28	†	†

*p(F2/F1) and p(F2/P1) refer to the probability of failing 8YR Auditory Memory Index (F2) if the indicated SLH index was failed (F1) or passed (P1).
†P not calculated.

pendix 6. The moderate correlations with 8YR language measures suggest that a general language ability is related to 8YR Auditory Memory. This suggestion is supported by the P values which predict failure on both measures from two to almost ten times as frequently as failure on the 8YR Auditory Memory Index and success on the language measures. Some of the language indexes contained a variable common to the 8YR Auditory Memory Index. For example, Understanding a Story was a component of both 8YR Language Comprehension and 8YR Auditory Memory; this commonality would contribute to a higher correlation. Yet, other 8YR indexes such as Word Identification (Dunn, 1965) and Written Communication did not contain common variables, and the r's remained at a moderate level.

**Relationship of NCPP* Variables
to the Auditory Memory Indexes
and Key Variables**

Three techniques were employed in an effort to predict SLH outcomes from antecedent events and conditions. These

---

* The non-SLH variables in the NINCDS Collaborative Perinatal Project (NCPP).

were: (1) a correlational screen of 676 biological, psychological, and sociological variables; (2) a cross-tabulation procedure which yielded conditional probabilities for failing or passing selected antecedents and the indexes; and (3) multi-category tables for certain variables which did not lend themselves to dichotomization.

3YR Findings

At the 3YR level, most of the correlations produced were <.10. Cross-tabulations yielded little additional information when variables through the 4YR level were studied. Conditional probabilities and correlations are presented in Table 8-8.

Multi-category tables were prepared for 13 other variables. No notable differences were observed between groups when Number of Cigarettes Smoked per Day, Number of Prior Pregnancies, One-Minute Apgar, and Parity were studied. In only the most favorable of three groupings did child's Hemoglobin and Five-Minute Apgar show differences. These were 5% less failure for a Hemoglobin of more than 18 mg% and 6% less failure for Five-Minute Apgar

Table 8-8

Conditional probabilities and correlations between 3YR Auditory Memory and selected NCPP variables.

	r	p(F2/F1)*	p(F2/P1)*
At-Birth NCPP Variables			
Diabetes: Gravida (Only During Pregnancy)	<.10	.41	.33
Diabetes: Gravida (Onset at 15 or Older)	<.10	.38	.33
Diabetes: Gravida (Onset Before Age 15)	<.10	.46	.33
Acute Toxemia	<.10	.31	.32
Chronic Hypertensive Disease	<.10	.29	.32
Convulsions During Pregnancy: During Only	<.10	.27	.33
Gestation at Registration	<.10	.42	.33
Blood Pressure: 24 Weeks to Labor	<.10	.30	.33
Weight Gain: (Fail = Little)	<.10	.32	.33
Weight Gain: Pounds (Fail = Too Much)	<.10	.34	.33
Height of Mother	<.10	.35	.33
Age of Gravida (Pass = 18-35; Fail = 36-58)	<.10	.34	.32
Age of Gravida (Pass = 18-35; Fail = 10-17)	<.10	.37	.32
Husband or FOB† Present	<.10	.35	.32
Occupation of Father: White Collar	<.10	.35	.25
Housing Density (Pass = 0.1-1.5,Fail = 1.6-8.0 Per Room)	<.10	.32	.33
Per Capita Income at Birth	<.10	.35	.29
Delivery type: Vertex	<.10	.33	.36
Delivery type: Breech	<.10	.41	.33
Delivery type: C/S	<.10	.34	.33
Gestational Age: Normal vs. Postmature	<.10	.17	.15
Gestational Age: Normal vs. Premature	<.10	.16	.15
Birthweight: Normal vs. High	<.10	.33	.32
Birthweight: Normal vs. Low	<.10	.39	.32
Direct Coombs' Test: child	<.10	.28	.33
Eight-Month NCPP Variables			
Bayley 8-Month Motor score	<.10	.45	.31
Bayley 8-Month Mental score	<.10	.41	.32
Bayley Gross Motor Development	<.10	.20	.15
Bayley Fine Motor Development	<.10	.19	.15
1YR NCPP Variables			
Ped-12: Infection, Inflammations (Number)	<.10	.35	.32
Ped-12: Neurologic Abnormalities (Number)	<.10	.37	.31
Ped-12: Syndromes (Number)	<.10	.42	.33
4YR NCPP Variables			
4YR IQ >70	.14	.05	.02
4YR IQ (Marginals) 70-80	<.10	.15	.09
Repeat Two Digits	<.10	.02	.01
Short Attention Span	<.10	.22	.16
Adequate Attention Span	<.10	.66	.73
Above Average Attention Span	<.10	.01	.02

*p(F2/F1) and p(F2/P1) refer to the probability of failing 3YR Auditory Memory (F2) if the NCPP variable was failed (F1) or passed (P1).

†FOB = father of baby.

scores of eight or more. Conversely, only the lowest grouping for one-year head circumference (≤44 cm) performed differently, with 3% more failure. Increasing neonatal head circumference showed a trend toward better performance on the index for girls, but boys performed slightly better only in the largest head circumference group.

Children delivered by mid forceps performed better than the low forceps group and the latter better than the outlet forceps group. There were only two children in this sample who were delivered by high forceps. Both passed 3YR Auditory Memory. This finding probably reflects the obstetrical practice at particular institutions and, thus, is confounded by socioeconomic status and race. Increased education of both parents had a small but systematically favorable influence on 3YR performance. The results concerning the effect of Socioeconomic Index, when studied by this method, confirmed previous findings of little difference in groups one to three (0.0 to 5.9) and better performance for groups four and five (6.0 to 9.5).

8YR Findings

Correlational outcomes for 8YR Digits and 8YR Auditory Memory were slightly higher than for 3YR Auditory Memory when the early variables were studied, although again most were <.10. Probability analyses did not add significant early predictive information although there was some suggestion of relationship with the Bayley scores at eight months and syndromes observed at one year. At four years, IQ, Very Brief Attention Span, and Perseveration appeared to be related to 8YR Digits and 8YR Auditory Memory, the association with the 8YR Auditory Memory Index being stronger.

The 7YR variables were most predictive of 8YR outcome with several moderate correlations and impressive P values

including WISC IQ (Wechsler, 1949), the Auditory-Vocal Association Test (McCarthy and Kirk, 1963), and WISC Digit Span. Activity level and Very Brief Attention Span, which had low correlations, demonstrated high association when probabilities were calculated. Definite Neurological Abnormalities, which had a correlation of <.10, did show a relationship to 8YR Auditory Memory in the cross-tabulation analysis. Correlations and all calculated probabilities for 8YR Auditory Memory and for 8YR Digits are shown in Tables 8-9 and 8-10. Additional correlational data are found in Appendix 6.

Eleven variables entered into multicategory tables with 3YR Auditory Memory were used identically at the 8YR level. Number of Prior Pregnancies and One-Minute Apgar scores were omitted. There were negligible differences in outcome for both 8YR Auditory Memory and 8YR Digits when Parity, Number of Cigarettes Smoked, Apgar Score, and Bilirubin Level were studied. Children with a Hemoglobin of more than 18 mg% performed slightly poorer on 8YR Auditory Memory than children with lower Hemoglobin values, the reverse of the findings at 3YR. On 8YR Digits, 5% more children with Hemoglobin of 0 to 12 mg% failed than in the higher two Hemoglobin groupings. Children in these groups were almost equivalent on 8YR Digits performance. Clearly, no predictive statements can be made from study of these variables.

Increasing neonatal Head Circumference showed a small trend toward better performance on 8YR Digits and 8YR Auditory Memory for boys, but with a difference of only 4.5% between the lowest and highest groups. Girls in the highest group performed 3% better on the 8YR Auditory Memory Index than the lowest group, but a consistent trend was not found for 8YR Digits. One-year Head Circumference appeared to show more association with 8YR Auditory Memory,

Table **8-9**

Conditional probabilities and correlations between 8YR Auditory Memory and selected NCPP variables.

	r	p(F2/F1)*	p(F2/P1)*
At-Birth NCPP Variables			
Diabetes: Gravida (Only During Pregnancy)	<.10	.05	.12
Pass = No			
Diabetes: Gravida (Onset at 15 or Older)	<.10	.04	.12
Pass = No			
Diabetes: Gravida (Onset Before Age 15)	<.10	.11	.12
Pass = No			
Acute Toxemia	<.10	.13	.12
Chronic Hypertensive Disease	<.10	.15	.12
Gestation at Registration	−.14	.15	.12
Blood Pressure: 24 Weeks to Labor	<.10	.15	.12
Age of Gravida (10-17 vs. 18-35)	<.10	.15	.12
Age of Gravida (18-35 vs. 36-58)	<.10	.12	.12
Weight Gain: Little = Fail	<.10	.13	.11
Weight Gain: Much = Fail	<.10	.12	.11
Height of Mother	<.10	.14	.12
Housing Density	−.20	.18	.10
(Pass = 0.1-1.5; Fail = 1.6-8.0 per room)			
Husband or FOB Present	<.10	.15	.11
Occupation of Father: White Collar	.21	.14	.06
Birthweight: Normal vs. Low	<.10	.18	.12
Birthweight: Normal vs. High	<.10	.10	.12
Gestational Age: Normal vs. Postmature	<.10	.10	.09
Gestational Age: Normal vs. Premature	<.10	.14	.09
Direct Coombs' Test: child	<.10	.08	.13
Delivery type: Vertex	<.10	.12	.13
Delivery type: Breech	<.10	.15	.12
Delivery type: C/S	<.10	.12	.12
Per Capita Income at Birth	.21	.16	.08
Eight-Month NCPP Variables			
Bayley 8-Month Motor score	.13	.21	.11
Bayley 8-Month Mental score	.14	.23	.11
Bayley Gross Motor Development	−.11	.17	.09
Bayley Fine Motor Development	−.11	.16	.09
1YR NCPP Variables			
Ped-12: Syndromes (Number)	<.10	.25	.12
Ped-12: Infection, Inflammations (Number)	<.10	.13	.12
Ped-12: Neurologic Abnormalities (Number)	<.10	.16	.11
4YR NCPP Variables			
Very Brief Attention Span	−.13	.40	.11
Short Attention Span	−.15	.18	.10
Adequate Attention Span	.19	.09	.20
Above Average Attention Span	<.10	.11	.12
Highly Perseverative Attention Span	<.10	.53	.12
4YR IQ > 70	.48	.49	.10
4YR IQ (Marginals) (Fail 70-80)	<.10	.23	.08

181

Table 8-9 (continued)

Conditional probabilities and correlations between 8YR Auditory Memory and selected NCPP variables.

	r	p(F2/F1)*	p(F2/P1)*
7YR NCPP Variables			
Wechsler: Full Scale IQ<70	.49	.64	.10
Wechsler: Full Scale IQ (Marginals)			
Fail = 70-80	<.10	.33	.08
Wechsler: Verbal IQ Pass = 80-155	.43	.42	.08
Wechsler: Performance IQ Pass = 80-156	.32	.31	.10
Auditory Vocal Association Test: Raw Score	.48	.42	.08
Wechsler: Digit Span Scaled Score Fail = 0-5	.46	.40	.09
Bender Gestalt	−.28	.26	.08
Non-Neurologic Abnormalities: None = Pass	<.10	.13	.12
Non-Neurologic Abnormalities:			
None or Minor = Pass	<.10	.18	.12
Neurologic Abnormalities: Pass = None	−.15	.24	.10
Neurologic Abnormalities:			
Pass = None or Suspicious	<.10	.33	.11
Extreme Overactivity Level	<.10	.35	.12
Nature of Activity: Extremely Impulsive	<.10	.54	.12
Highly Perseverative Attention Span	<.10	.24	.12
Very Brief Attention Span	<.10	.55	.12
Short Attention Span	−.15	.21	.11
Adequate Attention Span	.14	.10	.20
Above Average Attention Span	<.10	.14	.12
WRAT: Speech Class	.15	.14	.12
Mother's Occupation: Laborer, Farmer	.20	.13	.12

*p(F2/F1) and p(F2/P1) refer to the probability of failing 8YR Auditory Memory (F2) if the NCPP variable was failed (F1) or passed (P1).

with about 6% more children failing if the head was ≤44 cm in circumference. The other two groups were comparable in performance. However, for 8YR Digits the differences were only about 1% between groups. Slight trends toward better performance with larger 4YR head circumference were noted, but differences were small.

The 8YR Auditory Memory findings relative to type of forceps delivery mirrored the findings on 3YR Auditory Memory. Differences were small; children delivered by mid forceps performed 3% better on 8YR Auditory Memory than those delivered by outlet forceps. Differences were only 1% when 8YR Digits was the outcome variable. High forceps was

used for six deliveries of children included in the 8YR Auditory Memory distribution and seven in the 8YR Digits distribution. Of these, one failed 8YR Auditory Memory and two failed 8YR Digits. While this finding results in a much higher percentage of failure, the N is so small that only a suggestion of risk may be made.

Educational level of both parents and Socioeconomic Index increases had small but systematically favorable effects on performance on 8YR Digits and 8YR Auditory Memory. Since these variables appeared to be promising predictors, they were selected, together with several other variables, for a regression analysis which is described in the following section.

Table 8-10

Conditional probabilities and correlations between 8YR Digits and selected NCPP variables.

	r	p(F2/F1)*	p(F2/P1)*
At-Birth NCPP Variables			
Age of Gravida (10-17 vs. 18-35)	<.10	.16	.13
Age of Gravida (18-35 vs. 36-58)	<.10	.15	.13
Acute Toxemia	<.10	.13	.14
Chronic Hypertensive Disease	<.10	.15	.13
Gestation at Registration	−.10	.15	.13
Blood Pressure: 24 Weeks to Labor	<.10	.15	.13
Convulsions During Pregnancy Only	<.10	.16	.13
Weight Gain: Little	<.10	.14	.11
Weight Gain: Too Much	<.10	.14	.11
Height of Mother	<.10	.15	.13
Delivery type: Vertex	<.10	.13	.14
Delivery type: Breech	<.10	.16	.13
Delivery type: C/S	<.10	.13	.13
Housing Density			
(Pass = 0.1-1.5, Fail = 1.6-8.0 per room)	<.10	.16	.11
Per Capita Income at Birth	.11	.16	.10
Husband or FOB Present	<.10	.16	.12
Occupation of Father: White Collar	.15	.14	.08
Direct Coombs' Test: child	<.10	.10	.13
Birthweight: Normal vs. Low	<.10	.18	.13
Birthweight: Normal vs. High	<.10	.12	.13
Gestational Age: Normal vs. Postmature	<.10	.13	.11
Gestational Age: Normal vs. Premature	<.10	.14	.11
Eight-Month NCPP Variables			
Bayley Gross Motor Development	<.10	.18	.10
Bayley Fine Motor Development	<.10	.18	.11
Bayley 8-Month Mental score	<.10	.21	.12
Bayley 8-Month Motor score	<.10	.21	.12
1YR NCPP Variables			
Ped-12: Neurologic Abnormalities (Number)	<.10	.16	.12
Ped-12: Syndromes (Number)	<.10	.30	.13
Ped-12: Infection, Inflammations (Number)	<.10	.15	.12
4YR NCPP Variables			
Very Brief Attention Span	<.10	.37	.12
Adequate Attention Span	.14	.11	.20
Highly Perseverative Attention Span	<.10	.37	.13
4YR IQ Pass = ≥ 70	.31	.38	.11
4YR IQ (Marginals) 70-80	<.10	.22	.10

Table **8-10** *(continued)*

Conditional probabilities and correlations between 8YR Digits
and selected NCPP variables.

	r	p(F2/F1)*	p(F2/P1)*
7YR NCPP Variables			
Neurologic Abnormalities:			
Pass = None or suspicious	−.13	.34	.12
Neurologic Abnormalities: Pass = None	<.10	.24	.11
Non-Neurologic Abnormalities: Pass = None	<.10	.15	.12
Non-Neurologic Abnormalities:			
Pass = None or Minor	<.10	.24	.13
Bender Gestalt Test	−.23	.25	.10
Wechsler: Digit Span Scaled Score	.53	.44	.10
Wechsler: Verbal IQ	.18	.34	.10
Wechsler: Performance IQ	.10	.25	.11
Wechsler: Full Scale IQ	.21	.49	.12
Wechsler: IQ (Marginals) 70-80	<.10	.29	.10
Auditory Vocal Association Test: Raw Score	.31	.31	.11
WRAT: Speech Class	<.10	.20	.13
Extreme Overactivity Level	<.10	.36	.13
Nature of Activity: Extremely Impulsive	<.10	.51	.13

*p(F2/F1) and p(F2/P1) refer to the probability of failing 8YR Digits (F2) if the NCPP
variable was failed (F1) or passed (P1).

Multiple Regression Analysis

3YR Findings

Two regression analyses were undertaken for 3YR Auditory Memory. In the first, Birthweight, Gestational Age, Education of Mother, Education of Father, Per Capita Income, Father's Occupation, and the child's race and sex were entered. In the second analysis, eight-month Bayley Mental and Motor scores were added to the above. The multiple R's were low, .14 for the first analysis and .15 for the second with only 2% of the variance accounted for. These data are shown in Table 8-11.

8YR Findings

These two analyses were repeated for 8YR Digits and 8YR Auditory Memory. In addition, three more regressions were accomplished. One added 4YR IQ to the at-birth and eight-month variables, another utilized only 3YR indexes, and the last included 3YR indexes and the at-birth variables. Inspection of Tables 8-12 and 8-13 reveals that, in each instance, 8YR Auditory Memory was predicted better than 8YR Digits. The 3YR indexes and at-birth variables best predicted 8YR Digits with a multiple R = .342 and R^2 = .117. Eight-month variables, at-birth variables, and 4YR IQ predicted almost as well, with R = .336 and R^2 = .113. This relationship was reversed for 8YR Auditory Memory where 4YR IQ added significantly to the prediction with R = .494 and accounted for 24% of the variance.

Inspection of the beta weights shows the 3YR Language Comprehension beta weight to be considerably higher for 8YR Auditory Memory than for 8YR Digits. Beta weights were higher for 3YR Auditory Memory when 8YR Digits was the outcome studied. These findings strongly suggest that the 8YR Auditory Memory Index taps a more general language ability than 8YR Digits.

Table 8-11

Multiple correlations between the 3YR Auditory Memory Index and independent variables with beta coefficients.

	At-Birth NCPP variables	At-Birth NCPP variables plus 8-month NCPP variables
Multiple R	.144	.151
R Square	.0203	.023
Birthweight	.0310	.0219
Gestational Age	.00264	−.00284
Education of Mother	.0178	.0175
Per Capita Income	.0611	.0570
Education of Father	.0576	.0555
Occupation of Father	.0421	.0419
8-Month Mental Score		−.0187
8-Month Motor Score		.0567
4YR IQ		
Race-sex Marker I	−.100	−.0956
Race-sex Marker II	−.0774	−.0761
Race-sex Marker III	.0717	.0714

Table 8-12

Multiple correlations between the 8YR Auditory Memory Index and independent variables with beta coefficients.

	At-Birth NCPP variables	At-Birth NCPP variables plus 8-Month NCPP variables	At-Birth NCPP variables plus 8-month NCPP variables plus 4YR IQ	3YR indexes	3YR indexes plus At-Birth NCPP variables
Multiple R	.330	.347	.494	.324	.411
R Square	.109	.121	.244	.105	.169
3YR Speech Mechanism				−.00538	.0000980
3YR Hypernasality				−.0120	−.0142
3YR Fluency				−.0255	−.00722
3YR Articulation				.0873	.0678
3YR Intelligibility				.0842	.0746
3YR Language Comprehension				.158	.104
3YR Sentence Complexity				.0713	.0674
3YR Auditory Memory				.0977	.0858
3YR Hearing Screen				−.00727	.00340
Birthweight	.0566	.0312	.00836		.0311
Gestational Age	.00694	−.00832	−.00389		.0151
Education of Mother	.113	.113	.0504		.0839
Per Capita Income	.0668	.0563	.0188		.0369
Education of Father	.114	.110	.0608		.113
Occupation of Father	.0529	.0558	.0255		.0467
8-Month Mental Score		.0867	.0407		
8-Month Motor Score		.0395	−.00256		
4YR IQ			.428		
Race-sex Marker I	.0554	.0635	.0121		.0513
Race-sex Marker II	.0638	.0662	−.0506		.0165
Race-sex Marker III	−.0688	−.0690	.0343		−.0166

Special Studies

The extensive data collected both in terms of numbers of subjects examined and numbers of variables recorded made possible the study of several interesting subgroups. The 8YR Auditory Memory Index and 8YR Digits performances of children with adverse birth conditions, mental retardation, hearing loss, cerebral palsy, and stuttering were studied. In addition, children from various types of family situations were isolated and compared to the ALL 8YR population. These included adopted children, children living with relatives, natural parents or foster parents, and twins. Singletons* and

siblings† were also included in the analysis and contrasted with twins. The N's, means, and standard deviations for all of these groups on 8YR Auditory Memory are presented in Table 8-14.

Table 8-14 reveals no differences as large as one standard deviation between these special groups and the ALL 8YR population with the exception of the mental retardation with syndromes group. Interesting differences emerged, however. Children with hearing problems, cerebral palsy, and adverse neonatal conditions did less well than the ALL 8YR group. Mental retardation apparently was the most adverse condition.

---

* Singletons are children without brothers or sisters at birth and at seven years.

† Siblings are the two oldest children in the study who are not the result of a multiple birth.

Table 8-13

Multiple correlations between 8YR Digits and independent variables with beta coefficients.

	At-Birth NCPP variables	At-Birth NCPP variables plus 8-Month NCPP variables	At-Birth NCPP variables plus 8-Month NCPP variables plus 4YR IQ	3YR indexes	3YR indexes plus At-Birth NCPP variables
Multiple R	.213	.226	.336	.304	.342
R Square	.045	.051	.113	.093	.117
3YR Speech Mechanism				.0184	.0132
3YR Hypernasality				−.000774	−.00341
3YR Fluency				−.0108	−.00494
3YR Articulation				.0291	.0209
3YR Intelligibility				.112	.0926
3YR Language Comprehension				.0501	.0378
3YR Sentence Complexity				.0817	.0733
3YR Auditory Memory				.169	.158
3YR Hearing Screen				−.00276	−.0000360
Birthweight	.0676	.0528	.0366		.0505
Gestational Age	−.00567	−.0147	−.0115		−.00181
Education of Mother	.0874	.0871	.0428		.0657
Per Capita Income	.0277	.0220	−.00459		.0121
Education of Father	.0542	.0526	.0176		.0525
Occupation of Father	.0725	.0746	.0531		.0666
8-Month Mental Score		.0781	.0455		
8-Month Motor Score		−.00171	−.0316		
4YR IQ			.304		
Race-sex Marker I	−.0690	−.0652	−.102		−.0903
Race-sex Marker II	.0423	.0431	−.0399		−.0102
Race-sex Marker III	−.0433	−.0431	.0302		.0137

Table **8-14**

Performance on 8YR Auditory Memory Index by special subgroups.

Sample	N	Mean	SD
Cleft Palate	24	170	41
Stutterers	35	141	57
Cerebral Palsy	83	142	59
Mental Retardation Syndromes	53	91	41
Premature (≤36 weeks			
≤2,500 grams)	917	160	41
True Distress (Apgar <4)	869	167	44
Low Birthweight (≤1,500 grams)	100	149	47
Conductive Hearing Loss	1,024	165	43
Sensorineural Hearing Loss	447	161	43
Adopted Children	243*	172	36
Foster Children	277*	158	44
Children Living With Relatives	621*	161	40
Children Living With At Least			
One Biological Parent	23,931*	170	41
Singletons	879	176	39
Siblings	3,880	171	41
Twins	370	153	44
All 8YR	20,137	170	41

*N based on 3YR and 8YR combined; mean and SD based on those given the 8YR test.

It is not surprising that children with cleft palate do as well as the ALL 8YR population. The types of articulatory errors associated with cleft palate did not seriously affect speech intelligibility on the materials used in the memory tests. The hesitations and repetitions observed in children who stutter could affect performance on repetition of digits and syllables. This group scored quite poorly and similarly to the cerebral palsy group.

Table 8-15 presents means and standard deviations on 8YR Digits for the same special groups. In general, the same pattern of performance emerged as was observed for 8YR Auditory Memory. Cleft palate cases did not do as well on 8YR Digits and so must have excelled on some of the other memory tests to score as well as the ALL 8YR group on Auditory Memory.

Reference to Figures 8-9 and 8-10 provides illustration of similar patterns of performance on 8YR Auditory Memory and 8YR Digits for singletons, siblings, and twins. On both tests, singletons performed better than children with siblings, and twins performed least well. A trend toward better performance with rising socioeconomic status is seen for all three groups on 8YR Auditory Memory. This trend is not as consistent for 8YR Digits but is present.

Other family situations are also of interest. Children living with at least one biological parent performed as well as the ALL 8YR sample on 8YR Auditory Memory and 8YR Digits, followed by children living with relatives and those living with foster parents. While adopted children scored higher than any other group on 8YR Auditory Memory, they scored lowest on 8YR Digits. It may be that an enriched environment associated with usually being the first child in the adoptive family and the rise in socioeconomic status which usually accompanies adoption (Yarrow et al., 1973) has more effect on the 8YR Auditory Memory Index than on 8YR Digits. As stated earlier, the 8YR Auditory Memory Index appears to be more related to other language measures

187

Table 8-15

Performance on 8YR Digits by special subgroups.

Sample	N	Mean	SD
Cleft Palate	24	30	12
Stutterers	35	27	13
Cerebral Palsy	83	28	12
Mental Retardation Syndromes	53	18	13
Premature (≤36 weeks ≤2,500 grams)	917	31	10
True Distress (Apgar<4)	869	33	10
Low Birthweight (≤1,500 grams)	100	29	10
Conductive Hearing Loss	1,024	32	10
Sensorineural Hearing Loss	447	32	10
Adopted Children	243*	31	9
Foster Children	277*	30	10
Children Living With Relatives	621*	33	9
Children Living With at Least One Biological Parent	23,931*	34	10
Singletons	879	34	9
Siblings	3,880	34	10
Twins	370	31	10
All 8YR	20,137	34	10

*N based on 3YR and 8YR combined; means and SD based on those given the 8YR test.

than 8YR Digits and probably measures a more general language competence.

Normative data for 8YR Auditory Memory and 8YR Digits by IQ, sex, and race are presented numerically in Tables 8-16 and 8-17 and graphically in Figures 8-11 and 8-12. These analyses excluded mentally retarded children with syndromes. As would be expected, the scores increased as IQ increased. Black Females appeared to have some advantage on 8YR Digits, but race and sex groups performed similarly on 8YR Auditory Memory without a consistent advantage for any one group.

Discussion

In this study, the digit and syllable memory span tests represent an imitative task for children which appears to have little cultural bias. While there were trends towards better performance at three years for Black Females and the two highest Socioeconomic Index groups,

and a more consistent SEI trend at eight with Whites and Females performing slightly better, differences were small. This finding is interesting in that almost all of the other tests in the SLH battery showed greater racial differences and favored Whites. Differences favoring Whites over Blacks were noticeable on the sentence material (Number of Concepts and Understanding a Story). The lower scores of Blacks on these tests, of course, reduced the total 8YR Auditory Memory Index score. This finding is in agreement with Seitz (1974), who found poorer recall of standard English sentence material by Black children and conversely, poorer recall of nonstandard English by White children. These tests, included as tests of longer term memory, are probably biased toward standard English listeners and speakers. The better performance of Females and Blacks at three and, in particular, Black Females may represent different styles of learning for these groups (Kirk, 1972) and may

188

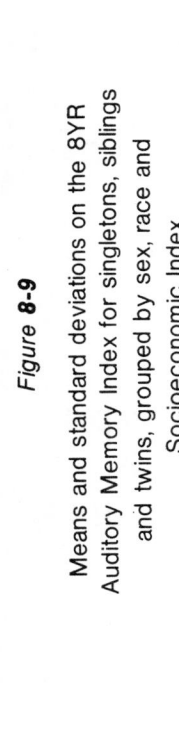

Figure 8-9

Means and standard deviations on the 8YR
Auditory Memory Index for singletons, siblings
and twins, grouped by sex, race and
Socioeconomic Index

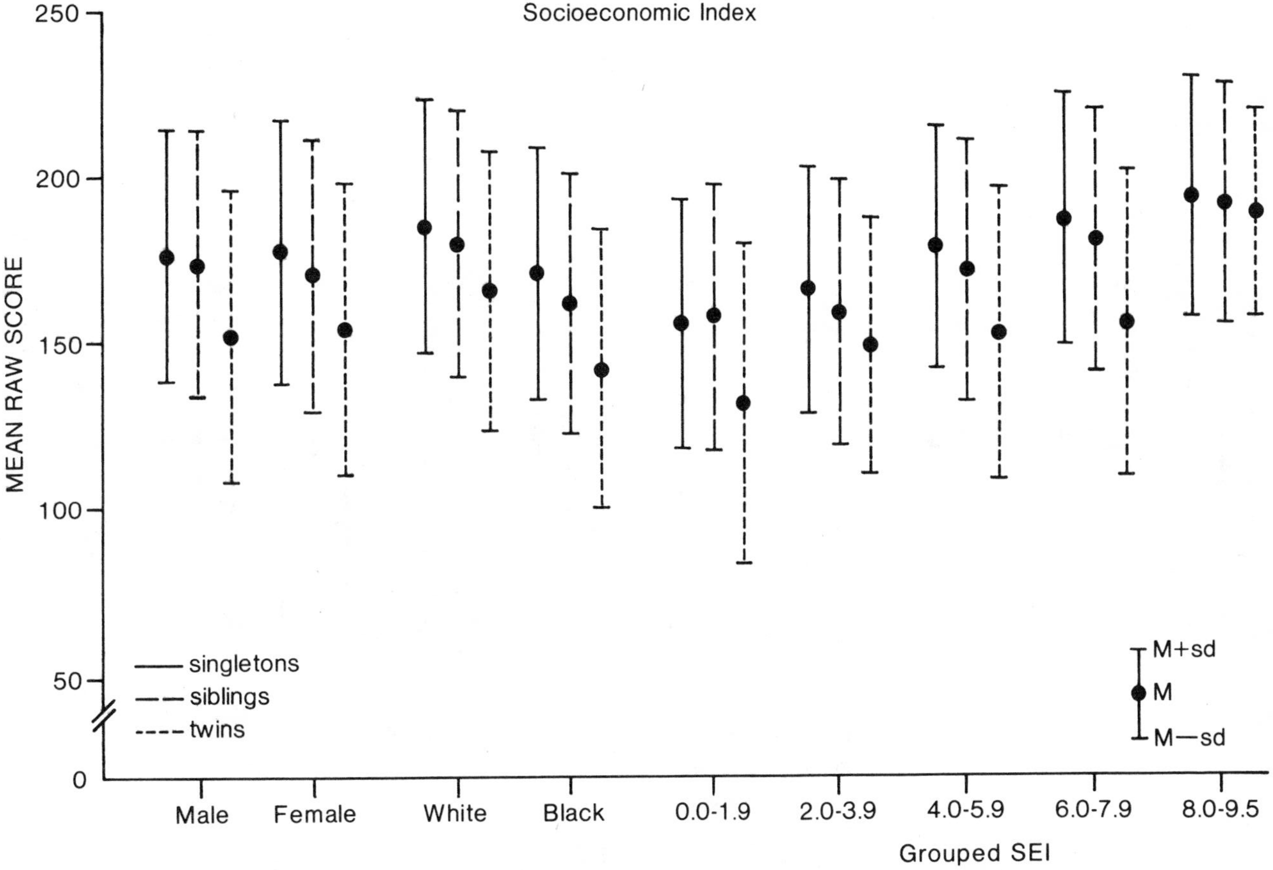

189

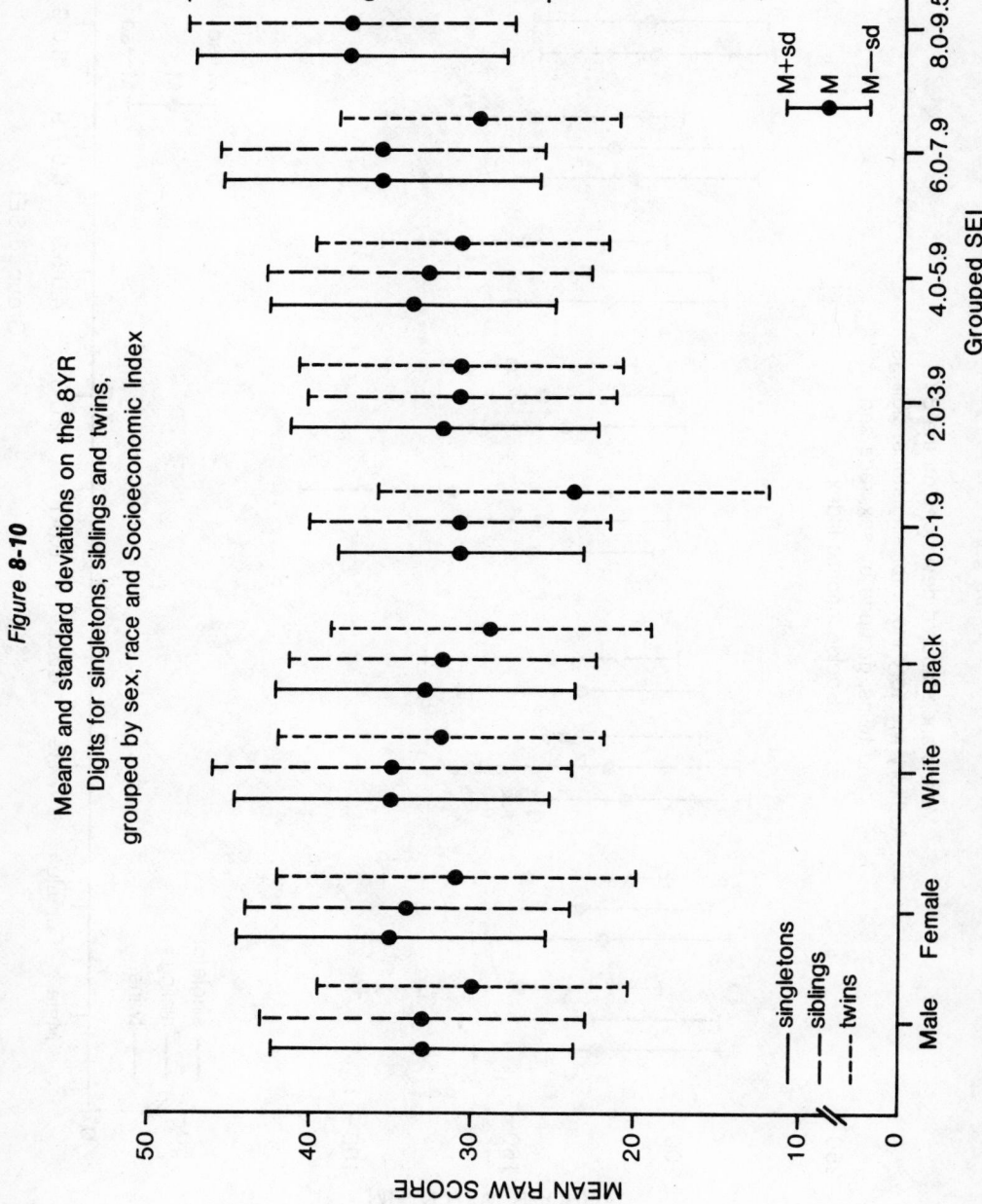

Figure 8-10

Means and standard deviations on the 8YR
Digits for singletons, siblings and twins,
grouped by sex, race and Socioeconomic Index

Table 8-16

Mean scores on 8YR Auditory Memory by grouped IQ, sex and race.

	≤39	40-49	50-59	60-69	70-79	80-89	90-99	100-109	110-119	WISC IQ 120+
White Male	9.0*	43.5*	69.3*	116.0	137.3	148.9	167.1	181.1	191.8	208.6
White Female	60.0*	23.5*	87.3*	103.0	124.3	149.9	166.5	181.6	198.1	212.0
Black Male	43.7*	64.8*	87.5	114.5	137.2	152.7	167.8	182.2	193.4	208.3
Black Female	24.0*	NA†	86.5	111.2	135.0	150.4	167.5	182.3	192.8	210.9

*Based on <20 cases.
†Not applicable: no cases.

191

Table 8-17

Mean scores on 8YR Digits by grouped IQ, sex and race.

	≤39	40-49	50-59	60-69	70-79	80-89	90-99	100-109	110-119	WISC IQ 120+
White Male	0*	8.6*	13.5*	21.7	24.2	27.9	31.1	34.0	36.8	40.0
White Female	15.0*	2.5*	15.0*	22.8	25.0	29.7	32.7	35.6	38.7	41.8
Black Male	10.0*	19.4*	21.1	26.7	28.6	30.6	33.1	35.6	37.1	40.5
Black Female	4.3*	2.5*	22.4	27.2	29.5	31.8	34.6	36.6	39.3	40.8

*Based on <20 cases.

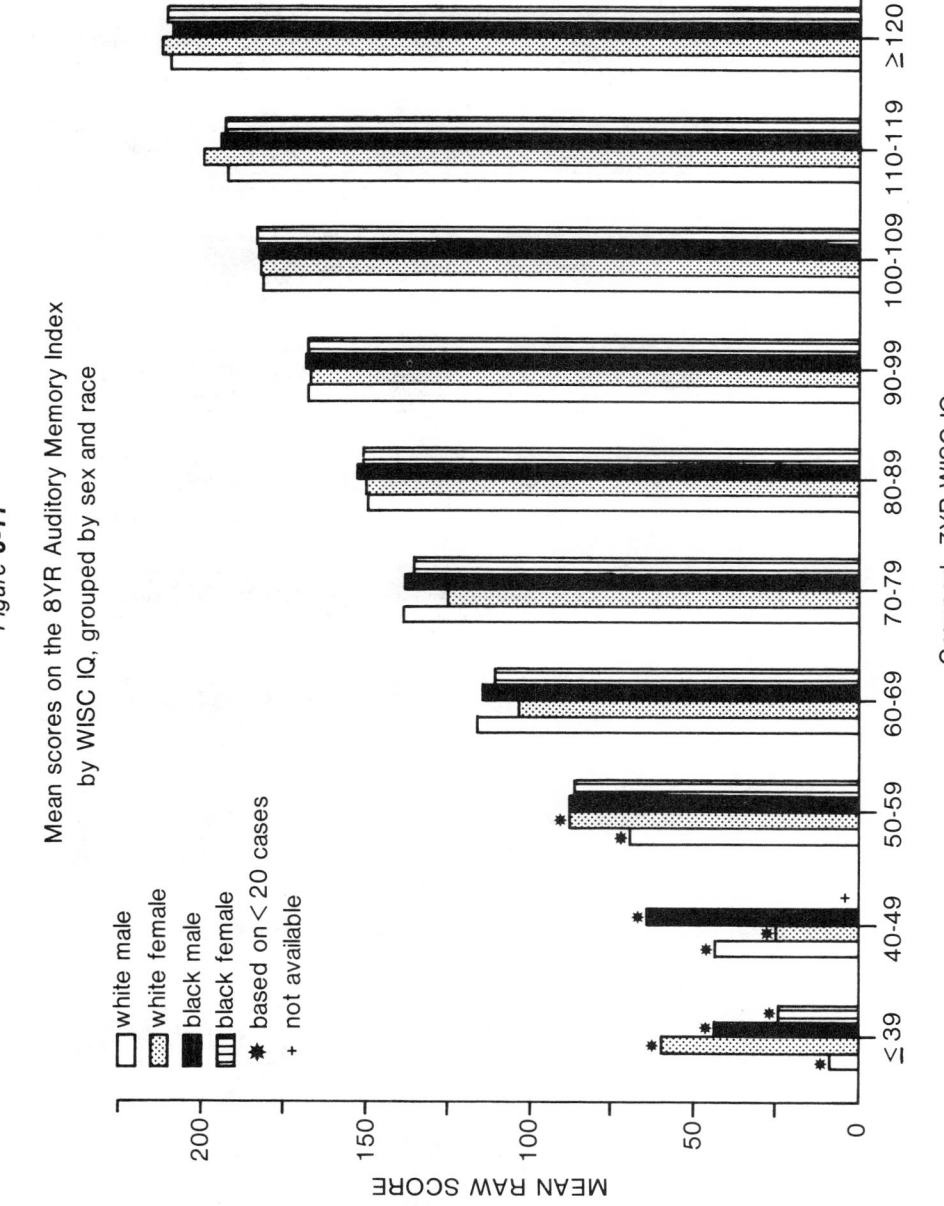

Figure *8-11*

Mean scores on the 8YR Auditory Memory Index
by WISC IQ, grouped by sex and race

white male
white female
black male
black female
* based on < 20 cases
+ not available

MEAN RAW SCORE

Grouped 7YR WISC IQ

193

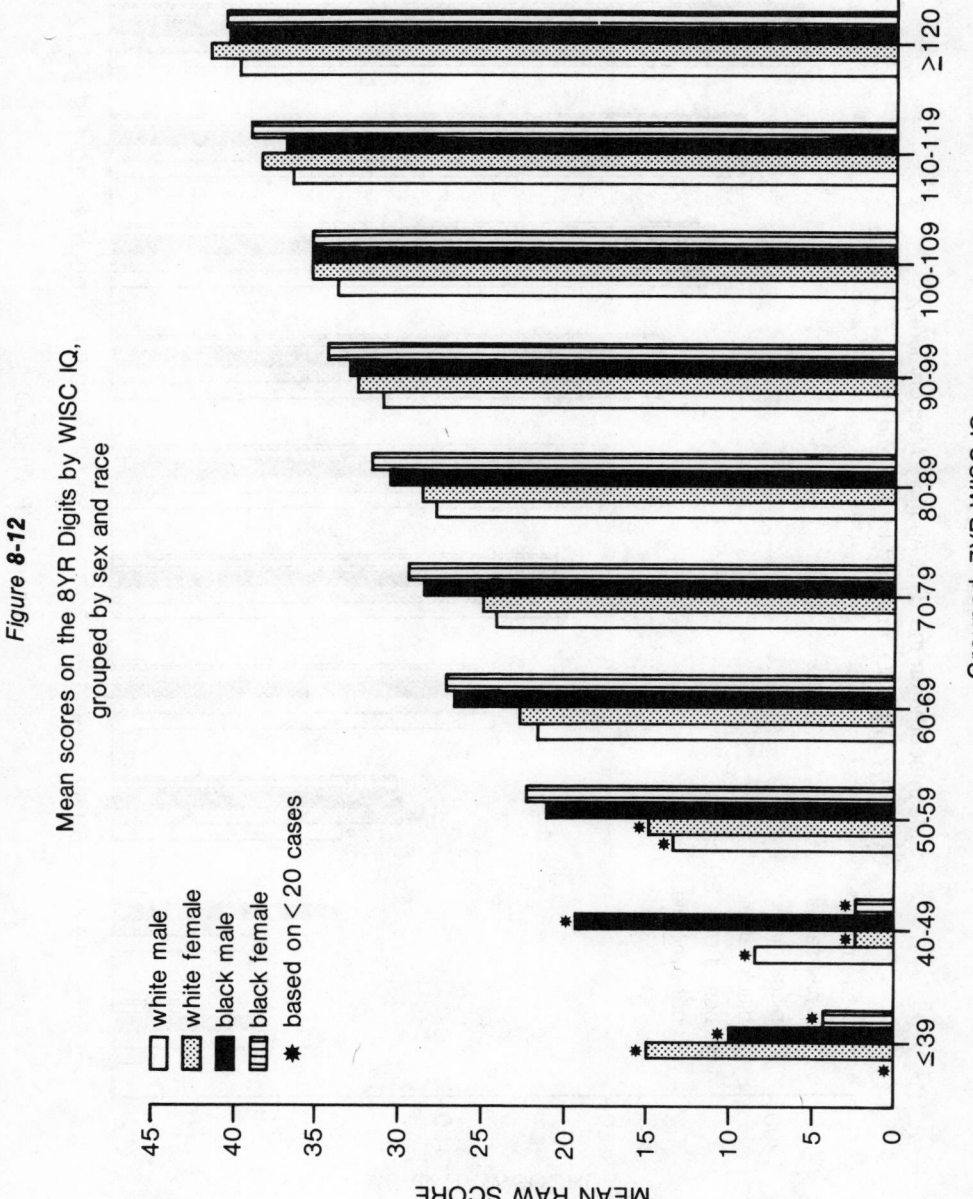

Figure **8-12**

Mean scores on the 8YR Digits by WISC IQ,
grouped by sex and race

194

also represent maturational and motivational differences between sex and race at this age level (Hertzig et al., 1968).

It should be reemphasized that differences between race and sex and Socioeconomic Index groups were small, particularly on digit and syllable materials. A phonological level of processing is suggested by Wickelgren (1965, 1966), who hypothesizes that vowels and consonants are coded in short-term memory as a set of distinctive features rather than as single speech sounds or as a group. When more grammatically related memory tests are added, processing must go beyond the phonological level to a more general language ability.

The relationships between auditory memory span and language abilities have been studied previously and a number of studies show a positive relationship, including the works of Graham (1968a, 1968b), Monsees (1968), Epstein (1964), Weiner (1969), and Salzinger, Salzinger, and Hobson (1967). Menyuk (1969), in studying young children without sensory or basic intellectual defects, also felt that grammatical competence is limited if a child has a restricted short-term memory. She states: "It has been postulated that as memory capacity or storage capacity increases, normal-speaking children expand the rules in their grammar, observe more contextual constraints, and, in some instances, reorganize rules to achieve greater definition and economy. . . . If the 3.0-year-old child could not keep in short-term memory storage more than a two-to-three-morpheme-length utterance, it is difficult to see how this developing process of a deepening analysis could be carried out, since only a very limited amount of data could be handled at one time." (Menyuk, 1969, p. 142.)

In the present study, relationships were found between auditory memory variables and indexes and the language tests including reading and writing. Correlations were higher than between auditory memory variables and articulation, another frequently researched area. Winitz (1969) provided a review of the major studies of the relationship between auditory memory and articulation and points out that the findings are equivocal. One of the problems, in our opinion, is the wide variation in materials and methodology which makes comparisons difficult. This study is not an exception, as the material were specially constructed for the SLH battery and have not, to our knowledge, been used in other published research.

Auditory memory was not predicted well by most NCPP variables except for attentional variables, IQ, and definite neurological abnormalities at seven as related to the 8YR outcome. The positive relationship of general intelligence and attention to memory span has been well documented. Belmont and Butterfield (1968), and Bush and Cohen (1970) provide examples. The findings of this study are in agreement with such previous investigations. The subjects who were abnormal neurologically may have had clusters and signs which would have been interesting to study in relation to attentional and memory variables. This area is worthy of further study.

The most salient findings of this investigation appear to be the relationships of auditory memory to other SLH variables and the relatively culture-free aspects of the auditory memory tests. It is suggested that the auditory memory span tests, and particularly the 8YR Auditory Memory Index, are clinically useful screening measures for general language competence in children and should be employed as such.

Summary

1. This study was based on 19,885 three-year-old children and 20,137 eight-year-olds who had speech, language, and hearing examinations at those age levels. Auditory

195

memory indexes were developed for both the three and eight-year-old levels. Digits at eight years was retained as a separate key variable. The 3YR index included digits, syllables, and the Spondaic Word Test, which consisted of words familiar to the three-year-old and is basically a word repetition task. At the 3YR level, missingness of data was a concern and either syllable or digit repetition of the same length was accepted as equivalent. This decision was supported by correlational studies. The 8YR index included tests of digit and syllable memory and also two tests of longer term memory: Connected Discourse (Number of Concepts Recalled) and Understanding a Story.

2. Blacks and Females performed better than Whites and Males on 3YR digit and syllable tests, with a clear Socioeconomic Index effect only for the highest group. Blacks and Females also had better performance on the Spondaic Word Test, but there was a consistent trend toward better performance with increasing socioeconomic status. At eight years, Females and Whites had slightly better mean scores for digits, syllables, and Number of Concepts Recalled. The performance of Whites and Males was slightly better on Understanding a Story. For all 8YR Auditory Memory Index variables, there were small but consistent improvements in mean scores with rising SEI status.

3. The individual 3YR and 8YR auditory memory variables were correlated with all other SLH variables. The highest correlation for 3YR variables was between Three-Digit Series and Three-Syllable Series with r = .57. Two-Digit Series and Two-Syllable Series yielded an r = .44. Other combinations of digits and syllables produced r's of .33 to .36. The Spondaic Word Test correlated at .13 to .14 with digits and syllables, and at .17 to .25 with 3YR language measures. These were higher r's than between digit and syllable tests and language tests. All other r's between 3YR Auditory Memory Index variables and other 3YR SLH variables were <.25, and most <.15. The correlation between Three-Digit Series or Three-Syllable Series at three and 8YR Digits was .25. The remainder of the 3YR/8YR correlations were low with the majority <.10.

The 8YR variables yielded somewhat higher correlations. Correlation coefficients of >.30 included 8YR Digits with 8YR Syllables, r = .44; 8YR Digits with Oral Reading, r = .33; 8YR Digits with Silent Reading, r = .31; 8YR Digits with Writing to Dictation, r = .32; Understanding a Story with Morphology, r = .33; and Understanding a Story with Connected Discourse (Number of Concepts Recalled), r = .33.

4. The 3YR Auditory Memory Index correlated with its component variables from .18 (Spondaic Word Test) to .76 (Three-Syllable Series) with r's for Three-Digit Series, Two-Digit Series, and Two-Syllable Series being .67, .53, and .57, respectively.

The 8YR Auditory Memory Index correlated at .55 with 8YR Digits and .57 with 8YR Syllables. The r for Understanding A Story was .75, and for Connected Discourse (number of concepts recalled) r = .68.

5. All indexes were correlated and cross-tabulations of particular interest were prepared. Correlations of 3YR Auditory Memory with other 3YR indexes were low, with Sentence Complexity (r = .22) and Intelligibility (r = .21) being the high-

est. The 3YR/8YR correlations were also low. Correlations with 8YR Digits and 8YR Auditory Memory were .23 and .17, respectively.

Moderate to moderately high correlations (.45 to .77) were found between 8YR Auditory Memory and 8YR language indexes. Probabilities of failure on 8YR Auditory Memory were doubled if 3YR Language Comprehension, 3YR Sentence Complexity, or 3YR Auditory Memory were failed rather than passed. The probability of failure on 8YR Auditory Memory was three times greater if 8YR Written Communication was failed than if it was passed; and for 8YR Language Comprehension, the probability rises tenfold.

6. A total of 676 biological, psychological, and sociological variables were entered into a correlational screen with SLH indexes. Almost all r's were < .10 for 3YR Auditory Memory and the remainder also were low. This was true also for 8YR Auditory Memory when early variables were studied. At four years, IQ had a moderate correlation; and at seven, there were also moderate correlations for IQ and the Auditory-Vocal Association Test with 8YR Auditory Memory.

7. Selected NCPP variables were studied in cross-tabulations. Early variables did not appear to be significantly predictive although there is some suggestion of relationships with Bayley scores and syndromes at one year. At 7YR, psychological tests, activity and attentional observations, and neurological abnormalities were predictive of 8YR outcome.

8. Two multiple regression analyses were undertaken for 3YR Auditory Memory using selected variables through the eight-month level. The multiple R's were .14 and .15. These analyses were repeated for 8YR Digits and 8YR Auditory Memory, and three additional regressions were accomplished adding three-year and four-year variables. Performance on 8YR Digits was best predicted by 3YR indexes and at-birth variables, with a multiple $R = .336$ and $R^2 = .113$. Performance on 8YR Auditory Memory was best predicted by at-birth variables, eight-month variables, and 4YR IQ; $R = .494$ and 24% of the variance was explained.

9. The 8YR performance of several subgroups was studied. Children with hearing loss, cerebral palsy, adverse neonatal conditions, mental retardation, and stutters did less well than the ALL 8YR population on both 8YR indexes. Differences were small, less than one standard deviation except for the mental retardation group. Cleft palate subjects performed as well as the ALL 8YR group on 8YR Auditory Memory but not as well on 8YR Digits. Singletons performed better than children with siblings, and twins performed least well on both indexes. Children living with at least one biological parent performed at the ALL 8YR mean for both indexes. Children living with relatives or foster parents did less well. Adopted children scored higher than any other group on 8YR Auditory Memory but lowest on 8YR Digits.

References

1. Belmont, J.M., and Butterfield, E.C. The relations of short term memory to development and intelligence. In L.P. Lipsit and H. Reese, Eds. *Advances in Child Development and Behavior.* New York: Academic Press, 1968.

2. Bush, E.S., and Cohen, L.B. The

effects of relevant and irrelevant labels on short-term memory in nursery school children. *Psychonomic Sci.* 18:228–229, 1970.

3. Dunn, L.M. *Peabody Picture Vocabulary Test Manual.* Circle Pines, Minnesota: American Guidance Service, 1965.

4. Durrell, D.D., and Sullivan, H.B. *Durrell-Sullivan Reading Capacity and Achievement Tests.* New York: Harcourt, Brace and World, 1945.

5. Epstein, A.G. Auditory memory span for language. *Folia Phoniatr.* 16:271–289, 1964.

6. Graham, N.C. Memory span and language proficiency. *J. Learning Dis.* 1:16–20, 1968a.

7. Graham, N.C. Short term memory and syntactic structure in educationally subnormal children. *Lang. Speech* 11:209–219, 1968b.

8. Gray, W.S. *Gray Oral Reading Tests.* Indianapolis, Indiana: Bobbs-Merrill, 1967.

9. Hertzig, M.E., Birch, H.G., Thomas, A., and Mendez, O.A. Class and ethnic differences in the responsiveness of preschool children to cognitive demands. *Monographs of the Society for Research in Child Development.* 33:(4, Serial No. 117), 1968.

10. Kirk, S.A. Ethnic differences in psycholinguistic abilities. *Except. Child.* 39: No. 2.112–118, 1972.

11. Lassman, F.M., and Englebart, E.S. Methodology in digit memory testing of college students. *J. Speech Hear Res.* 10:268–276, 1967.

12. McCarthy, J.J., and Kirk, S.A. *The Construction, Standardization and Statistical Characteristics of the Illinois Test of Psycholinguistic Abilities. Experimental Edition.* Urbana, Illinois: University of Illinois Press, 1963.

13. Menyuk, P. *Sentences Children Use.* Cambridge: MIT Press, 1969.

14. Monsees, E.K. Temporal sequence and expressive language disorders. *Except. Child.* 35:141–147, 1968.

15. Salzinger, S., Salzinger, K., and Hobson, S. the effect of syntactical structure on immediate memory for word sequences in middle and lower class children. *J. Psychol.* 67:147–159, 1967.

16. Seitz, V. The effects of integrated versus segregated school attendance on short-term memory for standard and non-standard English. Paper presented at the American Psychological Association, New Orleans, 1974.

17. Wechsler, D. *The Wechsler Intelligence Scale for Children.* New York: The Psychological Corp., 1949.

18. Weiner, P.S. The cognitive function of language deficient children. *J. Speech Hear. Res.* 1:53–64, 1969.

19. Wickelgren, W.A. Distinctive features and errors in short-term memory for English vowels. *J. Acoust. Soc. Am.* 38:583–588, 1965.

20. Wickelgren, W.A. Distinctive features and errors in short-term memory for English consonants. *J. Acoust. Soc. Am.* 39:388–398, 1966.

21. Winitz, H. *Articulatory Acquisition and Behavior.* New York: Appleton-Century-Crofts, 1969.

22. Yarrow, L.S., Goodwin, M.S., Manheimer, H., and Milowe, I.D. Infancy experiences and cognitive and personality development at ten years. In L.J. Stone, H.T. Smith, and L.B. Murphy, Eds. *The Competent Infant.* New York: Basic Books. 1973.

## CHAPTER 9

Speech Mechanism

Frederic L. Darley, Ph.D.
Warren H. Fay, Ph.D.

For a complete understanding of the communicative behaviors of the children being studied, some scrutiny was necessarily directed to the physiologic basis of their speech performance. Did the children demonstrate problems in neuromuscular control of the peripheral apparatus serving speech functions? Were any deviations from normal reflected ultimately in their vocal and articulatory skills? Were such deviations associated with antecedent or concurrent factors important as causes or maintainers of the communicative deficit? Is it possible to predict the appearance at three years or at eight years of aberrations of the speech mechanism from neonatal or infant conditions or behaviors?

To obtain answers to these questions the three-year-old children were shown how to retract and protrude their lips and how to protrude the tongue in the midline, lateralize it while protruding it, and elevate it to the alveolar ridge. Their imitation of these maneuvers was rated pass or fail, and notation was made of asymmetries or grimaces observed during their execution. The elevation of the soft palate while they prolonged "ah" was similarly rated. Their oral diadochokinesis was rated pass or unsustained as the children tried to produce at least three repetitions per second of "buh" and "tuh," tests of lip and tongue movement respectively. All of these observations, with the exception of oral diadochokinesis, were repeated at age eight and performances were similarly rated.

Performance on Speech Mechanism Tests

Frequency Distributions

Table 9-1 summarized the 3YR performance on the eight tasks comprising the speech mechanism examination. The tasks were such that between 11% and 17% of the children tested could not co-operate or perform well enough to allow valid observations (designated as Not in Data File or NIDF). Only small percentages of the children adequately tested were unsuccessful on the tasks of Lip Retraction (2%), Lip Protrusion (5%), and Midline Tongue Protrusion (1%). Lateralization of the protruded tongue was performed unsuccessfully by 15% of the total group, with boys (18%) experiencing more difficulty than girls (12%) and Blacks (20%) experiencing more difficulty than Whites (9%). Tongue Elevation proved even harder; 38% of the total group unsuccessfully performed this task; again, the boys (42%) failed more often than the girls (34%) and the Blacks (42%) more often than the Whites (32%). Limited mobility of the soft palate on elevation was noted in 3% of the total group. On both lip and tongue diadochokinesis 5% of the total group failed to sustain the required duration of syllable repetitions. On none of the eight measures did important differences appear between the various socioeconomic groups, except for lateralization of the protruded tongue. The lower Socioeconomic Index (SEI) groups (16% to 20%) failed on this task more often than the higher SEI groups (11%).

Table 9-2 presents the 8YR performance on the six tasks comprising the speech mechanism examination. Very small percentages failed on Lip Retraction (1%), Lip Protrusion (1%), Midline Tongue Protrusion (less than 1%), Lateral Tongue Protrusion (1%), Tongue Eleva-

tion (2%), and Soft Palate Elevation (2%). No important sex, race, or socioeconomic differences appeared.

Intercorrelations of Variables

Intercorrelations were computed between all speech, language, and hearing (SLH) variables at the 3YR and at the 8YR levels and between the 3YR and 8YR levels.

At the 3YR level, only two of the eight speech mechanism variables evidenced a high degree of relationship: Diadochokinesis for lips and for tongue correlated .74, suggesting that these two variables measure, to a considerable degree, an underlying motorical capacity. Lateral Tongue Protrusion and Tongue Elevation correlated .32. All other correlations were ≤.12.

These 3YR measures were not highly correlated, in turn, with certain speech production measures that one might think would be related. Oral Diadochokinesis was correlated with Intelligibility .14 for lips, .13 for the tongue. Adequacy of Soft Palate Elevation was weakly related (.10) to judgments of Hypernasality of voice. Tongue Lateralization was related to correctness of Articulation only .20 for Initial Consonants and .28 for Final Consonants. Tongue Elevation correlated .15 with Articulation of Initial Consonants and .22 with Articulation of Final Consonants. Though the relationship was not a close one, it is of interest that Lateral Tongue Protrusion was somewhat more closely related to correctness of Articulation than was Tongue Elevation.

At the 8YR level, no measures showed a high degree of relationship. Lateral Tongue Protrusion correlated .27 with Tongue Elevation and .23 with Midline Tongue Protrusion; Tongue Elevation correlated .23 with Midline Tongue Protrusion. Other relationships between the six measures were ≤.14.

Likewise, correlations between these

Table **9-1**

3YR Speech Mechanism performance (%) by race, sex, Socioeconomic Index and total of the ALL 3YR sample.

Outcome	Male	Female	White	Black	SEI 0.0-1.9	2.0-3.9	4.0-5.9	6.0-7.9	8.0-9.5	Total
Lip Retraction (11% NIDF)*										
Unsuccessful	2	2	1	3	2	3	2	1	1	2
Asymmetrical (left or right)	2	2	0	2	2	2	2	0	0	2
Pass with grimace	1	1	1	1	2	1	1	1	1	1
N	8,835	8,887	7,671	10,051	1,707	5,940	5,134	3,043	1,898	17,722
Lip Protrusion (11% NIDF)										
Unsuccessful	6	4	5	5	5	5	5	4	5	5
N	8,801	8,851	7,615	10,037	1,703	5,934	5,113	3,017	1,885	17,652
Midline Tongue Protrusion (11% NIDF)										
Unsuccessful	1	1	1		1	1	1	0	1	1
Asymmetrical (left or right)	1	0	0	2	2	2	0	0	0	1
Pass with tremor	1	1	1	0	1	1	1	0	0	1
N	8,855	8,885	7,658	10,082	1,708	5,963	5,144	3,027	1,898	17,740
Lateral Tongue Protrusion (14% NIDF)										
Unsuccessful	18	12	9	20	20	17	16	11	11	15
Mandible moves with tongue	5	5	4	6	7	5	5	4	3	3
Head moves to same side	4	2	3	3	3	4	3	2	2	3
N	8,429	8,615	7,429	9,615	1,634	5,700	4,925	2,932	1,853	17,044
Tongue Elevation (16% NIDF)										
Unsuccessful	42	34	32	42	40	38	38	35	43	38
Pass with head movement	0	0	1	0	1	0	0	1	1	1
N	8,233	8,375	7,209	9,399	1,608	5,570	4,789	2,827	1,814	16,608
Soft Palate Elevation (17% NIDF)										
Limited mobility	3	4	5	2	3	3	3	4	3	3
Asymmetrical elevation	1	0	1	1	0	0	1	1	0	1
N	8,176	8,288	6,895	7,569	1,585	5,567	4,763	2,793	1,756	16,464
Lip Diadochokinesis (16% NIDF)										
Unsustained	6	4	6	4	4	5	5	5	3	5
N	8,258	8,430	7,070	9,618	1,611	5,595	4,806	2,865	1,811	16,688
Tongue Diadochokinesis (17% NIDF)										
Unsustained	6	4	6	4	5	5	5	5	3	5
N	8,147	8,344	6,959	9,532	1,587	5,535	4,738	2,836	1,795	16,491

*NIDF = not in data file.

Table **9-2**

8YR Speech Mechanism performance (%) by race, sex, Socioeconomic Index and total of the ALL 8YR sample.

| | | | | | | | | SEI | | | |
Outcome	Male	Female	White	Black	0.0-1.9	2.0-3.9	4.0-5.9	6.0-7.9	8.0-9.5	Total
Lip Retraction (1.4% NIDF)*										
Fail	1	0	1	1	1	1	1	0	0	1
Pass with concomitant movement	1	0	1	0	0	0	0	1	1	0
N	9,989	9,869	10,092	9,766	1,600	5,900	5,980	4,077	2,301	19,858
Lip Protrusion (1.4% NIDF)										
Fail	1	0	1	1	1	1	1	0	0	1
N	10,026	9,886	10,112	9,800	1,606	5,917	5,992	4,092	2,305	19,912
Midline Tongue Protrusion (1.3% NIDF)										
Fail	1	0	0	1	0	1	1	0	0	0
Pass with concomitant movement	1	1	1	0	0	1	1	1	0	1
N	10,027	9,886	10,113	9,800	1,606	5,918	5,992	4,092	2,305	19,913
Lateral Tongue Protrusion (1.4% NIDF)										
Fail	1	1	1	1	1	1	1	1	1	1
Pass with concomitant movement	16	14	17	12	13	13	15	16	18	15
Fail with concomitant movement	1	0	0	1	1	0	0	0	0	0
N	10,026	9,886	10,112	9,800	1,606	5,917	5,992	4,092	2,305	19,912
Tongue Elevation (1.6% NIDF)										
Fail	2	2	1	3	3	2	2	2	1	2
Pass with concomitant movement	2	1	2	1	1	1	2	2	2	2
N	9,966	9,852	10,081	9,737	1,596	5,887	5,969	4,067	2,299	19,818
Soft Palate Elevation (1.7% NIDF)										
Abnormal	2	2	2	1	1	2	1	1	1	2
N	9,959	9,848	10,080	9,727	1,594	5,881	5,965	4,065	2,302	19,807

*NIDF = not in data file.

8YR measures and various speech production measures were low. The highest were between Soft Palate Elevation and judgments of Hypernasality (.14), Lateral Tongue Protrusion and Articulation adequacy (.11), Lip Retraction and Intelligibility (.11), and Lateral Tongue Protrusion and Intelligibility (.11).

Can one predict 8YR Speech Mechanism measures from similar 3YR measures? The answer is negative. All of the 48 correlations were ≤.09. Nor can one predict 8YR Speech Production measures from 3YR Speech Mechanism measures. The highest correlation was .14, between 3YR Lateral Tongue Protrusion and 8YR Articulation.

Speech Mechanism Indexes

Construction of Indexes

Four indexes were constructed, two for the 3YR and two for the 8YR Speech Mechanism measures, grouping together variables that might collectively constitute more comprehensive measures for discerning relationships among the data. (See Appendix 4 for specific rules for construction of the indexes and ordering their outcomes).

The indexes, their component variables, and the correlations of each index with the component variables were as follows:

1. 3YR Speech Mechanism   **r**

Lip Retraction	.17
Lip Diadochokinesis	.84
Tongue Diadochokinesis	.96

It appears that Tongue Diadochokinesis was the primary contributor to the variance for this index, correlating almost perfectly with the index. The additional descriptive power achieved by the development of this index appears to be negligible.

2. 3YR Hypernasality

Hypernasal voice quality was desig-nated a key variable. It was originally intended that Soft Palate Elevation would be an additional component variable in this index, but too many scores were missing to permit its reliable use. The examiner's auditory perception of present hypernasality was judged more important than his observation of the elevation of the palate.

3. 8YR Speech Mechanism   **r**

Lip Retraction	.24
Lip Protrusion	.21
Midline Tongue Protrusion	.34
Lateral Tongue Protrusion	.44
Tongue Elevation	.96

Tongue Elevation turned out to be the principal contributor to the variance of this index. The descriptive utility of the index was not substantially increased by adding the four other variables.

4. 8YR Palatal Function/   **r**
Hypernasality

Soft Palate Elevation	.59
Voice Quality: Resonance (Hypernasal)	.38

This index appeared to be weighted significantly by both its component variables.

Index Frequency Distributions

For each index, frequency distributions were constructed showing range of scores, means, standard deviation, median, and mode (Appendix 5) and are presented in Tables 9-3 to 9-6. The groups represented in these tables are the ALL 3YR and ALL 8YR samples. Corresponding data from the 3YR/8YR sample are almost identical. Institutional variability on these measures proved to be negligible.

1. 3YR Speech Mechanism Outcomes of this index ranged from 0 (total failure) to 7 (complete pass). Table 9-3 summarizes the data from this index. It shows that the mean scores fell between 6 and 7 for the total group and for all subsets of the

Table 9-3

Averages and standard deviations for ALL 3YR performance on 3YR Speech Mechanism by sex, race and Socioeconomic Index.

	Actual Range	Mean	SD	Median	Mode	N	NIDF*
Sex: Male	0-7	6.56	1.42	7	7	8,156	1,903
Female	0-7	6.70	1.19	7	7	8,321	1,505
Race: White	0-7	6.57	1.43	7	7	6,906	1,677
Black	0-7	6.67	1.21	7	7	9,571	1,731
SEI: 0.0-1.9	0-7	6.61	1.35	7	7	1,600	361
2.0-3.9	0-7	6.59	1.38	7	7	5,545	1,280
4.0-5.9	0-7	6.62	1.32	7	7	4,735	1,027
6.0-7.9	0-7	6.65	1.28	7	7	2,817	501
8.0-9.5	0-7	6.79	1.00	7	7	1,780	239
Total	**0-7**	**6.63**	**1.31**	**7**	**7**	**16,477**	**3,408**

*NIDF = not in data file.

Table 9-4

Percentage hypernasal children for ALL 3YR sample on 3YR Hypernasality by sex, race and Socioeconomic Index.

	Actual Range	Hypernasal (%)	N	NIDF*
Sex: Male	0-1	1.3	9,524	535
Female	0-1	1.0	9,384	442
Race: White	0-1	1.4	8,300	283
Black	0-1	0.9	10,608	694
SEI: 0.0-1.9	0-1	1.1	1,835	126
2.0-3.9	0-1	1.1	6,384	441
4.0-5.9	0-1	1.4	5,455	307
6.0-7.9	0-1	1.3	3,230	88
8.0-9.5	0-1	0.5	2,004	15
Total	**0-1**	**1.1**	**18,908**	**977**

*NIDF = not in data file.

group. No clinically important differences appeared with regard to sex, race, or socioeconomic status. These data are graphically presented in Figure 9-1.

2. *3YR Hypernasality* Outcomes were either 0 (presence of hypernasality) or 1 (absence of hypernasality). Table 9-4 shows that in approximately 1% of the total group hypernasality was noted, and this percentage was the same for all subsets of sex, race, and socioeconomic status.

3. *8YR Speech Mechanism* Outcomes ranged from 0 (fail all component variables) to 8 (pass all component variables). Table 9-5 shows that the mean for the total group was 7.88; the means for the various subgroups by sex, race, and socioeconomic status were close to that and differ from each other by no more than 0.1 scale value. Figure 9-2 presents these data graphically.

4. *8YR Palatal Function/Hypernasality* Outcomes ranged from 0 (abnormal pala-

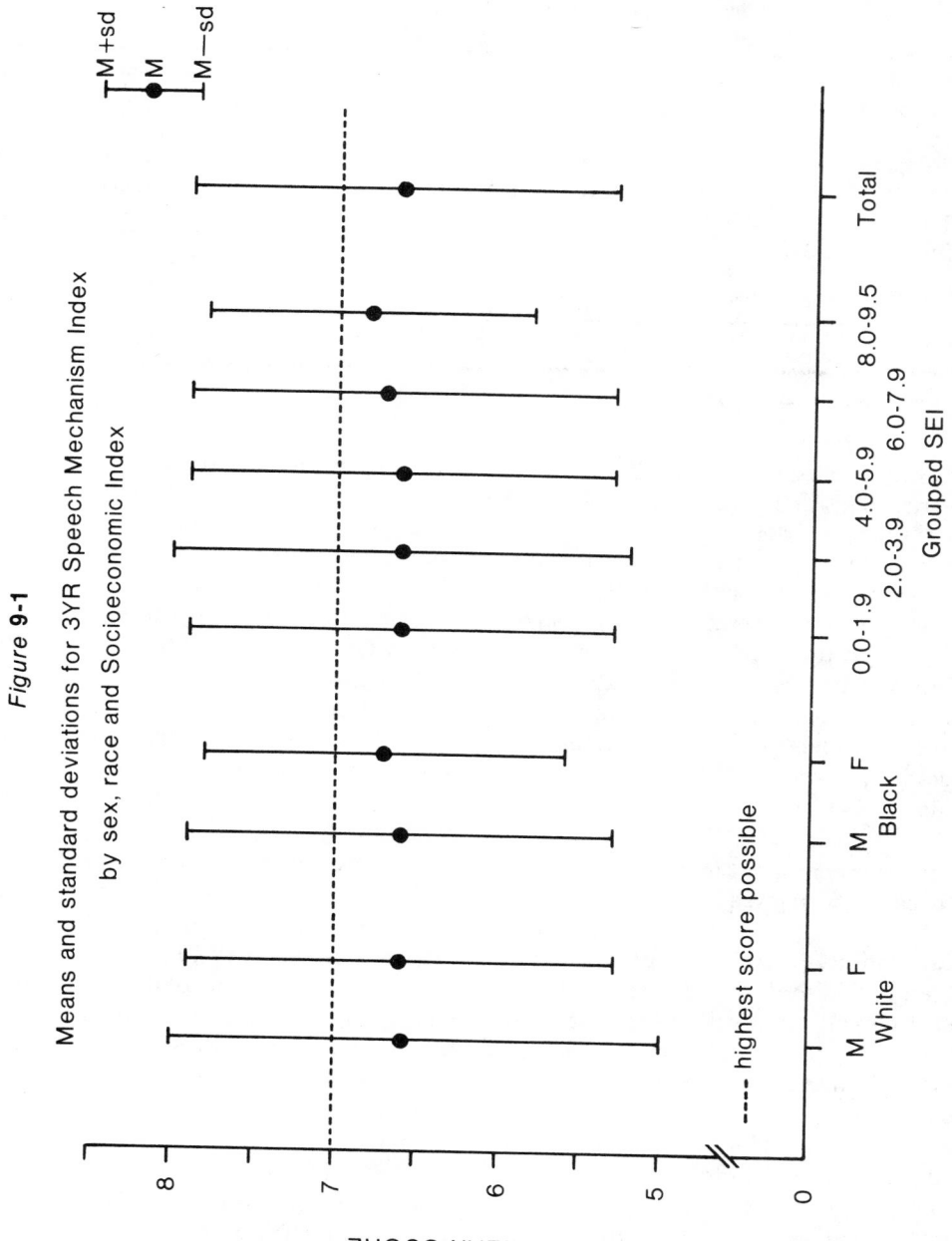

Figure **9-1**

Means and standard deviations for 3YR Speech Mechanism Index
by sex, race and Socioeconomic Index

205

Table 9-5

Averages and standard deviations for ALL 8YR performance on 8YR Speech Mechanism by sex, race and Socioeconomic Index.

	Actual Range	Mean	SD	Median	Mode	N	NIDF*
Sex: Male	0-8	7.85	0.77	8	8	9,955	179
Female	0-8	7.91	0.57	8	8	9,846	157
Race: White	0-8	7.90	0.60	8	8	10,074	74
Black	0-8	7.86	0.75	8	8	9,727	262
SEI: 0.0-1.9	2-8	7.82	0.84	8	8	1,596	35
2.0-3.9	2-8	7.88	0.69	8	8	5,879	121
4.0-5.9	0-8	7.88	0.67	8	8	5,965	108
6.0-7.9	1-8	7.89	0.66	8	8	4,065	57
8.0-9.5	0-8	7.92	0.55	8	8	2,296	15
Total	0-8	7.88	0.68	8	8	19,801	336

*NIDF = not in data file.

tal function in association with observed hypernasality) to 3 (normal palatal function without observed hypernasality). Table 9-6 shows that the mean for the total group was 2.96 with negligible variation within the sex, race, and socioeconomic subgroups.

Values presented in these tables are used for comparison of the total study sample with certain subsets of children selected for special study, described below.

Intercorrelations and Cross-tabulations of Indexes

Correlations were computed for all 3YR and 8YR indexes. In addition, in order to explicate further the obtained correlations, cross-tabulations were produced and, in the case of four-fold tables, probabilities were calculated. This procedure related a child's pass or fail* on a speech mechanism index to his pass or fail on another SLH index. Sometimes, when a correlation is small, the cross-tabulation procedure can show that one

---

* Failure was defined as a score falling in the lowest decile or, in the case of a restricted range, closest to the lowest decile.

can still predict to what degree failure on one variable will lead to failure on another variable; this probability can be contrasted with the probability that if the child passes on one variable he will fail on the other one. Consideration of the correlations together with the two probabilities gives more information than the correlations alone.

3YR Indexes The correlations of 3YR Speech Mechanism with other 3YR indexes were quite small. Table 9-7, Part I, contains the highest correlations found and those of special interest together with subsequent cross-tabulations. Other correlations were ≤.10, including all correlations between 3YR Hypernasality and other indexes. None of the correlations was high enough to warrant use of 3YR Speech Mechanism or 3YR Hypernasality as a predictor of communication performance. However, the conditional probabilities indicated that failure on these 3YR indexes may be related to some aspects of poor communication performance. Failing 3YR Speech Mechanism was twice as likely (.25) to be associated with failure on 3YR Articulation as was passing 3YR Speech Mechanism (.12). The probability of failing 3YR Sentence Complexity was nearly three times as great

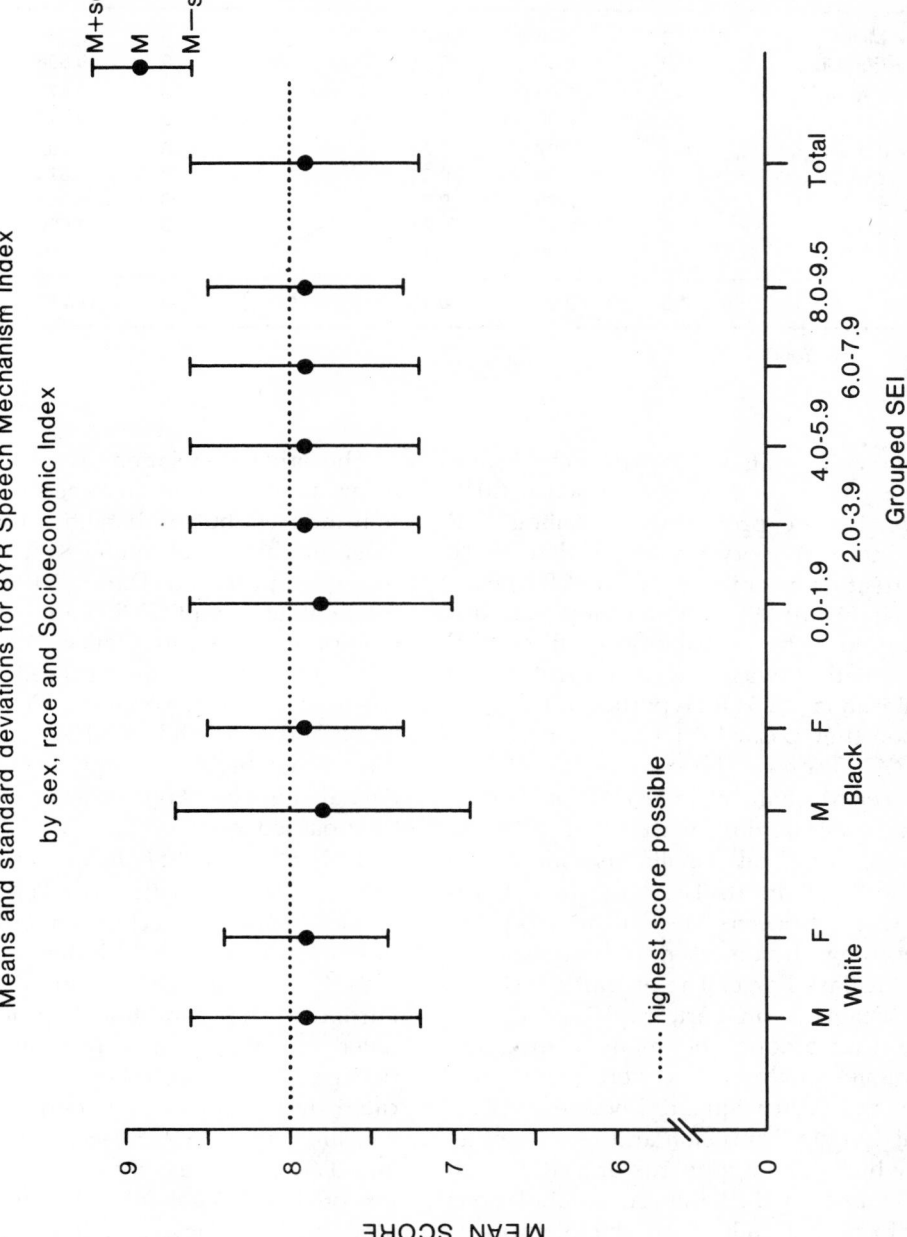

Figure **9-2**

Means and standard deviations for 8YR Speech Mechanism Index by sex, race and Socioeconomic Index

207

Table **9-6**

Averages and standard deviations for ALL 8YR performance on 8YR Palatal Function/
Hypernasality by sex, race and Socioeconomic Index.

	Actual Range	Mean	SD	Median	Mode	N	NIDF*
Sex: Male	0-3	2.96	0.26	3	3	9,949	185
Female	0-3	2.97	0.23	3	3	9,838	165
Race: White	0-3	2.95	0.29	3	3	10,072	76
Black	0-3	2.98	0.20	3	3	9,715	274
SEI: 0.0-1.9	0-3	2.97	0.23	3	3	1,592	39
2.0-3.9	0-3	2.96	0.27	3	3	5,874	126
4.0-5.9	0-3	2.96	0.25	3	3	5,961	112
6.0-7.9	0-3	2.97	0.24	3	3	4,060	62
8.0-9.5	0-3	2.98	0.19	3	3	2,300	11
Total	**0-3**	**2.96**	**0.25**	**3**	**3**	**19,787**	**350**

*NIDF = not in data file.

when children failed 3YR Speech Mechanism (.19) as when they passed it (.07). Likewise the probability of failing 3YR Auditory Memory was more than twice as great when children failed 3YR Speech Mechanism (.29) as when they passed it (.13). And the probability of failing 3YR Articulation was twice as great when children failed 3YR Hypernasality (.25) as when they passed it (.12).

8YR Indexes The correlations of 8YR Speech Mechanism and 8YR Palatal Function/Hypernasality with other 8YR indexes were all small, as shown in Table 9-7, Part II. The largest (.20) was between Speech Mechanism and the Neurologic Involvement Index developed by the Task Force. The magnitude of this coefficient is, in part, explained by the fact that among the many component variables of this index were Lip Retraction and Protrusion and Midline and Lateral Tongue Protrusion and Elevation, all of which are components of 8YR Speech Mechanism. But the cross-tabulations confirm that failure on the Neurologic Involvement Index was four times as likely to be associated with failing 8YR Speech Mechanism (.40) as with passing it (.10).

The other correlations were too small to predict failure on any speech production indexes, but probabilities were considerably higher of failing 8YR Articulation (Templin and Darley, 1960), 8YR Intelligibility, and 8YR Language Production if the children failed 8YR Speech Mechanism than if they passed it. Likewise, probabilities of failing 8YR Articulation and 8YR Intelligibility were two to three times higher if children failed 8YR Palatal Function/Hypernasality than if they passed it.

3YR Index and 8YR Index Correlations The correlations of the two 3YR indexes related to speech mechanism and hypernasality and all the 8YR indexes approximated zero, as shown in Table 9-7, Part III. The conditional probabilities failed to suggest any relationship between these indexes beyond that indicated by the correlation coefficients. We conclude that 3YR Speech Mechanism and 3YR Hypernasality are poor predictors of speech mechanism function, articulation proficiency, and intelligibility at eight years, and that 3YR Fluency, 3YR Articulation, and 3YR Intelligibility also are poor predictors of 8YR speech mechanism function.

Table **9-7**

Correlations and conditional probabilities for indexes related to speech mechanism function.

Index 1	Index 2	r	p(F2/F1)*	p(F2/P1)*
	I. 3YR vs. 3YR			
3YR Speech Mechanism	3YR Hypernasality	.04	.02	.01
3YR Speech Mechanism	3YR Articulation	.13	.25	.12
3YR Speech Mechanism	3YR Intelligibility	.18	.11	.03
3YR Speech Mechanism	3YR Language Comprehension	.13	.15	.06
3YR Speech Mechanism	3YR Sentence Complexity	.16	.19	.07
3YR Speech Mechanism	3YR Auditory Memory	.15	.29	.13
3YR Hypernasality	3YR Articulation	.05	.25	.12
3YR Hypernasality	3YR Intelligibility	.09	.07	.02
	II. 8YR vs. 8YR			
8YR Speech Mechanism	8YR Pal. Func/Hypernasality	.05	.07	.02
8YR Speech Mechanism	8YR Articulation	.12	.28	.13
8YR Speech Mechanism	8YR Intelligibility	.13	.17	.05
8YR Speech Mechanism	8YR Language Production	.10	.24	.10
8YR Speech Mechanism	8YR Neurologic Involvement	.20	.40	.10
8YR Pal. Func/Hypernasality	8YR Articulation	.09	.27	.12
8YR Pal. Func/Hypernasality	8YR Intelligibility	.12	.18	.06
	III. 3YR vs. 8YR			
3YR Speech Mechanism	8YR Speech Mechanism	.04	.07	.04
3YR Speech Mechanism	8YR Pal. Func/Hypernasality	.01	.04	.03
3YR Speech Mechanism	8YR Articulation	.07	.20	.12
3YR Speech Mechanism	8YR Intelligibility	.08	.10	.05
3YR Hypernasality	8YR Speech Mechanism	.00	.06	.05
3YR Hypernasality	8YR Pal. Func/Hypernasality	.02	.04	.03
3YR Hypernasality	8YR Articulation	.03	.19	.13
3YR Hypernasality	8YR Intelligibility	.01	.08	.06
3YR Fluency	8YR Speech Mechanism	.00	.06	.04
3YR Articulation	8YR Speech Mechanism	.06	.07	.04
3YR Intelligibility	8YR Speech Mechanism	.05	.10	.04

*p(F2/F1) and p(F2/P1) refer to the probability of failing (scoring in or closest to the lowest decile) the variable in Index 2 (F2) if the variable in Index 1 was failed (F1) or passed (P1).

Correlations Between Indexes and Noncomponent SLH Variables

Correlations were computed also between the four indexes pertaining to speech mechanism and all SLH variables which were not components of those indexes. Only two correlations were of sufficient magnitude to note. One was a correlation of .20 between 3YR Speech Mechanism and the evaluation made by the speech examiner of the intelligibility of the child's speech during administration of the 8YR test battery. The other was a correlation of .17 between 3YR Speech Mechanism and the 3YR Summary Score representing the totality of a child's verbal expression skills (Naming Objects, Sentence Length, Sentence Structure, Relevance of content, Word Order, and Use of Pronouns). All other correlations were ≤.15.

Relationship of NCPP Variables to Indexes

Correlation Screen and Cross-tabulations

What conditions in the biological, psychological, and social background of the children are related to and predictive of dysfunction of their speech mechanism? To answer this question, selected NCPP* variables were correlated with the four indexes pertaining to speech mechanism function. Unfortunately, this statistic proved not useful in yielding the answer in this study, involving as it did an extremely large sample which did not meet the requirement of normal bivariate distribution. None of the obtained correlations was of a magnitude worth discussing ($r \leq .13$) except for a peculiar set of correlations between 3YR Hypernasality and an array of seemingly irrelevant variables, to be discussed below.

Again recourse was made to cross-tabulations, which permit a contrast between the likelihood of failing on an index when one has (a) failed or (b) passed an antecedent NCPP measure. For example, if a White Male child fails the eight-month Bayley item Enjoys Sound Production (Bayley, 1958), the probability is .50 that he will fail 3YR Speech Mechanism; in contrast, the probability is only .29 that a White Male child who passes this Bayley item will fail the index. Evaluation of these two probabilities gives more information than does the correlation of $<.10$.

3YR Speech Mechanism Table 9-8 presents the interesting cross-tabulations of NCPP variables and 3YR Speech Mechanism. Only items for which substantial numbers occurred in all cells are reported. Several signs emerged from the children's communicative and other behavior that may serve as cues to the pos-

sibility that they have some speech mechanism dysfunction. Even though the number of children who failed on these particular measures was in some cases quite small, probabilities that failure signals a speech mechanism problem were such that one would be well advised to scrutinize those children particularly. Nine measures derived from administration of the eight-month Bayley scales provided such cues (Part I, Table 9-8). Some relate to judgments of the child's vocalization. If a child failed to vocalize to a social stimulus, the probability was .63 that he would fail 3YR Speech Mechanism; this is 2.5 times the risk than if he passed the item (probability .25). If he failed to vocalize two syllables, the probability was .57 that he would fail 3YR Speech Mechanism, the risk being over twice that if he vocalized two syllables (.25). Similar contrasts are seen with regard to the child's failure to enjoy sound production (particularly true among White Male children, for whom the probabilities were .50 and .29), and failure to vocalize attitudes (particularly among children in the highest socioeconomic groups, where probabilities were of the order of .50 and .17).

Other Bayley items relate to the child's response to sound. Probabilities of failure on 3YR Speech Mechanism were much greater in cases of failure to turn head to sound of a bell or a rattle or failure to search with eyes for sound than in cases where these measures were passed. The Bayley final diagnosis (failure to pass as "normal" or "suspect") and the Bayley motor score similarly cued the likelihood of failure on 3YR Speech Mechanism. It is of some interest that the Bayley Fine Motor Development and Gross Motor Development judgments both correlated with 3YR Speech Mechanism $<.10$; the conditional probabilities were such that failure on these Bayley measures did not provide a cue that there may be speech mechanism dysfunction.

Certain physical signs may also be

---

* Non-SLH variables in the NINCDS Collaborative Perinatal Project (NCPP).

Table 9-8

Correlations and conditional probabilities for NCPP variables and 3YR Speech Mechanism.

NCPP Variables	r	p(F2/F1)*	p(F2/P1)*
I. Eight-Month Bayley Measures			
Bayley: Vocalizes to a Social Stimulus	<.10	.63	.25
Bayley: Vocalizes Two Syllables	<.10	.57	.25
Bayley: Enjoys Sound Production	<.10	.36	.24
Bayley: Vocalizes Attitudes	<.10	.32	.25
Bayley: Turns Head to Sound of Bell	<.10	.58	.25
Bayley: Turns Head to Sound of Rattle	<.10	.58	.25
Bayley: Searches with Eyes for Sound	<.10	.70	.25
Bayley: Final diagnosis	<.10	.46	.25
Bayley: Motor Score	<.10	.36	.24
II. Physical Signs			
Newborn: Syndromes	<.10	.64	.25
12-Month: Syndromes	<.10	.39	.25
12-Month: Eye Conditions	<.10	.34	.25
12-Month: Skeletal Conditions	<.10	.36	.25
7YR: Neurologic Abnormalities	<.10	.35	.23
7YR: Neurologic Abnormalities (Suspicious)	<.10	.49	.24
III. Family Factors			
Mental retardation: Gravida	<.10	.32	.25
Mental retardation: Father	<.10	.38	.25
Diabetes: Gravida (onset before age 15)	<.10	.39	.25
Prior Siblings with Sensory Defects or Trouble Speaking	<.10	.44	.26
Prior Siblings with Cleft Palate	<.10	.38	.26
Prior Siblings with Head or Spine Congenital Malformations	<.10	.37	.26
Prior Siblings with Motor Defects of Infectious Etiology	<.10	.34	.26

*p(F2/F1) and p(F2/P1) refer to the probability of failing 3YR Speech Mechanism (F2) if the NCPP variable was failed (F1) or passed (P1).

early indicators of possible speech mechanism dysfunction (Part II, Table 9-8). These include identification of a syndrome (for example, Down's, Pierre-Robin, and so forth) at birth and in the 12-month pediatric summary; reporting of deviant eye conditions in the 12-month pediatric summary (particularly in the case of lower socioeconomic group children where probabilities are around .42 and .26); and finding of abnormal skeletal conditions during the first year (especially in the case of Black children and children in the lower socioeconomic group). The failure on 3YR Speech Mechanism also was seen likely to be related to the identification or the suspicion of neurologic abnormalities at seven years, particularly in lower socioeconomic groups.

Certain family factors were associated with heightened risk of failing 3YR Speech Mechanism (Part III, Table 9-8). These included mental retardation on the part of both the mother and the father, diabetes of early onset in the mother, as well as incidence among older siblings of trouble speaking, cleft palate, head or spine congenital malformation, and motor defects of infectious etiology.

3YR Hypernasality Table 9-9 presents the correlations of appreciable magnitude together with additional interesting cross-tabulations of NCPP variables and 3YR Hypernasality. Sizeable correlations were obtained with several 7YR psychological test variables and some variables pertaining to characteristics of the mother and the home situation. It turns out that these correlations were spuriously high, apparent artifacts of the existence of a small group of children with judged hypernasality who were also judged by a psychological examiner to present certain behavioral deviations and family characteristics. The cross-tabulations shown make it clear that failing 3YR Hypernasality was no more likely to be associated with these behavioral deviations or family characteristics than was passing 3YR Hypernasality. Our conclusion is that the apparent relationships suggested by the correlation coefficients should be discounted.

The last four entries in Table 9-9 show that three eight-month Bayley motor measures and a one-year summary measure reporting neurologic abnormalities all failed to predict failure on 3YR Hypernasality.

8YR Speech Mechanism Table 9-10 presents the interesting cross-tabulations of NCPP variables and 8YR Speech Mechanism. As at the 3YR level, so at this level we find that several of the children's communicative and other behaviors at earlier ages can serve as cues to the possibility of speech mechanism dysfunction (Part I, Table 9-10). Failures on six of the eight-month Bayley items pertaining to vocalization and response to sound were associated with considerably higher probabilities of failure on 8YR Speech Mechanism than were found when those Bayley items are passed. If the 4YR Stanford-Binet (Terman and Merrill, 1960) examiner reported the child to be nonverbal, the probability of the child's failing 8YR Speech Mechanism (.25) was five times greater than if he had not been so described (.05). Likewise, judgments of both extreme impulsivity and being ex-

Table **9-9**

Correlations and conditional probabilities for NCPP variables and 3YR Hypernasality.

NCPP Variables	r	p(F2/F1)*	p(F2/P1)*
WISC Verbal IQ	.50	.13	.12
WISC Performance IQ	.43	.14	.11
WISC Full-Scale IQ	.49	.05	.04
7YR Psych.: Cooperation: Extreme Negativism	.39	.00	.00
7YR Psych.: Dependency: Extremely Self-reliant	.52	.00	.00
7YR Psych.: Goal Orientation: No effort	.41	.00	.00
7YR Psych.: Extremely Inactive	.37	.00	.00
7YR Psych.: Nature of Activity: Variable	.74	.00	.00
7YR Psych.: Extremely Assertive, Willful	.46	.01	.00
7YR Psych.: Very Hostile	.59	.00	.00
7YR Psych.: Echolalia	.47	.01	.00
Mother's Occupation: Service Work	.44	.76	.80
Mother's Occupation: Farmer, Laborer	.85	.00	.00
Bayley: 8-Month Motor Score	<.10	.12	.07
Bayley: Fine Motor Development	<.10	.02	.01
Bayley: Gross Motor Development	<.10	.02	.01
Ped. 12: Neurologic Abnormalities	<.10	.09	.05

*p(F2/F1) and p(F2/P1) refer to the probability of failing 3YR Hypernasality (F2) if the NCPP variable was failed (F1) or passed (P1).

Table **9-10**

Correlations and conditional probabilities for NCPP variables and 8YR Speech Mechanism.

NCPP Variables	r	p(F2/F1)*	p(F2/P1)*
I. Observed Behaviors			
Bayley: Vocalizes to a Social Stimulus	<.10	.25	.06
Bayley: Vocalizes Two Syllables	<.10	.19	.06
Bayley: Vocalizes Attitudes	<.10	.12	.06
Bayley: Turns Head to Sound of Bell	<.10	.20	.06
Bayley: Turns Head to Sound of Rattle	<.10	.22	.06
Bayley: Searches with Eyes for Sound	<.10	.29	.06
S-B: Communication: Nonverbal	<.10	.25	.05
S-B: Level of Activity: Extremely Impulsive	<.10	.15	.05
S-B: Irritability: Extremely Phlegmatic	<.10	.16	.05
S-BII: Picture Vocabulary	<.10	.32	.05
S-BII: Word Combination	<.10	.30	.05
S-BII-6: Picture Vocabulary	<.10	.16	.05
7YR WISC: Full-Scale IQ	<.10	.19	.05
7YR Psych.: Tester's Report: Little/None Communication	<.10	.22	.06
7YR Psych.: Echolalia	<.10	.21	.06
7YR Mother's Report: Child Has Trouble Speaking	<.10	.20	.06
7YR WRAT: In Non-Graded Special Class	<.10	.34	.06
II. Physical Signs			
Blindness	<.10	.20	.06
Newborn: Abnormal Conditions and Presumed Anoxia	<.10	.20	.06
Newborn: Presumed Anoxia and Trauma	<.10	.21	.06
Newborn: Syndromes	<.10	.28	.06
7YR Neurologic Abnormalities	<.10	.17	.05
III. Family Factors			
Mental Retardation: Gravida	<.10	.22	.06

*p(F2/F1) and p(F2/P1) refer to the probability of failing 8YR Speech Mechanism (F2) if the NCPP variable was failed (F1) or passed (P1).

tremely phlegmatic were three times more likely to be associated with failure on 8YR Speech Mechanism than were contrary judgments. Poor performance on two subtests of the Stanford-Binet at level II (Picture Vocabulary and Word Combination) and one subtest at level II-6 (Picture Vocabulary) was much more likely to be associated with failure on 8YR Speech Mechanism than was good performance.

Five observations at the 7YR level also were cues worth following up. These included the WISC Full-Scale IQ (Wechsler, 1949) and the examiner's reports of little or no communication and of echolalia (the latter being an especially important cue among Black children). In fact, it turns out that both the examiner's report of little or no communication and the mother's report that the child had trouble speaking were better predictors of failure on 8YR Speech Mechanism than was failure on 3YR Speech Mechanism. The report made in connection with administration of the Wide Range Achievement Test (Jastak and Jastak, 1965) that the child was in a nongraded special class was associated with failure on 8YR Speech Mechanism (.34) almost six times more frequently than the report that he was not in such a special class (.06).

Physical signs noted earlier in the child's life may signal 8YR Speech Mechanism dysfunction (Part II, Table 9-10). These include blindness, the report at birth of presumed anoxia, trauma, and specific syndromes (for example, Down's), and the report of neurological abnormalities at the time of the 7YR examination.

If the mother was mentally retarded, the likelihood (.22) of the child failing 8YR Speech Mechanism was about four times as great as when the mother was not mentally retarded (.06) (Part III, Table 9-10).

8YR Palatal Function/Hypernasality Table 9-11 shows the cross-tabulations for NCPP variables that one might expect to be related to failure on 8YR Palatal Function/Hypernasality. Only one of these variables turned out to be a useful predictor of failure on this index. If the examiner who administered the WRAT at seven years noted that the child was receiving speech therapy, the probability of failure on 8YR Palatal Function/Hypernasality (.17) was four times the probability of failure if he was not receiving speech therapy (.04). None of the Bayley scores, IQ measures, or reports of neurological abnormalities at 7YR proved to be useful predictors, nor did any NCPP variables related to circumstances of pregnancy, birth, or neonatal life.

Multiple Regression Analysis

A multiple correlation procedure was used to assess the degree of relationship between several NCPP variables (designated independent variables) and the four speech mechanism indexes (each designated a dependent variable). At the 3YR level, the following NCPP variables were selected to serve as independent variables: Birthweight, Gestational Age, Education of Gravida, Per Capita Income, Education of Father, Occupation of Father, race, and sex. In a second analysis

two eight-month variables from the Bayley were added: Eight-Month Mental Score and Eight-Month Motor Score.

Table 9-12 presents for the 3YR speech mechanism indexes the multiple R's, R^2's, and the beta coefficients for the several independent variables. The multiple R's are low (.11 and .05). The smallness of R^2's shows that practically none of the variance of these two indexes was determined by the independent variables selected. The addition of the two eight-month Bayley scores did not alter the multiple R's; it only reduced slightly the beta coefficients for the socioeconomic variables (Education of Gravida, Per Capita Income, Education of Father, Occupation of Father) and race and sex variables which are positively correlated with intelligence of the child.

At the 8YR level, five multiple correlations were computed: (1) using the nine At-Birth NCPP variables listed above; (2) using these nine plus two Bayley scores (Eight-Month Mental Score and Eight-Month Motor Score); (3) using these 11 plus 4YR IQ; (4) using the nine 3YR indexes; and (5) using the nine 3YR indexes plus the original nine At-Birth NCPP variables. Table 9-13 presents for the 8YR Speech Mechanism the multiple R's, R^2's and the beta coefficients for the independent variables, and Table 9-14 presents the same for 8YR Palatal Function/Hypernasality. Once again it can be seen that the multiple R's are low, none being larger than .12. The very small R^2's show that almost none of the variance of these two 8YR indexes was determined by the independent variables selected. The addition of intelligence indicators altered the multiple R's negligibily; it served to reduce the magnitude of the beta coefficients for socioeconomic, race, and sex variables, which are positively correlated with the child's intelligence. The addition of 3YR variables added little to the prediction.

In summary, none of the multiple correlations is large enough to serve predictive or diagnostic purposes.

214

Table **9-11**

Correlations and conditional probabilities for NCPP variables and 8YR Palatal Function/Hypernasality.

NCPP Variables	r	p(F2/F1)*	p(F2/P1)*
Bayley: Motor Score	<.10	.06	.04
Bayley: Fine Motor Development	<.10	.03	.02
Bayley: Gross Motor Development	<.10	.04	.02
Ped. 12: Neurologic Abnormalities	<.10	.05	.03
4YR Stanford-Binet IQ	<.10	.10	.03
7YR WISC: Verbal IQ	<.10	.07	.03
7YR WISC: Performance IQ	<.10	.06	.04
7YR WISC: Full-Scale IQ	<.10	.12	.04
7YR Neurologic Abnormalities	<.10	.07	.03
7YR Neurologic Abnormalities (Suspicious)	<.10	.11	.04
7YR WRAT: In Speech Class	<.10	.17	.04

*p(F2/F1) and p(F2/P1) refer to the probability of failing 8YR Palatal Function/Hypernasality (F2) if the NCPP variable was failed (F1) or passed (P1).

Table **9-12**

Multiple correlations between the 3YR Speech Mechanism Indexes and selected independent variables with beta coefficients.

	3YR Speech Mechanism		3YR Hypernasality	
	At-Birth NCPP variables	At-Birth NCPP variables plus 8-Month NCPP variables	At-Birth NCPP variables	At-Birth NCPP variables plus 8-Month NCPP variables
Multiple R	.106	.109	.0501	.0526
R Square	.0112	.0118	.00251	.00277
Birthweight	.0322	.0259	.0148	.0113
Gestational Age	−.00431	−.00817	−.00282	−.00496
Education of Gravida	.0229	.00227	.0207	.0205
Per Capita Income	.0450	.0420	.00338	.00176
Education of F.O.B.*	.0181	.0175	.00309	.00242
Occupation of F.O.B.*	.0240	.0240	.0231	.0203
8-Month Mental Score		.0130		−.00302
8-Month Motor Score		.0173		.0184
Race-Sex Marker I	−.0920	−.0897	−.0253	−.0236
Race-Sex Marker II	−.0244	−.0238	−.0309	−.0305
Race-Sex Marker III	.0154	.0154	.00919	.00910

*Father of the baby.

Table **9-13**

Multiple correlations between 8YR Speech Mechanism and selected independent variables with beta coefficients.

	At-Birth NCPP variables	At-Birth NCPP variables plus 8-Month NCPP variables	At-Birth NCPP variables plus 8-Month NCPP variables plus 4YR IQ	3YR indexes	3YR indexes plus At-Birth NCPP variables
Multiple R	.075	.091	.106	.089	.115
R Square	.006	.008	.011	.008	.013
3YR Speech Mechanism				.0220	.0246
3YR Hypernasality				−.00198	−.00171
3YR Fluency				.00580	.00548
3YR Articulation				.0452	.0411
3YR Intelligibility				−.00399	−.00516
3YR Language Comprehension				.0297	.0145
3YR Sentence Complexity				.0127	.0132
3YR Auditory Memory				.0354	.0400
3YR Hearing Screen				.0160	.0185
Birthweight	.00773	−.00492	−.00841		.0175
Gestational Age	.0272	.0197	.0203		.0163
Education of Gravida	.0292	.0289	.0194		.0238
Per Capita Income	−.0187	−.0241	−.0298		−.0327
Education of F.O.B.*	.0202	.0176	.0101		.0117
Occupation of F.O.B.*	−.00615	−.00489	−.00952		−.0230
8-Month Mental Score		.0300	.0230		
8-Month Motor Score		.0313	.0249		
4YR IQ			.0653		
Race-Sex Marker I	−.0125	−.00799	−.0158		.0171
Race-Sex Marker II	.0461	.0476	.0298		.0557
Race-Sex Marker III	−.0534	−.0537	−.0380		−.0702

*Father of the baby.

Special Studies

A number of ancillary questions were developed for which it was believed the extensive data available could provide some answers. These questions pertain to the characteristics and performance of specific subsets of children selected because of anatomic or neuromuscular distinctiveness, intelligence, family status, circumstance of birth, or speech disorder. The following section explores the questions with respect to the Speech Mechanism indexes.

Intelligence

Children in the ALL 8YR sample who took the 7YR WISC were grouped by IQ into ten ranges, and means for the 8YR indexes were calculated for each IQ group. Table 9-15 shows the scores of the children on 8YR Speech Mechanism and 8YR Palatal Function/Hypernasality. Figure 9-3 graphically displays the scores on 8YR Speech Mechanism.

The lowest two IQ groups (IQ scores up to 49) performed somewhat inferiorly on the oral tasks, but the groups with IQ

Table   9-14

Multiple correlations between 8YR Palatal Function/Hypernasality and selected independent variables with beta coefficients.

	At-Birth NCPP variables	At-Birth NCPP variables plus 8-Month NCPP variables	At-Birth NCPP variables plus 8-Month NCPP variables plus 4YR IQ	3YR indexes	3YR indexes plus At-Birth NCPP variables
Multiple R	.050	.075	.086	.061	.086
R Square	.003	.006	.007	.004	.007
3YR Speech Mechanism				.000656	−.00397
3YR Hypernasality				.0169	.0159
3YR Fluency				.00334	.00263
3YR Articulation				.00449	.00571
3YR Intelligibility				.00839	.00129
3YR Language Comprehension				.00987	.0209
3YR Sentence Complexity				.0337	.0309
3YR Auditory Memory				.0178	.0125
3YR Hearing Screen				.0176	.0154
Birthweight	.0148	.0216	.0188		.0135
Gestational Age	.00282	−.00854	−.00799		.00265
Education of Gravida	.0207	.0243	.0167		.0141
Per Capita Income	.00338	.0192	.0146		.0101
Education of F.O.B.*	.00309	.0132	.00713		.0113
Occupation of F.O.B.*	.0231	.00328	−.000440		.0104
8-Month Mental Score		.0129	.00725		
8-Month Motor Score		.00661	.00145		
4YR IQ			.0525		
Race-Sex Marker I	−.0253	−.0614	−.0677		−.0468
Race-Sex Marker II	−.0309	−.0416	−.0559		.00129
Race-Sex Marker III	.00919	.0401	.0527		.0350

*Father of the baby.

of 50 and above performed (means from 7.7 to 7.9) essentially like the ALL 8YR sample, whose mean score on 8YR Speech Mechanism was 7.88 (see Table 9-5). On 8YR Palatal Function/Hypernasality all the groups except White Males at the lowest level performed like the ALL 8YR sample (mean = 2.96, Table 9-6). It should be noted that the lowest IQ groups were small.

A separate analysis was made of 53 children who were mentally retarded (7YR WISC IQ ≤70) and were also reported to present specific syndromes (for example, Down's, Pierre-Robin, Marfan's). The mean IQ of this group was 51 (SD = 15). Their mean score on 8YR Speech Mechanism was 7.3 (SD = 1.7), 0.5 scale value below the mean for ALL 8YR. On 8YR Palatal Function/Hypernasality their mean score was 2.6 (SD = .92), 0.6 scale value below the mean for ALL 8YR.

Family Status

All 8YR children were categorized as singletons, siblings, and twins. Singletons are children without brothers or sis-

Table **9-15**

Means for ALL 8YR Children on the 8YR Speech Mechanism Indexes according to IQ level.

						Grouped 7YR WISC IQ				
	≤39	40-49	50-59	60-69	70-79	80-89	90-99	100-109	110-119	120+
8YR Speech Mechanism										
White Male	2.3*	8.0*	7.3*	7.8	7.7	7.8	7.9	7.9	7.9	7.9
White Female	5.0*	5.3*	7.8*	7.8	7.9	7.9	7.9	7.9	8.0	8.0
Black Male	6.6*	6.3*	7.4	7.6	7.7	7.8	7.9	7.9	8.0	8.0
Black Female	6.6*	6.3*	7.5	7.8	7.8	7.9	7.9	7.9	7.9	7.9
8YR Palatal Function/Hypernasality										
White Male	2.0*	3.0*	2.7*	2.8	2.8	2.9	2.9	3.0	3.0	3.0
White Female	3.0*	3.0*	2.9*	2.8	2.9	2.9	3.0	3.0	3.0	3.0
Black Male	2.8*	2.9*	2.8	3.0	3.0	3.0	3.0	3.0	3.0	3.0
Black Female	2.8*	3.0*	3.0	2.9	3.0	3.0	3.0	3.0	3.0	3.0

*Based on fewer than 20 cases.

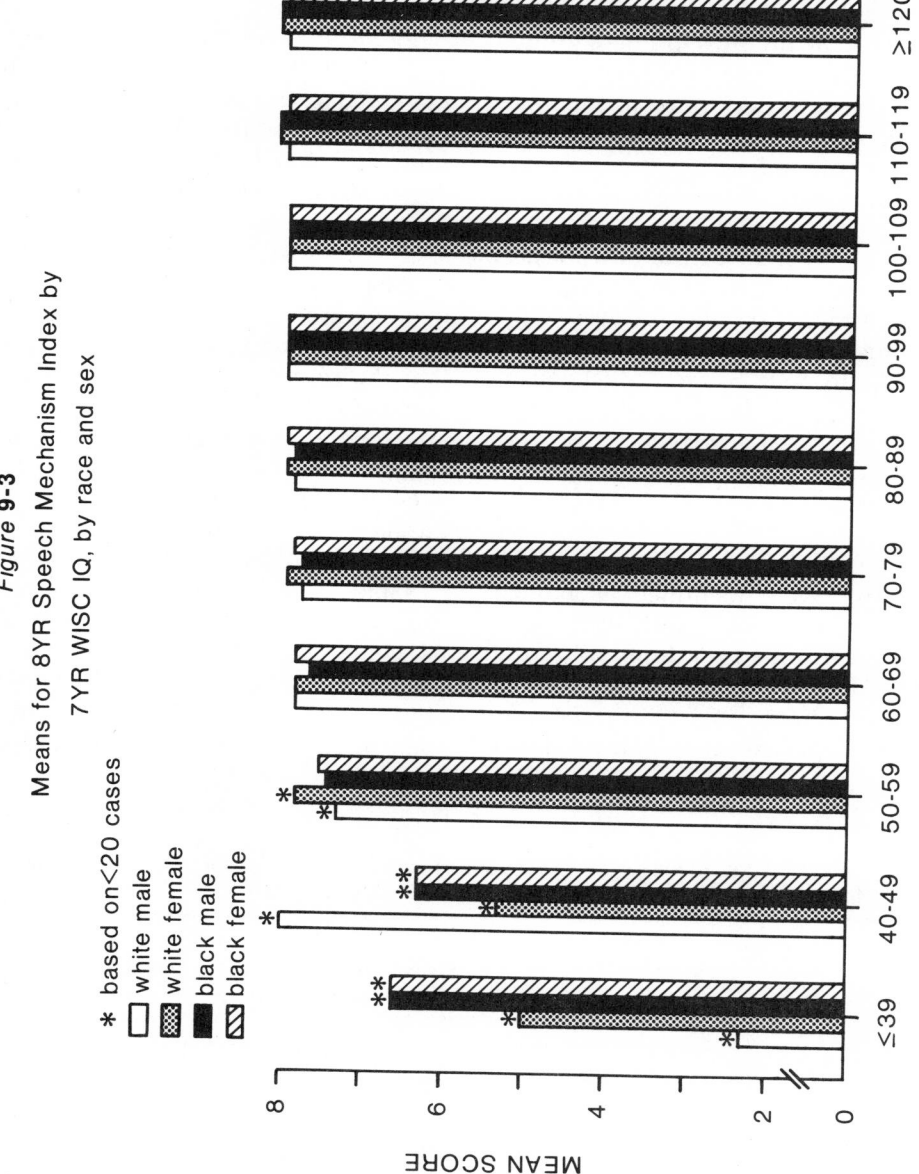

Figure 9-3

Means for 8YR Speech Mechanism Index by
7YR WISC IQ, by race and sex

* based on <20 cases

□ white male
▦ white female
■ black male
▨ black female

MEAN SCORE

Grouped 7YR WISC IQ

≤39 40-49 50-59 60-69 70-79 80-89 90-99 100-109 110-119 ≥120

ters at birth and at seven years; siblings are the two oldest children in the study who are not the result of a multiple birth. A further division was made of children according to whether they were adopted, living with foster parents, living with relatives other than parents, or living with at least one natural parent. Table 9-16 summarizes the findings for these groups on the two 8YR Speech Mechanism Indexes. All groups performed in a manner closely comparable to the total ALL 8YR sample on both indexes; no clinically significant differences among the various groups are discernible.

Table 9-17 further divides the singletons, siblings, and twins subgroups according to race, sex, and socioeconomic status, and Figure 9-4 displays the data pertaining to 8YR Speech Mechanism. Again, no clinically important differences between subgroups emerged.

Cleft Palate Group

Twenty-four children from the ALL 8YR sample were identified as having unrepaired or repaired clefts of the palate. They performed no differently from the total ALL 8YR sample on 8YR Speech Mechanism (mean = 7.9, SD = .34). As would be expected, they earned lower and more variable scores on 8YR Palatal Function/Hypernasality. Their mean score of 2.3 (SD = 1.2) is contrasted with the ALL 8YR mean of 2.96 (SD = .25), where a perfect score would be 3.0.

Cerebral Palsy Group

Eighty-nine of the ALL 3YR sample and 83 of the ALL 8YR sample were identified as children with cerebral palsy. Since such children's neuromotor dysfunction often implicates the speech mechanism, their performance on the four speech mechanism indexes was of special interest.

Table 9-18 presents the scores on the two 3YR indexes for the 89 three-year-old cerebral palsied children. It can be seen that the cerebral palsied children exhibited marked difficulty in executing the lip and tongue movements required in the speech mechanism examination. However, their performance on 3YR Hypernasality was not judged to be substantially different from that of ALL 3YR.

Table 9-19 summarizes the performance on 8YR Speech Mechanism of the 83 eight-year-old cerebral palsied children, as a total group and subdivided according to the degree of severity of their neuromotor involvement and clini-

Table **9-16**

Means and standard deviations for the 8YR Speech Mechanism Indexes for ALL 8YR children categorized according to family status.

	N	8YR Speech Mechanism		8YR Palatal Function/Hypernasality	
		Mean	SD	Mean	SD
Singletons	879	7.9	.75	3.0	.24
Siblings	3,880	7.9	.69	3.0	.23
Twins	370	7.9	.64	3.0	.23
Adopted	243*	8.0	.20	3.0	.23
In foster homes	277*	7.8	.84	2.9	.40
With other relative	621*	7.9	.74	3.0	.25
With at least one natural parent	23,931*	7.9	.68	3.0	.25

*N is based on 3YR and 8YR combined; mean and SD based on those given the 8YR test.

Table 9-17

Means and standard deviations for the 8YR Speech Mechanism Indexes for ALL 8YR children categorized according to family status and subdivided according to sex, race and Socioeconomic Index.

| | 8YR Speech Mechanism | | | | | | 8YR Palatal Function/Hypernasality | | | | | |
| | Singletons | | Siblings | | Twins | | Singletons | | Siblings | | Twins | |
	Mean	SD	Mean	SD	Mean	SD	Mean	SD	Mean	SD	Mean	SD
Male	7.8	.83	7.8	.80	7.8	.87	3.0	.25	3.0	.23	2.9	.31
Female	7.9	.66	8.0	.56	8.0	.30	3.0	.23	3.0	.22	3.0	.10
White	7.9	.58	7.9	.60	7.9	.60	3.0	.26	3.0	.24	3.0	.29
Black	7.8	.87	7.8	.80	7.9	.68	3.0	.22	3.0	.19	3.0	.16
SEI 0.0-1.9	7.8	.76	7.8	.86	7.6	1.1	2.9	.29	3.0	.28	2.9	.38
SEI 2.0-3.9	7.9	.70	7.9	.70	7.9	.61	3.0	.23	3.0	.25	3.0	.27
SEI 4.0-5.9	7.8	.76	7.9	.70	7.9	.63	3.0	.29	3.0	.21	3.0	.20
SEI 6.0-7.9	7.9	.65	7.9	.74	8.0	.00	3.0	.18	3.0	.21	3.0	.17
SEI 8.0-9.5	7.8	.97	7.9	.43	7.9	.86	3.0	.18	3.0	.20	3.0	.00

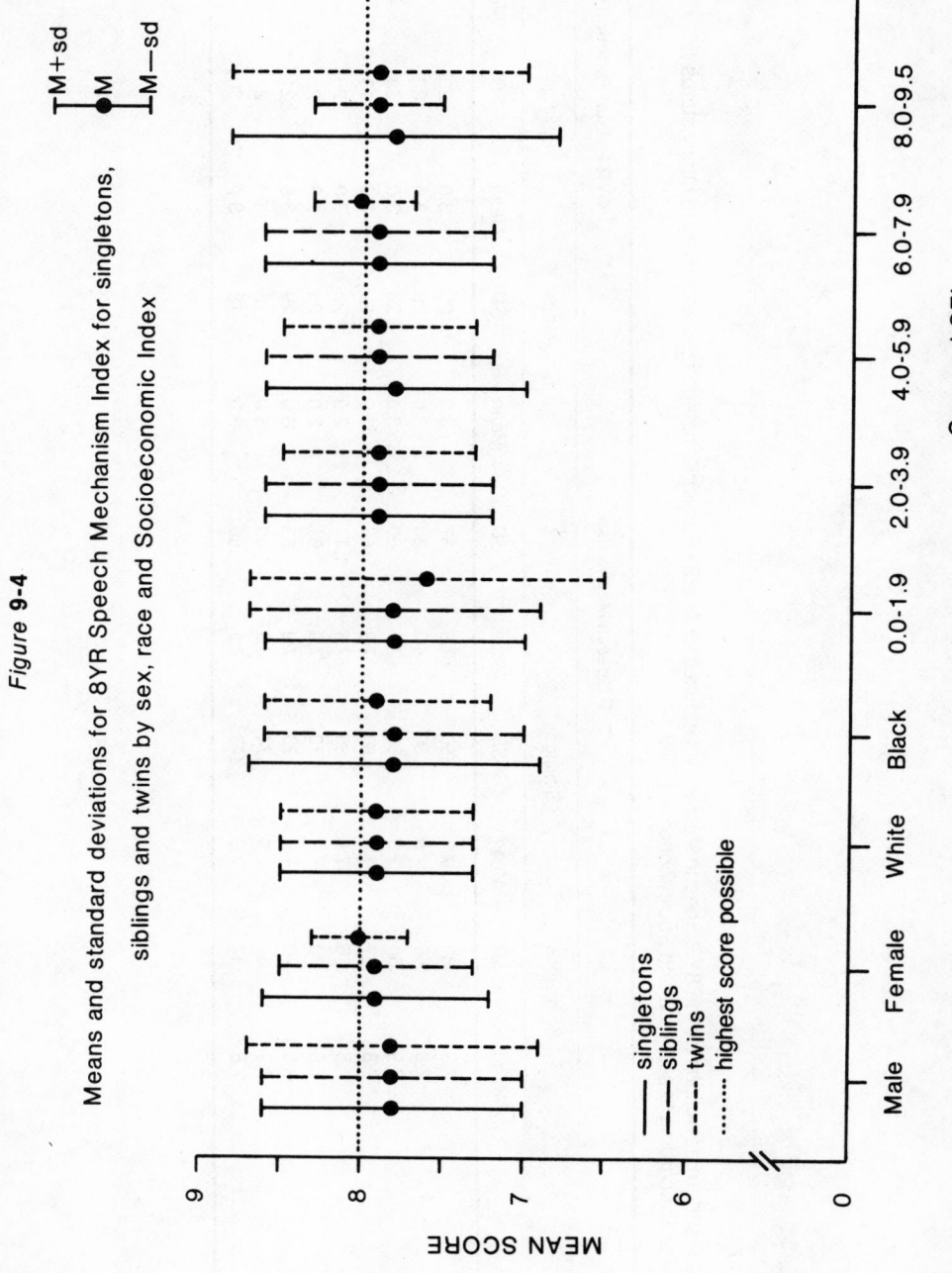

Figure **9-4**

Means and standard deviations for 8YR Speech Mechanism Index for singletons, siblings and twins by sex, race and Socioeconomic Index

222

Table **9-18**

Means and standard deviations for 89 cerebral palsied children on the 3YR Speech Mechanism Indexes, by race, sex and Socioeconomic Index. Comparable data for the ALL 3YR sample are shown below.

| | | White Male | White Female | Black Male | Black Female | Socioeconomic Index† | | | | | |
						1	2	3	4	5	Total
Cerebral Palsy Subsample											
3YR Speech Mechanism	Mean	5.0*	4.4*	5.0*	4.7*	4.9*	4.7*	5.4*	4.0*	3.0*	4.8
	SD	2.9	3.0	2.8	3.6	3.2	3.1	2.8	2.8	.0	2.9
3YR Hypernasality (percentage passing)		100	92	100	86	86	100	95	100	100	96
All 3YR Sample											
3YR Speech Mechanism	Mean	6.5	6.6	6.6	6.7	6.6	6.6	6.6	6.6	6.8	6.6
	SD	1.5	1.3	1.3	1.1	1.3	1.4	1.3	1.3	1.0	1.3
3YR Hypernasality (percentage passing)		99	99	99	99	99	99	99	99	99	99

*Based on fewer than 20 cases.
†SEI:1 0.0-1.9
2 2.0-3.9
3 4.0-5.9
4 6.0-7.9
5 8.0-9.5

Table **9-19**

Means and standard deviations for 8YR Speech Mechanism Index for 83 cerebral palsied children according to severity of neuromotor involvement and clinical type of cerebral palsy, by sex, race and Socioeconomic Index.

| | N | | White Male | White Female | Black Male | Black Female | Socioeconomic Index† | | | | | Total |
							1	2	3	4	5	
Total Group	83	Mean	7.1	6.4	6.6*	6.0*	5.5*	6.4	7.0	7.8*	6.8*	6.7
		SD	1.9	2.8	2.1	2.8	2.6	2.2	2.4	.77	2.5	2.2
Mild	44	Mean	6.9	8.0*	7.7*	6.3*	7.0*	6.5*	7.2*	7.7*	8.0*	7.1
		SD	2.1	.0	.67	2.6	1.9	2.3	2.0	1.0	.0	1.9
Moderate and Severe	39	Mean	7.5*	5.6*	5.1*	5.0*	2.8*	6.3*	6.5*	8.0*	6.3*	6.2
		SD	1.4	3.2	2.4	4.2	.5	2.2	3.2	.0	2.9	2.5
Hemiparesis	31	Mean	7.9*	7.7*	7.0*	6.8*	5.5*	7.5*	7.9*	8.0*	8.0*	7.5
		SD	.28	.58	1.8	2.5	2.9	.76	.35	.0	.0	1.3
Spastic Diplegia	21	Mean	6.0*	8.0*	6.5*	5.5*	7.3*	6.3*	5.8*	8.0*	††	6.6*
		SD	3.1	.0	1.9	3.5	1.2	2.7	3.0	.0	††	2.3
Spastic Quadriplegia	11	Mean	6.0*	5.5*	3.0*	2.0*	2.7*	5.5*	8.0*	5.0*	††	5.0*
		SD	2.4	3.5	.0	.0	.58	3.5	.0	.0	††	2.6
Dyskinesia/ Ataxia	25	Mean	6.6*	3.5*	5.4*	8.0*	4.3*	5.5*	6.0*	8.0*	5.5*	5.8
		SD	2.4	3.3	2.6	.0	2.5	2.5	3.5	.0	3.5	2.7
Mixed	9	Mean	4.3*	3.7*	3.3*	††	3.0*	5.0*	3.3*	††	††	3.8*
		SD	3.2	4.0	.58	††	.0	2.6	4.2	††	††	2.6

*Based on fewer than 20 cases.
†SEI: 1 0.0-1.9
    2 2.0-3.9
    3 4.0-5.9
    4 6.0-7.9
    5 8.0-9.5
†† = Not available.

cal type of cerebral palsy. Comparing the mean values shown with the mean for ALL 8YR (7.9, SD = .68), we can see that the children showed clinically significant impairment of the ability to execute lip and tongue movements volitionally. The motor disability was most marked in the lower socioeconomic division of the total group (mean 5.5). It was understandably more marked in those whose total neuromotor involvement was judged to be moderate or severe (mean 6.2) than in those in whom it was judged to be mild (mean 7.1). It was most marked in the group of mixed clinical type (mean 3.8) and in the group with spastic quadriplegia (mean 5.0), only slightly less marked in the dyskinesia/ataxia group (mean 5.8). The spastic diplegia group showed less oral impairment (mean 6.6), and the hemiparesis group approximated the ALL 8YR performance (mean 7.5).

The group differences are clear and appear to be of clinical significance. They might have been even clearer had all of the cerebral palsied children identified at three years been available for retesting at eight years. Of 125 cerebral palsied children for whom data at both age levels were not available, 119 originally were diagnosed as moderate or severe. The 8YR data, then, are not as fully representative of the population of cerebral palsied children as one would wish.

Table 9-20 presents similar data pertaining to 8YR Palatal Function/ Hypernasality. The cerebral palsied children were less deviant with regard to palatal function than with regard to lip and tongue function, and largely resembled the ALL 8YR sample whose mean score was 2.96 (SD = .25). The spastic diplegia subgroup was most deviant (mean 2.7), but group differences do not appear to be clinically significant.

Other Communication Disorders

A group of 35 stuttering children was singled out for study at the 8YR level, as were groups of children with conductive hearing loss (monaural and binaural losses combined, N = 1024) and sensorineural hearing loss (monaural and binaural losses combined, N = 447). The latter were compared with the group of normal hearing eight-year-old children (N = 18,438).

Table 9-21 shows that the stuttering group was not clinically different from the ALL 8YR sample on the two 8YR Speech Mechanism indexes. The children with hearing losses could not be distinguished from either the normal hearing children or the ALL 8YR sample on these indexes. A further study of the hearing groups showed negligible differences when they were analyzed according to sex, race, and socioeconomic status.

Unusual Birth Conditions

A group of 917 children born prematurely (birthweight ≤2500 grams and gestation ≤36 weeks) were studied. Table 9-22 shows that the premature group, as well as the ALL 8YR subgroups divided according to birthweight, performed on both 8YR speech mechanism indexes in a manner not distinguishable from the total ALL 8YR sample.

Discussion

Many three-year-old children were unable to cooperate in performance of the required lip and tongue movements and diadochokinetic maneuvers. The data obtained from those who would or could cooperate proved generally unrevealing with regard to their expressive speech abilities at that time, even with regard to their articulation. And the three-year data were of no value in predicting either speech mechanism function or speech skills at eight years. A review of all the outcomes of the tests of speech mechanism function at ages three and eight leads to the conclusions that (1) these tests are more difficult to administer suc-

Table 9-20

Means and standard deviations for 8YR Palatal Function/Hypernasality for cerebral palsied children according to severity of neuromotor involvement and clinical type of cerebral palsy, by race, sex and Socioeconomic Index.

	N		White Male	White Female	Black Male	Black Female	Socioeconomic Index† 1	2	3	4	5	Total
Total Group	83	Mean	2.9	2.9*	2.9*	2.8*	2.9*	2.8	2.9*	2.9*	3.0*	2.9
		SD	.59	.30	.32	.45	.32	.69	.24	.50	.0	.48
Mild	44	Mean	2.9	3.0*	2.9*	3.0*	3.0*	2.8*	2.9*	3.0*	3.0*	2.9
		SD	.64	.0	.30	.0	.0	.87	.29	.0	.0	.49
Moderate and Severe	39	Mean	2.9*	2.9*	2.9*	2.0*	2.7*	2.8*	3.0*	2.7*	3.0*	2.8
		SD	.53	.38	.38	.0	.58	.42	.0	.76	.0	.47
Hemiparesis	31	Mean	3.0*	2.7*	2.9*	3.0*	3.0*	2.9*	2.9*	3.0*	3.0*	2.9
		SD	.0	.58	.35	.0	.0	.35	.33	.0	.0	.26
Spastic Diplegia	21	Mean	2.3*	3.0*	3.0*	2.5*	3.0*	2.4*	3.0*	2.5*	††	2.7*
		SD	1.3	.0	.0	.71	.0	1.1	.0	1.0	††	.84
Spastic Quadriplegia	11	Mean	3.0*	3.0*	††	††	3.0*	3.0*	3.0*	3.0*	††	3.0*
		SD	.0	.0	††	††	.0	.0	.0	.0	††	.0
Dyskinesia/ Ataxia	25	Mean	3.0*	3.0*	2.9*	††	2.8*	3.0*	3.0*	3.0*	3.0*	3.0
		SD	.0	.0	.38	††	.50	.0	.0	.0	.0	.22
Mixed	9	Mean	3.0*	3.0*	3.0*	††	3.0*	3.0*	3.0*	††	††	3.0*
		SD	.0	.0	.0	††	.0	.0	.0	††	††	.0

*Based on fewer than 20 cases.

†SEI: 1 0.0-1.9
    2 2.0-3.9
    3 4.0-5.9
    4 6.0-7.9
    5 8.0-9.5

†† = Not available.

Table **9-21**

Means and standard deviations for 8YR Speech Mechanism Indexes for stutterers and children with hearing losses compared to ALL 8YR sample and all normal hearing 8YR sample.

	N	8YR Speech Mechanism		8YR Palatal Function/ Hypernasality	
		Mean	SD	Mean	SD
Stutterers	35	7.6	1.4	2.9	.35
Conductive Hearing Loss	1,024	7.8	.80	2.9	.36
Sensorineural Hearing Loss	447	7.9	.71	2.9	.39
Normal Hearing	18,438	7.9	.64	2.9	.23
ALL 8YR	20,137	7.9	.68	3.0	.25

Table **9-22**

Means and standard deviations for the 8YR Speech Mechanism Indexes for children born prematurely and for subgroups of 8YR sample by birthweight.

	N	8YR Speech Mechanism		8YR Palatal Function/ Hypernasality	
		Mean	SD	Mean	SD
Premature	917	7.8	.82	2.9	.30
≤1,500 gm	100	7.7	1.1	2.9	.45
1,501-2,500 gm	1,905	7.9	.73	3.0	.26
2,501-3,500 gm	12,948	7.9	.68	3.0	.25
3,501-4,500 gm	4,998	7.9	.64	3.0	.23
4,501 gm +	166	7.9	.65	3.0	.32
ALL 8YR	20,137	7.9	.68	3.0	.25

cessfully at three years, and (2) they yield information that throws little light on the communication skills of young children except in cases of anatomical or physiological impairment.

Early observations of the child may portend dysfunction of the speech mechanism even though dependable direct measures of a young child's speech mechanism are lacking. Eight-month observations of limited vocalization and failure to respond to sound are especially telling cues. The presence of identified syndromes, deviant eye conditions, deviant skeletal conditions, and suspected neurological abnormalities also lead to the expectation of a higher than average incidence of speech mechanism dysfunction.

Measures of speech mechanism function made at eight years are no better than 3YR measures in predicting speech skills; all correlations are low and conditional probabilities are of little help. Regrettably, measures of oral diadochokinesis were not obtained at eight years, so information is lacking that has been found useful at older age levels.

The finding that 3YR and 8YR speech mechanism measures correlate poorly with speech production measures in the general population of children was not unexpected. Winitz (1969) reviewed the literature on the relationship between

227

oral and facial motor skills and articulatory proficiency. Most of the studies which have shown a significant relationship (that is, significant differences between control groups with adequate articulation and experimental groups with defective articulation) have used measures of movements involved in producing speech (for example, repetition of words or syllables); these measures Winitz considers unfair to the articulatory defective. Six studies involving children have yielded contradictory findings. Mase (1946) found that only one of five tests of oral diadochokinesis (lip rounding) significantly differentiated his groups. Reid (1947a, 1947b) found that none of her five measures yielded significant correlations with articulation proficiency when chronological age was held constant. Clark (1959) found that normal subjects did significantly better than articulatory defective subjects on two tests (open lips, touch tongue to lollipop, draw tongue back into mouth, close lips; bite lower lip, purse lips, and say *oo*.) Prins (1962a, 1962b) found no group differences on repetition of /pʌ/ and /tʌ/; only one group of children with omission errors did significantly more poorly than a control group on repetition of /kʌ/ and /pʌtʌ/; and three different defective groups (omission errors, interdentalizations, and phonemic substitutions) all performed more poorly than his control group on repetition of /pʌtʌkʌ/. Shelton et al. (1966) found that children who could hold their tongue tips in contact with the alveolar ridge for five seconds on three trials had fewer articulatory errors than those who failed the task, but many children without articulation errors could not hold the tongue position for five seconds for all three trials. Yoss and Darley (1974) found that a group of articulatory defective children identified as presenting a developmental apraxia of speech were significantly poorer than other articulatory defective children in maintaining the correct syllable sequence at a normal rate in repeating /pʌtʌkʌ/.

Obviously articulation skill depends upon many complexly interrelated factors other than oral muscle function. We understand that speech mechanism measures are unlikely to single out decisively poor articulators or speakers who are low in intelligibility from a large population of children. But measures of speech mechanism function do help to identify children with neuromotor impairments and with anatomical deficiencies of the speech apparatus. The data from the present study reaffirm that cerebral palsied children show clinically significant impairment of volitional lip and tongue movements, especially those children whose total neuromotor involvement is judged to be moderate or severe. This finding confirms the findings of Heltman and Peacher (1943), who related the articulatory skill of a group of spastic cerebral palsied children to their oral diadochokinetic rates on five jaw, lip, and tongue maneuvers; they reported a correlation of −.64 between diadochokinetic rate and number of misarticulations, increased to −.76 when age was held constant. Other investigators who studied adult dysarthric subjects reported contradictory findings; Canter (1965) found that oral diadochokinesis correlated highly with speech adequacy in parkinsonian patients, but Kreul (1972) and Ewanowski (1964) reported that their parkinsonian subjects could not be differentiated from normal subjects on oral diadochokinetic measures. Portnoy (1976) found both spastic and ataxic dysarthric subjects to have oral diadochokinetic rates significantly slower than those of normal speakers.

Our cerebral palsied children did better on 8YR Palatal Function/Hypernasality than expected, resembling the ALL 8YR sample. Netsell (1969) reported various patterns of palatopharyngeal dysfunction among cerebral palsied subjects. But our cleft palate children, as expected, earned lower and more variable scores on 8YR Palatal Function/Hypernasality than did the ALL

8YR sample. This is in accord with many studies (for example, Spriesterbach, Moll, and Morris, 1961) of cleft palate subjects, the main cause of whose communication problems (hypernasality, nasal emission of air, distortion of pressure consonants, and substitutions of the glottal plosive for pressure consonants) is incompetence of the palatopharyngeal mechanism. Our cleft palate children, however, did not differ from ALL 8YR on 8YR Speech Mechanism. This finding of essentially normal lip and tongue function is also in accord with earlier research on cleft palate children (Spriesterbach, Moll, and Morris, 1961).

We conclude that measures of lip, tongue, and palate movement and hypernasality will, in the majority of children, reveal little or nothing that explains their speech production status at the time or in future years. But these measures are important in helping to identify children with neurological impairment or anatomical deficiencies and in determining what specific dysfunctions must be dealt with in an intervention program.

Summary

Examinations of the speech mechanism were performed on ALL 3YR and ALL 8YR children, with the following outcomes:

1. Valid measures could not be obtained at 3YR from between 11% and 17% of the children. Those who could or would cooperate well enough displayed little difficulty on Lip Protrusion and Lip Retraction, Midline Tongue Protrusion, Soft Palate Elevation, and oral diadochokinesis, but substantial percentages failed Lateral Tongue Protrusion (15%) and Tongue Elevation (38%). Boys failed more often than girls and Blacks more often than Whites, but no socioeconomic group differences emerged.

2. At 8YR, only 1% to 2% failed speech mechanism measures. No important sex, race, or socioeconomic differences were found.

3. Single speech mechanism measures were not highly correlated with each other at either age level. The highest were 3YR diadochokinesis for lips and tongue (.74), 3YR Lateral Tongue Protrusion and Tongue Elevation (.32), and 8YR Lateral Tongue Protrusion and Tongue Elevation (.27).

4. Single speech mechanism measures were not highly correlated with speech production measures at either age level, most being of a magnitude $\leq.20$.

5. The creation of four speech mechanism indexes (3YR Speech Mechanism, 3YR Hypernasality, 8YR Speech Mechanism, and 8YR Palatal Function/Hypernasality) by grouping related variables into more comprehensive measures failed to add precision either to description or to prediction of speech production measures.

6. Cross-tabulations showed that failures on 3YR Articulation, 3YR Sentence Complexity, and 3YR Auditory Memory were much more likely to occur if children failed 3YR Speech Mechanism indexes than if they passed them. Similarly, failures on 8YR Articulation, 8YR Intelligibility, and 8YR Language Production were much more frequently associated with failing 8YR Speech Mechanism than with passing it.

7. 3YR Speech Mechanism and 3YR Hypernasality are poor predictors of Speech Mechanism function, Articulation, and Intelligibility at eight years.

8. All four speech mechanism indexes yielded low correlations with all individual NCPP variables thought possibly to be related to them.

9. Cross-tabulations showed that among possible NCPP predictors of failure on 3YR Speech Mechanism were failure at eight months to Vocalize to a Social Stimulus, to Vocalize Two Syllables, to Vocalize Attitudes, to Turn Head to Sound of Bell or Rattle, and to Search With Eyes for Sound. Other possible predictors were the Bayley final diagnosis and motor score; incidence of syndromes, eye conditions, skeletal conditions, and neurological abnormalities; mental retardation on the part of parents; and incidence among siblings of speaking and other motor defects, cleft palate, and head or spine malformations.

10. Cross-tabulations showed that among possible predictors of failure on 8YR Speech Mechanism were eight-month Bayley measures of vocalization and response to sound; 4YR reports of being nonverbal, extremely impulsive, or highly phlegmatic; 7YR Full Scale WISC IQ and examiner's reports of little or no communication and of echolalia; the mother's report at 7YR that the child has trouble speaking; incidence of blindness, syndromes, and neurological abnormalities; and mental retardation of the mother.

11. Multiple regression analysis yielded multiple R's and independent variable beta weights too small to serve diagnostic or predictive purposes.

12. Children with cleft palate performed at a clinically significantly lower level than ALL 8YR Palatal Function/Hypernasality but not on 8YR Speech Mechanism.

13. Children identified as cerebral palsied performed at a clinically significantly lower level on both 3YR and 8YR Speech Mechanism than the total group of children at both ages, but on both 3YR and 8YR indexes of Palatal Function/Hypernasality they resembled the total group. Those whose neuromotor involvement was judged to be moderate and severe and those of mixed, spastic hemiplegic, and dyskinesia/ataxia clinical types were most deviant on speech mechanism measures.

14. Children with IQ below 50 performed inferiorly on 8YR speech mechanism indexes, but children in all other IQ ranges approximated ALL 8YR measures.

15. Studies failed to show differences from the total population on speech mechanism indexes of: (a) children categorized according to family status (singletons, siblings, twins, adopted, in foster homes, living with relatives, living with parents), (b) stuttering children, (c) children with conductive or sensorineural hearing losses, (d) premature children, or (e) children categorized according to birthweight.

16. Measures of speech mechanism function are of little use in predicting current or future speech production proficiency, but they help identify children with anatomical deficiencies or neurological impairment and help determine what dysfunctions warrant attention in a remedial program.

References

1. Bayley, N. *COLR Research Form of the Bayley Scales of Mental and Motor Development.* Bethesda, Maryland: Perinatal Research Branch, NINDB-NIH, 1958.

2. Canter, G.J. Speech characteristics of patients with Parkinson's disease. III. Articulation, diadochokinesis, and overall speech adequacy. *J. Speech Hear. Disord.* 30:217–224, 1965.

3. Clark, R.M. Maturation and speech development, Part I. *Logos* 2:49–54, 1959.

4. Ewanowski, S.J. Selected motor-speech behavior of patients with Parkinsonism. Ph.D. dissertation, University of Wisconsin, 1964.

5. Heltman, H.J., and Peacher, G.M. Misarticulation and diadochokinesis in the spastic paralytic. *J. Speech Hear. Disord.* 8:137–145, 1943.

6. Jastak, J.F., and Jastak, S.R. *The Wide Range Achievement Test (WRAT)*. Wilmington, Del.: Guidance Associates, 1965.

7. Kreul, J.E. Neuromuscular control examination (NMC) for Parkinsonism; vowel prolongations and diadochokinetic and reading rates. *J. Speech Hear. Res.* 15:72–83, 1972.

8. Mase, D.J. Etiology of articulatory speech defects. *Teachers College Contributions to Education,* No. 921. New York: Columbia University, 1946.

9. Netsell, R. Evaluation of velopharyngeal function in dysarthria. *J. Speech Hear. Disord.* 34:113–122, 1969.

10. Portnoy, R.A. Computer measurements and listener ratings of syllable repetitions in normal and dysarthric subjects. Ph.D. dissertation, University of Missouri, 1976.

11. Prins, T.D. Analysis of correlations among various articulatory deviations. *J. Speech Hear. Res.* 5:152–160, 1962a.

12. Prins, T.D. Motor and auditory abilities in different groups of children with articulatory deviations. *J. Speech Hear. Res.* 5:161–168, 1962b.

13. Reid, G. The etiology and nature of functional articulatory defects in elementary school children. *J. Speech Disord.* 12:143–150, 1947a.

14. Reid, G. The efficacy of speech re-education of functional articulatory defectives in the elementary school. *J. Speech Disord.* 12:301–313, 1947b.

15. Shelton, R.L., Arndt, W.B., Krueger, A.L., and Huffman, E. Identification of persons with articulation errors from observation of non-speech movements. *Am. J. Phys. Med.* 45:143–150, 1966.

16. Spriesterbach, D.C., Moll, K.L., and Morris, H.L. Subject classification and articulation of speakers with cleft palates. *J. Speech Hear. Res.* 4:362–372, 1961.

17. Templin, M.C., and Darley, F.L. *The Templin-Darley Tests of Articulation.* Iowa City, Iowa: University of Iowa Press, 1960.

18. Terman, L.M., and Merrill, M.A. *Stanford-Binet Intelligence Scale.* Boston: Houghton Mifflin, 1960.

19. Wechsler, D. *The Wechsler Intelligence Scale for Children.* New York: The Psychological Corp., 1949.

20. Winitz, H. *Articulatory Acquisition and Behavior.* New York: Meredith Corp., 1969.

21. Yoss, K.A., and Darley, F.L. Developmental apraxia of speech in children with defective articulation. *J. Speech Hear. Res.* 17:399–416, 1974.

## CHAPTER 10

Speech Production

Harris Winitz, Ph.D.
Frederic L. Darley, Ph.D.

The genesis of faulty speech production continues to demand the attention and interest of speech pathologists. A primary ingredient in the continuing wish to promote further study is the realization that past investigations have fallen short of ideal research goals. The sample size has often been too small and the age at which the children were studied was generally limited to one point in time.

This investigation contains neither of these two problems. The sample size is large, perhaps excessively so from the viewpoint of the single investigator. In no previous investigation have so many children been subjects of a longitudinal investigation stretching from birth to eight years, the age range during which articulation development unfolds.

A great number of developmental, psychological, and medical tests were administered to the children. Assessments of speech production were derived from measures of articulation, intelligibility, voice characteristics, and fluency.

At the three-year level, tests of speech, language, and hearing (SLH) were devised by expert judgment, and several at the eight-year level were similarly constructed (see Chapter 3). A number of standardized tests were also included in the eight-year battery. In the areas of speech and language, these inlcuded: The Templin-Darley Tests of Articulation, 50-Item Screening Test (Templin and Darley, 1960); the Auditory-Vocal Automatic Test (Morphology) of the Illinois Test of Psycholinguistic Abilities (McCarthy and Kirk, 1963); the Gray Oral Reading Tests (Gray, 1967); the Peabody Picture Vocabulary Test (Dunn, 1965) which is referred to here as Word Identification; and the Durrell-Sullivan Reading Capacity and Achievement Tests (Durrell and Sullivan, 1945), used to assess Silent Reading and Understanding A Story.

The analysis took several forms. Frequency distributions will be discussed first. Next, intercorrelations of the speech production measures and selected independent variables will be summarized. Then the results obtained through the use of speech production indexes will be reviewed. Finally, the results of the cross-tabulations will be reported.

Performance on Speech Production Tests Frequency Distributions

3YR Findings

Table 10-1 summarizes the 3YR performance on the several measures of voice, articulation, and fluency (see also Appendix 3). For a certain proportion of the children, ranging from about 5% to 11% depending on the task, valid test observations were not made. These invalid tests are recorded as not in the data file (NIDF).

Three evaluations of voice were made: Pitch, Loudness, and Quality. Almost all children were considered to demonstrate Adequate Pitch (98%) and Adequate Loudness (96%). The children performed less well on Voice Quality. Of the total population, 89% were rated as Adequate Voice Quality, 1% Hypernasal, 1% Hyponasal, and 7% Hoarse.

The results of the 60-item articulation test are shown in Table 10-1 and Figure 10-1, which also display percent of errors by word position. Generally Males performed less well than Females (the difference was 10% for Initial Consonants), and Whites outperformed Blacks on consonants but not on vowels. About 63% of the total population was regarded as having normal articulation.

Intelligibility scores (Table 10-1 and Figure 10-2) indicate that only 46% of the children can be regarded as having no difficulty in being understood. Less than 5% of the sample were regarded as unintelligible. About 1% were regarded as having no speech at all.

Fluency distribution scores are given in Table 10-1. Only 9% of the children were regarded as having abnormal amounts of dysfluency and only 1% reflected some Struggle Behavior.

8YR Findings

Table 10-2 summarizes 8YR performance on the several speech production measures. For a small proportion of the children (usually less than 2%), reliable test observations could not be made. Only 2% of the 8YR population appeared to have a pitch problem, Too High (1%) or Too Low (1%). Similarly, 2% of the 8YR population were rated Loudness as Too Soft. A higher frequency of children had phonation and resonance problems; Hoarseness (9%) and Breathiness (1%) were observed, as well as Hypernasality (1%) and Hyponasality (6%).

Means are reported in Table 10-2 for scores on the Templin-Darley 50-item screening test. Females (mean 46) scored slightly higher than Males (mean 45), and Whites (mean 47) were slightly ahead of Blacks (mean 44). The average score of 46 for eight-year-olds is well within the limits established by Templin (1957). Intelligibility scores (Table 10-2) indicate that only 5% of the sample were considered to have some difficulty and 1% considerable difficulty in being understood.

Rate and fluency are reported in Table 10-2. Only 1% of the population sample was considered Irregular in Rate. Other deviations in rate were found in

Table 10-1

3YR Speech Production performance by sex, race, Socioeconomic Index and total sample.

Outcome	Male Freq.	Male %	Female Freq.	Female %	White Freq.	White %	Black Freq.	Black %	SEI 0.0-1.9 Freq.	%	SEI 2.0-3.9 Freq.	%	SEI 4.0-5.9 Freq.	%	SEI 6.0-7.9 Freq.	%	SEI 8.0-9.5 Freq.	%	Totals Freq.	%
Speech Production																				
Voice: Pitch (5% NIDF)*																				
Adequate	9,326	98†	9,203	98	8,117	98	10,412	98	1,794	98	6,235	98	5,354	98	3,171	98	1,975	99	18,529	98
Unusual Fluctuations	29	0	19	0	27	0	21	0	6	0	20	0	16	0	4	0	2	0	48	0
Too High	70	1	70	1	80	1	60	1	15	1	55	1	34	1	25	1	11	1	140	1
Too Low	57	1	58	1	43	1	72	1	13	1	48	1	33	1	13	0	8	0	115	1
Monotone	21	0	19	0	15	0	25	0	4	0	13	0	9	0	10	0	4	0	40	0
Combination of Codes	10	0	4	0	7	0	7	0	1	0	5	0	4	0	2	0	2	0	14	0
Voice: Loudness (5% NIDF)																				
Adequate	9,142	96	9,019	96	8,013	97	10,148	96	1,747	95	6,084	95	5,238	96	3,141	97	1,951	97	18,161	96
Too Soft	351	4	339	4	258	3	432	4	80	4	287	4	200	4	76	2	47	2	690	4
Too Loud	20	0	15	0	19	0	16	0	3	0	9	0	10	0	10	0	3	0	35	0
Unusual Fluctuations	12	0	5	0	6	0	11	0	2	0	6	0	6	0	2	0	1	0	17	0
Unusual Fluctuations and Too Loud	1	0	0	0	0	0	1	0	0	0	0	0	0	0	0	0	0	0	1	0
Voice: Quality (6% NIDF)																				
Adequate	8,376	88	8,544	91	7,684	93	9,236	87	1,558	85	5,617	88	4,878	89	2,978	92	1,889	94	16,920	89
Hypernasal	113	1	86	1	108	1	91	1	18	1	63	1	66	1	41	1	11	1	199	1
Hyponasal	137	1	114	1	133	2	118	1	17	1	74	1	85	2	49	2	26	1	251	1
Hoarseness	782	8	566	6	282	3	1,066	10	222	12	561	9	376	7	131	4	58	3	1,348	7
Hyponasal and Hoarseness	27	0	19	0	20	0	26	0	5	0	16	0	10	0	10	0	5	0	46	0
Hypernasal and Hoarseness	9	0	9	0	9	0	9	0	3	0	5	0	8	0	2	0	0	0	18	0
Articulation: Initial Consonants (5% NIDF)																				
Normal	5,326	60	6,229	70	5,424	70	6,131	61	922	54	3,560	60	3,291	64	2,235	73	1,547	80	11,555	65
Suspect	2,589	29	2,135	24	1,784	23	2,940	29	546	32	1,795	30	1,407	28	653	21	323	17	4,724	27
Abnormal	922	10	556	6	524	7	954	10	236	14	587	10	418	8	167	5	70	4	1,478	8

*NIDF = Not in data file.
†Not all columns sum to 100% because of rounding.

234

Table **10-1** *(continued)*

3YR Speech Production performance by sex, race, Socioeconomic Index and total sample.

	Male		Female		White		Black		Socioeconomic Index 0.0-1.9		2.0-3.9		4.0-5.9		6.0-7.9		8.0-9.5		Totals	
Outcome	Freq.	%	Freq.	%	Freq.	%	Freq.	%	Freq.	%	Freq.	%	Freq.	%	Freq.	%	Freq.	%	Freq.	%
Articulation: Final Consonants (11% NIDF)*																				
Normal	5,151	58	5,747	64	6,117	79	4,781	48	753	44	3,065	52	3,040	59	2,308	76	1,732	89	10,898	61
Suspect	1,930	22	1,800	20	1,112	14	2,618	26	440	26	1,482	25	1,168	23	494	16	146	8	3,730	21
Abnormal	1,746	20	1,367	15	493	6	2,620	26	509	30	1,392	23	904	18	247	8	61	3	3,113	18
Articulation: Vowels and Diphthongs (11% NIDF)																				
Normal	7,844	89	8,197	92	6,937	90	9,104	91	1,493	88	5,328	90	4,620	90	2,804	92	1,796	93	16,041	90
Suspect	905	10	676	8	712	9	869	9	197	12	567	10	455	9	227	7	135	7	1,581	9
Abnormal	77	1	42	0	72	1	47	0	13	1	43	1	37	1	19	1	7	0	119	1
Intelligibility of Speech (6% NIDF)																				
No Difficulty	3,779	40	4,887	53	4,002	49	4,664	44	712	39	2,643	42	2,445	45	1,659	52	1,207	61	8,666	46
Some Difficulty	3,346	36	3,051	33	2,618	32	3,779	36	700	39	2,293	36	1,827	34	1,017	32	560	28	6,397	34
Considerable Difficulty	1,858	20	1,183	13	1,286	16	1,755	17	325	18	1,158	18	940	17	429	13	189	10	3,041	16
Verbalized but Unintelligible	329	3	124	1	237	3	216	2	49	3	165	3	151	3	67	2	21	1	453	2
No Speech	89	1	53	1	75	1	67	1	23	1	52	1	45	1	16	1	6	0	142	1
Dysfluent Events (6% NIDF)																				
None	8,508	91	8,612	93	7,409	90	9,711	93	1,675	93	5,881	93	4,998	93	2,881	90	1,685	85	17,120	92
Some	789	8	626	7	720	9	695	7	105	6	391	6	352	7	287	9	280	14	1,415	8
Many	97	1	58	1	73	1	82	1	16	1	39	1	39	1	38	1	23	1	155	1
Struggle Behavior (6% NIDF)																				
None	9,308	99	9,218	99	8,115	99	10,411	99	1,780	99	6,267	99	5,345	99	3,166	99	1,968	100	18,526	99
Some	53	1	52	1	37	0	68	1	14	1	36	1	29	1	18	1	8	0	105	1
Many	10	0	3	0	5	0	8	0	2	0	4	0	4	0	4	0	0	0	13	0

*NIDF = Not in data file.

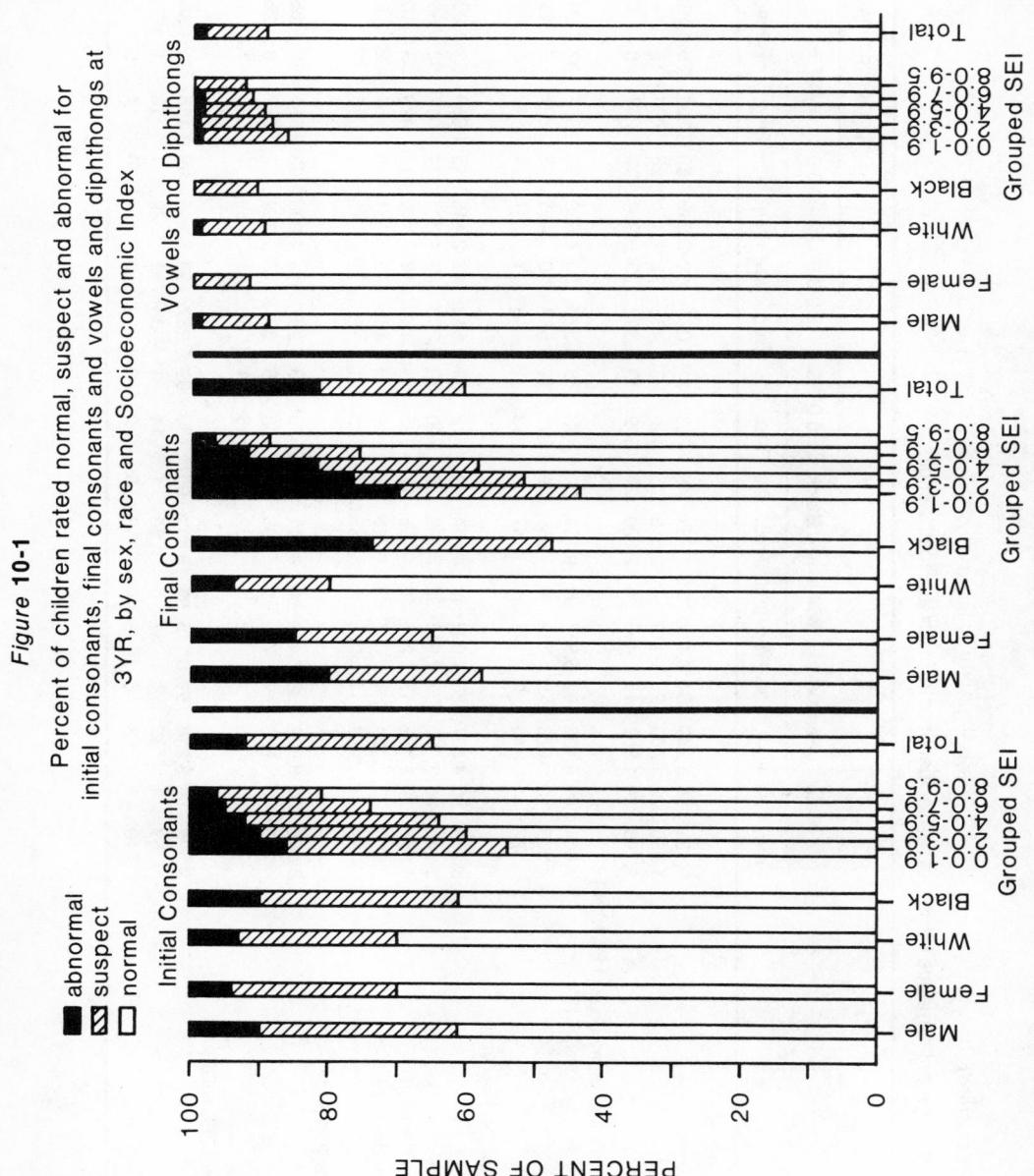

Figure **10-1**

Percent of children rated normal, suspect and abnormal for initial consonants, final consonants and vowels and diphthongs at 3YR, by sex, race and Socioeconomic Index

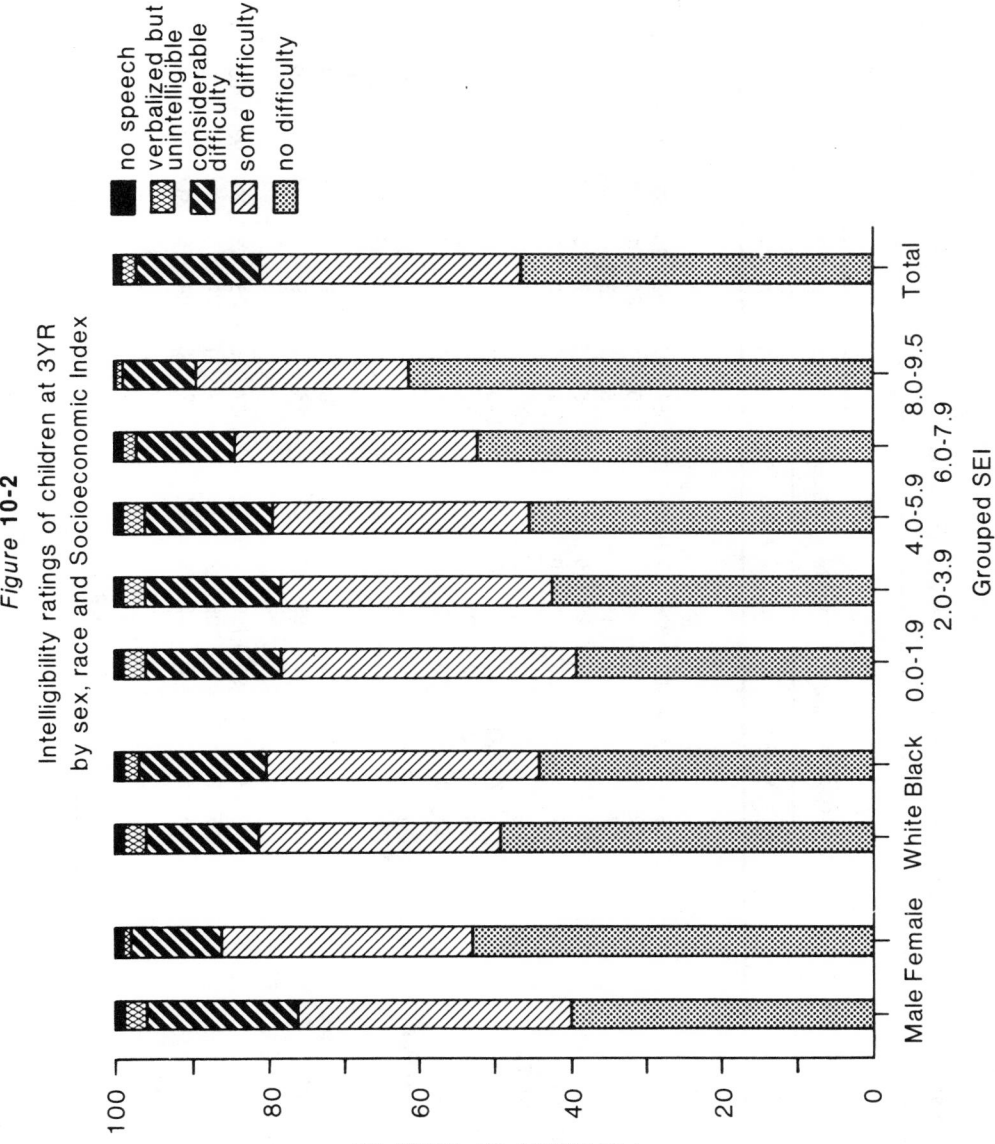

Figure **10-2**

Intelligibility ratings of children at 3YR
by sex, race and Socioeconomic Index

237

Table 10-2

8YR Speech Production performance by sex, race, Socioeconomic Index and total sample.

Outcome	Male		Female		White		Black		Socioeconomic Index 0.0-1.9		2.0-3.9		4.0-5.9		6.0-7.9		8.0-9.5		Totals	
	Freq.	%	Freq.	%	Freq.	%	Freq.	%	Freq.	%	Freq.	%	Freq.	%	Freq.	%	Freq.	%	Freq.	%
Speech Production																				
Voice: Pitch (1% NIDF)*																				
Adequate	9,758	97†	9,682	98	9,828	97	9,612	98	1,557	97	5,792	98	5,837	98	3,994	98	2,260	98	19,440	98
Too High	109	1	37	0	105	1	41	0	15	1	36	1	49	1	29	1	17	1	146	1
Too Low	87	1	121	1	116	1	92	1	18	1	63	1	72	1	38	1	17	1	208	1
Monotonous	23	0	16	0	23	0	16	0	5	0	7	0	13	0	10	0	4	0	39	0
Combination of Codes	7	0	4	0	5	0	6	0	2	0	0	0	4	0	4	0	1	0	11	0
Voice: Loudness (1% NIDF)																				
Adequate	9,718	97	9,608	97	9,829	97	9,497	97	1,543	96	5,722	97	5,823	97	3,981	97	2,257	98	19,326	97
Too Soft	239	2	239	2	231	2	247	3	54	3	157	3	134	2	93	2	40	2	478	2
Too Loud	21	0	15	0	18	0	18	0	1	0	13	0	12	0	7	0	3	0	36	0
Voice Quality: Phonation (2% NIDF)																				
Adequate	8,618	86	8,931	90	8,953	89	8,596	88	1,377	86	5,059	85	5,286	88	3,727	91	2,100	91	17,549	88
Breathiness	97	1	86	1	68	1	10	1	10	1	56	1	60	1	36	1	21	1	183	1
Hoarseness	1,117	11	749	8	888	9	978	10	178	11	685	12	564	9	273	7	166	7	1,866	9
Combination of Codes	118	1	69	1	95	1	92	1	26	2	69	1	44	1	39	1	9	0	187	1
Voice Quality: Resonance (2% NIDF)																				
Adequate	9,273	92	9,243	93	9,156	91	9,360	96	1,527	95	5,525	93	5,590	93	3,792	93	2,082	90	18,516	93
Hypernasality	118	1	88	1	136	1	70	1	17	1	72	1	64	1	39	1	14	1	206	1
Hyponasality	584	6	523	5	780	8	327	3	52	3	294	5	317	5	245	6	199	9	1,107	6
Articulation: Score (2% NIDF)																				
Mean	45		46		47		44		43		44		46		47		48		46	
Standard Deviation	7.1		5.4		5.9		6.4		7.3		7.0		6.0		5.4		4.7		6.4	

*NIDF = Not in data file.

†Not all columns sum to 100% because of rounding.

238

Table 10-2 (continued)

8YR Speech Production performance by sex, race, Socioeconomic Index and total sample.

	Male		Female		White		Black		Socioeconomic Index										Totals	
									0.0-1.9		2.0-3.9		4.0-5.9		6.0-7.9		8.0-9.5			
Outcome	Freq.	%	Freq.	%	Freq.	%	Freq.	%	Freq.	%	Freq.	%	Freq.	%	Freq.	%	Freq.	%	Freq.	%
Speech Production																				
*Rate of Speech Sounds (2% NIDF)**																				
Adequate	9,802	98	9,781	99	9,958	98	9,625	98	5,810	97	5,894	98	4,032	98	2,283	99	1,564	98	19,583	98
Too Fast	27	0	12	0	22	0	17	0	2	0	12	0	12	0	8	0	5	0	39	0
Too Slow	46	0	26	0	34	0	38	0	12	0	22	0	18	0	14	0	6	0	72	0
Irregular	89	1	37	0	57	1	69	1	16	0	44	1	47	1	15	1	4	0	126	1
Combination of Codes	6	0	2	0	4	0	4	0	1	0	3	0	2	0	1	0	1	0	8	0
Intelligibility (2% NIDF)																				
No Difficulty	9,289	93	9,515	96	9,741	96	9,063	93	5,461	90	5,671	93	3,690	95	2,274	97	1,708	99	18,804	95
Some Difficulty	581	6	286	3	292	3	575	6	352	8	261	6	126	4	103	3	25	1	867	4
Considerable Difficulty	103	1	50	1	49	0	104	1	68	2	40	1	31	1	12	0	2	0	153	1
Verbalized but Unintelligible	22	0	10	0	11	0	21	0	14	0	8	0	7	0	3	0	0	0	32	0
No Speech	9	0	6	0	5	0	10	0	6	0	3	0	3	0	3	0	0	0	15	0
Dysfluent Events (1% NIDF)																				
None	9,492	95	9,581	97	9,859	98	9,214	94	5,612	93	5,765	95	3,963	96	2,243	97	1,490	97	19,073	96
Some	464	5	267	3	211	2	520	5	264	6	205	4	106	3	99	3	57	2	731	4
Many	40	0	14	0	19	0	35	0	23	1	12	0	10	0	8	0	1	0	54	0
Struggle Behavior (1% NIDF)																				
None	9,866	99	9,796	99	10,006	99	9,656	99	5,835	99	5,921	99	4,047	99	2,282	99	1,577	99	19,662	99
Some	107	1	55	1	61	1	101	1	18	1	53	1	52	1	23	1	16	1	162	1
Many	17	0	10	0	18	0	9	0	3	0	9	0	7	0	5	0	3	0	27	0

*NIDF = Not in data file.

239

another 1% of the sample. With regard to dysfluent behavior, 4% of the children were evaluated as exhibiting some Dysfluent Events, and 1% had some degree of Struggle Behavior. In general, children at 8YR who were Male, Black, and/or from lower Socioeconomic Index (SEI) families were rated as somewhat less fluent. This is in contrast to the 3YR findings where Males, Whites, and higher SEI groups were judged to be less fluent.

Intercorrelations of Variables

Intercorrelations were computed for all speech, language, and hearing (SLH) variables for the ALL 3YR, ALL 8YR, and 3YR/8YR groups.

3YR Correlations

The intercorrelations of SLH variables for the 3YR level are given in Appendix 6.

There were low positive correlations between hearing scores and the measures of speech production, articulation, intelligibility, and voice. Generally these correlations did not exceed .15.

The several articulation measures showed interrelationships: $r = .58$ between Initial Consonants and Final Consonants; $r = .30$ between Initial Consonants and Vowels and Diphthongs; and $r = .26$ between Final Consonants and Vowels and Diphthongs. Intelligibility also evidenced moderate correlations with articulation measures, ranging from .37 (Vowels and Diphthongs) to .47 (Initial Consonants).

Articulation was positively correlated with several of the language measures. The expressive language summary score correlated .25 with Initial Consonants, .24 with Final Consonants, and .25 with Vowels and Diphthongs. The correlational matrix indicated relatively high correlations between Intelligibility and the language measures. In particular, the Expressive Language Summary score and Intelligibility correlated .52.

The moderately high relationships between language and articulation and between language and intelligibility can be given several interpretations. One possibility is that the examiners were biased by poor articulation performance when evaluating language capabilities. Another interpretation is that articulatory insufficiencies reflect an underlying linguistic deficit, perhaps a deficiency in the rules which govern phonological strings or in the realization of phonological-phonetic strings.

8YR Correlations

The intercorrelations between SLH variables at the 8YR level are also given in Appendix 6. Generally there were low correlations between hearing and articulation, and hearing and intelligibility measures. The highest correlation was .28 between Articulation and Discrimination for the left ear. It must be remembered that the sample consisted of largely normal-hearing children, and almost all of those who had hearing impairments had problems which were mild in degree (see Chapter 6). Thus, speech production and hearing variables would be expected to have low correlations in this sample.

Articulation and Intelligibility were correlated (.52), indicating that these two measures overlap in the functions which they test. Articulation also correlated with a number of the language measures: Word Identification (.36), Orientation (.31), Understanding a Story (.19), Oral Reading (.30), Silent Reading (.29), Morphology subtest of the ITPA (.45), Connected Discourse (.22), and Writing from Dictation (.38). The relationships between each of these measures and Intelligibility were not as high, ranging from $r = .12$ for Understanding a Story to $r = .29$ for Writing from Dictation.

The rather high relationship ($r = .45$) between Morphology and Articulation is of interest. The morphology subtest of the ITPA consists of a large number of

240

plurals and past tense markers, requiring the articulatory production of /s/, /z/, /t/ and /d/. In the instructions for the morphology test, it is stated that no penalty should be given for misarticulations. Distortions, most likely lisps, would be considered correct. In this regard, there is the important consideration that substitutions which resemble the target morpheme (that is, substitutions of a distorted quality) might be scored as correct. Additionally, there is the possibility that substitutions which do not resemble the target morpheme might be scored as errors. For example, /s/ would not be an acceptable distortion for the phonetically similar /z/ in *knives* and *leaves,* as is the case in some dialects when the terminal consonant of the singular form remains voiceless (*leafs* and *knifes*); and /k/, of course, would not be an acceptable distortion for /g/ to form the past tense of *hang.* In this last instance, *hunk* would be an incorrect response for *hung.*

In addition to methodological concerns, there are other considerations in interpreting the correlation between Morphology and Articulation. Morphology and Intelligibility correlated .28, considerably less than the .45 obtained between Morphology and Articulation. Redundancy is characteristic of natural languages. In running speech, the utterance *two book* might not affect a scorer's intuitive understanding of sentential meaning. For this reason, the absence of morphological markers may contribute more to the articulation score than to the intelligibility score.

The various measures of voice (Pitch, Loudness, Phonation, and Resonance) evidenced intercorrelations of low magnitude. Of these several voice measures, only Pitch showed a correlation of >.10 with measures of Bone Conduction taken from left and right ears at 500 Hz, 1000 Hz, and 2000 Hz. The r varied from .15 to .20.

Fluency, as measured by Dysfluent Events and Struggle Behavior, evidenced

its highest correlation with Rate of Speech (.17 for Dysfluent Events and .15 for Struggle Behavior).

3YR/8YR Correlations

Of major significance for diagnostic purposes is the relationship between speech production scores at 3YR and 8YR. High correlations would suggest that children maintain their relative ranking across a five-year span. Stability is essential in order to identify accurately children at 3YR who will exhibit speech and language disorders at 8YR. It should be mentioned, however, that the relationship between 3YR and 8YR SLH variables needs to be considered relative to the relationship between biological, psychological and sociological (NCPP)* variables and the 8YR SLH variables. Conceivably, the relative rankings of SLH variables across age levels may not be maintained because a deficiency in physiological or psychological functioning may not manifest itself until after three years of age.

Identification of high risk children (children who will develop speech and voice disorders) can potentially be made from either the SLH variables or the NCPP variables. An NCPP variable that predicts a deficiency in one or more SLH measures is valuable since knowledge of an early medical or psychological problem may prevent an SLH disorder. An SLH variable that has high predictability from another SLH variable is useful because it directs attention to those children who should be carefully observed during the years when language and speech are developing rapidly.

The observations reported in this section involve the 3YR/8YR SLH relationships. Low positive correlations were obtained between the several articulation measures and Intelligibility at 3YR with the Templin-Darley Screening Test given at 8YR and are as follows:

---

* Non-SLH variables in the NINCDS Collaborative Perinatal Project (NCPP).

	8YR Articulation	8YR Intelligibility
3YR Initial Consonants	.30	.16
3YR Final Consonants	.35	.16
3YR Vowels and Diphthongs	.20	.16
3YR Intelligibility	.29	.25

The magnitude of these correlations precludes their use for predictive purposes. It is interesting to observe that the measures for initial and final consonants predict articulation performance best at 8YR.

Some additional correlations with the 8YR Speech Production measures were of interest. Correlations of low magnitude were obtained between the several language measures and Articulation. The highest correlations obtained were .22 between the 3YR Language Expression Summary Item Score and 8YR Articulation, and .20 between the 3YR Language Expression Summary Item Score and 8YR Intelligibility. The relationships between memory span (3YR Digits and 3YR Syllables) and 8YR Articulation were low; the highest was $r = .08$ for Two Syllables at 3YR. These findings are in agreement with past results, summarized by Winitz (1969). Previous research has generally indicated that the best predictor of articulation is the prior articulation score. All correlations for the 3YR/8YR voice measures were ≤.05. Fluency measures at 3YR and 8YR correlated ≤.06.

Speech Production Indexes

Construction of Indexes and Correlations with SLH Variables

Each index was developed by consultation within the Scientific Management Panel, which assigned component variables to indexes according to "natural groupings."

Ideally, an index should consist of natural groupings of component variables and each variable should evidence only a moderate relationship with the index. If one component variable correlates highly with the index, little preci-

sion is gained by generating the index. As will be observed, there is overlap among the several indexes with regard to component variables. The construction of the indexes has been described in Chapter 5 and Appendix 4.

The indexes, the component variables, and the correlation of the indexes with the component variables are indicated in Table 10-3 for the 3YR and 8YR level. Indexes for 8YR Articulation, 8YR Intelligibility, and 3YR Intelligibility are not included since these indexes consisted of a single (key) variable.

From Table 10-3 it can be observed that Initial Consonants were more highly correlated (.87) with 3YR Articulation than were Vowels and Diphthongs (.59). Also, Dysfluent Events correlated more highly (.98) with 3YR Fluency than did Struggle Behavior (.54).

For the 8YR indexes it may be noted that for the fluency measure, Dysfluent Events ($r = .94$) was the primary contributor.

Frequency Distributions

For each of the five speech production indexes, frequency distributions were generated. These findings are summarized in Appendix 5 and Table 10-4. A brief summary of these findings follows.

3YR Articulation

Only scores derived for Initial Consonants and Vowels and Diphthongs were included in the index of articulation. Final consonants were excluded, as it was believed that their inclusion would unfairly contribute to lower scores for the Black children because final consonants

242

Table **10-3**

Correlations between 3YR Articulation, 3YR Fluency and 8YR Fluency indexes and their component variables.

Indexes and Variables		r
3YR Articulation:	Initial Consonants	.87
	Vowels and Diphthongs	.59
3YR Fluency:	Dysfluent Events	.98
	Struggle Behavior	.54
8YR Fluency:	Dysfluent Events	.94
	Struggle Behavior	.70
	Rate of Speech Sounds	.30

Table **10-4**

Means, standard deviations and ranges for ALL 3YR and 8YR performance on 3YR and 8YR speech production indexes.

	Mean	SD	Range
3YR Articulation			
Male	6.88	1.99	0-8
Female	7.24	1.61	0-8
White	7.19	1.71	0-8
Black	6.93	1.91	0-8
3YR Intelligibility			
Male	2.14	.86	0-3
Female	2.37	.76	0-3
White	2.24	.81	0-3
Black	2.27	.83	0-3
3YR Fluency			
Male	2.90	.34	0-3
Female	2.92	.31	0-3
White	2.93	.30	0-3
Black	2.82	.35	0-3
8YR Articulation			
Male	44.44	7.35	0-50
Female	46.11	5.51	0-50
White	46.96	6.21	0-50
Black	43.75	6.50	0-50
8YR Fluency			
Male	6.85	.66	0-7
Female	6.92	.47	0-7
White	6.84	.67	0-7
Black	6.94	.45	0-7

are often omitted in Black dialect. As can be observed in Appendix 5 and Figure 10-3, there were minor fluctuations among the subgroups. Higher scores were achieved by Females and Whites. Also, articulation scores were directly related to increases in SEI.

8YR Articulation

The trends observed at three years were repeated at eight years (Appendix 5 and Figure 10-4). Better scores were obtained for Whites, Females, and children with high SEI ratings.

243

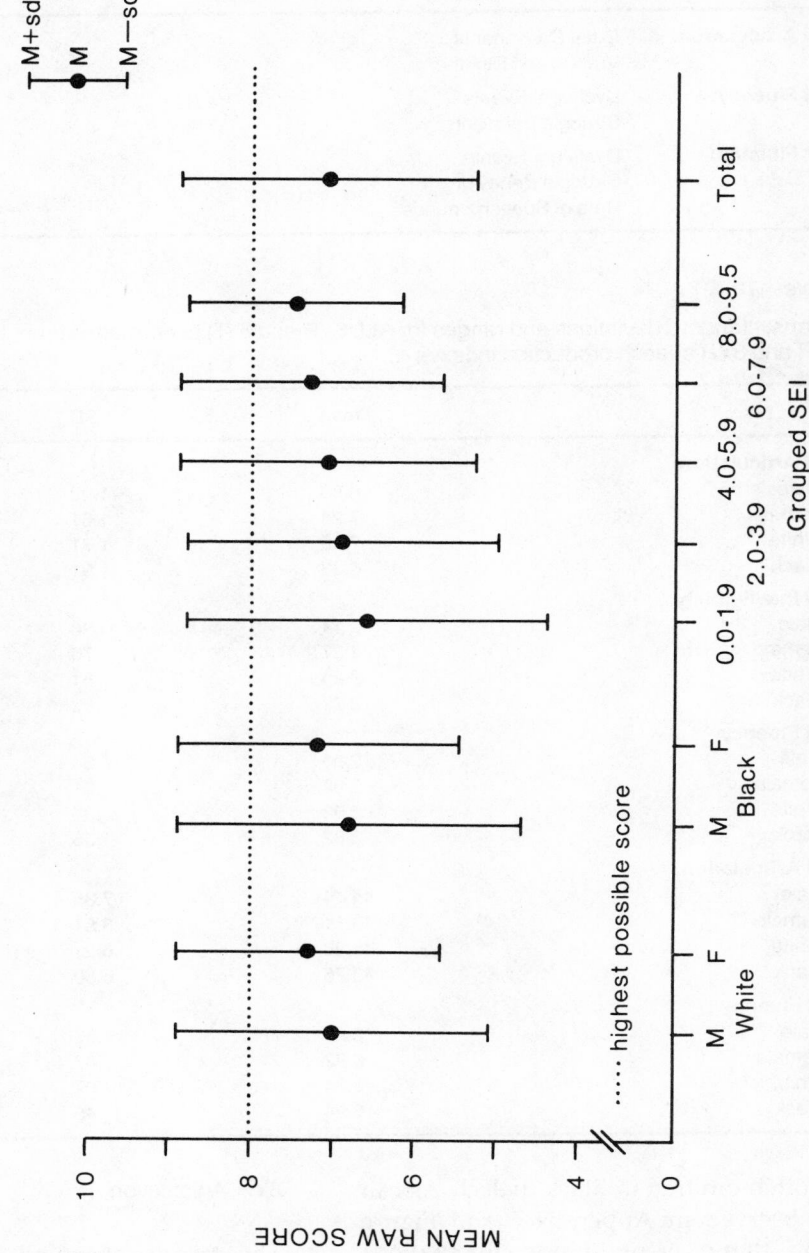

Figure **10-3**

Means and standard deviations for the 3YR Articulation Index by sex, race and Socioeconomic Index

244

Figure 10-4

Means and standard deviations for the 8YR Articulation Index
by sex, race and Socioeconomic Index

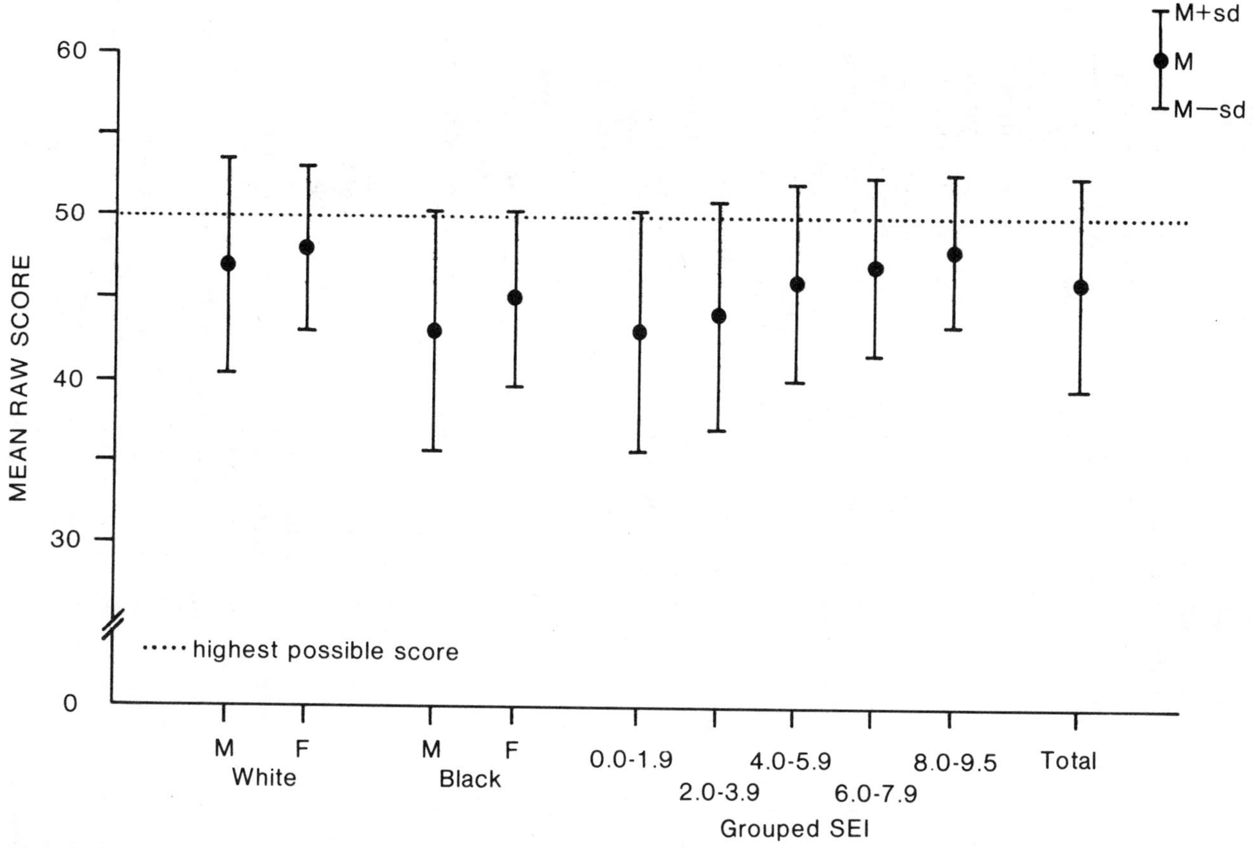

245

3YR Intelligibility

The distribution for 3YR Intelligibility is listed in Appendix 5 and Figure 10-5. Only minor fluctuations were observed across the subsamples.

Of interest is the finding that the proportion of children classified as "no speech" never exceeded 1% for each of the several populations (Appendix 5). However, the "no speech" classification was not part of this intelligibility index.

8YR Intelligibility

Scores for intelligibility at eight years are given in Appendix 5 and Figure 10-6. As can be observed in Figure 10-6, scores for the several subgroups were similar.

3YR and 8YR Fluency

At both the 3YR and 8YR levels, the fluency indexes did not appear to be related to race, sex, or SEI (Appendix 5, Figures 10-7 and 10-8).

Intercorrelations of Indexes

Intercorrelations among indexes are summarized in Appendix 6. This discussion will briefly highlight these findings.

Intercorrelations of 3YR Indexes At the 3YR level the indexes showed low intercorrelations. The highest r was between 3YR Sentence Complexity and Intelligibility (.43). One surprising finding was that the relationships between Speech Mechanism and Intelligibility and between Speech Mechanism and Articulation were not increased by the componential additions in the indexes.

Intercorrelations of 8YR Indexes Positive correlations were found between 8YR Articulation and Intelligibility (.52), Language Comprehension (.25), Written Communication (.36), Language Production (.48), Concept Development (.42), Communicative Effectiveness (.44), Auditory Processing (.44), and Word Identification (.37).

Intelligibility and Language Production correlated at .40. In some instances, the correlations reported above reflect evaluations of the same basic skills; in other instances, underlying and related deficiencies may be reflected by the correlations.

Intercorrelations of 3YR/8YR Indexes Intercorrelations computed between 3YR and 8YR indexes showed that 3YR Articulation correlated with 8YR Articulation (.31), 8YR Intelligibility (.20), 8YR Auditory Memory (.19), 8YR Word Identification (.20), 8YR Written Communication (.19), 8YR Language Production (.25), 8YR Concept Development (.25), 8YR Communicative Effectiveness (.24), and 8YR Auditory Processing (.26). The 3YR intelligibility measure showed similar relationships, of which the higher correlations were as follows: 8YR Articulation (.27), Written Communication (.27), 8YR Concept Development (.27), 8YR Communicative Effectiveness (.27), and Auditory Processing (.30).

The above 3YR/8YR correlations are not of sufficient magnitude to be clinically useful for predictive purposes; however, they suggested possible sources of study for the cross-tabulations and correlations to be reported below.

Correlations and Cross-Tabulations of SLH Indexes and NCPP Variables

In order to determine whether conditions in the biological, psychological, and social background of the children are predictive of speech production dysfunctions, correlations were computed between selected NCPP variables and the speech production indexes. In addition, cross-tabulations were produced, yielding the proportion of children who failed* on an SLH index relative to a pass or fail on another SLH index or NCPP variable.

---

* Failure was defined as a score falling in the lowest decile or, in the case of a restricted range, closest to the lowest decile.

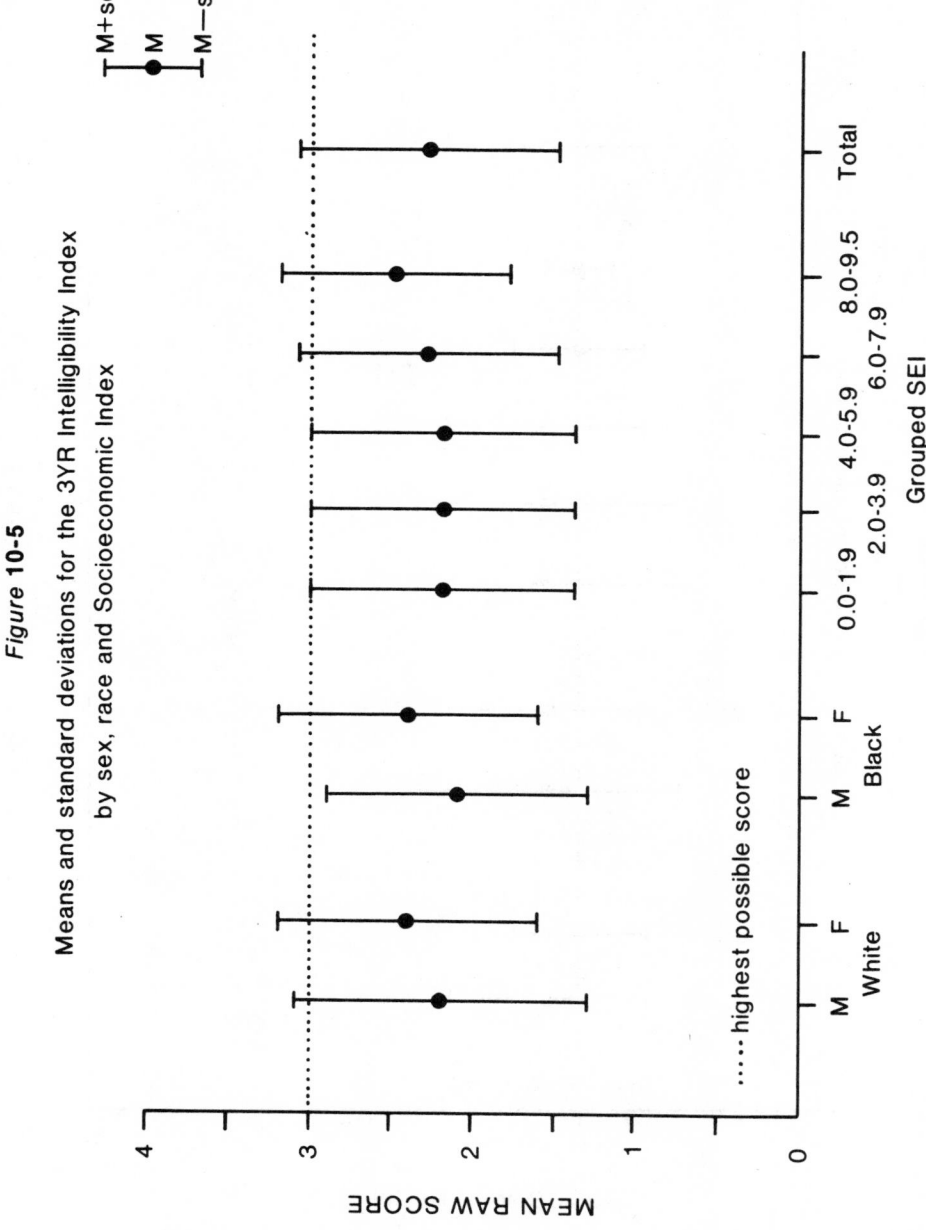

Figure **10-5**

Means and standard deviations for the 3YR Intelligibility Index
by sex, race and Socioeconomic Index

247

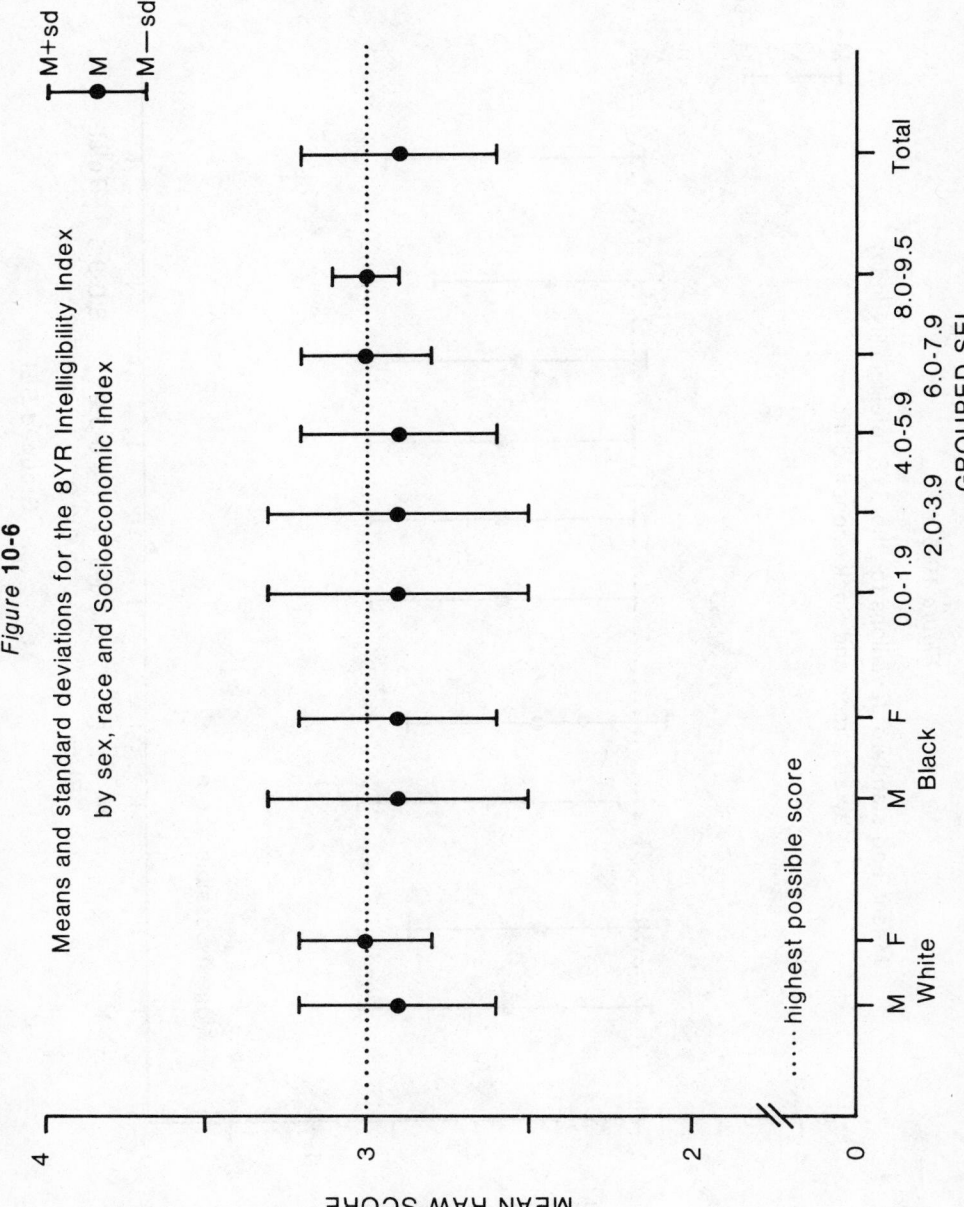

Figure **10-6**

Means and standard deviations for the 8YR Intelligibility Index
by sex, race and Socioeconomic Index

248

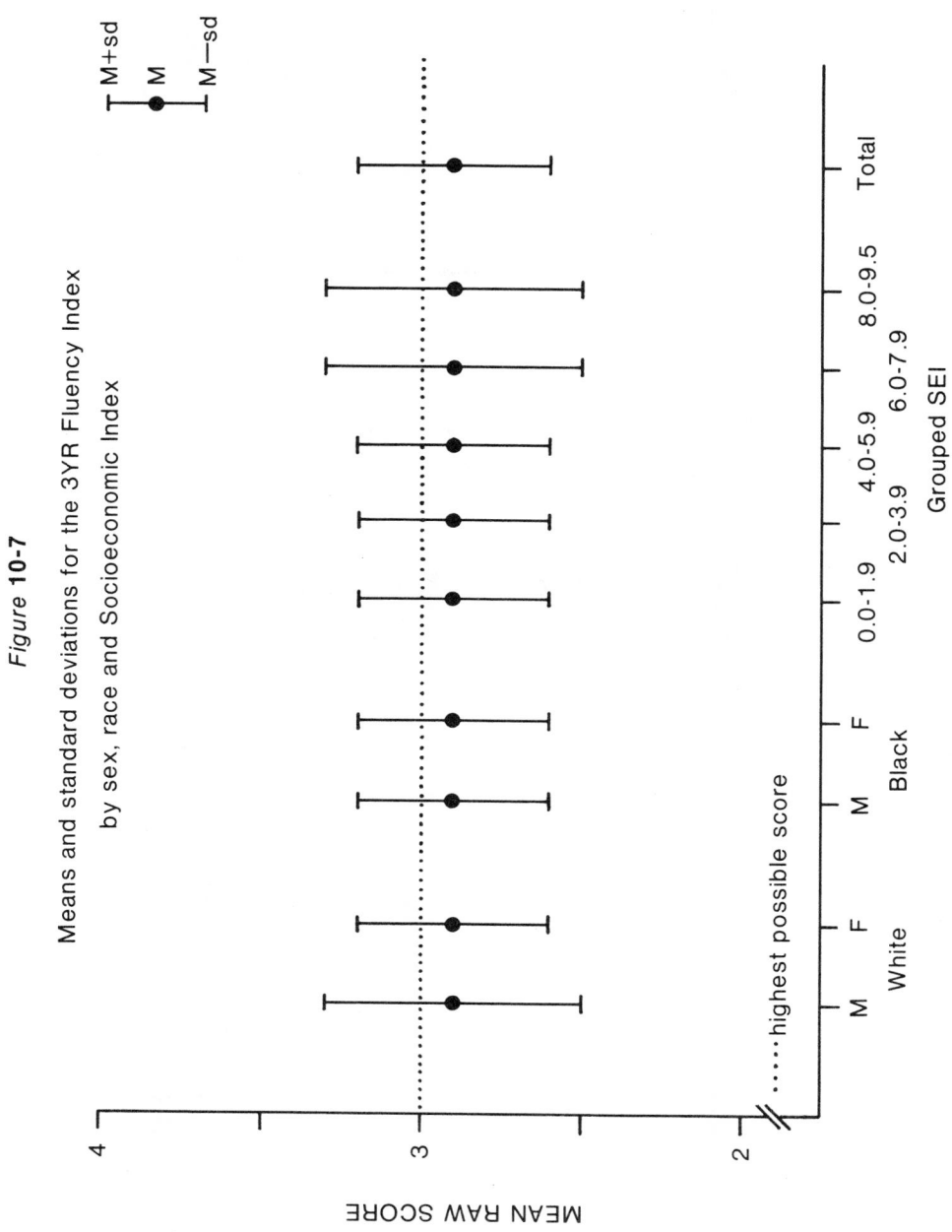

Figure **10-7**

Means and standard deviations for the 3YR Fluency Index
by sex, race and Socioeconomic Index

249

Figure **10-8**

Means and standard deviations for the 8YR Fluency Index
by sex, race and Socioeconomic Index

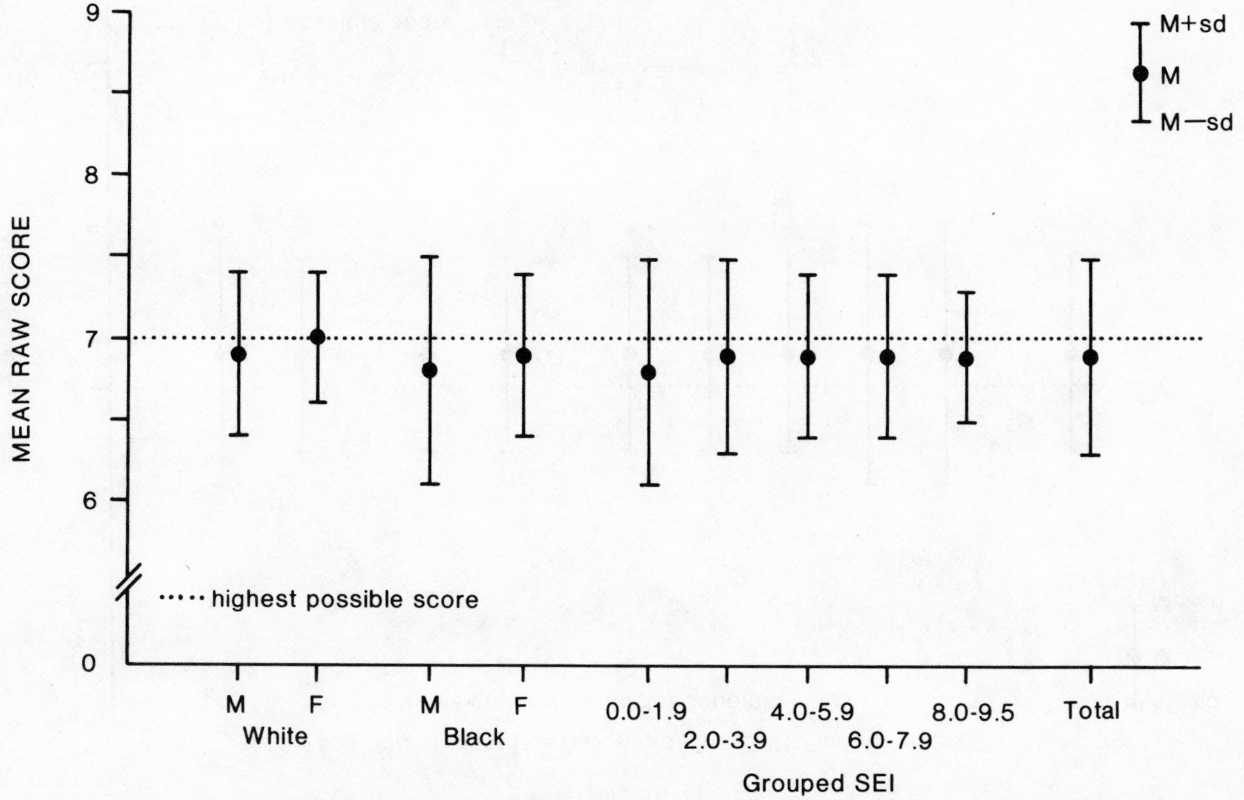

250

In this chapter, conditional probabilities are not reported when the total number of failures for the independent variables (for example, Bayley tests, IQ) fell below 100, with the exception of a small number of variables of particular interest.

3YR NCPP Variables and Speech Production Outcome

Conditional probabilities for 3YR Articulation and Intelligibility and the selected NCPP variables are given in Tables 10-5 and 10-6. Correlations are also indicated. The tables are further explained by the following example.

Of the total number of 18,682 children who were tested on the 3YR articulation test and the Bayley Eight-Month Motor Scale, 703 children failed both tests. The proportion of children who failed the 3YR articulation test relative to the total number of failures on the Bayley is $\frac{703}{1937}$, or .36. In other words, of all those who failed the Bayley, 36% failed the 3YR articulation test. This kind of proportion is denoted by p(F2/F1), an abbreviation for the proportion of children who failed the second test among those who failed the first test. Also of interest is the proportion of children who failed the articulation test but who passed the Bayley Eight-Month Motor Scale. This proportion is denoted by p(F2/P1). In this case, its value is $\frac{3288}{16745}$, or .20. The difference between the p(F2/F1) and p(F2/P1) is .16

Table **10-5**

Correlations and conditional probabilities for 3YR Articulation and selected NCPP variables.

Variables	r	p(F2/F1)*	p(F2/P1)*
Bayley 8-Month Motor Score	.10	.36	.20
Bayley 8-Month Mental Score			
Total Population	—†	.34	.20
Black Male	—	.41	.26
Low SEI	—	.38	.27
High SEI	—	.25	.10
Bayley 8-Month			
Fine Motor Development	—	.19	.11
Gross Motor Development	—	.20	.11
Social Emotional Development	—	.15	.12
Head Turns to Sound of Bell	—	.60	.21
Head Turns to Sound of Rattle	—	.64	.21
Neurological Abnormalities (number)(given at 1YR)	—	.27	.19
3YR Speech Mechanism (pass = 6-8; fail = 0-5)	.11	.25	.12
Stanford-Binet II-6: Naming Objects	−.10	.26	.12
Stanford-Binet III: Picture Vocabulary	−.17	.28	.11
Stanford-Binet III-6: Comprehension	−.18	.18	.09
Stanford-Binet IV: Picture Vocabulary	−.14	.15	.07
Stanford-Binet IV: Pictorial Identification	−.15	.17	.09
Stanford-Binet VII: Comprehension IV	—	.12	.03
4YR IQ (Marginals)(pass = 81-175; fail = 70-80)	.24	.36	.11
4YR IQ (pass = 71-175; fail = 25-70)	.24	.23	.10
Duration of Attention Span: Very Brief	—	.26	.12
7YR Neurological Abnormalities (pass = none or suspicious)	—	.09	.02
7YR Neurological Abnormalities (pass = no abnormalities)	—	.29	.15
Occupation of Father: White-Collar	.11	.24	.14

*p(F2/F1) and p(F2/P1) refer to the probability of failing 3YR Articulation (F2) when the NCPP variable is failed (F1) or passed (P1).
†< .10.

Table 10-6

Correlations and conditional probabilities for 3YR Intelligibility and selected NCPP variables.

Variables	r	p(F2/F1)*	p(F2/P1)*
Bayley: 8-Month Motor Score	.13	.20	.08
Bayley: Head Turns to Sound of Bell	.00	.45	.09
Bayley: Head Turns to Sound of Rattle	.00	.47	.09
4YR IQ	.33	.25	.03
Stanford-Binet II-6 Picture Vocabulary	.00	.18	.02
Stanford-Binet III-6 Comprehension	−.23	.04	.01
Stanford-Binet IV Picture Vocabulary	−.20	.03	.01
Stanford-Binet IV Opposite Analogies	−.21	—†	—
Stanford-Binet IV-6 Comprehension III	−.20	.03	.01
Stanford-Binet V Definitions	−.21	—	—

*p(F2/F1) and p(F2/P1) refer to the probability of failing 3YR Articulation (F2) when the NCPP variable is failed (F1) or passed (P1).
†p not calculated.

which, in our opinion, is not of clinical significance.

In summary, the proportion of children who failed the articulation test and who failed the Bayley was greater than the proportion of children who failed the articulation test but who passed the Bayley test; the difference is .16.

The 3YR correlations and conditional probabilities will now be discussed. In general, the correlations are too low for predictive purposes. With regard to the conditional probabilities, the variables included for consideration were those for which the correlations suggested further inspection and those which have held high interest among clinical researchers. The conditional probabilities (Tables 10-5 and 10-6) for the early auditory tests are of interest. The Bayley tests for sound orientation (bell and rattle stimuli) resulted in $p(F2/F1) \leq .60$ and $\leq .64$ for 3YR articulation. Of the total number of 123 children who failed the Bayley bell localizing task, 74 children also failed the 3YR articulation test. Thus, 60% of those children who failed this auditory screening test also failed the articulation test, a finding not in agreement with the findings of Bordley and Hardy (1972). However, 3990 children failed the 3YR Articu-

lation Index, so we conclude that failure in articulation was not predicted well for the entire sample by this auditory screening test in spite of the fact that some articulation errors may reflect auditory insufficiencies.

Generally, hearing tests reported in this investigation (Chapter 6) did not predict articulation failure, a result that evokes concern regarding the value of the hearing tests for predicting articulation problems on a general population.

The analysis for 3YR Fluency produced one especially interesting finding. Fluency pass scores decreased as socioeconomic levels increased. The pass percentages across SEI were as follows: 0.0 to 1.9, 93%; 2.0 to 3.9, 93%; 4.0 to 5.9, 91%; 6.0 to 7.9, 89%; 8.0 to 9.5, 84%. It may be concluded from this finding that dysfluencies are related to the socioeconomic level of the parents.

The correlations and the conditional probabilities for 8YR Articulation are given in Table 10-7. Language and articulation showed a moderate relation, as the Stanford-Binet level II-6 Picture Vocabulary p(F2/F1) is .40; p(F2/P1) is .12. The first probability predicts that 40% of the children who fail the Stanford-Binet level II-6 Picture Vocabulary (given at

252

Table 10-7

Correlations and conditional probabilities for 8YR Articulation and selected NCPP variables.

Variables	r	p(F2/F1)*	p(F2/P1)*
Housing Density (Birth)	−.12	.15	.14
Birth SEI	.23	—†	—†
Race of Child: White	.25	—	—
Race of Child: Black	−.25	—	—
Per Capita Income	.20	.17	.10
4YR IQ	.35	.39	.12
4YR Graham Block Sort	.23	.14	.13
7YR Neurological Abnormality	−.21	.27	.11
7YR SEI	−.23	—	—
Stanford-Binet II-6: Picture Vocabulary	−.21	.40	.12
Stanford-Binet III: Picture Vocabulary	−.24	.29	.11
Stanford-Binet III: Picture Memory	−.20	—	—
Stanford-Binet III-6: Response to Pictures	−.23	—	—
Stanford-Binet III-6: Discrimination of Animal Pictures	−.23	—	—
Stanford-Binet III-6: Comprehension	−.25	.18	.10
Stanford-Binet IV: Picture Vocabulary	−.20	.15	.08
Stanford-Binet IV: Naming Objects from Memory	−.20	—	—
Stanford-Binet IV: Opposite Analogies	−.23	—	—
Stanford-Binet IV: Pictorial Identification	−.22	.17	.10
Stanford-Binet IV-6: Pictorial Similarities/Differences	−.20	—	—
Stanford-Binet IV-6: Comprehension III	−.21	.16	.09
Stanford-Binet V: Definitions	−.22	—	—
Bender Gestalt Test: Total Score	−.25	.23	.11
Wechsler: Verbal IQ	.15	.29	.11
Wechsler: Performance IQ	.15	.28	.12
Wechsler: 7YR IQ (71-154 = pass; 25-70 = fail)	—†	.50	.12
Wechsler: Information Scaled Score	.25	—	—
Wechsler: Vocabulary Scaled Score	.32	—	—
Wechsler: Digit Span Scaled Score	.25	—	—
Wechsler: Picture Arrangement Scaled Score	.26	—	—
Wechsler: Block Design Scaled Score	.23	—	—
Wechsler: Full Scale IQ	.22	.50	.12
Auditory-Vocal Association Test: Raw Score	.40	.31	.11
Goodenough-Harris Drawing Test: Raw Score	.21	—	—
WRAT: Spelling — Raw Score	.31	—	—
WRAT: Reading — Raw Score	.32	—	—
WRAT: Math — Raw Score	.33	—	—
7YR Psych: Other Obvious Speech Defects	−.38	—	—
Housing Density (7YR)	−.21	—	—
Total Income Prior 3 Months (7YR)	.20	—	—
Occupation of Mother: Service Work	.20	—	—
3YR Sentence Complexity	.18	.27	.11
3YR Speech Mechanism	.15	.20	.12
8YR Speech Mechanism	.22	.28	.13

*p(F2/F1) and p(F2/P1) refer to the probability of failing 8YR Articulation (F2) when the NCPP variable is failed (F1)
  or passed (P1).
†not calculated.

4YRS) will also fail the articulation test (8YR). The remaining measures of intellectual functioning suggest a relation between 8YR Articulation and intelligence. For the 7YR WISC the proportions were p(F2/F1) = .50 and p(F2/P1) = .12, and for the 4YR Stanford-Binet p(F2/F1) was .39 and p(F2/P1) was .12.

The conditional probabilities and correlations for intelligibility of speech and selected NCPP variables are listed in Table 10-8. The conditional probability analysis revealed definite relationships between 8YR Intelligibility and IQ, language measures, neurological abnormalities, and speech training variables, although correlations were low (.21 to .32). An interesting finding, not indicated in Table 10-8, is that presence of cleft lip or palate at birth does not invariably predict intelligibility at 8YR. Of the children with this impairment at birth, 21% (or 10 of 47) were regarded as unintelligible.

Multiple Regression

3YR Speech Production Measures

Multiple correlation was used to measure the degree of relationship between given dependent variables, each SLH index, and several NCPP variables designated as the independent variables. The values for the standardized regression weights, the beta values, are used to compare the relative contribution of each NCPP variable.

The following measures served as predictors for 3YR Speech Production: Birthweight, race, sex, Eight-Month Mental and Motor Scores, Occupation of the Father, Per Capita Income, Gestational Age, Education of Gravida, and Education of Father of Baby (FOB). Two multiple correlations were computed: with and without Eight-Month Mental and Motor Scores. These correlations for 3YR Articulation, 3YR Fluency, and 3YR Intelligibility are reported in Table 10-9 and Appendix 6.

As can be observed in Table 10-9 and Appendix 6, the higher multiple correlations were for 3YR Articulation and 3YR Intelligibility. The primary contributors to these correlations, judging from the beta weights, are Eight-Month Mental and Motor Scores, Per Capita Income, Education of Gravida and FOB, and the Race-Sex Markers. The relative contribution of the Race-Sex Marker was greater for 3YR Intelligibility than for articulation.

Table **10-8**

Correlations and conditional probabilities for 8YR Intelligibility and selected NCPP variables.

Variables	r	p(F2/F1)*	p(F2/P1)*
4YR IQ	.21	.27	.05
7YR Neurological Abnormality	−.22	.17	.05
Nature of Communication: Non-Verbal	−.22	.41	.06
Wechsler: Verbal IQ	.27	.19	.04
Wechsler: Performance IQ	.27	.18	.05
Wechsler: Full Scale IQ	.32	.39	.05
Auditory-Vocal Association Test: Raw Score	.22	.21	.04
WRAT: Special Speech Class	.24	.37	.06
WRAT: Math	.22	—†	—†
WRAT: Adequacy of Exam	−.23	—	—

*p(F2/F1) and p(F2/P1) refer to the probability of failing 8YR Intelligibility (F2) when the NCPP variable is failed (F1) or passed (P1).
†not calculated.

254

Table *10-9*

Multiple correlations for 3YR Articulation, 3YR Intelligibility and 3YR Fluency and selected independent variables with beta coefficients.

	3YR Articulation		3YR Intelligibility		3YR Fluency	
	At-Birth NCPP variables	At-Birth NCPP variables plus 8-Month NCPP variables	At-Birth NCPP variables	At-Birth NCPP variables plus 8-Month NCPP variables	At-Birth NCPP variables	At-Birth NCPP variables plus 8-Month NCPP variables
Multiple R	.181	.200	.230	.250	.0869	.0890
R Square	.0329	.0399	.0531	.0626	.00756	.00793
Birthweight	.0327	.0126	.0483	.0242	-.00237	-.00622
Gestational Age	.0123	-.000153	.0129	-.00189	.00594	.00354
Education of Gravida	.0426	.0418	.0628	.0619	-.0107	-.0109
Per Capita Income	.0729	.0633	.0531	.0417	-.0421	-.0440
Education of F.O.B.	.0578	.0562	.0813	.0784	-.0151	-.0152
Occupation of F.O.B.	.0140	.0139	.0330	.0328	-.0355	-.0355
8-Month Mental Score		.0531		.0336		.0194
8-Month Motor Score		.0459		.0803		.00109
Race-Sex Marker I	-.0677	-.0607	-.152	.142	-.0331	-.0321
Race-Sex Marker II	.0477	.0494	.0648	.0673	.0386	.0388
Race-Sex Marker III	-.0777	-.0775	-.0683	.0684	-.0147	-.0146

255

8YR Speech Production Measures

The multiple correlations for 8YR Articulation and 8YR Intelligibility are included in Tables 10-10 and 10-11. At the 8YR level, five multiple correlations were completed: (1) using the ten At-Birth NCPP variables used for the 3YR analysis; (2) using these ten plus two Bayley scores (Eight-Month Mental Score and Eight-Month Motor Score); (3) using these 12 plus 4YR IQ; (4) using nine 3YR indexes; and (5) using the nine 3 YR indexes plus the original ten At-Birth NCPP variables. The R's were somewhat higher than at 3YR. Judging from the beta weights, Per Capita Income and education were not significantly related to articulation performance. Race and sex show the highest beta weights. Inclusion of 3YR indexes and At-Birth NCPP variables provided R's of .447 for articulation and .293 for intelligibility.

8YR Fluency Stuttering generally stabilizes by eight years of age (Johnson, 1955). Accordingly, it is at this age level, rather than at 3YR, that disordered fluency should be indicative of pathological behavior. The results of the multiple correlation analysis are given in Table 10-12, which indicates that none of the five correlations exceeds .133. We conclude that, in this study, fluency was not well predicted by early physical, social, and psychological measures, and speech and language behavior assessed at 3YR.

Special Studies

Articulation

Over the past 30 years children who evidence articulatory errors have been studied intensively. Generally, the research has failed to identify factors which contribute to the etiology of articulation disorders. Often the data were gathered for small groups of subjects for whom almost no background information was available. This investigation provides data for large numbers of subjects for whom background data are available. In the following section the 8YR Articulation scores will be examined relative to effects of true distress (Apgar), Birthweight, Parity, Education of Gravida, race, SEI, family status, and special disorders.

Five-Minute Apgar Score

Of particular interest is the relation between Apgar scores and articulation. The articulation percentage pass rates obtained for three levels of Apgar scores were as follows: 0 to 3, 87.7%; 4 to 7, 84.9%; 8 to 10, 87.9%. Thus, there appears to be no relation between Apgar scores and articulation performance.

Birthweight

A group of 917 children born prematurely (birthweight ≤2500 grams and gestation ≤36 weeks) was studied. In Table 10-13 the 8YR Articulation scores are reported for the total group and for subgroups according to Birthweight. It may be observed that prematurely born children and those with birthweight ≤2500 grams evidence a slight performance deficit. The difference is small and clearly not of clinical significance.

Parity

The number of offspring (parity) in a family may in some way affect the quality and quantity of social and communicative interaction between child and parents. Data were available for parity comparisons at each level of SEI. In Table 10-14 the proportion of passes on 8YR Articulation for parity ranging from 0 to 9 is indicated for each level of SEI.

The distribution of scores presented in Table 10-14 strongly suggests that large family size predicts a greater number of articulation failures (scoring in the lowest decile) when the SEI of the family is evaluated as low.

Table **10-10**

Multiple correlations between 8YR Articulation and selected independent variables with beta coefficients.

	At-Birth NCPP variables		At-Birth NCPP variables plus 8-Month NCPP variables		At-Birth NCPP variables plus 8-Month NCPP variables plus 4YR IQ		3YR Indexes		3YR Indexes plus At-Birth NCPP variables	
	β	B	β	B	β	B	β	B	β	B
Multiple R	.321		.344		.397		.373		.447	
R Square	.103		.119		.158		.139		.200	
Constant		38.29		30.65		27.29		33.04		27.58
3YR Speech Mechanism							.00509	.0263	.0137	.0707
3YR Hypernasality							−.00145	−.0956	−.000909	−.0601
3YR Fluency							.0191	.386	.0303	.614
3YR Articulation							.219	.790	.195	.703
3YR Intelligibility							.0871	.698	.0801	.642
3YR Language Comprehension							.130	.461	.0657	.233
3YR Sentence Complexity							.0921	.549	.0926	.552
3YR Auditory Memory							−.0242	−.330	−.0201	−.274
3YR Hearing Screen							−.0139	−.238	.00107	.0183
Birthweight	.0366	.000431	.00643	.758E-4*	−.00643	−.757E-4*			.0164	.000199
Gestational Age	.0207	.0427	.00277	.00571	.00527	.0108			.0245	.0515
Education of Gravida	.0810	.215	.0802	.213	.0452	.120			.0584	.156
Per Capita Income	.0750	.000437	.0623	.000363	.0412	.00240			.0304	.000181
Education of F.O.B.	.0626	.136	.0569	.123	.0292	.0634			.0663	.143
Occupation of F.O.B.	−.0139	−.197	−.0108	−.153	−.0278	−.394			−.0417	−.610
8-Month Mental Score			.0825	.0945	.0567	.0649				
8-Month Motor Score			.0648	.0892	.0412	.0567				
4YR IQ					.241	.0916				
Race-Sex Marker I	.0512	.457	.0615	.549	.0326	.291			.0834	.767
Race-Sex Marker II	.192	1.731	.195	1.762	.130	1.169			.153	1.434
Race-Sex Marker III	−.229	−2.072	−.230	−2.076	−.172	−1.552			−.212	−1.908

*The E ± xx refers to a power of 10 by which the preceding number should be multiplied. See Appendix 7.

Table **10-11**

Multiple correlations between 8YR Intelligibility and selected variables with beta coefficients.

	At-Birth NCPP variables		At-Birth NCPP variables plus 8-Month NCPP variables		At-Birth NCPP variables plus 8-Month NCPP variables plus 4YR IQ		3YR Indexes		3YR Indexes plus At-Birth NCPP variables	
	β	B	β	B	β	B	β	B	β	B
Multiple R	.154		.198		.245		.277		.293	
R Square	.0236		.0392		.0601		.0768		.0860	
Constant		2.70		2.35		2.24		2.40		2.24
3YR Speech Mechanism							.0281	.00675	.0295	.00708
3YR Hypernasality							-.0104	-.0319	-.0107	-.0329
3YR Fluency							.00101	.000951	.00439	.00414
3YR Articulation							.126	.0211	.117	.0196
3YR Intelligibility							.0341	.0127	.0275	.0102
3YR Language Comprehension							.0711	.0117	.0507	.00835
3YR Sentence Complexity							.122	.0339	.122	.0337
3YR Auditory Memory							.0454	.0288	.0453	.0288
3YR Hearing Screen							.0188	.0149	.0235	.0187
Birthweight	.0294	.159E-4*	-.00102	-.549E-6*	-.0104	-.562E-5*			.00925	.523E-5*
Gestational Age	.0169	.00160	-.00120	-.000113	.000619	.583E-4*			.0219	.00214
Education of Gravida	.0605	.00734	.0597	.00724	.0341	.00414			.0364	.00453
Per Capita Income	.0292	.780E-5*	.0164	.437E-5*	.000977	.261E-6*			.00397	.110E-5*
Education of F.O.B.	.0358	.00355	.0299	.00297	.00961	.000955			.0329	.00331
Occupation of F.O.B.	.00797	.00517	.0111	.00721	-.00134	.000866			-.0162	-.0110
8-Month Mental Score			.0806	.00422	.0617	.00323				
8-Month Motor Score			.0680	.00428	.0507	.00319				
4YR IQ					.176	.00306				
Race-Sex Marker I	-.0225	-.00922	-.0120	-.00492	-.0332	-.0136			.0125	.00537
Race-Sex Marker II	.0626	.0259	.0661	.0273	.0181	.00747			.0398	.0174
Race-Sex Marker III	-.0885	-.0366	-.0891	-.0368	-.0467	-.0193			-.0772	-.0323

*The E ± xx refers to a power of 10 by which the preceding number should be multiplied. See Appendix 7.

Table **10-12**

Multiple correlations between 8YR Fluency and selected independent variables with beta coefficients.

	At-Birth NCPP variables		At-Birth NCPP variables plus 8-Month NCPP variables		At-Birth NCPP variables plus 8-Month NCPP variables plus 4YR IQ		3YR Indexes		3YR Indexes plus At-Birth NCPP variables	
	β	B	β	B	β	B	β	B	β	B
Multiple R	.0946		.103		.114		.0840		.133	
R Square	.00894		.0106		.0130		.00706		.0177	
Constant		6.81		6.61		6.54		6.35		6.34
3YR Speech Mechanism							-.00749	-.00339	-.00406	-.00184
3YR Hypernasality							.00245	.0142	.00308	.0179
3YR Fluency							.0508	.0901	.0532	.0944
3YR Articulation							.0272	.00859	.0182	.00575
3YR Intelligibility							.00222	.00156	-.000397	-.000279
3YR Language Comprehension							.0336	.0105	.0102	.00316
3YR Sentence Complexity							.0141	.00738	.0142	.00742
3YR Auditory Memory							.0152	.0182	.0189	.0225
3YR Hearing Screen							.0270	.0405	.0324	.0486
Birthweight	-.00589	-.596E-5*	-.0159	-.161E-4*	-.0191	-.193E-4*			-.00417	-.445E-5*
Gestational Age	.00620	.00110	.000262	.464E-4*	.000879	.000156			-.00123	-.000227
Education of Gravida	.00168	.000383	.00143	.000326	-.00725	.00165			-.00546	-.00128
Per Capita Income	.00197	.987E-6*	-.00227	-.114E-5*	-.00749	.376E-5*			-.00195	-.102E-5*
Education of F.O.B.	.0274	.00512	.0254	.00474	.0186	.00346			.0316	.00600
Occupation of F.O.B.	-.00583	-.00710	-.00482	-.00587	-.00904	-.0110			-.0115	-.0148
8-Month Mental Score			.0246	.00242	.0182	.00179				
8-Month Motor Score			.0239	.00283	.0181	.00214				
4YR IQ					.0596	.00195				
Race-Sex Marker I	.0157	.0120	.0192	.0147	.0120	.00923			.0299	.0241
Race-Sex Marker II	.0741	.0575	.0753	.0584	.0590	.0458			.0813	.0669
Race-Sex Marker III	-.0934	-.0726	-.0936	-.0727	-.0792	-.0616			-.116	-.0916

*The E ± xx refers to a power of 10 by which the preceding number should be multiplied. See Appendix 7.

259

Table **10-13**

Performance on 8YR Articulation test of children born prematurely and subgroups of 8YR samples by Birthweight.

Group	N	Mean	SD
Prematures	917	44	7.2
≤1,500 grams	100	42	10.3
1,501-2,500 grams	1,905	45	7.1
2,501-3,500 grams	12,948	46	6.3
3,501-4,500 grams	4,998	46	6.0
4,501+ grams	166	46	7.3
ALL 8YR	**20,137**	**46**	**6.4**

Table **10-14**

Proportion of 8YR Articulation passes for each SEI level by Parity. The number of subjects is indicated in parenthesis.

					Socioeconomic Index
Parity	0.0-1.9	2.0-3.9	4.0-5.9	6.0-7.9	8.0-9.5
0	88.9	94.1	89.9	91.5	93.0
	(24)	(80)	(89)	(97)	(66)
1	81.9	85.5	90.7	90.8	90.1
	(204)	(982)	(1,225)	(954)	(573)
2	76.7	83.4	88.4	89.6	87.7
	(165)	(786)	(873)	(626)	(327)
3	81.8	83.7	86.5	90.9	89.7
	(126)	(592)	(682)	(389)	(165)
4	80.7	83.5	84.4	89.7	92.7
	(117)	(425)	(422)	(243)	(89)
5	78.3	82.7	88.3	88.0	84.8
	(65)	(345)	(286)	(139)	(39)
6	83.1	81.8	86.9	81.5	100.0
	(49)	(184)	(172)	(75)	(21)
7	70.8	80.6	82.2	85.2	86.7
	(34)	(133)	(88)	(46)	(13)
8	63.0	75.2	78.8	89.2	50.0
	(17)	(88)	(52)	(33)	(2)
9	72.2	83.1	84.2	93.3	100.0
	(13)	(49)	(32)	(14)	(2)

Education of Gravida

The education of the mother appears to be correlated with articulation performance. The following percentages of passes were obtained for three levels of education: 0 to 8 years of schooling, 82.3%; 9 to 12 years of schooling, 88.1%; 13 and more years of schooling, 91.1%. Possibly, the level of education influences the way in which mothers stimulate and communicate with children.

Special Groups

Indicated in Table 10-15 are the 8YR Articulation mean scores categorized by race, sex, SEI, family status, presence of stuttering, and selected organic dis-

Table 10-15

Performance on 8YR Articulation by ALL 8YR children categorized according to sex, race, Socioeconomic Index, family status, disorders of stuttering, mental retardation with syndromes, hearing loss, cerebral palsy and cleft palate.

Group	N	Mean	SD
White Male	5,142	47	6.6
White Female	4,948	48	5.0
Black Male	4,848	43	7.3
Black Female	4,915	45	5.3
SEI 0.0-1.9	1,599	43	7.3
SEI 2.0-3.9	5,901	44	7.0
SEI 4.0-5.9	5,972	46	6.0
SEI 6.0-7.9	4,080	47	5.4
SEI 8.0-9.5	2,301	48	4.7
Singletons	879	47	5.5
Siblings	3,880	46	6.5
Twins	370	45	7.0
Foster Parents	277*	44	8.7
Adopted	243*	47	5.8
Stutterers	35	38	13
Cerebral Palsy	83	38	15
Cleft Palate	24	38	12
Mental Retardation with Syndromes	53	29	15
Conductive Hearing Loss	1,024	44	8.1
Sensorineural Hearing Loss	447	43	9.0
Normal Hearing	18,438	46	6.0

*N based on 3YR and 8YR combined; mean and SD based on those given the 8YR Test.

orders. Differences among the averages of major groups are very small. The effect of family status across race, sex, and SEI is graphed in Figure 10-9.

Cerebral palsied children and children with cleft palate score significantly below normal children. A surprising finding is that stutterers evidence articulation scores which are well below the average score. Children with syndromes who were mentally retarded had dramatically lower articulation scores. The distribution of 8YR Articulation mean scores by grouped IQ is shown in Table 10-16. It is clear that increasing IQ results in increased articulation ability. Differences are small, however, in the normal IQ range.

Stuttering

Table 10-17 shows the average scores on 8YR speech and language indexes for 35 stutterers as well as for the total group. On every measure stutterers performed less well than the average of all groups combined. There is conflicting opinion as to the interpretation of these scores (Johnson, 1955; Van Riper, 1971). It can be argued either that stutterers are innately different from nonstutterers and/or that the stuttering itself negatively affects performance skills.

Discussion

These results indicate that no single factor studied can be said to reflect a significant degree of causality or association with regard to speech production. Low but positive relationships were obtained between speech performance, the articulation and intelligibility measures, and some of the nonphysical variables, primarily SEI and intelligence. Articulation errors appeared not to be consistently

Figure 10-9

Means and standard deviations for 8YR Articulation for singletons, siblings and twins by sex, race and Socioeconomic Index

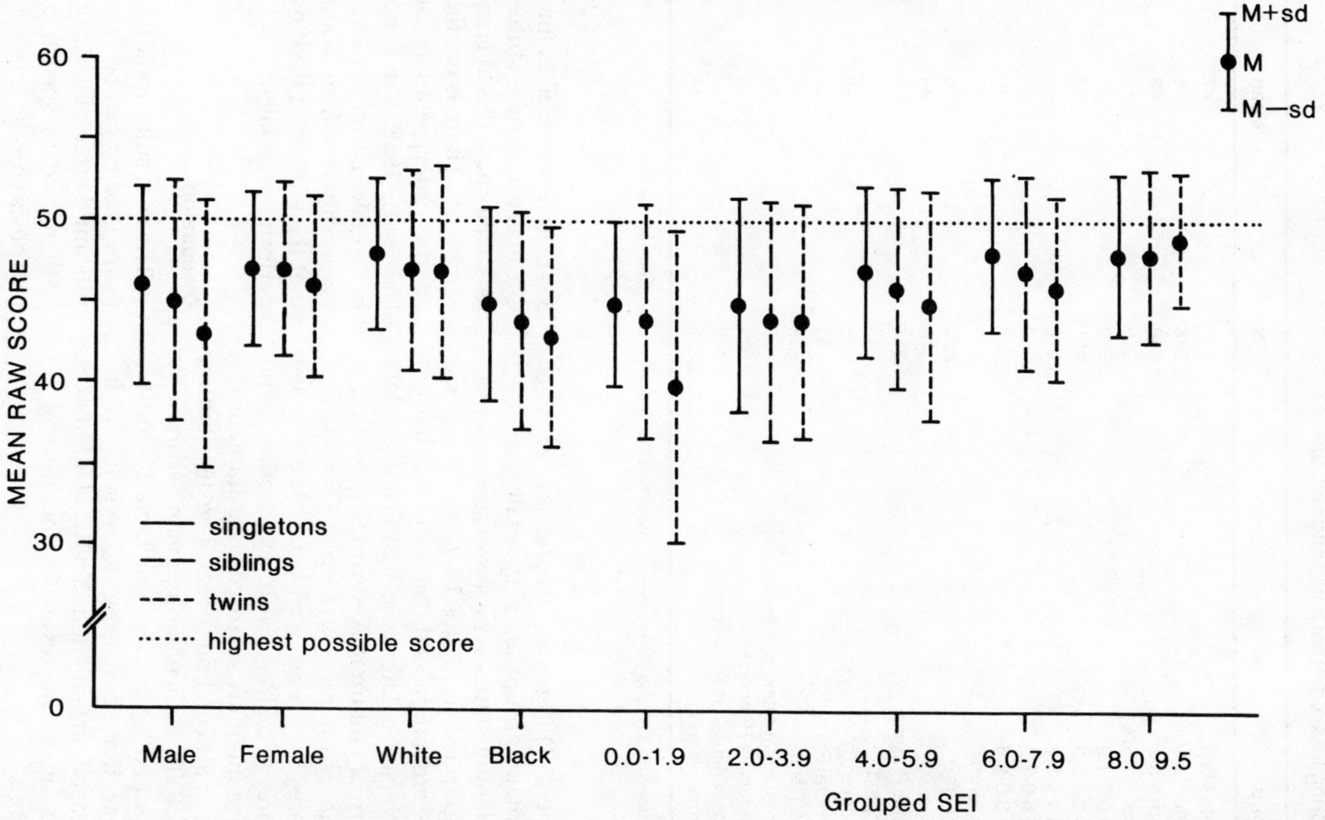

262

Table 10-16

Mean scores on 8YR Articulation by grouped WISC IQ, sex and race.

IQ	41-50	51-60	61-70	71-80	81-90	91-100	101-110	111-120	>120
White Male	28	26	39	42	45	47	47	48	48
White Female	33	32	43	44	47	48	48	49	48
Black Male	28	34	37	41	43	44	46	47	48
Black Female	20	36	40	43	45	46	47	48	49
N	22	92	397	1,670	3,467	5,268	4,540	2,374	919

Table 10-17

Comparison between stutterers and ALL 8YR sample on several speech and language indexes.

8YR Indexes	Stutterers		ALL 8YR	
	Mean	SD	Mean	SD
8YR Speech Mechanism	7.6	1.4	7.9	.68
8YR Intelligibility	2.5	.79	2.9	.29
8YR Articulation	38	13	46	6.4
8YR Language Comprehension	122	52	153	45
8YR Auditory Memory Span	141	57	170	41
8YR Digits	27	13	34	10
8YR Word Identification	55	13	62	9.9
8YR Written Communication	163	71	202	57
8YR Language Production	662	147	727	102
8YR Concept Development	35	14	42	10

related to a single physical or behavioral variable with the exception of the Bayley scale item Turns to Sound of Bell. No clear predictors emerged from an analysis of the physical variables; this is in agreement with findings reported in Winitz (1969). Winitz summarized the results of a large number of studies and concluded that social variables are more strongly related to articulation growth than are physical variables, except for clearly relevant organic deficiencies. The cleft palate and cerebral palsied children in this study demonstrated impairment in articulation. Articulation scores show a slight relationship to social experience and background; SEI and Education of Gravida correlate with articulation development.

Speech development is the result of a complex interaction between physical maturity and environment. Children classified as mentally retarded evidenced severe deficiencies in intelligibility and articulation. Although physical variables were nonpredictive for the general population, true prematures and low birthweight children evidenced a slight performance deficit in articulation.

Our investigation of fluency also failed to indicate specific variables or sets of variables that contribute to poor fluency. However, when stutterers were examined as a group they performed less well

263

than the total sample on several language and speech measures. It is not known whether the stutterers' depressed scores reflected a general inability to perform well, or whether a past history of stuttering adversely affected performance.

Summary

Voice, articulation, and fluency measures were obtained for children at three years and eight years of age. The findings are summarized below.

1. Voice evaluations (Pitch, Loudness, and Quality) indicated that a small proportion of the 3YR children, usually less than 8%, performed abnormally. At eight years, hoarseness was the only disorder of voice that reflected a significant frequency of abnormality, about 9%.

2. At three years, 35% to 39% of the children were regarded as having articulation scores for consonants that were abnormal or suspect, but only 11% had abnormal or suspect vowel production. Less than 5% of the sample were regarded as unintelligible. At eight years, there were small differences in the articulation scores of the several subgroups. Articulation was slightly lower for Blacks, Males, and children of low and moderately low SEI. At eight years, about 1% of the sample were considered to be difficult to understand.

3. A fairly strong relationship was noted between articulation and intelligibility. Articulation showed a weak relationship with some of the language measures.

4. Interrelationships among the several voice measures were weak.

5. The intercorrelations among the fluency measures of Rate, Struggle Behavior, and Dysfluent Events were low.

6. Correlations computed between 3YR and 8YR Speech Production measures were too small to be of value in making predictions.

7. Three speech production indexes (3YR Articulation, 3YR Intelligibility, and 8YR Fluency) were devised by grouping related variables into more comprehensive measures. It was found that Initial Consonants contributed more than Vowels and Diphthongs to the 3YR Articulation Index; Dysfluent Events and Struggle Behavior contributed strongly to the Fluency Index. Intercorrelations between the 3YR and 8YR indexes were generally of the same magnitude as those obtained for the single speech production measures.

8. The intercorrelations between SLH indexes and NCPP variables were generally small and not of predictive value. Among those relationships that showed small, positive correlations were 4YR IQ with 3YR Articulation, 7YR IQ with 8YR Intelligibility, SEI with 8YR Articulation, Auditory-Vocal Association Test with 8YR Articulation, and several social variables (Occupation of Mother, Housing Density, Per Capita Income) with 8YR Articulation. School achievement, as measured by the WRAT spelling, reading, and arithmetic tests showed a weak positive relationship with 8YR Articulation.

9. With few exceptions, conditional probabilities supported correlational findings. The Bayley tests for sound orientation were predictors of performance on the 3YR Articulation test. The likelihood of reduced articulation scores and intelligibility at 3YR is greater if one fails the Bayley sound tests (bell and rattle). WISC IQ at 7YR seemed predictive of 8YR Articulation and 8YR Intelligibility.

10. Multiple regression analysis yielded R's too small for definitive diagnostic or predictive purposes.

SEI variables and 4YR IQ contribute most to the variance of the articulation and intelligibility scores.

11. Children with cleft palate, cerebral palsy, and mental retardation performed at a lower level on 3YR and 8YR articulation tests, considered clinically significant.

12. Children identified as stutterers performed at a clinically significant lower level on articulation and on measures of language.

13. Family status influenced 8YR Articulation. Adopted children performed better than foster children. Singletons scored higher than children with siblings, and twins scored lowest. Whites generally performed slightly better than Blacks and Females slightly better than Males on 8YR Articulation. Performance improved consistently for all groups as SEI increased.

14. Adverse birth conditions (low 5-minute Apgar score and low birthweight) did not distinguish children on 8YR Articulation sufficiently for clinical prediction.

References

1. Bordley, J.E., and Hardy, J.B. A hearing survey of preschool children. *Trans. Am. Acad. Ophthalmol. Otolaryngol.* 76:349–354, 1972.

2. Dunn, L.M. *Peabody Picture Vocabulary Test Manual.* Circle Pines, Minnesota: American Guidance Service, 1965.

3. Durrell, D.D., and Sullivan, H.B. *Durrell-Sullivan Reading Capacity and Achievement Tests.* New York: Harcourt, Brace and World, 1945.

4. Gray, W.S. *Gray Oral Reading Tests.* Indianapolis, Indiana: Bobbs-Merrill, 1967.

5. Johnson, W. (Ed.) *Stuttering in Children and Adults.* Minneapolis: University of Minnesota Press, 1955.

6. McCarthy, J.J., and Kirk, S.A. *The Construction, Standardization and Statistical Characteristics of the Illinois Test of Psycholinguistic Ability. Experimental Edition.* Urbana, Ill.: University of Illinois Press, 1963.

7. Templin, M.C., and Darley, F.L. *The Templin-Darley Test of Articulation.* Iowa City, Iowa: University of Iowa Press, 1960.

8. Van Riper, C. *The Nature of Stuttering.* Englewood Cliffs, N.J.: Prentice-Hall, 1971.

9. Winitz, H. *Articulatory Acquisition and Behavior.* New York: Appleton-Century-Crofts, 1969.

10. Winitz, H. *From Syllable to Conversation.* Baltimore: University Park Press, 1975.

11

Language

Dolores K. Vetter, Ph.D.
Warren H. Fay, Ph.D.
Harris Winitz, Ph.D.

Language Variables

The NINCDS Collaborative Perinatal Project was designed to include an evaluation of the language behavior of the children at two different ages. Each evaluation was composed of tests selected to assess various aspects of language behavior.

The 3YR speech, language, and hearing (SLH) examination which was administered to 19,885 children evaluated the general areas of language reception and language expression with five tests. Language comprehension was measured through the Identification of Familiar Objects, Understanding Action Words, and Understanding Words Indicating Space Relationships and Directions. Language expression was measured by Naming Objects and the Use of Phrases or Sentences. The tests are described in Chapter 3, and the manual for administration containing the scoring criteria is found in Appendix 1. Frequency distributions for SLH variables are found in Appendix 3.

Within the area of language comprehension, or reception, performance on the tests indicated an order of difficulty: 93% of the children passed Identification of Familiar Objects; 89% passed Understanding Action Words; and 78% passed Understanding Space Relationships and Directions. Although there were consistent differences between Males and Females, the differences were only 2% to 3% favoring the Female (Figure 11-1). A higher percentage of White children than Black children passed the tests (Figure 11-2). This finding may reflect cultural differences inherent in the test construction. Socioeconomic Index (SEI) level appeared to be highly related to the percentage passing. Fewer children passed in the lower SEI groups than in the higher groups (Figure 11-3). Because the lower SEI groups contained a higher proportion of Black children and the upper SEI groups a higher proportion of White children, it is not possible to determine whether race and SEI effects were due to one or both of these factors.

Within the area of language expression, 85% of the children passed Naming Objects. Females achieved higher scores than Males with a difference of 6% in the number who passed this test (Figure 11-1). Differences due to race were only 2% (Figure 11-2). Fewer children passed in the lower SEI groups than in the upper groups (Figure 11-3).

The second test of language expression was Use of Phrases or Sentences. This test did not use a standard procedure for eliciting conversation from the child; scores were based on observations by the examiner throughout the 3YR examination. Judgments of pass or fail were made on five scales relating to sentence length and structure, word order, relevance, and use of pronouns. If the child passed any four of these, he scored a pass on the Summary Evaluation. Figures 11-1, 11-2, and 11-3 contain information concerning performance on this test. Again, more Females passed than did Males (2% to 6%). The percentage of Black children who passed was slightly greater than the percentage of White children on the Summary Evaluation (1%) and on three of the five scales (1% to 2%). Trends in SEI noted previously were repeated in these scales and in the Summary Evaluation. The data for both of these tests of language expression suggest that it is SEI

rather than race which influences expressive ability.

The SLH examination at eight years evaluated language comprehension and language expression (see Chapter 3) on a sample of 20,137 children. Language comprehension was assessed by Word Identification (Peabody Picture Vocabulary Test, Form B, Dunn, 1965), Orientation, and Understanding a Story. Language expression was measured by Morphology, using the Auditory-Vocal Automatic Test (AVAT) of the Illinois Test of Psycholinguistic Abilities (ITPA) (McCarthy and Kirk, 1963) and evaluations of Connected Discourse. The test Connected Discourse consisted of the examiner's telling a story illustrated by sequential line drawings, then asking the child to retell the story. The child's story was rated on five scales and the number of concepts recounted. Figures 11-4 through 11-13 contain descriptive statistics for these variables.

The Word Identification (Figure 11-4) mean for the total group was 62.45 and the standard deviation (SD) was 9.98. This is slightly lower than the mean of the seven-year-six-month to eight-year-five-month White standardization group (Dunn, 1965). There has been no standardization for Black children. In the Collaborative Perinatal Project (NCPP), the mean for White children was 67.65, SD 8.45, and the mean for Black children was 57.08, SD 8.45. Males performed slightly better than Females, and the trend was toward higher performance as socioeconomic level increased.

Orientation (Figure 11-5) had a mean for the total sample of 7.68, SD 2.12. Differences between Males and Females were small but were larger between Black children and White children. The SEI effect was rather pronounced; lower socioeconomic level children performed more poorly than higher SEI children.

Figure 11-6 shows the performance of the children on Understanding A Story. The mean for the total sample was 3.01,

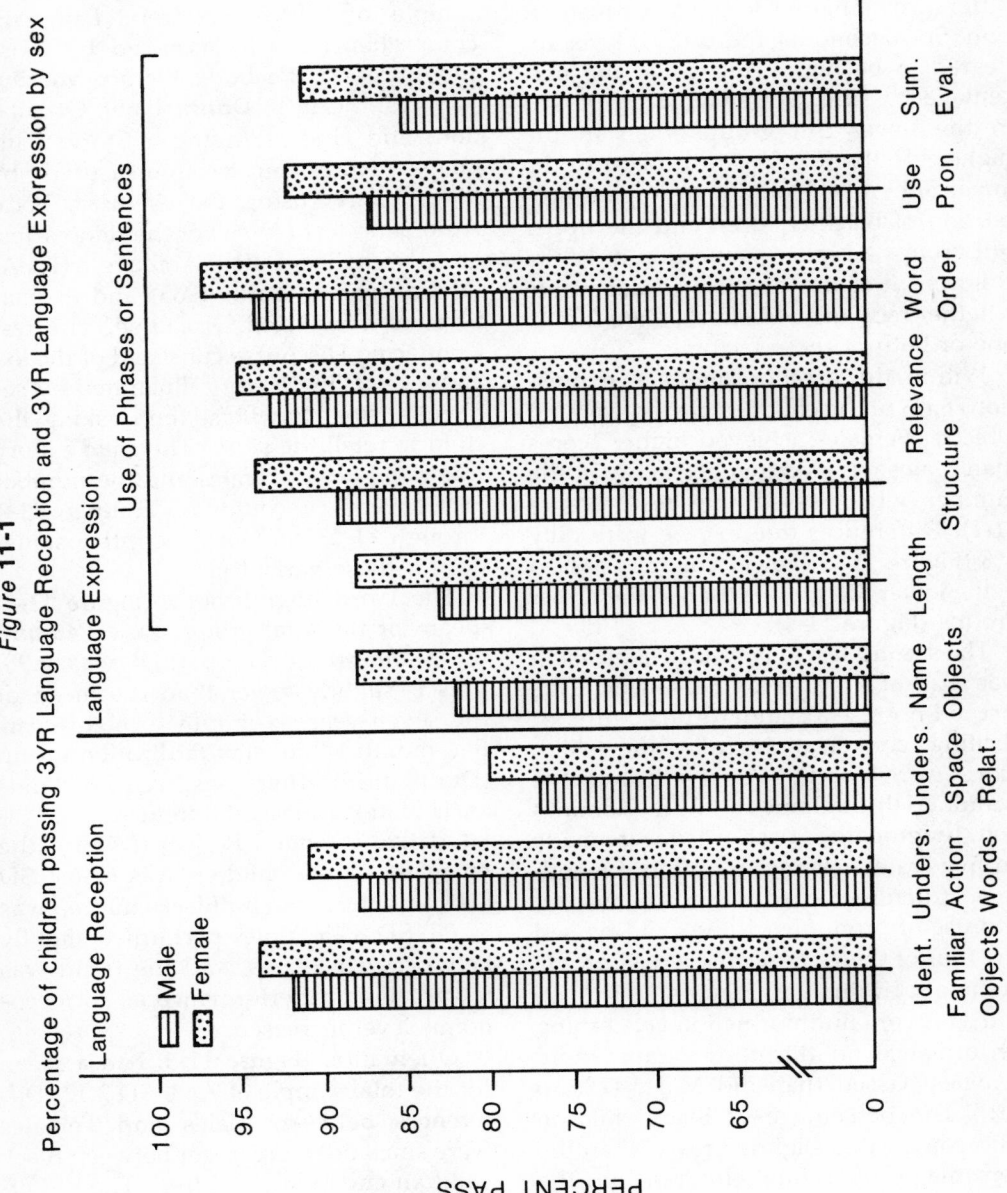

Figure 11-1

Percentage of children passing 3YR Language Reception and 3YR Language Expression by sex

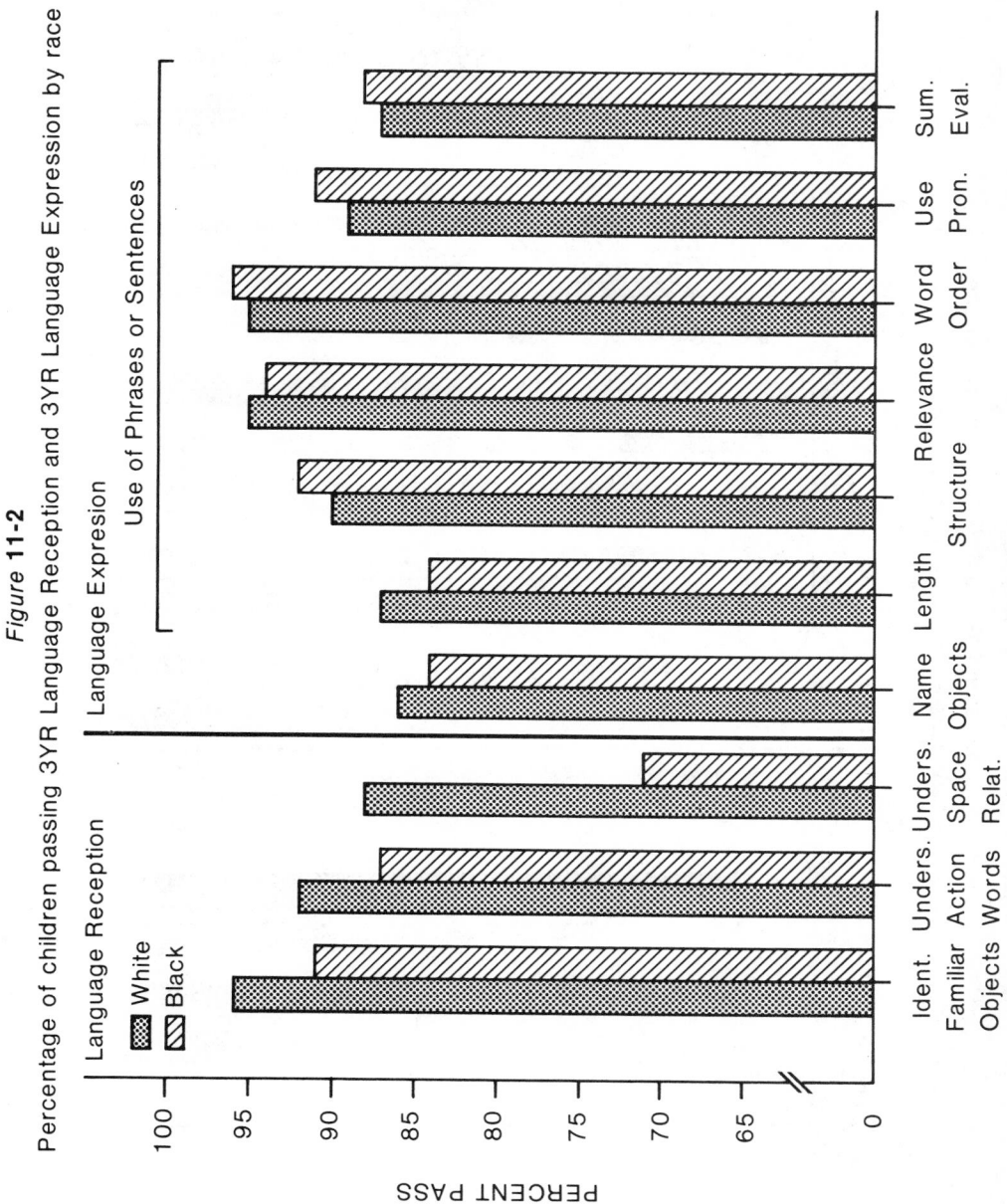

Figure 11-2

Percentage of children passing 3YR Language Reception and 3YR Language Expression by race

269

Figure 11-3

Percentage of children passing 3YR Language Reception and 3YR Language Expression by Socioeconomic Index

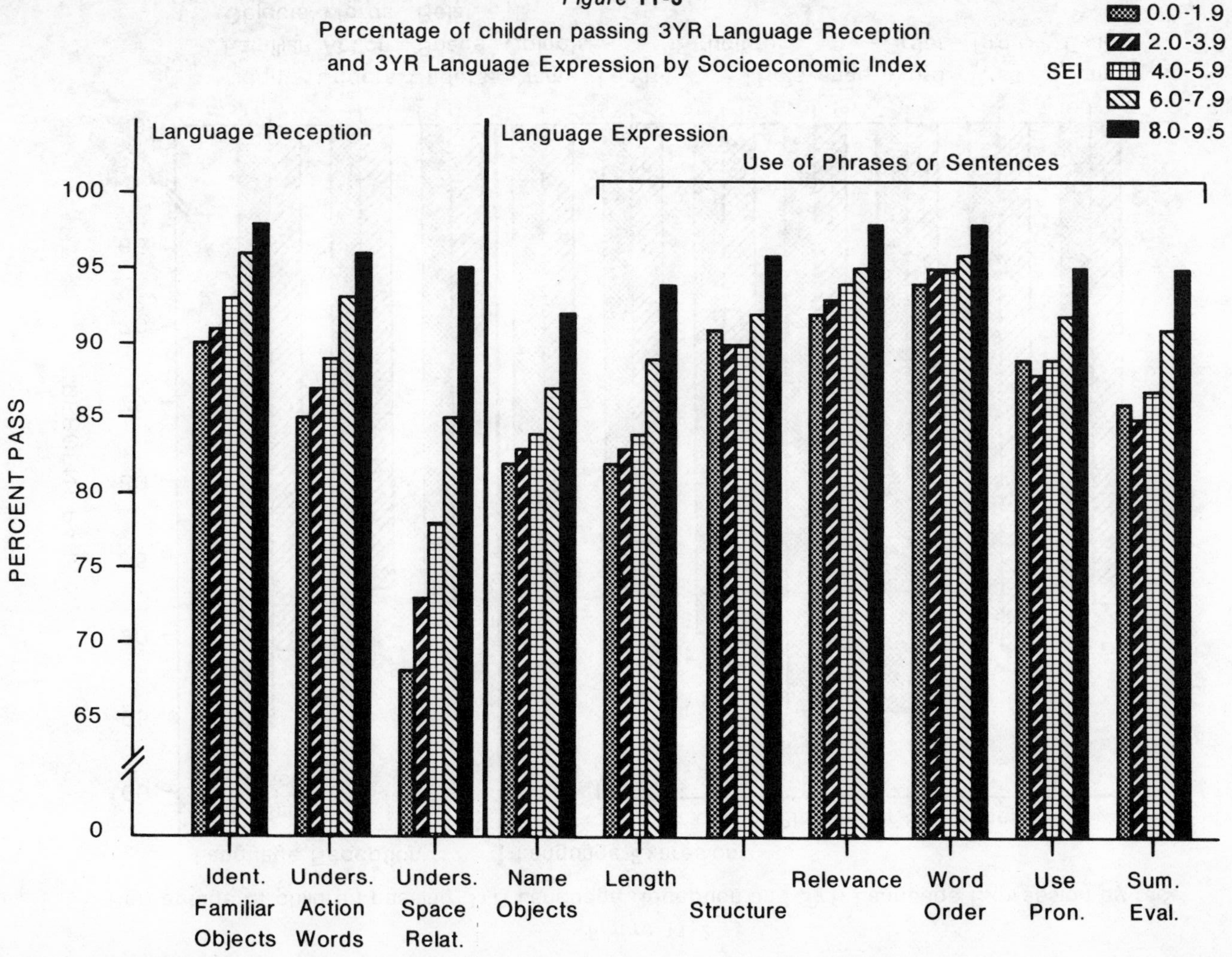

270

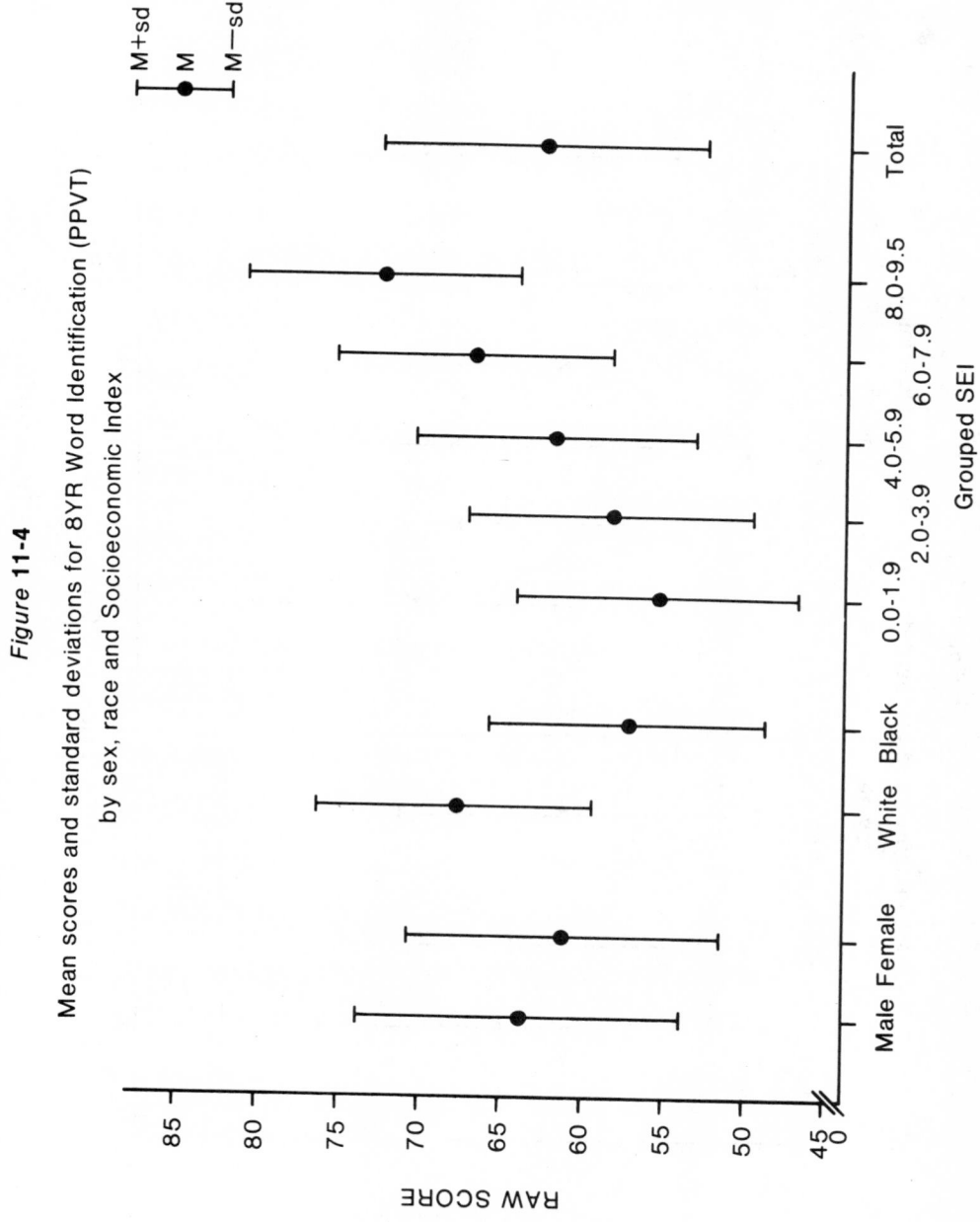

Figure 11-4

Mean scores and standard deviations for 8YR Word Identification (PPVT) by sex, race and Socioeconomic Index

271

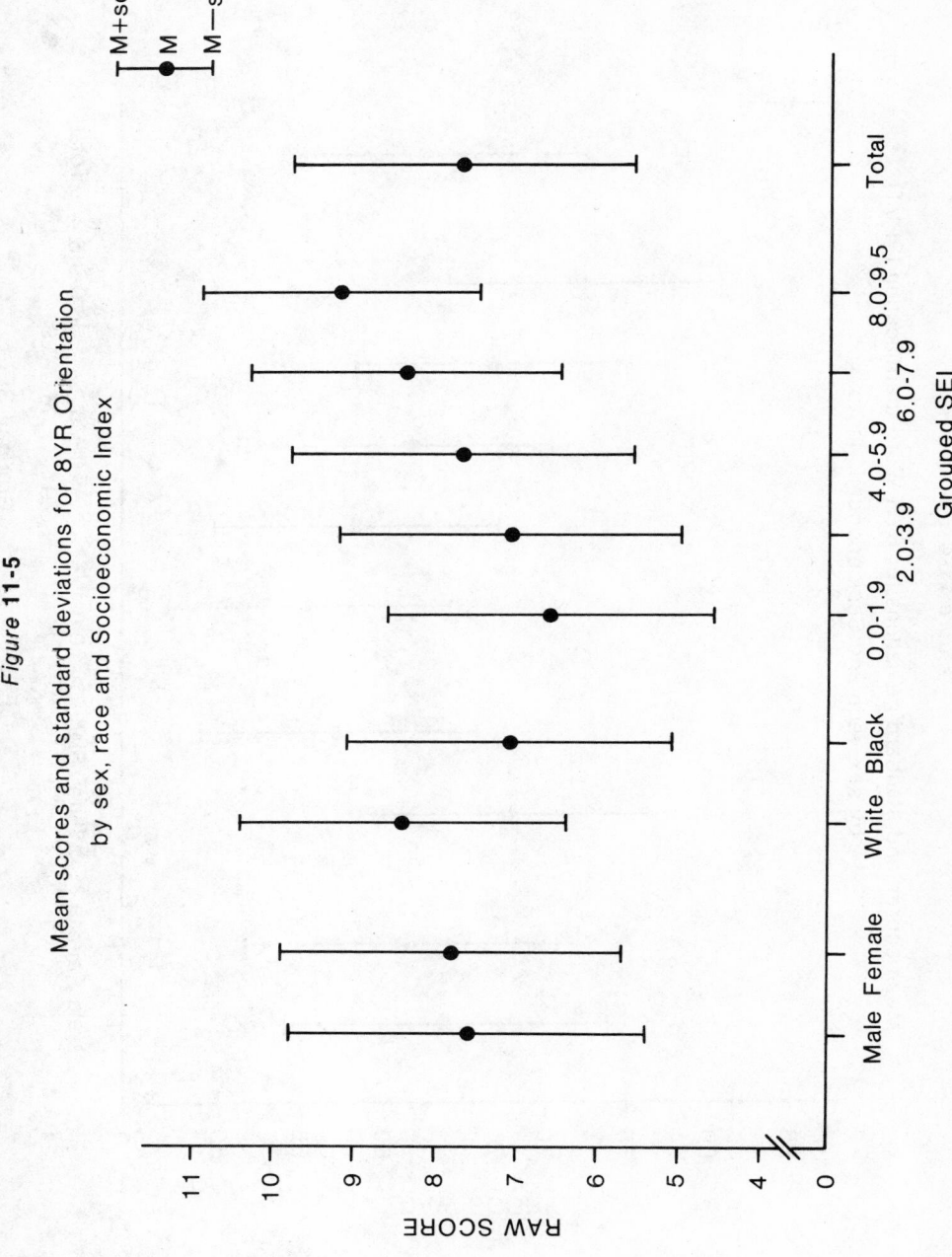

Figure **11-5**

Mean scores and standard deviations for 8YR Orientation
by sex, race and Socioeconomic Index

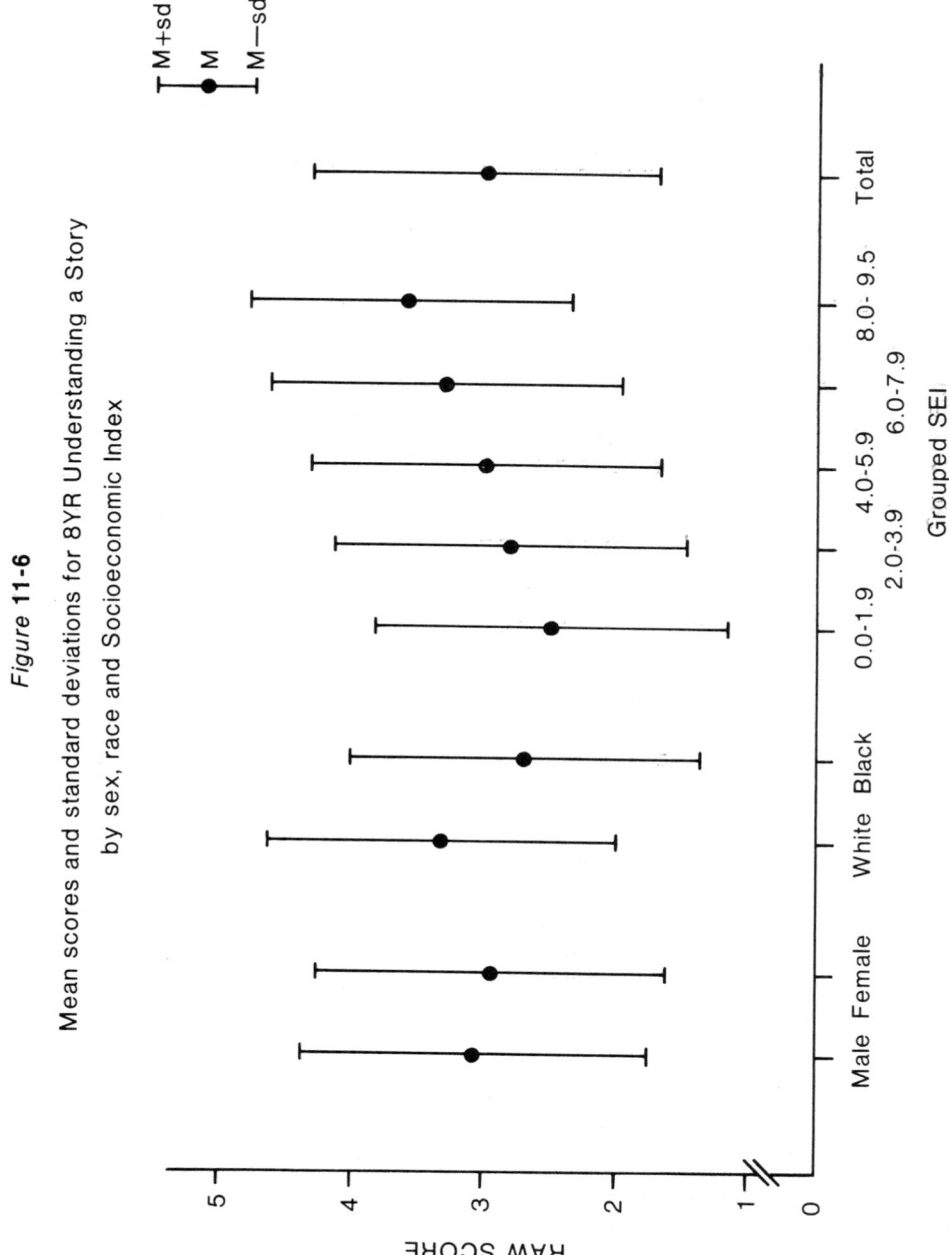

Figure **11-6**

Mean scores and standard deviations for 8YR Understanding a Story by sex, race and Socioeconomic Index

SD 1.32. It can be seen that Males performed slightly better than Females and that White children performed better than Black children. The SEI effect was present but was not as pronounced as in the Word Identification or Orientation tests.

The first 8YR test of language expression was Morphology (Figure 11-7). The mean for the total sample was 14.34, SD 4.73, which is slightly lower than that reported by McCarthy and Kirk (1963) in the standardization data for the comparable age group. Male and Female means were similar, in agreement with the McCarthy and Kirk data. Because standardization was conducted solely on White children, it is not possible to compare the present study data with the earlier data. In this study, however, White children performed better than Black children. Social class was defined differently by McCarthy and Kirk than it was in the present study, but the effect of SEI shown in Figure 11-7 is consistent with the data for social class reported by these authors.

There appear to be no substantial sex differences on any of the parameters of Connected Discourse (Figures 11-8 through 11-13). Females did slightly better than Males, but the differences are inconsequential. Differences between White and Black children were also slight, particularly when the categories of Excellent and Adequate are combined. Even differences in SEI were small, although the trend is in the expected direction. The confounding of race with SEI makes it impossible to infer a causal influence by either of these factors on language expression at age eight years. Whatever influence they may have produces less effect on judgments of Connected Discourse than it does on Morphology.

Correlations Among 3YR Variables

The intercorrelations among the 3YR Language Comprehension measures ranged from .30 to .39 (Appendix 6). The magnitude of the correlations suggests that they measure slightly different aspects of language comprehension. The correlations between the 3YR Language Comprehension and Expression measures were also relatively small (.14 to .27). This finding might be interpreted as indicating some overlap between the processes of language reception and language expression, but there is considerable variance which they do not share. The intercorrelations among the 3YR Language Expression measures were in general considerably higher (.24 to .75). The lower correlations occurred between the test Naming Objects and the various ratings of overall language expression such as Sentence Structure, Relevance, and Word Order. While it had been expected that the several ratings of language expression would correlate strongly with the Summary Item Score because of the part-whole relationship, the correlations among the ratings themselves were also quite high, indicating an association between ratings of Length of Expression, Relevance, and Grammar.

For normal-hearing children the 3YR Spondaic Word Test is essentially a language imitation task. The correlations between the various language comprehension and expression measures and the 3YR Spondaic Word Test ranged from .16 to .25. The other correlations of interest are those between the language measures and Articulation and Intelligibility. The correlations between Language Comprehension and Articulation were relatively low (.10 to .32) and those between Language Expression and Articulation were similar (.12 to .28).

The correlations between Intelligibility and Language Comprehension were smaller (.22 to .26) than those with Language Expression (.34 to .52). These higher correlations suggest that the examiners may have used Intelligibility as an aid in making judgments of Language Expression.

274

Figure 11-7

Mean scores and standard deviations for 8YR Morphology (AVAT) by sex, race and Socioeconomic Index

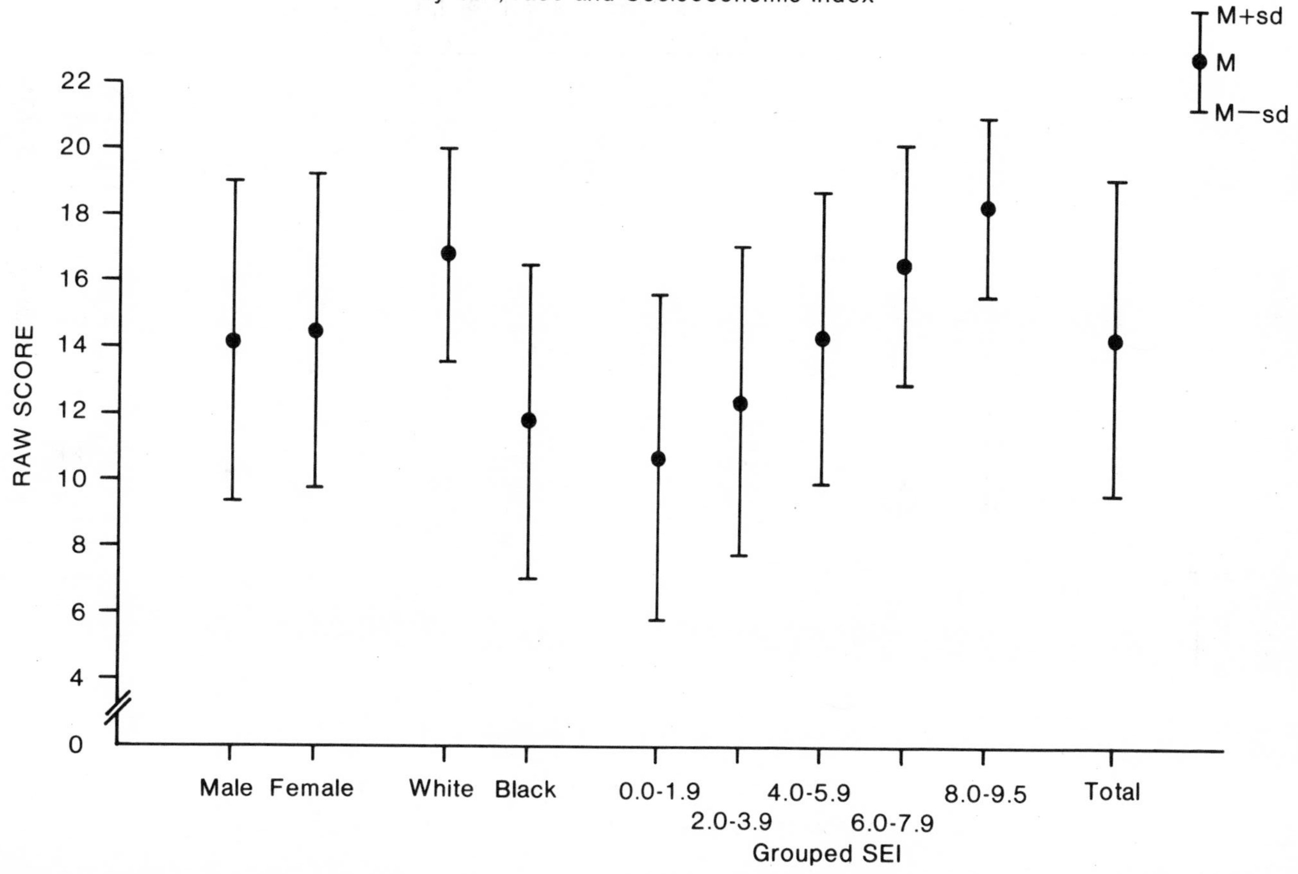

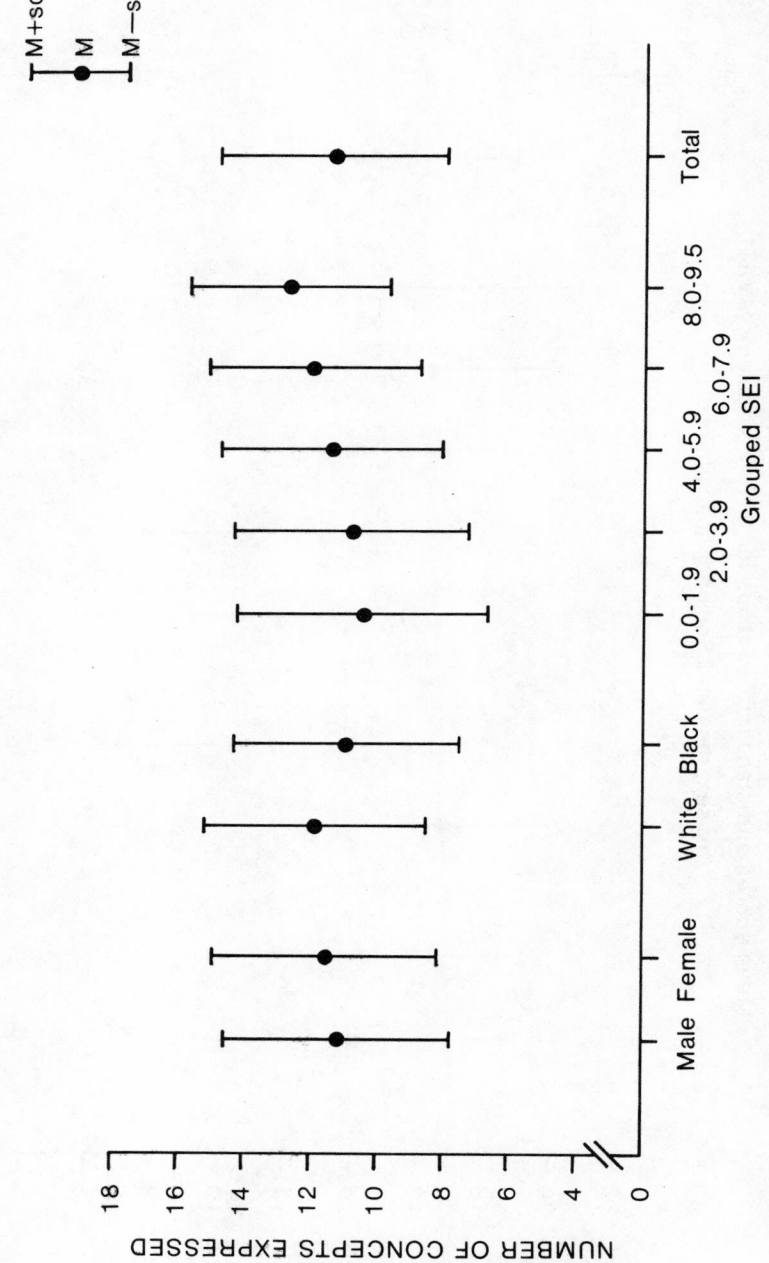

Figure 11-8

Mean scores and standard deviations for 8YR Number of Concepts Expressed in Connected Discourse by sex, race and Socioeconomic Index

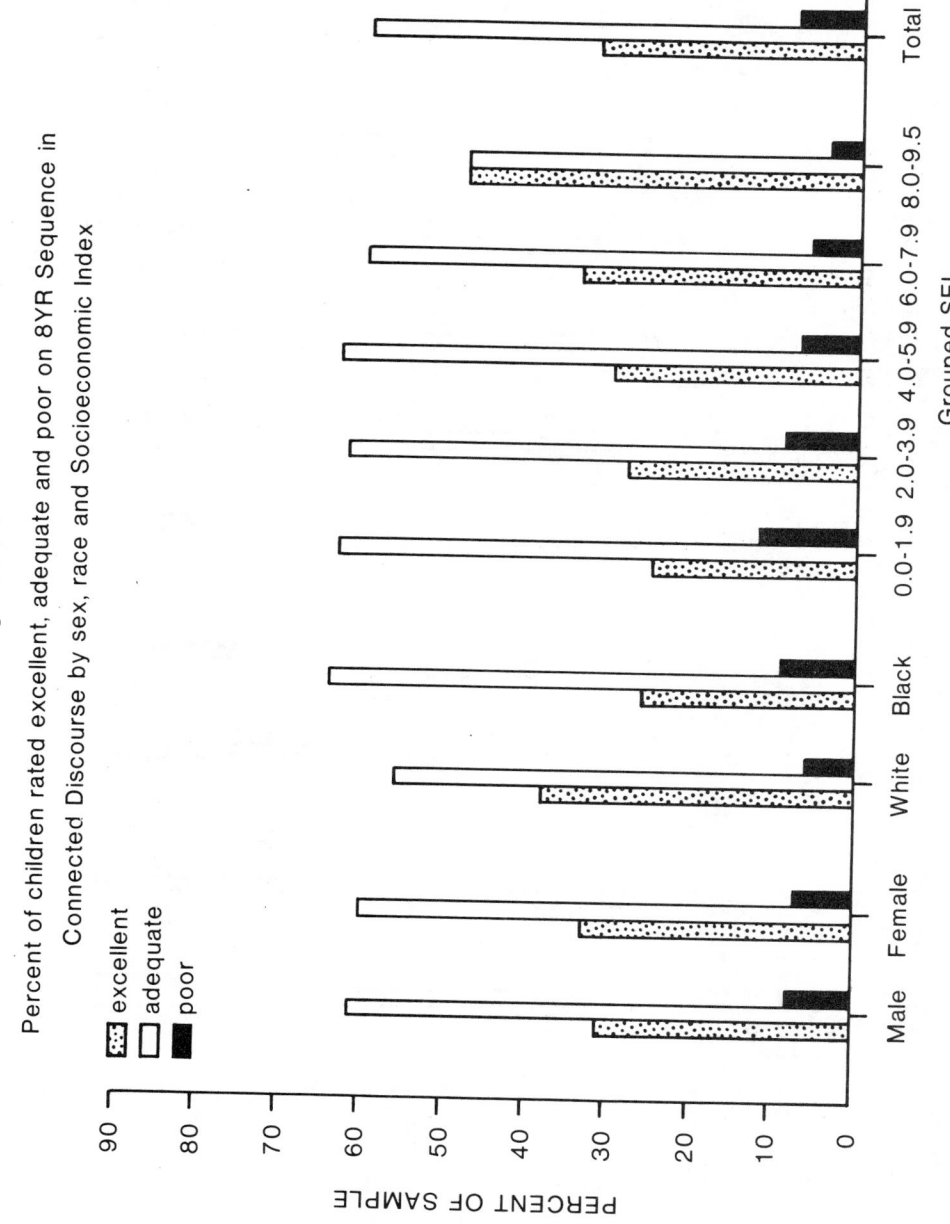

Figure **11-9**

Percent of children rated excellent, adequate and poor on 8YR Sequence in Connected Discourse by sex, race and Socioeconomic Index

277

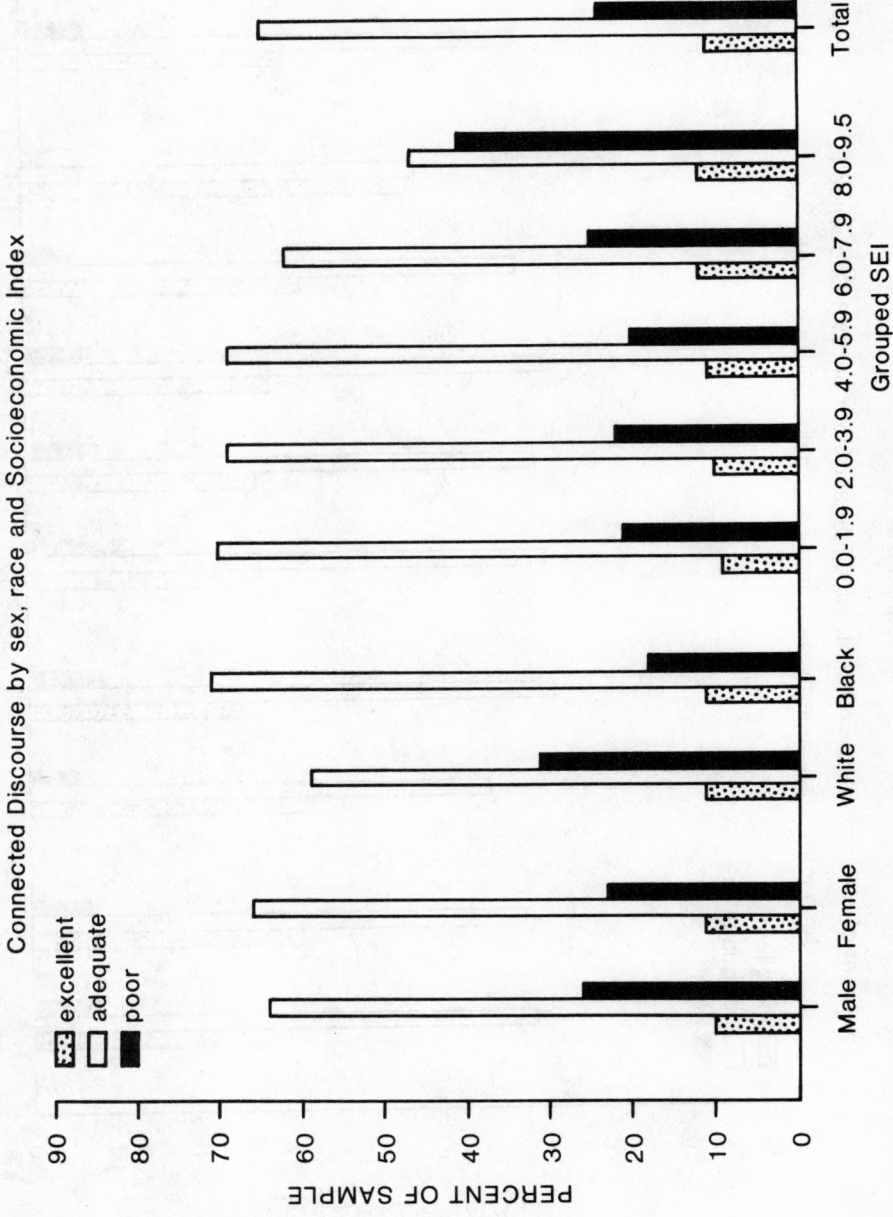

Figure 11-10

Percent of children rated excellent, adequate and poor on 8YR Elaboration in Connected Discourse by sex, race and Socioeconomic Index

excellent
adequate
poor

PERCENT OF SAMPLE

90 80 70 60 50 40 30 20 10 0

Male Female   White Black   0.0-1.9 2.0-3.9 4.0-5.9 6.0-7.9 8.0-9.5   Total

Grouped SEI

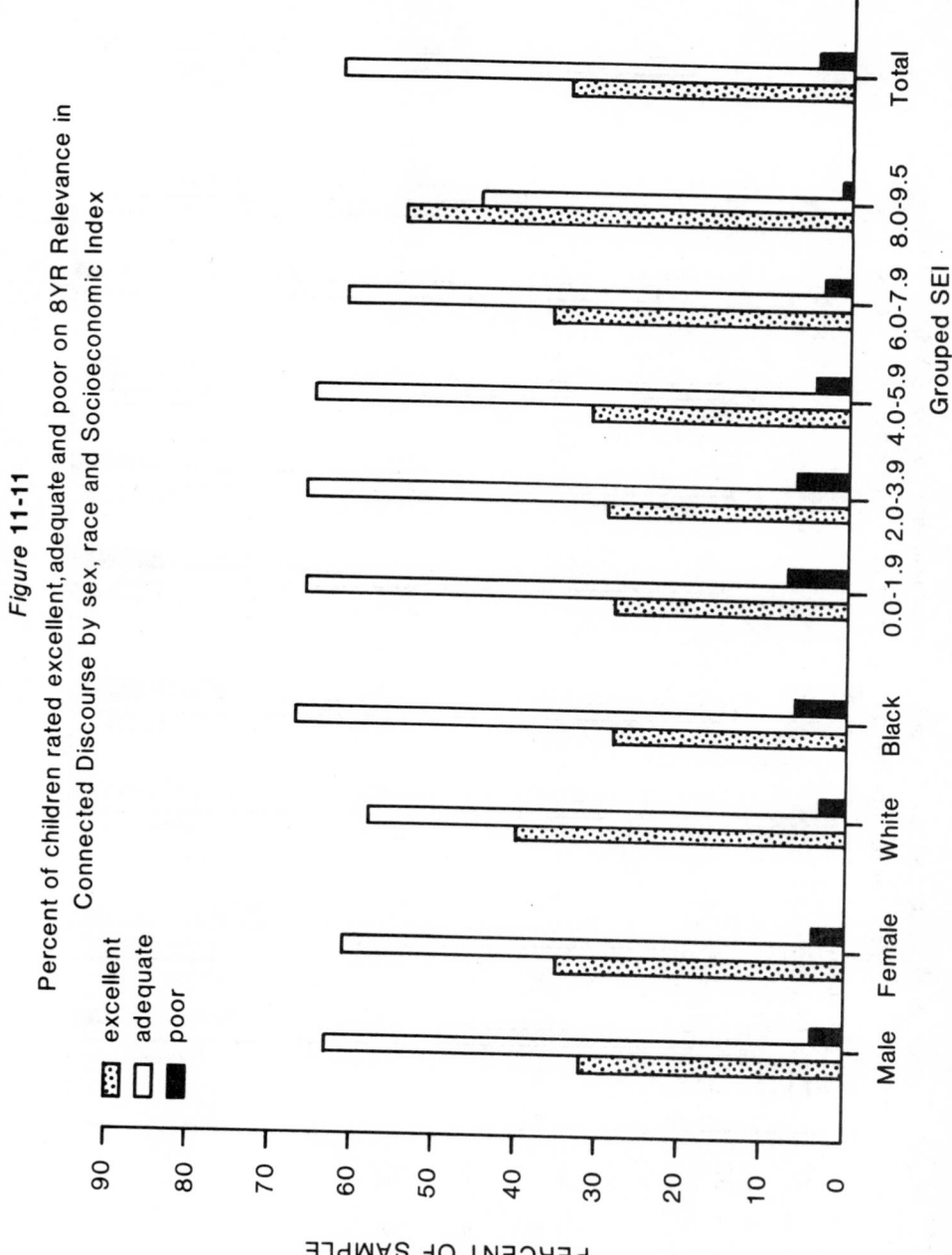

Figure **11-11**

Percent of children rated excellent, adequate and poor on 8YR Relevance in Connected Discourse by sex, race and Socioeconomic Index

excellent
adequate
poor

PERCENT OF SAMPLE

90 80 70 60 50 40 30 20 10 0

Male Female White Black 0.0-1.9 2.0-3.9 4.0-5.9 6.0-7.9 8.0-9.5 Total

Grouped SEI

Figure **11-12**

Percent of children rated excellent, adequate and poor on 8YR Grammar in
Connected Discourse by sex, race and Socioeconomic Index

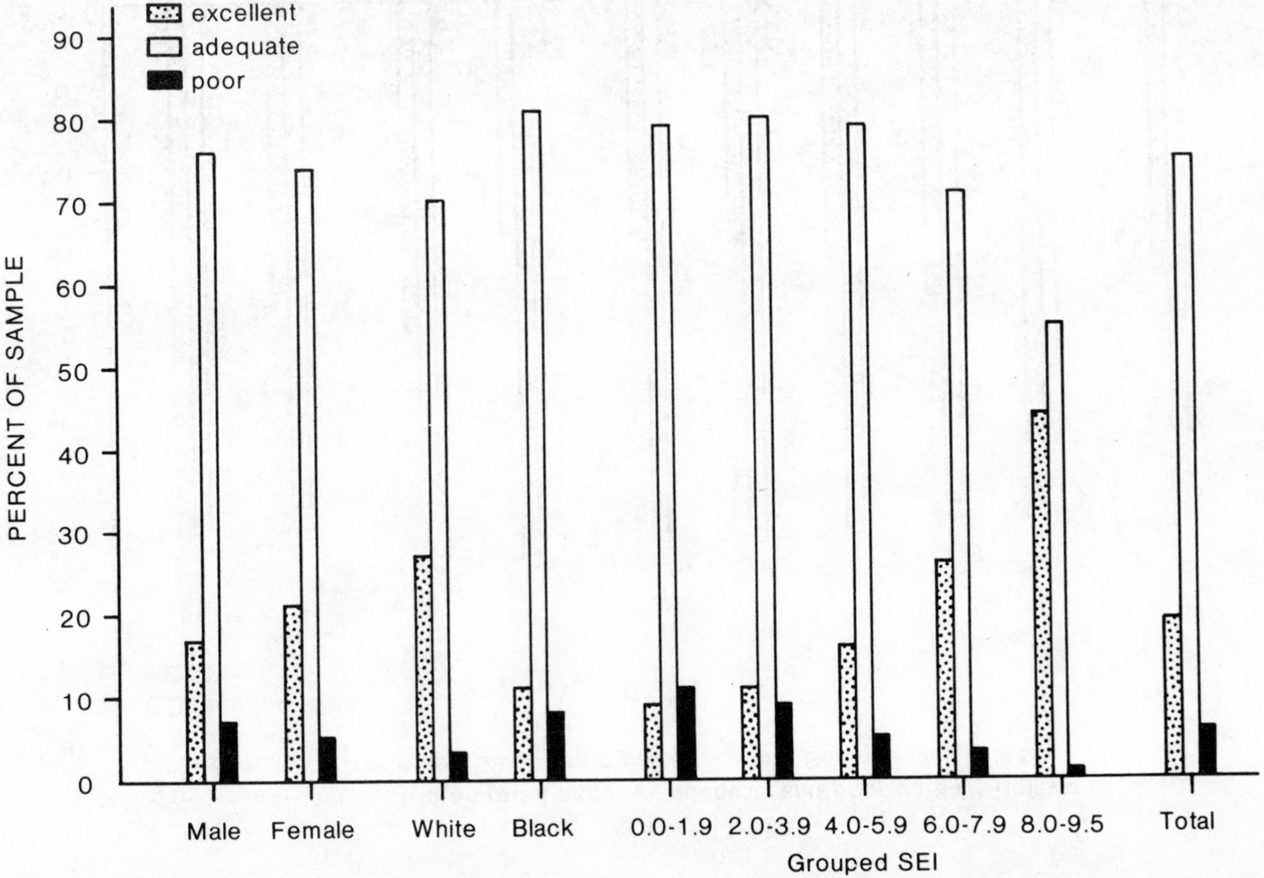

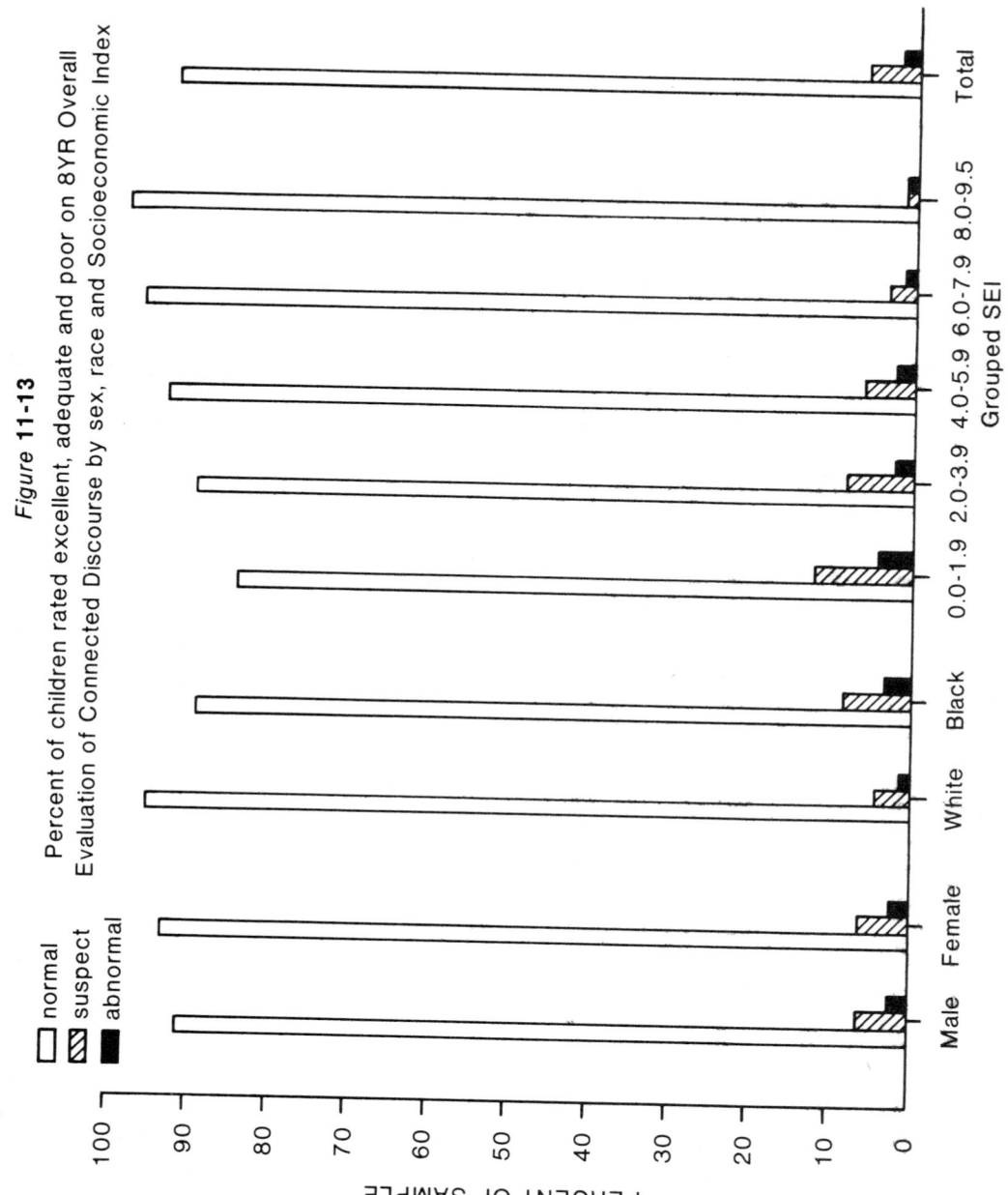

Figure **11-13**

Percent of children rated excellent, adequate and poor on 8YR Overall Evaluation of Connected Discourse by sex, race and Socioeconomic Index

281

The 8YR measures of Language Comprehension were intercorrelated .34 to .55 (Appendix 6) and the measures of Language Expression were .41. The correlations among comprehension and expression measures ranged from .33 to .71. These values reflect closer associations between comprehension and expression at eight years than those found at age three years. The highest correlation was between the two tests upon which there has been extensive prior research, Word Identification (PPVT) and Morphology (subtest of ITPA), with an r of .71.

Correlations between oral language and reading and writing were low to moderate (.23 to .56). The three lowest correlations were .25 between Understanding A Story and Oral Reading (Gray, 1967), .28 with Silent Reading (Durrell and Sullivan, 1945), and .23 with Writing from Dictation.

Correlations between Intelligibility and the language measures were less impressive at eight years (.12 to .28) than they were at three years. This difference probably reflects a ceiling effect and a consequent reduction in variability of the rating scale for Intelligibility in eight-year-old children. Articulation correlated highest with Morphology (.45) and with Word Identification (.36) and, to a lesser degree, with the other measures of language comprehension and expression (.19 to .31).

Correlations Between 3YR and 8YR Variables

When correlations were calculated for the various language measures at three years and at eight years (Appendix 6), none of the values was large (.05 to .33). This finding was not surprising since the tests and measurements were not the same in the two examinations.

3YR Indexes

Two indexes were formulated to reflect the various aspects of language behavior sampled at age three years. A language comprehension index was constructed from Identification of Familiar Objects, Understanding Action Words, and Understanding Space Relationships and Directions. These three tests appeared to be ordered in difficulty, as noted previously. This ordering was preserved in the criteria for outcomes on the index. The frequency distributions for all indexes are presented in Appendix 5; rules for the construction of all indexes are found in Appendix 4. Means and standard deviations for 3YR Language Comprehension are contained in Figure 11-14. Differences between Males and Females on 3YR Language Comprehension were small, while those between White children and Black children and among SEI groups were slightly larger. The combination of the three tests within a single index of 3YR Language Comprehension produced a frequency distribution which was slightly skewed, but in which the variability was increased because of the combination of the three measurements.

The 3YR Sentence Complexity Index was constructed from the five judgments of the child's verbal expression made by the examiner and based upon observations during the entire testing session. Means and standard deviations are graphed in Figure 11-15. There were essentially no differences between the means of the various subgroups. The construction of this index appears to have provided a less variable measure of the child's language production than the individual items did. Only 1% of the children were judged to have no speech, so the data on this index are based on an adequate sample.

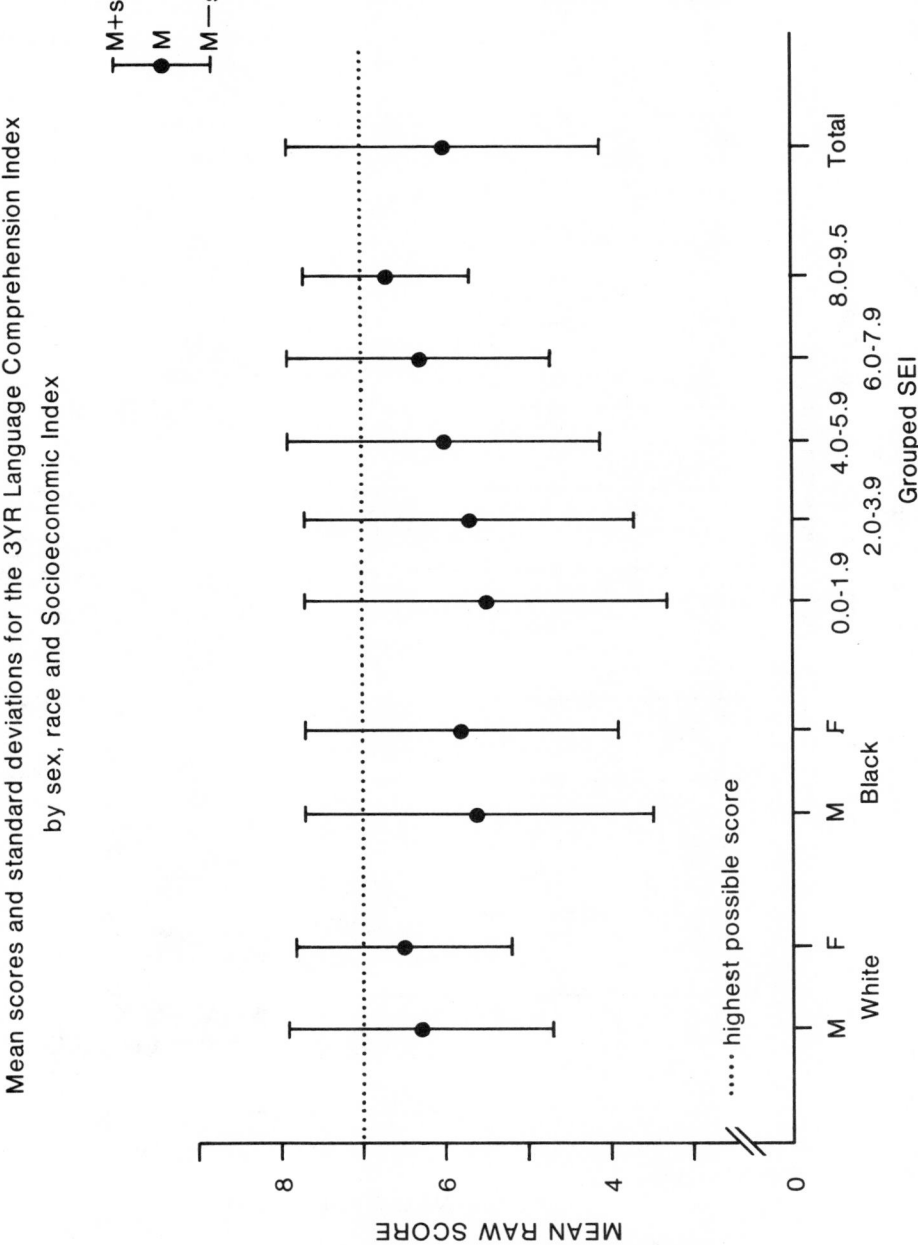

Figure **11-14**

Mean scores and standard deviations for the 3YR Language Comprehension Index
by sex, race and Socioeconomic Index

283

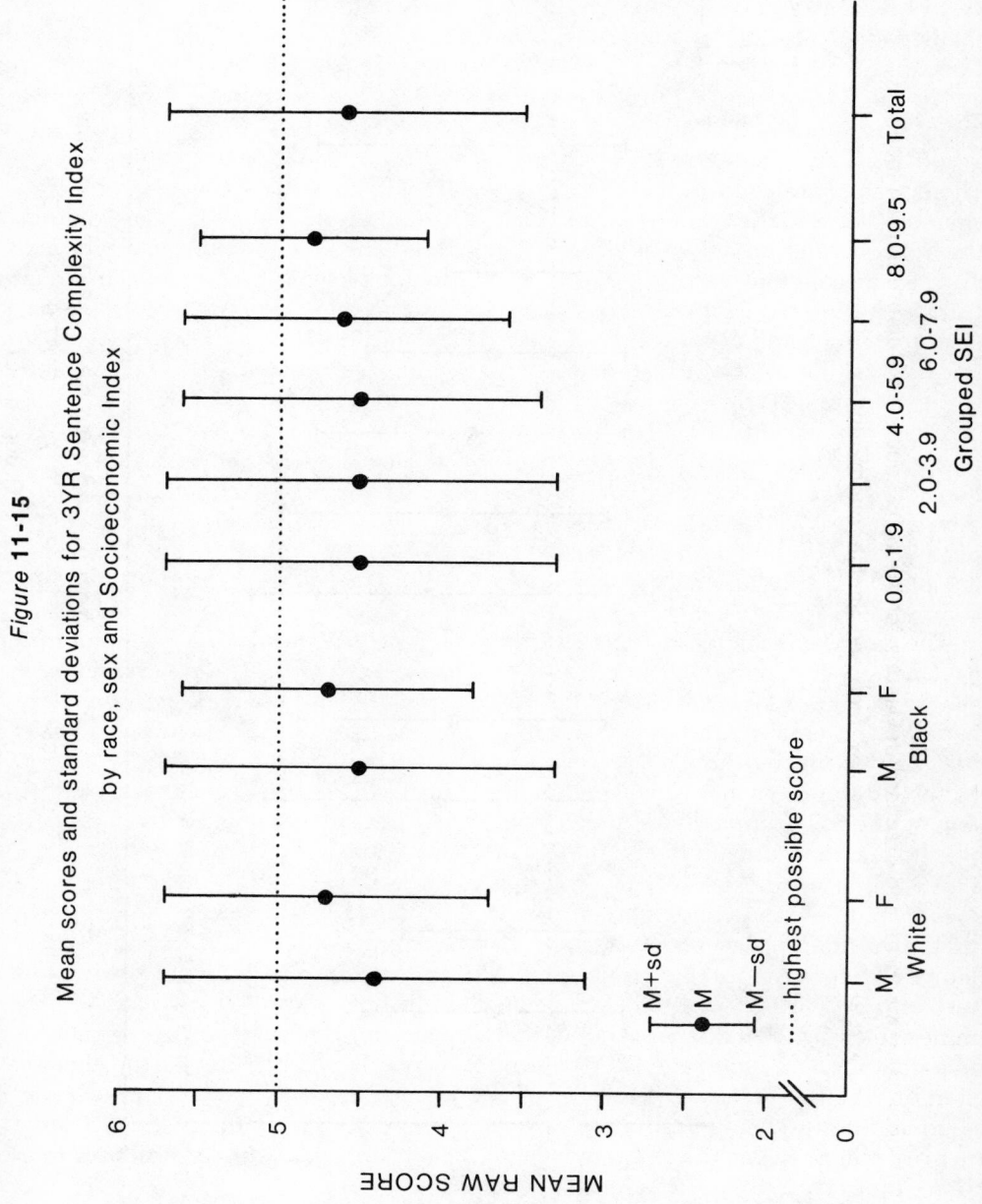

Figure **11-15**

Mean scores and standard deviations for 3YR Sentence Complexity Index
by race, sex and Socioeconomic Index

284

The four 8YR language indexes constructed were 8YR Language Comprehension, 8YR Language Production, 8YR Word Identification (Peabody Picture Vocabulary Test as a key variable), and 8YR Concept Development.

The 8YR Language Comprehension Index was composed of Word Identification (PPVT) and Understanding A Story. There was some concern that the inclusion of Word Identification would bias the index because of its sensitivity to race and socioeconomic factors. Therefore, Understanding A Story was weighted prior to being combined with Word Identification in the index. The weighting of Understanding A Story was justified also because the test involves several skills required in everyday language comprehension situations. In addition, the vocabulary employed is familiar to persons of all SEI groups and both races, allowing a more valid measurement of language comprehension.

The means and standard deviations for 8YR Language Comprehension are presented in Figure 11-16. Males performed better than Females, and White children had higher means than Black children. Notable differences in means were found among the SEI groups. Even though care was taken to avoid the construction of indexes that were especially favorable to White middle-class children, it appears that such attempts were not successful. However, because of the confounding of race and SEI, it is not possible to determine which factor influences the normative data for 8YR Language Comprehension or whether both factors play a role.

In addition to being used as a component of the 8YR Language Comprehension Index, 8YR Word Identification (PPVT) was also retained independently as a key variable, or unidimensional index, primarily because it was a well-standardized test. Extensive literature exists on the Peabody Picture Vocabulary Test and it seemed appropriate to use these data comparatively. The normative data for 8YR Word Identification as an index (Figure 11-17) are identical to the data for it as a single SLH variable (Figure 11-4), although values differ in the figures because of differences in race and sex grouping.

The 8YR Language Production Index was composed of Morphology, several parameters of Connected Discourse, 8YR Intelligibility, 8YR Articulation, Echolalia, and Lack of Spontaneous Communication. The construction of this index was an attempt to devise a global index taking into account various aspects of the language production process. Each component selected for inclusion in the index is a factor which a listener might use in judging a child's language production.

Means and standard deviations for 8YR Language Production are presented in Figure 11-18. Females performed better than Males, and White children performed better than Black children. Performance improved as SEI increased.

The 8YR Concept Development Index was constructed from test items which appeared to be related to the development of concepts, including items from Morphology, Orientation, and Connected Discourse. Inclusion of an index of concept development was thought to be of interest because current theories (Sinclair-deZwart, 1973; Bloom, 1973; Brown, 1973) have made a good case for the proposition that language acquisition has as its base a cognitive framework. Concepts were not measured independently on the 8YR SLH examination, so it was not possible to test the theories directly; but since some data were available, even if intertwined with language behaviors, it seemed reasonable to examine them.

Means and standard deviations for Concept Development are displayed graphically in Figure 11-19. Differences were extremely small between Males and Females but were larger between Black

285

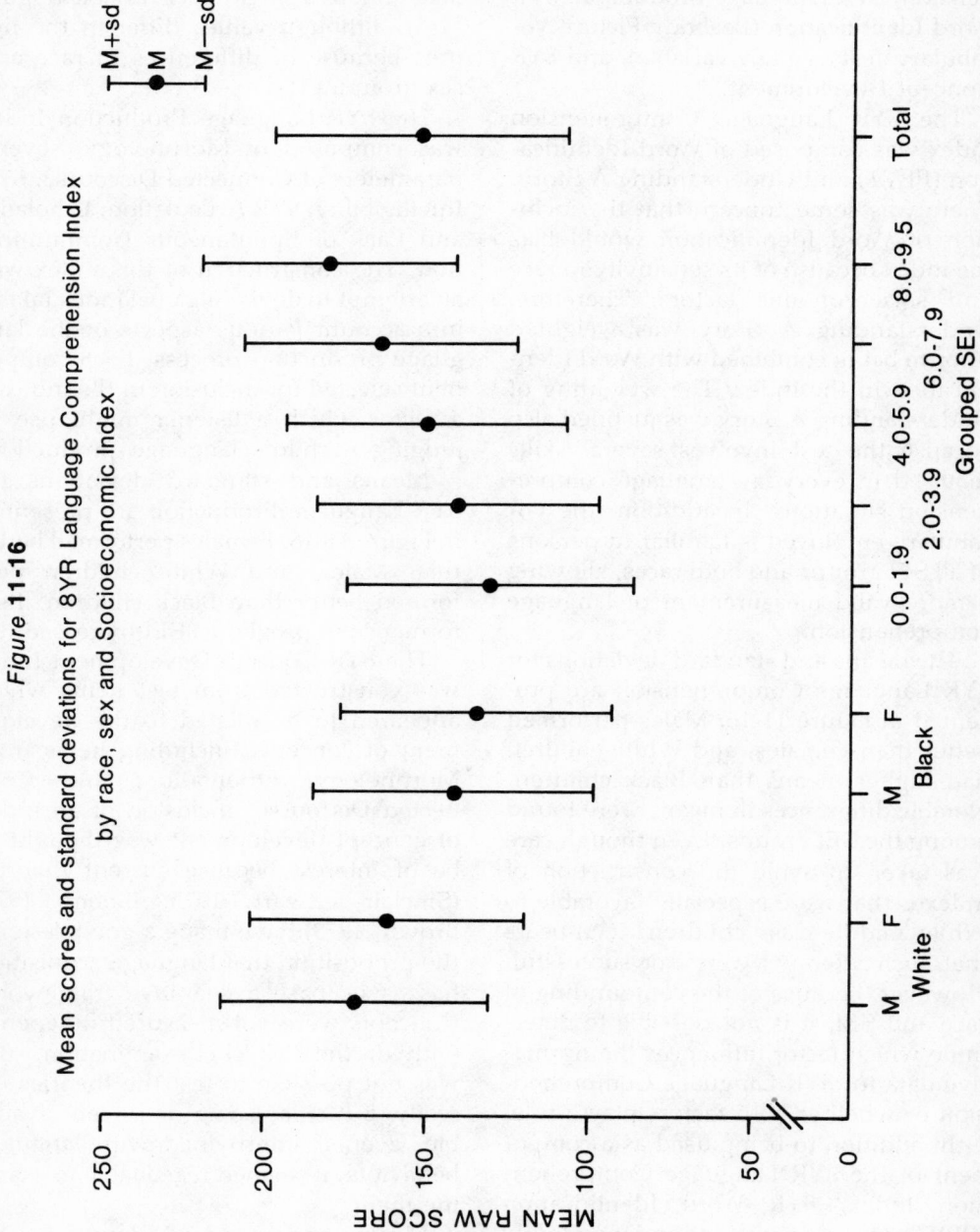

Figure 11-16

Mean scores and standard deviations for 8YR Language Comprehension Index by race, sex and Socioeconomic Index

286

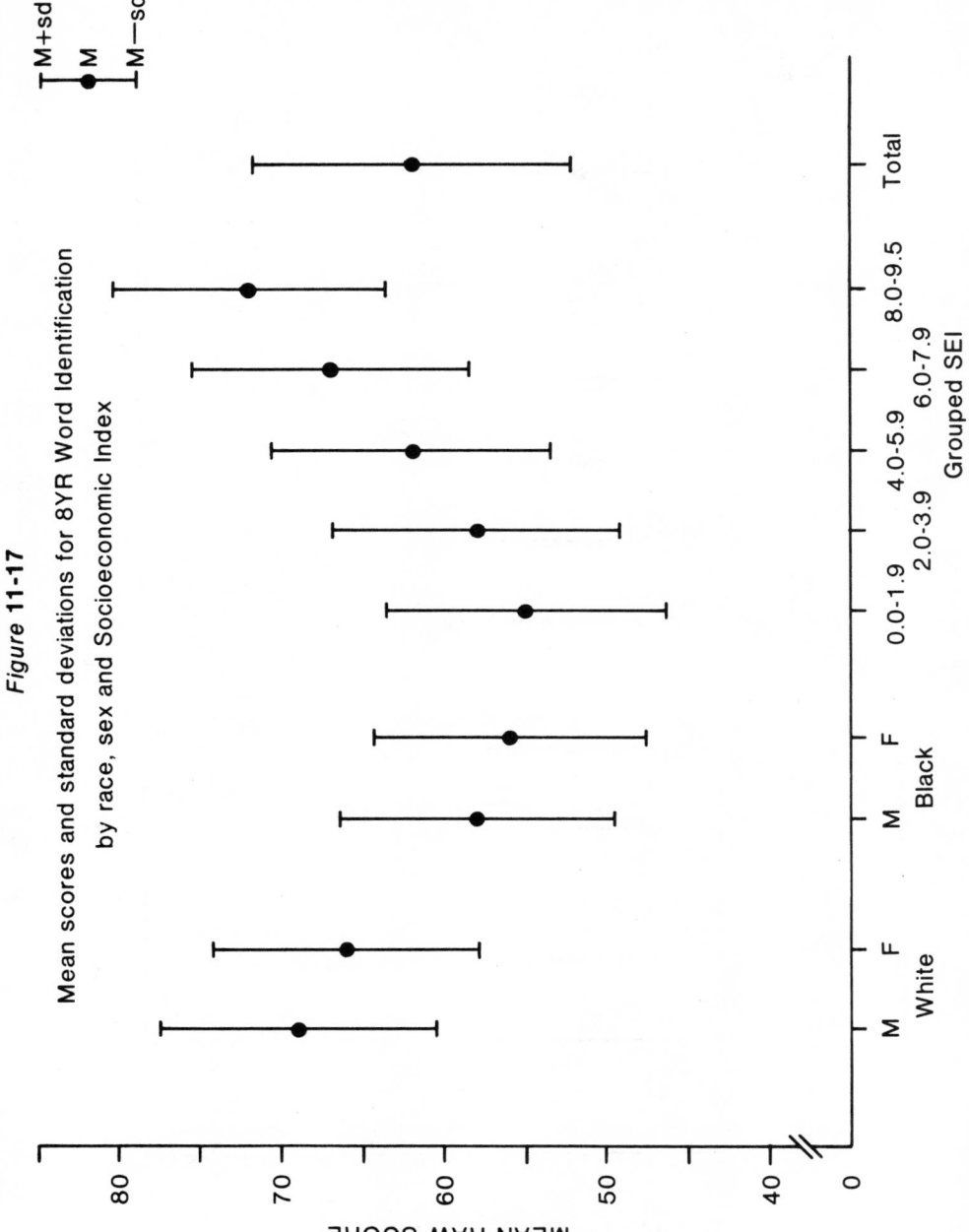

Figure **11-17**

Mean scores and standard deviations for 8YR Word Identification by race, sex and Socioeconomic Index

287

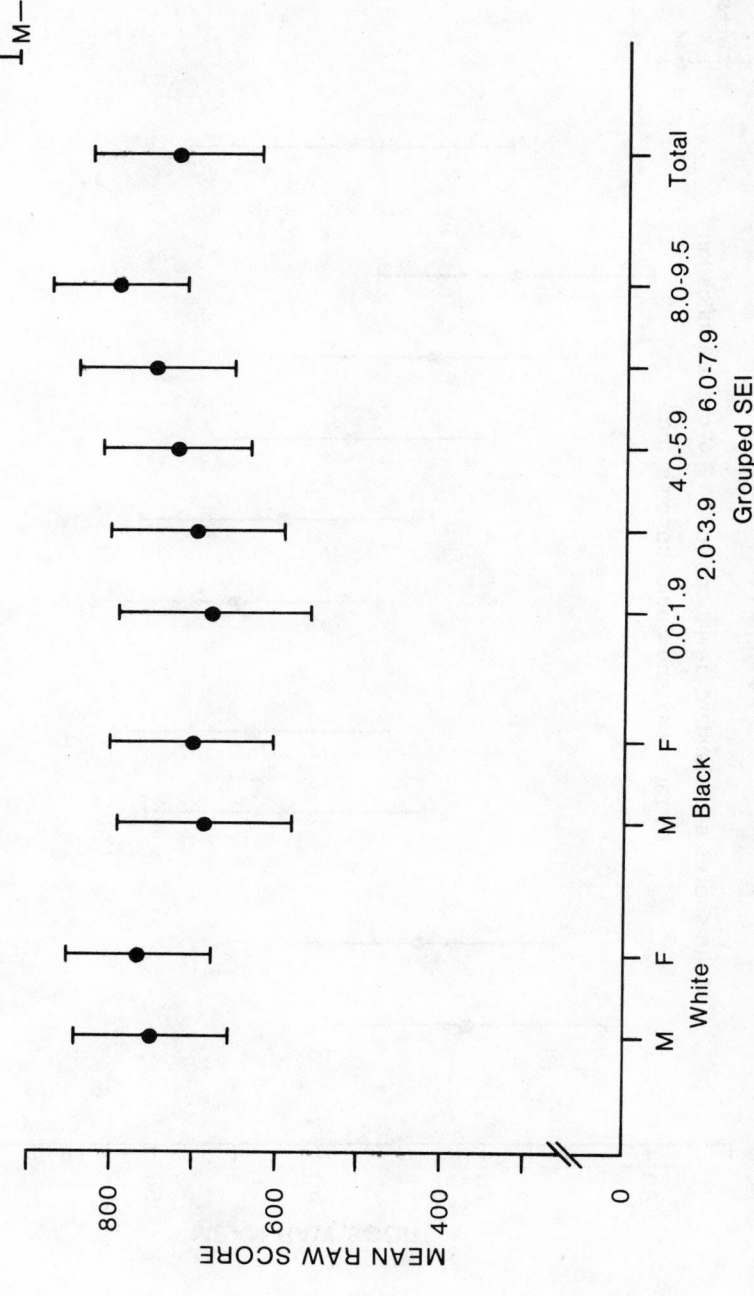

Figure **11-18**

Mean scores and standard deviations for 8YR Language Production Index
by race, sex and Socioeconomic Index

288

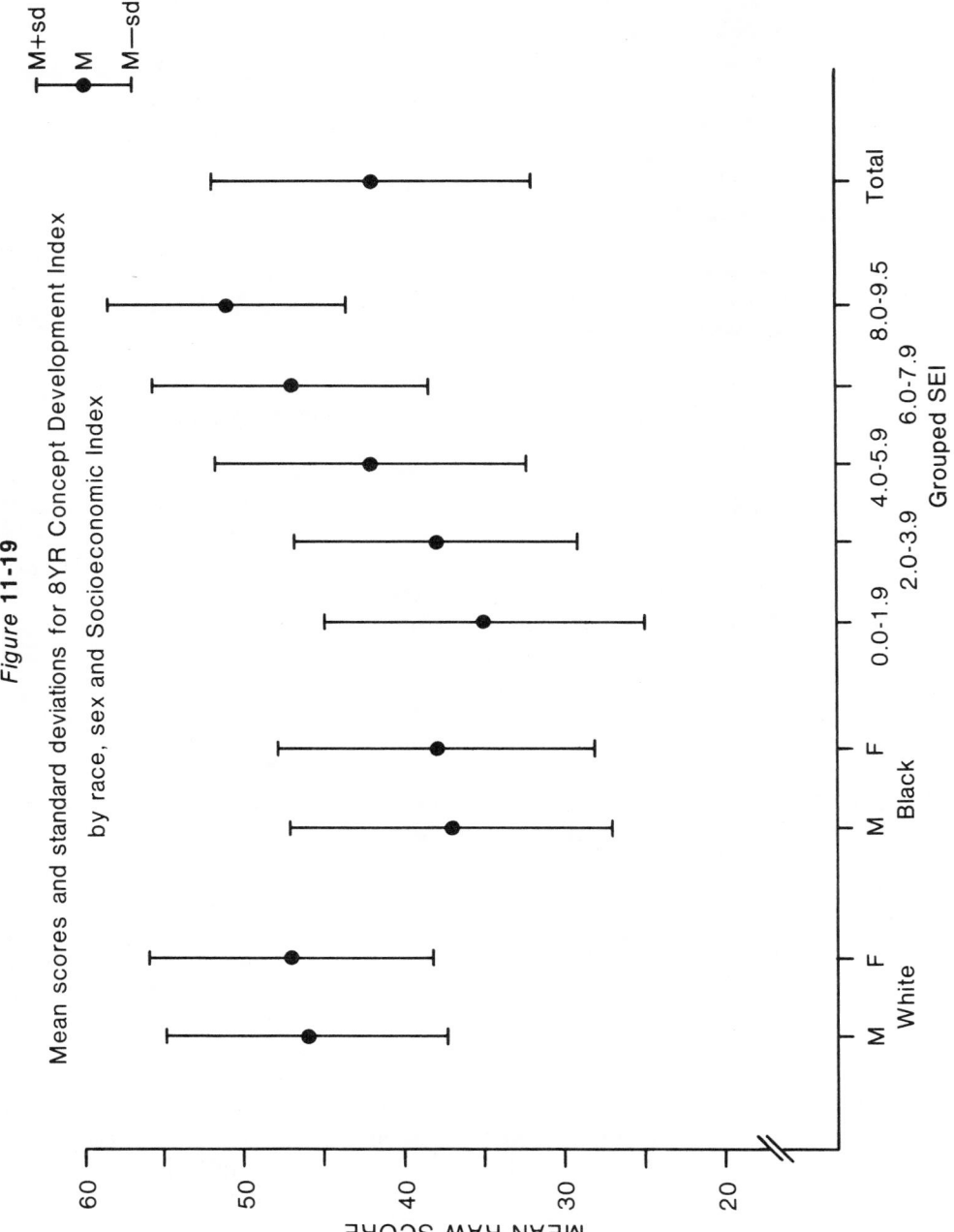

Figure **11-19**

Mean scores and standard deviations for 8YR Concept Development Index by race, sex and Socioeconomic Index

and White children. The progressive change in means was pronounced as SEI increased. A possible interpretation of the differences between groups on this index is that the language component of these items was being measured more effectively than the underlying concepts.

· Correlations Between Indexes and Variables

The correlations between 3YR Language Comprehension and the components from which it was constructed were .56 with Identification of Familiar Objects, .68 with Understanding Action Words, and .88 with Understanding Space Relations. The highest correlation with other tests at the 3YR level was .35, and most of the correlations were below .20. The higher correlations were with measures of Language Production, Articulation, and Intelligibility.

Correlations of 3YR Sentence Complexity with its five components ranged from .72 to .84 (Appendix 6). It also correlated .89 with the Summary Item Score because of the part-whole relationship of the tests with the Summary Item Score. The other measure of 3YR language expression, Naming Objects, correlated .31 with 3YR Sentence Complexity. The correlations with other speech, language, and hearing comprehension measures ranged from |.00| to |.52|, with all correlations below .25 except that with Intelligibility of Speech (.52). This finding again raises the possibility that the intelligibility of the child's speech had some effect on the ratings which the child received on Sentence Structure, Grammar, Sentence Length, Relevance, and Use of Pronouns.

The 8YR Language Comprehension Index had relatively high correlations with its components Word Identification (.60) and Understanding A Story (.98). The latter correlation is understandable because of the heavy weighting given to this component in the attempt to reduce the cultural bias of the PPVT in the index.

The correlation of 8YR Word Identification Index with other SLH variables were the same as discussed previously because 8YR Word Identification was studied both as a key variable and as a component variable.

The 8YR Language Production Index had correlations of .65 with Morphology, .60 with Connected Discourse, .40 with 8YR Intelligibility, and .48 with 8YR Articulation (Templin and Darley, 1960). Correlations with other variables were small except for those with other language measures, auditory memory, reading, and writing variables (Appendix 6).

Correlations Among Indexes

The correlations between 3YR Language Comprehension and the other 3YR indexes ranged from −.02 to .31, and the 8YR indexes from −.10 to .34. The range of correlation values was similar for 3YR Sentence Complexity with the 3YR indexes (.04 to .43); with the 8YR indexes the range was smaller (−.06 to .25). It appears that the construction and use of indexes did not predict language behavior from age three to age eight years much better than did use of the individual variables.

In general, the intercorrelations among the 8YR indexes were much larger than among the 3YR indexes, probably because several indexes were constructed from commonly shared tests or portions of tests. For example, 8YR Language Comprehension was correlated with 8YR Auditory Memory with an r of .77; both indexes contain Understanding A Story as a component. The higher correlations indicate that some indexes may be measuring the same underlying abilities. Correlations between the 8YR language indexes and indexes constructed from components which were mutually exclusive ranged in value from |.00| to |.66|.

Correlation Screen and Multiple Regression

The correlation screen for all the 3YR indexes showed low correlations between antecedent variables and both of the language indexes ($r < .20$). The correlations increased slightly when predicting events at four years and seven years of age (Appendix 7).

The multiple regression analyses, using a combination of antecedent NCPP* variables (see Appendix 8), yielded multiple R's of .25 between 3YR Language Comprehension and At-Birth variables and .28 between 3YR Language Comprehension and At-Birth plus 8-Month NCPP variables. The multiple correlations were lower for 3YR Sentence Complexity. They were .16 when At-Birth NCPP variables were used and .21 when At-Birth NCPP variables plus 8-Month NCPP variables were used. These multiple correlations are low and none accounts for more than 7.6% of the variance. Even with small correlations, however, it is possible to identify those factors which were weighted the heaviest in the prediction equation: 8-Month Bayley Mental and Motor Scores (Bayley, 1958), Occupation and Education of Father, and race and sex.

In general, the predictions of 8YR Word Identification in the correlation screen were much better than those of 8YR Language Comprehension, which contains Word Identification as a component. It may be that the memory ability required by Understanding A Story, the other component of 8YR Language Comprehension, contributed to the lower correlations. When specific NCPP variables were used to predict these two indexes, correlations were higher for those NCPP variables which are socioeconomic indi-

cators; for example, Education of Gravida, Education of Father, and Per Capita Income.

Multiple regression analyses yielded values ranging from .25, when only 3YR indexes were used as independent variables, to .51 when At-Birth NCPP variables, 8-Month NCPP variables, and the Stanford-Binet (Terman and Merrill, 1960) 4YR IQ were used to predict 8YR Language Comprehension. If early identification is desired, the multiple correlation resulting from the use of At-Birth NCPP variables and 8-Month NCPP variables is probably the best ($R = .43$). The addition of 4YR IQ increased the R from .43 to .51, but waiting until age four years for an IQ estimate may be considered unacceptable when contemplating initiation of a remedial program for a child at an early age. Obviously IQ can be measured prior to age four; but these predictions hold only for data as gathered in this study. Furthermore, if the beta weights of the two prediction equations are studied (Appendix 7), it can be seen that when 4YR IQ is added, the largest changes in weights occur for the Race-Sex Markers, Education of Gravida, and Education of Father. These changes probably reflect the intercorrelation of these NCPP variables with 4YR IQ and are not likely to alter appreciably over a four-year period.

The multiple regression employing all the 3YR indexes as independent variables did not improve the prediction of 8YR Language Comprehension ($R = .25$) over its prediction by 3YR Language Comprehension alone ($r = .23$). When At-Birth NCPP variables were added to 3YR indexes as independent variables, the R increased to .46. This prediction equation accounts for only 2.9% more variance than does the equation involving measures made at eight months of age and at birth. Therefore, the prediction equation employing the variables measured early in a child's life appears to be almost as

---

* Non-SLH variables in the NINCDS Collaborative Perinatal Project (NCPP).

useful for determining early intervention as the equation using later variables.

As in the case of the single variable predictions, the multiple regression analyses yielded much higher correlations (R = .37 to .75) for 8YR Word Identification. The amount of variance explained by the various combinations of NCPP variables followed a pattern which was higher than, but otherwise identical to, the pattern for 8YR Language Comprehension. The 3YR indexes produced the smallest multiple correlation (R = .37), and At-Birth NCPP variables together with 8-Month NCPP variables and 4YR IQ produced the largest multiple correlation (R = .75). When it was added to the prediction equation, 4YR IQ had a relatively large effect, increasing the explained variance by 9.1%. This result is not surprising, given the reported correlation between the PPVT and IQ (Dunn, 1965). The beta weights which changed substantially were those of Race-Sex Markers, Education of Gravida, Education of Father, and Per Capita Income, reflecting their intercorrelations with IQ.

The correlation screen yielded values for 8YR Language Production similar to those obtained for 8YR Language Comprehension. NCPP variables which yielded the higher correlations for the comprehension index generally yielded the higher correlations for the production index as well; a similar tendency was noted for variables yielding lower correlations with the two indexes. Of the early antecedent variables, those related to socioeconomic factors yielded the higher correlations. Of the later antecedent variables, higher correlations were obtained from variables measured on the 7YR Psychology examination: the WISC (Wechsler, 1949), the WRAT (Jastak and Jastak, 1965), and the Auditory-Vocal Association Test from the ITPA.

Multiple regression analyses yielded values slightly higher (R = .39 to .54) for 8YR Language Production than those obtained for 8YR Language Comprehen-sion. The optimum equation for prediction of language production problems early in the child's life again contained the At-Birth NCPP variables and the 8-Month NCPP variables (R = .44), although more variance was accounted for in the equations involving 4YR IQ (R = .52) or the At-Birth NCPP variables and 3YR indexes (R = .54). Waiting until age three or four years to gather additional information seems unprofitable in view of the slight improvement in prediction which it provides. The beta weights that change are mainly those related to socioeconomic factors, and these are not likely to shift markedly over the period of a few years.

The correlation screen yielded moderate correlations between various socioeconomic-related variables and 8YR Concept Development. In every instance where socioeconomic factors were included in the prediction equations, the beta weights for these variables were higher. When 4YR IQ was a variable, the weights for the Education of Gravida, Education of Father, and Per Capita Income were reduced while the weighting for 4YR IQ was high, reflecting their intercorrelations. The prediction equation which included 4YR IQ had the highest multiple correlation associated with it (R = .69) and accounted for 47.9% of the variance. The multiple regression analyses based on variables measured early in the child's life yielded multiple correlations of .55 for the At-Birth NCPP variables and .56 for the At-Birth NCPP variables plus 8-Month NCPP variables.

Cross-Tabulations and Correlations

Fourfold Tables

In order to explicate further the correlations obtained, cross-tabulations were produced, and in the case of fourfold tables probabilities were calculated. The tabulations contained the child's pass or fail measure on an antecedent event and his subsequent pass or fail* on an SLH outcome. Conditional probabilities were calculated for the situation where a failure on an antecedent variable was followed by a failure on a subsequent variable, and for the situation where the child passed the antecedent measure and then failed the subsequent one. Scrutiny of both probabilities provides an indication of the discrimination possible using the specific antecedent variable and leads to a clearer interpretation of the data than is possible by means of the correlations alone. For example, when the Bayley item Vocalizes to a Social Stimulus is failed by the child, the probability is .50 that the child will fail 3YR Language Comprehension. In contrast, the probability is only .13 that a child who passes this Bayley item will fail 3YR Language Comprehension. Evaluation of these two probabilities provides more information than using only the correlation of <.10.

Multiple Category Tables

Some NCPP variables did not lend themselves readily to dichotomization, for example, the Socioeconomic Index (SEI). In those instances, grouping was done by reference to the literature or by the recommendation of consultants. The most appropriate statistic for comparisons was the percentage of children failing the index in each of several categories. If the percent failing is compared across all categories, statements concerning the effect of the NCPP variable can be made, and a better understanding of the correlation between the variable and the index can be obtained.

---

* Fail was defined as an SLH index score falling in the lowest decile or, in the case of a restricted range, closest to the lowest decile.

3YR Language Indexes

3YR Language Comprehension

Most of the correlations of antecedent variables with 3YR Language Comprehension (Appendix 7) were small (≤.19). Tables 11-1 and 11-2 contain the correlations and subsequent cross-tabulations of NCPP variables and 3YR Language Comprehension. Failure on 3YR Language Comprehension was defined as a score of 3 or less on the index (see Appendix 4).

Education of the Gravida and Education of Father demonstrate a clear association with 3YR Language Comprehension. In both cases, as the amount of education increased the failure rate of the children on 3YR Language Comprehension decreased markedly (Table 11-2), even though there was only a small positive correlation (.16). Other NCPP variables related to socioeconomic level had correlations of similar magnitude (Table 11-1). The associated probabilities for Overcrowding, Occupation of Father, and Per Capita Income were small, but their directions were consistent with previous research. If the child's father was a white-collar worker, the probability was .06 that he would fail 3YR Language Comprehension. If his father was not a white-collar worker, the probability increased 2.5 times to .15 that he would fail 3YR Language Comprehension. The SEI used in the NINCDS Collaborative Perinatal Project reflected the composite effect of the above factors on the child's performance on 3YR Language Comprehension. In Table 11-2 it can be seen that as SEI level increased from low to high, the failure rate on 3YR Language Comprehension decreased from 13.4% to 1.9%. This appears to be a much more substantial change than the magnitude of the correlation would suggest.

Low birthweight and low gestational age are two factors frequently considered indicative of poor outcomes in children (Bierman et al., 1963; Dann, Levine, and

293

Table 11-1

Correlations and cross-tabulations for 3YR Language Comprehension and selected NCPP variables.

	r	p(F2/F1)*	p(F2/P1)*
At-Birth NCPP Variables			
Housing Density (Overcrowding)	−.10	.16	.11
Per Capita Income	.14	.16	.09
Occupation of Father of the Baby: White-Collar	.16	.15	.06
Gravida: Mentally Retarded	<.10	.18	.13
Gravida: Acute Toxemia	<.10	.15	.13
Gravida: Chronic Hypertensive Disease	<.10	.20	.13
Father of Baby: Mentally Retarded	<.10	.08	.13
Birthweight: Normal versus Low Birthweight	.11	.18	.12
Gestation: Normal versus Short	<.10	.11	.08
8-Month NCPP Variables			
Bayley Mental Score	.12	.23	.12
Bayley Motor Score	.14	.24	.12
Bayley Item: Vocalizes to Social Stimulus	<.10	.50	.13
Bayley Item: Vocalizes Two Syllables	<.10	.44	.13
Bayley Item: Enjoys Sound Production	<.10	.25	.12
Fine Motor Development	−.12	.15	.07
Gross Motor Development	−.13	.15	.07
1YR NCPP Variable			
Neurological Abnormality	−.11	.18	.11

*p(F2/F1) and p(F2/P1) refer to the probability of failing 3YR Language Comprehension (F2) when the NCPP variable is failed (F1) or passed (P1).

Table 11-2

Correlations and percent of children failing 3YR Language Comprehension by education of parents and Socioeconomic Index.

NCPP Variables	r	% Fail
Education of Mother	.16	
Years in School		
0-8		12.2
9-12		8.2
13+		3.1
Education of Father	.16	
Years in School		
0-8		11.1
9-12		8.6
13+		3.0
Socioeconomic Index at Birth	.19	
0.0-1.9		13.4
2.0-3.9		10.4
4.0-5.9		8.2
6.0-7.9		5.3
8.0-9.5		1.9

294

New, 1964). In the case of 3YR Language Comprehension, although the correlations were low (≤.11), the probabilities indicated some increase in risk when birthweight was low or when the child was born at or before 36 weeks gestation.

At eight months of age, each study child was given a psychological examination. The Bayley Mental and Motor scales were administered and the examiner made a number of judgments about the child's behavior. The Bayley Mental and Motor scales yielded correlations (.12 and .14, respectively) and probabilities that were similar (Table 11-1). The probability of failing 3YR Language Comprehension approximately doubled if the child's performance on the Bayley was in the lowest 10% on either scale. Specific items on the Bayley, however, yielded better conditional probabilities than either full scale, although correlations were low (<.10). If the child failed to vocalize to a social stimulus, the probability was .50 that he would fail 3YR Language Comprehension. This is almost four times the risk than if he had passed the item. If he failed to vocalize two syllables, the probability was .44 that he would fail 3YR Language Comprehension, a risk three times greater than if he had vocalized two syllables. These values are sufficiently high and seem to discriminate well enough to be useful as clinical indicators of a need for early remediation.

3YR Sentence Complexity

Correlations between NCPP variables and 3YR Sentence Complexity were generally lower than with 3YR Language Comprehension (Appendix 7). Education of Gravida and Education of Father had correlations of <.10 with 3YR Sentence Complexity. These variables did, however, show an effect on the index (Table 11-4). As the amount of parental education increased, the percentage of children failing 3YR Sentence Complexity decreased from over 11% to 4.1%. Failure

on 3YR Sentence Complexity was defined as a score of 3 or lower (see Appendix 4). Occupation of Father, Per Capita Income, and Overcrowding, all with r <.10, had associated probabilities which showed slight increases in the risk of failing 3YR Sentence Complexity (Table 11-3). As the SEI increased, there was a more gradual reduction in the percent failing 3YR Sentence Complexity (Table 11-4) even though the correlation was less than .10. If either parent was reported to be mentally retarded, the probability was .32 or higher that the child would fail 3YR Sentence Complexity; otherwise the probability of failure was .16.

The Bayley Mental and Motor scales at eight months had correlations and probabilities associated with 3YR Sentence Complexity similar to those occurring with 3YR Language Comprehension. Likewise, the individual items relating to vocalization provided good prediction of failing 3YR Sentence Complexity (Table 11-3). Failure to achieve a rating of normal or better on either fine or gross motor development at age eight months doubled the risk of failing this index.

8YR Language Indexes

For the most part, the NCPP variables had higher correlations with the 8YR language indexes than with the 3YR language indexes. This finding may be due to the longer time for the variables to act on the child's performance, to the greater ease of testing older children, or because more standardized tests were used to evaluate the language abilities of the eight-year-old children than were used at the earlier age. Whatever the magnitude of the correlations, the cross-tabulations and their associated probabilities appear to reveal the usefulness of the NCPP variables in prediction more effectively than the correlation alone does. In some instances when the correlation was high, the cross-tabulation procedure suggested the spurious nature of

Table 11-3

Correlations and cross-tabulations for 3YR Sentence Complexity with selected NCPP variables.

	r	p(F2/F1)*	p(F2/P1)*
At-Birth NCPP Variables			
Housing Density (Overcrowding)	<.10	.18	.15
Per Capita Income	<.10	.19	.13
Occupation of Father of the Baby: White-Collar	<.10	.17	.10
Gravida: Mentally Retarded	<.10	.32	.16
Gravida: Acute Toxemia	<.10	.15	.15
Gravida: Chronic Hypertensive Disease	<.10	.17	.14
Father of Baby: Mentally Retarded	<.10	.38	.16
Birthweight: Normal versus Low Birthweight	<.10	.22	.16
Gestation: Normal versus Short	<.10	.11	.09
8-Month NCPP Variables			
Bayley Mental Score	.14	.26	.15
Bayley Motor Score	.15	.30	.15
Bayley Item: Vocalizes to Social Stimulus	<.10	.55	.16
Bayley Item: Vocalizes Two Syllables	<.10	.51	.16
Bayley Item: Enjoys Sound Production	<.10	.26	.15
Fine Motor Development	−.14	.18	.08
Gross Motor Development	−.15	.18	.08
1YR NCPP Variable			
Neurological Abnormality	−.15	.22	.14

*p(F2/F1) and p(F2/P1) refer to the probability of failing 3YR Sentence Complexity (F2) when the NCPP variable is failed (F1) or passed (P1).

Table 11-4

Correlations and percent of children failing 3YR Sentence Complexity by education of parents and Socioeconomic Index.

NCPP Variables	r	% Fail
Education of Mother	<.10	
Years in School		
0-8		11.5
9-12		10.0
13+		4.1
Education of Father	<.10	
Years in School		
0-8		11.8
9-12		9.4
13+		4.1
Socioeconomic Index at Birth	<.10	
0.0-1.9		10.9
2.0-3.9		11.3
4.0-5.9		10.2
6.0-7.9		7.8
8.0-9.5		3.9

the statistic. For example, Occupation of Mother when the child was seven was correlated .73 with 8YR Word Identification, but cross-tabulations revealed that there were only 53 mothers working as a laborer or farmer. The correlation was probably inflated because of the way these cases were distributed. Even though the risk of failure was almost twice as large when the mother was a laborer-farmer as when she was not, the occurrence was such a rare event in the total sample that it seems unprofitable to pursue.

In other cases, the magnitude of the correlation was confirmed by the probabilities associated with the cross-tabulations. For example, 8YR Concept Development was correlated .70 with the Auditory-Vocal Association Test at age seven years. The probability was .58 that if the child failed the seven year test he would also fail 8YR Concept Development, but only .08 if he passed the test.

8YR Language Comprehension

Overcrowding, Per Capita Income, and Occupation of Father produced correlations of $-.25$, .27, and .23, respectively (Table 11-5). The associated probabilities indicated that there was at least twice the risk of failing 8YR Language Comprehension if Overcrowding existed, Per Capita Income was low, or if the father was not a white-collar worker (Table 11-5). This was borne out by the percent failing in each SEI group. Since SEI does not change drastically over time, the same finding was demonstrated using SEI at seven years of age (Table 11-6). Failure on 8YR Language Comprehension was defined as a score of 91 or lower (see Appendix 4).

There was almost three times the chance that the child would fail 8YR Language Comprehension if the mother was reported to be mentally retarded than if she was not. The report that the father of the baby was mentally retarded did not

appear to have the same risk attached (Table 11-5). This difference may be due to inaccuracies in the report or because the father may be less involved in the child's early language acquisition process.

Some individual Bayley items predicted 8YR Language Comprehension better than the total mental and motor scores even though the correlations were of almost the same magnitude (Table 11-5). Judgments of fine and gross motor development, also recorded at eight months of age, did not predict as well at eight years as they did for 3YR Language Comprehension.

The 4YR IQ, as measured by the Stanford-Binet, was correlated .45, and the 7YR IQ, as measured by the WISC, was correlated .40 with 8YR Language Comprehension (Table 11-5). The magnitude of these correlations undoubtedly reflects the measurement of language abilities by intelligence tests. More specifically it probably reflects the variance shared by the PPVT and the Stanford-Binet or the WISC (Dunn, 1965), since the PPVT is a component of 8YR Language Comprehension. Various subtests or scales from the intelligence tests also were correlated with 8YR Language Comprehension and subjected to the cross-tabulation procedure when there was reason to examine the relationships (Table 11-5). According to the probabilities calculated, none of the subtests or scales was as good a predictor as either of the full-scale IQs.

Judgments of the child's attention span and activity level at both age four and age seven years correlated weakly with 8YR Language Comprehension, but appeared to predict reasonably well on the basis of the probabilities calculated (Table 11-5). In addition, if the child was judged echolalic at four years of age, the risk of failing 8YR Language Comprehension was twice that of being judged not echolalic. If he was judged echolalic at age seven years, there was almost five times the risk of his failing 8YR Language

Table **11-5**

Correlations and cross-tabulations for 8YR Language Comprehension with selected NCPP variables.

	r	p(F2/F1)*	p(F2/P1)*
At-Birth NCPP Variables			
Housing Density (Overcrowding)	−.25	.20	.10
Per Capita Income	.27	.18	.08
Occupation of Father of the Baby: White-Collar	.23	.14	.06
Gravida: Mentally Retarded	<.10	.38	.13
Gravida: Acute Toxemia	<.10	.14	.12
Gravida: Chronic Hypertensive Disease	<.10	.17	.12
Father of Baby: Mentally Retarded	<.10	.16	.13
Birthweight: Normal versus Low Birthweight	.12	.18	.12
Gestation: Normal versus Short	<.10	.14	.10
8-Month NCPP Variables			
Bayley Mental Score	.11	.23	.11
Bayley Motor Score	.12	.20	.12
Bayley Item: Vocalizes to Social Stimulus	<.10	.44	.12
Bayley Item: Vocalizes Two Syllables	<.10	.36	.12
Bayley Item: Enjoys Sound Production	−.11	.25	.12
Fine Motor Development	<.10	.15	.10
Gross Motor Development	−.10	.15	.10
1YR NCPP Variables			
Neurological Abnormality	<.10	.16	.11
4YR NCPP Variables			
4YR IQ	.45	.43	.10
Stanford-Binet: III-6 Comprehension	−.32	.21	.07
Stanford-Binet: IV-6 Comprehension III	−.27	.16	.06
Stanford-Binet: VII Comprehension IV	<.10	.12	.03
Stanford-Binet: VIII Comprehension IV	<.10	.12	.06
Very Brief Attention Span	−.11	.34	.11
Highly Perseverative Attention Span	<.10	.33	.12
Echolalia	<.10	.24	.12
7YR NCPP Variables			
Bender Gestalt	−.26	.22	.09
WISC: Comprehension Scaled Score	.27	.24	.11
WISC: Verbal IQ	.40	.35	.09
WISC: Performance IQ	.32	.30	.10
WISC: Full Scale IQ	.40	.55	.11
Auditory-Vocal Association Test	.46	.38	.09
Highly Perseverative Attention Span	<.10	.27	.13
Level of Activity: Extreme Overactivity	<.10	.30	.12
Nature of Activity: Extreme Overactivity	<.10	.54	.12
Very Hostile	.18	.19	.13
Echolalia	<.10	.50	.12
WRAT: Speech Class	.11	.11	.12
Neurological Abnormality	<.10	.20	.11

*p(F2/F1) and p(F2/P1) refer to the probability of failing 8YR Language Comprehension (F2) when the NCPP variable is failed (F1) or passed (P1).

Table **11-6**

Correlations and percent of children failing 8YR Language Comprehension by education of parents and Socioeconomic Index.

NCPP Variables	r	% Fail
Education of Mother	.28	
Years in School		
0-8		17.8
9-12		10.5
13+		2.6
Education of Father	.29	
Years in School		
0-8		15.4
9-12		10.3
13+		2.6
Socioeconomic Index at Birth	.33	
0.0-1.9		20.2
2.0-3.9		15.6
4.0-5.9		10.5
6.0-7.9		5.0
8.0-9.5		2.0
Socioeconomic Index at 7YR	.32	
0.0-1.9		19.2
2.0-3.9		14.7
4.0-5.9		10.1
6.0-7.9		5.9
8.0-9.5		1.9

Comprehension. While the occurrence of echolalia was infrequent at age seven years, 50% of the children displaying this behavior fell in the bottom 10% of the 8YR Language Comprehension frequency distribution of scores.

Two other tests given on the psychological examination were analyzed with respect to 8YR Language Comprehension. The Bender Gestalt yielded a correlation of −.26; the negative value reflects the difference in directionality of the scales. The Auditory-Vocal Association Test correlated .46 with 8YR Language Comprehension. If a child failed either test, he was at two to four times greater risk of failing the comprehension index (Table 11-5).

8YR Word Identification (PPVT)

Correlations of NCPP variables with 8YR Word Identification were generally larger than those with 8YR Language Comprehension (Appendix 6), even though 8YR Word Identification is a component of 8YR Language Comprehension. These higher correlations are due in part to the construction and standardization of the PPVT (Dunn 1965). As stated earlier, the use of 8YR Word Identification as a key variable afforded a check on the language evaluation since so much previous research has been done on the PPVT. Failure on 8YR Word Identification was defined as a score of 51 or lower (see Appendix 4).

The influence of socioeconomic level on the PPVT has been known from previous research (Milgram and Ozer, 1967; Jeruchimowicz, Costello, and Bagur, 1971; Teasdale and Katz, 1968). In the present study, Education of Gravida and Education of Father correlated higher with 8YR Word Identification than with any other language index, with r's of .42

and .43, respectively (Table 11-8). Occupation of Father, Per Capita Income, and Housing Density produced correlations of .36 or better (Table 11-7). Reflecting all of these factors, the SEI at birth correlated .51 with 8YR Word Identification. Virtually the same correlation (.49) was noted for SEI at seven years of age (Table 11-8). Performance on the PPVT appears, therefore, to be strongly associated with socioeconomic variables.

The Bayley Mental and Motor scores obtained at eight months yielded correlations of .16 with 8YR Word Identification. The associated probabilities were about the same as for the other language indexes. The individual items from the Bayley scales yielded low correlations (Table 11-7), but the probability of a child's failing 8YR Word Identification when failing Vocalizes to a Social Stimulus at eight months was .50. Likewise, if the child failed Vocalizes Two Syllables at eight months, the probability was .49 that he would fail 8YR Word Identification. In both instances, the probability was only .14 that the child would fail 8YR Word Identification if he passed these Bayley items.

The correlations between 8YR Word Identification and intelligence test results were .64 for the Stanford-Binet and .51 for the WISC. These values are consistent with those reported previously (Dunn, 1965). Various intelligence subtests and scales had substantially lower correlations, but failure on any increased the probability of failure on 8YR Word Identification (Table 11-7).

The judgments of attention span at both four years and seven years predicted with reasonable success the children's failures on 8YR Word Identification. If short attention span persists to age eight years, it suggests the possibility that those children were hard to test. Yet all the children with a score on 8YR Word Identification were judged as having been given an adequate examination. It seems more likely that short attention

span or perseverative behavior is related to an underlying dysfunction which also produces poor performance on 8YR Word Identification. Echolalia reported at four and seven years also predicted poor performance on 8YR Word Identification, as it did for 8YR Language Comprehension.

The correlation between the judgment Very Hostile at age seven years and 8YR Word Identification was .50. However, when the associated probabilities are examined (Table 11-7), it can be seen that the judgment was not a good predictor of later performance on 8YR Word Identification even though the correlation was a moderate one. The cross-tabulation reveals that there were only 21 cases judged as Very Hostile; of these, only two failed 8YR Word Identification.

8YR Language Production

The effect of socioeconomic variables on 8YR Language Production was similar to that on 8YR Language Comprehension. The correlations and the cross-tabulation probabilities were almost identical for the two indexes. Failure on 8YR Language Production was defined as a score of 611 or less (see Appendix 4). The percentage of children failing 8YR Language Production decreased as the education of either parent increased (Table 11-10). Per Capita Income, Housing Density, and the Occupation of Father predicted with the same accuracy as they did for 8YR Language Comprehension (Table 11-5). The overall effect of socioeconomic factors at birth was such that failure on the index decreased from 20% to 1.5% as the SEI level increased (Table 11-10). The same pattern was observed for SEI at seven years of age, but the slope was somewhat less steep.

Maternal mental retardation appeared to be a potent predictor of failure on 8YR Language Production. If the mother was reported to be mentally retarded, the conditional probability was .49 that the child would fail the index, as opposed to

Table 11-7

Correlations and cross-tabulations for 8YR Word Identification with selected NCPP variables.

	r	p(F2/F1)*	p(F2/P1)*
At-Birth NCPP Variables			
Housing Density (Overcrowding)	−.36	.26	.10
Per Capita Income	.41	.22	.07
Occupation of Father of the Baby: White-Collar	.36	.16	.05
Gravida: Acute Toxemia	<.10	.16	.13
Gravida: Chronic Hypertensive Disease	<.10	.18	.13
Birthweight: Normal versus Low Birthweight	.20	.23	.14
Gestation: Normal versus Short	.14	.20	.11
8-Month NCPP Variables			
Bayley Mental Score	.16	.27	.13
Bayley Motor Score	.16	.22	.13
Bayley Item: Vocalizes to Social Stimulus	<.10	.50	.14
Bayley Item: Vocalizes Two Syllables	<.10	.49	.14
Bayley Item: Enjoys Sound Production	−.14	.32	.13
Fine Motor Development	−.13	.18	.11
Gross Motor Development	−.14	.17	.12
1YR NCPP Variable			
Neurological Abnormality	−.12	.17	.13
4YR NCPP Variables			
4YR IQ	.64	.54	.12
Stanford-Binet: II Picture Vocabulary	<.10	.53	.13
Stanford-Binet: II-6 Picture Vocabulary	−.22	.57	.12
Stanford-Binet: III Picture Vocabulary	−.33	.46	.10
Stanford-Binet: IV Picture Identification	−.43	.22	.06
Very Brief Attention Span	−.13	.37	.13
Highly Perseverative Attention Span	<.10	.53	.14
Echolalia	−.11	.31	.13
7YR NCPP Variables			
Bender Gestalt	−.20	.31	.10
WISC: Vocabulary Scaled Score	.35	.46	.09
WISC: Verbal IQ	.61	.46	.10
WISC: Performance IQ	.45	.38	.11
WISC: Full Scale IQ	.51	.66	.12
Auditory-Vocal Association Test	.30	.50	.10
Muscle Balance: Not seen, off table	.52	.07	.14
Highly Perseverative Attention Span	<.10	.37	.14
Degree of Cooperation: Extremely Negative	.34	.40	.14
Nature of Activity: Variable	.57	.47	.14
Very Hostile	.50	.10	.14
Echolalia	.35	.54	.14
WRAT: Speech Class	.40	.14	.14
Mother's Occupation: Laborer, Farmer	.73	.26	.14
Neurological Abnormality	−.14	.23	.12

*p(F2/F1) and p(F2/P1) refer to the probability of failing 8YR Word Identification (F2) when the NCPP variable is failed (F1) or passed (P1).

Table 11-8

Correlations and percent of children failing 8YR Word Identification by education of parents and Socioeconomic Index.

NCPP Variables	r	% Fail
Education of Mother	.42	
Years in School		
0-8		25.0
9-12		11.7
13+		1.9
Education of Father	.43	
Years in School		
0-8		19.5
9-12		11.3
13+		1.9
Socioeconomic Index at Birth	.51	
0.0-1.9		29.8
2.0-3.9		20.1
4.0-5.9		11.0
6.0-7.9		4.0
8.0-9.5		0.8
Socioeconomic Index at 7YR	.49	
0.0-1.9		26.7
2.0-3.9		18.8
4.0-5.9		10.7
6.0-7.9		4.5
8.0-9.5		1.0

only 14% for children with normal mothers. Paternal retardation did not have the same predictive power.

Failure on the Bayley Mental and Motor Scales was associated with twice the risk of failing 8YR Language Production as passing those scales (Table 11-9). Two of the individual Bayley items predicted failure even better than did the full scales. The probabilities were .42 and .45, respectively, that if the child at eight months failed to vocalize to a social stimulus or failed to vocalize two syllables he would fail 8YR Language Production. These probabilities are more than three times greater than those associated with passing the two Bayley items. With such prognostic potential, these items might be used profitably to indicate need for remediation early in the child's life.

The 4YR IQ correlated .48 with 8YR Language Production and yielded conditional probabilities which predict well.

The risk was almost five times greater that the child would fail the index if he had a low IQ (<70) than if he had a normal or high IQ. The data on 7YR IQ were similar. The correlation between the full scale WISC IQ and 8YR Language Production was .32, and the associated probabilities indicated that the risk of failure was more than five times greater for children with low IQ (<70) than for the normal or superior children. Judgments of attention span and activity at both four and seven years of age showed low correlations with 8YR Language Production, but they appeared to be predictive nevertheless. Table 11-9 contains conditional probabilities which indicate that the perseverative or overactive child was much less likely to pass the language production index than other children. Echolalia was also indicative of failure on 8YR Language Production, but it predicted less well at age four than at age seven.

Table 11-9

Correlations and cross-tabulations for 8YR Language Production with selected NCPP variables.

	r	p(F2/F1)*	p(F2/P1)*
At-Birth NCPP Variables			
Housing Density (Overcrowding)	−.24	.21	.11
Per Capita Income	.27	.19	.08
Occupation of Father of the Baby: White-Collar	.25	.15	.06
Gravida: Mentally Retarded	<.10	.49	.14
Gravida: Acute Toxemia	<.10	.13	.12
Gravida: Chronic Hypertensive Disease	<.10	.19	.12
Father of Baby: Mentally Retarded	<.10	.19	.13
Birthweight: Normal versus Low Birthweight	.12	.20	.13
Gestation: Normal versus Short	.10	.15	.09
8-Month NCPP Variables			
Bayley Mental Score	.11	.24	.12
Bayley Motor Score	.15	.24	.12
Bayley Item: Vocalizes to Social Stimulus	<.10	.42	.13
Bayley Item: Vocalizes Two Syllables	<.10	.45	.13
Bayley Item: Enjoys Sound Production	<.10	.23	.13
Fine Motor Development	−.13	.18	.09
Gross Motor Development	−.14	.17	.09
1YR NCPP Variable			
Neurological Abnormality	−.10	.18	.11
4YR NCPP Variables			
4YR IQ	.48	.51	.11
Very Brief Attention Span	−.11	.38	.12
Highly Perseverative Attention Span	<.10	.63	.13
Echolalia	−.11	.29	.13
7YR NCPP Variables			
Bender Gestalt	−.35	.27	.09
WISC: Verbal IQ	.25	.42	.10
WISC: Performance IQ	.23	.36	.11
WISC: Full Scale IQ	.32	.66	.12
Auditory-Vocal Association Test	.55	.44	.10
Highly Perseverative Attention Span	<.10	.37	.14
Level of Activity: Extreme Overactivity	<.10	.34	.13
Nature of Activity: Extreme Overactivity	<.10	.54	.14
Very Hostile	<.10	.19	.14
Echolalia	−.14	.53	.13
WRAT: Speech Class	<.10	.31	.13
Neurological Abnormality	−.17	.27	.11

*p(F2/F1) and p(F2/P1) refer to the probability of failing 8YR Language Production (F2) when the NCPP variable is failed (F1) or passed (P1).

8YR Concept Development

SEI at birth and at seven years of age exhibited a more pronounced association with 8YR Concept Development than with either 8YR Language Comprehension or 8YR Language Production (Table 11-12). As might be expected, the amount of education of either parent also demonstrated a marked relation to the failure rate on this index. Failure on 8YR Concept Development was defined as a score of 29 or less (see Appendix 4). Children whose fathers were not white-collar workers or whose families were below the poverty level were three times as likely to fail as other children (Table 11-11).

303

Table 11-10

Correlations and percent of children failing 8YR Language Production by education of parents and Socioeconomic Index.

NCPP Variables	r	% Fail
Education of Mother	.30	
Years in School		
0-8		19.0
9-12		10.0
13+		2.5
Education of Father	.31	
Years in School		
0-8		16.6
9-12		9.8
13+		2.5
Socioeconomic Index at Birth	.33	
0.0-1.9		20.0
2.0-3.9		15.2
4.0-5.9		9.8
6.0-7.9		6.1
8.0-9.5		1.5
Socioeconomic Index at 7YR	.34	
0.0-1.9		18.2
2.0-3.9		15.0
4.0-5.9		9.9
6.0-7.9		5.7
8.0-9.5		1.8

The report of maternal mental retardation put a child at more risk of failure than the report of paternal mental retardation. As with the 8YR Language Comprehension, this finding may be due to inaccuracies in reporting, to differences in the amount of time spent with the child, or to differences in the influence of the parents on the child.

The eight-month Bayley scales, and particularly certain specific items, appeared to predict performance on 8YR Concept Development at least as well as they predicted the other language indexes. There was more than three times the risk involved if the child failed either of the two vocalization items than if he passed them.

As might be expected, 8YR Concept Development correlated .65 with 4YR IQ and .43 with 7YR full scale IQ. The associated probability of failing 8YR Concept Development was about six times greater if the child had a low IQ than if his IQ was normal or above on either of the intelligence tests. Various subtests or scales of both intelligence tests were evaluated separately and, in all cases, predicted well the children's failure on the index. However, the Stanford-Binet IQ and the full scale WISC IQ predicted better than the individual subtests.

Judgments of attention span, activity, and echolalia at four and seven years of age demonstrated relatively high conditional probabilities. If a child had a brief attention span, was perseverative or overactive, or was echolalic at either age, he was much more likely to fail 8YR Concept Development than if these behaviors were not noted.

Special Studies

The extensive amount of data gathered by the NINCDS Collaborative Project

304

Table 11-11

Correlations and cross-tabulations for 8YR Concept Development with selected NCPP variables.

	r	p(F2/F1)*	p(F2/P1)*
At-Birth NCPP Variables			
Housing Density (Overcrowding)	−.33	.24	.10
Per Capita Income	.37	.21	.07
Occupation of Father of the Baby: White-Collar	.33	.16	.05
Gravida: Mentally Retarded	<.10	.41	.14
Gravida: Acute Toxemia	<.10	.14	.12
Gravida: Chronic Hypertensive Disease	<.10	.19	.12
Father of Baby: Mentally Retarded	<.10	.23	.14
Birthweight: Normal versus Low Birthweight	.17	.22	.14
Gestation: Normal versus Short	.13	.19	.10
8-Month NCPP Variables			
Bayley Mental Score	.17	.29	.12
Bayley Motor Score	.16	.24	.12
Bayley Item: Vocalizes to Social Stimulus	<.10	.44	.14
Bayley Item: Vocalizes Two Syllables	<.10	.43	.14
Bayley Item: Enjoys Sound Production	−.13	.31	.13
Fine Motor Development	−.13	.19	.11
Gross Motor Development	−.14	.19	.10
1YR NCPP Variable			
Neurological Abnormality	−.12	.18	.12
4YR NCPP Variables			
4YR IQ	.65	.63	.11
4YR Graham Block Sort	.39	.34	.11
Stanford-Binet: II-6 Identification of Objects by Use	−.22	.53	.12
Very Brief Attention Span	−.15	.46	.13
Highly Perseverative Attention Span	<.10	.60	.13
Echolalia	−.13	.33	.13
7YR NCPP Variables			
Bender Gestalt	−.47	.36	.09
WISC: Information Scaled Score	.57	.52	.11
WISC: Coding Scaled Score	.19	.29	.12
WISC: Verbal IQ	.35	.54	.08
WISC: Performance IQ	.31	.44	.10
WISC: Full Scale IQ	.43	.78	.12
Auditory-Vocal Association Test	.70	.58	.08
Highly Perseverative Attention Span	<.10	.47	.14
Level of Activity: Extreme Overactivity	<.10	.38	.14
Nature of Activity: Extreme Overactivity	<.10	.60	.14
Echolalia	−.13	.54	.14
WRAT: Speech Class	<.10	.17	.14
Neurological Abnormality	−.18	.28	.11

*p(F2/F1) and p(F2/P1) refer to the probability of failing 8YR Concept Development (F2) when the NCPP variable is failed (F1) or passed (P1).

Table 11-12

Correlations and percent of children failing 8YR Concept Development by education of parents and Socioeconomic Index.

NCPP Variables	r	% Fail
Education of Mother	.38	
Years in School		
0-8		22.5
9-12		11.4
13+		1.8
Education of Father	.38	
Years in School		
0-8		18.8
9-12		10.6
13+		2.4
Socioeconomic Index at Birth	.46	
0.0-1.9		26.3
2.0-3.9		19.3
4.0-5.9		10.3
6.0-7.9		4.0
8.0-9.5		1.2
Socioeconomic Index at 7YR	.45	
0.0-1.9		24.7
2.0-3.9		18.0
4.0-5.9		10.1
6.0-7.9		4.4
8.0-9.5		1.1

made it possible to raise a number of supplementary questions. For example, how do children at various levels of intelligence function on the indexes? Other questions asked how certain subsamples performed. For example, how did children with hearing losses or with cleft palates perform on the indexes? The following section explores the various questions with respect to the language indexes.

Intelligence

The full scale WISC IQ scores at seven years of age were grouped by ten-point intervals and the mean for each race-sex group was calculated. Figures 11-20 through 11-23 display bar graphs of these data for each of the four language indexes at eight years of age.

The 8YR Language Comprehension Index correlated .40 with the WISC full scale IQ. Figure 11-20 shows that the relationship between these two measures was monotonic when sample size was large enough to stabilize the mean. Furthermore, the monotonic relation existed within the race-sex groups for an IQ of 50 and above. With intelligence controlled, Males performed better than Females, and White children had higher means than Black children on 8YR Language Comprehension.

The results for 8YR Word Identification were similar to those for 8YR Language Comprehension, but the correlation between 8YR Word Identification and the WISC full scale IQ was somewhat higher at .51. In Figure 11-21 it can be seen that the same monotonic relationship existed between IQ and 8YR Word Identification. This finding was expected not only because Word Identification is a component of 8YR Language Comprehension, but also because of previous findings (Dunn,

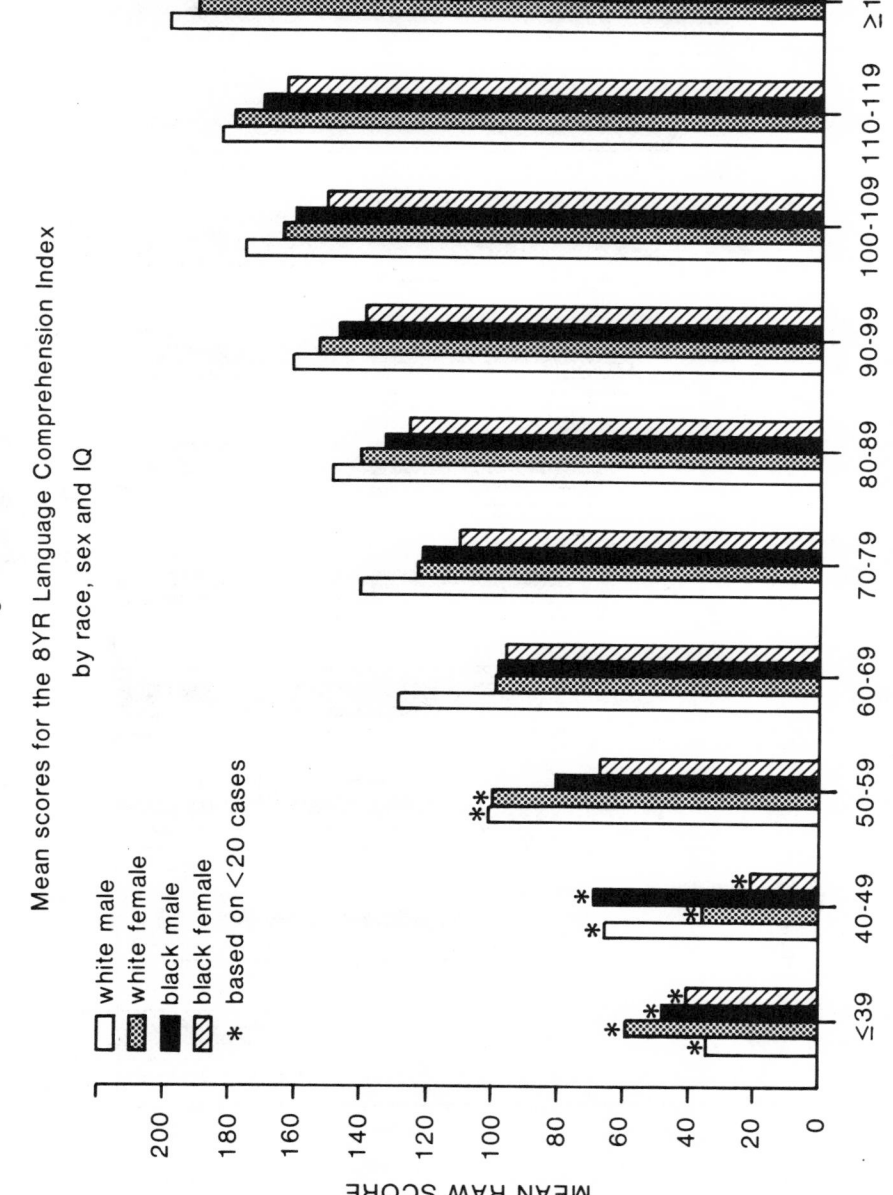

Figure **11-20**

Mean scores for the 8YR Language Comprehension Index
by race, sex and IQ

☐ white male
▨ white female
■ black male
▧ black female
* based on <20 cases

MEAN RAW SCORE

Grouped 7YR WISC IQ

≤39 40-49 50-59 60-69 70-79 80-89 90-99 100-109 110-119 ≥120

307

Figure **11-21**
Mean scores for 8YR Word Identification
by race, sex and IQ

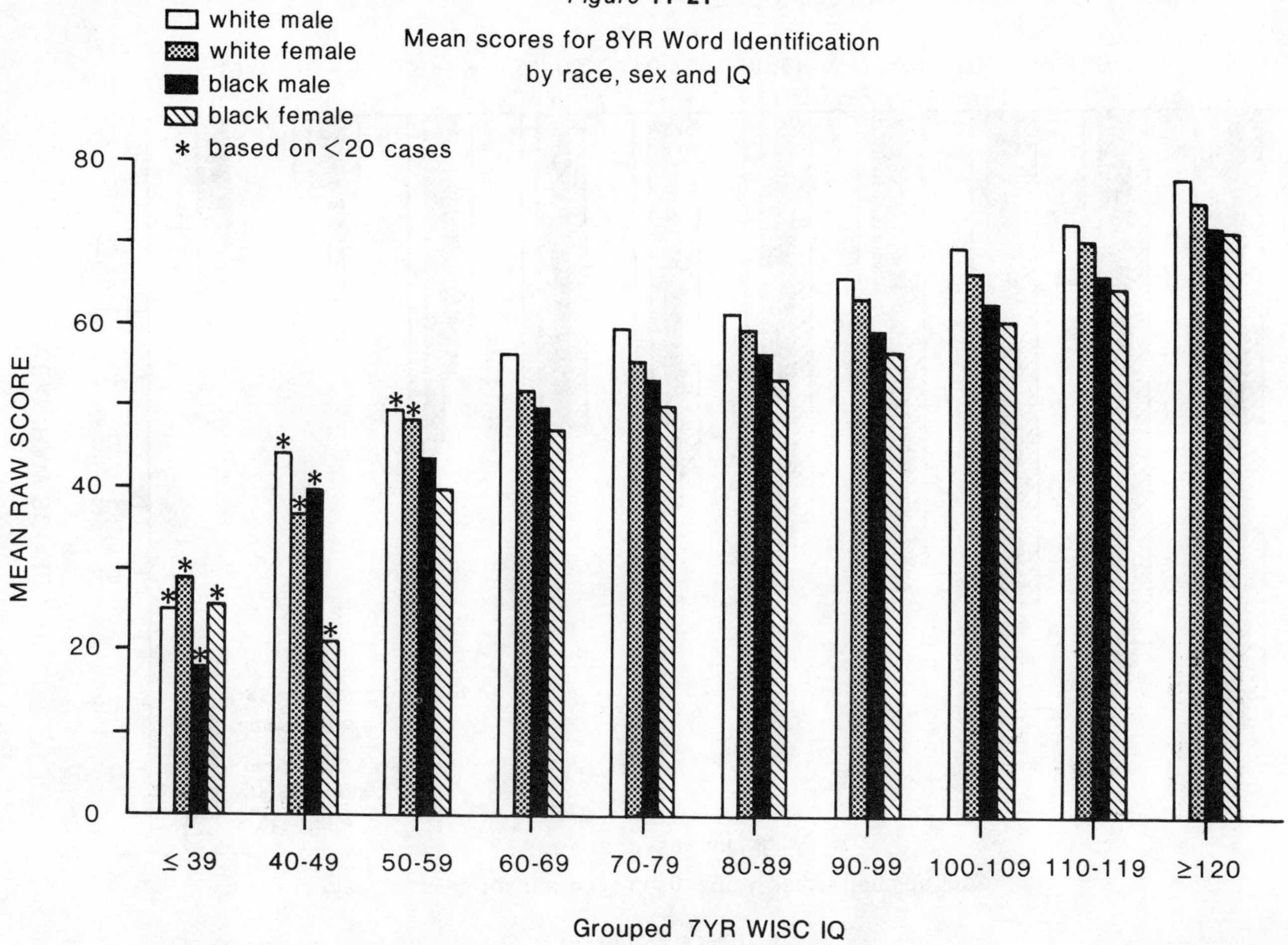

Legend:
□ white male
▨ white female
■ black male
▧ black female
* based on <20 cases

Y-axis: MEAN RAW SCORE
X-axis: Grouped 7YR WISC IQ

X-axis categories: ≤39, 40-49, 50-59, 60-69, 70-79, 80-89, 90-99, 100-109, 110-119, ≥120

308

1965). Females performed better than Males, and differences between races were somewhat smaller than for 8YR Language Comprehension.

The correlation between the full scale WISC IQ and 8YR Language Production was .32. Figure 11-22 shows that there is a consistent increase in performance on 8YR Language Production as intelligence increases. When sample size was large enough (>20) to stabilize the means of the race-sex groups and intelligence was controlled, Females performed better than Males and White children performed slightly better than Black children.

The 8YR Concept Development Index was correlated .43 with the WISC full scale IQ. An overall monotonic relationship existed with mean 8YR Concept Development increasing as IQ increased (Figure 11-23), but there were some reversals within the race-sex groups. White Males performed better than White Females for some of the lower IQ groups but did more poorly when IQ exceeded 80. Within the sample of Black children, Males consistently performed more poorly than Females.

Singletons, Siblings, and Twins

There has been speculation in the literature about the language acquisition and performance of children raised singly as opposed to those with siblings (Davis, 1937). Other literature has discussed the language of twins (Day, 1932; Mittler, 1971). It was possible to determine which children had no siblings at enrollment into the NINCDS Collaborative Perinatal Project or during the eight years they were followed in the project. These are defined as singletons; there were 879 in the ALL 8YR sample. When a child who was enrolled in the study had a sibling also enrolled in the study, and data were available for both children, these children were labeled siblings; there were 1940 sets of siblings in the ALL 8YR sample. There were also 185 sets of twins in the ALL 8YR sample for whom data were available for both children.

Figure 11-24 displays the means and standard deviations for singletons, siblings, and twins on 8YR Language Comprehension. The general trend was for singletons to perform better than either siblings or twins regardless of sex, race, or SEI. Siblings invariably had higher mean scores than twins. Although many of the mean differences were small, the trend was clearly evident and it was maintained within SEI groups.

The data yielded similar results for 8YR Word Identification (Figure 11-25), but the mean differences between singletons and twins were larger (using the standard deviation as the referent). Again, the SEI did not alter the order of differences among groups.

Means for 8YR Language Production did not appear to be as closely associated with the status of the child as for the two comprehension indexes (Figure 11-26). Differences between singletons and siblings were smaller but twins still performed poorest. Changes in SEI lessened the difference between twins and the other two groups.

Differences between singletons and siblings in 8YR Concept Development (Figure 11-27) were small, but they were appreciably larger between twins and both of the other two groups. As in the case of 8YR Language Production, increases in SEI lessened the differences between twins and both siblings and singletons for 8YR Concept Formation.

Children with Parents or Parent-Surrogates

A number of children in the NINCDS Collaborative Perinatal Project were not living with their biological parents at the time of the 8YR Speech, Language, and Hearing Examination. Because of interest in the contribution of heredity and environment to the child's development

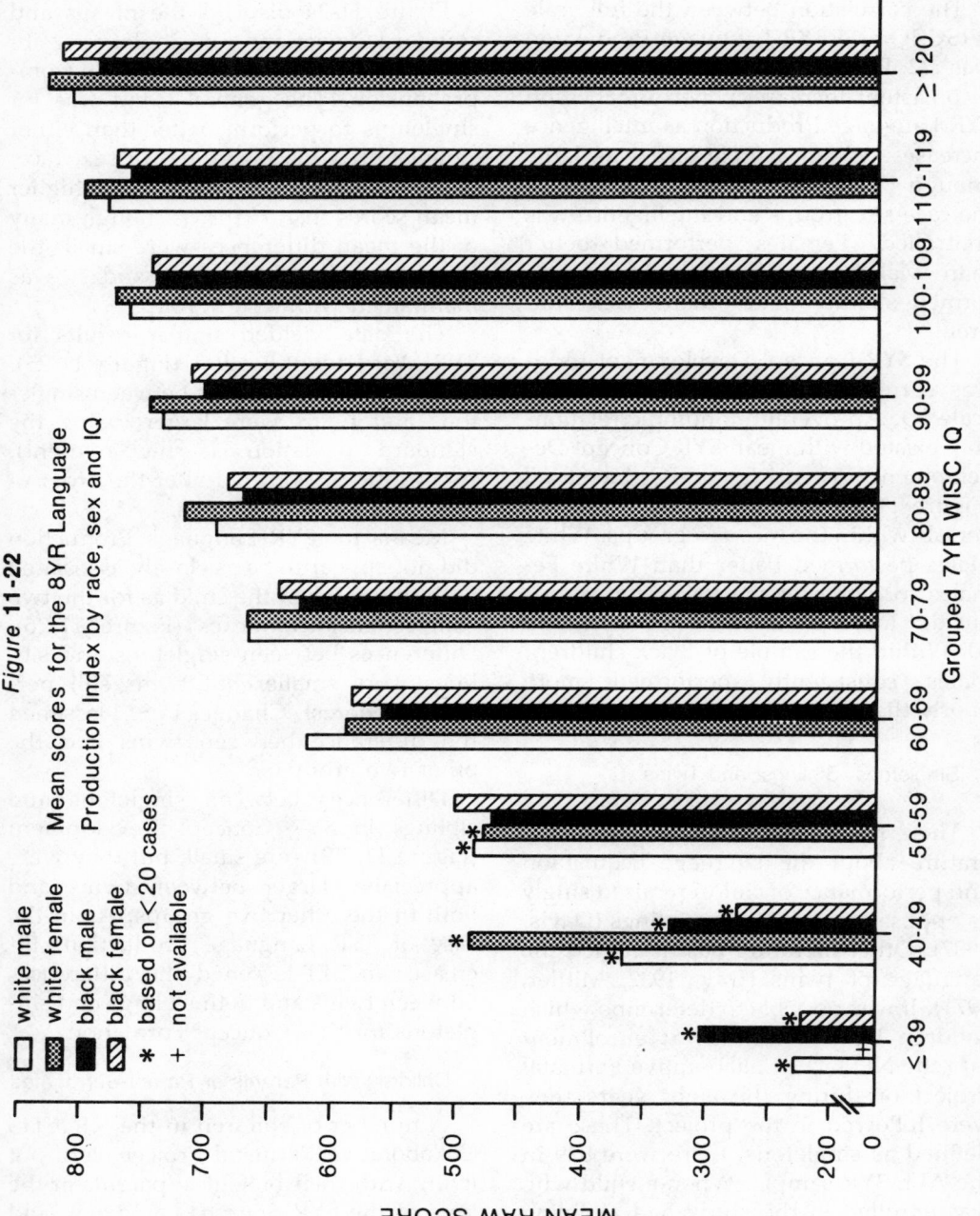

Figure 11-22

Mean scores for the 8YR Language
Production Index by race, sex and IQ

white male
white female
black male
black female
* based on <20 cases
+ not available

MEAN RAW SCORE

Grouped 7YR WISC IQ

310

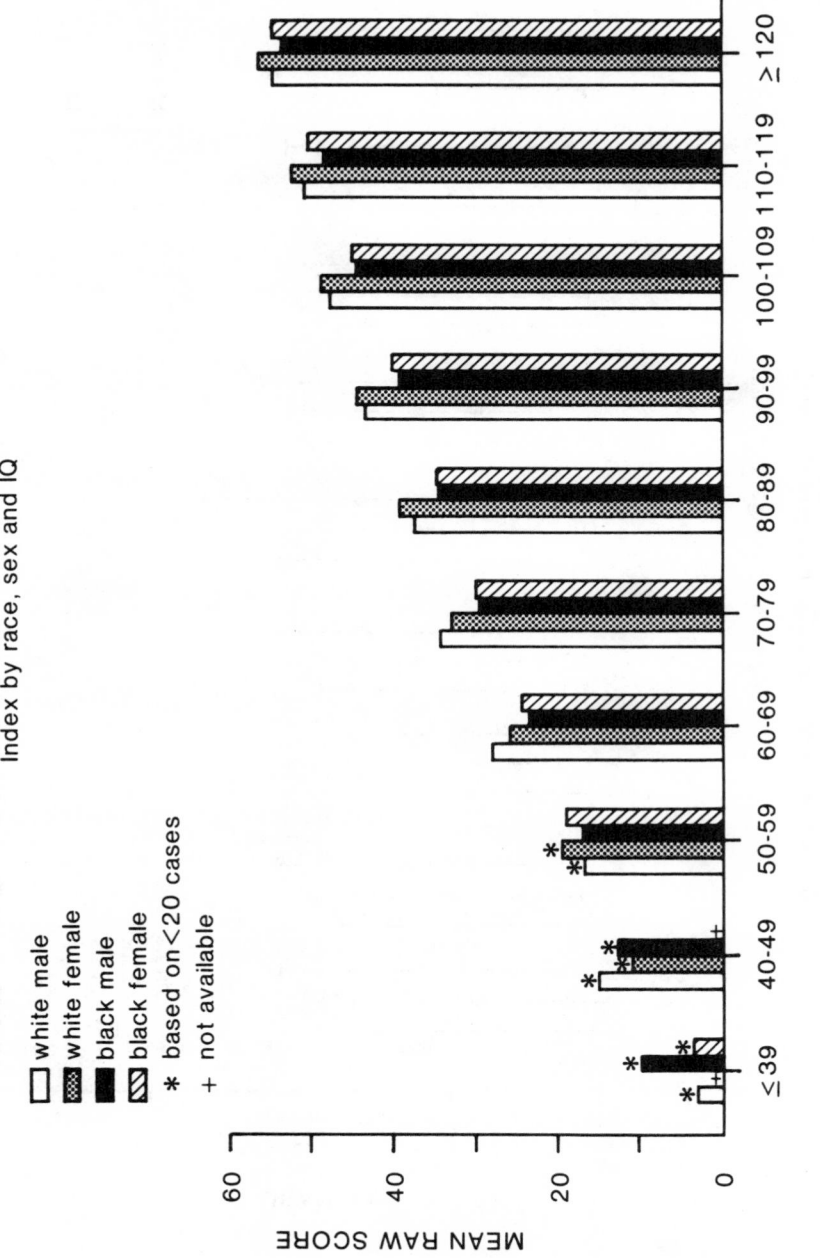

Figure **11-23**

Mean scores for the 8YR Concept Development

Index by race, sex and IQ

white male
white female
black male
black female
* based on <20 cases
+ not available

MEAN RAW SCORE

Grouped 7YR WISC IQ

311

Figure **11-24**

Mean scores for the 8YR Language Comprehension Index
for singletons, siblings and twins

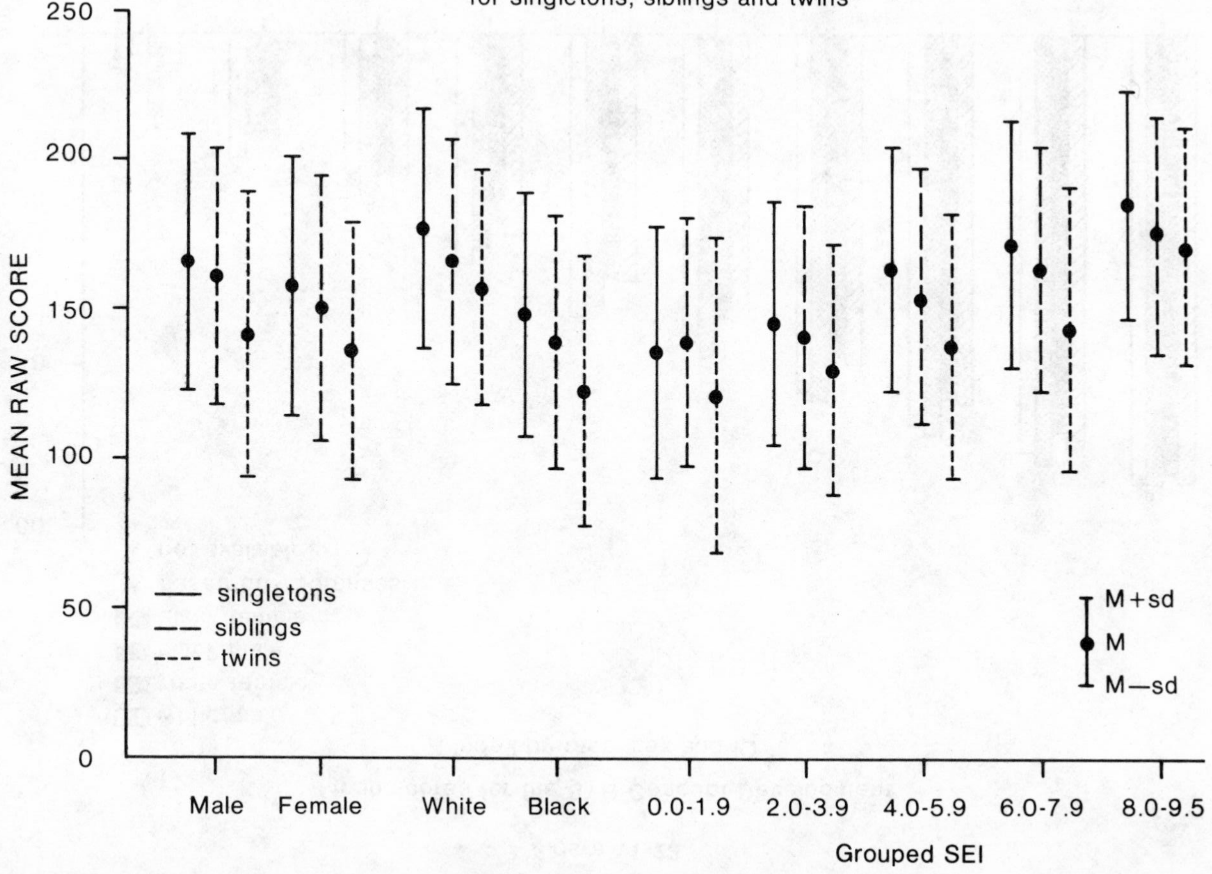

312

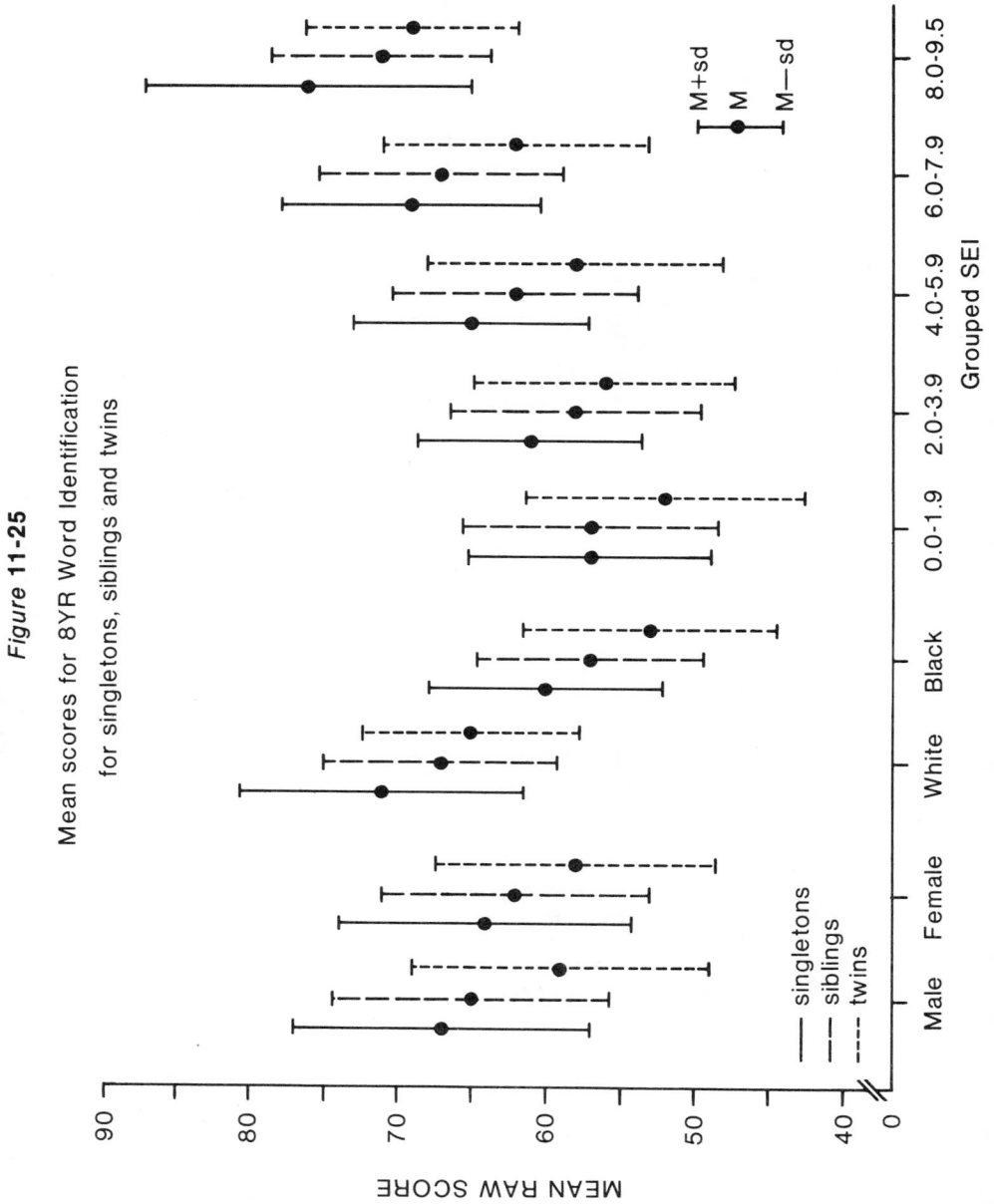

Figure **11-25**

Mean scores for 8YR Word Identification

for singletons, siblings and twins

313

Figure **11-26**

Mean scores for the 8YR Language Production Index
for singletons, siblings and twins

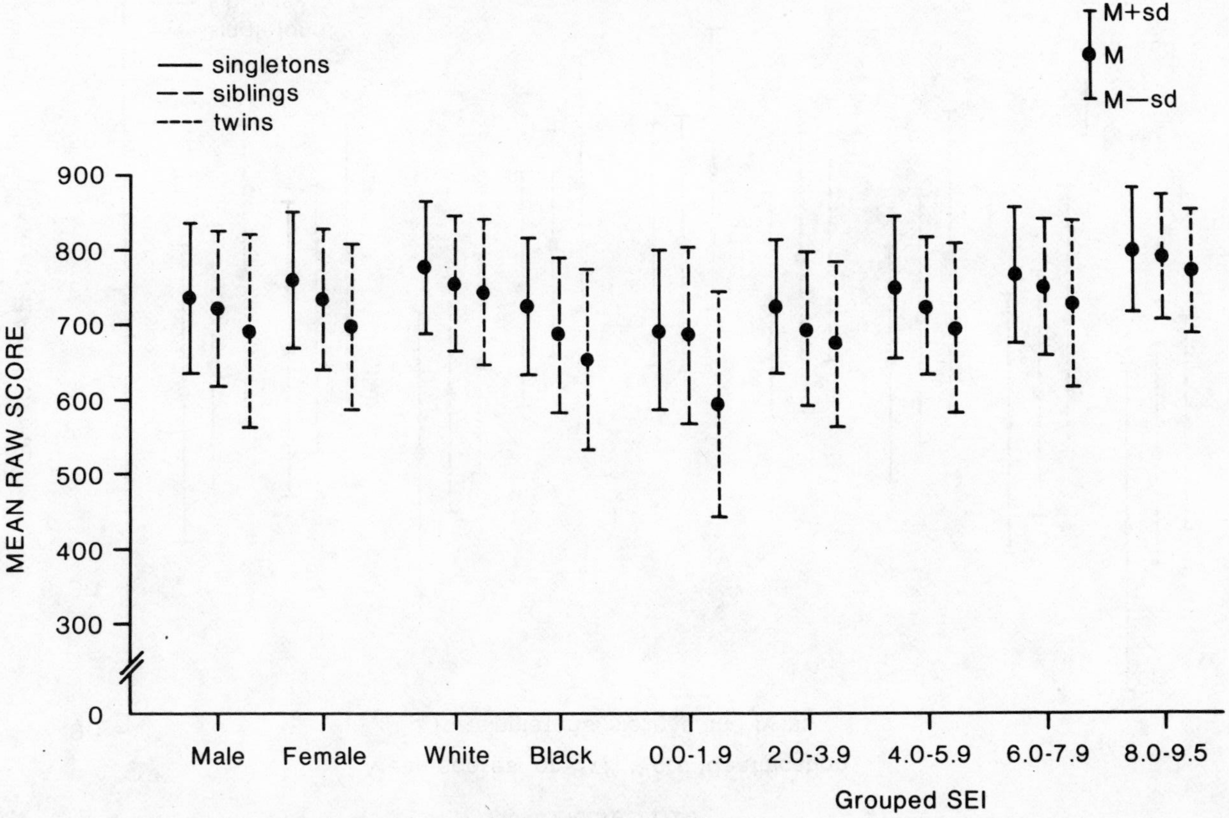

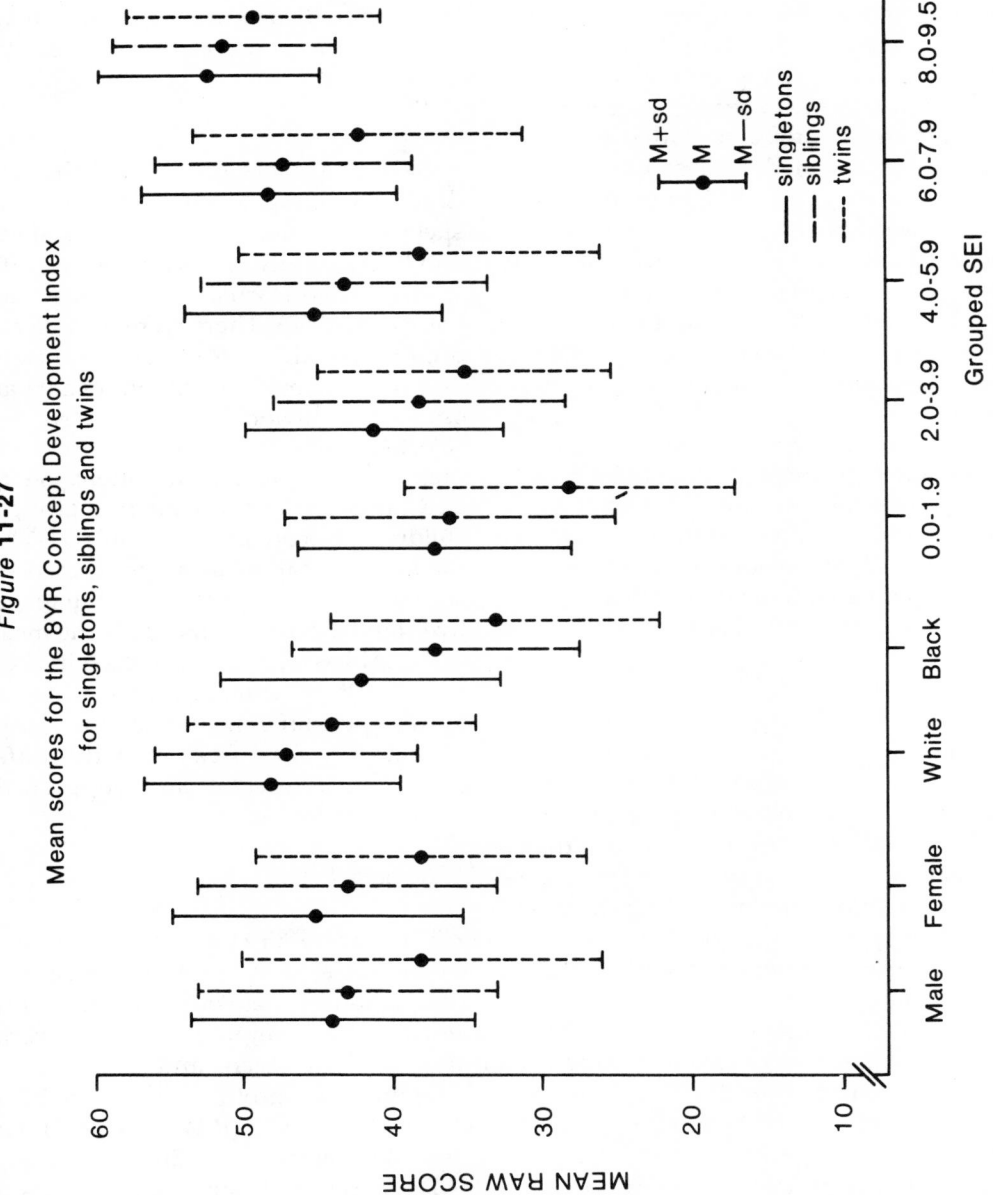

Figure **11-27**

Mean scores for the 8YR Concept Development Index
for singletons, siblings and twins

(Eells et al., 1951; Jensen, 1968), it seemed important to evaluate the performance of adopted and foster children, those living with at least one biological parent, and those living with other relatives. Table 11-13 contains the means and standard deviations for these four groups of children on each of the four language indexes. Children living with at least one biological parent constitute the comparison group. It can be seen that adopted children performed consistently better, and children in foster homes or living with relatives performed consistently poorer than children living with at least one biological parent. The performance of the adopted children is attributable to the improvement in socioeconomic factors that generally accompanies adoption (Yarrow et al., 1973). That is, the child acquires more opportunities for language stimulation because of his higher SEI group. The lower means of the other two groups may be due to increased stress which the child experiences in a foster or other-relative placement as well as to the SEI level of the placement.

Cleft Palate

There were 24 children with cleft palate in the ALL 8YR sample. Since it has been reported in the literature that these children may perform more poorly than normal children in speech and language (Faircloth and Faircloth, 1972; Morris, 1962; Spriestersbach, Darley, and Morris, 1958), it was of interest to compare the performance of the children with cleft palates to the ALL 8YR sample. Table 11-14 contains the means and standard deviations on the four 8YR language indexes for children with cleft palates and for the total ALL 8YR sample. It can be seen that cleft palate children performed better on 8YR Language Comprehension and more poorly on 8YR Word Identification, 8YR Language Production, and 8YR Concept Development than the ALL 8YR sample. However, none of the differ-

ences exceeded one-third the respective standard deviations. Because of the small sample size, it is not reasonable to conclude that these differences are other than normal fluctuations due to sampling. However, they might conceivably be attributed to hearing loss which was confounded in the cleft palate sample.

Stutterers

Several authors have noted that children exhibiting dysfluencies in their speech may also be delayed in speech and language behaviors (Van Riper, 1971; Andrews and Harris, 1964; deHirsch and Langford, 1950). There were only 35 children in the ALL 8YR sample who exhibited some or many dysfluent events and struggle behavior. These children were selected as the sample of stutterers. The means and standard deviations on the 8YR language indexes for this group of children are contained in Table 11-14. It can be seen that the mean performance of stutterers was about one-half the respective standard deviations below the means of the ALL 8YR sample on each index. It is difficult to conclude that these are meaningful differences since the sample of stutterers was small, but the differences are consistent and support the cited literature.

Cerebral Palsy

There were 83 children diagnosed as cerebral palsied in the ALL 8YR sample. The various types of problems represented in the sample ranged in severity from mild to severe and constituted a heterogeneous group. The mean IQ of the group on the 7YR WISC was 73 with a standard deviation of 20.

The means and standard deviations on the 8YR language indexes for the cerebral palsy group are contained in Table 11-14. The means for the cerebral palsy group were consistently lower than the means for the ALL 8YR sample and were con-

Table 11-13

Sample sizes, means and standard deviations on the 8YR Language Indexes for singletons, siblings, twins, adopted and foster children, children living with relatives or with at least one biological parent.

Sample	N	8YR Language Comprehension		8YR Word Identification		8YR Language Production		8YR Concept Development	
		Mean	SD	Mean	SD	Mean	SD	Mean	SD
Singletons	879	162	43	65	10.0	749	96	45	9.6
Siblings	1,940 sets	155	44	63	9.3	728	100	43	10.2
Twins	185 sets	138	46	59	10.0	696	120	38	11.6
Adopted Children	243*	165	42	66	7.7	750	95	45	8.8
Foster Children	277*	145	46	59	9.6	706	113	39	11
Children Living with Relatives	621*	142	43	58	8.8	698	103	37	10
Children Living with at least one Biological Parent	23,931*	154	45	63	9.9	729	101	43	10

*N is based on 3YR and 8YR combined.

Table 11-14

Sample sizes, means and standard deviations on the 8YR Language Indexes for groups of children with special study characteristics.

Sample	N	8YR Language Comprehension		8YR Word Identification		8YR Language Production		8YR Concept Development	
		Mean	SD	Mean	SD	Mean	SD	Mean	SD
Cleft Palate	24	160	36	60	8.5	709	104	39	10
Stutterers	35	122	52	55	13	662	147	35	14
Cerebral Palsy	83	133	58	56	18	662	141	36	15
Mental Retardation Syndromes	53	85	43	42	17	517	185	19	9.1
Premature (≤36 weeks and ≤2,500 gms)	917	144	44	59	9.7	701	108	39	11
True Distress (Apgar <4)	617	148	44	60	9.0	722	115	41	10
Low Birthweight (<1,500 gms)	100	138	43	55	12	660	127	34	12
ALL 8YR	20,137	153	45	62	9.9	727	102	42	10

siderably more variable. However, the means for the cerebral palsy group were consistently higher than those with 7YR WISC IQ's between 71 and 80 (Figures 11-20 through 11-23), which might be considered more appropriate as a control group. It would appear that the disabilities of the children in the cerebral palsy group have also caused their scores on the WISC to be depressed. Overall, the cerebral palsy group did not perform as poorly as might have been predicted, given their known physical disabilities and intellectual level.

Mental Retardation with Syndromes

There were 53 children with 7YR WISC IQ's lower than 70 who were diagnosed as having the characteristics of a syndrome, such as Down's Syndrome, Pierre-Robin, or some other. It is shown in Table 11-14 that these children performed substantially more poorly than the ALL 8YR sample. Their mean IQ on the 7YR WISC was 51 (SD 15) and their performance was similar to that of the 51 to 60 IQ group of mental retardation without syndromes (Figures 11-20 through 11-23).

Prematurity

Children born at 36 weeks gestation or younger and weighing 2500 grams or less were designated as premature. Because premature children have been said to have poorer outcomes than full-term children (Drillien, 1964; deHirsch, Langford, and Jansky, 1965), it was of interest to compare their performance on the indexes. Table 11-14 contains means and standard deviations for the 917 premature infants in the ALL 8YR sample. Although the performance of the premature group was poorer than the ALL 8YR sample on all four indexes, no difference exceeded one-third the size of the standard deviation. These data may be interpreted as supporting Wright's position

that a majority of prematures ". . . eventually reach developmental levels which are within normal limits . . ." (1971, p. 278).

True Distress

There were 617 children who received a score of less than four on the 5-minute Apgar. These children were in distress at or immediately following delivery, and the distress persisted for at least five minutes. The performance of these children was only slightly poorer than the performance of the ALL 8YR sample (Table 11-14). The children who survived this early distress did so with little effect on their language behavior at eight years of age.

Low Birthweight

As in the case of prematurity, children with low birthweight are considered to be at risk in terms of later performance (Knobloch, Rider, and Harper, 1956; Dann, Levine, and New, 1964; Drillien, 1967). There were 100 children in the ALL 8YR sample whose birthweight was below 1500 grams. In general, the mean performance of this group of children was about one-half a standard deviation lower than the mean performance of the ALL 8YR sample on each language index (Table 11-14). Children with birthweights between 1500 and 2500 grams (N = 1905) produced mean scores which were intermediate between the low birthweight group (1500 grams) and the ALL 8YR sample. These data support statements in the literature about the performance abilities of low birthweight children.

Hearing Loss

Children with hearing losses have restricted auditory input, and they frequently are found to perform poorly on speech and language tasks (Moores, 1972; Davis, 1974). The ALL 8YR sample contained 1024 children with conductive hearing losses, 447 with sensorineural hearing losses, and 18,438 with normal hearing. The criteria for conductive and sensorineural hearing losses are given in Appendix 4. Children with normal hearing had neither a conductive nor a sensorineural hearing loss.

Figure 11-28 displays the mean performance for each hearing group by race, sex, and SEI for 8YR Language Comprehension. The sensorineural loss group performed more poorly than the other two groups except in the highest SEI group. The relationships among the groups change as a function of increasing SEI. Neither hearing loss group performed as poorly with respect to the normal hearing group in SEI 8.0 to 9.5 as they did in the lower SEI groups. It can be postulated that opportunity for educational and social experiences occurs in the upper socioeconomic levels which tends to improve performance by the hearing-impaired on 8YR Language Comprehension.

The effect of SEI on the hearing loss groups is not as obvious for 8YR Word Identification (Figure 11-29). For this index the relative ordering of sensorineural loss, conductive loss, and normal hearing maintained the same relationship.

Performance on 8YR Language Production (Figure 11-30) was quite similar to 8YR Language Comprehension for the three hearing groups. Children with sensorineural losses performed the most poorly, followed by the conductive loss group and the normal hearing group. An increase in SEI appeared to reduce the differences among the groups, as it did with 8YR Language Comprehension, and probably for the same reason suggested.

The means on 8YR Concept Development (Figure 11-31) for the hearing groups followed a pattern similar to that of the other language indexes. The group of children with a sensorineural loss had the lowest mean score, followed by the

conductive loss group and the normal hearing group. The effects of SEI on the hearing groups were also similar.

In general, it appears that the findings reported in the research literature have been supported in that children with the more severe hearing loss (sensorineural) performed more poorly than normal hearing children, and that children with a less severe hearing loss (conductive) scored means that were intermediate.

Discussion and Summary

Descriptive Statistics

The descriptive statistics and frequency distributions of the 3YR and 8YR language variables and indexes provide information on three questions:

1. Are there differences in performance between Males and Females?
2. Are there differences in performance between White and Black Children?
3. Are there differences in the performance of socioeconomic groups?

At three yeas of age, Females perform better than Males, although the differences are small. At eight years of age differences do not reflect consistently superior performance by either Males or Females. These findings support data presented in previous literature (Harms and Spiker, 1959; Templin, 1957) for a number of different speech and language measures. They also suggest that differences between boys and girls have lessened or become nonexistent since the early studies were done (Maccoby and Jacklin, 1974).

Current research (Bloom, 1973; Brown, 1973) has disregarded any potential differences implied by the previous literature and has assumed that the language acquisition process is the same for both sexes. Performance measured by the 3YR and 8YR examinations provides some support for this assumption.

320

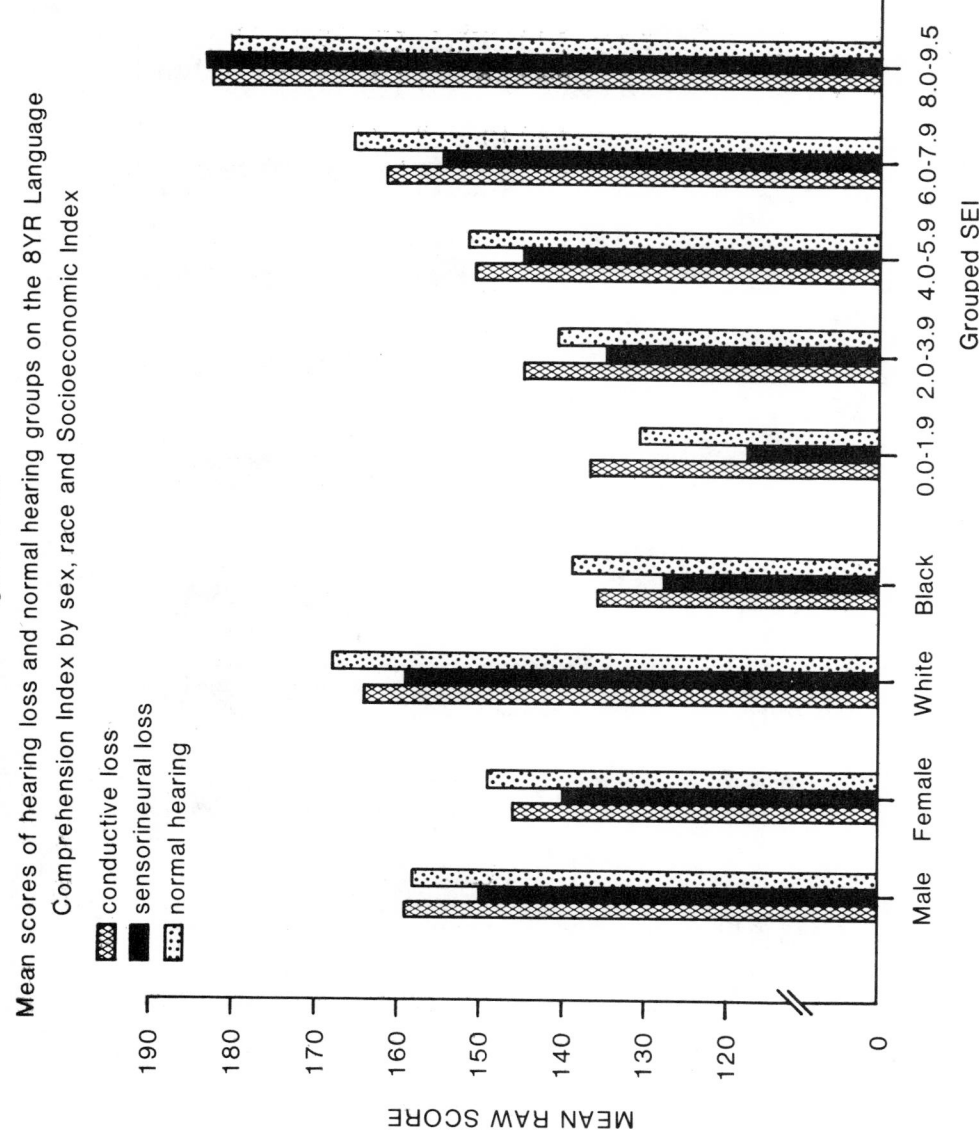

Figure **11-28**

Mean scores of hearing loss and normal hearing groups on the 8YR Language
Comprehension Index by sex, race and Socioeconomic Index

321

Figure **11-29**

Mean scores of hearing loss and normal hearing groups on 8YR Word Identification by sex, race and Socioeconomic Index

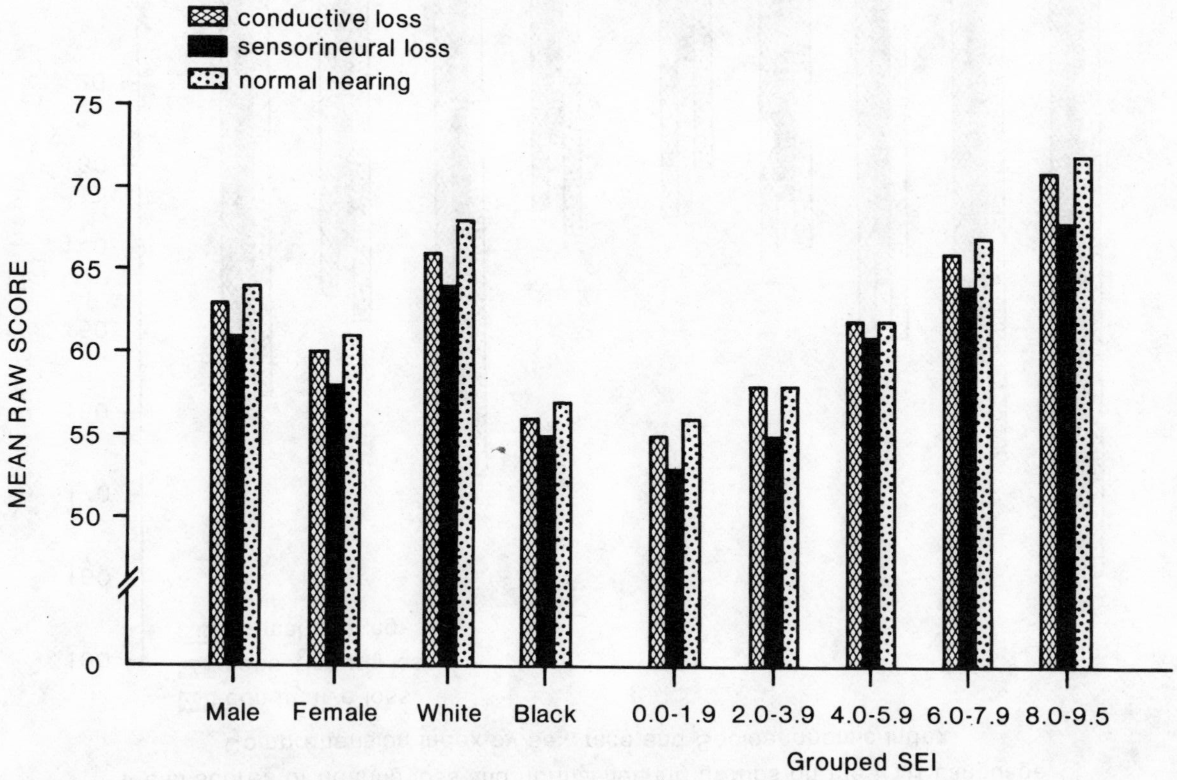

322

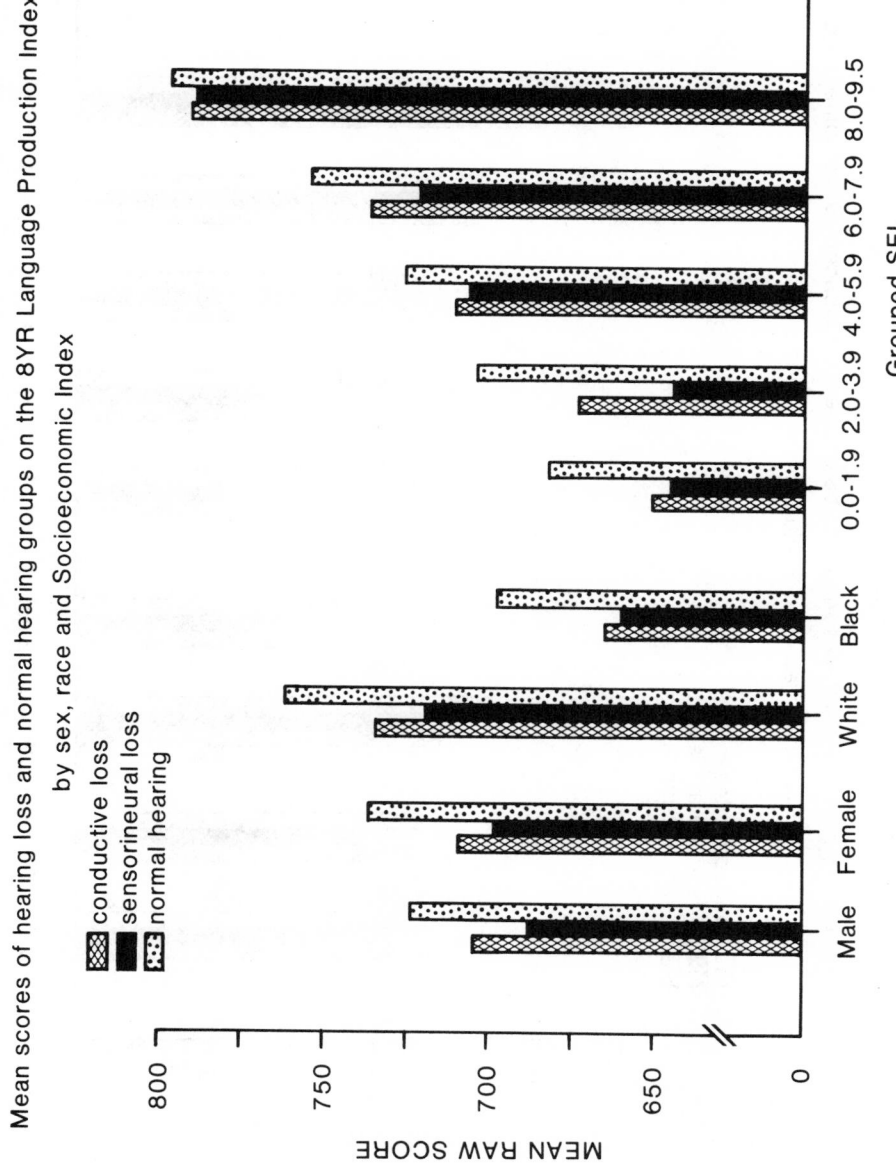

Figure 11-30

Mean scores of hearing loss and normal hearing groups on the 8YR Language Production Index by sex, race and Socioeconomic Index

conductive loss
sensorineural loss
normal hearing

MEAN RAW SCORE

800 750 700 650 0

Male Female White Black 0.0-1.9 2.0-3.9 4.0-5.9 6.0-7.9 8.0-9.5

Grouped SEI

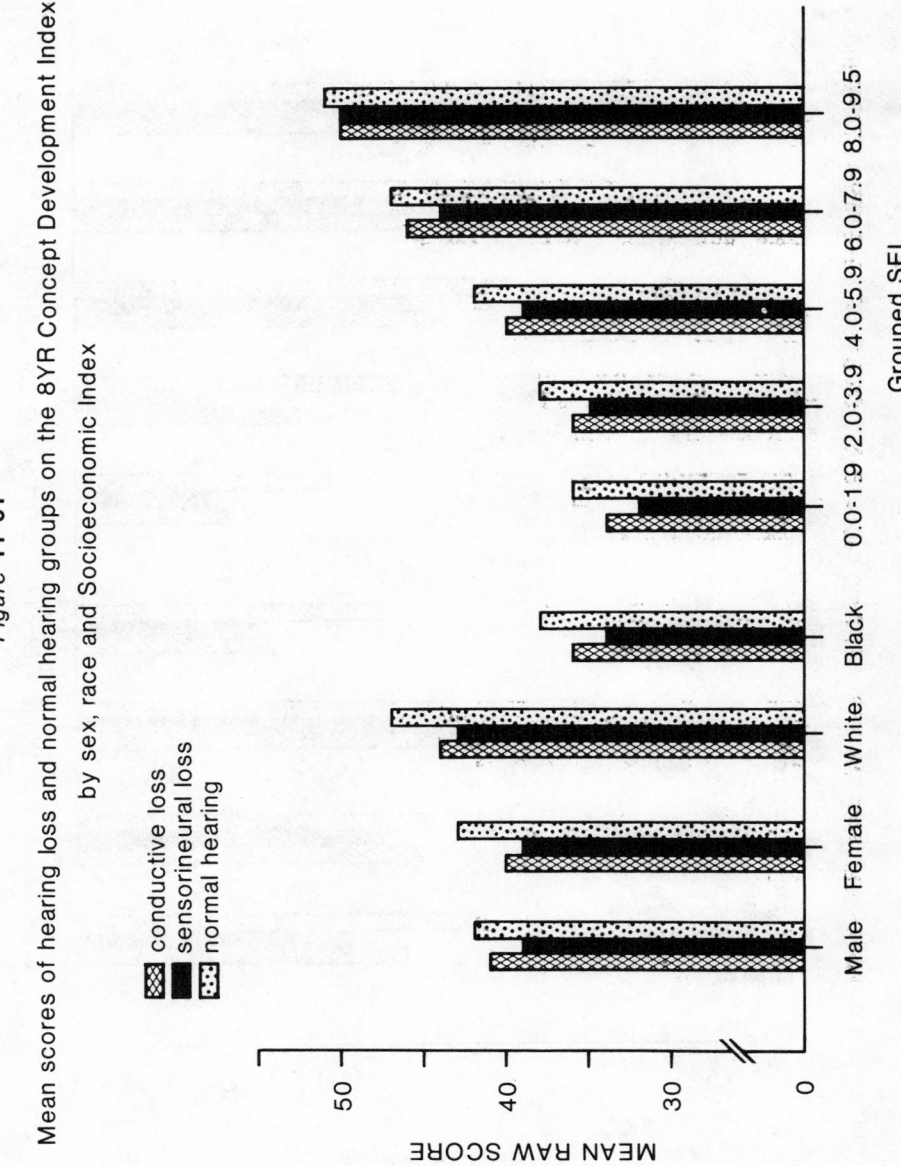

Figure **11-31**

Mean scores of hearing loss and normal hearing groups on the 8YR Concept Development Index by sex, race and Socioeconomic Index

324

Discussion of differences between the performance of White children and the performance of Black children must acknowledge several qualifying factors: (1) most of the SLH examiners were white; (2) no information is available on how many of the Black children in the sample spoke Black English as opposed to standard English; (3) there was confounding of race and socioeconomic level in the analyses; and (4) most of the tests used were standardized on White children only.

It has long been recognized that children in a testing situation may perform more poorly with a strange examiner and that race differences between examiner and child also may cause poorer performance (Cronbach, 1960; Forrester and Klaus, 1964). The examiners for the SLH examinations were predominantly white females. It seems appropriate, therefore, to interpret performance differences between the White and Black children with this in mind.

The second factor of concern when interpreting race differences in performance is the dialect(s) spoken by the children. Literature published since 1960 has emphasized that Black children may speak a nonstandard dialect of English (Labov, 1970; Baratz, 1970). Black English, as any other dialect, is a well-formed, highly-structured system of language which native speakers and listeners produce and comprehend; it is, however, different in many ways from standard English (Stewart, 1970). The differences that exist between the two dialects may be tested by various measuring instruments and may be interpreted as a poorer performance by the speaker of Black English. When the language tests of the SLH examinations were selected and pretested, distinctions between Black English and standard English had not been published and, therefore, were not taken into account in test selection. Other differences in the children's cultural experiences were also relatively unknown, but it was assumed that these differences would be averaged out by social class and geographical selection factors.

Those language tests involving examiner judgments of the child's oral productions would be affected most by the child using Black English. These would be the judgments of sentence structure, sentence length, word order, relevance, and use of pronouns on the 3YR SLH examination, and the Morphology test and the Connected Discourse test on the 8YR SLH examination. The child's comprehension of the examiner's standard English productions would also influence his scores on the language comprehension measures. Any differences between Black and White children should be interpreted with the knowledge that dialect differences probably existed and may have influenced the findings.

The final factor which must be taken into account for these data is that race and socioeconomic level were confounded within the analyses. There were more Black children than White children in the lowest SEI group, while the reverse was true for the highest SEI group in the sample (see Chapter 4).

A study which was successful in evaluating children of different ethnic groups and in differing social classes was conducted by Stodolsky and Lesser (1967). They found that the absolute level of ability on verbal, reasoning, number, and spatial-conceptualization tests was determined by socioeconomic level, but that the pattern of abilities was related to the child's ethnic group. Children in the lower socioeconomic level of each ethnic group scored significantly lower than children in their corresponding middle-class sample. Since these children were tested in their native language by examiners who were also native speakers of the language, the effects of socioeconomic level are clearly separate from ethnic heritage. If the Stodolsky and Lesser data are valid, then any interpretation of the confounded race and SEI data in the

NINCDS Collaborative Perinatal Project should place more weight on the effects of SEI and less on the effects of race.

Prediction and Risk

The SLH data were analyzed to see how well outcomes at ages three and eight could be predicted from early antecedent events. Cross-tabulations and conditional probabilities were also calculated to provide an estimate of how antecedent events were related to poor outcomes at the same two ages.

Predictions of the 8YR language indexes were better than those of the other indexes at either age. The independent variables related to race, sex, and socioeconomic factors contributed most to the predictions. When 4YR IQ was added to the multiple regression analyses, the correlation coefficients increased and the change in beta weights reflected the partial correlations between IQ and race, sex, and socioeconomic factors. Using the variables measured at birth and eight months as independent variables in the prediction equation would enable clinicians to identify children prior to one year of age, with some confidence, as potentially at risk for language problems at eight years. Since race, sex, and socioeconomic factors tend to be stable over time, the increased predictive power which the IQ estimate contributes is not of sufficient magnitude to warrant the use of equations which include 4YR IQ.

The early factors related to socioeconomic level with higher beta weights in the multiple regression analyses also yielded conditional probabilities which indicated children at risk for language problems. These cross-tabulation analyses showed a clearer effect at eight years of age than at three.

Other factors, such as a mother who was ill during the pregnancy or who was mentally retarded, also were related to the performance outcome of the child.

Perhaps the most interesting of these other factors were two particular items from the Bayley Scale of Mental and Motor Development administered at eight months of age. Failure of these items, Vocalizes to a Social Stimulus and Vocalizes Two Syllables, were associated with risks of later poor language performance that were three or more times greater than if the items had been passed by the child. These are particularly important items the relevance of which was masked in the over-all mental score. The ease with which these two items can be administered and their indication of potential risk if the child fails the items give them particular clinical usefulness and significance.

Special Studies

Data were analyzed for several subgroups of children who, according to previous findings, often evidence language delay. Descriptive statistics were developed for children who varied on physical, sensory, or psychological parameters.

The analyses supported several previously reported findings: (1) that performance on language measures improved as intelligence increased; (2) that mentally retarded children with syndromes performed like their IQ controls; and (3) that children with cerebral palsy performed consistently better than their IQ scores would suggest, perhaps because their motor disabilities depressed the intelligence score.

Children who had low birthweights, were premature, or had low Apgar scores performed less well than the ALL 8YR sample. The differences were small but this finding seems to support the current literature (Wright, 1971; Drillien, 1967). Children with cleft palates and those who stuttered did not perform in a way that could be considered significantly inferior to the ALL 8YR sample; therefore, these data are in conflict with the previous literature (Faircloth and Faircloth, 1972;

Morris, 1962; Spriestersbach, Darley, and Morris, 1958; Van Riper, 1971; Andrews and Harris, 1964; deHirsch and Langford, 1950). The discrepancies between these data and the previous literature may be due to sampling error because of the small samples studied.

Children with hearing losses performed at a lower level than those with normal hearing. In general, children with sensorineural losses (usually more severe) performed the poorest, while those with conductive losses were intermediate and normal hearing children performed best. For both 8YR Language Comprehension and 8YR Language Production, performance of both hearing loss groups moved closer to the performance of normal hearing children as SEI increased. This may be due to: (1) more opportunity for educational and social experiences which the upper SEI groups afford; (2) better health care which permits the higher SEI child to attend school more regularly; or (3) the greater value the higher SEI parent places on oral communication.

Analyses were also done for groups of children where child rearing practices were potentially different. The findings indicated that adopted children performed better than children living with at least one biological parent or those in foster homes. This could be accounted for partially by the increase in SEI and all the benefits accruing to it, which accompanied adoption. Children placed in foster homes performed the poorest, and it was speculated that their lowered performance was due to increased stress as well as socioeconomic factors in the placement.

Data on twins, singletons, and siblings supported previous literature (Davis, 1937; Day, 1932; Mittler, 1971). In general, singletons performed best, followed by siblings and, finally, twins. Higher socioeconomic status appeared to lessen the differences between twins and the two other groups.

Conclusions regarding most of the special study groups must be tempered somewhat because of the relatively small samples available for study. No tests of statistical significance were applied between the ALL 8YR sample and the special groups because they were thought to be inappropriate (see Chapter 5). The descriptive normative data, however, should be valuable to the clinician concerned with any of these distinctive groups of children.

Conclusions

In summary, the data on the language outcomes from the SLH examinations appear to provide: (1) useful descriptive statistics; (2) index outcomes which are predicted from variables measured prior to one year of age; and (3) probabilities which indicate other variables as predictive of children who are potentially at risk on later language performance measures.

References

1. Andrews, G., and Harris, M. *The Syndrome of Stuttering.* London: Heinemann, 1964.

2. Baratz, J.C. Teaching reading in an urban negro school system. In F. Williams, Ed. *Language and Poverty.* Chicago: Markham, 1970.

3. Bayley, N. *COLR Research Form of the Bayley Scales of Mental and Motor Development.* Bethesda, Maryland: Perinatal Research Branch, NINDB-NIH, 1958.

4. Bierman, J.M., Siegal, E., French, F.E., and Conner, A. The community impact of handicaps of perinatal or natal origin. *Publ. Health Rep.* 78:839–855, 1963.

5. Bloom, L. *One Word At A Time.* The Hague: Mouton, 1973.

6. Brown, R. *A First Language: The Early Stages.* Cambridge: Harvard University Press, 1973.

7. Cronbach, L.J. *Essentials of Psychological Testing.* 2nd Ed. New York: Harper, 1960.

8. Dann, M., Levine, S.Z., and New, E.V. A long term follow-up study of small premature infants. *Pediatrics* 33:945–955, 1964.

9. Davis, E.A. The development of linguistic skills in twins, singletons with siblings, and only children from age 5 to 10 years. *Univ. Minn. Child Welf. Monogr. Ser.* No. 14, 1937.

10. Davis, J. Performance of young hearing-impaired children on a test of basic concepts. *J. Speech Hear. Res.* 17:343–351, 1974.

11. Day, E.J. The development of language in twins: 1. A comparison of twins and single children. *Child Development* 3:179–199, 1932.

12. deHirsch, K., and Langford, W.S. Clinical note on stuttering and cluttering in young children. *Pediatrics* 5:934–940, 1950.

13. deHirsch, K., Langford, W.S., and Jansky, J.J. Comparison of prematurely and maturely-born children. *Am. J. Orthopsychiatry* 35:357–358, 1965.

14. Drillien, C.M. *The Growth and Development of the Prematurely Born Infant.* Baltimore: Williams and Wilkins, 1964.

15. Drillien, C.M. The incidence of mental and physical handicaps in school age children of very low birthweigt. *Pediatrics* 39:238–247, 1967.

16. Dunn, L.M. *Peabody Picture Vocabulary Test Manual.* Circle Pines, Minnesota: American Guidance Service, 1965.

17. Durrell, D.D., and Sullivan, H.B. *Durrell-Sullivan Reading Capacity and Achievement Tests.* New York: Harcourt, Brace and World, 1945.

18. Eells, K., Davis, A. Havighurst, R.J., Herrick, V.E., and Tyler, R.W. *Intelligence and Cultural Differences.* Chicago: University of Chicago Press, 1951.

19. Faircloth, S.R., and Faircloth, M.A. Delayed language and linguistic variations. In K.R. Bzoch, Ed. *Communicative Disorders Related to Cleft Lip and Palate.* Boston: Little, Brown, 1972.

20. Forrester, B.J., and Klaus, R.A. The effect of the examiner on intelligence test scores of Negro kindergarten children. *Peabody Papers in Human Development.* 2:1–7, 1964.

21. Gray, W.S. *Gray Oral Reading Tests.* Indianapolis, Indiana: Bobbs-Merrill, 1967.

22. Harms, I.E., and Spiker, C.C. Factors associated with the performance of young children on intelligence scales and tests of speech development. *J. Genet. Psychol.*, 94:3–22, 1959.

23. Jastak, J.F., and Jastak, S.R. *The Wide Range Achievement Test (WRAT).* Wilmington, Delaware: Guidance Associates, 1965.

24. Jensen, A. Social class, race and genetics: Implications for education. *Am. Educ. Res. J.* 5:1–42, 1968.

25. Jeruchimowicz, R., Costello, J., and Bagur, J.S. Knowledge of action and object words: A comparison of lower- and middle-class negro preschoolers. *Child Development* 42:455–464, 1971.

26. Knobloch, H., Rider, R., and Harper, P. Neuro-psychiatric sequelae of prematurity. *JAMA* 161:581–585, 1956.

27. Labov, W. The logic of nonstandard English. In F. Williams, Ed. *Language and Poverty.* Chicago: Markham, 1970.

28. Maccoby, E.E., and Jacklin, C.N. *The Psychology of Sex Differences.* Palo Alto: Stanford University Press, 1974.

29. McCarthy, J.J., and Kirk, S.A. *The Construction, Standardization and Statistical Characteristics of the Illinois Test of Psycholinguistic Ability. Experimental Edition.* Urbana, Illinois: University of Illinois Press, 1963.

30. Milgram, N.A., and Ozer, M.N. Peabody Picture Vocabulary Test scores of preschool children. *Psychol. Rep.*, 20:784–799, 1967.

31. Mittler, P. *The Study of Twins.* Middlesex, England: Penguin, 1971.

32. Moores, D. Language disabilities of hearing-impaired children. In J.V. Irwin, and M. Marge, Eds. *Principles of Childhood Language Disabilities.* New York: Appleton-Century-Crofts, 1972.

33. Morris, H.L. Communication skills

of children with cleft lips and palates. *J. Speech Hear. Res.* 5:79–90, 1962.

34. Sinclair-deZwart, H. Language acquisition and cognitive development. In T.E. Moore, Ed. *Cognitive Development and the Acquisition of Language.* New York: Academic Press, 1973.

35. Spriestersbach, D.C., Darley, F.L., and Morris, H.L. Language skills in children with cleft palates. *J. Speech Hear. Res.* 1:279–285, 1958.

36. Stewart, W.A. Toward a history of American Negro Dialect. In F. Williams, Ed. *Language and Poverty.* Chicago: Markham, 1970.

37. Stodolsky, S., and Lesser, G. Learning patterns in the disadvantaged. *Harvard Educ. Rev.* 37:546–593, 1967.

38. Teasdale, G.R., and Katz, F.M. Psycholinguistic abilities of children from different ethnic and socioeconomic backgrounds. *Australian J. Psychol.* 20:155–159, 1968.

39. Templin, M.C. *Certain Language Skills in Children.* Minneapolis: University of Minnesota Press, 1957.

40. Templin, M.C., and Darley, F.L. *The Templin-Darley Tests of Articulation.* Iowa City, Iowa: University of Iowa Press, 1960.

41. Terman, L.M., and Merrill, M.A. *Stanford-Binet Intelligence Scale.* Boston: Houghton Mifflin, 1960.

42. Van Riper, C. *The Nature of Stuttering.* Englewood Cliffs, N.J.: Prentice-Hall, 1971.

43. Wechsler, D. *The Wechsler Intelligence Scale for Children.* New York: The Psychological Corp., 1949.

44. Wright, L. The theoretical and research base for a program of early stimulation care and training of premature infants. In J. Hellmuth, Ed. *Exceptional Infant: Studies in Abnormalities*, Vol. 2. New York: Brunner/Mazel, 1971.

45. Yarrow, L.J., Goodwin, M.S., Manheimer, H., and Milowe, I.D. Infancy experiences and cognitive and personality development at ten years. In L.J. Stone, H.T. Smith, and L.B. Murphy, Eds. *The Competent Infant.* New York: Basic Books, 1973.

## CHAPTER 12

Written Communication: Reading, Writing, and Spelling

Elaine S. LaBenz, M.A.
Kenneth F. Swaiman, M.D.
Allen R. Sullivan, Ph.D.

The outcomes of reading, writing, and spelling were combined to form a Written Communication Index at the 8YR level only. There are no comparable measures contained in the 3YR examinations, nor are these skills commonly acquired at this age level. The 8YR variables included were Writing to Dictation and the Gray Oral Reading Test (Gray, 1963).* Silent Reading (Durrell and Sullivan, 1939) was not included in the index because of the large number of children who failed to pass any item on the test. Two measures from the Wide Range Achievement Test (WRAT) (Jastak and Jastak, 1965) administered at the seven-year level were included in the index, specifically the spelling and reading (word recognition) subtests. The rationale for these inclusions will be explained within the section on index construction. Frequency distributions of these variables show marked sex, race, and Socioeconomic Index (SEI) differences and will be discussed separately.

Analyses reported here are based on the ALL 8YR population; that is, all Black

---

* Manuals and forms for all tests including unstandardized or adapted tests such as Silent Reading and Writing to Dictation are found in Appendix I.

and White children who attempted the 8YR examination within the proper age limits. Negligible differences were found in outcomes when this sample was compared to the 3YR/8YR sample which included children who had taken both the 3YR and 8YR examinations. The use of the ALL 8YR sample is further justified in that it yields a larger N, 20,137, as opposed to 12,464 for the 3YR/8YR sample.

Written Communication Variables

Oral Reading

A range of 0 to 54 for the total passage score was theoretically possible; the actual range was 0 to 53. The test was administered and scored as specified in the Gray manual (Gray, 1963). This probably resulted in some bias toward standard English speakers, as articulatory substitutions and omissions common to Black English speakers would decrease the score obtained (Hunt, 1974–1975). Figure 12-1 points out sex, race, and socioeconomic differences, with Females performing better than Males, Whites better than Blacks, and a systematic trend of better performance with increasing socioeconomic status. Since this is a widely used test which was standardized on a relatively limited number of White subjects, the means and standard deviations for Black and White subjects by sex and SEI groups are of interest and are presented in Table 12-1.

Silent Reading

This test was adapted from the Durrell-Sullivan Reading Capacity and Achievement Tests: Primary Test: Form A (Durrell and Sullivan, 1939), and had a theoretical and actual range of 0 to 5. The race, sex, and SEI trends observed in the Gray Oral Reading Test distributions also exist for the Silent Reading Test and are shown in Figure 12-2. The mean for the total sample was 2.2 (questions answered correctly), SD = 1.76. This test was apparently too difficult for many children in the sample, as 25% of the subjects were unable to answer even one of the questions correctly.

Writing to Dictation

This test, composed of letters, words, and simple sentences totaling 14 items, showed no more than one point mean difference between sexes and races. Scores increased systematically with SEI, ranging from a mean of 10.4 for the lowest group to 13.2 for the highest SEI group. The mean for the total group was 11.8, SD = 2.70. There apparently was a ceiling effect on this test, as 36% of the subjects achieved a perfect score. Distributions are shown in Figure 12-3.

Wide Range Achievement Test (WRAT) Spelling

WRAT Spelling (Jastak and Jastak, 1965) consisted of written spelling tasks which became progressively more difficult. The theoretical range on this test is 0 to 65 points; the actual range in this study was 0 to 55. The mean for the total group was 24.6, SD = 5.9. There were small differences between race, sex, and SEI groups with the same trends observed earlier for other Written Communiction variables. The means and standard deviations are presented numerically in Table 12-2 and graphically in Figure 12-4.

Wide Range Achievement Test (WRAT) Reading

The Reading subtest of the WRAT (Jastak and Jastak, 1965) measures letter recognition and single word reading skills. Trends toward better performance for Whites, Females, and higher SEI groups are more observable on this scale than on the narrower scale of the WRAT Spelling subtest. The theoretical range on

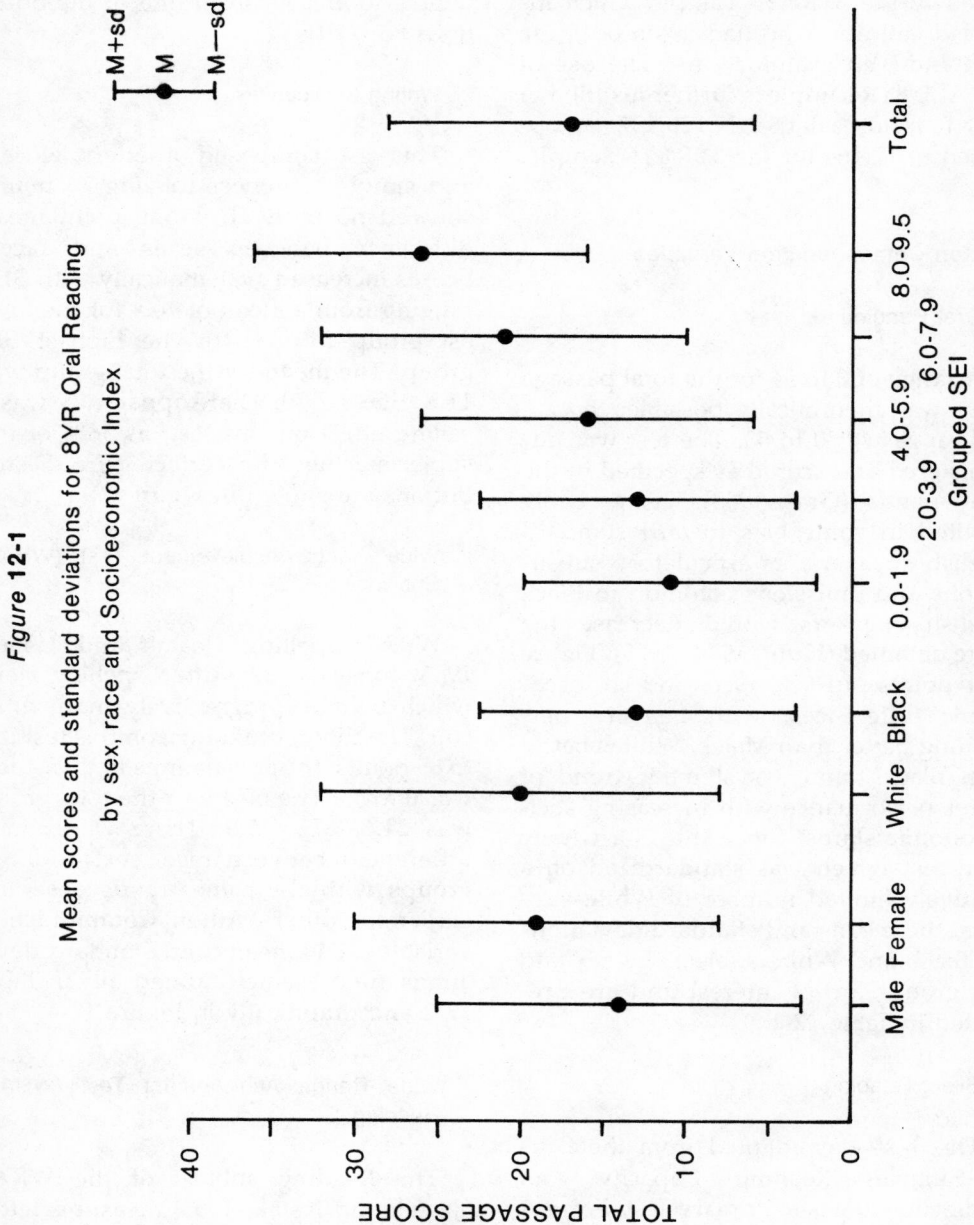

Figure **12-1**

Mean scores and standard deviations for 8YR Oral Reading by sex, race and Socioeconomic Index

332

Table **12-1**

Total passage score on the Gray Oral Reading Test by sex, race and Socioeconomic Index.

	N	Mean	SD
Male	9,996	14.3	10.8
Female	9,865	18.9	11.1
White	10,084	20.2	11.5
Black	9,777	12.8	9.5
SEI 0.0-1.9	1,601	10.6	8.8
SEI 2.0-3.9	5,903	12.5	9.5
SEI 4.0-5.9	5,980	15.6	10.5
SEI 6.0-7.9	4,081	20.7	10.9
SEI 8.0-9.5	2,296	26.2	10.3
Total	**19,861**	**16.6**	**11.2**

Table **12-2**

Means and standard deviations for WRAT Spelling by sex, race and Socioeconomic Index.

	N	Mean	SD
White Male	5,018	25.1	5.9
White Female	4,846	26.9	6.0
Black Male	4,722	22.4	5.4
Black Female	4,794	23.9	5.3
SEI 0.0-1.9	1,539	21.6	5.2
SEI 2.0-3.9	5,743	22.8	5.4
SEI 4.0-5.9	5,851	24.3	5.4
SEI 6.0-7.9	4,007	26.4	5.7
SEI 8.0-9.5	2,240	28.8	5.7
Total	**19,380**	**24.6**	**5.9**

this test is 0 to 100 and the actual range 0 to 82, with a mean of 35.4, SD = 11.8. See Table 12-3 and Figure 12-5 for breakdowns by sex, race, and SEI.

Intercorrelations of Speech, Language, and Hearing (SLH) Variables

The highest correlation found for the Written Communication variables was, not surprisingly, between Oral Reading and Silent Reading. The magnitude of this correlation was .74, followed by a correlation of .70 between Oral Reading and Writing to Dictation. Oral Reading correlated moderately (.56) with Orientation, .54 with Morphology (McCarthy and Kirk, 1963), and .45 with the Peabody Picture Vocabulary Test (PPVT) (Dunn, 1965). There were lower correlations with Connected Discourse (.32), Digits (.33) and Articulation (.30). All other 8YR SLH variables correlated with Oral Reading below .30.

Inspection of Silent Reading correlations with other 8YR SLH variables revealed a pattern remarkably similar to those found with Oral Reading with r's within .00 to .04 points of those reported above. One exception was the correlation between Silent Reading and Writing to Dictation, which dropped to .61.

Writing to Dictation correlated .53 with Orientation, .48 with Morphology, .37 with the PPVT, and .32 with Digits. An r of .38 was found between Writing to Dic-

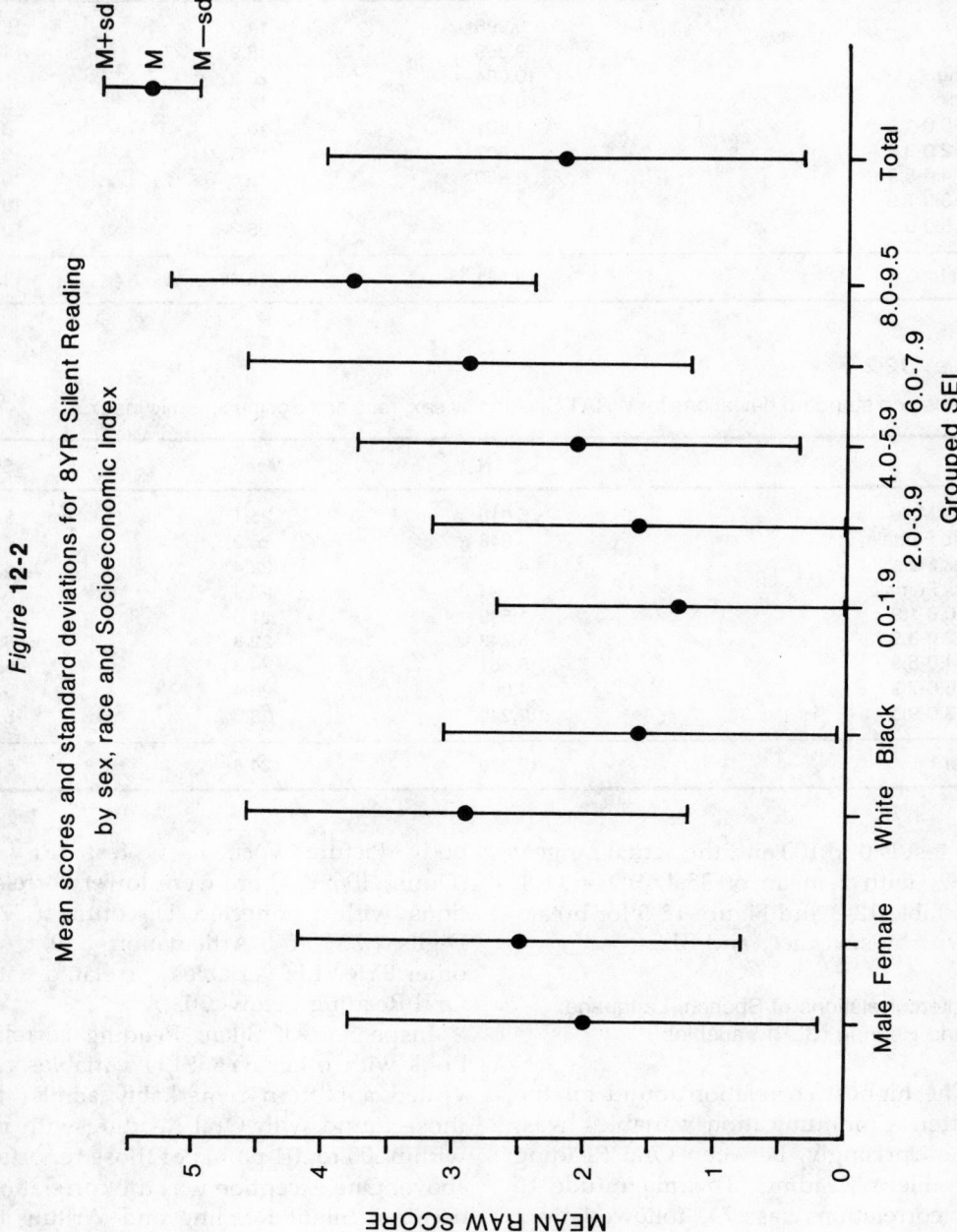

Figure 12-2

Mean scores and standard deviations for 8YR Silent Reading by sex, race and Socioeconomic Index

334

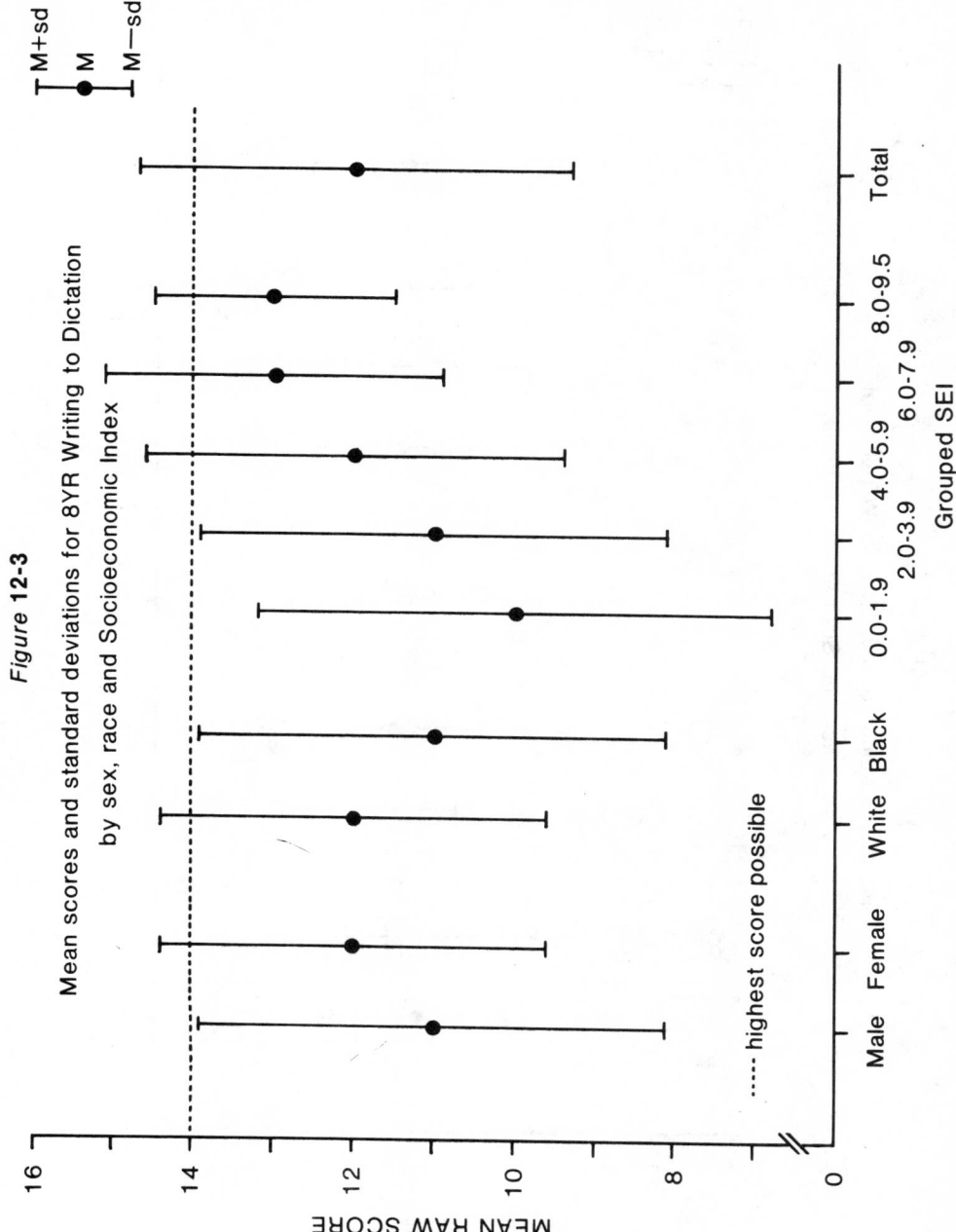

Figure **12-3**

Mean scores and standard deviations for 8YR Writing to Dictation by sex, race and Socioeconomic Index

335

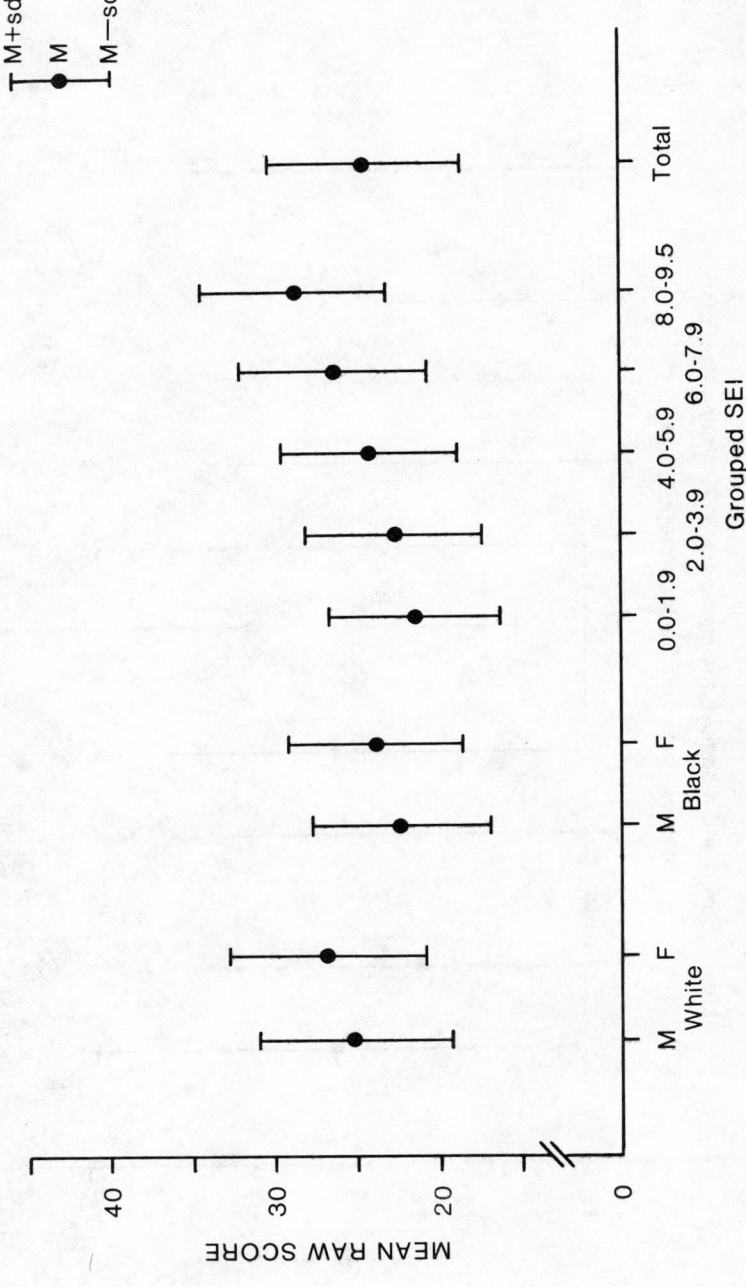

Figure **12-4**

Means and standard deviations for WRAT Spelling

by sex, race and Socioeconomic Index

336

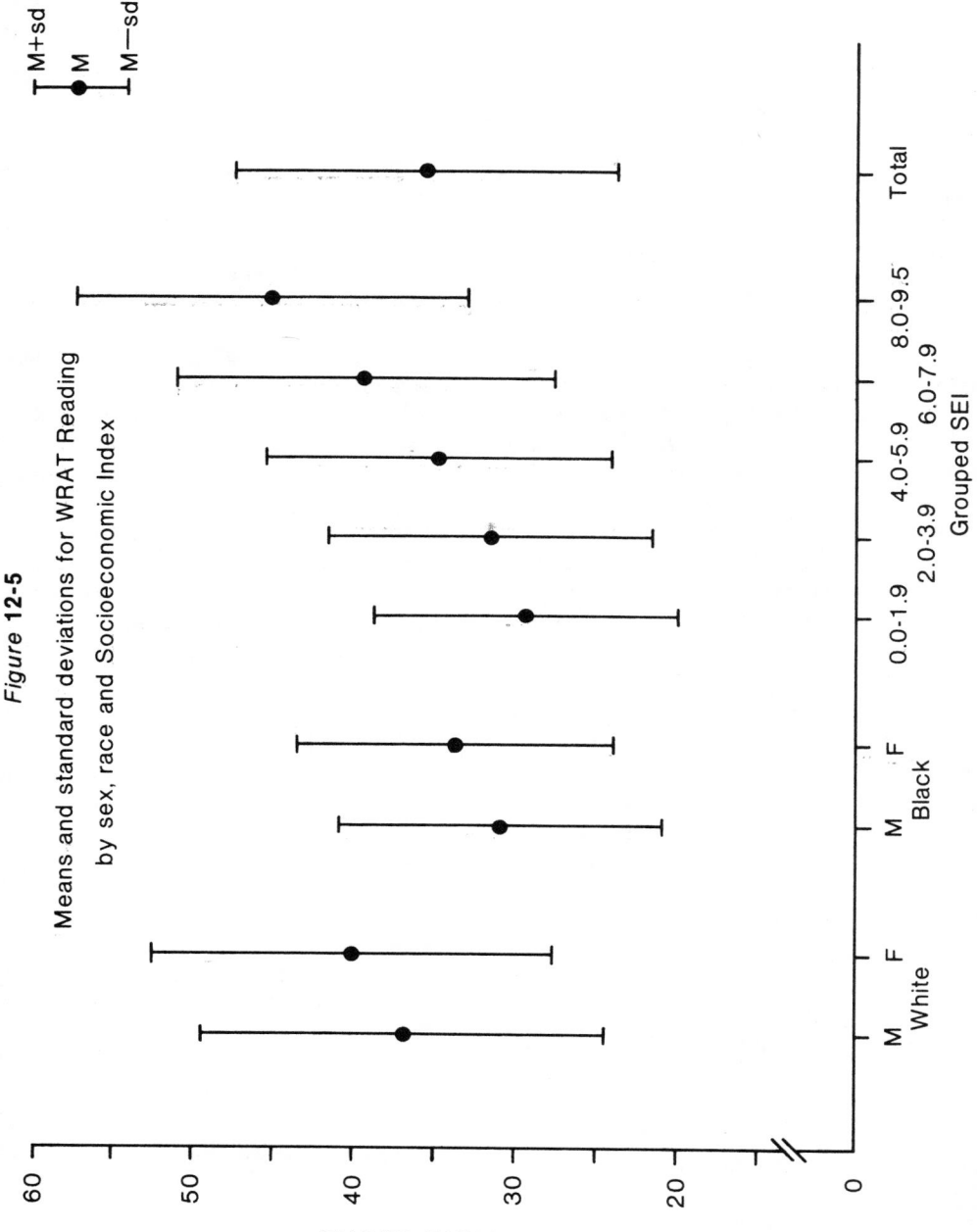

Figure **12-5**

Means and standard deviations for WRAT Reading
by sex, race and Socioeconomic Index

337

Table 12-3

Means and standard deviations for WRAT Reading by sex, race and Socioeconomic Index.

	N	Mean	SD
White Male	5,016	36.9	12.5
White Female	4,843	40.0	12.4
Black Male	4,729	30.9	10.0
Black Female	4,796	33.7	9.8
SEI 0.0-1.9	1,538	29.3	9.4
SEI 2.0-3.9	5,741	31.5	10.0
SEI 4.0-5.9	5,860	34.7	10.7
SEI 6.0-7.9	4,007	39.2	11.7
SEI 8.0-9.5	2,238	45.0	12.1
Total	**19,384**	**35.4**	**11.8**

tation and Articulation. All other r's were below .30. For Oral Reading, Writing to Dictation, and Silent Reading there were very low correlations with Pure-Tone Hearing (r < .10). Correlations with Discrimination, an ability which some have thought to be prerequisite to learning the code, ranged from .17 to .22. It is possible that discrimination testing at an earlier point in the child's life would be somewhat more predictive.

Several 3YR variables were also correlated with the 8YR Written Communication variables. The highest correlation was .30 with 3YR Final Consonants and Silent Reading; 3YR Initial Consonants, Final Consonants, and Intelligibility correlated at .20 to .29 with the 8YR Written Communication variables. The remainder yielded r's of ≤.12.

Correlations were not calculated for the seven-year reading and spelling variables except with Oral Reading, Writing to Dictation, and the SLH indexes. These findings will be discussed under Intercorrelations of Indexes. All correlational outcomes between SLH variables and indexes are found in Appendix 6.

Written Communication Index

Construction of the Index

In order to improve the sampling of specific skills of the children and also to provide a greater range of scores for the analyses, it was decided to include the 7YR WRAT reading and spelling subtests. These subtests extend down to the earliest levels of reading and spelling whereas the 8YR SLH battery did not.

A decision was also made to eliminate the Silent Reading test on which so many children scored zero. In the lowest SEI group, 40% of the children had a zero score. The Gray Oral Reading test posed a lesser problem; 9% of the total scoring zero, although 17% of the lowest SEI group scored zero.

Raw scores for each of the four components were given equal weight and yielded a scale which ranged from 0 to 399.92. Specific details are contained in Appendix 4.

Correlations of the Written Communication Index and the Component Variables

The Written Communication Index correlated with its component variables as follows: Oral Reading, .91; Writing to Dictation, .86; WRAT Spelling, .84; and WRAT Reading, .85.

Correlations were also calculated between the individual variables contained in the Written Communication Index. These r's were also high and are presented in Table 12-4.

Table **12-4**

Intercorrelations of the variables composing the Written Communication Index.

	Oral Reading	Writing to Dictation	WRAT Spelling
Oral Reading			
Writing to Dictation	.70		
WRAT Spelling	.69	.63	
WRAT Reading	.74	.66	.88

Descriptive Statistics

Table 12-5 and Figure 12-6 present the means and standard deviations for the index by race, sex, and SEI groups. The expected trend of increasing scores with increasing socioeconomic status is noted. Whites and Females have higher means than Males and Blacks, respectively. It was pointed out in Chapter 4 that the Black sample was markedly skewed toward the lower SEI groups, and the confounding variable of quality of education for these children could not be dealt with in this study. Racial differences were not studied with SEI controlled, so the findings of racial differences must be interpreted cautiously. Sex differences and SEI trends seem quite clear and are in agreement with previous studies. Institutional differences also reflected the composition of the samples, with lower mean scores for samples in institutions where the mean SEI was lower.

Intercorrelations of Indexes*

The Written Communication Index had very low correlations with 3YR indexes. Only three correlated above .20; Intelligibility, .27; Language Comprehension, .24; and Sentence Complexity, .23. Intercorrelations of the 3YR and 8YR indexes are found in Appendix 6.

Written Communication and 8YR indexes had some moderate to high intercorrelations with nine of them at levels above .30. These are shown in Table 12-6. The highest correlations were with Auditory Processing (.84) and Communicative Effectiveness (.81). The inclusion of the

---

* All SLH indexes are defined in Appendix 4 and are discussed in the appropriate substantive chapters.

Table **12-5**

Means and standard deviations for the Written Communication Index by sex, race and Socioeconomic Index.

	N	Mean	SD
Male	9,471	191.74	57.28
Female	9,422	213.45	53.79
White	9,672	219.29	56.28
Black	9,221	185.03	51.42
SEI 0.0-1.9	1,488	168.91	52.22
SEI 2.0-3.9	5,576	181.57	52.36
SEI 4.0-5.9	5,693	199.36	52.54
SEI 6.0-7.9	3,926	223.78	50.57
SEI 8.0-9.5	2,210	248.77	46.48
Total	**18,893**	**202.57**	**56.61**

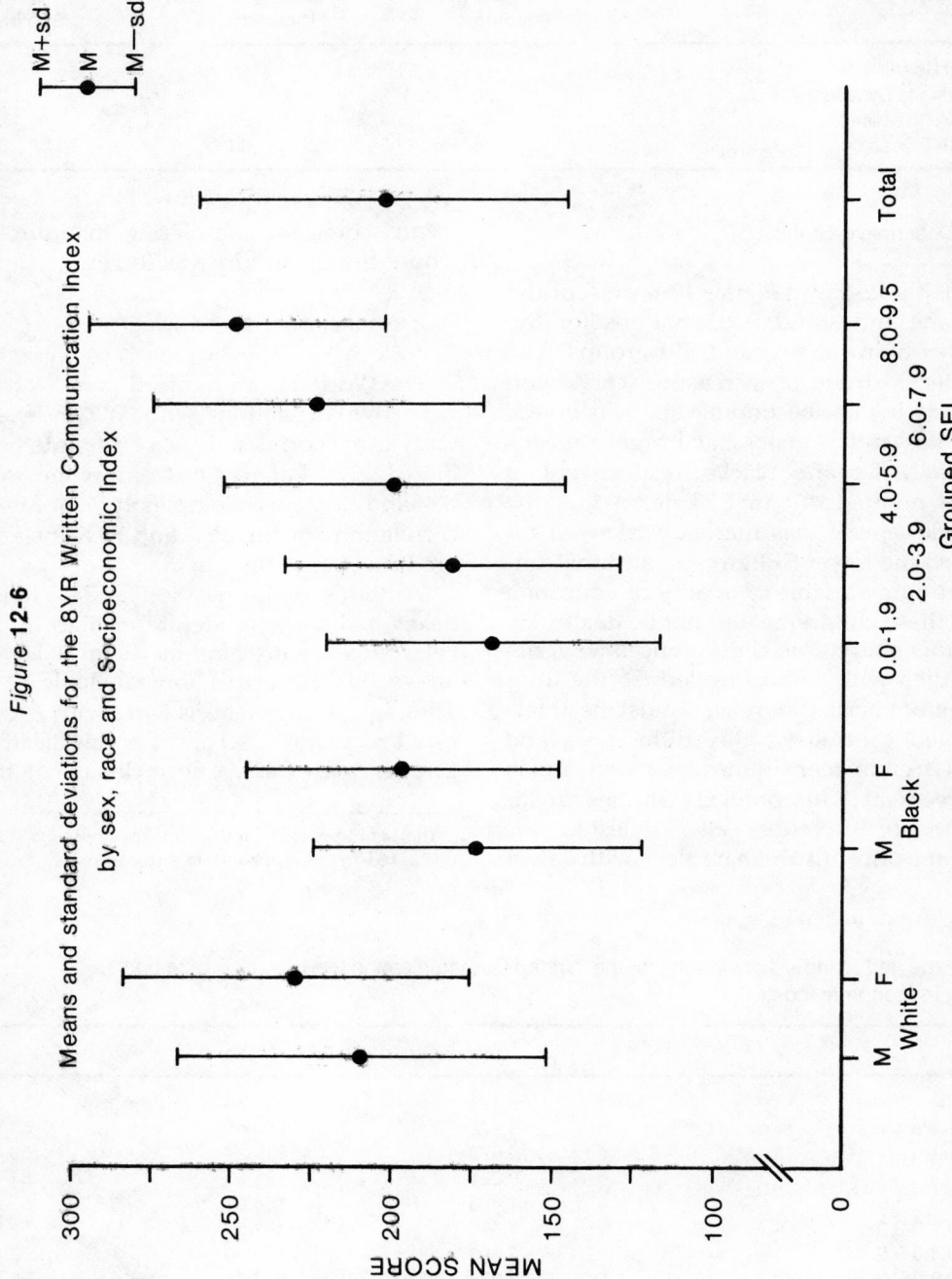

Figure **12-6**

Means and standard deviations for the 8YR Written Communication Index
by sex, race and Socioeconomic Index

Table 12-6

Intercorrelations >.30 for the Written Communication Index with 8YR indexes.

	r
Auditory Processing	.84
Communicative Effectiveness	.81
Concept Development	.66
Word Identification	.49
Language Production	.48
Auditory Memory	.45
Digits	.36
Articulation	.36
Language Comprehension	.34

reading variables in the Communicative Effectiveness Index and the inclusion of Oral Reading and Writing to Dictation in the Auditory Processing Index account partially for this high correlation. These indexes also contain a large number of tests from the entire 8YR battery including those with the higher independent correlations with Written Communication. It is suggested that a general language competence, as reflected in moderate correlations with Concept Development, Word Identification, Language Production, and Auditory Memory, is associated with competence in Written Communication.

The WRAT subtests were not entered into correlation matrixes with individual SLH variables other than with Oral Reading and Writing to Dictation. The WRAT subtests were, however, correlated with the SLH indexes, and there were eight r's > .30. Correlations were slightly higher for WRAT Reading than for WRAT Spelling. None of these correlations was as high as those of the Written Communication Index to the other indexes and ranged from .30 to .70. These correlational outcomes are also found in Appendix 6.

Cross-tabulations of Indexes

As a further check on the relatedness of performance on one index to performance on another, cross-tabulations were prepared and conditional probabilities calculated. The indexes chosen for these analyses were those which conceptually were expected to be more predictive of the Written Communication outcome than the correlations suggested.

Correlations between the 3YR speech and language indexes and the 8YR Written Communication Index were particularly low, but the cross-tabulation procedure indicated that failure at eight years was two to three times as likely if the child failed at three than if he passed at three. This also held true at eight years when failure occurred on the 8YR Articulation, Language Comprehension, Auditory Memory, or Word Identification indexes. Correlations and probabilities are presented in Table 12-7.

Relationship of NCPP Variables to the Written Communication Index

Correlation Screen and Cross-tabulations

The prediction of Written Communication skills from earlier communication skills is of considerable interest and entailed the detailed 3YR/8YR analysis described earlier. However, the main focus of the study was on prediction of outcome at the earliest possible time in the child's life. For this reason, biological

Table **12-7**

Correlations and conditional probabilities for selected indexes and the Written Communication Index.

	r	p(F2/F1)*	p(F2/P1)*
3YR Articulation	.19	.25	.13
3YR Intelligibility	.27	.42	.15
3YR Language Comprehension	.24	.32	.14
3YR Sentence Complexity	.23	.33	.13
3YR Auditory Memory	.18	.20	.12
8YR Articulation	.36	.34	.13
8YR Language Comprehension	.34	.34	.14
8YR Auditory Memory	.45	.39	.13
8YR Word Identification	.49	.34	.13

*p(F2/F1) and p(F2/P1) refer to the probability of failing Written Communication (F2) when other SLH variables are failed (F1) or passed (P1).

measurements of the mother and child as well as psychological, behavioral, and social variables (NINCDS Collaborative Perinatal Project or NCPP variables), totaling 676, were chosen for a correlational screen procedure.

In general, the single biological and psychological-behavioral items yielded unimpressive correlations. This finding is hardly surprising considering that the shape of the distribution is markedly skewed with the great majority of children being normal. The highest correlations were as expected with SEI, parents' education, and IQ. Some of the biological and behavioral variables (for example, motor development and attention span) thought to be related to failure in Written Communication produced low correlations. Again, further information was sought by means of cross-tabulations of failure on the Written Communication Index and NCPP variables of particular interest.

Failure on the index was defined as a score falling in the lowest decile or, in the case of a restricted range, closest to the lowest decile. Most of the variables could be dichotomized and probabilities calculated. For some variables such as Head Circumference and education of parents, multi-category tables were prepared.

Resultant P values and r's are shown in Table 12-8 for the variables which were

cross-tabulated. Several eight-month behavioral variables and hydrocephalus were subjected to this procedure but, due to very small N's and some missing cells, results are not reported here.

Mental retardation in the mother, while yielding an r of <.10, resulted in over three times the risk of the child failing Written Communication than if the mother was not mentally retarded. Trends are noted in some of the at-birth biological variables, but generally the predictions of failure are not very different whether the conditions did or did not exist. Some of the variables for which prediction of failure on Written Communication was about twice as high if the condition existed were low Bayley scores, presence of syndromes, prematurity, low income, and father's occupation.

Attentional and activity level variables were also of interest, and the differences between the two probabilities were greater. Very Brief Attention Span or Extremely Impulsive ratings at four, and Very Brief Attention Span or Extreme Overactivity at seven appear to be among the more effective predictors of failure on the Written Communication Index.

Neurological abnormalities at seven were studied in two ways. When the fail group included only those judged to be clearly neurologically abnormal, the P for the F2/F1 group was .42. The inclusion in

Table **12-8**

Correlations and conditional probabilities for selected NCPP Variables and Written Communication.

	r	p(F2/F1)*	p(F2/P1)*
At-Birth NCPP Variables			
Gravida: Special Class, Slow Learners	<.10	.28	.16
Gravida: Mentally Retarded	<.10	.52	.16
Gravida: Seizures, Eclampsia Only	<.10	.25	.16
Gravida: Seizures, Age 15 or Older	<.10	.21	.16
Prior Stillbirths and Neonatal Deaths (Number)	<.10	.26	.17
Prior Abortions (Number)	<.10	.19	.17
Gestation at Registration	.23	.21	.16
Blood Pressure: 24 Weeks to Labor	<.10	.21	.16
Convulsions During Pregnancy: During Only	<.10	.18	.16
Convulsions During Pregnancy: Before and During			No Cases
Convulsions During Pregnancy: During and Postpartum			No Cases
Housing Density: pass 0.1 to 1.5	−.26	.23	.14
fail 1.6 to 8.0	−.25		
Number Complications of this Pregnancy	<.10	.16	.16
X-Ray Exposure: Abdomino-Pelvic Area	<.10	.14	.17
Polyhydramnios	<.10	.13	.15
Diabetes: Gravida (Only During Pregnancy)	<.10	.12	.16
Diabetes: Gravida (Onset at 15 or Older)	<.10	.18	.16
Diabetes: Gravida (Onset Before Age 15)	<.10	.14	.16
Weight Gain: Pounds (Fail = Little or Loss)	<.10	.18	.14
Weight Gain: Pounds (Fail = Too Much)	<.10	.18	.14
Height of Mother (Inches)	<.10	.19	.17
Chronic Hypertensive Disease	<.10	.20	.15
Acute Toxemia	<.10	.16	.15
Abruptio Placenta	<.10	.17	.16
Placenta Previa: Partial	<.10	.16	.16
Method of Delivery Type: C/S	<.10	.17	.16
Method of Delivery Type: Breech	<.10	.21	.16
Method of Delivery Type: Vertex	<.10	.16	.19
Gravida: Mental Illness	<.10	.17	.16
Age of Gravida: Young vs. Normal	<.10	.21	.16
Age of Gravida: Normal vs. Old	<.10	.15	.16
Age of F.O.B.:† Years pass = 18-35	<.10	.15	.14
fail = 36-66			
Age of F.O.B.: Years (a) pass = 18-50 (b) 18-35	<.10	.17	.15
fail = 51-66 14-17	<.10	.15	.14
Husband Living at Home	.19	.22	.15
Husband or F.O.B. Present	.19	.22	.15
F.O.B.: Mental Illness	<.10	.15	.16
Occupation of Father: Blue-Collar	−.30	.09	.18
Occupation of Father: White-Collar	.31	.18	.09
Per Capita Income at Birth	.35	.22	.10
Number Children under 8 Supported/Cared for (At Birth)	−.21	.26	.15
Birthweight: Grams (Normal vs. Low)	.12	.25	.15
Birthweight: Grams (Normal vs. High)	.10	.15	.15
Gestational Age: (Normal vs. Premature)	<.10	.16	.09
Gestational Age: (Normal vs. Postmature)	<.10	.12	.09
Direct Coombs' Test: Child	<.10	.09	.17

*p(F2/F1) and p(F2/P1) refer to the probability of failing Written Communication (F2)
 when NCPP variables are failed (F1) or passed (P1).
†Father of Baby.

343

Table *12-8* (continued)

Correlations and conditional probabilities for selected NCPP Variables and Written Communication.

	r	p(F2/F1)*	p(F2/P1)*
8-Month NCPP Variables			
Bayley 8-Month Motor Score	.13	.28	.14
Bayley 8-Month Mental Score	.13	.29	.14
Bayley: Fine Motor Development	−.13	.20	.09
Bayley: Gross Motor Development	−.13	.20	.09
Bayley: Social Emotional Development	.10	.17	.10
1YR NCPP Variables			
Ped-12: Negative Social, Environmental Conditions	<.10	.22	.15
Ped-12: Neurological Abnormalities (Number)	−.11	.21	.14
Ped-12: Syndromes (Number)	<.10	.35	.16
Ped-12: Infection, Inflammations (Number)	<.10	.19	.15
4YR NCPP Variables			
Stanford-Binet IQ: pass >70	.54	.57	.13
Stanford-Binet IQ: (Marginals) fail = 70-80	Not calculated	.32	.11
Unusual Amount of Activity	<.10	.23	.14
Extremely Impulsive: a. nature	<.10	.36	.15
b. level	<.10	.39	.15
Normal Activity	.13	.13	.21
Little Activity	<.10	.18	.15
Extreme Inactivity	<.10	.27	.15
Above Average Attention Span	<.10	.11	.15
Adequate Attention Span	.21	.12	.27
Short Attention Span	−.19	.26	.13
Very Brief Attention Span	−.13	.47	.14
Communication: Only to Direct Questions	−.12	.19	.14
Communication: Spontaneous Conversation	.10	.13	.19
Deviant Behavior: Crying	<.10	.27	.15
Child in Nursery School: pass = yes	−.11	.16	.11
7YR NCPP Variables			
7YR Neuro Abnorms: pass = normal or suspect	<.10	.42	.14
7YR Neuro Abnorms: pass = none	<.10	.34	.12
7YR Non-Neuro Abnorms: a. none or minor	<.10	.30	.15
b. none	<.10	.17	.14
Child Lives with Parent	.20	.13	.22
Overcrowding: (fail = 1.5 or more)	<.10	.22	.13
Mother Occupied as Laborer, Farmer	.13	.25	.15
Child's Sibs: Male Liveborn (Number)	−.23	.25	.13
Child's Sibs: Female Liveborn (Number)	−.11	.21	.14
Child's Sibs: Prematures (Number)	−.16	.24	.14
Child's Sibs: Convulsions (Number)	<.10	.21	.14
Child's Sibs: Retardation (Number)	−.21	.30	.12
Short Attention Span	−.20	.30	.11
Adequate Attention Span	.19	.10	.27
Above Average Attention Span	<.10	.15	.13
Highly Perseverative Attention Span	<.10	.45	.13
Extreme Overactivity (level)	<.10	.47	.13
Unusual Amount of Activity	−.11	.30	.13
Extreme Overactivity (nature)	<.10	.63	.13
Meaningless Smiling, Laughing	<.10	.40	.13

*p(F2/F1) and p(F2/P1) refer to the probability of failing Written Communication (F2)
when NCPP variables are failed (F1) or passed (P1).

Table *12-8* *(continued)*

Correlations and conditional probabilities for selected NCPP Variables and Written Communication.

	r	p(F2/F1)*	p(F2/P1)*
7YR NCPP Variables (continued)			
Crying	<.10	.31	.14
Occasionally Withdraws	−.15	.21	.11
Attempts to Cope	.14	.11	.22
Quite Upset	<.10	.23	.13
Extreme Acting Out	<.10	.52	.13
Very Brief Attention Span	<.10	.75	.13
Handedness	<.10	.16	.13
Bender Gestalt Test: Total Score	−.47	.40	.08
Wechsler Prorated: Verbal IQ	.47	.45	.09
Wechsler Prorated: Performance IQ	.45	.47	.10
7YR WISC Full Scale IQ >70	.54	.78	.11
7YR WISC Full Scale IQ (Marginals) 70-80	<.10	.42	.08
Auditory-Vocal Association Test: Raw Score	.53	.46	.09
Speech Therapy	.14	.14	.13

*p(F2/F1) and p(F2/P1) refer to the probability of failing Written Communication (F2)
when NCPP variables are failed (F1) or passed (P1).

the fail group of the children rated as suspect neurologically resulted in a P of .34, which is still about three times as high as if there were no minor or major signs. Handedness had an r of <.10 and differences in the P values were negligible. In the sample, 88% of the subjects were judged to be right handed, 12% left handed at seven years of age.

Psychological tests yielded impressive P value contrasts and moderate correlations. Interestingly, the Stanford-Binet (Terman and Merrill, 1960) at four years and the WISC (Wechsler, 1949) at seven years correlated identically (.54) with Written Communication. However, if a child had an IQ below normal, the probability of failure was considerably higher when the IQ at seven years was used than when the four-year IQ was used. The Bender Gestalt Test (Koppitz, 1964) and the Auditory-Vocal Association Test of the Illinois Test of Psycholinguistic Abilities (ITPA) (McCarthy and Kirk, 1963) administered at seven also appeared to be among the better predictors. The Bender Gestalt Test appears to have quite different predictive value by race and sex. Failure on the Bender Gestalt

and Written Communication occurred most often for White Males and least often for Black Females. There were the usual SEI trends with fewer failures in higher groups. This finding does not, of course, explain the race-sex differences, which are quite striking and are presented in Table 12-9.

Multi-category tables revealed negligible differences in failure rate on Written Communication when cigarettes smoked per day, forceps deliveries, and bilirubin levels were studied. Head Circumference and Five-Minute Apgar scores were studied in three-category tables which showed noticeable differences for the lowest categories only.

Children who were singletons (only children) or had only one sibling at birth performed best and were similar in performance. There was a definite trend toward poorer performance as the number of siblings increased up to nine. Beyond that number, the failure rate trend is inconsistent and the N so small that no conclusions can be drawn for very large families. The increase in performance with increasing socioeconomic status and education of parents was further con-

Table 12-9

Conditional probabilities for failing Written Communication, given fail or pass on the Bender Gestalt Test.

	p(F2/F1)*	p(F2/P1)*
White Male	.50	.08
White Female	.39	.03
Black Male	.49	.16
Black Female	.29	.06

*p(F2/F1) and p(F2/P1) refer to the probability of failing Written Communication (F2) when the Bender Gestalt Test is failed (F1) or passed (P1).

firmed by multi-category tables. These again appear to be among the most powerful predictors studied.

Multiple Regression Analysis

The technique of multiple regression was used to evaluate the contribution of independent variables which seemed likely to be predictive of communication outcome. Five analyses were undertaken. In the first, Birthweight, Gestational Age, education of both mother and father, Per Capita Income, race and sex of the child, and the occupation of the father were entered. The second regression included the above variables plus the eight-month mental and motor scores of the Bayley (Bayley, 1958). To these, the Stanford-Binet IQ at four years was added for the third analysis. Another analysis involved entry of the 3YR indexes only, and the last included the 3YR indexes plus the At-Birth variables from the first analysis. Results are shown in Table 12-10.

Inspection of the multiple R's and R^2's reveals little change when the 8-Month variables are added to the At-Birth variables. The R's equal .519 and .526, respectively, with 27% and 28% of the variance being explained. The 3YR indexes alone were the least powerful predictors with an R of .349 and R^2 of .122.

The most predictive of the combinations was At-Birth and 8-Month variables plus 4YR IQ. With this grouping R was .614 and 38% of the variance was ex-

plained. The 3YR indexes with At-Birth variables ranked second and yielded an R of .564 with an R^2 of .318. If prediction of a deficit in Written Communication is attempted using only At-Birth variables, only very broad generalizations may be made.

We must conclude that new and clinically useful predictors do not emerge from the early variables, and that performance measures taken later in the child's life will be useful.

Special Studies

The large number of subjects enrolled and the many variables coded for each subject made it possible to examine the performance of certain subgroups. Index outcomes were used. The performance of twins, siblings (the two oldest siblings enrolled in the study), cerebral palsied children, cleft palate children, hearing impaired children, children of low birthweight, prematures, those in true distress, children who were judged to stutter, and those who lived with a natural parent, as opposed to those who did not, were studied. In addition, children for whom the seven-year WISC IQ was available were grouped by ten-point IQ intervals and means were reported. The findings expressed as means and standard deviations are shown in Table 12-11 and Figure 12-7, with the exception of the intelligence study which is summarized in Table 12-12 and Figure 12-8.

Table **12-10**

Multiple correlations between Written Communication and independent variables with beta coefficients.

	At-Birth NCPP variables	At-Birth NCPP variables plus 8-Month NCPP variables	At-Birth NCPP variables plus 8-Month NCPP variables plus 4YR IQ	3YR Indexes	3YR Indexes plus At-Birth NCPP variables
Multiple R	.519	.526	.614	.349	.564
R Square	.269	.276	.376	.122	.318
3YR Speech Mechanism				.0124	.0117
3YR Hypernasality				.00897	−.0119
3YR Fluency				−.0316	−.00720
3YR Articulation				.0579	.0162
3YR Intelligibility				.144	.103
3YR Language Comprehension				.139	.0537
3YR Sentence Complexity				.0874	.0735
3YR Auditory Memory				.0902	.0726
3YR Hearing Screen				−.0237	−.0000734
Birthweight	.0767	.0575	.0369		.0588
Gestational Age	−.00814	−.0197	−.0157		.000544
Education of Gravida	.153	.152	.0960		.139
Per Capita Income	.162	.154	.120		.138
Education of F.O.B.	.126	.123	.0787		.136
Occupation of F.O.B	.0754	.0777	.0504		.0750
8-Month Mental Score		.0706	.0292		
8-Month Motor Score		.0253	−.0127		
4YR IQ			.386		
Race-Sex Marker I	−.0434	−.0374	−.0838		−.0787
Race-Sex Marker II	.226	.228	.122		.162
Race-Sex Marker III	−.246	−.246	−.153		−.190

It can be observed that children with organic problems, adverse birth conditions, and stutter performed less well than the ALL 8YR population. Twins performed less well than siblings and siblings poorer than singletons. As would be expected, the higher the child's IQ, the higher was his score on the Written Communication Index.

The performance of adopted children is especially interesting in that this is the only group whose mean exceeded that of the ALL 8YR population. It is possible that the rise in SEI associated with adoption accounts for this (Yarrow et al., 1963).

In the studies where the sample size permitted, results by SEI were obtained. These included the singleton/sibling/twin study, the hearing loss groups, and the cerebral palsy group. In each of these analyses, the mean performance im-

Table **12-11**

Performance on the Written Communication Index by special subgroups.

Sample	N	Mean	SD
Cleft Palate	24	158	67
Stutterers	35	163	71
Cerebral Palsy	83	154	81
Mental Retardation Syndromes	53	79	46
Premature ($\leq$36 weeks $\leq$2,500 grams)	917	184	63
True Distress (Apgar <4)	617	191	55
Low Birthweight ($\leq$1,500 grams)	100	159	65
Conductive Hearing Loss	1,024	193	59
Sensorineural Hearing Loss	447	187	58
Adopted Children	243*	205	52
Foster Children	277*	174	56
Children Living with Relatives	621*	182	51
Children Living with at Least One Biological Parent	23,931*	203	27
ALL 8YR	20,137	203	57

*N based on 3YR and 8YR samples combined.

Table **12-12**

Mean scores on the Written Communication Index by grouped IQ, sex and race.

	<39	40-49	50-59	60-69	70-79	80-89	90-99	100-109	110-119	120+
White Male	—	23.0*	37.0*	94.5	124.6	158.7	188.0	215.8	234.4	261.7
White Female	—	20.0*	45.6*	105.2	147.5	186.2	213.8	236.4	255.3	280.0
Black Male	1.0*	41.6*	66.5	104.0	134.2	157.0	183.4	200.7	219.8	248.1
Black Female	—	9.0*	78.2	121.2	155.7	184.0	203.5	224.3	240.1	266.2

*Based on fewer than 20 cases.

proved with increasing SEI status. The cerebral palsy group yielded fewer than 20 cases for each of the SEI groups and was heterogeneous with regard to the nature and extent of impairment. Nonetheless, the same trend was evident when SEI was studied. The special studies, then, besides providing normative information and pointing out the effects of the special conditions, are again confirmatory of the powerful effects of SEI on the child's performance, regardless of his condition.

Discussion

The focus of this study was on the identification of early predictors of deficits in reading, writing, and spelling. The more reliable predictors appeared to be variables measured after the first year of life, and these are of clinical usefulness. If a child can be identified as at risk at age three, four, or even seven, there remains the possibility of intervention which can prevent a general education deficit with all of its ensuant problems.

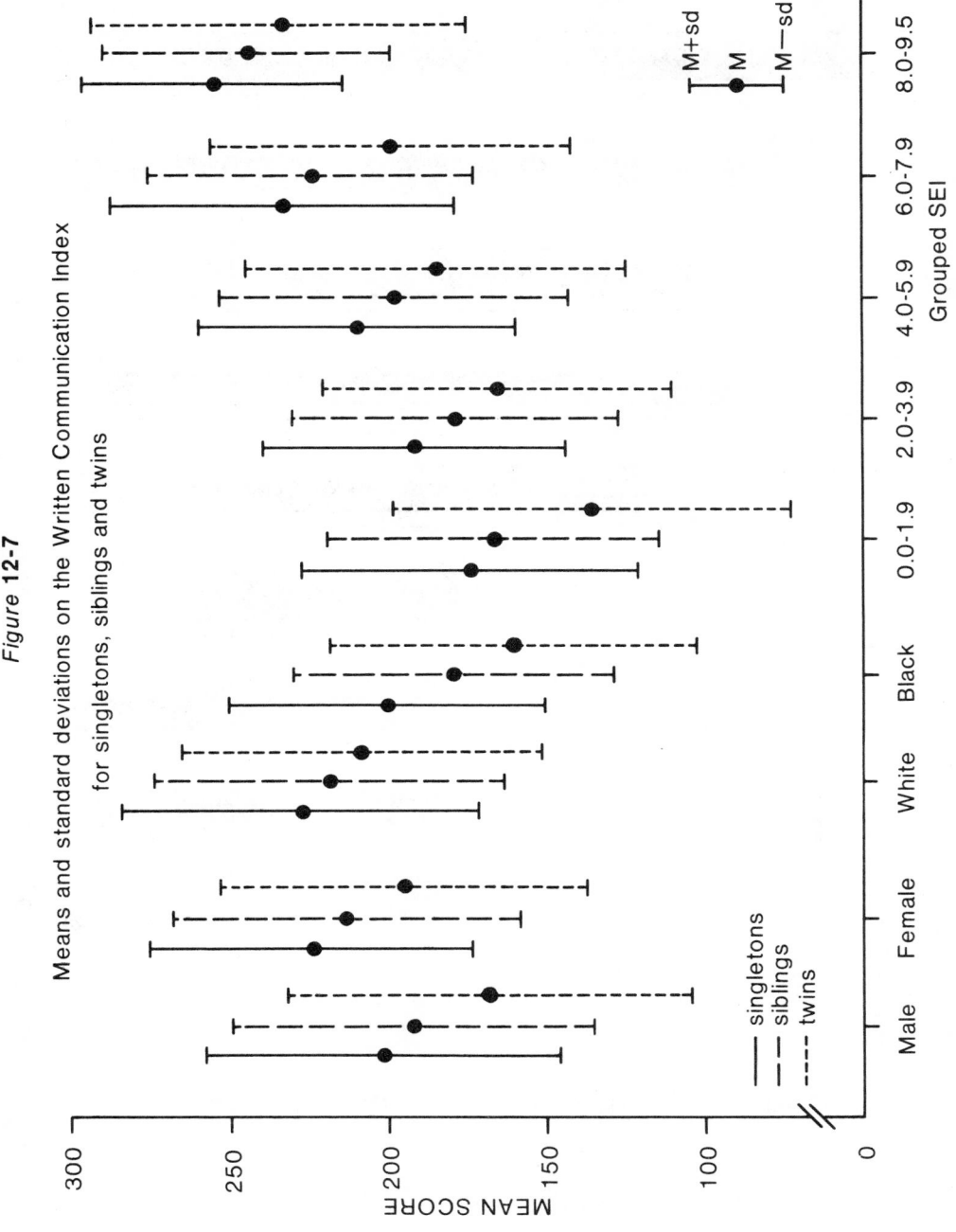

Figure **12-7**

Means and standard deviations on the Written Communication Index
for singletons, siblings and twins

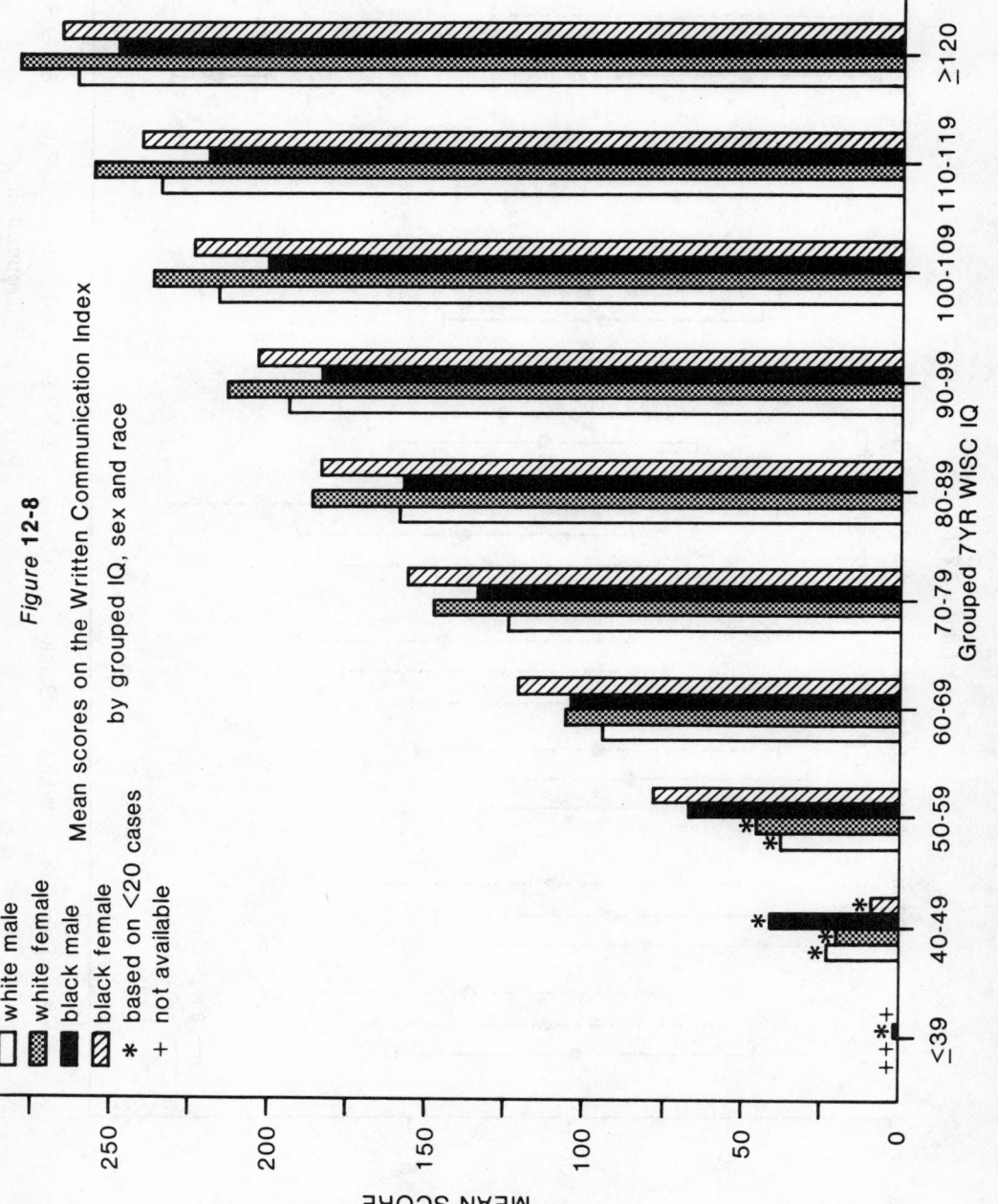

Figure **12-8**

Mean scores on the Written Communication Index
by grouped IQ, sex and race

□ white male
▨ white female
■ black male
▧ black female
* based on <20 cases
+ not available

MEAN SCORE

Grouped 7YR WISC IQ

<39 40-49 50-59 60-69 70-79 80-89 90-99 100-109 110-119 ≥120

350

The early variables studied, including Birthweight, Gestational Age, neonatal distress, and complications of pregnancy and delivery, yielded findings that are not convincingly predictive. Recent prospective studies which tend to confirm the lack of impact of perinatal difficulties on reading achievement include those of Robinson and Robinson (1965), Colligen (1974), and Fraser and Wilks (1959). Studies which seemed to confirm the negative effects of perinatal problems include the work of Rubin, Rosenblatt, and Balow (1973), Davie, Butler, and Goldstein (1972), Denhoff, Hainsworth, and Hainsworth (1972), Menkes et al. (1972), Wiener (1970), deHirsch, Jansky, and Langford (1966), Corah et al. (1965), and Douglas (1960).

The lack of significant association of prematurity (gestation less than 36 weeks and birthweight below 2500 grams) with deficiency on the Written Communication Index, as judged by correlation with the 8YR group as a whole, parallels findings of some previous reports and is at variance with others. However, there appears to be greater agreement with carefully designed prospective longitudinal research than with retrospective studies.

Balow, Rubin, and Rosen (1975) have reviewed the literature extensively. The authors pointed out problems of methodology such as the different outcomes studied (for example, reading tests and judgments of reading ability) and varying research design. These problems are also well described by Applebee (1971). There is obvious difficulty in comparing retrospective, retrospective follow-up, and prospective studies, and varying methods of statistical treatment of data, but they conclude: ". . . despite a lack of clearly established causal chains leading from perinatal insult to reading difficulty, the weight of the accumulated evidence supports, at the minimum, the hypothesis that low birthweight, as well as certain pregnancy and birth complications, are related to impaired reading ability." (Balow et al., 1975, p. 41.)

The present study was unique because of the numbers of children studied and the precision of data collection. While there is some evidence of adverse perinatal events affecting the outcome on the Written Communication Index, we must conclude that in this study these events, singly, are ineffective predictors. Rather, the hypothesis is supported that deficits in Written Communication are the result of multiple causes; environmental and later developmental factors are most predictive.

The predictive value of some behavioral measures are of particular interest. The addition of certain language and speech related measures (particularly 3YR Intelligibility and 4YR IQ) to the multiple regression analyses and in the cross-tabulations, while yielding modest values, produced results which are nonetheless supportive of earlier studies which found speech and language delay to be related to reading problems. For example, Lyle (1970) found when studying antenatal, perinatal, and speech variables in relation to reading retardation, that early speech problems were most predictive.

The moderate-to-high correlations and P values of the Written Communication Index with several of the 8YR Language Indexes is consistent with the findings of Hardy, Mellits, and Willig (1971), who studied a subset of the NINCDS Collaborative Project subjects. While different statistical methods were used, they concluded that: ". . . there was a consistent relationship between oral language and the written form of language. . . ." (Hardy et al., 1971, p. 51.) The theory that oral language proficiency is related to reading, writing, and spelling is well known. Researchers as early as Orton (1937) and Wepman (1962) provide articulate statements regarding these interrelationships, but also emphasize the multiplicity of factors which may relate to reading retardation. These include sensory, perceptual, and environmental factors.

351

The importance of SEI as a predictor of language proficiency diminishes the value of many studies not controlled for the SEI variable. A number of the sample groups in Table 12-11 are clearly related to socioeconomic status (that is, adopted children, foster children, children living with relatives, children living with at least one biological parent). Other categories are less clearly linked to SEI, but nevertheless a relationship exists (that is, mental retardation, prematurity, low birthweight).

In conclusion, the well-known effects of socioeconomic status were confirmed by this study. The effects of same/different race examiners and educational opportunity were not explored and only speculation is offered. Perinatal and neonatal observations, for the most part, were limited in predictive value. However, the findings do suggest a number of measures that, taken at a later time or taken with At-Birth measures, are of clinical value.

Summary

1. This study was based on 20,137 Black and White children. The variables in the Written Communication Index included two tests administered at seven years, WRAT Spelling and WRAT Reading; and two tests administered at eight years, Oral Reading and Writing to Dictation. Silent Reading was not included in the index because 25% of the children failed to answer any of the questions correctly.

2. There were systematic SEI and race effects for each of the individual variables and the index. Trends were toward better performance for Whites, Females, and higher SEI groups.

3. The individual Written Communication Index variables were correlated with all other SLH variables. Among the higher correlations were r's of .74 between Oral Reading and Silent Reading and .70 between Oral Reading and Writing to Dictation. Oral Reading correlated moderately with Orientation (.56), Morphology (.54), and Word Identification (PPVT) (.45). Lower correlations were found for Connected Discourse (.32), Digits (.33), and Articulation (.30). All other correlations were <.30. Silent Reading correlated with these variables within 0 to .04 points of the Oral Reading correlations, the only exception being Writing to Dictation which had an r of .61.

   Writing to Dictation correlated .53 with Orientation, .48 with Morphology, .34 with Word Identification, .32 with Digits, and .38 with Articulation. All other r's were <.30. The WRAT variables were not entered into the individual SLH variable correlation matrix.

4. The Written Communication Index correlated with its component variables .84 to .91, with Oral Reading being the highest correlation. The intercorrelations of these variables ranged from .63 (WRAT Spelling to Writing to Dictation) to .88 (WRAT Spelling to WRAT Reading).

5. Cross-tabulations and correlations between indexes were prepared. The 3YR Articulation, Intelligibility, Language Comprehension, Sentence Complexity indexes correlated .18 to .27 with Written Communication. However, the cross-tabulation procedure indicated that scoring in the lowest decile on Written Communication was two to three times as likely if the child failed at three than if he passed at three. This remained true if he failed 8YR Articulation, Language Comprehension, Auditory Memory or Word Identification. The r's between these indexes and Written Communication ranged from .34 to .49.

6. A total of 676 psychological, behavioral, social, and biological variables were entered into a correlational screen with the Written Communication Index as the outcome. The highest correlations were between SEI, parents' education, four and seven year IQ, the Bender Gestalt, and the Auditory Vocal Association Test. Correlations for the early biological and behavioral observations were low.

7. Selected variables were studied in cross-tabulations for possible predictive value. Among the early variables, Bayley scores, syndromes, and several SEI variables emerged as promising. Attentional problems, overactivity, and neurological abnormality at seven were among the more powerful predictors. Handedness did not show a relationship to Written Communication. The variables listed in the preceding section which showed predictive value were also shown to be predictive in this analysis.

8. Five multiple regression analyses were undertaken using selected perinatal, eight-month, and three and four year variables. The most predictive combination was birth and eight-month variables plus four-year IQ, with R = .614 and 38% of the variance explained. The 3YR indexes with At-Birth variables ranked second, with R = .564 and R^2 = .318.

9. Several subgroups of children with special problems or situations were studied. Children with organic problems or adverse birth conditions and those judged to stutter performed less well than the ALL 8YR population. Twins performed less well than siblings, and siblings less well than singletons. As IQ increased, so did the score on the index. Adopted children were the only group whose mean exceeded that of the ALL 8YR group. This finding may be due to an associated rise in SEI. The N permitted distributions by SEI for several groups and the trend, regardless of the child's condition, was toward better performance with increasing socioeconomic status.

References

1. Applebee, A.N. Research in reading retardation: Two critical problems. *J. Child Psychol. Psychiatry* 12:91–113, 1971.

2. Balow, B., Rubin, R., and Rosen, J.J. Perinatal events as precursors of reading disability. *Reading Res. Qtly.* 1:36–71, 1975.

3. Bayley, N. *COLR Research Form of the Bayley Scale of Mental and Motor Development.* Bethesda, Maryland: Perinatal Research Branch, NINDB-NIH. 1958.

4. Colligen, R.C. Psychometric deficits related to perinatal stress. *J. Learning Dis.* 7:154–160, 1974.

5. Corah, N.L., James, E.J., Painter, P., Stern, J.A., and Thurston, D. Effects of perinatal anoxia after seven years. *Psych. Monographs.* 79:No. 596, 1965.

6. Davie, R., Butler, N., and Goldstein, H. *From Birth to Seven: A Report of the National Child Development Study.* London: Longmar, 1972.

7. deHirsch, K., Jansky, J., and Langford, W.S. Comparisons between prematurely and maturely born children at three age levels. *Am. J. Orthopsychiatry* 36:616–628, 1966.

8. Denhoff, E., Hainsworth, P.K., and Hainsworth, M.L. The child at risk for learning disorders: Can he be identified during the first year of life? *Clin. Pediatr.* 11:164–170, 1972.

9. Douglas, J.W.B. "Premature" children at primary schools. *Brit. Med. J.* 1:1008–1013, 1960.

10. Durrell, D.D., and Sullivan, H.B. *Durrell-Sullivan Reading Capacity and Achievement Tests: Primary Test; Form A.*

New York: Harcourt, Brace and World, 1939.

11. Fraser, M.S., and Wilks, J. The residual effects of neonatal asphyxia. *J. Obstet. Gynecol. Br. Empire* 66:748–752, 1959.

12. Gray, W.S. *Gray Oral Reading Test, Form A.* Indianapolis, Indiana: Bobbs-Merrill, 1963.

13. Hardy, M.P., Mellits, E.D., and Willig, S.N. Reading: A Function of Language Usage. *Johns Hopkins Med. J.* 129:43–53, 1971.

14. Hunt, B.C. Black dialect and 3rd and 4th graders' performance on the Gray Oral Reading Test. *Reading Res. Qtly.* 1:103–231, 1974–1975.

15. Jastak, J.F., and Jastak, S.R. *The Wide Range Achievement Test (WRAT).* Wilmington, Delaware: Guidance Associates, 1965.

16. Koppitz, E.M. *The Bender Gestalt Test for Young Children.* New York: Grune and Stratton, 1964.

17. Lyle, J.G. Certain antenatal, perinatal and developmental variables and reading retardation in middle-class boys. *Child Development* 41:481–491, 1970.

18. McCarthy, J.J., and Kirk, S.A. *The Construction, Standardization and Statistical Characteristics of the Illinois Test of Psycholinguistic Abilities, Experimental Edition.* Urbana, Illinois: University of Illinois Press, 1963.

19. Menkes, J.H., Welcher, D.W., Levi, H.S., Dallas, J., and Gretsky, N.E. Relationship of elevated blood tyrosine to the ultimate intellectual performance of premature infants. *Pediatrics* 49:218–224, 1972.

20. Orton, S.T. *Reading, Writing and Speech Problems in Children.* New York: Norton and Co., 1937.

21. Robinson, N.M., and Robinson, H.B. A follow-up study of children of low birthweight and control children at school age. *Pediatrics* 52:352–363, 1965.

22. Rubin, R.A., Rosenblatt, C., and Balow, B. Psychological and educational sequelae of prematurity. *Pediatrics* 52:352–363, 1973.

23. Terman, L.M., and Merrill, M.A. *Stanford-Binet Intelligence Scale.* Boston: Houghton-Mifflin, 1960.

24. Wechsler, D. *The Wechsler Intelligence Scale for Children.* New York: The Psychological Corp., 1949.

25. Wepman, J.M. Dyslexia: Its relationship to language acquisition and concept formation. In J. Money, Ed. *Reading Disability.* Baltimore, Maryland: Johns Hopkins University Press, 1962.

26. Wiener, C. The relationship of birthweight and length of gestation to intellectual development at ages 8 to 10 years. *J. Pediatr.* 76:694–699, 1970.

27. Yarrow, L.S., Goodwin, M.S., Manheimer, H., and Milowe, I.D. Infancy experiences and cognitive and personality development at ten years. In L.J. Stone, H.L. Smith, and L.B. Murphy, Eds. *The Competent Infant.* New York: Basic Books, 1973.

## CHAPTER 13

Overview: Perinatal, Medical, and Growth Factors

Robert O. Fisch, M.D.

One objective of the collaborative study was to learn the causes of communication disorders and to ascertain which perinatal factors affect later speech, language, and hearing competency. Therefore, it seems proper to start with conditions of pregnancy, labor and delivery, the socioeconomic level, and the parents' biological factors such as age and genetic history, and then to relate other medical and psychosocial variables with speech, language, and hearing performance at different ages. Among the questions which need to be answered are the following:

1. Which factors influence performance?
2. Which are the earliest warning signs?
3. Which are the best predictors?
4. What can we learn from this study in order to prevent handicaps and improve performance?

This chapter attempts to summarize perinatal, medical, growth, and other biological factors as related to SLH performance. Chapter 14 summarizes the relationships among psychosocial factors and SLH outcomes.

There are a few summary statements which should be presented here. First, small correlations (above .10 and ranging to .21) were found between 3YR and 8YR SLH performance and maternal age, blood type, metabolic condition, mental condition, prior pregnancy outcome, x-ray exposure during gestation, marital status, and smoking habits; the father of the baby's (FOB) age, sensory defects, and mental condition; and malformations and sensory defects in siblings.

In addition to single correlations, a multiple regression analysis was used (Appendix 8) to analyze the influence of race, sex, Birthweight, Gestational age, eight-month mental and motor scores (Bayley, 1958), father's education and occupation, the mother's education and Per Capita Income. Among these, the independent variables of race, sex, and socioeconomic status (SEI) proved to be the most important predictors of later performance. These results will be amplified in the following sections.

Maternal Factors

Age

The children were divided into three groups according to the mother's age at the time of her registration during pregnancy: group one, under 18 years of age; group two, 18 to 35 years of age; and group three, over 35 years of age. Comparisons were made between groups one and two and between groups three and two (Table 13-1).

3YR SLH Indexes Neither group one nor three had a higher probability of failure* than group two.

8YR SLH Indexes Group one had a slightly higher probability of failure than group two in nine of the 8YR Indexes: Written Communication, Concept Development, Digits, Auditory Memory, Hearing Severity, Language Production, Language Comprehension, Fluency, and Word Identification. Group three was similar to group two.

A woman's age may affect the course of pregnancy and the well-being of the

offspring (Israel and Deutschberger, 1964). The *best* age for childbearing as documented by low prenatal mortality or morbidity is between 18 and 25 years. However, the *best* maternal age might not necessarily be the most favorable age for child rearing. Children of younger mothers have lower IQ's (Broman, Nichols, and Kennedy, 1975). For all age groups, a higher SEI status indicated a lower probability of a failure in SLH performance, regardless of age. Maternal age apparently had minimal influence on later SLH performance, even though the younger mother probably had received less education. This finding may be explained by one or more of the following possibilities: (1) group one mothers received further education after the birth of their children; (2) the children grew up in another environment; (3) maternal age had negligible influence inasmuch as group three did not differ from group two; and/or (4) performance differences were reduced by other factors as the child matured.

Parity

Parity, determined during a prenatal interview, was defined as the number of prior pregnancies of 20 weeks or more gestation. Higher parity appears to be associated with a nonlinear increase in the probability of SLH failure at three and eight years in almost all indexes except for 3YR Fluency (Table 13-2). This greater probability of failure appears to persist for each sex, race, and SEI group. Parity is somewhat reduced, as expected, in the higher socioeconomic groups. Although there is increased parity in the lower socioeconomic groups, the probability of failure rises with the number of pregnancies regardless of socioeconomic status.

Height

The mother's height was measured to the nearest inch, without shoes, during the prenatal examination. The children

---

* Failure on an SLH index was defined as a score falling in the lowest decile or, in the case of a restricted range, closest to the lowest decile.

356

Table **13-1**

Correlations and conditional probabilities for SLH indexes and age of mother.

Indexes (F2)	r	Mother <18 years (F1) vs. Mother 18-35 years (P1)		Mother >35 years (F1) vs. Mother 18-35 years (P1)	
		p(F2/F1)*	p(F2/P1)*	p(F2/F1)	p(F2/P1)
3YR Speech Mechanism	<.10	.27	.25	.27	.25
3YR Hypernasality	<.10	.07	.06	.07	.06
3YR Fluency	<.10	.13	.14	.15	.14
3YR Articulation	<.10	.23	.22	.23	.22
3YR Intelligibility	<.10	.09	.09	.11	.09
3YR Language Comprehension	<.10	.19	.12	.13	.12
3YR Sentence Complexity	<.10	.16	.16	.18	.16
3YR Auditory Memory	<.10	.37	.32	.34	.32
3YR Hearing Screen	<.10	.20	.19	.21	.19
8YR Speech Mechanism	<.10	.06	.06	.06	.06
8YR Palatal Function and Hypernasality	<.10	.04	.04	.05	.04
8YR Fluency	<.10	.07	.06	.06	.06
8YR Articulation	<.10	.13	.14	.14	.14
8YR Intelligibility	<.10	.07	.07	.07	.07
8YR Language Comprehension	<.10	.15	.13	.12	.13
8YR Auditory Memory	<.10	.15	.12	.12	.12
8YR Digits	<.10	.16	.13	.15	.13
8YR Word Identification	.11	.23	.14	.12	.14
8YR Written Communication	<.10	.21	.16	.15	.16
8YR Language Production	<.10	.17	.13	.14	.13
8YR Concept Development	<.10	.22	.13	.12	.13
8YR Hearing Severity	<.10	.23	.21	.20	.21
8YR Total Conductive Loss	<.10	.07	.07	.08	.07
8YR Total Sensorineural Loss	<.10	.04	.04	.05	.04
Neurological Involvement	<.10	.22	.18	.19	.18
Communicative Effectiveness	<.10	.21	.15	.16	.15
Auditory Processing	<.10	.26	.20	.20	.20

*p(F2/F1) and p(F2/P1) refer to the probability of failing (i.e., scoring in the lowest decile) the SLH index (F2) when the antecedent variable was failed (F1) or passed (P1).

were divided for study into two groups according to maternal height: group one, 40 to 60 inches; and group two, 61 or more inches (Table 13-3). Comparisons were drawn between the two groups.

3YR Indexes Group one had a slightly higher probability of failure than group two.

8YR Indexes Group one also had a slightly higher probability of failure in speech and language, but did as well as group two in hearing tests.*

---

* Similarly, 4YR IQ increased with maternal height among white children (Broman et al., 1975).

Weight Gain During Pregnancy

The mother was weighed during each prenatal examination. Children were divided for study into three groups according to their mother's maximum weight gain during pregnancy: group one gained ≤14 pounds (or lost weight), group two gained from 15 to 25 pounds, and group three gained >25 pounds (Table 13-4). Comparisons were made between groups one and two and between groups three and two.

3YR Indexes Comparisons between groups one and two and between groups

Table **13-2**

Failure (%) in SLH performance by parity of the mother.

Index	0	1	2	3	4	5	6	7	8	9*
3YR Speech Mechanism	7.7	8.9	9.4	11.8	10.7	14.1	11.2	10.0	14.4	14.7
3YR Hypernasality	0.5	1.2	1.1	1.4	1.6	1.0	1.1	1.4	0.8	1.9
3YR Fluency	8.0	8.6	8.1	7.2	6.9	8.0	7.7	8.5	6.6	3.4
3YR Articulation	7.3	11.6	13.9	13.1	15.1	14.0	14.8	14.0	17.1	20.7
3YR Intelligibility	1.4	1.6	2.6	3.2	2.9	2.7	3.4	2.3	1.7	4.0
3YR Language Comprehension	6.7	7.2	7.3	8.5	8.1	8.4	7.4	9.1	8.7	10.2
3YR Sentence Complexity	6.8	8.1	9.9	10.4	12.2	10.2	11.7	11.8	10.1	16.9
3YR Auditory Memory	13.6	14.8	14.5	15.1	15.8	16.1	16.9	17.4	17.6	14.4
3YR Hearing Screen	13.9	11.3	11.9	12.5	11.7	12.4	11.9	13.8	10.5	12.7
8YR Speech Mechanism	3.4	3.7	4.0	4.1	5.0	5.0	4.4	4.7	8.1	5.3
8YR Palatal Function and Hypernasality	1.0	2.1	2.5	2.4	2.4	2.4	2.2	1.8	1.6	0.8
8YR Fluency	2.1	4.0	3.6	4.6	5.4	5.2	5.0	3.9	5.6	5.3
8YR Articulation	8.2	11.2	13.7	13.6	14.8	15.0	15.8	19.3	23.3	16.7
8YR Intelligibility	2.8	4.4	5.1	6.3	5.7	7.8	7.9	8.5	14.5	9.1
8YR Language Comprehension	5.7	9.2	11.0	13.0	11.2	13.3	15.6	14.8	13.8	13.0
8YR Auditory Memory	7.0	9.0	10.1	11.0	10.6	12.6	12.5	15.4	18.5	9.8
8YR Digits	9.6	11.1	10.7	11.7	13.5	14.1	13.0	12.9	16.9	13.6
8YR Word Identification	6.5	11.1	11.8	13.0	13.7	16.2	17.6	20.9	21.5	19.1
8YR Written Communication	8.7	8.5	10.3	12.0	14.7	16.9	17.0	20.9	24.1	26.4
8YR Language Production	7.3	8.5	10.3	12.1	11.3	14.7	15.4	16.7	22.9	14.7
8YR Concept Development	7.3	10.0	11.6	13.3	11.6	15.4	15.5	20.6	23.4	20.6
8YR Hearing Severity	5.4	4.2	5.2	5.7	5.1	6.5	7.3	5.2	4.8	6.1
Neurological Involvement	8.9	10.7	12.0	12.1	11.9	13.9	12.6	14.0	14.5	11.7
Communicative Effectiveness	6.2	8.5	10.7	12.0	11.7	15.4	18.8	18.7	25.4	23.2
Auditory Processing	8.5	9.3	11.6	13.7	15.4	18.2	17.2	21.6	25.2	27.1

*Percent failing where parity is above nine is not shown due to small Ns ($\leq$56).

Table **13-3**

Correlations and conditional probabilities for SLH indexes and height of mother.

| Indexes (F2) | r | Mother 40-60 in. (F1) vs. Mother ≥61 in. (P1) | |
		p(F2/F1)*	p(F2/P1)*
3YR Speech Mechanism	<.10	.26	.25
3YR Hypernasality	<.10	.07	.06
3YR Fluency	<.10	.14	.14
3YR Articulation	<.10	.24	.22
3YR Intelligibility	<.10	.11	.09
3YR Language Comprehension	<.10	.15	.13
3YR Sentence Complexity	<.10	.19	.16
3YR Auditory Memory	<.10	.35	.33
3YR Hearing Screen	<.10	.21	.19
8YR Speech Mechanism	<.10	.08	.06
8YR Palatal Function and Hypernasality	<.10	.05	.04
8YR Fluency	<.10	.07	.06
8YR Articulation	<.10	.15	.14
8YR Intelligibility	<.10	.09	.07
8YR Language Comprehension	<.10	.15	.13
8YR Auditory Memory	<.10	.14	.12
8YR Digits	<.10	.15	.13
8YR Word Identification	<.10	.18	.15
8YR Written Communication	<.10	.19	.17
8YR Language Production	<.10	.17	.14
8YR Concept Development	<.10	.17	.15
8YR Hearing Severity	<.10	.21	.21
8YR Total Conductive Loss	<.10	.07	.07
8YR Total Sensorineural Loss	<.10	.04	.04
Neurological Involvement	<.10	.20	.19
Communicative Effectiveness	<.10	.19	.16
Auditory Processing	<.10	.25	.21

*p(F2/F1) and p(F2/P1) refer to the probability of failing the SLH index (F2) when the antecedent variable was failed (F1) or passed (P1).

three and two revealed no notable differences.

8YR Indexes Groups one and three had a slightly higher probability of failure on all SLH indexes than group two. There were minimal differences between the groups; and we may conclude that, although low or excessive weight gain is not usually regarded as favorable, neither appeared to influence later SLH performance.

As expected, an inverse relationship existed between SEI and the probability of failure on SLH indexes. Air travel and radiation during pregnancy, high blood pressure, toxemia, and diabetes (regardless of duration) did not affect 3YR and 8YR SLH performance.

Mental Retardation

A threefold increase in the probability of failure in 8YR Written Communication, Language Production, Language Comprehension, Concept Development, and Speech Mechanism (Table 13-5) existed among children of mentally retarded mothers, as compared with those whose mothers were not so afflicted. Although maternal retardation was not found in

Table 13-4

Correlations and conditional probabilities for SLH indexes and weight gain during pregnancy.

Indexes (F2)	r	Weight ≤14 lbs. (F1) vs. Weight 15-25 lbs. (P1)		Weight >25 lbs. (F1) vs. Weight 15-25 lbs. (P1)	
		p(F2/F1)*	p(F2/P1)*	p(F2/F1)	p(F2/P1)
3YR Speech Mechanism	<.10	.25	.25	.25	.25
3YR Hypernasality	<.10	.06	.06	.06	.06
3YR Fluency	<.10	.14	.14	.14	.14
3YR Articulation	<.10	.23	.21	.21	.21
3YR Intelligibility	<.10	.09	.09	.09	.09
3YR Language Comprehension	<.10	.13	.13	.13	.13
3YR Sentence Complexity	<.10	.17	.16	.17	.16
3YR Auditory Memory	<.10	.32	.33	.34	.33
3YR Hearing Screen	<.10	.19	.18	.20	.18
8YR Speech Mechanism	<.10	.06	.05	.06	.05
8YR Palatal Function and Hypernasality	<.10	.04	.04	.04	.04
8YR Fluency	<.10	.06	.05	.07	.05
8YR Articulation	<.10	.14	.13	.14	.13
8YR Intelligibility	<.10	.07	.06	.07	.06
8YR Language Comprehension	<.10	.14	.12	.13	.12
8YR Auditory Memory	<.10	.13	.11	.12	.11
8YR Digits	<.10	.14	.11	.14	.11
8YR Word Identification	<.10	.17	.13	.14	.13
8YR Written Communication	<.10	.18	.14	.18	.14
8YR Language Production	<.10	.15	.13	.14	.13
8YR Concept Development	<.10	.16	.13	.14	.13
8YR Hearing Severity	<.10	.22	.20	.22	.20
8YR Total Conductive Loss	<.10	.08	.07	.07	.07
8YR Total Sensorineural Loss	<.10	.05	.04	.04	.04
Neurological Involvement	<.10	.19	.18	.19	.18
Communicative Effectiveness	<.10	.18	.14	.16	.14
Auditory Processing	<.10	.23	.19	.21	.19

*p(F2/F1) and p(F2/P1) refer to the probability of failing the SLH index (F2) when the antecedent variable was failed (F1) or passed (P1).

the highest socioeconomic group, it resulted in a higher probability of failure across all other socioeconomic groups. Further study of possible genetic influence is suggested.

Other factors such as motor defects, mental illness, and retardation of the mother's and father's siblings, as well as the father's physical defects, had no discernible influence on SLH performance at three and eight years.

Gestational Age

Gestational age at delivery was calculated from the first day of the last menstrual period reported by the mother. The children were divided for study into three groups according to their gestational age: group one, less than 38 weeks (premature); group two, 38 to 42 weeks (mature); and group three, over 42 weeks (postmature). Comparisons were made between groups one and two (Table 13-6) and between groups three and two (Table 13-7).

3YR Indexes Both group one and group three had a probability of failure similar to that of group two.

8YR Indexes Group one had a slightly higher probability of failure than group two for several indexes (Word Identifica-

Table 13-5

Correlations between SLH indexes and conditional probabilities of failure by Socioeconomic Index and total when the child's mother is mentally retarded.

Indexes (F2)	SEI r	0.0-1.9 p(F2/F1)*	0.0-1.9 p(F2/P1)*	2.0-3.9 p(F2/F1)	2.0-3.9 p(F2/P1)	4.0-5.9 p(F2/F1)	4.0-5.9 p(F2/P1)	6.0-7.9 p(F2/F1)	6.0-7.9 p(F2/P1)	8.0-9.5 p(F2/F1)	8.0-9.5 p(F2/P1)	Total p(F2/F1)	Total p(F2/P1)
3YR Speech Mechanism	<.10	.29	.27	.29	.28	.50	.26	0	.23	†	.17	.32	.25
3YR Language Comprehension	<.10	.14	.19	.29	.16	.13	.13	0	.09	†	.04	.18	.13
3YR Sentence Complexity	<.10	.24	.20	.43	.20	.38	.17	0	.12	†	.06	.32	.16
8YR Speech Mechanism	<.10	.14	.08	.26	.06	.24	.06	.33	.05	†	.03	.22	.06
8YR Language Comprehension	<.10	.23	.23	.30	.18	.71	.12	.33	.07	†	.04	.38	.13
8YR Written Communication	<.10	.59	.30	.44	.22	.59	.16	.33	.09	†	.06	.52	.16
8YR Language Production	<.10	.50	.24	.41	.19	.65	.13	.33	.09	†	.03	.49	.14
8YR Concept Development	<.10	.41	.29	.33	.22	.53	.13	.33	.06	†	.03	.41	.14

*p(F2/F1) and p(F2/P1) refer to the probability of failing the SLH index (F2) when the mother was mentally retarded (F1) or not mentally retarded (P1).
†No cases.

Table **13-6**

Correlations and conditional probabilities for SLH indexes and Gestational Age by Socioeconomic Index and by total; Mature (P1) vs. Premature (F1).

Indexes (F2)	SEI r	SEI p(F2/F1)*	SEI p(F2/P1)*	0.0-1.9 p(F2/F1)	0.0-1.9 p(F2/P1)	2.0-3.9 p(F2/F1)	2.0-3.9 p(F2/P1)	4.0-5.9 p(F2/F1)	4.0-5.9 p(F2/P1)	6.0-7.9 p(F2/F1)	6.0-7.9 p(F2/P1)	8.0-9.5 p(F2/F1)	8.0-9.5 p(F2/P1)	Total p(F2/F1)	Total p(F2/P1)
3YR Speech Mechanism	<.10	.09	.11	.12	.11	.09	.10	.10	.09	.09	.09	.06	.06	.10	.10
3YR Hypernasality	<.10	.01	.01	.01	.01	.02	.01	.01	.01	.01	.01	.00	.01	.01	.01
3YR Fluency	<.10	.04	.07	.06	.07	.06	.07	.12	.09	.09	.09	.11	.15	.07	.08
3YR Articulation	<.10	.18	.19	.17	.13	.13	.12	.10	.08	.08	.08	.08	.07	.15	.12
3YR Intelligibility	<.10	.04	.02	.02	.03	.03	.03	.02	.02	.02	.01	.01	.01	.03	.02
3YR Language Comprehension	<.10	.14	.13	.11	.10	.12	.07	.08	.05	.05	.04	.04	.02	.11	.08
3YR Sentence Complexity	<.10	.12	.11	.11	.11	.11	.10	.10	.07	.07	.09	.09	.03	.11	.09
3YR Auditory Memory	<.10	.16	.16	.16	.18	.17	.16	.15	.12	.12	.11	.11	.08	.16	.15
3YR Hearing Screen	<.10	.12	.10	.10	.12	.12	.12	.13	.12	.12	.14	.12	.12	.12	.12
8YR Speech Mechanism	<.10	.08	.05	.06	.04	.05	.05	.05	.04	.04	.05	.05	.02	.06	.04
8YR Palatal Function & Hypernasality	<.10	.02	.02	.02	.03	.03	.02	.03	.02	.02	.02	.02	.02	.02	.02
8YR Fluency	<.10	.09	.06	.06	.05	.05	.04	.03	.03	.03	.05	.05	.02	.05	.04
8YR Articulation	<.10	.24	.17	.17	.15	.14	.11	.11	.09	.09	.09	.16	.09	.16	.12
8YR Intelligibility	<.10	.14	.09	.08	.07	.07	.05	.03	.03	.03	.00	.09	.01	.07	.05
8YR Language Comprehension	<.10	.23	.19	.18	.15	.13	.10	.08	.05	.05	.02	.09	.02	.14	.10
8YR Auditory Memory	<.10	.20	.17	.16	.13	.13	.09	.09	.05	.05	.03	.03	.03	.14	.09
8YR Digits	<.10	.21	.16	.16	.14	.14	.11	.11	.08	.08	.05	.05	.06	.14	.11
8YR Word Identification	.14	.38	.28	.26	.19	.17	.10	.11	.10	.09	.05	.20	.01	.14	.11
8YR Written Communication	<.10	.27	.23	.19	.16	.15	.09	.09	.06	.06	.03	.16	.01	.16	.09
8YR Language Production	.10	.26	.18	.18	.14	.13	.10	.09	.06	.10	.03	.15	.01	.15	.09
8YR Concept Development	.13	.32	.25	.26	.17	.15	.09	.09	.06	.06	.02	.19	.01	.19	.10
8YR Hearing Severity	<.10	.05	.07	.07	.05	.05	.05	.05	.05	.05	.03	.05	.05	.05	.05
8YR Total Conductive Loss	<.10	.04	.06	.06	.06	.05	.05	.05	.05	.05	.04	.05	.04	.05	.05
8YR Total Sensorineural Loss	<.10	.03	.02	.03	.02	.02	.02	.02	.02	.02	.01	.03	.02	.03	.02
Neurological Involvement	<.10	.18	.14	.15	.13	.11	.11	.11	.10	.10	.09	.13	.07	.11	.11
Communicative Effectiveness	.12	.31	.24	.23	.16	.14	.09	.09	.07	.07	.01	.17	.01	.17	.09
Auditory Processing	.13	.33	.28	.26	.18	.16	.10	.10	.06	.06	.03	.19	.01	.19	.10

*p(F2/F1) and p(F2/P1) refer to the probability of failing the SLH index (F2) when the antecedent variable was failed (F1) or passed (P1).

Table 13-7

Correlations and conditional probabilities for SLH indexes and Gestational Age by Socioeconomic Index and by total; Mature (P1) vs. Postmature (F1).

Indexes (F2)	SEI r	SEI p(F2/F1)*	SEI p(F2/P1)*	0.0-1.9 p(F2/F1)	0.0-1.9 p(F2/P1)	2.0-3.9 p(F2/F1)	2.0-3.9 p(F2/P1)	4.0-5.9 p(F2/F1)	4.0-5.9 p(F2/P1)	6.0-7.9 p(F2/F1)	6.0-7.9 p(F2/P1)	8.0-9.5 p(F2/F1)	8.0-9.5 p(F2/P1)	Total p(F2/F1)	Total p(F2/P1)
3YR Speech Mechanism	<.10	.10	.11	.12	.11	.09	.10	.08	.10	.09	.09	.04	.06	.10	.10
3YR Hypernasality	<.10	.01	.01	.00	.01	.01	.01	.03	.01	.01	.01	.01	.01	.01	.01
3YR Fluency	<.10	.05	.07	.04	.07	.07	.07	.08	.07	.09	.09	.15	.15	.07	.08
3YR Articulation	<.10	.20	.19	.13	.13	.10	.12	.11	.12	.08	.08	.05	.07	.12	.12
3YR Intelligibility	<.10	.05	.02	.03	.03	.04	.03	.03	.03	.08	.02	.01	.01	.03	.02
3YR Language Comprehension	<.10	.12	.13	.11	.10	.08	.07	.05	.07	.05	.05	.00	.02	.08	.08
3YR Sentence Complexity	<.10	.09	.11	.13	.11	.12	.10	.07	.10	.07	.07	.03	.03	.08	.08
3YR Auditory Memory	<.10	.14	.16	.18	.18	.20	.16	.16	.16	.12	.12	.08	.08	.11	.09
3YR Hearing Screen	<.10	.15	.10	.10	.12	.14	.12	.14	.12	.12	.12	.16	.12	.13	.12
8YR Speech Mechanism	<.10	.05	.05	.03	.04	.04	.05	.02	.05	.04	.04	.03	.02	.03	.04
8YR Palatal Function & Hypernasality	<.10	.01	.02	.03	.03	.02	.02	.03	.02	.02	.02	.02	.02	.03	.02
8YR Fluency	<.10	.06	.06	.05	.05	.04	.04	.03	.04	.03	.03	.04	.02	.04	.04
8YR Articulation	<.10	.11	.17	.13	.15	.10	.11	.11	.11	.09	.09	.10	.09	.11	.12
8YR Intelligibility	<.10	.11	.09	.07	.07	.05	.05	.04	.05	.03	.03	.02	.01	.06	.05
8YR Language Comprehension	<.10	.20	.19	.14	.15	.09	.10	.05	.10	.05	.05	.01	.02	.10	.10
8YR Auditory Memory	<.10	.20	.17	.13	.13	.10	.09	.06	.09	.05	.05	.02	.03	.10	.09
8YR Digits	<.10	.14	.16	.15	.14	.15	.11	.09	.11	.08	.08	.05	.06	.13	.11
8YR Word Identification	.14	.22	.28	.17	.19	.10	.10	.05	.10	.03	.03	.02	.01	.12	.11
8YR Written Communication	<.10	.17	.23	.17	.16	.14	.09	.05	.09	.04	.04	.02	.01	.12	.09
8YR Language Production	.10	.16	.18	.15	.14	.10	.09	.06	.09	.06	.06	.02	.01	.11	.09
8YR Concept Development	.13	.23	.25	.19	.17	.10	.09	.05	.10	.04	.04	.02	.01	.12	.10
8YR Hearing Severity	<.10	.06	.07	.06	.05	.05	.05	.07	.05	.05	.05	.03	.05	.06	.05
8YR Total Conductive Loss	<.10	.06	.06	.05	.06	.06	.05	.05	.05	.05	.05	.03	.04	.05	.05
8YR Total Sensorineural Loss	<.10	.04	.02	.03	.02	.03	.02	.03	.02	.02	.02	.02	.02	.03	.02
Neurological Involvement	<.10	.20	.14	.14	.13	.11	.11	.09	.11	.10	.10	.09	.07	.12	.11
Communicative Effectiveness	.12	.20	.24	.15	.16	.12	.09	.05	.09	.05	.03	.01	.01	.11	.09
Auditory Processing	.13	.19	.28	.21	.18	.09	.10	.05	.10	.03	.03	.02	.01	.12	.10

*p(F2/F1) and p(F2/P1) refer to the probability of failing the SLH index (F2) when the antecedent variable was failed (F1) or passed (P1).

tion, Written Communication, Language Production, Concept Development, Communicative Effectiveness, and Auditory Processing). Group three had a negligibly higher probability of failure than group two. However, the probability of failure diminished with higher SEI.*

Duration of labor (<4 hours and >16 hours), membrane rupture (≥24 hours prior delivery), and cord and placenta pathology were associated with only slightly higher failure rates on 3YR and 8YR SLH indexes.

Method of Delivery

Children were divided into three groups according to the method by which they were delivered: group one, vertex; group two, breech; group three, caesarean section. Comparisons were made between group one and groups two and three combined; between group two and groups one and three combined; and between group three and groups one and two combined (Table 13-8).

3YR and 8YR Indexes No systematic or sizeable differences in the probability of failure on SLH indexes were found among any groups.

Vertex Delivery with Forceps

Children were divided into four groups according to the type of application of forceps used for their deliveries: group one, outlet forceps; group two, low forceps; group three, midforceps; and group four, high forceps (Table 13-9). Comparisons were made between each group and the no forceps group.

3YR Indexes No differences in the percentage of failure were observed between any of the first three groups. There were no 3YR cases in the fourth group (high forceps).

---

*A positive relationship between gestational age and 4YR IQ was shown previously for each race and sex group by Broman et al. (1975).

8YR Indexes Although usage of high forceps (group four) was limited, the percentage of failure rate was relatively high for eight of the 8YR indexes, varying from two- to fivefold over any other group. The second highest percentage of failure was observed for group one.

The usage of high forceps is extremely limited, but associated poor performance suggests that this method of delivery should be avoided. Outlet forceps are sometimes used electively to control the birth process; yet the second highest percentage of failure was associated with this group. This finding may reflect the obstetrical practice at certain institutions and thus be confounded by race and SEI effects.

Apgar Scores

Apgar scores were observed routinely at one, two, and five minutes after birth. Although scores were the best predictors (together with birthweight) of neonatal death (Drage, Kennedy, and Schwarz, 1964), they did not predict 4YR IQ (Broman et al., 1975) and SLH performance with the exception of five-minute Apgar scores of 0 to 3 which were related to a higher percentage of failure on the 3YR and 8YR hearing examination. The failure rates for the 3YR Hearing Screen were 15.8%, 12.9%, and 11.5% for five-minute Apgar scores of 0 to 3, 4 to 7, and 8 to 10, respectively. For the 8YR Hearing Severity Index, the corresponding failure rates were 9.1%, 4.9%, and 5.0%.

Sex

In all 3YR and most 8YR indexes (except 8YR Language Comprehension and Word Identification) Females of each race had a lower probability of failure than Males. The superior performance of Females, regardless of race or SEI, is one of the more interesting and consistent findings. However, Black Females did not score as well as White Males. Neither sex

Table **13-8**

Correlations and conditional probabilities for SLH indexes and method of delivery.

Indexes (F2)	Vertex (P1)			Breech (P1)			C-Section (P1)	
	r	p(F2/F1)*	p(F2/P1)*	r	p(F2/F1)	p(F2/P1)	p(F2/F1)	p(F2/P1)
3YR Speech Mechanism	<.10	.25	.27	<.10	.30	.25	.26	.25
3YR Hypernasality	<.10	.06	.06	<.10	.06	.06	.06	.06
3YR Fluency	<.10	.14	.14	<.10	.16	.14	.13	.06
3YR Articulation	<.10	.22	.24	<.10	.27	.22	.23	.14
3YR Intelligibility	<.10	.09	.11	<.10	.12	.09	.10	.22
3YR Language Comprehension	<.10	.13	.15	<.10	.15	.13	.15	.09
3YR Sentence Complexity	<.10	.16	.20	<.10	.20	.16	.20	.13
3YR Auditory Memory	<.10	.33	.36	<.10	.41	.33	.34	.16
3YR Hearing Screen	<.10	.19	.21	<.10	.22	.19	.20	.33
8YR Speech Mechanism	<.10	.06	.06	<.10	.08	.06	.05	.06
8YR Palatal Function and Hypernasality	<.10	.04	.04	<.10	.05	.04	.03	.04
8YR Fluency	<.10	.06	.05	<.10	.05	.06	.05	.06
8YR Articulation	<.10	.14	.14	<.10	.15	.14	.13	.14
8YR Intelligibility	<.10	.07	.07	<.10	.08	.07	.06	.07
8YR Language Comprehension	<.10	.13	.14	<.10	.13	.13	.14	.13
8YR Auditory Memory	<.10	.12	.13	<.10	.15	.12	.12	.12
8YR Digits	<.10	.13	.14	<.10	.16	.13	.13	.13
8YR Word Identification	<.10	.14	.15	<.10	.16	.14	.14	.14
8YR Written Communication	<.10	.16	.19	<.10	.21	.16	.17	.16
8YR Language Production	<.10	.14	.14	<.10	.16	.14	.12	.14
8YR Concept Development	<.10	.14	.15	<.10	.15	.14	.14	.14
8YR Hearing Severity	<.10	.15	.17	<.10	.19	.15	.15	.15
8YR Total Conductive Loss	<.10	.07	.08	<.10	.10	.07	.07	.07
8YR Total Sensorineural Loss	<.10	.04	.04	<.10	.05	.04	.03	.04
Neurological Involvement	<.10	.19	.19	<.10	.21	.19	.18	.19
Auditory Processing	<.10	.10	.10	<.10	.13	.10	.08	.10

*p(F2/F1) and p(F2/P1) refer to the probability of failing the SLH index (F2) when the antecedent variable was failed (F1) or passed (P1).

365

Table 13-9

Correlations and failure rate (%) on SLH indexes for vertex delivery with type of application of forceps.

Indexes	r	Type of Forceps			
		Outlet	Low	Mid	High
3YR Speech Mechanism	<.10	9.2	10.5	10.0	*
3YR Hypernasality	<.10	1.2	1.6	1.0	*
3YR Fluency	<.10	9.1	9.4	13.9	*
3YR Articulation	<.10	11.3	10.5	8.3	*
3YR Intelligibility	<.10	2.2	2.4	2.1	*
3YR Language Comprehension	<.10	8.2	8.4	4.1	*
3YR Sentence Complexity	<.10	8.4	8.5	7.4	*
3YR Auditory Memory	<.10	15.8	13.0	10.2	*
3YR Hearing Screen	<.10	12.8	13.3	13.2	*
8YR Speech Mechanism	<.10	4.5	3.5	4.2	14.3
8YR Palatal Function and Hypernasality	<.10	2.4	1.7	1.4	14.3
8YR Fluency	<.10	4.1	3.0	2.5	*
8YR Articulation	<.10	10.5	10.7	10.8	*
8YR Intelligibility	<.10	4.3	2.8	3.0	*
8YR Language Comprehension	.10	9.1	7.4	4.7	*
8YR Auditory Memory	<.10	9.5	7.5	6.2	16.7
8YR Digits	<.10	10.6	10.1	9.6	28.6
8YR Word Identification	.16	11.0	7.6	4.1	*
8YR Written Communication	.11	8.0	6.7	4.8	14.3
8YR Language Production	<.10	8.6	7.3	5.2	*
8YR Concept Development	.13	10.8	7.8	3.5	14.3
8YR Hearing Severity	<.10	5.0	4.8	5.1	*
Neurological Involvement	<.10	11.3	9.6	9.6	28.6
Communicative Effectiveness	.15	8.1	6.8	2.8	16.7
Auditory Processing	.14	8.9	8.1	3.8	*

*No cases.

predominates in the 8YR sensorineural hearing loss rate (Appendix 6).

The Collaborative Study revealed that females have higher 4YR IQ than males for each race and sex group (Broman et al., 1975). There is a considerable amount of literature on sex-related performance differences (Tyler, 1956). Although conclusions may differ, studies have revealed that Males were usually superior on tests of mathematical reasoning, spatial relationships and science, while Females were superior in verbal fluency, most types of memory, speech, and dexterity.

Other Factors

Newborn symptoms and complications such as apnea, respiratory distress syndrome, and even high bilirubin concentration did not influence 3YR and 8YR SLH performance. Actually, the highest incidence of sensorineural hearing loss occurred among babies whose bilirubin concentration never rose above 5 mg%.

Previous studies suggested that there is a relationship between bilirubin concentrations and abnormal developmental status at eight months (Boggs, Hardy, and Frazier, 1967; Scheidt et al., 1977) and twelve months of age (Hardy and Peeples, 1971; Scheidt et al., 1977). Among Blacks, very high bilirubin levels of more than 14 mg% have been associated with lower IQ's at four years of age; there was a smaller negative association with IQ among whites (Broman, Nichols, and Kennedy, 1975). Cognitive development and school achievement tests given at ages four through seven years confirmed an association between elevated neonatal bilirubin levels with early developmental deficit, but failed to support the hypothesis that elevated bilirubin levels are predictive of long-term cognitive impairment (Rubin, Balow, and Fisch, 1978).

Late neurological, psychological, and auditory sequelae might have occurred in children with lower levels of bilirubin (Hyman et al., 1969). However, incidence of sensorineural hearing loss subsequent to hyperbilirubinemia was 4.2%; this incidence was similar to that found among unselected children (Keaster, Hyman, and Harris, 1969). From this finding we can speculate that: (1) those who had severe complications and high bilirubin values expired and were not available for follow-up; (2) high bilirubin concentration levels may not be associated with higher incidence of sensorineural hearing loss; and/or (3) unrecognized factors confound the relationship between hyperbilirubinemia and hearing loss.

Children with syndromes identified at birth or during the first year of life had a higher failure rate in most 3YR and 8YR SLH performance evaluations, as expected.

Growth Measurements

Birthweight

Birthweight was measured within one hour after birth. Children were divided into three groups according to birthweight: group one, less than 2500 grams; group two, 2501 to 4000 grams; group

three, more than 4000 grams. Comparisons were made between groups one and two and between groups three and two (Table 13-10).

3YR Indexes Group one had a higher probability of failure than group two. The differences were small. This was true for each sex and race. Socioeconomic level did not seem to be influential. The probability of failure for groups three and two were not different.

8YR Indexes In this analysis, correlations between birthweight and performance were low. However, if we compare the extremes, children with birthweights less than 1500 grams with those over 4500 grams, the larger children did better on the following indexes: Intelligibility, Articulation, Language Comprehension, Language Production, Auditory Memory, Digits, Word Identification, Written Communication, Concept Development, Hearing Severity, Neurological Involvement, Communicative Effectiveness, and Auditory Processing. These differences, however, were less than one standard deviation.* The conclusion is that large babies have no obviously unfavorable outcome, and they perform better in some ways than very small babies.

Head Circumference

Head circumference was measured to the nearest centimeter during the first day of life. Male newborns were divided into three groups according to head circumference: group one, ≤33 cm; group two, 34 to 36 cm; and group three, ≥37 cm. Female newborns were also divided into three groups: group one, ≤33 cm; group two, 34 to 35 cm; and group three, ≥36 cm. Comparisons were made between groups one and two and between groups three and two (Table 13-11).

3YR and 8YR Indexes Group one had

---

* Significant correlations between 4YR IQ and birth weight were found earlier by Broman et al. (1975).

Table **13-10**

Correlations and conditional probabilities for SLH indexes and birthweight.

Indexes (F2)	r	Normal (P1) vs. Low (F1)		Normal (P1) vs. High (F1)	
		p(F2/F1)*	p(F2/P1)*	p(F2/F1)	p(F2/P1)
3YR Speech Mechanism	<.10	.29	.25	.25	.25
3YR Hypernasality	<.10	.08	.06	.06	.06
3YR Fluency	<.10	.17	.14	.15	.14
3YR Articulation	<.10	.28	.21	.20	.21
3YR Intelligibility	<.10	.13	.08	.10	.08
3YR Language Comprehension	.11	.18	.12	.10	.12
3YR Sentence Complexity	<.10	.22	.16	.17	.16
3YR Auditory Memory	<.10	.39	.32	.33	.32
3YR Hearing Screen	<.10	.22	.19	.20	.19
8YR Speech Mechanism	<.10	.07	.06	.05	.06
8YR Palatal Function and Hypernasality	<.10	.05	.04	.04	.04
8YR Fluency	<.10	.07	.06	.07	.06
8YR Articulation	<.10	.17	.13	.13	.13
8YR Intelligibility	<.10	.09	.06	.06	.06
8YR Language Comprehension	.12	.18	.12	.09	.12
8YR Auditory Memory	.10	.18	.12	.10	.12
8YR Digits	<.10	.18	.13	.12	.13
8YR Word Identification	.20	.23	.14	.08	.14
8YR Written Communication	.12	.25	.15	.15	.15
8YR Language Production	.12	.20	.13	.11	.13
8YR Concept Development	.17	.22	.14	.10	.14
8YR Hearing Severity	<.10	.25	.21	.18	.21
8YR Total Conductive Loss	<.10	.09	.07	.07	.07
8YR Total Sensorineural Loss	<.10	.05	.04	.04	.04
Neurological Involvement	<.10	.22	.18	.18	.18
Communicative Effectiveness	.16	.24	.15	.11	.15
Auditory Processing	.17	.31	.20	.16	.20

*p(F2/F1) and p(F2/P1) refer to the probability of failing the SLH index (F2) when the antecedent variable was failed (F1) or passed (P1).

only a marginally higher percentage of failure on most indexes than group two. Group three did not differ materially from group two. Head size at one year of age has been found to be a good predictor of the 4YR IQ (Nelson and Deutschberger, 1970).

Four Year Measurements

Weight

Correlation coefficients between 4YR weight and SLH indexes were generally low. These did not reach values of .10 except for 8YR Language Comprehension, Concept Development, Word Identification, Written Communication, Communicative Effectiveness, and Auditory Processing. None of the correlations exceeded .20 (Table 13-12).

Height

All correlations between 4YR height and SLH indexes were less than .10 (Table 13-12).

Table 13-11

Failure rate (%) by head circumference (cm) at birth by race and sex.

	White						Black					
	Males			Females			Males			Females		
Indexes	≤33	34-36	≥37	≤33	34-35	≥36	≤33	34-36	≥37	≤33	34-35	≥36
3YR Speech Mechanism	13.3	10.5	12.3	9.8	8.5	8.3	11.3	11.4	13.0	7.7	8.2	6.1
3YR Hypernasality	1.4	1.3	0.6	1.7	1.3	1.4	1.0	1.3	2.6	0.7	0.7	*
3YR Fluency	9.7	11.2	10.6	8.7	6.7	6.2	7.0	7.4	6.5	6.2	7.1	5.7
3YR Articulation	13.7	12.5	14.6	9.5	8.3	5.6	17.2	16.2	18.4	11.0	10.1	7.5
3YR Intelligibility	4.0	4.1	5.8	1.7	1.6	1.0	3.5	2.4	5.8	1.6	0.7	0.4
3YR Language Comprehension	6.7	5.2	6.7	4.2	2.9	4.7	13.3	11.6	9.9	10.6	9.0	6.8
3YR Sentence Complexity	14.5	12.3	16.6	8.4	5.9	6.3	13.5	9.6	10.6	6.6	6.3	6.8
3YR Auditory Memory	19.0	19.0	18.6	16.5	14.5	13.2	14.9	13.4	13.2	13.1	11.8	9.2
3YR Hearing Screen	12.5	14.0	15.8	15.2	14.9	13.4	11.3	9.4	12.3	10.2	9.9	8.0
8YR Speech Mechanism	5.8	4.3	4.4	3.0	2.6	1.5	6.0	5.1	5.6	3.8	4.2	2.4
8YR Palatal Function and Hypernasality	4.3	3.0	2.2	3.4	2.6	2.4	2.1	1.4	2.8	1.3	1.2	2.4
8YR Fluency	3.4	3.5	4.4	1.7	1.5	2.7	7.6	7.4	11.4	4.4	4.3	8.5
8YR Articulation	15.1	12.9	10.5	8.0	7.4	8.3	19.6	18.2	21.1	10.2	9.7	11.2
8YR Intelligibility	5.7	4.3	7.4	2.8	1.6	0.5	10.5	8.5	10.6	4.9	5.1	4.0
8YR Language Comprehension	3.8	3.4	3.5	7.2	5.5	5.0	15.6	15.0	15.0	18.9	17.1	16.1
8YR Auditory Memory	8.8	5.9	5.3	9.1	6.3	7.2	14.9	13.4	14.5	13.4	11.8	10.2
8YR Digits	16.2	12.1	8.7	11.1	8.2	9.6	15.5	12.7	15.5	11.3	8.8	7.6
8YR Word Identification	2.1	1.7	1.3	5.3	3.5	2.2	18.6	16.0	16.9	29.8	26.1	22.9
8YR Written Communication	13.5	8.1	9.5	5.8	3.6	4.8	23.8	18.4	16.3	10.7	7.3	5.1
8YR Language Production	5.6	5.1	4.9	5.3	3.7	2.5	20.1	16.5	15.7	15.5	13.5	13.9
8YR Concept Development	5.2	3.5	4.0	4.6	3.0	2.7	24.5	20.3	18.1	20.7	16.3	13.4
8YR Hearing Severity	6.0	6.3	5.3	5.2	4.2	4.9	4.9	5.2	2.1	4.9	3.7	5.9

*No cases.

Table **13-12**

Correlations between SLH indexes and weight (Kgm) and height (cm) at four years.

Indexes	Weight at 4YR (Kgm)	Height at 4YR (cm)
3YR Speech Mechanism	<.10	<.10
3YR Hypernasality	<.10	<.10
3YR Fluency	<.10	<.10
3YR Articulation	<.10	<.10
3YR Intelligibility	<.10	<.10
3YR Language Comprehension	<.10	<.10
3YR Sentence Complexity	<.10	<.10
3YR Auditory Memory	<.10	<.10
3YR Hearing Screen	<.10	<.10
8YR Speech Mechanism	<.10	<.10
8YR Palatal Function and Hypernasality	<.10	<.10
8YR Fluency	<.10	<.10
8YR Articulation	<.10	<.10
8YR Intelligibility	<.10	<.10
8YR Language Comprehension	.12	<.10
8YR Auditory Memory	<.10	<.10
8YR Digits	<.10	<.10
8YR Word Identification	.20	<.10
8YR Written Communication	.12	<.10
8YR Language Production	<.10	<.10
8YR Concept Development	.15	<.10
8YR Hearing Severity	<.10	<.10
8YR Total Conductive Loss	<.10	<.10
8YR Total Sensorineural Loss	<.10	<.10
Neurological Involvement	<.10	<.10
Communicative Effectiveness	.15	<.10
Auditory Processing	.16	<.10

Weight/Height Ratio Index

Children were divided into three groups according to their weight/height ratio index: group one, lowest decile; group two, middle 80%; and group three, upper decile. Comparisons were made between groups one and two and between groups three and two (Table 13-13). For the 8YR indexes, group one generally showed a higher failure rate than group two. Group three had a lower percentage of failure than group two for most of the indexes, except for White Males.

Head Circumference

Children were divided by sex and race into three groups according to their occi-pito-frontal circumferences at four years. The groups were composed of Males, ≤48 cm, 49 to 52 cm, and ≥53 cm; and Females, ≤47 cm, 48 to 52 cm, and ≥53 cm. Comparisons were made between groups one and two and between groups three and two (Table 13-14).

8YR Indexes With few exceptions, group one had a somewhat higher percentage of failure for all indexes than group two for each race and sex. Group three had failure rates closer to group two than group one. Black Males in group three had a lower percentage of failure than Black Males in groups one or two. This finding is in basic agreement with Fisch et al. (1976), who found that greater weight, height, and head circumference were observed at four and seven years of age in children with superior intelligence as measured at seven years of age.

Table **13-13**

Failure rate (%) by weight/height ratio at four years.

	White						Black					
	Males			Females			Males			Females		
Indexes	0.0-.146	.147-.184	.185-1.0	0.0-.142	.143-.181	.182-1.0	0.0-.142	.143-.179	.180-1.0	0.0-.136	.137-.177	.178-1.0
8YR Speech Mechanism	5.6	4.6	4.8	4.1	2.5	1.5	5.9	5.6	5.7	7.0	3.6	4.7
8YR Palatal Function and Hypernasality	5.3	3.0	1.4	3.9	2.9	2.5	3.6	1.6	0.7	1.0	1.5	1.6
8YR Fluency	2.9	3.6	2.9	1.6	1.8	1.5	8.7	7.1	10.0	5.1	4.4	3.6
8YR Articulation	16.7	12.8	11.9	9.3	7.9	5.7	21.8	18.7	16.5	13.4	9.6	7.0
8YR Intelligibility	5.0	4.3	4.0	3.9	1.7	1.2	12.1	8.7	8.2	7.3	4.6	3.9
8YR Language Comprehension	3.4	3.2	4.8	8.1	6.0	6.2	18.0	15.6	11.0	26.1	17.6	17.7
8YR Auditory Memory	8.6	6.1	6.5	11.7	7.3	6.7	17.2	13.7	11.1	17.8	12.4	11.0
8YR Digits	18.9	12.6	8.9	15.2	8.7	6.9	18.3	13.8	12.2	13.3	10.2	4.4
8YR Word Identification	3.7	1.2	2.1	8.9	3.4	3.2	25.6	16.8	11.2	38.1	27.8	18.0
8YR Written Communication	15.1	8.5	6.4	7.7	3.9	3.8	27.4	19.7	16.0	14.5	8.8	5.2
8YR Language Production	7.4	4.5	5.2	6.4	3.7	3.5	20.3	18.7	15.1	17.5	14.8	11.9
8YR Concept Development	5.6	3.2	4.8	6.0	3.2	3.0	29.0	22.0	16.3	28.1	18.7	10.2
8YR Hearing Severity	6.4	5.8	7.6	5.1	4.6	3.7	5.9	5.1	5.0	5.4	4.4	4.1
Neurological Involvement	13.4	11.3	11.1	10.9	7.5	6.9	15.4	15.2	14.6	11.6	11.0	11.5
Communicative Effectiveness	6.3	2.9	2.2	4.6	2.8	2.5	29.1	22.4	14.2	27.9	14.3	10.2
Auditory Processing	7.2	4.7	3.4	7.4	3.7	3.5	30.1	24.7	16.1	22.8	15.3	9.6

Table **13-14**

Failure rate (%) by head circumference (cm) at four years of age.

	White						Black					
	Males			Females			Males			Females		
Indexes	≤48	49-52	≥53	≤47	48-52	≥53	≤48	49-52	≥53	≤47	48-52	≥53
8YR Speech Mechanism	5.4	4.7	4.1	5.6	2.3	2.6	6.4	5.6	4.2	7.0	3.8	4.5
8YR Palatal Function and Hypernasality	3.7	3.1	2.7	5.6	2.8	1.3	2.0	1.8	1.0	0.4	1.5	0.6
8YR Fluency	2.3	3.5	3.8	3.4	1.6	3.8	8.0	7.4	9.0	4.9	4.2	7.1
8YR Articulation	14.8	12.8	12.9	11.6	7.5	11.5	22.3	18.7	13.2	15.3	9.4	7.1
8YR Intelligibility	5.7	4.2	4.1	5.6	1.5	2.6	14.4	8.5	5.2	8.0	4.7	3.2
8YR Language Comprehension	5.7	3.2	3.0	13.2	5.8	3.9	18.7	15.1	12.7	19.0	18.5	17.5
8YR Auditory Memory	9.9	6.1	6.6	16.9	7.0	6.5	17.6	13.7	8.6	18.5	12.3	14.2
8YR Digits	22.8	12.3	9.3	19.6	8.5	6.4	21.7	13.5	7.1	16.1	9.5	8.4
8YR Word Identification	5.7	1.2	1.7	12.0	3.3	1.3	23.6	16.5	13.7	37.9	27.4	22.1
8YR Written Communication	21.5	8.3	5.1	10.2	3.9	5.2	32.3	18.7	14.7	20.3	8.4	5.4
8YR Language Production	7.6	4.7	3.9	12.9	3.3	3.8	25.9	17.9	11.5	23.7	14.3	11.1
8YR Concept Development	8.1	3.2	3.9	11.6	2.9	2.6	28.5	21.7	16.3	27.3	18.4	13.0
8YR Hearing Severity	7.4	6.1	4.9	8.9	4.3	2.6	3.5	5.4	5.2	7.7	4.2	4.6

Seven Year Measurements

Weight and Height

Children were measured wearing only underpants and a hospital gown. Correlation coefficients (Table 13-15) between 7YR weight and 8YR SLH indexes were uniformly low. The only correlations which exceeded .10 were with Concept Development (.11), Word Identification (.14), and Auditory Processing (.11). All correlations between 7YR height and 8YR SLH indexes fell below .10.

Weight/Height Ratio Index

Children were divided into three groups according to their weight/height ratio: group one, lowest decile; group two, middle 80%; and group three, highest decile. Comparisons were made between groups one and two and between groups three and two (Table 13-15).

Group one had a higher percentage of failure than group two on all but one index (8YR Fluency, White Males). Group three had a lower percentage of failure than group two on almost all indexes.

Head Circumference

Children were divided into three groups according to 7YR occipito-frontal circumference: group one, ≤49 cm (lowest decile); group two, 50 to 53 cm; and group three, ≥54 cm (highest decile). Comparisons were made between groups one and two and between groups three and two (Table 13-16). Group one had a higher percentage of failure than group two on almost all indexes. Group three had a lower percentage of failure on more of the indexes than group two.

Conclusions

Among the growth measurements from birth on, small head size appears to be the strongest correlate of poor performance. Weight had a low correlation, and height alone had a negligible correlation with 3YR and 8YR SLH performance. On the 8YR SLH examinations, children who were lean at four and seven years of age performed somewhat more poorly, that is, had higher failure rate, and the children who were obese at four and seven years of age performed somewhat better than the children of medium weight in group two. This finding supports previous observations of a relationship between 4YR and 7YR IQ and body habitus of the Collaborative Study children (Fisch, Bilek, and Ulstrom, 1975).

Neurological Abnormalities

One Year of Age

Children were divided into two groups based on the results of neurological examination at one year and on other medical records obtained during the first year of life. Group one were children with definite neurological abnormality; group two were children who were neurologically normal (Table 13-17). Group one had a slightly higher probability of failure on all indexes regardless of race, sex, or SEI. Correlations between SLH indexes and neurological abnormality did not exceed .15 for any index.

Seven Years of Age

Children were divided according to results of neurological examination at age seven. Group one was composed of children with definite neurological abnormality, and group two of children who were neurologically normal or only suspected of abnormality. Both groups were compared (Table 13-18). Group one had a somewhat higher probability of failure than group two on all 8YR indexes, a probability of failure approximately two to three times greater than group two on all indexes. The results of this analysis

Table **13-15**

Failure rate (%) by weight/height ratio at seven years of age.

	White						Black					
	Males			Females			Males			Females		
Indexes	0.0-.170	.171-.224	.225-1.0	0.0-.165	.166-.227	.228-1.0	0.0-.167	.168-.220	.221-1.0	0.0-.160	.161-.225	.226-1.0
8YR Speech Mechanism	5.0	4.6	4.4	3.6	2.6	2.1	6.9	5.6	4.4	6.7	3.5	4.7
8YR Palatal Function & Hypernasality	5.2	3.3	1.2	4.0	3.0	2.5	2.5	1.6	1.5	1.6	1.3	2.0
8YR Fluency	2.3	3.7	3.4	2.5	1.7	1.2	9.9	7.3	9.3	8.0	4.5	3.4
8YR Articulation	16.9	13.1	11.4	10.1	7.6	5.7	26.1	18.2	15.4	15.1	9.8	6.5
8YR Intelligibility	5.5	4.6	5.8	2.9	1.9	2.0	17.6	8.8	7.2	7.3	5.0	3.2
8YR Language Comprehension	4.2	3.6	2.2	9.3	5.8	5.8	20.5	15.1	9.8	27.8	17.1	11.5
8YR Auditory Memory	8.3	6.5	5.4	10.9	7.2	6.5	20.1	13.9	8.8	21.1	11.8	8.4
8YR Digits	20.6	12.9	8.6	13.5	9.2	9.7	19.6	13.5	10.6	14.8	9.8	7.0
8YR Word Identification	3.4	1.6	1.6	8.1	3.9	2.7	28.3	16.2	7.4	36.9	27.5	14.7
8YR Written Communication	15.1	9.3	6.6	7.9	4.5	3.8	30.8	20.1	12.6	15.0	9.2	3.1
8YR Language Production	6.4	5.1	4.7	6.8	3.9	5.0	25.8	18.0	11.9	18.4	14.8	10.6
8YR Concept Development	6.0	3.8	3.7	6.0	3.4	3.3	34.6	20.8	11.1	28.3	18.3	8.6
8YR Hearing Severity	8.2	6.0	6.3	5.4	4.7	3.3	7.5	4.9	2.5	5.4	4.4	3.7
Neurological Involvement	15.9	11.1	12.2	8.4	8.3	7.2	17.1	14.7	14.9	12.1	11.0	9.6
Communicative Effectiveness	6.2	3.5	2.1	5.4	2.9	2.1	35.1	21.6	11.1	25.6	14.9	7.2
Auditory Processing	8.5	5.1	4.2	7.5	4.2	3.1	37.8	23.0	15.0	24.5	15.1	7.7

Table 13-16

Failure rate (%) by head circumference (cm) at seven years of age.

| | White | | | | | | Black | | | | | |
| | Males | | | Females | | | Males | | | Females | | |
Indexes	≤49	50-53	≥54	≤49	50-52	≥53	≤49	50-53	≥54	≤49	50-53	≥54
8YR Speech Mechanism	8.5	4.6	3.9	4.1	2.4	3.1	5.8	5.6	5.7	5.2	3.7	5.1
8YR Palatal Function & Hypernasality	9.0	3.1	2.8	5.1	2.6	3.1	2.6	1.6	1.9	1.0	1.5	1.0
8YR Fluency	2.4	3.5	4.1	2.0	1.5	2.3	6.6	7.8	7.8	4.9	4.6	5.8
8YR Articulation	19.0	13.2	12.7	10.5	7.0	8.1	24.2	18.0	19.4	14.7	9.5	7.8
8YR Intelligibility	7.6	4.7	5.3	4.2	1.6	2.1	15.0	9.2	8.0	7.3	4.8	3.8
8YR Language Comprehension	6.7	3.7	1.9	10.9	5.6	4.3	20.4	14.5	14.4	21.4	17.5	12.1
8YR Auditory Memory	16.1	6.4	5.3	14.1	6.6	5.9	19.3	13.7	11.8	15.8	12.3	7.2
8YR Digits	31.0	13.2	8.5	16.1	8.8	7.6	20.7	13.5	10.9	14.1	9.6	6.8
8YR Word Identification	6.7	1.7	0.9	10.2	3.4	2.0	25.7	16.0	13.3	34.5	26.8	17.5
8YR Written Communication	25.5	9.6	6.2	10.6	3.7	3.8	35.5	19.8	12.7	18.5	8.2	3.2
8YR Language Production	10.9	5.1	4.6	8.6	3.7	3.1	25.3	17.8	14.6	19.4	14.4	9.9
8YR Concept Development	12.6	3.7	3.4	8.8	2.8	2.8	30.6	20.8	15.7	25.7	17.7	11.6
8YR Hearing Severity	10.6	6.1	5.7	5.8	4.6	3.5	5.6	4.7	6.0	4.5	4.6	2.4
Neurological Involvement	15.1	11.3	12.8	11.9	7.5	7.7	17.6	14.6	16.2	14.4	10.3	11.2
Communicative Effectiveness	9.5	3.6	2.2	7.6	2.3	1.7	34.8	21.3	15.8	25.5	14.0	9.9
Auditory Processing	16.0	5.3	3.3	11.1	3.3	2.8	35.7	23.1	17.8	24.3	14.5	7.6

Table **13-17**

Correlations and conditional probabilities for SLH indexes and neurological abnormalities at one year.

Indexes (F2)	r	Abnormal (F1) p(F2/F1)*	Normal (P1) p(F2/P1)*
3YR Speech Mechanism	<.10	.30	.23
3YR Hypernasality	<.10	.09	.05
3YR Fluency	<.10	.17	.13
3YR Articulation	<.10	.27	.19
3YR Intelligibility	−.10	.13	.07
3YR Language Comprehension	−.11	.18	.11
3YR Sentence Complexity	−.15	.22	.14
3YR Auditory Memory	<.10	.37	.31
3YR Hearing Severity	<.10	.23	.17
8YR Speech Mechanism	<.10	.08	.05
8YR Palatal Function and Hypernasality	<.10	.05	.03
8YR Fluency	<.10	.07	.05
8YR Articulation	−.11	.17	.12
8YR Intelligibility	−.10	.10	.05
8YR Language Comprehension	<.10	.16	.11
8YR Auditory Memory	<.10	.16	.11
8YR Digits	<.10	.16	.12
8YR Word Identification	−.12	.17	.13
8YR Written Communication	−.11	.21	.14
8YR Language Production	−.10	.18	.11
8YR Concept Development	−.12	.18	.12
8YR Hearing Severity	<.10	.17	.14
8YR Total Conductive Loss	<.10	.09	.07
8YR Total Sensorineural Loss	<.10	.05	.03
Neurological Involvement	<.10	.22	.17
Communicative Effectiveness	−.13	.14	.09
Auditory Processing	−.11	.12	.09

*p(F2/F1) and p(F2/P1) refer to the probability of failing the SLH index (F2) when the antecedent variable was failed (F1) or passed (P1).

indicate that the seven year neurological examination is a better predictor of later SLH performance than the one year neurological examination.

Summary

The following factors appeared to be associated favorably with SLH performance: maternal age ≥18 years; lower parity; maternal height >61 in; weight gain during pregnancy from 15 to 25 pounds; full-term neonate; birthweight ≥2500 grams; larger head circumference (at birth and later age); obesity; and normal neurological findings.

The following factors seemed unfavorably associated with SLH performance: maternal age <18 years; higher parity; maternal height ≤60 in; weight gain during pregnancy <15 pounds or >25 pounds; maternal mental retardation; prematurity; high forceps used; birthweight <2500 grams; microcephaly (at birth and later age); leanness; and abnormal neurological findings.

Females in each race performed better than corresponding Males on the SLH examination.

References

1. Bayley, N. *COLR Research Form of the Bayley Scales of Mental and Motor Development*. Bethesda, Maryland: Perinatal

Table **13-18**

Correlations and conditional probabilities for 8YR SLH indexes and neurological abnormalities at seven years of age.

Indexes (F2)		Abnormal (F1)	Normal (P1)
	r	p(F2/F1)*	p(F2/P1)*
8YR Speech Mechanism	<.10	.11	.05
8YR Palatal Function and Hypernasality	<.10	.07	.03
8YR Fluency	<.10	.10	.05
8YR Articulation	−.21	.27	.11
8YR Intelligibility	−.22	.17	.05
8YR Language Comprehension	<.10	.20	.11
8YR Auditory Memory	−.15	.24	.10
8YR Digits	−.13	.24	.11
8YR Word Identification	−.14	.23	.12
8YR Written Communication	−.20	.34	.12
8YR Language Production	−.17	.27	.11
8YR Concept Development	−.18	.28	.11
8YR Hearing Severity	<.10	.21	.14
8YR Total Conductive Loss	<.10	.12	.06
8YR Total Sensorineural Loss	<.10	.08	.03
Neurological Involvement	<.10	.27	.17
Communicative Effectiveness	−.17	.24	.08
Auditory Processing	−.19	.15	.09

*p(F2/F1) and p(F2/P1) refer to the probability of failing the SLH index (F2) when the antecedent variable was failed (F1) or passed (P1).

Research Branch, NINDB-NIH, 1958.

2. Boggs, T., Hardy, J., and Frazier, T. Correlation of neonatal serum total bilirubin concentrations and developmental status at age eight months. *J. Pediatr.* 71:553–560, 1967.

3. Broman, S.H., Nichols, P.L., and Kennedy, W.A. *Preschool IQ: Prenatal and Early Developmental Correlates.* Hillsdale, N.J.: Lawrence Erlbaum Associates, 1975.

4. Drage, J.S., Kennedy, C., and Schwarz, B.K. The Apgar score as an index of neonatal mortality. A report from the Collaborative Study of Cerebral Palsy. *Obstet. Gynecol.* 24:222–230, 1964.

5. Fisch, R.O., Bilek, M.K., Horrobin, J.M., and Chang, P.N. Children with superior intelligence at 7 years of age. A prospective study of the influence of perinatal, medical and socioeconomic factors. *Am. J. Dis. Child.* 130:481–487, 1976.

6. Fisch, R.O., Bilek, M., and Ulstrom, R. Obesity and leanness at birth and their relationship to body habitus in later childhood. *Pediatrics* 56:521–528, 1975.

7. Hardy, J., and Peeples, P. Serum bilirubin levels in newborn infants: Distributions and associations with neurological abnormalities during the first year of life. *Johns Hopkins Med. J.* 128:265–272, 1971.

8. Hyman, C.B., Keaster, J., Hanson, V., Harris, E., Sedgwick, R., Wursten, H., and Wright, A.R. CNS abnormalities after neonatal hemolytic disease or hyperbilirubinemia. *Am. J. Dis. Child.* 117:395–405, 1969.

9. Israel, L.S., and Deutschberger, J. Relation of mother's age to obstetric performance. *Obstet. Gynecol.* 24:411–417, 1964.

10. Keaster, J., Hyman, C.B., and Harris, E. Hearing problems subsequent to neonatal hemolytic disease or hyperbilirubinemia. *Am. J. Dis. Child.* 117:406–410, 1969.

11. Nelson, K.B., and Deutschberger,

J. Head size at one year as a predictor of four-year IQ. *Dev. Med. Child. Neurol.* 4:487–495, 1970.

12. Rubin, R.A., Balow, B., and Fisch, R.O. Neonatal serum bilirubin levels related to cognitive development at ages four through seven. In press, *J Pediatr.*, 1979.

13. Scheidt, P.C., Mellits, D.A., Hardy, J.B., Drage, J.S., and Boggs, T. Toxicity to bilirubin in neonates: Infant development during first year in relation to maximum neonatal serum bilirubin concentration. *J. Pediatr.* 91:292–297, 1977.

14. Tyler, L.E. *The Psychology of Human Differences.* New York: Appleton-Century-Crofts, 1956, pp. 247–275.

CHAPTER **14**

Overview: Psychosocial Factors

Dolores K. Vetter, Ph.D.

The variables indicative of socioeconomic level (Appendix 8) have the greatest predictive value of all the potential factors affecting a child's speech, language, and hearing. As described previously (Chapter 4), information about education, income, and other demographic variables was obtained from the mother prior to the birth of the child and again when the child was seven years of age. Education, occupation, and income were combined into a Socioeconomic Index (SEI) similar to the index used by the U.S. Bureau of the Census (Myrianthopoulos and French, 1968).

Comparisons of SEI at birth and SEI at seven years of age indicated that relatively small changes occurred in the seven-year period and that most changes were in the direction of adjacent SEI levels (Table 14-1). These data are comparable to the percentages calculated for the total NCPP population (Nichols, 1976). Children with SEI of 2.0 to 3.9, 4.0 to 5.9, or 6.0 to 7.9 at birth, tended to remain in the same group at seven years of age. If socioeconomic factors changed in their families, the changes did not shift their SEI appreciably. They were usually classified in the adjacent higher or lower socioeconomic group at seven years of age. Almost two-thirds of the children who were in the highest SEI (8.0 to 9.5) at birth remained in that group at seven years of age, while 27.8% shifted down to SEI 6.0 to 7.9 and the remaining 9.3%

Table 14-1

Percentage of 3YR/8YR sample cross-tabulated for Socioeconomic Index at birth and at seven years of age.

7YR SEI	Birth SEI				
	0.0-1.9	2.0-3.9	4.0-5.9	6.0-7.9	8.0-9.5
0.0-1.9	27.7	11.3	4.9	2.0	.3
2.0-3.9	49.9	48.3	28.8	11.2	2.2
4.0-5.9	19.4	32.3	42.5	31.2	6.8
6.0-7.9	3.0	7.3	22.1	43.3	27.8
8.0-9.5	.1	.8	1.7	12.3	62.9

were distributed in the three lowest SEI groups. The greatest changes occurred among the children classified in the lowest SEI group at birth; 27.7% remained in that group at seven years of age and 49.9% rose into the SEI group of 2.0 to 3.9. The residual 22.5% were classified in the other three groups.

These small changes are not surprising when the variables composing the Socioeconomic Index are considered. At the time of registration into the study, the mean education of both mothers and fathers of the study children was about 11 years. Given that mothers had a mean age of 24.2 and fathers a mean age of about 28 years when the study child was born, there is little expectation of change in education since most people have completed their education at these ages. Nichols' data (1976) for the total NCPP population support this proposition. Furthermore, income classification was adjusted for inflation before the SEI was calculated (Nichols, 1976). The similarity between SEI calculated at birth and at seven years is seen in Tables 14-2 and 14-3 where, for the sake of comparison, the percentages of children failing the 8YR indexes is given. Because greater availability of SEI data at birth was anticipated early in the analysis of SLH data, a decision was made to use this earlier SEI classification. The decision received additional support from the similarity in SLH outcomes based on either SEI classi-

fication. Frequency distributions and descriptive statistics presented in previous chapters are based on SEI data obtained at birth.

The association between membership in a particular socioeconomic group and performance on the indexes is demonstrated by the smaller percentages of children failing* in the higher SEI groups (Tables 14-2 and 14-3). Some indexes show a decrease in failures of as much as 25% from the lowest to the highest SEI group; others change very little across SEI. A comparison of the data in Tables 14-2 and 14-3 shows small differences between the two SEI measures; more than two-thirds of the differences are 0.6% or less. Correlations are also virtually identical for both measures. These findings support the notion that SEI effects are stable and long-lasting.

Specific Factors Related to Socioeconomic Level

When multiple regression analyses were done, the variables which composed the SEI were entered as separate independent variables rather than using the SEI as a single independent variable. Therefore, it was possible to evaluate the relative weights of these factors in pre-

---

* Failure was defined as any value falling in the lowest decile, or, in the case of a restricted range, closest to the lowest decile of scores for an index.

Table 14-2

Correlations between SLH indexes and birth Socioeconomic Index and percentages failing each index within each SEI group.

Index	r	Failure rate (%) by Socioeconomic Index at birth				
		0.0-1.9	2.0-3.9	4.0-5.9	6.0-7.9	8.0-9.5
8YR Speech Mechanism	<.10	5.5	4.2	4.5	3.7	2.6
8YR Palatal Function and Hypernasality	<.10	1.9	2.8	2.3	2.3	1.8
8YR Fluency	<.10	6.9	5.1	4.1	3.1	2.7
8YR Articulation	.23	17.7	15.0	11.4	9.3	8.8
8YR Intelligibility	.11	10.1	7.2	5.1	2.9	1.2
8YR Language Comprehension	.33	19.6	15.2	10.2	4.9	1.9
8YR Auditory Memory	.28	17.2	13.7	9.8	5.9	2.4
8YR Digits	.18	16.5	14.4	11.7	8.3	5.7
8YR Word Identification	.51	28.9	19.6	10.8	3.9	.8
8YR Written Communication	.43	21.3	15.6	9.6	4.1	1.3
8YR Language Production	.33	18.9	14.5	9.4	5.9	1.5
8YR Concept Development	.46	25.3	18.8	10.0	3.9	1.2
8YR Hearing Severity	<.10	5.7	5.3	4.8	5.1	4.3
Neurological Involvement	.19	14.0	12.5	9.9	9.1	7.3
Communicative Effectiveness	.47	22.9	16.0	9.3	3.2	.7
Auditory Processing	.43	24.8	17.7	9.8	3.1	.8

Table 14-3

Correlations between SLH indexes and 7YR Socioeconomic Index and percentages failing each index within each SEI group.

Index	r	Failure rate (%) by Socioeconomic Index at 7YR				
		0.0-1.9	2.0-3.9	4.0-5.9	6.0-7.9	8.0-9.5
8YR Speech Mechanism	<.10	5.4	4.8	4.3	3.6	2.6
8YR Palatal Function and Hypernasality	<.10	2.5	2.3	2.5	2.6	2.0
8YR Fluency	<.10	5.8	4.9	4.4	3.2	3.1
8YR Articulation	.23	17.5	15.2	11.4	9.1	8.9
8YR Intelligibility	.10	8.9	7.0	5.1	3.0	1.9
8YR Language Comprehension	.32	19.2	14.7	10.1	5.9	1.9
8YR Auditory Memory	.29	17.2	13.8	9.8	5.8	2.7
8YR Digits	.17	15.5	14.3	12.0	9.1	5.6
8YR Word Identification	.49	26.7	18.8	10.7	4.5	1.0
8YR Written Communication	.42	22.7	16.1	9.4	4.5	1.6
8YR Language Production	.34	18.2	15.0	9.9	5.7	1.8
8YR Concept Development	.45	24.7	18.0	10.1	4.4	1.1
8YR Hearing Severity	<.10	6.1	5.0	5.4	4.7	4.2
Neurological Involvement	.21	15.3	12.7	11.2	10.6	7.0
Communicative Effectiveness	.50	24.1	16.2	8.7	4.0	1.0
Auditory Processing	.49	26.7	18.1	10.6	3.9	.8

dicting a given SLH outcome. In order to provide a fuller evaluation of factors related to SEI and their association with SLH indexes, conditional probabilities were calculated for dichotomous variables and failure rates were calculated for variables having three or more categories.

Education of Mother and of Father

Table 14-4 contains the percentages of children failing each index according to the amount of education the mother had completed prior to the birth of the child. It also contains the correlation between the mother's education and the child's performance on each index. Similarly, Table 14-5 contains failure rates based upon the amount of education of the fa-

ther of the baby. Although the correlations are generally of low magnitude, a study of the tables reveals that the failure rate decreases as the amount of education of either parent increases. The similarity in findings suggests a high correlation between the educational levels of the parents.

It should be noted that all of the indexes except 3YR Fluency and Hearing show decreases in failure rates as parental education increases. The failure rate for 3YR Fluency is the reverse of the rates for other indexes. At age three years the failure rate is highest when the parents had completed 13 years or more of education, but this is not evident when the child is eight years old. This is not an artifact of small sample size. One might

Table **14-4**

Correlations between SLH indexes and education of mother, and percentages of children failing each index relative to mother's education.

Index	r	Years of Mother's Education		
		0-8YRS	9-12YRS	13YRS & Over
3YR Speech Mechanism	<.10	11.2	10.2	6.3
3YR Hypernasality	<.10	1.5	1.2	.6
3YR Fluency	<.10	6.5	7.5	12.0
3YR Articulation	.13	16.7	12.3	6.7
3YR Intelligibility	.14	3.8	2.4	.9
3YR Language Comprehension	.16	12.2	8.2	3.1
3YR Sentence Complexity	<.10	11.5	10.0	4.1
3YR Auditory Memory	<.10	16.8	16.1	9.0
3YR Hearing Screen	<.10	11.6	11.9	12.3
8YR Speech Mechanism	<.10	5.1	4.3	2.7
8YR Palatal Function and Hypernasality	<.10	2.7	2.3	2.2
8YR Fluency	<.10	5.8	4.2	3.3
8YR Articulation	.19	17.7	11.9	8.9
8YR Intelligibility	.11	9.8	4.8	2.2
8YR Language Comprehension	.28	17.8	10.5	2.6
8YR Auditory Memory	.26	16.5	10.2	2.4
8YR Digits	.16	16.6	11.8	5.3
8YR Word Identification	.42	25.0	11.7	1.9
8YR Written Communication	.36	21.2	10.3	2.0
8YR Language Production	.30	19.0	10.0	2.5
8YR Concept Development	.38	22.5	11.4	1.8
8YR Hearing Severity	<.10	5.5	5.2	4.2
Neurological Involvement	.18	14.5	11.5	7.4
Communicative Effectiveness	.42	21.1	10.2	1.7
Auditory Processing	.42	24.5	11.5	1.4

Table **14-5**

Correlations between SLH indexes and education of father, and percentages of children failing each index relative to father's education.

| Index | r | Years of Father's Education | | |
		0-8YRS	9-12YRS	13YRS & Over
3YR Speech Mechanism	<.10	12.0	9.9	6.8
3YR Hypernasality	<.10	1.2	1.4	.6
3YR Fluency	<.10	6.5	7.6	12.7
3YR Articulation	.14	16.8	12.1	6.9
3YR Intelligibility	.14	3.5	2.4	1.1
3YR Language Comprehension	.16	11.1	8.6	3.0
3YR Sentence Complexity	<.10	11.8	9.4	4.1
3YR Auditory Memory	<.10	17.9	15.5	9.4
3YR Hearing Screen	<.10	11.8	12.0	11.9
8YR Speech Mechanism	<.10	4.8	4.3	2.6
8YR Palatal Function and Hypernasality	<.10	2.5	2.3	2.1
8YR Fluency	<.10	6.0	3.8	3.3
8YR Articulation	.19	17.1	11.3	8.9
8YR Intelligibility	<.10	8.4	4.6	1.8
8YR Language Comprehension	.29	15.4	10.3	2.6
8YR Auditory Memory	.27	15.4	10.0	3.1
8YR Digits	.16	16.3	11.2	6.0
8YR Word Identification	.43	19.5	11.3	1.9
8YR Written Communication	.37	17.8	9.6	2.0
8YR Language Production	.31	16.6	9.8	2.5
8YR Concept Development	.38	18.8	10.6	2.4
8YR Hearing Severity	<.10	6.6	5.0	4.5
Neurological Involvement	.17	13.5	11.0	8.0
Communicative Effectiveness	.43	17.9	9.6	1.6
Auditory Processing	.42	19.5	10.6	1.8

speculate that the high percentage of failure in three-year-old children of parents with the most education, and therefore the higher socioeconomic level, is due to increased parental stress on fluency at this time in the child's life (Morgenstern, 1956). In any case, the effect is transient except for a small number of children.

Education of the mother and of the father were entered as independent variables in the multiple regression analyses (Appendix 8). Prediction of outcomes for the 3YR indexes was not generally successful. For those indexes mentioned previously as being particularly sensitive to parental education, however, the beta weights of either or both of these variables tended to be larger than other independent variables in the equations. For the 8YR indexes, the beta weights were considerably larger than they were for the 3YR indexes. In general, the Race-Sex Markers were the only independent variables which were weighted more heavily in the prediction equations than was the education of the parents.

Occupation of Father (White-Collar)
and Per Capita Income

Since the father's occupation and income are correlated, these variables will be discussed together. Tables 14-6 and 14-7 contain the correlations and cross-tabulations between Occupation of the Father (Table 14-6) and Per Capita Income (Table 14-7) and various SLH outcomes. The correlations with Per Capita Income are slightly larger than those with the Occupation of the Father (White-Collar)

Table 14-6

Correlations and conditional probabilities for SLH indexes and Occupation of Father: White Collar.

Index	r	p(F2/F1)*	p(F2/P1)*
3YR Speech Mechanism	<.10	.27	.20
3YR Hypernasality	<.10	.07	.03
3YR Fluency	<.10	.14	.16
3YR Articulation	.11	.24	.14
3YR Intelligibility	.11	.10	.05
3YR Language Comprehension	.16	.15	.06
3YR Sentence Complexity	<.10	.17	.10
3YR Auditory Memory	<.10	.35	.25
3YR Hearing Screen	<.10	.20	.16
8YR Speech Mechanism	<.10	.06	.04
8YR Palatal Function and Hypernasality	<.10	.04	.03
8YR Fluency	<.10	.06	.04
8YR Articulation	.13	.14	.10
8YR Intelligibility	<.10	.07	.03
8YR Language Comprehension	.23	.14	.06
8YR Auditory Memory	.21	.14	.06
8YR Digits	.15	.14	.08
8YR Word Identification	.36	.16	.05
8YR Written Communication	.31	.18	.09
8YR Language Production	.25	.15	.06
8YR Concept Development	.33	.16	.05
8YR Hearing Severity	<.10	.16	.12
8YR Total Conductive Loss	<.10	.07	.07
8YR Total Sensorineural Loss	<.10	.04	.03
Neurological Involvement	.16	.20	.14
Communicative Effectiveness	.37	.12	.03
Auditory Processing	.36	.10	.08

*p(F2/F1) and p(F2/P1) refer to the probability of failing the SLH index (F2) when the antecedent variable is failed (F1) or passed (P1).

probably because the former variable was continuous while the latter was discrete. The restricted variability tended to slightly lower the correlations with the Occupation of the Father (White-Collar). The highest correlations were obtained with 8YR Word Identification (Peabody Picture Vocabulary Test, Dunn, 1965) as a key variable and with other indexes which had Word Identification as a component. Since the Peabody Picture Vocabulary Test (PPVT) is known to be sensitive to socioeconomic level (Milgram and Ozer, 1967; Jeruchimowicz, Costello, and Bagur, 1971; Teasdale and Katz, 1968), the magnitudes of these correlations were not unexpected.

For the purpose of calculating conditional probabilities, father's occupation and Per Capita Income were dichotomized. Occupation of the Father was separated into white-collar workers and all others. Per Capita Income was divided at $901; that is, those families whose annual income was $900 or less per person were considered to have low per capita income, those with $901 or higher were placed in the remaining income group. This point was chosen because it was consistent with the poverty level established by governmental agencies.

The cross-tabulations indicate that when the child is three years of age he seems to be at slightly greater risk on 3YR Intelligibility, 3YR Articulation, 3YR Language Comprehension, and 3YR Sen-

Table **14-7**

Correlations and conditional probabilities for SLH indexes and Per Capita Income at Birth.

Index	r	p(F2/F1)*	p(F2/P1)*
3YR Speech Mechanism	<.10	.27	.22
3YR Hypernasality	<.10	.08	.04
3YR Fluency	<.10	.15	.14
3YR Articulation	.14	.25	.17
3YR Intelligibility	.11	.11	.07
3YR Language Comprehension	.14	.16	.09
3YR Sentence Complexity	<.10	.19	.13
3YR Auditory Memory	<.10	.35	.29
8YR Speech Mechanism	<.10	.07	.05
8YR Palatal Function and Hypernasality	<.10	.05	.03
8YR Fluency	<.10	.07	.05
8YR Articulation	.20	.17	.10
8YR Intelligibility	<.10	.09	.04
8YR Language Comprehension	.27	.18	.08
8YR Auditory Memory	.21	.16	.08
8YR Digits	.11	.16	.10
8YR Word Identification	.41	.22	.07
8YR Written Communication	.35	.22	.10
8YR Language Production	.27	.19	.08
8YR Concept Development	.37	.21	.07
Neurological Involvement	.16	.21	.16
Communicative Effectiveness	.42	.17	.04
Auditory Processing	.40	.11	.09

*p(F2/F1) and p(F2/P1) refer to the probability of failing the SLH index (F2) when the antecedent variable is failed (F1) or passed (P1).

tence Complexity if his father was not a white-collar worker or if the Per Capita Income for the family was low. When the child is eight years of age, the risk is still at least double that he will fail 8YR Intelligibility, 8YR Language Comprehension, 8YR Auditory Memory, 8YR Word Identification, 8YR Written Communication, 8YR Language Production, 8YR Concept Development, and Communicative Effectiveness if his father is not a white-collar worker or if Per Capita Income is low. Occupation of the Father and Per Capita Income tended to have their highest beta weights in those multiple regression equations used in predicting the 8YR indexes mentioned above.

Housing Density

Housing Density was a variable indicating the number of people per room in the child's dwelling, essentially an index of overcrowding. After consideration of the British Perinatal Study (Davie, Butler, and Goldstein, 1972) and other literature (Bloom, Whiteman, and Deutsch, 1967), it was decided to use the value of 1.5 as the cutoff for Housing Density (that is, if there were more than 1.5 persons per room, the house was considered overcrowded). Table 14-8 contains the correlations and cross-tabulations for Housing Density and a number of SLH outcomes. For 3YR and 8YR Articulation, 3YR and 8YR Language Comprehension, 8YR Auditory Memory, 8YR Word Identification, 8YR Written Communication, 8YR Language Production, 8YR Concept Development, and the three Task Force indexes the correlations range from -.10 to -.36 with the majority greater than -.25. These findings are in accord with Deutsch (1967), who has suggested that as over-

Table 14-8

Correlations and conditional probabilities for SLH indexes and Housing Density (overcrowding).

Index	r	p(F2/F1)*	p(F2/P1)*
3YR Speech Mechanism	<.10	.27	.24
3YR Hypernasality	<.10	.08	.05
3YR Fluency	<.10	.16	.14
3YR Articulation	−.14	.27	.19
3YR Intelligibility	<.10	.11	.08
3YR Language Comprehension	−.10	.16	.11
3YR Sentence Complexity	<.10	.18	.15
3YR Auditory Memory	<.10	.32	.33
3YR Hearing Screen	<.10	.18	.19
8YR Speech Mechanism	<.10	.07	.05
8YR Palatal Function and Hypernasality	<.10	.04	.04
8YR Fluency	<.10	.08	.05
8YR Articulation	−.22	.18	.12
8YR Intelligibility	<.10	.10	.05
8YR Language Comprehension	−.25	.20	.10
8YR Auditory Memory	−.20	.18	.10
8YR Digits	<.10	.16	.11
8YR Word Identification	−.36	.26	.10
8YR Written Communication	−.25	.23	.14
8YR Language Production	−.24	.21	.11
8YR Concept Development	−.33	.24	.10
8YR Hearing Severity	<.10	.18	.14
8YR Total Conductive Loss	<.10	.07	.07
8YR Total Sensorineural Loss	<.10	.05	.04
Neurological Involvement	−.13	.22	.17
Communicative Effectiveness	−.33	.20	.07
Auditory Processing	−.34	.11	.09

*p(F2/F1) and p(F2/P1) refer to the probability of failing the SLH index (F2) when the antecedent variable is failed (F1) or passed (P1).

crowding increases, performance worsens on speech and language tasks. The conditional probabilities bear out these associations by indicating that the risk of failing any of the above indexes is at least 1.5 times greater if there is overcrowding than if Housing Density is less than 1.5. Housing Density was not entered into the multiple regression analyses since it did not have an average absolute correlation with the SLH indexes greater than .10 (Chapter 5 and Appendix 7).

Psychological Measurements at 8 Months

At eight months of age the children in the NINCDS Collaborative Perinatal Project (NCPP) were given the research form of the Bayley Infant Scales of Mental and Motor Development and judgments were made of fine and gross motor development. The procedure for administering the Bayley Test was well standardized and structured (Bayley, 1958, 1969). The judgments of motor development were based upon observation of the child during the entire eight-month psychological evaluation and were made on a four-point scale: abnormal, suspect, normal, and advanced.

Fine and Gross Motor Development

Correlations and cross-tabulations for judgments of gross and fine motor development are presented in Tables 14-9 and

Table *14-9*

Correlations and conditional probabilities for SLH indexes and gross motor development at eight months of age.

Index	r	p(F2/F1)*	p(F2/P1)*
3YR Speech Mechanism	<.10	.14	.09
3YR Hypernasality	<.10	.02	.01
3YR Fluency	<.10	.09	.08
3YR Articulation	<.10	.20	.11
3YR Intelligibility	−.13	.06	.02
3YR Language Comprehension	−.13	.15	.07
3YR Sentence Complexity	−.15	.18	.08
3YR Auditory Memory	<.10	.20	.15
3YR Hearing Screen	<.10	.13	.11
8YR Speech Mechanism	<.10	.07	.04
8YR Palatal Function and Hypernasality	<.10	.04	.02
8YR Fluency	<.10	.06	.04
8YR Articulation	−.13	.20	.11
8YR Intelligibility	−.13	.11	.04
8YR Language Comprehension	−.10	.15	.10
8YR Auditory Memory	−.11	.17	.09
8YR Digits	<.10	.18	.10
8YR Word Identification	−.14	.17	.12
8YR Written Communication	−.13	.20	.09
8YR Language Production	−.14	.17	.09
8YR Concept Development	−.14	.19	.10
8YR Hearing Severity	<.10	.19	.15
8YR Total Conductive Loss	<.10	.07	.05
8YR Total Sensorineural Loss	<.10	.03	.02
Neurological Involvement	<.10	.14	.11
Communicative Effectiveness	−.14	.18	.10

*p(F2/F1) and p(F2/P1) refer to the probability of failing the SLH index (F2) when the antecedent variable is failed (F1) or passed (P1).

14-10. The correlations are small ($\leq |.15|$) for both variables and the conditional probabilities are also unremarkable. These findings are consistent with an earlier NINCDS Collaborative Perinatal Project study (Broman, Nichols, and Kennedy, 1975) in which the judgments of gross and fine motor development did not qualify for use as predictors of 4YR IQ.

Bayley Scales of Mental and Motor Development

Tables 14-11 and 14-12 contain the correlations and cross-tabulations for the Bayley Mental and Motor Scales with SLH outcomes. The correlations range from less than .10 to .17. These values are only slightly lower than correlations with 4YR IQ reported by Broman et al. (1975).

The data were cross-tabulated after dichotomizing the Bayley Mental and Motor Scores. The arbitrary cutoffs chosen were about one standard deviation below the means of the two scales. Therefore, a child had to score above 74 on the Mental Scale and above 27 on the Motor Scale in order to be tabulated in the pass group. If a child failed the Bayley Motor Scale, there was twice the risk that he would fail 3YR and 8YR Intelligibility, 3YR Language Comprehension, 3YR Sentence Complexity, 8YR Written Communication, 8YR Language Production, and 8YR Concept Development than if he passed the Motor Scale (Table 14-11). Similar findings are presented in Table

Table 14-10

Correlations and conditional probabilities for SLH indexes and fine motor development at eight months of age.

Index	r	p(F2/F1)*	p(F2/P1)*
3YR Speech Mechanism	<.10	.14	.10
3YR Hypernasality	<.10	.02	.01
3YR Fluency	<.10	.08	.08
3YR Articulation	<.10	.19	.11
3YR Intelligibility	−.13	.06	.02
3YR Language Comprehension	−.12	.15	.07
3YR Sentence Complexity	−.14	.18	.08
3YR Auditory Memory	<.10	.19	.15
3YR Hearing Screen	<.10	.13	.11
8YR Speech Mechanism	<.10	.06	.04
8YR Palatal Function and Hypernasality	<.10	.03	.02
8YR Fluency	<.10	.06	.04
8YR Articulation	−.12	.19	.12
8YR Intelligibility	−.12	.10	.04
8YR Language Comprehension	<.10	.15	.10
8YR Auditory Memory	−.11	.16	.09
8YR Digits	<.10	.18	.11
8YR Word Identification	−.13	.18	.11
8YR Written Communication	−.13	.20	.09
8YR Language Production	−.13	.18	.09
8YR Concept Development	−.13	.19	.11
8YR Hearing Severity	<.10	.21	.15
8YR Total Conductive Loss	<.10	.07	.05
8YR Total Sensorineural Loss	<.10	.04	.02
Neurological Involvement	<.10	.15	.11
Communicative Effectiveness	−.14	.19	.09

*p(F2/F1) and p(F2/P1) refer to the probability of failing the SLH index (F2) when the antecedent variable is failed (F1) or passed (P1).

14-12 for the Bayley Mental Scale except that performance on 8YR Language Comprehension, 8YR Word Identification, and 8YR Auditory Memory is also at increased risk.

Previous investigation (Willerman, Broman, and Fiedler, 1970; Ireton, Thwing, and Gravem, 1970) has found that lower performance on the Bayley Scales is associated with lower IQ's at four years of age. Willerman et al. (1970) found that infants in the lowest quartile on the Bayley Mental and Motor Scales comprised 11% of their total population but they comprised 58% of the children with IQ's below 79. They also found that children who came from lower SEI groups were most likely to be retarded than children from higher SEI groups

and that, within each SEI level, infants in the lowest quartile on the Bayley Scales scored consistently lower on 4YR IQ. Ireton et al. (1970) found that they were better able to predict low IQ at four years with the Bayley Mental Scale than with low SEI as the predictor. They also suggest that the relationship between low Mental Scale Score and low IQ cannot be explained by SEI, since in their analysis no relationship between SEI and Mental Scale Score was found. This literature is relevant to the SLH indexes, since intelligence is the variable whose correlations are the highest with the SLH outcomes; and the child's tasks on an intelligence test are similar to the tasks he faces during the speech, language, and hearing evaluations.

Table **14-11**

Correlations and conditional probabilities for SLH indexes and the Bayley Motor Score at eight months of age.

Index	r	p(F2/F1)*	p(F2/P1)*
3YR Speech Mechanism	<.10	.36	.24
3YR Hypernasality	<.10	.12	.05
3YR Fluency	<.10	.22	.13
3YR Articulation	.10	.36	.20
3YR Intelligibility	.13	.20	.08
3YR Language Comprehension	.14	.24	.12
3YR Sentence Complexity	.15	.30	.15
3YR Auditory Memory	<.10	.45	.31
8YR Speech Mechanism	<.10	.10	.05
8YR Palatal Function and Hypernasality	<.10	.06	.04
8YR Fluency	<.10	.09	.06
8YR Articulation	.14	.23	.12
8YR Intelligibility	.13	.14	.05
8YR Language Comprehension	.12	.20	.12
8YR Auditory Memory	.13	.21	.11
8YR Digits	<.10	.21	.12
8YR Word Identification	.16	.22	.13
8YR Written Communication	.13	.28	.14
8YR Language Production	.15	.24	.12
8YR Concept Development	.16	.24	.12
Neurological Involvement	<.10	.24	.18
Communicative Effectiveness	.16	.20	.09
Auditory Processing	.16	.13	.09

*p(F2/F1) and p(F2/P1) refer to the probability of failing the SLH index (F2) when the antecedent variable is failed (F1) or passed (P1).

Items from the Bayley Scales

Several items from the Bayley Scales were of particular interest because of their potential to predict outcomes on the speech, language, and hearing indexes. These items were analyzed individually to assess their value.

Turns Head to Sound of Bell
or to Sound of Rattle

Because of the importance of hearing to speech and language development (DiCarlo, 1964; Dale, 1976), it would be helpful to have an early indicator of potential hearing difficulty. Although head-turning is a developmental stage in localizing sound (Northern and Downs, 1974), it is not purely a test of hearing acuity. It is apparent in Tables 14-13 and 14-14, however, that failure to localize either sound is associated with considerable risk of failure on 3YR and 8YR Speech Mechanism, 3YR Articulation, and 3YR Intelligibility. Failure to localize the sound may be due to factors other than hearing impairment; among other things, it could be the result of mental retardation or neurological disorder. For these analyses, it was not possible to determine why the child did not localize.

A study on a subsample of the NINCDS Collaborative Perinatal Project was conducted by Bordley and Hardy (1972). One of their primary objectives was to determine if they could predict hearing loss on the 8YR SLH examination from responses to broad-spectrum acoustic stimuli at 48 hours, four months, and 12 months. They were unsuccessful in predicting hearing loss inasmuch as 98% of the children failing the hearing

Table **14-12**

Correlations and conditional probabilities for SLH indexes and the Bayley Mental Score
at eight months of age.

Index	r	p(F2/F1)*	p(F2/P1)*
3YR Speech Mechanism	<.10	.33	.24
3YR Hypernasality	<.10	.11	.05
3YR Fluency	<.10	.21	.14
3YR Articulation	<.10	.34	.20
3YR Intelligibility	<.10	.18	.08
3YR Language Comprehension	.12	.23	.12
3YR Sentence Complexity	.14	.26	.15
3YR Auditory Memory	<.10	.41	.32
8YR Speech Mechanism	<.10	.10	.05
8YR Palatal Function and Hypernasality	<.10	.06	.04
8YR Fluency	<.10	.10	.06
8YR Articulation	.15	.23	.13
8YR Intelligibility	.13	.14	.06
8YR Language Comprehension	.11	.23	.11
8YR Auditory Memory	.14	.23	.11
8YR Digits	<.10	.21	.12
8YR Word Identification	.16	.27	.13
8YR Written Communication	.13	.29	.14
8YR Language Production	.11	.24	.12
8YR Concept Development	.17	.29	.12
Neurological Involvement	<.10	.25	.18
Communicative Effectiveness	.16	.22	.09
Auditory Processing	.16	.14	.09

*p(F2/F1) and p(F2/P1) refer to the probability of failing the SLH index (F2) when the antecedent variable is failed (F1)
or passed (P1).

Table **14-13**

Correlations and conditional probabilities for selected SLH indexes and the Bayley item Turns Head
to Sound of Bell at eight months of age.

Index	r	p(F2/F1)*	p(F2/P1)*
3YR Speech Mechanism	<.10	.58	.26
3YR Articulation	<.10	.60	.21
3YR Intelligibility	<.10	.45	.09
8YR Speech Mechanism	<.10	.20	.06

*p(F2/F1) and p(F2/P1) refer to the probability of failing selected SLH indexes (F2) when the antecedent variable is failed (F1)
or passed (P1).

test at eight years of age had given normal responses to the neonatal testing.

Vocalization Items

Previous studies (Cameron, Livson,
and Bayley, 1967; McCall, Hogarty, and
Hurlburt, 1972) have reported significant
correlations between vocalization items
and later intelligence for girls, but not for
boys. Three vocalization items from the
Bayley Scales were among those analyzed for relationship to later speech and
language indexes. Enjoys Sound Production (Table 14-15), Vocalizes to a Social
Stimulus (Table 14-16), and Vocalizes Two

Table **14-14**

Correlations and conditional probabilities for selected SLH indexes and the Bayley item Turns Head to Sound of Rattle at eight months of age.

Index	r	p(F2/F1)*	p(F2/P1)*
3YR Speech Mechanism	<.10	.58	.25
3YR Articulation	<.10	.64	.21
3YR Intelligibility	<.10	.47	.09
8YR Speech Mechanism	<.10	.22	.06

*p(F2/F1) and p(F2/P1) refer to the probability of failing selected SLH indexes (F2) when the antecedent variable is failed (F1) or passed (P1).

Table **14-15**

Correlations and conditional probabilities for selected SLH indexes and the Bayley item Enjoys Sound Production at eight months of age.

Index	r	p(F2/F1)*	p(F2/P1)*
3YR Speech Mechanism	<.10	.36	.24
3YR Language Comprehension	<.10	.25	.12
3YR Sentence Complexity	<.10	.26	.15
8YR Speech Mechanism	<.10	.09	.05
8YR Language Comprehension	−.11	.25	.12
8YR Word Identification	−.14	.32	.13
8YR Language Production	<.10	.23	.13
8YR Concept Development	−.13	.31	.13

*p(F2/F1) and p(F2/P1) refer to the probability of failing selected SLH indexes (F2) when the antecedent variable is failed (F1) or passed (P1).

Table **14-16**

Correlations and conditional probabilities for selected SLH indexes and the Bayley item Vocalizes to Social Stimulus at eight months of age.

Index	r	p(F2/F1)*	p(F2/P1)*
3YR Speech Mechanism	<.10	.63	.25
3YR Language Comprehension	<.10	.50	.13
3YR Sentence Complexity	<.10	.55	.16
8YR Speech Mechanism	<.10	.25	.06
8YR Language Comprehension	<.10	.44	.12
8YR Word Identification	<.10	.50	.14
8YR Language Production	<.10	.42	.13
8YR Concept Development	<.10	.44	.14

*p(F2/F1) and p(F2/P1) refer to the probability of failing selected SLH indexes (F2) when the antecedent variable is failed (F1) or passed (P1).

Syllables (Table 14-17) yielded correlations ranging from less than .10 to −.14 with the various SLH indexes listed. Nevertheless, the risk of failing the index is at least 1.5 times greater if the infant failed the item than if he passed the item. When the cross-tabulations are studied within race and sex (not shown), the risk factor is about the same for Males and Females as it is for the total sample.

Stanford-Binet 4YR IQ

When the child was four years old, he was given the Stanford-Binet Intelligence Scale, Form L-M (Terman and Merrill, 1960). The prenatal and early developmental correlates of this measure have been presented and discussed by Broman et al. (1975). Table 14-18 contains the means and standard deviations for the ALL 3YR, 3YR/8YR, ALL 8YR samples and, for comparison purposes, it also contains the same information from the Broman et al. (1975) study. The means and standard deviations are stable within race-sex groups. The means do not vary more than 2.1 IQ points, and the greatest difference between standard deviations is 0.7. Females and Whites had higher mean IQ's than Males and Blacks. Broman et al. (1975) used race, sex, and socioeconomic status as control variables. They found that the best predictors of 4YR IQ among White children were maternal education, SEI, nonverbal intelligence test score of the mother, Bayley Mental and Motor Scores, number of

Table **14-17**

Correlations and conditional probabilities for selected SLH indexes and the Bayley item Vocalizes Two Syllables at eight months of age.

Index	r	p(F2/F1)*	p(F2/P1)*
3YR Speech Mechanism	<.10	.57	.24
3YR Language Comprehension	<.10	.44	.13
3YR Sentence Complexity	<.10	.51	.16
8YR Speech Mechanism	<.10	.19	.06
8YR Language Comprehension	<.10	.36	.12
8YR Word Identification	<.10	.49	.14
8YR Language Production	<.10	.45	.13
8YR Concept Development	<.10	.43	.14

*p(F2/F1) and p(F2/P1) refer to the probability of failing selected SLH indexes (F2) when the antecedent variable is failed (F1) or passed (P1).

Table **14-18**

Means and standard deviations by race-sex combinations for the ALL 3YR, 3YR/8YR, ALL 8YR and Broman et al. (1975) samples on the 4YR Stanford-Binet IQ Test.

Sample	White Male		White Female		Black Male		Black Female	
	Mean	SD	Mean	SD	Mean	SD	Mean	SD
ALL 3YR	101.1	16.0	104.7	16.6	89.2	13.7	91.5	13.4
3YR/8YR	101.7	16.0	105.5	16.5	89.3	13.6	91.6	13.2
ALL 8YR	103.2	16.1	106.8	16.4	89.9	13.9	91.9	13.7
Broman, et al. (1975)	102.8	16.5	106.5	16.7	90.2	13.9	92.5	13.9

prenatal visits by the mother, and length of gestation at registration for prenatal care. Black children's IQ's were predicted best by the Bayley Mental and Motor Scores, SEI, and maternal education. These factors are also the best predictors of the speech, language, and hearing indexes.

Table 14-19 contains the correlations and conditional probabilities for 4YR IQ and the SLH indexes. Correlations range from .24 to .41 for 3YR Articulation, 3YR Intelligibility, and the two language indexes at three years of age. The conditional probabilities indicate that if the child failed 3YR Articulation, 3YR Intelligibility, 3YR Language Comprehension, or 3YR Sentence Complexity the risk is three to eight times greater that he would have an IQ below 80 at four years of age than if he passed these indexes. It was a rare event for the child to pass any of the 3YR indexes and then to fail (IQ < 80) 4YR IQ. Because the speech, language, and hearing evaluation was administered a year prior to the Stanford-Binet, the 3YR indexes have potential as warning indicators of intellectual deficit. A speech and language pathologist might well consider an intellectual evaluation for a three-year-old who had severe problems with articulation, language comprehension, or language production. These data provide support for such a practice.

When 4YR IQ is used to predict 8YR SLH indexes, correlations range from less than |.10| to |.67|. These are among the stronger associations found in the study.

Table 14-19

Correlations and conditional probabilities for SLH indexes and 4YR IQ (Stanford-Binet).

Index	r	p(F2/F1)*	p(F2/P1)*
3YR Speech Mechanism	.11	.07	.03
3YR Hypernasality	<.10	.08	.04
3YR Fluency	<.10	.02	.04
3YR Articulation	.24	.10	.02
3YR Intelligibility	.33	.25	.03
3YR Language Comprehension	.41	.21	.03
3YR Sentence Complexity	.26	.15	.03
3YR Auditory Memory	.14	.05	.02
3YR Hearing Screen	<.10	.06	.03
8YR Speech Mechanism	<.10	.16	.05
8YR Palatal Function and Hypernasality	<.10	.10	.03
8YR Fluency	<.10	.15	.05
8YR Articulation	.35	.39	.12
8YR Intelligibility	.21	.27	.05
8YR Language Comprehension	.45	.43	.10
8YR Auditory Memory	.48	.49	.10
8YR Digits	.31	.38	.11
8YR Word Identification	.64	.54	.12
8YR Written Communication	.54	.57	.13
8YR Language Production	.48	.51	.11
8YR Concept Development	.65	.63	.11
8YR Hearing Severity	−.13	.33	.20
8YR Total Conductive Loss	<.10	.15	.06
8YR Total Sensorineural Loss	<.10	.10	.03
Neurological Involvement	.27	.33	.17
Communicative Effectiveness	.65	.62	.13
Auditory Processing	.67	.70	.17

*p(F2/F1) and p(F2/P1) refer to the probability of failing the SLH indexes (F2) when the 4YR IQ is failed (F1) or passed (P1).

393

Most of the 8YR indexes show moderate correlations. The conditional probabilities indicate that if a child's IQ is 80 or lower he is at three to five times greater risk of failing 8YR SLH indexes than if his IQ is above 80. An exception is 8YR Hearing Severity; the conditional probabilities are .20 if the child passed 4YR IQ and .33 if he failed 4YR IQ (IQ < 80) that he would fail 8YR Hearing Severity.

The relationship of 4YR IQ to SLH indexes is illustrated in the multiple regression analyses (Appendix 8). The 4YR IQ was not used in the prediction equations for the 3YR SLH indexes because they antedated the administration of the Stanford-Binet, and reverse predictons are not of interest clinically. When 4YR IQ was used to predict 8YR SLH indexes, the beta weights were large. In only two instances, 8YR Palatal Function and Hypernasality and 8YR Fluency, are the beta weights for other independent variables larger; in these cases the Race-Sex Markers are weighted slightly more than 4YR IQ.

Psychological Measurements at Seven Years

At seven years of age the children in the NINCDS Collaborative Perinatal Project received the Wide Range Achievement Test (WRAT) (Jastak and Jastak, 1965), the Goodenough-Harris Drawing Test (Harris, 1963), the Bender Gestalt Test (Koppitz, 1964), the Auditory-Vocal Association subtest of the Illinois Test of Psycholinguistic Abilities (ITPA) (McCarthy and Kirk, 1963), and the Wechsler Intelligence Scale for Children (WISC) (Wechsler, 1949). Performance on these tests was of particular interest since the children were just getting started in school and academic achievement as well as intelligence could be evaluated. The WRAT Spelling and Reading Scores from the 7YR psychological testing were included in the construction of 8YR Written Communication (Chapter 12); because of its standardiza-

tion, this achievement test was thought to yield reliable measures and would increase the stability of the index as well as extend its range.

Auditory-Vocal Association Test

The Auditory-Vocal Association subtest of the experimental version of the ITPA (McCarthy and Kirk, 1963) is essentially a verbal analogies test. Previous research has found that subtests using the auditory-vocal channel are more affected by social class than are those using the visual-motor channel (Mittler and Ward, 1970; Teasdale and Katz, 1968). Sex differences are normally not found on the subtest (McCarthy and Kirk, 1963). Kirk (1972) reported that Ryckman (1965) found that performance of Black children is best on the Auditory-Vocal Sequential Memory subtest; performance on the Auditory-Vocal Association subtest appears to be at age level for middle class Black children; lower class Black children perform more poorly.

Table 14-20 contains the correlations and conditional probabilities for the Auditory-Vocal Association subtest and the 8YR SLH indexes. Correlations range from less than .10 to .71. Indexes reflecting articulation, receptive and expressive language abilities, auditory memory, and written communication have the higher correlations. The magnitude of the correlations are similar to those of comparable variables reported by McCarthy and Olson (1964). The mean for the seven-year-old children of the standardization sample used by McCarthy and Kirk (1963) was 18.92 with a standard deviation of 3.15. When the cross-tabulations were prepared, a raw score of 13 or less, about two standard deviations below the mean, was designated a fail while a raw score of 14 and above was a pass. If a child failed the Auditory-Vocal Association Test, the risk was from two and a half to five times greater that he would fail one of the previously mentioned in-

Table **14-20**

Correlations and conditional probabilities for selected SLH indexes and the Auditory-Vocal Association subtest at seven years of age.

Index	r	p(F2/F1)*	p(F2/P1)*
3YR Speech Mechanism	<.10	.26	.19
8YR Speech Mechanism	<.10	.11	.05
8YR Palatal Function and Hypernasality	<.10	.05	.04
8YR Fluency	.10	.12	.05
8YR Articulation	.40	.31	.11
8YR Intelligibility	.22	.21	.04
8YR Language Comprehension	.46	.38	.09
8YR Auditory Memory	.48	.42	.08
8YR Digits	.31	.31	.11
8YR Word Identification	.30	.50	.10
8YR Written Communication	.53	.46	.09
8YR Language Production	.55	.44	.10
8YR Concept Development	.70	.58	.08
Neurological Involvement	.17	.30	.17
Communicative Effectiveness	.68	.52	.06
Auditory Processing	.71	.15	.09

*p(F2/F1) and p(F2/P1) refer to the probability of failing selected SLH indexes (F2) when the Auditory-Vocal Association subtest is failed (F2) or passed (P1).

dexes than if he passed the test. There are only minor variations in conditional probabilities within race, sex, and SEI. A general statement can be made that the risk is approximately the same regardless of race, sex, or SEI.

Bender Gestalt Test for Young Children

The Bender Gestalt Test for Young Children is a visual-motor test which is said to reflect biological principles of sensory-motor action, and to depend upon the developmental level of the child and any existing pathological state (Bender, 1938). Koppitz (1964) constructed scoring systems for the Bender Gestalt which allow for the evaluation of perceptual maturity and possible neurological disability or emotional disorders in young children. The Koppitz scoring system was used when the Bender Gestalt was administered to the seven-year-old children in the NINCDS Collaborative Perinatal Project. The error mean of children in the normative study age group 6–6 year to 6–11 year was 6.4, SD = 3.8; and in the age group 7-0 year to 7-5 year it

was 4.8, SD = 3.6. The mean of the children in the present study, who were tested within two months of their seventh birthday, was 7.2 errors. The slightly better performance of the children in the normative study probably reflects differences in sampling between the two studies.

The correlations and conditional probabilities for the Bender Gestalt Test and various 8YR SLH indexes are presented in Table 14-21. The correlations are negative because the Bender gestalt is scored for errors and the SLH indexes were constructed using correct responses. The correlations range from less than .10 to −.50. Bender (1938) has suggested that performance on her visual-motor test is closely related to language ability and to intelligence. The higher correlations between the Bender Gestalt Test and the SLH indexes support this statement. In addition, these correlations are similar to some reported by Koppitz (1964) in her studies of the relationships of the Bender Gestalt to intelligence and to school achievement.

Table 14-21

Correlations and conditional probabilities for selected SLH indexes and the Bender Gestalt
Test at seven years of age.

Index	r	p(F2/F1)*	p(F2/P1)*
8YR Speech Mechanism	<.10	.07	.04
8YR Palatal Function and Hypernasality	<.10	.02	.02
8YR Fluency	<.10	.08	.04
8YR Articulation	−.25	.23	.11
8YR Intelligibility	−.13	.15	.04
8YR Language Comprehension	−.26	.22	.09
8YR Auditory Memory	−.28	.26	.08
8YR Digits	−.23	.25	.10
8YR Word Identification	−.20	.31	.10
8YR Written Communication	−.47	.40	.08
8YR Language Production	−.35	.27	.09
8YR Concept Development	−.47	.36	.09
Neurological Involvement	−.17	.17	.11
Communicative Effectiveness	−.48	.34	.08
Auditory Processing	−.50	†	†

*p(F2/F1) and p(F2/P1) refer to the probability of failing selected SLH indexes (F2) when the Bender Gestalt Test
is failed (F1) or passed (P1).
†Conditional probabilities could not be calculated because no children who took the Bender Gestalt Test failed
Auditory Processing.

The conditional probabilities were calculated using children with scores from 0
to 12 as the pass group and 13 to 20 as the
fail group ($\cong$ mean ±2SD). If the child
failed the Bender Gestalt Test, there was
at least three times the risk that he would
fail 8YR Auditory Memory, 8YR Word
Identification, 8YR Written Communication, 8YR Language Production, 8YR
Concept Development, and Communicative Effectiveness than if he passed the
Bender Gestalt Test. These findings appear to provide additional support for
Bender's (1938) statement about the relationships between her test and language
abilities.

Wechsler Intelligence Scale for Children (WISC)

The WISC was scored for Verbal IQ
and Performance IQ as well as Full Scale
IQ. Tables 14-22 and 14-23 contain the
correlations and conditional probabilities
for the Verbal IQ and the Performance
IQ, and Table 14-24 contains similar information for the Full Scale IQ.
Correlations between the IQ measures

and the 3YR SLH indexes yield values
from less than .10 to .50. The high correlations with 3YR Hypernasality are values
of interest. As noted in Chapter 10, study
of the cross-tabulations of these variables
indicates that there is some spurious factor operating to increase the size of these
correlations. The most likely factor is the
marginal distribution for 3YR Hypernasality. Clearly the conditional probabilities do not indicate that if a child
failed 3YR Hypernasality he was at
greater risk of failing 7YR IQ.
The correlations between 7YR IQ
measures and the 8YR indexes range
from less than .10 to .61. As might have
been expected, the correlations between
the 7YR Verbal IQ and most 8YR indexes
are larger than the corresponding correlations with the 7YR Performance IQ except for Articulation and Intelligibility
which are identical. Correlations between
Full Scale IQ and the SLH indexes range
from <.10 to .54; they appear to be more
similar to the correlations with Verbal IQ
than to the correlations with Performance IQ.

Table **14-22**

Correlations and conditional probabilities for selected SLH indexes and the WISC 7YR Verbal IQ.

Index	r	p(F2/F1)*	p(F2/P1)*
3YR Speech Mechanism	<.10	.18	.11
3YR Hypernasality	.50	.13	.12
8YR Speech Mechanism	<.10	.11	.05
8YR Palatal Function and Hypernasality	<.10	.07	.03
8YR Fluency	<.10	.11	.05
8YR Articulation	.15	.29	.11
8YR Intelligibility	.27	.19	.04
8YR Language Comprehension	.40	.35	.09
8YR Auditory Memory	.43	.42	.08
8YR Digits	.18	.34	.10
8YR Word Identification	.61	.46	.10
8YR Written Communication	.47	.45	.09
8YR Language Production	.25	.42	.10
8YR Concept Development	.35	.54	.08
Neurological Involvement	.53	.29	.17
Communicative Effectiveness	.39	.48	.06
Auditory Processing	.23	.16	.08

*p(F2/F1) and p(F2/P1) refer to the probability of failing selected SLH indexes (F2) when the WISC 7YR Verbal IQ is failed (F1) or passed (P1).

Table **14-23**

Correlations and conditional probabilities for selected SLH indexes and the WISC 7YR Performance IQ.

Index	r	p(F2/F1)*	p(F2/P1)*
3YR Speech Mechanism	<.10	.16	.10
3YR Hypernasality	.43	.14	.11
8YR Speech Mechanism	<.10	.11	.05
8YR Palatal Function and Hypernasality	<.10	.06	.04
8YR Fluency	<.10	.12	.05
8YR Articulation	.15	.28	.12
8YR Intelligibility	.27	.18	.05
8YR Language Comprehension	.32	.30	.10
8YR Auditory Memory	.32	.31	.10
8YR Digits	.10	.25	.11
8YR Word Identification	.45	.38	.11
8YR Written Communication	.45	.47	.10
8YR Language Production	.23	.36	.11
8YR Concept Development	.31	.44	.10
Neurological Involvement	.47	.27	.17
Communicative Effectiveness	.37	.40	.08
Auditory Processing	.21	.15	.09

*p(F2/F1) and p(F2/P1) refer to the probability of failing selected SLH indexes (F2) when the WISC 7YR Performance IQ is failed (F1) or passed (P1).

Table 14-24

Correlations and conditional probabilities for selected SLH indexes and the WISC 7YR Full Scale IQ.

Index	r	p(F2/F1)*	p(F2/P1)*
3YR Speech Mechanism	<.10	.05	.03
3YR Hypernasality	.49	.05	.04
3YR Articulation	.11	.09	.02
3YR Intelligibility	.23	.18	.03
8YR Speech Mechanism	<.10	.19	.05
8YR Palatal Function and Hypernasality	<.10	.12	.04
8YR Fluency	<.10	.19	.05
8YR Articulation	.22	.50	.12
8YR Intelligibility	.32	.39	.05
8YR Language Comprehension	.40	.55	.11
8YR Auditory Memory	.49	.64	.10
8YR Digits	.21	.49	.12
8YR Word Identification	.51	.66	.12
8YR Written Communication	.54	.78	.11
8YR Language Production	.32	.66	.12
8YR Concept Development	.43	.78	.12
8YR Hearing Severity	<.10	.36	.21
8YR Total Conductive Loss	<.10	.18	.07
8YR Total Sensorineural Loss	.34	.14	.03
Neurological Involvement	.50	.42	.18
Communicative Effectiveness	.50	.79	.14
Auditory Processing	.31	.87	.18

*p(F2/F1) and p(F2/P1) refer to the probability of failing selected SLH indexes (F2) when the WISC 7YR Full Scale IQ is failed (F1) or passed (P1).

Conditional probabilities displayed in Table 14-24 clearly indicate that if a child has a WISC IQ below 80, there is considerably greater likelihood that the child will fail SLH indexes. The conditional probabilities by race, sex, and SEI are similar to those for the total population.

3YR SLH Indexes

The relationship between the 3YR SLH indexes and the 8YR SLH indexes was examined in several ways. Initially, correlations were calculated between each 3YR index and each 8YR index (Table 14-25). Conditional probabilities were also calculated in those instances where further explanation of the relationship seemed to be indicated, and can be found in the relevant chapters. Finally, the 3YR SLH indexes were used as the independent variables to predict each 8YR SLH index (Table 14-26).

3YR Speech Mechanism

Correlations between 3YR Speech Mechanism and the 8YR SLH indexes range in value from |.00| to |.09| (Table 14-25). One might have expected that 3YR Speech Mechanism would have shown stronger relationships with 8YR Speech Mechanism, 8YR Articulation, and 8YR Intelligibility. However, these findings are consistent with Winitz's (1969) summary of the relevant literature. Conditional probabilities indicate that if the child failed 3YR Speech Mechanism there is almost twice the risk that the child will fail 8YR Speech Mechanism, 8YR Articulation, and 8YR Intelligibility than if he had passed 3YR Speech Mechanism. Therefore, 3YR Speech Mechanism may have some potential as an early warning indicator.

Table **14-25**

Correlations between 3YR SLH indexes and 8YR SLH indexes.

	3YR Speech Mechanism	3YR Hypernasality	3YR Fluency	3YR Articulation	3YR Intelligibility	3YR Language Comprehension	3YR Sentence Complexity	3YR Auditory Memory	3YR Hearing
8YR Speech Mechanism	.04	.00	.00	.06	.05	.05	.04	.05	.03
8YR Palatal Function and Hypernasality	.01	.02	.00	.02	.04	.03	.05	.03	.03
8YR Fluency	.01	.01	.05	.04	.04	.05	.04	.03	.03
8YR Articulation	.07	.03	.01	.31	.27	.22	.22	.07	.03
8YR Intelligibility	.08	.01	-.01	.20	.19	.16	.21	.12	.06
8YR Language Comprehension	.01	.02	-.05	.13	.13	.23	.12	.05	.01
8YR Auditory Memory	.07	.01	-.03	.19	.23	.24	.20	.17	.04
8YR Digits	.09	.02	-.02	.14	.22	.15	.19	.23	.04
8YR Word Identification	.05	.02	-.08	.20	.20	.33	.17	.09	.01
8YR Written Communication	.09	.02	-.04	.19	.27	.24	.23	.18	.03
8YR Language Production	.06	.04	-.01	.25	.24	.32	.20	.15	.01
8YR Concept Development	.07	.01	-.04	.25	.27	.34	.23	.14	.04
8YR Hearing Severity	-.03	-.03	.00	-.06	-.07	-.10	-.06	.00	-.09
8YR Total Conductive Loss	.03	.02	.00	.03	.06	.05	.06	.04	.07
8YR Total Sensorineural Loss	.00	.00	-.01	.03	.05	.04	.05	.01	.05
Neurological Involvement	.04	.01	-.01	.12	.11	.11	.08	.06	.03
Communicative Effectiveness	.07	.02	-.05	.24	.27	.32	.23	.15	.02
Auditory Processing	.09	.02	-.05	.26	.30	.33	.25	.19	.03

Table **14-26**

Multiple correlations for 8YR SLH indexes with 3YR SLH indexes as the independent variables.

Index	R
8YR Speech Mechanism	.089
8YR Palatal Function and Hypernasality	.061
8YR Fluency	.084
8YR Articulation	.373
8YR Intelligibility	.277
8YR Language Comprehension	.252
8YR Auditory Memory	.324
8YR Digits	.304
8YR Word Identification	.370
8YR Written Communication	.349
8YR Language Production	.387
8YR Concept Development	.409
8YR Hearing Severity	.143
8YR Total Conductive Loss	.098
8YR Total Sensorineural Loss	.076
Neurological Involvement	.155
Communicative Effectiveness	.395
Auditory Processing	.427

3YR Hypernasality

Correlations and conditional probabilities are unremarkable for 3YR Hypernasality and the 8YR SLH indexes. Correlations distribute themselves between |.00| and |.04| and conditional probabilities indicate that little can be said about performance on the 8YR SLH indexes based upon whether or not the child passed 3YR Hypernasality.

3YR Fluency

Correlations between 3YR Fluency and various 8YR SLH indexes range from |.00| to |.08|. Conditional probabilities indicate that the risk of failing the 8YR SLH indexes does not change appreciably regardless of the child's passing or failing 3YR Fluency. These findings are, in part, a result of the marginal distribution of 3YR Fluency, since only 102 children failed the index.

3YR Articulation

Although articulation was measured by different instruments at the two ages,

it was expected that there would be a moderate correlation between the indexes of articulation (Winitz, 1969). As Table 14-25 shows, the correlation between 3YR Articulation and 8YR Articulation is .31; and the conditional probabilities indicate that a child who failed 3YR Articulation is at three times greater risk of failing 8YR Articulation than is a child who passed 3YR Articulation. Other correlations of interest are those between 3YR Articulation and 8YR Intelligibility (.20), 8YR Word Identification (.20), 8YR Language Production (.25), and 8YR Concept Development (.25). In each of these instances, the child is at least twice the risk of failing the 8YR SLH index if he failed 3YR Articulation than if he had passed it.

3YR Intelligibility

Correlations between 3YR Intelligibility and the 8YR SLH indexes range between |.04| and |.30|. Although the correlation between the intelligibility measures at the two ages is not large (.19), a child who failed 3YR Intelligibility is at almost six times higher risk than a child who had passed 3YR Intelligibility.

Correlations with other 8YR SLH indexes which have components reflecting the expressive aspects of communication (Appendix 4) are .27 with 8YR Articulation, .24 with 8YR Language Production, .27 with 8YR Concept Development, and .27 with 8YR Written Communication. Children who failed 3YR Intelligibility were at almost three times greater risk of failing these indexes than were children who had passed 3YR Intelligibility.

3YR Language Comprehension

The measurements of language comprehension differed in the SLH examinations at three years and at eight years of age. Therefore, the two indexes of language comprehension are constructed from different components (Appendix 4) and their correlation is .23. The child is at twice the risk of failing 8YR Language Comprehension if he failed 3YR Language Comprehension than if he had passed it. The correlation with the other index of language comprehension, 8YR Word Identification, is .33 and the risk is similar to that for 8YR Language Comprehension. Correlations with 8YR Language Production and 8YR Concept Development are .32 and .34, respectively, but correlations with other 8YR SLH indexes are smaller.

3YR Sentence Complexity

The 3YR Sentence Complexity Index was constructed from ratings of the child's expressive language made by the examiner throughout the 3YR SLH examination (Appendix 4). The correlations between 3YR Sentence Complexity and 8YR SLH indexes are distributed from |.04| to |.25|. The correlations between 3YR Sentence Complexity and 8YR Language Production and with 8YR Concept Development are .20 and .23, respectively, and the risk of failing these in-

dexes is two and a half times greater if the child failed 3YR Sentence Complexity than if he had passed it. Correlations between 3YR Sentence Complexity and 8YR Articulation and 8YR Intelligibility are .22 and .21, respectively. These values are similar to the correlations between the articulation and the intelligibility indexes at both ages. These findings suggest the possibility that scores on 3YR Sentence Complexity may reflect the examiner's attention to articulation and intelligibility while rating the language produced by the child.

3YR Auditory Memory

Performance on 3YR Auditory Memory is correlated .23 with 8YR Digits and .17 with 8YR Auditory Memory. Children who failed 3YR Auditory Memory are at two or more times the risk of failing either 8YR Digits or 8YR Auditory Memory than are children who had passed 3YR Auditory Memory.

3YR Hearing

Correlations and conditional probabilities for 3YR Hearing and the 8YR SLH indexes are unremarkable. The values of the correlations range from |.00| to |.09|, and the conditional probabilities indicate that little can be said about the child's performance on the 8YR SLH indexes based upon whether or not he passed 3YR Hearing. The correlations between 3YR Hearing and 8YR Hearing Severity, 8YR Total Conductive Loss, and 8YR Total Sensorineural Loss are less than |.09|. These findings are consistent with the conclusions drawn by Bordley and Hardy (1972) from studying a subsample of the NINCDS Collaborative Perinatal Project.

Multiple Regression Analyses

A multiple regression analysis was employed to investigate the efficacy of predicting each 8YR SLH index, using the 3YR SLH indexes as independent variables. Table 14-26 contains the list of the 8YR SLH indexes and their respective multiple correlations (R). The beta weights for the 3YR SLH indexes within each prediction equation are contained in Appendix 8.

The indexes for 8YR Speech Mechanism, 8YR Palatal Function and Hypernasality, 8YR Fluency, 8YR Hearing Severity, 8YR Total Conductive Loss, 8YR Total Sensorineural Loss and Neurological Involvement are predicted poorly by the 3YR SLH indexes; less than 3% of the variance is explained in their respective predictions. The remaining multiple correlations, with values ranging from .252 to .427, indicate more success in prediction. These values, however, are only slightly larger than the highest zero-order correlation for the 8YR SLH indexes (Table 14-25). For example, the multiple correlation for 8YR Language Comprehension is .252 and its highest zero-order correlation is .23 with 3YR Language Comprehension. When using correlational techniques, the usefulness of the 3YR SLH indexes as predictors of 8YR SLH indexes must be questioned, because no prediction equation accounted for more than 18.2% of the variance. The use of risk tables (conditional probabilities) offers a more useful approach to prediction.

In sum, variables indicative of socioeconomic level, whether determined at birth or at seven years, have the strongest relationship to speech, language, and hearing abilities at eight years of age. Other variables which have predictive value include race, sex, Birthweight, Gestational Age, Bayley mental and motor scores at eight months, IQ at four years and seven years, and the Bender Gestalt Test. Individual items of particular usefulness for prediction of SLH outcome at eight years include vocalization items from the Bayley Scales, the Auditory-Vocal Association subtest of the ITPA, and several of the 3YR SLH in-

dexes. Correlational methods appear to be less useful for predictive purposes than calculated conditional probabilities.

References

1. Bayley, N. *COLR Research Form of the Bayley Scales of Mental and Motor Development.* Bethesda, Maryland: Perinatal Research Branch, NINDB-NIH, 1958.

2. Bayley, N. *Manual for the Bayley Scales of Infant Development.* New York: The Psychological Corp., 1969.

3. Bender, L. A visual motor Gestalt Test and its clinical use. *Am. Orthopsychiat. Ass. Res. Mon.* No. 3, 1938.

4. Bloom, R.D., Whiteman, M., and Deutsch, M. Race and social class as separate factors related to social environment. In M. Deutsch, Ed. *The Disadvantaged Child.* New York: Basic Books, 1967.

5. Bordley, J.E., and Hardy, J.B. A hearing survey on preschool children. *Trans. Am. Acad. Ophthalmol. Otolaryngol.* 76:349–354, 1972.

6. Broman, S.H., Nichols, P.L., and Kennedy, W.A. *Preschool IQ: Prenatal and Early Developmental Correlates.* Hillsdale, N.J.: Lawrence Erlbaum Associates, 1975.

7. Cameron, J., Livson, N., and Bayley, N. Infant vocalizations and their relationship to mature intelligence. *Science* 157:331–333, 1967.

8. Dale, P.S. *Language Development.* New York: Holt, Rinehart and Winston, 1976.

9. Davie, R., Butler, N., and Goldstein H. *From Birth to Seven.* London: Longman, 1972.

10. Deutsch, M., Ed. *The Disadvantaged Child.* New York: Basic Books, 1967.

11. DiCarlo, L.M. *The Deaf.* Englewood Cliffs, N.J.: Prentice-Hall, 1964.

12. Dunn, L.M. *Peabody Picture Vocabulary Test Manual.* Circle Pines, Minnesota: American Guidance Service, 1965.

13. Harris, D.B. *Children's Drawings as Measures of Intellectual Maturity.* New York: Harcourt, Brace and World, 1963.

14. Ireton, H., Thwing, E., and

Gravem, H. Infant mental development and neurological status, family socioeconomic status and intelligence at age four. *Child Development* 41:937–945, 1970.

15. Jastak, J.F., and Jastak, S.R. *The Wide Range Achievement Test (WRAT).* Wilmington, Delaware: Guidance Associates, 1965.

16. Jeruchimowicz, R., Costello, J., and Bagur, J.S. Knowledge of action and object words: A comparison of lower- and middle-class Negro preschoolers. *Child Development* 42:455–464, 1971.

17. Kirk, S.A. Ethnic differences in psycholinguistic abilities. *Except. Child.* 112–118, 1972.

18. Koppitz, E.M. *The Bender Gestalt Test for Young Children.* New York: Grune and Stratton, 1964.

19. McCall, R.B., Hogarty, P.S., and Hurlburt, N. Transitions in infant sensorimotor development and the prediction of childhood IQ. *Am. Psychol.* 27:728–748, 1972.

20. McCarthy, J.J., and Kirk, S.A. *The Construction, Standardization and Statistical Characteristics of the Illinois Test of Psycholinguistic Abilities. Experimental Edition.* Urbana, Illinois: University of Illinois Press, 1963.

21. McCarthy, J.J., and Olson, J.L. *Validity studies on the Illinois Test of Psycholinguistic Abilities. Experimental Edition.* Urbana, Illinois: University of Illinois Press, 1964.

22. Milgram, N.A., and Ozer, M.N. Peabody Picture Vocabulary Test scores of preschool children. *Psychol. Rep.* 20:779–784, 1967.

23. Mittler, P., and Ward, J. The use of the Illinois Test of Psycholinguistic Abilities on British four-year-old children: A normative and factorial study. *Br. J. Educ. Psychol.* 40:43–53, 1970.

24. Morgenstern, J.J. Socioeconomic factors in stuttering. *J. Speech Hear. Disord.* 21:25–33, 1956.

25. Myrianthopoulos, N.C., and French, K.S. An application of the U.S. Bureau of the Census socioeconomic index to a large diversified patient population. *Soc. Sci. Med.* 2:283–299, 1968.

26. Nichols, P.L. The development and use of an index of socioeconomic status in longitudinal research. Personal communication, 1976.

27. Northern, J.L., and Downs, M.P. *Hearing in Children.* Baltimore: Williams and Wilkins, 1974.

28. Ryckman, D.B. The psychological process of disadvantaged children. Ph.D. dissertation. University of Illinois, 1965.

29. Teasdale, G.R., and Katz, F.M. Psycholinguistic abilities of children from different ethnic and socioeconomic backgrounds. *Australian J. Psychol.* 20:155–159, 1968.

30. Terman, L.M., and Merrill, M.A. *Stanford-Binet Intelligence Scale.* Boston: Houghton Mifflin, 1960.

31. Wechsler, D. *The Wechsler Intelligence Scale for Children.* New York: The Psychological Corp., 1949.

32. Willerman, L., Broman, S.H., and Fiedler, M. Infant development, preschool IQ and social class. *Child Development* 41:69–77, 1970.

33. Winitz, H. *Articulatory Acquisition and Behavior.* New York: Meredith Corp., 1969.

CHAPTER 15

Summary

Paul J. LaBenz, Sc.D.

Speech, language, and hearing (SLH) data were collected as part of the Collaborative Perinatal Project (NCPP) of the National Institute of Neurological and Communicative Disorders and Stroke. Clinical populations and a group of private patients were sampled at twelve medical institutions located largely in eastern and southern states. Data from SLH examinations administered at 3YR and 8YR were analyzed for interrelationships and for associations with findings in other areas of the NCPP study. These include variables relating to pregnancy, labor, and delivery; family characteristics; and the physical, mental, and behavioral characteristics of the children. Relationships among the variables were studied to provide clues to the etiology of communicative disorders and to uncover findings which might be clinically applicable as well as predictive of outcome. The results of these analyses and the interpretation of their significance and applicability are the substance of this report.

The cohort chosen for analytic study included all White and Black children who were given valid SLH examinations within age limits specified in the study protocols, and for whom there were sufficient prenatal, socioeconomic, and other non-SLH data. The selection criteria yielded a cohort of 27,558 children consisting of three subsamples: (1) those tested at 3YR (19,885); (2) those tested at

8YR (20,137); and (3) those tested at both ages (12,464). These subsamples were compared with the children who took neither test (11,225) on selected SLH and NCPP variables and were described statistically by race, sex, and Socioeconomic Index (SEI) for each medical institution and in total. They appeared to be similar in all respects one to another and, except for SEI and race, to the group not given either of the SLH examinations.

The speech, language, and hearing examination administered at 3YR covered Language Comprehension and Language Expression, Hearing, Speech Mechanism, Speech Production, and Memory for Digits and Syllables. The battery was devised especially for use in the NCPP study, and its component tests were largely unstandardized. At the 8YR level, the same general SLH areas were examined but in greater detail with more standardized tests. Reading and writing were assessed at 8YR but not at 3YR.

The SLH data were examined for quality as it pertains to availability of the data, reasonableness of values, and stability of findings. Examiner variability was evaluated on the basis of test-retest results obtained from the NCPP quality control program. Institutional variability was studied, with particular emphasis on two data-gathering institutions which used atypical sampling methods at the 3YR level. Intercorrelations were calculated for the 3YR SLH variables and the 8YR SLH variables, using data on the population examined at both ages (3YR/8YR). The quality of most SLH variables appeared satisfactory in general. The NCPP variables were scrutinized by consultants and the NCPP staff for validity, reliability, redundancy, and missing data. This resulted in the selection of a list of 676 NCPP variables for study.

In order to facilitate study of the relationships with NCPP variables, key SLH variables were identified and a number of composite indexes were constructed to serve as summary descriptors. The SLH variables were evaluated by consultants and staff for acceptability as potential components of indexes and were combined according to criteria recommended on the basis of expert judgment. Frequency distributions and descriptive statistics were generated for each index, and intercorrelations were obtained among indexes and between indexes and individual SLH variables. Additionally, the method of principal components was used with the same variables to obtain different weightings. This resulted in another set of indexes which correlated well with the indexes constructed by the consultant panel. Three other comprehensive indexes proposed by another task force also were subjected to the same evaluative process. A total of 27 SLH indexes and key variables emerged, and these were used to construct a correlation screen with the 676 NCPP variables selected earlier. Multiple regression analyses, using early variables which survived the correlation screen, yielded equations with varying predictive abilities. Correlations of residuals yielded no potential variables as additions to the multiple regression analyses. In addition, conditional probabilities were calculated to assess the risk of SLH failure given success or failure on certain other antecedent variables.

Two multiple regression analyses were performed using the 3YR SLH indexes as outcomes. One used data at birth, and the other used at-birth plus 8-month mental and motor scores. In general, these predictors explained less than 8% of the variance. The better predictions were for 3YR Articulation, Intelligibility, Language Comprehension, and Sentence Complexity. Addition of the 8-month data did not materially improve prediction.

Five multiple regression analyses were done using the 8YR indexes as outcomes. In addition to the two sets of predictor variables used for 3YR outcome, the 4YR IQ and 3YR indexes were used in various combinations. Best predictions occurred for 8YR Word Identification (.75), Concept Development (.69), Written Communication (.61), Language Production (.54), Language Comprehension (.51), Auditory Memory (.49), and Articulation (.45).

The 4YR IQ demonstrated (by means of large beta coefficients) pronounced effects in almost every multiple regression in which it was entered. The 8-month variables contributed very little to any of the predictions, and 3YR indexes alone were not successful predictors of 8YR indexes. A combination of at-birth variables and 3YR indexes performed slightly better in predicting more than half the 8YR outcomes than did a combination of at-birth variables with 8-month scores and 4YR IQ.

Measures of lip, tongue, and palate movement revealed little about communication skills such as Articulation, or about speech intelligibility, at 3YR or at 8YR for most children. They were useful to help identify children with neuromotor impairments and anatomical deficiencies of the speech apparatus. Higher than average incidence of speech mechanism dysfunction occurred in identified syndromes, deviant eye and skeletal conditions, and suspected neurological abnormalities.

Social variables, such as SEI and mother's education, were more strongly related to articulation development than were physical variables other than clearly organic deficiencies. Premature children showed a slight performance deficit in articulation. No specific variables or sets of variables could be identified as predictive of poor fluency of speech. Failure on Articulation and Intelligibility at 3YR was predicted best by behavior on sound orientation items in the Bayley Test at eight months. Speech production at 8YR could not be predicted reliably by performance at 3YR.

In accord with reports in the literature, sex differences in language performance favoring females were not consistently found at eight years. Race differences were confounded by SEI and other effects tending to favor performance by Whites. Race, sex, SEI, and IQ contributed most to predicting the 8YR language indexes. Failure on 8-month Bayley vocalization items increased by two to three times the risk of later poor language performance. Poorer language performance was associated with lower IQ, low birthweight, prematurity, low Apgar scores, and hearing loss. Children with dysfluent speech or cleft palates were not inferior in language. Single children performed better than those with siblings, and adopted children did better than those with biological parents or children in foster homes.

Written communication (reading, writing, spelling) likewise showed systematic improvement with increasing IQ, SEI, and education of the parents. Performance was better also for Whites, Females, singletons, and adopted children. Scores were poorer for Blacks, Males, stutterers, siblings, twins, and those with adverse birth conditions or organic problems. Highest correlations were found to occur with SEI, parental education, IQ at 4YR and 7YR, and performance on the Bender Gestalt and the Auditory-Vocal Association Test (ITPA). Low correlations were found with early physiological and behavioral observations. Handedness showed no relationship to performance. Single adverse perinatal events were ineffective predictors of written communication ability; environmental and later developmental multiple factors, including SEI, were better predictors.

Digit and syllable memory span tests were found to be relatively free of cultural bias. Race, sex, and SEI differences were small. Performance was related to reading and writing and other language tests and to speech articulation. Performance was not predicted well by other variables except for IQ, attentional variables, and neurological abnormality.

Hearing tests at 3YR revealed that 4.3% (N = 16,000) failed one or more frequencies in either or both ears. Spondee words were failed by 7.7%. No systematic relationships were found between hearing at 3YR and other 3YR SLH variables or with NCPP variables. However, failure of the 3YR Pure-Tone Hearing Screen was predictive of loss in hearing sensitivity at 8YR.

Mean air conduction thresholds at 8YR were comparable to those reported in other studies. Discrimination scores were higher for Whites and for higher SEI ratings. Abnormal conditions of the ears observed during the first year of life were not highly indicative of hearing loss at 8YR. Of 1186 children judged otoscopically abnormal at 7YR, about 100 appeared in the monaural or binaural conductive categories at 8YR, and less than half as many in the sensorineural loss group. Only about 1% of children falling outside the normal range in the conductive categories were judged "deaf" in the 12-month pediatric examination, as compared with about 20% in the sensorineural group.

Relationships between 8YR hearing and antecedent medical and nonmedical factors were generally weak; the strongest was between the binaural sensorineural category and infectious diseases during pregnancy (r = .20). Relationships between 8YR hearing and other SLH performance were stronger, particularly with Articulation (−.66), Intelligibility (−.66), and Word Identification (−.52). Only short attention span appeared to be related to monaural loss indexes. Weak relationships were found for conductive binaural loss and the Direct Coombs' Test (−.23), bilirubin level (.21), and Observable Ear Condition (.25 to .33). Early responses to sound at eight months showed only weak association with the binaural indexes at 8YR.

Hearing was found to be worse in the poorer ear during colder months but no geographic effects were noted. Average hearing levels improved with higher birthweight. There was greater incidence of hearing loss among foster children than among adopted children. A small difference (1.5 dB) in hearing sensitivity was found in favor of singletons compared with twins and children with siblings. Greater than average loss in the poorer ear occurred for children diagnosed as Cleft Palate (14.7 dB, n = 24), Mentally Retarded (14.3 dB, n = 53), Cerebral Palsy (11.3 dB, n = 83), and dysfluent (11.4 dB, n = 35). Premature children with true distress (5-minute Apgar) were similar to the total sample in poorer ear sensitivity.

Higher relative risks for sensorineural hearing loss in children was suggested for certain drugs administered to mothers during pregnancy. These include: (a) several sulfa drugs (sulfathiazole, sulfacetamide, sulfabenzamide, sulfamethoxypridazine), (b) phenothiazines (promazine or buclizine), (c) streptomycin, (d) methamphetamine, and (e) 17 tranquilizers. The analyses were controlled variously for SEI, hyperemesis, hematuria, bacterial infection, prior stillbirth or neonatal death, short gestation, no weight gain in pregnancy, smoking, second trimester bleeding, and hypertension, although most characteristics of pregnancy were weakly or not at all associated with hearing loss. High relative risks were indicated for some other drugs as well (antidepressants, general anesthetics, nonbarbiturate anticonvulsants, and antihypertension agents), but too few cases precluded analysis.

In brief, perinatal and physical factors associated with favorable SLH outcome included the following: low parity, maternal age equal to or greater than 18 years, maternal height greater than 61 inches, weight gain in pregnancy 15 to 25 pounds, full term infant, no forceps used, birthweight equal to or greater than 2500 gm, larger head circumference, obesity, Female, and normal neurological findings. Factors associated with less favorable SLH outcome included the following: high parity, maternal age less than 18 years, maternal height less than 60 inches, weight gain in pregnancy less than 15 or more than 25 pounds, prematurity, breech delivery, forceps used, birthweight less than 2500 gm, microcephaly, leanness, maternal mental retardation, Male, and abnormal neurological findings.

Psychosocial factors associated with SLH outcome at 8YR included SEI, race, sex, mental and motor scores at eight months, IQ at four and seven years, and performance on the Bender Gestalt test. Other useful indicators were performance on vocalization items of the Bayley Scales, the Auditory-Vocal Association Test of the ITPA, and some 3YR SLH indexes. Variables indicative of socioeconomic level have the strongest relationship to SLH outcome at 8YR. Correlational methods appeared to be less useful for predictive purposes than calculated conditional probabilities regarding outcome.

Manuals and Protocols for the SLH Examinations

A. Manual for Administration of the Speech, Language and Hearing Examination (3YR).
B. Speech, Language and Hearing Examination Forms (PS-10 through PS-17).
C. Manual for Administration of the Final Speech, Language and Hearing Examination (8YR).
D. Final Speech, Language and Hearing Examination Forms (PS-40 through PS-45).

MANUAL FOR ADMINISTRATION
OF THE SPEECH, LANGUAGE AND
HEARING EXAMINATION

(for Forms PS-10 thru PS-17, inclusive, Rev. 4-64)

COLLABORATIVE STUDY OF CEREBRAL PALSY, MENTAL RETARDATION, AND
OTHER NEUROLOGICAL AND SENSORY DISORDERS OF
INFANCY AND CHILDHOOD

APRIL 1964

I. General Instructions

A. Introduction:
In the administration of the Speech, Language and Hearing Examination, it is important that the examiners follow instructions carefully to insure uniformity in testing procedures. Examiners should, therefore, make every attempt to get to know the instrument well before actually administering it to patients routinely. It is therefore recommended that they practice giving this examination until a smooth and natural sequence is achieved.

B. Arrangement and Contents of the Examination:
The Speech, Language and Hearing Examination is composed of a series of subtests. The major functions being tested, i.e., language reception, language expression, etc., are designated as areas and are referred to in this way in the specific instructions of this manual. Each of these areas may be composed of several subtests called subareas which may measure the function being tested by different means. Language reception, for example, is broken down into two subareas dealing with verbal comprehension for one, and alternate comprehension for the other; or an area such as auditory memory is broken down into two subareas dealing with the recall of digits and the recall of nonsense syllables. Each subarea is broken down into a number of items, under which are generally included several subitems. The subitems consist of the actual commands, questions, or procedures used by the examiner in testing the child. In all cases, wherever possible, the examination should be administered in the following sequence:

1. Language Reception
2. Language Expression
3. Hearing Tests
4. Speech Mechanism
5. Speech Production
6. Auditory Memory for Digits and Nonsense Syllables

Each subarea of the examination should be administered as a unit with specific emphasis placed on the function under test. For example, in testing hearing acuity with the spondee word list, the attention of the examiner should be directed to determining whether the utterances of the child are recognizable as the specific words on the tape, rather than judging how well the child articulates.

Although the recommended sequence for administration of the examination will be appropriate for the majority of cases, there are some instances in which it may be necessary to change it. For example, if upon initial presentation of the first series of subtests the examiner suspects that the child is suffering from a slight or possible severe hearing loss, it may be good procedure to administer the hearing tests first before testing the other functions. The examiner must note in the comments section any departure from the established sequence.

C. General Scoring Procedure:
Particular attention should be paid to the scoring procedures used in this examination. As a general rule, if the examiner has any doubt about whether the child has given a satisfactory response to a specific item, it is advisable that he mark the item as failed with notations made in the comments section of the scoring record. This step may provide important information for modification of the examination or resolution of some of the problems encountered with specific subtests or items.

D. Guidelines to Employ in Testing Preschool Children:

1. Make sure that the child is physically comfortable, i.e., he is seated in a comfortable chair and is able to manipulate any pictures or objects presented to him on a table suitable to his own sitting level.

2. Never test if the child is in obvious distress. Delay testing until the child is comfortable.

3. Generally exclude observers, although for children of this age it may be necessary to have the mother present. However, she should remain in the background and should not be allowed in any way to interfere with the performance of the child.

4. A few toys (which are not similar to the test materials) may be used to aid the examiner in putting the child at ease. Before the formal examination begins, these toys should be removed from sight and reach.

5. The examiner may indicate approval of the child and should avoid expressions of dissatisfaction.

6. The testing room should be free from distractions and as free as possible from ambient noise.

April 1964

7. The materials should be within easy reach of the examiner, although they should be hidden from the child.

8. The procedure and the specific instructions to the child should be memorized as part of an attempt to achieve standardized testing. However, it is advisable to keep the manual readily at hand for reference. All scoring should be done inconspicuously and all sections of each scoring record should be completed to avoid confusion and misinterpretation upon final analysis. It is also suggested that immediately following the examination, and given sufficient time, that examiners recheck each scoring record for completeness.

9. Under circumstances where the examiner has not been able to elicit a response from the child in either subareas of a major area and/or to specific items of a subarea, there is a tendency to score the subarea or item as "fail" and sometimes the area as "suspect" or "abnormal." The comments have not clearly differentiated the child whose performance has been elicited from the child whose cooperation has not been obtained. Clearly distinguishing these differences is necessary to enable more effective processing of data. It is recommended that when the cooperation of the child has not been obtained after all considered efforts to do so have not succeeded, the examiner should proceed as follows:

   a. Do not score in "pass" or "fail" boxes.

   b. Document carefully in the comments section the failure to cooperate or any other behavior explaining the lack of response.

   c. On the Summary Sheet, PS-17, do not score an inadequate examination of any area (9-13) as "abnormal." Do not check any of the alternatives "normal," "suspect," or "abnormal." Instead, write an appropriate comment explaining that an adequate examination of the area was not accomplished and the reasons why.

   d. However, if the examiner has succeeded in obtaining the child's cooperation in at least 4 of the 5 major areas (excluding Auditory Memory) of the examination, he may exercise his clinical judgment in estimating how the child would have performed on the remaining area, and evaluate him accordingly as "normal," "suspect," or "abnormal." This

practice may be accomplished only when an adequate Hearing Test has been accomplished. It should be emphasized that this procedure should be used rarely, only with extreme caution, and must be fully documented whenever used. This procedure cannot be employed for the Verbal Expression Area.

10. If the examiner is unable to obtain the child's cooperation or has not enough responses to make an adequate evaluation, he must make provisions to readminister this area or subarea during the same testing session at a point when the child is likely to be more cooperative. Avoid successive administration of the same area or subarea.

11. The examination should be administered in the sequence of the manual. However, under very unusual circumstances, departures from this sequence may be adopted if the examiner feels he can thereby obtain a more representative performance from the child.

12. Whenever there is any deviation from the manual in the administration or scoring of the examination, this must be justified in the form of detailed and pertinent explanations in the comment section. Unless careful documentation is furnished in this way, the coders in the Central Office will earmark such deviations as errors with consequent corruption of the data and lengthy delays in data processing. Grossly deviant records without explanation will be returned to the Collaborative Institution.

13. All records must be edited carefully and completely prior to transmission to the Central Office. This means that all scoring entries must be completed and special measures taken to insure that correct scoring criteria have been applied. This is especially important for such areas as Hearing and Speech Production where scoring criteria are more complex.

14. Copies of all examination records even though incomplete or inadequate should be forwarded to the Central Office.

II. Facilities

A. Specifications for Examination Room:

1. A quiet room away from the main sources of ambient noise is necessary.

2. The dimensions of the room should be at least 8' x 10'.

April 1964

3. The ambient noise level within the room used for testing hearing should not exceed 40 db. on an ASA accepted sound level meter using the "B" scale.

4. If a sound-conditioned room is not available, the following suggestions for room selection and modification will provide additional sound control:

   a. Choose a room away from pedestrian traffic in halls and removed from street traffic, isolated from other noises within the building by distance or by the presence of intervening room or closet.

   b. Sound conditioning of the room will be improved by drapes, acoustic tile on ceilings and walls, carpeting, and by the use of storm windows if there is outside exposure.

   c. All room air conditioners should be turned off during the tests of hearing.

5. The examiner should study the ambient noise level in the room over a period of hours to become familiar with the effect of temporary noises such as footsteps, motor noises, etc., on the sound level meter.

6. He should wait before presenting the auditory signal to the child if there is a passing increase in noise level.

7. Record the ambient noise level at the time of the hearing test in the appropriate place on the scoring form.

B. Furniture Selection and Placement:

1. An examination table should be used of sufficient width and length to accommodate placement of materials during test presentations.

2. Heights of table and chairs should be appropriate for three-year-old children.

3. For the hearing test, the loud speaker must be three feet from the ears of the child as he faces it. This distance must be strictly maintained for intensity levels to be kept at appropriate values.

4. The loud speaker should face the center of the room from a position close to a wall. It should be placed on a low table or shelf so that the center of the loud speaker is oriented perpendicular to and at the same height as the ears of the seated child.

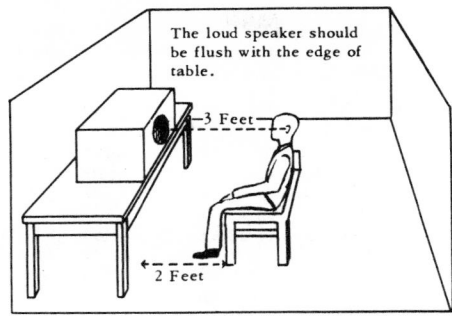

The loud speaker should be flush with the edge of table.

3 Feet

2 Feet

5. Make a line on the floor two feet from and parallel to the face of the loud speaker. Make this line permanent with masking tape, paint, or other suitable means. For the hearing test, place the front legs of the child's chair on this line.

6. The tape recorder used in the hearing test should be placed on a shelf or table to one side, to avoid distracting the child. The examiner sits between child and tape recorder so that he is within easy reach of the child and the controls. If possible, the recorder should be out of the child's vision.

7. A table must be available to accommodate a pure tone audiometer. The examiner and child should face each other, but the child should not be permitted to see the manipulation of the controls.

III. Specific Instructions for Hearing Tests

A. Introduction: The purpose of the hearing tests is to determine whether there are significant problems of auditory sensitivity. Two kinds of measurements are made to check this:
   1. Speech hearing for familiar spondaic words.
   2. Pure tone screening for the three critical speech frequencies.

Since reasonably normal hearing in at least one ear is necessary for the acquisition of language and speech, every effort must be made by the tester to determine whether or not the child can hear at soft levels. The examiner needs great skill in eliciting the child's interest and cooperation in listening intently because some children with normal hearing have difficulty in centering attention at soft levels. The tester also needs to be

April 1964

acutely aware of ambient noise levels. If there are disturbing bursts of interfering noises, he should wait before presenting a signal.

B. **Calibration of Equipment:** Equipment must be calibrated before the child enters the test room as follows:

1. Plug loud speaker into Wollensak Tape Recorder.

2. Turn on tape recorder and allow it to warm up for approximately two minutes.

3. Adjust tone control to Hi-Fi position.

4. Play 1000 cycle calibrating tone with the switch on the loud speaker in the Hi position. Increase the volume on the tape recorder until the needle on the loud speaker calibrating dial is at the line. This is meter setting Hi.

5. Meter setting Lo is obtained by changing the switch on the loud speaker to Lo position. Do not change the volume on the tape recorder.

C. **Acoustic Values:** Meter setting Hi is equivalent to 72 db. over one microbar at a distance of three feet as measured by an acoustic engineer with a general radio sound pressure level meter. This is equivalent to a moderate conversational voice (approximately 58 db., regarding normal speech-hearing threshold).

When the switch is changed to the Lo setting, the output is reduced by 30 db. to the level of a very quiet voice (approximately 28 db., regarding normal speech-hearing threshold). This is called meter setting Lo.

D. **Description of Materials Recorded on Tape:**

1. For the verbal response test, there are four lists of familiar spondaic words. There is a five second interval between each word.

a. <u>List I</u> (Meter setting Hi)

cowboy
baseball
hot dog

b. <u>List II</u> (Meter setting Hi)

doorbell
flashlight
goldfish
lipstick
football
sidewalk
toothpaste
oatmeal
cupcake
bathtub

c. <u>List III</u> (Meter setting Lo)

mailman
seesaw
ice cream
lipstick
haircut
toothbrush
outside
sailboat
airplane
birthday

d. <u>List IV</u> (Meter setting Lo)

popcorn
icebox
pancake
pork chop
ashtray
ice cream
toothbrush
birthday
hairbrush
airport

2. For the picture pointing test (nonverbal response) there are four lists of familiar spondaic words. Three of the lists employ five different words and each word is used twice. They are recorded at seven second intervals. The limited number presents the child with a spread of six pictures which he can visually manage. The increased time interval allows time for the child to point to the appropriate picture.

April 1964

a. List V (Meter setting Hi)

cowboy
baseball
hot dog

b. List VI (Meter setting Hi)

bathtub
ice cream
seesaw
redbird
hairbrush
ice cream
redbird
hairbrush
seesaw
bathtub

c. List VII (Meter setting Lo)

mailman
bluebird
toothbrush
sailboat
airplane
sailboat
airplane
mailman
toothbrush
bluebird

d. List VIII (Meter setting Lo)

popgun
goldfish
necktie
flashlight
teaspoon
teaspoon
goldfish
popgun
flashlight
necktie

IV. Miscellaneous Instructions

A. **Alternative Testing:** The remaining pages of this manual contain information about each of the areas and subareas. Each area of the examination, except in unusual cases, should be administered in the order in which it appears. It should be noted that there are areas in which alternative testing is provided. For example, in the language reception area there is both a verbal comprehension subarea and an alternate comprehension subarea. The instructions regarding these subareas indicate that only one subarea is to be used initially in testing the child. Thus, if the child can respond satisfactorily on the verbal comprehension subarea, it would not be necessary to administer the alternate comprehension subarea. The examiner may return to a subarea which the child did not attempt on first presentation.

B. **Summary of Test Performance and Additional Observations:** A "Summary of Test Performance" (PS-17) and a series of items which have been labeled "Additional Observations" (PS-16) are included in the scoring record. The "Summary of Test Performance" is a condensed report for quick and ready reference regarding the child's level of performance on the major areas of the examination. The "Additional Observations" are to be filled out by the examiner to describe the state of health of the child on the day of the examination, and also permits the examiner to record any noticeable physical abnormalities or behavioral deviations.

C. **Summary of Areas and Subareas:** Procedures for summary scoring of individual subareas are explained under the paragraph labeled "Scoring" at the end of each set of specific instructions for the subarea. Instructions for summary scoring of the total functional area, e.g., language reception, language expression, etc., are described in the last section of each area and are "boxed in" for ready identification.

D. **Comments Section:** A comments section pertinent to each item has been included on the scoring record to enable the examiner to record any unusual occurrences, behavior, or actions of the child that he (the examiner) considers indicative of a possible disorder or pathological entity. The examiner should take such comments into account when filling out the summary scoring sheet at the end of the scoring record.

E. **Age of Children For Testing:**

1. It is desirable that the child be tested between the age range of two years, 11 months and three years, one month.

2. Under special circumstances, such as caseload and scheduling difficulties, the child may be tested as late as three years, two months of age. The record forms of any child tested after the age of three years, two months should nevertheless be transmitted to the Central Office.

April 1964

3. It is recommended that testing of children beyond the age of three years, two months be initiated at the discretion of the supervisor of the speech, language and hearing section at the Collaborative Institution. Generally, testing after three years, four months of age should be done only if the child has been referred as impaired by another section of the Collaborative Institution.

F. Instructions for Global Scoring: The following criteria are to be employed in evaluating the child's performance on the total examination:

Normal: Five major areas scored as normal.

Four major areas scored as normal and remaining major areas scored as suspect.

Suspect: Two or more suspect scores in the five major areas.

An abnormal score in any of the five major areas and any combination of suspect and normal in the remaining four major areas.

Abnormal: Abnormal scores in two or more of the five major areas.

G. Instructions for Determining Adequacy of the Examination: Adequacy means that the performance of the child has met the requirements to score pass or fail, normal, suspect or abnormal, according to the level of the examination. An examination is judged to be inadequate when any one of the following events occur:

1. When the child's cooperation cannot be obtained.
2. If there is inadequacy judged on any two of the five major areas of the examination (excluding Auditory Memory).

AREA: Language Reception (PS-10)

SUBAREA: Verbal Comprehension

Purpose: To determine whether the child has the ability to comprehend spoken commands and spoken questions as indicated by his responses. An alternative group of items has been provided for further testing of the child who fails to complete *all* of the items in this section successfully.

Materials Required for All Items: Small toy objects will be further specified in the items comprising this section of the examination.

Scoring: Scoring requirements are described for each item respectively.

Item 1: Identification of Familiar Objects

Purpose: To ascertain whether the child is able to form correct associations for a series of familiar objects.

Materials: Box without lid, car, man and flag.

Procedure: Place the toy objects on the table in a row, from the child's left to right, in the order shown above. Make sure that there is adequate spacing between the toy objects so that there is no doubt possible about which object the child points to on request. If the child then fails to respond, go on to each succeeding item. (If the child has a motor handicap involving the use of his hands or arms which prevents him from pointing, hold up two objects sufficiently apart to observe whether he looks at the one named. Repeat the procedure with all four objects. Be sure to use different pairs of objects chosen at random so that the child does not use a given object as a clue.) Regardless of which procedure is used, introduce each request in the order shown as follows:
1. "SHOW ME THE CAR."
2. "SHOW ME THE BOX."
3. "SHOW ME THE FLAG."
4. "SHOW ME THE MAN."

Scoring: The child must pass three of the four subitems in this group to be given a passing score. A pass score for each subitem should be given if the child points to, or picks up, the object corresponding to the word which designates it. A fail score is given when the child either points to, or picks up, the wrong object.

Item 2: Understanding Action Words

Purpose: To determine whether the child comprehends the meaning of common "action" words, as they relate to several well-known objects.

Materials: Box without lid, car, man and flag.

- 6 -

Procedure: Place the toy objects on the table in a row, from the child's left to right, in the above order allowing approximately two to three inches between objects. Introduce each of the following commands in the order they are shown below. Allow the child time to respond to the command. Repeat each command once if the child does not respond readily.

1. "PICK UP THE MAN."
2. "MAKE THE MAN JUMP."
3. "PUSH THE CAR."
4. "SHAKE THE BOX."
5. "WAVE THE FLAG."

Scoring: The child must pass three of the five subitems in this group to achieve a passing score. A pass score in this instance is represented by the child selecting the appropriate object and applying the correct action to it as indicated by the command. A fail score is indicated if the child does the following:

1. Selects *incorrect object* and carries out *inappropriate action.*
2. Selects *incorrect object* and carries out *appropriate action.*
3. Selects *correct object* and carries out *inappropriate action.*

Item 3: Understanding Words Indicating Space Relationships and Direction

Purpose: To determine whether the child has any understanding of words dealing with space relationships and direction.

Materials: Table, box, truck, cat and cup.

Procedure: Place the toy objects on the table in a row, from the child's left to right, in the above order. Give each of the commands in the order shown below. Allow child time to respond. If child does not respond readily, repeat each command once.

1. "PUT THE CAT (KITTY) IN THE BOX."
2. "PUT THE CAT (KITTY) ON TOP OF THE TABLE." or "PUT THE CAT (KITTY) ON TOP OF THE TOY TABLE."
3. "PUT THE CAT (KITTY) UNDER THE TABLE." or "PUT THE CAT (KITTY) UNDER THE TOY TABLE."
4. "PUSH THE TRUCK BACKWARDS."
5. "TURN THE CUP UPSIDE DOWN." or "TURN THE CUP OVER."

Scoring: The child must pass three of the five subitems in this group to achieve a passing score. A pass score is represented by the child selecting the appropriate object and putting it in the proper place. A fail score is indicated if the child does the following:

1. Selects *incorrect object* and carries out *inappropriate action.*
2. Selects *incorrect object* and carries out *appropriate action.*
3. Selects *correct object* and carries out *inappropriate action.*

SUBAREA: Alternate Comprehension

Purpose: This subarea is to be administered if the child fails two or all three items in the verbal comprehension subarea. In this subarea discontinue testing the child as soon as he passes any one of the four items given in the designated sequence. Please note that no changes will be necessary in the summary total score for the major area as a whole since the child has already been designated as "abnormal" based on his verbal comprehension score. Note that if the child fails the verbal comprehension subarea, you <u>must</u> <u>administer</u> the alternate comprehension subarea even though you comment that the child is a "verbal" child. The objective of the language reception area is not to determine the child's media of communication, but to evaluate his ability to associate signs and symbols leading to effective comprehension.

Materials Required for All Items: Fer-Will Object Kit, King Company, 2414 West Lawrence Ave., Chicago 25, Ill.

1. Composite picture card illustrating cup, fork, spoon, toothbrush, shoe and dog.

2. Corresponding objects.

3. Set of corresponding single pictures presented on table as shown at right:

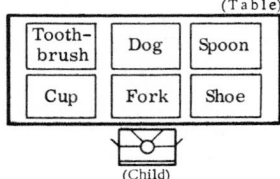

(Table)

Tooth-brush	Dog	Spoon
Cup	Fork	Shoe

(Child)

April 1964

417

Item 1: Word and Picture Identification

Purpose: To determine the comprehension of an auditory symbol referring to the corresponding visual symbol.

Materials: Composite picture card showing toothbrush, dog, spoon, cup, shoe and fork.

Procedures: Place the composite picture card on the table with the pictures facing the child. Say the word "CUP" with a rising inflection. If the child does not respond by pointing to the appropriate picture, say the word again in the same way and simultaneously make a sweeping, searching gesture over the pictures. Repeat the same procedure with each of the other pictures, following the order as shown on the scoring record. (If the child has a motor handicap involving the use of his hands or arms which prevents him from pointing, hold up two single pictures sufficiently apart to observe whether he looks at the one named. This procedure should be followed with all five pictures. Be sure to use different pairs of pictures chosen at random so that the child does not use a given picture as a clue.)

Scoring: Each subitem of this grouping is scored as pass or fail. Pass is defined as a definite identification of the picture named by pointing. Fail is defined as any response such as, for example, pointing to the wrong picture, repetition of the word, or no response in any way from the child. The child must pass all six subitems in this group to pass the item. If Item 1 is passed, discontinue the test.

Item 2: Word and Object Identification

Purpose: To determine the comprehension of a verbal symbol referring to the corresponding object.

Materials: Shoe, fork, cup, toothbrush, dog and spoon.

Procedure: Place the objects on the table in a row, following the order of presentation as shown above. Say the word "CUP" with a rising inflection. If the child does not respond by touching the cup or picking it up, say the word again in the same way and simultaneously pick up the object in order to demonstrate the desired response. Replace the cup in the same spot and repeat the word in the same way accompanied by a hand gesture without indicating the object, ("GIVE ME"). Repeat the request without demonstration with each of the other objects. (If the child has a motor handicap involving the use of his hands or arms which prevents him from pointing, hold up two objects sufficiently apart to observe whether he looks at the one named. Repeat the procedure with all five objects. Be sure to use different pairs of objects chosen at random so that the child does not use a given object as a clue.)

Scoring: Each subitem of this grouping is scored as pass or fail. Pass is defined as a definite identification of the object named by pointing, picking it up, touching it, or pantomiming its use. Fail is defined as a response other than the above; for example, pointing to the wrong object, repetition of the word, or no response. The child must pass all six subitems in the group to pass the item. If Item 2 is passed, discontinue the test.

Item 3: Pantomime and Object Identification

Purpose: To determine the comprehension of pantomime describing the use of object.

Materials: Toothbrush, spoon and cup.

Procedure: Place the objects on the table in a row, in the order shown above. Indicate through appropriate pantomime that you would like the child to identify the cup. For example, without picking up or touching the cup, pretend you are drinking from a cup and then look searchingly at the objects. The child should identify the object by pointing to it or by touching or picking it up. Repeat the procedure for the toothbrush and spoon. All the objects should always be replaced in the same order in front of the child even after he has identified one of them.

Scoring: Each subitem of the grouping is scored as pass or fail. Pass is defined as the ability to identify an object after its use is pantomimed by touching it or picking it up. Fail is defined as the incorrect identification of the object or as echoing the examiner's pantomime without picking the object up or touching it. The child must pass all three subitems in this group to pass the item. If Item 3 is passed, discontinue the test.

April 1964

Item 4: Matching Object to Picture

Purpose: To determine the ability to associate an object with the corresponding visual representation.

Materials: Composite picture card showing shoe, cup, fork, spoon, dog and toothbrush. Corresponding objects.

Procedure: Place the composite picture card on the table facing the child. Demonstrate what is wanted by placing the *object shoe* on the *picture shoe.* Remove the *object shoe* from the *picture shoe.* This constitutes a practice trial and should not be scored. The object shoe is therefore not used again. In the order shown above under "Materials" proceed to hand the child each succeeding object (one at a time) and ask him by word or pantomime to place the object on the corresponding picture. Be careful not to indicate the exact spot on which the child is to place the object. The child gets only one trial for each object.

Scoring: Each subitem of this grouping is scored as pass or fail. Pass is defined as the ability to match the object with the picture correctly. Fail is defined as the incorrect matching of object to picture or no response in any way from the child. The child must pass five of the six subitems in this group to pass the item.

Summary Scoring Instructions for the Language Reception Area (For entry on the "Final Summary of Test Performance" on the scoring record.)

1. The following procedure is to be used in recording a summary total score for performance in this area in terms of "normal," "suspect," or "abnormal" evaluations:

   Normal   : Child passes all of the three verbal comprehension items.
   Suspect   : Child passes any two out of the three verbal comprehension items.
   Abnormal : Child fails two or all of the three verbal comprehension items.

2. If the child receives a summary total score of "abnormal" for the language reception area (i.e., he fails two or all three verbal comprehension items), continue testing by administering the items in the alternate comprehension subarea. To repeat, please note that if the child is marked "normal" or "suspect" on the verbal comprehension subarea, it is not necessary to administer the alternate comprehension subarea.

AREA: Language Expression (PS-11)

SUBAREA: Verbal Expression

Purpose: To determine the ability of the child to communicate or express himself in words appropriate to his age level and to the materials presented to him.

Item 1: Naming Objects

Purpose: To determine whether the child can express himself verbally by giving the names to a series of objects that are presented to him.

Materials: Chair, scissors, dog, key and button.

Procedure: Present the objects one at a time. Have the child name each. Say, "WHAT IS THIS?" or "WHAT DO YOU CALL THIS?". Present in the following order:

1. Chair
2. Scissors
3. Dog
4. Key
5. Button

April 1964

Item 1: Naming Objects (Continued)

Scoring: The child must name four out of the five objects to be credited with a passing score. The object must be named. Perfect articulation is not necessary but the word must be recognizable. Responses in terms of use or descriptions are considered to be failures, but plural for singular and familiar childish names are considered satisfactory. If the child is inattentive or remains silent throughout successive presentations of the subitems, he should be scored as failed and his action should be further described in the comments section of the scoring record.

Item 2: Use of Phrases or Sentences

Purpose: To determine the child's ability to use phrases and sentences.

Materials: Chair, scissors, dog, etc., and any other materials or objects which seem appropriate such as pictures, games, etc.

Procedure: There is no standard procedure for evoking a flow of conversation from the child. Following, however, are suggestions to stimulate the child to express himself, but do not necessarily have to be used. The examiner may utilize objects, pictures, questions, and any other means to elicit verbal expression. The examiner may have to evaluate the child's performance by eavesdropping on the child's conversation with his parent or during play. Record verbatim as many responses or spontaneous utterances as possible throughout the examination. At least three different phrases or sentences, including the longest one, must be recorded.

Picture: "WHAT IS HAPPENING IN THE PICTURE?"
Question: "HOW DID YOU COME HERE TODAY?"

Scoring: The summary evaluation on the scoring record should be marked in accordance with the following instructions:

Pass: Any four of the five items on the checklist rated pass.

Fail: Anything below the requirement for pass.

Observations of deficiencies in language expression should not be limited to Item 2 solely, but should be noted, if possible, throughout the examination. The examiner must be sure that his judgments are based on an adequate sampling of the child's performance.

Definitions:

1. Sentence or Phrase Length
   Pass: Four words or more
   Fail: Three words or less

2. Sentence Structure
   Pass: Subject and predicate used correctly most of the time
   Fail: Subject and predicate used incorrectly most of the time

3. Relevance
   Pass: Response makes sense in relation to question or situation most of the time
   Fail: Response has doubtful meaning in relation to question or situation most of the time

4. Word Order
   Pass: Correct grammatical sequence most of the time
   Fail: Transposition of words in a sentence most of the time

5. Pronouns
   Pass: Uses pronouns correctly most of the time
   Fail: Uses no pronouns or uses them incorrectly most of the time

SUBAREA: Alternate Expression (Single-Word and Pantomime)

Purpose: This subarea is to be administered if the child is rated as "abnormal" on the verbal expression sub-area. (See page 12 for summary scoring instructions for the language expression area.) In this subarea, discontinue testing the child as soon as he passes any one item in the sequence shown below. Please note that no changes will be necessary in the summary total score for the major area as a whole since the child has already been designated as "abnormal" based on his verbal expression score.

Materials Required for All Items: Fer-Will Object Kit

1. Composite picture card illustrating cup, fork, spoon, toothbrush, shoe and dog.

2. Corresponding objects.

3. Sets of corresponding single pictures.

Item 1: Identification of Pictures Through Pantomime

Purpose: To determine the ability of the child to identify through pantomime (or by naming) the picture of a given object.

Materials: Composite picture card which includes cup, fork, shoe, spoon, dog and toothbrush. However, only toothbrush, cup and shoe are used for this item.

Procedure: Place the picture card on the table facing the child. If the child has any understanding of words, point to the picture of the toothbrush and say: "WHAT'S THIS?" The child should respond by trying to say "toothbrush" or by pantomiming the use of the object. Repeat the process for cup and shoe. (In the case of the shoe, the child may also point to his own.) If the child does not seem to understand spoken language, point to each picture questioningly as though to ask, "What's this?" and observe whether the child pantomimes use of the object.

Scoring: Each subitem is scored as pass or fail. Pass is defined as the ability to name or pantomime the use of the object depicted after the examiner says: "WHAT'S THIS?" or after the examiner points to a picture questioningly. Fail is defined as inappropriate pantomime, incorrect identification of the object, imitating the examiner's pointing, or no response in any way from the child. If Item 1 is passed, discontinue the test.

Item 2: Identification of Objects through Pantomime

Purpose: To determine the ability of the child to identify through pantomime (or by naming) a given object.

Materials: Toothbrush, cup and shoe.

Procedure: Place the objects on the table in a row facing the child. If the child has any understanding of words, point to the toothbrush and say: "WHAT'S THIS?" The child may respond by making a recognizable verbal attempt or by pantomiming the use of the object. Repeat the procedure for the cup and shoe. In the case of the shoe, the child may point to his own. If the child does not seem to understand spoken language, hold up each object in turn, ask: "WHAT'S THIS?" and at the same time look at it questioningly. Observe whether the child pantomimes its use or tries to name it.

Item 2: Identification of Objects Through Pantomime (Continued)

Scoring: Each subitem is scored as pass or fail. Pass is defined as making a recognizable attempt to name the object, the ability to pantomime the use of an object (or in the case of the shoe, pointing to his own) after the examiner says: "WHAT'S THIS?" or after the examiner holds up an object and looks at it questioningly. Fail is defined as inappropriate pantomime, incorrect identification of the object, echoing the movements of the examiner, or no response in any way from the child.

Summary Scoring Instructions for the Language Expression Area (For entry on the "Final Summary of Test Performance" on the scoring record.)

1. The following procedure is to be used in recording a summary total score for performance in this area in terms of "normal," "suspect," or "abnormal" evaluations:

   Normal   : Child passes Item 1 and passes Item 2 of the verbal expression subarea.
   Suspect   : Child passes Item 1 and fails Item 2 of the verbal expression subarea.
                   Child fails Item 1 and passes Item 2 of the verbal expression subarea.
   Abnormal : Child fails Item 1 and fails Item 2 of the verbal expression subarea.

2. If the child receives a summary total score of "abnormal" for the language expression area (i.e., he is rated as "abnormal" on the verbal expression subarea) continue testing by administering the items in the alternate expression subarea. Please note that if the child is marked "normal" or "suspect" on the verbal expression subarea, it is not necessary to administer the alternate expression subarea.

AREA: Hearing Tests (PS-13)

SUBAREA: Spondaic Word Test

Purpose: To determine whether the child can hear spondaic words at the soft level.

Materials: Wollensak tape recorder, taped spondaic words, loud-speaker with calibrating meter, sound level meter, test booklet with pictures of spondaic words, scoring record, and the chart of test sequences.

Procedure: The specific details involving the arrangement and calibration of equipment, ambient noise levels, etc., that are delineated in sections II and III at the beginning of the manual must be noted carefully.

The equipment has been calibrated, and with the meter setting on Hi, and the child on a chair facing the loud-speaker say to the child, "NOW I AM GOING TO TURN ON THE RADIO. YOU WILL HEAR A LADY TALKING. YOU LISTEN AND TELL ME WHAT SHE SAYS." Before the Lo setting words are played say to the child, "NOW THE LADY IS GOING TO WHISPER THE WORDS TO YOU. BE VERY QUIET, LISTEN AND TELL ME WHAT SHE SAYS."

Included in this section is a chart which delineates all possible sequences for presenting the spondaic word test, depending upon each child's responses. The majority of children will pass List I and thereby follow either of the first two possible sequences shown on the chart. A careful study of the chart should be made before the tester administers the spondaic word test routinely.

April 1964

AREA: Hearing Tests (PS-13) (Continued)

Scoring:

Definition of Pass

List I, correct repetition of all three words

List II, III, IV, correct repetition of any five consecutive words or seven out of ten words

LIST V, correct pointing to all three pictures

LIST VI, VII, VIII, correct pointing to any five consecutive pictures or seven out of ten pictures

Definition of Fail

Anything less than the number of words or pictures required for pass.

Summary Score for the Spondaic Word Test Subarea:

Pass: Child passes either List III, IV, VII or VIII respectively. (Passes any one of the low-setting lists.)

Fail: Child does not pass any of the low-setting lists.

EXPLANATION OF THE CHART OF TEST SEQUENCES — SPONDAIC WORD EXAM

In an effort to conserve time and maintain the child's interest, List I has only three words given at the Hi level. If all three are passes, experience has shown that one can expect the child to immediately proceed to the lists at the Lo level. The procedure for administering the spondaic word exam is contingent upon the child's passing or failing List I (Hi).

/CHILD PASSES LIST I/

Omit List II (Hi), proceed to List III (Lo). If the child passes the latter, he passes the exam, STOP, go on to next subarea (pure tone exam). If the child fails List III (Lo), go on to List IV (Lo). If the child passes or fails List IV, STOP, go on to next subarea (pure tone exam).

/CHILD ATTEMPTS LIST I AND FAILS/

Proceed to List II (Hi). If the child passes List II, go on to List III (Lo). If he passes List III, STOP, go on to next subarea (pure tone exam). If the child fails List III, go on to List IV (Lo). If the child passes or fails List IV, STOP, go on to next subarea (pure tone exam).

If the child fails List II (Hi), go on to List III (Lo). If the child passes List III, he passes the exam, STOP, go on to next subarea (pure tone exam). If the child fails List II (Hi) and fails List III (Lo), go on to List V (Hi). If he passes or fails List V, proceed to List VII (Lo). If he passes or fails List VII, STOP, go on to next subarea (pure tone exam).

/CHILD DOES NOT ATTEMPT LIST I AND FAILS/

Proceed to List V (Hi). If the child passes List V, omit List VI (Hi), proceed to List VII (Lo). If the child passes the latter, he passes the exam, STOP, go on to next subarea (pure tone exam). If the child fails List VII, go on to List VIII (Lo). If the child passes or fails List VIII, STOP, go on to next subarea (pure tone exam).

If the child fails List V, go on to List VI (Hi). If the child passes List VI, go on to List VII (Lo). If he passes List VII, STOP, he passes the exam, go on to next subarea (pure tone exam). If the child fails List VII, go on to List VIII (Lo). If the child passes or fails List VIII, STOP, go on to next subarea (pure tone exam). If the child fails List V and fails List VI, go on to List VII (Lo). If he passes or fails List VII, STOP, go on to next subarea (pure tone exam).

April 1964

423

CHART OF TEST SEQUENCES — SPONDAIC WORD EXAM

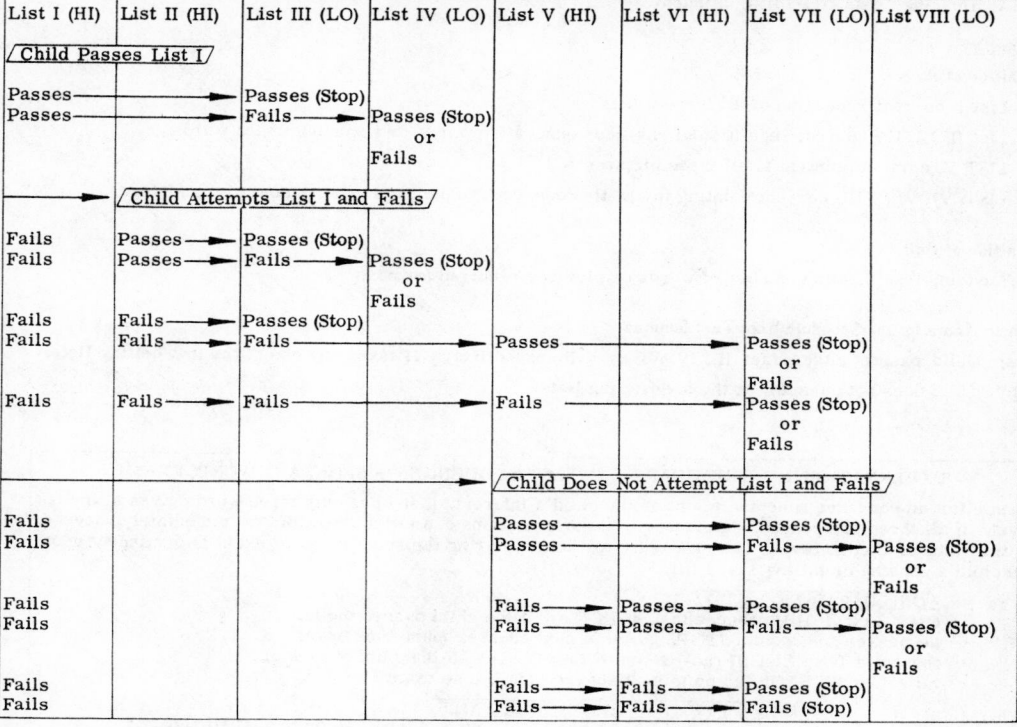

List I (HI)	List II (HI)	List III (LO)	List IV (LO)	List V (HI)	List VI (HI)	List VII (LO)	List VIII (LO)
Child Passes List I							
Passes	→	Passes (Stop)					
Passes	→	Fails →	Passes (Stop) or Fails				
Child Attempts List I and Fails							
Fails	Passes →	Passes (Stop)					
Fails	Passes →	Fails →	Passes (Stop) or Fails				
Fails	Fails →	Passes (Stop)					
Fails	Fails →	Fails ————→		Passes ————→		Passes (Stop) or Fails	
Fails	Fails →	Fails ————→		Fails ————→		Passes (Stop) or Fails	
Child Does Not Attempt List I and Fails							
Fails				Passes ————→		Passes (Stop)	
Fails				Passes ————→		Fails →	Passes (Stop) or Fails
Fails				Fails →	Passes →	Passes (Stop)	
Fails				Fails →	Passes →	Fails →	Passes (Stop) or Fails
Fails				Fails →	Fails →	Passes (Stop)	
Fails				Fails →	Fails →	Fails (Stop)	

SUBAREA: Pure Tone Screening

Purpose: To determine whether the child can hear pure tones at 20 db in relation to "audiometer zero."

Materials: A pure tone screening audiometer with two headphones held by a headband. A diagnostic audiometer may be used if it is available. A room with appropriate sound conditioning as described in "general instructions" of the manual.

Procedure:

a. Training and Warm-Up Period: The examiner may use any method which can obtain consistent responses to the sound stimulus. The following suggestions may be useful with particular children:

1. The examiner may wish to wear the headphones first, indicating visibly that the sound is heard.
2. Sometimes the child who rejects the wearing of the headband will accept one receiver held against one ear by the parent or the examiner. The receiver should be held snugly over the external meatus with care that arm and hand movements do not develop noises under the headphones.
3. The examiner may wish to train the youngster to react to sound from the receivers while they are still on the table and before being placed on the head.
4. One technique may begin with the examiner offering the stimulus at a comfortable loudness level (40 db). The examiner then says, "THE SOUND HAS GONE AWAY. TELL ME THE MINUTE IT COMES BACK." The stimulus is then offered at 20 db. The time interval between tones should be varied.
5. Play audiometry techniques may be used where the sound serves to signal permission for some action by the child, e.g., dropping a block into a box, etc.
6. Sounds of comfortable loudness often make learning the game easier to accomplish. Avoid using intensities above an indicated 70 db when the receiver is on the ear.

April 1964

SUBAREA: Pure Tone Screening Test — (Continued)

b. Test Period:

    1. Obtain reliable responses to tones presented at 20 db re.: audiometer zero in the following frequency sequence:

        Right Ear: 2000, 1000, 500
        Left Ear: 500, 1000, 2000

        Observe the response to each frequency separately. The examiner should be satisfied that a reliable response has been obtained for each frequency.

Scoring: Child's response must meet conventional criterion of latency with the stimulus. The examiner must take into account the possible occurrence of "response" by the child in the absence of the stimulus.

Summary Score for Pure Tone Screening Test Subarea:

Pass: Child indicates he hears all three frequencies in the ear under test at 20 db.

Fail: Child fails to respond to one or more frequencies in the ear under test.

If the receiver had to be held by parent or examiner during the test period, record this fact under comments.

Summary Scoring Instructions for the Hearing Tests Area (For entry on the "Final Summary of Test Performance" on the scoring record.)

The following are the criteria for evaluating the child's hearing:

Normal:
    1. Child passes both speech-hearing and pure tone tests.
    2. Child passes speech-hearing test, refuses pure tone test, and passes all other areas of the examination.
    3. Child passes pure tone test, refuses speech-hearing test, and passes all other areas of the examination.
Suspect:
    1. Child fails either speech-hearing or pure tone test, but not both.
    2. Child passes either speech-hearing test or pure tone test, but refuses the other test of hearing, and fails one or more of the other areas of the examination.
Abnormal:
    1. Child fails both speech-hearing test and pure tone test.

NOTE: If the child refuses to cooperate on the speech-hearing and pure tone tests, this is considered an inadequate test of the Hearing Area and will have to be given again during this administration of the Speech, Language and Hearing Examination or at a later date.

AREA: Speech Mechanism (PS-14)

SUBAREA: Examination of the Speech Mechanism

Purpose: To determine if deficiency is present in muscle functioning of articulators and if there are any structural abnormalities of the articulators. The examiner can use any order he desires within this area.

Materials Required for All Items: Flashlight (examination of the soft palate).

Item 1: Examination of the Lips

  A. Retraction

    Procedure: Demonstrate by retracting lips as for smiling and ask the child to imitate. Give two demonstrations if needed to make the instructions clear.

    Scoring: Retraction is scored as "pass" or "other" with additional boxes for describing specific deficiencies or abnormalities which may be observed. "Pass" is defined as the ability to imitate the examiner. "Other" is provided to describe deficiencies or abnormalities not listed with the deficiencies already included in this section of the scoring record.

                            April 1964

Item 1: Examination of the Speech Mechanism — (Continued)

B. **Protrusion**

Procedure: Demonstrate by puckering lips as for blowing and ask the child to imitate. Provide two or three demonstrations if necessary.

Scoring: Protrusion is scored as "pass" with additional boxes for describing specific deficiencies or abnormalities which may be observed. "Pass" is defined as the ability to imitate protrusion of the lips. "Other" is provided to describe deficiencies or abnormalities not listed with the deficiencies already included in this section of the scoring record.

Item 2: **Examination of the Tongue**

A. **Mid-Line Protrusion**

Procedure: Demonstrate by protruding the tongue. Provide two or three demonstrations.

Scoring: Protrusion is scored as "pass" or "other" with additional boxes for describing specific deficiencies or abnormalities which may be observed. "Pass" is defined as the ability to protrude tongue in imitation of the examiner. "Other" is provided to describe deficiencies or abnormalities not listed with the deficiencies already included in this section on the scoring record.

B. **Lateral Protrusion**

Procedure: Demonstrate by protruding tongue and moving it from one corner of the mouth to the other, outside the mouth. Provide two or three demonstrations if necessary.

Scoring: Lateral protrusion is scored as "pass" or "other," with additional boxes for describing specific deficiencies or abnormalities which may be observed. "Pass" is defined as the ability to protrude the tongue to the left and right. "Other" is provided to describe deficiencies or abnormalities not listed with the deficiencies already included in this section of the scoring record.

C. **Elevation**

Procedure: Demonstrate by elevating tongue to alveolar ridge. Provide two or three demonstrations if necessary.

Scoring: Elevation is scored as "pass" or "other," with additional boxes for describing specific deficiencies or abnormalities which may be observed. "Pass" is defined as the ability to elevate tongue to alveolar ridge in imitation of the examiner. "Other" is provided to describe deficiencies or abnormalities not listed with those already included in this section.

Item 3: **Examination of the Soft Palate**

A. **Elevation**

Procedure: Ask the child to open his mouth and say "ah" a sufficient number of times for you to make adequate observations of his palatal elevation.

Scoring: This item is scored as "pass" or "other" with additional boxes for describing specific deficiencies or abnormalities which may be observed. "Pass" is defined as the ability of the child to elevate the soft palate. "Other" is provided to describe deficiencies or abnormalities not listed with those already included in this section.

Item 4: **Diadochokinesis**

A. **Lips**

Procedure: The purpose of this section is to observe the child's ability to perform sustained, rapid movements of the lips. Demonstrate by repeating "buh" for one second at the rate of 6 to 7 "buhs" per second. Provide two or three demonstrations if necessary.

Scoring: This item is scored as "pass" or "other" with an additional box for describing a specific deficiency which may be observed. "Pass" is defined as the ability of the child to repeat "buh" clearly at least three or four times within a one-second period. "Other" is provided to describe deficiencies or abnormalities not listed with those already included in the section.

- 16 -

April 1964

426

Item 4: Diadochokinesis — (Continued)

B. Tongue

Procedure: Demonstrate by repeating "tuh" for one second at the rate of 6 to 7 "tuhs" per second. Provide two or three demonstrations if necessary.

Scoring: This item is scored as "pass" or "other" with an additional box for describing a specific deficiency which may be observed. "Pass" is defined as the ability of the child to repeat "tuh" at least three or four times within a one-second period. "Other" is provided to describe a deficiency not listed with those already included in the section.

Summary Scoring Instructions for the Speech Mechanism Area (For entry on the "Final Summary of Test Performance" on the scoring record.)

The following are the criteria for evaluating the child's speech mechanism:

Normal : Passes all items or fails only one specific item.
Suspect : Fails two or more specific subitems in different item categories and passes all others.
Abnormal : Fails three or more specific subitems in three or more item categories.

Note: These failures are determined on the basis of the whole test, rather than the number of failures within each item. So, for a child to be rated "suspect" for example, he would have to fail any subitem in each of two major items such as "lips" and "tongue," or "tongue" and "soft palate," etc.

AREA: Speech Production (PS-15)

SUBAREA: Voice

Purpose: To determine if there are significant deviations in pitch, loudness and quality.

Materials: None

Procedure: No specific procedures are used. Certain observations must be made during the examination. Special deficiencies applicable to each of the vocal characteristics are given on the scoring record. Boxes are provided for the examiner to check. "Adequate" means that there is nothing unusual noted concerning the voice. "Other" is provided to describe characteristics other than those included in the section.

Scoring: The following procedure is to be used in scoring this subarea:

Normal : No impairments checked in pitch, loudness or quality items.
Suspect : Impairment(s) checked in pitch, loudness or quality respectively.
Abnormal : Impairments checked in pitch and loudness, pitch and quality, loudness and quality, or all three items.

SUBAREA: Articulation

Purpose: To measure the child's articulation as evidenced by his ability to repeat individual words after these words are spoken by the examiner. Vowels, diphthongs, and single consonants which appear in initial and final positions in English are evaluated.

Materials: Wordlist.

Procedure: Say to the child: "I AM GOING TO SAY SOME WORDS AND I WANT YOU TO SAY THEM RIGHT AFTER ME."

April 1964

SUBAREA: Articulation — (Continued)

Scoring: All 60 underlined sounds in the 34 test words are to be evaluated. If it is necessary to elicit a verbal response from a child a second time (because of not being able to hear the child, extreme uncertainty as to whether or not the sound was correctly or incorrectly articulated, etc.) base the judgment of the adequacy of articulation on the second verbalization alone. If there is any question as to whether the sound was correctly articulated, count it wrong. Each underlined sound on the scoring record is evaluated according to the following code:

1. + = Correct articulation
2. — = Incorrect articulation
3. O = Omission
4. NR = No response

A sound is judged "incorrect" whenever any sound other than the test sound is substituted. It is judged "omission" if no sound is substituted. "No response" indicates that the test word was not elicited from the child. If upon administering the articulation subarea test the child, although responding to the first few words on the test, balks or refuses to continue or does not respond at all, the examiner should take careful note of the child's speech in connected discourse, as observed throughout the examination (particularly in the verbal expression subarea) and may evaluate him as "normal" on the articulation subarea if few or no articulatory deficiencies have been noted.

However, if articulation is checked as a remark to the intelligibility subarea rating of 2, 3, 4, or 5, then the examiner may, depending upon his judgment, mark the articulation subarea as "suspect" or "abnormal," if he has been unable to administer the articulation list.

1. **Initial consonants**
   Normal   : 15 or above
   Suspect   : 11 - 14
   Abnormal : 10 or less

2. **Final consonants**
   Normal   : 11 or above
   Suspect   : 6 - 10
   Abnormal : 5 or less

3. **Vowels and diphthongs**
   Normal   : 14 or above
   Suspect   : 10 - 13
   Abnormal : 9 or less

4. **All tested sounds**
   Normal   : All three categories normal, or, two normal and one suspect category.
   Suspect   : Suspect or abnormal on any one and suspect on at least one other of the remaining categories, or normal on any two categories and abnormal on the remaining category.
   Abnormal : Abnormal on two or more categories.

SUBAREA: Intelligibility of Speech

Purpose: To evaluate the intelligibility of the connected speech of the child. The evaluation should be based on his complete performance on the examination as well as the examiner's observations in general conversation with the child.

Materials: Checklist with associated definitions.

Procedure: Observation.

SUBAREA: Intelligibility of Speech — (Continued)

Scoring: The highest level of intelligibility of connected speech manifested by the child should be entered in the checklist.

How well can you understand this child:

☐₁ No difficulty in understanding what he says regardless of any deviations which may or may not be present in articulation, voice quality, pitch, rhythm, etc. However, such deviations must be listed in the comments column.

☐₂ Some difficulty in understanding what the child says.

☐₃ Considerable difficulty in understanding what the child says.

☐₄ The child has verbalized but is unintelligible.

☐₅ No speech.

☐₈ Other.

If 2, 3, 4 or 5 are checked, indicate the types of deviation you observed in detail. The ratings 3, 4 or 5 are considered impairments in intelligibility and should be recorded as "abnormal" on the scoring record. A rating of 2 should be recorded as "suspect" on the scoring record. If there are impairments noted regarding the intelligibility of speech, the following list may assist you in making your comments:

Impairments In:
1. Rhythm
2. Rate
3. Loudness
4. Pitch
5. Quality
6. Stress
7. Articulation

SUBAREA: Fluency of Speech Production

Purpose: To determine whether the child exhibits dysfluencies (for example, repetitions, prolongation, hesitation, insertion, arrest, etc.) in his speech and whether some struggle or special effort to produce speech accompanies these events.

Materials: Checklist.

Procedure: Observations are made throughout the test. The examiner's attention is called to the opportunity to evaluate this subarea while administering the verbal expression items.

Scoring: The following criteria should be applied for this subarea:

Normal: 1. If "none" is checked for dysfluent events and struggle behavior.
            2. If "some observed" is checked for dysfluent events but "none" is checked for struggle behavior.

Suspect: 1. If "some observed" is checked for both dysfluent events and struggle behavior.
            2. If "none" is checked for dysfluent events but "some observed" is checked for struggle behavior.
            3. If "many observed" is checked for dysfluent events, and "none observed" is checked for struggle behavior.
            4. If "none observed" is checked for dysfluent events and "many observed" is checked for struggle behavior.

Abnormal: 1. If "many observed" is checked for both dysfluent events and struggle behavior.
            2. If "many observed" is checked for dysfluent events and "some observed" is checked for struggle behavior.
            3. If "some observed" is checked for dysfluent events and "many observed" is checked for struggle behavior.

April 1964

SUBAREA: Fluency — (Continued)

> **Summary Scoring Instructions for the Speech Production Area** (For entry in the "Final Summary of Test Performance" on the scoring record.)
>
> The following are the criteria for evaluating the child's performance in the speech production area:
>
> **Normal:**
> 1. Normal ratings on all subareas.
> 2. Suspect rating on voice subarea alone or suspect rating on articulation subarea alone or suspect rating on fluency of speech production subarea alone with normal ratings on all other areas.
>
> **Suspect:**
> 1. Suspect rating on intelligibility subarea alone.
> 2. Suspect ratings on voice and articulation subareas together.
> 3. Suspect ratings on voice and fluency subareas together, or fluency and articulation subareas together.
> 4. Abnormal rating on voice subarea alone.
> 5. Abnormal rating on articulation subarea alone.
>
> **Abnormal:**
> 1. Abnormal rating on intelligibility subarea alone.
> 2. Abnormal rating on fluency subarea alone.
> 3. Abnormal ratings on any other two subareas.

AREA: Auditory Memory for Digits and Nonsense Syllables (PS-12)

SUBAREA: Recall of Digits

Purpose: Although auditory memory has been designated as a major area of this examination, it has not been included as a category in the "Final Summary of Test Performance." The examiner is required to administer this test area to every child, regardless of performance on other major areas of the test battery.

Item 1: Two-Digit Series

Purpose: To measure span of auditory memory and the ability to remember the details of auditory stimuli in sequence.

Materials: List of digits, scoring form, stop watch.

Procedure: There are four series of digits. Whenever the child has repeated one series in correct order, proceed to the three-digit series. Pronounce the digits distinctly and with uniform emphasis at the rate of one per second. Each series is to be given only once. Do not repeat any series for the child. Say to the child: "LISTEN; SAY 3-1. NOW, SAY 4-2." etc.

1. "4 - 2."
2. "8 - 5."
3. "6 - 1."
4. "3 - 8."

Scoring: The following definitions of the terms used in the scoring procedure applies to both the two-digit and three-digit series:
1. **Pass:** Child repeats one set of digits correctly and in given sequence. (See scoring record.)
2. **Fail:** Child does not repeat any of the sets of digits correctly or in given sequence.

The important point in scoring a response is whether the digits are recognized and repeated in correct sequence. The emphasis is not upon correct articulation but upon recognizable recall in sequence. Therefore, if the child, for example, should say "foh-foo" or "oh-oo" instead of "4 - 2" this is to be scored as a correct response. If the child should repeat the same number of sound units as the series presented but you cannot recognize the numbers, score as a failing response. Although it is not necessary to record verbatim responses to items that are passed in this area, it is important that the examiner record all verbatim responses to items that are failed.

Item 2: Three-Digit Series

Purpose: To measure span of auditory memory and the ability to remember the details of auditory stimuli in sequence.

Materials: List of three-digit series, scoring form, stop watch.

Procedure: There are four series of digits. Pronounce the digits distinctly and with uniform emphasis at the rate of one per second. Each series is to be given only once. Do not repeat any series for the child. Whenever the child has repeated one series in correct order, proceed to the subarea recall of nonsense syllables.

1. "3 - 6 - 2."
2. "8 - 3 - 1."
3. "6 - 2 - 8."
4. "2 - 4 - 1."

Scoring: The following definitions of the terms used in the scoring procedure apply to both the two-digit and three-digit series.

1. Pass: Child repeats one set of digits correctly and in given sequence.
2. Fail: Child does not repeat any of the sets of digits correctly or in given sequence.

The important point in scoring a response is whether the digits are recognized and repeated in correct sequence. The emphasis is not upon correct articulation but upon recognizable recall in sequence. Therefore, if the child, for example, should say "fee-fih-oo" or "ee-ih-oo" instead of "3 - 6 - 2," this is to be scored as a correct response. If he should repeat the same number of sound units as the series presented, but you can not understand him, score as failing response. Record verbatim child's response on scoring form. Place check mark in the appropriate column.

SUBAREA: Recall of Nonsense Syllables

Item 1: Two-Syllable Series

Materials: List of nonsense syllables, scoring form, stop watch.

Procedure: There are four series of paired nonsense syllables. Pronounce the syllables distinctly and with uniform emphasis at the rate of one per second. Each series is to be given only once. Do not repeat any series for the child. Say to the child: "LISTEN AGAIN AND SAY WHAT I SAY."

1. "POO-BAH."
2. "DEE-BOO."
3. "MOW-DAH."
4. "TAH-DOY."

Scoring: The following definitions of the terms in the scoring procedures apply both to the two-series and the three-series nonsense syllables.

1. Pass: Child repeats one set of nonsense syllables correctly and in given sequence.
2. Fail: Child does not repeat any of the sets of nonsense syllables or in given sequence.

The important point in scoring a response is whether the nonsense syllables are recognizable and repeated in correct sequence. The emphasis is not upon correct articulation but on correct recall in sequence. The child may omit the consonants but if the vowel is recognizable, this is to be scored as a correct response. Therefore, if the child, for example, should say "oo-ah" for "boo-bah" this is a correct response. Record verbatim the child's response on scoring form. Place a check mark in appropriate column.

April 1964

Item 2: Three-Syllable Series

Materials: List of three-syllable series, scoring form, stop watch.

Procedure: There are four series of nonsense syllables. Pronounce the syllables distinctly and with uniform emphasis at the rate of one per second. Each series is to be given only once. Do not repeat any series for the child. Say to the child: "NOW LISTEN AGAIN AND SAY WHAT I SAY." Whenever the child has repeated one series in correct order, discontinue testing.

1. "PAH-BOO-DEE."
2. "MOW-DAH-POO."
3. "TAH-BOW-DOY."
4. "DEE-GAH-TAY."

Scoring: The following definitions of the terms used in the scoring procedure apply both to the two-series and the three-series nonsense syllables.

1. **Pass:** Child repeats one set of nonsense syllables correctly and in given sequence.
2. **Fail:** Child does not repeat any of the sets of nonsense syllables correctly or in given sequence.

The important point in scoring a response is whether the nonsense syllables are recognizable and repeated in correct sequence. The emphasis is not upon correct articulation but on correct recall in sequence. The child may omit the consonants but if the vowel is recognizable, this is to be scored as a correct response. Therefore, if the child, for example, should say "ah-oo-ee" for "pah-boo-dee" this is a correct response. Record verbatim child's response on scoring form. Place a check mark in appropriate column.

April 1964

SPEECH, LANGUAGE AND HEARING EXAMINATION
LANGUAGE RECEPTION

2. NAME OF CHILD

3. DATE OF BIRTH	4. AGE	5. SEX	6. RACE

MO. | DAY | YEAR		☐ MALE ☐ FEMALE
		  1 2
			☐ W ☐ N ☐ OR ☐ PR
			 1 2 3 4
			☐ OTHER
			  8

7. EXAMINED BY	8. DATE OF EXAM
	MO. | DAY | YEAR

---

9. VERBAL COMPREHENSION

10. COMMENTS

1. IDENTIFICATION OF FAMILIAR OBJECTS

Objects   Pass   Fail

	Pass	Fail
CAR	☐	☐
BOX	☐	☐
FLAG	☐	☐
MAN	☐	☐

SUMMARY ITEM SCORE (PASS = 3 CORRECT RESPONSES)

Pass	Fail
☐ 1	☐ 0

2. UNDERSTANDING ACTION WORDS

Action Words   Pass   Fail

	Pass	Fail
PICK UP MAN	☐	☐
MAN JUMP	☐	☐
PUSH CAR	☐	☐
SHAKE BOX	☐	☐
WAVE FLAG	☐	☐

SUMMARY ITEM SCORE (PASS = 3 CORRECT RESPONSES)

Pass	Fail
☐ 1	☐ 0

3. UNDERSTANDING SPACE RELATIONSHIPS

Objects and Relationships   Pass   Fail

	Pass	Fail
CAT IN BOX	☐	☐
CAT ON TABLE	☐	☐
CAT UNDER TABLE	☐	☐
PUSH TRUCK BACKWARDS	☐	☐
CUP UPSIDE DOWN	☐	☐

SUMMARY ITEM SCORE (PASS = 3 CORRECT RESPONSES)

Pass	Fail
☐ 1	☐ 0

DO NOT ADMINISTER REMAINING ITEMS
IF CHILD PASSES AT LEAST 2 OF THE 3
VERBAL COMPREHENSION ITEMS   ☐
8888

COLLABORATIVE RESEARCH
PERINATAL RESEARCH BRANCH, NINDB, NIH
BETHESDA 14, MD.

REV. 4-64

PAGE
1 OF 3

PS-10

433

COLR-3151-10
REV. 4-64

SPEECH, LANGUAGE AND HEARING EXAMINATION
LANGUAGE RECEPTION

12. EXAMINED BY	13. DATE OF EXAM	
	MO. | DAY | YEAR	

---

14. ALTERNATE COMPREHENSION

1. WORD AND PICTURE IDENTIFICATION

Pictures   Pass   Fail

	Pass	Fail
CUP	☐	☐
DOG	☐	☐
TOOTHBRUSH	☐	☐
SPOON	☐	☐
FORK	☐	☐
SHOE	☐	☐

SUMMARY ITEM SCORE (PASS = 6 CORRECT RESPONSES)

	Pass	Fail
	☐ 1	☐ 0

DO NOT ADMINISTER REMAINING ITEMS   ☐ 888
IF CHILD PASSES ITEM 1

2. WORD AND OBJECT IDENTIFICATION

Objects   Pass   Fail

	Pass	Fail
CUP	☐	☐
FORK	☐	☐
SHOE	☐	☐
SPOON	☐	☐
DOG	☐	☐
TOOTHBRUSH	☐	☐

SUMMARY ITEM SCORE (PASS = 6 CORRECT RESPONSES)

	Pass	Fail
	☐ 1	☐ 0

DO NOT ADMINISTER REMAINING ITEMS   ☐ 88
IF CHILD PASSES ITEM 2

COLR—3151-10
REV. 4-64

SPEECH, LANGUAGE AND HEARING EXAMINATION
LANGUAGE RECEPTION

16. PATIENT IDENTIFICATION

17. EXAMINED BY	18. DATE OF EXAM	
	MO.	DAY	YEAR

14. ALTERNATE COMPREHENSION (continued)

3. PANTOMIME AND OBJECT IDENTIFICATION

Objects and Pantomime	Pass	Fail
CUP	☐	☐
TOOTHBRUSH	☐	☐
SPOON	☐	☐

SUMMARY ITEM SCORE (PASS = 3 CORRECT RESPONSES)

	Pass	Fail
	☐ 1	☐ 0

DO NOT ADMINISTER ITEM 4
IF CHILD PASSES ITEM 3   ☐ 8

4. MATCHING OBJECT TO PICTURE

Objects and Pictures	Pass	Fail
SHOE	☐	☐
CUP	☐	☐
FORK	☐	☐
SPOON	☐	☐
DOG	☐	☐
TOOTHBRUSH	☐	☐

SUMMARY ITEM SCORE (PASS = 5 CORRECT RESPONSES)

	Pass	Fail
	☐ 1	☐ 0

19. COMMENTS

COLLABORATIVE RESEARCH
PERINATAL RESEARCH BRANCH, NINDB, NIH
BETHESDA 14, MD.

435

COLR-3151-11
REV. 4-64

SPEECH, LANGUAGE AND HEARING EXAMINATION
LANGUAGE EXPRESSION

2. NAME OF CHILD

3. DATE OF BIRTH			4. AGE	5. SEX	6. RACE
MO.	DAY	YEAR		☐ MALE ☐ FEMALE 1　　　2	☐ W ☐ N ☐ OR ☐ PR 1　2　3　4 ☐ OTHER 6

7. EXAMINED BY	8. DATE OF EXAM.		
	MO.	DAY	YEAR

---

9. VERBAL EXPRESSION

10. COMMENTS

1. NAMING OBJECTS

Objects	Pass	Fail
CHAIR	☐	☐
SCISSORS	☐	☐
DOG	☐	☐
KEY	☐	☐
BUTTON	☐	☐

SUMMARY ITEM SCORE (PASS = 4 CORRECT RESPONSES)

Pass	Fail
☐ 1	☐ 0

2. USE OF PHRASES OR SENTENCES
CHECKLIST FOR USE OF PHRASES OR SENTENCES
(SEE MANUAL FOR DEFINITION OF TERMS "SENTENCE OR
PHRASE LENGTH," "SENTENCE STRUCTURE," ETC., AS
WELL AS SCORING DEFINITIONS)

	Pass	Fail
SENTENCE OR PHRASE LENGTH	☐ 1	☐ 0
SENTENCE STRUCTURE	☐ 1	☐ 0
RELEVANCE	☐ 1	☐ 0
WORD ORDER	☐ 1	☐ 0
USE OF PRONOUNS	☐ 1	☐ 0

SUMMARY ITEM SCORE *(See Manual for Instructions)*

Pass	Fail
☐ 1	☐ 0

DO NOT ADMINISTER REMAINING ITEMS
IF CHILD PASSES AT LEAST 1 OF THE 2
VERBAL EXPRESSION ITEMS

☐
88

COLR—3151-11
REV. 4-64

SPEECH, LANGUAGE AND HEARING EXAMINATION
LANGUAGE EXPRESSION

11. PATIENT IDENTIFICATION

12. EXAMINED BY	13. DATE OF EXAM		
	MO.	DAY	YEAR

---

14. ALTERNATE EXPRESSION (ALTERNATE TEST ITEMS)

15. COMMENTS

1. IDENTIFICATION OF PICTURES THROUGH PANTOMIME

Pictures	Pass		Fail
	Named	Pantomimed	
TOOTHBRUSH	☐	☐	☐
CUP	☐	☐	☐
SHOE	☐	☐	☐

SUMMARY ITEM SCORE (PASS = 3 CORRECT RESPONSES)

	Pass		Fail
	Named	Pantomimed	
	☐	☐	☐
	1	2	0

DO NOT ADMINISTER ITEM 2
IF CHILD PASSES ITEM 1   ☐
                                8

2. IDENTIFICATION OF OBJECTS THROUGH PANTOMIME

Objects	Pass		Fail
	Named	Pantomimed	
TOOTHBRUSH	☐	☐	☐
CUP	☐	☐	☐
SHOE	☐	☐	☐

SUMMARY ITEM SCORE (PASS = 3 CORRECT RESPONSES)

	Pass		Fail
	Named	Pantomimed	
	☐	☐	☐
	1	2	0

COLLABORATIVE RESEARCH
PERINATAL RESEARCH BRANCH, NINDB, NIH
BETHESDA 14, MD.

REV. 4-64

PAGE
2 OF 2

PS-11

437

COLR–3151-12
REV. 4-64

SPEECH, LANGUAGE AND HEARING EXAMINATION
AUDITORY MEMORY FOR
DIGITS AND NONSENSE SYLLABLES

1. PATIENT IDENTIFICATION

2. NAME OF CHILD

3. DATE OF BIRTH	4. AGE	5. SEX	6. RACE
MO. | DAY | YEAR		☐MALE ☐FEMALE 1 2	☐W ☐N ☐OR ☐PR 1 2 3 4 ☐OTHER 8

7. EXAMINED BY	8. DATE OF EXAM
	MO. | DAY | YEAR

---

9. RECALL OF DIGITS

1. TWO-DIGIT SERIES

2-Digit Series	Verbatim Response	Pass	Fail
4,2	_____ _____	☐	☐
8,5	_____ _____	☐	☐
6,1	_____ _____	☐	☐
3,8	_____ _____	☐	☐

SUMMARY ITEM SCORE (PASS = 1 CORRECT RESPONSE)

Pass	Fail
☐	☐
1	0

2. THREE-DIGIT SERIES

3-Digit Series	Verbatim Response	Pass	Fail
3,6,2	_____ _____ _____	☐	☐
8,3,1	_____ _____ _____	☐	☐
6,2,8	_____ _____ _____	☐	☐
2,4,1	_____ _____ _____	☐	☐

SUMMARY ITEM SCORE (PASS = 1 CORRECT RESPONSE)

Pass	Fail
☐	☐
1	0

---

10. RECALL OF NONSENSE SYLLABLES

1. TWO-SYLLABLE SERIES

2-Syllable Series	Verbatim Response	Pass	Fail
POO, BAH	_____ _____	☐	☐
OEE, BOO	_____ _____	☐	☐
MOW, DAH	_____ _____	☐	☐
TAH, DOY	_____ _____	☐	☐

SUMMARY ITEM SCORE (PASS = 1 CORRECT RESPONSE)

Pass	Fail
☐	☐
1	0

2. THREE-SYLLABLE SERIES

3-Syllable Series	Verbatim Response	Pass	Fail
PAH, BOO, DEE	_____ _____ _____	☐	☐
MOW, DAH, POO	_____ _____ _____	☐	☐
TAH, BOW, DOY	_____ _____ _____	☐	☐
DEE, GAH, TAY	_____ _____ _____	☐	☐

SUMMARY ITEM SCORE (PASS = 1 CORRECT RESPONSE)

Pass	Fail
☐	☐
1	0

11. COMMENTS

COLLABORATIVE RESEARCH
PERINATAL RESEARCH BRANCH, NINDB, NIH
BETHESDA 14, MD.

REV. 4-64

PS-12

COLR-3151-13
REV. 4-64

SPEECH, LANGUAGE AND HEARING EXAMINATION
HEARING TEST

2. NAME OF CHILD

3. DATE OF BIRTH			4. AGE	5. SEX	6. RACE	

MO.	DAY	YEAR		☐ MALE ☐ FEMALE
				  1 2
					☐ W ☐ N ☐ OR ☐ PR
					 1 2 3 4
					☐ OTHER
					     8	

7. EXAMINED BY	8. DATE OF EXAM		
	MO.	DAY	YEAR

1. PATIENT IDENTIFICATION

9. SPONDAIC WORD TEST (VERBAL)

1. METER SETTING HI (LIST 1)   10. AMBIENT NOISE LEVEL_____ DB.

11. COMMENTS

	Pass	Fail
COWBOY	☐	☐
BASEBALL	☐	☐
HOT DOG	☐	☐

SUMMARY SCORE (PASS = ALL 3 WORDS REPEATED CORRECTLY)

	Pass	Fail
	☐ 1	☐ 0

2. METER SETTING HI (LIST 11)

	Pass	Fail
DOORBELL	☐	☐
FLASHLIGHT	☐	☐
GOLDFISH	☐	☐
LIPSTICK	☐	☐
FOOTBALL	☐	☐
SIDEWALK	☐	☐
TOOTHPASTE	☐	☐
OATMEAL	☐	☐
CUPCAKE	☐	☐
BATHTUB	☐	☐

SUMMARY SCORE (PASS = ANY 5 CONSECUTIVE WORDS
REPEATED CORRECTLY OR 7 OF 10
WORDS REPEATED CORRECTLY)

	Pass	Fail
	☐ 1	☐ 0

COLLABORATIVE RESEARCH
PERINATAL RESEARCH BRANCH, NINDB, NIH
BETHESDA 14, MARYLAND

REV. 4-64   PAGE
                   1 OF 5   **PS-13**

439

SPEECH, LANGUAGE AND HEARING EXAMINATION
HEARING TEST

12. PATIENT IDENTIFICATION

13. EXAMINED BY	14. DATE OF EXAM		
	MO.	DAY	YEAR

9. SPONDAIC WORD TEST (VERBAL CONTINUED)

15. COMMENTS

3. METER SETTING LO (LIST III)

	Pass	Fail
MAILMAN	☐	☐
SEESAW	☐	☐
ICE CREAM	☐	☐
LIPSTICK	☐	☐
HAIRCUT	☐	☐
TOOTHBRUSH	☐	☐
OUTSIDE	☐	☐
SAILBOAT	☐	☐
AIRPLANE	☐	☐
BIRTHDAY	☐	☐

SUMMARY SCORE (PASS = ANY 5 CONSECUTIVE WORDS REPEATED CORRECTLY OR 7 OF 10 WORDS REPEATED CORRECTLY)

Pass	Fail
☐	☐
1	0

4. METER SETTING LO (LIST IV)

	Pass	Fail
POPCORN	☐	☐
ICEBOX	☐	☐
PANCAKE	☐	☐
PORKCHOP	☐	☐
ASHTRAY	☐	☐
ICE CREAM	☐	☐
TOOTHBRUSH	☐	☐
BIRTHDAY	☐	☐
HAIRBRUSH	☐	☐
AIRPORT	☐	☐

SUMMARY SCORE (PASS = ANY 5 CONSECUTIVE WORDS REPEATED CORRECTLY OR 7 OF 10 WORDS REPEATED CORRECTLY)

Pass	Fail
☐	☐
1	0

COLLABORATIVE RESEARCH
PERINATAL RESEARCH BRANCH, NINDB, NIH
BETHESDA 14, MARYLAND

REV. 4-64

PAGE
2 OF 5

PS-13

COLR—3151-13
REV. 4-64

SPEECH, LANGUAGE AND HEARING EXAMINATION
HEARING TEST

16. PATIENT IDENTIFICATION

17. EXAMINED BY	18. DATE OF EXAM		
	MO.	DAY	YEAR

9. SPONDAIC WORD TEST (NONVERBAL)

19. AMBIENT NOISE LEVEL_____DB.

5. METER SETTING HI (LIST V)

	Pass	Fail
COWBOY	☐	☐
BASEBALL	☐	☐
HOT DOG	☐	☐

SUMMARY SCORE (PASS = ALL 3 PICTURES IDENTIFIED
        CORRECTLY)

Pass	Fail
☐ 1	☐ 0

6. METER SETTING HI (LIST VI)

	Pass	Fail
BATHTUB	☐	☐
ICE CREAM	☐	☐
SEESAW	☐	☐
REDBIRD	☐	☐
HAIRBRUSH	☐	☐
ICE CREAM	☐	☐
REDBIRD	☐	☐
HAIRBRUSH	☐	☐
SEESAW	☐	☐
BATHTUB	☐	☐

SUMMARY SCORE (PASS = ANY 5 CONSECUTIVE PICTURES
        IDENTIFIED CORRECTLY OR 7 OF 10
        PICTURES IDENTIFIED CORRECTLY)

Pass	Fail
☐ 1	☐ 0

20. COMMENTS

COLLABORATIVE RESEARCH
PERINATAL RESEARCH BRANCH, NINDB, NIH
BETHESDA 14, MD.

REV. 4-64   PAGE
               3 OF 5

PS-13

441

COLR-3151-13
REV. 4-64

SPEECH, LANGUAGE AND HEARING EXAMINATION
HEARING TEST

21. PATIENT IDENTIFICATION

22. EXAMINED BY	23. DATE OF EXAM		
	MO.	DAY	YEAR

9. SPONDAIC WORD TEST (NONVERBAL CONTINUED)

25. COMMENTS

7. METER SETTING LO (LIST VII)

	Pass	Fail
MAILMAN	☐	☐
BLUEBIRD	☐	☐
TOOTHBRUSH	☐	☐
SAILBOAT	☐	☐
AIRPLANE	☐	☐
SAILBOAT	☐	☐
AIRPLANE	☐	☐
MAILMAN	☐	☐
TOOTHBRUSH	☐	☐
BLUEBIRD	☐	☐

SUMMARY SCORE (PASS = ANY 5 CONSECUTIVE PICTURES IDENTIFIED CORRECTLY OR 7 OF 10 PICTURES IDENTIFIED CORRECTLY)

Pass	Fail
☐ 1	☐ 0

8. METER SETTING LO (LIST VIII)

	Pass	Fail
POPGUN	☐	☐
GOLDFISH	☐	☐
NECKTIE	☐	☐
FLASHLIGHT	☐	☐
TEASPOON	☐	☐
TEASPOON	☐	☐
GOLDFISH	☐	☐
POPGUN	☐	☐
FLASHLIGHT	☐	☐
NECKTIE	☐	☐

SUMMARY SCORE (PASS = ANY 5 CONSECUTIVE PICTURES IDENTIFIED CORRECTLY OR 7 OF 10 PICTURES IDENTIFIED CORRECTLY)

Pass	Fail
☐ 1	☐ 0

24. SUMMARY TOTAL SCORE FOR SPONDAIC WORD TEST SUBAREA

Pass	Fail
☐ 1	☐ 0

COLLABORATIVE RESEARCH
PERINATAL RESEARCH BRANCH, NINDB, NIH
BETHESDA 14, MD.

REV. 4-64

PAGE 4 OF 5

PS-13

442

26. PATIENT IDENTIFICATION

SPEECH, LANGUAGE AND HEARING EXAMINATION
HEARING TEST

27. EXAMINED BY	28. DATE OF EXAM
	MO.	DAY	YEAR

29. PURE TONE SCREENING TEST

32. COMMENTS

1. TRIAL ONE   30. AMBIENT NOISE LEVEL_____ DB.

Sequence of Tones (at 20 db.)	Ear	Pass	Fail
2000 CYCLES	RIGHT	☐	☐
1000 CYCLES	RIGHT	☐	☐
500 CYCLES	RIGHT	☐	☐
500 CYCLES	LEFT	☐	☐
1000 CYCLES	LEFT	☐	☐
2000 CYCLES	LEFT	☐	☐

31. SUMMARY TOTAL SCORE FOR PURE TONE SCREENING TEST
SUBAREA

	Pass	Fail
RIGHT EAR	☐ 1	☐ 0
LEFT EAR	☐ 1	☐ 0

COLLABORATIVE RESEARCH
PERINATAL RESEARCH BRANCH, NINDB, NIH
BETHESDA 14, MD.

REV. 4-64   PAGE
5 OF 5

PS-13

443

COLR—3151-14
REV. 4-64

SPEECH, LANGUAGE AND HEARING EXAMINATION
SPEECH MECHANISM

1. PATIENT IDENTIFICATION

2. NAME OF CHILD

3. DATE OF BIRTH	4. AGE	5. SEX	6. RACE
MO. DAY YEAR		☐ MALE ☐ FEMALE 1 2	☐ W ☐ N OR ☐ PR 1 2 3 4 ☐ OTHER 8

7. EXAMINED BY:	8. DATE OF EXAM
	MO. DAY YEAR

9. EXAMINATION OF THE SPEECH MECHANISM

1. EXAMINATION OF THE LIPS

A. RETRACTION

☐ PASS
1
☐ PASS WITH GRIMACE
2
☐ PASS WITH TREMOR
3
☐ PULLS TO LEFT
4
☐ PULLS TO RIGHT
5
☐ DOES NOT SUCCEED IN RETRACTING
6
☐ OTHER (Describe)
8

B. PROTRUSION

☐ PASS
1
☐ PASS WITH GRIMACE
2
☐ PASS WITH TREMOR
3
☐ DEVIATES TO LEFT
4
☐ DEVIATES TO RIGHT
5
☐ DOES NOT SUCCEED IN PROTRUDING
6
☐ OTHER (Describe)
8

2. EXAMINATION OF THE TONGUE

A. MID-LINE PROTRUSION

☐ PASS
1
☐ PASS WITH HEAD MOVEMENT
2
☐ PASS WITH TREMOR
3
☐ DEVIATES TO LEFT
4
☐ DEVIATES TO RIGHT
5
☐ DOES NOT SUCCEED IN PROTRUDING
6
☐ OTHER (Describe)
8

B. LATERAL PROTRUSION

☐ PASS
1
☐ PASS WITH GRIMACE
2
☐ PASS WITH TREMOR
3
☐ HEAD MOVES TO SAME SIDE
4
☐ MANDIBLE MOVES WITH TONGUE
5
☐ DOES NOT SUCCEED IN LATERAL PROTRUSION
6
☐ OTHER (Describe)
8

10. COMMENTS

COLLABORATIVE RESEARCH
PERINATAL RESEARCH BRANCH, NINDB, NIH
BETHESDA 14, MD.

REV. 4-64

PAGE
1 OF 2

PS-14

444

COLR—3151-14
REV. 4-64

SPEECH, LANGUAGE AND HEARING EXAMINATION
SPEECH MECHANISM

11. PATIENT IDENTIFICATION

12. EXAMINED BY	13. DATE OF EXAM		
	MO.	DAY	YEAR

9. EXAMINATION OF THE SPEECH MECHANISM (continued)

14. COMMENTS

   2. EXAMINATION OF THE TONGUE (continued)

     C. ELEVATION

      ☐ PASS
      1

      ☐ PASS WITH HEAD MOVEMENT
      2

      ☐ PASS WITH TREMOR
      3

      ☐ DOES NOT SUCCEED IN ELEVATION
      6

      ☐ OTHER (Describe)
      8

   3. EXAMINATION OF THE SOFT PALATE

     A. ELEVATION

      ☐ PASS
      1

      ☐ LIMITED MOTILITY
      2

      ☐ ASYMMETRICAL ELEVATION
      3

      ☐ CLEFT, REPAIRED OR UNREPAIRED
      4

      ☐ OTHER (Describe)
      8

   4. DIADOCHOKINESIS

     A. LIPS

      ☐ PASS
      1

      ☐ UNSUSTAINED
      2

      ☐ OTHER
      8

     B. TONGUE

      ☐ PASS
      1

      ☐ UNSUSTAINED
      2

      ☐ OTHER (Describe)
      8

COLLABORATIVE RESEARCH
PERINATAL RESEARCH BRANCH, NINDB, NIH
BETHESDA 14, MD.

REV. 4-64

PAGE
2 OF 2

PS-14

445

SPEECH, LANGUAGE AND HEARING EXAMINATION
SPEECH PRODUCTION

1. PATIENT IDENTIFICATION

2. NAME OF CHILD

3. DATE OF BIRTH	4. AGE	5. SEX		6. RACE			
MO. | DAY | YEAR		☐ MALE ☐ FEMALE		☐ W ☐ N ☐ OR ☐ PR			
		1 2		1 2 3 4			
				☐ OTHER			
				8			

7. EXAMINED BY	8. DATE OF EXAM
	MO. | DAY | YEAR

---

9. VOICE

1. PITCH

☐ ADEQUATE
1

☐ UNUSUAL FLUCTUATIONS
2

☐ TOO HIGH
3

☐ TOO LOW
4

☐ MONOTONE
5

☐ OTHER (Describe)
8

2. LOUDNESS

☐ ADEQUATE
1

☐ TOO SOFT
2

☐ TOO LOUD
3

☐ UNUSUAL FLUCTUATIONS
4

☐ OTHER (Describe)
8

3. QUALITY

☐ ADEQUATE
1

☐ HYPERNASAL
2

☐ HYPONASAL
3

☐ HOARSENESS
4

☐ OTHER (Describe)
8

SUMMARY SCORE

NORMAL	SUSPECT	ABNORMAL
☐	☐	☐
0	1	2

10. COMMENTS

COLLABORATIVE RESEARCH
PERINATAL RESEARCH BRANCH, NINDB, NIH
BETHESDA 14, MD.

REV. 4-64

PAGE
1 OF 4

PS-15

446

SPEECH, LANGUAGE AND HEARING EXAMINATION
SPEECH PRODUCTION

11. PATIENT IDENTIFICATION

12. EXAMINED BY	13. DATE OF EXAM.		
	MO.	DAY	YEAR

14. ARTICULATION

CODE—
- + = CORRECT ARTICULATION
- – = INCORRECT ARTICULATION
- O = OMISSION
- NR = NO RESPONSE

Test Word	Initial (Consonants)	Final (Consonants)	Vowels & Diphthongs	Test Word	Initial	Final (Consonants)	Vowels & Diphthongs
1. MOUTH	m ___	θ ___		18. HOUSE	h ___		aʊ ___
2. NOSE	n ___		oʊ ___	19. WET	w ___		ɛ ___
3. PEACH	p ___	tʃ ___		20. YARN	j ___		
4. TOYS	t ___		ɔi ___	21. WHITE	ʍ ___	t ___	
5. CAR	k ___	r ___		22. CHEESE	tʃ ___	z ___	
6. BIRD	b ___		ɝ ___	23. JUMP	dʒ ___		
7. DISH	d ___	ʃ ___		24. PIN		n ___	ɪ ___
8. GAME	g ___	m ___		25. SING		ŋ ___	
9. FEET	f ___		i ___	26. BOOK		k ___	ʊ ___
10. THUMB	θ ___		ʌ ___	27. TUB		b ___	
11. SOCK	s ___		a ___	28. KNIFE		f ___	aɪ ___
12. SHIP	ʃ ___	p ___		29. MOVE		v ___	
13. VAN	v ___		æ ___	30. BATHE		ð ___	
14. THIS	ð ___	s ___		31. ROUGE		ʒ ___	
15. ZOO	z ___		u ___	32. BALL		l ___	ɔ ___
16. RED	r ___	d ___		33. CAGE	dʒ ___	dʒ ___	eɪ ___
17. LEG	l ___	g ___		34. YOU			ju ___

15. SUMMARY EVALUATION

	Normal	Suspect	Abnormal
INITIAL CONSONANTS	☐ 0	☐ 1	☐ 2
FINAL CONSONANTS	☐ 0	☐ 1	☐ 2
VOWELS AND DIPHTHONGS	☐	☐ 1	☐ 2
SUMMARY SCORE: ALL TESTED SOUNDS	☐ 0	☐ 1	☐ 2

INSTRUCTIONS FOR SCORING CATEGORIES:

INITIAL CONSONANTS:	NORMAL = 15 OR ABOVE; SUSPECT = 11-14; ABNORMAL = 10 OR LESS
FINAL CONSONANTS:	NORMAL = 11 OR ABOVE; SUSPECT = 6-10; ABNORMAL = 5 OR LESS
VOWELS AND DIPHTHONGS:	NORMAL = 14 OR ABOVE; SUSPECT = 10-13; ABNORMAL = 9 OR LESS
ALL TESTED SOUNDS:	NORMAL = ALL 3 CATEGORIES NORMAL OR, 2 NORMAL AND 1 SUSPECT CATEGORY;
	SUSPECT = SUSPECT OR ABNORMAL ON ANY 1 CATEGORY AND SUSPECT ON AT LEAST 1 OF THE REMAINING CATEGORIES, OR NORMAL ON ANY TWO CATEGORIES AND ABNORMAL ON THE REMAINING CATEGORY
	ABNORMAL = ABNORMAL ON 2 OR MORE CATEGORIES

COLLABORATIVE RESEARCH
PERINATAL RESEARCH BRANCH, NINDB, NIH
BETHESDA 14, MD.

447

SPEECH, LANGUAGE AND HEARING EXAMINATION
SPEECH PRODUCTION

16. PATIENT IDENTIFICATION

17. EXAMINED BY

18. DATE OF EXAM
MO. | DAY | YEAR

19. INTELLIGIBILITY OF SPEECH

HOW WELL CAN YOU UNDERSTAND THIS CHILD? *(Check only one of the following)*

Description

☐ NO DIFFICULTY IN UNDERSTANDING WHAT HE SAYS RE-
1 GARDLESS OF ANY DEVIATIONS WHICH MAY BE PRESENT
IN ARTICULATION, VOICE QUALITY, PITCH, RHYTHM, ETC.

☐ SOME DIFFICULTY IN UNDERSTANDING WHAT THE CHILD
2 SAYS.

☐ CONSIDERABLE DIFFICULTY IN UNDERSTANDING WHAT THE
3 CHILD SAYS.

☐ THE CHILD HAS VERBALIZED, BUT IS UNINTELLIGIBLE.
4

☐ NO SPEECH
5

☐ OTHER
8

INSERT CHECKS IN THE FOLLOWING LIST ONLY IF SCALE
VALUES 2, 3, 4 OR 5 ARE MARKED.

RHYTHM ☐   QUALITY ☐

RATE ☐   STRESS ☐

LOUDNESS ☐   ARTICULATION ☐

PITCH ☐   OTHER ☐

SUMMARY SCORE
Normal ☐   Suspect ☐   Abnormal ☐
0   1   2

20. COMMENTS

COLLABORATIVE RESEARCH
PERINATAL RESEARCH BRANCH, NINDB, NIH
BETHESDA 14, MD.

REV. 4-64

PAGE
3 OF 4

PS-15

COLR—3151-15
REV. 4-64

SPEECH, LANGUAGE AND HEARING EXAMINATION
SPEECH PRODUCTION

21. PATIENT IDENTIFICATION

22. EXAMINED BY	23. DATE OF EXAM
	MO. | DAY | YEAR

24. FLUENCY OF SPEECH PRODUCTION

1. DYSFLUENT EVENTS

NONE	SOME OBSERVED	MANY OBSERVED
☐	☐	☐
0	1	2

2. STRUGGLE BEHAVIOR

NONE	SOME OBSERVED	MANY OBSERVED
☐	☐	☐
0	1	2

SUMMARY SCORE	NORMAL	SUSPECT	ABNORMAL
	☐	☐	☐
	0	1	2

25. COMMENTS

COLLABORATIVE RESEARCH
PERINATAL RESEARCH BRANCH, NINDB, NIH
BETHESDA 14, MD.

REV. 4-64

PAGE
4 OF 4

PS-15

449

COLR—3151-16
REV. 4-64

SPEECH, LANGUAGE AND HEARING EXAMINATION
ADDITIONAL OBSERVATIONS

1. PATIENT IDENTIFICATION

2. NAME OF CHILD

3. DATE OF BIRTH	4. AGE	5. SEX	6. RACE
MO.	DAY	YEAR			

5. SEX ☐ MALE ☐ FEMALE
1   2

6. RACE ☐ W ☐ N ☐ OR ☐ PR
1   2   3   4
☐ OTHER
8

7. EXAMINED BY

8. DATE OF EXAM
MO.   DAY   YEAR

9. STATE OF HEALTH ON DAY OF EXAMINATION. MAKE NOTE OF ANY CONDITION WHICH MAY AFFECT THE CHILD'S TEST PER-FORMANCE, E.G., HEARING AID, GLASSES OR OTHER PROSTHESES, RESPIRATORY CONDITION, RUNNING EARS, ETC.

11. COMMENTS

10. OBSERVABLE PHYSICAL ANOMALIES

1. HEAD – NONE ☐ 0
EXTREMELY SMALL ☐ 1
EXTREMELY LARGE ☐ 2
PECULIAR SHAPE ☐ 3
OTHER (Describe) ☐ 8

2. FACE – NONE ☐ 0
ASYMMETRY ☐ 1
MASK-LIKE ☐ 2
GRIMACES ☐ 3
TICS ☐ 4
OTHER (Describe) ☐ 8

3. EARS – NONE ☐ 0
ATRESIA ☐ 1
OTHER (Describe) ☐ 8

4. EYES – NONE ☐ 0
STRABISMUS ☐ 1
NYSTAGMUS ☐ 2
OTHER (Describe) ☐ 8

5. MOUTH – NONE ☐ 0
CLEFT LIP ☐ 1
DROOLING ☐ 2
MOUTH BREATHER ☐ 3
OTHER (Describe) ☐ 8

COLLABORATIVE RESEARCH
PERINATAL RESEARCH BRANCH, NINDB, NIH
BETHESDA 14, MD.

REV. 4-64

PAGE
1 OF 2

PS-16

450

COLR—3151-16
REV. 4-64

SPEECH, LANGUAGE AND HEARING EXAMINATION
ADDITIONAL OBSERVATIONS

12. PATIENT IDENTIFICATION

13. EXAMINED BY	14. DATE OF EXAM		
	MO.	DAY	YEAR

10. OBSERVABLE PHYSICAL ANOMALIES (continued)

6. HANDS AND ARMS — NONE ☐ 0

          IMPAIRED FUNCTION *(Describe)* ☐ 1

          OTHER *(Describe)* ☐ 8

7. LEGS   NONE ☐ 0

          IMPAIRED FUNCTION *(Describe)* ☐ 1

          OTHER *(Describe)* ☐ 8

15. UNUSUAL BEHAVIOR OBSERVED DURING TEST PERIOD

NONE ☐ 00

PURPOSELESS HAND MOTIONS ☐ 01

UNUSUAL POSTURING ☐ 02

EXCESSIVE CRYING ☐ 03

EXCESSIVE LAUGHING ☐ 04

HYPERACTIVITY ☐ 05

HYPOACTIVITY ☐ 06

WITHDRAWN ☐ 07

PERSEVERATION ☐ 08

ECHOLALIA ☐ 09

SPONTANEOUS COMMUNICATION, LIMITED OR LACKING ☐ 10

OTHER *(Describe)* ☐ 11

16. COMMENTS *(Please describe in further detail any behavior category that is checked.)*

COLLABORATIVE RESEARCH
PERINATAL RESEARCH BRANCH, NINDB, NIH
BETHESDA 14, MD.

REV. 4-64

PAGE
2 OF 2

PS-16

451

COLR-3151-17
REV. 4-64

SPEECH, LANGUAGE AND HEARING EXAMINATION
FINAL SUMMARY OF TEST PERFORMANCE

1. PATIENT IDENTIFICATION

2. NAME OF CHILD

3. DATE OF BIRTH			4. AGE	5. SEX		6. RACE
MO.	DAY	YEAR		☐ MALE ☐ FEMALE		☐ W ☐ N OR ☐ PR
				1 2		1 2 3 4
						☐ OTHER
						8

7. EXAMINED BY	8. DATE OF EXAM		
	MO.	DAY	YEAR

---

9. LANGUAGE RECEPTION
☐ NORMAL   ☐ SUSPECT   ☐ ABNORMAL
0   1   2

10. LANGUAGE EXPRESSION
☐ NORMAL   ☐ SUSPECT   ☐ ABNORMAL
0   1   2

11. HEARING
☐ NORMAL   ☐ SUSPECT   ☐ ABNORMAL
0   1   2

12. SPEECH MECHANISM
☐ NORMAL   ☐ SUSPECT   ☐ ABNORMAL
0   1   2

13. SPEECH PRODUCTION
☐ NORMAL   ☐ SUSPECT   ☐ ABNORMAL
0   1   2

14. GLOBAL SCORING *
☐ NORMAL   ☐ SUSPECT   ☐ ABNORMAL
0   1   2

15. AUDITORY MEMORY

	Pass	Fail		Pass	Fail
2-DIGIT	☐ 1	☐ 0	2-NONSENSE SYLLABLE	☐ 1	☐ 0
3-DIGIT	☐ 1	☐ 0	3-NONSENSE SYLLABLE	☐ 1	☐ 0

16. ADEQUACY OF EXAMINATION
☐ ADEQUATE   ☐ INADEQUATE (Describe)
0   1

17. REFERRAL
☐ NO REFERRAL INDICATED
0

☐ REFERRED FOR FURTHER PROFESSIONAL EXAMINATION
1

18. COMMENTS

---

*INSTRUCTIONS FOR GLOBAL SCORING:

NORMAL = 5 MAJOR AREAS SCORED AS NORMAL.
4 MAJOR AREAS SCORED AS NORMAL AND REMAINING MAJOR AREA SCORED AS SUSPECT.

SUSPECT = ANY COMBINATION OF NORMAL AND SUSPECT SCORES IN THE 5 MAJOR AREAS BUT NO ABNORMAL SCORES.
AN ABNORMAL SCORE IN ANY OF THE 5 MAJOR AREAS AND ANY COMBINATION OF SUSPECT AND NORMAL
IN THE REMAINING 4 MAJOR AREAS.

ABNORMAL: ABNORMAL SCORES IN 2 OR MORE OF THE 5 MAJOR AREAS.

COLLABORATIVE RESEARCH
PERINATAL RESEARCH BRANCH, NINDB, NIH
BETHESDA 14, MD.

REV. 4-64

PS-17

MANUAL FOR ADMINISTRATION
OF THE FINAL SPEECH, LANGUAGE AND
HEARING EXAMINATION

(for Forms PS–40 thru PS–45, inclusive)

COLLABORATIVE STUDY OF CEREBRAL PALSY, MENTAL RETARDATION, AND
OTHER NEUROLOGICAL AND SENSORY DISORDERS OF
INFANCY AND CHILDHOOD

APRIL 1970

MANUAL FOR ADMINISTRATION OF THE FINAL SPEECH, LANGUAGE AND HEARING EXAMINATION
(for Forms PS-40 thru PS-45, inclusive)

I. INTRODUCTION

An important objective of the Collaborative Study is to discover some of the causes of neurological defect identifiable, in some instances, as: (1) disturbances of motor function; (2) disturbances of mental function; (3) disabilities in learning, whether general or specific; (4) disturbances in symbolization and auditory function; and (5) disturbances of visual function. Since verbal communication encómpasses all of these functions, examining the verbal communication of the child plays an important role in the assessment of the neurological status of each child in the Collaborative Project. The 3-Year Speech, Language and Hearing Examination was designed to sample each of these aspects of verbal communication at a time when most children have begun to use language as a communication tool. Age three was chosen for this first examination because it was felt that the children whose language development was delayed, for whatever reason, would not yet have developed emotional overlays or negative compensatory mechanism.

Age 8 was chosen for the next speech, language and hearing examination because by this age most children: (1) can articulate all sounds in the English language correctly (Templin and others); (2) can use most of the grammatical and syntactic forms in their mother tongue; (3) can respond to formal audiometric testing in a satisfactory manner; and (4) have developed at least in an elementary way, the basic communicative skills including reading, writing, and spelling.

II. GENERAL INSTRUCTIONS

A. Introduction

In the administration of the speech, language and hearing examination, it is important that the examiners follow instructions carefully to insure uniformity in testing procedures. Examiners should, therefore, make every attempt to get to know the instrument well before actually administering it to patients routinely. It is therefore recommended that they practice giving this examination until a smooth and natural sequence is achieved.

B. Arrangement and Contents of the Examination

The examination is composed of a series of subtests. The major functions being tested, i.e., language comprehension, language expression, etc., are designated as AREAS and are referred to in this way in the specific instructions of this manual. Each of these areas may be composed of several subtests called SUBAREAS which may measure the function being tested by different means. Language comprehension, for example, is broken down into two subareas dealing with auditory verbal comprehension for one, and visual verbal comprehension for the other. Each subarea is broken down into a number of items, under which are generally included several sub-items. In all cases, wherever possible, the examination should be administered in the following sequence:

1. Hearing and Auditory Memory
2. Language Comprehension
3. Language Expression
4. Speech Mechanism
5. Speech Production

Each subarea of the examination should be administered as a unit with specific emphasis placed on the function under test.

Although the recommended sequence for administration of the examination will be appropriate for the majority of cases, there are some instances in which it may be necessary to change it. The examiner must note in the comments section any departure from the established sequence.

C. *Guidelines to Employ in Testing*

1. Make sure that the child is physically comfortable, i.e., he is seated in a comfortable chair and is able to manipulate any pictures or objects presented to him on a table suitable to his own sitting level.

2. Never test if the child is in obvious distress. Delay testing until the child is comfortable.

3. Generally exclude observers.

4. A few toys (which are not similar to the test materials) may be used to aid the examiner in putting the child at ease. Before the formal examination begins, these toys should be removed from sight and reach.

5. The examiner may indicate approval of the child and should avoid expressions of dissatisfaction.

6. The testing room should be free from distractions and as free as possible from ambient noise (see specification in item 5, page 3).

7. The materials should be within easy reach of the examiner, although they should be out of sight of the child.

8. Mark each test "adequate" or "not adequate" in appropriate box.

9. The procedure and the specific instructions to the child should be memorized as part of an attempt to achieve standardized testing. However, it is advisable to keep the manual readily at hand for reference. All scoring should be done inconspicuously and all sections of each scoring record should be completed to avoid confusion and misinterpretation upon final analysis. It is also suggested that examiners recheck each scoring record for completeness immediately following the examination.

10. Under circumstances where the examiner has not been able to elicit a response from the child, score according to the following procedures:

    a. Do not score in "pass" or "fail" boxes.

    b. Document carefully in the comments section the failure to cooperate or any other behavior explaining the lack of response.

    c. Do not score an inadequate examination of any area as abnormal. Instead, write an appropriate comment explaining that an adequate examination of the area was not accomplished and the reasons why.

11. If the examiner is unable to obtain the child's cooperation or has not enough responses to make an adequate evaluation, he must make provisions to readminister this area or subarea during the same testing session at a point when the child is likely to be more cooperative. Avoid successive administration of the same area or subarea.

April 1970

12. The examination should be administered in the sequence enumerated on page 1 of this manual. However, under very unusual circumstances, departures from this sequence may be adopted if the examiner feels he can thereby obtain a more representative performance from the child.

13. Whenever there is any deviation from the manual in the administration or scoring of the examination, this must be justified in the form of detailed and pertinent explanations in the comments section. Unless careful documentation is furnished in this way, the coders in the Central Office will earmark such deviations as errors with consequent corruption of the data and lengthy delays in data processing. Grossly deviant records without explanations will be returned to the Collaborative Institution.

14. All records must be edited carefully and completely by the examiner and supervisor prior to transmission to the Perinatal Research Branch. This means that all scoring entries must be completed and special measures taken to insure that correct scoring criteria have been applied.

15. Copies of all examination records even though incomplete or inadequate should be forwarded to the Central Office.

III. FACILITIES

A. Specifications for Examination Room

1. A quiet room away from the main sources of ambient noise is necessary.

2. The dimensions of the room should be at least 8' x 10'.

3. The ambient noise level within the room used for testing hearing should not exceed 40 dB on the ASA accepted sound level meter using the "B" scale.

4. If a sound-conditioned room is not available, the following suggestions for room selection and modification will provide additional sound control:

   a. Choose a room away from pedestrian traffic in halls and removed from street traffic, isolated from other noises within the building by distance or by the presence of intervening room or closet.

   b. Sound conditioning of the room will be improved by drapes, acoustic tile on ceiling and walls, carpeting, and by the use of storm windows if there is outside exposure.

   c. All room air conditioners should be turned off during the tests of hearing.

5. The examiner should study the ambient noise level in the room over a period of hours to become familiar with the effect of temporary noises such as footsteps, motor noises, etc., on the sound level meter.

6. He should wait before presenting the auditory signal to the child if there is a passing increase in noise level.

7. He should record the ambient noise level at the time of the hearing test in the appropriate place on the scoring form.

B. *Furniture Selection and Placement*

1. An examination table should be used of sufficient width and length to accommodate placement of materials during test presentations.

2. Heights of table and chairs should be appropriate for 8-year-old children.

3. The tape recorder used in the hearing test should be placed on a shelf or table to one side, to avoid distracting the child. The examiner sits between the child and the tape recorder so that he is within easy reach of the child and controls. If possible, the recorder should be out of the child's vision.

4. A table must be available to accommodate a pure tone audiometer. The child should not be permitted to see the manipulation of the controls.

IV. SPECIFIC INSTRUCTIONS

AREA: Hearing (PS-40)

SUBAREA: Pure Tone Audiometry — Air Conduction

Purpose: To determine the hearing level by air conduction for each ear separately.

Materials: A pure tone audiometer calibrated to ISO standards. Binaural earphones held snugly against the ears by a headband. Masking circuit producing a broadband flat spectrum (white noise) with control of output level. Test room appropriately sound-treated as described in "General Instructions" of the manual.

Procedure: GENERAL

1. Test the better ear first if there is information as to disparity between ears. Otherwise:

   a. Test the right ear first if the child was born on an <u>even</u>-numbered day of the month;

   b. Test the left ear first if the child was born on an <u>odd</u>-numbered day of the month.

2. When conducting threshold determinations, test tones should be presented for approximately one second.

3. Tone presentations should be spaced by varying intervals of silence.

4. Tones should be off (interrupted) when the level is being varied by means of the hearing level control (attenuator).

5. The child must not be allowed to see manipulations of the audiometer controls while being tested.

6. The child should be reminded from time to time to hold up his hand when and as long as he hears the test tones.

7. Audiometer calibration must be maintained.

April 1970
PS-40

SPECIFIC:

Seat the child comfortably and tell him "YOU ARE GOING TO HEAR SOME MUSICAL SOUNDS THAT GO BEEP, BEEP, BEEP. SOME OF THE SOUNDS ARE GOING TO BE SO SOFT OR FAINT THAT YOU WILL HAVE TO LISTEN VERY CAREFULLY TO HEAR THEM. I WANT TO FIND OUT THE SOFTEST, FAINTEST SOUNDS YOU CAN HEAR. AS SOON AS YOU HEAR A BEEP SOUND HOLD UP YOUR HAND LIKE THIS (demonstrate). KEEP YOUR HAND UP AS LONG AS YOU CAN HEAR THE SOUND. BUT PUT YOUR HAND DOWN AS SOON AS IT GOES AWAY. REMEMBER NOW, HOLD UP YOUR HAND AS LONG AS YOU HEAR IT, EVEN IF IT'S VERY, VERY FAINT; PUT YOUR HAND DOWN AS SOON AS IT GOES AWAY. DO YOU UNDERSTAND?" Repeat instructions as necessary to insure understanding of the task.

Then pick up the earphones and say "THE SOUNDS WILL COME FROM THESE PHONES WHICH I'M GOING TO PUT NEXT TO YOUR EAR; SO DON'T MOVE THEM AFTER I PUT THEM ON." Place the headset on the child's head gently, being careful that: (1) the right phone is on the right ear; (2) the earphones are in proper relation to the external auditory canals; (3) the child's hair and pinnae do not block the path of sound transmission; and (4) the earphone cushions fit snugly but comfortably over his ears.

Obtain reliable threshold responses by the ascending method as outlined below:

1. Present a tone of 1000 Hz to the first ear under test at a hearing level of 30 dB. If there is no response to the tone at this level, increase the level by successive 10 dB steps until a response is elicited.

2. After the initial response to tone, reduce the level by steps of 10 dB until no response occurs.

3. Increase the level by steps of 5 dB until the child responds again.

4. Reduce the level again by 10 dB steps until he fails to respond.

5. Increase the level by 5 dB until he again responds.

6. Repeat steps 4 and 5 as necessary to determine threshold. The threshold is designated as the lowest hearing level at which the majority of responses to ascending presentations occurs. A minimum of two responses to three presentations is required at this lowest level. Occasionally, four, five or more presentations will be necessary to determine threshold reliability.

7. Repeat the threshold determination procedure (steps 1-6) for the other frequencies in the order indicated: 1000, 2000, 4000, 8000, 1000, 500, 250 Hz.

8. Switch the audiometer to test the other ear in the same manner, except that the threshold at 1000 Hz need be obtained only once.

NOTE:

1. In rare instances (anticipated to be less than 1% of all cases), when threshold cannot be obtained by the prescribed ascending method, a descending procedure may be employed. Present the tone initially at the 30 dB hearing level. If the child does not respond, increase the hearing level by 20 dB steps until he responds. Then decrease in successive 10 dB steps until he fails to respond. Threshold is designated as the lowest level at which he responds. This should be repeated, if possible, in the interest of reliability.

– 5 –

2. If the Air Conduction threshold at any frequency is 40 dB or more poorer in one ear than in the other at the same frequency, the better ear should be masked with noise and the measurement on the worse ear repeated. Say to the child: "NOW I AM GOING TO PUT A HISSING NOISE IN THIS EAR (pointing to the ear to be masked). TRY NOT TO PAY ATTENTION TO THE HISSING NOISE. LISTEN FOR THE MUSICAL (beeping) TONE IN YOUR OTHER EAR (pointing to test ear), AND HOLD UP YOUR HAND WHEN YOU HEAR IT. REMEMBER NOW, HOLD UP YOUR HAND ONLY WHEN YOU HEAR THE TONES, NOT WHEN YOU HEAR THE HISSING NOISE."

Masking noise should then be introduced at the lowest level possible and increased gradually to a level of 60 dB Sound Pressure Level (SPL). While the masking noise continues at this level, determine threshold by the method prescribed.

Then increase the masking noise by 10 dB (to 70 dB SPL), and present the test tone at the threshold level just determined. If the tone is heard in spite of the increase in masking consider that threshold has been determined.

If the tone is not heard when masking is increased, raise the level of tone in steps of 5 dB until the child responds.

Increase the masking level again by 10 dB (to 80 dB SPL) and present the test tone at the previously heard level. If the tone is now heard at the same level in spite of the increase in masking regard this level of tone as the threshold. However, if the threshold for the tone heard at the previous level of masking does not shift in proportion to the increase in masking level (i.e., 10 dB threshold increase with 10 dB masking level increase), the threshold for tone has very likely been determined. An increase of only 5 dB for the tone when masking was increased by 10 dB can be disregarded if it occurs only once or occurs inconsistently when masking level is raised to 70 and/or 80 dB.

If the ear which is being masked is within 10 dB of audiometric normal threshold in the frequency range 500-2000 Hz, masking levels should be limited to 80 dB SPL to avoid distressing the child. But if the ear being masked is found to have reduced sensitivity by air conduction, it may be necessary to increase the level of masking above 80 dB SPL. In this event the amount of masking used may be increased in proportion to the amount of air conduction loss in that ear when the loss is averaged at the frequencies 500, 1000 and 2000 Hz. Indicate on the record for the ear masked the amount of masking used, if any, at each test frequency.

SUBAREA: Abnormal Auditory Adaptation

Purpose: To screen for the presence of abnormal auditory adaptation in each ear separately.

Materials: Pure tone audiometer and stopwatch.

Procedure: This screening test is done most conveniently following the pure tone air conduction test. The earphones may be left on the child's ears after the air conduction test unless they must be removed because he requires rest or because they interfere with hearing the instructions.

Say to the child: "NOW WE WILL DO SOMETHING DIFFERENT. YOU WILL LISTEN TO A VERY LONG SOUND, NOT A SHORT BEEP SOUND. RAISE YOUR HAND WHEN THE SOUND BEGINS—KEEP IT UP AS LONG AS YOU HEAR THE SOUND—AND PUT IT DOWN THE MOMENT THE SOUND GOES AWAY. REMEMBER, THIS SOUND WILL LAST MUCH LONGER THAN THE OTHERS. KEEP YOUR HAND UP AS LONG AS YOU HEAR IT."

Repeat the instructions if necessary.

April 1970
PS-40

Place the earphones carefully over the child's ears if he is not wearing them. Set the audiometer to 4000 Hz at a hearing level 20 dB higher than his previously measured threshold for that frequency in the ear under test.

Turn on the steady tone by placing the Interrupter Switch at the Normally On position and begin timing with the stopwatch the instant he raises his hand. If he lowers his hand before one minute elapses, note the time in seconds but continue to present the tone while inquiring "CAN YOU STILL HEAR IT?", as the child may have stopped signaling because of inattention. If he raises his hand again upon inquiry, ask him "ARE YOU SURE?" If he seems certain in his response and indicates that he has heard the tone for a full minute, mark him "pass" for the ear tested (right or left) at 4000 Hz. At the end of one minute turn off the tone and note whether or not the child lowers his hand. If he does not lower his hand, proceed to the other tests of hearing and come back to this later. If this behavior is the same at retest, consider the test as inadequate and note this in the Comments Section.

Test the other ear similarly at 4000 Hz at 20 dB above its measured threshold.

If the tone is heard for less than a full minute at 4000 Hz in either ear, record the time in seconds during which the tone was heard in that ear and mark him "fail" for the ear tested.

Failure to hear 4000 Hz for a full minute in either ear requires that the test be repeated in that ear at 500 Hz at a level 20 dB above the measured threshold for that frequency. The procedure and scoring are the same as for 4000 Hz.

SUBAREA: Pure Tone Audiometry — Bone Conduction

Purpose: To determine the presence of sensorineural components when air conduction pure tone testing indicates impaired sensitivity.

Materials: Same as for pure tone air conduction audiometry with the addition of a bone conduction vibrator (hearing aid type) held by a headband and calibrated to physiologic norms.

Procedure: Thresholds for pure tones must be measured by bone conduction when the air conduction threshold at any of the frequencies 500, 1000, 2000 or 4000 Hz in either ear is found to be poorer than audiometric normal (zero dB hearing level, ISO) by more than 15 dB. Test by bone conduction only the ear showing such deviation in air conduction, but test bone conduction at all frequencies (500 to 4000 Hz) in that ear. If both ears have air conduction thresholds greater than 15 dB at any frequency from 500 to 4000 Hz, then both ears must be tested by bone conduction. Test in the order 500, 1000, 2000, 4000 Hz.

The bone conduction vibrator should be applied to the mastoid region on the side to be tested. It should be seated firmly on the skin of the mastoid region without contacting the pinna, and should be held snugly in place by the headband. The headband should exert force of about one pound against the vibrator. Be sure that the child's hair does not intervene between the vibrator and the skin of the mastoid. Earphones should then be placed on the child's head in a manner such that the ear _not_ to be tested by bone conduction is fully covered by the earphone which will present the masking noise. The other earphone should be pushed forward on the head so that it rests on the cheekbone, leaving the ear to be tested uncovered while helping to support the masking earphone on the head.

April 1970
PS-40

Say to the child: "NOW YOU ARE GOING TO HEAR SOME OF THE SAME MUSICAL (beeping) TONES YOU HEARD BEFORE. BUT SOMETIMES YOU ARE ALSO GOING TO HEAR A HISSING NOISE IN THIS EAR (point to the ear covered by the masking earphone). TRY NOT TO PAY ATTENTION TO THE HISSING NOISE, EVEN IF IT GETS LOUD. HOLD UP YOUR HAND ONLY WHEN YOU CAN HEAR THE MUSICAL TONE IN THIS EAR (point to test ear) EVEN THOUGH IT MIGHT BE A TINY, FAINT SOUND." Repeat and elaborate instructions as necessary. Use the ascending method outlined for air conduction audiometry. Use the descending method only if the ascending method cannot be used successfully and note this on the record. First present the test tone at 30 dB hearing level without masking. Increase the level of the tone if it is not heard. The child may indicate that he hears it in the non-test (covered) ear. Nod reassuringly if this occurs, and introduce masking noise gradually from the lowest level possible to a level of 60 dB SPL. Present the tone again at 30 dB (or higher if necessary). With the masking noise on, determine threshold for the test tone.

Then increase the masking level by 10 dB (to 70 dB SPL). Present the tone at the measured threshold level. If the tone is not heard when masking was increased, increase the level of the tone in 5 dB steps until it is heard. The increase in tone level should not exceed 10 dB if masking is causing the shift in threshold.

Response to tone at the same threshold level in spite of the increase in masking level suggests that threshold has been measured. Additional confidence is gained by increasing the masking level by another 10 dB step (to 80 dB SPL); if the child responds to the same level of tone as previously, or at a level no more than 5 dB higher than he did with the previous masking level, consider this tone level his threshold and record it.

Be sure to turn the masking noise off or to an inaudible level while recording the result, and allow a moment of rest before testing another frequency with masking.

NOTE:

1. Do not use more than 80 dB SPL of masking noise unless the ear being masked also has a loss in air conduction sensitivity. In this case the amount of masking used may be increased in proportion to the amount of existing air conduction loss averaged at the frequencies 500, 1000 and 2000 Hz in that ear. Masking noise must not be raised to levels which cause obvious distress to the child, or which introduce the risk of over masking (i.e., masking the threshold of the ear under test).

2. Should the child not respond to the test tone at the limit of audiometer output (usually 50-60 dB in the range 500-4000 Hz), the threshold is recorded with a plus sign (+) appended to the maximum level of bone conduction used (e.g., 60+). The bone conduction threshold value should never be greater than the air conduction threshold value obtained at the same frequency. If it is, the apparatus is not calibrated correctly or the child has not responded properly. In either case the test result is not correct and the measurement must be repeated.

SUBAREA: Discrimination Test

Purpose: To determine the ability with each ear separately to repeat words heard at the level of faint conversational speech.

Materials: A speech audiometer or puretone audiometer with tape-recorder input and switching to enable testing each ear separately. A tape-recorder and tape-recorded PB-K word lists including demonstration samples of 5 words.

Procedure: Set the audiometer having level control to a level 30 dB above the measured threshold level for 1000 Hz in the ear to be tested. Say to the child: "YOU ARE GOING TO HEAR A PERSON SAYING SOME

April 1970
PS-40

Manual for Administration of the Final Speech, Language and Hearing Examination

WORDS VERY SOFTLY. LISTEN CAREFULLY AND TELL ME THE WORDS YOU HEAR. EVEN IF YOU'RE NOT SURE ABOUT IT SOMETIMES, TELL ME WHAT THE WORD SOUNDS LIKE TO YOU. TELL ME THE WORDS LOUD ENOUGH SO I CAN HEAR THEM. LISTEN CAREFULLY SO YOU WON'T MISS ANY. ARE YOU READY?"

Begin the recording with the sample words to determine whether or not he understands the task and can comply. If he complains that the words are too loud, lower the level by 5 dB steps as necessary and note this fact on the record form under Comment. If he states that the speech is too faint urge him to try responding. Repeat the sample as necessary to elicit response. Should no response occur then raise the level in steps of 5 dB as necessary until he begins to respond, and note this fact on the record. Do not change the level of presentation unless discrimination cannot otherwise be tested.

Obtain and record a discrimination score for each ear separately, assigning a value of 4% for each word in the test lists repeated correctly. Use any of the lists of 25 words for testing either ear, but do not use the same list more than once for any child.

Enter the hearing levels (dB) at which lists are presented and the discrimination scores (percent) in the summary table. Also indicate which lists were used for testing.

SUBAREA: Auditory Memory

Purpose: To determine the subject's memory for digits and for words.

Materials: List of digits, list of syllables, stopwatch.

Procedure: Examiner presents digits and syllables at the rate of one per second monitored with stopwatch. Examiner should introduce the digit test by saying: "I AM GOING TO SAY SOME NUMBERS. LISTEN CAREFULLY AND WHEN I AM THROUGH SAY THEM RIGHT AFTER ME." Record verbatim responses for each presentation.

Examiner should introduce the nonsense word test by saying: "NOW I AM GOING TO SAY SOME NONSENSE WORDS. LISTEN CAREFULLY AND WHEN I AM THROUGH, SAY THEM RIGHT AFTER ME."

Discontinue after failure of both items at the same series length.

Scoring: The score for digits and for syllables is the longest series of digits (digit span) and of syllables (syllable span) repeated correctly. If both series of the same length have been repeated correctly, increase the score by 0.5. For example, the child who correctly repeats one of the six-digit items but fails the other six-digit item, as well as both of the seven-digit items, receives a score of 6; the child who correctly repeats both of the six-digit items, but fails both of the seven-digit items, receives a score of 6.5.

AREA: Language Comprehension (PS-41)

SUBAREA: Auditory Verbal Comprehension

Purpose: To determine whether the child has adequate auditory verbal comprehension by assessment of his vocabulary development, ability to comprehend verbal concept dealing with time and space, and ability to comprehend verbally presented materials.

Scoring: Scoring requirements are described for each item respectively.

– 9 –

April 1970
PS-41

Item 1: WORD IDENTIFICATION (PEABODY PICTURE VOCABULARY TEST)[1]

Purpose: 1. To determine whether the child can demonstrate auditory verbal comprehension of single words by identifying appropriate pictures.

2. To determine the child's vocabulary age.

Materials: Peabody Picture Vocabulary Test—Form B, manual of administration and Booklet of Plates.

Procedure: The directions for administration of the Peabody Picture Vocabulary Test should be adhered to closely. See pages 6, 7 and 8 of the PPVT manual. The instructions for introducing the test are those specified for subjects below 8 years of age with the subject pointing to the appropriate picture. The suggested starting point for the examination is Plate 40. Basals and ceilings are to be established in accordance with the directions specified on page 8. Refer to the Peabody manual for establishing a basal age if the first few items, beginning with item 40, are failed by the child.

Scoring: See instructions in PPVT manual under "Recording Responses" and "Scoring the Test." By use of Table 2 on page 12 therein, find the Vocabulary Age for the raw score obtained by the child.

Item 2: ORIENTATION

Purpose: To assess the child's verbal concepts of time, direction and laterality.

Materials: Twelve sentences listed below.

Procedure: Ask the questions as stated, pausing 10 to 20 seconds for an answer, if necessary. If an answer is not given within 10 to 20 seconds, repeat the question once only, again pausing 10 to 20 seconds for an answer, if necessary. Note under Comments each question asked twice. The point is to get an answer for each question, but within a few seconds and as spontaneously as possible. Record the answer verbatim. Enter total of Pass responses.

Time:

	1.	When is your birthday?
(Detroit)[2]	2.	How many birthdays do you have in a year? ans. 1
(Detroit)[2]	3.	Are you older than your mother? ans. No.
(Hawthorn)[3]	4.	In what month does the Fourth of July come? ans. July
(Hawthorn)[3]	5.	What season of the year comes just before winter? ans. Fall, autumn
(Hawthorn)[3]	6.	Tell me the names of the days you go to school. ans. Monday-Friday

[1]Peabody Picture Vocabulary Test. Copyright 1959 by Lloyd M. Dunn. All rights reserved. Published by American Guidance Service, Inc., Minneapolis, Minnesota. Reproduced by permission.

[2]Portions of the Detroit Test of Learning Aptitude are reproduced by permission of the publishers, The Bobbs-Merrill Co., Inc., Indianapolis, Indiana. Copyright 1959. All rights reserved.

[3]Portions of the Hawthorne Test reproduced by permission.

April 1970
PS-41

Direction:

(Detroit)[2]   7.   Put one hand on your head and the other behind you.

8.   Suppose you were on the eighth floor of a building. If you took the elevator to the third floor, which way would the elevator go?
ans. Down

Laterality:

(Benton)[4]   9.   Show me your left hand.

10.   Show me your right eye.

11.   Point to my right ear.

12.   Point to my left hand.

Item 3: UNDERSTANDING A STORY

Purpose: To evaluate a child's ability to follow a story read aloud and answer questions verbally.

Materials: Story Number II (Durrell-Sullivan Reading Capacity Test)[5] reproduced below in the manual.

Procedure: Read story aloud (approximately 40 seconds) with expression. The story may be read only once. Instruct the child: "LISTEN CAREFULLY WHILE I TELL YOU A STORY BECAUSE I WILL ASK YOU SOME QUESTIONS ABOUT IT. READY?" Record the child's answers verbatim.

Mother had promised Ned and Ted a trip to the zoo during vacation. So one bright sunny morning they got on the bus and started on their trip. When they reached the zoo, they went to see the large animals first. There was a huge grizzly bear pacing his cage. The boys enjoyed him very much. At noon they had a picnic luncheon. When lunch was over they visited the monkey houses, where they saw the funny little animals performing all kinds of tricks. Later, just before going home, they visited the lions' cage. The mother lion was there with her cub. She was sitting near the edge of the cage, looking so fierce that the boys were very glad she was behind strong bars.

Questions:	Correct Responses:
1. How did the boys and their mother go to the zoo?	1. bus
2. What animal did the boys enjoy looking at very much?	2. grizzly bear, bear
3. What did they do at noontime?	3. picnic, picnic luncheon, lunch, they ate
4. What did they do after they finished eating?	4. visited monkey houses, saw monkeys
5. What was the last thing the boys saw at the zoo?	5. visited the lion's cage, saw the lion

[4]Portion of the Benton Test reproduced by permission.

[5]From Durrell-Sullivan Reading Capacity and Achievement Tests: Primary Test: Form A. Copyright 1939, 1937 by Harcourt, Brace & World, Inc. All rights reserved. Reproduced by permission.

April 1970
PS-41

Scoring: Give one point for each correct answer. It is assumed that a child could have answered all 5 questions for Story I correctly. The age and grade equivalents for Story II are as follows:

Score	Grade Equivalent	Age
0	Below Norms	
1	1.8	7-0
2	1.9	7-1
3	2.0	7-2
4	2.1	7-3
5	2.2	7-5

SUBAREA: Reading

Purpose: To determine whether the child has adequate visual verbal reading comprehension by assessment of his oral reading competence, and silent reading competence.

Scoring: Scoring requirements are described for each item respectively.

Item 1: ORAL READING (Paragraph)

Purpose: To assess ease and accuracy of the child's oral reading and to analyze the kinds of errors present.

Materials: Gray Oral Reading Test, Form A[6], manual of directions, first five reading passages, stopwatch (appropriate sections of record booklet adapted and incorporated into scoring form). A sixth reading passage has been included and may be used by the examiner if he has any doubt about the level of performance achieved by the child.

Procedure: Examiner should begin by saying: "I HAVE SOME STORIES WHICH I WOULD LIKE YOU TO READ OUT LOUD FOR ME. READ THEM THE WAY YOU WOULD TO YOUR TEACHER AND THE CHILDREN IN YOUR CLASS."

Show the child the first passage on a card, saying: "WHEN I SAY 'BEGIN', PLEASE READ OUT LOUD THE STORY ON THE CARD. READY. BEGIN."

Passage Number		Difficulty
1 ⎫		Pre-Primer
2 ⎬ Grade I		Primer
3 ⎭		Book I
4		Grade II
5		Grade III
6		Grade IV

Timing should start with the word BEGIN and continue until the last word of the passage is read.

[6]Selections from Gray Oral Reading Test, Form A, are reproduced by permission of the publishers, The Bobbs-Merrill Co., Indianapolis, Indiana. Copyright © 1963. All rights reserved.

April 1970
PS-41

"HERE IS THE NEXT CARD. GET READY TO READ. BEGIN." Continue until the pupil has made seven or more errors on each of two successive passages. After reading one passage with seven or more errors, if the pupil makes seven errors early in the next passage, discontinue by saying: "THAT'S A VERY HARD ONE. YOU NEEDN'T READ ANY MORE OF IT."

Record the time to the nearest second for reading each passage in the space provided for this purpose on the record blank. If a pupil notes that you are recording the time and as a result he tries to read more rapidly, tell him to read at his usual rate because he reads better that way.

Recording Errors: As each pupil reads, note carefully any errors he makes and record them in the scoring record. The following legend is useful in making a continuing record of errors:

1. *Aid:* When the pupil hesitates for <u>five seconds</u> without making any audible effort to pronounce the word, or <u>ten seconds</u> if he appears to be trying to pronounce it, the examiner pronounces the word. The error is marked by underlined parentheses.

    Example: (geologists)

2. *Gross mispronunciation of a word:* A gross mispronunciation is one in which the pupil's pronunciation bears so little resemblance to the proper pronunciation that the examiner must be looking at the word to recognize it. Such an error is marked by drawing a straight line under the entire word and writing the pupil's pronunciation phonetically.

    fratific
    Example: traffic

3. *Partial Mispronunciation:* When a word is partially mispronounced, specific types of errors should be noted and recorded as follows:

    a. When the examiner pronounces a part of a word for the pupil, enclose that part in underlined parentheses.

       Example: re (gard)   (1 error)

    b. Wrong sound of letters or groups of letters. Underline the part mispronounced and write the error or errors above it.

       Examples: veins, than, dazzling, himself   (1 error for each)

    c. Omission of one or more elements.

       Examples: house (s), st (r) aight, (al) most   (1 error for each)

    d. Insertion of an element

       al
       Example: already for ready, marked ∧ ready   (1 error)

    e. Wrong syllabication.

       Examples: pier/ced, alm/ost   (1 error)

— 13 —

f.   Wrong accent.

   Example: re′cord   instead of   record′   (1 error)

g.   Inversion.

   Example: on for no,   marked (n/o)   (1 error)

4.   *Omission of a word or group of words:* Circle the omitted word or group of words.

   Examples: I saw a (hungry) dog on the street.   (1 error)

   They fly passengers, (freight and mail)   from one city to another.   (1 error)

5.   *Insertion of a word or group of words:* Place an insert mark and write the word(s) above the point at which they were added.

   Examples: The   clear   sky was bright blue.   (1 error)
                    ∧
                         pretty little
   He called his   ∧   dog.   (1 error)

6.   *Substitution of one meaningful word or several for others:*

                              many
   Examples: The sun shone into _my_ large window .... (1 error)
                   there was
   Once _upon a time_ a boy .... (3 errors)
                sat on
   A boy _had a_ wagon .... (2 errors)
                sat on
   A boy _had_ a wagon .... (1 error)

The number of errors depends on the number of words replaced by the substitution.

7.   *Repetition of one or more word(s):* (Except when due to stuttering'0 Underline with a wavy line.

   Examples: _The_ boy ran away.   (1 error)

   The boy ran _far into_ the woods.   (1 error)

Repetition of the same word or group of words more than once counts as only one error.

Example: They played _for a_ long time. (2 repetitions of 2 words but only 1 error.)

In case the repetition is to correct an error, mark the repetition and cross out the corrected error.

                live
Example: _His_ pet bird sat on mother's hat.   (1 error, repetition only)

   If there is no repetition in correcting mistakes, no errors are recorded.

8.   *Inverting or changing word order:* Mark as in the example.

   Example: He ran   rapidly   there.   (1 error)

April 1970
PS-41

Scoring: The examiner should complete scoring as soon as possible, using the procedure outlined below:

1. Record below each passage:

   a. Time in seconds;
   b. Number of errors (all types) made;
   c. Passage score (0-9) derived from Table 1 (Passage Scores) on page 7 of the Gray manual, using the time (in seconds) and the number of errors (all types) for each passage;
   d. Specific types of errors.

2. Record on the Scoring Summary (page 7 of the scoring record):

   a. Times, errors and scores for individual passages;
   b. Total obtained by adding all individual passage scores;
   c. Grade Equivalent obtained from the Gray manual tables of tentative norms (Revised 1967). For Boys use Table 2 (Form A) on page 8; for Girls use Table 6 (Form A) on page 12. The Grade Equivalent is shown adjacent to the Total Passage Score;
   d. Specific types of errors for each passage;
   e. Specific types of errors total for all passages.

Item 2. SILENT READING (Paragraph)

Purpose: To sample the child's comprehension of written language by having him read a paragraph silently and then answer written questions by choosing one of five alternatives for each question.

Materials: Durrell-Sullivan Reading Capacity and Achievement Tests.[7] Primary Achievement A, Test 2. Sample Paragraph and Paragraph 1.

Procedure: "PUT YOUR FINGER ON THE SHORT STORY AT THE TOP OF THIS PAGE. (Examiner points to sample story.) YOU ARE GOING TO READ IT TO YOURSELF. WHEN YOU ARE THROUGH, I AM GOING TO ASK YOU TO ANSWER SOME QUESTIONS ABOUT THE STORY. READY—READ TO YOURSELF. WHEN YOU ARE THROUGH, RAISE YOUR HAND."

When the child is finished, say: "PUT YOUR FINGER ON QUESTION 1 UNDER THE STORY. (Examiner demonstrates on her copy.) QUESTION 1 SAYS: 'WHAT DID HELEN AND HER BROTHER DO?' WHICH NUMBER TELLS THE RIGHT ANSWER? (Pause) YES, 2 IS RIGHT. SO MAKE A RING AROUND THE NUMBER 2." (Indicate)

"PUT YOUR FINGER ON QUESTION 2. READ THE QUESTION. WHAT IS THE CORRECT ANSWER? YES, 3 IS CORRECT; SO DRAW A CIRCLE AROUND THE 3." Check to see that the child is recording the answers correctly. Assist him if he needs help.

"WE WILL TRY TO SEE IF YOU CAN MARK THE NEXT QUESTION CORRECTLY. PUT YOUR FINGER ON QUESTION 3. (Indicate) READ AND ANSWER THE QUESTION. (Pause) DID YOU PUT A RING AROUND THE RIGHT NUMBER? THE ANSWER, OF COURSE, IS NUMBER 5."

"YOU DO EXACTLY THE SAME THING TO THE OTHER STORY ON THIS PAGE. (Examiner points to Test Paragraph) YOU CAN BEGIN NOW."

---

[7]From Durrell-Sullivan Reading Capacity and Achievement Tests: Primary Test: Form A. Copyright 1939, 1937 by Harcourt, Brace & World, Inc. All rights reserved. Reproduced by permission.

April 1970
PS-41

Manual for Administration of the Final Speech, Language and Hearing Examination

Scoring: Give one point for each correct answer. The age and grade equivalents are as follows:

Score	Grade Equivalent	Age
0	Below Norms	
1	1.9	7-1
2	2.1	7-3
3	2.2	7-5
4	2.4	7-7
5	2.5	7-8

SUBAREA: Morphology

Purpose: To sample child's knowledge of linguistic form.

Item 1: KNOWLEDGE OF GRAMMATICAL RULES

Purpose: To sample child's repertoire of grammatical rules by having him complete each test statement with a common inflected word.

Materials: Illinois Test of Psycholinguistic Abilities[8]
Experimental Edition: (Auditory-Vocal Automatic Test).
Examiner's Manual and Picture Test Book

Procedure: Present the demonstration item in the Picture Test Book to S and Say:

"HERE (point) IS A BED. HERE (point) ARE TWO____."

Wait for S to complete the statement.[†] If S responds incorrectly, supply the correct response and repeat the statement; if S responds correctly, begin the test immediately. If Ss mental age is less than 7-0, begin with item 1; if over 7-0, begin with item 5. Continue testing until the ceiling level of six consecutive failures, or the end of the test is reached (whichever is first).

For Ss beginning with item 5, the basal level is reached when six consecutive items are passed. If S fails to pass the first six items administered (5-10 inclusive), continue testing until the ceiling or end of the test is reached, and then administer progressively easier items beginning with item 4 (4, 3, 2, 1) until the basal level is established or no items remain (whichever is first).

No help is given on test items except for the verb items (3, 5, 6, 11, 14, 17, 22)[‡] where one follow-up question for each such item is required when S fails to respond, or responds incorrectly. There are two general forms of this question; one is asked to attempt to elicit the progressive (-ing) form of the verb (item 3), and the other is asked to elicit the past tense form of the verb (items 5, 6, 11, 14, 17, 22).

---

[8]From The Illinois Test of Psycholinguistic Abilities. Copyright 1961 by Samuel A. Kirk and James J. McCarthy. Published by the University of Illinois Press, Urbana, Illinois. All rights reserved. Reproduced by permission.
[†]Occasionally young Ss will completely lack a final "s". See scoring procedures for procedure to be followed.
[‡]Marked with an asterisk on following pages.

Progressive Form: "NO, WHAT IS THE MAN DOING; HE IS____."

If S fails to respond correctly to <u>this</u> question, simply record the failure and go on to the next item.

Past Tense Form: "NO, WHAT DID____DO TO THE____? HE (SHE)____."
In item 11, for example, S may answer "finished." At this point E says

"NO, WHAT DID MOTHER DO TO THE LETTER? SHE____."

If S fails to respond correctly to <u>this</u> question, simply record the failure and go on to the next item.

TEST STATEMENTS

Demonstration. HERE IS A BED. HERE ARE TWO_____.

1. HERE IS AN APPLE. HERE ARE TWO_____.

2. HERE IS A HAT. HERE ARE TWO_____.

*3. THIS MAN LIKES TO EAT. HERE HE IS _____.

4. HERE IS A DRESS. HERE ARE TWO_____.

*5. FATHER IS OPENING THE CAN. NOW THE CAN HAS BEEN_____.

*6. THIS MAN IS GOING TO WRECK HIS CAR. NOW THE CAR IS_____.

7. THIS STICK IS LONG. THIS STICK IS EVEN_____.

8. THIS BOX IS BIG. THIS BOX IS EVEN_____.

9. ALL THESE POTATOES ARE BIG, BUT THIS ONE IS THE _____.

10. THIS MAN IS PAINTING. HE IS A _____.

*11. MOTHER IS WRITING A LETTER. THIS IS THE LETTER SHE_____.

12. THIS MAN HAS MANY PIPES. THIS MAN HAS EVEN_____.

13. HERE IS A MAN. HERE ARE TWO_____.

*14. MOTHER IS POLISHING THE COFFEE POT. NOW THE COFFEE POT HAS BEEN_____.

15. HERE IS A LEAF. HERE ARE TWO_____.

16. HERE IS A KNIFE. HERE ARE TWO_____.

*17. FATHER IS HANGING A PICTURE. NOW THE PICTURE HAS BEEN_____.

18. THIS CAKE LOOKS GOOD. THIS ONE LOOKS EVEN_____.

19. THESE PENCILS ALL LOOK GOOD, BUT THIS ONE LOOKS THE_____.

April 1970
PS-41

20. HERE IS A THIEF. HERE ARE TWO _____ .

21. HERE IS A MOUSE. HERE ARE TWO _____ .

*22. THE THIEF IS STEALING THE JEWELS. THERE ARE THE JEWELS HE _____ .

Item 2. SCORING

Score later using the correct responses and common errors listed below. Allow credit for all items below the basal level. The raw score is the number of items answered correctly. In judging unlisted responses, allow credit when S gives a meaningfully incorrect but grammatically correct response (e.g., smallest for item 9, where the _____ est suffix is required).

In the past tense items (5, 6, and 14) S may give a meaningfully and grammatically correct substitute for the listed correct response; he is not given credit for this response unless the inflections are phonetically identical. For example, in item 14, "cleaned" for "polished" is not given credit because "cleaned" ends with a "d" sound and "polished" (the correct response) ends with a "t" sound. "Refinished" would be a creditable substitute for "polished."

The intent of this test is to assess grammatical, and not articulatory, ability. Therefore, articulation errors are acceptable if the grammatical form is correct. It is unfortunate that the simplest inflection in English, the addition of a final "s," is also one of the last speech sounds to develop. However, most children who do not have an "s" have a substitute sound for "s" which is close enough to it to differentiate the singular case from the plural. In the standardization sample it was found that this test could be administered if the child had speech — that is, his approximations were clear enough to make a judgment about the correctness or incorrectness of his response. There is one exception to this. In a few cases, S had neither the final "s" sound nor an "s" substitute which made it impossible to answer items 1, 2, 4, 9, 14, 15, 16, 19, and 20. In such cases, the following procedure is suggested.

If, in talking to S, prior to the test, E suspects the lack of a final "s," he should ask S to repeat the following words: ball, balls, cat, cats, mess, messes. If S repeats all words correctly assume he has a final "s," use standard test procedure, and mark all test items wrong unless correctly inflected.

If, however, the plural and singular forms of these words sound alike, administer only the following 13 ("non-s") items: 3, 5, 6, 7, 8, 10, 11, 12, 13, 17, 18, 21, and 22. Administer all the items in this list unless S gets six consecutive items wrong; then stop testing.

To score, (1) obtain the proportion of correct responses among the thirteen "non-s" items, (2) multiply this by nine, and (3) add the product to the number of correct "non-s" responses to obtain the raw score.

EXAMPLE:　　(1)　　S gets 5 "non-s" items correct
　　　　　　　　　　= 5/13 or about .38 of them correct

　　　　　　　(2)　　.38 x 9 = 3.42 = (rounded) 3.00

　　　　　　　(3)　　Raw score = 3 + 5 = 8

This procedure is used only for children with no final "s." The great majority of children are scored according to the standard procedure given under the specific instructions for this test.

April 1970
PS-41

Item No.	One Point Credit	No Credit
Demonstration	beds	bed
1	apples	apple, red, ball
2	hats, caps	hat, cap
3	eating	eat, eat that, going to eat, eats, sit, eats eggs, ate
4	dresses	dress, two of them clothes
5	(d) opened	open, beans, opens can, took thing off, broke it, poured, get the soup, turn, top come off, put peas in
6	(t) wrecked, smashed	wreck, break, broken, hit in the dirt, breaked, crashing into mud, busted, going to crash, crashed
7	longer, smaller, bigger, larger, longer than that, shorter, taller	long, short, big, King, broken, bent, large, tall
8	bigger, taller, larger, smaller, longer, shorter	big, little, long, short
9	biggest, largest, fattest, littlest, longest, smallest, tallest	little, bigger one, potato, big one, big, King, small, larger, real potato, bumpy one, mashed
10	painter, worker, paint worker, carpenter, painter-man	painting the gate, paintman, George, painting, dirty, daddy, guy, gate, painting man, man, work man, working man, big one
11	wrote, has written	writted, pencil, write, writes, did, is writing, was writing
12	more	many-many, any pipes, two, 2 and 3 and 4, others, some pipes, whole bunch, pipes, a lot of pipes, many, many pipes, 600, some amount
13	men	man, mans, mens, two daddies
14	(t) polished, refinished, finished, washed, wiped	shiny, polish it, polish-ed, polishes coffee pot, clean, all finish, all done, shined, prepared, shine it, cleaned, was polishing it, fulled, pretty, painted, new, scrubbed
15	leaves, tree leaves	leafs, leaf, leafy, trees, flowers
16	knives	knifes, knife, knifey
17	hung, hung up	hanged, hanged up, hunged up, hang-ed, put up, hanging, already up, painted, nailed, done, hammered it

April 1970
PS-41

Item No.	One Point Credit	No Credit
18	better	gooder, good, chocolate, bigger, cake awful, pretty, different
19	best	goodest, baddest, better, biggest, good, shiny one, tallest, prettiest, bigger, terrible, not good, larger, gooder
20	thieves	thiefs, thief, thies, mans, bandits, robbers, hats, men, bad mans
21	mice	mouses, meese, mouse, more
22	stole, has stolen	stealed, stoled, stealing, thiefed, found, steal

Translate into Language Age Norms from Table A.

TABLE A	
Auditory-Vocal Automatic Test	
RAW SCORE	LANGUAGE AGE
0	Below Norms
1	Below Norms
2	2- 4
3	2- 9
4	3- 1
5	3- 6
6	3-10
7	4- 3
8	4- 7
9	5- 0
10	5- 4
11	5- 9
12	6- 1
13	6- 6
14	6-10
15	7- 3
16	7- 7
17	8- 0
18	8- 4
19	8- 9
20	9- 1
21	9- 6
22	Above Norms

Where no credit is listed for a given score, indicate this on the subject's record form with the words "below norms" or "above norms" as appropriate.

April 1970
PS-41

AREA: Language Expression (PS-42)

SUBAREA: None

Item 1: CONNECTED DISCOURSE

Purpose: To evaluate the child's capacity to engage in connected discourse upon presentation of an appropriate, structured stimulus as shown in the following procedure.

Materials: Paragraph consisting of story of "Peter and Spot," illustrations, checklist, and rating scales.

Procedure: Place the illustrations on the table in front of the child. Be sure that they are right side up from his point of view. Say: "HERE ARE SOME PICTURES ABOUT PETER AND HIS DOG SPOT." Allow the child to examine the illustrations for 30 seconds. After 30 seconds, or sooner if the child looks up to suggest that he has examined the pictures sufficiently, say: "NOW I AM GOING TO TELL YOU A STORY ABOUT PETER AND HIS DOG SPOT. WHEN I FINISH, I AM GOING TO ASK YOU TO TELL ME ABOUT IT. ARE YOU READY?" Examiner tells the story. Remove the pictures and say: "NOW TELL ME THE STORY." Examiner should press for maximal response by saying: "TELL ME MORE ABOUT THE STORY."

> One day Peter said "Goodby" to his dog Spot in front of his house and ran off to catch the school bus. In the middle of the arithmetic lesson everyone heard a strange scratching on the classroom door. The teacher, whose name was Miss Smith, opened the door to see who was there and in came Spot. Spot ran right to Peter and curled up under his chair. Miss Smith said, "If Spot will be very quiet he can stay until after lunch and ride home on the bus with Peter."

Scoring: While the child is telling the story, the examiner should tally each of the concepts the child expresses by marking the checklist shown in the scoring record. Additional notations concerning marked deviations from normal, expressive modes, errors in sequence, relevance, or grammar, should also be indicated by comments opposite the checklist to enable the examiner to evaluate the child's performance more objectively.

The summary evaluation of the adequacy of the child's connected discourse consists of the following items:

1. *Number of concepts* (18 in number)

   Excellent = (13 - 18)
   Adequate = (6 - 12)
   Poor   = (1 - 5)

2. *Sequence*

   Excellent = All of the ideas presented were in sequence
   Adequate = most of the ideas presented were in sequence
   Poor   = very few of the ideas presented were in sequence

April 1970
PS-42

3. *Elaboration*

    Excellent = Adds a great many details
    Adequate = adds some details
    Poor   = adds no details

4. *Relevance*

    Excellent = All utterances related to story
    Adequate = most utterances related to story
    Poor   = very few utterances related to story

5. *Grammar*

    Excellent = Correct usage all of the time
    Adequate = Correct usage most of the time
    Poor   = never demonstrates correct usage or only does so infrequently

An overall evaluation of the child's connected discourse should involve use of the checklist supplemented by (a) the clinical observations of the examiner during administration of this item and (b) observations of any spontaneous connected discourse elicited from the child at any time during the examination. Examiner should make his overall evaluation and check one of the following categories: Normal, Suspect, or Abnormal.

If the child is checked as "Suspect" or "Abnormal," detailed justification for assigning these categories should be made in the comments section of the scoring record.

Item 2: WRITING FROM DICTATION

Purpose: To determine the ability of the child to identify the auditory stimulus with the equivalent written symbol.

Materials: Lined paper, pencil, list 1, letters and numbers; list 2, words; list 3, sentences.

Procedure: Give the child a pencil and the scoring form (page 5 of PS-42) and say "USE THIS PENCIL AND PAPER TO WRITE DOWN WHAT I'M GOING TO TELL YOU. START ON THE FIRST LINE OF THE PAPER (indicate) AND USE A DIFFERENT LINE FOR EACH THING I TELL YOU TO WRITE. DO THE BEST YOU CAN AND WRITE ONLY THE THINGS I TELL YOU TO WRITE. PRINT IF YOU LIKE. ARE YOU READY?"

Dictate the first item on List 1, saying "WRITE THE LETTER L". When the child has written the item, proceed to the next, etc. Dictate numbers with the introductory phrase "WRITE THE NUMBER 6", etc. Dictate the first item on List 2, saying "WRITE THE WORD 'BOOK' ". When the child has written the item, proceed to the next, etc. Dictate the first item on List 3, saying "WRITE THE SENTENCE 'SEE THE DOG' ". When the child has written the item, proceed to the next, etc.

    List 1 – L S C P 6 3 9 5
    List 2 – book bed girl was
    List 3 – See the dog. Look at the boy.

Enter the child's name and NINDS number on the scoring record after the child has finished writing all of the dictated items.

April 1970
PS-42

Scoring: Score Pass any item which is legible and without error. Score Fail any item which is illegible or contains one or more errors as defined.

1. *Illegible* elements are those which cannot be identified as letters or numerals.

2. *Reversal* is the inversion of a single letter or numeral. Reversal applies only to the letter. not to its position within a word.

   Examples:

d for b	ꓘ for k	bɘd (e is reversed)
b for d	ꟼ for P	looꓘ (k is reversed)
Ɛ for 3	ɡ for g	ɡirl (g is reversed)
ƨ for 5	⅃ for L	bog (d is reversed)
ɔ for c		doy (b is reversed)
		dook (B is reversed)

3. *Substitution is:*

   (a) the replacement of a letter or numeral by another;
   (b) the replacement of one word by another, or a group of letters for a word (these letters need not constitute a formal word);
   (c) substitution of one phrase by another phrase.

   Examples:

where	for	was	bay	for	boy
when	for	was	bad	for	bed
whens	for	was	goog	for	dog
went	for	was	lool	for	book
withe	for	was	that	for	at
gog	for	dog	waz	for	was
doy	for	dog	whrth	for	was
bat	for	bed	add	for	at
gitl	for	girl	not	for	at
wiet	for	at			

4. *Addition* is the adding of one or more letters to a word, or words to a phrase which otherwise would stand correct. That is, if the added elements were deleted the word or phrase would then be correct except possibly for errors in sequence (see example under Combinations). In the case of words, whenever the number of added letters equals or exceeds the number of letters in the correct word, the error is considered a word substitution rather than an error or addition (see example under Substitutions).

   Examples: *(letters in parentheses are the additions)*

girl(e)	boo(l)k	look(e)
gir(e)l	boy(s)	wa(i)s
was(h)	the(n)	w(h)as

5. *Omission* is the absence of a letter, numeral, word or phrase which has not been replaced by another letter, numeral, word or phrase.

Examples:

gil	for	girl	see dog	for	see the dog
be	for	bed	look at boy	for	look at the boy

6. *Sequence error:* Transposition of letters within a word or words within a phrase.

Examples:

kool	for	look	glir	for	girl	god	for	dog
saw	for	was	koob	for	book	deb	for	bed
aws	for	was	teh	for	the			
gril	for	girl	ta	for	at			

look the at boy   for   look at the boy

In addition, the examiners should complete observations item A concerning the hand used for writing.

Record under Comments the number of passes for each list and the total number of passes for all lists, thus:

	Lists			Total
	1	2	3	
No. Passes	☐	☐	☐	☐

AREA: Speech Mechanism (PS-43)

SUBAREA: Examination of the Speech Mechanism

Purpose: To determine the adequacy of the structure of the oral mechanism and the functioning of the articulators. The sequence of examination of subitems is optional.

Materials: Flashlight (Examination of the soft palate)

Scoring: For examination of the lips and tongue there are two categories for scoring, Pass and Fail. "Pass" is defined as the ability to imitate the examiner. "Fail" is defined as partial or complete restriction of the lips or tongue (whichever is being examined) in the attempt to imitate the examiner. The "Unknown" box indicates that the examiner was unable to elicit a response from the child pertinent to the instruction. The box on the scoring record designated as "Concomitant Movement" should be checked, where applicable, and a full description entered under Comments. Please note that the specific act the child performs in imitation of the examiner is to be scored as "Pass" or "Fail": regardless of whether or not the imitative action itself had concomitant movement.

Separate scoring requirements for Concomitant Movements and Examination of the Soft Palate are given in the respective items.

April 1970
PS-43

Item 1: EXAMINATION OF THE LIPS

A. *Retraction*

Procedure: Demonstrate by retracting lips as for smiling and ask the child to imitate. Give two demonstrations if necessary.

B. *Protrusion*

Procedure: Demonstrate by protruding the lips as for blowing and ask the child to imitate. Give two demonstrations if necessary.

Item 2: EXAMINATION OF THE TONGUE

A. *Mid-Line Protrusion*

Procedure: Demonstrate by protruding the tongue. Give two demonstrations if necessary.

B. *Lateral Protrusion*

Procedure: Demonstrate by protruding tongue and moving it from one corner of the mouth to the other, outside of the mouth. Give two demonstrations if necessary.

C. *Elevation*

Procedure: Demonstrate by elevating tongue to alveolar ridge. Give two demonstrations if necessary.

Item 3: CONCOMITANT MOVEMENTS

If concommitant movements are observed during the child's performance of the actions specified in items 1 and 2 preceding, note these under Comments. Summarize in the section of the scoring record designated "Concomitant Movements" while performing: "retraction of the lips . . . etc." The concomitant movements are as follows: (1) lateral movements of the head, (2) backward movement of the head; and (3) grimaces.

Item 4: EXAMINATION OF THE SOFT PALATE

Procedure: Ask the child to open his mouth and say "ah" a sufficient number of times for you to make adequate observations of his palatal function.

Scoring: "Normal" is defined as vigorous movement of the soft palate. "Abnormal" is defined as manifestly weak or asymmetrical movements, absence of movement, or obvious lack of velo-pharyngeal approximation.

AREA: Speech Production (PS-44)

SUBAREA: Rate and Fluency of Connected Speech

Purpose: To assess rate and fluency of connected speech.

Procedure: No specific procedures are prescribed. The fluency of words or connected speech should be observed throughout the administration of the examination and in non-test conversation. Boxes are provided on the scoring sheet for the examiner to indicate his rating. "Adequate" means there is nothing unusual noted about the characteristic under consideration.

Item 1: RATE OF SPEECH SOUNDS IN SEQUENCE

Indicate Adequate, Too Fast for Intelligibility, Too Slow, Irregular/Inconsistent, or Other. If Other is marked, describe the observation.

Item 2a: FLUENCY OF SPEECH PRODUCTION

Determine whether the child exhibits dysfluencies (for example, repetitions, prolongations, hesitations, arrest, etc.) in his speech. If present, describe under Comments.

Item 2b:

Determine whether some struggle or special effort to produce speech accompanies dysfluent events. If present, describe under Comments.

Item 2c:

Ask the child the following question(s): "DO YOU BELIEVE YOU HAVE TROUBLE IN TALKING?" Record "yes" or "no" to this question. If the child answers affirmatively, inquire further as follows: "WHAT KIND OF TROUBLE DO YOU HAVE?" and then ask "WHAT DO YOU CALL IT?" Record his answers verbatim in the space provided.

SUBAREA: Voice

Purpose: To determine presence of deviations in voice function.

Procedure: No specific procedures are prescribed. Voice production during the examination should be observed by the examiner for deviations according to the definitions below. Boxes are provided for the examiner to check. "Adequate" means that there is nothing unusual about the characteristic under consideration.

Item 1: PITCH

Indicate Adequate, Too high for age and/or sex, Too low for age and/or sex, Monotonous, or Other. If Other is marked, describe the observation.

Item 2: LOUDNESS

Indicate Adequate, Too soft, Too loud, or Other.

Item 3a: VOICE QUALITY (Phonation)

Indicate Adequate, Breathiness (vibration of vocal folds with escape of air), Hoarseness (includes such qualities as harsh, hoarse, grating, rasping), or Other.

Item 3b: VOICE QUALITY (Resonance)

Indicate Adequate, Hyper-nasality and/or excessive nasal emission of air, Hypo-nasality, or Other.

April 1970
PS-44

SUBAREA: Intelligibility of Speech

Purpose: To evaluate the intelligibility of the <u>connected speech</u> of the child.

Procedure: No specific procedures are prescribed. The evaluation should be based on the child's verbal performance, on the examination up to this point as well as the examiner's observations in general conversation with the child.

NOTE: This evaluation should be completed <u>prior</u> to administration of the articulation evaluation which follows.

Describe by checking only one of the following items.

1. No difficulty in understanding what he says regardless of any deviations which may or may not be present in articulation, voice quality, pitch, rhythms, etc.

2. Some difficulty in understanding what the child says.

3. Considerable difficulty in understanding what the child says.

4. The child has verbalized but is essentially unintelligible.

5. No speech.

8. Other. (if "Other" is marked, describe the observation under Comments.)

Summarize the evaluation by completing the checklist on the scoring record.

SUBAREA: Articulation

Purpose: To measure the child's articulatory skill as evidenced by his ability to produce phonemes within the context of individual words elicited by picture stimulation.

Materials: The "Screening Test" (first 50 pictures, first 16 cards) of the Templin-Darley <u>Tests of Articulation</u>.[9]

Procedure: For each test word a single line drawing is presented to the child telling him that you have some drawings and that you want him to tell you what each is a picture of. Show him each of the 16 cards in order. Many children will continue to name the pictures with little prompting. Others will need to be asked about each picture. In order to avoid a monotonous repetition of "What is this?" use the questions and statements printed on the backs of the cards. These contain neither the test word nor the test sound. If the child does not say the desired test word spontaneously, say it for him and ask him to repeat it.

Recording of responses: Space is provided after each test sound to record the response of the child. For each single consonant, vowel, or diphthong make an entry in the appropriate space using the following symbols:

1. If the child produced the sound correctly, indicate this fact with a check mark ($\sqrt{}$).

2. If he <u>substitutes</u> another phoneme, enter the phonetic symbol representing the phoneme he uttered.

[9]From the Templin-Darley Tests of Articulation. Copyright 1960 by The University of Iowa, Iowa City, Iowa. All rights reserved. Reproduced by permission.

April 1970
PS-44

3. If he omits a test sound in producing the test word indicate the omission with a dash (−).

4. If he distorts a sound (that is, produces the sound faultily although his production can be recognized as being an example of the desired phoneme), enter an (X).

5. If the child does not attempt to produce the desired test word, enter (nr), signifying "no response."

In the case of the consonant blends adapt the code above so that errors and correct articulation will be readily identifiable for any given sound element. Thus, if one blend is produced correctly while the other is omitted, transcribe phonetically the correctly produced phoneme and use a dash to indicate the omitted one.

Sample Scoring Sheet:

		I	M	F
7.	ð	√	√	−
3.	r	w	w	
9.	ʃ	x	x	x
14.	pr	pw		

Scoring with Norms: Count those screening items correctly produced and enter the total in the space provided on the scoring record.

Indicate whether performance is Normal, Suspect, or Abnormal on the basis of the total correct responses using the following values:

Normal   − 45-50
Suspect   − 40-44
Abnormal − 39 or less

NOTE: These tentative values are subject to adjustment based on experience with score distributions.

April 1970
PS-44

COLR-3151-40
4-70

FINAL SPEECH, LANGUAGE AND HEARING EXAMINATION
HEARING

2. NAME OF CHILD

3. DATE OF BIRTH	4. AGE	5. SEX	6. RACE
MO. | DAY | YEAR		☐ MALE ☐ FEMALE	☐ W ☐ N OR 1 2 3 ☐ PR ☐ OTHER 4 8

7. EXAMINED BY	8. DATE OF EXAM
	MO. | DAY | YEAR

9. PURE TONE AUDIOMETRY – AIR CONDUCTION

	250	500	1000	2000	4000	8000	Method Used:
Right (Mask L.)							☐ Ascending
Left (Mask R.)							☐ Descending

TEST ADEQUACY   ☐ ADEQUATE (1)   ☐ NOT ADEQUATE (explain) (2)

Masking Level Used in dB: SPL

Right						
Left						

10. ABNORMAL AUDITORY ADAPTATION

	4000 Hz			500 Hz		
	PASS	FAIL	SECONDS	PASS	FAIL	SECONDS
Right						
Left						

TEST ADEQUACY   ☐ ADEQUATE (1)   ☐ NOT ADEQUATE (explain) (2)

11. PURE TONE AUDIOMETRY – BONE CONDUCTION
(omit when AC < 20 dB HL (ISO) 500-4000 Hz)

	500	1000	2000	4000	Method Used:
Right (Mask L.)					☐ Ascending
Left (Mask R.)					☐ Descending

TEST ADEQUACY   ☐ NOT APPLICABLE (0)   ☐ ADEQUATE (1)   ☐ NOT ADEQUATE (explain) (2)

Masking Level Used in dB: SPL

Right				
Left				

12. COMMENTS

13. PATIENT IDENTIFICATION

FINAL SPEECH, LANGUAGE AND HEARING EXAMINATION

HEARING

14. DISCRIMINATION TEST

15. COMMENTS

PB-K List 1   PB-K List 2

Sample:	gun	*Sample:*	ball
	this		three
	chew		rest
	cloud		shoe
	best		left

List 1-A	List 1-B	List 2-A	List 2-B
1. please	1. smile	1. tire	1. most
2. great	2. bath	2. seed	2. thick
3. sled	3. slip	3. purse	3. if
4. pants	4. ride	4. quick	4. them
5. rat	5. end	5. room	5. sheep
6. bad	6. pink	6. bug	6. air
7. pinch	7. thank	7. that	7. set
8. such	8. take	8. sell	8. dad
9. bus	9. cart	9. low	9. ship
10. need	10. scab	10. rich	10. case
11. ways	11. lay	11. those	11. you
12. five	12. class	12. ache	12. may
13. mouth	13. me	13. black	13. choose
14. rag	14. dish	14. else	14. white
15. put	15. neck	15. nest	15. frog
16. fed	16. beef	16. jay	16. bush
17. fold	17. few	17. raw	17. clown
18. hunt	18. use	18. true	18. cab
19. no	19. did	19. had	19. hurt
20. box	20. hit	20. cost	20. pass
21. are	21. pond	21. vase	21. grade
22. teach	22. hot	22. press	22. blind
23. slice	23. own	23. fit	23. drop
24. is	24. bead	24. bounce	24. leave
25. tree	25. shop	25. wide	25. nuts

Check correct responses. Number of correct responses × 4 = discrimination score in %.

	Hearing Level in dB	Discrimination Percent	List Used
Right			
Left			

TEST ADEQUACY   ☐ ADEQUATE   ☐ NOT ADEQUATE *(explain)*.
                1   2

16. PATIENT IDENTIFICATION

FINAL SPEECH, LANGUAGE AND HEARING EXAMINATION
HEARING

17. AUDITORY MEMORY

1. Memory for Digits (Forward)

Verbatim Response	Pass	Fail
72	☐	☐
68	☐	☐
941	☐	☐
536	☐	☐
6149	☐	☐
8351	☐	☐
92174	☐	☐
31685	☐	☐
457182	☐	☐
635214	☐	☐
8679143	☐	☐
5263814	☐	☐
43973258	☐	☐
26769381	☐	☐
818735243	☐	☐
682937684	☐	☐
1862835746	☐	☐
3276215849	☐	☐

Score [_____]

TEST ADEQUACY ☐ ADEQUATE ☐ NOT ADEQUATE (explain)
1   2

18. COMMENTS

484

FINAL SPEECH, LANGUAGE AND HEARING EXAMINATION
HEARING TEST

19. PATIENT IDENTIFICATION

17. AUDITORY MEMORY (Continued)

2. Memory for Nonsense Syllables (Forward)

	Verbatim Response	Pass	Fail
doy poo		☐	☐
kah mow		☐	☐
dee mow pah		☐	☐
boo dah tay		☐	☐
bow gah dee tah		☐	☐
doy boo mow kah		☐	☐
tah dee gah bow tay		☐	☐
poo kah dee bah doy		☐	☐
pah doy poo dee tah bow		☐	☐
gah tay boo day mow dah		☐	☐

Score [   ]

TEST
ADEQUACY   ☐ ADEQUATE   ☐ NOT ADEQUATE (explain)
                    1   2

20. COMMENTS

COLLABORATIVE RESEARCH
PERINATAL RESEARCH BRANCH, NINDS, NIH
BETHESDA, MD. 20014

FINAL SPEECH, LANGUAGE AND HEARING EXAMINATION

LANGUAGE COMPREHENSION

1. PATIENT IDENTIFICATION

2. NAME OF CHILD

3. DATE OF BIRTH	4. AGE	5. SEX		6. RACE		
MO. DAY YEAR		☐ MALE 1 ☐ FEMALE 2		☐ W 1 ☐ N 2 ☐ OR 3 ☐ PR 4 ☐ OTHER 8		

7. EXAMINED BY	8. DATE OF EXAM.
	MO. DAY YEAR

9. AUDITORY VERBAL COMPREHENSION

*1. Word Identification (PPVT)

A. ITEM RESP. KEY WORD

1 _____ (2) table	37 _____ (3) wasp	73 _____ (3) cobbler	112 _____ (1) tangent
2 _____ (4) bus	38 _____ (2) barber	74 _____ (2) autumn	113 _____ (4) sconce
3 _____ (2) horse	39 _____ (3) parachute	75 _____ (3) dissatisfaction	114 _____ (4) hoary
4 _____ (3) dog	40 _____ (4) saddle	76 _____ (4) scholar	115 _____ (1) pendant
5 _____ (4) shoe	41 _____ (3) temperature	77 _____ (1) oasis	116 _____ (1) prodigy
6 _____ (4) finger	42 _____ (1) captain	78 _____ (3) soldering	117 _____ (2) casement
7 _____ (3) boat	43 _____ (2) whale	79 _____ (3) astonishment	118 _____ (1) quiescent
8 _____ (2) children	44 _____ (4) cash	80 _____ (1) tread	119 _____ (4) talon
9 _____ (1) bell	45 _____ (1) balancing	81 _____ (2) thatched	120 _____ (1) chevron
10 _____ (4) turtle	46 _____ (3) cobweb	82 _____ (1) jurisprudence	121 _____ (4) feline
11 _____ (2) climbing	47 _____ (3) pledging	83 _____ (2) sapling	122 _____ (2) cairn
12 _____ (1) lamp	48 _____ (1) argument	84 _____ (3) arch	123 _____ (4) convergence
13 _____ (3) sitting	49 _____ (3) hydrant	85 _____ (4) dwelling	124 _____ (3) apothecary
14 _____ (2) jacket	50 _____ (4) binocular	86 _____ (1) lubricating	125 _____ (2) indigent
15 _____ (1) pulling	51 _____ (1) locomotive	87 _____ (2) pedestrian	126 _____ (4) edifice
16 _____ (2) ring	52 _____ (2) hive	88 _____ (3) vale	127 _____ (3) scallion
17 _____ (1) nail	53 _____ (4) reel	89 _____ (3) jubilant	128 _____ (1) infirm
18 _____ (2) hitting	54 _____ (1) insect	90 _____ (2) laden	129 _____ (1) emaciate
19 _____ (3) tire	55 _____ (1) gnawing	91 _____ (2) pursuit	130 _____ (2) catapult
20 _____ (3) ladder	56 _____ (2) weapon	92 _____ (4) goblet	131 _____ (2) arable
21 _____ (1) snake	57 _____ (3) bannister	93 _____ (2) rodent	132 _____ (4) orifice
22 _____ (1) river	58 _____ (1) idol	94 _____ (3) confiding	133 _____ (3) renovate
23 _____ (4) ringing	59 _____ (1) globe	95 _____ (4) reclining	134 _____ (1) precarious
24 _____ (4) baking	60 _____ (3) walrus	96 _____ (1) frisking	135 _____ (2) dromedary
25 _____ (2) cone	61 _____ (1) filing	97 _____ (2) moat	136 _____ (1) pedagogue
26 _____ (3) engineer	62 _____ (3) shears	98 _____ (3) salutation	137 _____ (1) sepal
27 _____ (4) peeking	63 _____ (1) horror	99 _____ (2) barrier	138 _____ (3) lethargic
28 _____ (1) kite	64 _____ (4) chef	100 _____ (3) foal	139 _____ (4) delectation
29 _____ (1) rat	65 _____ (4) harvesting	101 _____ (4) incandescent	140 _____ (3) embellish
30 _____ (1) time	66 _____ (3) construction	102 _____ (3) cornucopia	141 _____ (1) osculation
31 _____ (4) sail	67 _____ (4) observatory	103 _____ (2) ascending	142 _____ (2) cincture
32 _____ (2) ambulance	68 _____ (4) assistance	104 _____ (1) summit	143 _____ (3) barrister
33 _____ (2) trunk	69 _____ (2) erecting	105 _____ (3) caster	144 _____ (3) carrion
34 _____ (4) skiing	70 _____ (3) thoroughbred	106 _____ (2) lobe	145 _____ (2) lanate
35 _____ (2) hook	71 _____ (2) casserole	107 _____ (3) patriarch	146 _____ (4) chirography
36 _____ (1) tweezers	72 _____ (4) ornament	108 _____ (3) sampler	147 _____ (1) mendicant
		109 _____ (3) ingenious	148 _____ (1) saltation
		110 _____ (1) repose	149 _____ (2) florescence
		111 _____ (3) constrain	150 _____ (4) culver

B. CALCULATION

Errors _____ Raw Score _____ Vocabulary Age _____

TEST ADEQUACY   ☐ ADEQUATE 1   ☐ NOT ADEQUATE (explain) 2

10. COMMENTS (Attach a CP-5 if more space is required.)

COLLABORATIVE RESEARCH
PERINATAL RESEARCH BRANCH, NINDS, NIH
BETHESDA, MD. 20014

*Peabody Picture Vocabulary Test. Copyright 1959 by Lloyd M. Dunn. All rights reserved. Published by American Guidance Service, Inc., Minneapolis, Minnesota. Reproduced by permission.

(4-70)   PAGE 1 OF 10   PS-41

486

11. PATIENT IDENTIFICATION

FINAL SPEECH, LANGUAGE AND HEARING EXAMINATION
LANGUAGE COMPREHENSION

9. AUDITORY VERBAL COMPREHENSION *(Continued)*
2. Orientation

12. COMMENTS

	Verbatim Response	Pass	Fail
1. When is your birthday?	_____	☐	☐
*2. How many birthdays do you have in a year?	_____	☐	☐
*3. Are you older than your mother?	_____	☐	☐
4. In what month does the Fourth of July come?	_____	☐	☐
5. What season of the year comes just before winter?	_____	☐	☐
6. Tell me the names of the days you go to school?	_____	☐	☐
*7. Put one hand on your head and the other behind you.		☐	☐
8. Suppose you were on the eighth floor of a building. If you took the elevator to the third floor, which way would the elevator go?	_____	☐	☐
9. Show me your left hand.		☐	☐
10. Show me your right eye.		☐	☐
11. Point to my right ear.		☐	☐
12. Point to my left hand.		☐	☐

Total ☐

TEST ADEQUACY ☐ ADEQUATE ☐ NOT ADEQUATE *(explain)*
1   2

COLLABORATIVE RESEARCH
PERINATAL RESEARCH BRANCH, NINDS, NIH
BETHESDA, MD. 20014

(4-70) PAGE
2 OF 10

PS-41

487

COLR–3151–41
4-70

FINAL SPEECH, LANGUAGE AND HEARING EXAMINATION
LANGUAGE COMPREHENSION

9. AUDITORY VERBAL COMPREHENSION (continued)

3A. UNDERSTANDING A STORY*

14. COMMENTS

Pass Fail

1. How did the boys and their mother go to the zoo?   ☐   ☐

Record verbatim response: _____

_____

2. What animal did the boys enjoy looking at very much?   ☐   ☐

Record verbatim response: _____

_____

3. What did they do at noontime?   ☐   ☐

Record verbatim response: _____

_____

4. What did they do after they finished eating?   ☐   ☐

Record verbatim response: _____

_____

5. What was the last thing the boys saw at the zoo?   ☐   ☐

Record verbatim response: _____

_____

3B. CALCULATION

Raw Score _____

Grade Equivalent _____

Age Equivalent _____

TEST
ADEQUACY   ☐ ADEQUATE   ☐ NOT ADEQUATE
             1   2   (explain)

COLLABORATIVE RESEARCH
PERINATAL RESEARCH BRANCH, NINDS, NIH
BETHESDA, MD. 20014

15. PATIENT IDENTIFICATION

FINAL SPEECH, LANGUAGE AND HEARING EXAMINATION

LANGUAGE COMPREHENSION

16. READING

1. Oral Reading (Paragraphs)*

A. Look, Mother, look.

See me go.

I go up.

I come down.

Come here, Mother.

Come and play with me.

B. A boy said, "Run, little girl.

Run with me to the boat."

They ran and ran.

"This is fun," said the boy.

"Look," said the girl.

"I see something in the boat.

It is my kitten.

She wants to play."

Time (seconds) _____

Total Errors _____

Passage Score _____

TYPES OF ERRORS	NUMBER
1. Aid	
2. Gross Mispronunciation	
3. Partial Mispronunciation	
4. Omission	
5. Insertion	
6. Substitution	
7. Repetition	
8. Inversion	
Total Errors	

Time (seconds) _____

Total Errors _____

Passage Score _____

TYPES OF ERRORS	NUMBER
1. Aid	
2. Gross Mispronunciation	
3. Partial Mispronunciation	
4. Omission	
5. Insertion	
6. Substitution	
7. Repetition	
8. Inversion	
Total Errors	

17. COMMENTS

A.

B.

COLLABORATIVE RESEARCH
PERINATAL RESEARCH BRANCH, NINDS, NIH
BETHESDA, MD. 20014

18. PATIENT IDENTIFICATION

FINAL SPEECH, LANGUAGE AND HEARING EXAMINATION
LANGUAGE COMPREHENSION

16. READING (Continued)

1. Oral Reading (Paragraphs)

C. One morning a boy made a boat. "Where can I play with it?"

he asked.

Father said, "Come with me in the car!

We will take your boat with us."

Soon the boy called, "Please stop. I see water.

May I play here?"

"Yes," said Father. "Have a good time."

Time (seconds) _____

Total Errors _____

Passage Score _____

TYPES OF ERRORS	NUMBER
1. Aid	
2. Gross Mispronunciation	
3. Partial Mispronunciation	
4. Omission	
5. Insertion	
6. Substitution	
7. Repetition	
8. Inversion	
Total Errors	

D. One day five children went out to play in the beautiful white

snow. They played for a long time and then began to make

snow animals.

One of the animals was a dog. Soon the dog next door

came out of the house. When he saw the snow dog he

said, "Bow-wow."

The children laughed. "Now we have a dog that can bark."

Time (seconds) _____

Total Errors _____

Passage Score _____

TYPES OF ERRORS	NUMBER
1. Aid	
2. Gross Mispronunciation	
3. Partial Mispronunciation	
4. Omission	
5. Insertion	
6. Substitution	
7. Repetition	
8. Inversion	
Total Errors	

19. COMMENTS

C.

D.

COLLABORATIVE RESEARCH
PERINATAL RESEARCH BRANCH, NINDS, NIH
BETHESDA, MD. 20014

20. PATIENT IDENTIFICATION

FINAL SPEECH, LANGUAGE AND HEARING EXAMINATION
LANGUAGE COMPREHENSION

16. READING (Continued)

1. Oral Reading (Paragraphs) *

E.   It was pet day at the fair. The children were waiting for
the parade of animals to begin. They had trained their pets
to do many different tricks. Among them was a tall boy
whose goat made trouble for him. It kicked and tried hard
to break away. When it heard the band it became quiet.
During the parade it danced so well that it won a prize.

OPTIONAL

F.   Airplane pilots have many important jobs. They fly passengers,
freight, and mail from one city to another. Sometimes they
make dangerous rescues in land and sea accidents, and drop
food where people or herds are starving. They bring strange
animals from dense jungles to our zoos. They also serve as
traffic police and spot speeding cars on highways.

Time (seconds) _____

Total Errors _____

Passage Score _____

TYPES OF ERRORS	NUMBER
1. Aid _____	
2. Gross Mispronunciation _____	
3. Partial Mispronunciation _____	
4. Omission _____	
5. Insertion _____	
6. Substitution _____	
7. Repetition _____	
8. Inversion _____	
Total Errors	

Time (seconds) _____

Total Errors _____

Passage Score _____

TYPES OF ERRORS	NUMBER
1. Aid _____	
2. Gross Mispronunciation _____	
3. Partial Mispronunciation _____	
4. Omission _____	
5. Insertion _____	
6. Substitution _____	
7. Repetition _____	
8. Inversion _____	
Total Errors	

21. COMMENTS

E.

F.

*Selections from Gray Oral Reading Test, Form A, are
reproduced by permission of the publishers, The
Bobbs-Merrill Co., Inc., Indianapolis, Indiana. Copyright © 1963. All rights reserved.

(4-70) PAGE
6 OF 10

PS-41

491

COLR-3151-41
4-70

FINAL SPEECH, LANGUAGE AND HEARING EXAMINATION
LANGUAGE COMPREHENSION

22. PATIENT IDENTIFICATION

16. READING *(Continued)*

1. Oral Reading (Paragraph)

G (1) SUMMARY:

Passage	Time (in seconds)	No. of Errors	Passage Scores
A			
B			
C			
D			
E			
F			
		Total Passage Score	
		Grade Equivalent	

(2) TYPES OF ERRORS	PASSAGE A	B	C	D	E	F	TOTAL
1. Aid							
2. Gross Mispronunciation							
3. Partial Mispronunciation							
4. Omission							
5. Insertion							
6. Substitution							
7. Repetition							
8. Inversion							

TEST ADEQUACY ☐ ADEQUATE 1 ☐ NOT ADEQUATE 2 *(explain)*

23. COMMENTS

FINAL SPEECH, LANGUAGE AND HEARING EXAMINATION

LANGUAGE COMPREHENSION

16. READING (Continued)

2. Silent Reading

A. SAMPLE PARAGRAPH (MEANING)*

   One warm, sunny day Helen and her brother went on a trip to the beach.
Their mother and aunt went with them. They took their bathing suits so that they
could all go into the water. When noontime came, they had lunch on the sand.
After lunch the children gathered sea shells. They saw a starfish and some funny
little crabs.

			P	F
1. What did Helen and her brother do?	1 2 3 4 5	went to see their aunt went to the seashore went on a train went for crabs went fishing	☐	☐
2. The weather was—	1 2 3 4 5	quiet funny fair gloomy rainy	☐	☐
3. The best name for this story is—	1 2 3 4 5	Helen and Her Aunt Gathering Shells Eating Lunch Outdoors One Warm Day A Trip to the Beach	☐	☐

TEST
ADEQUACY   ☐ ADEQUATE   ☐ NOT ADEQUATE (explain)
                    1   2

COLLABORATIVE RESEARCH
PERINATAL RESEARCH BRANCH, NINDS, NIH
BETHESDA, MD. 20014
*From Durrell-Sullivan Reading Capacity and Achieve-
ment Tests: Primary Test: Form A. Copyright 1939,
1937 by Harcourt, Brace & World, Inc. All rights reserved. Reproduced by permission.

FINAL SPEECH, LANGUAGE AND HEARING EXAMINATION
LANGUAGE COMPREHENSION

16. READING (Continued)

    2. Silent Reading (Continued)

    B. TEST PARAGRAPH *

        Mary and John go to camp as soon as school closes in the summer. They go on the train and stay until it is time for school to open again in the fall. They have a happy time at camp because there are many other boys and girls there too. They ride, swim, and play games together every day.

			P	F
1. When do Mary and John go to camp?	1 2 3 4 5	before school when school is over in the fall when school starts every day	☐	☐
2. Which word tells what kind of a time the children have at camp?	1 2 3 4 5	lonesome sad joyous funny weary	☐	☐
3. How do the children travel to camp?	1 2 3 4 5	on a train on a bus in an automobile on a car in an airplane	☐	☐
4. The best name for this story would be—	1 2 3 4 5	Close of School Playing Games A Trip on the Train A Summer at Camp The Boys at Camp	☐	☐
5. Mary and John enjoy camp life because they—	1 2 3 4 5	are glad to be away for the summer like the ride on the train are glad to be out of school like to study nature have fun playing games with other children	☐	☐

TEST
ADEQUACY   ☐ ADEQUATE   ☐ NOT ADEQUATE
              1   2   (explain)

COLLABORATIVE RESEARCH
PERINATAL RESEARCH BRANCH, NINDS, NIH
BETHESDA, MD. 20014

COLR—3151-41
4-70

FINAL SPEECH, LANGUAGE AND HEARING EXAMINATION
LANGUAGE COMPREHENSION

27. MORPHOLOGY

Auditory-Vocal Automatic Test *

	Pass	Fail
1.	☐	☐
2.	☐	☐
3.	☐	☐
4.	☐	☐
5.	☐	☐
6.	☐	☐
7.	☐	☐
8.	☐	☐
9.	☐	☐
10.	☐	☐
11.	☐	☐
12.	☐	☐
13.	☐	☐
14.	☐	☐
15.	☐	☐
16.	☐	☐
17.	☐	☐
18.	☐	☐
19.	☐	☐
20.	☐	☐
21.	☐	☐
22.	☐	☐

Raw Score ☐

Age Level Score ☐

28. COMMENTS

TEST ADEQUACY

☐ ADEQUATE
1

☐ NOT ADEQUATE (explain)
2

COLLABORATIVE RESEARCH
PERINATAL RESEARCH BRANCH, NINDS, NIH
BETHESDA, MD. 20014

(4-70)   PAGE
10 OF 10   **PS-41**

495

FINAL SPEECH, LANGUAGE AND HEARING EXAMINATION
LANGUAGE EXPRESSION

1. PATIENT IDENTIFICATION

2. NAME OF CHILD

3. DATE OF BIRTH	4. AGE	5. SEX	6. RACE
MO.	DAY	YEAR			MALE FEMALE 1 2	W 1 N 2 OR 3 PR 4 OTHER 8

7. EXAMINED BY	8. DATE OF EXAM.
	MO. DAY YEAR

NOTE: Items 9, 10 and 11 of the Trial 10-66 version are no longer used and have been deleted from the 4-70 printing.

12. CONNECTED DISCOURSE

One day Peter said "Goodby" to his dog Spot in front of his house and ran off to catch the school bus. In the middle of the arithmetic lesson everyone heard a strange scratching on the classroom door. The teacher, whose name was Miss Smith, opened the door to see who was there and in came Spot. Spot ran right to Peter and curled up under his chair. Miss Smith said, "If Spot will be very quiet he can stay until after lunch and ride home on the bus with Peter".

CHECKLIST: *(number of concepts and other observations)*

(Insert check mark (√) in column if child expresses concept)

Concept	√	13. COMMENTS
said goodby		
to dog Spot		
in front of house		
ran off		
to catch school bus		
arithmetic lesson		
strange scratching		
on classroom door		
teacher		
Miss Smith		
opened door		
in came Spot		
Spot ran to Peter		
curled up under his chair		
Miss Smith said		
if Spot quiet		
can stay until after lunch		
ride home in bus with Peter		
Total number of concepts expressed		

COLLABORATIVE RESEARCH
PERINATAL RESEARCH BRANCH, NINDS, NIH
BETHESDA, MD. 20014
(4-70)
PAGE
1 OF 4
PS-42

496

14. PATIENT IDENTIFICATION

FINAL SPEECH, LANGUAGE AND HEARING EXAMINATION
LANGUAGE EXPRESSION

---

15. SUMMARY EVALUATION

16. COMMENTS

1. Number of Concepts (N-18)

   Excellent (13-18).. ☐ 0

   Adequate (6-12) .... ☐ 1

   Poor (1-5) .... ☐ 2

2. Sequence

   Excellent .... ☐ 0

   Adequate.. ☐ 1

   Poor .... ☐ 2

3. Elaboration

   Excellent .... ☐ 0

   Adequate.. ☐ 1

   Poor .... ☐ 2

4. Relevance

   Excellent .... ☐ 0

   Adequate.. ☐ 1

   Poor .... ☐ 2

5. Grammar

   Excellent .... ☐ 0

   Adequate.. ☐ 1

   Poor .... ☐ 2

6. Overall Evaluation of Child's Connected Discourse
   (see manual under "Scoring" page 21).

   Normal   ☐ 0

   Suspect   ☐ 1

   Abnormal   ☐ 2

   TEST
   ADEQUACY   ☐ ADEQUATE 1   ☐ NOT ADEQUATE 2 (explain)

COLR—3151-42
4-70

FINAL SPEECH, LANGUAGE AND HEARING EXAMINATION
LANGUAGE EXPRESSION

18. WRITING FROM DICTATION

	Pass	Fail

1. List 1 —

L .... ☐ ☐
S... ☐ ☐
C... ☐ ☐
P... ☐ ☐
6... ☐ ☐
3... ☐ ☐
9... ☐ ☐
5... ☐ ☐

2. List 2 —

book... ☐ ☐
bed... ☐ ☐
girl... ☐ ☐
was.. ☐ ☐

3. List 3 —

See the dog. .... ☐ ☐
Look at the boy. .... ☐ ☐

4. Summary

	LISTS			TOTAL
	1	2	3	
A. NO. PASSES	☐	☐	☐	☐

B. TYPES OF ERRORS

	LISTS		
	1	2	3
Illegible			
Reversal			
Substitution			
Addition			
Omission			
Sequence Error			

5. TEST ADEQUACY   ☐ ADEQUATE   ☐ NOT ADEQUATE (explain)

6. Observations (enter descriptions in Comments)

A. HAND USED TO WRITE WITH   ☐ RIGHT   ☐ LEFT   ☐ UNDETERMINED

19. COMMENTS

CHILD'S NAME _____   NINDB # _____

FINAL SPEECH, LANGUAGE AND HEARING EXAMINATION
SPEECH MECHANISM

1. PATIENT IDENTIFICATION

2. NAME OF CHILD

3. DATE OF BIRTH	4. AGE	5. SEX	6. RACE
MO. DAY YEAR		☐ MALE ☐ FEMALE 1 2	☐ W ☐ N ☐ OR 1 2 3 ☐ PR ☐ OTHER 4 8

7. EXAMINED BY	8. DATE OF EXAM.
	MO. DAY YEAR

9. EXAMINATION OF THE SPEECH MECHANISM

10. COMMENTS

1. Examination of the Lips

  A. RETRACTION

    ☐ Pass
    1

    ☐ Fail
    2

    ☐ Concomitant Movement
    3

    ☐ Unknown
    9

  B. PROTRUSION

    ☐ Pass
    1

    ☐ Fail
    2

    ☐ Concomitant Movement
    3

    ☐ Unknown
    9

2. Examination of the Tongue

  A. MID-LINE PROTRUSION

    ☐ Pass
    1

    ☐ Fail
    2

    ☐ Concomitant Movement
    3

    ☐ Unknown
    9

500

11. PATIENT IDENTIFICATION

FINAL SPEECH, LANGUAGE AND HEARING EXAMINATION
SPEECH MECHANISM

9. EXAMINATION OF THE SPEECH MECHANISM *(Continued)*

12. COMMENTS

  2. Examination of the Tongue *(Continued)*

    B. LATERAL PROTRUSION

    ☐ Pass
     1

    ☐ Fail
     2

    ☐ Concomitant Movement
     3

    ☐ Unknown
     9

    C. ELEVATION

    ☐ Pass
     1

    ☐ Fail
     2

    ☐ Concomitant Movement
     3

    ☐ Unknown
     9

  3. Concomitant Movements Present While Performing:

	None	Head Lateral	Head Backward	Grimaces
A. Retraction of the Lips............	☐ 0	☐ 1	☐ 2	☐ 3
B. Protrusion of the Lips............	☐ 0	☐ 1	☐ 2	☐ 3
C. Mid-Line Protrusion of the Tongue.....................................	☐ 0	☐ 1	☐ 2	☐ 3
D. Lateral Protrusion of the Tongue.....................................	☐ 0	☐ 1	☐ 2	☐ 3
E. Elevation of the Tongue	☐ 0	☐ 1	☐ 2	☐ 3
F. Other *(describe)*	☐ 0	☐ 1	☐ 2	☐ 3

  4. Examination of the Soft Palate

    ☐ Normal
     0

    ☐ Abnormal
     1

    ☐ Unknown
     9

COLLABORATIVE RESEARCH
PERINATAL RESEARCH BRANCH, NINDS, NIH
BETHESDA, MD. 20014

COLR—3151-44
4-70

FINAL SPEECH, LANGUAGE AND HEARING EXAMINATION

SPEECH PRODUCTION

1. PATIENT IDENTIFICATION

2. NAME OF CHILD

3. DATE OF BIRTH	4. AGE	5. SEX	6. RACE
MO. DAY YEAR		☐ MALE ☐ FEMALE 1 2	☐ W ☐ N ☐ OR 1 2 3 ☐ PR ☐ OTHER 4 8

7. EXAMINED BY	8. DATE OF EXAM.
	MO. DAY YEAR

---

9. RATE AND FLUENCY OF CONNECTED SPEECH

1. Rate of Speech Sounds in Sequence

  ☐ Adequate
    1

  ☐ Too Fast for Intelligibility
    2

  ☐ Too Slow
    3

  ☐ Irregular/Inconsistent
    4

  ☐ Other *(describe)*
    8

2. A. Fluency of Speech Production (dysfluent events)

  ☐ None
    0

  ☐ Some
    1

  ☐ Many
    2

2. B. Struggle Behavior (or special effort) to produce speech, accompanying dysfluent events.

  ☐ None
    0

  ☐ Some
    1

  ☐ Many
    2

2. C. Do you believe you have trouble in talking?

  ☐ Yes
    1

  ☐ No
    2

If "yes" what kind of trouble do you have? *(record verbatim)*

_____

_____

What do you call it? *(record verbatim)* _____

_____

_____

10. COMMENTS

502

11. PATIENT IDENTIFICATION

FINAL SPEECH, LANGUAGE AND HEARING EXAMINATION

SPEECH PRODUCTION

12. VOICE

13. COMMENTS

1. Pitch

☐ Adequate
1

☐ Too high for age and/or sex
2

☐ Too low for age and/or sex
3

☐ Monotonous
4

☐ Other (describe)
8

2. Loudness

☐ Adequate
1

☐ Too soft
2

☐ Too loud
3

☐ Other (describe)
8

3a. Voice Quality (Phonation)

☐ Adequate
1

☐ Breathiness
2

☐ Hoarseness
3

☐ Other (describe)
8

3b. Voice Quality (Resonance)

☐ Adequate
1

☐ Hyper-Nasality and/or excessive nasal emission of air
2

☐ Hypo-Nasality
3

☐ Other (describe)
8

COLLABORATIVE RESEARCH
PERINATAL RESEARCH BRANCH, NINDS, NIH
BETHESDA, MD. 20014

(4-70)

PAGE
2 of 4

PS-44

503

14. PATIENT IDENTIFICATION

FINAL SPEECH, LANGUAGE AND HEARING EXAMINATION

SPEECH PRODUCTION

15. INTELLIGIBILITY

How well can you understand this child? *(Check only one of the following)*

DESCRIPTION

☐ No difficulty in understanding what he says regardless of
1   any deviations which may or may not be present in articulation, voice quality, pitch rhythms, etc.

☐ Some difficulty in understanding what the child says
2

☐ Considerable difficulty in understanding what the child says
3

☐ The child has verbalized, but is essentially unintelligible
4

☐ No speech
5

☐ Other *(describe)*
8

CHECKLIST

	Absent	Present
1. Inappropriate Rhythm	☐ 0	☐ 1
2. Inappropriate Rate	☐ 0	☐ 1
3. Inappropriate Stress	☐ 0	☐ 1
4. Inappropriate Loudness	☐ 0	☐ 1
5. Voice Quality Deviations	☐ 0	☐ 1
6. Articulatory Inprecision	☐ 0	☐ 1
7. Telegraphic	☐ 0	☐ 1
8. Difficulty in the Sequence of Sounds and/or Words *(describe)*	☐ 0	☐ 1

16. COMMENTS

COLLABORATIVE RESEARCH
PERINATAL RESEARCH BRANCH, NINDS, NIH
BETHESDA, MD. 20014

(4-70)   PAGE
3 OF 4   **PS-44**

504

17. PATIENT IDENTIFICATION

FINAL SPEECH, LANGUAGE AND HEARING EXAMINATION

SPEECH PRODUCTION

---

18. ARTICULATION*

Mark correct sound (✓); substitutions (with sound substituted); omitted sounds (—); distorted sounds (x); no response (nr)

19. COMMENTS

	r-blends	s-blends
1. ʒ _____	14. pr- _____	27. sm- _____
2. ju _____	15. br- _____	28. sn- _____
I M F	16. tr- _____	29. sp- _____
3. r _____ _____	17. dr- _____	30. st- _____
4. l _____	18. kr- _____	31. sk- _____
5. v _____	19. gr- _____	32. sl- _____
6. θ _____ _____ _____	20. fr- _____	33. sw- _____
7. ð _____ _____ _____	21. θr- _____	Other 2-element Blends
8. z _____	22. ∫r- _____	34. tw- _____
9. ∫ _____ _____ _____		35. kw- _____
10. ʒ _____	l-blends	
11. j _____ _____	23. pl- _____	3-element Blends
12. t∫ _____ _____ _____	24. kl- _____	36. spl- _____
13. dʒ _____ _____	25. gl- _____	37. spr- _____
	26. fl- _____	38. str- _____
		39. skr- _____

Total Number (score) produced correctly ☐

Summary Score: ☐ Normal
              0

               ☐ Suspect
              1

               ☐ Abnormal
              2

COLLABORATIVE RESEARCH
PERINATAL RESEARCH BRANCH, NINDS, NIH
BETHESDA, MD. 20014

(4-70)   PAGE
         4 OF 4   **PS-44**

COLR—3151-45
4-70

FINAL SPEECH, LANGUAGE AND HEARING EXAMINATION
ADDITIONAL OBSERVATIONS

2. NAME OF CHILD

3. DATE OF BIRTH	4. AGE	5. SEX	6. RACE
MO. : DAY : YEAR		☐ MALE ☐ FEMALE 1 2	☐ W ☐ N ☐ OR 1 2 3 ☐ PR ☐ OTHER 4 8

7. EXAMINED BY	8. DATE OF EXAM.
	MO. : DAY : YEAR

1. PATIENT IDENTIFICATION

9. STATE OF HEALTH ON DAY OF EXAMINATION (*Comment on any condition which may affect the child's test performance, e.g., hearing aid, glasses or other prostheses, respiratory condition, running ears, etc.*)

10. OBSERVABLE ANOMALIES

1. Head   ☐ None   Yes
   - 0
   - EXTREMELY SMALL   ☐ 1
   - EXTREMELY LARGE   ☐ 2
   - PECULIAR SHAPE (*describe*)   ☐ 3
   - OTHER (*describe*)   ☐ 8

2. Face   ☐ None
   - 0
   - ASYMMETRY   ☐ 1
   - MASK-LIKE   ☐ 2
   - GRIMACES   ☐ 3
   - OTHER (*describe*)   ☐ 8

3. Ears   ☐ None
   - 0
   - ATRESIA   ☐ 1
   - OTHER (*describe*)   ☐ 8

4. Eyes   ☐ None
   - 0
   - STRABISMUS   ☐ 1
   - NYSTAGMUS   ☐ 2
   - OTHER (*describe*)   ☐ 8

11. COMMENTS

506

COLR-3151-45
4-70

12. PATIENT IDENTIFICATION

FINAL SPEECH, LANGUAGE AND HEARING EXAMINATION
ADDITIONAL OBSERVATIONS

10. OBSERVABLE ANOMALIES *(continued)*

13. COMMENTS

5. Mouth

	No	Yes
a. TONGUE AND PALATE		
CLEFT PALATE	☐ 0	☐ 1
CLEFT PALATE (repaired)	☐ 0	☐ 1
VERY HIGH HARD PALATE	☐ 0	☐ 1
VERY SHORT SOFT PALATE	☐ 0	☐ 1
VERY SHORT LINGUAL FRENULUM	☐ 0	☐ 1
CLEFT LIP	☐ 0	☐ 1
b. TEETH AND JAW		
MALOCCLUSION (i.e. overbite, underbite, crossbite, openbite, etc.)	☐ 0	☐ 1
MISSING TEETH *(describe)*	☐ 0	☐ 1
c. DROOLING	☐ 0	☐ 1
MOUTH BREATHER	☐ 0	☐ 1
OTHER *(describe)*	☐ 0	☐ 1

6. Hands and Arms ☐ None 0

IMPAIRED FUNCTION	☐ 1
OTHER *(describe)*	☐ 2

7. Legs ☐ None 0

IMPAIRED FUNCTION	☐ 1
OTHER *(describe)*	☐ 2

8. General Awkwardness ☐ No 0   ☐ 1

507

14. PATIENT IDENTIFICATION

FINAL SPEECH, LANGUAGE AND HEARING EXAMINATION
ADDITIONAL OBSERVATIONS

15. GENERAL BEHAVIOR ABERRATIONS OBSERVED DURING TEST PERIOD

	No	Yes
Purposeless Hand Motions	☐ 0	☐ 1
Unusual Posturing	☐ 0	☐ 1
Excessive Crying	☐ 0	☐ 1
Excessive Laughing	☐ 0	☐ 1
Hyperactivity	☐ 0	☐ 1
Hypoactivity	☐ 0	☐ 1
Lack of Spontaneous Communication	☐ 0	☐ 1
Withdrawal	☐ 0	☐ 1
Distractibility	☐ 0	☐ 1
Negativism	☐ 0	☐ 1
Perseveration	☐ 0	☐ 1
Echolalia	☐ 0	☐ 1
Impulsivity	☐ 0	☐ 1
Echopraxia	☐ 0	☐ 1
Motor Disinhibition	☐ 0	☐ 1
Short Attention Span	☐ 0	☐ 1
Tics	☐ 0	☐ 1
Tremors	☐ 0	☐ 1
Other (describe)	☐ 0	☐ 1

16. COMMENTS

COLLABORATIVE RESEARCH
PERINATAL RESEARCH BRANCH, NINDS, NIH
BETHESDA, MD. 20014

508

List of NCPP Variables Used as Predictors in the Correlation Screen

The following is a list of the 901 NCPP variables used in the SLH study as described in Chapter 5. The valid codes for each are given; numerical values used in computer analyses are given for categorical variables. All invalid codes were grouped together and appear as blanks for each variable. The far right column gives the source for each variable, which is either the Variable File (VF), a special tape, or a form number. The column for codes includes the following terminology:

dich: dichotomous, i.e., 0 = no, 1 = pass
p/f: 0 = fail, 1 = pass
as given: refers to a variable measured on a continuous scale; the units of measurement (pounds, cms, "number") and the actual range of values, when known, are indicated

Sequence number	Variable name	Codes	Source
1	Age of gravida (years)	10–58 = as given	VF
2	Gestation at registration (weeks)	1–50 = as given	VF
	Marital status at birth:		
3	single	dich	VF
4	married, common law	dich	VF
5	widowed, divorced, separated	dich	VF
6	Prior pregnancies (number)	0–28 = as given	VF
7	Parity: nonaborted prior pregnancies of 20 weeks or greater Gestation (number)	0–28 = as given	VF
8	Prior perinatal loss (number)	0–7 = as given 8 = 8 or more	VF
9	Prior viable births (number)	0 = prior births but no viables 1–7 = as given 8 = 8 or more	VF
10	Cigarettes per day at registration (number)	0 = none (includes nonsmokers) 1–60 = as given 61 = 61 or more	VF
11	Cigarette smoking: status at registration	0 = nonsmoker 1 = smoker	VF
12	Height of mother (inches)	40–80 = as given	VF
13	Prepregnancy weight (pounds)	50–360 = as given	VF
14	Weight gain: gravida (pounds)	−149 to 132 = as given	VF
15	Lowest hemoglobin: gravida	1 = 5.9 and less 2 = 6.0–7.9 3 = 8.0–9.9 4 = 10.0–11.9 5 = 12.0 and greater	VF
16	Blood pressure (systolic ≥ 160 or diastolic ≥ 110): postpartum	1 = first two weeks only 2 = third to eighth weeks only 3 = first to eighth weeks only	VF
17	24 weeks to labor	dich	VF
18	up to 24 weeks	0 = no 1 = yes 2 = regularly after 23rd week	VF
19	intrapartum	dich	VF
	Convulsions during pregnancy:		
20	before pregnancy only	dich	VF
21	during pregnancy only	dich	VF
22	before and during pregnancy only	dich	VF
23	post partum only	dich	VF
24	before pregnancy and post partum only	dich	VF
25	during pregnancy and post partum only	dich	VF
26	before pregnancy, during pregnancy, post partum	dich	VF
	OB-60 summary of number of conditions:		
27	metabolic and endocrine	0–7 = as given 8 = 8 or more	VF
28	urinary tract	0–7 = as given	VF

Sequence number	Variable name	Codes	Source
		8 = 8 or more	
29	neurologic and psychiatric	0–7 = as given	VF
		8 = 8 or more	
30	complications of this pregnancy	0–7 = as given	VF
		8 = 8 or more	
31	infectious diseases during pregnancy	0–7 = as given	VF
		8 = 8 or more	
32	Education of gravida (years) at registration	0–18 = as given	VF
33	Annual family income: grouped at registration	1 = no income	VF
		2 = $1–$1999	
		3 = $2000–$3999	
		4 = $4000–$5999	
		5 = $6000–$7999	
		6 = $8000–$9999	
		7 = $10,000 or more	
34	Housing density: number of persons per room (overcrowding)	1–75 = 0.1 to 7.5 as given	VF
		80 = 8.0 or more	
35	Gravida in home for unwed mothers	dich	VF
	Seizures, convulsions, epilepsy of prior siblings of study child:		
36	with fever	dich	VF
37	without fever	dich	VF
38	with and without fever	dich	VF
39	Socioeconomic index at birth	0–95 = 0.0 to 9.5 as given	VF
	Race (mother and child):		
40	White	dich	VF
41	Black	dich	VF
42	Number of confining illnesses during year before registration	0–7 = as given	VF
	X-ray exposures:	8 = 8 or more	
43	abdomino-pelvic area during year before registration	dich	VF
44	other areas during year before registration	dich	VF
	Blood type (gravida):		
52	Age of father of baby at registration (years)	12–65 = as given	VF
		66 = 66 or older	
53	Education of husband or father of baby at registration (years)	0–18 = as given	VF
63	Prior prematures (number)	0–6 = as given	VF
		7 = 7 or more	
64	Prior abortions (number)	0–6 = as given	VF
		7 = 7 or more	
65	Prior stillbirths and neonatal deaths (number)	0–7 = as given	VF
		8 = 8 or more	
	Conditions of prior siblings of study child:		
66	congenital malformation: cleft lip or palate	dich	VF
67	congenital malformation: heart	dich	VF
68	congenital malformation: head or spine	dich	VF
69	motor defect: injury	dich	VF
70	motor defect: infection	dich	VF
71	sensory defect: blind	dich	VF
72	sensory defect: deaf	dich	VF
73	sensory defect: trouble speaking	dich	VF
74	retardation and disturbance: physical retardation	dich	VF
75	retardation and disturbance: mental retardation	dich	VF
	Conditions of gravida:		
76	malformations	dich	VF
77	sensory defect: seeing	dich	VF

511

Sequence number	Variable name	Codes	Source
78	sensory defect: hearing	dich	VF
79	sensory defect: seeing and hearing	dich	VF
80	sensory defect: speaking	dich	VF
81	sensory defect: seeing and speaking	dich	VF
82	sensory defect: hearing and speaking	dich	VF
83	sensory defect: seeing, hearing, and speaking	dich	VF
84	seizures: before age 15	dich	VF
85	seizures: age 15 or older	dich	VF
86	seizures: throughout lifetime	dich	VF
87	seizures: age unknown	dich	VF
88	seizures: eclampsia only	dich	VF
89	motor defects: injury	dich	VF
90	motor defects: infection	dich	VF
91	motor defects: injury and infection	dich	VF
92	mental retardation	dich	VF
93	special class for slow learners, ungraded	dich	VF
94	mental illness	dich	VF
	Conditions of father of baby:		
95	malformations	dich	VF
96	sensory defect: seeing	dich	VF
97	sensory defect: hearing	dich	VF
98	sensory defect: seeing and hearing	dich	VF
99	sensory defect: speaking	dich	VF
100	sensory defect: seeing and speaking	dich	VF
101	sensory defect: hearing and speaking	dich	VF
102	sensory defect: seeing, hearing, and speaking	dich	VF
103	seizures	dich	VF
104	motor defects	dich	VF
105	mental retardation	dich	VF
106	special class for slow learners, ungraded	dich	VF
107	mental illness	dich	VF
108	diabetes: onset before age 15	dich	VF
109	diabetes: onset at age 15 or older	dich	VF
110	diabetes: age at onset unknown	dich	VF
111	Bayley 8-month mental score	0–106 = as given	VF
112	Bayley 8-month motor score	0–43 = as given	VF
113	Bayley 8-month examination: final diagnosis	2 = normal 3 = suspect 4 = abnormal	VF
114	Stanford-Binet 4-year IQ	25–175 = as given	VF
115	Placental weight (grams)	1–2000 = as given	VF
	Sex of study child:		
116	male	dich	VF
117	female	dich	VF
	One-minute Apgar:		
118	heart rate	0 = absent 1 = slow 2 = 100 or over	VF
119	respiratory effort	0 = absent 1 = weak cry 2 = crying lustily	VF
120	muscle tone	0 = flaccid 1 = some flexion 2 = well flexed	VF
121	reflex irritability	0 = no response 1 = some motion 2 = cry	VF

512

Sequence number	Variable name	Codes	Source
122	color	0 = blue pale 1 = blue hands and feet 2 = entirely pink	VF
123	score	0–10 = as given	VF
	Five-minute Apgar:		
124	heart rate	0 = absent 1 = slow 2 = 100 or over	VF
125	respiratory effort	0 = absent 1 = weak cry 2 = crying lustily	VF
126	muscle tone	0 = flaccid 1 = some flexion 2 = well flexed	VF
127	reflex irritability	0 = no response 1 = some motion 2 = cry	VF
128	color	0 = blue pale 1 = blue hands and feet 2 = entirely pink	VF
129	score	0–10 = as given	VF
130	Procedures: positive pressure	0 = not used 1 = used	VF
131	Stage of dysmaturity	0 = none 1 = stage 1 2 = stage 2 3 = stage 3	VF
132	Direct Coombs' test: child	1 = positive 2 = negative	VF
133	Lowest hemoglobin: child (grams)	2–62 = as given	VF
134	Maximum serum bilirubin (grams)	0 = less than 1 1–53 = as given	VF
	PED-8 summary of number of conditions:		
135	neurologic abnormality	0–8 = as given 9 = 9 or more	VF
136	central nervous system malformations and related skeletal conditions	0–8 = as given 9 = 9 or more	VF
137	musculoskeletal abnormality	0–8 = as given 9 = 9 or more	VF
138	eye conditions	0–8 = as given 9 = 9 or more	VF
139	ear conditions	0–8 = as given 9 = 9 or more	VF
140	upper respiratory tract and mouth conditions	0–8 = as given 9 = 9 or more	VF
141	thoracic abnormality	0–8 = as given 9 = 9 or more	VF
142	respiratory abnormality	0–8 = as given 9 = 9 or more	VF
143	cardiovascular conditions	0–8 = as given 9 = 9 or more	VF
144	alimentary tract malformations and other conditions	0–8 = as given 9 = 9 or more	VF
145	abnormal liver, bile ducts, spleen	0–8 = as given	VF

513

Sequence number	Variable name	Codes	Source
146	genitourinary conditions	9 = 9 or more 0–8 = as given	VF
147	neoplastic disease and/or other tumors	9 = 9 or more 0–8 = as given	VF
148	hematologic conditions	9 = 9 or more 0–8 = as given	VF
149	skin conditions and malformations	9 = 9 or more 0–8 = as given	VF
150	infection	9 = 9 or more 0–8 = as given	VF
151	syndromes	9 = 9 or more. 0–8 = as given	VF
152	other endocrine or metabolic disease	9 = 9 or more 0–8 = as given	VF
153	procedures	9 = 9 or more 0–8 = as given	VF
	other conditions and presumptive etologic conditions:	9 = 9 or more	
154	other conditions only	dich	VF
155	presumed anoxia only	dich	VF
156	presumed trauma only	dich	VF
157	presumed anoxia and trauma	dich	VF
158	other conditions and presumed anoxia	dich	VF
159	other conditions and presumed trauma	dich	VF
160	other conditions, presumed anoxia, and presumed trauma	dich	VF
161	Head circumference: 1YR (cms)	23–79 = as given	VF
	PED-12 summary of number of conditions:		
162	neurologic abnormality	0–8 = as given	VF
163	related central nervous system and skeletal conditions	9 = 9 or more 0–8 = as given	VF
164	musculoskeletal abnormality	9 = 9 or more 0–8 = as given	VF
165	eye conditions	9 = 9 or more 0–8 = as given	VF
166	ear conditions	9 = 9 or more 0–8 = as given	VF
167	upper respiratory tract and mouth conditions	9 = 9 or more 0–8 = as given	VF
168	thoracic conditions	9 = 9 or more 0–8 = as given	VF
169	lower respiratory tract abnormality	9 = 9 or more 0–8 = as given	VF
170	cardiovascular conditions	9 = 9 or more 0–8 = as given	VF
171	alimentary tract conditions	9 = 9 or more 0–8 = as given	VF
172	abnormal liver, bile duct, and/or spleen	9 = 9 or more 0–8 = as given	VF
173	genitourinary conditions	9 = 9 or more 0–8 = as given	VF
174	neoplastic disease and/or other tumors	9 = 9 or more 0–8 = as given	VF
175	hematologic conditions	9 = 9 or more 0–8 = as given	VF
176	skin conditions and malformations	9 = 9 or more 0–8 = as given 9 = 9 or more	VF

Sequence number	Variable name	Codes	Source
177	syndromes	0–8 = as given 9 = 9 or more	VF
178	other endocrine and metabolic disease	0–8 = as given 9 = 9 or more	VF
179	infection and inflammation	0–8 = as given 9 = 9 or more	VF
180	trauma due to physical agents and intoxications	0–8 = as given 9 = 9 or more	VF
181	disturbances in homeostasis	0–8 = as given 9 = 9 or more	VF
182	other conditions	0–8 = as given 9 = 9 or more	VF
183	procedures	0–8 = as given 9 = 9 or more	VF
184	social and environmental conditions	0–8 = as given 9 = 9 or more	VF
185	Birthweight (grams)	1–7400 = as given	VF
186	Gestation at delivery (weeks) blood type (child):	1–50 = as given	VF
187	O	dich	VF
188	A	dich	VF
189	B	dich	VF
190	AB	dich	VF
191	Rh factor: child	1 = positive 2 = negative	VF
192	Graham Block Sort, raw score total (4YR)	0–45 = as given	VF
193	Dominance: hand (4YR)	1 = right 2 = left	VF
194	Dominance: leg (4YR)	1 = right 2 = left	VF
195	Dominance: eye (4YR)	1 = right 2 = left	VF
196	Dominance: overall summary (4YR)	1 = right 2 = left	VF
197	Neurological abnormalities: 7YR	0 = none 1 = suspicious 2 = definite	VF
198	Head circumference: neonatal (cm)	14–46 = as given	VF
199	Head circumference: 4 months (cm)	27–60 = as given	VF
200	Head circumference: 8 months (cm)	as given	VF
201	Head circumference: 3 years (cm)	as given	VF
202	Head circumference: 4 years (cm)	as given	VF
203	Head circumference: 7 years (cm)	as given	VF
204	Weight: 1 year (kg)	as given	VF
205	Weight: 3 years (kg)	as given	VF
206	Weight: 4 years (kg)	as given	VF
207	Weight: 7 years (kg)	as given	VF
208	Body length at birth (cm)	15–63 = as given	VF
209	Body length: 4 months (cm)	25–80 = as given	VF
210	Body length: 8 months (cm)	as given	VF
211	Body length: 1 year (cm)	48–90 = as given	VF
212	Body length: 3 years (cm)	as given	VF
213	Body length: 4 years (cm)	as given	VF
214	Body length: 7 years (cm)	90–150 = as given	VF
215	Mother/mother surrogate intelligence (SRA) Method of delivery type:	60–140 = as given	VF
216	vertex	dich	VF

Sequence number	Variable name	Codes	Source
217	breech	dich	VF
218	caesarean section	dich	VF
219	Abruptio placenta	0 = no	VF
		1 = partial	
		2 = complete	
	Cord pathology:		
220	true knot	0 = tight	VF
		1 = loose	
		2 = none	
221	velamentous insertion	dich	VF
222	varices	dich	VF
223	ruptured cord vessel	dich	VF
224	other	dich	VF
225	cord around body	0 = tight	VF
		1 = loose	
		2 = none	
226	loose cord around neck (number of times)	0–7 = as given	VF
227	tight cord around neck (number of times)	0–6 = as given	VF
		7 = 7 or more	
	Placenta previa:		
228	total	dich	VF
229	partial	dich	VF
230	marginal	dich	VF
231	low implantation	dich	VF
	Prolapsed cord:		
232	occult	dich	VF
233	into vagina	dich	VF
234	through introitus	dich	VF
235	Vertex delivery with forceps: application	1 = class I-outlet	VF
		2 = class II-low	
		3 = class III-mid	
		4 = class IV-high	
236	Vertex delivery with forceps application: unsuccessful attempt	dich	VF
237	Acute toxemia	0 = none	VF
		1 = possible pre-eclampsia	
		2 = pre-eclampsia, mild	
		3 = pre-eclampsia, severe	
		4 = eclampsia	
238	Chronic hypertensive disease	dich	VF
239	Polyhydramnios	dich	VF
240	Duration: first and second stages of labor (hours and minutes)	0–9959 = as given	VF
241	Marginal sinus rupture	dich	VF
242	Weight: 4 months (grams)	as given	VF
243	Weight: 8 months (grams)	as given	VF
244	7YR socioeconomic index	0–97 = 0.0 to 9.7 as given	PRB 7YR SEI tape
245	Date of birth: mother surrogate	month, day, year as given	PS-26
	Race (mother surrogate):		
246	White	dich	PS-26
247	Negro	dich	PS-26
248	Oriental	dich	PS-26
249	Puerto Rican	dich	PS-26
	Relationship to child:		

516

Sequence number	Variable name	Codes	Source
250	mother	dich	PS-26
251	adoptive mother	dich	PS-26
252	foster mother	dich	PS-26
253	guardian	dich	PS-26
254	Rash or skin trouble: gravida	dich	OB-8
255	Operation: gravida	dich	OB-8
256	Air travel by gravida	dich	OB-8
257	Number of children under 8 years supported at registration	0–10 = as given	FHH-1 & 3
258	Physical defects: gravida	0 = none 1 = head and/or spine	GEN-7
259	Sensory defects: siblings and gravida (number)	0–6 = as given 7 = 7 or more	GEN-7
	Sensory defects:		
260	mother of gravida	dich	GEN-7
261	father of gravida	dich	GEN-7
262	mother and father of gravida	dich	GEN-7
	Diabetes (gravida):		
263	onset before age 15	dich	GEN-7
264	onset at age 15 or older	dich	GEN-7
265	occurred only during pregnancy	dich	GEN-7
266	Diabetes: siblings of gravida (number)	0–6 = as given 7 = 7 or more	GEN-7
	Diabetes:		
267	mother of gravida	dich	GEN-7
268	father of gravida	dich	GEN-7
269	mother and father of gravida	dich	GEN-7
270	Seizures: siblings of gravida (number)	0–6 = as given 7 = 7 or more	GEN-7
	Seizures:		
271	mother of gravida	dich	GEN-7
272	father of gravida	dich	GEN-7
273	mother and father of gravida	dich	GEN-7
274	Motor defect: siblings of gravida (number)	0–6 = as given 7 = 7 or more	GEN-7
	Motor defect:		
275	mother of gravida	dich	GEN-7
276	father of gravida	dich	GEN-7
277	mother and father of gravida	dich	GEN-7
278	Mental retardation: siblings of gravida (number)	0–6 = as given 7 = 7 or more	GEN-7
	Mental retardation:		
279	mother of gravida	dich	GEN-7
280	father of gravida	dich	GEN-7
281	mother and father of gravida	dich	GEN-7
282	Mental illness: siblings of gravida (number)	0–6 = as given 7 = 7 or more	GEN-7
	Mental illness:		
283	mother of gravida	dich	GEN-7
284	father of gravida	dich	GEN-7
285	mother and father of gravida	dich	GEN-7
286	Physical defects: father of baby	0 = none 1 = head and/or spine	GEN-8
287	Sensory defects: siblings of father of baby (number)	0–6 = as given 7 = 7 or more	GEN-8

517

Sequence number	Variable name	Codes	Source
	Sensory defects:		
288	mother of father of baby	dich	GEN-8
289	father of father of baby	dich	GEN-8
290	mother and father of father of baby	dich	GEN-8
291	Diabetes: siblings of father of baby (number)	0–6 = as given 7 = 7 or more	GEN-8
	Diabetes:		
292	mother of father of baby	dich	GEN-8
293	father of father of baby	dich	GEN-8
294	mother and father of father of baby	dich	GEN-8
295	Seizures: siblings of father of baby (number)	0–6 = as given 7 = 7 or more	GEN-8
	Seizures:		
296	mother of father of baby	dich	GEN-8
297	father of father of baby	dich	GEN-8
298	mother and father of father of baby	dich	GEN-8
299	Motor defect: siblings of father of baby (number)	0–6 = as given 7 = 7 or more	GEN-8
	Motor defect:		
300	mother of father of baby	dich	GEN-8
301	father of father of baby	dich	GEN-8
302	mother and father of father of baby	dich	GEN-8
303	Mental retardation: siblings of father of baby (number)	0–6 = as given 7 = 7 or more	GEN-8
	Mental retardation:		
304	mother of father of baby	dich	GEN-8
305	father of father of baby	dich	GEN-8
306	mother and father of father of baby	dich	GEN-8
307	Mental illness: siblings of father of baby (number)	0–6 = as given 7 = 7 or more	GEN-8
	Mental illness:		
308	mother of father of baby	dich	GEN-8
309	father of father of baby	dich	GEN-8
310	mother and father of father of baby	dich	GEN-8
	8-Month psychological examination (Bayley):		
311	searches with eyes for sound	p/f	PS-1
312	vocalizes to social stimulus	p/f	PS-1
313	vocalizes two syllables	p/f	PS-1
314	reacts to disappearance of face	p/f	PS-1
315	plays with rattle	p/f	PS-1
316	aware of strange situation	p/f	PS-1
317	inspects own hands	p/f	PS-1
318	turns head to sound of bell	p/f	PS-1
319	turns head to sound of rattle	p/f	PS-1
320	discriminates strangers	p/f	PS-1
321	vocalizes attitudes	p/f	PS-1
322	recovers rattle in crib	p/f	PS-1
323	turns head after dropped objects	p/f	PS-1
324	enjoys frolic play	p/f	PS-1
325	picks up cube directly and easily	p/f	PS-1
326	enjoys sound production	p/f	PS-1
327	attends to scribbling	p/f	PS-1
328	looks for dropped object	p/f	PS-1
329	manipulates bell	p/f	PS-1
330	vocalizes four different syllables	p/f	PS-1
331	responds to social play	p/f	PS-1
332	rings bell imitatively	p/f	PS-1

518

Sequence number	Variable name	Codes	Source
333	responds to name	p/f	PS-1
334	says da-da	p/f	PS-1
335	adjusts to words	p/f	PS-1
	speed of response:		
336	very slow, does not approach object	dich	PS-3
337	approaches objects, but only after they have been in front of him for a long time	dich	PS-3
338	approaches objects after looking at them briefly	dich	PS-3
339	quickly approaches presented objects	dich	PS-3
340	very fast, anticipates examiner's moves	dich	PS-3
341	varies greatly	dich	PS-3
	intensity of response:		
342	does not look at or handle objects	dich	PS-3
343	when given objects, holds them, but does not play with them	dich	PS-3
344	some manipulations of objects	dich	PS-3
345	plays with objects actively	dich	PS-3
346	exerts considerable force in manipulating objects	dich	PS-3
347	varies greatly	dich	PS-3
	duration of response:		
348	attends to object very briefly	dich	PS-3
349	spends short time with objects	dich	PS-3
350	spends moderate time with objects	dich	PS-3
351	spends fairly long time with objects	dich	PS-3
352	spends very long time with objects	dich	PS-3
353	varies greatly	dich	PS-3
	persistence in pursuit:		
354	makes no attempt to get objects	dich	PS-3
355	makes one or two attempts, then gives up	dich	PS-3
356	makes several brief attempts, but gives up when encounters difficulty	dich	PS-3
357	makes frequent attempts to reach goal, does not give up easily	dich	PS-3
358	makes very frequent and vigorous attempts, does not give up easily	dich	PS-3
359	varies greatly	dich	PS-3
	intensity of social response:		
360	does not respond to initiation of social contact	dich	PS-3
361	responds only to direct approach, no interest in persons	dich	PS-3
362	as interested in social contact as in object manipulation	dich	PS-3
363	behavior strongly affected by persons, more interested in persons than objects	dich	PS-3
364	very strong-over-reacts to persons	dich	PS-3
365	varies greatly	dich	PS-3
	nature of social response to examiner:		
366	avoids, draws back, turns to mother	dich	PS-3
367	hesitates, is apprehensive of examiner	dich	PS-3
368	accepts, is passivee, but responds	dich	PS-3
369	friendly, responds easily to most test situations	dich	PS-3
370	invites, instigates social contact	dich	PS-3
371	varies greatly	dich	PS-3
	nature of social response to mother:		
372	ignores mother during free play, resists contact with mother	dich	PS-3
373	hesitates, cooperates in certain tests	dich	PS-3
374	accepts, responds adequately to assistance by mother	dich	PS-3
375	enjoys contact with mother	dich	PS-3

519

Sequence number	Variable name	Codes	Source
376	demands, clings to mother	dich	PS-3
377	varies greatly	dich	PS-3
	activity level:		
378	hypoactive, no self-initiated moves	dich	PS-3
379	little activity, seldom moves	dich	PS-3
380	responds appropriately	dich	PS-3
381	much activity, in action much of the time	dich	PS-3
382	hyperactive, constantly in motion	dich	PS-3
383	varies greatly	dich	PS-3
384	physical development	1 = advanced	PS-3
		2 = normal	
		3 = suspect	
		4 = abnormal	
385	mental development	1 = advanced	PS-3
		2 = normal	
		3 = suspect	
		4 = abnormal	
386	fine motor development	1 = advanced	PS-3
		2 = normal	
		3 = suspect	
		4 = abnormal	
387	gross motor development	1 = advanced	PS-3
		2 = normal	
		3 = suspect	
		4 = abnormal	
388	social emotional development	1 = advanced	PS-3
		2 = normal	
		3 = suspect	
		4 = abnormal	
	deviant behavior:		
389	present in at least one of first five observations	dich	PS-4
390	unusual and meaningless hand motions	dich	PS-4
391	head rolling or banging	dich	PS-4
392	rocking	dich	PS-4
393	meaningless smiling and laughing	dich	PS-4
394	excessive crying	dich	PS-4
395	combination of deviant behaviors	dich	PS-4
	obvious defects:		
396	mongolism	dich	PS-4
397	hydrocephalus	dich	PS-4
398	microcephalus	dich	PS-4
399	asymmetry of skull	dich	PS-4
400	very obese or very small	dich	PS-4
401	skin condition	dich	PS-4
402	combination of obvious defects	dich	PS-4
403	sits alone momentarily	p/f	PS-2
	expression of affection by mother:		
404	negative	dich	PS-5
405	occasionally negative	dich	PS-5
406	warm	dich	PS-5
407	frequently caressed child	dich	PS-5
408	extravagant	dich	PS-5
409	variable	dich	PS-5
	evaluation of child by mother:		
410	critical	dich	PS-5
411	generally negative	dich	PS-5
412	accepting	dich	PS-5

520

Sequence number	Variable name	Codes	Source
413	ignores less desirable behavior	dich	PS-5
414	effusive	dich	PS-5
415	variable	dich	PS-5
	handling of child by mother:		
416	rough	dich	PS-5
417	awkward and clumsy	dich	PS-5
418	considerate	dich	PS-5
419	very gently	dich	PS-5
420	overly cautious	dich	PS-5
421	variable	dich	PS-5
	management of child by mother:		
422	no facilitation	dich	PS-5
423	followed suggestions, held child	dich	PS-5
424	orienting	dich	PS-5
425	frequently interfered	dich	PS-5
426	overdirecting	dich	PS-5
427	variable	dich	PS-5
	reaction to child's needs by mother:		
428	unresponsive	dich	PS-5
429	slow in responding	dich	PS-5
430	recognized	dich	PS-5
431	responded immediately	dich	PS-5
432	absorbed	dich	PS-5
433	variable	dich	PS-5
	reaction to child's performance by mother:		
434	indifferent	dich	PS-5
435	brief interest	dich	PS-5
436	interested	dich	PS-5
437	excessive pride	dich	PS-5
438	defensive	dich	PS-5
439	variable	dich	PS-5
	mother's focus of attention:		
440	child	dich	PS-5
441	involved self with child	dich	PS-5
442	situation	dich	PS-5
443	occasionally interrupted	dich	PS-5
444	self	dich	PS-5
445	variable	dich	PS-5
	child's appearance:		
446	unkempt	dich	PS-5
447	helter-skelter	dich	PS-5
448	appropriate	dich	PS-5
449	somewhat overdressed	dich	PS-5
450	overdressed	dich	PS-5
451	variable	dich	PS-5
	4YR psychological examination (Stanford-Binet):		
	year II:		
452	three-hole form board	dich	PS-20
453	identifying parts of the body	dich	PS-20
454	picture vocabulary	dich	PS-20
455	word combination	dich	PS-20
456	alternate	p/f	PS-20
	year II-6:		
457	identifying objects by use	dich	PS-20
458	naming objects	dich	PS-20
459	picture vocabulary	dich	PS-20
460	repeating 2 digits	dich	PS-20

521

Sequence number	Variable name	Codes	Source
461	alternate	p/f	PS-20
	year III:		
462	picture vocabulary	dich	PS-20
463	block building	dich	PS-20
464	picture memories	dich	PS-20
465	copying a circle	dich	PS-20
466	alternate	p/f	PS-20
	year III-6:		
467	comparison of balls	dich	PS-20
468	discrimination of animal pictures	dich	PS-20
469	response to pictures	dich	PS-20
470	comprehension	dich	PS-20
471	alternate	p/f	PS-20
	year IV:		
472	picture vocabulary	dich	PS-20
473	naming objects from memory	dich	PS-20
474	opposite analogies	dich	PS-20
475	pictorial identification	dich	PS-20
476	alternate	p/f	PS-20
	year IV-6:		
477	opposite analogies	dich	PS-20
478	pictorial similarities/differences	dich	PS-20
479	three commissions	dich	PS-20
480	comprehension III	dich	PS-20
481	alternate	p/f	PS-20
	year V:		
482	picture completion	dich	PS-20
483	definitions	dich	PS-20
484	copying a square	dich	PS-20
485	patience: rectangles	dich	PS-20
486	alternate	p/f	PS-20
	year VI:		
487	vocabulary	dich	PS-20
488	differences	dich	PS-20
489	number concepts	dich	PS-20
490	opposite analogies	dich	PS-20
491	alternate	p/f	PS-20
	year VII:		
492	similarities	dich	PS-20
493	copying a diamond	dich	PS-20
494	comprehension IV	dich	PS-20
495	repeating 5 digits	dich	PS-20
496	alternate	p/f	PS-20
	year VIII:		
497	vocabulary	dich	PS-20
498	verbal absurdities	dich	PS-20
499	similarities/differences	dich	PS-20
500	comprehension IV	dich	PS-20
501	alternate	p/f	PS-20
	year IX:		
502	memory for designs	dich	PS-20
503	rhymes	dich	PS-20
504	making change	dich	PS-20
505	repeating 4 digits reversed	dich	PS-20
506	alternate	p/f	PS-20
	year X:		
507	vocabulary	dich	PS-20

522

Sequence number	Variable name	Codes	Source
508	abstract words	dich	PS-20
509	word naming	dich	PS-20
510	repeating 6 digits	dich	PS-20
511	alternate	p/f	PS-20
	orientation to testing situation, emotional reactivity:		
512	extremely flat	dich	PS-23
513	somewhat flat	dich	PS-23
514	normal	dich	PS-23
515	mood more variable than average	dich	PS-23
516	extreme instability	dich	PS-23
	orientation to testing situation, degree of irritability:		
517	extremely phlegmatic	dich	PS-23
518	rarely annoyed	dich	PS-23
519	normally reactive	dich	PS-23
520	frequently irritable	dich	PS-23
521	extremely irritable	dich	PS-23
522	variable	dich	PS-23
	orientation to examiner, degree of cooperation:		
523	extreme negativism	dich	PS-23
524	resistive	dich	PS-23
525	cooperative	dich	PS-23
526	accepts directions more easily	dich	PS-23
527	extremely suggestible	dich	PS-23
528	variable	dich	PS-23
	orientation to examiner, degree of dependency		
529	very self-reliant	dich	PS-23
530	rarely needs help	dich	PS-23
531	dependent in appropriate situation	dich	PS-23
532	demands more attention	dich	PS-23
533	constant need for attention	dich	PS-23
534	variable	dich	PS-23
	orientation to test materials, duration of attention span:		
535	very brief	dich	PS-23
536	short time	dich	PS-23
537	adequate	dich	PS-23
538	more than average	dich	PS-23
539	highly perseverative	dich	PS-23
540	variable	dich	PS-23
	orientation to test materials, goal orientation:		
541	no effort	dich	PS-23
542	brief attempt	dich	PS-23
543	able to keep goal in mind	dich	PS-23
544	keeps goals and questions in mind	dich	PS-23
545	compulsive absorption	dich	PS-23
546	variable	dich	PS-23
	orientation to test materials, response to directions:		
547	unwilling or unable to follow specific directions	dich	PS-23
548	some responsiveness	dich	PS-23
549	responds to directions	dich	PS-23
550	shows little deviation from examiner's directions	dich	PS-23
551	completely dependent upon specific directions	dich	PS-23
552	variable	dich	PS-23
	activity, level of activity:		
553	extreme inactivity	dich	PS-23
554	little activity	dich	PS-23
555	normal amount of activity	dich	PS-23
556	unusual amount of activity	dich	PS-23

Sequence number	Variable name	Codes	Source
557	extremely impulsive	dich	PS-23
558	variable	dich	PS-23
	activity, nature of activity:		
559	extreme rigidity	dich	PS-23
560	some rigidity	dich	PS-23
561	flexible behavior	dich	PS-23
562	behavior frequently impulsive	dich	PS-23
563	extremely impulsive	dich	PS-23
564	variable	dich	PS-23
	nature of communication:		
565	nonverbal	dich	PS-23
566	content confined to directed questions	dich	PS-23
567	content includes spontaneous conversation	dich	PS-23
568	answers questions, contains some spontaneous conversation	dich	PS-23
569	content irrelevant and inappropriate	dich	PS-23
	deviant or stereotyped behavior:		
570	dropping, throwing, pushing off table	dich	PS-24
571	excessive/persistent thumb sucking	dich	PS-24
572	excessive/persistent nail biting	dich	PS-24
573	unusual/meaningless hand motions	dich	PS-24
574	meaningless smiling and laughing	dich	PS-24
575	excessive crying	dich	PS-24
576	echolalia	dich	PS-24
577	child in nursery school?	0 = yes 1 = no	
578	Minimum temperature: neonate	degrees as given	PED-3
579	No temperature below 95° axillary or 96° rectal	dich	PED-3
580	Neonatal minimum temperature: zone	1 = axillary 2 = rectal	PED-3
581	Visual acuity: without glasses, left eye	1 = 20/20 2 = 20/30 3 = 20/40 4 = 20/50 5 = 20/70 6 = 20/100 7 = 20/200	PED-75
582	Blind	dich	PED-75
583	Visual acuity: without glasses, right eye	1 = 20/20 2 = 20/30 3 = 20/40 4 = 20-50 5 = 20/70 6 = 20/100 7 = 20/200	PED-75
	Muscle balance, without glasses:		
584	yes, on table	dich	PED-75
585	off table but no picture	dich	PED-75
586	not seen or off table	dich	PED-75
587	Visual acuity: with glasses, left eye	1 = 20/30 2 = 20/30 3 = 20/40 4 = 20/50 5 = 20/70 6 = 20/100 7 = 20/200	PED-75

524

Sequence number	Variable name	Codes	Source
588	Visual acuity: with glasses, right eye	1 = 20/20	PED-75
		2 = 20/30	
		3 = 20/40	
		4 = 20/50	
		5 = 20/70	
		6 = 20/100	
		7 = 20/200	
	Muscle balance, with glasses:		
589	yes, on table	dich	PED-75
590	off table but no picture	dich	PED-75
591	not seen or off table	dich	PED-75
592	Age at 7YR psychological examination (years and months)	as given	PS-30
593	Bender Gestalt test: total score	0–30 = as given	PS-30
594	Ears: size, shape, position	0 = normal	PED-76
		8 = other	
595	Ears: otoscopic examination	0 = normal	PED-76
		8 = other	
596	WISC verbal: information scaled score	0–20 = as given	PS-31
597	WISC verbal: comprehension scaled score	0–20 = as given	PS-31
598	WISC verbal: vocabulary scaled score	0–20 = as given	PS-31
599	WISC verbal: digit span scaled score	0–20 = as given	PS-31
600	WISC performance: picture arrangement scaled score	0–20 = as given	PS-31
601	WISC performance: block design scaled score	0–20 = as given	PS-31
602	WISC performance: coding scaled score	0–20 = as given	PS-31
603	WISC prorated: verbal IQ	45–155 = as given	PS-31
604	WISC prorated: performance IQ	44–156 = as given	PS-31
605	WISC prorated: full scale IQ	25–154 = as given	PS-31
606	WISC prorated: full scale IQ below norms	dich	PS-31
607	WISC prorated: adequacy of examination	1 = adequate	PS-31
		2 = not adequate	
608	Auditory Vocal Association Test: raw score	0–26 = as given	PS-32
609	Auditory Vocal Association Test: adequacy of examination	1 = adequate	PS-32
		2 = not adequate	
610	Goodenough-Harris Draw-a-Person Test: raw score	1–73 = as given	PS-33
611	Tactile Finger Recognition Test: total	0–10 = as given	PS-34
612	WRAT: months of schooling	1–59 = as given	PS-35
613	WRAT: child in a nongraded, special class	dich	PS-35
614	WRAT: child does not attend school	dich	PS-35
615	WRAT: child repeating a grade	dich	PS-35
616	WRAT: child never attended school	dich	PS-35
617	WRAT: child in special speech class	dich	PS-35
618	WRAT: spelling raw score	0–55 = as given	PS-35
619	WRAT: reading raw score	0–84 = as given	PS-35
620	WRAT: arithmetic raw score	0–49 = as given	PS-35
621	WRAT: adequacy of examination	1 = adequate	PS-35
		2 = inadequate	
	7YR psychological examination, behavior profile: separation from mother:		
622	no concern, eager to leave	dich	PS-36
623	very little concern	dich	PS-36
624	appropriate initial reticence	dich	PS-36
625	more than usual amount of concern	dich	PS-36
626	very upset, cries, clings to mother	dich	PS-36
627	variable	dich	PS-36
	fearfulness:		
628	none	dich	PS-36

525

Sequence number	Variable name	Codes	Source
629	very little fear	dich	PS-36
630	normal amount of caution	dich	PS-36
631	inhibited and uneasy	dich	PS-36
632	very fearful and apprehensive	dich	PS-36
633	variable	dich	PS-36
	rapport with examiner:		
634	exceptionally shy, withdrawn	dich	PS-36
635	shy	dich	PS-36
636	initial shyness, at ease	dich	PS-36
637	very friendly	dich	PS-36
638	extreme friendliness	dich	PS-36
639	variable	dich	PS-36
	self confidence:		
640	lacking, extremely self-critical	dich	PS-36
641	distrusts own ability	dich	PS-36
642	adequate	dich	PS-36
643	more amount than usual	dich	PS-36
644	very self-confident	dich	PS-36
645	variable	dich	PS-36
	emotional reactivity:		
646	extremely flat	dich	PS-36
647	somewhat flat	dich	PS-36
648	normal	dich	PS-36
649	mood more variable than average	dich	PS-36
650	extreme instability	dich	PS-36
651	variable	dich	PS-36
	degree of cooperation:		
652	extreme negativism	dich	PS-36
653	resistive	dich	PS-36
654	cooperative	dich	PS-36
655	accepts direction more easily	dich	PS-36
656	extremely suggestible	dich	PS-36
657	variable	dich	PS-36
	level of frustration tolerance:		
658	withdraws completely	dich	PS-36
659	occasionally withdraws	dich	PS-36
660	attempts to cope with situation	dich	PS-36
661	becomes quite upset	dich	PS-36
662	extreme acting out behavior	dich	PS-36
663	variable	dich	PS-36
	degree of dependency:		
664	very self-reliant	dich	PS-36
665	rarely needs reassurance	dich	PS-36
666	appropriate dependency	dich	PS-36
667	demands more attention than average	dich	PS-36
668	constant need for attention	dich	PS-36
669	variable	dich	PS-36
	duration of attention span:		
670	very brief	dich	PS-36
671	short	dich	PS-36
672	adequate	dich	PS-36
673	more than average	dich	PS-36
674	highly perseverative	dich	PS-36
675	variable	dich	PS-36
	goal orientation:		
676	no effort to reach goal	dich	PS-36

Sequence number	Variable name	Codes	Source
677	brief attempt	dich	PS-36
678	able to keep goal in mind	dich	PS-36
679	keeps goal and questions in mind	dich	PS-36
680	compulsive absorption	dich	PS-36
681	variable	dich	PS-36
	level of activity:		
682	extreme inactivity	dich	PS-36
683	little activity	dich	PS-36
684	normal amount of activity	dich	PS-36
685	unusual amount of activity	dich	PS-36
686	extreme overactivity	dich	PS-36
687	variable	dich	PS-36
	nature of activity:		
688	extreme inactivity, passivity	dich	PS-36
689	little activity	dich	PS-36
690	normal amount	dich	PS-36
691	unusual amount	dich	PS-36
692	extreme overactivity	dich	PS-36
693	variable	dich	PS-36
	nature of communication:		
694	little or none	dich	PS-36
695	confined to answering directed questions	dich	PS-36
696	readily answers questions	dich	PS-36
697	answers freely	dich	PS-36
698	difficult to follow child's thinking	dich	PS-36
699	variable	dich	PS-36
	assertiveness:		
700	extremely assertive, willful	dich	PS-36
701	quite forceful	dich	PS-36
702	self-assertive but accepts situation	dich	PS-36
703	passive acceptance	dich	PS-36
704	extreme passivity	dich	PS-36
705	variable	dich	PS-36
	hostility:		
706	very hostile	dich	PS-36
707	unusual amount of hostility	dich	PS-36
708	no unusual amount	dich	PS-36
709	very agreeable	dich	PS-36
710	ingratiating	dich	PS-36
711	variable	dich	PS-36
	Deviant or stereotyped behavior (7YR):		
712	excessive, persistent thumb sucking	0 = absent 1 = present	PS-37
713	excessive, persistent nail biting	0 = absent 1 = present	PS-37
714	unusual, meaningless hand motioning	0 = absent 1 = present	PS-37
715	meaningless smiling and laughing	0 = absent 1 = present	PS-37
716	crying	0 = absent 1 = present	PS-37
717	echolalia	0 = absent 1 = present	PS-37
718	other obvious speech difficulties	0 = absent 1 = present	PS-37
719	Handedness (7YR)	1 = right 2 = left	PS-37

Sequence number	Variable name	Codes	Source
720	Nonneurological abnormalities (7YR)	0 = none 1 = minor 3 = definite	PED-76
	With whom child lives at age 7:		
721	mother and father, stepmother and father, mother and stepfather	dich	FHH-9
722	mother only	dich	FHH-9
723	father only	dich	FHH-9
724	other relatives	dich	FHH-9
725	foster home	dich	FHH-9
726	adoptive parents	dich	FHH-9
727	other residence	dich	FHH-9
728	institutionalized due to mental retardation	dich	FHH-9
729	institutionalized due to cerebral palsy	dich	FHH-9
730	institutionalized due to behavioral problem	dich	FHH-9
731	institutionalized due to seizures	dich	FHH-9
732	institutionalized due to congenital malformation	dich	FHH-9
733	institutionalized due to a combination of factors	dich	FHH-9
734	Foster parent, adoptive parent, guardian: age (years)	20 = under 21 21–65 = as given 66 = 66 and over	FHH-9
	Foster parent, adoptive parent, guardian: race		
735	White	dich	FHH-9
736	Negro	dich	FHH-9
737	Oriental	dich	FHH-9
738	Puerto Rican	dich	FHH-9
739	Foster parent, adoptive parent, guardian: years of regular school completed	0–12 = as given 13–16 = 1–4 years college completed 17 = some graduate or professional school 18 = degree (graduate or professional school)	FHH-9
	Marital status of foster parent, adoptive parent, guardian:		
740	single	dich	FHH-9
741	married, common-law	dich	FHH-9
742	widowed, divorced, separated	dich	FHH-9
743	Number of rooms in household of foster parent, adoptive parent, guardian	1–19 = as given 20 = 20 or more	FHH-9
744	Number of persons living in household of foster parent, adoptive parent, guardian	2–19 = as given 20 = 20 or more	FHH-9
745	Number of children under 8 years living in household of foster parent, adoptive parent, guardian	0–19 = as given 20 = 20 or more	FHH-9
	Occupation of foster mother, adoptive mother, guardian:		
746	not working or never worked	dich	FHH-9
747	retired on pension and/or widow's pension	dich	FHH-9
748	no occupation reported except welfare	dich	FHH-9
749	professional and technical	dich	FHH-9
750	college, professional, or graduate school student	dich	FHH-9
751	proprietors, managers, officials, officers of the Armed Forces, farm owners	dich	FHH-9
752	clerical and kindred workers	dich	FHH-9

Sequence number	Variable name	Codes	Source
753	sales workers	dich	FHH-9
754	craftsmen, foremen, and kindred workers	dich	FHH-9
755	operators and kindred workers	dich	FHH-9
756	private household workers	dich	FHH-9
757	service workers (other than private household)	dich	FHH-9
758	laborers, farmers	dich	FHH-9
759	students (but not college, professional, or graduate school)	dich	FHH-9
	Occupation of husband of foster mother, adoptive mother, guardian:		
760	not working or never worked	dich	FHH-9
761	retired on pension or husband deceased	dich	FHH-9
762	no occupation reported except welfare	dich	FHH-9
763	professional and technical	dich	FHH-9
764	college, professional, or graduate school student	dich	FHH-9
765	proprietors, managers, officials, officers of the Armed Forces, farm owners	dich	FHH-9
766	clerical and kindred workers	dich	FHH-9
767	sales workers	dich	FHH-9
768	craftsmen, foremen, and kindred workers	dich	FHH-9
769	operators and kindred workers	dich	FHH-9
770	private household workers	dich	FHH-9
771	service workers (other than private household)	dich	FHH-9
772	laborers, farmers	dich	FHH-9
773	students (but not college, professional, or graduate school)	dich	FHH-9
774	Foster parent, adoptive parent, guardian: total family income for last year	0 = none 5 = under $1000 15 = $1000–$1999 25 = $2000–$2999 35 = $3000–$3999 45 = $4000–$4999 55 = $5000–$5999 65 = $6000–$6999 75 = $7000–$7999 85 = $8000–$8999 95 = $9000–$9999 96 = $10,000 or more	FHH-9
	Mother's marital status when child age 7:		
775	single	dich	FHH-9
776	married, common-law	dich	FHH-9
777	widowed, divorced, separated	dich	FHH-9
778	Number of moves in last 7 years	0–40 = as given	FHH-9
779	Mother in dormitory or institution when child age 7	dich	FHH-9
780	Overcrowding when child age 7	1–75 = 0.1 to 7.5 person per room 80 = 8.0 or more persons per room	FHH-9
781	Presence of husband who is father of child in household when child age 7	dich	FHH-9
782	Presence of father of child who is not husband in household when child age 7	dich	FHH-9
783	Presence of husband who is not father of child in household when child age 7	dich	FHH-9
784	Presence of no husband or father of child in household when child age 7	dich	FHH-9
785	Mother to school since child born	dich	FHH-9

529

Sequence number	Variable name	Codes	Source
786	Age of child when mother employed (years)	1 = less than 1 2 = 1 but less than 2 3 = 2 but less than 3 4 = 3 but less than 4 5 = 4 but less than 5 6 = 5 but less than 6 7 = 6 and over	FHH-9
787	Total months mother employed	0–97 = as given 98 = 98 or more	FHH-9
	Occupation of mother when child age 7:		
788	none	dich	FHH-9
789	retired on pension and/or widow's pension	dich	FHH-9
790	no occupation reported except welfare	dich	FHH-9
791	professional and technical	dich	FHH-9
792	college, professional, or graduate school student	dich	FHH-9
793	proprietors, managers, officials, officers of the Armed Forces, farm owners	dich	FHH-9
794	clerical and kindred workers	dich	FHH-9
795	sales workers	dich	FHH-9
796	craftsmen, foremen, and kindred workers	dich	FHH-9
797	operators and kindred workers	dich	FHH-9
798	private household workers	dich	FHH-9
799	service workers (other than private household)	dich	FHH-9
800	laborers, farmers	dich	FHH-9
801	students (but not college, professional, or graduate school)	dich	FHH-9
	Occupation of father (current or last job) when child age 7:		
802	none	dich	FHH-9
803	retired on pension	dich	FHH-9
804	no occupation reported except welfare	dich	FHH-9
805	professional and technical	dich	FHH-9
806	college, professional or graduate school student who is fellow, research or teaching assistant	dich	FHH-9
807	college, professional or graduate school student with full or part-time nonacademic job	dich	FHH-9
808	college, professional or graduate school student on co-op program	dich	FHH-9
809	proprietors, managers, officials, officers of the Armed Forces, farm owners	dich	FHH-9
810	clerical and kindred workers	dich	FHH-9
811	sales workers	dich	FHH-9
812	craftsmen, foremen, and kindred workers	dich	FHH-9
813	operators and kindred workers	dich	FHH-9
814	private household workers	dich	FHH-9
815	service workers (other than private household)	dich	FHH-9
816	laborers, farmers	dich	FHH-9
817	students (but not college, professional, or graduate school)	dich	FHH-9
818	Total income: prior 3 months when child age 7	0 = none 5 = under $250 15 = $250–$499 25 = $500–$749 35 = $750–$999 45 = $1000–$1249	FHH-9

Sequence number	Variable name	Codes	Source
		55 = $1250–$1499	
		65 = $1500–$1749	
		75 = $1750–$1999	
		85 = $2000–$2249	
		95 = $2250–$2499	
		96 = $2500 or more	
819	Number of persons cared for when child age 7	1–19 = as given 20 = 20 and over	FHH-9
	Total number of children in family:		
820	fetal death under 20 weeks	0–7 = as given 8 = 8 or more	FHH-9
821	fetal death 20 weeks and over	0–7 = as given 8 = 8 or more	FHH-9
822	liveborn male	0–7 = as given 8 = 8 or more	FHH-9
823	liveborn female	0–7 = as given 8 = 8 or more	FHH-9
824	prematures	0–7 = as given 8 = 8 or more	FHH-9
825	dead 27 days or younger	0–7 = as given 8 = 8 or more	FHH-9
826	dead 28 days or older	0–7 = as given 8 = 8 or more	FHH-9
827	condition: Rh	0–7 = as given 8 = 8 or more	FHH-9
828	condition: congenital malformation	0–7 = as given 8 = 8 or more	FHH-9
829	condition: convulsions	0–7 = as given 8 = 8 or more	FHH-9
830	condition: motor deficit	0–7 = as given 8 = 8 or more	FHH-9
831	condition: sensory defect	0–7 = as given 8 = 8 or more	FHH-9
832	condition: retardation	0–7 = as given 8 = 8 or more	FHH-9
	Rh trouble present in siblings since birth of study child:		
833	incompatibility: fetal death	dich	FHH-9
834	incompatibility: liveborn, no transfusion	dich	FHH-9
835	incompatibility: liveborn, exchange transfusion	dich	FHH-9
836	severe jaundice and transfusion: no incompatibility	dich	FHH-9
	Malformations present in siblings since birth of study child:		
837	cleft lip or palate	dich	FHH-9
838	club foot	dich	FHH-9
839	fingers or toes	dich	FHH-9
840	heart	dich	FHH-9
841	head or spine	dich	FHH-9
842	Number of child deaths since birth of study child	0–7 = as given 8 = 8 or more	FHH-9
	Retardation and disturbances present in siblings since birth of study child:		
843	physical retardation	dich	FHH-9
844	mental retardation	dich	FHH-9
845	severe behavioral problem	dich	FHH-9
	Seizures, convulsions, epilepsy:		
846	mother of child	dich	FHH-9
847	father of child	dich	FHH-9

Sequence number	Variable name	Codes	Source
848	study child	dich	FHH-9
849	children subsequent to study child	dich	FHH-9
850	children prior to study child	dich	FHH-9
851	other relatives	dich	FHH-9
852	combination of relatives	dich	FHH-9
	Motor defect, injury:		
853	mother of child	dich	FHH-9
854	father of child	dich	FHH-9
855	study child	dich	FHH-9
856	children subsequent to study child	dich	FHH-9
857	children prior to study child	dich	FHH-9
858	other relatives	dich	FHH-9
859	combination of relatives	dich	FHH-9
	Motor defect, infectious diseases:		
860	mother of child	dich	FHH-9
861	father of child	dich	FHH-9
862	study child	dich	FHH-9
863	children subsequent to study child	dich	FHH-9
864	children prior to study child	dich	FHH-9
865	other relatives	dich	FHH-9
866	combination of relatives	dich	FHH-9
	Sensory defects, blindness:		
867	mother of child	dich	FHH-9
868	father of child	dich	FHH-9
869	study child	dich	FHH-9
870	children subsequent to study child	dich	FHH-9
871	children prior to study child	dich	FHH-9
872	other relatives	dich	FHH-9
873	combination of relatives	dich	FHH-9
	Sensory defects, deafness:		
874	mother of child	dich	FHH-9
875	father of child	dich	FHH-9
876	study child	dich	FHH-9
877	children subsequent to study child	dich	FHH-9
878	children prior to study child	dich	FHH-9
879	other relatives	dich	FHH-9
880	combination of relatives	dich	FHH-9
	Sensory defects, trouble speaking:		
881	mother of child	dich	FHH-9
882	father of child	dich	FHH-9
883	study child	dich	FHH-9
884	children subsequent to study child	dich	FHH-9
885	children prior to study child	dich	FHH-9
886	other relatives	dich	FHH-9
887	combination of relatives	dich	FHH-9
	Sugar diabetes:		
888	mother of child	dich	FHH-9
889	father of child	dich	FHH-9
890	study child	dich	FHH-9
891	children subsequent to study child	dich	FHH-9
892	children prior to study child	dich	FHH-9
893	other relatives	dich	FHH-9
894	combination of relatives	dich	FHH-9
	Nervous problem requiring hospitalization, psychiatric treatment, or other therapy:		
895	mother of child	dich	FHH-9
896	father of child	dich	FHH-9

532

Sequence number	Variable name	Codes	Source
897	study child	dich	FHH-9
898	children subsequent to study child	dich	FHH-9
899	children prior to study child	dich	FHH-9
900	other relatives	dich	FHH-9
901	combination of relatives	dich	FHH-9

Descriptive Statistics and Frequency Distributions by Race, Sex, SEI, and Total for SLH Variables

Descriptive Statistics and Frequency Distributions of 3YR and 8YR SLH Variables by Sex, Race, grouped SEI, and Total Sample Size.

Code	Male Freq.	Male %	Female Freq.	Female %	White Freq.	White %	Black Freq.	Black %	0.0-1.9 Freq.	0.0-1.9 %	2.0-3.9 Freq.	2.0-3.9 %	4.0-5.9 Freq.	4.0-5.9 %	6.0-7.9 Freq.	6.0-7.9 %	8.0-9.5 Freq.	8.0-9.5 %	Totals Freq.	Totals %
3YR SLH Variables (from PS-10 to 17)																				
Language Reception: Verbal Comprehension																				
Identification of Familiar Objects																				
Fail	735	8	582	6	297	4	1,020	9	182	10	586	9	376	7	138	4	35	2	1,317	7
Pass	8,969	92	8,911	94	8,044	96	9,836	91	1,698	90	5,930	91	5,186	93	3,105	96	1,961	98	17,880	93
NIDF	355		333		242		446		81		309		200		75		23		688	
Understanding Action Words																				
Fail	1,139	12	887	9	643	8	1,383	13	280	15	843	13	613	11	218	7	72	4	2,026	11
Pass	8,468	88	8,497	91	7,601	92	9,364	87	1,573	85	5,613	87	4,869	89	2,998	93	1,912	96	16,965	89
NIDF	452		442		339		555		108		369		280		102		35		894	
Understanding Space Relationships																				
Fail	2,247	23	1,852	20	957	12	3,142	29	588	32	1,728	27	1,210	22	469	15	104	5	4,099	22
Pass	7,368	77	7,540	80	7,314	88	7,594	71	1,271	68	4,722	73	4,284	78	2,748	85	1,883	95	14,908	78
NIDF	444		434		312		566		102		375		268		101		32		878	
Language Expression: Verbal Expression																				
Naming Objects																				
Fail	1,723	18	1,164	12	1,161	14	1,726	16	336	18	1,111	17	873	16	415	13	152	8	2,887	15
Pass	7,835	82	8,225	88	7,131	86	8,929	84	1,491	82	5,317	83	4,609	84	2,810	87	1,833	92	16,060	85
NIDF	501		437		291		647		134		397		280		93		34		938	
Sentence Length																				
Fail	1,585	17	1,087	12	1,061	13	1,611	16	313	18	1,071	17	832	16	339	11	117	6	2,672	14
Pass	7,675	83	8,098	88	7,073	87	8,700	84	1,457	82	5,116	83	4,496	84	2,840	89	1,864	94	15,773	86
NIDF	799		641		449		991		191		638		434		139		38		1,440	
Sentence Structure																				
Fail	1,040	11	577	6	827	10	790	8	163	9	604	10	513	10	263	8	74	4	1,617	9
Pass	8,198	89	8,599	94	7,287	90	9,510	92	1,603	91	5,570	90	4,807	90	2,913	92	1,904	96	16,797	91
NIDF	821		650		469		1,002		195		651		442		142		41		1,471	
Relevance																				
Fail	652	7	422	5	417	5	657	6	138	8	431	7	317	6	152	5	36	2	1,074	6
Pass	8,592	93	8,758	95	7,702	95	9,648	94	1,628	92	5,746	93	5,006	94	3,026	95	1,944	98	17,350	94
NIDF	815		646		464		997		195		648		439		140		39		1,461	
Word Order																				
Fail	572	6	292	3	426	5	438	4	101	6	326	5	260	5	134	4	43	2	864	5
Pass	8,668	94	8,885	97	7,694	95	9,859	96	1,663	94	5,849	95	5,061	95	3,044	96	1,936	98	17,553	95
NIDF	819		649		463		1,005		197		650		441		140		40		1,468	

Descriptive Statistics and Frequency Distributions of 3YR and 8YR SLH Variables by Sex, Race, grouped SEI, and Total Sample Size.

Code	Male Freq.	%	Female Freq.	%	White Freq.	%	Black Freq.	%	0.0-1.9 Freq.	%	2.0-3.9 Freq.	%	4.0-5.9 Freq.	%	6.0-7.9 Freq.	%	8.0-9.5 Freq.	%	Totals Freq.	%
3YR SLH Variables (from PS-10 to 17) (continued)																				
Language Expression: Verbal Expression (continued)																				
Use of Pronouns																				
Fail	1,162	13	735	8	931	11	966	9	198	11	733	12	596	11	266	8	104	5	1,897	10
Pass	8,063	87	8,433	92	7,180	89	9,316	91	1,566	89	5,431	88	4,718	89	2,908	92	1,873	95	16,496	90
NIDF	834		658		472		1,020		197		661		448		144		42		1,492	
Summary Item Score																				
Fail	1,451	15	848	9	1,043	13	1,256	12	260	14	941	15	713	13	295	9	90	5	2,299	12
Pass	8,110	85	8,544	91	7,277	87	9,377	88	1,572	86	5,476	85	4,774	87	2,931	91	1,901	95	16,654	88
NIDF	498		434		263		669		129		408		275		92		28		932	
Auditory Memory: Recall																				
2 Digits																				
Fail	574	7	533	6	509	7	598	6	111	7	452	8	346	7	152	5	46	2	1,107	7
Pass	7,841	93	8,049	94	6,696	93	9,194	94	1,529	93	5,231	92	4,500	93	2,783	95	1,847	98	15,890	93
NIDF	1,644		1,244		1,378		1,510		321		1,142		916		383		126		2,888	
3 Digits																				
Fail	2,250	27	2,125	25	2,035	29	2,340	24	425	26	1,626	29	1,359	29	682	24	283	15	4,375	26
Pass	5,979	73	6,293	75	4,937	71	7,335	76	1,194	74	3,952	71	3,378	71	2,181	76	1,567	85	12,272	74
NIDF	1,830		1,408		1,611		1,627		342		1,247		1,025		455		169		3,238	
2 Syllables																				
Fail	397	5	368	4	353	5	412	4	82	5	327	6	232	5	94	3	30	2	765	5
Pass	7,874	95	8,071	96	6,672	95	9,273	96	1,539	95	5,272	94	4,526	95	2,786	97	1,822	98	15,945	95
NIDF	1,788		1,387		1,558		1,617		340		1,226		1,004		438		167		3,175	
3 Syllables																				
Fail	1,869	23	1,698	20	1,798	26	1,769	18	346	22	1,313	24	1,099	24	538	19	271	15	3,567	22
Pass	6,224	77	6,600	80	5,000	74	7,824	82	1,261	78	4,181	76	3,568	76	2,279	81	1,535	85	12,824	78
NIDF	1,966		1,528		1,785		1,709		354		1,331		1,095		501		213		3,494	
Hearing																				
Spondaic Word Test: Summary Total Score																				
Fail	763	9	578	7	612	8	729	7	178	11	536	9	368	7	175	6	84	4	1,341	8
Pass	7,941	91	8,189	93	7,037	92	9,093	93	1,487	89	5,289	91	4,695	93	2,835	94	1,824	96	16,130	92
NIDF	1,355		1,059		934		1,480		296		1,000		699		308		111		2,414	

Descriptive Statistics and Frequency Distributions of 3YR and 8YR SLH Variables by Sex, Race, grouped SEI, and Total Sample Size.

Code	Male Freq.	%	Female Freq.	%	White Freq.	%	Black Freq.	%	0.0-1.9 Freq.	%	2.0-3.9 Freq.	%	4.0-5.9 Freq.	%	6.0-7.9 Freq.	%	8.0-9.5 Freq.	%	Totals Freq.	%
3YR SLH Variables (from PS-10 to 17) (continued)																				
Hearing (continued)																				
Pure-Tone Screen: Summary Score, Right Ear																				
Fail	357	4	310	4	320	4	347	4	71	4	236	4	193	4	102	4	65	4	667	4
Pass	8,244	96	8,169	96	6,964	96	9,449	96	1,595	96	5,536	96	4,730	96	2,801	96	1,751	96	16,413	96
NIDF	1,458		1,347		1,299		1,506		295		1,053		839		415		203		2,805	
Pure-Tone Screen: Summary Score, Left Ear																				
Fail	386	4	342	4	344	5	384	4	71	4	257	4	209	4	111	4	80	4	728	4
Pass	8,202	96	8,109	96	6,921	95	9,390	96	1,589	96	5,501	96	4,702	96	2,793	96	1,726	96	16,311	96
NIDF	1,471		1,375		1,318		1,528		301		1,067		851		414		213		2,846	
Speech Mechanism																				
Lips: Retraction																				
Pass	8,422	95	8,539	96	7,418	97	9,543	95	1,621	95	5,627	95	4,908	96	2,954	97	1,851	98	16,961	96
Pass with grimace	105	1	90	1	82	1	113	1	29	2	71	1	54	1	25	1	16	1	195	1
Pass with tremor	1	0	1	0	0	0	2	0	2	0	0	0	0	1	0	0	0	0	2	0
Pulls to left	47	1	47	1	34	0	60	1	9	1	39	1	29	1	11	0	6	0	94	1
Pulls to right	50	1	58	1	30	0	78	1	19	1	42	1	30	1	14	0	3	0	108	1
Unsuccessful	210	2	152	2	107	1	255	3	28	2	161	3	113	2	38	1	22	1	362	2
NIDF	1,224		939		912		1,251		254		885		628		275		121		2,163	
Lips: Protrusion																				
Pass	8,244	94	8,404	95	7,173	94	9,475	94	1,601	94	5,589	94	4,789	94	2,879	95	1,790	95	16,648	94
Pass with grimace	40	1	45	1	46	1	39	0	9	1	29	0	34	1	9	0	4	0	85	0
Pass with tremor	3	0	3	0	2	0	4	0	4	0	3	0	2	0	0	0	0	0	6	0
Deviates to left	12	0	11	0	8	0	15	0	1	0	8	0	11	0	0	0	0	0	23	0
Deviates to right	10	0	16	0	6	0	20	0	2	0	10	0	10	0	2	0	3	0	26	0
Unsuccessful	492	6	372	4	380	5	434	5	89	5	295	5	267	5	127	4	86	5	864	5
NIDF	1,258		975		968		1,265		258		891		649		301		134		2,233	
Tongue: Mid-Line Protrusion																				
Pass	8,596	97	8,694	98	7,494	98	9,796	97	1,666	98	5,775	97	5,007	97	2,974	98	1,868	98	17,290	97
Pass with head movement	14	0	14	0	14	0	14	0	1	0	11	0	10	0	4	0	2	0	28	0
Pass with tremor	54	1	48	1	54	1	48	0	9	1	34	1	37	1	13	0	9	0	102	1
Deviates to left	42	0	37	0	25	0	54	1	9	1	33	1	23	0	9	0	5	0	79	0
Deviates to right	54	1	35	0	24	0	65	1	9	1	43	1	22	0	14	0	1	0	89	1
Unsuccessful	95	1	57	1	47	1	105	1	14	1	67	1	45	1	13	1	13	1	152	1
NIDF	1,204		941		925		1,220		253		862		618		291		121		2,145	

Descriptive Statistics and Frequency Distributions of 3YR and 8YR SLH Variables by Sex, Race, grouped SEI, and Total Sample Size.

Code	Male Freq.	Male %	Female Freq.	Female %	White Freq.	White %	Black Freq.	Black %	0.0-1.9 Freq.	0.0-1.9 %	2.0-3.9 Freq.	2.0-3.9 %	4.0-5.9 Freq.	4.0-5.9 %	6.0-7.9 Freq.	6.0-7.9 %	8.0-9.5 Freq.	8.0-9.5 %	Totals Freq.	Totals %
3YR SLH Variables (from PS-10 to 17) (continued)																				
Speech Mechanism (continued)																				
Tongue: Lateral Protrusion																				
Pass	6,144	73	6,836	79	6,233	84	6,747	70	1,133	69	4,170	73	3,717	75	2,425	83	1,535	83	12,980	76
Pass with grimace	20	0	15	0	15	0	20	0	2	0	17	0	10	0	1	0	5	0	35	0
Pass with tremor	34	0	42	0	31	0	45	0	6	0	38	1	21	0	8	0	3	0	76	0
Head moves to same side	304	4	200	2	188	3	316	3	52	3	200	4	139	3	67	2	46	2	504	3
Inaudible moves with tongue	380	5	456	5	266	4	570	6	109	7	294	5	262	5	118	4	53	3	836	5
Unsuccessful	1,547	18	1,066	12	696	9	1,917	20	332	20	981	17	776	16	313	11	211	11	2,613	15
NIDF	1,630		1,211		1,154		1,687		327		1,125		837		386		166		2,841	
Tongue: Elevation																				
Pass	4,704	57	5,492	66	4,813	67	5,383	57	948	59	3,441	62	2,964	62	1,830	65	1,013	56	10,196	61
Pass with head movement	53	1	41	0	54	1	40	0	11	1	27	0	22	0	17	1	17	1	94	1
Pass with tremor	6	0	8	0	5	0	9	0	2	0	7	0	2	0	1	0	2	0	14	0
Unsuccessful	3,470	42	2,834	34	2,337	32	3,967	42	647	40	2,095	38	1,801	38	979	35	782	43	6,304	38
NIDF	1,826		1,451		1,374		1,903		353		1,255		973		491		205		3,277	
Soft Palate: Elevation																				
Pass	7,867	96	7,953	96	6,518	95	9,302	97	1,530	97	5,349	96	4,571	96	2,675	96	1,695	97	15,820	96
Limited mobility	250	3	292	4	311	5	231	2	43	3	186	3	160	3	101	4	52	3	542	3
Asymmetrical elevation	48	1	36	0	58	1	26	0	9	1	24	0	27	1	16	1	8	0	84	1
Cleft, repaired or unrepaired	6	0	5	0	6	0	5	0	2	0	5	0	3	0	0	0	1	0	11	0
Limited mobility and cleft	1	0	0	0	1	0	0	0	0	0	0	0	0	0	1	0	0	0	11	0
Asymmetrical elevation and cleft	1	0	0	0	0	0	1	0	0	0	0	0	0	0	0	0	0	0	1	0
Limited mobility and asymmetrical elevation			0	0	1	0	0	0	0	0	1	0	2	0	0	0	0	0	5	0
NIDF	1,883		1,538		1,688		1,733		376		1,258		999		525		263		3,421	
Diadochokinesis: Lips																				
Pass	7,800	94	8,104	96	6,643	94	9,261	96	1,542	96	5,306	95	4,564	95	2,736	95	1,756	97	15,904	95
Unsustained	458	6	326	4	427	6	357	4	69	4	289	5	242	5	129	5	55	3	784	5
NIDF	1,801		1,396		1,513		1,684		350		1,230		956		453		208		3,197	
Diadochokinesis: Tongue																				
Pass	7,688	94	8,016	96	6,529	94	9,175	96	1,515	95	5,248	95	4,509	95	2,694	95	1,738	97	15,704	95
Unsustained	459	6	328	4	430	6	357	4	72	5	287	5	229	5	142	5	57	3	787	5
NIDF	1,912		1,482		1,624		1,770		374		1,290		1,024		482		224		3,394	
Speech Production																				
Voice: Pitch																				
Adequate	9,326	98	9,203	98	8,117	98	10,412	98	1,794	98	6,235	98	5,354	98	3,171	98	1,975	99	18,529	98
Unusual fluctuations	29	0	19	0	27	0	21	0	6	0	20	0	16	0	4	0	2	0	48	0
Too high	70	1	70	1	80	1	60	1	15	1	55	1	34	1	25	1	11	1	140	1

Descriptive Statistics and Frequency Distributions of 3YR and 8YR SLH Variables by Sex, Race, grouped SEI, and Total Sample Size.

Code	Male Freq.	Male %	Female Freq.	Female %	White Freq.	White %	Black Freq.	Black %	0.0-1.9 Freq.	0.0-1.9 %	2.0-3.9 Freq.	2.0-3.9 %	4.0-5.9 Freq.	4.0-5.9 %	6.0-7.9 Freq.	6.0-7.9 %	8.0-9.5 Freq.	8.0-9.5 %	Totals Freq.	Totals %
3YR SLH Variables (from PS-10 to 17) (continued)																				
Speech Production (continued)																				
Voice: Pitch (continued)																				
Too Low	57	1	58	1	43	1	72	1	13	1	48	1	33	1	13	0	8	0	115	1
Monotone	21	0	19	0	15	0	25	0	4	0	13	0	9	0	10	0	4	0	40	0
Combination of codes	10	0	4	0	7	0	7	0	1	0	5	0	4	0	2	0	2	0	14	0
NIDF	546		453		294		705		128		449		312		93		17		999	
Voice: Loudness																				
Adequate	9,142	96	9,019	96	8,013	97	10,148	96	1,747	95	6,084	95	5,238	96	3,141	97	1,951	97	18,161	96
Too soft	351	4	339	4	258	3	432	4	80	4	287	4	200	4	76	2	47	2	690	4
Too loud	20	0	15	0	19	0	16	0	3	0	9	0	10	0	10	0	3	0	35	0
Unusual fluctuations	12	0	5	0	6	0	11	0	2	0	6	0	6	0	2	0	0	0	17	0
Unusual fluctuations and too loud	1	0	0	0	0	0	1	0	1	0	0	0	0	0	0	0	0	0	1	0
NIDF	533		448		287		694		128		439		308		89		17		981	
Voice: Quality																				
Adequate	8,376	88	8,544	91	7,684	93	9,236	87	1,558	85	5,617	88	4,878	89	2,978	92	1,889	94	16,920	89
Hypernasal	113	1	86	1	108	1	91	1	18	1	63	1	66	1	41	1	11	1	199	1
Hyponasal	137	1	114	1	133	2	118	1	17	1	74	1	85	2	49	2	26	1	251	1
Hoarseness	782	8	566	6	282	3	1,066	10	222	12	561	9	376	7	131	4	58	3	1,348	7
Hyponasal and hoarseness	27	0	19	0	20	0	26	0	5	0	16	0	10	0	10	0	5	0	46	0
Hypernasal and hoarseness	9	0	9	0	9	0	9	0	3	0	5	0	8	0	2	0	0	0	18	0
NIDF	615		488		347		756		138		489		339		107		30		1,103	
Articulation: Initial Consonants																				
Normal	5,326	60	6,229	70	5,424	70	6,131	61	922	54	3,560	60	3,291	64	2,235	73	1,547	80	11,555	65
Suspect	2,589	29	2,135	24	1,784	23	2,940	29	546	32	1,795	30	1,407	28	653	21	323	17	4,724	27
Abnormal	922	10	556	6	524	7	954	10	236	14	587	10	418	8	167	5	70	4	1,478	8
NIDF	1,222		906		851		1,277		257		883		646		263		79		2,128	
Articulation: Final Consonants																				
Normal	5,151	58	5,747	64	6,117	79	4,781	48	753	44	3,065	52	3,040	59	2,308	76	1,732	89	10,898	61
Suspect	1,930	22	1,800	20	1,112	14	2,613	26	440	26	1,482	25	1,168	23	494	16	146	8	3,730	21
Abnormal	1,746	20	1,367	15	493	6	2,620	26	509	30	1,392	23	904	18	247	8	61	3	3,113	18
NIDF	1,232		912		861		1,283		259		886		650		269		80		2,144	
Articulation: Vowels and Diphthongs																				
Normal	7,844	89	8,197	92	6,937	90	9,104	91	1,493	88	5,328	90	4,620	90	2,804	92	1,796	93	16,041	90
Suspect	905	10	676	8	712	9	869	9	197	12	567	10	455	9	227	7	135	7	1,581	9
Abnormal	77	1	42	0	72	1	47	0	13	1	43	1	37	1	19	1	7	0	119	1
NIDF	1,233		911		862		1,282		258		887		650		268		81		2,144	

Descriptive Statistics and Frequency Distributions of 3YR and 8YR SLH Variables by Sex, Race, grouped SEI, and Total Sample Size.

Code	Male Freq.	%	Female Freq.	%	White Freq.	%	Black Freq.	%	0.0-1.9 Freq.	%	2.0-3.9 Freq.	%	4.0-5.9 Freq.	%	6.0-7.9 Freq.	%	8.0-9.5 Freq.	%	Totals Freq.	%
3YR SLH Variables (from PS-10 to 17) (continued)																				
Speech Production (continued)																				
Intelligibility of Speech																				
No difficulty	3,779	40	4,887	53	4,002	49	4,664	44	712	39	2,643	42	2,445	45	1,659	52	1,207	61	8,666	46
Some difficulty	3,346	36	3,051	33	2,618	32	3,779	36	700	39	2,293	36	1,827	34	1,017	32	560	28	6,397	34
Considerable difficulty	1,858	20	1,183	13	1,286	16	1,755	17	325	18	1,158	18	940	17	429	13	189	10	3,041	16
Verbalized but unintelligible	329	3	124	1	237	3	216	2	49	3	165	3	151	3	67	2	21	1	453	2
No Speech	89	1	53	1	75	1	67	1	23	1	52	1	45	1	16	1	6	0	142	1
NIDF	658		528		365		821		152		514		354		130		36		1,186	
Dysfluent Events																				
None	8,508	91	8,612	93	7,409	90	9,711	93	1,675	93	5,881	93	4,998	93	2,881	90	1,685	85	17,120	92
Some	789	8	626	7	720	9	695	7	105	6	391	6	352	7	287	9	280	14	1,415	8
Many	97	1	58	1	73	1	82	1	16	1	39	1	39	1	38	1	23	1	155	1
NIDF	665		530		381		814		165		514		373		112		31		1,195	
Struggle Behavior																				
None	9,308	99	9,218	99	8,115	99	10,411	99	1,780	99	6,267	99	5,345	99	3,166	99	1,968	100	18,526	99
Some	53	1	52	1	37	0	68	1	14	1	36	1	29	1	18	1	8	0	105	1
Many	10	0	3	0	5	0	8	0	2	0	3	0	4	0	4	0	0	0	13	0
NIDF	688		553		426		815		165		519		384		130		43		1,241	
Unusual Behavior Observed During Test Period																				
Echolalia	978	10	686	7	382	4	1,282	11	235	12	655	10	501	9	230	7	43	2	1,664	8
Spontaneous communication, limited or lacking	1,836	18	1,460	15	1,099	13	2,197	20	398	20	1,434	21	947	17	388	12	129	6	3,296	17

Descriptive Statistics and Frequency Distributions of 3YR and 8YR SLH Variables by Sex, Race, grouped SEI, and Total Sample Size.

8YR SLH Variables (from PS-40 to 45)

Pure-Tone Audiometry: Air Conduction

Right Ear, 500 Hz

Code	Male Freq.	Male %	Female Freq.	Female %	White Freq.	White %	Black Freq.	Black %	0.0-1.9 Freq.	%	2.0-3.9 Freq.	%	4.0-5.9 Freq.	%	6.0-7.9 Freq.	%	8.0-9.5 Freq.	%	Totals Freq.	%
0dB	1,583	16	1,559	16	1,684	17	1,458	15	247	15	1,054	18	991	16	598	15	252	11	3,142	16
5	2,370	24	2,439	25	2,464	24	2,345	24	354	22	1,260	21	1,415	23	1,090	27	690	30	4,809	24
10	3,155	31	3,099	31	3,011	30	3,243	33	494	31	1,843	31	1,861	31	1,296	32	760	33	6,254	31
15	2,402	24	2,345	24	2,313	23	2,434	25	440	27	1,479	25	1,442	24	890	22	496	22	4,747	24
20	195	2	182	2	214	2	163	2	29	2	107	2	119	2	81	2	41	2	377	2
25	166	1	126	1	195	2	97	1	16	1	101	2	84	1	64	2	27	1	292	1
30	79	0	74	1	77	1	76	1	14	1	48	0	47	1	37	1	7	0	153	1
35	39	0	50	1	46	0	43	0	9	1	29	0	33	1	11	0	7	0	89	1
40	32	0	22	0	27	0	27	0	2	0	20	0	20	0	8	0	4	0	54	0
45	18	0	13	0	22	0	9	0	3	0	8	0	7	0	7	0	6	0	31	0
50	5	0	4	0	5	0	4	0			1		4		4				9	0
55	8	0	8	0	11	0	5	0	2		5		4		3		1		16	0
60	6	0	3	0	5	0	4	0	1		1		3		1				9	0
65	3	0	1	0	2	0	2	0			3		1		1				4	0
70	3	0	4	0	6	0	0	0	2		1		1				2		7	0
75	1	0	1	0	2	0	2	0					2						2	0
80	1	0	2	0	1	0	4	0	1		3				1				3	0
85	3	0	1	0	0	0	1	0			1		0		2				4	0
90	2	0	0	0	1	0	0	0			2		1		0				2	0
95 or more	4	0	8	0	4	0	8	0	2		7		0				1	0	12	0
NIDF	59		62		58		63		15		28		39		25		14		121	
mean	9.7		9.5		9.6		9.6		9.9		9.7		9.5		9.4		9.4		9.6	
standard deviation	7.3		7.2		7.4		7.1		7.6		7.7		7.0		7.1		6.6		7.2	

Right Ear, 1,000 Hz

Code	Male Freq.	Male %	Female Freq.	Female %	White Freq.	White %	Black Freq.	Black %	0.0-1.9 Freq.	%	2.0-3.9 Freq.	%	4.0-5.9 Freq.	%	6.0-7.9 Freq.	%	8.0-9.5 Freq.	%	Totals Freq.	%
0dB	3,114	31	3,226	32	3,930	39	2,410	24	409	25	1,722	29	1,974	33	1,481	36	754	33	6,340	32
5	3,218	32	3,147	32	3,090	31	3,275	33	511	32	1,811	30	1,848	31	1,307	32	888	39	6,365	32
10	2,230	22	2,212	22	1,782	18	2,660	27	421	26	1,478	25	1,337	22	801	20	405	18	4,442	22
15	1,092	11	1,039	10	870	9	1,261	13	214	13	719	12	665	11	358	9	175	8	2,131	11
20	139	1	107	1	141	1	105	1	19	1	78	1	75	1	53	1	21	1	246	1
25	106	1	73	1	99	1	80	1	7	0	56	1	56	1	40	1	20	1	179	1
30	59	0	50	0	58	1	51	1	15	1	39	1	28	0	15	0	12	1	109	1
35	41	0	31	0	41	0	31	0	11	1	18	0	21	0	11	0	11	1	72	1
40	24	0	20	0	29	0	15	0	1	0	18	0	12	0	10	0	3	0	44	0
45	13	0	9	0	15	0	7	0	2	0	3	0	8	0	7	0	3	0	22	0
50	11	0	8	0	8	0	11	0	1	0	10	0	5	0	2	0	2	0	19	0
55	3	0	7	0	7	0	3	0	1	0	4	0	1	0	3	0	1	0	10	0
60	5	0	0	0	3	0	2	0	1	0		0		0		0		0	5	0

Descriptive Statistics and Frequency Distributions of 3YR and 8YR SLH Variables by Sex, Race, grouped SEI, and Total Sample Size.

8YR SLH Variables (from PS-40 to 45) (continued)
Pure-Tone Audiometry: Air Conduction (continued)

Code	Male Freq	Male %	Female Freq	Female %	White Freq	White %	Black Freq	Black %	0.0-1.9 Freq	0.0-1.9 %	2.0-3.9 Freq	2.0-3.9 %	4.0-5.9 Freq	4.0-5.9 %	6.0-7.9 Freq	6.0-7.9 %	8.0-9.5 Freq	8.0-9.5 %	Totals Freq	Totals %
Right Ear, 1,000 Hz (continued)																				
65dB	0	0	1	0	0	0	1	0	0	0	0	0	0	0	0	0	1	0	1	0
70	2	0	3	0	5	0	0	0	0	0	2	0	1	0	2	0	0	0	5	0
75	3	0	0	0	1	0	2	0	0	0	2	0	0	0	1	0	0	0	3	0
80	3	0	0	0	2	0	1	0	0	0	0	0	2	0	0	0	1	0	3	0
85	4	0	1	0	4	0	1	0	0	0	2	0	2	0	0	0	1	0	5	0
90	0	0	1	0	0	0	1	0	0	0	1	0	0	0	0	0	0	0	1	0
95 or more	7	0	9	0	5	0	11	0	2	0	7	0	3	0	2	0	2	0	16	0
NIDF	60		59		58		61		15		29		36		25		14		119	
mean	7.0		6.7		6.2		7.5		7.6		7.4		6.7		6.3		6.2		6.9	
standard deviation	7.3		6.9		7.2		6.9		7.3		7.5		6.7		7.0		6.8		7.1	
Right Ear, 2,000 Hz																				
0dB	3,595	36	3,624	36	4,570	45	2,649	27	426	26	1,864	31	2,215	37	1,751	43	963	42	7,219	36
5	3,061	30	3,026	30	3,010	30	3,077	31	471	29	1,772	30	1,734	29	1,281	31	829	36	6,087	30
10	1,982	20	1,980	20	1,473	15	2,489	25	415	26	1,360	23	1,234	20	637	16	316	14	3,962	20
15	1,079	11	1,043	10	743	7	1,379	14	246	15	756	13	673	11	312	8	135	6	2,122	11
20	122	1	83	1	97	1	108	1	15	1	79	1	61	1	39	1	11	0	205	1
25	83	1	56	1	63	0	76	1	15	1	43	1	44	1	26	1	11	0	139	1
30	48	0	42	0	35	0	55	1	13	1	25	0	26	0	17	0	9	0	90	0
35	28	0	28	0	31	0	25	0	4	0	19	0	14	0	12	0	7	0	56	0
40	20	0	15	0	17	0	18	0	4	0	12	0	11	0	4	0	4	0	35	0
45	11	0	13	0	10	0	14	0	2	0	12	0	5	0	3	0	2	0	24	0
50	8	0	10	0	11	0	7	0	2	0	5	0	5	0	4	0	2	0	18	0
55	5	0	3	0	5	0	3	0	0	0	1	0	4	0	2	0	1	0	8	0
60	5	0	4	0	4	0	5	0	0	0	5	0	1	0	1	0	2	0	9	0
65	6	0	0	0	4	0	2	0	1	0	3	0	1	0	1	0	0	0	6	0
70	4	0	2	0	3	0	3	0	0	0	1	0	1	0	3	0	0	0	6	0
75	2	0	0	0	1	0	1	0	0	0	0	0	1	0	1	0	0	0	2	0
80	2	0	0	0	0	0	2	0	0	0	1	0	0	0	1	0	0	0	2	0
85	4	0	4	0	7	0	1	0	0	0	3	0	2	0	1	0	2	0	8	0
90	1	0	1	0	1	0	1	0	0	0	0	0	0	0	0	0	2	0	2	0
95 or more	8	0	9	0	6	0	11	0	1	0	7	0	3	0	2	0	4	0	17	0
NIDF	60		60		57		63		14		30		37		25		14		120	
mean	6.6		6.3		5.5		7.5		7.7		7.2		6.4		5.6		5.3		6.5	
standard deviation	7.4		6.9		7.0		7.2		7.4		7.7		6.8		6.8		6.9		7.2	

Descriptive Statistics and Frequency Distributions of 3YR and 8YR SLH Variables
by Sex, Race, grouped SEI, and Total Sample Size.

8YR SLH Variables (from PS-40 to 45) (continued)
Pure-Tone Audiometry: Air Conduction (continued)

Right Ear, 4,000 Hz

Code	Male Freq.	%	Female Freq.	%	White Freq.	%	Black Freq.	%	0.0-1.9 Freq.	%	2.0-3.9 Freq.	%	4.0-5.9 Freq.	%	6.0-7.9 Freq.	%	8.0-9.5 Freq.	%	Totals Freq.	%
0dB	3,280	33	3,277	33	4,276	42	2,281	23	380	24	1,706	29	1,982	33	1,537	38	952	41	6,557	33
5	2,190	22	2,145	22	2,201	22	2,134	22	305	19	1,193	20	1,314	22	948	23	575	25	4,335	22
10	2,187	22	2,212	22	1,802	18	2,597	26	433	27	1,403	24	1,299	20	802	20	462	20	4,399	22
15	1,815	18	1,838	18	1,257	12	2,396	24	405	25	1,319	22	1,113	18	592	14	224	10	3,653	18
20	132	1	137	1	121	1	148	1	27	2	92	2	77	1	51	1	22	1	269	1
25	171	2	136	1	155	2	152	2	23	1	102	2	92	2	70	2	20	1	307	2
30	74	1	47	0	57	1	64	1	11	1	33	1	41	1	22	1	14	1	121	1
35	61	1	50	1	64	1	47	0	6	0	35	1	35	1	28	1	7	0	111	1
40	44	0	25	0	39	0	30	0	9	1	20	0	19	0	15	0	6	0	69	0
45	41	0	26	0	44	0	23	0	7	0	23	0	23	0	9	0	5	0	67	0
50	21	0	15	0	23	0	13	0	4	0	11	0	14	0	3	0	4	0	36	0
55	13	0	9	0	12	0	10	0	3	0	6	0	11	0	2	0	0	0	22	0
60	10	0	6	0	11	0	5	0	0	0	5	0	4	0	4	0	3	0	16	0
65	8	0	1	0	5	0	4	0	0	0	4	0	2	0	3	0	0	0	9	0
70	2	0	1	0	3	0	0	0	1	0	0	0	0	0	2	0	0	0	3	0
75	6	0	2	0	4	0	4	0	1	0	4	0	1	0	2	0	0	0	8	0
80	3	0	2	0	4	0	0	0	0	0	0	0	1	0	0	0	0	0	1	0
85	2	0	2	0	5	0	0	0	0	0	1	0	0	0	2	0	0	0	5	0
90	2	0	2	0	1	0	3	0	1	0	2	0	1	0	0	0	0	0	4	0
95 or more	10	0	9	0	7	0	12	0	1	0	10	0	1	0	0	0	2	0	19	0
NIDF	63		63		61		65		14		31		40		27		14		126	
mean	8.3		7.9		7.0		9.2		9.5		8.9		8.1		7.3		6.3		8.1	
standard deviation	8.9		8.0		8.7		8.1		8.4		8.9		8.3		8.3		7.5		8.4	

Left Ear, 500 Hz

Code	Male Freq.	%	Female Freq.	%	White Freq.	%	Black Freq.	%	0.0-1.9 Freq.	%	2.0-3.9 Freq.	%	4.0-5.9 Freq.	%	6.0-7.9 Freq.	%	8.0-9.5 Freq.	%	Totals Freq.	%
0dB	1,569	16	1,639	16	1,678	17	1,530	15	263	16	1,102	18	1,017	17	577	14	249	11	3,208	16
5	2,423	24	2,458	25	2,466	24	2,415	24	358	22	1,286	22	1,454	24	1,099	27	684	30	4,881	24
10	3,049	30	2,989	30	2,934	29	3,104	31	470	29	1,761	29	1,754	29	1,321	32	732	32	6,038	30
15	2,442	24	2,334	23	2,359	23	2,417	24	432	27	1,461	24	1,483	25	885	22	515	22	4,776	24
20	200	2	165	2	203	2	162	2	39	2	122	2	95	2	67	2	42	2	365	2
25	172	2	139	1	200	2	111	1	21	1	97	2	99	2	64	2	30	1	311	2
30	91	1	81	1	102	1	70	1	9	1	60	1	53	1	28	1	22	1	172	1
35	47	0	55	1	62	1	40	0	9	1	29	0	36	1	19	0	9	0	102	1
40	24	0	28	0	28	0	24	0	4	0	14	0	19	0	10	0	5	0	52	0
45	20	0	17	0	23	0	14	0	0	0	11	0	8	0	14	0	2	0	37	0
50	6	0	9	0	9	0	6	0	3	0	5	0	3	0	3	0	1	0	15	0

Descriptive Statistics and Frequency Distributions of 3YR and 8YR SLH Variables by Sex, Race, grouped SEI, and Total Sample Size.

	Male		Female		White		Black		0.0-1.9		2.0-3.9		4.0-5.9		6.0-7.9		8.0-9.5		Totals	
Code	Freq.	%	Freq.	%	Freq.	%	Freq.	%	Freq.	%	Freq.	%	Freq.	%	Freq.	%	Freq.	%	Freq.	%
8YR SLH Variables (from PS-40 to 45) (continued)																				
Pure-Tone Audiometry: Air Conduction (continued)																				
Left Ear, 500 Hz (continued)																				
55dB	3	0	8	0	5	0	12	0	2	0	9	0	4	0	1	0	1	0	17	0
60	3	0	5	0	5	0	3	0	1	0	2	0	3	0	1	0	1	0	8	0
65	2	0	2	0	2	0	2	0	0	0	1	0	1	0	2	0	0	0	4	0
70	3	0	1	0	4	0	0	0	0	0	1	0	2	0	0	0	1	0	4	0
75	2	0	0	0	1	0	1	0	1	0	0	0	0	0	0	0	0	0	2	0
80	1	0	1	0	2	0	0	0	0	0	1	0	0	0	1	0	0	0	2	0
85	2	0	0	0	0	0	2	0	0	0	0	0	0	0	2	0	0	0	2	0
90	3	0	1	0	1	0	3	0	0	0	2	0	2	0	2	0	0	0	4	0
95 or more	4	0	9	0	5	0	8	0	2	0	6	0	2	0	1	0	2	0	13	0
NIDF	62		62		59		65		15		30		40		24		15		124	
mean	9.7		9.5		9.7		9.5		9.9		9.7		9.5		9.5		9.6		9.6	
standard deviation	7.3		7.4		7.5		7.2		7.7		7.7		7.1		7.4		6.8		7.4	
Left Ear, 1,000 Hz																				
0dB	3,071	30	3,330	33	3,860	38	2,541	26	440	27	1,807	30	1,961	32	1,412	34	781	34	6,401	32
5	3,230	32	3,149	32	3,089	31	3,290	33	484	30	1,820	30	1,858	31	1,369	33	848	37	6,379	32
10	2,205	22	2,135	21	1,761	17	2,579	26	422	26	1,364	23	1,327	22	813	20	414	18	4,340	22
15	1,150	11	961	10	929	9	1,182	12	208	13	737	12	643	11	350	9	173	8	2,111	11
20	128	1	117	1	134	1	111	1	20	1	69	1	82	1	51	1	23	1	245	1
25	114	1	94	1	131	1	77	1	12	1	59	1	67	1	42	1	28	1	208	1
30	50	0	56	1	56	1	50	1	11	1	39	1	32	1	14	0	10	0	106	1
35	46	0	33	0	44	0	35	0	5	0	32	1	21	0	15	0	6	0	79	0
40	28	0	25	0	33	0	20	0	4	0	15	0	19	0	9	0	6	0	53	0
45	19	0	15	0	18	0	16	0	4	0	11	0	10	0	8	0	1	0	34	0
50	8	0	6	0	8	0	6	0	1	0	5	0	3	0	4	0	1	0	14	0
55	7	0	3	0	6	0	4	0	0	0	3	0	1	0	3	0	1	0	10	0
60	6	0	3	0	6	0	2	0	2	0	3	0	2	0	3	0	1	0	9	0
65	2	0	4	0	7	0	1	0	0	0	2	0	2	0	1	0	1	0	6	0
70	1	0	3	0	5	0	3	0	1	0	0	0	3	0	0	0	0	0	4	0
75	2	0	0	0	1	0	1	0	1	0	1	0	0	0	1	0	0	0	2	0
80	2	0	0	0	0	0	0	0	0	0	0	0	1	0	0	0	0	0	2	0
85	2	0	0	0	2	0	0	0	0	0	1	0	1	0	0	0	0	0	2	0
90	2	0	0	0	2	0	2	0	0	0	0	0	0	0	0	0	0	0	2	0
95 or more	8	0	11	0	6	0	13	0	2	0	7	0	2	0	5	0	3	0	19	0
NIDF	53		58		55		56		14		25		37		21		14		111	
mean	7.1		6.7		6.4		7.4		7.6		7.3		6.9		6.5		6.2		6.9	
standard deviation	7.5		7.1		7.4		7.1		7.5		7.5		7.1		7.4		6.9		7.3	

Descriptive Statistics and Frequency Distributions of 3YR and 8YR SLH Variables by Sex, Race, grouped SEI, and Total Sample Size.

8YR SLH Variables (from PS-40 to 45) (continued)
Pure-Tone Audiometry: Air Conduction (continued)

Left Ear, 2,000 Hz

Code	Male Freq.	Male %	Female Freq.	Female %	White Freq.	White %	Black Freq.	Black %	0.0–1.9 Freq.	0.0–1.9 %	2.0–3.9 Freq.	2.0–3.9 %	4.0–5.9 Freq.	4.0–5.9 %	6.0–7.9 Freq.	6.0–7.9 %	8.0–9.5 Freq.	8.0–9.5 %	Totals Freq.	Totals %
0dB	3,335	33	3,576	36	4,420	44	2,491	25	394	24	1,789	30	2,084	35	1,699	41	945	41	6,911	35
5	3,019	30	2,933	29	2,983	30	2,969	30	472	29	1,710	29	1,703	28	1,252	31	815	35	5,952	30
10	2,009	20	2,004	20	1,480	15	2,533	26	406	25	1,376	23	1,252	21	661	16	318	14	4,013	20
15	1,316	13	1,119	11	864	9	1,571	16	277	17	850	14	794	13	354	9	160	7	2,435	12
20	131	1	101	1	120	1	112	1	14	1	91	2	64	1	40	1	23	1	232	1
25	100	1	75	1	80	1	95	1	25	2	57	1	56	1	29	1	8	0	175	1
30	47	0	42	0	42	0	47	0	8	0	31	1	26	0	20	0	4	0	89	0
35	43	0	32	0	33	0	42	0	7	0	23	0	21	0	14	0	10	0	75	0
40	16	0	23	0	17	0	22	0	4	0	16	0	10	0	6	0	3	0	39	0
45	11	0	6	0	3	0	14	0	1	0	8	0	3	0	2	0	2	0	17	0
50	9	0	5	0	9	0	5	0			4	0	3	0	4	0	2	0	14	0
55	10	0	5	0	8	0	7	0	2	0	2	0	5	0	1	0	2	0	15	0
60	6	0	4	0	8	0	2	0			5	0	3	0	2	0	1	0	10	0
65	4	0	1	0	2	0	3	0	2	0					2	0			5	0
70	3	0	6	0	7	0	2	0			1	0	4	0	2	0	1	0	9	0
75	4	0	1	0	4	0	1	0							2	0			5	0
80	3	0	1	0	4	0			1	0	1	0	2	0	4	0			4	0
85	3	0					3	0											3	0
90	1	0					1	0											1	0
95 or more	8	0	11	0	7	0	12	0	0	0	1	0	1	0	5	0	3	0	19	0
NIDF	56		58		56		58		14		8		39		21		14		114	
mean	7.0		6.5		5.8		7.8		8.2		7.5		6.8		6.0		5.5		6.8	
standard deviation	7.6		7.1		7.3		7.3		7.8		7.6		7.0		7.6		6.8		7.4	

Left Ear, 4,000 Hz

Code	Male Freq.	Male %	Female Freq.	Female %	White Freq.	White %	Black Freq.	Black %	0.0–1.9 Freq.	0.0–1.9 %	2.0–3.9 Freq.	2.0–3.9 %	4.0–5.9 Freq.	4.0–5.9 %	6.0–7.9 Freq.	6.0–7.9 %	8.0–9.5 Freq.	8.0–9.5 %	Totals Freq.	Totals %
0dB	2,961	29	3,180	32	3,892	39	2,249	23	371	23	1,627	27	1,894	31	1,419	35	830	36	6,141	31
5	2,248	22	2,256	22	2,290	23	2,214	22	335	21	1,287	22	1,262	21	972	24	648	28	4,504	23
10	2,230	22	2,145	22	1,824	18	2,551	26	387	24	1,378	23	1,328	22	861	21	421	18	4,375	22
15	1,974	20	1,881	19	1,458	14	2,397	24	419	26	1,300	22	1,221	20	622	15	293	13	3,855	19
20	163	2	135	1	162	2	136	1	27	2	94	2	92	2	54	1	31	1	298	2
25	195	2	132	1	175	2	152	2	39	2	103	2	90	1	64	2	31	1	327	2
30	75	1	72	1	79	1	68	1	13	1	58	1	37	1	27	1	12	1	147	1
35	69	1	41	0	62	1	48	0	8	0	41	1	35	1	18	0	8	0	110	1
40	36	0	31	0	34	0	33	0	6	0	28	0	18	0	9	0	6	0	67	0
45	34	0	25	0	38	0	21	0	4	0	19	0	18	0	13	0	5	0	59	0
50	27	0	9	0	20	0	16	0	2	0	9	0	9	0	12	0	4	0	36	0

546

Descriptive Statistics and Frequency Distributions of 3YR and 8YR SLH Variables by Sex, Race, grouped SEI, and Total Sample Size.

Code	Male Freq.	Male %	Female Freq.	Female %	White Freq.	White %	Black Freq.	Black %	0.0-1.9 Freq.	0.0-1.9 %	2.0-3.9 Freq.	2.0-3.9 %	4.0-5.9 Freq.	4.0-5.9 %	6.0-7.9 Freq.	6.0-7.9 %	8.0-9.5 Freq.	8.0-9.5 %	Totals Freq.	Totals %
8YR SLH Variables (from PS-40 to 45) (continued)																				
Pure-Tone Audiometry: Air Conduction (continued)																				
Left Ear, 4,000 Hz (continued)																				
55dB	18	0	10	0	17	0	11	0	1	0	8	0	10	0	7	0	2	0	28	0
60	5	0	5	0	7	0	3	0	1	0	3	0	5	0	1	0	0	0	10	0
65	10	0	3	0	7	0	6	0	1	0	1	0	6	0	5	0	0	0	13	0
70	7	0	2	0	6	0	3	0	0	0	2	0	3	0	3	0	1	0	9	0
75	5	0	2	0	5	0	2	0	1	0	1	0	2	0	2	0	1	0	7	0
80	4	0	0	0	1	0	3	0	0	0	1	0	1	0	2	0	0	0	4	0
85	1	0	0	0	0	0	1	0	0	0	0	0	0	0	1	0	0	0	1	0
90	2	0	1	0	1	0	2	0	0	0	1	0	0	0	0	0	1	0	3	0
95 or more	9	0	13	0	11	0	11	0	2	0	9	0	4	0	4	0	3	0	22	0
NIDF	61		60		59		62		14		30		38		25		14		121	
mean	8.7		8.0		7.5		9.2		9.5		8.9		8.3		7.7		7.0		8.3	
standard deviation	9.0		8.1		8.8		8.1		8.2		8.7		8.4		8.8		8.0		8.5	
Adequacy of Exam																				
Adequate	9,992	99	9,879	99	10,029	100	9,842	99	1,607	99	5,922	99	5,992	99	4,065	99	2,285	100	19,871	99
Not Adequate	66	1	55	1	43	0	78	1	10	1	40	1	36	1	28	1	7	0	121	1
NIDF	76		69		76		69		14		38		45		29		19		145	
Abnormal Auditory Adaptation																				
Right Ear, 4,000 Hz																				
Pass	9,595	98	9,340	97	9,759	98	9,176	97	1,484	96	5,598	97	5,687	97	3,924	98	2,242	99	18,935	97
Fail	221	2	283	3	195	2	309	3	59	4	167	3	166	3	86	2	26	1	504	3
Test not required	115		122		37		200		25		86		88		31		7		237	
NIDF	203		258		157		304		63		149		132		81		36		461	
Right Ear, 500 Hz																				
Pass	232	95	283	91	181	90	334	94	66	96	174	91	167	91	82	93	26	100	515	92
Fail	13	5	29	9	20	10	22	6	3	4	17	9	16	9	6	7	0	0	42	8
Test not required	9,717		9,498		9,798		9,417		1,522		5,701		5,782		3,960		2,250		19,215	
NIDF	172		193		149		216		40		108		108		74		35		365	
Left Ear, 4,000 Hz																				
Pass	9,651	98	9,452	98	9,809	99	9,294	98	1,513	97	5,643	98	5,753	98	3,951	98	2,243	99	19,103	98
Fail	163	2	217	2	148	1	232	2	39	3	131	2	125	2	61	2	24	1	380	2
Test not required	116		122		38		200		25		86		89		31		7		238	
NIDF	204		212		153		263		54		140		106		79		37		416	

547

Descriptive Statistics and Frequency Distributions of 3YR and 8YR SLH Variables by Sex, Race, grouped SEI, and Total Sample Size.

	Male		Female		White		Black		0.0-1.9		2.0-3.9		4.0-5.9		6.0-7.9		8.0-9.5		Totals	
Code	Freq.	%	Freq.	%	Freq.	%	Freq.	%	Freq.	%	Freq.	%	Freq.	%	Freq.	%	Freq.	%	Freq.	%
8YR SLH Variables (from PS-40 to 45) (continued)																				
Abnormal Auditory Adaptation (continued)																				
Left Ear, 500 Hz																				
Pass	190	94	223	92	154	92	259	93	42	93	139	90	138	95	70	92	24	96	413	93
Fail	13	6	20	8	13	8	20	7	3	7	16	10	7	5	6	8	1	4	33	7
Test not required	9,758		9,582		9,833		9,507		1,547		5,732		5,837		3,974		2,250		19,340	
NIDF	173		178		148		203		39		113		91		72		36		351	
Adequacy of Exam																				
Adequate	9,814	99	9,673	99	9,947	100	9,540	99	1,560	98	5,782	99	5,866	99	4,011	99	2,268	99	19,487	99
Not adequate	61	1	95	1	48	0	108	1	25	2	58	1	34	1	25	1	14	1	156	1
Test not required	114		122		36		200		25		85		88		31		7		236	
NIDF	145		113		117		141		21		75		85		55		22		258	
Pure-Tone Audiometry: Bone Conduction																				
Right Ear, 500 Hz																				
0dB	254	31	171	25	267	32	158	24	24	20	144	30	135	29	87	29	35	25	425	28
5	171	21	139	20	170	20	140	21	27	22	99	20	96	21	58	19	30	22	310	21
10	144	18	154	22	163	20	135	20	22	18	88	18	90	20	61	20	37	27	298	20
15	120	15	111	16	111	13	120	18	28	23	72	15	71	15	49	16	11	8	231	15
20	51	6	56	8	57	7	50	7	7	6	34	7	39	8	19	6	8	6	107	7
25	34	4	23	3	29	3	28	4	6	5	25	5	9	2	10	3	7	5	57	4
30	9	1	10	1	7	1	12	2	6	5	6	1	6	1	3	1	3	2	19	1
35	6	1	8	1	7	1	7	1	1	1	5	1	5	1	2	1	1	1	14	1
40	8	1	5	1	9	1	4	1	1	1	4	1	3	1	3	1	2	1	13	1
45	8	1	3		2		3		1	1	2		1		3	1	1		5	0
50	2	0	3		2		3		0		2		0		0		1		5	0
55	2	0	0		0		0		1		0		0		2		0		5	0
60 or more	3	0	2	0	4	0	1	0	0		1		1		0		1		5	0
Test not required	9,183		9,190		9,193		9,180		1,476		5,441		5,527		3,774		2,155		18,373	
NIDF	139		122		121		140		33		75		86		49		18		261	
mean	9.7		11		9.4		11		12		9.9		9.6		10		11		10	
standard deviation	10		10		10		10		12		9.8		9.7		11		11		10	
Right Ear, 1,000 Hz																				
0dB	206	25	167	24	226	27	147	22	23	19	131	27	116	25	71	24	32	23	373	25
5	205	25	141	21	208	25	138	21	36	30	91	19	101	22	84	28	34	25	346	23
10	148	18	139	20	149	18	138	21	20	16	108	22	85	19	50	17	24	17	287	19
15	129	16	124	18	131	16	122	18	22	18	77	16	81	18	50	17	23	17	253	17
20	46	6	46	7	43	5	49	7	9	7	31	6	33	7	11	4	8	6	92	6

548

Descriptive Statistics and Frequency Distributions of 3YR and 8YR SLH Variables by Sex, Race, grouped SEI, and Total Sample Size.

Code	Male Freq.	%	Female Freq.	%	White Freq.	%	Black Freq.	%	0.0-1.9 Freq.	%	2.0-3.9 Freq.	%	4.0-5.9 Freq.	%	6.0-7.9 Freq.	%	8.0-9.5 Freq.	%	Totals Freq.	%
8YR SLH Variables (from PS-40 to 45) (continued)																			
Pure-Tone Audiometry: Bone Conduction (continued)																			
Right Ear, 1,000 Hz (continued)																			
25dB	30	4	23	3	26	3	27	4	2	2	15	3	19	4	11	4	6	4	53	4
30	12	1	15	2	13	2	14	2	3	3	9	2	4	1	7	2	4	3	27	2
35	7	1	10	1	10	1	7	1	1	1	6	1	4	1	3	1	3	2	17	1
40	4	0	4	1	3	0	5	1	0	0	3	1	3	1	1	0	1	1	8	1
45	4	0	3	0	2	0	5	1	2	2	3	1	0	0	1	0	1	1	7	0
50	4	0	3	0	3	0	4	1	2	2	4	1	0	0	2	1	0	0	7	0
55	5	1	1	0	5	1	1	0	1	1	2	0	2	0	1	0	0	0	6	0
60 or more	12	1	9	1	10	1	11	2	2	2	5	1	7	2	5	2	2	1	21	1
Test not required	9,184		9,191		9,194		9,181		1,476		5,441		5,529		3,774		2,155		18,375	
NIDF	138		127		125		140		33		74		89		51		18		265	
mean	10		11		9.9		12		12		11		10		10		11		11	
standard deviation	11		11		11		11		12		11		10		11		11		11	
Right Ear, 2,000 Hz																			
0dB	240	30	194	28	262	32	172	26	28	23	133	28	134	30	94	32	45	33	434	29
5	227	28	169	25	237	29	159	24	31	26	118	24	120	26	79	27	48	35	396	27
10	121	15	123	18	129	16	115	17	25	21	82	17	81	18	41	14	15	11	244	16
15	93	12	85	12	83	10	95	14	16	13	71	15	51	11	31	10	9	7	178	12
20	51	6	42	6	48	6	45	7	4	3	33	7	29	6	20	7	7	5	93	6
25	23	3	29	4	23	3	29	4	10	8	11	2	13	3	13	4	5	4	52	3
30	9	1	14	2	10	1	13	2	0	0	7	1	5	1	6	2	1	1	23	2
35	10	1	5	1	4	0	11	2	1	1	7	1	5	1	2	1	0	0	15	1
40	5	1	3	0	6	1	2	0	2	2	1	0	2	0	1	0	1	1	8	1
45	5	1	3	0	3	0	5	1	1	1	4	1	1	0	1	0	2	0	8	1
50	3	0	2	0	3	0	2	0	0	0	1	0	2	0	1	0	0	0	5	0
55	2	0	2	0	3	0	1	0	1	1	0	0	2	0	0	0	0	0	4	0
60 or more	19	2	11	2	16	2	14	2	1	1	9	2	8	2	7	2	5	4	30	2
Test not required	9,184		9,191		9,194		9,181		1,476		5,441		5,529		3,774		2,155		18,375	
NIDF	142		130		127		145		35		77		91		51		18		272	
mean	9.9		10		9.2		11		11		10		9.6		9.9		9.4		10	
standard deviation	12		11		11		12		11		11		11		12		13		12	

Descriptive Statistics and Frequency Distributions of 3YR and 8YR SLH Variables by Sex, Race, grouped SEI, and Total Sample Size.

8YR SLH Variables (from PS-40 to 45) (continued)

Pure-Tone Audiometry: Bone Conduction (continued)

Right Ear, 4,000 Hz

Code	Male Freq.	%	Female Freq.	%	White Freq.	%	Black Freq.	%	0.0-1.9 Freq.	%	2.0-3.9 Freq.	%	4.0-5.9 Freq.	%	6.0-7.9 Freq.	%	8.0-9.5 Freq.	%	Totals Freq.	%
0dB	194	24	143	21	192	23	145	22	23	19	111	23	102	22	68	23	33	24	337	23
5	190	23	140	20	201	24	129	19	33	27	91	19	92	20	82	28	32	23	330	22
10	128	16	107	16	129	16	106	16	17	14	85	18	82	18	39	13	12	9	235	16
15	122	15	136	20	137	17	121	18	21	17	83	17	83	18	44	15	27	20	258	17
20	45	6	62	9	50	6	57	9	12	10	37	8	34	7	14	5	10	7	107	7
25	46	6	42	6	43	5	45	7	4	3	30	6	22	5	20	7	12	9	88	6
30	18	2	12	2	10	1	20	3	3	2	10	2	9	2	7	2	1	1	30	2
35	13	2	16	2	21	3	8	1	3	2	9	2	12	3	5	2	1	1	29	2
40	14	2	5	1	8	1	11	2	0	0	7	1	4	1	5	2	3	2	19	1
45	6	1	3	0	7	1	2	0	2	1	1	0	4	1	2	1			9	1
50	6	1	4	1	6	1	4	1	1	2	6	1	5	1	1	0	1	1	10	1
55	9	1	3	0	5	1	7	1	2	1	1	0		0		0	1	1	12	1
60 or more	21	3	11	2	18	2	14	2	1	2	8	2	9	2	2	1	4	3	32	2
Test not required	9,184		9,192		9,195		9,181		1,476		5,441		5,529		3,775		2,155		18,376	
NIDF	138		127		126		139		34		79		84		50		18		265	
mean	13		12		12		13		12		12		13		12		13		13	
standard deviation	14		12		13		13		12		12		13		13		14		13	

Left Ear, 500 Hz

Code	Male Freq.	%	Female Freq.	%	White Freq.	%	Black Freq.	%	0.0-1.9 Freq.	%	2.0-3.9 Freq.	%	4.0-5.9 Freq.	%	6.0-7.9 Freq.	%	8.0-9.5 Freq.	%	Totals Freq.	%
0dB	248	29	152	22	249	27	151	23	27	20	135	27	123	28	76	24	39	24	400	26
5	182	21	141	20	201	22	122	19	23	17	99	20	85	19	78	25	38	24	323	21
10	164	19	154	22	172	19	146	22	37	27	99	20	97	22	51	16	34	21	318	20
15	139	16	115	17	139	15	115	18	23	17	79	16	76	17	53	17	23	14	254	16
20	67	8	66	9	75	8	58	9	12	9	53	11	32	7	25	8	11	7	133	9
25	23	3	29	4	32	4	20	3	3	2	14	3	20	5	9	3	6	4	52	3
30	13	2	13	2	13	1	13	2	4	3	9	2	4	1	8	3	1	0	26	2
35	6	1	4	1	5	1	5	1	2	1	4	1	1	0	3	1	0	1	10	1
40	6	1	4	1	6	1	4	1	1	1	4	1	1	0	3	1	2	1	10	1
45	3	0	4	1	3	0	4	1	1	1	1	0	0	0	0	0	1	1	7	0
50	3	0	5	1	4	0	4	1	2	1	2	0	2	0	1	0	1	1	8	1
55	3	0	1	0	2	0	2	0	0	0	1	0	0	0	0	0	2	1	4	0
60 or more	4	0	7	1	6	1	5	1	1	1	4	1	1	0	3	1	2	1	11	1
Test not required	9,132		9,186		9,121		9,197		1,464		5,419		5,542		3,763		2,130		18,318	
NIDF	141		122		120		143		31		77		88		46		21		263	
mean	9.7		9.9		9.9		11		12		10		9.5		11		11		10	
standard deviation	9.6		10		9.8		10		11		10		8.4		11		11		10	

Descriptive Statistics and Frequency Distributions of 3YR and 8YR SLH Variables by Sex, Race, grouped SEI, and Total Sample Size.

Code	Male Freq	Male %	Female Freq	Female %	White Freq	White %	Black Freq	Black %	0.0-1.9 Freq	0.0-1.9 %	2.0-3.9 Freq	2.0-3.9 %	4.0-5.9 Freq	4.0-5.9 %	6.0-7.9 Freq	6.0-7.9 %	8.0-9.5 Freq	8.0-9.5 %	Totals Freq	Totals %
8YR SLH Variables (from PS-40 to 45) (continued)																				
Pure-Tone Audiometry: Bone Conduction (continued)																				
Left Ear, 1,000 Hz																				
0dB	200	23	143	21	214	24	129	20	24	18	122	24	105	24	64	21	28	18	343	22
5	207	24	150	22	222	25	135	21	23	17	114	23	90	20	90	29	40	25	357	23
10	171	20	137	20	189	21	119	18	30	23	94	19	86	20	64	21	34	21	308	20
15	137	16	117	17	136	15	118	18	26	20	86	17	80	18	38	12	24	15	254	16
20	54	6	62	9	58	6	58	9	14	11	42	8	26	6	19	6	15	9	116	7
25	31	4	37	5	35	4	33	5	3	2	19	4	23	5	14	5	9	6	68	4
30	18	2	14	2	10	1	22	3	6	5	6	1	13	3	5	2	2	1	32	2
35	11	1	8	1	11	1	8	1	2	2	5	1	7	2	3	1	2	1	19	1
40	7	1	4	1	7	1	4	1	1	1	2	0	4	0	3	1	1	1	11	1
45	7	1	8	1	8	1	7	1	1	1	8	2	0	0	4	1	2	1	15	1
50	2	0	2	0	1	0	3	0	0	0	2	0	1	0	1	0	0	0	4	0
55	1	0	1	0	2	0	0	0	0	0	0	0	0	0	0	0	0	0	2	0
60 or more	10	1	9	1	8	1	11	2	3	2	4	1	4	1	5	2	3	2	19	1
Test not required	9,132		9,186		9,121		9,197		1,464		5,419		5,542		3,763		2,130		18,318	
NIDF	146		125		126		145		34		77		91		48		21		271	
mean	11		12		10		12		13		11		11		11		12		11	
standard deviation	11		11		10		11		12		10		10		11		11		11	
Left Ear, 2,000 Hz																				
0dB	231	27	184	27	259	29	156	24	32	24	137	27	108	25	96	31	42	26	415	27
5	209	25	198	29	262	29	145	23	32	24	117	23	126	29	77	25	55	34	407	26
10	141	17	112	16	132	15	121	19	24	18	89	18	68	15	46	15	26	16	253	16
15	123	14	89	13	122	14	90	14	20	15	69	14	66	15	38	12	19	12	212	14
20	62	7	49	7	56	6	55	9	12	9	41	8	36	8	17	6	5	3	111	7
25	26	3	24	3	23	3	27	4	5	4	14	3	16	4	11	4	4	2	50	3
30	14	2	11	2	7	1	18	3	1	1	14	3	5	1	3	1	2	1	25	2
35	10	1	5	1	7	1	8	1	3	2	5	1	2	0	3	1	0	0	15	1
40	6	1	4	1	2	0	8	1	0	0	2	0	3	1	4	1	2	1	10	1
45	6	1	4	1	7	1	3	0	0	0	3	1	1	0	3	1	1	1	10	1
50	6	1	0	0	5	1	1	0	0	0	1	0	1	0	1	0	1	0	6	0
55	1	0	4	1	3	0	2	0	0	0	3	1	0	0	0	0	0	0	5	0
60 or more	16	2	9	1	13	1	12	2	4	2	5	1	6	1	8	3	4	2	25	2
Test not required	9,135		9,187		9,124		9,198		1,464		5,420		5,544		3,764		2,130		18,322	
NIDF	148		126		126		148		36		80		90		49		19		274	
mean	11		9.7		9.4		11		10		10		10		11		9.7		10	
standard deviation	12		11		11		12		10		11		10		13		12		11	

551

Descriptive Statistics and Frequency Distributions of 3YR and 8YR SLH Variables
by Sex, Race, grouped SEI, and Total Sample Size.

Code	Male Freq.	Male %	Female Freq.	Female %	White Freq.	White %	Black Freq.	Black %	0.0-1.9 Freq.	0.0-1.9 %	2.0-3.9 Freq.	2.0-3.9 %	4.0-5.9 Freq.	4.0-5.9 %	6.0-7.9 Freq.	6.0-7.9 %	8.0-9.5 Freq.	8.0-9.5 %	Totals Freq.	Totals %
8YR SLH Variables (from PS-40 to 45) (continued)																				
Pure-Tone Audiometry: Bone Conduction (continued)																				
Left Ear, 4,000 Hz																				
0dB	201	23	157	23	216	24	142	22	37	28	111	22	95	21	72	23	43	27	358	23
5	177	20	149	22	204	22	122	19	22	16	102	20	100	23	64	20	38	24	326	21
10	142	16	109	16	164	18	87	13	24	18	73	15	71	16	60	19	23	14	251	16
15	142	16	118	17	148	16	112	17	17	13	96	19	74	17	45	14	28	17	260	17
20	64	7	62	9	64	7	62	10	16	12	43	9	38	9	22	7	7	4	126	8
25	41	5	40	6	34	4	47	7	8	6	33	7	21	5	13	4	6	4	81	5
30	16	2	18	3	14	2	20	3	3	2	16	3	8	2	3	1	4	2	34	2
35	20	2	10	1	14	2	16	2	2	1	7	1	8	2	10	3	3	2	30	2
40	15	2	4	1	10	1	9	1	1	1	6	1	7	2	5	2	0	0	19	1
45	13	2	7	1	13	1	7	1	2	1	4	1	8	2	3	1	3	2	20	1
50	7	1	3	0	8	1	2	0	0	0	2	0	4	1	3	1	1	1	10	1
55	5	1	2	0	4	0	3	0	1	1	1	0	2	0	2	1	1	1	7	0
60 or more	21	2	10	1	15	2	16	2	1	1	7	1	8	2	11	4	4	2	31	2
Test not required	9,133	0	9,186		9,122		9,197		1,464		5,420		5,541		3,764		2,130		18,319	
NIDF	137		128		118		147		33		79		88		45		20		265	
mean	13		12		12		14		12		12		13		13		12		13	
standard deviation	13		12		12		13		11		12		13		14		13		13	
Adequacy of Exam																				
Adequate	1,179	94	966	95	1,200	95	945	95	191	95	688	95	622	95	428	94	216	95	2,145	95
Not adequate	69	6	50	5	64	5	55	6	10	5	36	5	35	5	26	6	12	5	119	5
Not applicable	8,718		8,823		8,770		8,771		1,383		5,165		5,309		3,620		2,064		17,541	
NIDF	168		164		114		218		47		111		107		48		19		332	
Discrimination Percent																				
Right Ear																				
0%	3	0	1	0	2	0	2	0	0	0	1	0	0	0	2	0	1	0	4	0
4	1	0	0	0	0	0	1	0	0	0	1	0	0	0	0	0	0	0	1	0
8	0	0	0	0	0	0	0	0	0	0	0	0	0	0	0	0	0	0	0	0
12	0	0	0	0	0	0	0	0	0	0	0	0	0	0	0	0	0	0	1	0
16	1	0	1	0	0	0	2	0	0	0	2	0	2	0	0	0	0	0	0	0
20	2	0	0	0	3	0	1	0	0	0	2	0	0	0	0	0	1	0	2	0
24	2	0	2	0	0	0	2	0	0	0	2	0	1	0	1	0	0	0	4	0
28	2	0	0	0	0	0	3	0	0	0	2	0	0	0	0	0	0	0	3	0
32	1	0	0	0	1	0	0	0	0	0	0	0	0	0	0	0	0	0	2	0
36	7	0	1	0	3	0	5	0	0	0	4	0	2	0	1	0	0	0	8	0
40	3	0	5	0	3	0	5	0	1	0	3	0	3	0	1	0	0	0	8	0

Descriptive Statistics and Frequency Distributions of 3YR and 8YR SLH Variables
by Sex, Race, grouped SEI, and Total Sample Size.

8YR SLH Variables (from PS-40 to 45) (continued)
Discrimination Percent (continued)
Right Ear (continued)

Code	Male Freq.	Male %	Female Freq.	Female %	White Freq.	White %	Black Freq.	Black %	0.0-1.9 Freq.	0.0-1.9 %	2.0-3.9 Freq.	2.0-3.9 %	4.0-5.9 Freq.	4.0-5.9 %	6.0-7.9 Freq.	6.0-7.9 %	8.0-9.5 Freq.	8.0-9.5 %	Totals Freq.	Totals %
44%	7	0	5	0	5	0	7	0	2	0	4	0	5	0	0	0	1	0	12	0
48	13	0	5	0	10	0	8	0	2	0	12	0	4	0	0	0	0	0	18	0
52	10	0	9	0	6	0	13	0	3	0	6	0	8	0	3	0	2	0	19	0
56	14	0	17	0	15	0	16	0	7	0	14	0	7	0	5	0	0	0	31	0
60	20	0	23	0	7	0	36	0	6	0	19	0	13	0	5	0	0	0	43	0
64	39	0	26	0	22	0	43	0	8	0	28	0	25	0	4	0	0	0	65	0
68	57	1	49	1	25	0	81	1	21	1	45	1	27	0	8	0	5	0	106	1
72	72	1	62	1	37	0	97	1	18	1	62	1	41	1	10	0	3	0	134	1
76	166	2	135	1	64	1	237	2	54	3	142	2	71	1	31	1	3	0	301	2
80	278	3	246	3	114	1	410	4	74	5	240	4	147	3	48	1	15	1	524	3
84	498	5	478	5	234	2	742	8	137	9	384	7	308	5	111	3	36	2	976	5
88	881	9	964	10	547	6	1,298	13	232	15	717	12	573	10	227	6	96	4	1,845	9
92	1,601	16	1,683	17	1,312	13	1,972	20	341	22	1,095	19	1,007	17	567	14	274	12	3,284	17
96	2,593	26	2,503	26	2,858	29	2,238	23	347	22	1,442	25	1,509	26	1,121	28	677	30	5,096	26
100	3,518	36	3,444	36	4,562	46	2,400	25	316	20	1,552	27	2,095	36	1,853	46	1,146	51	6,962	36
NIDF	344		341		317		368		61		220		224		129		51		685	
mean	94		94		96		92		91		92		94		96		97		94	
standard deviation	8.2		7.5		6.6		8.6		8.8		8.9		7.7		6.2		5.4		7.9	
Left Ear																				
0%	2	0	0	0	2	0	0	0	0	0	1	0	0	0	1	0	0	0	2	0
4	0	0	0	0	0	0	0	0	0	0	0	0	0	0	0	0	0	0	0	0
8	0	0	0	0	0	0	1	0	0	0	0	0	1	0	0	0	0	0	1	0
12	0	0	1	0	0	0	0	0	0	0	0	0	0	0	0	0	0	0	0	0
16	2	0	0	0	3	0	0	0	0	0	2	0	0	0	1	0	0	0	3	0
20	0	0	0	0	0	0	0	0	0	0	0	0	0	0	0	0	0	0	0	0
24	2	0	1	0	2	0	1	0	0	0	2	0	0	0	0	0	1	0	3	0
28	2	0	0	0	2	0	0	0	0	0	0	0	2	0	0	0	0	0	2	0
32	2	0	1	0	1	0	2	0	0	0	3	0	0	0	0	0	0	0	3	0
36	2	0	7	0	4	0	5	0	1	0	2	0	4	0	2	0	0	0	9	0
40	7	0	10	0	9	0	8	0	0	0	12	0	2	0	2	0	1	0	17	0
44	6	0	4	0	6	0	4	0	2	0	5	0	3	0	0	0	0	0	10	0
48	13	0	7	0	9	0	11	0	2	0	10	0	6	0	1	0	1	0	20	0
52	16	0	10	0	13	0	13	0	1	0	9	0	13	0	3	0	0	0	26	0
56	10	0	18	0	14	0	14	0	3	0	16	0	4	0	5	0	0	0	28	0
60	32	0	24	0	18	0	38	0	10	1	24	0	15	0	6	0	1	0	56	0
64	24	1	34	0	14	0	44	0	8	1	26	0	15	0	9	0	0	0	58	0
68	55	1	43	0	36	0	62	1	17	1	43	1	28	0	6	0	4	0	98	1

Descriptive Statistics and Frequency Distributions of 3YR and 8YR SLH Variables by Sex, Race, grouped SEI, and Total Sample Size.

Code	Male Freq.	%	Female Freq.	%	White Freq.	%	Black Freq.	%	0.0-1.9 Freq.	%	2.0-3.9 Freq.	%	4.0-5.9 Freq.	%	6.0-7.9 Freq.	%	8.0-9.5 Freq.	%	Totals Freq.	%
8YR SLH Variables (from PS-40 to 45) (continued)																				
Discrimination Percent (continued)																				
Left Ear (continued)																				
72%	77	1	67	1	45	0	99	1	19	1	61	1	49	1	11	0	4	0	144	1
76	118	1	138	1	44	0	212	2	39	2	123	2	70	1	19	0	5	0	256	1
80	290	3	241	2	105	1	426	4	83	5	243	4	155	3	36	1	14	1	531	3
84	504	5	485	5	226	2	763	8	150	10	410	7	283	5	97	2	49	2	989	5
88	910	9	937	10	576	6	1,271	13	221	14	721	12	556	10	248	6	101	4	1,847	9
92	1,629	17	1,670	17	1,330	14	1,969	20	329	21	1,094	19	1,028	18	562	14	286	13	3,299	17
96	2,570	26	2,665	28	2,901	29	2,334	24	332	21	1,451	25	1,594	27	1,155	29	703	31	5,235	27
100	3,514	36	3,301	34	4,475	46	2,340	24	355	23	1,520	26	2,022	35	1,826	46	1,092	48	6,815	35
NIDF	347		338		313		372		59		222		223		132		49		685	
mean	94		94		96		92		91		92		94		96		96		94	
standard deviation	8.0		7.7		7.0		8.2		8.5		10		7.6		6.3		5.1		7.8	
Adequacy of Exam																				
Adequate	9,764	99	9,642	99	9,810	99	9,596	99	1,570	100	5,766	99	5,838	99	3,977	99	2,255	99	19,406	99
Not adequate	74	1	61	1	85	1	50	1	6	0	36	1	36	1	38	1	19	1	135	1
NIDF	296		300		253		343		55		198		199		107		37		596	
Auditory Memory																				
Digits: Total Pass Score																				
2.0 or less	22	0	16	0	12	0	26	0	5	0	16	0	12	0	3	0	2	0	38	0
2.5	13	0	20	0	15	0	18	0	3	0	14	0	10	0	4	0	0	0	33	0
3.0	89	1	56	1	81	1	64	1	21	1	58	1	44	1	18	0	4	0	145	1
3.5	249	2	197	2	232	2	214	2	51	3	185	3	131	2	61	1	18	1	446	2
4.0	980	10	682	7	810	8	852	9	190	12	595	10	515	9	256	6	106	5	1,662	8
4.5	1,567	16	1,443	15	1,469	15	1,541	16	290	18	961	16	955	16	560	14	244	11	3,010	15
5.0	2,496	25	2,230	23	2,263	22	2,463	25	419	26	1,467	25	1,462	24	924	23	454	20	4,726	24
5.5	1,602	16	1,788	18	1,590	16	1,800	18	261	16	1,059	18	994	17	688	17	388	17	3,390	17
6.0	1,504	15	1,662	17	1,777	18	1,389	14	181	11	787	13	950	16	753	18	495	22	3,166	16
6.5	481	5	603	6	585	6	499	5	73	5	278	5	300	5	260	6	173	8	1,084	5
7.0	687	7	791	8	823	8	655	7	78	5	353	6	429	7	364	9	254	11	1,478	7
7.5	158	2	205	2	217	2	146	1	20	1	73	1	94	2	96	2	80	3	363	2
8.0	112	1	127	1	174	2	65	1	3	0	36	1	57	1	76	2	67	3	239	1
8.5	11	0	17	0	18	0	10	0	1	0	5	0	9	0	8	0	5	0	28	0
9.0	11	0	11	0	13	0	9	0	0	0	9	0	7	0	4	0	2	0	22	0
9.5	0	0	4	0	4	0	0	0	0	0	0	0	0	0	2	0	1	0	4	0
10.0	2	0	4	0	6	0	0	0	0	0	0	0	1	0	2	0	3	0	6	0
10.5	1	0	0	0	1	0	0	0	0	0	0	0	0	0	0	0	0	0	1	0
NIDF	149		147		58		238		35		104		102		42		13		296	

Descriptive Statistics and Frequency Distributions of 3YR and 8YR SLH Variables
by Sex, Race, grouped SEI, and Total Sample Size.

	Male		Female		White		Black		0.0-1.9		2.0-3.9		4.0-5.9		6.0-7.9		8.0-9.5		Totals	
Code	Freq.	%	Freq.	%	Freq.	%	Freq.	%	Freq.	%	Freq.	%	Freq.	%	Freq.	%	Freq.	%	Freq.	%
8YR SLH Variables (from PS-40 to 45) (continued)																				
Auditory Memory (continued)																				
Digits: Total Pass Score (continued)																				
Adequate	9,973	100	9,836	100	10,072	100	9,737	100	1,594	100	5,892	100	5,957	100	4,073	100	2,293	100	19,809	100
mean	5.3		5.4		5.4		5.3		5.1		5.2		5.3		5.5		5.7		5.4	
standard deviation	1.0		1.0		1.0		.95		.94		.97		.98		1.0		1.0		1.0	
Nonsense Syllables: Total Pass Score																				
2.0 or less	372	4	327	3	282	3	417	4	82	5	256	4	214	4	96	2	51	2	699	4
2.5	451	5	392	4	468	5	375	4	69	4	270	5	241	4	164	4	99	4	843	4
3.0	2,128	21	1,907	19	2,095	21	1,940	20	337	21	1,305	22	1,229	21	758	19	406	18	4,035	20
3.5	2,285	23	2,254	23	2,338	23	2,201	23	380	24	1,370	23	1,380	23	912	22	497	22	4,539	23
4.0	2,839	28	2,863	29	2,827	28	2,875	29	462	29	1,648	28	1,694	28	1,204	29	694	30	5,702	29
4.5	1,488	15	1,560	16	1,517	15	1,531	16	215	13	814	14	939	16	703	17	377	16	3,048	15
5.0	336	3	425	4	420	4	341	3	47	3	190	3	211	4	184	5	129	6	761	4
5.5	50	1	62	1	71	1	41	0	3	0	28	0	34	0	26	1	21	1	112	1
6.0	36	0	53	1	61	1	28	0	1	0	12	0	24	0	29	1	23	1	89	0
6.5	3	0	10	0	11	0	2	0	0	0	1	0	4	0	6	0	2	0	13	0
NIDF	146		150		58		238		35		106		103		40		12		296	
Adequate	9,974	100	9,836	100	10,068	100	9,742	100	1,592	100	5,891	100	5,959	100	4,076	100	2,292	100	19,810	100
mean	3.7		3.7		3.7		3.7		3.6		3.6		3.7		3.8		3.8		3.7	
standard deviation	.71		.72		.72		.71		.70		.71		.71		.71		.73		.71	
Language Comprehension																				
Word Identification (PPVT): Raw Score																				
0	0	0	0	0	0	0	1	0	0	0	1	0	0	0	0	0	0	0	1	0
1	2	0	1	0	0	0	0	0	0	0	1	0	0	0	0	0	0	0	2	0
2	0	0	0	0	1	0	0	0	0	0	0	0	0	0	0	0	0	0	0	0
3	0	0	0	0	0	0	3	0	0	0	2	0	0	0	0	0	0	0	3	0
4	2	0	1	0	0	0	1	0	1	0	1	0	0	0	0	0	0	0	3	0
5	0	0	0	0	0	0	0	0	0	0	0	0	0	0	0	0	0	0	1	0
6	1	0	1	0	0	0	2	0	0	0	2	0	0	0	0	0	0	0	2	0
7	0	0	0	0	0	0	0	0	0	0	0	0	0	0	0	0	0	0	0	0
8	0	0	0	0	0	0	0	0	0	0	0	0	0	0	0	0	0	0	0	0
9	3	0	0	0	1	0	2	0	1	0	2	0	0	0	1	0	0	0	3	0
10	2	0	3	0	0	0	5	0	1	0	3	0	2	0	0	0	0	0	5	0
11	0	0	1	0	0	0	2	0	0	0	0	0	0	0	0	0	0	0	2	0
12	1	0	0	0	0	0	1	0	1	0	1	0	0	0	0	0	0	0	1	0
13	0	0	0	0	0	0	1	0	0	0	0	0	1	0	0	0	0	0	1	0

555

Descriptive Statistics and Frequency Distributions of 3YR and 8YR SLH Variables
by Sex, Race, grouped SEI, and Total Sample Size.

8YR SLH Variables (from PS–40 to 45) (continued)
Language Comprehension (continued)
Word Identification (PPVT): Raw Score (continued)

Code	Male Freq.	Male %	Female Freq.	Female %	White Freq.	White %	Black Freq.	Black %	0.0–1.9 Freq.	0.0–1.9 %	2.0–3.9 Freq.	2.0–3.9 %	4.0–5.9 Freq.	4.0–5.9 %	6.0–7.9 Freq.	6.0–7.9 %	8.0–9.5 Freq.	8.0–9.5 %	Totals Freq.	Totals %
14	0	0	1	0	1	0	0	0	1	0	0	0	0	0	0	0	0	0	1	0
15	1	0	0	0	0	0	1	0	1	0	0	0	0	0	0	0	0	0	1	0
16	0	0	1	0	0	0	1	0	0	0	1	0	0	0	0	0	0	0	1	0
17	2	0	2	0	0	0	4	0	1	0	1	0	2	0	0	0	0	0	4	0
18	1	0	0	0	0	0	1	0	0	0	1	0	0	0	0	0	0	0	1	0
19	3	0	1	0	1	0	3	0	1	0	1	0	2	0	0	0	0	0	4	0
20	0	0	2	0	0	0	2	0	0	0	2	0	0	0	0	0	0	0	2	0
21	1	0	0	0	1	0	0	0	0	0	1	0	0	0	0	0	0	0	1	0
22	2	0	0	0	0	0	2	0	0	0	2	0	0	0	0	0	0	0	2	0
23	2	0	0	0	1	0	1	0	0	0	1	0	1	0	0	0	0	0	2	0
24	2	0	0	0	0	0	2	0	1	0	1	0	0	0	0	0	0	0	2	0
25	0	0	2	0	2	0	0	0	0	0	1	0	1	0	0	0	0	0	2	0
26	1	0	1	0	0	0	2	0	2	0	0	0	0	0	0	0	0	0	2	0
27	3	0	2	0	0	0	5	0	2	0	1	0	2	0	0	0	0	0	5	0
28	0	0	0	0	0	0	0	0	0	0	0	0	0	0	0	0	0	0	0	0
29	2	0	5	0	2	0	5	0	3	0	3	0	0	0	1	0	0	0	7	0
30	2	0	3	0	1	0	4	0	1	0	2	0	2	0	0	0	0	0	5	0
31	3	0	4	0	1	0	6	0	1	0	5	0	1	0	0	0	0	0	7	0
32	2	0	4	0	1	0	5	0	2	0	1	0	2	0	1	0	0	0	6	0
33	6	0	5	0	1	0	10	0	2	0	5	0	1	0	3	0	0	0	11	0
34	5	0	7	0	2	0	10	0	7	0	1	0	3	0	1	0	0	0	12	0
35	4	0	9	0	1	0	12	0	3	0	8	0	0	0	2	0	0	0	13	0
36	5	0	10	0	2	0	13	0	3	0	5	0	5	0	2	0	0	0	15	0
37	7	0	11	0	4	0	14	0	5	0	4	0	6	0	3	0	0	0	18	0
38	14	0	18	0	3	0	29	0	4	0	17	0	8	0	3	0	0	0	32	0
39	10	0	22	0	1	0	31	0	13	1	13	0	6	0	0	0	0	0	32	0
40	18	0	29	0	2	0	45	0	11	1	20	1	11	0	4	0	1	0	47	0
41	29	0	35	0	3	0	61	1	7	0	30	1	24	0	2	0	1	0	64	0
42	36	0	50	1	8	0	78	1	16	1	47	1	18	0	3	0	2	0	86	0
43	53	1	76	1	9	0	120	1	23	1	66	1	33	1	7	0	0	0	129	1
44	59	1	108	1	13	0	154	2	37	2	85	1	39	1	6	0	0	0	167	1
45	56	1	122	1	12	0	166	2	46	3	78	1	48	1	6	0	0	0	178	1
46	64	1	145	1	20	0	189	2	47	3	103	2	44	1	15	0	0	0	209	1
47	83	1	161	2	28	0	216	2	50	3	126	2	52	1	13	0	3	0	244	1
48	82	1	159	2	29	0	212	2	43	3	98	2	81	1	19	0	0	0	241	1
49	114	1	176	2	43	0	247	3	43	3	133	2	92	2	20	0	2	0	290	1

556

Descriptive Statistics and Frequency Distributions of 3YR and 8YR SLH Variables by Sex, Race, grouped SEI, and Total Sample Size.

8YR SLH Variables (from PS-40 to 45) (continued)
Language Comprehension (continued)
Word Identification (PPVT): Raw Score (continued)

Code	Male Freq.	Male %	Female Freq.	Female %	White Freq.	White %	Black Freq.	Black %	0.0-1.9 Freq.	%	2.0-3.9 Freq.	%	4.0-5.9 Freq.	%	6.0-7.9 Freq.	%	8.0-9.5 Freq.	%	Totals Freq.	%
50	118	1	229	2	49	0	298	3	66	4	158	3	88	1	34	1	1	0	347	2
51	1??	1	175	2	60	1	239	2	39	2	148	3	85	1	23	1	4	0	299	2
52	136	1	213	2	58	1	291	3	61	4	147	2	98	2	37	1	6	0	349	2
53	182	2	207	2	58	1	331	3	70	4	155	3	127	2	36	1	1	0	389	2
54	245	2	261	3	86	1	420	4	68	4	245	4	149	3	41	1	3	0	506	3
55	299	3	306	3	111	1	494	5	100	6	255	4	190	3	53	1	7	0	605	3
56	294	3	380	4	136	1	538	6	83	5	299	5	220	4	62	2	10	0	674	3
57	354	4	407	4	159	2	602	6	82	5	342	6	249	4	80	2	8	0	761	4
58	416	4	437	4	243	2	610	6	91	6	355	6	267	4	115	3	25	1	853	4
59	410	4	457	5	304	3	563	6	89	6	330	6	312	5	118	3	18	1	867	4
60	386	4	459	5	326	3	519	5	67	4	309	5	311	5	131	3	27	1	845	4
61	405	4	369	4	347	3	427	4	47	3	291	5	263	4	141	4	32	1	774	4
62	468	5	423	4	422	4	469	5	53	3	314	5	303	5	177	4	44	2	891	4
63	418	4	372	4	442	4	348	4	54	3	205	3	273	5	202	5	56	2	790	4
64	408	4	365	4	442	4	331	3	54	3	181	3	284	5	188	5	66	3	773	4
65	376	4	347	4	462	5	261	3	28	2	173	3	259	4	191	5	72	3	723	4
66	370	4	349	4	495	5	224	2	30	2	156	3	250	4	201	5	82	4	719	4
67	357	4	330	3	480	5	207	2	30	2	159	3	210	4	190	5	98	4	687	3
68	383	4	347	4	551	6	179	2	23	1	148	3	235	4	216	5	108	5	730	4
69	371	4	347	4	557	5	161	2	11	1	137	2	215	4	218	5	137	6	718	3
70	337	3	309	3	516	5	130	1	21	1	108	2	191	3	200	5	126	5	646	3
71	326	3	312	3	534	5	104	1	12	1	83	1	188	3	205	5	150	7	638	3
72	317	3	238	2	455	5	100	1	11	1	89	2	143	2	185	5	127	6	555	3
73	268	3	208	2	412	4	64	1	6	0	46	1	121	2	153	4	150	7	476	2
74	266	3	170	2	378	3	58	1	5	0	47	1	105	2	158	4	121	5	436	2
75	234	2	143	1	344	3	33	0	4	0	29	0	95	2	111	3	138	6	377	2
76	199	2	97	1	271	3	25	0	6	0	25	0	74	1	96	2	95	4	296	1
77	162	2	99	1	245	2	16	0	4	0	22	0	45	1	89	2	101	4	261	1
78	146	1	61	1	194	2	13	0	4	0	15	0	32	1	69	2	87	4	207	1
79	113	1	71	1	173	2	11	0	2	0	20	0	24	0	63	2	75	3	184	1
80	99	1	37	0	131	1	5	0	2	0	10	0	23	0	39	1	62	3	136	1
81	63	1	36	0	90	1	9	0	2	0	3	0	17	0	32	1	45	2	99	0
82	34	0	14	0	43	0	5	0	0	0	4	0	6	0	12	0	26	1	48	0
83	30	0	16	0	45	0	1	0	0	0	4	0	4	0	20	0	21	1	46	0
84	22	0	7	0	29	0	0	0	1	0	1	0	2	0	13	0	12	1	29	0
85	13	0	9	0	21	0	1	0	0	0	0	0	6	0	8	0	8	0	22	0

557

Descriptive Statistics and Frequency Distributions of 3YR and 8YR SLH Variables
by Sex, Race, grouped SEI, and Total Sample Size.

Code	Male Freq.	Male %	Female Freq.	Female %	White Freq.	White %	Black Freq.	Black %	0.0-1.9 Freq.	0.0-1.9 %	2.0-3.9 Freq.	2.0-3.9 %	4.0-5.9 Freq.	4.0-5.9 %	6.0-7.9 Freq.	6.0-7.9 %	8.0-9.5 Freq.	8.0-9.5 %	Totals Freq.	Totals %
8YR SLH Variables (from PS-40 to 45) (continued)																				
Language Comprehension (continued)																				
Word Identification (PPVT): Raw Score (continued)																				
86	24	0	10	0	33	0	1	0		0	3	0	5	0	11	0	15	1	34	0
87	23	0	7	0	28	0	2	0		0	2	0	4	0	7	0	17	1	30	0
88	7	0	2	0	8	0	1	0		0	0	0	2	0	5	0	2	0	9	0
89	22	0	4	0	25	0	1	0		0	1	0	1	0	9	0	16	1	26	0
90	11	0	3	0	12	0	2	0		0	1	0	3	0	4	0	6	0	14	0
91	14	0	6	0	20	0	0	0		0	0	0	3	0	6	0	10	0	20	0
92	9	0	3	0	11	0	1	0		0	1	0	1	0	2	0	9	0	12	0
93	10	0	3	0	13	0	0	0		0	0	0	0	0	4	0	9	0	13	0
94	8	0	4	0	12	0	0	0		0	1	0	1	0	3	0	7	0	12	0
95	7	0	7	0	14	0	0	0		0	0	0	1	0	3	0	10	0	14	0
96	3	0	3	0	6	0	0	0		0	1	0	1	0	1	0	4	0	6	0
97	8	0	5	0	13	0	0	0		0	0	0	2	0	3	0	8	0	13	0
98	4	0	6	0	7	0	3	0		0	2	0	0	0	3	0	5	0	10	0
99	1	0	1	0	2	0	0	0		0	0	0	0	0	0	0	2	0	2	0
100	2	0	5	0	7	0	0	0		0	0	0	0	0	2	0	5	0	7	0
101	1	0	0	0	1	0	0	0		0	0	0	0	0	0	0	1	0	1	0
102	3	0	0	0	3	0	0	0		0	1	0	0	0	2	0	0	0	3	0
103	0	0	0	0	0	0	0	0		0	0	0	0	0	0	0	0	0	0	0
104	1	0	1	0	2	0	0	0		0	0	0	0	0	0	0	2	0	2	0
105	2	0	0	0	2	0	0	0		0	0	0	0	0	1	0	0	0	2	0
106	2	0	1	0	2	0	1	0		0	1	0	0	0	0	0	2	0	3	0
107	0	0	0	0	1	0	0	0		0	0	0	0	0	0	0	1	0	1	0
108	1	0	1	0	1	0	0	0		0	0	0	1	0	1	0	0	0	1	0
109	0	0	0	0	1	0	0	0		0	0	0	0	0	0	0	1	0	1	0
110	1	0	1	0	1	0	0	0		0	1	0	1	0	1	0	1	0	2	0
111	0	0	0	0	1	0	0	0		0	0	0	0	0	0	0	0	0	0	0
112	2	0	1	0	1	0	0	0		0	0	0	0	0	1	0	1	0	2	0
113	0	0	0	0	2	0	0	0		0	0	0	0	0	0	0	0	0	0	0
114	0	0	0	0	0	0	0	0		0	0	0	0	0	0	0	0	0	0	0
115	0	0	0	0	0	0	0	0		0	0	0	0	0	0	0	0	0	0	0
116	3	0	0	0	3	0	0	0		0	0	0	0	0	1	0	2	0	3	0
117	0	0	0	0	0	0	0	0		0	0	0	0	0	0	0	0	0	0	0
118	0	0	0	0	0	0	0	0		0	0	0	0	0	0	0	0	0	0	0
119	0	0	0	0	0	0	0	0		0	0	0	0	0	0	0	0	0	0	0
120	0	0	0	0	0	0	0	0		0	0	0	0	0	0	0	0	0	0	0
121	0	0	0	0	0	0	0	0		0	0	0	0	0	0	0	0	0	0	0

Descriptive Statistics and Frequency Distributions of 3YR and 8YR SLH Variables
by Sex, Race, grouped SEI, and Total Sample Size.

8YR SLH Variables (from PS-40 to 45) (continued)
Language Comprehension (continued)
Word Identification (PPVT): Raw Score (continued)

Code	Male Freq.	%	Female Freq.	%	White Freq.	%	Black Freq.	%	0.0-1.9 Freq.	%	2.0-3.9 Freq.	%	4.0-5.9 Freq.	%	6.0-7.9 Freq.	%	8.0-9.5 Freq.	%	Totals Freq.	%
122																				
123																				
124																				
125																				
126																				
127																				
128																				
129																				
130																				
131																				
132																				
133																				
134																				
135																				
136																				
137																				
138																				
139																				
140																				
141																				
142																				
143																				
144																				
145																				
146																				
147																				
148																				
149																				
150																				
NIDF	131		144		55		220		31		97		94		41		12		275	
Adequate	9,927	99	9,782	99	10,014	99	9,695	99	1,585	99	5,855	99	5,940	99	4,053	100	2,276	100	19,709	99
mean	64		61		68		57		55		58		62		67		72		62	
standard deviation	10		9.7		8.5		8.4		8.7		8.8		8.7		8.5		8.4		10	

559

Descriptive Statistics and Frequency Distributions of 3YR and 8YR SLH Variables by Sex, Race, grouped SEI, and Total Sample Size.

8YR SLH Variables (from PS-40 to 45) (continued)
Language Comprehension (continued)
Orientation: Total Score

Code	Male Freq.	%	Female Freq.	%	White Freq.	%	Black Freq.	%	0.0-1.9 Freq.	%	2.0-3.9 Freq.	%	4.0-5.9 Freq.	%	6.0-7.9 Freq.	%	8.0-9.5 Freq.	%	Totals Freq.	%
0	14	0	4	0	5	0	13	0	1	0	8	0	5	0	3	0	1	0	18	0
1	20	0	8	0	5	0	23	0	5	0	14	0	7	0	2	0	0	0	28	0
2	76	1	45	0	29	0	92	1	26	2	57	1	30	1	7	0	1	0	121	1
3	182	2	142	1	102	1	222	2	57	4	151	3	81	1	28	1	7	0	324	2
4	486	5	401	4	249	2	638	7	143	9	401	7	264	4	67	2	12	1	887	4
5	877	9	759	8	498	5	1,138	12	224	14	695	12	521	9	161	4	35	3	1,636	8
6	1,182	12	1,174	12	748	7	1,608	16	299	19	958	16	735	12	301	7	63	3	2,356	12
7	1,502	15	1,476	15	1,135	11	1,843	19	308	19	1,081	18	925	15	507	12	157	7	2,978	15
8	1,509	15	1,530	16	1,401	14	1,638	17	225	14	939	16	1,001	17	641	16	233	10	3,039	15
9	1,363	14	1,392	14	1,619	16	1,136	12	150	9	682	12	924	15	660	16	339	15	2,755	14
10	1,193	12	1,275	13	1,684	17	734	8	98	6	498	8	691	12	707	17	474	21	2,468	12
11	839	8	898	9	1,319	13	418	4	40	3	261	4	480	8	519	13	437	19	1,737	9
12	755	8	757	8	1,301	13	211	2	24	2	154	3	316	5	478	12	540	23	1,512	8
NIDF	136		142		53		225		31		101		93		41		12		278	
Adequate	9,985	100	9,851	100	10,080	100	9,756	100	1,596	100	5,897	100	5,978	100	4,072	100	2,293	100	19,836	100
mean	7.6		7.8		8.3		7.1		6.6		7.0		7.7		8.4		9.2		7.7	
standard deviation	2.2		2.1		2.0		2.0		2.0		2.1		2.1		1.9		1.7		2.1	

Understanding a Story: Raw Score

Code	Male Freq.	%	Female Freq.	%	White Freq.	%	Black Freq.	%	0.0-1.9 Freq.	%	2.0-3.9 Freq.	%	4.0-5.9 Freq.	%	6.0-7.9 Freq.	%	8.0-9.5 Freq.	%	Totals Freq.	%
0	284	3	357	4	189	2	452	5	94	6	262	4	183	3	77	2	25	1	641	3
1	935	9	1,134	12	690	7	1,379	14	264	17	782	13	647	11	286	7	90	4	2,069	10
2	1,981	20	2,229	23	1,694	17	2,516	26	465	29	1,436	24	1,310	22	713	17	286	12	4,210	21
3	2,711	27	2,741	28	2,735	27	2,717	28	387	24	1,696	29	1,685	28	1,129	28	555	24	5,452	27
4	2,382	24	2,139	22	2,734	27	1,787	18	274	17	1,120	19	1,337	22	1,075	26	715	31	4,521	23
5	1,698	17	1,258	13	2,049	20	907	9	115	7	599	10	815	14	800	20	627	27	2,956	15
NIDF	143		145		57		231		32		105		96		42		13		288	
Adequate	9,977	100	9,843	100	10,080	100	9,740	100	1,596	100	5,886	100	5,970	100	4,073	100	2,295	100	19,820	100
mean	3.1		2.9		3.3		2.7		2.5		2.8		3.0		3.3		3.6		3.0	
standard deviation	1.3		1.3		1.3		1.3		1.3		1.3		1.3		1.3		1.2		1.3	

Oral Reading: Total Passage Score

Code	Male Freq.	%	Female Freq.	%	White Freq.	%	Black Freq.	%	0.0-1.9 Freq.	%	2.0-3.9 Freq.	%	4.0-5.9 Freq.	%	6.0-7.9 Freq.	%	8.0-9.5 Freq.	%	Totals Freq.	%
0	1,211	12	539	5	620	6	1,130	12	279	17	779	13	527	9	146	4	19	1	1,750	9
1	181	2	82	1	71	1	192	2	35	2	123	2	77	1	25	1	3	0	263	1
2	297	3	136	1	130	1	303	3	60	4	175	3	142	2	45	1	11	0	433	2
3	189	2	98	1	87	1	200	2	43	3	110	2	89	1	37	1	8	0	287	1
4	242	2	127	1	119	1	250	3	43	3	148	3	126	2	46	1	6	0	369	2

Descriptive Statistics and Frequency Distributions of 3YR and 8YR SLH Variables
by Sex, Race, grouped SEI, and Total Sample Size.

8YR SLH Variables (from PS-40 to 45) (continued)
Oral Reading: Total Passage Score (continued)

Code	Male Freq.	Male %	Female Freq.	Female %	White Freq.	White %	Black Freq.	Black %	0.0-1.9 Freq.	%	2.0-3.9 Freq.	%	4.0-5.9 Freq.	%	6.0-7.9 Freq.	%	8.0-9.5 Freq.	%	Totals Freq.	%
5	285	3	172	2	142	1	315	3	67	4	187	3	148	2	38	1	17	1	457	2
6	333	3	198	2	169	2	362	4	68	4	221	4	159	3	67	2	16	1	531	3
7	406	4	246	2	209	2	443	5	82	5	260	4	203	3	87	2	20	1	652	3
8	416	4	348	4	247	2	517	5	79	5	311	5	256	4	98	2	20	1	764	4
9	463	5	380	4	318	3	525	5	85	5	352	6	262	4	116	3	28	1	843	4
10	327	3	267	3	234	2	360	4	59	3	214	4	192	3	107	3	22	1	594	3
11	346	3	331	3	262	2	415	4	75	5	221	4	217	4	125	3	39	2	677	3
12	271	3	280	3	224	2	327	3	45	3	194	3	183	3	92	2	37	2	551	3
13	310	3	286	3	254	3	342	3	63	4	192	3	185	3	120	3	36	2	596	3
14	279	3	277	3	230	2	326	3	44	3	185	3	180	3	103	3	44	2	556	3
15	274	3	293	3	281	3	286	3	48	3	174	3	177	3	127	3	41	2	567	3
16	280	3	284	3	279	3	285	3	35	2	177	3	172	3	134	3	46	2	564	3
17	239	2	272	3	259	3	252	3	40	2	156	3	168	3	98	2	49	2	511	3
18	263	3	280	3	287	3	255	3	37	2	159	3	163	3	124	3	60	3	543	3
19	257	3	269	3	273	3	253	3	24	1	136	2	181	3	124	3	61	3	526	3
20	277	3	315	3	322	3	270	3	35	2	171	3	198	3	131	3	57	2	592	3
21	256	3	306	3	323	3	239	2	27	2	147	2	183	3	121	3	84	4	562	3
22	243	2	325	3	349	3	219	2	35	2	137	2	171	3	146	4	79	3	568	3
23	242	2	294	3	319	3	217	2	35	2	116	2	177	3	133	3	75	3	536	3
24	215	2	304	3	305	3	214	2	26	2	111	2	159	3	121	3	102	4	519	3
25	206	2	307	3	328	3	185	2	33	2	100	2	147	3	150	4	83	4	513	3
26	211	2	307	3	349	3	169	2	15	1	92	2	162	3	150	4	99	4	518	3
27	173	2	248	2	280	3	141	1	15	1	79	1	133	2	110	3	84	4	421	2
28	158	2	250	3	280	3	128	1	12	1	78	1	120	2	125	3	73	3	408	2
29	149	1	241	2	275	3	115	1	12	1	81	1	91	2	114	3	92	4	390	2
30	139	1	229	2	258	3	110	1	6	0	60	1	90	2	120	3	92	4	368	2
31	113	1	210	2	243	2	80	1	7	0	43	1	89	1	105	3	79	3	323	2
32	100	1	169	2	204	2	65	1	9	1	30	1	65	1	90	2	75	3	269	1
33	97	1	173	2	216	2	54	1	5	0	31	1	67	1	102	2	65	3	270	1
34	77	1	140	1	169	2	48	0	2	0	32	1	53	1	62	2	68	3	217	1
35	62	1	127	1	157	2	32	0	1	0	24	0	41	1	65	2	58	3	189	1
36	66	1	119	1	142	1	43	0	4	0	21	0	38	1	58	1	64	3	185	1
37	69	1	103	1	147	1	28	0	2	0	18	0	44	1	57	1	51	2	172	1
38	56	1	91	1	128	1	19	0	4	0	13	0	29	0	46	1	55	2	147	1
39	25	0	87	1	95	1	17	0	2	0	17	0	23	0	36	1	34	1	112	1
40	39	0	56	1	75	1	20	0	2	0	9	0	22	0	26	1	36	2	95	0
41	32	0	78	1	103	1	7	0	0	0	2	0	20	0	35	1	53	2	110	1

Descriptive Statistics and Frequency Distributions of 3YR and 8YR SLH Variables by Sex, Race, grouped SEI, and Total Sample Size.

	Male		Female		White		Black		0.0–1.9		2.0–3.9		4.0–5.9		6.0–7.9		8.0–9.5		Totals	
Code	Freq.	%	Freq.	%	Freq.	%	Freq.	%	Freq.	%	Freq.	%	Freq.	%	Freq.	%	Freq.	%	Freq.	%
8YR SLH Variables (from PS–40 to 45) (continued)																				
Oral Reading: Total Passage Score (continued)																				
42	25	0	54	1	70	1	9	0	0	0	4	0	13	0	22	1	40	2	79	0
43	30	0	48	0	74	1	4	0	0	0	6	0	12	0	29	1	31	1	78	0
44	14	0	34	0	47	0	1	0	0	0	1	0	6	0	22	1	19	1	48	0
45	15	0	24	0	36	0	3	0	0	0	2	0	9	0	17	0	11	0	39	0
46	10	0	17	0	24	0	3	0	0	0	2	0	6	0	4	0	15	1	27	0
47	9	0	13	0	22	0	0	0	0	0	1	0	6	0	3	0	12	1	22	0
48	3	0	19	0	22	0	0	0	0	0	0	0	3	0	9	0	10	0	22	0
49	8	0	5	0	13	0	0	0	0	0	0	0	1	0	4	0	8	0	13	0
50	5	0	2	0	7	0	0	0	0	0	1	0	0	0	1	0	5	0	7	0
51	3	0	3	0	5	0	1	0	1	0	0	0	1	0	1	0	3	0	6	0
52	0	0	1	0	1	0	0	0	0	0	0	0	0	0	1	0	0	0	1	0
53	0	0	0	0	0	0	0	0	0	0	0	0	0	0	0	0	0	0	0	0
54	0	0	0	0	0	0	0	0	0	0	0	0	0	0	0	0	0	0	0	0
NIDF	138		138		64		212		30		97		93		41		15		276	
Adequate	9,922	99	9,815	100	10,014	100	9,723	100	1,591	99	5,866	99	5,939	99	4,055	100	2,286	100	19,737	100
mean	14		19		20		13		11		13		16		21		26		17	
standard deviation	11		11		12		9.5		8.8		9.5		10		11		10		11	
Silent Reading: Test Paragraph Total Score																				
0	3,154	32	1,950	20	1,661	17	3,443	35	658	41	2,130	36	1,609	27	603	15	104	5	5,104	26
1	1,366	14	1,313	13	893	9	1,786	18	332	21	1,047	18	844	14	363	9	93	4	2,679	14
2	1,484	15	1,497	15	1,269	13	1,712	18	251	16	1,011	17	1,002	17	540	13	177	8	2,981	15
3	1,453	15	1,658	17	1,746	17	1,365	14	205	13	797	14	1,014	17	761	19	334	15	3,111	16
4	1,411	14	1,885	19	2,286	23	1,010	10	111	7	607	10	914	15	964	24	700	30	3,296	17
5	1,092	11	1,547	16	2,205	22	434	4	40	3	287	5	581	10	840	21	891	39	2,639	13
NIDF	174		153		88		239		34		121		109		51		12		327	
Adequate	9,705	98	9,698	99	9,943	99	9,460	97	1,521	96	5,719	98	5,856	99	4,026	99	2,281	100	19,403	98
mean	2.0		2.5		2.9		1.6		1.3		1.6		2.1		2.9		3.8		2.2	
standard deviation	1.8		1.7		1.7		1.5		1.4		1.6		1.7		1.7		1.4		1.8	
Morphology (Auditory Vocal Automatic Test): Raw Score																				
0	39	0	18	0	9	0	48	0	16	1	23	0	16	0	1	0	1	0	57	0
1	54	1	41	0	11	0	84	1	25	2	47	1	20	0	3	0	0	0	95	0
2	92	1	60	1	10	0	142	1	40	3	64	1	38	1	10	0	0	0	152	1

Descriptive Statistics and Frequency Distributions of 3YR and 8YR SLH Variables by Sex, Race, grouped SEI, and Total Sample Size.

Code	Male Freq.	Male %	Female Freq.	Female %	White Freq.	White %	Black Freq.	Black %	0.0-1.9 Freq.	0.0-1.9 %	2.0-3.9 Freq.	2.0-3.9 %	4.0-5.9 Freq.	4.0-5.9 %	6.0-7.9 Freq.	6.0-7.9 %	8.0-9.5 Freq.	8.0-9.5 %	Totals Freq.	Totals %
8YR SLH Variables (from PS-40 to 45) (continued)																				
Morphology (Auditory Vocal Automatic Test): Raw Score (continued)																				
3	147	1	134	1	17	0	264	3	62	4	125	2	71	1	21	1	2	0	281	1
4	110	1	79	1	11	0	178	2	35	2	93	2	48	1	10	0	3	0	189	1
5	147	2	134	1	19	0	262	2	73	5	145	2	54	1	9	0	0	0	281	1
6	189	2	193	2	17	0	365	4	90	6	179	3	89	1	21	1	3	0	382	2
7	244	2	234	2	35	0	443	5	98	6	227	4	129	2	21	1	3	0	478	2
8	340	3	323	3	45	0	618	6	110	7	312	5	196	3	41	1	4	0	663	3
9	387	4	376	4	78	1	685	7	120	8	362	6	218	5	59	1	4	0	763	4
10	378	4	411	4	111	1	678	7	93	6	363	6	245	4	84	2	4	0	789	4
11	458	5	471	5	173	2	756	8	127	8	412	7	293	5	85	2	12	1	929	5
12	578	6	492	5	291	3	779	8	96	6	466	8	354	6	120	3	34	1	1,070	5
13	595	6	630	6	474	5	751	8	96	6	477	8	432	7	182	4	38	2	1,225	6
14	782	8	805	8	804	8	783	8	114	7	508	9	585	10	297	7	83	4	1,587	8
15	776	8	751	8	911	9	616	6	103	6	473	8	508	9	331	8	112	5	1,527	8
16	945	9	886	9	1,243	12	588	6	85	5	434	7	592	10	503	12	217	9	1,831	9
17	997	10	922	9	1,392	14	527	5	85	5	416	7	620	10	519	13	279	12	1,919	10
18	877	9	832	8	1,299	13	410	4	55	3	324	5	490	8	487	12	353	15	1,709	9
19	739	7	752	8	1,152	11	339	3	36	2	231	4	412	7	458	11	354	15	1,491	8
20	517	5	549	6	847	8	219	2	20	1	120	2	292	5	357	9	277	12	1,066	5
21	357	4	441	4	652	6	146	1	14	1	69	1	165	3	274	7	276	12	798	4
22	233	2	318	3	481	5	70	1	6	0	21	0	102	2	183	4	239	10	551	3
NIDF	153		151		66		238		32		109		104		46		13		304	
Adequate	9,919	100	9,802	100	10,034	100	9,687	100	1,586	99	5,859	100	5,935	100	4,053	100	2,288	100	19,721	100
mean	14		14		17		12		11		12		14		17		18		14	
standard deviation	4.8		4.7		3.2		4.7		4.9		4.6		4.4		3.6		2.7		4.7	
Connected Discourse																				
Number of Concepts Expressed																				
0	91	1	68	1	55	1	104	1	28	2	63	1	49	1	14	0	5	0	159	1
1	43	0	32	0	31	0	44	0	7	0	35	1	18	0	12	0	3	0	75	0
2	49	1	58	1	49	0	58	1	19	1	42	1	23	0	20	0	3	0	107	1
3	83	1	76	1	56	1	103	1	28	2	64	1	43	1	15	0	9	0	159	1
4	144	1	125	1	129	1	140	1	34	2	103	2	67	1	50	1	15	1	269	1
5	194	2	177	2	146	1	225	2	42	3	132	2	118	2	58	1	21	1	371	2
6	308	3	295	3	271	3	332	3	64	4	223	4	174	3	96	2	46	2	603	3
7	451	5	432	4	389	4	494	5	77	5	352	6	271	5	131	3	52	2	883	4
8	578	6	564	6	491	5	651	7	121	8	407	7	330	6	200	5	84	4	1,142	6

Descriptive Statistics and Frequency Distributions of 3YR and 8YR SLH Variables by Sex, Race, grouped SEI, and Total Sample Size.

Code	Male Freq.	Male %	Female Freq.	Female %	White Freq.	White %	Black Freq.	Black %	0.0-1.9 Freq.	0.0-1.9 %	2.0-3.9 Freq.	2.0-3.9 %	4.0-5.9 Freq.	4.0-5.9 %	6.0-7.9 Freq.	6.0-7.9 %	8.0-9.5 Freq.	8.0-9.5 %	Totals Freq.	Totals %
8YR SLH Variables (from PS-40 to 45) (continued)																				
Connected Discourse (continued)																				
Number of Concepts Expressed (continued)																				
9	783	8	718	7	647	6	854	9	156	10	510	9	499	8	238	6	98	4	1,501	8
10	986	10	909	9	873	9	1,022	11	162	10	614	10	588	10	365	9	166	7	1,895	10
11	1,134	11	1,005	10	1,017	10	1,122	12	171	11	679	12	660	11	423	10	206	9	2,139	11
12	1,180	12	1,189	12	1,185	12	1,184	12	175	11	707	12	745	13	485	12	257	11	2,369	12
13	1,220	12	1,174	12	1,268	13	1,126	12	182	11	628	11	792	13	491	12	301	13	2,394	12
14	1,062	11	1,138	12	1,263	13	937	10	145	9	534	9	601	10	556	14	364	16	2,200	11
15	868	9	920	9	1,079	11	709	7	86	5	432	7	509	9	457	11	304	13	1,788	9
16	503	5	601	6	706	7	398	4	56	4	224	4	300	5	300	7	224	10	1,104	6
17	204	2	286	3	310	3	180	2	29	2	102	2	129	2	119	3	111	5	490	2
18	66	1	57	1	87	1	36	0	6	0	18	0	31	1	40	1	28	1	123	1
NIDF	187		179		96		270		43		131		126		52		14		366	
mean	11		11		12		11		10		11		11		12		13		11	
standard deviation	3.4		3.4		3.3		3.4		3.6		3.5		3.3		3.2		3.0		3.4	
Sequence																				
Excellent	3,052	31	3,240	33	3,775	38	2,517	26	390	25	1,644	28	1,772	30	1,385	34	1,101	48	6,292	32
Adequate	6,015	61	5,832	60	5,636	56	6,211	64	990	63	3,625	62	3,704	63	2,415	60	1,113	48	11,847	60
Poor	810	8	698	7	593	6	915	9	183	12	553	9	437	7	253	6	82	4	1,508	8
NIDF	257		233		144		346		68		178		160		69		15		490	
Elaboration																				
Excellent	1,006	10	1,121	11	1,063	11	1,064	11	135	9	568	10	641	11	506	12	277	12	2,127	11
Adequate	6,348	64	6,404	66	5,869	59	6,883	71	1,095	70	3,995	69	4,063	69	2,518	62	1,081	47	12,752	65
Poor	2,524	26	2,245	23	3,072	31	1,697	18	333	21	1,260	22	1,209	20	1,029	25	938	41	4,769	24
NIDF	256		233		144		345		68		177		160		69		15		489	
Relevance																				
Excellent	3,200	32	3,408	35	3,953	40	2,655	28	432	28	1,661	29	1,808	31	1,468	36	1,239	54	6,608	34
Adequate	6,237	63	5,972	61	5,785	58	6,424	67	1,025	66	3,838	66	3,854	65	2,458	61	1,034	45	12,209	62
Poor	441	4	391	4	268	3	564	6	106	7	324	6	253	4	126	3	23	1	832	4
NIDF	256		232		142		346		68		177		158		70		15		488	
Grammar																				
Excellent	1,720	17	2,071	21	2,729	27	1,062	11	147	9	660	11	927	16	1,049	26	1,008	44	3,791	19
Adequate	7,506	76	7,225	74	6,958	70	7,773	81	1,237	79	4,668	80	4,688	79	2,871	71	1,267	55	14,731	75
Poor	650	7	475	5	316	3	809	8	179	11	495	9	299	5	132	3	20	1	1,125	6
NIDF	258		232		145		345		68		177		159		70		16		490	

Descriptive Statistics and Frequency Distributions of 3YR and 8YR SLH Variables by Sex, Race, grouped SEI, and Total Sample Size.

Code	Male Freq.	Male %	Female Freq.	Female %	White Freq.	White %	Black Freq.	Black %	0.0-1.9 Freq.	0.0-1.9 %	2.0-3.9 Freq.	2.0-3.9 %	4.0-5.9 Freq.	4.0-5.9 %	6.0-7.9 Freq.	6.0-7.9 %	8.0-9.5 Freq.	8.0-9.5 %	Totals Freq.	Totals %
8YR SLH Variables (from PS-40 to 45) (continued)																				
Connected Discourse (continued)																				
Overall Evaluation																				
Normal	9,102	91	9,133	93	9,524	95	8,711	89	1,336	84	5,233	89	5,515	93	3,893	96	2,258	98	18,235	92
Suspect	636	6	549	6	412	4	773	8	187	12	499	8	339	6	135	3	25	1	1,185	6
Abnormal	210	2	154	2	111	1	253	3	68	4	146	2	98	2	40	1	12	1	364	2
NIDF	186		167		101		252		40		122		121		54		16		353	
Adequate	9,889	99	9,781	100	10,004	99	9,666	100	1,631	100	5,835	100	5,919	99	4,056	100	2,291	100	19,670	100
Writing from Dictation: Total Score, Lists 1-3																				
0	49	0	30	0	22	0	57	1	13	1	29	0	29	0	7	0	1	0	79	0
1	32	0	13	0	15	0	30	0	6	0	27	1	9	0	1	0	2	0	45	0
2	46	0	17	0	24	0	39	0	9	1	31	1	16	0	5	0	2	0	63	0
3	57	1	19	0	30	0	46	0	14	1	32	1	24	0	6	0	0	0	76	0
4	106	1	44	0	47	0	103	1	34	2	66	1	37	1	12	0	1	0	150	1
5	167	1	59	1	73	1	153	2	47	3	100	2	61	1	14	0	4	0	226	1
6	307	3	115	1	156	2	266	3	79	5	198	3	106	2	31	1	8	0	422	2
7	423	4	212	2	221	2	414	4	96	6	264	4	201	3	65	2	9	0	635	3
8	656	7	337	3	331	3	662	7	140	9	444	8	285	5	103	3	21	1	993	5
9	639	6	418	4	385	4	672	7	129	8	451	8	330	6	122	3	25	1	1,057	5
10	796	8	520	5	489	5	827	8	143	9	525	9	405	7	195	5	48	2	1,316	7
11	843	8	738	7	645	6	936	10	147	9	548	9	539	9	254	6	93	4	1,581	8
12	1,200	12	1,080	11	1,030	10	1,250	13	188	12	736	12	740	12	443	11	173	8	2,280	12
13	1,754	18	1,865	19	1,948	19	1,671	17	258	16	980	17	1,120	19	837	21	424	18	3,619	18
14	2,898	29	4,381	44	4,658	46	2,621	27	288	18	1,459	25	2,062	35	1,983	49	1,487	65	7,279	37
NIDF	161		155		74		242		40		110		109		44		13		316	
Adequate	9,926	100	9,833	100	10,041	100	9,718	100	1,584	99	5,877	100	5,940	100	4,066	100	2,292	100	19,759	100
mean	11		12		12		11		10		11		12		13		13		12	
standard deviation	2.9		2.4		2.4		2.9		3.2		2.9		2.6		2.1		1.5		2.7	
Speech Mechanism																				
Lips: Retraction																				
Pass	9,849	99	9,796	99	9,958	99	9,687	99	1,575	98	5,847	99	5,915	99	4,032	99	2,276	99	19,645	99
Fail	74	1	34	0	58	1	50	1	17	1	39	1	32	1	13	0	7	0	108	1
Pass with concomitant movement	59	1	35	0	68	1	26	0	7	0	13	0	28	0	29	1	17	1	94	0
Fail with concomitant movement	7	0	4	0	8	0	3	0	1	0	1	0	5	0	3	0	1	0	11	0
NIDF	145		134		56		223		31		100		93		45		10		279	

Descriptive Statistics and Frequency Distributions of 3YR and 8YR SLH Variables
by Sex, Race, grouped SEI, and Total Sample Size.

Code	Male Freq.	Male %	Female Freq.	Female %	White Freq.	White %	Black Freq.	Black %	0.0-1.9 Freq.	%	2.0-3.9 Freq.	%	4.0-5.9 Freq.	%	6.0-7.9 Freq.	%	8.0-9.5 Freq.	%	Totals Freq.	%
8YR SLH Variables (from PS–40 to 45) (continued)																				
Speech Mechanism (continued)																				
Lips: Protrusion																				
Pass	9,880	99	9,795	99	9,983	99	9,692	99	1,586	99	5,851	99	5,916	99	4,039	99	2,283	99	19,675	99
Fail	71	1	47	0	64	1	54	1	12	1	37	1	42	1	16	0	11	0	118	1
Pass with concomitant movement	29	0	21	0	39	0	11	0	0	0	8	0	16	0	20	0	6	0	50	0
Fail with concomitant movement	6	0	4	0	4	0	6	0	2	0	2	0	4	0			0	0	10	0
NIDF	148		136		58		226		31		102		95		45		11		284	
Tongue: Mid-Line Protrusion																				
Pass	9,856	98	9,784	99	9,965	99	9,675	99	1,585	99	5,832	99	5,900	98	4,038	99	2,285	99	19,640	99
Fail	61	1	28	0	36	0	53	1	7	0	30	1	32	1	14	0	6	0	89	0
Pass with concomitant movement	76	1	56	1	89	1	43	0	8	0	40	1	48	1	27	1	9	0	132	1
Fail with concomitant movement	3	0	2	0	4	0	1	0	0	0	3	0	1	0	0	0	0	0	5	0
NIDF	138		133		54		217		30		95		92		43		11		271	
Tongue: Lateral Protrusion																				
Pass	8,209	82	8,389	85	8,218	81	8,380	86	1,348	84	5,024	85	4,961	83	3,389	83	1,876	81	16,598	83
Fail	115	1	75	1	79	1	111	1	19	1	61	1	60	1	34	1	16	1	190	1
Pass with concomitant movement	1,607	16	1,367	14	1,765	17	1,209	12	213	13	789	13	925	15	641	16	406	18	2,974	15
Fail with concomitant movement	55	1	37	0	29	0	63	1	20	1	26	0	29	0	12	0	5	0	92	0
NIDF	148		135		57		226		31		100		98		46		8		283	
Tongue: Elevation																				
Pass	9,510	95	9,560	97	9,696	96	9,374	96	1,533	96	5,678	96	5,737	96	3,893	96	2,229	97	19,070	96
Fail	245	2	151	2	149	2	247	3	46	3	122	2	116	2	86	2	26	1	396	2
Pass with concomitant movement	175	2	127	1	209	2	93	1	10	0	73	1	100	2	81	2	38	2	302	2
Fail with concomitant movement	36	0	14	0	27	0	23	0	7	0	14	0	16	0	7	0	6	0	50	0
NIDF	168		151		67		252		35		113		104		55		12		319	
Soft Palate Function																				
Normal	9,807	98	9,699	98	9,866	98	9,640	99	1,578	99	5,771	98	5,878	99	4,005	99	2,274	99	19,506	98
Abnormal	152	2	149	2	214	2	87	1	16	1	110	2	87	1	60	1	28	1	301	2
NIDF	175		155		68		262		37		119		108		57		9		330	
Speech Production																				
Rate of Speech Sounds																				
Adequate	9,802	98	9,781	99	9,958	98	9,625	98	1,564	97	5,810	98	5,894	98	4,032	99	2,283	99	19,583	98
Too fast	27	0	12	0	17	0	17	0	2	0	12	0	12	0	8	0	5	0	39	0
Too slow	46	0	26	0	34	0	38	0	12	1	22	0	18	0	14	0	6	0	72	0
Irregular	89	1	37	0	57	1	69	1	16	1	44	1	47	1	15	0	4	0	126	1
Combination of codes	6	0	2	0	4	0	4	0	1	0	3	0	2	0	1	0	1	0	8	0
NIDF	164		145		73		236		36		109		100		52		12		309	

Descriptive Statistics and Frequency Distributions of 3YR and 8YR SLH Variables by Sex, Race, grouped SEI, and Total Sample Size.

8YR SLH Variables (from PS-40 to 45) (continued)

Speech Production (continued)

Code	Male Freq.	%	Female Freq.	%	White Freq.	%	Black Freq.	%	0.0-1.9 Freq.	%	2.0-3.9 Freq.	%	4.0-5.9 Freq.	%	6.0-7.9 Freq.	%	8.0-9.5 Freq.	%	Totals Freq.	%
Dysfluent Events																				
None	9,492	95	9,581	97	9,859	98	9,214	94	1,490	93	5,612	95	5,765	96	3,963	97	2,243	97	19,073	96
Some	464	5	267	3	211	2	520	5	99	6	264	4	205	3	106	3	57	2	731	4
Many	40	0	14	0	19	0	35	0	10	1	23	0	12	0	8	0	1	0	54	0
NIDF	138		141		59		220		32		101		91		45		10		279	
Struggle Behavior																				
None	9,866	99	9,796	99	10,006	99	9,656	99	1,577	99	5,835	99	5,921	99	4,047	99	2,282	99	19,662	99
Some	107	1	55	1	61	1	101	1	18	1	53	1	52	1	23	1	16	1	162	1
Many	17	0	10	0	18	0	9	0	3	0	9	0	7	0	5	0	3	0	27	0
NIDF	144		142		63		223		33		103		93		47		10		286	
Voice: Pitch																				
Adequate	9,758	97	9,682	98	9,828	97	9,612	98	1,557	97	5,792	98	5,837	97	3,994	98	2,260	98	19,440	98
Too high	109	1	37	0	105	1	41	0	15	1	36	1	49	1	29	1	17	1	146	1
Too low	87	1	121	1	116	1	92	1	18	1	63	1	72	1	38	1	17	1	208	1
Monotonous	23	0	16	0	23	0	16	0	5	0	7	0	13	0	10	0	4	0	39	0
Combination of codes	7	0	4	0	5	0	6	0	2	0	0	0	4	0	1	0	1	0	11	0
NIDF	150		143		71		222		34		102		98		47		12		293	
Voice: Loudness																				
Adequate	9,718	97	9,608	97	9,829	97	9,497	97	1,543	96	5,722	97	5,823	97	3,981	97	2,257	98	19,326	97
Too soft	239	2	239	2	231	2	247	3	54	3	157	3	134	2	93	2	40	2	478	2
Too loud	21	0	15	0	18	0	18	0	1	0	13	0	12	0	7	0	3	0	36	0
NIDF	156		141		70		227		33		108		104		41		11		297	
Voice Quality: Phonation																				
Adequate	8,618	86	8,931	90	8,953	89	8,596	88	1,377	86	5,059	85	5,286	88	3,727	91	2,100	91	17,549	88
Breathiness	97	1	86	1	115	1	68	1	10	1	56	1	60	1	36	1	21	1	183	1
Hoarseness	1,117	11	749	8	888	9	978	10	178	11	685	12	564	9	273	7	166	7	1,866	9
Combination of codes	118	1	69	1	95	1	92	1	26	2	69	1	44	1	39	1	9	0	187	1
NIDF	184		168		97		255		40		131		119		47		15		352	
Voice Quality: Resonance																				
Adequate	9,273	92	9,243	93	9,156	91	9,360	96	1,527	95	5,525	93	5,590	93	3,792	93	2,082	90	18,516	93
Hypernasality	118	1	88	1	136	1	70	1	17	1	72	1	64	1	39	1	14	1	206	1
Hyponasality	584	6	523	5	780	8	327	3	52	3	294	5	317	5	245	6	199	9	1,107	6
NIDF	159		149		76		232		35		109		102		46		16		308	

Descriptive Statistics and Frequency Distributions of 3YR and 8YR SLH Variables by Sex, Race, grouped SEI, and Total Sample Size.

8YR SLH Variables (from PS-40 to 45) (continued)

Speech Production (continued)

Code	Male Freq.	Male %	Female Freq.	Female %	White Freq.	White %	Black Freq.	Black %	0.0-1.9 Freq.	0.0-1.9 %	2.0-3.9 Freq.	2.0-3.9 %	4.0-5.9 Freq.	4.0-5.9 %	6.0-7.9 Freq.	6.0-7.9 %	8.0-9.5 Freq.	8.0-9.5 %	Totals Freq.	Totals %
Intelligibility																				
No difficulty	9,289	93	9,515	96	9,741	96	9,063	93	1,438	90	5,461	93	5,671	95	3,960	97	2,274	99	18,804	95
Some difficulty	581	6	286	3	292	3	575	6	126	8	352	6	261	4	103	3	25	1	867	4
Considerable difficulty	103	1	50	1	49	0	104	1	31	2	68	1	40	1	12	0	2	0	153	1
Verbalized but unintelligible	22	0	10	0	11	0	21	0	7	0	14	0	8	0	3	0	0	0	32	0
No speech	9	0	6	0	5	0	10	0	0	0	6	0	3	0	3	0	3	0	15	0
NIDF	130		136		50		216		29		99		90		41		7		266	
Articulation: Score																				
0	5	0	5	0	6	0	4	0	2	0	6	0	0	0	2	0	0	0	10	0
1	0	0	1	0	0	0	1	0	0	0	0	0	1	0	0	0	0	0	1	0
2	3	0	0	0	1	0	2	0	1	0	1	0	0	0	1	0	0	0	3	0
3	4	0	0	0	2	0	2	0	0	0	3	0	0	0	1	0	0	0	4	0
4	7	0	6	0	7	0	6	0	4	0	4	0	2	0	3	0	0	0	13	0
5	9	0	2	0	4	0	7	0	1	0	5	0	2	0	2	0	1	0	11	0
6	6	0	1	0	4	0	3	0	0	0	3	0	4	0	0	0	0	0	7	0
7	5	0	1	0	2	0	4	0	1	0	4	0	2	0	0	0	0	0	6	0
8	5	0	1	0	1	0	5	0	1	0	4	0	1	0	0	0	0	0	6	0
9	7	0	2	0	2	0	7	0	0	0	3	0	4	0	1	0	0	0	9	0
10	8	0	6	0	5	0	9	0	3	0	5	0	3	0	3	0	0	0	14	0
11	7	0	2	0	3	0	6	0	2	0	4	0	3	0	0	0	0	0	9	0
12	12	0	2	0	5	0	9	0	0	0	10	0	4	0	0	0	0	0	14	0
13	10	0	3	0	6	0	7	0	1	0	6	0	5	0	1	0	0	0	13	0
14	7	0	3	0	6	0	4	0	0	0	2	0	5	0	3	0	0	0	10	0
15	5	0	2	0	5	0	2	0	0	0	4	0	2	0	0	0	1	0	7	0
16	9	0	7	0	7	0	9	0	0	0	8	0	5	0	2	0	1	0	16	0
17	10	0	5	0	5	0	11	0	3	0	9	0	5	0	0	0	0	0	16	0
18	15	0	5	0	6	0	14	0	3	0	9	0	5	0	3	0	0	0	20	0
19	15	0	6	0	8	0	13	0	3	0	10	0	6	0	1	0	1	0	21	0
20	12	0	3	0	5	0	10	0	3	0	9	0	2	0	1	0	0	0	15	0
21	15	0	7	0	7	0	15	0	5	0	7	0	9	0	1	0	0	0	22	0
22	19	0	8	0	7	0	20	0	7	0	13	0	3	0	3	0	1	0	27	0
23	25	0	9	0	10	0	24	0	9	0	12	0	7	0	5	0	1	0	34	0
24	25	0	9	0	11	0	23	0	6	0	16	0	6	0	6	0	1	0	34	0
25	40	0	6	0	15	0	31	0	7	0	22	0	11	0	3	0	3	0	46	0
26	27	0	6	0	9	0	24	0	7	0	9	0	8	0	7	0	2	0	33	0

Descriptive Statistics and Frequency Distributions of 3YR and 8YR SLH Variables by Sex, Race, grouped SEI, and Total Sample Size.

Code	Male Freq.	%	Female Freq.	%	White Freq.	%	Black Freq.	%	0.0-1.9 Freq.	%	2.0-3.9 Freq.	%	4.0-5.9 Freq.	%	6.0-7.9 Freq.	%	8.0-9.5 Freq.	%	Totals Freq.	%
8YR SLH Variables (from PS-40 to 45) (continued)																				
Speech Production (continued)																				
Articulation: Score (continued)																				
27	36	0	19	0	17	0	38	0	8	1	25	0	13	0	6	0	3	0	55	0
28	41	0	26	0	32	0	35	0	10	1	21	0	20	0	10	0	6	0	67	0
29	50	1	18	0	20	0	48	0	10	1	26	0	19	0	8	0	5	0	68	0
30	48	0	19	0	28	0	39	0	5	0	30	1	14	0	12	0	6	0	67	0
31	59	1	46	0	36	0	69	1	17	1	39	1	34	1	11	0	4	0	105	1
32	66	1	33	0	29	0	70	1	16	1	37	1	31	1	10	0	5	0	99	1
33	81	1	49	0	47	0	83	1	20	1	41	1	38	1	28	1	3	0	130	1
34	83	1	51	1	44	0	90	1	13	1	58	1	38	1	20	0	5	0	134	1
35	127	1	61	1	71	1	117	1	18	1	82	1	57	1	14	0	17	1	188	1
36	125	1	76	1	97	1	104	1	18	1	74	1	56	1	34	1	19	1	201	1
37	147	1	92	1	114	1	125	1	20	1	86	1	77	1	37	1	19	1	239	1
38	231	2	159	2	249	2	141	1	26	2	97	2	113	2	92	2	62	3	390	2
39	191	2	119	1	132	1	178	2	40	3	98	2	81	1	55	1	36	2	310	2
40	174	2	116	1	94	1	196	2	36	2	117	2	79	1	40	1	18	1	290	1
41	214	2	162	2	109	1	267	3	53	3	148	3	99	2	49	1	27	1	376	2
42	284	3	211	2	116	1	379	4	67	4	209	4	147	2	48	1	24	1	495	2
43	371	4	297	3	140	1	528	5	105	5	278	5	201	3	62	2	22	1	668	3
44	438	4	414	4	154	2	698	7	120	8	372	6	244	4	93	2	23	1	852	4
45	565	6	593	6	176	2	982	10	158	10	509	9	335	6	125	3	31	1	1,158	6
46	649	6	731	7	254	3	1,126	12	162	10	563	10	427	7	175	4	53	2	1,380	7
47	765	8	777	8	327	3	1,215	12	175	11	575	10	530	9	201	5	61	3	1,542	8
48	705	7	886	9	517	5	1,074	11	142	9	560	9	550	9	251	6	88	4	1,591	8
49	868	9	1,045	11	992	10	921	9	115	7	579	10	652	11	396	10	171	7	1,913	10
50	3,360	34	3,754	38	6,146	61	968	10	177	11	1,089	18	2,013	34	2,256	55	1,579	69	7,114	36
NIDF	144		140		58		226		32		99		101		42		10		284	
mean	45		46		47		44		43		44		46		47		48		46	
standard deviation	7.1		5.4		5.9		6.4		7.3		7.0		6.0		5.4		4.7		6.4	
Observed Aberrations																				
Lack of spontaneous communication	769	8	695	7	426	4	1,038	11	166	10	551	9	469	8	228	6	50	2	1,464	7
Echolalia	51	1	25	0	23	0	53	1	7	0	34	1	22	0	9	0	4	0	76	0

569

Rules for the Construction of the SLH Indices

References: 3YR Variables from **The Collaborative Study on Cerebral Palsy, Mental Retardation, and Other Neurological and Sensory Disorders of Infancy and Childhood: Part IX-B**, March 1966, DHEW (page and form references below) 8YR Variables from **The Collaborative Study on Cerebral Palsy, Mental Retardation, and Other Neurological and Sensory Disorders of Infancy and Childhood: Part IX-C**, April 1970, DHEW (page and form references below)

3YR Speech Mechanism
Component Variables

Component Variables	Original Coded Values	Ordered Outcomes[1]	Missingness Profile
a. Lips: Retraction (p.53, PS-14)	Pass = 1,2,3 Fail = 4,5,6,8 Not Administered = 9	(0) Fail a,b,c (1) Pass a; Fail b,c (2) Pass b; Fail a,c (3) Pass a,b; Fail c (4) Pass c; Fail a,b (5) Pass a,c; Fail b (6) Pass b,c; Fail a (7) Pass a,b,c	(0) No Component Missing (1) a Missing (2) b Missing (3) a,b Missing (4) c Missing (5) a,c Missing (6) b,c Missing (7) a,b,c Missing
b. Diadochokinesis: Lips (p.54, PS-14)	Pass = 1 Fail = 2,8 Not Administered = 9		
c. Diadochokinesis: Tongue (p.54, PS-14)	Pass = 1 Fail = 2,8 Not Administered = 9		

3YR Hypernasality
Component Variable

Component Variable	Original Coded Values	Ordered Outcomes	Missingness Profile
a. Voice: Quality, Hypernasal (p.55, PS-15)	Absence = 1,3,4,5,8 Presence = 2,6 Not Examined = 9	(0) Hypernasality (1) No Hypernasality	(0) Component Present (1) Component Missing

3YR Fluency
Component Variables

Component Variables	Original Coded Values	Ordered Outcomes	Missingness Profile
a. Dysfluent Events (p.58, PS-15)	None = 0 Some = 1 Many = 2 Unknown = 9	(0) Many a; Some or Many b (1) Some a; Some or Many b (2) Some a; None b (3) None a; None b	(0) No Component Missing (1) a Missing (2) b Missing (3) a,b Missing
b. Struggle Behavior (p.58, PS-15)	None = 0 Some = 1 Many = 2 Unknown = 9	Note: All possible combinations of the variables are not relevant outcomes for the index.	

[1] For all indexes,
Blank - Not in Data File

3YR Articulation
Component Variables

a. Articulation: Initial
   Consonants
   (p.56, PS-15)

b. Articulation: Vowels
   and Diphthongs
   (p.56, PS-15)

Original Coded Values

Normal = 0
Suspect = 1
Abnormal = 2
Not Administered = 9
Normal = 0
Suspect = 1
Abnormal = 2
Not Administered = 9

Ordered Outcomes

(0) Abnormal a; Abnormal b
(1) Abnormal a; Suspect b
(2) Abnormal a; Normal b
(3) Suspect a; Abnormal b
(4) Normal a; Abnormal b
(5) Suspect a; Suspect b
(6) Normal a; Suspect b
(7) Suspect a; Normal b
(8) Normal a; Normal b

Missingness Profile

(0) No Component Missing
(1) a Missing
(2) b Missing
(3) a,b Missing

3YR Intelligibility
Component Variable

a. Intelligibility
   (p.57, PS-15)

Original Coded Values

No Difficulty = 1
Some Difficulty = 2
Considerable Difficulty = 3
Verbalized but Unintelligible = 4
No Speech = 5
Other = 8
Unknown = 9

Note: Intelligibility will only
be used for those children who
could be rated.

Ordered Outcomes

(0) Verbalized but Unintelligible
(1) Considerable Difficulty
(2) Some Difficulty
(3) No Difficulty

Missingness Profile

(0) Component Useable
(1) Component Missing or
    Not Useable

3YR No Speech
Component Variable

a. Intelligibility:
   No Speech
   (p.57, PS-15)

Original Coded Values

Presence = 5
Absence = 1,2,3,4
Unknown = 8,9

Ordered Outcomes

(0) Presence a
(1) Absence a

Missingness Profile

(0) Component Present
(1) Component Missing

3YR Language Comprehension
Component Variables

a. Identification of
   Familiar Objects
   (p.43, PS-10)
b. Understanding Action
   Words
   (p.43, PS-10)
c. Understanding Space
   Relationships
   (p.43, PS-10)

Original Coded Values

Pass = 1
Fail = 0
Unknown, Not Administered = 9
Pass = 1
Fail = 0
Unknown, Not Administered = 9
Pass = 1
Fail = 0
Unknown, Not Administered = 9

Ordered Outcomes

(0) Fail a,b,c
(1) Pass a; Fail b,c
(2) Pass b; Fail a,c
(3) Pass c; Fail a,b
(4) Pass a,b; Fail c
(5) Pass a,c; Fail b
(6) Pass b,c; Fail a
(7) Pass a,b,c

Missingness Profile

(0) No Component Missing
(1) a Missing
(2) b Missing
(3) a,b Missing
(4) c Missing
(5) a,c Missing
(6) b,c Missing
(7) a,b,c, Missing

3YR Sentence Complexity

Component Variables	Original Coded Values	Outcome Combinations	Missingness Profile
a. Sentence Structure (p.46, PS-11)	Pass = 1 Fail = 0 Unknown = 9	equation: a+b+c+d+e	(0) No Component Missing
		Note: Scores run from worst (0) to best (5).	(1) a Missing
b. Word Order (p.46, PS-11)	Pass = 1 Fail = 0 Unknown = 9		(2) b Missing
			(3) a,b Missing
c. Sentence Length (p.46, PS-11)	Pass = 1 Fail = 0 Unknown = 9		(4) c Missing
			(5) a,c Missing
d. Relevance (p.46, PS-11)	Pass = 1 Fail = 0 Unknown = 9		(6) b,c Missing
			(7) a,b,c Missing
e. Use of Pronouns (p.46, PS-11)	Pass = 1 Fail = 0 Unknown = 9		(8) d Missing
			(9) a,d Missing
			(10) b,d Missing
			(11) a,b,d Missing
			(12) c,d Missing
			(13) a,c,d Missing
			(14) b,c,d Missing
			(15) a,b,c,d Missing
			(16) e Missing
			(17) a,e Missing
			(18) b,e Missing
			(19) a,b,e Missing
			(20) c,e Missing
			(21) a,c,e Missing
			(22) b,c,e Missing
			(23) a,b,c,e Missing
			(24) d,e Missing
			(25) a,d,e Missing
			(26) b,d,e Missing
			(27) a,b,d,e Missing
			(28) c,d,e Missing
			(29) a,c,d,e Missing
			(30) b,c,d,e Missing
			(31) a,b,c,d,e Missing

3YR Auditory Memory Component Variables

a. 2 Digits
(p.59, PS-12)

b. 3 Digits
(p.59, PS-12)

c. 2 Syllables
(p.59, PS-12)

d. 3 Syllables
(p.59, PS-12)

e. Spondaic Word Test
(p.48-51, PS-13)

Original Coded Values

Pass = 1
Fail = 0
No Response = 2
Unknown = 9

Pass = 1
Fail = 0
No Response = 2
Unknown = 9

Pass = 1
Fail = 0
No Response = 2
Unknown = 9

Pass = 1
Fail = 0
No Response = 2
Unknown = 9

Pass = Pass Hi or Lo List
Fail = Fail Both Hi and Lo
Lists

Ordered Outcomes

(0) Fail a,b,c,d,e
(1) Pass e; Fail a,b,c,d
(2) Pass a or c; Fail b and
d; Pass or Fail e
(3) Pass b or d; Pass or Fail
a and/or c; Pass or Fail e

Note: All possible combinations
of these variables are not
relevant for the index.

Missingness Profile

(0) No Component Missing
(1) a Missing
(2) b Missing
(3) a,b Missing
(4) c Missing
(5) a,c Missing
(6) b,c Missing
(7) a,b,c Missing
(8) d Missing
(9) a,d Missing
(10) b,d Missing
(11) a,b,d Missing
(12) c,d Missing
(13) a,c,d Missing
(14) b,c,d Missing
(15) a,b,c,d Missing
(16) e Missing
(17) a,e Missing
(18) b,e Missing
(19) a,b,e Missing
(20) c,e Missing
(21) a,c,e Missing
(22) b,c,e Missing
(23) a,b,c,e Missing
(24) d,e Missing
(25) a,d,e Missing
(26) b,d,e Missing
(27) a,b,d,e Missing
(28) c,d,e Missing
(29) a,c,d,e Missing
(30) b,c,d,e Missing
(31) a,b,c,d,e Missing

3YR Hearing Screen
Component Variables

a. Pure-Tone Screen:
   Right Ear
   (p.52, PS-13)
b. Pure-Tone Screen:
   Left Ear
   (p.52, PS-13)
c. Spondaic Word Test:
   Summary Total Score
   (p.51, PS-13)

Original Coded Values

Pass = 1
Fail = 0
Unknown = 9
Pass = 1
Fail = 0
Unknown = 9
Pass = 1
Fail = 0
Unknown = 9

Ordered Outcomes

(0) Fail a,b,c
(1) Pass a or b or c
(2) Pass a and b; Ignore c

Note: For outcome (1) the
pure tone in the other
ear could be "fail" or
"unknown." If values of
component variables are a
combination of fail and
"unknown" or missing, no
index is generated.

Missingness Profile

(0) No Component Missing
(1) a Missing
(2) b Missing
(3) a,b Missing
(4) c Missing
(5) a,c Missing
(6) b,c Missing
(7) a,b,c Missing

Note: Index is sometimes generated
despite some missing component
variables.

8YR Speech Mechanism
Component Variables

a. Lips: Retraction
   (p.67, PS-43)
b. Lips: Protrusion
   (p.67, PS-43)
c. Tongue: Mid-line
   Protrusion
   (p.67, PS-43)
d. Tongue: Lateral
   Protrusion
   (p.68, PS-43)
e. Tongue: Elevation
   (p.68, PS-43)

Original Coded Values

Pass = 1,3
Fail = 2,4
Unknown = 9
Pass = 1,3
Fail = 2,4
Unknown = 9
Pass = 1,3
Fail = 2,4
Unknown = 9
Pass = 1,3
Fail = 2,4
Unknown = 9
Pass = 1,3
Fail = 2,4
Unknown = 9

Ordered Outcomes

(0) Fail a,b,c,d,e
(1) Fail any 3 of a,b,c,d;
    Fail e
(2) Fail any 2 of a,b,c,d;
    Fail e
(3) Fail any 1 of a,b,c,d;
    Fail e
(4) Fail all a,b,c,d; Pass e
    or Pass all a,b,c,d;
    Fail e
(5) Pass any 1 of a,b,c,d;
    Pass e
(6) Pass any 2 of a,b,c,d;
    Pass e
(7) Pass any 3 of a,b,c,d;
    Pass e
(8) Pass a,b,c,d,e

Missingness Profile

(0) No Component Missing
(1) a Missing
(2) b Missing
(3) a,b Missing
(4) c Missing
(5) a,c Missing
(6) b,c Missing
(7) a,b,c Missing
(8) d Missing
(9) a,d Missing
(10) b,d Missing
(11) a,b,d Missing
(12) c,d Missing
(13) a,c,d Missing
(14) b,c,d Missing
(15) a,b,c,d Missing
(16) e Missing
(17) a,e Missing
(18) b,e Missing
(19) a,b,e Missing
(20) c,e Missing
(21) a,c,e Missing
(22) b,c,e Missing
(23) a,b,c,e Missing
(24) d,e Missing
(25) a,d,e Missing
(26) b,d,e Missing
(27) a,b,d,e Missing
(28) c,d,e Missing
(29) a,c,d,e Missing
(30) b,c,d,e Missing
(31) a,b,c,d,e Missing

8YR Palatal Function and Hypernasality

Component Variables

a. Soft Palate Function (p.68, PS-43)

b. Voice Quality: Resonance (Hypernasal) (p.70, PS-44)

Original Coded Values

Normal = 0
Abnormal = 1
Unknown = 9

Absence = 1,3,8
Presence = 2
Unknown = 9

Ordered Outcomes

(0) Abnormal a and Presence b
(1) Normal a and Presence b
(2) Abnormal a and Absence b
(3) Normal a and Absence b

Missingness Profile

(0) No Component Missing
(1) a Missing
(2) b Missing
(3) a,b Missing

8YR Fluency

Component Variables

a. Dysfluent Events (p.69, PS-44)

b. Struggle Behavior (p.69, PS-44)

c. Rate of Speech Sounds (p.69, PS-44)

Original Coded Values

None = 0
Some = 1
Many = 2
Unknown = 9

None = 0
Some = 1
Many = 2
Unknown = 9

Presence = 2,4
Absence = 1,3,5,8
Unknown = 9

Ordered Outcomes

(0) Many a; Some or Many b; Presence c
(1) Many a; Some or Many b; Absence c
(2) Some a; Some or Many b; Presence c
(3) Some a; Some or Many b; Absence c
(4) Some a; None b; Presence c
(5) Some a; None b; Absence c
(6) None a; None b; Presence c
(7) None a; None b; Absence c

Note: All possible combinations of the variables are not relevant outcomes for the index.

Missingness Profile

(0) No Component Missing
(1) a Missing
(2) b Missing
(3) a,b Missing
(4) c Missing
(5) a,c Missing
(6) b,c Missing
(7) a,b,c Missing

8YR Articulation

Component Variable

a. Articulation (Templin-Darley) (p.72, PS-44)

Original Coded Values

Raw Score = 0-50
Unknown = 99

Ordered Outcomes

Outcomes are ordered by raw score: low (0) to high (50)

Missingness Profile

(0) Component Present
(1) Component Missing

577

8YR Intelligibility
Component Variable

a. Intelligibility
(p.71, PS-44)

Original Coded Values

No Difficulty = 1
Some Difficulty = 2
Considerable Difficulty = 3
Verbalized but Unintelligible = 4
No Speech = 5
Other = 8
Unknown = 9

Note: Intelligibility will only be used for those children who could be rated.

Ordered Outcomes

(0) Verbalized but Unintelligible
(1) Considerable Difficulty
(2) Some Difficulty
(3) No Difficulty

Missingness Profile

(0) Component Useable
(1) Component Missing or Not Useable

8YR Language Comprehension
Component Variables

a. Word Identification
(p.53, PS-41)

b. Understanding a Story
(p.55, PS-41)

a'. Adequacy of
Component a
(p.53, PS-41)

b'. Adequacy of
Component b
(p.55, PS-41)

Original Coded Values "X" [+]

Raw Score = 0-150
Unknown = 999

Raw Score = 0-5
Unknown = 9

Adequate = 1
Not Adequate = 2
Unknown = 9

Adequate = 1
Not Adequate = 2
Unknown = 9

Weighted Values

as is

b = 30X
 = 0,30,...,150

Outcome Combinations

equation: a+b

Note: Scores run from worst (0) to best (300).

Missingness Profile

(0) No Component Missing
(1) a Missing
(2) b Missing
(3) a,b Missing

Note: For all component variables with adequacy measured, missing for the variable includes both not adequate and unknown adequacy codes.

8YR Auditory Memory
Component Variables

a. Digits: Total Pass
(p.51, PS-40)

b. Syllables: Total Pass
(p.52, PS-40)

c. Understanding a Story
(p.55, PS-41)

d. Connected Discourse:
Number of Concepts
(p.63, PS-42)

a'. Adequacy of
Component a
(p.51, PS-40)

b'. Adequacy of
Component b
(p.52, PS-40)

c'. Adequacy of
Component c
(p.55, PS-41)

Original Coded Values "X"

Raw Score = 20-105
Unknown = 999

Raw Score = 20-65
Unknown = 99

Raw Score = 0-5
Unknown = 9

Raw Score = 0-18
Unknown = 99

Adequate = 1
Not Adequate = 2
Unknown = 9

Adequate = 1
Not Adequate = 2
Unknown = 9

Adequate = 1
Not Adequate = 2
Unknown = 9

Weighted Values

a = X - 20
 = 0-85

b = 1.89(X-20)
 = 0-85.05

c = 17X
 = 0,17,...,85

d = 4.72X
 = 0,4.72,...,84.96

Outcome Combinations

equation: [a+b+c+d]

Note: Scores run from worst (0) to best (340).

Missingness Profile

(0) No Component Missing
(1) a Missing
(2) b Missing
(3) a,b Missing
(4) c Missing
(5) a,c Missing
(6) b,c Missing
(7) a,b,c Missing
(8) d Missing
(9) a,d Missing
(10) b,d Missing
(11) a,b,d Missing
(12) c,d Missing
(13) a,c,d Missing
(14) b,c,d Missing
(15) a,b,c,d Missing

[+] Where X = valid codes or scores

578

8YR Digits

Component Variable	Original Coded Values "X"	Weighted Values	Ordered Outcomes	Missingness Profile
a. Digits: Total Pass (p.51, PS-40) a'. Adequacy of Component a (p.51, PS-40)	Raw Score = 20-105 Unknown = 999 Adequate = 1 Not Adequate = 2 Unknown = 9	$a = X-20$ $= 0-85$	Scores run from worst (0) to best (85).	(0) Component Present (1) Component Missing

8YR Word Identification

Component Variable	Original Coded Values "X"	Weighted Values	Ordered Outcomes	Missingness Profile
a. Word Identification (p.53, PS-41) a'. Adequacy of Component a (p.53, PS-41)	Raw Score = 0-150 Unknown = 999 Adequate = 1 Not Adequate = 2 Unknown = 9	No Change	Outcomes are ordered by raw score: low (0) to high (150).	(0) Component Present (1) Component Missing

Written Communication

Component Variables	Original Coded Values "X"	Weighted Values	Outcome Combinations	Missingness Profile
a. Oral Reading: Total Passage Score (p.56-59, PS-41) b. Writing from Dictation: Total Score (p.65-66, PS-42) c. WRAT Reading: Total Points (p.39, PS-35) d. WRAT Spelling: Total Points (p.38, PS-35) a'. Adequacy of Component a (p.59, PS-41) b'. Adequacy of Component b (p.65, PS-42) c'. Adequacy of Components c and d (p.37, PS-35)	Raw Score = 0-54 Unknown = 99 Raw Score = 0-14 Unknown = 99 Raw Score = 0-84 Unknown = 99 Raw Score = 0-55 Unknown = 99 Adequate = 1 Not Adequate = 2 Unknown = 9 Adequate = 1 Not Adequate = 2 Unknown = 9 Adequate = 1 Not Adequate = 2 Unknown = 9	$a = 1.85X$ $= 0,...,99.90$ $b = 7.14X$ $= 0,...,99.96$ $c = 1.19X$ $= 0,...,99.96$ $d = 1.82X$ $= 0,...,100.10$	equation: $[a+b+c+d]$ Note: Scores run from worst (0) to best (399).	(0) No Component Missing (1) a Missing (2) b Missing (3) a,b Missing (4) c Missing (5) a,c Missing (6) b,c Missing (7) a,b,c Missing (8) d Missing (9) a,d Missing (10) b,d Missing (11) a,b,d Missing (12) c,d Missing (13) a,c,d Missing (14) b,c,d Missing (15) a,b,c,d Missing

8YR Language Production

Component Variables	Original Coded Values "X"	Weighted Values	Outcome Combinations	Missingness Profile
a. Morphology (p.62, PS-41)	Raw Score = 0-22 Unknown = 99	a = 4.55X = 0,....100.10	equation: [a+b+c+d+e+f+g+h+i+j]	(0-9) Number of Components Missing
b. Connected Discourse: Sequence (p.64, PS-42)	Excellent = 0 Adequate = 1 Poor = 2 Unknown = 9	b = 100-50X	Note: Scores run from worst (0) to best (900).	
c. Connected Discourse: Relevance (p.64, PS-42)	Excellent = 0 Adequate = 1 Poor = 2 Unknown = 9	c = 100-50X		
d. Connected Discourse: Grammar (p.64, PS-42)	Excellent = 0 Adequate = 1 Poor = 2 Unknown = 9	d = 100-50X		
e. Connected Discourse: Overall Evaluation (p.64, PS-42)	Normal = 0 Suspect = 1 Abnormal = 2 Unknown = 9	e = 100-50X		
f. Echolalia (p.75, PS-45)	Absence = 0 Presence = 1 Unknown = 9	f = 100-100X		
g. Lack of Spontaneous Communication (p.75, PS-45)	Absence = 0 Presence = 1 Unknown = 9	g = 100-100X		
h. 8YR Intelligibility Index	Outcomes = 0-3 (see above)	h = 33.33X = 0,....99.99		
i. 8YR Articulation Index	Outcomes = 0-50 (see above)	i = 2X = 0,2,4,....100		
a'. Adequacy of Component a (p.62, PS-41)	Adequate = 1 Not Adequate = 2 Unknown = 9	Note: Reverse scales on b,c,d e,f,g.		
b'. Adequacy of Component b,c,e (p.64, PS-42)	Adequate = 1 Not Adequate = 2 Unknown = 9			

8YR Concept Development
Component Variables

Component Variables	Original Coded Values "X"	Weighted Values	Outcomes Combinations	Missingness Profile
a. Orientation: Total Score (p.54, PS-41)	Raw Score = 0-12 Unknown = 99	$a = 1.83X$ = 0,1.83,...21.96	equation: $[a+b+c]$	(0) No Component Missing
b. Morphology (p.62, PS-41)	Raw Score = 0-22 Unknown = 99	No change	Note: Scores run from worst (0) to best (65).	(1) a Missing
c. Connected Discourse: Number of Concepts (p.63, PS-42)	Raw Score = 0-18 Unknown = 99	$c = 1.22X$ = 0,1.22,...21.96		(2) b Missing
a'. Adequacy of Component a (p.54, PS-41)	Adequate = 1 Not Adequate = 2 Unknown = 9			(3) a,b Missing
b'. Adequacy of Component b (p.62, PS-41)	Adequate = 1 Not Adequate = 2 Unknown = 9			(4) c Missing
				(5) a,c Missing
				(6) b,c Missing
				(7) a,b,c Missing

8YR Hearing Severity
Component Variables

Component Variables	Original Coded Values	Ordered Outcomes	Missingness Profile
a. Pure-Tone, Air: 500Hz, Right Ear	For a to h: Threshold of 0 = 01	$(a+c+e+g)/4 = x$	(0-8) Number of Component Variables Missing
b. Pure-Tone, Air: 500Hz, Left Ear	Threshold as given = 05-90	$(b+d+f+h)/4 = x'$	(9) Test Coded Inadequate
c. Pure-Tone, Air: 1000Hz, Right Ear	Threshold of 95 or more = 95	Note: Outcome = maximum (x,x').	Note: This is identical to the Missingness Profile for 8YR Hearing Acuity
d. Pure-Tone, Air: 1000Hz, Left Ear	Unknown = 99	Reverse scale: scores run from best (0) to worst (95).	
e. Pure-Tone, Air: 2000Hz, Right Ear			
f. Pure-Tone, Air: 2000Hz, Left Ear			
g. Pure-Tone, Air: 4000Hz, Right Ear			
h. Pure-Tone, Air: 4000Hz, Left Ear			
a'. Adequacy of Components a to h	Adequate = 1 Not Adequate = 2 Unknown = 9		

Note: All variables found on p.49, PS-40.

8YR Hearing Acuity

Component Variables	Original Coded Values	Ordered Outcomes	Missingness Profile
a. Pure-Tone, Air: 500Hz, Right Ear	For a to h:	$(a+c+e+g)/4 = x$	Note: See Missingness Profile for 8YR Hearing Severity.
b. Pure-Tone, Air: 500Hz, Left Ear	Threshold of 0 = 01	$(b+d+f+h)/4 = x'$	
c. Pure-Tone, Air: 1000Hz, Right Ear	Threshold as given = 05-90		
d. Pure-Tone, Air: 1000Hz, Left Ear	Threshold of 95 or more = 95	Note: Outcome = minimum (x,x'). Reverse scale: scores run from best (0) to worst (95).	
e. Pure-Tone, Air: 2000Hz, Right Ear	Unknown = 99		
f. Pure-Tone, Air: 2000Hz, Left Ear			
g. Pure-Tone, Air: 4000Hz, Right Ear			
h. Pure-Tone, Air: 4000Hz, Left Ear			
a'. Adequacy of components a to h	Adequate = 1		
Note: All variables found on p.49, PS-40.	Not Adequate = 2		
	Unknown = 9		

8YR Monaural Conductive Loss

Component Variables	Original Coded Values	Ordered Outcomes
a. Pure-Tone, Air: 500Hz, Right Ear	For a to d:	(0) Monaural Conductive Loss
b. Pure-Tone, Air: 500Hz, Left Ear	Threshold of 0 = 01	(1) No Monaural Conductive Loss
c. Pure-Tone, Air: 1000Hz, Right Ear	Threshold as given = 05-90	
d. Pure-Tone, Air: 1000Hz, Left Ear	Threshold of 95 or more = 95	Note: Algorithm for arriving at outcome follows 8YR Binaural Conductive Loss.
e. Pure-Tone, Bone: 500Hz, Right Ear	Unknown = 99	
f. Pure-Tone, Bone: 500Hz, Left Ear		
g. Pure-Tone, Bone: 1000Hz, Right Ear	For e to h:	
h. Pure-Tone, Bone: 1000Hz, Left Ear	Test Not Required = 0	
a'. Adequacy of Pure-Tone, Air	Threshold of 0 = 01	
b'. Adequacy of Pure-Tone, Bone	Threshold as given = 05-55	
Note: All variables found on p.49, PS-40.	Threshold of 60 or more = 60	
	Test Required, Not Given = 88	
	Unknown = 99	
	Adequate = 1	
	Not Adequate = 2	
	Unknown = 9	
	Not Applicable = 0	
	Adequate = 1	
	Not Adequate = 2	
	Unknown = 9	

8YR Binaural Conductive Loss

Component Variables	Original Coded Values	Ordered Outcomes
a. Pure-Tone, Air: 500Hz, Right Ear	For a to d:	(0) Binaural Conductive Loss
b. Pure-Tone, Air: 500Hz, Left Ear	Threshold of 0 = 01	(1) No Binaural Conductive Loss
c. Pure-Tone, Air: 1000Hz, Right Ear	Threshold as given = 05-90	
d. Pure-Tone, Air: 1000Hz, Left Ear	Threshold of 95 or more = 95	Note: Algorithm for arriving at outcome follows.
	Unknown = 99	
e. Pure-Tone, Bone: 500Hz, Right Ear	For e to h:	
f. Pure-Tone, Bone: 500Hz, Left Ear	Test Not Required = 0	
g. Pure-Tone, Bone: 1000Hz, Right Ear	Threshold of 0 = 01	
h. Pure-Tone, Bone: 1000Hz, Left Ear	Threshold as given = 05-55	
	Threshold of 60 or more = 60	
	Test Required, Not Given = 88	
	Unknown = 99	
a'. Adequacy of Pure-Tone, Air	Adequate = 1	
	Not Adequate = 2	
	Unknown = 9	
b'. Adequacy of Pure-Tone, Bone	Not Applicable = 0	
	Adequate = 1	
	Not Adequate = 2	
	Unknown = 9	

Note: All variables found on p.49, PS-40.

Algorithm: 8YR Monaural Conductive Loss, 8YR Binaural Conductive Loss

1. Check adequacy of Pure-Tone, Air. If a' coded not adequate or if any of variables a through d coded unknown, then both indexes blank (not in data file). Otherwise,
2. Check missingness of variables a through d. If any are missing, then both indexes blank. Otherwise,
3. If all variables a through d ≤ 15dB, then there is no monaural conductive loss and there is no binaural conductive loss. Otherwise,
4. Check adequacy of Pure-Tone, Bone. If b' coded not adequate or if any of variables e through h coded unknown, then both indexes blank. Otherwise,
5. Check missingness of variables e through h. If any are missing, then both indexes blank. Otherwise,
6. Calculate $X = \frac{(a-e) + (c-g)}{2}$ and $Y = \frac{(b-f) + (d-h)}{2}$.

7. If either $X > 10dB$ or $Y > 10dB$, but not both, then there is a monaural conductive loss and there is no binaural conductive loss. Otherwise,
8. If both $X > 10dB$ and $Y > 10dB$, then there is no monaural conductive loss and there is binaural conductive loss. Otherwise,
9. If both $X ≤ 10dB$ and $Y ≤ 10dB$, then there is no monaural conductive loss and there is no binaural conductive loss.

8YR Monaural Sensorineural Loss
Component Variables

a. Pure-Tone, Air: 500Hz, Right Ear
b. Pure-Tone, Air: 500Hz, Left Ear
c. Pure-Tone, Air: 1000Hz, Right Ear
d. Pure-Tone, Air: 1000Hz, Left Ear
e. Pure-Tone, Air: 2000Hz, Right Ear
f. Pure-Tone, Air: 2000Hz, Left Ear
g. Pure-Tone, Air: 4000Hz, Right Ear
h. Pure-Tone, Air: 4000Hz, Left Ear
i. Pure-Tone, Bone: 500Hz, Right Ear
j. Pure-Tone, Bone: 500Hz, Left Ear
k. Pure-Tone, Bone: 1000Hz, Right Ear
l. Pure-Tone, Bone: 1000Hz, Left Ear
m. Pure-Tone, Bone: 2000Hz, Right Ear
n. Pure-Tone, Bone: 2000Hz, Left Ear
o. Pure-Tone, Bone: 4000Hz, Right Ear
p. Pure-Tone, Bone: 4000Hz, Left Ear
a'. Adequacy of Pure-Tone, Air

b'. Adequacy of Pure-Tone, Bone

Note: All variables found on p.49, PS-40.

Original Coded Values

For a to h:
Threshold of 0 = 01
Threshold as given = 05-90
Threshold of 95 or more = 95
Unknown = 99

For i to p:
Test not required = 0
Threshold of 0 = 01
Threshold as given = 05-55
Threshold of 60 or more = 60
Test required, not given = 88
Unknown = 99

Adequate = 1
Not Adequate = 2
Unknown = 9
Not Applicable = 0
Adequate = 1
Not Adequate = 2
Unknown = 9

Ordered Outcomes

(0) Monaural Sensorineural Loss
(1) No Monaural Sensorineural Loss

Note: Algorithm for arriving at outcome follows 8YR Binaural Sensorineural Loss.

8YR Binaural Sensorineural Loss
Component Variables

a. Pure-Tone, Air: 500Hz, Right Ear
b. Pure-Tone, Air: 500Hz, Left Ear
c. Pure-Tone, Air: 1000Hz, Right Ear
d. Pure-Tone, Air: 1000Hz, Left Ear
e. Pure-Tone, Air: 2000Hz, Right Ear
f. Pure-Tone, Air: 2000Hz, Left Ear
g. Pure-Tone, Air: 4000Hz, Right Ear
h. Pure-Tone, Air: 4000Hz, Left Ear
i. Pure-Tone, Bone: 500Hz, Right Ear
j. Pure-Tone, Bone: 500Hz, Left Ear
k. Pure-Tone, Bone: 1000Hz, Right Ear
l. Pure-Tone, Bone: 1000Hz, Left Ear
m. Pure-Tone, Bone: 2000Hz, Right Ear
n. Pure-Tone, Bone: 2000Hz, Left Ear
o. Pure-Tone, Bone: 4000Hz, Right Ear
p. Pure-Tone, Bone: 4000Hz, Left Ear
a'. Adequacy of Pure-Tone, Air

b'. Adequacy of Pure-Tone, Bone

Note: All variables found on p.49, PS-40.

Original Coded Values

For a to h:
Threshold of 0 = 01
Threshold as given = 05-90
Threshold of 95 or more = 95
Unknown = 99

For i to p:
Test not required = 0
Threshold of 0 = 01
Threshold as given = 05-55
Threshold of 60 or more = 60
Test required, not given = 88
Unknown = 99

Adequate = 1
Not Adequate = 2
Unknown = 9
Not Applicable = 0
Adequate = 1
Not Adequate = 2
Unknown = 9

Ordered Outcomes

(0) Binaural Sensorineural Loss
(1) No Binaural Sensorineural Loss

Note: Algorithm for arriving at outcomes follows.

585

Algorithm: 8YR Monaural Sensorineural Loss, 8YR Binaural Sensorineural Loss

1. Check adequacy of Pure-Tone, Air. If a' coded not adequate or if any of variables a through h coded unknown, then both indexes blank (not in data file). Otherwise,
2. Check missingness of variables a through h. If any one missing, then both indexes blank. Otherwise,
3. If all variables a through h ≤ 15dB, then there is no monaural sensorineural loss and there is no binaural sensorineural loss, Otherwise,
4. Check adequacy of Pure-Tone, Bone. If b' coded not adequate or if any of variables i through p coded unknown, then both indexes blank. Otherwise,
5. Check missingness of variables i through p. If any one missing, then both indexes blank. Otherwise,
6. Check condition 1: at least two of the variables a,c,e.g ≥ 30dB
   condition 2: at least two of the variables b,d,f,h ≥ 30dB
   condition 3: at least two of the variables a,c,e.g < 30dB
   condition 4: at least two of the variables b,d,f,h < 30dB

Calculate $X = \dfrac{(a\text{-}1) + (c\text{-}k) + (e\text{-}m) + (g\text{-}o)}{4}$ and $Y = \dfrac{(b\text{-}j) + (d\text{-}l) + (f\text{-}n) + (h\text{-}p)}{4}$.

7. If either condition 1 is true and X ≤ 10dB or condition 2 is true and Y ≤10dB, but not both, then there is monaural sensorineural loss and there is no binaural sensorineural loss. Otherwise,
8. If both condition 1 is true and X ≤ 10dB and condition 2 is true and Y ≤ 10dB, then there is no monaural sensorineural loss and there is binaural sensorineural loss. Otherwise,
9. If both condition 3 is true and/or X > 10dB and condition 4 is true and/or Y > 10dB, then there is no monaural sensorineural loss and there is no binaural sensorineural loss.

8YR Monaural Mixed (Component of Sensorineural) Loss

Component Variables	Original Coded Values	Ordered Outcomes
a. Pure-Tone, Air: 500Hz, Right Ear	For a to h:	(0) Monaural Mixed (Component of Sensorineural) Loss
b. Pure-Tone, Air: 500Hz, Left Ear	Threshold of 0 = 01	(1) No Monaural Mixed (Component of Sensorineural) Loss
c. Pure-Tone, Air: 1000Hz, Right Ear	Threshold as given = 05-90	
d. Pure-Tone, Air: 1000Hz, Left Ear	Threshold of 95 or more = 95	
e. Pure-Tone, Air: 2000Hz, Right Ear	Unknown = 99	Note: Algorithm for arriving at outcome follows 8YR Binaural Sensorineural Loss.
f. Pure-Tone, Air: 2000Hz, Left Ear		
g. Pure-Tone, Air: 4000Hz, Right Ear		
h. Pure-Tone Air: 4000Hz, Left Ear		
i. Pure-Tone, Bone: 500Hz, Right Ear	For i to p:	
j. Pure-Tone, Bone: 500Hz, Left Ear	Test not required = 0	
k. Pure-Tone, Bone: 1000Hz, Right Ear	Threshold of 0 = 01	
l. Pure-Tone, Bone: 1000Hz, Left Ear	Threshold as given = 05-55	
m. Pure-Tone, Bone: 2000Hz, Right Ear	Threshold of 60 or more = 60	
n. Pure-Tone, Bone: 2000Hz, Left Ear	Test required, not given = 88	
o. Pure-Tone, Bone: 4000Hz, Right Ear	Unknown = 99	
p. Pure-Tone, Bone: 4000Hz, Left Ear		
a'. Adequacy of Pure-Tone, Air	Adequate = 1	
	Not Adequate = 2	
	Unknown = 9	
b'. Adequacy of Pure-Tone, Bone	Not Applicable = 0	
	Adequate = 1	
Note: All variables found on p.49, PS-40.	Not Adequate = 2	
	Unknown = 9	

8YR Binaural Mixed (Component of Sensorineural) Loss

Component Variables	Original Coded Values	Ordered Outcomes
a. Pure-Tone, Air: 500Hz, Right Ear	For a to h: Threshold of 0 = 01 Threshold as given = 05-90 Threshold of 95 or more = 95 Unknown = 99	(0) Binaural Mixed (Component of Sensorineural) Loss (1) No Binaural Mixed (Component of Sensorineural) Loss
b. Pure-Tone, Air: 500Hz, Left Ear		
c. Pure-Tone, Air: 1000Hz, Right Ear		Note: Algorithm for arriving at outcomes follows.
d. Pure-Tone, Air: 1000Hz, Left Ear		
e. Pure-Tone, Air: 2000Hz, Right Ear		
f. Pure-Tone, Air: 2000Hz, Left Ear		
g. Pure-Tone, Air: 4000Hz, Right Ear		
h. Pure-Tone, Air: 4000Hz, Left Ear		
i. Pure-Tone, Bone: 500Hz, Right Ear	For i to p: Test not required = 0 Threshold of 0 = 01 Threshold as given = 05-55 Threshold of 60 or more = 60 Test required, not given = 88 Unknown = 99	
j. Pure-Tone, Bone: 500Hz, Left Ear		
k. Pure-Tone, Bone: 1000Hz, Right Ear		
l. Pure-Tone, Bone: 1000Hz, Left Ear		
m. Pure-Tone, Bone: 2000Hz, Right Ear		
n. Pure-Tone, Bone: 2000Hz, Left Ear		
o. Pure-Tone, Bone: 4000Hz, Right Ear		
p. Pure-Tone, Bone: 4000Hz, Left Ear		
a'. Adequacy of Pure-Tone, Air	Adequate = 1 Not Adequate = 2 Unknown = 9	
b'. Adequacy of Pure-Tone, Bone	Not Applicable = 0 Adequate = 1 Not Adequate = 2 Unknown = 9	
Note: All variables found on p.49, PS-40.		

Algorithm: 8YR Monaural Mixed (Component of Sensorineural) Loss, 8YR Binaural Mixed (Component of Sensorineural) Loss

1. Check adequacy of Pure-Tone, Air. If a' coded not adequate or if any of variables a through h coded unknown, then both indexes blank (not in data file). Otherwise,

2. Check missingness of variables a through h. If any one missing, then both indexes blank. Otherwise,

3. If all variables a through h ≤ 15dB, then there is no monaural mixed (component of sensorineural) loss and there is no binaural mixed (component of sensorineural) loss. Otherwise,

4. Check adequacy of Pure-Tone, Bone. If b' coded not adequate or if any of variables i through p coded unknown, then both indexes blank. Otherwise,

5. Check missingness of variables i through p. If any one missing, then both indexes blank. Otherwise,

6. Check condition 1: at least two of the variables a,c,e,g > 30dB
   condition 2: at least two of the variables b,d,f,h > 30dB
   condition 3: at least two of the variables a,c,e,g ≤ 30dB
   condition 4: at least two of the variables b,d,f,h ≤ 30dB
   condition 5: at least 2 of the variables i,k,m,o > 20dB
   condition 6: at least 2 of the variables j,l,n,p > 20dB
   condition 7: at least 2 of the variables i,k,m,o ≤ 20dB
   condition 8: at least 2 of the variables j,l,n,p ≤ 20dB

Calculate $X_1 = (a-i)$
$X_2 = (c-k)$
$X_3 = (e-m)$
$X_4 = (g-o)$
$X_5 = (b-j)$
$X_6 = (d-l)$
$X_7 = (f-n)$
$X_8 = (h-p)$

7. If either conditions 1 and 5 are true and any two of X_1 through $X_4 \geq$ 10dB or conditions 2 and 6 are true and any two of X_5 through $X_8 \geq$ 10dB, but not both, then there is a monaural mixed (component of sensorineural) loss and there is no binaural mixed (component of sensorineural) loss. Otherwise,

8. If both conditions 1 and 5 are true and any two of X_1 through $X_4 \geq$ 10dB and conditions 2 and 6 are true and any two of X_5 through $X_8 \geq$ 10dB, then there is no monaural mixed (component of sensorineural) loss and there is a binaural mixed (component of sensorineural) loss. Otherwise,

9. If both conditions 3 and/or 7 are true and/or any two of X_1 through $X_4 <$ 10dB and conditions 4 and/or 8 are true and/or any two of X_5 through $X_8 <$ 10dB, then there is no monaural mixed (component of sensorineural) loss and there is no binaural mixed (component of sensorineural) loss.

COMBINATIONS OF HEARING LOSSES

Criteria for monaural and binaural conductive loss, monaural and binaural sensorineural loss, and monaural and binaural mixed (component of sensorineural) loss were applied separately. After identifying all losses separately, the following recodings and combinations were made, so that each subject is coded as having only one type of loss.

1. A monaural mixed (component of sensorineural) loss is coded as a monaural sensorineural loss if no other condition is present.

589

A binaural mixed (component of sensorineural) loss is coded as a binaural sensorineural loss if no other condition is present.

2. A subject exhibiting a monaural sensorineural loss in one ear and a monaural mixed (component of sensorineural) loss in the other is coded as having a binaural sensorineural loss.

3. A subject exhibiting a monaural sensorineural loss in one ear and a monaural mixed (component of sensorineural) loss in the same ear is coded as having a monaural sensorineura loss.

4. A subject exhibiting both a binaural mixed (component of sensorineural) loss and a binaural sensorineural loss is coded as having a binaural sensorineural loss.

5. A subject exhibiting   a binaural conductive loss and
a monaural sensorineural loss and/or
a monaural mixed (component of sensorineural) loss

or

A subject exhibiting a monaural conductive loss in one ear and
a monaural sensorineural loss and/or
a monaural mixed (component of sensorineural) loss
in the other ear

is coded as having a monaural sensorineural loss for all analyses involving medical antecedents and as having a binaural heterogeneous loss for all analyses involving non-medical antecedents or outcomes. In both cases conductive component is omitted, since the sensorineural component was considered to have more impact.

8YR Total Conductive Loss Component Indexes

Component Indexes	Original Codes	Ordered Outcomes	Missingness Profile
a. Monaural Conductive Loss	Loss = 0	(0) Conductive Loss ($a = 0$ and/or $b = 0$)	(0) No Component Missing
b. Binaural Conductive Loss	No Loss = 1	(1) No Conductive Loss ($a = 1$ and $b = 1$)	(1) Both Components Missing

8YR Total Sensorineural Loss Component Indexes

Component Indexes	Original Codes	Ordered Outcomes	Missingness Profile
a. Monaural Sensorineural Loss	Loss = 0	(0) Sensorineural Loss ($a = 0$ and/or $b = 0$)	(0) No Component Missing
b. Binaural Sensorineural Loss	No Loss = 1	(1) No Sensorineural Loss ($a = 1$ and $b = 1$)	(1) Both Components Missing

Neurological Involvement[2]

Component Variables	Original Codes	Recoding Algorithm	Component Outcomes
a. Pure-Tone, Air: 500Hz, Right Ear 1000Hz, Right Ear 2000Hz, Right Ear 4000Hz, Right Ear 8000Hz, Right Ear 500Hz, Left Ear 1000Hz, Left Ear 2000Hz, Left Ear 4000Hz, Left Ear 8000Hz, Left Ear Note: Low frequencies = 500, 1000, 2000; high frequencies = 4000, 8000. All variables found on p.49, PS-40.	Threshold of 0 = 01 Threshold as Given = 05-90 Threshold of 95 or More = 95 Unknown = 99	1. Calculate: $\bar{X}_{LR}$ = mean, low frequencies, right ear $\bar{X}_{HR}$ = mean, high frequencies, right ear $\bar{X}_{LL}$ = mean, low frequencies, left ear $\bar{X}_{HL}$ = mean, high frequencies, left ear 2. $\bar{Y}_R = \bar{X}_{HR} - \bar{X}_{LR}$ $\bar{Y}_L = \bar{X}_{HL} - \bar{X}_{LL}$ 3. $Y = \text{maximum}(Y_R, Y_L)$	(0) $Y > 16$ dB (1) $Y \leq 16$ dB
a'. Adequacy of Component a (p.49, PS-40)	Adequate = 1 Not Adequate = 2 Unknown = 9 Test not required = 0		
b. Abnormal Auditory Adaptation 4000 Hz, Right Ear 4000 Hz, Left Ear (p.49, PS-40)	Pass = 1 Fail = 2 Inadequate Test = 8 Unknown = 9	Pass = 0,1 Fail = 2 Unknown = 8,9	(0) Fail Either or Both Ears (1) Pass Both Ears
b'. Adequacy of Component b (p.49, PS-40)	Adequate = 1 Not Adequate = 2 Unknown = 9 Test Not Required = 00		
c. Pure-Tone, Bone: 500Hz, Right Ear 1000Hz, Right Ear 2000Hz, Right Ear 4000Hz, Right Ear 500Hz, Left Ear 1000Hz, Left Ear 2000Hz, Left Ear 4000Hz, Left Ear Note: All variables found on p.49, PS-40.	Threshold of 0 = 01 Threshold As Given = 05-55 Threshold of 60 or more = 60 Test Required, Not Given = 88 Unknown = 99 Note: If Pure-Tone, Bone not required, use Air thresholds for indicated frequencies.	1. Calculate: $\bar{X}_R$ = mean, all frequencies, right ear $\bar{X}_L$ = mean, all frequencies, left ear 2. $X = \text{maximum}(\bar{X}_R, \bar{X}_L)$	(0) X = 50.5-60 (1) X = 40.5-50 (2) X = 30.5-40 (3) X = 20.5-30 (4) X = 10.5-20 (5) X = 0-10

[2] Algorithm for arriving at index outcomes follows description of component variables. All variables are from 8YR SLH test battery.

591

Neurological Involvement — (Cont'd.)

Component Variables	Original Codes	Recoding Algorithm	Component Outcomes
c'. Adequacy of Component c (p.49, PS-40)	Adequate = 0,1 Not Adequate = 2 Unknown = 9		
d. Discrimination Test: Right Ear, Percent Left Ear, Percent (p.50, PS-40)	Percent as Given = 0-96 100% = 97 Unknown = 99	1. Calculate: X = Right Ear % — Left Ear %	(0) X = 17 or More (1) X = 0-16
d'. Adequacy of Component d (p.50, PS-40)	Adequate = 1 Not Adequate = 2 Unknown = 9		
e. Orientation Items 9,10,11,12 (p.54, PS-41)	For each item: Pass = 1 Fail = 2 Unknown = 9		(0) Fail All Items (1) Pass One Item (2) Pass Two Items (3) Pass Three Items (4) Pass Four Items
e'. Adequacy of Component e (p.54, PS-41)	Adequate = 1 Not Adequate = 2 Unknown = 9		
f. Lips: Retraction Protrusion (p.67, PS-43)	Pass = 1 Fail = 2 Pass with Concomitant Movement = 3 Fail with Concomitant Movement = 4 Unknown = 9	For each subcomponent: Pass = 1,3 Fail = 2,4	(0) Fail Both (1) Pass Either (2) Pass Both
g. Tongue: Midline Protrusion Lateral Protrusion Elevation (p.67-68, PS-43)	Pass = 1 Fail = 2 Pass with Concomitant Movement = 3 Fail with Concomitant Movement = 4 Unknown = 9	For each subcomponent: Pass = 1,3 Fail = 2,4	(0) Fail All Subcomponents (1) Pass One Subcomponent (2) Pass Two Subcomponents (3) Pass Three Subcomponents

Algorithm: Neurological Involvement
1. Check adequacies of variables a through e. If any of a' through e' coded not adequate or unknown or if any of variables a through g missing or coded unknown, then index outcome blank. Otherwise,
2. Index outcome equals the sum of all component outcomes a through g. Scores run from 0 to 17.

Communicative Effectiveness[3]

Component Variables	Original Codes	Recoding Algorithm	Component Outcomes
a. Understanding a Story (p.55, PS-41)	Raw Score = 0-5 Unknown = 9	Score = 30X where X = raw score	Score = 0,30,60,90,120,150
a'. Adequacy of Component a (p.55, PS-41)	Adequate = 1 Not Adequate = 2 Unknown = 9		
b. Word Identification (p.53, PS-41)	Raw Score = 0-150 Unknown = 999	No Change	Score = 0-150
b'. Adequacy of Component b (p.53, PS-41)	Adequate = 1 Not Adequate = 2 Unknown = 9		
c. Intelligibility (p.71, PS-44)	No Difficulty = 1 Some Difficulty = 2 Considerable Difficulty = 3 Verbalized, Unintelligible = 4 No Speech = 5 Other = 8 Unknown = 9	Score = 50(4-X) where X = 1,2,3,4	Score = 0,50,100,150
d. Silent Reading (p.60-61, PS-41)	Non-Reader = 0 As Given = 1-5 Unknown = 9	Score = 30X where X = 1,2,3,4,5	Score = 0,30,60,90,120,150
d'. Adequacy of Component d (p.60-61, PS-41)	Adequate = 1 Not Adequate = 2 Unknown = 9		
e. Oral Reading (p.56-59, PS-41)	Raw Score = 0-54 Unknown = 99	Score = 2.78X where X = raw score	Score = 0-150
e'. Adequacy of Component e (p.59, PS-41)	Adequate = 1 Not Adequate = 2 Unknown = 9		
f. Morphology (p.62, PS-41)	Raw Score = 0-22 Unknown = 99	Score = 6.82X where X = raw score	Score = 0-150
f'. Adequacy of Component f (p.62, PS-41)	Adequate = 1 Not Adequate = 2 Unknown = 9		

[3] Algorithm for arriving at index outcomes follows description of component variables. All variables are from 8YR SLH test battery.

Algorithm: Communicative Effectiveness
1. Check adequacies of variables where possible. If any coded not adequate or unknown or if any of variables a through f missing or coded unknown, then index outcome blank. Otherwise,
2. Index outcome equals the sum of all component outcomes a through f. Scores run from 0 to 900.

Auditory Processing[4]

Component Variables	Original Codes	Recoding Algorithm	Component Outcomes
a. Pure-Tone, Air: 500Hz, Right Ear 1000Hz, Right Ear 2000Hz, Right Ear 500Hz, Left Ear 1000Hz, Left Ear 2000Hz, Left Ear (p.49, PS-40)	Threshold of 0 = 01 Threshold as Given = 05-90 Threshold of 95 or More = 95 Unknown = 99	1. Calculate: $\bar{X}_{LR}$ = mean, low frequencies, right ear $\bar{X}_{LL}$ = mean, low frequencies, left ear 2. X_L = minimum $(\bar{X}_{LR}, \bar{X}_{LL})$	(0) 90 < X_L ≤ 95 (1) 80 < X_L ≤ 90 (2) 70 < X_L ≤ 80 (3) 60 < X_L ≤ 70 (4) 50 < X_L ≤ 60 (5) 40 < X_L ≤ 50 (6) 30 < X_L ≤ 40 (7) 20 < X_L ≤ 30 (8) 10 < X_L ≤ 20 (9) 0 ≤ X_L ≤ 10
b. Pure-Tone, Air: 2000Hz, Right Ear 4000Hz, Right Ear 2000Hz, Left Ear 4000Hz, Left Ear (p.49, PS-40)	Threshold of 0 = 01 Threshold as Given = 05-90 Threshold of 95 or More = 95 Unknown = 99	1. Calculate: $\bar{X}_{HR}$ = mean, high frequencies, right ear $\bar{X}_{HL}$ = mean, high frequencies, left ear 2. X_H = minimum $(\bar{X}_{HR}, \bar{X}_{HL})$	(0) 90 < X_H ≤ 95 (1) 80 < X_H ≤ 90 (2) 70 < X_H ≤ 80 (3) 60 < X_H ≤ 70 (4) 50 < X_H ≤ 60 (5) 40 < X_H ≤ 50 (6) 30 < X_H ≤ 40 (7) 20 < X_H ≤ 30 (8) 10 < X_H ≤ 20 (9) 0 ≤ X_H ≤ 10
b'. Adequacy of Components a and b (p.49, PS-40)	Adequate = 1 Not Adequate = 2 Unknown = 9		
c. Abnormal Auditory Adaptation 4000Hz, Right Ear 4000Hz, Left Ear (p.49, PS-40)	Test not required = 0 Pass = 1 Fail = 2 Inadequate Test = 8 Unknown = 9	Pass = 0,1 Fail = 2 Unknown = 8,9	(0) Fail Both Ears (1) Pass Either Ear (2) Pass Both Ears
c'. Adequacy of Component c (p.49, PS-40)	Adequate = 1 Not Adequate = 2 Unknown = 9		
d. Discrimination Test: Right Ear, Percent Left Ear, Percent (p.50, PS-40)	Percent As Given = 0-96 100% = 97 Unknown = 99	X = maximum (right ear%, left ear%)	(0) X ≤ 76% (1) X > 76%
d'. Adequacy of Component d (p.50, PS-40)	Adequate = 1 Not Adequate = 2 Unknown = 9		
e. Digits (p.51, PS-40)	Raw Score = 20(5)105 Unknown = 999	Score = (X-20)/10 where X = raw score	Score = 0-8.5

[4] Algorithm for arriving at index outcomes follows description of component variables. All variables are from 8YR SLH test battery.

Auditory Processing (Cont'd.)

Component Variables	Original Codes	Recoding Algorithm	Component Outcomes
e'. Adequacy of Component e (p.51, PS-40)	Adequate = 1 Not Adequate = 2 Unknown = 9		Score = 0-4.5
f. Syllables (p.52, PS-40)	Raw Score = 20(5)65 Unknown = 99	Score = (X-20)/10 where X = raw score	
f'. Adequacy of Component f (p.52, PS-40)	Adequate = 1 Not Adequate = 2 Unknown = 9		
g. Word Identification (p.53, PS-41)	Raw Score = 0-150 Unknown = 999	No Change	(0) Raw Score < 33 (1) Raw Score = 33-42 (2) Raw Score = 43-52 (3) Raw Score = 53-62 (4) Raw Score = 63-72 (5) Raw Score = 73-82 (6) Raw Score = 83-92 (7) Raw Score > 92
g'. Adequacy of Component g (p.53, PS-41)	Adequate = 1 Not Adequate = 2 Unknown = 9		
h. Orientation (p.54, PS-41)	Raw Score = 0-12 Unknown = 99	No Change	Score = 0-12
h'. Adequacy of Component h (p.54, PS-41)	Adequate = 1 Not Adequate = 2 Unknown = 99		
i. Understanding a Story (p.55, PS-41)	Raw Score = 0-5 Unknown = 9	No Change	Score = 0-5
i'. Adequacy of Component i (p.55, PS-41)	Adequate = 1 Not Adequate = 2 Unknown = 9		
j. Oral Reading (p.56-59, PS-41)	Raw Score = 0-54 Unknown = 99	Score = X/10 where X = raw score	Score = 0-5.4
j'. Adequacy of Component j (p.59, PS-41)	Adequate = 1 Not Adequate = 2 Unknown = 9		
k. Morphology (p.62, PS-41)	Raw Score = 0-22 Unknown = 99	Score = X/2 where X = raw score	Score = 0-11
k'. Adequacy of Component k (p.62, PS-41)	Adequate = 1 Not Adequate = 2 Unknown = 9		
l. Connected Discourse: Overall Evaluation (p.64, PS-42)	Normal = 0 Suspect = 1 Abnormal = 2 Unknown = 9	Reverse values of original codes	(0) Abnormal (1) Suspect (2) Normal

595

Auditory Processing (Cont'd.)

Component Variables	Original Codes	Recoding Algorithm	Component Outcomes
l'. Adequacy of Component l (p.64, PS-42)	Adequate = 1 Not Adequate = 2 Unknown = 9		
m. Writing From Dictation (p.65, PS-42)	Raw Score = 0-14 Unknown = 99	No Change	Score = 0-14
m'. Adequacy of Component m (p.65, PS-42)	Adequate = 1 Not Adequate = 2 Unknown = 9		

Algorithm: Auditory Processing

1. Check adequacies of variables. If b' through m' coded not adequate or unknown or if any of variables a through m missing or coded unknown, then index outcome blank. Otherwise,
2. Index outcome equals the sum of all component outcomes a through m. Scores run from 0 to 90.

596

Descriptive
Statistics and
Frequency
Distributions by
Race, Sex, SEI,
and Total for
SLH Indices.

Descriptive Statistics and Frequency Distributions of 3YR and 8YR Indexes
by Sex, Race, grouped SEI, and Total Sample Size

		Male	Female	White	Black	SEI 0.0-1.9	SEI 2.0-3.9	SEI 4.0-5.9	SEI 6.0-7.9	SEI 8.0-9.5	Total
3YR Speech Mechanism	Mean	6.6	6.7	6.6	6.7	6.6	6.6	6.6	6.7	6.8	6.6
	Std. dev.	1.4	1.2	1.4	1.2	1.4	1.4	1.3	1.3	1.0	1.3
	% NIDF	19	15	20	15	18	19	18	15	12	17
3YR Hypernasality	% Hypernasal	1.3	1.0	1.4	0.9	1.1	1.1	1.4	1.3	0.5	1.1
	% NIDF	5	4	3	6	6	6	5	3	1	5
3YR Fluency	Mean	2.9	2.9	2.9	2.9	2.9	2.9	2.9	2.9	2.9	2.9
	Std. dev.	.33	.30	.33	.31	.30	.29	.30	.35	.38	.32
	% NIDF	8	6	6	8	9	8	7	5	3	7
3YR Articulation	Mean	6.9	7.2	7.2	7.0	6.6	6.9	7.1	7.3	7.5	7.1
	Std. dev.	2.0	1.6	1.7	1.9	2.2	1.9	1.8	1.6	1.3	1.8
	% NIDF	12	9	10	11	13	13	11	8	4	11
3YR Intelligibility	Mean	2.1	2.4	2.3	2.2	2.2	2.2	2.2	2.4	2.5	2.3
	Std. dev.	.85	.76	.83	.80	.82	.82	.83	.79	.71	.81
	% NIDF	7	6	5	8	9	8	7	4	2	7
3YR No Speech	% No Speech	0.9	0.6	0.9	0.6	1.3	0.8	0.8	0.5	0.3	0.8
	% NIDF	7	5	4	7	8	8	6	4	2	6
3YR Language Comprehension	Mean	5.9	6.1	6.4	5.7	5.5	5.8	6.0	6.3	6.7	6.0
	Std. dev.	2.0	1.8	1.5	2.0	2.2	2.0	1.9	1.6	1.0	1.9
	% NIDF	5	5	4	6	8	8	5	4	2	5
3YR Sentence Complexity	Mean	4.5	4.7	4.6	4.6	4.5	4.5	4.5	4.6	4.8	4.6
	Std. dev.	1.2	0.94	1.1	1.1	1.2	1.2	1.1	1.0	0.74	1.1
	% NIDF	8	7	6	9	10	10	8	4	2	8
3YR Auditory Memory	Mean	2.8	2.8	2.8	2.9	2.8	2.8	2.8	2.9	2.9	2.8
	Std. dev.	.46	.44	.48	.43	.48	.49	.46	.40	.30	.45
	% NIDF	23	19	23	19	23	23	22	18	13	21
3YR Hearing Screen	Mean	1.9	1.9	1.8	1.9	1.9	1.9	1.9	1.9	1.9	1.9
	Std. dev.	.39	.37	.40	.35	.37	.38	.37	.38	.38	.38
	% NIDF	9	7	8	8	10	10	8	5	3	8

3YR Indexes: Frequency Distributions

Code	Male Freq	Male %	Female Freq	Female %	White Freq	White %	Black Freq	Black %	0.0-1.9 Freq	0.0-1.9 %	2.0-3.9 Freq	2.0-3.9 %	4.0-5.9 Freq	4.0-5.9 %	6.0-7.9 Freq	6.0-7.9 %	8.0-9.5 Freq	8.0-9.5 %	Totals Freq	Totals %
3YR Speech Mechanism																				
0	40	0	27	0	25	0	42	0	6	0	33	1	21	0	6	0	1	0	67	0
1	335	4	236	3	317	5	254	3	58	4	210	4	169	4	96	3	38	2	571	3
2	12	0	7	0	5	0	14	0	1	0	8	0	6	0	4	0	0	0	19	0
3	184	2	116	1	137	2	163	2	38	2	105	2	80	2	55	2	22	1	300	2
4	8	0	6	0	2	0	12	0	4	0	5	0	4	0	1	0	0	0	14	0
5	117	1	82	1	89	1	110	1	13	1	72	1	62	1	37	1	15	1	199	1
6	234	3	215	3	129	2	320	3	43	3	191	3	135	3	52	2	28	2	449	3
7	7,726	89	7,632	92	6,202	90	8,656	90	1,437	90	4,921	89	4,258	90	2,566	91	1,676	94	14,858	90
	8,156		8,321		6,906		9,571		1,600		5,545		4,735		2,817		1,780		16,477	
3YR Hypernasality																				
0	122	1	95	1	117	1	100	1	21	1	68	1	74	1	43	1	11	1	217	1
1	9,402	99	9,289	99	8,183	99	10,508	99	1,814	99	6,316	99	5,381	99	3,187	99	1,993	99	18,691	99
	9,524		9,384		8,300		10,608		1,835		6,384		5,455		3,230		2,004		18,908	
3YR Fluency																				
0	26	0	18	0	19	0	25	0	4	0	10	0	15	0	12	0	3	0	44	0
1	30	0	28	0	18	0	40	0	9	1	23	0	14	0	8	0	4	0	58	0
2	759	8	597	6	701	9	655	6	96	5	368	6	337	6	279	9	276	14	1,356	7
3	8,479	91	8,581	93	7,360	91	9,700	93	1,672	94	5,871	94	4,984	93	2,861	91	1,672	86	17,060	92
	9,294		9,224		8,098		10,420		1,781		6,272		5,350		3,160		1,955		18,518	
3YR Articulation																				
0	51	1	27	0	51	1	27	0	8	0	33	1	23	0	9	0	5	0	78	0
1	313	4	163	2	205	3	271	3	74	4	186	3	140	3	51	2	25	1	476	3
2	554	6	364	4	263	3	655	7	153	9	368	6	253	5	105	3	39	2	918	5
3	19	0	8	0	17	0	10	0	3	0	6	0	9	0	8	0	1	0	27	0
4	7	0	7	0	4	0	10	0	2	0	4	0	5	0	2	0	1	0	14	0
5	377	4	292	3	291	4	378	4	81	5	240	4	196	4	89	3	63	3	669	4
6	215	2	221	2	216	3	220	2	42	2	141	2	119	2	87	3	47	2	436	2
7	2,190	25	1,833	21	1,474	19	2,549	25	462	27	1,546	26	1,201	23	556	18	258	13	4,023	23
8	5,100	58	6,000	67	5,200	67	5,900	59	878	52	3,414	57	3,166	62	2,143	70	1,499	77	11,100	63
	8,826		8,915		7,721		10,020		1,703		5,938		5,112		3,050		1,938		17,741	
3YR Intelligibility																				
0	329	4	124	1	237	3	216	2	49	3	165	3	151	3	67	2	21	1	453	2
1	1,858	20	1,183	13	1,286	16	1,755	17	325	18	1,158	19	940	18	429	14	189	10	3,041	16
2	3,346	36	3,051	33	2,618	32	3,779	36	700	39	2,293	37	1,827	34	1,017	32	560	28	6,397	34
3	3,779	41	4,887	53	4,002	49	4,664	45	712	40	2,643	42	2,445	46	1,659	52	1,207	61	8,666	47
	9,312		9,245		8,143		10,414		1,786		6,259		5,363		3,172		1,977		18,557	

3YR Indexes: Frequency Distributions

		Male		Female		White		Black		0.0-1.9		2.0-3.9		4.0-5.9		6.0-7.9		8.0-9.5		Totals	
	Code	Freq.	%	Freq.	%	Freq.	%	Freq.	%	Freq.	%	Freq.	%	Freq.	%	Freq.	%	Freq.	%	Freq.	%
3YR No Speech	0	89	1	53	1	75	1	67	1	23	1	52	1	45	1	16	1	6	0	142	1
	1	9,312	99	9,245	99	8,143	99	10,414	99	1,786	99	6,259	99	5,363	99	3,172	99	1,977	100	18,557	99
		9,401		9,298		8,218		10,481		1,809		6,311		5,408		3,188		1,983		18,699	
3YR Language Comprehension	0	351	4	210	2	146	2	415	4	84	5	230	4	162	3	67	2	18	1	561	3
	1	325	3	246	3	163	2	408	4	184	6	224	3	170	3	62	2	11	1	571	3
	2	164	2	149	2	48	1	265	2	44	2	148	2	89	2	27	1	5	0	313	2
	3	54	1	61	1	28	0	87	1	14	1	61	1	24	0	12	0	4	0	115	1
	4	1,380	14	1,232	13	591	7	2,021	19	350	19	1,106	17	776	14	311	10	69	3	2,612	14
	5	384	4	347	4	294	4	437	4	73	4	307	5	242	4	72	2	37	2	731	4
	6	145	2	141	2	62	1	224	2	36	2	132	2	88	2	24	1	6	0	286	2
	7	6,736	71	6,944	74	6,881	84	6,799	64	1,133	62	4,193	66	3,898	72	2,625	82	1,831	92	13,680	72
		9,539		9,330		8,213		10,656		1,838		6,401		5,449		3,200		1,981		18,869	
3YR Sentence Complexity	0	399	4	203	2	267	3	335	3	74	4	232	4	184	3	87	3	25	1	602	3
	1	124	1	53	1	101	1	76	1	22	1	67	1	46	1	30	1	12	1	177	1
	2	228	2	136	1	192	2	172	2	37	2	145	2	121	2	46	2	15	1	364	2
	3	367	4	235	3	271	3	331	3	59	3	251	4	191	4	77	2	24	1	602	3
	4	1,049	11	971	11	756	9	1,264	12	217	12	767	12	646	12	290	9	100	5	2,020	11
	5	7,046	76	7,557	83	6,511	80	8,092	79	1,352	77	4,694	76	4,120	78	2,639	83	1,798	91	14,603	80
		9,213		9,155		8,098		10,270		1,761		6,156		5,308		3,169		1,974		18,368	
3YR Auditory Memory	0	42	1	35	0	39	1	38	0	12	1	32	1	23	1	7	0	3	0	77	0
	1	113	1	111	1	90	1	134	1	22	1	103	2	67	1	28	1	4	0	224	1
	2	1,097	14	1,009	13	1,066	16	1,040	11	204	13	779	15	665	15	326	12	132	8	2,106	13
	3	6,509	84	6,845	86	5,372	82	7,982	87	1,280	84	4,336	83	3,747	83	2,375	87	1,616	92	13,354	85
		7,761		8,000		6,567		9,194		1,518		5,250		4,502		2,736		1,755		15,761	
3YR Hearing Screen	0	153	2	93	1	114	1	132	1	27	2	97	2	63	1	38	1	21	1	246	1
	1	917	10	1,010	11	1,021	13	906	9	168	9	610	10	566	11	352	11	231	12	1,927	11
	2	8,094	88	8,011	88	6,794	86	9,311	90	1,572	89	5,442	89	4,644	88	2,746	88	1,701	87	16,105	88
		9,164		9,114		7,929		10,349		1,767		6,149		5,273		3,136		1,953		18,278	

Descriptive Statistics and Frequency Distributions of 3YR and 8YR Indexes by Sex, Race, grouped SEI, and Total Sample Size

		Male	Female	White	Black	0.0-1.9	2.0-3.9	4.0-5.9	6.0-7.9	8.0-9.5	Total
									SEI		
8YR Speech Mechanism	Mean	7.9	7.9	7.9	7.9	7.8	7.9	7.9	7.9	7.9	7.9
	Std. dev.	.77	.57	.60	.75	.84	.69	.67	.66	.55	.68
	% NIDF	2	2	1	3	2	2	2	1	1	2
8YR Palatal Function and Hypernasality	Mean	3.0	3.0	3.0	3.0	3.0	3.0	3.0	3.0	3.0	3.0
	Std. dev.	.26	.23	.29	.20	.23	.27	.25	.24	.19	.25
	% NIDF	2	2	1	3	2	2	2	2	<1	2
8YR Fluency	Mean	6.9	6.9	6.9	6.9	6.8	6.9	6.9	6.9	6.9	6.9
	Std. dev.	.62	.45	.46	.62	.67	.60	.54	.47	.43	.55
	% NIDF	2	2	1	3	3	2	2	1	<1	2
8YR Articulation	Mean	45	46	47	44	43	44	46	47	48	46
	Std. dev.	7.1	5.4	5.9	6.4	7.3	7.0	6.0	5.4	4.7	6.4
	% NIDF	1	1	1	2	2	2	2	1	<1	1
8YR Intelligibility	Mean	2.9	3.0	3.0	2.9	2.9	2.9	2.9	3.0	3.0	2.9
	Std. dev.	.33	.24	.24	.34	.42	.35	.28	.21	.12	.29
	% NIDF	1	1	1	2	2	2	2	1	<1	1
8YR Language Comprehension	Mean	157	148	167	138	131	141	151	165	181	153
	Std. dev.	45	44	42	43	44	43	43	42	39	45
	% NIDF	2	2	1	3	3	3	2	2	2	2
8YR Auditory Memory	Mean	170	170	178	162	154	160	169	180	192	170
	Std. dev.	41	41	40	40	41	40	39	39	36	41
	% NIDF	2	2	3	2	3	3	3	2	1	2
8YR Digits	Mean	33	34	34	33	31	32	33	35	37	34
	Std. dev.	10	10	10	9.5	9.3	9.7	9.8	10	10	10
	% NIDF	2	2	1	3	2	2	2	1	1	2
8YR Word Identification	Mean	64	61	68	57	55	58	62	67	72	62
	Std. dev.	10	9.7	8.4	8.4	8.6	8.8	8.6	8.5	8.4	9.9
	% NIDF	2	2	1	3	3	2	2	2	2	2
8YR Written Communication	Mean	192	213	219	185	169	182	199	224	249	203
	Std. dev.	57	54	56	51	52	52	53	51	46	57
	% NIDF	7	6	5	8	7	7	6	5	4	6

Descriptive Statistics and Frequency Distributions of 3YR and 8YR Indexes
by Sex, Race, grouped SEI, and Total Sample Size

		Male	Female	White	Black	0.0-1.9	2.0-3.9	4.0-5.9	6.0-7.9	8.0-9.5	Total
										SEI	
8YR Language Production	Mean	722	734	760	695	680	701	724	753	796	728
	Std. dev.	104	100	90	103	114	102	95	92	81	102
	% NIDF	4	3	3	5	4	4	4	3	2	4
8YR Concept Development	Mean	42	43	47	38	35	38	42	47	51	42
	Std. dev.	11	10	8.9	10	10	9.9	9.7	8.7	7.5	10
	% NIDF	3	3	2	4	4	3	3	3	1	3
8YR Hearing Severity	Mean	8.8	8.4	8.0	9.2	9.7	9.1	8.5	8.1	7.7	8.6
	Std. dev.	7.6	6.9	7.5	7.0	7.3	7.7	6.8	7.5	6.8	7.3
	% NIDF	1	1	1	2	2	1	1	1	1	1
8YR Hearing Acuity	Mean	5.8	5.5	4.9	6.4	6.5	6.1	5.6	5.1	4.8	5.6
	Std. dev.	5.3	5.0	5.3	4.9	5.1	5.5	4.9	5.0	5.0	5.1
	% NIDF	1	1	1	2	2	1	1	1	1	1
8YR Monaural Conductive Loss	% Loss	3.9	3.3	4.2	3.0	4.1	3.7	3.6	3.5	3.1	3.6
	% NIDF	2	2	2	2	3	2	2	2	2	2
8YR Binaural Conductive Loss	% Loss	1.5	1.2	1.8	0.9	0.9	1.6	1.2	1.5	1.1	1.3
	% NIDF	2	2	2	2	3	2	2	2	2	2
8YR Monaural Sensorineural Loss	% Loss	1.5	1.4	1.6	1.3	1.4	1.4	1.7	1.4	0.9	1.4
	% NIDF	2	2	2	2	2	2	2	2	2	2
8YR Binaural Sensorineural Loss	% Loss	0.3	0.3	0.3	0.3	0.1	0.3	0.3	0.3	0.4	0.3
	% NIDF	2	2	2	2	2	2	2	2	1	2
8YR Monaural Mixed (Component of Sensorineural) Loss	% Loss	0.7	0.8	0.8	0.7	0.6	0.9	0.7	0.8	0.5	0.7
	% NIDF	2	2	2	2	2	2	2	2	1	2
8YR Binaural Mixed (Component of Sensorineural) Loss	% Loss	0.2	0.1	0.2	0.1	0.1	0.1	0.1	0.2	0.2	0.1
	% NIDF	2	2	2	2	2	2	2	2	1	2
8YR Total Conductive Loss	% Loss	5.7	4.7	6.3	4.1	5.3	5.5	5.1	5.3	4.4	5.2
	% NIDF	2	2	2	2	3	2	2	2	2	2

Descriptive Statistics and Frequency Distributions of 3YR and 8YR Indexes
by Sex, Race, grouped SEI, and Total Sample Size

		Male	Female	White	Black	SEI 0.0-1.9	2.0-3.9	4.0-5.9	6.0-7.9	8.0-9.5	Total
8YR Total Sensorineural Loss	% Loss	2.4	2.2	2.4	2.1	2.1	2.4	2.3	2.3	1.6	2.3
	% NIDF	2	2	2	2	2	2	2	2	1	2
Neurological Involvement	Mean	15	15	15	15	15	15	15	15	16	15
	Std. dev.	1.4	1.3	1.4	1.3	1.4	1.3	1.3	1.4	1.3	1.4
	% NIDF	8	8	7	10	10	9	8	8	5	8
Communicative Effectiveness	Mean	504	525	574	452	422	457	505	573	642	515
	Std. dev.	132	129	117	115	112	114	120	114	94	131
	% NIDF	7	5	4	8	9	7	6	5	3	6
Auditory Processing	Mean	62	63	66	59	56	59	62	67	71	63
	Std. dev.	9.2	8.6	7.9	8.3	8.5	8.3	8.1	7.2	6.0	9.0
	% NIDF	10	10	9	11	12	11	10	9	7	10

8YR Indexes: Frequency Distributions

8YR Speech Mechanism

Code	Male Freq.	Male %	Female Freq.	Female %	White Freq.	White %	Black Freq.	Black %	0.0-1.9 Freq.	0.0-1.9 %	2.0-3.9 Freq.	2.0-3.9 %	4.0-5.9 Freq.	4.0-5.9 %	6.0-7.9 Freq.	6.0-7.9 %	8.0-9.5 Freq.	8.0-9.5 %	Totals Freq.	Totals %
0	1	0	1	0	1	0	1	0	0	0	0	0	1	0	0	0	1	0	2	0
1	2	0	0	0	1	0	1	0	0	0	0	0	0	0	1	0	0	0	2	0
2	27	0	7	0	8	0	26	1	3	0	16	0	9	0	4	0	2	0	34	0
3	67	1	33	0	37	0	63	2	22	1	34	1	25	0	12	0	7	0	100	1
4	183	2	123	1	129	1	177	2	28	2	84	1	96	2	76	2	22	1	306	2
5	5	0	3	0	5	0	3	0	2	0	0	0	3	0	3	0	0	0	8	0
6	19	0	9	0	14	0	14	0	2	0	10	0	7	0	6	0	2	0	28	0
7	204	2	151	2	179	2	176	2	39	2	109	2	130	2	50	1	27	1	355	2
8	9,447	95	9,519	97	9,700	96	9,266	95	1,499	94	5,626	96	5,693	95	3,913	96	2,235	97	18,966	96
	9,955		9,846		10,074		9,727		1,596		5,879		5,965		4,065		2,296		19,801	

8YR Palatal Function and Hypernasality

Code	Male Freq.	Male %	Female Freq.	Female %	White Freq.	White %	Black Freq.	Black %	0.0-1.9 Freq.	0.0-1.9 %	2.0-3.9 Freq.	2.0-3.9 %	4.0-5.9 Freq.	4.0-5.9 %	6.0-7.9 Freq.	6.0-7.9 %	8.0-9.5 Freq.	8.0-9.5 %	Totals Freq.	Totals %
0	18	0	16	0	29	0	5	0	1	0	15	0	13	0	4	0	1	0	34	0
1	100	1	69	1	106	1	63	1	15	1	55	1	51	1	35	1	13	1	169	1
2	134	1	133	1	185	2	82	1	15	1	95	2	74	1	56	1	27	1	267	1
3	9,697	97	9,620	98	9,752	97	9,565	98	1,561	98	5,709	97	5,823	98	3,965	98	2,259	98	19,317	98
	9,955		9,838		10,072		9,715		1,592		5,874		5,961		4,060		2,300		19,787	

8YR Fluency

Code	Male Freq.	Male %	Female Freq.	Female %	White Freq.	White %	Black Freq.	Black %	0.0-1.9 Freq.	0.0-1.9 %	2.0-3.9 Freq.	2.0-3.9 %	4.0-5.9 Freq.	4.0-5.9 %	6.0-7.9 Freq.	6.0-7.9 %	8.0-9.5 Freq.	8.0-9.5 %	Totals Freq.	Totals %
0	11	0	3	0	6	0	8	0	0	0	0	0	5	0	2	0	0	0	14	0
1	13	0	8	0	6	0	15	0	4	0	8	0	4	0	4	0	1	0	21	0
2	8	0	5	0	8	0	5	0	2	0	4	0	5	0	0	0	1	0	13	0
3	70	1	33	0	41	0	62	1	12	1	33	1	33	1	15	0	10	0	103	1
4	25	0	9	0	15	0	19	0	6	0	9	0	11	0	5	0	3	0	34	0
5	357	4	220	2	146	1	431	4	79	5	216	4	155	3	84	2	43	2	577	3
6	65	1	31	0	46	0	50	1	9	1	30	1	37	1	15	0	5	0	96	0
7	9,397	94	9,531	97	9,790	97	9,138	94	1,475	93	5,570	95	5,711	96	3,941	97	2,231	97	18,928	96
	9,946		9,840		10,058		9,728		1,587		5,877		5,961		4,067		2,294		19,786	

8YR Articulation

Code	Male Freq.	Male %	Female Freq.	Female %	White Freq.	White %	Black Freq.	Black %	0.0-1.9 Freq.	0.0-1.9 %	2.0-3.9 Freq.	2.0-3.9 %	4.0-5.9 Freq.	4.0-5.9 %	6.0-7.9 Freq.	6.0-7.9 %	8.0-9.5 Freq.	8.0-9.5 %	Totals Freq.	Totals %
0	5	0	5	0	6	0	4	0	2	0	6	0	0	0	2	0	0	0	10	0
1	0	0	0	0	0	0	1	0	0	0	0	0	1	0	0	0	0	0	1	0
2	3	0	0	0	1	0	2	0	1	0	3	0	0	0	1	0	0	0	3	0
3	4	0	6	0	7	0	2	0	0	0	4	0	2	0	1	0	0	0	4	0
4	7	0	2	0	4	0	6	0	4	0	4	0	2	0	3	0	1	0	13	0
5	9	0	1	0	4	0	7	0	0	0	5	0	4	0	2	0	0	0	11	0
6	6	0	1	0	2	0	3	0	0	0	3	0	2	0	0	0	0	0	7	0
7	5	0	0	0	1	0	4	0	4	0	4	0	1	0	0	0	0	0	6	0
8	5	0	1	0	2	0	5	0	0	0	4	0	0	0	0	0	0	0	6	0
9	7	0	2	0	2	0	7	0	1	0	3	0	4	0	1	0	0	0	9	0

8YR Articulation (continued)

Code	Male Freq.	%	Female Freq.	%	White Freq.	%	Black Freq.	%	0.0-1.9 Freq.	%	2.0-3.9 Freq.	%	4.0-5.9 Freq.	%	6.0-7.9 Freq.	%	8.0-9.5 Freq.	%	Totals Freq.	%
10	8	0	6	0	5	0	9	0	3	0	5	0	3	0	3	0	0	0	14	0
11	7	0	2	0	3	0	6	0	2	0	4	0	3	0	0	0	0	0	9	0
12	12	0	2	0	5	0	9	0	0	0	10	0	4	0	0	0	0	0	14	0
13	10	0	3	0	6	0	7	0	1	0	6	0	5	0	0	0	1	0	13	0
14	7	0	3	0	6	0	4	0	0	0	2	0	5	0	3	0	0	0	10	0
15	5	0	2	0	5	0	2	0	0	0	4	0	2	0	0	0	1	0	7	0
16	9	0	7	0	7	0	9	0	2	0	8	0	5	0	1	0	0	0	16	0
17	10	0	6	0	5	0	11	0	0	0	9	0	5	0	3	0	0	0	16	0
18	15	0	5	0	6	0	14	0	3	0	9	0	5	0	0	0	1	0	20	0
19	15	0	6	0	8	0	13	0	3	0	10	0	6	0	1	0	0	0	21	0
20	12	0	3	0	5	0	10	0	3	0	9	0	2	0	1	0	0	0	15	0
21	15	0	7	0	7	0	15	0	5	0	7	0	9	0	1	0	0	0	22	0
22	19	0	8	0	7	0	20	0	7	0	13	0	3	0	3	0	1	0	27	0
23	25	0	9	0	10	0	24	0	9	1	12	0	7	0	5	0	1	0	34	0
24	25	0	9	0	11	0	23	0	6	0	16	0	5	0	6	0	1	0	34	0
25	40	0	6	0	15	0	31	0	7	0	22	0	11	0	3	0	3	0	46	0
26	27	0	6	0	9	0	24	0	7	0	9	0	8	0	7	0	2	0	33	0
27	36	0	19	0	17	0	38	0	8	1	25	0	13	0	6	0	3	0	55	0
28	41	0	26	0	32	0	35	0	10	1	21	0	20	0	10	0	6	0	67	0
29	50	1	18	0	20	0	48	0	10	1	26	0	19	0	8	0	5	0	68	0
30	48	0	19	0	28	0	39	0	5	0	30	1	14	0	12	0	6	0	67	0
31	59	1	46	0	36	0	69	1	17	1	39	1	34	1	11	0	4	0	105	1
32	66	1	33	0	29	0	70	1	16	1	37	1	31	1	10	0	5	0	99	0
33	81	1	49	0	47	0	83	1	20	1	41	1	38	1	28	1	3	0	130	1
34	83	1	51	1	44	0	90	1	13	1	58	1	38	1	20	0	5	0	134	1
35	127	1	61	1	71	1	117	1	18	1	82	1	57	1	14	0	17	1	188	1
36	125	1	76	1	97	1	104	1	18	1	74	1	56	1	34	1	19	1	201	1
37	147	1	92	1	114	1	125	1	20	1	86	1	77	1	37	1	19	1	239	1
38	231	2	159	2	249	2	141	1	26	2	97	2	113	2	92	2	62	3	390	2
39	191	2	119	1	132	1	178	2	40	3	98	2	81	1	55	1	36	2	310	2
40	174	2	116	2	94	1	196	2	36	2	117	2	79	1	40	1	18	1	290	1
41	214	2	162	2	109	1	267	3	53	3	148	2	99	2	49	1	27	1	376	2
42	284	3	211	2	116	1	379	4	67	4	209	4	147	3	48	1	24	1	495	2
43	371	4	297	3	140	1	528	5	105	7	278	5	201	3	62	2	22	1	668	3
44	438	4	414	4	154	2	698	7	120	8	372	6	244	4	93	2	23	1	852	4
45	565	6	593	6	176	2	982	10	158	10	509	9	335	6	125	3	31	1	1,158	6
46	649	6	731	7	254	3	1,126	12	162	10	563	10	427	7	175	4	53	3	1,380	7
47	765	8	777	8	327	3	1,215	12	175	11	575	10	530	9	201	5	61	3	1,542	8
48	705	7	886	9	517	5	1,074	11	142	9	560	9	550	9	251	6	88	4	1,591	8
49	868	9	1,045	11	992	10	921	9	115	7	579	10	652	11	396	10	171	7	1,913	10

8YR Articulation (continued)

Code	Male Freq.	%	Female Freq.	%	White Freq.	%	Black Freq.	%	0.0-1.9 Freq.	%	2.0-3.9 Freq.	%	4.0-5.9 Freq.	%	6.0-7.9 Freq.	%	8.0-9.5 Freq.	%	Totals Freq.	%
50	3,360	34	3,754	38	6,146	61	968	10	177	11	1,089	18	2,013	34	2,256	55	1,579	68	7,114	36
	9,990		9,863		10,090		9,763		1,599		5,901		5,972		4,080		2,301		19,853	

8YR Intelligibility

Code	Male Freq.	%	Female Freq.	%	White Freq.	%	Black Freq.	%	0.0-1.9 Freq.	%	2.0-3.9 Freq.	%	4.0-5.9 Freq.	%	6.0-7.9 Freq.	%	8.0-9.5 Freq.	%	Totals Freq.	%
0	22	0	10	0	11	0	21	0	7	0	14	0	8	0	3	0	0	0	32	0
1	103	1	50	1	49	0	104	1	31	2	68	1	40	1	12	0	2	0	153	1
2	581	6	286	3	292	3	575	6	126	8	352	6	261	4	103	3	25	1	867	4
3	9,289	93	9,515	96	9,741	97	9,063	93	1,438	90	5,461	93	5,671	95	3,960	97	2,274	99	18,804	95
	9,995		9,861		10,093		9,763		1,602		5,895		5,980		4,078		2,301		19,856	

8YR Language Comprehension

Code	Male Freq.	%	Female Freq.	%	White Freq.	%	Black Freq.	%	0.0-1.9 Freq.	%	2.0-3.9 Freq.	%	4.0-5.9 Freq.	%	6.0-7.9 Freq.	%	8.0-9.5 Freq.	%	Totals Freq.	%
0-1	0	0	0	0	0	0	0	0	0	0	0	0	0	0	0	0	0	0	0	0
2-3	0	0	1	0	0	0	1	0	0	0	1	0	0	0	0	0	0	0	1	0
4-5	3	0	1	0	0	0	4	0	1	0	3	0	0	0	0	0	0	0	4	0
6-7	1	0	0	0	0	0	1	0	0	0	1	0	0	0	0	0	0	0	1	0
8-9	0	0	0	0	0	0	0	0	0	0	0	0	0	0	0	0	0	0	0	0
10-11	2	0	0	0	0	0	2	0	1	0	1	0	1	0	0	0	0	0	2	0
12-13	0	0	1	0	0	0	1	0	0	0	0	0	0	0	0	0	0	0	1	0
14-15	0	0	0	0	0	0	0	0	0	0	0	0	0	0	0	0	0	0	0	0
16-17	0	0	0	0	1	0	1	0	0	0	0	0	1	0	0	0	0	0	1	0
18-19	2	0	1	0	0	0	2	0	1	0	2	0	0	0	1	0	0	0	3	0
20-21	0	0	1	0	0	0	1	0	0	0	1	0	1	0	0	0	0	0	1	0
22-23	1	0	1	0	2	0	2	0	0	0	0	0	2	0	0	0	0	0	2	0
24-25	2	0	1	0	0	0	1	0	0	0	1	0	0	0	1	0	0	0	3	0
26-27	3	0	1	0	1	0	4	0	3	0	1	0	2	0	0	0	0	0	4	0
28-29	2	0	3	0	1	0	4	0	1	0	2	0	2	0	0	0	0	0	5	0
30-31	3	0	1	0	1	0	3	0	2	0	2	0	1	0	0	0	0	0	4	0
32-33	2	0	4	0	1	0	5	0	2	0	3	0	1	0	1	0	0	0	6	0
34-35	3	0	4	0	2	0	5	0	3	0	3	0	2	0	0	0	0	0	7	0
36-37	2	0	2	0	1	0	3	0	0	0	0	0	4	0	1	0	0	0	4	0
38-39	7	0	8	0	2	0	13	0	1	0	8	0	7	0	2	0	0	0	15	0
40-41	12	0	8	0	4	0	16	0	1	0	6	0	5	0	2	0	2	0	20	0
42-43	17	0	17	0	3	0	31	0	5	0	21	0	11	0	4	0	1	0	34	0
44-45	17	0	35	0	7	0	45	0	13	0	26	0	14	0	2	0	0	0	52	0
46-47	16	0	26	0	8	0	34	0	7	0	17	0	10	0	4	0	0	0	42	0
48-49	11	0	25	0	7	0	29	0	8	0	15	0	9	0	3	0	1	0	36	0
50-51	15	0	21	0	9	0	27	0	7	0	15	0	9	0	4	0	0	0	36	0
52-53	13	0	24	0	2	0	35	0	6	0	22	0	9	0	0	0	0	0	37	0
54-55	31	0	23	0	8	0	46	0	9	0	26	0	15	0	4	0	1	0	54	0
56-57	25	0	28	0	18	0	35	0	3	0	26	0	20	0	3	0	0	0	53	0
58-59	22	0	28	0	18	0	32	0	10	0	22	0	12	0	5	0	1	0	50	0
60-61	20	0	26	0	18	0	28	0	4	0	19	0	15	0	6	0	1	0	46	0
62-63	20	0	15	0	16	0	19	0	4	0	9	0	10	0	9	0	3	0	35	0
64-65	14	0	20	0	15	0	19	0	3	0	8	0	15	0	6	0	2	0	34	0

8YR Indexes: Frequency Distributions

8YR Language Comprehension (continued)

Code	Male Freq.	Male %	Female Freq.	Female %	White Freq.	White %	Black Freq.	Black %	0.0-1.9 Freq.	0.0-1.9 %	2.0-3.9 Freq.	2.0-3.9 %	4.0-5.9 Freq.	4.0-5.9 %	6.0-7.9 Freq.	6.0-7.9 %	8.0-9.5 Freq.	8.0-9.5 %	Totals Freq.	Totals %
66-67	14	0	31	0	20	0	25	0	6	0	9	0	14	0	12	0	4	0	45	0
68-69	13	0	20	0	11	0	22	1	8	1	9	0	10	0	3	0	3	0	33	0
70-71	20	0	26	0	4	0	42	9	11	1	18	1	15	0	2	0	0	0	46	0
72-73	28	0	48	1	14	0	62	1	13	1	39	1	14	0	6	0	4	0	76	0
74-75	26	0	50	1	4	0	72	1	19	1	38	1	16	0	2	0	1	0	76	1
76-77	39	0	70	1	17	0	92	1	23	1	51	1	26	0	8	0	1	0	109	1
78-79	45	0	71	1	14	0	102	1	19	1	48	1	39	1	10	0	0	0	116	1
80-81	47	1	88	1	18	0	117	1	23	2	64	1	38	1	9	0	1	0	135	1
82-83	52	1	67	1	21	0	98	1	28	2	49	1	27	0	14	0	1	0	119	1
84-85	107	1	88	1	20	0	175	2	26	1	92	2	63	1	11	0	3	0	195	1
86-87	80	1	100	1	40	0	140	1	16	1	79	1	65	1	18	0	2	0	180	1
88-89	103	1	110	1	73	1	140	1	23	1	95	2	67	1	20	0	8	0	213	1
90-91	77	1	85	1	83	1	79	1	9	1	57	1	60	1	32	1	4	1	162	1
92-93	72	1	84	1	75	1	81	1	14	1	54	1	48	1	35	1	5	0	156	1
94-95	55	1	79	1	74	1	60	1	12	1	27	0	54	1	33	1	8	0	134	1
96-97	50	1	57	1	76	1	31	0	8	1	17	0	34	0	35	1	13	1	107	1
98-99	44	0	42	0	61	1	25	0	9	1	19	0	25	0	20	0	13	1	86	0
100-101	37	0	45	0	38	0	44	0	6	0	26	0	23	0	17	0	10	0	82	0
102-103	45	0	39	0	20	0	64	1	15	1	28	0	28	0	8	0	5	0	84	0
104-105	56	1	92	1	23	0	125	1	30	2	55	1	50	1	9	0	4	0	148	1
106-107	56	1	93	1	23	0	126	1	26	2	80	1	26	0	12	0	5	0	149	1
108-109	69	1	117	1	37	0	149	2	32	2	80	1	57	1	14	0	3	0	186	1
110-111	80	1	131	1	38	0	173	2	37	2	93	2	53	1	24	1	4	0	211	1
112-113	102	1	130	1	38	0	194	2	43	3	87	2	72	1	29	1	1	0	232	2
114-115	141	1	162	2	51	1	252	3	52	3	127	2	94	2	28	1	2	0	303	2
116-117	187	2	211	2	74	1	324	3	55	3	170	3	135	3	37	1	1	0	398	2
118-119	217	2	239	2	155	2	301	3	49	3	185	3	150	3	59	2	13	1	456	2
120-121	172	2	204	2	145	1	231	2	24	2	124	2	143	2	70	2	15	1	376	2
122-123	186	2	172	2	174	2	184	2	30	2	107	2	127	2	73	2	21	1	358	2
124-125	143	1	145	1	171	2	117	1	19	1	69	1	99	2	73	2	28	1	288	1
126-127	122	1	116	1	171	2	67	1	12	1	72	1	73	1	63	2	18	1	238	1
128-129	118	1	123	1	171	2	70	1	7	0	59	1	78	1	50	1	47	2	241	1
130-131	97	1	100	1	150	2	47	0	9	1	34	1	56	1	55	1	43	2	197	1
132-133	84	1	76	1	103	1	57	1	7	0	38	1	44	1	40	1	31	1	160	1
134-135	73	1	73	1	77	1	69	1	17	1	41	1	32	1	36	1	20	1	146	1
136-137	60	1	97	1	50	0	107	1	27	2	63	1	33	1	23	1	11	0	157	1
138-139	56	1	93	1	47	0	102	1	15	1	55	1	41	1	24	1	14	1	149	1
140-141	78	1	110	1	49	0	139	1	24	2	85	1	45	1	20	0	14	1	188	1
142-143	96	1	124	1	38	0	182	2	37	2	94	2	68	1	17	1	4	0	220	1
144-145	160	2	171	2	74	1	257	3	45	3	150	3	102	2	31	1	3	0	331	2

8YR Indexes: Frequency Distributions

8YR Language Comprehension (continued)

Code	Male Freq.	Male %	Female Freq.	Female %	White Freq.	White %	Black Freq.	Black %	0.0-1.9 Freq.	0.0-1.9 %	2.0-3.9 Freq.	2.0-3.9 %	4.0-5.9 Freq.	4.0-5.9 %	6.0-7.9 Freq.	6.0-7.9 %	8.0-9.5 Freq.	8.0-9.5 %	Totals Freq.	Totals %
146-147	166	2	253	3	81	1	338	3	46	3	188	3	134	2	42	1	9	0	419	2
148-149	236	2	269	3	151	1	354	4	40	3	206	4	176	3	74	2	9	0	505	3
150-151	256	3	253	3	210	3	299	3	36	2	206	4	174	3	81	2	12	1	509	3
152-153	255	3	259	3	258	3	256	3	29	1	168	3	172	3	115	3	30	1	514	3
154-155	229	2	202	2	244	2	187	2	22	1	108	2	157	3	107	3	37	3	431	3
156-157	237	2	198	2	298	3	137	1	14	1	92	2	149	3	119	3	61	3	435	2
158-159	224	2	198	2	328	3	94	1	10	1	78	1	123	2	146	4	65	3	422	2
160-161	181	2	158	2	278	3	61	1	7	0	59	1	105	2	101	2	67	3	339	2
162-163	144	1	130	1	227	2	47	0	6	0	40	1	72	1	93	2	63	3	274	1
164-165	135	1	86	1	185	2	36	0	6	0	32	1	58	1	66	2	59	3	221	1
166-167	86	1	81	1	118	1	49	1	12	1	26	0	46	1	42	1	41	2	167	1
168-169	89	1	54	1	85	1	58	1	9	1	35	1	38	1	29	1	32	1	143	1
170-171	72	1	57	1	67	1	62	1	13	1	41	1	31	1	21	1	23	1	129	1
172-173	49	0	58	1	25	0	82	1	14	1	39	1	39	1	10	0	5	0	107	1
174-175	76	1	98	1	43	0	131	1	30	2	74	1	44	1	16	0	10	0	174	1
176-177	131	1	141	2	69	1	203	2	33	3	125	2	73	1	33	1	8	0	272	2
178-179	174	2	166	2	109	1	231	2	43	3	114	2	116	2	54	1	13	1	340	2
180-181	170	2	192	2	146	1	216	2	28	2	128	2	133	2	54	1	19	1	362	2
182-183	223	2	173	2	225	3	171	2	18	1	108	2	148	2	93	2	29	2	396	2
184-185	217	2	185	2	257	3	145	2	22	1	98	2	138	2	99	2	45	2	402	2
186-187	178	2	176	2	245	2	109	1	15	1	76	1	121	2	92	2	50	2	354	2
188-189	219	2	204	2	313	3	110	1	11	1	87	1	129	2	130	3	66	3	423	2
190-191	209	2	196	2	323	3	82	1	11	1	60	1	116	2	136	3	82	4	405	2
192-193	185	2	147	2	281	3	51	1	2	0	50	1	85	1	101	2	94	4	332	2
194-195	162	2	115	1	244	2	33	0	3	0	24	0	65	1	94	2	91	3	277	1
196-197	122	1	59	1	163	2	18	0	6	0	23	0	26	0	55	1	71	3	181	1
198-199	101	1	56	1	123	1	34	0	4	0	22	0	26	0	52	1	53	2	157	1
200-201	51	1	42	0	68	1	25	0	3	0	14	0	19	0	23	1	34	1	93	0
202-203	33	0	27	0	32	0	28	0	1	0	13	0	13	0	16	0	17	1	60	0
204-205	46	0	30	0	31	0	45	0	6	0	27	1	22	0	17	0	4	0	76	0
206-207	76	1	61	1	45	0	92	1	10	1	51	1	44	1	19	0	13	1	137	1
208-209	86	1	81	1	59	1	108	1	17	1	57	1	56	1	28	1	9	0	167	1
210-211	102	1	76	1	83	1	95	1	11	1	64	1	55	1	33	1	15	1	178	1
212-213	133	1	90	1	121	1	102	1	12	1	72	1	64	1	56	2	19	1	223	1
214-215	142	1	95	1	159	2	78	1	9	1	51	1	82	1	64	2	31	1	237	1
216-217	136	1	119	1	170	2	85	1	13	1	52	1	76	1	73	2	41	2	255	1
218-219	145	1	131	1	213	2	63	1	5	0	52	1	92	2	78	2	49	2	276	1
220-221	150	2	151	2	257	3	44	0	6	0	36	1	90	2	91	2	78	3	301	2
222-223	172	2	111	1	234	2	49	1	8	1	31	1	66	1	98	2	80	4	283	1
224-225	144	1	84	1	201	2	27	0	2	0	21	0	53	1	69	2	83	4	228	1

608

Code	Male Freq	Male %	Female Freq	Female %	White Freq	White %	Black Freq	Black %	0.0-1.9 Freq	0.0-1.9 %	2.0-3.9 Freq	2.0-3.9 %	4.0-5.9 Freq	4.0-5.9 %	6.0-7.9 Freq	6.0-7.9 %	8.0-9.5 Freq	8.0-9.5 %	Totals Freq	Totals %
8YR Language Comprehension (continued)																				
226-227	127	1	72	1	183	2	16	0	3	0	15	0	42	1	68	2	71	3	199	1
228-229	82	1	44	0	124	1	2	0	2	0	9	0	15	0	39	1	61	3	126	1
230-231	58	0	28	0	79	0	7	0	2	0	7	0	17	0	26	0	34	1	86	0
232-233	31	0	14	0	43	0	2	0	0	0	1	0	4	0	17	0	23	1	45	0
234-235	15	0	4	0	19	0	0	0	1	0	0	0	2	0	8	0	8	0	19	0
236-237	19	0	8	0	26	0	1	0	0	0	1	0	3	0	8	0	15	1	27	0
238-239	9	0	3	0	11	0	1	0	0	0	0	0	1	0	3	0	8	0	12	0
240-241	13	0	3	0	15	0	1	0	0	0	1	0	2	0	6	0	7	0	16	0
242-243	9	0	2	0	10	0	0	0	0	0	0	0	1	0	1	0	9	0	11	0
244-245	1	0	4	0	5	0	0	0	0	0	0	0	0	0	1	0	4	0	5	0
246-247	5	0	1	0	6	0	1	0	0	0	0	0	2	0	2	0	2	0	6	0
248-249	2	0	5	0	6	0	0	0	0	0	1	0	0	0	1	0	5	0	7	0
250-251	2	0	2	0	4	0	0	0	0	0	0	0	2	0	2	0	2	0	4	0
252-253	2	0	0	0	2	0	0	0	0	0	1	0	0	0	1	0	0	0	2	0
254-255	2	0	1	0	2	0	1	0	0	0	0	0	0	0	1	0	1	0	2	0
256-257	1	0	0	0	1	0	1	0	0	0	1	0	0	0	0	0	0	0	2	0
258-259	2	0	1	0	1	0	0	0	0	0	1	0	0	0	1	0	1	0	1	0
260-261	0	0	0	0	2	0	0	0	0	0	0	0	0	0	0	0	0	0	2	0
262-263	0	0	0	0	0	0	0	0	0	0	1	0	1	0	1	0	0	0	0	0
264-265	3	0	0	0	3	0	0	0	0	0	0	0	0	0	1	0	2	0	3	0
	9,899		9,759		9,997		9,661		1,581		5,834		5,926		4,045		2,272		19,658	
8YR Auditory Memory																				
0-1	2	0	0	0	1	0	1	0	0	0	0	0	2	0	0	0	0	0	2	0
2-3	0	0	0	0	0	0	0	0	0	0	0	0	0	0	0	0	0	0	0	0
4-5	2	0	0	0	2	0	0	0	0	0	2	0	2	0	0	0	0	0	2	0
6-7	0	0	1	0	0	0	1	0	0	0	0	0	0	0	0	0	0	0	0	0
8-9	3	0	0	0	3	0	0	0	0	0	2	0	1	0	1	0	0	0	4	0
10-11	0	0	1	0	0	0	1	0	0	0	0	0	0	0	0	0	0	0	1	0
12-13	0	0	0	0	2	0	0	0	0	0	4	0	0	0	0	0	0	0	0	0
14-15	2	0	3	0	0	0	3	0	0	0	0	0	1	0	0	0	0	0	5	0
16-17	0	0	0	0	1	0	1	0	0	0	1	0	0	0	0	0	0	0	1	0
18-19	1	0	0	0	0	0	1	0	0	0	0	0	0	0	0	0	0	0	1	0
20-21	4	0	0	0	1	0	3	0	0	0	2	0	2	0	0	0	0	0	4	0
22-23	3	0	0	0	0	0	3	0	2	0	0	0	1	0	0	0	0	0	3	0
24-25	0	0	1	0	0	0	1	0	0	0	1	0	0	0	0	0	0	0	1	0
26-27	1	0	0	0	0	0	2	0	2	0	0	0	0	0	0	0	0	0	2	0
28-29	2	0	2	0	2	0	2	0	0	0	2	0	1	0	0	0	0	0	4	0
30-31	0	0	0	0	0	0	0	0	0	0	0	0	0	0	0	0	0	0	0	0
32-33	4	0	2	0	5	0	1	0	2	0	3	0	1	0	0	0	0	0	6	0
34-35	1	0	3	0	0	0	4	0	1	0	3	0	0	0	0	0	0	0	4	0
36-37	3	0	2	0	1	0	4	0	2	0	2	0	0	0	1	0	0	0	5	0

8YR Indexes: Frequency Distributions

8YR Auditory Memory (continued)

Code	Male Freq	Male %	Female Freq	Female %	White Freq	White %	Black Freq	Black %	0.0-1.9 Freq	0.0-1.9 %	2.0-3.9 Freq	2.0-3.9 %	4.0-5.9 Freq	4.0-5.9 %	6.0-7.9 Freq	6.0-7.9 %	8.0-9.5 Freq	8.0-9.5 %	Totals Freq	Totals %
38-39	4	0	2	0	4	0	2	0	0	0	2	0	3	0	0	0	1	0	6	0
40-41	3	0	0	0	0	0	3	0	0	0	0	0	3	0	0	0	0	0	3	0
42-43	5	0	5	0	4	0	6	0	2	0	4	0	1	0	2	0	1	0	10	0
44-45	1	0	1	0	1	0	1	0	0	0	1	0	0	0	1	0	0	0	2	0
46-47	3	0	2	0	2	0	3	0	2	0	2	0	0	0	1	0	0	0	5	0
48-49	8	0	8	0	4	0	12	0	4	0	7	0	4	0	1	0	0	0	16	0
50-51	6	0	1	0	3	0	4	0	2	0	1	0	1	0	2	0	1	0	7	0
52-53	8	0	6	0	4	0	10	0	2	0	7	0	2	0	3	0	0	0	14	0
54-55	6	0	2	0	4	0	4	0	0	0	5	0	3	0	0	0	0	0	8	0
56-57	7	0	5	0	4	0	8	0	1	0	5	0	4	0	1	0	1	0	12	0
58-59	5	0	1	0	1	0	5	0	0	0	4	0	1	0	1	0	0	0	6	0
60-61	8	0	8	0	5	0	11	0	1	0	8	0	3	0	3	0	0	0	16	0
62-63	13	0	9	0	6	0	16	0	5	0	8	0	3	0	3	0	1	0	22	0
64-65	10	0	8	0	7	0	11	0	4	0	8	0	4	0	3	0	0	0	18	0
66-67	7	0	17	0	11	0	13	0	6	0	8	0	7	0	3	0	0	0	24	0
68-69	7	0	4	0	7	0	4	0	5	0	2	0	3	0	1	0	0	0	11	0
70-71	20	0	14	0	9	0	25	0	7	0	11	0	11	0	3	0	2	0	34	0
72-73	8	0	14	0	11	0	11	0	1	0	11	0	3	0	4	0	1	0	22	0
74-75	17	0	12	0	9	0	20	0	7	0	13	0	8	0	3	0	1	0	29	0
76-77	22	0	24	0	17	0	29	0	6	0	16	0	7	0	1	0	0	0	46	0
78-79	12	0	14	0	10	0	16	0	5	0	12	0	3	0	3	0	1	0	26	0
80-81	18	0	21	0	14	0	25	0	7	0	13	0	9	0	6	0	0	0	39	0
82-83	31	0	18	0	21	0	28	0	7	0	21	0	9	0	4	0	1	0	49	0
84-85	27	0	25	0	10	0	42	0	7	0	19	0	16	0	9	0	0	0	52	0
86-87	33	0	22	0	17	0	38	0	9	0	26	0	18	0	3	0	1	0	55	0
88-89	38	0	32	0	19	0	51	1	8	0	33	0	15	0	4	0	2	0	70	0
90-91	28	0	22	0	17	0	33	0	11	0	21	0	20	0	6	0	2	0	50	0
92-93	44	0	28	0	24	0	48	0	6	0	25	0	15	0	4	0	0	0	72	0
94-95	24	0	30	0	20	0	34	0	21	0	24	0	14	0	7	0	2	0	54	0
96-97	27	0	34	0	29	0	32	0	9	0	31	0	17	0	12	0	1	0	61	0
98-99	42	0	41	0	23	0	60	1	6	0	32	0	13	0	10	0	0	0	83	0
100-101	60	1	47	0	33	0	74	1	11	0	44	1	31	0	7	0	3	0	107	1
102-103	44	0	52	1	31	0	65	1	14	0	40	1	31	0	13	0	1	0	96	0
104-105	40	0	40	0	28	0	52	1	9	0	29	0	38	1	5	0	2	0	80	0
106-107	28	0	40	0	28	0	40	0	14	0	23	0	28	0	8	0	5	0	68	0
108-109	63	1	65	1	39	0	89	1	9	0	57	1	42	1	16	0	4	0	128	1
110-111	68	1	66	1	56	1	78	1	18	0	48	1	41	1	11	0	3	0	134	1
112-113	66	1	83	1	60	1	89	1	15	0	59	1	44	1	24	0	3	0	149	1
114-115	73	1	85	1	58	1	100	1	13	0	70	1	49	1	18	0	8	0	158	1
116-117	54	1	60	1	42	0	72	1	9	0	52	1	31	0	19	0	3	0	114	1

8YR Indexes: Frequency Distributions

8YR Auditory Memory (continued)

Code	Male Freq.	%	Female Freq.	%	White Freq.	%	Black Freq.	%	0.0-1.9 Freq.	%	2.0-3.9 Freq.	%	4.0-5.9 Freq.	%	6.0-7.9 Freq.	%	8.0-9.5 Freq.	%	Totals Freq.	%
118-119	55	1	68	1	49	0	74	1	13	1	58	1	33	1	16	0	3	0	123	1
120-121	85	1	88	1	70	1	103	1	29	2	56	1	54	1	21	1	13	1	173	1
122-123	90	1	114	1	86	1	118	1	23	1	67	1	77	1	29	1	8	0	204	1
124-125	114	1	120	1	91	1	143	1	30	2	88	2	70	1	34	1	12	1	234	1
126-127	91	1	115	1	83	1	123	1	22	1	79	1	63	1	34	1	8	0	206	1
128-129	75	1	82	1	61	1	96	1	19	1	65	1	41	1	23	1	9	0	157	1
130-131	103	1	109	1	64	1	148	2	33	2	77	1	62	1	28	1	12	1	212	1
132-133	131	1	118	1	112	1	137	1	33	1	88	2	64	1	51	1	13	1	249	1
134-135	161	2	155	2	121	1	195	2	44	3	121	2	87	1	46	1	18	1	316	2
136-137	148	1	168	2	140	1	176	2	29	2	105	2	104	2	57	1	21	1	316	2
138-139	149	2	120	1	96	1	173	2	23	1	109	2	93	2	31	1	13	1	269	1
140-141	92	1	121	1	91	1	122	1	19	1	89	2	63	1	28	1	14	1	213	1
142-143	135	1	129	1	121	1	143	1	22	1	103	2	71	1	46	1	22	1	264	1
144-145	141	1	139	1	123	1	157	2	24	2	91	2	94	2	52	1	19	1	280	1
146-147	185	2	166	2	155	2	196	2	31	2	126	2	114	2	59	1	21	1	351	2
148-149	149	2	187	2	138	1	198	2	39	2	107	2	113	2	60	1	17	1	336	2
150-151	158	2	155	2	152	2	161	2	24	1	110	2	97	2	55	1	27	1	313	2
152-153	161	2	140	1	126	1	175	2	20	1	113	2	102	2	45	1	21	1	301	2
154-155	135	1	144	1	120	1	159	2	20	1	86	1	86	2	57	1	30	1	279	2
156-157	179	2	188	2	170	2	197	2	22	2	111	2	131	2	75	2	28	1	367	2
158-159	205	2	204	2	186	2	223	2	42	3	123	2	133	2	71	2	40	2	409	2
160-161	214	2	196	2	191	2	219	2	31	2	142	2	125	2	82	2	30	1	410	2
162-163	179	2	175	2	172	2	182	2	37	2	111	2	116	2	66	2	24	1	354	2
164-165	198	2	152	2	166	2	184	2	25	2	124	2	95	2	65	2	41	2	350	2
166-167	143	1	141	1	127	1	157	2	26	2	99	2	86	2	51	1	22	1	284	1
168-169	195	2	189	2	175	2	209	2	18	1	116	2	111	2	86	2	34	1	384	2
170-171	230	2	239	2	235	2	234	2	18	1	150	3	144	2	91	2	46	2	469	2
172-173	196	2	231	2	222	2	205	2	38	2	125	2	120	2	113	3	39	2	427	2
174-175	199	2	199	2	196	2	202	2	30	2	116	2	128	2	85	2	33	1	398	2
176-177	164	2	181	2	173	2	172	2	36	2	97	2	112	2	75	2	35	2	345	2
178-179	160	2	153	2	169	2	144	1	18	1	78	1	113	2	63	2	41	2	313	2
180-181	243	2	191	2	214	2	220	2	18	1	131	2	142	2	85	2	58	3	434	2
182-183	196	2	216	2	226	2	186	2	33	2	110	2	126	2	89	2	54	2	412	2
184-185	252	3	214	2	245	2	221	2	23	1	137	2	152	3	97	2	57	3	466	2
186-187	188	2	173	2	215	2	146	2	18	1	93	2	111	2	88	2	51	2	361	2
188-189	126	1	138	1	139	1	125	2	27	2	75	1	73	1	46	1	43	2	264	1
190-191	162	2	134	2	182	2	114	1	12	1	72	1	79	1	82	2	51	2	296	2
192-193	202	2	182	2	221	2	163	2	28	2	93	2	131	2	74	2	58	3	384	2
194-195	191	2	182	2	221	2	152	2	32	2	84	2	119	2	93	2	45	3	373	2
196-197	165	2	186	2	205	2	146	2	24	2	80	1	112	2	78	2	57	3	351	2

8YR Indexes: Frequency Distributions

8YR Auditory Memory (continued)

Code	Male Freq.	Male %	Female Freq.	Female %	White Freq.	White %	Black Freq.	Black %	0.0-1.9 Freq.	0.0-1.9 %	2.0-3.9 Freq.	2.0-3.9 %	4.0-5.9 Freq.	4.0-5.9 %	6.0-7.9 Freq.	6.0-7.9 %	8.0-9.5 Freq.	8.0-9.5 %	Totals Freq.	Totals %
198-199	156	2	151	2	184	2	123	2	14	1	76	1	91	2	81	2	45	2	307	2
200-201	140	1	108	1	156	2	92	1	15	1	57	1	77	1	58	1	41	2	248	1
202-203	129	1	134	1	148	1	115	1	14	1	70	1	77	1	59	1	43	2	263	1
204-205	200	2	181	2	246	2	135	1	22	1	93	2	96	2	103	3	67	3	381	2
206-207	155	2	154	2	186	2	123	1	20	1	66	1	92	2	79	2	52	2	309	2
208-209	170	2	138	1	191	2	117	1	14	1	63	1	95	2	79	2	57	3	308	2
210-211	123	1	130	1	160	2	93	1	8	1	61	1	63	1	67	2	54	3	253	1
212-213	76	1	82	1	86	1	72	1	15	1	39	1	39	1	42	1	23	1	158	1
214-215	128	1	126	1	169	2	85	1	10	1	44	1	69	1	68	2	63	3	254	1
216-217	121	1	116	1	158	2	79	1	11	1	48	1	71	1	58	1	49	2	237	1
218-219	148	1	123	1	171	2	100	1	7	1	53	1	71	1	68	2	72	3	271	1
220-221	87	1	86	1	103	1	70	1	7	0	40	1	50	1	45	1	31	1	173	1
222-223	94	1	79	1	105	1	68	1	6	0	34	1	52	1	50	1	31	1	173	1
224-225	64	1	75	1	96	1	43	0	7	0	28	1	36	1	37	1	25	1	139	1
226-227	66	1	73	1	87	1	52	1	4	0	24	1	38	1	48	1	44	2	214	1
228-229	114	1	100	1	146	1	68	1	8	1	34	1	71	1	57	1	31	1	107	1
230-231	52	1	55	1	73	1	34	1	5	0	18	0	21	1	32	1	41	2	169	1
232-233	88	1	81	1	118	1	51	1	7	1	33	1	33	1	55	2	14	1	67	1
234-235	30	0	37	0	52	0	15	0	0	0	12	0	22	0	18	1	11	0	63	0
236-237	24	1	39	1	44	1	19	1	7	1	13	0	17	0	22	1	34	1	134	1
238-239	75	1	59	1	94	1	40	0	2	0	18	0	34	1	41	1	6	0	62	0
240-241	31	0	31	0	42	0	20	0	4	0	11	0	20	1	23	1	39	1	121	1
242-243	54	1	67	1	85	1	36	1	0	0	14	0	30	1	34	1	12	1	38	0
244-245	14	0	24	0	26	0	12	0	1	0	6	0	11	0	9	0	16	1	66	0
246-247	27	0	39	0	47	0	19	0	0	0	9	0	16	0	24	1	14	1	53	0
248-249	27	0	26	0	40	0	13	0	1	0	7	0	15	0	16	0	7	1	21	0
250-251	10	0	11	0	15	0	6	0	0	0	5	0	2	0	7	0	20	0	68	0
252-253	44	0	24	0	46	1	22	0	1	0	9	0	15	0	23	1	12	1	12	0
254-255	1	0	11	0	10	0	2	0	0	0	1	0	3	0	3	0	5	0	34	0
256-257	17	0	17	0	24	0	10	0	0	0	6	0	5	0	17	0	6	0	16	0
258-259	7	0	9	0	13	0	3	0	0	0	3	0	3	0	6	0	4	0	12	0
260-261	3	0	9	0	8	0	4	0	0	0	1	0	0	0	4	0	6	0	25	0
262-263	10	0	15	0	20	0	5	0	1	0	3	0	4	0	9	0	8	0	6	0
264-265	4	0	2	0	4	0	2	0	0	0	0	0	2	0	1	0	3	0	34	0
266-267	16	0	18	0	29	0	5	0	0	0	5	0	11	0	10	0	8	0	5	0
268-269	2	0	3	0	3	0	2	0	0	0	2	0	0	0	0	0	1	0	3	0
270-271	2	0	1	0	3	0	0	0	0	0	2	0	2	0	0	0	1	0	12	0
272-273	5	0	7	0	9	0	3	0	0	0	2	0	3	0	2	0	5	0	0	0
274-275	0	0	1	0	1	0	0	0	0	0	0	0	0	0	0	0	1	0	7	0
276-277	2	0	5	0	5	0	2	0	0	0	2	0	1	0	2	0	2	0	7	0

8YR Indexes: Frequency Distributions

Code	Male Freq.	%	Female Freq.	%	White Freq.	%	Black Freq.	%	0.0-1.9 Freq.	%	2.0-3.9 Freq.	%	4.0-5.9 Freq.	%	6.0-7.9 Freq.	%	8.0-9.5 Freq.	%	Totals Freq.	%
8YR Auditory Memory (continued)																				
278-279	1	0	0	0	1	0	0	0	0	0	0	0	0	0	0	0	1	0	1	0
280-281	2	0	5	0	6	0	1	0	0	0	1	0	1	0	2	0	3	0	7	0
282-283	0	0	2	0	2	0	0	0	0	0	0	0	2	0	0	0	0	0	2	0
284-285	0	0	4	0	3	0	1	0	0	0	0	0	1	0	1	0	1	0	4	0
286-287	4	0	4	0	7	0	1	0	0	0	1	0	2	0	3	0	3	0	8	0
288-289	1	0	2	0	2	0	1	0	0	0	0	0	0	0	1	0	1	0	3	0
290-291	6	0	3	0	7	0	2	0	0	0	1	0	1	0	6	0	2	0	9	0
292-293	0	0	0	0	0	0	0	0	0	0	0	0	0	0	0	0	0	0	0	0
294-295	1	0	1	0	2	0	0	0	0	0	0	0	0	0	1	0	1	0	2	0
296-297	0	0	0	0	0	0	0	0	0	0	0	0	0	0	0	0	0	0	1	0
298-299	0	0	2	0	1	0	0	0	0	0	0	0	0	0	1	0	1	0	2	0
300-301	0	0	0	0	2	0	0	0	0	0	0	0	0	0	0	0	0	0	0	0
302-303	0	0	0	0	0	0	0	0	0	0	0	0	0	0	0	0	0	0	0	0
304-305	0	0	0	0	0	0	0	0	0	0	0	0	0	0	0	0	0	0	0	0
306-307	0	0	0	0	0	0	0	0	0	0	0	0	0	0	0	0	0	0	0	0
308-309	0	0	0	0	0	0	0	0	0	0	0	0	0	0	0	0	0	0	0	0
310-311	0	0	0	0	1	0	0	0	0	0	0	0	0	0	0	0	0	0	1	0
312-313	0	0	0	0	0	0	0	0	0	0	0	0	0	0	0	0	0	0	0	0
314-315	0	0	0	0	0	0	0	0	0	0	0	0	0	0	0	0	0	0	0	0
316-317	0	0	1	0	1	0	0	0	0	0	0	0	0	0	0	0	0	0	0	0
318-319	0	0	0	0	0	0	0	0	0	0	0	0	0	0	1	0	0	0	0	0
320-321	0	0	0	0	0	0	0	0	0	0	0	0	0	0	0	0	0	0	0	0
322-323	0	0	0	0	0	0	0	0	0	0	0	0	0	0	0	0	0	0	0	0
324-325	0	0	0	0	0	0	0	0	0	0	0	0	0	0	0	0	0	0	0	0
326-327	0	0	0	0	0	0	0	0	0	0	0	0	0	0	0	0	0	0	0	0
328-329	0	0	0	0	0	0	0	0	0	0	0	0	0	0	0	0	0	0	0	0
330-331	0	0	0	0	0	0	0	0	0	0	0	0	0	0	0	0	0	0	0	0
332-333	0	0	0	0	0	0	0	0	0	0	0	0	0	0	0	0	0	0	0	0
334-335	1	0	0	0	1	0	0	0	0	0	0	0	0	0	1	0	0	0	1	0
	9,894		9,758		9,996		9,656		1,574		5,842		5,910		4,046		2,280		19,652	
8YR Digits																				
0	22	0	14	0	12	0	24	0	5	0	15	0	11	0	3	0	2	0	36	0
5	13	0	19	0	15	0	17	0	3	0	14	0	9	0	4	0	2	0	32	0
10	88	1	55	1	79	1	64	1	20	1	57	1	44	1	18	0	4	0	143	1
15	249	2	197	2	232	2	214	2	51	3	185	3	131	2	61	1	18	1	446	2
20	978	10	682	7	810	8	850	9	190	12	594	10	514	9	256	6	106	5	1,660	8
25	1,566	16	1,442	15	1,468	15	1,540	16	290	18	961	16	954	16	559	14	244	11	3,008	15
30	2,492	25	2,224	23	2,257	22	2,459	25	418	26	1,466	25	1,457	24	922	23	453	20	4,716	24
35	1,602	16	1,786	18	1,588	16	1,800	18	261	16	1,059	18	994	17	687	17	387	17	3,388	17
40	1,502	15	1,658	17	1,775	18	1,385	14	181	11	786	13	948	16	751	18	494	22	3,160	16
45	481	5	603	6	585	6	499	5	73	5	278	5	300	5	260	6	173	8	1,084	5

8YR Digits (continued)

Code	Male Freq.	Male %	Female Freq.	Female %	White Freq.	White %	Black Freq.	Black %	0.0-1.9 Freq.	0.0-1.9 %	2.0-3.9 Freq.	2.0-3.9 %	4.0-5.9 Freq.	4.0-5.9 %	6.0-7.9 Freq.	6.0-7.9 %	8.0-9.5 Freq.	8.0-9.5 %	Totals Freq.	Totals %
50	686	7	788	8	820	8	654	7	78	5	353	6	426	7	364	9	253	11	1,474	7
55	158	2	204	2	216	2	146	1	20	1	73	1	94	2	96	2	79	3	362	2
60	111	1	127	1	173	2	65	1	3	0	36	1	57	1	75	2	67	3	238	1
65	11	0	17	0	18	0	10	0	1	0	5	0	9	0	8	0	5	0	28	0
70	11	0	11	0	13	0	9	0		0	9	0	7	0	4	0	2	0	22	0
75	0	0	4	0	4	0	0	0	0		0		0		2	0		0	4	0
80	2	0	4	0	6	0	0	0	0		0			0	2	0	3	0	6	0
85	1	0	0	0	1	0	0	0	0		0		1	0		0		0	1	0
	9,973		9,835		10,072		9,736		1,594		5,891		5,957		4,073		2,293		19,808	

8YR Word Identification

Code	Male Freq.	Male %	Female Freq.	Female %	White Freq.	White %	Black Freq.	Black %	0.0-1.9 Freq.	0.0-1.9 %	2.0-3.9 Freq.	2.0-3.9 %	4.0-5.9 Freq.	4.0-5.9 %	6.0-7.9 Freq.	6.0-7.9 %	8.0-9.5 Freq.	8.0-9.5 %	Totals Freq.	Totals %
0	0	0	1	0	0	0	1	0	0	0	1	0	0	0	0	0	0	0	1	0
1	1	0	0	0	0	0	1	0	0	0	0	0	0	0	0	0	0	0		0
2	0	0	0	0	0	0	0	0	0	0	0	0	0	0	0	0	0	0		0
3	0	0	0	0	0	0	0	0	0	0	0	0	0	0	0	0	0	0		0
4	2	0	1	0	0	0	3	0	0	0	2	0	0	0	0	0	0	0	3	0
5	1	0	0	0	0	0	1	0	0	0	0	0	0	0	0	0	0	0	1	0
6	0	0	0	0	0	0	2	0	1	0	0	0	0	0	0	0	0	0		0
7	0	0	0	0	0	0	0	0	0	0	0	0	0	0	0	0	0	0	2	0
8	0	0	0	0	0	0	0	0	0	0	2	0	0	0	0	0	0	0	0	0
9	3	0	2	0	1	0	4	0	1	0	0	0	2	0	0	0	0	0	3	0
10	2	0	0	0	0	0	1	0	0	0	1	0	0	0	0	0	0	0	4	0
11	1	0	0	0	0	0	1	0	1	0	0	0	1	0	0	0	0	0	1	0
12	0	0	0	0	0	0	1	0	0	0	0	0	0	0	0	0	0	0	1	0
13	1	0	0	0	0	0	1	0	0	0	1	0	1	0	0	0	0	0		0
14	0	0	1	0	0	0	0	0	0	0	0	0	0	0	0	0	0	0	1	0
15	1	0	0	0	0	0	1	0	1	0	1	0	1	0	0	0	0	0	1	0
16	0	0	1	0	0	0	0	0	0	0	0	0	0	0	0	0	0	0	0	0
17	2	0	1	0	0	0	3	0	1	0	2	0	1	0	0	0	0	0	1	0
18	0	0	1	0	0	0	1	0	2	0	0	0	1	0	0	0	0	0	1	0
19	2	0	2	0	0	0	3	0	0	0	0	0	1	0	0	0	0	0	3	0
20	0	0	0	0	0	0	2	0	3	0	0	0	0	0	0	0	0	0	1	0
21	0	0	1	0	0	0	2	0	0	0	1	0	1	0	0	0	0	0	3	0
22	1	0	0	0	0	0	0	0	0	0	2	0	1	0	0	0	0	0	2	0
23	0	0	0	0	0	0	2	0	0	0	0	0	0	0	0	0	0	0	0	0
24	2	0	2	0	0	0	1	0	0	0	0	0	0	0	0	0	0	0	2	0
25	2	0	0	0	0	0	2	0	1	0	1	0	2	0	0	0	0	0	2	0
26	1	0	1	0	0	0	5	0	2	0	0	0	0	0	1	0	0	0	2	0
27	3	0	2	0	0	0	0	0	0	0	3	0	0	0	0	0	0	0	2	0
28	0	0	0	0	0	0	5	0	3	0	0	0	0	0	0	0	0	0	5	0
29	2	0	5	0	0	0	5	0	0	0	2	0	2	0	0	0	0	0	7	0
30	2	0	3	0	1	0	4	0	1	0	1	0	2	0	1	0	0	0	5	0

8YR Indexes: Frequency Distributions

8YR Word Identification (continued)

Code	Male Freq.	%	Female Freq.	%	White Freq.	%	Black Freq.	%	0.0-1.9 Freq.	%	2.0-3.9 Freq.	%	4.0-5.9 Freq.	%	6.0-7.9 Freq.	%	8.0-9.5 Freq.	%	Totals Freq.	%
31	3	0	4	0	1	0	6	0	1	0	5	0	1	0	0	0	0	0	7	0
32	2	0	4	0		0	5	0	1	0	1	0	2	0	1	0	1	0	6	0
33	6	0	5	0	1	0	10	0	2	0	8	0	1	0	0	0	0	0	11	0
34	5	0	7	0	2	0	10	0	2	0	7	0	3	0	0	0	0	0	12	0
35	4	0	8	0	1	0	11	0	7	0	5	0	0	0	0	0	0	0	12	0
36	4	0	10	0	1	0	13	0	3	0	5	0	5	0	3	0	1	0	14	0
37	7	0	11	0	4	0	14	0	5	0	4	0	6	0	3	0	0	0	18	0
38	14	0	18	0	3	0	29	0	4	0	4	0	8	0	3	0	0	0	32	0
39	10	0	22	0	1	0	31	0	13	1	17	0	8	0	0	0	0	0	32	0
40	18	0	29	0	2	0	45	1	13	1	13	0	6	0	4	0	1	0	47	0
41	29	0	34	1	3	0	60	1	11	1	20	0	11	0	2	0	1	0	63	1
42	36	0	50	1	8	0	78	1	16	1	29	0	24	1	3	0	2	1	86	1
43	53	1	76	1	9	0	120	1	23	1	47	1	18	1	7	0	0	0	129	1
44	58	1	106	1	13	0	151	2	36	2	66	1	33	1	5	0	1	0	164	1
45	56	1	121	1	12	0	165	2	46	3	84	1	38	1	6	0	0	0	177	1
46	64	1	143	2	19	0	188	2	46	3	77	1	43	1	15	0	3	0	207	1
47	81	1	159	2	28	0	212	2	49	3	103	2	51	1	13	0	3	0	240	1
48	82	1	157	2	29	0	210	2	42	3	124	2	51	1	19	0	2	0	239	1
49	113	1	175	2	43	0	245	3	42	3	97	2	81	1	20	0	0	0	288	1
50	118	1	228	2	49	0	297	3	66	4	132	2	92	2	34	1	2	0	346	2
51	123	1	175	2	60	1	238	2	39	2	158	3	87	2	23	1	1	0	298	2
52	135	1	211	2	57	1	289	3	61	4	146	2	85	1	37	1	4	0	346	2
53	180	2	206	2	58	1	328	3	68	4	155	3	97	2	36	1	1	0	386	2
54	244	2	258	3	86	1	416	4	68	4	243	4	126	2	41	1	3	0	502	3
55	299	3	302	3	110	1	491	5	99	6	254	4	147	3	53	1	7	0	601	3
56	290	3	379	4	135	1	534	6	82	5	296	5	188	3	62	2	10	0	669	3
57	347	3	406	4	158	2	595	6	81	5	338	6	219	4	80	2	8	0	753	4
58	414	4	435	4	241	2	608	6	91	6	353	6	246	4	114	3	25	1	849	4
59	405	4	454	5	302	3	557	6	89	6	326	6	266	4	116	3	18	1	859	4
60	384	4	459	5	326	3	517	5	67	4	307	5	310	5	131	3	27	1	843	4
61	402	4	368	4	345	4	425	4	46	3	289	5	311	5	141	4	32	1	770	4
62	463	5	419	4	418	4	464	5	52	3	311	5	262	4	176	5	43	2	882	4
63	413	4	369	4	440	4	342	3	54	3	202	3	300	5	201	5	55	2	782	4
64	405	4	362	4	437	4	330	3	53	3	180	3	270	5	186	5	72	3	767	4
65	375	4	346	4	461	5	260	3	28	2	171	3	259	4	191	5	66	3	721	4
66	366	4	344	4	486	5	224	2	30	2	152	3	249	4	199	5	80	4	710	4
67	356	4	328	3	478	5	206	2	30	2	159	3	208	4	190	5	97	4	684	3
68	381	4	345	4	548	5	178	2	23	1	147	3	234	4	214	5	108	5	726	4
69	365	4	340	3	546	5	159	2	11	1	135	2	213	4	212	5	134	6	705	4
70	335	3	307	3	513	5	129	1	21	1	108	2	190	3	197	5	126	6	642	3

615

8YR Indexes: Frequency Distributions

8YR Word Identification (continued)

Code	Male Freq.	Male %	Female Freq.	Female %	White Freq.	White %	Black Freq.	Black %	0.0-1.9 Freq.	0.0-1.9 %	2.0-3.9 Freq.	2.0-3.9 %	4.0-5.9 Freq.	4.0-5.9 %	6.0-7.9 Freq.	6.0-7.9 %	8.0-9.5 Freq.	8.0-9.5 %	Totals Freq.	Totals %
71	325	3	312	3	533	5	104	1	12	1	83	1	188	3	204	5	150	7	637	3
72	317	3	236	2	453	5	100	1	11	1	89	2	142	2	184	5	127	6	553	3
73	267	3	207	2	411	4	63	1	6	0	46	1	120	2	153	4	149	7	474	2
74	266	3	167	2	375	4	58	1	5	0	47	1	105	2	157	4	119	5	433	2
75	231	2	142	1	340	3	33	0	4	0	29	0	94	1	110	3	136	6	373	2
76	198	2	96	1	269	3	25	0	6	0	25	0	74	1	95	2	94	4	294	1
77	162	2	99	1	245	2	16	0	4	0	22	0	45	1	89	2	101	4	261	1
78	146	1	60	1	193	2	13	0	4	0	15	0	32	1	69	2	86	4	206	1
79	113	1	70	1	172	2	11	0	2	0	20	0	23	0	63	2	75	3	183	1
80	98	1	37	0	130	1	5	0	2	0	10	0	23	1	38	1	62	3	135	1
81	62	1	35	0	88	1	9	0	0	0	3	0	17	0	32	1	43	2	97	0
82	34	0	13	0	42	0	5	0	0	0	4	0	6	0	12	0	25	1	47	0
83	29	0	15	0	43	0	1	0	1	0	1	0	4	0	19	0	20	1	44	0
84	22	0	7	0	29	0	0	0	0	0	1	0	2	0	13	0	12	1	29	0
85	13	0	9	0	21	0	1	0	1	0	0	0	6	0	8	0	8	0	22	0
86	24	0	9	0	32	0	1	0	0	0	3	0	5	0	11	0	14	1	33	0
87	23	0	7	0	28	0	2	0	0	0	2	0	4	0	7	0	17	1	30	0
88	7	0	2	0	8	0	1	0	0	0	0	0	2	0	5	0	2	0	9	0
89	22	0	4	0	25	0	1	0	0	0	1	0	1	0	9	0	16	1	26	0
90	10	0	3	0	11	0	2	0	0	0	0	0	3	0	4	0	5	0	13	0
91	14	0	6	0	20	0	0	0	0	0	1	0	3	0	6	0	10	1	20	0
92	9	0	3	0	11	0	1	0	0	0	0	0	1	0	2	0	9	1	12	0
93	10	0	3	0	13	0	0	0	0	0	0	0	0	0	4	0	9	0	13	0
94	8	0	4	0	12	0	0	0	0	0	0	0	1	0	3	0	7	0	12	0
95	7	0	7	0	14	0	0	0	0	0	0	0	0	0	3	0	10	1	14	0
96	3	0	3	0	6	0	0	0	0	0	0	0	1	0	1	0	4	0	6	0
97	8	0	5	0	13	0	0	0	0	0	0	0	2	0	3	0	8	0	13	0
98	3	0	6	0	6	0	3	0	0	0	0	0	1	0	2	0	4	0	9	0
99	1	0	1	0	2	0	0	0	0	0	0	0	0	0	0	0	2	0	2	0
100	2	0	5	0	7	0	0	0	0	0	2	0	0	0	2	0	5	0	7	0
101	1	0	0	0	1	0	0	0	0	0	0	0	0	0	0	0	1	0	1	0
102	3	0	0	0	3	0	0	0	0	0	0	0	0	0	2	0	0	0	3	0
103	0	0	1	0	2	0	0	0	0	0	0	0	0	0	0	0	2	0	2	0
104	1	0	1	0	2	0	0	0	0	0	0	0	0	0	1	0	1	0	2	0
105	2	0	0	0	2	0	0	0	0	0	0	0	0	0	0	0	2	0	2	0
106	2	0	1	0	2	0	1	0	0	0	0	0	0	0	1	0	2	0	3	0
107	0	0	1	0	1	0	0	0	0	0	0	0	0	0	0	0	1	0	1	0
108	1	0	0	0	1	0	0	0	0	0	0	0	0	0	0	0	1	0	1	0
109	1	0	0	0	1	0	0	0	0	0	0	0	0	0	1	0	0	0	1	0
110	0	0	1	0	1	0	0	0	0	0	0	0	0	0	0	0	1	0	1	0

8YR Word Identification (continued)

Code	Male Freq.	Male %	Female Freq.	Female %	White Freq.	White %	Black Freq.	Black %	0.0-1.9 Freq.	0.0-1.9 %	2.0-3.9 Freq.	2.0-3.9 %	4.0-5.9 Freq.	4.0-5.9 %	6.0-7.9 Freq.	6.0-7.9 %	8.0-9.5 Freq.	8.0-9.5 %	Totals Freq.	Totals %
111	2	0	0	0	2	0	0	0	0	0	0	0	0	0	1	0	1	0	2	0
112	0	0	0	0	0	0	0	0	0	0	0	0	0	0	0	0	0	0	0	0
113	0	0	0	0	0	0	0	0	0	0	0	0	0	0	0	0	0	0	0	0
114	0	0	0	0	3	0	0	0	0	0	0	0	0	0	1	0	2	0	3	0
115	3	0	0	0	0	0	0	0	0	0	0	0	0	0	0	0	0	0	0	0
116	0	0	0	0	0	0	0	0	0	0	0	0	0	0	0	0	0	0	0	0
117	0	0	0	0	0	0	0	0	0	0	0	0	0	0	0	0	0	0	0	0
118	0	0	0	0	0	0	0	0	0	0	0	0	0	0	0	0	0	0	0	0
119	0	0	0	0	0	0	0	0	0	0	0	0	0	0	0	0	0	0	0	0
120	0	0	0	0	0	0	0	0	0	0	0	0	0	0	0	0	0	0	0	0
121	0	0	0	0	0	0	0	0	0	0	0	0	0	0	0	0	0	0	0	0
122	0	0	0	0	0	0	0	0	0	0	0	0	0	0	0	0	0	0	0	0
123	0	0	0	0	0	0	0	0	0	0	0	0	0	0	0	0	0	0	0	0
124	0	0	0	0	0	0	0	0	0	0	0	0	0	0	0	0	0	0	0	0
125	0	0	0	0	0	0	0	0	0	0	0	0	0	0	0	0	0	0	0	0
126	0	0	0	0	0	0	0	0	0	0	0	0	0	0	0	0	0	0	0	0
127	0	0	0	0	0	0	0	0	0	0	0	0	0	0	0	0	0	0	0	0
128	0	0	0	0	0	0	0	0	0	0	0	0	0	0	0	0	0	0	0	0
129	0	0	0	0	0	0	0	0	0	0	0	0	0	0	0	0	0	0	0	0
130	0	0	0	0	0	0	0	0	0	0	0	0	0	0	0	0	0	0	0	0
131	0	0	0	0	0	0	0	0	0	0	0	0	0	0	0	0	0	0	0	0
132	0	0	0	0	0	0	0	0	0	0	0	0	0	0	0	0	0	0	0	0
133	0	0	0	0	0	0	0	0	0	0	0	0	0	0	0	0	0	0	0	0
134	0	0	0	0	0	0	0	0	0	0	0	0	0	0	0	0	0	0	0	0
135	0	0	0	0	0	0	0	0	0	0	0	0	0	0	0	0	0	0	0	0
136	0	0	0	0	0	0	0	0	0	0	0	0	0	0	0	0	0	0	0	0
137	0	0	0	0	0	0	0	0	0	0	0	0	0	0	0	0	0	0	0	0
138	0	0	0	0	0	0	0	0	0	0	0	0	0	0	0	0	0	0	0	0
139	0	0	0	0	0	0	0	0	0	0	0	0	0	0	0	0	0	0	0	0
140	0	0	0	0	0	0	0	0	0	0	0	0	0	0	0	0	0	0	0	0
141	0	0	0	0	0	0	0	0	0	0	0	0	0	0	0	0	0	0	0	0
142	0	0	0	0	0	0	0	0	0	0	0	0	0	0	0	0	0	0	0	0
143	0	0	0	0	0	0	0	0	0	0	0	0	0	0	0	0	0	0	0	0
144	0	0	0	0	0	0	0	0	0	0	0	0	0	0	0	0	0	0	0	0
145	0	0	0	0	0	0	0	0	0	0	0	0	0	0	0	0	0	0	0	0
146	0	0	0	0	0	0	0	0	0	0	0	0	0	0	0	0	0	0	0	0
147	0	0	0	0	0	0	0	0	0	0	0	0	0	0	0	0	0	0	0	0
148	0	0	0	0	0	0	0	0	0	0	0	0	0	0	0	0	0	0	0	0
149	0	0	0	0	0	0	0	0	0	0	0	0	0	0	0	0	0	0	0	0
150	0	0	0	0	0	0	0	0	0	0	0	0	0	0	0	0	0	0	0	0
	9,927		9,781		10,014		9,694		1,585		5,855		5,939		4,053		2,276		19,708	

8YR Indexes: Frequency Distributions

Written Communication

Code	Male Freq.	Male %	Female Freq.	Female %	White Freq.	White %	Black Freq.	Black %	0.0–1.9 Freq.	0.0–1.9 %	2.0–3.9 Freq.	2.0–3.9 %	4.0–5.9 Freq.	4.0–5.9 %	6.0–7.9 Freq.	6.0–7.9 %	8.0–9.5 Freq.	8.0–9.5 %	Totals Freq.	Totals %
0-1	1	0	0	0	0	0	1	0	1	0	0	0	0	0	0	0	0	0	1	0
2-3	1	0	0	0	1	0	1	0	1	0	0	0	0	0	1	0	1	0	2	0
4-5	0	0	1	0	0	0	0	0	0	0	0	0	0	0	0	0	0	0	0	0
6-7	0	0	0	0	0	0	0	0	0	0	0	0	0	0	0	0	0	0	0	0
8-9	2	0	2	0	1	0	3	0	0	0	1	0	2	0	1	0	0	0	4	0
10-11	0	0	2	0	0	0	0	0	0	0	0	0	0	0	0	0	0	0	0	0
12-13	2	0	0	0	1	0	1	0	1	0	0	0	0	0	1	0	0	0	2	0
14-15	1	0	0	0	0	0	1	0	0	0	0	0	1	0	0	0	0	0	1	0
16-17	1	0	0	0	1	0	1	0	1	0	0	0	0	0	0	0	0	0	1	0
18-19	2	0	1	0	0	0	3	0	0	0	1	0	2	0	0	0	0	0	3	0
20-21	3	0	2	0	3	0	2	0	1	0	3	0	0	0	1	0	0	0	5	0
22-23	1	0	2	0	2	0	1	0	0	0	2	0	0	0	1	0	0	0	3	0
24-25	3	0	2	0	1	0	4	0	3	0	2	0	0	0	0	0	0	0	5	0
26-27	3	0	1	0	3	0	1	0	0	0	2	0	2	0	0	0	0	0	4	0
28-29	3	0	1	0	1	0	3	0	0	0	1	0	2	0	1	0	0	0	4	0
30-31	1	0	3	0	1	0	3	0	0	0	4	0	0	0	0	0	0	0	4	0
32-33	1	0	1	0	0	0	2	0	0	0	2	0	0	0	0	0	0	0	2	0
34-35	1	0	2	0	1	0	2	0	1	0	1	0	1	0	0	0	0	0	3	0
36-37	6	0	0	0	1	0	5	0	2	0	2	0	1	0	1	0	0	0	6	0
38-39	5	0	1	0	2	0	4	0	2	0	3	0	1	0	0	0	0	0	6	0
40-41	5	0	0	0	1	0	4	0	0	0	1	0	0	0	0	0	0	0	5	0
42-43	3	0	2	0	3	0	2	0	1	0	4	0	2	0	2	0	0	0	5	0
44-45	4	0	4	0	3	0	5	0	4	0	2	0	3	0	0	0	0	0	8	0
46-47	4	0	4	0	2	0	3	0	1	0	1	0	0	0	1	0	0	0	5	0
48-49	2	0	1	0	1	0	2	0	3	0	0	0	1	0	0	0	0	0	3	0
50-51	6	0	4	0	2	0	8	0	2	0	4	0	3	0	1	0	0	0	10	0
52-53	7	0	3	0	2	0	8	0	1	0	8	0	0	0	1	0	0	0	10	0
54-55	8	0	2	0	3	0	7	0	2	0	4	0	3	0	0	0	1	0	10	0
56-57	6	0	3	0	4	0	5	0	3	0	3	0	5	0	0	0	0	0	9	0
58-59	9	0	4	0	5	0	8	0	5	0	7	0	4	0	0	0	0	0	13	0
60-61	8	0	8	0	3	0	13	0	1	0	10	0	1	0	2	0	1	0	16	0
62-63	11	0	2	0	8	0	5	0	3	0	4	0	5	0	0	0	1	0	13	0
64-65	13	0	3	0	8	0	8	0	3	0	7	0	5	0	1	0	0	0	16	0
66-67	12	0	4	0	4	0	12	0	2	0	4	0	7	0	1	0	2	0	16	0
68-69	6	0	2	0	6	0	2	0	3	0	0	0	2	0	1	0	0	0	8	0
70-71	11	0	2	0	4	0	9	0	3	0	8	0	2	0	0	0	0	0	13	0
72-73	14	0	9	0	8	0	15	0	8	0	9	0	5	0	1	0	0	0	23	0
74-75	16	0	10	0	6	0	20	0	3	0	13	0	8	0	2	0	0	0	26	0
76-77	14	0	8	0	10	0	12	0	4	0	8	0	7	0	3	0	0	0	22	0
78-79	19	0	5	0	7	0	17	0	6	0	12	0	5	0	1	0	0	0	24	0

Written Communication (continued)

Code	Male Freq.	Male %	Female Freq.	Female %	White Freq.	White %	Black Freq.	Black %	0.0-1.9 Freq.	0.0-1.9 %	2.0-3.9 Freq.	2.0-3.9 %	4.0-5.9 Freq.	4.0-5.9 %	6.0-7.9 Freq.	6.0-7.9 %	8.0-9.5 Freq.	8.0-9.5 %	Totals Freq.	Totals %
80-81	16	0	8	0	9	0	15	0	4	0	14	0	4	0	1	0	1	0	24	0
82-83	25	0	8	0	11	0	22	0	4	0	14	0	10	0	4	0	1	0	33	0
84-85	28	0	10	0	12	0	26	0	5	0	22	0	9	0	2	0	0	0	38	0
86-87	29	0	11	0	15	0	25	0	9	1	15	0	14	0	2	0	0	0	40	0
88-89	36	0	15	0	15	0	36	0	10	1	25	0	16	0	0	0	0	0	51	0
90-91	20	0	10	0	17	0	13	0	6	0	10	0	12	0	2	0	0	0	30	0
92-93	34	0	12	0	14	0	32	0	17	1	17	0	9	0	3	0	1	0	46	0
94-95	35	0	23	0	14	0	44	0	12	1	31	1	12	0	3	0	0	0	58	0
96-97	31	0	14	0	17	0	28	0	9	1	20	1	10	0	3	0	1	1	45	0
98-99	45	0	22	0	21	0	46	0	6	0	40	1	17	0	4	0	0	0	67	0
100-101	54	1	28	0	36	0	46	0	10	1	41	1	20	0	11	0	3	1	82	0
102-103	44	0	26	0	25	0	45	0	12	1	35	1	16	0	7	0	0	0	70	0
104-105	46	1	25	0	23	0	48	1	9	1	32	1	24	0	5	0	1	0	71	0
106-107	54	1	30	0	26	0	58	1	16	1	37	1	25	1	4	0	2	0	84	0
108-109	58	1	16	0	28	0	46	0	15	1	32	1	18	0	7	0	2	0	74	0
110-111	62	1	36	0	26	0	72	1	12	1	43	1	33	1	10	0	0	0	98	1
112-113	63	1	33	0	38	0	58	1	11	1	43	1	29	1	10	0	3	0	96	1
114-115	55	1	26	0	29	0	52	1	15	1	35	1	20	0	10	0	3	0	81	1
116-117	69	1	32	0	35	0	66	1	12	1	50	1	28	0	10	0	1	0	101	1
118-119	66	1	28	0	25	0	69	1	12	1	46	1	31	1	8	0	3	0	94	1
120-121	74	1	31	0	37	0	68	1	10	1	57	1	29	1	3	0	2	0	105	1
122-123	78	1	30	0	30	0	78	1	21	1	33	1	37	1	8	0	1	0	108	1
124-125	90	1	36	0	45	0	81	1	20	1	45	1	43	1	17	0	0	0	126	1
126-127	82	1	44	0	43	0	83	1	22	1	57	1	38	1	15	0	3	0	126	1
128-129	72	1	48	1	36	0	84	1	12	1	54	1	37	1	9	0	0	0	120	1
130-131	74	1	38	0	44	0	68	1	18	1	55	1	24	0	13	0	4	0	112	1
132-133	71	1	38	0	31	0	78	1	17	1	50	1	34	1	13	0	2	0	109	1
134-135	73	1	41	0	43	0	71	1	11	1	46	1	42	1	7	0	3	0	114	1
136-137	85	1	52	1	49	1	88	1	24	1	54	1	46	1	12	0	3	0	137	1
138-139	90	1	50	1	57	1	83	1	17	1	63	1	47	1	11	0	2	0	140	1
140-141	73	1	47	0	38	0	82	1	16	1	52	1	39	1	11	0	2	0	120	1
142-143	92	1	63	1	49	1	106	1	22	1	72	1	47	1	14	0	2	0	155	1
144-145	84	1	46	0	43	0	87	1	20	1	52	1	38	1	16	0	4	0	130	1
146-147	96	1	63	1	57	1	102	1	17	1	65	1	49	1	26	1	2	0	159	1
148-149	95	1	60	1	61	1	94	1	17	1	68	1	46	1	16	0	8	0	155	1
150-151	94	1	54	1	58	1	90	1	19	1	62	1	41	1	7	0	2	0	148	1
152-153	104	1	60	1	55	1	109	1	13	1	56	1	63	1	11	0	2	0	164	1
154-155	110	1	78	1	63	1	125	2	33	2	57	1	57	1	23	1	9	0	188	1
156-157	104	1	57	1	61	1	100	1	16	1	58	1	62	1	34	1	7	0	161	1
158-159	117	1	64	1	57	1	124	1	20	1	68	1	58	1	27	1	8	0	181	1

8YR Indexes: Frequency Distributions

Written Communication (continued)

Code	Male Freq.	%	Female Freq.	%	White Freq.	%	Black Freq.	%	0.0-1.9 Freq.	%	2.0-3.9 Freq.	%	4.0-5.9 Freq.	%	6.0-7.9 Freq.	%	8.0-9.5 Freq.	%	Totals Freq.	%
160-161	101	1	88	1	61	1	128	1	21	1	77	1	71	1	15	0	5	0	189	1
162-163	111	1	88	1	69	1	130	1	20	1	88	2	62	1	24	1	5	0	199	1
164-165	97	1	66	1	67	1	96	1	19	1	55	1	53	1	29	1	7	0	163	1
166-167	98	1	69	1	62	1	105	1	21	1	66	1	54	1	22	1	4	0	167	1
168-169	93	1	86	1	63	1	116	1	17	1	69	1	59	1	30	1	4	0	179	1
170-171	107	1	78	1	78	1	107	1	17	1	67	2	57	1	38	1	6	0	185	1
172-173	106	1	106	1	77	1	135	1	19	1	87	1	68	1	31	1	7	0	212	1
174-175	105	1	88	1	79	1	114	1	12	1	72	2	55	1	34	1	13	1	193	1
176-177	110	1	109	1	83	1	136	1	17	1	87	2	73	1	35	1	12	1	219	1
178-179	128	1	94	1	75	2	147	2	24	2	89	1	73	1	34	1	9	0	222	1
180-181	132	1	109	1	109	1	132	1	20	1	78	2	87	1	42	1	10	0	241	1
182-183	104	1	98	1	78	1	124	1	22	1	84	1	60	2	32	1	6	0	202	1
184-185	123	1	109	1	79	1	153	2	23	2	77	1	76	1	47	1	10	0	232	1
186-187	125	1	116	1	101	1	140	2	19	2	88	2	76	1	40	1	14	1	241	1
188-189	125	1	105	1	110	1	120	1	18	1	68	1	93	1	39	1	11	0	230	1
190-191	125	1	128	1	95	1	158	2	25	2	85	2	91	2	42	1	17	1	253	1
192-193	126	1	123	1	114	1	135	1	11	1	83	2	75	2	49	1	17	1	249	1
194-195	114	1	124	1	100	1	138	1	12	1	92	2	87	2	34	1	14	1	238	1
196-197	128	1	111	1	107	1	132	1	21	1	84	2	80	1	43	1	20	1	239	1
198-199	119	1	121	1	98	1	142	2	26	2	81	2	66	1	53	1	19	1	240	1
200-201	140	1	131	1	139	1	132	1	34	2	90	2	77	1	57	1	21	1	271	1
202-203	120	1	145	2	114	1	151	2	20	1	75	1	88	2	51	1	17	1	265	1
204-205	103	1	128	1	100	1	131	1	26	2	76	1	78	1	42	1	15	1	231	1
206-207	116	1	140	1	109	1	147	2	25	2	77	1	91	2	46	1	16	1	256	1
208-209	129	1	151	2	131	1	149	2	22	2	78	1	96	2	60	2	21	1	280	1
210-211	131	1	149	2	132	1	148	2	14	1	84	2	86	2	65	2	23	1	280	1
212-213	125	1	113	1	119	1	119	1	23	2	73	1	67	1	62	2	22	1	238	1
214-215	141	1	138	1	137	1	142	2	13	1	65	1	92	2	67	2	32	1	279	1
216-217	119	1	135	1	121	1	133	1	19	1	72	1	72	1	68	2	29	1	254	1
218-219	138	1	156	2	159	2	135	1	14	1	83	1	91	1	64	2	37	2	294	2
220-221	118	1	147	2	137	1	128	1	14	1	73	1	83	1	62	2	33	1	265	1
222-223	115	1	171	2	155	2	131	1	15	1	89	1	89	2	53	1	40	2	286	2
224-225	127	1	162	2	168	2	121	1	14	1	77	1	92	2	71	2	35	2	289	2
226-227	137	1	153	2	171	2	119	1	17	1	55	1	110	2	71	2	37	2	290	2
228-229	108	1	151	2	127	1	132	1	9	1	65	1	86	2	69	2	30	1	259	1
230-231	119	1	151	2	150	2	120	1	11	1	59	1	86	1	75	2	39	2	270	2
232-233	118	1	130	1	155	2	93	1	15	1	62	1	71	1	63	2	37	2	248	2
234-235	121	1	127	1	154	2	94	1	16	1	56	1	68	1	67	2	41	1	248	1
236-237	91	1	151	2	143	2	99	1	14	1	54	1	77	1	59	2	38	2	242	1
238-239	108	1	138	1	151	2	95	1	17	1	36	1	86	2	69	2	38	2	246	1

8YR Indexes: Frequency Distributions

Written Communication (continued)

Code	Male Freq.	Male %	Female Freq.	Female %	White Freq.	White %	Black Freq.	Black %	0.0-1.9 Freq.	0.0-1.9 %	2.0-3.9 Freq.	2.0-3.9 %	4.0-5.9 Freq.	4.0-5.9 %	6.0-7.9 Freq.	6.0-7.9 %	8.0-9.5 Freq.	8.0-9.5 %	Totals Freq.	Totals %
240-241	89	1	152	2	145	1	96	1	9	1	66	1	64	1	64	2	38	2	241	1
242-243	86	1	126	1	124	1	88	1	5	0	45	1	72	1	57	1	33	1	212	1
244-245	90	1	117	1	132	1	75	1	11	1	47	1	72	1	49	1	28	1	207	1
246-247	79	1	119	1	125	1	73	1	9	1	44	1	49	1	54	1	42	2	198	1
248-249	107	1	104	1	146	2	65	1	6	0	52	1	58	1	57	1	38	2	211	1
250-251	80	1	122	1	134	1	68	1	5	0	35	1	62	1	63	2	37	2	202	1
252-253	67	1	122	1	128	1	61	1	9	1	35	1	57	1	53	1	35	2	189	1
254-255	76	1	111	1	123	1	64	1	8	1	41	1	54	1	54	1	30	2	187	1
256-257	87	1	111	1	157	2	41	0	1	0	29	1	57	1	67	2	44	2	198	1
258-259	71	1	115	1	140	1	46	1	2	0	24	1	59	1	61	2	40	2	186	1
260-261	59	1	109	1	102	1	66	1	7	0	30	1	52	1	46	1	33	1	168	1
262-263	60	1	110	1	130	1	40	0	0	0	21	1	47	1	52	1	50	2	170	1
264-265	59	1	101	1	112	1	48	1	2	0	18	0	48	1	56	1	36	2	160	1
266-267	53	1	94	1	111	1	36	0	5	0	19	0	36	1	50	1	37	2	147	1
268-269	66	1	77	1	122	1	21	0	1	0	15	0	42	1	49	1	36	2	143	1
270-271	58	1	80	1	103	1	35	0	4	0	19	0	31	1	43	1	41	1	138	1
272-273	54	1	70	1	96	1	28	0	2	0	16	0	33	1	40	1	33	2	124	1
274-275	38	0	84	1	95	1	27	0	3	0	19	0	29	1	35	1	36	2	122	1
276-277	43	0	60	1	73	1	30	0	4	0	14	0	19	0	41	1	25	1	103	1
278-279	43	0	77	1	94	1	26	0	3	0	18	0	33	1	32	1	34	2	120	1
280-281	39	0	66	1	91	1	14	0	0	0	10	0	27	0	35	1	33	2	105	1
282-283	39	0	63	1	87	1	15	0	2	0	6	0	24	0	33	1	37	2	102	1
284-285	46	0	66	1	93	1	19	0	0	0	14	0	22	0	37	1	39	2	112	1
286-287	27	0	52	1	63	1	16	0	2	0	9	0	21	0	23	1	24	1	79	0
288-289	42	0	65	1	85	1	22	0	1	0	12	0	26	0	30	1	38	2	107	1
290-291	24	0	60	1	68	1	16	0	1	0	8	0	10	0	27	1	38	2	84	0
292-293	41	0	65	1	83	1	23	0	1	0	9	0	31	0	32	1	33	2	106	0
294-295	29	0	55	1	72	1	12	0	0	0	5	0	18	0	27	1	34	2	84	0
296-297	17	0	37	0	48	0	6	0	1	0	4	0	8	0	21	1	20	1	54	0
298-299	25	0	49	1	67	1	7	0	1	0	7	0	15	0	28	1	23	1	74	0
300-301	18	0	40	0	48	0	10	0	0	0	3	0	13	0	19	0	23	1	58	0
302-303	20	0	29	0	40	0	9	0	0	0	3	0	12	0	17	0	17	1	49	0
304-305	17	0	23	0	31	0	9	0	0	0	6	0	8	0	14	0	12	1	40	0
306-307	17	0	32	0	42	0	7	0	0	0	2	0	10	0	16	0	21	1	49	0
308-309	18	0	24	0	37	0	5	0	0	0	1	0	7	0	15	0	19	1	42	0
310-311	15	0	24	0	36	0	3	0	1	0	4	0	7	0	13	0	15	1	39	0
312-313	10	0	26	0	29	0	7	0	0	0	0	0	7	0	12	0	16	1	36	0
314-315	16	0	17	0	31	0	2	0	0	0	4	0	3	0	11	0	15	1	33	0
316-317	10	0	22	0	31	0	1	0	0	0	1	0	5	0	9	0	17	1	32	0
318-319	6	0	17	0	19	0	4	0	1	0	2	0	2	0	7	0	11	0	23	0

8YR Indexes: Frequency Distributions

Code	Male Freq.	Male %	Female Freq.	Female %	White Freq.	White %	Black Freq.	Black %	0.0-1.9 Freq.	0.0-1.9 %	2.0-3.9 Freq.	2.0-3.9 %	4.0-5.9 Freq.	4.0-5.9 %	6.0-7.9 Freq.	6.0-7.9 %	8.0-9.5 Freq.	8.0-9.5 %	Totals Freq.	Totals %
Written Communication (continued)																				
320-321	10	0	19	0	26	0	3	0	0	0	4	0	2	0	12	0	11	0	29	0
322-323	12	0	10	0	21	0	1	0	0	0	2	0	4	0	6	0	10	0	22	0
324-325	9	0	18	0	24	0	3	0	0	0	3	0	5	0	10	0	9	0	27	0
326-327	8	0	12	0	19	0	1	0	0	0	3	0	4	0	8	0	8	0	20	0
328-329	3	0	18	0	18	0	3	0	0	0	4	0	1	0	8	0	8	0	21	0
330-331	6	0	7	0	11	0	2	0	0	0	1	0	1	0	8	0	3	0	13	0
332-333	8	0	7	0	12	0	3	0	0	0	0	0	5	0	4	0	6	0	15	0
334-335	3	0	5	0	7	0	1	0	0	0	0	0	1	0	4	0	3	0	8	0
336-337	5	0	4	0	9	0	0	0	0	0	0	0	0	0	4	0	5	0	9	0
338-339	1	0	5	0	5	0	1	0	1	0	1	0	0	0	2	0	2	0	6	0
340-341	2	0	1	0	3	0	0	0	0	0	0	0	1	0	0	0	3	0	3	0
342-343	2	0	4	0	5	0	1	0	0	0	0	0	0	0	2	0	3	0	6	0
344-345	3	0	7	0	10	0	0	0	0	0	0	0	1	0	2	0	7	0	10	0
346-347	1	0	5	0	6	0	0	0	0	0	0	0	0	0	0	0	5	0	6	0
348-349	2	0	1	0	3	0	1	0	0	0	0	0	1	0	2	0	3	0	3	0
350-351	0	0	4	0	3	0	1	0	0	0	0	0	0	0	0	0	2	0	4	0
352-353	2	0	1	0	1	0	1	0	0	0	1	0	1	0	2	0	2	0	3	0
354-355	0	0	1	0	0	0	1	0	0	0	0	0	0	0	0	0	0	0	2	0
356-357	0	0	1	0	1	0	0	0	0	0	0	0	0	0	1	0	1	0	1	0
358-359	1	0	2	0	3	0	1	0	0	0	0	0	1	0	0	0	1	0	3	0
360-361	0	0	0	0	0	0	0	0	0	0	0	0	0	0	0	0	0	0	0	0
362-363	0	0	1	0	1	0	1	0	0	0	0	0	1	0	2	0	0	0	2	0
364-365	1	0	2	0	3	0	0	0	0	0	2	0	1	0	0	0	0	0	3	0
366-367	3	0	1	0	4	0	1	0	0	0	0	0	0	0	0	0	4	0	4	0
368-369	0	0	0	0	0	0	0	0	0	0	0	0	0	0	0	0	0	0	0	0
370-371	1	0	0	0	0	0	0	0	0	0	0	0	0	0	1	0	0	0	1	0
372-373	0	0	0	0	1	0	0	0	0	0	0	0	0	0	0	0	0	0	0	0
374-375	0	0	1	0	0	0	0	0	0	0	0	0	0	0	0	0	1	0	1	0
376-377	0	0	0	0	1	0	0	0	0	0	0	0	0	0	0	0	0	0	0	0
378-379	0	0	0	0	0	0	0	0	0	0	0	0	0	0	0	0	0	0	0	0
380-381	0	0	0	0	0	0	0	0	0	0	0	0	0	0	0	0	0	0	0	0
382-383	1	0	0	0	1	0	0	0	0	0	0	0	0	0	0	0	1	0	1	0
	9,471		9,422		9,672		9,221		1,488		5,576		5,693		3,926		2,210		18,893	
8YR Language Production																				
100-103	2	0	0	0	0	0	2	0	0	0	0	0	0	0	0	0	0	0	0	0
104-107	1	0	0	0	0	0	1	0	0	0	0	0	1	0	0	0	0	0	1	0
108-111	0	0	0	0	0	0	0	0	0	0	0	0	0	0	0	0	0	0	0	0
112-115	0	0	0	0	0	0	0	0	0	0	0	0	0	0	0	0	0	0	0	0
116-119	0	0	1	0	0	0	1	0	0	0	1	0	0	0	0	0	0	0	1	0
120-123	0	0	0	0	0	0	0	0	0	0	0	0	0	0	0	0	0	0	0	0
124-127	0	0	0	0	0	0	0	0	0	0	0	0	0	0	0	0	0	0	0	0

8YR Language Production (continued)

Code	Male Freq.	Male %	Female Freq.	Female %	White Freq.	White %	Black Freq.	Black %	0.0-1.9 Freq.	0.0-1.9 %	2.0-3.9 Freq.	2.0-3.9 %	4.0-5.9 Freq.	4.0-5.9 %	6.0-7.9 Freq.	6.0-7.9 %	8.0-9.5 Freq.	8.0-9.5 %	Totals Freq.	Totals %
128-131	0	0	0	0	0	0	0	0	0	0	0	0	0	0	0	0	0	0	0	0
132-135	1	0	0	0	1	0	0	0	0	0	0	0	1	0	0	0	0	0	1	0
136-139	0	0	0	0	0	0	0	0	0	0	0	0	0	0	0	0	0	0	0	0
140-143	0	0	1	0	0	0	0	0	0	0	0	0	0	0	0	0	0	0	1	0
144-147	0	0	0	0	1	0	0	0	1	0	0	0	0	0	0	0	0	0	0	0
148-151	1	0	0	0	0	0	1	0	1	0	0	0	0	0	0	0	0	0	1	0
152-155	2	0	0	0	0	0	2	0	0	0	1	0	1	0	0	0	0	0	2	0
156-159	1	0	0	0	0	0	1	0	0	0	0	0	1	0	0	0	0	0	1	0
160-163	1	0	1	0	1	0	1	0	0	0	1	0	1	0	0	0	0	0	2	0
164-167	2	0	1	0	2	0	0	0	1	0	1	0	0	0	0	0	0	0	3	0
168-171	1	0	0	0	0	0	1	0	0	0	1	0	1	0	0	0	0	0	1	0
172-175	1	0	1	0	1	0	1	0	1	0	0	0	0	0	0	0	0	0	2	0
176-179	1	0	0	0	0	0	0	0	0	0	1	0	1	0	0	0	0	0	0	0
180-183	0	0	0	0	0	0	0	0	1	0	0	0	0	0	0	0	0	0	0	0
184-187	0	0	0	0	0	0	0	0	0	0	0	0	0	0	0	0	0	0	0	0
188-191	0	0	2	0	1	0	1	0	0	0	0	0	0	0	0	0	0	0	2	0
192-195	2	0	0	0	1	0	0	0	0	0	1	0	2	0	0	0	0	0	2	0
196-199	2	0	0	0	0	0	1	0	0	0	0	0	0	0	0	0	0	0	2	0
200-203	0	0	0	0	0	0	0	0	0	0	0	0	1	0	0	0	0	0	0	0
204-207	0	0	0	0	1	0	0	0	0	0	0	0	0	0	2	0	0	0	3	0
208-211	1	0	2	0	0	0	3	0	1	0	2	0	0	0	1	0	0	0	3	0
212-215	1	0	2	0	0	0	3	0	0	0	0	0	1	0	0	0	0	0	3	0
216-219	2	0	0	0	0	0	2	0	0	0	1	0	0	0	0	0	0	0	2	0
220-223	1	0	0	0	0	0	1	0	0	0	0	0	0	0	1	0	0	0	1	0
224-227	0	0	0	0	0	0	0	0	0	0	0	0	0	0	0	0	0	0	0	0
228-231	1	0	0	0	1	0	0	0	1	0	0	0	0	0	0	0	0	0	1	0
232-235	0	0	0	0	0	0	0	0	0	0	0	0	0	0	0	0	0	0	0	0
236-239	0	0	0	0	0	0	0	0	0	0	1	0	1	0	0	0	0	0	0	0
240-243	2	0	1	0	1	0	2	0	1	0	0	0	0	0	1	0	0	0	2	0
244-247	0	0	0	0	0	0	0	0	0	0	3	0	0	0	0	0	0	0	1	0
248-251	0	0	1	0	0	0	0	0	0	0	1	0	0	0	0	0	0	0	0	0
252-255	3	0	0	0	1	0	4	0	1	0	2	0	0	0	1	0	0	0	4	0
256-259	2	0	0	0	0	0	2	0	0	0	0	0	0	0	0	0	0	0	2	0
260-263	2	0	0	0	0	0	1	0	0	0	2	0	0	0	0	0	0	0	2	0
264-267	1	0	1	0	1	0	0	0	0	0	0	0	0	0	1	0	0	0	1	0
268-271	2	0	1	0	1	0	2	0	1	0	2	0	0	0	0	0	0	0	3	0
272-275	1	0	0	0	0	0	2	0	0	0	2	0	1	0	0	0	0	0	2	0
276-279	4	0	0	0	1	0	3	0	0	0	2	0	0	0	2	0	1	0	4	0
280-283	2	0	0	0	0	0	2	0	0	0	2	0	1	0	0	0	0	0	2	0
284-287	2	0	3	0	1	0	4	0	1	0	1	0	2	0	1	0	0	0	5	0

8YR Indexes: Frequency Distributions

8YR Language Production (continued)

Code	Male Freq.	Male %	Female Freq.	Female %	White Freq.	White %	Black Freq.	Black %	0.0-1.9 Freq.	0.0-1.9 %	2.0-3.9 Freq.	2.0-3.9 %	4.0-5.9 Freq.	4.0-5.9 %	6.0-7.9 Freq.	6.0-7.9 %	8.0-9.5 Freq.	8.0-9.5 %	Totals Freq.	Totals %
288-291	1	0	0	0	0	0	1	0	1	0	0	0	0	0	0	0	0	0	1	0
292-295	1	0	0	0	0	0	1	0	0	0	0	0	1	0	0	0	0	0	1	0
296-299	1	0	1	0	0	0	2	0	1	0	0	0	1	0	0	0	0	0	2	0
300-303	0	0	1	0	1	0	1	0	1	0	0	0	0	0	0	0	0	0	1	0
308-311	4	0	0	0	2	0	3	0	2	0	1	0	1	0	0	0	0	0	4	0
312-315	3	0	0	0	0	0	1	0	0	0	3	0	0	0	0	0	0	0	3	0
316-319	1	0	2	0	1	0	3	0	1	0	2	0	0	0	1	0	1	0	3	0
320-323	1	0	5	0	1	0	5	0	3	0	1	0	1	0	1	0	1	0	6	0
324-327	4	0	1	0	1	0	4	0	0	0	3	0	0	0	1	0	0	0	5	0
328-331	4	0	2	0	1	0	5	0	1	0	4	0	1	0	1	0	0	0	6	0
332-335	4	0	1	0	1	0	4	0	1	0	1	0	2	0	0	0	0	0	5	0
336-339	0	0	3	0	0	0	3	0	1	0	2	0	0	0	0	0	0	0	3	0
340-343	2	0	1	0	1	0	2	0	0	0	0	0	1	0	1	0	1	0	3	0
344-347	1	0	1	0	2	0	2	0	0	0	2	0	0	0	0	0	0	0	2	0
348-351	1	0	4	0	0	0	4	0	0	0	2	0	3	0	0	0	0	0	5	0
352-355	4	0	3	0	1	0	7	0	3	0	4	0	1	0	0	0	0	0	8	0
356-359	5	0	4	0	1	0	6	0	2	0	5	0	0	0	0	0	0	0	7	0
360-363	1	0	4	0	2	0	7	0	1	0	5	0	1	0	1	0	1	0	9	0
364-367	3	0	1	0	0	0	2	0	0	0	1	0	1	0	1	0	0	0	2	0
368-371	3	0	2	0	1	0	4	0	1	0	3	0	0	0	1	0	0	0	5	0
372-375	2	0	3	0	2	0	3	0	1	0	2	0	1	0	0	0	0	0	5	0
376-379	6	0	2	0	1	0	4	0	1	0	0	0	0	0	2	0	0	0	5	0
380-383	5	0	3	0	1	0	10	0	2	0	7	0	1	0	3	0	0	0	11	0
384-387	5	0	4	0	1	0	7	0	5	0	2	0	1	0	1	0	0	0	9	0
388-391	7	0	5	0	3	0	7	0	4	0	1	0	5	0	0	0	0	0	10	0
392-395	6	0	4	0	5	0	6	0	1	0	3	0	5	0	2	0	0	0	11	0
396-399	6	0	9	0	0	0	15	0	4	0	8	0	3	0	0	0	0	0	15	0
400-403	5	0	1	0	0	0	6	0	2	0	2	0	1	0	1	0	0	0	6	0
404-407	2	0	5	0	0	0	7	0	1	0	6	0	0	0	0	0	0	0	7	0
408-411	4	0	5	0	3	0	6	0	0	0	6	0	2	0	1	0	0	0	9	0
412-415	2	0	3	0	0	0	5	0	1	0	1	0	2	0	1	0	0	0	5	0
416-419	2	0	5	0	1	0	6	0	2	0	3	0	2	0	0	0	0	0	7	0
420-423	8	0	1	0	1	0	8	0	2	0	5	0	2	0	0	0	0	0	9	0
424-427	9	0	2	0	0	0	11	0	2	0	7	0	2	0	0	0	0	0	11	0
428-431	6	0	4	0	2	0	8	0	0	0	5	0	4	0	1	0	0	0	10	0
432-435	7	0	2	0	0	0	9	0	3	0	4	0	1	0	1	0	0	0	9	0
436-439	8	0	7	0	5	0	10	0	3	0	9	0	3	0	0	0	0	0	15	0
440-443	7	0	6	0	3	0	10	0	3	0	5	0	3	0	2	0	0	0	13	0
444-447	6	0	8	0	5	0	9	0	5	0	3	0	5	0	0	0	1	0	14	0
448-451	5	0	7	0	5	0	7	0	2	0	5	0	1	0	3	0	1	0	12	0

8YR Indexes: Frequency Distributions

8YR Language Production (continued)

Code	Male Freq.	Male %	Female Freq.	Female %	White Freq.	White %	Black Freq.	Black %	0.0-1.9 Freq.	0.0-1.9 %	2.0-3.9 Freq.	2.0-3.9 %	4.0-5.9 Freq.	4.0-5.9 %	6.0-7.9 Freq.	6.0-7.9 %	8.0-9.5 Freq.	8.0-9.5 %	Totals Freq.	Totals %
452-455	7	0	6	0	5	0	8	0	2	0	6	0	4	0	1	0	0	0	13	0
456-459	5	0	5	0	3	0	7	0	0	0	5	0	5	0	0	0	0	0	10	0
460-463	13	0	6	0	5	0	14	0	3	0	8	0	4	0	4	0	0	0	19	0
464-467	8	0	4	0	0	0	12	0	3	0	6	0	3	0	0	0	0	0	12	0
468-471	12	0	3	0	5	0	10	0	5	0	3	0	4	0	3	0	0	0	15	0
472-475	8	0	3	0	6	0	5	0	2	0	4	0	3	0	2	0	0	0	11	0
476-479	8	0	5	0	5	0	8	0	1	0	7	0	3	0	1	0	1	0	13	0
480-483	8	0	15	0	6	0	17	0	5	0	13	0	3	0	1	0	1	0	23	0
484-487	12	0	10	0	7	0	15	0	2	0	9	0	6	0	5	0	0	0	22	0
488-491	14	0	8	0	3	0	19	0	4	0	12	0	3	0	3	0	0	0	22	0
492-495	9	0	6	0	4	0	11	0	2	0	9	0	4	0	0	0	0	0	15	0
496-499	4	0	10	0	0	0	14	0	1	0	10	0	2	0	0	0	1	0	14	0
500-503	17	0	16	0	5	0	28	0	6	0	10	0	15	0	1	0	1	0	33	0
504-507	9	0	10	0	5	0	14	0	4	0	7	0	7	0	1	0	0	0	19	0
508-511	9	0	9	0	2	0	16	0	3	0	5	0	9	0	1	0	0	0	18	0
512-515	13	0	5	0	6	0	12	0	1	0	9	0	4	0	4	0	0	0	18	0
516-519	20	0	15	0	7	0	28	0	6	0	17	0	9	0	3	0	0	0	35	0
520-523	10	0	19	0	9	0	20	0	4	0	15	0	6	0	3	0	1	0	29	0
524-527	18	0	11	0	8	0	21	0	5	0	12	0	8	0	2	0	2	0	29	0
528-531	16	0	15	0	6	0	25	0	1	0	15	0	10	0	5	0	0	0	31	0
532-535	17	0	17	0	12	0	22	0	8	1	13	0	10	0	3	0	0	0	34	0
536-539	23	0	16	0	5	0	34	0	8	1	13	0	10	0	7	0	1	0	39	0
540-543	22	0	13	0	7	0	28	0	9	1	13	0	9	0	4	0	0	0	35	0
544-547	22	0	19	0	7	0	34	0	5	0	13	0	18	0	4	0	1	0	41	0
548-551	31	0	23	0	12	0	42	0	13	1	24	0	12	0	3	0	2	0	54	0
552-555	25	0	23	0	13	0	35	0	6	0	23	0	13	0	6	0	0	0	48	0
556-559	30	0	16	0	8	0	38	0	8	1	21	0	12	0	5	0	0	0	46	0
560-563	37	0	20	0	16	0	41	0	11	1	28	0	11	0	7	0	0	0	57	0
564-567	31	0	37	0	14	0	54	1	10	1	32	1	17	0	8	0	1	0	68	0
568-571	25	0	36	0	16	0	45	0	5	0	32	1	16	0	7	0	1	0	61	0
572-575	37	0	25	0	18	0	44	0	8	1	28	0	18	0	6	0	2	0	62	0
576-579	47	0	24	0	16	0	55	1	12	1	25	0	19	0	12	0	3	0	71	0
580-583	36	0	29	0	9	0	56	1	13	1	28	0	17	0	7	0	0	0	65	0
584-587	40	0	35	0	18	0	57	1	5	0	32	1	24	0	12	0	2	0	75	0
588-591	44	0	35	0	15	0	64	1	7	0	39	1	24	0	8	0	1	0	79	0
592-595	38	0	41	0	23	0	56	1	8	1	32	1	31	1	7	0	1	0	79	0
596-599	41	0	50	1	25	0	66	1	8	1	44	1	23	0	15	0	1	0	91	1
600-603	56	1	42	0	19	0	79	1	12	1	39	1	29	1	16	0	2	0	98	1
604-607	45	0	51	1	26	0	70	1	10	1	33	1	31	1	18	0	4	0	96	1
608-611	53	1	41	0	28	0	66	1	10	1	33	1	38	1	12	0	1	0	94	0

8YR Language Production (continued)

Code	Male Freq.	Male %	Female Freq.	Female %	White Freq.	White %	Black Freq.	Black %	0.0-1.9 Freq.	0.0-1.9 %	2.0-3.9 Freq.	2.0-3.9 %	4.0-5.9 Freq.	4.0-5.9 %	6.0-7.9 Freq.	6.0-7.9 %	8.0-9.5 Freq.	8.0-9.5 %	Totals Freq.	Totals %
612-615	46	0	41	0	21	0	66	1	14	1	36	1	24	0	12	0	1	0	87	0
616-619	62	1	50	1	43	0	69	1	20	1	37	1	32	1	19	0	4	0	112	1
620-623	74	1	58	1	44	0	88	1	16	1	50	1	50	1	10	0	6	0	132	1
624-627	67	1	60	1	36	0	91	1	15	1	49	1	39	1	21	1	3	0	127	1
628-631	61	0	46	0	29	0	78	1	15	1	39	1	36	0	13	0	4	0	107	1
632-635	45	1	45	0	14	0	76	1	6	0	37	1	29	0	13	0	5	0	90	0
636-639	52	1	52	1	28	0	76	1	14	1	43	1	29	1	13	0	5	0	104	1
640-643	74	1	37	0	33	0	78	1	10	1	54	1	33	1	12	0	2	0	111	1
644-647	77	1	61	1	35	0	103	1	17	1	60	1	45	1	15	0	1	0	138	1
648-651	78	1	48	0	31	0	95	1	16	1	49	1	48	1	11	0	2	0	126	1
652-655	89	1	52	1	29	0	112	1	19	1	59	1	45	1	14	0	4	0	141	1
656-659	81	1	70	1	31	0	120	1	25	2	64	1	49	1	9	0	4	0	151	1
660-663	84	1	65	1	49	0	100	1	24	1	60	1	43	1	18	0	4	0	149	1
664-667	81	1	97	1	23	0	155	2	21	1	92	2	49	1	9	0	7	0	178	1
668-671	134	1	120	1	69	1	185	2	39	3	117	2	65	1	28	1	5	0	254	1
672-675	132	1	121	1	82	1	171	2	37	2	85	2	79	1	40	1	12	1	253	1
676-679	162	2	132	1	55	1	239	2	34	2	135	2	82	2	34	1	9	0	294	2
680-683	175	2	169	2	82	1	262	3	36	2	150	3	104	2	43	1	11	0	344	2
684-687	159	2	148	2	69	1	238	2	31	2	126	2	104	2	35	1	11	0	307	2
688-691	169	2	151	2	82	1	238	3	31	2	123	2	105	2	52	1	9	0	320	2
692-695	183	2	197	2	92	1	288	3	42	3	150	3	131	2	42	1	15	1	380	2
696-699	203	2	164	2	104	1	263	3	43	3	142	2	125	2	41	1	16	1	367	2
700-703	195	2	226	2	129	1	292	3	35	2	169	3	138	2	62	2	17	1	421	2
704-707	219	2	229	2	172	2	276	3	35	2	159	3	155	3	77	3	22	1	448	2
708-711	236	2	261	3	263	3	234	2	32	2	167	3	177	3	101	3	20	1	497	3
712-715	264	3	260	3	300	3	224	2	32	2	154	3	186	3	113	3	39	2	524	3
716-719	322	3	324	3	398	4	248	3	45	3	150	3	223	4	171	4	57	3	646	3
720-723	399	4	376	4	549	6	226	2	38	2	161	3	255	4	237	6	84	4	775	4
724-727	343	4	366	4	523	5	186	2	24	2	146	3	246	4	202	5	91	4	709	4
728-731	318	3	297	3	446	5	169	2	31	2	119	2	169	3	185	5	111	5	615	3
732-735	100	1	92	1	73	1	119	1	16	1	56	1	59	1	39	1	22	1	192	1
736-739	253	3	282	3	385	4	150	2	14	1	106	2	169	3	159	4	87	4	535	3
740-743	230	3	200	2	298	3	132	1	20	1	68	1	143	2	131	3	68	3	430	2
744-747	140	1	158	2	199	2	99	1	17	1	47	1	77	1	97	2	60	3	298	2
748-751	123	1	139	1	165	2	97	1	14	1	60	1	56	1	71	2	61	3	262	1
752-755	72	1	81	1	59	1	94	1	15	1	53	1	62	1	16	0	7	0	153	1
756-759	74	1	76	1	70	1	80	1	16	1	59	1	50	1	18	0	7	0	150	1
760-763	90	1	87	1	97	1	80	1	18	1	52	1	61	1	30	1	16	1	177	1
764-767	56	1	67	1	39	0	84	1	11	1	48	1	43	1	18	0	3	0	123	1
768-771	122	1	108	1	128	1	102	1	18	1	73	1	79	1	42	1	18	1	230	1

8YR Indexes: Frequency Distributions

8YR Language Production (continued)

Code	Male Freq.	Male %	Female Freq.	Female %	White Freq.	White %	Black Freq.	Black %	0.0-1.9 Freq.	0.0-1.9 %	2.0-3.9 Freq.	2.0-3.9 %	4.0-5.9 Freq.	4.0-5.9 %	6.0-7.9 Freq.	6.0-7.9 %	8.0-9.5 Freq.	8.0-9.5 %	Totals Freq.	Totals %
772-775	90	1	105	1	122	1	73	1	11	1	61	1	65	1	40	1	18	1	195	1
776-779	125	1	118	1	153	2	90	1	14	1	68	1	67	1	61	2	33	1	243	1
780-783	113	1	116	1	170	2	59	1	14	1	64	1	73	1	46	1	32	1	229	1
784-787	93	1	97	1	117	1	73	1	8	1	46	1	59	1	44	1	33	1	190	1
788-791	79	1	91	1	102	1	68	1	11	1	41	1	49	1	46	1	23	1	170	1
792-795	91	1	86	1	101	1	76	1	17	1	46	1	42	1	43	1	29	1	177	1
796-799	67	1	49	1	33	0	83	1	12	1	36	1	43	1	21	1	4	0	116	1
800-803	69	1	87	1	77	1	79	1	15	1	45	1	38	1	30	0	28	1	156	1
804-807	58	1	55	1	37	0	76	1	11	1	34	1	45	1	18	0	5	0	113	1
808-811	75	1	64	1	66	1	73	1	8	1	46	1	50	1	23	1	12	1	139	1
812-815	83	1	82	1	94	1	71	1	16	1	45	1	62	1	25	1	17	1	165	1
816-819	101	1	112	1	133	1	80	1	14	1	70	1	67	1	43	1	19	1	213	1
820-823	124	1	100	1	153	2	71	1	7	0	55	1	70	1	59	1	33	1	224	1
824-827	115	1	102	1	162	2	55	1	13	1	51	1	76	1	39	1	38	2	217	1
828-831	119	1	128	1	180	2	67	1	11	1	49	1	56	1	60	1	71	3	247	1
832-835	46	0	37	1	43	0	40	0	6	0	23	0	23	0	12	0	19	1	83	0
836-839	98	1	99	1	157	2	40	0	4	0	45	1	43	1	51	1	54	2	197	1
840-843	72	1	81	1	115	1	38	0	8	0	27	0	38	1	44	1	36	2	153	1
844-847	56	0	69	1	89	1	36	0	7	0	21	0	17	0	39	1	41	2	125	1
848-851	44	0	56	0	71	1	29	0	2	0	19	0	27	1	25	1	27	1	100	1
852-855	51	1	47	0	43	0	55	1	4	0	34	1	32	0	12	0	16	1	98	1
856-859	41	0	51	1	46	1	46	0	3	0	23	0	28	0	25	1	13	1	92	0
860-863	62	1	62	1	77	1	47	0	7	0	36	1	33	1	28	1	20	1	124	1
864-867	46	0	52	1	54	1	44	0	7	0	38	1	17	0	23	1	13	1	98	1
868-871	61	1	94	1	104	1	51	1	6	0	41	1	44	1	40	1	24	1	155	1
872-875	85	1	129	1	147	1	67	1	7	0	34	1	51	1	69	2	53	2	214	1
876-879	149	2	143	1	229	2	63	1	10	1	45	1	80	1	78	2	79	3	292	2
880-883	120	1	160	2	234	2	46	0	4	0	38	1	63	1	91	2	84	4	280	1
884-887	141	1	190	2	273	3	58	1	8	1	30	1	64	1	118	3	111	5	331	2
888-891	113	1	174	2	237	2	50	1	5	0	20	0	65	1	95	2	102	4	287	1
892-895	112	1	152	2	216	2	48	1	7	0	24	0	51	1	68	2	114	5	264	1
896-899	15	0	14	0	17	0	12	0	1	0	2	0	10	0	7	0	9	0	29	0
900	77	1	128	1	186	2	19	0	1	0	9	0	36	1	64	2	95	4	205	1
	9,751		9,656		9,885		9,522		1,544		5,741		5,849		4,003		2,270		19,407	

8YR Concept Development

Code	Male Freq.	Male %	Female Freq.	Female %	White Freq.	White %	Black Freq.	Black %	0.0-1.9 Freq.	0.0-1.9 %	2.0-3.9 Freq.	2.0-3.9 %	4.0-5.9 Freq.	4.0-5.9 %	6.0-7.9 Freq.	6.0-7.9 %	8.0-9.5 Freq.	8.0-9.5 %	Totals Freq.	Totals %
0	0	0	0	0	0	0	0	0	0	0	0	0	0	0	0	0	0	0	0	0
1	9	0	1	0	3	0	7	0	0	0	5	0	4	0	0	0	1	0	10	0
2	1	0	0	0	0	0	1	0	0	0	0	0	0	0	0	0	0	0	1	0
3	2	0	0	0	1	0	1	0	0	0	0	0	1	0	1	0	0	0	2	0
4	4	0	2	0	1	0	5	0	2	0	3	0	1	0	0	0	0	0	6	0
5	2	0	2	0	0	0	4	0	2	0	1	0	1	0	0	0	0	0	4	0

8YR Indexes: Frequency Distributions

8YR Concept Development (continued)

Code	Male Freq.	Male %	Female Freq.	Female %	White Freq.	White %	Black Freq.	Black %	0.0-1.9 Freq.	0.0-1.9 %	2.0-3.9 Freq.	2.0-3.9 %	4.0-5.9 Freq.	4.0-5.9 %	6.0-7.9 Freq.	6.0-7.9 %	8.0-9.5 Freq.	8.0-9.5 %	Totals Freq.	Totals %
6	3	0	2	0	0	0	5	0	1	0	1	0	2	0	1	0	0	0	5	0
7	6	0	3	0	3	0	6	0	0	0	4	0	5	0	0	0	0	0	9	0
8	7	0	3	0	3	0	7	0	2	0	5	0	3	0	0	0	0	0	10	0
9	8	0	3	0	2	0	9	0	3	0	5	0	3	0	0	0	0	0	11	0
10	11	0	10	0	4	0	17	0	10	1	5	0	4	0	1	0	1	0	21	0
11	5	0	7	0	2	0	10	0	0	0	7	0	2	0	2	0	1	0	12	0
12	13	0	7	0	4	0	16	0	6	0	7	0	5	0	2	0	0	0	20	0
13	16	0	16	0	5	0	27	0	5	0	19	0	5	0	3	0	0	0	32	0
14	20	0	16	0	8	0	28	0	11	1	17	1	5	0	2	0	1	0	36	0
15	22	0	12	0	3	0	31	0	12	1	10	1	10	0	2	0	0	0	34	0
16	30	0	23	0	6	0	47	1	15	1	23	1	13	0	2	0	0	0	53	0
17	34	0	21	0	8	0	47	0	10	1	36	1	6	0	2	0	1	0	55	0
18	35	0	29	0	11	0	53	1	18	1	30	1	14	0	1	0	1	0	64	0
19	51	1	38	0	9	0	80	1	20	1	40	1	20	1	9	0	0	0	89	0
20	50	1	48	1	9	0	89	1	19	1	41	1	31	1	7	0	0	0	98	0
21	50	1	54	1	14	0	90	1	19	1	43	1	36	1	6	0	0	0	104	1
22	62	1	54	1	12	0	104	1	20	1	61	1	27	0	7	0	1	0	116	1
23	74	1	72	1	21	0	125	1	32	2	74	1	32	1	5	0	3	0	146	1
24	71	1	78	1	21	0	128	1	24	2	76	1	40	1	9	0	0	0	149	1
25	109	1	79	1	23	0	165	2	39	2	91	2	48	1	10	0	0	0	188	1
26	101	1	108	1	38	0	171	2	31	2	98	2	58	1	19	0	3	0	209	1
27	132	1	132	1	56	1	208	2	30	2	140	2	74	1	16	0	4	0	264	1
28	175	2	131	1	59	1	247	3	42	3	157	3	81	1	23	1	3	0	306	2
29	148	2	136	1	59	1	225	2	40	3	128	2	78	1	32	1	6	0	284	1
30	163	2	146	1	67	1	242	3	55	4	146	2	83	1	21	1	4	0	309	2
31	180	2	183	2	99	1	264	3	50	3	138	2	126	2	42	1	7	0	363	2
32	211	2	205	2	103	1	313	3	56	4	182	3	127	2	44	1	7	0	416	2
33	231	2	226	2	109	1	348	4	70	4	193	3	148	3	37	1	9	0	457	2
34	233	2	248	2	134	1	347	4	64	4	203	3	155	3	53	1	6	0	481	2
35	250	3	275	3	153	2	372	4	76	5	235	4	149	3	50	1	15	1	525	3
36	282	3	267	3	187	2	362	4	69	4	215	4	176	3	72	2	17	1	549	3
37	320	3	269	3	192	2	397	4	70	4	239	4	191	3	71	2	18	1	589	3
38	309	3	289	3	221	2	377	4	42	4	241	4	205	3	85	2	25	1	598	3
39	304	3	317	3	257	3	364	4	58	4	209	4	227	4	99	2	28	1	621	3
40	318	3	338	3	276	3	380	4	49	3	243	4	220	4	121	3	23	1	656	3
41	330	3	297	3	289	3	338	4	62	4	204	4	192	3	130	3	39	2	627	3
42	391	4	317	3	346	3	362	4	40	4	232	4	245	4	153	4	38	2	708	4
43	369	4	364	4	366	4	367	4	55	4	223	4	259	4	147	4	49	2	733	4
44	382	4	338	3	401	4	319	3	37	2	210	4	262	4	155	4	56	2	720	4
45	342	3	363	4	420	4	285	3	35	2	197	3	243	4	167	4	63	3	705	4

8YR Indexes: Frequency Distributions

Code	Male Freq.	%	Female Freq.	%	White Freq.	%	Black Freq.	%	0.0-1.9 Freq.	%	2.0-3.9 Freq.	%	4.0-5.9 Freq.	%	6.0-7.9 Freq.	%	8.0-9.5 Freq.	%	Totals Freq.	%
8YR Concept Development (continued)																				
46	374	4	344	4	417	4	301	3	38	2	194	3	226	4	174	4	86	4	718	4
47	398	4	395	4	492	5	301	3	45	3	168	3	272	5	214	5	94	4	793	4
48	326	3	325	3	431	4	220	2	30	2	142	2	211	4	164	4	104	5	651	3
49	370	4	325	3	469	5	226	2	30	2	148	3	232	4	171	4	114	5	695	4
50	330	3	317	3	442	5	205	2	28	2	130	2	187	3	188	5	114	5	647	3
51	314	3	348	4	477	5	185	2	20	1	128	2	183	3	209	5	122	5	662	3
52	305	3	307	3	462	5	150	2	7	0	97	2	181	3	198	5	129	6	612	3
53	266	3	274	3	410	4	130	1	10	1	75	1	140	2	182	5	133	6	540	3
54	239	2	268	3	383	4	124	1	21	1	78	1	129	2	145	4	134	6	507	3
55	235	2	254	3	394	4	95	1	8	1	63	1	118	2	153	4	147	6	489	2
56	200	2	205	2	330	3	75	1	9	1	44	1	102	2	132	3	118	5	405	2
57	152	2	193	2	283	3	62	1	4	0	31	1	85	1	118	3	107	5	345	2
58	137	1	169	2	256	3	50	1	5	0	26	0	61	1	105	3	109	5	262	1
59	117	1	145	1	221	2	41	0	6	0	23	0	57	1	89	2	87	4	170	1
60	69	1	101	1	139	1	31	0	5	0	16	0	32	1	53	1	64	3	167	1
61	64	1	103	1	146	1	21	0	5	0	10	0	27	0	54	1	74	3	114	1
62	51	1	63	1	103	1	11	0	2	0	5	0	21	0	33	1	55	2	114	1
63	31	0	51	1	74	1	8	0	0	0	6	0	12	0	24	1	40	2	82	0
64	17	0	22	0	34	0	5	0	0	0	3	0	10	0	11	0	15	1	39	0
65	3	0	6	0	9	0	0	0	0	0	1	0	2	0	3	0	3	0	9	0
	9,864		9,744		9,977		9,631		1,569		5,825		5,905		4,029		2,280		19,608	
8YR Hearing Severity																				
0	329	3	385	4	448	4	266	3	40	2	249	4	232	4	142	3	51	2	714	4
1	415	4	417	4	555	6	277	3	47	3	211	4	270	5	202	5	102	4	832	4
2	608	6	602	6	800	8	410	4	68	4	300	5	365	6	286	7	191	8	1,210	6
3	774	8	825	8	1,016	10	583	6	95	6	423	7	458	8	380	9	243	11	1,599	8
4	0	0	0	0	0	0	0	0	0	0	0	0	0	0	0	0	0	0	0	0
5	904	9	889	9	1,045	10	748	8	122	8	430	7	512	9	431	11	298	13	1,793	9
6	1,007	10	1,020	10	1,074	11	953	10	123	8	553	9	580	10	476	12	295	13	2,027	10
7	951	10	1,061	11	1,036	10	976	10	150	9	547	9	614	10	452	11	249	11	2,012	10
8	974	10	937	9	823	8	1,088	11	172	11	606	10	578	10	362	9	193	8	1,911	10
9	0	0	0	0	0	0	0	0	0	0	0	0	0	0	0	0	0	0	0	0
10	921	9	927	9	767	8	1,081	11	174	11	589	10	572	10	332	8	181	8	1,848	9
11	839	8	805	8	620	6	1,024	10	168	10	534	9	504	8	295	7	143	6	1,644	8
12	615	6	605	6	467	5	753	8	133	8	444	8	361	6	192	5	90	4	1,220	6
13	467	5	431	4	323	3	575	6	97	6	329	6	292	5	122	3	58	3	898	5
14	0	0	0	0	0	0	0	0	0	0	0	0	0	0	0	0	0	0	0	0
15	329	3	300	3	230	2	399	4	76	5	211	4	211	4	92	2	39	2	629	3
16	117	1	100	1	112	1	105	1	20	1	68	1	69	1	39	1	21	1	217	1
17	101	1	70	1	96	1	75	1	19	1	57	1	49	1	29	1	17	1	171	1
18	76	1	54	1	69	1	61	1	9	1	50	1	34	1	23	1	14	1	130	1

8YR Indexes: Frequency Distributions

8YR Hearing Severity (continued)

Code	Male Freq.	Male %	Female Freq.	Female %	White Freq.	White %	Black Freq.	Black %	0.0-1.9 Freq.	0.0-1.9 %	2.0-3.9 Freq.	2.0-3.9 %	4.0-5.9 Freq.	4.0-5.9 %	6.0-7.9 Freq.	6.0-7.9 %	8.0-9.5 Freq.	8.0-9.5 %	Totals Freq.	Totals %
19	0	0	0	0	0	0	0	0	0	0	0	0	0	0	0	0	0	0	0	0
20	76	1	55	1	60	1	71	1	15	1	44	1	35	1	28	1	9	0	131	1
21	56	1	41	0	58	1	39	0	7	0	27	0	25	0	26	0	12	1	97	0
22	49	0	48	0	57	1	40	0	7	0	32	1	32	1	19	0	7	0	97	0
23	30	0	38	0	34	0	34	0	5	0	20	0	20	0	12	0	11	0	68	0
24	0	0	0	0	0	0	0	0	0	0	0	0	0	0	0	0	0	0	0	0
25	38	0	31	0	43	0	26	0	4	0	22	0	20	0	15	0	8	0	69	0
26	27	0	16	0	23	0	20	0	7	0	14	0	10	0	4	0	8	0	43	0
27	34	0	22	0	29	0	27	0	5	0	16	0	19	0	14	0	2	0	56	0
28	15	0	21	0	15	0	21	0	1	0	14	0	12	0	5	0	4	0	36	0
29	0	0	0	0	0	0	0	0	0	0	0	0	0	0	0	0	0	0	0	0
30	22	0	21	0	27	0	16	0	3	0	15	0	8	0	12	0	5	0	43	0
31	27	0	16	0	24	0	19	0	4	0	12	0	18	0	7	0	2	0	43	0
32	15	0	15	0	12	0	18	0	4	0	8	0	11	0	5	0	2	0	30	0
33	29	0	13	0	23	0	19	0	6	0	8	0	14	0	8	0	6	0	42	0
34	0	0	0	0	0	0	0	0	0	0	0	0	0	0	0	0	0	0	0	0
35	8	0	8	0	10	0	6	0	0	0	6	0	6	0	0	0	3	0	16	0
36	8	0	8	0	7	0	9	0	3	0	5	0	3	0	5	0	0	0	16	0
37	13	0	10	0	14	0	9	0	2	0	6	0	6	0	4	0	5	0	23	0
38	9	0	15	0	11	0	13	0	5	0	6	0	5	0	7	0	1	0	24	0
39	0	0	0	0	0	0	0	0	0	0	0	0	0	0	0	0	0	0	0	0
40	14	0	8	0	11	0	11	0	3	0	5	0	8	0	5	0	1	0	22	0
41	9	0	7	0	7	0	9	0	0	0	9	0	4	0	2	0	1	0	16	0
42	12	0	4	0	12	0	4	0	1	0	3	0	8	0	2	0	2	0	16	0
43	8	0	5	0	8	0	5	0	0	0	7	0	4	0	2	0	0	0	13	0
44	0	0	0	0	0	0	0	0	0	0	0	0	0	0	0	0	0	0	0	0
45	8	0	5	0	6	0	7	0	2	0	3	0	3	0	3	0	2	0	13	0
46	3	0	4	0	2	0	5	0	1	0	4	0	1	0	1	0	0	0	7	0
47	2	0	4	0	4	0	2	0	0	0	2	0	1	0	0	0	2	0	6	0
48	3	0	3	0	6	0	0	0	1	0	2	0	1	0	2	0	1	0	6	0
49	0	0	0	0	0	0	0	0	0	0	0	0	0	0	0	0	0	0	0	0
50	4	0	2	0	4	0	2	0	1	0	4	0	0	0	0	0	1	0	6	0
51	0	0	0	0	0	0	0	0	0	0	0	0	0	0	0	0	0	0	0	0
52	3	0	3	0	3	0	3	0	1	0	2	0	1	0	1	0	1	0	6	0
53	2	0	1	0	2	0	1	0	0	0	0	0	1	0	1	0	0	0	3	0
54	0	0	0	0	0	0	0	0	0	0	0	0	0	0	0	0	0	0	0	0
55	2	0	1	0	2	0	1	0	1	0	1	0	0	0	0	0	1	0	3	0
56	1	0	2	0	2	0	1	0	0	0	1	0	2	0	0	0	0	0	3	0
57	0	0	2	0	1	0	1	0	0	0	1	0	0	0	1	0	0	0	2	0
58	2	0	2	0	2	0	2	0	0	0	2	0	1	0	1	0	0	0	4	0

8YR Indexes: Frequency Distributions

8YR Hearing Severity (continued)

Code	Male Freq.	Male %	Female Freq.	Female %	White Freq.	White %	Black Freq.	Black %	0.0-1.9 Freq.	0.0-1.9 %	2.0-3.9 Freq.	2.0-3.9 %	4.0-5.9 Freq.	4.0-5.9 %	6.0-7.9 Freq.	6.0-7.9 %	8.0-9.5 Freq.	8.0-9.5 %	Totals Freq.	Totals %
59	0	0	0	0	0	0	0	0	0	0	0	0	0	0	0	0	0	0	0	0
60	2	0	0	0	2	0	0	0	1	0	0	0	0	0	1	0	0	0	2	0
61	1	0	1	0	1	0	1	0	1	0	0	0	1	0	0	0	1	0	2	0
62	1	0	2	0	3	0	0	0	0	0	0	0	1	0	2	0	0	0	3	0
63	1	0	1	0	2	0	0	0	0	0	0	0	0	0	2	0	0	0	2	0
64	0	0	0	0	0	0	0	0	0	0	0	0	0	0	0	0	0	0	0	0
65	1	0	1	0	1	0	1	0	1	0	0	0	0	0	1	0	0	0	2	0
66	1	0	0	0	1	0	1	0	1	0	0	0	0	0	1	0	0	0	2	0
67	1	0	0	0	1	0	0	0	0	0	1	0	0	0	0	0	0	0	1	0
68	1	0	0	0	1	0	0	0	0	0	0	0	1	0	0	0	0	0	1	0
69	0	0	0	0	0	0	0	0	0	0	0	0	0	0	0	0	0	0	0	0
70	2	0	0	0	1	0	2	0	1	0	1	0	0	0	0	0	0	0	2	0
71	1	0	0	0	1	0	0	0	0	0	0	0	1	0	0	0	0	0	1	0
72	1	0	1	0	1	0	0	0	0	0	1	0	0	0	1	0	0	0	1	0
73	4	0	0	0	5	0	0	0	0	0	0	0	2	0	0	0	0	0	5	0
74	0	0	0	0	0	0	0	0	0	0	0	0	0	0	0	0	0	0	0	0
75	0	0	0	0	0	0	0	0	0	0	0	0	0	0	0	0	0	0	0	0
76	0	0	1	0	0	0	1	0	0	0	0	0	0	0	0	0	0	0	1	0
77	0	0	0	0	0	0	2	0	1	0	0	0	1	0	0	0	0	0	0	0
78	1	0	1	0	0	0	0	0	0	0	1	0	0	0	1	0	0	0	2	0
79	0	0	1	0	0	0	0	0	0	0	0	0	0	0	0	0	0	0	0	0
80	0	0	0	0	0	0	0	0	0	0	0	0	0	0	0	0	0	0	0	0
81	0	0	0	0	0	0	0	0	0	0	0	0	0	0	0	0	0	0	1	0
82	2	0	0	0	2	0	1	0	0	0	1	0	0	0	0	0	0	0	2	0
83	0	0	1	0	0	0	0	0	0	0	0	0	0	0	0	0	0	0	0	0
84	0	0	0	0	0	0	1	0	0	0	1	0	0	0	0	0	0	0	0	0
85	1	0	0	0	0	0	0	0	0	0	0	0	0	0	1	0	1	0	0	0
86	0	0	0	0	0	0	1	0	0	0	0	0	0	0	0	0	0	0	0	0
87	0	0	1	0	0	0	0	0	0	0	1	0	0	0	0	0	0	0	1	0
88	2	0	0	0	2	0	0	0	0	0	0	0	0	0	0	0	0	0	0	0
89	0	0	0	0	0	0	3	0	0	0	1	0	0	0	0	0	0	0	3	0
90	0	0	0	0	0	0	2	0	0	0	1	0	0	0	0	0	0	0	0	0
91	3	0	1	0	0	0	0	0	0	0	0	0	0	0	2	0	0	0	3	0
92	1	0	0	0	0	0	0	0	0	0	0	0	0	0	0	0	0	0	0	0
93	0	0	1	0	0	0	0	0	0	0	1	0	0	0	1	0	1	0	3	0
94	0	0	0	0	0	0	0	0	0	0	0	0	0	0	0	0	0	0	2	0
95	6	0	7	0	6	0	7	0	1	0	8	0	1	0	1	0	2	0	13	0
	9,987		9,877		10,026		9,838		1,606		5,918		5,990		4,065		2,285		19,864	

8YR Indexes: Frequency Distributions

8YR Hearing Acuity

Code	Male Freq.	Male %	Female Freq.	Female %	White Freq.	White %	Black Freq.	Black %	0.0-1.9 Freq.	0.0-1.9 %	2.0-3.9 Freq.	2.0-3.9 %	4.0-5.9 Freq.	4.0-5.9 %	6.0-7.9 Freq.	6.0-7.9 %	8.0-9.5 Freq.	8.0-9.5 %	Totals Freq.	Totals %
0	993	10	1,051	11	1,297	13	747	8	114	7	626	11	667	11	447	11	190	8	2,044	10
1	921	9	958	10	1,224	12	655	7	115	7	486	8	559	9	452	11	267	12	1,879	9
2	1,049	11	1,089	11	1,309	13	829	8	120	7	519	9	629	11	546	13	324	14	2,138	11
3	1,073	11	1,126	11	1,260	13	939	10	159	10	563	10	622	10	519	13	336	15	2,199	11
4	0	0	0	0	0	0	0	0	0	0	0	0	0	0	0	0	0	0	0	0
5	1,101	11	1,070	11	1,101	11	1,070	11	156	10	588	10	652	11	455	11	320	14	2,171	11
6	1,063	11	1,092	11	1,024	10	1,131	11	181	11	654	11	630	11	432	11	258	11	2,155	11
7	935	9	850	9	782	8	1,003	10	172	11	530	9	546	9	334	8	203	9	1,785	9
8	822	8	815	8	611	6	1,026	10	172	11	568	10	484	8	269	7	144	6	1,637	8
9	0	0	0	0	0	0	0	0	0	0	0	0	0	0	0	0	0	0	0	0
10	671	7	641	6	429	4	883	9	128	8	453	8	420	7	220	5	91	4	1,312	7
11	466	5	448	5	308	3	606	6	118	7	326	6	281	5	138	3	51	2	914	5
12	309	3	277	3	189	2	397	4	75	5	223	4	168	3	88	2	32	1	586	3
13	170	2	156	2	130	1	196	2	38	2	117	2	108	2	41	1	22	1	326	2
14	0	0	0	0	0	0	0	0	0	0	0	0	0	0	0	0	0	0	0	0
15	130	1	98	1	86	1	142	1	23	1	91	2	81	1	27	1	6	0	228	1
16	51	1	32	0	41	0	42	0	9	1	33	1	24	0	13	0	4	0	83	0
17	43	0	30	0	38	0	35	0	5	0	23	0	22	0	15	0	8	0	73	0
18	36	0	24	0	36	0	24	0	6	0	21	0	13	0	13	0	7	0	60	0
19	0	0	0	0	0	0	0	0	0	0	0	0	0	0	0	0	0	0	0	0
20	26	0	19	0	27	0	18	0	3	0	12	0	17	0	11	0	2	0	45	0
21	16	0	12	0	17	0	11	0	0	0	12	0	7	0	6	0	3	0	28	0
22	19	0	13	0	20	0	12	0	2	0	13	0	7	0	7	0	3	0	32	0
23	8	0	16	0	14	0	10	0	1	0	10	0	7	0	4	0	2	0	24	0
24	0	0	0	0	0	0	0	0	0	0	0	0	0	0	0	0	0	0	0	0
25	16	0	6	0	9	0	13	0	1	0	6	0	9	0	6	0	0	0	22	0
26	5	0	2	0	2	0	5	0	2	0	1	0	3	0	1	0	0	0	7	0
27	8	0	1	0	7	0	2	0	0	0	4	0	3	0	1	0	0	0	9	0
28	8	0	6	0	7	0	7	0	1	0	6	0	5	0	2	0	0	0	14	0
29	0	0	0	0	0	0	0	0	0	0	0	0	0	0	0	0	0	0	0	0
30	6	0	5	0	5	0	6	0	1	0	2	0	5	0	3	0	0	0	11	0
31	4	0	5	0	5	0	4	0	0	0	3	0	2	0	3	0	0	0	9	0
32	3	0	5	0	8	0	0	0	1	0	4	0	1	0	1	0	0	0	8	0
33	7	0	4	0	6	0	5	0	1	0	3	0	3	0	1	0	2	0	11	0
34	0	0	0	0	0	0	0	0	0	0	0	0	0	0	0	0	0	0	0	0
35	3	0	4	0	4	0	3	0	0	0	4	0	0	0	0	0	3	0	7	0
36	2	0	2	0	2	0	2	0	0	0	0	0	3	0	1	0	0	0	4	0
37	1	0	3	0	3	0	1	0	1	0	2	0	1	0	0	0	0	0	4	0
38	0	0	2	0	0	0	1	0	0	0	0	0	1	0	1	0	0	0	2	0
39	0	0	0	0	0	0	0	0	0	0	0	0	0	0	0	0	0	0	0	0
40	1	0	0	0	1	0	0	0	0	0	0	0	0	0	0	0	1	0	1	0

8YR Indexes: Frequency Distributions

8YR Hearing Acuity (continued)

Code	Male Freq.	Male %	Female Freq.	Female %	White Freq.	White %	Black Freq.	Black %	0.0-1.9 Freq.	0.0-1.9 %	2.0-3.9 Freq.	2.0-3.9 %	4.0-5.9 Freq.	4.0-5.9 %	6.0-7.9 Freq.	6.0-7.9 %	8.0-9.5 Freq.	8.0-9.5 %	Totals Freq.	Totals %
41	2	0	2	0	2	0	2	0	0	0	1	0	3	0	0	0	0	0	4	0
42	0	0	3	0	3	0	0	0	0	0	2	0	0	0	1	0	1	0	3	0
43	2	0	1	0	1	0	2	0	0	0	2	0	1	0	0	0	0	0	3	0
44	0	0	0	0	0	0	0	0	0	0	0	0	0	0	1	0	0	0	0	0
45	1	0	1	0	2	0	0	0	0	0	1	0	1	0	0	0	0	0	2	0
46	1	0	0	0	0	0	2	0	0	0	1	0	0	0	1	0	0	0	2	0
47	1	0	1	0	1	0	0	0	0	0	1	0	2	0	0	0	0	0	1	0
48	2	0	0	0	3	0	0	0	0	0	0	0	0	0	1	0	0	0	3	0
49	0	0	1	0	0	0	2	0	0	0	0	0	0	0	0	0	0	0	0	0
50	0	0	0	0	1	0	0	0	0	0	1	0	1	0	0	0	0	0	1	0
51	1	0	1	0	1	0	0	0	0	0	1	0	0	0	0	0	0	0	3	0
52	0	0	0	0	0	0	0	0	0	0	0	0	1	0	1	0	0	0	0	0
53	0	0	0	0	0	0	0	0	0	0	0	0	0	0	0	0	0	0	0	0
54	0	0	0	0	1	0	0	0	0	0	0	0	2	0	0	0	0	0	0	0
55	0	0	0	0	0	0	0	0	0	0	0	0	0	0	0	0	0	0	0	0
56	1	0	0	0	0	0	1	0	0	0	0	0	0	0	0	0	0	0	1	0
57	1	0	0	0	1	0	0	0	0	0	0	0	0	0	0	0	0	0	0	0
58	1	0	0	0	0	0	0	0	1	0	0	0	0	0	0	0	0	0	0	0
59	0	0	0	0	0	0	0	0	0	0	0	0	0	0	0	0	0	0	1	0
60	0	0	0	0	0	0	0	0	0	0	0	0	0	0	0	0	0	0	0	0
61	1	0	0	0	1	0	0	0	0	0	1	0	0	0	1	0	0	0	1	0
62	0	0	0	0	0	0	0	0	0	0	0	0	0	0	0	0	0	0	0	0
63	0	0	0	0	0	0	0	0	0	0	0	0	0	0	0	0	0	0	0	0
64	0	0	0	0	0	0	0	0	0	0	0	0	0	0	0	0	0	0	0	0
65	1	0	0	0	0	0	0	0	0	0	0	0	0	0	0	0	0	0	1	0
66	0	0	0	0	0	0	0	0	0	0	0	0	0	0	0	0	0	0	0	0
67	0	0	1	0	1	0	0	0	1	0	0	0	0	0	0	0	0	0	1	0
68	0	0	0	0	0	0	1	0	0	0	0	0	0	0	0	0	0	0	0	0
69	0	0	0	0	0	0	0	0	0	0	0	0	0	0	0	0	0	0	0	0
70	0	0	0	0	0	0	0	0	0	0	0	0	0	0	0	0	0	0	1	0
71	1	0	0	0	1	0	0	0	0	0	0	0	0	0	0	0	0	0	0	0
72	0	0	0	0	0	0	0	0	0	0	0	0	0	0	1	0	0	0	1	0
73	0	0	0	0	0	0	0	0	0	0	0	0	0	0	0	0	0	0	0	0
74	0	0	0	0	0	0	0	0	0	0	0	0	0	0	0	0	0	0	0	0
75	1	0	0	0	0	0	1	0	0	0	0	0	0	0	0	0	0	0	1	0
76	0	0	0	0	0	0	0	0	0	0	0	0	0	0	0	0	0	0	0	0
77	1	0	0	0	0	0	0	0	0	0	0	0	1	0	0	0	0	0	1	0
78	0	0	0	0	0	0	0	0	0	0	0	0	0	0	0	0	0	0	0	0
79	0	0	0	0	0	0	0	0	0	0	0	0	0	0	0	0	0	0	0	0
80	0	0	0	0	0	0	0	0	0	0	0	0	0	0	0	0	0	0	0	0

8YR Indexes: Frequency Distributions

		Male		Female		White		Black		0.0-1.9		2.0-3.9		4.0-5.9		6.0-7.9		8.0-9.5		Totals	
	Code	Freq.	%	Freq.	%	Freq.	%	Freq.	%	Freq.	%	Freq.	%	Freq.	%	Freq.	%	Freq.	%	Freq.	%
8YR Hearing Acuity (continued)																					
	81	2	0	0	0	2	0	0	0	0	0	0	0	0	0	0	0	1	0	2	0
	82	0	0	0	0	0	0	0	0	0	0	0	0	0	0	0	0	0	0	0	0
	83	0	0	0	0	0	0	0	0	0	0	0	0	0	0	0	0	0	0	0	0
	84	0	0	0	0	0	0	0	0	0	0	0	0	0	0	0	0	0	0	0	0
	85	0	0	0	0	0	0	0	0	0	0	0	0	0	0	0	0	0	0	0	0
	86	0	0	0	0	0	0	0	0	0	0	0	0	0	0	0	0	0	0	0	0
	87	0	0	0	0	0	0	0	0	0	0	0	0	0	0	0	0	0	0	0	0
	88	1	0	1	0	1	0	1	0	0	0	1	0	0	0	1	0	0	0	2	0
	89	0	0	0	0	0	0	0	0	0	0	0	0	0	0	0	0	0	0	0	0
	90	1	0	0	0	1	0	1	0	0	0	0	0	0	0	1	0	1	0	1	0
	91	0	0	0	0	0	0	0	0	0	0	0	0	0	0	0	0	0	0	0	0
	92	0	0	1	0	0	0	0	0	0	0	1	0	0	0	0	0	0	0	1	0
	93	1	0	0	0	0	0	0	0	0	0	0	0	0	0	0	0	0	0	0	0
	94	0	0	0	0	0	0	0	0	0	0	0	0	0	0	0	0	0	0	0	0
	95	0	0	3	0	2	0	1	0	1	0	1	0	0	0	0	0	1	0	3	0
		9,987		9,877		10,026		9,838		1,606		5,918		5,990		4,065		2,285		19,864	
8YR Monaural Conductive Loss	0	386	4	320	3	417	4	289	3	65	4	216	4	213	4	142	4	70	3	706	4
	1	9,522	96	9,477	97	9,527	96	9,472	97	1,522	96	5,654	96	5,727	96	3,891	96	2,205	97	18,999	96
		9,908		9,797		9,944		9,761		1,587		5,870		5,940		4,033		2,275		19,705	
8YR Binaural Conductive Loss	0	144	1	117	1	177	2	84	1	14	1	91	2	73	1	59	1	24	1	261	1
	1	9,764	99	9,680	99	9,767	98	9,677	99	1,573	99	5,779	98	5,867	99	3,974	99	2,251	99	19,444	99
		9,908		9,797		9,944		9,761		1,587		5,870		5,940		4,033		2,275		19,705	
8YR Monaural Sensorineural Loss	0	152	2	133	1	156	2	129	1	22	1	84	1	101	2	57	1	21	1	285	1
	1	9,783	98	9,706	99	9,824	98	9,665	99	1,576	99	5,808	99	5,860	98	3,987	99	2,258	99	19,489	99
		9,935		9,839		9,980		9,794		1,598		5,892		5,961		4,044		2,279		19,774	
8YR Binaural Sensorineural Loss	0	31	0	28	0	33	0	26	0	2	0	20	0	17	0	12	0	8	0	59	0
	1	9,904	100	9,811	100	9,947	100	9,768	100	1,596	100	5,872	100	5,944	100	4,032	100	2,271	100	19,715	100
		9,935		9,839		9,980		9,794		1,598		5,892		5,961		4,044		2,279		19,774	
8YR Monaural Mixed (Component of Sensorineural) Loss	0	70	1	76	1	75	1	71	1	10	1	51	1	40	1	34	1	11	0	146	1
	1	9,876	99	9,774	99	9,917	99	9,733	99	1,589	99	5,847	99	5,927	99	4,017	99	2,270	100	19,650	99
		9,946		9,850		9,992		9,804		1,599		5,898		5,967		4,051		2,281		19,796	
8YR Binaural Mixed (Component of Sensorineural) Loss	0	16	0	10	0	15	0	11	0	2	0	6	0	6	0	8	0	4	0	26	0
	1	9,930	100	9,840	100	9,977	100	9,793	100	1,597	100	5,892	100	5,961	100	4,043	100	2,277	100	19,770	100
		9,946		9,850		9,992		9,804		1,599		5,898		5,967		4,051		2,281		19,796	
8YR Total Conductive Loss	0	560	6	464	5	622	6	402	4	84	5	322	5	304	5	215	5	99	4	1,024	5
	1	9,336	94	9,326	95	9,311	94	9,351	96	1,502	95	5,541	95	5,627	95	3,817	95	2,175	96	18,662	95
		9,896		9,790		9,933		9,753		1,586		5,863		5,931		4,032		2,274		19,686	
8YR Total Sensorineural Loss	0	235	2	212	2	238	2	209	2	33	2	143	2	140	2	94	2	37	2	447	2
	1	9,700	98	9,627	98	9,742	98	9,585	98	1,565	98	5,749	98	5,821	98	3,950	98	2,242	98	19,327	98
		9,935		9,839		9,980		9,794		1,598		5,892		5,961		4,044		2,279		19,774	

8YR Indexes: Frequency Distributions

Neurological Involvement

Code	Male Freq.	Male %	Female Freq.	Female %	White Freq.	White %	Black Freq.	Black %	0.0–1.9 Freq.	0.0–1.9 %	2.0–3.9 Freq.	2.0–3.9 %	4.0–5.9 Freq.	4.0–5.9 %	6.0–7.9 Freq.	6.0–7.9 %	8.0–9.5 Freq.	8.0–9.5 %	Totals Freq.	Totals %
0	0	0	0	0	0	0	0	0	0	0	0	0	0	0	0	0	0	0	0	0
1	0	0	0	0	0	0	0	0	0	0	0	0	0	0	0	0	0	0	0	0
2	0	0	0	0	0	0	0	0	0	0	0	0	0	0	0	0	0	0	0	0
3	0	0	0	0	0	0	0	0	0	0	0	0	0	0	0	0	0	0	0	0
4	0	0	0	0	0	0	0	0	0	0	0	0	0	0	0	0	0	0	0	0
5	0	0	0	0	0	0	0	0	0	0	0	0	0	0	0	0	0	0	0	0
6	0	0	0	0	0	0	0	0	0	0	0	0	0	0	0	0	0	0	0	0
7	0	0	0	0	0	0	0	0	0	0	0	0	0	0	0	0	0	0	0	0
8	0	0	1	0	0	0	1	0	0	0	1	0	0	0	0	0	0	0	1	0
9	7	0	1	0	5	0	3	0	2	0	3	0	0	0	2	0	1	0	8	0
10	19	0	5	0	9	0	15	0	6	0	6	0	7	0	3	0	2	0	24	0
11	59	1	26	0	33	0	52	1	13	1	26	0	25	0	15	0	6	0	85	0
12	290	3	192	2	203	2	279	3	51	3	187	3	136	2	81	2	27	1	482	3
13	862	9	659	7	694	7	827	9	157	11	524	10	435	8	273	7	132	6	1,521	8
14	1,652	18	1,617	18	1,232	13	2,037	23	362	25	1,180	22	1,052	19	489	13	186	8	3,269	18
15	3,243	35	3,369	37	3,134	33	3,478	39	539	37	2,047	38	2,080	37	1,296	34	650	30	6,612	36
16	1,259	13	1,284	14	1,405	15	1,138	13	140	10	672	12	784	14	593	16	354	16	2,543	14
17	1,936	21	2,017	22	2,763	29	1,190	13	199	14	805	15	1,065	19	1,050	28	834	38	3,953	21
	9,327		9,171		9,478		9,020		1,469		5,451		5,584		3,802		2,192		18,498	

Communicative Effectiveness

Code	Male Freq.	Male %	Female Freq.	Female %	White Freq.	White %	Black Freq.	Black %	0.0–1.9 Freq.	0.0–1.9 %	2.0–3.9 Freq.	2.0–3.9 %	4.0–5.9 Freq.	4.0–5.9 %	6.0–7.9 Freq.	6.0–7.9 %	8.0–9.5 Freq.	8.0–9.5 %	Totals Freq.	Totals %
01-03	0	0	0	0	0	0	0	0	0	0	0	0	0	0	0	0	0	0	0	0
04-07	1	0	0	0	0	0	1	0	0	0	1	0	0	0	0	0	0	0	1	0
08-11	0	0	0	0	0	0	0	0	0	0	0	0	0	0	0	0	0	0	0	0
12-15	0	0	0	0	0	0	0	0	0	0	0	0	0	0	0	0	0	0	0	0
16-19	1	0	0	0	1	0	0	0	0	0	1	0	0	0	0	0	0	0	1	0
20-23	0	0	0	0	0	0	0	0	0	0	0	0	0	0	0	0	0	0	0	0
24-27	1	0	1	0	1	0	1	0	0	0	0	0	2	0	0	0	0	0	2	0
28-31	0	0	0	0	0	0	0	0	0	0	0	0	0	0	0	0	0	0	0	0
32-35	0	0	0	0	0	0	0	0	0	0	0	0	0	0	0	0	0	0	0	0
36-39	0	0	0	0	0	0	0	0	0	0	0	0	0	0	0	0	0	0	0	0
40-43	1	0	0	0	0	0	1	0	0	0	1	0	0	0	0	0	0	0	1	0
44-47	0	0	0	0	0	0	0	0	0	0	0	0	0	0	0	0	0	0	0	0
48-51	0	0	0	0	0	0	0	0	0	0	0	0	0	0	0	0	0	0	0	0
52-55	0	0	0	0	0	0	0	0	0	0	0	0	0	0	0	0	0	0	0	0
56-59	0	0	1	0	0	0	0	0	0	0	0	0	0	0	0	0	0	0	1	0
60-63	1	0	0	0	1	0	2	0	0	0	1	0	1	0	0	0	0	0	2	0
64-67	0	0	0	0	0	0	0	0	0	0	0	0	0	0	0	0	0	0	0	0
68-71	2	0	0	0	0	0	1	0	0	0	0	0	0	0	0	0	0	0	2	0
72-75	0	0	0	0	0	0	0	0	0	0	2	0	0	0	0	0	0	0	0	0
76-79	0	0	0	0	0	0	0	0	0	0	0	0	0	0	0	0	0	0	0	0
80-83	0	0	0	0	0	0	0	0	0	0	0	0	0	0	0	0	0	0	0	0
84-87	0	0	0	0	0	0	0	0	0	0	0	0	0	0	0	0	0	0	0	0

8YR Indexes: Frequency Distributions

Communicative Effectiveness (continued)

Code	Male Freq.	Male %	Female Freq.	Female %	White Freq.	White %	Black Freq.	Black %	0.0-1.9 Freq.	0.0-1.9 %	2.0-3.9 Freq.	2.0-3.9 %	4.0-5.9 Freq.	4.0-5.9 %	6.0-7.9 Freq.	6.0-7.9 %	8.0-9.5 Freq.	8.0-9.5 %	Totals Freq.	Totals %
88-91	0	0	0	0	0	0	0	0	0	0	0	0	0	0	0	0	0	0	0	0
92-95	1	0	0	0	0	0	1	0	0	0	0	0	1	0	0	0	0	0	1	0
96-99	1	0	1	0	0	0	2	0	2	0	0	0	0	0	0	0	0	0	2	0
100-103	1	0	0	0	0	0	1	0	0	0	0	0	1	0	0	0	0	0	1	0
104-107	1	0	0	0	1	0	0	0	0	0	0	0	0	0	0	0	1	0	1	0
108-111	2	0	0	0	1	0	1	0	1	0	1	0	1	0	0	0	0	0	2	0
112-115	2	0	1	0	1	0	2	0	0	0	1	0	1	0	0	0	0	0	3	0
116-119	1	0	1	0	1	0	1	0	2	0	0	0	1	0	0	0	0	0	2	0
120-123	2	0	2	0	1	0	3	0	0	0	1	0	2	0	0	0	0	0	4	0
124-127	1	0	0	0	0	0	1	0	0	0	0	0	0	0	0	0	0	0	1	0
128-131	1	0	0	0	0	0	1	0	0	0	1	0	1	0	0	0	0	0	1	0
132-135	1	0	1	0	1	0	1	0	1	0	0	0	0	0	0	0	0	0	2	0
136-139	2	0	2	0	1	0	3	0	0	0	2	0	0	0	0	0	0	0	4	0
140-143	2	0	0	0	1	0	1	0	1	0	3	0	1	0	0	0	0	0	2	0
144-147	1	0	1	0	0	0	2	0	0	0	0	0	1	0	0	0	0	0	2	0
148-151	4	0	0	0	0	0	4	0	0	0	0	0	1	0	0	0	0	0	4	0
152-155	3	0	1	0	2	0	2	0	3	0	3	0	0	0	0	0	0	0	4	0
156-159	4	0	1	0	0	0	5	0	3	0	3	0	1	0	0	0	0	0	5	0
160-163	3	0	3	0	2	0	4	0	1	0	1	0	1	0	0	0	0	0	6	0
164-167	5	0	2	0	1	0	6	0	2	0	1	0	0	0	0	0	0	0	7	0
168-171	4	0	2	0	1	0	5	0	2	0	4	0	1	0	0	0	0	0	6	0
172-175	7	0	2	0	0	0	9	0	4	0	1	0	1	0	1	0	0	0	9	0
176-179	2	0	3	0	0	0	5	0	1	0	0	0	2	0	0	0	0	0	5	0
180-183	6	0	3	0	1	0	8	0	5	0	3	0	3	0	1	0	0	0	9	0
184-187	4	0	1	0	2	0	3	0	3	0	1	0	1	0	3	0	0	0	5	0
188-191	5	0	2	0	0	0	7	0	2	0	3	0	0	0	0	0	0	0	7	0
192-195	6	0	2	0	4	0	4	0	1	0	2	0	1	0	1	0	0	0	8	0
196-199	4	0	3	0	0	0	7	0	0	0	5	0	2	0	2	0	0	0	7	0
200-203	6	0	4	0	1	0	9	0	3	0	1	0	2	0	0	0	0	0	10	0
204-207	2	0	5	0	3	0	4	0	2	0	3	0	4	0	0	0	0	0	7	0
208-211	8	0	4	0	1	0	11	0	3	0	5	0	4	0	1	0	0	0	12	0
212-215	9	0	4	0	3	0	10	0	4	0	6	0	2	0	0	0	0	0	13	0
216-219	8	0	9	0	4	0	13	0	2	0	10	0	3	0	1	0	1	0	17	0
220-223	15	0	12	0	1	0	26	0	5	0	12	0	3	0	0	0	1	0	27	0
224-227	9	0	7	0	4	0	12	0	5	0	7	0	9	0	1	0	0	0	16	0
228-231	7	0	4	0	2	0	9	0	5	0	7	0	2	0	0	0	0	0	11	0
232-235	19	0	12	0	6	0	25	0	8	0	15	0	5	0	2	0	0	0	31	0
236-239	16	0	9	0	7	0	18	0	6	0	15	0	4	0	3	0	0	0	25	0
240-243	15	0	9	0	2	0	22	0	4	0	14	0	4	0	0	0	0	0	24	0
244-247	13	0	11	0	5	0	19	0	7	0	10	0	6	0	2	0	1	0	24	0

8YR Indexes: Frequency Distributions

Communicative Effectiveness (continued)

Code	Male Freq.	Male %	Female Freq.	Female %	White Freq.	White %	Black Freq.	Black %	0.0-1.9 Freq.	0.0-1.9 %	2.0-3.9 Freq.	2.0-3.9 %	4.0-5.9 Freq.	4.0-5.9 %	6.0-7.9 Freq.	6.0-7.9 %	8.0-9.5 Freq.	8.0-9.5 %	Totals Freq.	Totals %
248-251	18	0	13	0	5	0	26	0	8	1	12	0	9	0	1	0	1	0	31	0
252-255	14	0	11	0	6	0	19	0	6	0	14	0	3	0	2	0	0	0	25	0
256-259	11	0	14	0	4	0	21	0	4	0	16	0	5	0	0	0	0	0	25	0
260-263	11	0	16	0	1	0	26	0	5	1	15	0	7	0	1	0	0	0	27	0
264-267	26	0	12	0	3	0	35	0	11	1	17	0	9	0	4	0	0	0	38	0
268-271	21	0	20	0	4	0	37	0	6	0	15	0	15	0	1	0	1	0	41	0
272-275	18	0	23	0	6	0	35	0	7	0	21	0	12	0	3	0	1	0	41	0
276-279	30	0	22	0	8	0	44	0	10	1	25	0	13	0	5	0	1	0	52	0
280-283	32	0	16	0	11	0	37	1	8	1	26	0	9	0	5	0	1	0	48	0
284-287	35	0	21	0	10	0	46	1	10	1	20	0	20	0	4	0	1	0	56	0
288-291	29	0	20	0	6	0	43	1	3	0	26	0	16	0	6	0	1	0	49	0
292-295	29	0	32	0	12	0	49	1	11	1	26	0	17	0	4	0	1	0	61	0
296-299	40	0	31	0	6	0	65	1	12	1	37	1	18	0	2	0	1	0	71	0
300-303	38	0	28	0	8	0	58	1	11	1	39	1	13	0	5	0	1	0	66	0
304-307	37	0	36	0	9	0	64	1	20	1	30	1	18	0	5	0	0	0	73	0
308-311	37	0	34	0	11	0	60	1	9	1	36	1	21	0	4	0	1	0	71	0
312-315	45	1	41	0	12	0	74	1	16	1	37	1	28	0	5	0	1	0	86	0
316-319	50	1	40	0	14	0	76	1	16	1	40	1	29	1	4	0	0	0	90	0
320-323	68	1	45	0	20	0	93	1	21	1	55	1	33	1	3	0	0	0	113	1
324-327	45	0	40	0	11	0	74	1	10	1	52	1	19	0	8	0	1	0	85	0
328-331	68	1	42	0	19	0	91	1	13	1	54	1	33	1	9	0	2	0	110	1
332-335	65	1	45	0	17	0	93	1	12	1	56	1	31	1	11	0	2	0	110	1
336-339	70	1	45	0	21	0	94	1	18	1	56	1	30	1	11	0	0	0	115	1
340-343	69	1	45	0	18	0	96	1	21	1	46	1	36	1	6	0	0	0	114	1
344-347	64	1	49	1	23	0	90	1	20	2	44	1	43	1	8	0	2	0	113	1
348-351	71	1	64	1	32	0	103	1	25	1	54	1	46	1	8	0	1	0	135	1
352-355	65	1	54	1	21	0	98	1	19	1	57	1	34	1	8	0	1	0	119	1
356-359	77	1	58	1	30	0	105	1	20	1	51	1	52	1	11	0	1	0	135	1
360-363	70	1	63	1	30	0	103	1	19	1	59	1	42	1	12	0	1	0	133	1
364-367	72	1	63	1	30	0	105	1	19	1	61	1	43	1	11	0	1	0	135	1
368-371	66	1	75	1	27	0	114	1	21	1	67	1	35	1	14	0	4	0	141	1
372-375	75	1	63	1	29	0	109	1	25	2	61	1	42	1	9	0	1	0	138	1
376-379	77	1	77	1	37	0	117	1	22	2	70	1	52	1	10	0	0	0	154	1
380-383	88	1	89	1	43	0	134	1	30	2	74	1	52	1	18	0	3	0	177	1
384-387	75	1	74	1	44	0	105	1	11	1	59	1	56	1	16	0	3	0	149	1
388-391	89	1	77	1	43	1	123	1	23	2	71	1	55	1	22	1	1	0	166	1
392-395	116	1	62	1	54	0	124	1	25	2	86	2	42	1	17	1	3	0	178	1
396-399	103	1	71	1	46	1	128	1	21	1	76	1	57	1	17	0	3	0	174	1
400-403	102	1	83	1	54	1	131	1	23	2	89	2	53	1	17	0	3	0	185	1
404-407	110	1	80	1	56	1	134	1	25	2	87	2	54	1	20	1	4	0	190	1

8YR Indexes: Frequency Distributions

Communicative Effectiveness (continued)

Code	Male Freq.	Male %	Female Freq.	Female %	White Freq.	White %	Black Freq.	Black %	0.0-1.9 Freq.	0.0-1.9 %	2.0-3.9 Freq.	2.0-3.9 %	4.0-5.9 Freq.	4.0-5.9 %	6.0-7.9 Freq.	6.0-7.9 %	8.0-9.5 Freq.	8.0-9.5 %	Totals Freq.	Totals %
408-411	99	1	98	1	55	1	142	2	24	2	89	2	57	1	24	1	3	0	197	1
412-415	105	1	97	1	62	1	140	2	22	2	84	2	61	1	29	1	6	0	202	1
416-419	98	1	109	1	68	1	139	2	22	1	92	2	59	1	30	1	4	0	207	1
420-423	95	1	87	1	54	1	128	1	18	1	78	1	55	1	29	1	2	0	182	1
424-427	110	1	81	1	70	1	121	1	16	1	83	1	59	1	29	0	4	0	191	1
428-431	72	1	91	1	54	1	109	1	21	1	64	1	62	1	14	1	2	0	163	1
432-435	110	1	89	1	72	1	127	1	19	1	91	1	61	1	21	1	7	0	199	1
436-439	101	1	93	1	76	1	118	1	27	2	70	2	59	1	30	1	8	0	194	1
440-443	104	1	91	1	70	1	125	1	22	1	68	1	71	1	28	1	6	0	195	1
444-447	96	1	94	1	62	1	128	1	19	1	76	1	64	1	30	1	1	0	190	1
448-451	99	1	101	1	67	1	133	1	21	1	72	1	76	1	27	1	4	0	200	1
452-455	118	1	94	1	78	1	134	1	18	1	84	2	67	1	36	1	7	0	212	1
456-459	109	1	92	1	79	1	122	1	22	1	75	1	72	1	24	1	8	0	201	1
460-463	83	1	94	1	61	1	116	1	20	1	67	1	61	1	22	1	7	0	177	1
464-467	118	1	92	1	91	1	119	1	12	1	80	1	83	1	28	1	7	0	210	1
468-471	91	1	83	1	69	1	105	1	21	1	60	1	64	1	26	1	3	0	174	1
472-475	102	1	105	1	82	1	125	1	19	1	70	1	83	1	31	1	4	0	207	1
476-479	86	1	92	1	73	1	105	1	12	1	69	1	70	1	24	1	3	0	178	1
480-483	101	1	93	1	85	1	109	1	8	1	68	1	79	1	31	1	8	0	194	1
484-487	106	1	96	1	89	1	113	1	19	1	65	1	73	1	35	1	10	0	202	1
488-491	88	1	82	1	82	1	88	1	12	1	60	1	58	1	32	1	8	0	170	1
492-495	101	1	80	1	89	1	92	1	26	2	48	1	55	1	41	1	11	0	181	1
496-499	100	1	75	1	93	1	82	1	11	1	58	1	63	1	33	1	10	0	175	1
500-503	101	1	81	1	95	1	87	1	15	1	54	1	59	1	37	1	17	1	182	1
504-507	83	1	89	1	76	1	96	1	12	1	51	1	64	1	37	1	8	0	172	1
508-511	82	1	95	1	81	1	96	1	8	1	54	1	79	1	33	1	3	0	177	1
512-515	77	1	92	1	92	1	77	1	8	1	63	1	52	1	37	1	9	0	169	1
516-519	77	1	100	1	81	1	96	1	14	1	57	1	58	1	37	1	11	0	177	1
520-523	92	1	105	1	114	1	83	1	19	1	49	1	66	1	44	1	19	1	197	1
524-527	101	1	111	1	108	1	104	1	15	1	82	1	68	1	37	1	10	0	212	1
528-531	82	1	97	1	83	1	96	1	6	0	61	1	61	1	43	1	8	0	179	1
532-535	100	1	79	1	87	1	92	1	14	1	46	1	66	1	41	1	12	1	179	1
536-539	75	1	95	1	94	1	76	1	12	1	51	1	53	1	38	1	16	1	170	1
540-543	91	1	86	1	99	1	78	1	13	1	46	1	66	1	36	1	16	1	177	1
544-547	94	1	123	1	121	1	96	1	8	1	73	1	64	1	53	1	19	1	217	1
548-551	81	1	104	1	111	1	74	1	10	1	47	1	62	1	54	1	12	1	185	1
552-555	97	1	90	1	105	1	82	1	12	1	39	1	74	1	45	1	16	1	187	1
556-559	81	1	96	1	99	1	78	1	7	0	55	1	53	1	40	1	22	1	177	1
560-563	80	1	100	1	115	1	65	1	5	0	43	1	62	1	52	1	18	1	180	1
564-567	76	1	87	1	94	1	69	1	7	0	37	1	55	1	44	1	20	1	163	1

8YR Indexes: Frequency Distributions

Communicative Effectiveness (continued)

Code	Male Freq.	%	Female Freq.	%	White Freq.	%	Black Freq.	%	0.0-1.9 Freq.	%	2.0-3.9 Freq.	%	4.0-5.9 Freq.	%	6.0-7.9 Freq.	%	8.0-9.5 Freq.	%	Totals Freq.	%
568-571	62	1	93	1	101	1	54	1	11	1	30	1	45	1	52	1	17	1	155	1
572-575	100	1	114	1	126	1	88	1	9	1	64	1	59	1	53	1	29	1	214	1
576-579	98	1	90	1	124	1	64	1	8	1	38	1	69	1	49	1	24	1	188	1
580-583	106	1	93	1	136	1	63	1	12	1	43	1	65	1	50	1	29	1	199	1
584-587	94	1	98	1	119	1	73	1	7	0	43	1	54	1	58	1	30	1	192	1
588-591	100	1	103	1	140	1	63	1	6	0	41	1	64	1	63	2	29	1	203	1
592-595	76	1	106	1	126	1	56	1	5	0	44	1	53	1	56	1	24	1	182	1
596-599	87	1	86	1	122	1	51	1	7	0	35	1	59	1	45	1	27	1	173	1
600-603	93	1	89	1	130	1	52	1	7	0	34	1	62	1	52	1	27	1	182	1
604-607	80	1	81	1	109	1	52	1	10	1	18	0	54	1	55	1	24	1	161	1
608-611	85	1	89	1	120	1	54	1	10	1	33	1	47	1	54	1	30	1	174	1
612-615	104	1	101	1	145	1	60	1	5	0	39	1	59	1	66	2	36	2	205	1
616-619	91	1	105	1	137	1	59	1	3	0	30	1	61	1	67	2	35	2	196	1
620-623	85	1	109	1	129	1	65	1	8	1	31	1	74	1	50	1	31	1	194	1
624-627	88	1	95	1	131	1	52	1	7	0	26	0	53	1	66	2	31	1	183	1
628-631	95	1	102	1	156	2	41	0	3	0	41	1	62	1	60	2	31	1	197	1
632-635	82	1	102	1	136	1	48	1	0	0	35	1	59	1	51	1	39	2	184	1
636-639	85	1	101	1	138	1	48	1	4	0	31	1	49	1	60	2	42	2	186	1
640-643	75	1	91	1	130	1	36	0	0	0	17	0	53	1	52	1	44	2	166	1
644-647	79	1	85	1	133	1	31	0	5	0	15	0	46	1	51	1	47	2	164	1
648-651	78	1	98	1	139	1	37	0	4	0	26	0	46	1	50	1	50	2	176	1
652-655	70	1	85	1	119	1	36	0	2	0	19	0	51	1	49	1	34	2	155	1
656-659	68	1	99	1	136	1	31	0	5	0	26	0	40	1	47	1	49	2	167	1
660-663	80	1	94	1	133	1	41	0	6	0	19	0	53	1	61	2	35	2	174	1
664-667	62	1	91	1	120	1	33	0	6	0	25	0	37	1	34	1	51	2	153	1
668-671	78	1	79	1	121	1	36	0	2	0	20	0	41	1	56	1	38	2	157	1
672-675	71	1	72	1	118	1	25	0	0	0	18	0	31	1	48	1	45	2	143	1
676-679	79	1	91	1	142	1	28	0	1	0	21	0	40	1	62	2	46	2	170	1
680-683	60	1	69	1	111	1	18	0	2	0	14	0	28	0	43	1	42	2	129	1
684-687	64	1	73	1	115	1	22	0	2	0	12	0	28	0	48	1	47	2	137	1
688-691	54	1	81	1	117	1	18	0	0	0	15	0	31	1	46	1	43	2	135	1
692-695	64	1	73	1	120	1	17	0	1	0	11	0	34	1	46	1	45	2	137	1
696-699	52	1	78	1	112	1	18	0	0	0	10	0	25	0	39	1	55	2	130	1
700-703	56	1	69	1	109	1	16	0	0	0	16	0	28	0	40	1	41	2	125	1
704-707	50	1	43	0	82	1	11	0	1	0	7	0	20	0	32	1	33	1	93	0
708-711	45	1	56	1	87	1	14	0	1	0	8	0	20	0	41	1	31	1	101	1
712-715	39	0	66	1	99	1	6	0	0	0	8	0	16	0	41	1	39	2	105	1
716-719	41	0	62	1	92	1	11	0	1	0	8	0	14	0	44	1	36	2	103	1
720-723	32	0	43	0	71	1	4	0	0	0	3	0	13	0	23	1	35	2	75	0
724-727	29	0	30	0	49	1	10	0	0	0	7	0	12	0	20	1	20	1	59	0

8YR Indexes: Frequency Distributions

Communicative Effectiveness (continued)

Code	Male Freq.	Male %	Female Freq.	Female %	White Freq.	White %	Black Freq.	Black %	0.0-1.9 Freq.	0.0-1.9 %	2.0-3.9 Freq.	2.0-3.9 %	4.0-5.9 Freq.	4.0-5.9 %	6.0-7.9 Freq.	6.0-7.9 %	8.0-9.5 Freq.	8.0-9.5 %	Totals Freq.	Totals %
728-731	37	0	41	0	69	1	9	0	0	0	3	0	10	0	28	1	37	2	78	0
732-735	24	0	32	0	51	1	5	0	0	0	3	0	13	0	23	1	17	1	56	0
736-739	31	0	43	0	72	1	2	0	0	0	3	0	14	0	21	1	36	2	74	0
740-743	32	0	37	0	57	1	12	0	0	0	3	0	13	0	23	0	30	1	69	0
744-747	21	0	31	0	47	0	5	0	2	0	2	0	9	0	17	0	22	1	52	0
748-751	19	0	27	0	43	0	3	0	0	0	4	0	7	0	14	0	21	1	46	0
752-755	24	0	24	0	43	0	5	0	0	0	2	0	7	0	15	0	24	1	48	0
756-759	15	0	35	0	45	1	5	0	0	0	1	0	10	0	11	0	28	1	50	0
760-763	17	0	34	0	50	1	1	0	0	0	1	0	6	0	22	1	22	1	51	0
764-767	13	0	28	0	39	0	2	0	0	0	0	0	3	0	13	0	25	1	41	0
768-771	9	0	17	0	24	0	2	0	0	0	1	0	6	0	5	0	15	1	26	0
772-775	16	0	20	0	34	0	2	0	0	0	0	0	3	0	12	0	20	1	36	0
776-779	8	0	13	0	20	0	1	0	0	0	2	0	2	0	7	0	12	1	21	0
780-783	11	0	18	0	28	0	1	0	0	0	2	0	1	0	10	0	16	1	29	0
784-787	14	0	7	0	20	0	1	0	0	0	2	0	0	0	5	0	12	1	21	0
788-791	6	0	9	0	15	0	0	0	0	0	1	0	3	0	2	0	11	0	15	0
792-795	5	0	6	0	11	0	0	0	0	0	0	0	3	0	1	0	6	0	11	0
796-799	9	0	6	0	14	0	1	0	0	0	0	0	3	0	5	0	9	0	15	0
800-803	8	0	3	0	11	0	0	0	0	0	0	0	1	0	5	0	6	0	11	0
804-807	2	0	2	0	4	0	0	0	0	0	0	0	0	0	0	0	4	0	4	0
808-811	2	0	2	0	4	0	0	0	0	0	0	0	0	0	2	0	2	0	4	0
812-815	2	0	4	0	6	0	0	0	0	0	0	0	0	0	1	0	5	0	6	0
816-819	3	0	0	0	3	0	0	0	0	0	2	0	1	0	2	0	0	0	3	0
820-823	2	0	1	0	3	0	0	0	0	0	0	0	0	0	2	0	1	0	3	0
824-827	2	0	0	0	2	0	0	0	0	0	0	0	0	0	1	0	1	0	2	0
828-831	1	0	2	0	2	0	1	0	0	0	0	0	0	0	1	0	1	0	3	0
832-835	1	0	0	0	2	0	0	0	0	0	0	0	0	0	0	0	0	0	2	0
836-839	0	0	1	0	0	0	0	0	0	0	0	0	0	0	0	0	1	0	0	0
840-843	0	0	0	0	0	0	0	0	0	0	0	0	0	0	0	0	0	0	0	0
844-847	0	0	0	0	0	0	0	0	0	0	0	0	0	0	0	0	0	0	0	0
848-851	0	0	0	0	0	0	0	0	0	0	0	0	0	0	0	0	0	0	0	0
852-855	1	0	0	0	1	0	0	0	0	0	0	0	0	0	0	0	1	0	1	0
	9,471		9,487		9,739		9,219		1,485		5,572		5,724		3,936		2,241		18,958	

Auditory Processing

Code	Male Freq.	Male %	Female Freq.	Female %	White Freq.	White %	Black Freq.	Black %	0.0-1.9 Freq.	0.0-1.9 %	2.0-3.9 Freq.	2.0-3.9 %	4.0-5.9 Freq.	4.0-5.9 %	6.0-7.9 Freq.	6.0-7.9 %	8.0-9.5 Freq.	8.0-9.5 %	Totals Freq.	Totals %
1	0	0	0	0	0	0	0	0	0	0	0	0	0	0	0	0	0	0	0	0
2	0	0	0	0	0	0	0	0	0	0	0	0	0	0	0	0	0	0	0	0
3	0	0	0	0	0	0	0	0	0	0	0	0	0	0	0	0	0	0	0	0
4	0	0	0	0	0	0	0	0	0	0	0	0	0	0	0	0	0	0	0	0
5	0	0	0	0	0	0	0	0	0	0	0	0	0	0	0	0	0	0	0	0
6	0	0	0	0	0	0	0	0	0	0	0	0	0	0	0	0	0	0	0	0
7	0	0	0	0	0	0	0	0	0	0	0	0	0	0	0	0	0	0	0	0

8YR Indexes: Frequency Distributions

Auditory Processing (continued)

Code	Male Freq.	Male %	Female Freq.	Female %	White Freq.	White %	Black Freq.	Black %	0.0-1.9 Freq.	0.0-1.9 %	2.0-3.9 Freq.	2.0-3.9 %	4.0-5.9 Freq.	4.0-5.9 %	6.0-7.9 Freq.	6.0-7.9 %	8.0-9.5 Freq.	8.0-9.5 %	Totals Freq.	Totals %
8	0	0	0	0	0	0	0	0	0	0	0	0	0	0	0	0	0	0	0	0
9	0	0	0	0	0	0	0	0	0	0	0	0	0	0	0	0	0	0	0	0
10	0	0	0	0	0	0	0	0	0	0	0	0	0	0	0	0	0	0	0	0
11	0	0	0	0	0	0	0	0	0	0	0	0	0	0	0	0	0	0	0	0
12	0	0	0	0	0	0	0	0	0	0	0	0	0	0	0	0	0	0	0	0
13	0	0	0	0	0	0	0	0	0	0	0	0	0	0	0	0	0	0	0	0
14	0	0	0	0	0	0	0	0	0	0	0	0	0	0	0	0	0	0	0	0
15	0	0	0	0	0	0	0	0	0	0	0	0	0	0	0	0	0	0	0	0
16	0	0	0	0	0	0	0	0	0	0	0	0	0	0	0	0	0	0	0	0
17	0	0	0	0	0	0	0	0	0	0	0	0	0	0	0	0	0	0	0	0
18	0	0	0	0	0	0	0	0	0	0	0	0	0	0	0	0	0	0	0	0
19	0	0	0	0	0	0	0	0	0	0	0	0	0	0	0	0	0	0	0	0
20	1	0	0	0	0	0	1	0	0	0	1	0	0	0	0	0	0	0	1	0
21	0	0	0	0	0	0	0	0	0	0	0	0	0	0	0	0	0	0	0	0
22	0	0	0	0	0	0	0	0	0	0	0	0	0	0	0	0	0	0	0	0
23	2	0	0	0	0	0	2	0	0	0	2	0	0	0	0	0	0	0	2	0
24	2	0	0	0	1	0	1	0	0	0	1	0	1	0	0	0	0	0	2	0
25	0	0	0	0	0	0	0	0	0	0	0	0	0	0	0	0	0	0	0	0
26	1	0	0	0	0	0	1	0	1	0	0	0	0	0	0	0	0	0	1	0
27	3	0	1	0	2	0	2	0	0	0	2	0	1	0	0	0	1	0	4	0
28	1	0	0	0	1	0	0	0	0	0	0	0	0	0	0	0	1	0	1	0
29	3	0	2	0	2	0	3	0	2	0	1	0	1	0	1	0	0	0	5	0
30	2	0	4	0	2	0	4	0	4	0	1	0	1	0	0	0	0	0	6	0
31	1	0	0	0	1	0	0	0	0	0	0	0	1	0	0	0	0	0	1	0
32	4	0	2	0	3	0	3	0	1	0	5	0	0	0	0	0	0	0	6	0
33	6	0	6	0	1	0	11	0	4	0	6	0	1	0	0	0	1	0	12	0
34	11	0	2	0	2	0	11	0	5	0	4	0	3	0	1	0	0	0	13	0
35	11	0	2	0	1	0	12	0	5	0	6	0	1	0	1	0	0	0	13	0
36	17	0	10	0	4	0	23	0	9	1	13	0	4	0	1	0	0	0	27	0
37	16	0	9	0	6	0	19	0	4	0	14	0	4	0	2	0	1	0	25	0
38	16	0	16	0	5	0	27	0	7	1	12	0	11	0	2	0	0	0	32	0
39	26	0	16	0	9	0	33	0	12	1	20	0	8	0	2	0	0	0	42	0
40	30	0	11	0	11	0	30	0	7	1	18	0	11	0	5	0	0	0	41	0
41	38	1	22	0	11	0	49	1	13	1	28	1	13	0	6	0	0	0	60	1
42	49	1	34	0	19	0	64	1	16	1	46	1	16	1	5	0	0	0	83	1
43	54	1	30	0	20	0	64	1	18	1	41	1	17	1	8	0	0	0	84	1
44	71	1	43	0	21	0	93	1	24	1	48	1	37	1	5	0	0	0	114	1
45	76	1	41	0	21	0	96	1	21	1	51	1	38	1	5	0	2	0	117	1
46	89	1	61	0	35	0	115	1	30	2	82	2	34	1	4	0	0	0	150	1
47	111	1	74	1	39	0	146	2	39	2	88	2	46	1	10	0	2	0	185	1

641

8YR Indexes: Frequency Distributions

Auditory Processing (continued)

Code	Male Freq.	Male %	Female Freq.	Female %	White Freq.	White %	Black Freq.	Black %	0.0-1.9 Freq.	0.0-1.9 %	2.0-3.9 Freq.	2.0-3.9 %	4.0-5.9 Freq.	4.0-5.9 %	6.0-7.9 Freq.	6.0-7.9 %	8.0-9.5 Freq.	8.0-9.5 %	Totals Freq.	Totals %
48	140	2	93	1	36	0	197	2	38	2	118	2	66	1	8	0	3	0	233	1
49	173	2	126	1	57	1	242	3	52	3	155	3	74	1	17	0	0	0	299	2
50	191	2	129	1	66	1	254	3	41	3	154	3	99	2	22	1	4	0	320	2
51	175	2	156	2	78	1	253	3	52	3	148	3	104	2	24	1	3	0	331	2
52	175	2	176	2	80	1	271	3	67	4	153	3	104	2	22	1	5	0	351	2
53	241	3	173	2	106	1	308	3	58	4	208	4	118	2	26	1	4	0	414	2
54	251	3	189	2	113	1	327	4	53	3	210	4	133	2	40	1	4	0	440	2
55	274	3	237	3	144	2	367	4	64	4	218	4	169	3	52	1	8	0	511	3
56	250	3	251	3	136	1	365	4	65	4	227	4	142	3	60	2	7	0	501	3
57	304	3	278	3	175	2	497	5	72	5	256	5	171	3	70	2	13	1	582	3
58	316	3	274	3	187	2	403	4	70	5	245	5	192	4	72	2	11	1	590	3
59	284	3	306	3	207	2	383	4	52	4	221	4	222	4	81	2	14	1	590	3
60	301	3	320	4	228	2	393	4	61	4	208	4	233	4	96	3	23	1	621	3
61	338	4	384	4	284	3	438	5	66	5	246	5	256	5	123	3	31	1	722	4
62	357	4	376	4	335	4	398	4	59	5	244	5	259	5	135	4	36	2	733	4
63	407	4	359	4	366	4	400	4	48	3	254	5	258	5	165	4	41	2	766	4
64	369	4	420	5	379	4	410	5	47	3	217	4	296	5	171	5	58	3	789	4
65	369	4	408	5	423	5	354	4	49	3	223	4	266	5	167	4	72	3	777	4
66	377	4	403	4	456	5	324	4	34	2	224	4	258	5	196	5	68	3	780	4
67	402	4	391	4	480	5	313	4	41	3	189	4	251	5	216	6	96	4	793	4
68	383	4	425	5	551	6	257	3	33	2	165	3	267	5	228	6	115	5	808	4
69	361	4	378	6	512	6	227	3	20	1	131	2	229	4	243	6	116	5	739	4
70	366	4	416	5	563	6	219	2	27	2	130	2	218	4	241	6	166	8	782	4
71	349	4	361	4	555	6	155	2	7	0	94	2	207	4	226	6	176	8	710	4
72	290	3	302	3	465	5	127	1	9	1	63	1	178	3	197	5	145	7	592	3
73	269	3	305	3	471	5	103	1	11	1	54	1	138	3	204	5	167	8	574	3
74	215	2	251	3	390	4	76	1	7	0	48	1	107	2	157	4	147	7	466	3
75	166	2	224	2	337	4	53	1	3	0	27	1	81	1	128	3	151	7	390	2
76	134	1	145	2	251	3	28	0	3	0	16	0	49	1	100	3	114	5	279	2
77	80	1	128	1	194	2	14	0	0	0	15	0	33	0	60	2	100	5	208	1
78	82	1	97	1	165	2	14	0	0	0	8	0	24	0	59	2	88	4	179	1
79	49	1	59	1	102	1	6	0	0	0	3	0	16	0	24	1	65	3	108	1
80	38	0	38	0	72	1	4	0	0	0	7	0	7	0	25	1	37	2	76	0
81	15	0	16	0	30	0	1	0	0	0	0	0	0	0	12	0	19	1	31	0
82	7	0	15	0	22	0	0	0	0	0	0	0	3	0	9	0	10	0	22	0
83	7	0	8	0	15	0	0	0	0	0	0	0	3	0	4	0	8	0	15	0
84	2	0	2	0	4	0	0	0	0	0	0	0	0	0	2	0	2	0	4	0
85	0	0	5	0	5	0	0	0	0	0	0	0	0	0	1	0	4	0	5	0
86	0	0	1	0	1	0	0	0	0	0	0	0	0	0	0	0	1	0	0	0
87	0	0	0	0	0	0	0	0	0	0	0	0	0	0	0	0	0	0	0	0
88	0	0	0	0	0	0	0	0	0	0	0	0	0	0	0	0	0	0	0	0
89	0	0	0	0	0	0	0	0	0	0	0	0	0	0	0	0	0	0	0	0
90	0	0	0	0	0	0	0	0	0	0	0	0	0	0	0	0	0	0	0	0
	9,146		9,013		9,258		8,901		1,428		5,366		5,484		3,740		2,141		18,159	

Correlation
Matrices
between 3YR
and 8YR SLH
Variables and
SLH Indices

Correlations : 3YR Indexes with 3YR Indexes and 3YR Indexes with 8YR Indexes

	3YR Speech Mechanism	3YR Hypernasality	3YR Fluency	3YR Articulation	3YR Intelligibility	3YR Language Comprehension	3YR Sentence Complexity	3YR Auditory Memory	3YR Hearing Screen
3YR Indexes									
3YR Speech Mechanism	.04								
3YR Hypernasality	-.01	-.01							
3YR Fluency	.13	.05	-.00						
3YR Articulation	.18	.09	.01	.50					
3YR Intelligibility	.13	.03	-.02	.20	.31				
3YR Language Comprehension	.16	.05	-.04	.27	.43	.29			
3YR Sentence Complexity	.15	.02	-.02	.13	.21	.18	.22		
3YR Auditory Memory	.09	.01	-.01	.07	.11	.10	.12	.07	
3YR Hearing Screen									
8YR Indexes									
8YR Speech Mechanism	.04	.00	.00	.06	.05	.05	.04	.05	.03
8YR Palate Func.. Hypernasality	.01	.02	.00	.02	.04	.03	.05	.03	.03
8YR Fluency	.01	.01	.05	.04	.04	.05	.04	.03	.03
8YR Articulation	.07	.03	.01	.31	.27	.22	.22	.07	.03
8YR Intelligibility	.08	.01	-.01	.20	.19	.16	.21	.12	.06
8YR Language Comprehension	.01	.02	-.05	.13	.13	.23	.12	.05	.01
8YR Auditory Memory	.07	.01	-.03	.19	.23	.24	.20	.17	.04
8YR Digits	.09	.02	-.02	.14	.22	.15	.19	.23	.04
8YR Word Identification	.05	.02	-.08	.20	.20	.33	.17	.09	.01
Written Communication	.09	.02	-.04	.19	.27	.24	.23	.18	.03
8YR Language Production	.06	.04	-.01	.25	.24	.32	.20	.15	.01
8YR Concept Development	.07	.01	-.04	.25	.27	.34	.23	.14	.04
8YR Hearing Severity	-.03	-.03	.00	-.06	-.07	-.10	-.06	-.00	-.09
8YR Total Conductive Loss	.03	.02	-.00	.03	.06	.05	.06	.04	.07
8YR Total Sensorineural Loss	.00	.00	-.01	.03	.05	.04	.05	.01	.05
Neurological Involvement	.04	.01	-.01	.12	.11	.11	.08	.06	.03
Communicative Effectiveness	.07	.02	-.05	.24	.27	.32	.23	.15	.02
Auditory Processing	.09	.02	-.05	.26	.30	.33	.25	.19	.03

644

Correlations: 8YR Indexes with 8YR Indexes

8YR Indexes

8YR Indexes	8YR Speech Mechanism	8YR Palate Func., Hypernasality	8YR Fluency	8YR Articulation	8YR Intelligibility	8YR Language Comprehension	8YR Auditory Memory	8YR Digits	8YR Word Identification	Written Communication	8YR Language Production	8YR Concept Development	8YR Hearing Severity	8YR Total Conductive Loss	8YR Total Sensorineural Loss	Neurological Involvement	Communicative Effectiveness	Auditory Processing
8YR Speech Mechanism																		
8YR Palate Func., Hypernasality	.05																	
8YR Fluency	.05	.04																
8YR Articulation	.12	.09	.12															
8YR Intelligibility	.13	.12	.14	.52														
8YR Language Comprehension	.05	-.00	.05	.25	.15													
8YR Auditory Memory	.07	.02	.04	.28	.21	.77												
8YR Digits	.05	.03	.07	.18	.16	.17	.55											
8YR Word Identification	.07	.01	.08	.37	.24	.60	.50	.24										
Written Communication	.05	.03	.08	.36	.24	.34	.45	.36	.49									
8YR Language Production	.10	.03	.08	.48	.40	.42	.54	.23	.53	.48								
8YR Concept Development	.08	.02	-.01	.42	.28	.54	.69	.33	.68	.66	.72							
8YR Hearing Severity	-.02	-.05	-.00	-.17	-.15	-.09	-.10	-.06	-.16	-.11	-.16	-.16						
8YR Total Conductive Loss	.02	.04	.00	.06	.06	-.00	.03	.03	.02	.04	.05	.04	-.62					
8YR Total Sensorineural Loss	.00	.03	.04	.07	.06	.03	.03	.02	.05	.04	.06	.05	-.47	.31				
Neurological Involvement	.20	.03	.09	.19	.11	.17	.21	.14	.26	.29	.24	.47	-.29	.10	.16			
Communicative Effectiveness	.07	.02	.09	.44	.33	.69	.67	.34	.71	.81	.62	.81	-.15	.03	.04	.31		
Auditory Processing	.06	.03	.09	.44	.27	.60	.69	.47	.71	.84	.63	.88	-.20	.07	.07	.45	.91	

Correlations: 3YR Indexes with 3YR SLH Variables

3YR Variables	3YR Speech Mechanism	3YR Hypernasality	3YR Fluency	3YR Articulation	3YR Intelligibility	3YR Language Comprehension	3YR Sentence Complexity	3YR Auditory Memory	3YR Hearing Screen
Ident. Familiar Objects	.08	.04	-.00	.11	.18	.56	.21	.10	.06
Understand Action Words	.12	.02	-.01	.14	.23	.68	.23	.13	.10
Understand Space Relations	.09	.02	-.02	.17	.26	.88	.22	.15	.07
Naming Objects	.13	.05	-.02	.19	.29	.35	.31	.18	.08
Sentence Length	.14	.03	-.05	.25	.36	.23	.78	.18	.08
Sentence Structure	.14	.05	-.03	.20	.36	.22	.84	.18	.11
Relevance	.11	.03	-.02	.17	.29	.28	.72	.15	.11
Word Order	.12	.03	-.02	.18	.29	.20	.82	.14	.10
Use of Pronouns	.12	.05	-.02	.20	.34	.21	.81	.18	.10
Summary Item Score	.17	.04	-.05	.26	.42	.29	.89	.23	.12
Recall 2 Digits	.11	.01	-.01	.13	.17	.16	.17	.53	.05
Recall 3 Digits	.14	.02	-.02	.12	.22	.18	.21	.67	.07
Recall 2 Syllables	.11	.00	-.02	.12	.15	.13	.16	.57	.04
Recall 3 Syllables	.15	.02	-.01	.12	.21	.17	.20	.76	.08
Spondaic Word Test	.12	.02	-.02	.15	.20	.23	.23	.18	.29
Pure Tone, Right Ear	.06	.01	-.00	.07	.09	.08	.12	.04	.85
Pure Tone, Left Ear	.06	.01	-.01	.07	.09	.08	.13	.04	.88
Lips: Retraction (3YR)	.17	.01	-.00	.04	.07	.08	.07	.04	.02
Lips: Protrusion (3YR)	.11	.03	.00	.08	.08	.09	.04	.07	.05
Tongue: Midline Pro. (3YR)	.06	.01	.00	.04	.05	.07	.04	.01	.03
Tongue: Lateral Pro. (3YR)	.07	.02	.01	.13	.12	.15	.05	.03	.02
Tongue: Elevation (3YR)	.06	.01	.03	.12	.11	.14	.01	.03	-.01
Soft Palate: Elevation	.06	.12	-.01	.02	.07	.03	.06	.03	-.05
Diadochokinesis: Lips	.84	.02	-.01	.09	.14	.10	.16	.14	.07
Diadochokinesis: Tongue	.96	.04	-.01	.08	.14	.10	.14	.14	.09
Voice: Pitch (3YR)	.05	.06	.01	.04	.10	.09	.08	.04	.06
Voice: Loudness (3YR)	.10	.03	-.01	.08	.19	.09	.16	.06	.07
Voice: Quality (3YR)	.03	.33	.00	.09	.15	.11	.02	-.00	.04
Initial Consonants	.12	.05	.00	.87	.51	.21	.25	.12	.06
Final Consonants	.13	.05	.00	.52	.48	.32	.25	.14	.04
Vowels and Diphthongs	.12	.03	-.00	.59	.35	.16	.24	.18	.06
Intelligibility(3YR)	.20	.08	-.00	.50	.83	.32	.52	.22	.12
Dysfluent Events (3YR)	-.00	-.00	.98	-.00	.01	-.02	-.04	-.01	-.01
Struggle Behavior (3YR)	.00	-.01	.54	.00	.02	-.00	.00	-.00	.00

Correlations: 8YR Indexes with 3YR SLH Variables

8YR Indexes

3YR Variables	8YR Speech Mechanism	8YR Palate Func., Hypernasality	8YR Fluency	8YR Articulation	8YR Intelligibility	8YR Language Comprehension	8YR Auditory Memory	8YR Digits	8YR Word Identification	Written Communication	8YR Language Production	8YR Concept Development	8YR Hearing Severity	8YR Total Conductive Loss	8YR Total Sensorineural Loss	Neurological Involvement	Communicative Effectiveness	Auditory Processing
Ident. Familiar Objects	.04	.04	.04	.15	.12	.12	.13	.09	.20	.15	.19	.18	-.08	.04	.03	.06	.18	.19
Understand Action Words	.03	.05	.03	.15	.13	.14	.15	.11	.20	.16	.20	.20	-.08	.05	.02	.08	.19	.21
Understand Space Relations	.04	.01	.04	.19	.11	.22	.23	.13	.31	.21	.29	.32	-.08	.03	.04	.10	.30	.31
Naming Objects	.06	.04	.04	.18	.15	.13	.20	.17	.18	.22	.20	.23	-.07	.04	.03	.08	.22	.25
Sentence Length	.03	.02	.02	.17	.16	.13	.15	.16	.17	.18	.18	.16	-.04	.04	.03	.08	.23	.25
Sentence Structure	.03	.04	.05	.15	.18	.07	.14	.12	.10	.14	.14	.18	-.03	.05	.05	.05	.17	.18
Relevance	.06	.06	.03	.18	.19	.10	.13	.14	.15	.17	.15	.15	-.07	.05	.04	.07	.17	.18
Word Order	.04	.04	.03	.19	.16	.07	.13	.15	.11	.23	.13	.16	-.06	.05	.03	.06	.15	.16
Use of Pronouns	.04	.04	.04	.18	.20	.10	.14	.19	.11	.13	.16	.22	-.04	.04	.04	.06	.16	.17
Summary Item Score	.04	.04	.02	.22	.08	.10	.19	.19	.15	.19	.20	.10	-.05	.06	.03	.07	.23	.25
Recall 2 Digits	.02	.01	.02	.07	.09	.05	.12	.13	.07	.12	.12	.14	-.01	.03	.01	.03	.11	.13
Recall 3 Digits	.03	.03	.02	.05	.11	.05	.17	.25	.09	.17	.16	.12	-.00	.04	.01	.04	.15	.19
Recall 2 Syllables	.03	.04	.01	.08	.08	.04	.11	.12	.07	.13	.11	.14	-.01	.04	.02	.06	.11	.13
Recall 3 Syllables	.03	.04	.02	.05	.13	.07	.17	.11	.06	.03	.12	.05	-.10	.05	.06	.07	.13	.17
Spondaic Word Test	.03	.05	.03	.13	.09	.03	.12	.05	.11	.02	.13	.04	-.15	.10	.06	.04	.04	.17
Pure Tone, Right Ear	.03	.03	.00	.08	.08	.02	.04	.04	.05	.04	.04	.05	-.13	.09	.06	.03	.03	.06
Pure Tone, Left Ear	.04	.05	.00	.06	.04	.01	.03	.03	.04	.05	.03	.06	-.13	.08	.04	.01	.03	.04
Lips: Retraction (3YR)	.02	-.00	.03	.07	.04	.02	.03	.00	.03	.10	.06	.03	-.00	.00	.00	.04	.05	.05
Lips: Protrusion (3YR)	.01	.00	.02	.05	.04	.13	.05	.03	.03	.03	.07	.19	-.00	.02	.02	.09	.04	.03
Tongue: Midline Pro. (3YR)	.10	.01	.03	.04	.04	-.05	.01	.01	.17	.02	.04	.13	-.04	.01	.01	.06	.16	.16
Tongue: Lateral Pro. (3YR)	.09	-.02	.02	.14	.00	-.02	.12	.02	.08	.08	.17	.00	-.05	.00	.02	-.01	.07	.08
Tongue: Elevation (3YR)	.08	.03	.03	.09	.01	.01	.07	.10	-.02	.07	.11	.06	.01	.03	-.00	-.02	.00	.00
Soft Palate: Elevation	.01	.01	-.02	.01	.04	-.02	.01	.08	.03	.04	.01	.05	-.01	.03	.01	.01	.05	.07
Diadochokinesis: Lips	.03	.03	.01	.04	.06	.01	.06	.03	.04	.05	.03	.04	-.02	.03	.01	.02	.05	.06
Diadochokinesis: Tongue	.02	.02	.01	.04	.04	.02	.07	.06	.08	.09	.09	.09	-.03	.03	.01	.01	.04	.09
Voice: Pitch (3YR)	.03	.03	.01	.07	.05	.05	.05	.01	.12	.09	.12	.12	-.06	.03	.00	.03	.09	.12
Voice: Loudness (3YR)	.00	.02	.04	.09	.16	.08	.21	.14	.24	.22	.27	.29	-.08	.04	.04	.13	.27	.30
Voice: Quality (3YR)	.05	.03	.06	.32	.16	.16	.28	.15	.42	.29	.39	.45	-.11	.03	.06	.18	.42	.44
Initial Consonants	.06	.02	.05	.37	.17	.28	.13	.14	.09	.12	.13	.13	-.02	.07	.01	.05	.13	.15
Final Consonants	.04	.01	.05	.19	.25	.06	.20	.21	.17	.25	.23	.23	-.09	.03	.05	.09	.24	.26
Vowels and Diphthongs	.07	.06	.06	.29	-.01	.11	.13	.15	.09	.12	.13	.13	-.02	.07	.01	.05	.13	.15
Intelligibility (3YR)	.01	-.01	.04	.01	.00	-.05	-.04	-.02	-.08	-.04	-.01	-.04	-.00	.00	-.02	-.01	-.05	.26
Dysfluent Events (3YR)	.01	-.01	.06	.01	-.01	-.05	-.04	-.02	-.08	-.04	-.01	-.04	-.00	.00	-.02	-.01	-.05	-.05
Struggle Behavior (3YR)	-.01	.00	.04	.01	.00	-.02	-.01	.01	-.01	-.00	.00	-.00	-.01	-.00	-.01	-.01	-.01	-.01

647

Correlations: 3YR Indexes with 8YR SLH Variables

8YR Variables	3YR Speech Mechanism	3YR Hypernasality	3YR Fluency	3YR Articulation	3YR Intelligibility	3YR Language Comprehension	3YR Sentence Complexity	3YR Auditory Memory	3YR Hearing Screen
Air Cond. Right 500	.03	.02	.01	.06	.07	.08	.05	−.01	.09
Air Cond. Right 1,000	.01	.01	.00	.06	.05	.09	.05	−.00	.10
Air Cond. Right 2,000	.01	.02	−.02	.05	.05	.09	.06	−.01	.07
Air Cond. Left 500	.02	.03	−.01	.04	.05	.06	.05	−.01	.08
Air Cond. Left 1,000	.01	.02	−.01	.04	.06	.09	.07	−.01	.10
Air Cond. Left 2,000	.02	.02	−.01	.05	.05	.10	.05	−.01	.07
Abn. Aud. Adapt. Right 4,000	.02	−.01	−.02	−.00	−.00	−.02	.02	.03	.01
Abn. Aud. Adapt. Right 500	−.06	−.03	.00	−.06	−.01	.04	.12	.01	.04
Abn. Aud. Adapt. Left 4,000	.01	−.04	.05	−.01	.01	−.01	.03	−.04	.01
Abn. Aud. Adapt. Left 500	−.07	.03	−.03	−.02	.01	−.02	.01	−.01	.02
Bone Cond. Right 500	.02	−.00	−.06	−.01	.06	.07	.12	.06	.15
Bone Cond. Right 1,000	.05	.03	−.03	.00	.06	.11	.21	.06	.17
Bone Cond. Right 2,000	−.00	.05	−.02	.02	.09	.11	.19	.03	.17
Bone Cond. Left 500	.01	−.02	.01	.02	.05	.13	.14	−.01	.10
Bone Cond. Left 1,000	−.02	−.01	−.00	−.01	.09	.13	.20	.05	.13
Bone Cond. Left 2,000	−.08	.01	−.02	−.01	.13	.11	.14	−.01	.12
Discrimination Pct Right	.06	.01	−.02	.18	.13	.17	.10	.05	.01
Discrimination Pct Left	.06	.01	−.03	.17	.13	.18	.09	.04	.01

Correlations: 3YR Indexes with 8YR SLH Variables

8YR Variables	3YR Speech Mechanism	3YR Hypernasality	3YR Fluency	3YR Articulation	3YR Intelligibility	3YR Language Comprehension	3YR Sentence Complexity	3YR Auditory Memory	3YR Hearing Screen
						3YR Indexes			
Digits	.09	.02	-.02	.14	.22	.15	.20	.23	.04
Syllables	.07	.00	-.00	.13	.17	.09	.13	.15	.02
Word Identification	.05	.02	-.07	.20	.20	.34	.17	.09	.01
Orientation	.06	.02	-.04	.10	.22	.26	.19	.13	.03
Understanding a Story	.01	.01	-.04	.17	.09	.17	.09	.04	.01
Oral Reading	.08	.03	-.03	.17	.25	.23	.20	.15	.02
Silent Reading	.07	.02	-.04	.18	.24	.24	.20	.14	.02
Morphology	.05	.00	-.04	.26	.25	.34	.20	.10	.01
Connected Discourse	.05	-.00	-.02	.14	.17	.21	.17	.11	.05
Writing from Dictation	.09	.02	-.03	.18	.25	.23	.23	.16	.04
Lips: Retraction (8YR)	.02	.01	-.01	.02	.03	.02	.04	.01	.04
Lips: Protrusion (8YR)	.04	-.01	.01	.01	.03	.00	.02	.03	.02
Tongue: Midline Pro. (8YR)	.00	-.01	-.01	-.00	.01	.02	.01	.00	.00
Tongue: Lateral Pro. (8YR)	.01	.02	-.01	.03	.02	.03	.03	.01	.01
Tongue: Elevation (8YR)	.04	.00	-.00	.06	.04	.05	.04	.05	.02
Soft Palate Function	.04	.00	-.02	-.01	.01	.03	.04	.01	.01
Rate of Speech Sounds	.06	.01	.01	.06	.07	.06	.10	.03	.03
Dysfluent Events (8YR)	-.00	.00	.05	.03	.03	.04	.03	.03	.03
Struggle Behavior (8YR)	.00	.00	.03	.02	.01	.03	.02	.02	.02
Voice: Pitch (8YR)	.02	-.00	-.00	.05	.05	.03	.07	.02	.01
Voice: Loudness (8YR)	-.00	-.01	-.00	.01	.02	.01	.02	.03	.01
Voice: Qual., Phonation	.02	.01	.01	.01	.03	-.01	.03	.03	-.00
Voice: Qual. Resonance	.04	.01	.01	.01	.03	.00	.03	.04	.04
Intelligibility (8YR)	.08	.01	-.01	.20	.19	.16	.21	.11	.05
Articulation	.07	.03	.01	.31	.27	.22	.22	.07	.03

649

Correlations: 8YR Indexes with 8YR SLH Variables

8YR Variables	8YR Speech Mechanism	8YR Palate Func., Hypernasality	8YR Fluency	8YR Articulation	8YR Intelligibility	8YR Language Comprehension	8YR Auditory Memory	8YR Digits	8YR Word Identification	8YR Written Communication	8YR Language Production	8YR Concept Development	8YR Hearing Severity	8YR Total Conductive Loss	8YR Total Sensorineural Loss	Neurological Involvement	Communicative Effectiveness	Auditory Processing
Air Cond. Right 500	.03	.05	.00	.13	.12	.07	.07	.03	.11	.05	.11	.10	−.73	.47	.31	.19	.08	.11
Air Cond. Right 1,000	.03	.04	.00	.15	.14	.10	.09	.04	.16	.09	.14	.14	−.77	.47	.32	.22	.14	.17
Air Cond. Right 2,000	.02	.04	.02	.16	.15	.11	.10	.06	.18	.12	.14	.16	−.73	.37	.33	.24	.16	.20
Air Cond. Left 500	.04	.06	.01	.12	.13	.05	.06	.03	.09	.05	.11	.09	−.74	.48	.29	.19	.08	.11
Air Cond. Left 1,000	.03	.05	.01	.15	.14	.09	.09	.05	.14	.09	.15	.14	−.78	.49	.31	.22	.13	.16
Air Cond. Left 2,000	.02	.04	.03	.17	.16	.12	.11	.07	.19	.13	.14	.17	−.74	.37	.31	.24	.18	.22
Abn. Aud. Adapt. Right 4,000	.04	.02	.02	.04	.02	.03	.04	.02	.05	.02	.05	.05	−.06	.03	.01	.15	.04	.06
Abn. Aud. Adapt. Right 500	.02	.07	.05	.09	.07	.07	.10	.11	.06	.05	.06	.10	.01	−.02	.02	.08	.08	.07
Abn. Aud. Adapt. Left 4,000	.02	.02	.01	.03	.02	.02	.03	.01	.05	.02	.04	.04	−.07	−.04	.02	.13	.04	.06
Abn. Aud. Adapt. Left 500	.07	−.00	.05	.12	.09	.11	.13	.06	.12	.05	.13	.13	−.07	−.04	.08	.14	.13	.12
Bone Cond. Right 500	.06	.05	−.01	.12	.20	.09	.05	.04	.15	.02	.14	.09	−.37	−.16	.34	.31	.08	.05
Bone Cond. Right 1,000	.03	.08	−.01	.18	.21	.08	.08	.09	.18	.08	.14	.11	−.47	−.09	.37	.33	.12	.10
Bone Cond. Right 2,000	.01	.11	−.01	.17	.21	.12	.10	.09	.21	.09	.13	.12	−.53	.00	.42	.37	.12	.13
Bone Cond. Left 500	.04	.05	.01	.16	.20	.10	.05	.04	.17	.05	.13	.12	−.38	−.17	.35	.32	.09	.07
Bone Cond. Left 1,000	.02	.05	.03	.18	.19	.10	.08	.07	.18	.07	.10	.11	−.45	−.11	.38	.34	.12	.11
Bone Cond. Left 2,000	−.02	.05	.03	.16	.19	.13	.11	.09	.17	.12	.13	.13	−.49	−.04	.40	.39	.15	.16
Discrimination Pct Right	.06	.07	.07	.29	.20	.22	.23	.13	.32	.25	.25	.32	−.10	.06	.11	.18	.30	.34
Discrimination Pct Left	.07	.08	.07	.29	.20	.22	.23	.14	.31	.24	.24	.32	−.11	.05	.11	.17	.30	.33

650

Correlations: 8YR Indexes with 8YR SLH Variables

8YR Variables	8YR Speech Mechanism	8YR Palate Func., Hypernasality	8YR Fluency	8YR Articulation	8YR Intelligibility	8YR Language Comprehension	8YR Auditory Memory	8YR Digits	8YR Word Identification	Written Communication	8YR Language Production	8YR Concept Development	8YR Hearing Severity	8YR Total Conductive Loss	8YR Total Sensorineural Loss	Neurological Involvement	Communicative Effectiveness	Auditory Processing
Digits	.05	.04	.04	.18	.17	.17	.55	1.00	.24	.36	.23	.33	−.06	.03	.02	.14	.34	.47
Syllables	.04	.04	.04	.17	.14	.14	.57	.46	.18	.23	.18	.24	−.06	.03	.02	.11	.24	.35
Word Identification	.07	.02	.07	.37	.25	.60	.50	.24	1.00	.49	.53	.68	−.17	.02	.05	.26	.71	.71
Orientation	.07	.02	.07	.33	.22	.42	.47	.30	.56	.62	.47	.82	−.12	.03	.04	.66	.67	.80
Understanding a Story	.05	−.01	.04	.19	.12	.98	.75	.13	.47	.27	.35	.44	−.07	−.00	.03	.13	.61	.50
Oral Reading	.05	.02	.08	.32	.20	.32	.41	.34	.43	.91	.45	.61	−.11	.03	.03	.28	.80	.77
Silent Reading	.06	.02	.05	.30	.18	.36	.42	.31	.47	.75	.45	.62	−.12	.03	.03	.27	.86	.72
Morphology	.08	.01	.09	.46	.28	.51	.52	.29	.50	.60	.65	.85	−.17	.03	.05	.30	.80	.82
Connected Discourse	.06	.03	.03	.22	.20	.37	.68	.21	.38	.34	.60	.72	−.10	.04	.04	.16	.45	.45
Writing from Dictation	.07	.04	.08	.38	.29	.29	.39	.32	.40	.86	.43	.57	−.11	.04	.04	.25	.66	.78
Lips: Retraction (8YR)	.24	.06	.03	.10	.10	.04	.05	.02	.04	.04	.09	.06	−.01	.01	.01	.11	.05	.05
Lips: Protrusion (8YR)	.21	.05	.04	.06	.05	.03	.05	.03	.03	.03	.04	.05	−.00	.01	−.00	.09	.04	.03
Tongue: Midline Pro. (8YR)	.34	.02	.02	.04	.06	.02	.02	.02	.01	.01	.03	.02	−.01	.01	−.00	.10	.01	.01
Tongue: Lateral Pro. (8YR)	.44	.02	.04	.11	.12	.04	.06	.05	.07	.04	.07	.06	−.02	.02	.01	.14	.06	.05
Tongue: Elevation (8YR)	.96	.03	.04	.09	.10	.04	.05	.04	.06	.01	.08	.07	−.02	.02	.00	.16	.05	.05
Soft Palate Function	.03	.59	.02	.04	.06	.00	.02	.03	.01	.01	.00	.01	−.02	.03	.02	.01	.01	.01
Rate of Speech Sounds	.07	.07	.30	.16	.26	.06	.09	.08	.08	.09	.13	.09	−.04	.02	.02	.03	.10	.09
Dysfluent Events (8YR)	.05	.03	.94	.11	.11	.05	.05	.02	.07	.08	.07	.08	−.02	−.01	.00	.05	.09	.09
Struggle Behavior (8YR)	.04	.03	.70	.05	.07	.02	.02	.02	.02	.03	.03	.03	−.01	−.00	−.01	.01	.03	.03
Voice: Pitch (8YR)	.05	.06	.01	.07	.12	.00	.02	.03	.02	.03	.07	.03	−.06	.03	−.03	.04	.02	.03
Voice: Loudness (8YR)	.05	.04	.02	.06	.17	.03	.05	.02	.04	.05	.11	.06	−.04	.04	.01	.03	.06	.05
Voice: Qual., Phonation	.05	.08	.03	.11	.11	−.03	.06	.05	.07	.11	.07	.09	−.05	.03	.02	.07	.10	.05
Voice: Qual., Resonance	.02	.38	.02	.06	.09	.03	.01	.03	−.04	.01	.01	.01	−.09	.11	−.06	.02	−.01	.11
Intelligibility (8YR)	.13	.13	.14	.52	.99	.15	.21	.16	.23	.24	.40	.28	−.15	.06	−.06	.11	.33	.27
Articulation	.12	.09	.12	1.00	.52	.25	.28	.18	.37	.36	.48	.42	−.17	.06	.07	.19	.44	.44

651

Correlations: 3YR SLH Variables with 8YR SLH Variables

3YR Variables

8YR Variables	Id. Fam. Objs.	Und. Act. Words	Und. Space Rel.	Naming Objs.	Sent. Length	Sent. Structure	Relevance	Word Order	Use Pronouns	Sum. Item Score	2 Digits	3 Digits	2 Syllables	3 Syllables	Spond. Word Test	Pure Tone, Right	Pure Tone, Left	Lips: Ret. (3YR)	Lips: Pro. (3YR)	Tongue: Mid.Pro. (3YR)
Air Cond. Right 500	.08	.07	.05	.07	.02	.02	.07	.06	.03	.03	.01	-.01	.01	.00	.08	.15	.11	.01	.01	.00
Air Cond. Right 1,000	.09	.08	.07	.06	.03	.02	.07	.06	.03	.04	.01	-.01	.01	-.01	.10	.16	.12	.01	.01	.02
Air Cond. Right 2,000	.08	.07	.07	.07	.04	.04	.07	.06	.04	.06	.03	-.01	.02	.01	.09	.13	.10	.01	.01	-.01
Air Cond. Left 500	.07	.06	.04	.05	.01	.02	.07	.07	.04	.02	.00	-.02	.00	-.00	.08	.12	.13	.00	-.01	.00
Air Cond. Left 1,000	.08	.08	.05	.06	.05	.04	.08	.08	.05	.06	.01	-.01	.00	.00	.09	.14	.14	.00	.00	.00
Air Cond. Left 2,000	.08	.07	.08	.06	.03	.02	.07	.06	.03	.04	.01	.00	.01	.02	.09	.11	.12	.00	.02	.00
Abn. Aud. Adapt. Right 4,000	.00	.00	-.03	.01	.01	.01	.03	.03	.02	.02	-.03	-.01	.06	.03	.03	.02	.01	-.01	-.02	-.01
Abn. Aud. Adapt. Right 500	.06	.00	.04	.17	.04	.06	.08	.16	.15	.08	-.03	-.02	-.01	.01	.07	.17	.11	-.05	.00	-.02
Abn. Aud. Adapt. Left 4,000	-.01	.01	-.01	.02	.00	.01	.04	.03	.03	.03	.01	-.00	-.01	.01	.02	.01	.03	-.01	.13	-.00
Abn. Aud. Adapt. Left 500	.00	-.02	-.02	.04	-.01	.02	-.03	.05	.01	-.03	.03	.00	-.01	-.02	.04	-.00	-.02	-.05	-.01	-.02
Bone Cond. Right 500	.07	.04	.08	.02	.07	.10	.15	.11	.06	.05	-.00	.00	.03	.00	.03	.21	.19	-.04	-.00	.04
Bone Cond. Right 1,000	.07	.10	.10	.08	.14	.18	.17	.19	.15	.11	.08	.08	.04	.06	.12	.21	.19	-.04	-.01	-.02
Bone Cond. Right 2,000	.08	.08	.10	.09	.13	.19	.12	.15	.17	.14	.04	.07	-.00	.07	.10	.17	.17	-.03	-.01	-.03
Bone Cond. Left 500	.12	.12	.12	.04	.07	.10	.21	.17	.07	.07	-.03	-.02	-.01	.05	.03	.16	.12	.00	-.01	-.01
Bone Cond. Left 1,000	.09	.11	.11	.08	.13	.15	.20	.21	.13	.12	-.02	-.03	-.05	.04	.02	.16	.14	-.02	-.01	-.01
Bone Cond. Left 2,000	.07	.09	.10	.10	.10	.11	.11	.15	.11	.09	-.05	.02	.04	.03	.05	.15	.14	.01	-.02	-.01
Discrimination Pct Right	.11	.10	.17	.09	.10	.06	.11	.07	.07	.09	.05	.04	.02	.03	.09	.03	.02	.03	.03	.04
Discrimination Pct Left	.09	.10	.18	.09	.10	.05	.10	.07	.04	.08	.04	.03	.04	.03	.08	.02	.03	.03	.03	.04
Digits	.10	.11	.13	.17	.17	.16	.12	.14	.16	.19	.13	.25	.13	.25	.11	.05	.04	.03	.03	.04
Syllables	.07	.11	.07	.13	.12	.11	.08	.10	.10	.13	.09	.16	.10	.16	.07	.04	.02	.03	.04	.00
Word Identification	.20	.20	.31	.18	.17	.10	.15	.11	.11	.16	.07	.09	.07	.06	.11	.05	.04	.03	.03	.02
Orientation	.15	.17	.24	.19	.19	.14	.15	.13	.14	.19	.09	.13	.10	.12	.11	.04	.03	.04	.03	.03

652

Correlations: 3YR SLH Variables with 8YR SLH Variables

8YR Variables	Id. Fam. Objs.	Und. Act. Words	Und. Space Rel.	Naming Objs.	Sent. Length	Sent. Structure	Relevance	Word Order	Use Pronouns	Sum. Item Score	2 Digits	3 Digits	2 Syllables	3 Syllables	Spond. Word Test	Pure Tone, Right	Pure Tone, Left	Lips: Ret. (3YR)	Lips: Pro. (3YR)	Tongue: Mid.Pro. (3YR)
Understanding a Story	.09	.11	.17	.11	.10	.06	.08	.05	.06	.08	.04	.03	.03	.03	.06	.03	.02	.00	.02	.01
Oral Reading	.14	.15	.20	.19	.20	.17	.13	.12	.15	.21	.11	.16	.09	.14	.11	.02	.02	.04	.04	.03
Silent Reading	.14	.14	.22	.18	.19	.15	.13	.12	.15	.20	.10	.16	.10	.13	.10	.04	.02	.05	.03	.02
Morphology	.19	.19	.33	.19	.21	.12	.17	.13	.13	.18	.08	.11	.07	.07	.11	.04	.04	.03	.04	.03
Connected Discourse	.11	.13	.20	.17	.16	.13	.13	.11	.12	.16	.07	.11	.08	.10	.10	.04	.04	.03	.06	.01
Writing from Dictation	.15	.17	.19	.22	.21	.18	.14	.16	.17	.23	.12	.16	.12	.15	.14	.04	.04	.03	.04	.03
Lips: Retraction (8YR)	.02	.03	.01	.02	.01	.03	.05	.04	.03	.02	.01	.02	.01	.03	.04	.01	.04	.01	.04	.01
Lips: Protrusion (8YR)	–.01	.00	.01	.01	.00	.02	.02	.03	.03	.01	.02	–.02	.01	–.01	.01	.00	.00	–.00	–.00	.07
Tongue: Midline Pro. (8YR)	.01	.03	.02	.02	.01	.01	.02	.01	.00	.03	.01	–.00	.00	–.01	.01	.00	.01	–.01	–.01	.10
Tongue: Lateral Pro. (8YR)	.04	.02	.03	.04	.03	.03	.04	.03	.03	.04	.02	.00	.00	.03	.01	.03	.02	.02	–.01	.08
Tongue: Elevation (8YR)	.04	.03	.04	.06	.03	.02	.05	.03	.02	.02	.02	.03	.03	.03	.03	.02	.03	.02	.02	.01
Soft Palate Function	.04	.04	.01	.03	.01	.03	.05	.06	.07	.08	.00	.02	.00	.03	.04	.03	.05	.03	.00	.00
Rate of Speech Sounds	.04	.06	.03	.07	.06	.08	.09	.09	.02	.03	.04	.04	.03	.03	.00	.01	.03	–.00	.02	.00
Dysfluent Events (8YR)	.04	.02	.03	.03	.01	.01	.04	.02	.07	.03	.02	.02	.02	.03	.00	.02	.03	–.00	–.00	.04
Struggle Behavior (8YR)	.02	.02	.02	.02	.01	.01	.02	.01	.01	.02	.02	.03	.01	.02	.01	.04	.01	–.00	–.00	.04
Voice: Pitch (8YR)	.02	.03	.01	.04	.04	.06	.04	.07	.06	.05	.03	.03	.02	.03	.02	.04	.03	.01	.00	.01
Voice: Loudness (8YR)	–.00	.01	–.00	.01	.01	.02	.03	.01	.02	.02	.03	.01	.02	.00	.00	.02	.02	.02	–.01	.07
Voice: Qual., Phonation	–.01	–.00	–.01	.02	.02	.02	.03	.04	.03	.03	.03	.03	.03	.03	.03	.02	.01	.04	–.01	.01
Voice: Qual., Resonance	.01	.02	–.01	.04	.01	.04	.04	.04	.03	.04	.01	.04	.02	.04	.06	.03	.04	.01	.02	–.01
Intelligibility (8YR)	.13	.14	.11	.16	.15	.16	.18	.19	.16	.20	.07	.08	.11	.07	.13	.09	.08	.04	.04	.04
Articulation	.15	.15	.19	.18	.17	.15	.18	.19	.18	.22	.07	.05	.08	.05	.13	.08	.06	.06	.05	.06

Correlations: 3YR SLH Variables with 8YR SLH Variables

8YR Variables	Tong.: Lat. Pro. (3YR)	Tong.: Elev (3YR)	Palate: Elev.	Diad.: Lips	Diad.: Tong.	Voice: Pitch (3YR)	Voice: Loud. (3YR)	Voice: Qual. (3YR)	Init. Cons.	Final Cons.	Vow. and Diph.	Intell. (3YR)	Dys. Events (3YR)	Strug. Behav. (3YR)
Air Cond. Right 500	.04	.05	.01	.01	.03	.04	.03	.03	.07	.06	.03	.09	.01	.00
Air Cond. Right 1,000	.05	.06	.00	.00	.01	.04	.02	.05	.07	.09	.01	.08	.00	-.00
Air Cond. Right 2,000	.05	.03	.01	.00	.00	.03	.04	.04	.07	.10	.01	.09	-.01	-.01
Air Cond. Left 500	.03	.04	-.01	-.00	.02	.04	.03	.04	.04	.05	.02	.08	-.01	.02
Air Cond. Left 1,000	.04	.04	-.01	.00	.01	.04	.04	.05	.06	.08	.01	.09	-.00	.02
Air Cond. Left 2,000	.04	.03	-.02	.01	.01	.04	.04	.05	.06	.10	.00	.08	-.01	.00
Abn. Aud. Adapt. Right 4,000	.01	-.02	.01	.01	.01	.02	.01	-.01	-.01	.01	-.00	.02	-.02	-.01
Abn. Aud. Adapt. Right 500	.05	-.00	.06	-.01	-.07	.01	.03	-.09	-.04	-.03	-.09	.02	-.00	NA
Abn. Aud. Adapt. Left 4,000	.01	-.00	.01	-.01	-.00	.01	-.01	-.01	-.01	.01	-.01	.02	.02	.00
Abn. Aud. Adapt. Left 500	.07	.01	.14	-.01	-.07	.12	-.01	-.04	-.02	.07	-.04	.05	-.04	.14
Bone Cond. Right 500	.00	.06	-.05	.00	.01	.07	.07	.09	-.01	.06	-.02	.09	-.05	-.02
Bone Cond. Right 1,000	-.01	.06	-.04	.02	.05	.07	.07	.03	.01	.06	.01	.14	-.02	-.02
Bone Cond. Right 2,000	-.02	-.01	-.03	.02	.01	.04	.09	.06	.02	.05	.02	.14	-.03	-.04
Bone Cond. Left 500	-.01	.02	-.03	-.04	-.00	.03	.06	.09	.03	.07	.01	.11	-.01	-.04
Bone Cond. Left 1,000	-.03	.01	-.04	-.03	-.01	.04	.07	.08	.01	.06	-.06	.12	-.03	.06
Bone Cond. Left 2,000	-.01	-.04	.01	-.05	-.09	-.01	.05	.06	.04	.09	-.08	.11	-.02	.03
Discrimination Pct Right	.16	.10	.01	.05	.04	.03	.06	.07	.20	.29	.08	.10	-.02	.00
Discrimination Pct Left	.16	.11	-.01	.04	.03	.02	.05	.09	.19	.29	.06	.10	-.02	-.01
Digits	.03	.00	.02	.10	.08	.03	.06	.01	.14	.15	.14	.21	-.00	-.01
Syllables	.03	.03	.02	.06	.06	.01	.04	-.00	.13	.12	.12	.16	-.00	-.00
Word Identification	.17	.08	-.02	.03	.03	.04	.08	.12	.24	.42	.08	.17	-.08	-.02
Orientation	.13	.07	-.00	.05	.04	.03	.06	.09	.23	.33	.10	.20	-.04	-.00

654

Correlations: 3YR SLH Variables with 8YR SLH Variables

8YR Variables	Tong.: Lat. Pro. (3YR)	Tong.: Elev (3YR)	Palate: Elev.	Diad.: Lips	Diad.: Tong.	Voice: Pitch (3YR)	Voice: Loud (3YR)	Voice: Qual. (3YR)	Init. Cons.	Final Cons.	Vow. and Diph.	Intell. (3YR)	Dys. Events (3YR)	Strug. Behav. (3YR)
Understanding a Story	.11	.04	-.02	.00	.00	.01	.04	.06	.12	.21	.04	.08	-.03	-.02
Oral Reading	.11	.03	.02	.07	.06	.04	.09	.10	.20	.29	.10	.22	-.03	.01
Silent Reading	.11	.03	.01	.06	.05	.03	.08	.09	.21	.30	.10	.21	-.04	.01
Morphology	.22	.13	-.01	.03	.03	.04	.08	.15	.30	.50	.11	.21	-.04	-.00
Connected Discourse	.11	.09	.03	.05	.04	.04	.07	.05	.15	.21	.09	.16	-.02	-.01
Writing from Dictation	.08	.03	.03	.08	.07	.04	.09	.08	.20	.24	.12	.25	-.03	-.01
Lips: Retraction (8YR)	.01	.01	.02	.01	.01	-.00	-.00	-.00	.02	.01	.01	.04	-.02	-.00
Lips: Protrusion (8YR)	.02	.00	-.01	.03	.01	.00	.01	-.01	.02	.01	.01	.03	.02	-.01
Tongue: Midline Pro. (8YR)	.05	.04	.02	-.00	.03	.03	.00	.00	-.00	.02	-.00	.01	.02	-.01
Tongue: Lateral Pro. (8YR)	.09	.07	.01	.02	.01	.01	.00	.01	.03	.04	.04	.04	.01	-.01
Tongue: Elevation (8YR)	.08	.07	.01	.03	.03	.01	.03	.00	.05	.05	.04	.06	-.01	-.01
Soft Palate Function	.02	-.01	.05	.01	.03	.01	.01	-.00	-.02	-.04	.01	.03	-.01	.00
Rate of Speech Sounds	.01	.01	-.01	.05	.04	.01	.02	.02	.05	.06	.08	.11	-.02	.05
Dysfluent Events (8YR)	.03	.03	-.02	-.00	.01	-.02	.01	.00	.03	.06	.04	.04	.06	.05
Struggle Behavior (8YR)	-.02	-.00	-.01	.01	-.00	-.01	-.01	.01	.02	.02	.05	.03	.03	-.01
Voice: Pitch (8YR)	-.02	-.01	-.00	.01	-.02	.02	-.01	.01	.03	.01	.04	.09	-.00	-.01
Voice: Loudness (8YR)	-.01	-.01	.01	-.01	-.01	.04	.04	.01	.01	.00	.01	.02	.00	-.01
Voice: Qual., Phonation	-.01	-.01	.01	.02	.02	.01	.03	.05	.00	-.00	.01	.04	.00	-.01
Voice: Qual., Resonance	-.01	.00	.06	.03	.04	.04	.01	.00	-.01	-.05	.05	.05	.02	.00
Intelligibility (8YR)	.04	.00	.01	.05	.06	.05	.06	.04	.16	.16	.16	.25	-.01	.01
Articulation	.14	.08	.00	.04	.04	.04	.07	.09	.30	.35	.20	.29	.01	.01

655

Correlations: 3YR SLH Variables with 3YR SLH Variables

3YR Variables

3YR Variables	Id. Fam. Objs.	Und. Act. Words	Und. Space Rel.	Naming Objs.	Sent. Length	Sent. Structure	Relevance	Word Order	Use Pronouns	Sum. Item Score	2 Digits	3 Digits	2 Syllables	3 Syllables	Spond. Word Test	Pure Tone, Right	Pure Tone, Left	Lips: Ret. (3YR)	Lips: Pro. (3YR)	Tongue: Mid.Pro. (3YR)
Ident. Familiar Objects																				
Understand Action Words	.39																			
Understand Space Relations	.30	.30																		
Naming Objects	.25	.27	.27																	
Sentence Length	.14	.16	.20	.24																
Sentence Structure	.15	.17	.17	.28	.57															
Relevance	.21	.23	.21	.29	.37	.46														
Word Order	.17	.17	.14	.29	.46	.63	.63													
Use of Pronouns	.16	.17	.16	.27	.51	.60	.43	.56												
Summary Item Score	.20	.24	.22	.33	.70	.80	.54	.62	.75											
Recall 2 Digits	.11	.12	.13	.18	.13	.14	.13	.12	.14	.18										
Recall 3 Digits	.11	.14	.15	.19	.17	.18	.13	.12	.19	.23	.36									
Recall 2 Syllables	.09	.09	.11	.16	.12	.13	.12	.09	.12	.17	.44	.33								
Recall 3 Syllables	.11	.13	.14	.18	.14	.15	.13	.13	.16	.20	.33	.57	.36							
Spondaic Word Test	.17	.19	.16	.20	.17	.18	.20	.17	.18	.25	.13	.13	.13	.14						
Pure Tone, Right Ear	.06	.07	.06	.07	.06	.09	.11	.10	.08	.10	.05	.04	.04	.03	.35					
Pure Tone, Left Ear	.04	.06	.05	.05	.07	.09	.10	.10	.09	.11	.08	.07	.02	.04	.33	.68				
Lips: Retraction (3YR)	.08	.08	.06	.08	.03	.03	.05	.02	.03	.05	.08	.07	.04	.07	.03	.03	.02			
Lips: Protrusion (3YR)	.06	.05	.05	.03	.01	.02	.02	.02	.02	.06	.04	.00	.02	-.01	.07	.04	.03	.12		
Tongue: Midline Pro. (3YR)	.08	.10	.16	.07	.06	-.01	.03	.01	.01	.04	.04	-.01	.01	-.00	.04	.01	.02	.04	.08	
Tongue: Lateral Pro. (3YR)	.10	.10	.13	.07	.07	-.01	.06	-.02	.04	.02	.04	-.02	.02	.02	.05	-.01	.01	.05	.09	.11
Tongue: Elevation (3YR)	.01	.03	.04	.08	.03	.04	.01	.01	.12	.00	.04	.06	.04	.04	.02	-.01	.02	.06	.10	.08
Soft Palate: Elevation	.07	.10	.08	.14	.12	.14	.10	.11	.09	.07	.06	.14	.06	.07	.05	.05	.06	.05	.06	.02
Diadochokinesis: Lips	.06	.08	.09	.12	.10	.12	.10	.10	.13	.16	.10	.12	.10	.13	.10	.05	.07	.09	.10	.02
Diadochokinesis: Tongue	.07	.11	.14	.05	.05	.13	.10	.09	.06	.14	.05	.05	.12	.12	.12	.04	.04	.05	.10	.03
Voice: Pitch (3YR)	.06	.07	.13	.07	.03	-.01	-.01	-.01	.01	.07	.04	.07	.06	.07	.07	.06	.05	.02	.08	.04
Voice: Loudness (3YR)	.08	.08	.08	.08	.12	.17	.15	.15	.19	.25	.11	.10	-.01	.05	.13	.05	.06	.05	.03	.06
Voice: Quality (3YR)	.10	.10	.09	.09	.10	.16	.17	.12	.17	.24	.13	.12	.11	-.02	.14	.04	.07	.09	.02	.01
Initial Consonants	.11	.08	.14	.04	.05	-.01	.01	-.01	.01	.01	.17	.16	.15	.10	.07	.07	.04	.04	.04	.04
Final Consonants	.18	.12	.20	.17	.25	.17	.15	.15	.19	.25	.19	.21	.18	.12	.13	.05	.05	.05	.02	.05
Vowels and Diphthongs	.10	.19	.32	.19	.28	.16	.17	.12	.17	.24	.13	.16	.15	.10	.14	.06	.04	.09	.04	.06
Intelligibility (3YR)	.22	.13	.11	.19	.20	.20	.16	.12	.19	.25	.17	.12	.11	.12	.15	.13	.12	.02	.07	.01
Dysfluent Events (3YR)	-.00	-.01	-.02	-.03	-.06	-.01	-.02	-.02	-.02	-.04	-.00	-.01	-.02	-.01	-.02	-.01	-.00	-.00	-.00	-.00
Struggle Behavior (3YR)	.00	-.01	-.01	-.01	-.00	.00	-.00	-.01	-.02	-.00	-.00	-.01	-.01	-.01	-.01	.02	-.01	-.00	-.01	-.01

Correlations: 3YR SLH Variables with 3YR SLH Variables

3YR Variables

3YR Variables	Tong.: Lat. Pro. (3YR)	Tong.: Elev (3YR)	Palate: Elev.	Diad.: Lips	Diad.: Tong.	Voice: Pitch (3YR)	Voice: Loud (3YR)	Voice: Qual. (3YR)	Init. Cons.	Final Cons.	Vow. and Diph.	Intell. (3YR)	Dys. Events (3YR)	Strug. Behav. (3YR)
Ident. Familiar Objs.														
Understand Action Words														
Understand Space Relations														
Naming Objects														
Sentence Length														
Sentence Structure														
Relevance														
Word Order														
Use of Pronouns														
Summary Item Score														
Recall 2 Digits														
Recall 3 Digits														
Recall 2 Syllables														
Recall 3 Syllables														
Spondaic Word Test														
Pure Tone, Right Ear														
Pure Tone, Left Ear														
Lips: Retraction (3YR)														
Lips: Protrusion (3YR)														
Tongue: Midline Pro. (3YR)														
Tongue: Lateral Pro. (3YR)														
Tongue: Elevation (3YR)	.32													
Soft Palate: Elevation	.01	.02												
Diadochokinesis: Lips	.02	.02	.03											
Diadochokinesis: Tongue	.03	.03	.02	.74										
Voice: Pitch (3YR)	.04	.03	.03	.03	.04									
Voice: Loudness (3YR)	.04	.10	.07	.08	.08	.16								
Voice: Quality (3YR)	.12	.15	.10	.00	.01	.12	.09							
Initial Consonants	.20	.22	.02	.07	.06	.03	.08	.13						
Final Consonants	.28	.07	.01	.08	.06	.04	.10	.10	.58					
Vowels and Diphthongs	.07	.07	.06	.10	.09	.04	.06	.03	.30	.26				
Intelligibility (3YR)	.09	.02	.08	.14	.13	.10	.19	.09	.47	.40	.37			
Dysfluent Events (3YR)	.01	-.01	.01	-.01	-.01	.01	-.00	.00	-.01	-.02	-.00	.02		
Struggle Behavior (3YR)	.00		-.01	.00	.00	.00	.00	.01	-.01	-.01	.01	.01	.30	

Correlations: 8YR SLH Variables with 8YR SLH Variables

8YR Variables

8YR Variables	Air Cond. Right 500	Air Cond. Right 1,000	Air Cond. Right 2,000	Air Cond. Left 500	Air Cond. Left 1,000	Air Cond. Left 2,000	Abn. Aud. Adapt. R. 4,000	Abn. Aud. Adapt. R. 500	Abn. Aud. Adapt. L. 4,000	Abn. Aud. Adapt. L. 500	Bone Cond. Right 500	Bone Cond. Right 1,000	Bone Cond. Right 2,000	Bone Cond. Left 500	Bone Cond. Left 1,000	Bone Cond. Left 2,000	Discrimination %, Right	Discrimination %, Left	Digits	Syllables
Air Cond. Right 500																				
Air Cond. Right 1,000	.75																			
Air Cond. Right 2,000	.60	.69																		
Air Cond. Left 500	.62	.53	.40																	
Air Cond. Left 1,000	.53	.59	.45	.76																
Air Cond. Left 2,000	.42	.46	.55	.60	.70															
Abn. Aud. Adapt. Right 4,000	.05	.04	.05	.04	.04	.04														
Abn. Aud. Adapt. Right 500	-.02	.01	.05	.04	.02	.03	.06													
Abn. Aud. Adapt. Left 4,000	.05	.05	.07	.05	.05	.06	.36	.21												
Abn. Aud. Adapt. Left 500	-.04	.05	.05	.09	.16	.18	.12	.57	.09											
Bone Cond. Right 500	.46	.39	.37	.38	.37	.36	.09	.01	.03	.09										
Bone Cond. Right 1,000	.46	.53	.48	.40	.44	.42	.06	.12	.06	.28	.74									
Bone Cond. Right 2,000	.39	.46	.63	.28	.35	.48	.04	-.03	.06	.12	.58	.71								
Bone Cond. Left 500	.42	.38	.36	.47	.39	.34	.03	-.04	.10	.34	.83	.70	.56							
Bone Cond. Left 1,000	.40	.43	.41	.43	.52	.44	.03	-.06	.06	.45	.70	.82	.66	.71						
Bone Cond. Left 2,000	.30	.34	.47	.32	.41	.59	-.02	-.04	.02	.34	.55	.62	.76	.55	.70					
Discrimination Pct Right	.07	.06	.16	.03	.05	.10	.07	.22	.07	.16	.10	.16	.27	.17	.15	.17				
Discrimination Pct Left	.05	.06	.06	.06	.03	.14	.05	.14	.01	.26	.12	.13	.15	.15	.11	.22	.53			
Digits	.04	.04	.11	.03	.04	.06	.02	.08	.03	.06	.05	.10	.10	.03	.06	.10	.11	.11		
Syllables	.04	.05	.05	.03	.04	.05	.05	.10	.03	.02	.03	.09	.11	.04	.07	.09	.09	.09	.44	
Word Identification	.11	.15	.16	.09	.13	.18	.04	.12	.05	.11	.20	.23	.22	.24	.23	.21	.34	.33	.21	.15
Orientation	.05	.08	.09	.05	.08	.11	.03	.14	.02	.11	.05	.07	.08	.11	.13	.11	.26	.25	.29	.18

Correlations: 8YR SLH Variables with 8YR SLH Variables

8YR Variables

8YR Variables	Air Cond. Right 500	Air Cond. Right 1,000	Air Cond. Right 2,000	Air Cond. Left 500	Air Cond. Left 1,000	Air Cond. Left 2,000	Abn. Aud. Adapt. R. 4,000	Abn. Aud. Adapt. R. 500	Abn. Aud. Adapt. L. 4,000	Abn. Aud. Adapt. L. 500	Bone Cond. Right 500	Bone Cond. Right 1,000	Bone Cond. Right 2,000	Bone Cond. Left 500	Bone Cond. Left 1,000	Bone Cond. Left 2,000	Discrimination %, Right	Discrimination %, Left	Digits	Syllables
Understanding a Story	.04	.06	.07	.03	.06	.08	.03	.07	.01	.10	.07	.06	.09	.09	.08	.15	.17	.18	.12	.11
Oral Reading	.03	.07	.09	.04	.08	.11	.01	.05	.01	.10	.04	.10	.07	.07	.10	.14	.22	.21	.33	.19
Silent Reading	.04	.07	.09	.04	.08	.11	.02	.09	.02	.09	.02	.07	.04	.05	.09	.12	.20	.20	.31	.17
Morphology	.10	.15	.16	.08	.13	.18	.05	.09	.04	.11	.15	.16	.14	.17	.17	.16	.34	.35	.26	.18
Connected Discourse	.08	.09	.07	.07	.11	.09	.03	.09	.02	.15	.06	.07	.05	.09	.12	.11	.17	.18	.21	.15
Writing from Dictation	.05	.08	.09	.05	.08	.10	.02	.07	.01	.12	.03	.09	.10	.05	.07	.10	.21	.22	.32	.18
Lips: Retraction (8YR)	.02	.02	.01	.02	.02	.01	.01	.18	.02	.23	-.01	-.02	-.01	.02	.03	-.03	.04	.03	.02	.03
Lips: Protrusion (8YR)	.01	.00	-.01	.02	.02	.00	.01	.06	.03	.06	-.03	-.00	-.03	-.02	-.05	-.04	.05	.05	.02	.01
Tongue: Midline Pro. (8YR)	.01	.02	.01	.02	.01	.01	.01	-.03	.01	.13	.04	-.00	-.03	.01	.03	.02	.01	.01	.01	-.00
Tongue: Lateral Pro. (8YR)	.05	.04	.02	.04	.04	.03	.01	.03	.01	.05	.09	.08	.07	.05	.03	.02	.06	.07	.05	.04
Tongue: Elevation (8YR)	.04	.03	.02	.03	.03	.03	.01	.09	.02	.09	.05	.01	.01	.08	.06	-.01	.05	.06	.04	.02
Soft Palate Function	.04	.04	.02	.05	.04	.04	.02	.07	.02	.09	.02	.10	.04	.01	.05	.01	.07	.09	.02	.04
Rate of Speech Sounds	.05	.05	.05	.06	.06	.06	.01	-.04	.00	-.04	.14	.12	.11	.11	.12	.08	.06	.06	.08	.05
Dysfluent Events (8YR)	-.00	.01	.02	.01	.01	.03	-.00	.05	.03	.06	-.01	.00	.01	-.01	.04	.01	.06	.06	.01	.03
Struggle Behavior (8YR)	.07	.07	.07	.01	.01	.02	-.01	.09	-.01	.20	-.00	.03	.02	.20	.15	.02	.02	.02	.03	-.01
Voice: Pitch (8YR)	.03	.02	.04	.08	.07	.07	.01	-.05	.01	.05	.15	.20	.18	.07	.03	.15	.02	.01	.03	.03
Voice: Loudness (8YR)	.03	.04	.04	.04	.03	.05	.03	.00	.01	.12	.07	.03	.09	.02	.01	.07	.06	.05	.04	.02
Voice: Qual., Phonation	.06	.05	.05	.06	.04	.05	.01	-.01	.00	-.04	.08	.07	.07	-.04	-.01	.01	.06	.05	.04	.04
Voice: Qual., Resonance	.12	.10	.07	.10	.10	.06	.01	.03	.03	.10	-.06	-.02	.02	.18	.20	.00	.01	.00	.02	.02
Intelligibility (8YR)	.14	.15	.15	.13	.14	.15	.02	.04	.03	.10	.20	.22	.22	.18	.19	.17	.18	.17	.16	.13
Articulation	.14	.16	.17	.13	.16	.17	.04	.09	.03	.15	.14	.22	.20	.18	.19	.16	.28	.27	.16	.15

Correlations: 8YR SLH Variables with 8YR SLH Variables

8YR Variables

8YR Variables	Word Identification	Orientation	Understand* a Story	Oral Reading	Silent Reading	Morphology	Connect.Discourse	Writing from Dictation	Lips: Ret. (8YR)	Lips: Pro. (8YR)	Tongue: Mid. Pro. (8YR)	Tongue: Lat. Pro. (8YR)	Tongue: Elev. (8YR)	Palate Function	Rate of Speech	Dysfluent Events (8YR)	Struggle Behavior (8YR)	Voice: Pitch (8YR)	Voice: Loudness (8YR)	Voice: Qual., Phonation	Voice: Qual., Resonance	Intelligibility (8YR)	Articulation
Air Cond. Right 500																							
Air Cond. Right 1,000																							
Air Cond. Right 2,000																							
Air Cond. Left 500																							
Air Cond. Left 1,000																							
Air Cond. Left 2,000																							
Abn. Aud. Adapt. Right 4,000																							
Abn. Aud. Adapt. Right 500																							
Abn. Aud. Adapt. Left 4,000																							
Abn. Aud. Adapt. Left 500																							
Bone Cond. Right 500																							
Bone Cond. Right 1,000																							
Bone Cond. Right 2,000																							
Bone Cond. Left 500																							
Bone Cond. Left 1,000																							
Bone Cond. Left 2,000																							
Discrimination Pct Right																							
Discrimination Pct Left																							
Digits																							
Syllables																							
Word Identification																							
Orientation	.55																						

Correlations: 8YR SLH Variables with 8YR SLH Variables

8YR Variables

8YR Variables	Word Identification	Orientation	Understand a Story	Oral Reading	Silent Reading	Morphology	Connect Discourse	Writing from Dictation	Lips: Ret. (8YR)	Lips: Pro. (8YR)	Tongue: Mid. Pro. (8YR)	Tongue: Lat. Pro. (8YR)	Tongue: Elev. (8YR)	Palate Function	Rate of Speech	Dysfluent Events (8YR)	Struggle Behavior (8YR)	Voice: Pitch (8YR)	Voice: Loudness (8YR)	Voice: Qual., Phonation	Voice: Qual., Resonance	Intelligibility (8YR)	Articulation
Understanding a Story	.44	.34																					
Oral Reading	.45	.56	.25																				
Silent Reading	.49	.56	.28	.74																			
Morphology	.71	.60	.41	.54	.55																		
Connected Discourse	.37	.36	.33	.32	.34	.41																	
Writing from Dictation	.37	.53	.23	.70	.61	.48	.31																
Lips: Retraction (8YR)	.05	.05	.04	.04	.04	.05	.05	.07															
Lips: Protrusion (8YR)	.02	.03	.03	.02	.02	.02	.03	.03	.14														
Tongue: Midline Pro. (8YR)	.02	.02	.02	.01	.02	.03	.02	.02	.08	.04													
Tongue: Lateral Pro. (8YR)	.08	.06	.05	.05	.05	.06	.05	.07	.08	.07	.23												
Tongue: Elevation (8YR)	.07	.06	.04	.04	.05	.07	.04	.06	.10	.06	.23	.27											
Soft Palate Function	.00	.01	-.01	.00	-.01	-.01	.01	.01	.06	.04	.00	.02	.02										
Rate of Speech Sounds	.09	.08	.04	.08	.07	.08	.10	.11	.05	.04	.05	.05	.04	.02									
Dysfluent Events (8YR)	.06	.06	.05	.08	.06	.09	.03	.08	.04	.04	.03	.03	.02	.02	.17								
Struggle Behavior (8YR)	.02	.01	.02	.03	.02	.03	.03	.05	.01	.03	.01	.04	.02	.03	.15	.44							
Voice: Pitch (8YR)	.03	.03	.01	.03	.01	.03	.03	.05	.04	.02	.03	.02	.05	.03	.08	.02	.02						
Voice: Loudness (8YR)	.04	.04	.03	.04	.04	.04	.06	.04	.04	.02	.03	.02	.04	.06	.08	.02	.02	.12					
Voice: Qual., Phonation	.06	.07	.01	.09	.08	.07	.04	.10	.04	.04	.03	.04	.03	.14	.03	.02	.01	.16	.12				
Voice: Qual., Resonance	-.07	-.02	-.03	-.02	-.02	-.06	.00	.01	.02	.04	.01	.04	.00	.06	.25	-.00	.01	.03	-.00	.07			
Intelligibility (8YR)	.24	.22	.12	.20	.18	.28	.20	.29	.11	.04	.07	.11	.09	.14	.15	.11	.08	.14	.18	.12	.07		
Articulation	.36	.31	.19	.30	.29	.45	.22	.38	.09	.04	.04	.11	.09	.03	.15	.14	.09	.09	.05	.09	.04	.52	

Correlation Matrices between 901 NCPP Variables and the 3YR and 8YR SLH Variables and SLH Indices

February 3, 1976

To: Scientific Management Panel
From: Minneapolis Study Staff
Re: Correlations of CPP Variables with SLH Indices

The following pages are reduced copies of computer output of the first screen correlations between CPP variables and the 27 SLH indices. The purpose of this memo is to explain how to read the output.

The CPP variables were divided into ten groups which have been numbered I to X. The first one or two pages of a group list the CPP variables by name numbered 1 to n; the next pages give the correlations with $|R| < .10$ suppressed. The numbers corresponding to the CPP variables are in a column on the left of the page. There are 16 variables to a page. Each variable has been separated by a horizontal line.

There are three rows of correlations for each variable plus a mean R* at the end of the third row. The arrangement of the indices within these three rows is attached. There are 10 in the first row, 10 in the second, and 7 in the third. To facilitate reading, a vertical line has been drawn between the fifth and sixth correlations in each line. Each of the 27 correlations is followed by the sample size, in parentheses, on which it is based.

The mean R's are written in scientific notation, that is, a number, followed by the letter E, followed by a "+" or "−" sign, followed by another number. The "E ± xx" refers to a power of 10 by which the preceeding number should be multiplied. In other words,

$$a.bcE \pm de = (a.bc)(10^{\pm de})$$

For example:

$$.57E + 00 = .57$$
$$.57E - 01 = .057$$
$$.57E - 02 = .0057$$
$$.57E - 03 = .00057$$

As the arrows show, if the exponent is negative the decimal point is moved to the left by the number of spaces indicated in the exponential term.

* The mean R is the average of the absolute values of the 27 individual correlations. For CPP variable n,

$$\text{mean } R = \frac{\sum_{i=1}^{27} |R_{ni}|}{27}, \text{ where i = index.}$$

664

Order of 27 SLH Indices on Computer Output, for each NCPP Variable.

NCPP Variable Number										(Line)
3YR Speech Mechanism	3YR Hyper-nasality	3YR Fluency	3YR Articulation	3YR Intelligibility	3YR Language Compre.	3YR Sentence Complexity	3YR Auditory Memory	3YR Hearing	8YR Speech Mechanism	(1)
8YR Palate, Hypnasal.	8YR Fluency	8YR Articulation	8YR Intelligibility	8YR Language Compre.	8YR Auditory Memory	8YR Digits	8YR Word Identification	Written Commun.	8YR Language Production	(2)
8YR Concept Development	8YR Hearing Severity	8YR Total Cond. Loss	8YR Total S-N Loss	Neuro. Involve.	Commun. Effect.	Auditory Process			Mean R	(3)

I. FIRST SCREEN CORRELATIONS
   INDICES WITH NCPP VARIABLES LISTED BELOW

NCPP VARIABLE 1 = YES-NO BOSTON
NCPP VARIABLE 2 = YES-NO BUFFALO
NCPP VARIABLE 3 = YES-NO CHARITY
NCPP VARIABLE 4 = YES-NO COLUMBIA
NCPP VARIABLE 5 = YES-NO JOHNS HOPKINS
NCPP VARIABLE 6 = YES-NO VIRGINIA
NCPP VARIABLE 7 = YES-NO MINNESOTA
NCPP VARIABLE 8 = YES-NO N.Y. MEDICAL
NCPP VARIABLE 9 = YES-NO OREGON
NCPP VARIABLE 10 = YES-NO PENNSYLVANIA
NCPP VARIABLE 11 = YES-NO PROVIDENCE
NCPP VARIABLE 12 = YES-NO TENNESSEE

1 .27(19608) .18(19853) .16(19658) .11(18498) .17(19650) .31(18958) .15(19808) .32(18159) .29(19708) .29(18893) Mean-R 1.06E-01

2 .21(19608) -.11(18518) .18(19658) .10(18498) .15(18869) .26(18958) .24(18159) .11(15761) .29(19708) .20(18893) .24(19407) Mean-R 1.05E-01

3 -.14(19608) -.16(19786) -.15(19853) -.14(19658) -.11(19650) -.16(18958) -.17(18159) -.17(19708) -.12(18893) -.14(19407) Mean-R 8.15E-02

4 Mean-R 3.48E-02

5 -.17(18869) -.15(18958) -.11(18159) -.14(15761) -.16(19708) -.14(18893) -.19(19407) Mean-R 6.86E-02

6 -.10(18958) -.11(19708) -.11(18893) Mean-R 5.13E-02

7 .16(19608) .13(19658) .10(18869) .15(18958) .14(18159) .20(19708) .16(19407) Mean-R 6.27E-02

8 Mean-R 1.75E-02

9 -.12(19864) -.16(18368) -.13(19808) -.23(15761) -.17(18893) Mean-R 6.28E-02

10 -.10(19608) -.15(18958) -.11(18159) -.15(19708) Mean-R 5.07E-02

11 -.18(19787) Mean-R 5.07E-02

12 -.34(19608) -.16(19853) -.19(17741) -.24(19658) -.12(18498) -.15(18869) -.18(19650) -.28(18958) -.29(18159) -.34(19708) -.13(18893) -.20(19407) Mean-R 1.13E-01

II. FIRST SCREEN CORRELATIONS
   INDICES WITH NCPP VARIABLES LISTED BELOW

NCPP VARIABLE 1 = AGE OF GRAVIDA
NCPP VARIABLE 2 = GESTATION AT REGISTRATION
NCPP VARIABLE 3 = MARITAL STATUS: SINGLE
NCPP VARIABLE 4 = MARITAL STATUS: MARRIED, COMMON LAW
NCPP VARIABLE 5 = MARITAL STATUS: WIDOWED, DIVORCED, SEPARATED
NCPP VARIABLE 6 = PRIOR PREGNANCIES, NUMBER
NCPP VARIABLE 7 = PARITY
NCPP VARIABLE 8 = PRIOR PERINATAL LOSS, NUMBER
NCPP VARIABLE 9 = PRIOR VIABLE BIRTHS, NUMBER
NCPP VARIABLE 10 = CIGARETS PER DAY, NUMBER
NCPP VARIABLE 11 = HEIGHT OF MOTHER: INCHES
NCPP VARIABLE 12 = PRE-PREGNANCY WEIGHT: POUNDS
NCPP VARIABLE 13 = WEIGHT GAIN: GRAVIDA
NCPP VARIABLE 14 = BLOOD PRESSURE: POST PARTUM
NCPP VARIABLE 15 = BLOOD PRESSURE: 24 WEEKS TO LABOR
NCPP VARIABLE 16 = BLOOD PRESSURE: UP TO 24 WEEKS
NCPP VARIABLE 17 = BLOOD PRESSURE: INTRA PARTUM
NCPP VARIABLE 18 = CONVULSIONS DURING PREGNANCY
NCPP VARIABLE 19 = NUMBER OF CONDITIONS: METABOLIC AND ENDOCRINE (OB-60)
NCPP VARIABLE 20 = NUMBER OF CONDITIONS: URINARY TRACT (OB-60)
NCPP VARIABLE 21 = NUMBER OF CONDITIONS = NEUROLOGIC AND PSYCHIATRIC (OB-60)
NCPP VARIABLE 22 = NUMBER OF COMPLICATIONS OF THIS PREGNANCY
NCPP VARIABLE 23 = NUMBER OF INFECTIOUS DISEASES DURING PREGNANCY
NCPP VARIABLE 24 = EDUCATION OF GRAVIDA
NCPP VARIABLE 25 = FAMILY INCOME
NCPP VARIABLE 26 = HOUSING DENSITY
NCPP VARIABLE 27 = GRAVIDA IN HOME FOR UNWED MOTHERS
NCPP VARIABLE 28 = ALL SIBS: SEIZURES WITH FEVER
NCPP VARIABLE 29 = ALL SIBS: SEIZURES WITHOUT FEVER
NCPP VARIABLE 30 = ALL SIBS: SEIZURES WITH AND WITHOUT FEVER
NCPP VARIABLE 31 = SOCIO-ECONOMIC INDEX
NCPP VARIABLE 32 = RACE OF CHILD, WHITE
NCPP VARIABLE 33 = RACE OF CHILD, BLACK
NCPP VARIABLE 34 = NUMBER OF CONFINING ILLNESSES, PAST 12 MONTHS
NCPP VARIABLE 35 = X-RAY EXPOSURE: ABDOMINO PELVIC AREA
NCPP VARIABLE 36 = X-RAY EXPOSURE: OTHER AREAS
NCPP VARIABLE 37 = BLOOD TYPE: GRAVIDA O
NCPP VARIABLE 38 = BLOOD TYPE: GRAVIDA A
NCPP VARIABLE 39 = BLOOD TYPE: GRAVIDA B
NCPP VARIABLE 40 = BLOOD TYPE: GRAVIDA AB
NCPP VARIABLE 41 = RH FACTOR: GRAVIDA
NCPP VARIABLE 42 = PER CAPITA INCOME
NCPP VARIABLE 43 = HUSBAND LIVING AT HOME
NCPP VARIABLE 44 = AGE OF FATER OF BABY: YEARS
NCPP VARIABLE 45 = EDUCATION OF HUSBAND OR F.O.B.: YEARS
NCPP VARIABLE 46 = HUSBAND OR F.O.B. PRESENT
NCPP VARIABLE 47 = OCCUPATION OF FATHER = NEVER WORKED
NCPP VARIABLE 48 = OCCUPATION OF FATHER: WHITE COLLAR
NCPP VARIABLE 49 = OCCUPATION OF FATHER: BLUE COLLAR
NCPP VARIABLE 50 = PRIOR PREMATURES

Row	Correlation (N) values	Mean-R
1	.11(19708)	3.09E-02
2	−.11(19834), −.23(19589), −.16(19639), −.14(19631) / −.26(18939), −.10(19789) / −.26(18141), −.24(19689), −.23(18874), −.14(19388)	9.13E-02
3	−.17(19608), −.11(19658), −.18(18958), −.18(18159), −.20(19708), −.14(18893), −.12(19407)	6.16E-02
4	.20(19608), .13(19658), .10(19650) / .22(18958), .22(18159), .22(19708), .19(18893), .13(19407)	7.57E-02
5	−.10(18958), −.11(18159), −.11(18893)	3.99E-02
6	−.11(19838), −.14(19592), −.11(19642), −.18(18942), −.17(18144), −.15(19692), −.18(18877), −.12(19392)	6.45E-02
7	−.12(14341), −.16(14157), −.12(14200), −.20(13646), −.19(13086), −.17(14242), −.20(13671), −.13(14000)	7.28E-02
8		1.59E-02
9	−.16(13976), −.12(14160), −.12(14020), −.10(14011) / −.20(13480), −.19(12924), −.17(14062), −.20(13505), −.13(13826)	7.33E-02
10	.12(19618)	3.72E-02
11		2.72E-02
12		1.84E-02

669

13									Mean-R	1.89E-02
14									Mean-R	2.85E-02
15									Mean-R	1.22E-02
16	-.19(19582)	-.10(19826)		-.13(19631)	-.12(19623)	-.21(18932)	-.19(19681)	-.21(18135)	-.19(18867) -.11(19381)	Mean-R 7.41E-02
17									Mean-R	3.36E-02
18									Mean-R	6.71E-03
19									Mean-R	1.73E-02
20									Mean-R	3.28E-02
21									Mean-R	1.81E-02
22									Mean-R	1.36E-02
23							.11(17493)	.11(18189)	Mean-R	3.91E-02
24	.38(19567)	.19(19811)	.13(17712) .11(19814)	.14(18524) .28(19616) .18(18460)	.16(18834) .26(19608) .42(18919)	.16(19766) .42(18121)	.42(19666)	.36(18856)	.30(19366)	Mean-R 1.61E-01

#									Mean-R
25	.33(18631)	.17(18859)	.10(16896)	.23(18667) .14(17567)	.13(17967) .19(18671) .37(18003)	.13(18814) .36(17247)	.37(18712)	.31(17959)	.23(18446)	Mean-R 1.33E-01
26	-.33(19495)	-.22(19739)	-.14(17655)	-.25(19541) -.13(18391)	-.10(18775) -.20(19536) -.33(18846)	-.34(18056)	-.36(19591)	-.25(18788)	-.24(19297)	Mean-R 1.26E-01
27										Mean-R 6.46E-03
28										Mean-R 8.35E-03
29										Mean-R 7.59E-03
30										Mean-R 7.60E-03
31	.46(19608)	.23(19853)	.15(17741) .11(19856)	.12(18557) .33(19658) .21(18498)	.19(18869) .28(19650) .51(18958)	.18(19808) .51(18159)	.51(19708)	.43(18893)	.33(19407)	Mean-R 1.86E-01
32	.43(19608)	.25(19853)		.33(19658) .19(18498)	.20(18869) .20(19650) .47(18958)	.43(18159)	.53(19708)	.30(18893)	.32(19407)	Mean-R 1.63E-01
33	-.43(19608)	-.25(19853)		-.33(19658) -.19(18498)	-.20(18869) -.20(19650) -.47(18958)	-.43(18159)	-.53(19708)	-.30(18893)	-.32(19407)	Mean-R 1.63E-01
34										Mean-R 3.48E-02
35										Mean-R 2.71E-02
36										Mean-R 1.69E-02

Row	Data	Mean-R
37		7.89E-03
38		2.20E-02
39		2.27E-02
40		4.46E-03
41		3.14E-02
42	.37(18576) .20(18803) .14(16841) .11(17611) .27(18612) .16(17515) .14(17906) .21(18615) .42(17951) .11(18758) .40(17198) .41(18657) .35(17909) .27(18392)	1.50E-01
43	.20(19583) .12(19633) .21(18935) .22(18136) .21(19683) .19(18870) .12(19382)	7.40E-02
44		1.45E-02
45	.38(15741) .19(15926) .14(14252) .14(14904) .29(15761) .17(14855) .16(15102) .27(15768) .43(15256) .16(15889) .42(14582) .43(15801) .37(15160) .31(15595)	1.65E-01
46	.20(19597) .12(19647) .21(18949) .21(18151) .21(19697) .19(18885) .12(19396)	7.37E-02
47		1.11E-02
48	.33(16306) .13(16496) .11(14696) .11(15395) .23(16327) .16(15371) .16(15619) .21(16329) .37(15784) .15(16457) .36(15091) .36(16369) .31(15710) .25(16150)	1.38E-01

49

-.33(16306)

-.13(16496)

-.11(14696) -.11(15395) -.15(15619)
             -.23(16327) -.21(16329) -.15(16457) -.36(16369) -.30(15710) -.25(16150)
             -.16(15371) -.36(15784) -.36(15091)

Mean-R 1.36E-01

50

-.11(14148)

             -.13(13642) -.13(13078)

-.12(14233) -.12(13667)

Mean-R 4.80E-02

III. FIRST SCREEN CORRELATIONS
   INDICES WITH NCPP VARIABLES LISTED BELOW

NCPP VARIABLE   1 = PRIOR ABORTION
NCPP VARIABLE   2 = PRIOR STILLBIRTHS AND NEONATAL DEATHS
NCPP VARIABLE   3 = ALL SIBS, PRIOR: CONG MALFORM, CLEFT LIP OR PALATE
NCPP VARIABLE   4 = ALL SIBS, PRIOR: CONG MALFORMATION, HEART
NCPP VARIABLE   5 = ALL SIBS, PRIOR: CONG MALFORM, HEAD OR SPINE
NCPP VARIABLE   6 = ALL SIBS, PRIOR: MOTOR DEFECTS, INJURY
NCPP VARIABLE   7 = ALL SIBS, PRIOR: MOTOR DEFECTS, INFECTION
NCPP VARIABLE   8 = ALL SIBS, PRIOR: SENSORY DEFECTS, BLIND
NCPP VARIABLE   9 = ALL SIBS, PRIOR: SENSORY DEFECTS, DEAF
NCPP VARIABLE   10 = ALL SIBS, PRIOR: SENSORY DEFECTS, TROUBLE SPEAKING
NCPP VARIABLE   11 = ALL SIBS, PRIOR: MENTAL RETARDATION
NCPP VARIABLE   12 = GRAVIDA: MALFORMATIONS
NCPP VARIABLE   13 = GRAVIDA: SENSORY DEFECTS, SEEING
NCPP VARIABLE   14 = GRAVIDA: SENSORY DEFECTS, HEARING
NCPP VARIABLE   15 = GRAVIDA: SEIZURES, BEFORE AGE 15
NCPP VARIABLE   16 = GRAVIDA: SEIZURES, AGE 15 OR OLDER
NCPP VARIABLE   17 = GRAVIDA: SEIZURES, BEFORE AND AFTER AGE 15
NCPP VARIABLE   18 = GRAVIDA: SEIZURES, AGE UNKNOWN
NCPP VARIABLE   19 = GRAVIDA: SEIZURES, ECLAMPSIA ONLY
NCPP VARIABLE   20 = GRAVIDA: MOTOR DEFECTS, INFECTION
NCPP VARIABLE   21 = GRAVIDA: MENTALLY RETARDED
NCPP VARIABLE   22 = GRAVIDA: SPECIAL CLASS FOR SLOW LEARNERS, UNGRADED
NCPP VARIABLE   23 = GRAVIDA: MENTAL ILLNESS
NCPP VARIABLE   24 = F.O.B.: MALFORMATIONS
NCPP VARIABLE   25 = F.O.B.: SENSORY DEFECTS, SEEING
NCPP VARIABLE   26 = F.O.B.: SENSORY DEFECTS, HEARING
NCPP VARIABLE   27 = F.O.B.: MENTALLY RETARDED
NCPP VARIABLE   28 = F.O.B.: MENTAL ILLNESS
NCPP VARIABLE   29 = F.O.B.: DIABETES, ONSET BEFORE AGE 15
NCPP VARIABLE   30 = F.O.B.: DIABETES, ONSET AT AGE 15 OR OLDER
NCPP VARIABLE   31 = EIGHT MONTH MENTAL SCORE
NCPP VARIABLE   32 = EIGHT MONTH MOTOR SCORE
NCPP VARIABLE   33 = EIGHT MONTH EXAM: FINAL DIAGNOSIS
NCPP VARIABLE   34 = FOUR YEAR I.Q.
NCPP VARIABLE   35 = PLACENTAL WEIGHT: GRAMS
NCPP VARIABLE   36 = SEX OF CHILD: MALE
NCPP VARIABLE   37 = SEX OF CHILD: FEMALE
NCPP VARIABLE   38 = ONE MINUTE APGAR: HEART RATE
NCPP VARIABLE   39 = ONE MINUTE APGAR: RESPIRATORY EFFORT
NCPP VARIABLE   40 = ONE MINUTE APGAR: MUSCLE TONE
NCPP VARIABLE   41 = ONE MINUTE APGAR: REFLEX IRRITABILITY
NCPP VARIABLE   42 = ONE MINUTE APGAR: COLOR
NCPP VARIABLE   43 = ONE MINUTE APGAR: SCORE
NCPP VARIABLE   44 = FIVE MINUTE APGAR: HEART RATE
NCPP VARIABLE   45 = FIVE MINUTE APGAR: RESPIRATORY EFFORT
NCPP VARIABLE   46 = FIVE MINUTE APGAR: MUSCLE TONE
NCPP VARIABLE   47 = FIVE MINUTE APGAR: REFLEX IRRITABILITY
NCPP VARIABLE   48 = FIVE MINUTE APGAR: COLOR
NCPP VARIABLE   49 = FIVE MINUTE APGAR: SCORE
NCPP VARIABLE   50 = PROCEDURES: POSITIVE PRESSURE
NCPP VARIABLE   51 = STAGE OF DYSMATURITY
NCPP VARIABLE   52 = DIRECT COOMBS TEST: CHILD
NCPP VARIABLE   53 = MAXIMUM SERUM BILIRUBIN (GRAMS)
NCPP VARIABLE   54 = PED-8: NEUROLOGIC ABNORMALITY
NCPP VARIABLE   55 = PED-8: CNS MALFORM AND RELATED SKELETAL COND
NCPP VARIABLE   56 = PED-8: MUSCULOSKELETAL ABNORMALITY
NCPP VARIABLE   57 = PED-8: EYE CONDITIONS
NCPP VARIABLE   58 = PED-8: EAR CONDITIONS
NCPP VARIABLE   59 = PED-8: UPPER RESPIRATORY TRACT AND MOUTH COND
NCPP VARIABLE   60 = PED-8: THORACIC ABNORMALITY
NCPP VARIABLE   61 = PED-8: RESPIRATORY ABNORMALITY
NCPP VARIABLE   62 = PED-8: CARDIOVASCULAR COND
NCPP VARIABLE   63 = PED-8: ALIMENTARY TRACT MALFORM AND OTHER COND

674

NCPP VARIABLE 64 = PED-8: ABNORMAL LIVER, BILE DUCTS, SPLEEN
NCPP VARIABLE 65 = PED-8: GENITOURINARY COND
NCPP VARIABLE 66 = PED-8: HEMATOLOGIC COND
NCPP VARIABLE 67 = PED-8: SKIN COND AND MALFORM
NCPP VARIABLE 68 = PED-8: INFECTION
NCPP VARIABLE 69 = PED-8: SYNDROMES
NCPP VARIABLE 70 = PED-8: OTHER ENDOCRINE OR METABOLIC DISEASE
NCPP VARIABLE 71 = PED-8: PROCEDURES
NCPP VARIABLE 72 = PED-8: OTHER CONDITIONS ONLY
NCPP VARIABLE 73 = PED-8: OTHER CONDS, PRESUMED ANOXIA ONLY
NCPP VARIABLE 74 = PED-8: OTHER CONDS, PRESUMED TRAUMA ONLY
NCPP VARIABLE 75 = PED-8: OTHER CONDS, PRESUMED ANOXIA AND TRAUMA
NCPP VARIABLE 76 = PED-8: OTHER CONDITIONS AND PRESUMED ANOXIA
NCPP VARIABLE 77 = HEAD CIRCUMFERENCE: 1 YEAR (CMS)
NCPP VARIABLE 78 = PED-12: NEUROLOGIC ABNORMALITY
NCPP VARIABLE 79 = PED-12: PEL CNS AND SKEL COND
NCPP VARIABLE 80 = PED-12: MUSCULOSKELETAL ABNORMALITY
NCPP VARIABLE 81 = PED-12: EYE CONDITIONS
NCPP VARIABLE 82 = PED-12: EAR CONDITIONS
NCPP VARIABLE 83 = PED-12: UPPER RESP TRACT AND MOUTH COND
NCPP VARIABLE 84 = PED-12: THORACIC COND
NCPP VARIABLE 85 = PED-12: LOWER RESP TRACT ABNORM
NCPP VARIABLE 86 = PED-12: CARDIOVASCULAR COND
NCPP VARIABLE 87 = PED-12: ALIMENTARY TRACT COND
NCPP VARIABLE 88 = PED-12: ABNORMAL LIVER, BILE DUCT, SPLEEN
NCPP VARIABLE 89 = PED-12: GENITOURINARY COND
NCPP VARIABLE 90 = PED-12: NEOPL DISEASE, OTHER TUMORS
NCPP VARIABLE 91 = PED-12: HEMATOLOGIC COND
NCPP VARIABLE 92 = PED-12: SKIN COND AND MALFORM
NCPP VARIABLE 93 = PED-12: SYNDROMES
NCPP VARIABLE 94 = PED-12: OTHER ENDOCRINE AND METABOLIC DISEASE
NCPP VARIABLE 95 = PED-12: INFECTION, INFLAMMATION
NCPP VARIABLE 96 = PED-12: TRAUMA, PHYS AGENTS, INTOX
NCPP VARIABLE 97 = PED-12: DISTURBANCES IN HOMEOSTASIS
NCPP VARIABLE 98 = PED-12: OTHER CONDITIONS
NCPP VARIABLE 99 = PED-12: PROCEDURES
NCPP VARIABLE 100 = PED-12: SOCIAL, ENVIRONMENTAL COND

	Mean-R	
1	Mean-R	8.68E-03
2	Mean-R	2.02E-02
3	Mean-R	1.64E-02
4	Mean-R	8.54E-03
5	Mean-R	7.56E-03
6	Mean-R	5.67E-03
7	Mean-R	8.56E-03
8	Mean-R	5.30E-03
9	Mean-R	5.60E-03
10	Mean-R	7.68E-03
11	Mean-R	9.20E-03
12	Mean-R	1.23E-02

676

13	Mean-R	8.86E-03
14	Mean-R	6.24E-03
15	Mean-R	1.22E-02
16	Mean-R	4.54E-03
17	Mean-R	1.24E-02
18	Mean-R	5.04E-03
19	Mean-R	1.16E-02
20	Mean-R	6.03E-03
21	Mean-R	2.01E-02
22	Mean-R	1.77E-02
23	Mean-R	1.03E-02
24	Mean-R	2.01E-02

677

									Mean-R
25									Mean-R 7.78E-03
26									Mean-R 5.43E-03
27									Mean-R 8.94E-03
28									Mean-R 1.10E-02
29									Mean-R 5.90E-03
30									Mean-R 6.48E-03
31	.17(18023)	.15(18246)	.13(18247)	.11(18074)	.12(17735) .14(18068) .15(17447)	.14(17270) .17(16701)	.16(18115)	.13(17429)	.11(17845)	Mean-R 8.76E-02
32	.16(18024)	.14(18246)	.10(16688) .13(18247)	.13(17444) .12(18074)	.14(17732) .13(18069) .16(17448)	.15(17267) .16(16699)	.16(18115)	.13(17430)	.15(17845)	Mean-R 9.16E-02
33	-.14(17989)	-.13(18210)	-.15(18211)	-.12(17430)	-.12(17715) -.11(18032) -.14(17414)	-.15(17254) -.14(16667)	-.14(18079)	-.14(17398)	-.12(17809)	Mean-R 8.76E-02
34	.11(15310) .65(17436) -.13(17608)	.35(17642)	.24(16496) .21(17635)	.33(17210) .45(17474) .27(16505)	.41(17475) .48(17475) .65(16870)	.26(17001) .31(17602) .67(16213)	.14(14656) .64(17511)	.54(16919)	.48(17270)	Mean-R 2.87E-01
35										Mean-R 3.59E-02
36	-.12(19853)		-.15(18557)				.14(19708)	-.19(18893)		Mean-R 6.24E-02

#					Mean-R
37	.12(19853)	.15(18557)	-.14(19708)	.19(18893)	6.24E-02
38					1.19E-02
39					1.62E-02
40					1.30E-02
41					1.82E-02
42	-.12(18410)			-.14(18509)	4.63E-02
43		-.11(17805)	-.11(17035)		1.75E-02
44					1.19E-02
45					2.68E-02
46					2.29E-02
47					2.37E-02
48	-.17(18511)	-.13(18559)	-.17(17895)	-.17(17148)	-.20(18607)	6.24E-02

49	
50	Mean-R 2.27E-02
51	Mean-R 1.08E-02
52	Mean-R 1.64E-02
53	Mean-R 2.03E-02
54	Mean-R 2.20E-02
55	Mean-R 4.87E-02
56	Mean-R 1.91E-02
57	Mean-R 1.08E-02
58	Mean-R 1.13E-02
59	Mean-R 2.07E-02
60	Mean-R 2.24E-02
	Mean-R 6.79E-03

61

62   Mean-R   2.60E-02

63   Mean-R   1.62E-02

64   Mean-R   1.36E-02

65   Mean-R   1.52E-02

66   Mean-R   1.03E-02

67   Mean-R   5.31E-03

68   Mean-R   2.03E-02

69   Mean-R   2.03E-02

−.12(19729)

70   Mean-R   3.84E-02

71   Mean-R   8.03E-03

72   Mean-R   4.46E-02

   Mean-R   1.37E-02

73   Mean-R   1.38E-02

74   Mean-R   7.40E-03

75   Mean-R   8.21E-03

76   Mean-R   6.02E-03

77   .11(18624)   .12(18673)   .10(18663)   .12(17260)   .17(18719)   Mean-R   4.97E-02
                          .10(18013)

78   -.12(19308)   -.11(19550)   -.10(19553)   -.10(18430)   -.11(18738)   -.15(18241)   -.12(19408)   -.11(18619)   -.10(19108)   Mean-R   7.41E-02

79   -.13(18673)   -.11(17881)   Mean-R   2.68E-02

80   Mean-R   1.81E-02

81   Mean-R   1.16E-02

82   Mean-R   2.60E-02

83   Mean-R   2.14E-02

84   Mean-R   8.06E-03

85   Mean-R   1.16E-02

86   Mean-R   1.82E-02

87   Mean-R   9.15E-03

88   Mean-R   8.26E-03

89   Mean-R   1.49E-02

90   Mean-R   3.16E-03

91   Mean-R   2.93E-02

92   Mean-R   1.92E-02

93   Mean-R   4.22E-02

94   Mean-R   1.04E-02

95   Mean-R   2.80E-02

96   Mean-R   5.55E-03

97

98

99

100

Mean-R 2.36E-02

Mean-R 9.26E-03

Mean-R 2.36E-02

Mean-R 3.76E-02

$-.12(15646)$

$-.10(18619)$

IV. FIRST SCREEN CORRELATIONS
   INDICES WITH NCPP VARIABLES LISTED BELOW

NCPP VARIABLE 1 = BIRTHWEIGHT (GRAMS)
NCPP VARIABLE 2 = GESTATION AT DELIVERY (WEEKS)
NCPP VARIABLE 3 = BLOOD TYPE CHILD O
NCPP VARIABLE 4 = BLOOD TYPE CHILD A
NCPP VARIABLE 5 = BLOOD TYPE CHILD B
NCPP VARIABLE 6 = BLOOD TYPE CHILD AB
NCPP VARIABLE 7 = RH FACTOR CHILD
NCPP VARIABLE 8 = FOUR YEAR PSYCH EXAM: GRAHAM BLOCK SORT (TOTAL SCORE)
NCPP VARIABLE 9 = FOUR YEAR PSYCH EXAM: DOMINANCE, LEG
NCPP VARIABLE 10 = FOUR YEAR PSYCH EXAM: DOMINANCE, EYE
NCPP VARIABLE 11 = SEVEN YEAR NEURO ABNORM
NCPP VARIABLE 12 = HEAD CIRCUM (NEONATAL)
NCPP VARIABLE 13 = HEAD CIRCUM: FOUR MOS (CMS)
NCPP VARIABLE 14 = HEAD CIRCUM: FOUR YRS (CMS)
NCPP VARIABLE 15 = HEAD CIRCUM: SEVEN YRS (CMS)
NCPP VARIABLE 16 = WEIGHT: ONE YR (KGMS)
NCPP VARIABLE 17 = WEIGHT: FOUR YRS (KGMS)
NCPP VARIABLE 18 = WEIGHT: SEVEN YRS (KGMS)
NCPP VARIABLE 19 = BODY LENGTH: BIRTH (CMS)
NCPP VARIABLE 20 = BODY LENGTH: FOUR MOS (CMS)
NCPP VARIABLE 21 = BODY LENGTH: ONE YEAR (CMS)
NCPP VARIABLE 22 = BODY LENGTH: FOUR YRS (CMS)
NCPP VARIABLE 23 = BODY LENGTH: SEVEN YRS (CMS)
NCPP VARIABLE 24 = METHOD OF DELIVERY TYPE VERTEX
NCPP VARIABLE 25 = METHOD OF DELIVERY TYPE BREECH
NCPP VARIABLE 26 = METHOD OF DELIVERY TYPE C/S
NCPP VARIABLE 27 = ASRUPLIO PLACENTA
NCPP VARIABLE 28 = CORD PATHOLOGY: TRUE KNOT
NCPP VARIABLE 29 = CORD PATHOLOGY: CORD AROUND BODY
NCPP VARIABLE 30 = CORD PATHOLOGY: LOOSE CORD AROUND NECK
NCPP VARIABLE 31 = CORD PATHOLOGY: TIGHT CORD AROUND NECK
NCPP VARIABLE 32 = PLACENTA PREVIA: PARTIAL
NCPP VARIABLE 33 = PLACENTA PREVIA: LOW IMPLANTATION
NCPP VARIABLE 34 = PROLAPSED CORD: OCCULT
NCPP VARIABLE 35 = PROLAPSED CORD: INTO VAGINA
NCPP VARIABLE 36 = PROLAPSED CORD: THROUGH INTROITUS
NCPP VARIABLE 37 = VERTEX DELIVERY WITH FORCEPS APPLICATION
NCPP VARIABLE 38 = ACUTE TOXEMIA
NCPP VARIABLE 39 = CHRONIC HYPERTENSIVE DISEASE
NCPP VARIABLE 40 = POLYHYDRANNIOS
NCPP VARIABLE 41 = DURATION 1ST + 2ND STAGES LABOR (HRS, MINS)
NCPP VARIABLE 42 = MARGINAL SINUS RUPTURE
NCPP VARIABLE 43 = WEIGHT: FOUR MOS (GMS)
NCPP VARIABLE 44 = SEVEN YEAR S.E.I.

Row	Values (N in parentheses)	Mean-R
1	.17(19590) .12(19641) .10(19632) .17(18143) .20(19691) .12(18875) .12(19389)	6.84E-02
2	.13(19522) .16(18942) .12(18877) .13(18079) .14(19623) .10(19322)	4.93E-02
3		8.05E-03
4		2.47E-02
5		2.45E-02
6		4.92E-03
7		2.54E-02
8	.39(17184) .23(17377) .14(16305) .19(16980) .25(17227) .13(16775) .34(17251) .34(16694) .29(17026)	1.71E-01
9	.14(17368) .25(17218) .27(17226) .18(17340)	1.38E-02
10	.18(16277) .39(16633) .41(15994)	1.53E-02
11	−.18(18952) −.21(19185) −.10(15787) −.14(16520) −.15(16812) −.16(16359) −.14(19040) −.20(18505) −.17(18757)	1.15E-01
12	.14(19373) .11(19423) .11(19414) .14(18732) .18(19473) .15(17940) .11(18669)	5.72E-02

Additional stacked values (uncertain row assignment): −.22(19186), −.15(18993), −.17(18359), −.13(19140), −.19(17573)

13	.16(18455)	.15(18508)	.13(18499) .15(17850)	.17(17084)	.21(18552)	.11(17827)		Mean-R	6.23E-02
14	.11(15787)		.12(15287)	.13(14682)	.16(15858)	.12(15330)		Mean-R	5.57E-02
15	.15(18919)	.14(18959)	.13(18959)	.11(19107) .18(17542)	.21(19006)	.15(18467)		Mean-R	6.84E-02
16	.15(18526)	.13(18573)	.11(18564) .14(17921)	.15(17174)	.21(18617)	.10(17895)	.10(18340)	Mean-R	6.29E-02
17	.15(15833)	.12(15866)	.16(15331)	.16(14725)	.20(15903)	.12(15371)		Mean-R	6.36E-02
18	.11(18945)		.10(18351)	.11(17569)	.14(19031)	.10(18496)		Mean-R	5.04E-02
19	.11(19311)		.11(18672)	.12(17881)	.14(19409)			Mean-R	4.51E-02
20	.17(18300)	.14(18355)	.11(18344) .15(17704)	.17(16938)	.21(18399)	.11(17680)	.11(18123)	Mean-R	6.58E-02
21	.14(18424)	.13(18470)	.14(17820)	.15(17074)	.21(18514)		.10(18237)	Mean-R	5.67E-02
22								Mean-R	4.16E-02
23								Mean-R	2.84E-02
24								Mean-R	7.98E-03

25	Mean-R 1.06E-02
26	Mean-R 5.79E-03
27	Mean-R 1.35E-02
28	Mean-R 5.02E-03
29	Mean-R 8.07E-03
30	Mean-R 1.65E-02
31	Mean-R 1.08E-02
32	Mean-R 5.13E-03
33	Mean-R 5.64E-03
34	Mean-R 8.16E-03
35	Mean-R 6.49E-03
36	Mean-R 4.82E-03

#	Values	Mean-R
37	.13(7522) .10(7569) .15(7339) .14(6995) .16(7582) .11(7308)	5.53E-02
38		2.53E-02
39		4.16E-02
40		1.25E-02
41		1.25E-02
42		2.97E-02
43	.21(18311) .17(18364) .10(17796) .14(18356) .19(17709) .21(16950) .26(18408) .14(17685) .14(18134)	6.33E-03 / 8.23E-02
44	.45(18898) .23(19125) .10(19126) .12(15815) .14(16551) .32(18932) .21(17851) .19(16821) .29(18937) .50(18294) .17(19084) .49(17508) .49(18980) .42(18399) .34(18703)	1.83E-01

V. FIRST SCREEN CORRELATIONS
   INDICES WITH NCPP VARIABLES LISTED BELOW

NCPP VARIABLE 1 = S.E.I. AT BIRTH
NCPP VARIABLE 2 = RASH OR SKIN TROUBLE: GRAVIDA
NCPP VARIABLE 3 = OPERATION: GRAVIDA
NCPP VARIABLE 4 = AIR TRAVEL BY GRAVIDA
NCPP VARIABLE 5 = PHYSICAL DEFECTS: GRAVIDA
NCPP VARIABLE 6 = SENSORY DEFECTS: SIBS OF GRAVIDA
NCPP VARIABLE 7 = DIABETES: GRAVIDA (ONSET BEFORE AGE 15)
NCPP VARIABLE 8 = DIABETES: GRAVIDA (ONSET AT 15 OR OLDER)
NCPP VARIABLE 9 = DIABETES: GRAVIDA (ONLY DURING PREGNANCY)
NCPP VARIABLE 10 = DIABETES: SIBS OF GRAVIDA
NCPP VARIABLE 11 = SEIZURES: SIBS OF GRAVIDA
NCPP VARIABLE 12 = MOTOR DEFECTS: SIBS OF GRAVIDA
NCPP VARIABLE 13 = MENTAL RETARDATION: SIBS OF GRAVIDA
NCPP VARIABLE 14 = MENTAL ILLNESS: SIBS OF GRAVIDA
NCPP VARIABLE 15 = PHYSICAL DEFECTS: FOB
NCPP VARIABLE 16 = SENSORY DEFECTS: SIBS OF FOB
NCPP VARIABLE 17 = MOTOR DEFECTS: SIBS OF FOB
NCPP VARIABLE 18 = MENTAL RETARDATION: SIBS OF FOB
NCPP VARIABLE 19 = MENTAL ILLNESS: SIBS OF FOB
NCPP VARIABLE 20 = BAYLEY: SEARCHES WITH EYES FOR SOUND
NCPP VARIABLE 21 = BAYLEY: VOCALIZES TO SOCIAL STIMULUS
NCPP VARIABLE 22 = BAYLEY: VOCALIZES TWO SYLLABLES
NCPP VARIABLE 23 = BAYLEY: REACTS TO DISAPPEARANCE OF FACE
NCPP VARIABLE 24 = BAYLEY: PLAYS WITH RATTLE
NCPP VARIABLE 25 = BAYLEY: AWARE OF STRANGE SITUATIONS
NCPP VARIABLE 26 = BAYLEY: INSPECTS OWN HANDS
NCPP VARIABLE 27 = BAYLEY: TURNS HEAD TO SOUND OF BELL
NCPP VARIABLE 28 = BAYLEY: TURNS HEAD TO SOUND OF RATTLE
NCPP VARIABLE 29 = BAYLEY: DISCRIMINATES STRANGERS
NCPP VARIABLE 30 = BAYLEY: VOCALIZES ATTITUDES
NCPP VARIABLE 31 = BAYLEY: RECOVERS RATTLE IN CRIB
NCPP VARIABLE 32 = BAYLEY: TURNS HEAD AFTER DROPPED OBJECT
NCPP VARIABLE 33 = BAYLEY: ENJOYS FROLIC PLAY
NCPP VARIABLE 34 = BAYLEY: PICKS UP CUBE DIRECTLY AND EASILY
NCPP VARIABLE 35 = BAYLEY: ENJOYS SOUND PRODUCTION
NCPP VARIABLE 36 = BAYLEY: ATTENDS TO SCRIBBLING
NCPP VARIABLE 37 = BAYLEY: LOOKS FOR DROPPED OBJECT
NCPP VARIABLE 38 = BAYLEY: MANIPULATES BELL
NCPP VARIABLE 39 = BAYLEY: RESPONDS TO SOCIAL PLAY
NCPP VARIABLE 40 = BAYLEY: RINGS BELL IMITATIVELY
NCPP VARIABLE 41 = SPEED OF RESPONSE: VERY SLOW
NCPP VARIABLE 42 = SPEED OF RESPONSE: APPROACHES AFTER LONG TIME
NCPP VARIABLE 43 = SPEED OF RESPONSE: APPROACHES AFTER LOOKING BRIEFLY
NCPP VARIABLE 44 = SPEED OF RESPONSE: APPROACHES QUICKLY
NCPP VARIABLE 45 = SPEED OF RESPONSE: VERY FAST
NCPP VARIABLE 46 = SPEED OF RESPONSE: VARIES GREATLY
NCPP VARIABLE 47 = INTENSITY OF RESPONSE: DOES NOT LOOK AT OR HANDLE OBJ.
NCPP VARIABLE 48 = INTENSITY OF RESPONSE: WHEN GIVEN-HOLDS, DOES NOT PLAY
NCPP VARIABLE 49 = INTENSITY OF RESPONSE: SOME MANIPULATIONS
NCPP VARIABLE 51 = INTENSITY OF RESPONSE: CONSIDERABLE FORCE IN MANIPULATION
NCPP VARIABLE 52 = INTENSITY OF RESPONSE: VARIES GREATLY
NCPP VARIABLE 53 = DURATION OF RESPONSE: ATTENDS TO OBJECTS VERY BRIEFLY
NCPP VARIABLE 54 = DURATION OF RESPONSE: SHORT TIME WITH OBJECTS
NCPP VARIABLE 55 = DURATION OF RESPONSE: MODERATE TIME WITH OBJECTS
NCPP VARIABLE 56 = DURATION OF RESPONSE: FAIRLY LONG TIME WITH OBJECTS
NCPP VARIABLE 57 = DURATION OF RESPONSE: VERY LONG TIME WITH OBJ.
NCPP VARIABLE 58 = DURATION OF RESPONSE: VARIES GREATLY
NCPP VARIABLE 59 = PERSISTANCE IN PURSUIT: NO ATTEMPT
NCPP VARIABLE 60 = PERSISTANCE IN PURSUIT: 1 OR 2 ATTEMPTS—GIVES UP
NCPP VARIABLE 61 = PERSISTANCE IN PURSUIT: SEVERAL BRIEF ATTEMPTS—GIVES UP
NCPP VARIABLE 62 = PERSISTANCE IN PURSUIT: FREQUENT, DOES NOT GIVE UP
NCPP VARIABLE 63 = PERSISTANCE IN PURSUIT: VERY FREQUENT AND VIGOROUS
NCPP VARIABLE 64 = PERSISTANCE IN PURSUIT: VARIES GREATLY

690

NCPP VARIABLE 65 = INTENSITY OF SOCIAL RESPONSE: NO RESPONSE
NCPP VARIABLE 66 = INTENSITY OF SOCIAL RESPONSE: RESPONSE TO DIRECT APPROACH
NCPP VARIABLE 67 = INTENSITY OF SOCIAL RESPONSE: SOCIAL/OBJECT INTEREST
NCPP VARIABLE 68 = INTENSITY OF SOCIAL RESPONSE: MORE INTEREST IN PERSONS
NCPP VARIABLE 69 = INTENSITY OF SOCIAL RESPONSE: VERY STRONG, OVER-REACTS
NCPP VARIABLE 70 = INTENSITY OF SOCIAL RESPONSE: VARIES GREATLY
NCPP VARIABLE 71 = NATURE OF SOC RESP. TO EXAMINER: AVOIDS, TURNS TO MOTHER
NCPP VARIABLE 72 = NATURE OF SOC RESP. TO EXAMINER: HESITATES, APPREHENSIVE
NCPP VARIABLE 73 = NATURE OF SOC RESP. TO EXAMINER: ACCEPTS, PASSIVE RESPONSE
NCPP VARIABLE 74 = NATURE OF SOC RESP. TO EXAMINER: FRIENDLY. RESPONDS EASILY
NCPP VARIABLE 75 = NATURE OF SOC RESP. TO EXAMINER: INSTIGATES SOCIAL CONTACTS
NCPP VARIABLE 76 = NATURE OF SOC RESP. TO EXAMINER: VARIES GREATLY
NCPP VARIABLE 77 = NATURE OF SOC RESP TO MOTHER: IGNORES, RESISTS CONTACT
NCPP VARIABLE 78 = NATURE OF SOC RESP TO MOTHER: HESITATES, COOPERATES
NCPP VARIABLE 79 = NATURE OF SOC RESP TO MOTHER: ACCEPTS, RESPONDS ADEQUATELY
NCPP VARIABLE 80 = NATURE OF SOC RESP TO MOTHER: ENJOYS CONTACT
NCPP VARIABLE 81 = NATURE OF SOC RESP TO MOTHER: CLINGS TO MOTHER
NCPP VARIABLE 82 = NATURE OF SOC RESP TO MOTHER: VARIES GREATLY
NCPP VARIABLE 83 = ACTIVITY LEVEL: HYPOACTIVE
NCPP VARIABLE 84 = ACTIVITY LEVEL: LITTLE ACTIVITY
NCPP VARIABLE 85 = ACTIVITY LEVEL: RESPONDS APPROPRIATELY
NCPP VARIABLE 86 = ACTIVITY LEVEL: MUCH ACTIVITY
NCPP VARIABLE 87 = ACTIVITY LEVEL: HYPERACTIVE
NCPP VARIABLE 88 = ACTIVITY LEVEL: VARIES GREATLY
NCPP VARIABLE 89 = MENTAL DEVELOPMENT
NCPP VARIABLE 90 = FINE MOTOR DEVELOPMENT
NCPP VARIABLE 91 = GROSS MOTOR DEVELOPMENT
NCPP VARIABLE 92 = SOCIAL EMOTIONAL DEVELOPMENT
NCPP VARIABLE 93 = DEVIANT BEHAVIOR: PRESENT IN AT LEAST 1/5 OBS.
NCPP VARIABLE 94 = DEVIANT BEHAVIOR: UNUSUAL AND MEANINGLESS HAND MOTIONS
NCPP VARIABLE 95 = DEVIANT BEHAVIOR: HEAD ROLLING OR BANGING
NCPP VARIABLE 96 = DEVIANT BEHAVIOR: ROCKING
NCPP VARIABLE 97 = DEVIANT BEHAVIOR: EXCESSIVE CRYING
NCPP VARIABLE 98 = DEVIANT BEHAVIOR: SOME DEVIANT BEHAVIORS
NCPP VARIABLE 99 = NUMBER OF CHILDREN UNDER 8 SUPPORTED (CARED FOR)

1	.46(19608)	.23(19853)	.13(17741) .11(19856)	.12(18557) .33(19658) .21(18498)	.19(18869) .28(19650) .51(18958)	.18(19808) .51(18159)	.51(19708)	.43(18893)	.33(19407)	Mean-R .19E+00
2										Mean-R .26E-01
3										Mean-R .10E-01
4						.10(19397)				Mean-R .38E-01
5										Mean-R .10E-01
6										Mean-R .61E-02
7										Mean-R .63E-02
8										Mean-R .48E-02
9										Mean-R .63E-02
10										Mean-R .11E-01
11										Mean-R .11E-01
12										Mean-R .97E-02

13

14   Mean-R .73E-02

15   Mean-R .10E-01

16   Mean-R .94E-02

17   Mean-R .91E-02

18   Mean-R .64E-02

19   Mean-R .70E-02

20   Mean-R .65E-02

21   Mean-R .21E-01

22   Mean-R .30E-01

23   Mean-R .35E-01

24   Mean-R .30E-01

      Mean-R .28E-01

693

Row	Values	Mean-R
25		.38E-01
26		.33E-01
27		.42E-01
28		.39E-01
29	-.10(18171)	.47E-01
30		.40E-01
31		.49E-01
32	-.11(18236)	.52E-01
33		
34	-.10(18230) -.10(17255)	.44E-01
35	-.13(17981) -.11(18029) -.12(17405) -.12(16660) -.14(18070)	.55E-01 .57E-01
36		.40E-01

Row	Correlations	Mean-R
37		Mean-R .55E-01
38	-.11(17368)	Mean-R .57E-01
39	-.10(17386) -.10(16644)	Mean-R .60E-01
40	-.12(15701) -.13(16288) -.10(15690)	Mean-R .35E-01
41	-.11(16404) -.12(15033)	Mean-R .38E-01
42		Mean-R .27E-01
43	-.12(16208)	Mean-R .12E-01
44		Mean-R .25E-01
45		Mean-R .12E-01
46		Mean-R .73E-02
47		Mean-R .29E-01
48		Mean-R .36E-01

49	Mean-R	.11E-01
50	Mean-R	.28E-01
51	Mean-R	.90E-02
52	Mean-R	.63E-02
53	Mean-R	.29E-01
54	Mean-R	.30E-01
55	Mean-R	.11E-01
56	Mean-R	.27E-01
57	Mean-R	.78E-02
58	Mean-R	.94E-02
59	Mean-R	.41E-01
60	Mean-R	.38E-01

61	Mean-R	.13E-01
62	Mean-R	.26E-01
63	Mean-R	.17E-01
64	Mean-R	.91E-02
65	Mean-R	.24E-01
66	-.11(17298)	Mean-R	.44E-01
67	Mean-R	.32E-01
68	Mean-R	.11E-01
69	Mean-R	.77E-02
70	Mean-R	.57E-02
71	Mean-R	.72E-02
72	Mean-R	.18E-01

73	Mean-R	.24E-01
74	Mean-R	.25E-01
75	Mean-R	.34E-01
76	Mean-R	.52E-02
77	Mean-R	.81E-02
78	Mean-R	.25E-01
79	Mean-R	.16E-01
80	Mean-R	.20E-01
81	Mean-R	.11E-01
82	Mean-R	.46E-02
83	Mean-R	.37E-01
84	Mean-R	.39E-01

85						Mean-R .14E-01
86						Mean-R .29E-01
87						Mean-R .90E-02
88						Mean-R .53E-02
89	-.15(17225)	-.13(17431) -.13(17429) -.11(17266)	-.13(17162) -.12(17262) -.15(16680)	-.12(16724) -.16(15977)	-.15(17306)	-.15(16678) -.13(17047) Mean-R .84E-01
90	-.13(17231)	-.12(17438) -.12(17436) -.13(16899)	-.12(17171) -.11(17268) -.14(16687)	-.14(16732) -.14(15984)	-.13(17314)	-.13(16686) -.13(17053) Mean-R .83E-01
91	-.14(17212)	-.13(17418) -.13(17416) -.13(16885) -.10(17253)	-.13(17156) -.11(17250) -.14(16667)	-.15(16718) -.14(15965)	-.14(17293)	-.13(16668) -.14(17034) Mean-R .87E-01
92					-.10(17303)	Mean-R .49E-01
93						Mean-R .10E-01
94						Mean-R .86E-02
95						Mean-R .87E-02
96						Mean-R .12E-01

97

98

99

Mean-R .10E-01

Mean-R .13E-01

Mean-R .87E-01

−.16(19507)   −.13(19501)   −.23(19557)   −.21(18751)   −.17(19264)

−.16(19703)   −.24(18813)   −.22(18026)

−.20(19459)

NCPP VARIABLE 1 = OBVIOUS DEFECTS: HYDROCEPHALUS
NCPP VARIABLE 2 = OBVIOUS DEFECTS: ASYMMETRY OF SKULL
NCPP VARIABLE 3 = OBVIOUS DEFECTS: VERY OBESE OR VERY SMALL
NCPP VARIABLE 4 = OBVIOUS DEFECTS: SKIN CONDITIONS
NCPP VARIABLE 5 = OBVIOUS DEFECTS: OTHER OBVIOUS DEFECTS
NCPP VARIABLE 6 = SITS ALONE MOMENTAILY
NCPP VARIABLE 7 = EXPRESSION OF AFFECTION BY MOTHER: NEGATIVE
NCPP VARIABLE 8 = EXPRESSION OF AFFECTION BY MOTHER: OCCASIONALLY NEGATIVE
NCPP VARIABLE 9 = EXPRESSION OF AFFECTION BY MOTHER: WARM
NCPP VARIABLE 10 = EXPRESSION OF AFFECTION BY MOTHER: FREQUENT CARESS
NCPP VARIABLE 11 = EXPRESSION OF AFFECTION BY MOTHER: EXTRAVAGANT
NCPP VARIABLE 12 = EVALUATION OF CHILD BY MOTHER: CRITICAL
NCPP VARIABLE 13 = EVALUATION OF CHILD BY MOTHER: GENERALLY NEG.
NCPP VARIABLE 14 = EVALUATION OF CHILD BY MOTHER: ACCEPTING
NCPP VARIABLE 15 = EVALUATION OF CHILD BY MOTHER: IGNORES UNDESIRABLE BEHAVIOR
NCPP VARIABLE 16 = EVALUATION OF CHILD BY MOTHER: EFFUSIVE
NCPP VARIABLE 17 = HANDLING OF CHILD BY MOTHER: ROUGH
NCPP VARIABLE 18 = HANDLING OF CHILD BY MOTHER: AWKWARD
NCPP VARIABLE 19 = HANDLING OF CHILD BY MOTHER: CONSIDERATE
NCPP VARIABLE 20 = HANDLING OF CHILD BY MOTHER: VERY GENTLY
NCPP VARIABLE 21 = HANDLING OF CHILD BY MOTHER: OVERLY CAUTIOUS
NCPP VARIABLE 22 = MANAGEMENT OF CHILD BY MOTHER: NO FACILITATION
NCPP VARIABLE 23 = MANAGEMENT OF CHILD BY MOTHER: FOLLOWED SUGGESTIONS, HELD
NCPP VARIABLE 24 = MANAGEMENT OF CHILD BY MOTHER: ORENTING
NCPP VARIABLE 25 = MANAGEMENT OF CHILD BY MOTHER: FREQUENTLY INTERFERRED
NCPP VARIABLE 26 = MANAGEMENT OF CHILD BY MOTHER: OVERDIRECTING
NCPP VARIABLE 27 = REACT. TO CHILDS NEEDS, MOTHER: UNRESPONSIVE
NCPP VARIABLE 28 = REACT. TO CHILDS NEEDS, MOTHER: SLOW RESPONSE
NCPP VARIABLE 29 = REACT. TO CHILDS NEEDS, MOTHER: RECOGNIZED
NCPP VARIABLE 30 = REACT. TO CHILDS NEEDS, MOTHER: IMMEDIATE RESPONSE
NCPP VARIABLE 31 = REACT. TO CHILDS NEEDS, MOTHER: ABSORBED
NCPP VARIABLE 32 = MOTHERS REAC. TO CHILDS PERFORM: INDIFFERENT
NCPP VARIABLE 33 = MOTHERS REAC. TO CHILDS PERFORM: BRIEF INTEREST
NCPP VARIABLE 34 = MOTHERS REAC. TO CHILDS PERFORM: INTERESTED
NCPP VARIABLE 35 = MOTHERS REAC. TO CHILDS PERFORM: EXCESSIVE PRIDE
NCPP VARIABLE 36 = MOTHERS REAC. TO CHILDS PERFORM: DEFENSIVE
NCPP VARIABLE 37 = MOTHERS FOCUS OF ATTENTION: CHILD
NCPP VARIABLE 38 = MOTHERS FOCUS OF ATTENTION: INVOLVED WITH CHILD
NCPP VARIABLE 39 = MOTHERS FOCUS OF ATTENTION: SITUATION
NCPP VARIABLE 40 = MOTHERS FOCUS OF ATTENTION: OCCASIONALLY INTERRUPTED
NCPP VARIABLE 41 = MOTHERS FOCUS OF ATTENTION: SELF
NCPP VARIABLE 42 = CHILDS APPEARANCE: UNKEMPT
NCPP VARIABLE 43 = CHILDS APPEARANCE: HELTER-SKELTER
NCPP VARIABLE 44 = CHILDS APPEARANCE: APPROPRIATE
NCPP VARIABLE 45 = CHILDS APPEARANCE: SOMEWHAT OVERDRESSED
NCPP VARIABLE 46 = CHILDS APPEARANCE: OVERDRESSED
NCPP VARIABLE 47 = YEAR II: THREE-HOLE FORM BOARD   (STANFORD-BINET)
NCPP VARIABLE 48 = YEAR II: IDENTIFYING PARTS OF THE BODY   (STANFORD-BINET)
NCPP VARIABLE 49 = YEAR II: PICTURE VOCABULARY   (STANFORD-BINET)
NCPP VARIABLE 50 = YEAR II: WORD COMBO.   (STANFORD-BINET)
NCPP VARIABLE 51 = YEAR II: ALTERNATE   (STANFORD-BINET)
NCPP VARIABLE 52 = YEAR II-6: IDENTIFYING OBJECTS BY USE   (STANFORD-BINET)
NCPP VARIABLE 53 = YEAR II-6: NAMING OBJECTS   (STANFORD-BINET)
NCPP VARIABLE 54 = YEAR II-6: PICTURE VOCABULARY   (STANFORD-BINET)
NCPP VARIABLE 55 = YEAR II-6: REPEATING 2 DIGITS   (STANFORD-BINET)
NCPP VARIABLE 56 = YEAR III: PICTURE VOCABULARY   (STANFORD-BINET)
NCPP VARIABLE 57 = YEAR III: BLOCK BUILDING   (STANFORD-BINET)
NCPP VARIABLE 58 = YEAR III: PICTURE MEMORIES   (STANFORD-BINET)
NCPP VARIABLE 59 = YEAR III: COPYING A CIRCLE   (STANFORD-BINET)
NCPP VARIABLE 60 = YEAR III-6: COMPARISON OF BALLS   (STANFORD-BINET)
NCPP VARIABLE 61 = YEAR III-6: DISCRIMINATION OF ANIMAL PICTURES   (STANFORD-BINET)
NCPP VARIABLE 62 = YEAR III-6: RESPONSE TO PICTURES   (STANFORD-BINET)
NCPP VARIABLE 63 = YEAR III-6: COMPREHENSION   (STANFORD-BINET)
NCPP VARIABLE 64 = YEAR IV: PICTURE VOCAB   (STANFORD-BINET)

701

```
NCPP VARIABLE 65 = YEAR IV: NAMING OBJECTS FROM MEMORY          (STANFORD-BINET)
NCPP VARIABLE 66 = YEAR IV: OPPOSITE ANALOGIES                  (STANFORD-BINET)
NCPP VARIABLE 67 = YEAR IV: PICTORIAL IDENTIFICATION            (STANFORD-BINET)
NCPP VARIABLE 68 = YEAR IV-6: OPPOSITE ANALOGIES               (STANFORD-BINET)
NCPP VARIABLE 69 = YEAR IV-6: PICTORIAL SIM/DIFF               (STANFORD-BINET)
NCPP VARIABLE 70 = YEAR IV-6: THREE COMMISSIONS                (STANFORD-BINET)
NCPP VARIABLE 71 = YEAR IV-6: COMPREHENSION III               (STANFORD-BINET)
NCPP VARIABLE 72 = YEAR V: PICTURE COMPLETION                  (STANFORD-BINET)
NCPP VARIABLE 73 = YEAR V: DEFINITIONS                         (STANFORD-BINET)
NCPP VARIABLE 74 = YEAR V: COPYING A SQUARE                    (STANFORD-BINET)
NCPP VARIABLE 75 = YEAR V: PAITENCE, RECTANGLES                (STANFORD-BINET)
NCPP VARIABLE 76 = YEAR VI: VOCABULARY                         (STANFORD-BINET)
NCPP VARIABLE 77 = YEAR VI: DIFFERENCES                        (STANFORD-BINET)
NCPP VARIABLE 78 = YEAR VI: NUMBER CONCEPTS                    (STANFORD-BINET)
NCPP VARIABLE 79 = YEAR VI: OPPOSITE ANALOGIES                 (STANFORD-BINET)
NCPP VARIABLE 80 = YEAR VII: SIMILARITIES                      (STANFORD-BINET)
NCPP VARIABLE 81 = YEAR VII: COPYING A DIAMOND                 (STANFORD-BINET)
NCPP VARIABLE 82 = YEAR VII: COMPREHENSION IV                  (STANFORD-BINET)
NCPP VARIABLE 83 = YEAR VII: REPEATING 5 DIGITS                (STANFORD-BINET)
NCPP VARIABLE 84 = YEAR VIII: VOCABULARY                       (STANFORD-BINET)
NCPP VARIABLE 85 = YEAR VIII: VERBAL ABSURDITIES               (STANFORD-BINET)
NCPP VARIABLE 86 = YEAR VIII: SIMS/DIFFS                       (STANFORD-BINET)
NCPP VARIABLE 87 = YEAR VIII: COMPREHENSION IV                 (STANFORD-BINET)
NCPP VARIABLE 88 = YEAR VIII: ALTERNATE                        (STANFORD-BINET)
NCPP VARIABLE 89 = YEAR IX: MEMORY FOR DESIGNS                 (STANFORD-BINET)
NCPP VARIABLE 90 = YEAR IX: RHYMES                             (STANFORD-BINET)
NCPP VARIABLE 91 = YEAR IX: MAKING CHANGE                      (STANFORD-BINET)
NCPP VARIABLE 92 = YEAR IX: REPEATING 4 DIGITS REVERSED        (STANFORD-BINET)
NCPP VARIABLE 93 = YEAR IX: ALTERNATE                          (STANFORD-BINET)
NCPP VARIABLE 94 = YEAR X: VOCABULARY                          (STANFORD-BINET)
NCPP VARIABLE 95 = YEAR X: ABSTRACT WORDS                      (STANFORD-BINET)
NCPP VARIABLE 96 = YEAR X: WORD NAMING                         (STANFORD-BINET)
NCPP VARIABLE 97 = YEAR X: REPEATING 6 DIGITS                  (STANFORD-BINET)
NCPP VARIABLE 98 = YEAR X: ALTERNATE
```

1	Mean-R	.92E-02
2	Mean-R	.11E-01
3	Mean-R	.27E-01
4	Mean-R	.54E-02
5	Mean-R	.17E-01
6	Mean-R	.60E-01
7	Mean-R	.10E-01
8	Mean-R	.28E-01
9	Mean-R	.17E-01
10	Mean-R	.14E-01
11	Mean-R	.89E-02
12	Mean-R	.71E-02

-.11(17260)

-.12(18235)

-.10(18234)

					Mean-R	
13					Mean-R	.75E-02
14					Mean-R	.89E-02
15					Mean-R	.11E-01
16					Mean-R	.99E-02
17					Mean-R	.83E-02
18					Mean-R	.26E-01
19					Mean-R	.19E-01
20					Mean-R	.11E-01
21					Mean-R	.11E-01
22					Mean-R	.78E-02
23	-.10(16392)			-.11(16473)	Mean-R	.24E-01
24	.11(16392)	.11(15885)	.11(15187)	.11(16473)	Mean-R	.43E-01
					Mean-R	.47E-01

704

25	Mean-R	.15E-01
26	Mean-R	.68E-02
27	Mean-R	.12E-01
28	Mean-R	.31E-01
29	Mean-R	.21E-01
30	Mean-R	.11E-01
31	Mean-R	.14E-01
32	Mean-R	.17E-01
33	Mean-R	.36E-01
34	Mean-R	.23E-01
35	Mean-R	.12E-01
36	Mean-R	.10E-01

		Mean-R	
37		Mean-R	.20E-01
38		Mean-R	.16E-01
39		Mean-R	.16E-01
40		Mean-R	.12E-01
41		Mean-R	.10E-01
42		Mean-R	.19E-01
43		Mean-R	.37E-01
44		Mean-R	.33E-01
45		Mean-R	.12E-01
46		Mean-R	.63E-02
47		Mean-R	.18E-01
48		Mean-R	.29E-01

49			-14(17545)							Mean-R .45E-01
50			-12(17488)							Mean-R .35E-01
51										Mean-R .14E-01
52	-22(17333)	-17(17527)	-14(17521)	-13(17113) -15(17372)	-17(17348) -17(17376) -20(16775)	-13(16880) -10(17495) -21(16128)	-20(17403)	-17(16831)	-20(17171)	Mean-R .11E+00
53	-26(17337)	-18(17532)	-10(16433) -15(17526)	-15(17114) -18(17377)	-19(17349) -21(17380) -25(16780)	-15(16880) -14(17500) -27(16129)	-23(17408)	-22(16834)	-21(17175)	Mean-R .13E+00
54	-23(17343)	-21(17538)	-13(16438) -19(17532)	-14(17119) -16(17383)	-18(17355) -18(17366) -21(16786)	-12(16886) -12(17506) -23(16135)	-22(17414)	-19(16840)	-21(17181)	Mean-R .12E+00
55	-13(17281)	-13(17471)	-14(17466)		-12(17291) -13(17324) -12(16730)	-11(16819) -10(17439) -14(16081)	-10(17348)	-12(16782)	-13(17122)	Mean-R .78E-01
56	-33(17350)	-24(17546)	-17(16446) -18(17540)	-18(17129) -24(17369) -10(16429)	-23(17364) -25(17393) -31(16792)	-15(16897) -15(17514) -34(16140)	-33(17420)	-26(16848)	-26(17188)	Mean-R .15E+00
57	-23(17348)	-16(17544)	-11(17538)	-10(17128) -15(17387)	-15(17369) -18(17391) -21(16788)	-11(16896) -13(17512) -23(16138)	-21(17418)	-19(16843)	-17(17184)	Mean-R .10E+00
58	-31(17332)	-20(17527)	-10(16434) -12(17521)	-15(17112) -23(17371)	-21(17349) -23(17375) -32(16776)	-10(16879) -14(17495) -33(16124)	-31(17402)	-27(16833)	-23(17171)	Mean-R .14E+00
59	-18(17428)	-13(17624)	-11(17618)	-13(17211) -11(17466)	-16(17452) -13(17470) -18(16864)	-10(16985) -11(17591) -19(16209)	-16(17499)	-16(16915)	-15(17264)	Mean-R .93E-01
60	-31(17342)	-16(17536)	-12(16440)	-16(17120) -20(17380) -12(16424)	-23(17354) -20(17386) -29(16784)	-13(16885) -13(17503) -31(16136)	-30(17411)	-23(16841)	-22(17181)	Mean-R .13E+00

No.									Mean-R
61	−37(17331)	−23(17525)	−15(16431) −14(17518)	−17(17106) −25(17369) −13(16414)	−25(17341) −26(17375) −35(16774)	−14(16874) −16(17492) −37(16127)	−29(16832)	−27(17170)	.16E+00
62	−31(17260)	−23(17452)	−16(16383) −15(17445)	−18(17048) −20(17296) −10(16345)	−21(17282) −24(17304) −29(16705)	−17(16816) −16(17420) −31(16062)	−26(16760)	−24(17101)	.15E+00
63	−46(17232) .10(17397)	−25(17422)	−18(16380) −14(17415)	−23(17043) −32(17269) −17(16316)	−31(17270) −32(17274) −45(16681)	−15(16809) −19(17389) −47(16036)	−35(16733)	−35(17074)	.19E+00
64	−40(17332)	−20(17524)	−14(16432)	−20(17109) −29(17368) −15(16412)	−23(17341) −29(17375) −40(16773)	−14(16875) −17(17491) −41(16126)	−32(16831)	−30(17171)	.17E+00
65	−29(17316)	−16(17508)	−11(16424) −11(17501)	−13(17098) −21(17352) −12(16398)	−21(17333) −24(17360) −28(16757)	−12(16864) −14(17475) −30(16113)	−23(16815)	−20(17155)	.13E+00
66	−44(17286)	−23(17475)	−16(16405) −12(17468)	−21(17079) −31(17320) −17(16372)	−27(17311) −32(17327) −43(16730)	−15(16843) −20(17442) −45(16091)	−33(16786)	−32(17125)	.19E+00
67	−42(17312)	−22(17503)	−15(16419)	−19(17089) −30(17347) −17(16392)	−26(17325) −29(17355) −42(16754)	−13(16856) −17(17470) −44(16108)	−33(16811)	−30(17151)	.18E+00
68	−41(17275)	−18(17464)	−13(16401)	−19(17076) −30(17309) −18(16362)	−21(17307) −30(17316) −42(16720)	−13(16840) −19(17431) −42(16079)	−32(16773)	−30(17115)	.17E+00
69	−39(17305)	−20(17496)	−13(16404)	−16(17075) −27(17340) −17(16387)	−23(17310) −27(17348) −41(16747)	−11(16842) −17(17463) −41(16101)	−33(16804)	−27(17144)	.16E+00
70	−37(17147)	−19(17334)	−12(16290)	−15(16952) −25(17178) −15(16233)	−22(17185) −27(17186) −34(16591)	−11(16722) −16(17301) −36(15954)	−26(16649)	−25(16989)	.15E+00
71	−39(17217)	−21(17408)	−15(16353) −11(17401)	−20(17021) −27(17253) −16(16304)	−24(17256) −28(17261) −38(16662)	−15(16788) −17(17375) −39(16022)	−30(16719)	−29(17057)	.17E+00
72	−27(17289)	−13(17481)	−10(16402)	−13(17075) −19(17324) −12(16371)	−15(17308) −20(17331) −29(16731)	−13(17448) −29(16085)	−25(16786)	−20(17128)	.12E+00

Row	Entries	Mean-R
73	−.43(17288), −.22(17479), −.17(16402), −.11(17472), −.21(17067), −.29(17322), −.16(16370), −.27(17302), −.30(17330), −.42(16732), −.15(16833), −.18(17446), −.43(16088), −.41(17353), −.33(16788), −.30(17128)	.18E+00
74	−.22(17345), −.10(17534), −.13(17378), −.14(16420), −.10(17401), −.14(17386), −.24(16780), −.12(17501), −.24(16135), −.21(17410), −.24(16834), −.14(17181)	.94E-01
75	−.15(17308), −.10(17343), −.12(17351), −.14(16749), −.15(16102), −.13(17374), −.11(16805)	.62E-01
76	−.27(17299), −.12(17489), −.13(17069), −.20(17333), −.12(16379), −.12(17302), −.20(17341), −.30(16741), −.13(17456), −.30(16094), −.33(17364), −.25(16797), −.20(17138)	.12E+00
77	−.26(17286), −.11(17476), −.12(17064), −.18(17320), −.12(16367), −.12(17298), −.18(17328), −.28(16731), −.12(17443), −.27(16083), −.29(17351), −.23(16784), −.18(17126)	.11E+00
78	−.18(17292), −.12(17326), −.11(16375), −.14(17334), −.20(16735), −.13(17449), −.20(16090), −.18(17357), −.20(16790), −.14(17131)	.79E-01
79	−.26(17284), −.11(17063), −.20(17316), −.12(16365), −.11(17295), −.20(17325), −.29(16728), −.14(17440), −.28(16082), −.32(17347), −.24(16781), −.20(17123)	.11E+00
80	−.11(17365)	.39E-01
81		.17E-01
82	−.11(16737), −.12(17359)	.40E-01
83	−.11(17290), −.13(17332), −.12(16733), −.15(17447), −.13(16085), −.11(17355), −.11(16788)	.54E-01
84	−.10(17297), −.12(16740), −.12(16092), −.15(17362), −.11(16795)	.46E-01

85	Mean-R	.75E-02
86	Mean-R	.14E-01
87	Mean-R	.17E-01
88	Mean-R	.70E-02
89	Mean-R	.67E-02
90	Mean-R	.71E-02
91	Mean-R	.64E-02
92	Mean-R	67E-02
93	Mean-R	.65E-02
94	Mean-R	.78E-02
95	Mean-R	.62E-02
96	Mean-R	.62E-02

97   Mean-R   .62E-02

98   Mean-R   .62E-02

VII. FIRST SCREEN CORRELATIONS
   INDICES WITH NCPP VARIABLES LISTED BELOW

NCPP VARIABLE 1 = EMOTIONAL REACTIVITY (SB): EXTREMELY FLAT
NCPP VARIABLE 2 = EMOTIONAL REACTIVITY (SB): SOMEWHAT FLAT
NCPP VARIABLE 3 = EMOTIONAL REACTIVITY (SB): NORMAL
NCPP VARIABLE 4 = EMOTIONAL REACTIVITY (SB): VARIES MORE THAN NORMAL
NCPP VARIABLE 5 = EMOTIONAL REACTIVITY (SB): EXTREME INSTABILITY
NCPP VARIABLE 6 = IRRITABILITY (SB): EXTREMELY PHLEGMATIC
NCPP VARIABLE 7 = IRRITABILITY (SB): RARELY ANNOYED
NCPP VARIABLE 8 = IRRITABILITY (SB) 2: NORMALLY REACTIVE
NCPP VARIABLE 9 = IRRITABILITY (SB): FREQUENTLY IRRITABLE
NCPP VARIABLE 10 = IRRITABILITY (SB): EXTREMELY IRRITABLE
NCPP VARIABLE 11 = DEGREE OF COOPERATION (SB): EXTREME NEGATIVISM
NCPP VARIABLE 12 = DEGREE OF COOPERATION (SB): RESISTIVE
NCPP VARIABLE 13 = DEGREE OF COOPERATION (SB): COOPERATIVE
NCPP VARIABLE 14 = DEGREE OF COOPERATION (SB): ACCEPTS DIRECTIONS MORE EASILY
NCPP VARIABLE 15 = DEGREE OF COOPERATION (SB): EXTREMELY SUGGESTIBLE
NCPP VARIABLE 16 = DEPENDENCY (SB): VERY SELF-RELIANT
NCPP VARIABLE 17 = DEPENDENCY (SB): RARELY NEEDS HELP
NCPP VARIABLE 18 = DEPENDENCY (SB): DEPENDENT IN APPROPRIATE SITUATION
NCPP VARIABLE 19 = DEPENDENCY (SB): DEMANDS MORE ATTENTION
NCPP VARIABLE 20 = DEPENDENCY (SB): CONSTANT NEED FOR ATTENTION
NCPP VARIABLE 21 = DURATION OF ATTENTION SPAN (SB): VERY BRIEF
NCPP VARIABLE 22 = DURATION OF ATTENTION SPAN (SB): SHORT TIME
NCPP VARIABLE 23 = DURATION OF ATTENTION SPAN (SB): ADEQUATE
NCPP VARIABLE 24 = DURATION OF ATTENTION SPAN (SB): MORE THAN AVERAGE
NCPP VARIABLE 25 = DURATION OF ATTENTION SPAN (SB): HIGHLY PERSEVERATIVE
NCPP VARIABLE 26 = GOAL ORIENTATION (SB): NO EFFORT
NCPP VARIABLE 27 = GOAL ORIENTATION (SB): BRIEF ATTEMPT
NCPP VARIABLE 28 = GOAL ORIENTATION (SB): ABLE TO KEEP GOAL IN MIND
NCPP VARIABLE 29 = GOAL ORIENTATION (SB): KEEPS GOAL AND QUESTIONS IN MIND
NCPP VARIABLE 30 = RESPONSE TO DIRECTIONS (SB): WONT FOLLOW SPECIFIC DIRECTION
NCPP VARIABLE 31 = RESPONSE TO DIRECTIONS (SB): SOME RESPONSIVENESS
NCPP VARIABLE 32 = RESPONSE TO DIRECTIONS (SB): RESPONDS TO DIRECTIONS
NCPP VARIABLE 33 = RESPONSE TO DIRECTIONS (SB): LITTLE DEVIATION FROM DIRECTION
NCPP VARIABLE 34 = RESPONSE TO DIRECTIONS (SB): COMPLETELY DEPENDENT ON DIRECTION
NCPP VARIABLE 35 = LEVEL OF ACTIVITY (SB): EXTREME INACTIVITY
NCPP VARIABLE 36 = LEVEL OF ACTIVITY (SB): LITTLE ACTIVITY
NCPP VARIABLE 37 = LEVEL OF ACTIVITY (SB): NORMAL ACTIVITY
NCPP VARIABLE 38 = LEVEL OF ACTIVITY (SB): UNUSUAL AMOUNT OF ACTIVITY
NCPP VARIABLE 39 = LEVEL OF ACTIVITY (SB): EXTREMELY IMPULSIVE
NCPP VARIABLE 40 = NATURE OF ACTIVITY (SB): EXTREME RIGIDITY
NCPP VARIABLE 41 = NATURE OF ACTIVITY (SB): SOME RIGIDITY
NCPP VARIABLE 42 = NATURE OF ACTIVITY (SB): FLEXIBLE BEHAVIOR
NCPP VARIABLE 43 = NATURE OF ACTIVITY (SB): FREQUENTLY IMPULSIVE
NCPP VARIABLE 44 = NATURE OF ACTIVITY (SB): EXTREMELY IMPULSIVE
NCPP VARIABLE 45 = NATURE OF ACTIVITY (SB): VARIABLE
NCPP VARIABLE 46 = NATURE OF COMMUNICATION (SB): NONVERBAL
NCPP VARIABLE 47 = NATURE OF COMMUNICATION (SB): ONLY TO DIRECTED QUESTIONS
NCPP VARIABLE 48 = NATURE OF COMMUNICATION (SB): INCLUDES SPON CONVERSATION
NCPP VARIABLE 49 = NATURE OF COMMUNICATION (SB): ANSWERS AND SPON CONTENT
NCPP VARIABLE 51 = DEVIANT BEHAVIOR (SB): DROPPING OFF TABLE
NCPP VARIABLE 52 = DEVIANT BEHAVIOR (SB): THUMB SUCK
NCPP VARIABLE 53 = DEVIANT BEHAVIOR (SB): NAIL BITE
NCPP VARIABLE 54 = DEVIANT BEHAVIOR (SB): HAND MOTIONS
NCPP VARIABLE 55 = DEVIANT BEHAVIOR (SB): SMILING AND LAUGHING
NCPP VARIABLE 56 = DEVIANT BEHAVIOR (SB): CRYING
NCPP VARIABLE 57 = DEVIANT BEHAVIOR (SB): ECHOLALIA
NCPP VARIABLE 58 = CHILD IN NURSERY SCHOOL
NCPP VARIABLE 59 = NO MIN TEMP BELOW 95 (AXILLARY), 96 (RECTAL)

#														Mean-R
1					-.11(16290)									.47E-01
2	-.16(17519)	-.10(17732)	-.12(17562)	-.12(17559) -.14(16947)	-.11(16290)	-.14(17605)	-.10(16996)	-.16(17348)						.69E-01
3	.22(17519)	.14(17732)	.11(17731)	.12(17246) .15(17562)	.13(17514) .17(17559) .19(16947)	.11(17042) .11(17694) .21(16290)	.18(17605)	.16(16996)	.19(17348)					.10E+00
4														.45E-01
5														.33E-01
6														.38E-01
7														.20E-01
8	.12(17506)			.10(17546)		.11(16277)	.11(17590)	.11(17334)						.62E-01
9														.49E-01
10														.30E-01
11														.31E-01
12	-.12(17520)			-.10(17559) -.11(16946)	-.12(16289)									.59E-01

Row										Mean-R
13										.38E-01
14										.26E-01
15										.19E-01
16	.16(17539)									.25E-01
17										.33E-01
18										.53E-01
19	-.11(17470)					-.11(16246)				.58E-01
20				-.10(17510)						.50E-01
21	-.15(17468)		-.12(17678)	-.11(17512)	-.13(17485) -.13(17508) -.13(16901)		-.13(17554)	-.13(16950)	-.11(17299)	.77E-01
22	-.20(17468)	-.12(17679)		-.12(17224) -.11(17512)	-.13(17485) -.15(17508) -.19(16901)	-.11(17642) -.21(16245)	-.15(17554)	-.19(16950)	-.14(17299)	.93E-01
23	.23(17468)	.14(17679)	.10(16495) .12(17678)	.15(17224) .14(17512)	.16(17485) .19(17508) .22(16901)	.11(17018) .14(17642) .24(16245)	.18(17554)	.21(16950)	.17(17299)	.11E+00
24										.14E-01

											Mean-R	
25	.13(17535)										Mean-R	.39E-01
26	-.11(17478)						-.11(17565)				Mean-R	.55E-01
27	-.26(17478)	-.15(17690)	-.11(16497) -.13(17688)	-.17(17236) -.16(17523) -.10(16538)	-.18(17494) -.21(17518) -.25(16910)	-.12(17031) -.16(17652) -.27(16255)	-.12(16255) -.20(17565)	-.24(16961)	-.19(17309)		Mean-R	.13E+00
28	.22(17478)	.14(17690)	.10(16497) .13(17688)	.15(17236) .14(17523)	.17(17494) .18(17518) .21(16910)	.11(17031) .14(17652) .23(16255)	.17(17565)	.20(16961)	.16(17309)		Mean-R	.11E+00
29	.11(17478)				.11(16910)		.10(17565)				Mean-R	.47E-01
30	-.11(17510)	-.11(17721)		-.12(17508) -.11(17550)	-.10(17041) -.10(16281)		-.11(17597)				Mean-R	.64E-01
31	-.20(17510)	-.12(17723)	-.10(17721)	-.13(17244) -.12(17554)	-.13(17508) -.17(17550) -.18(16939)	-.12(17685) -.20(16281)	-.15(17597)	-.17(16990)	-.15(17338)		Mean-R	.97E-01
32	.24(17510)	.15(17723)	.11(16502) .13(17721)	.16(17244) .16(17554)	.16(17508) .21(17550) .21(16939)	.13(17041) .13(17685) .23(16281)	.20(17597)	.18(16990)	.20(17338)		Mean-R	.12E+00
33											Mean-R	.22E-01
34											Mean-R	.23E-01
35											Mean-R	.39E-01
36										-.10(17335)	Mean-R	.40E-01

715

37	.17(17506)		.10(17718)	.10(17241)	.11(17507).12(17546).15(16934)	.16(16279)	.13(17591)	.13(16987)	.15(17335)	Mean-R .77E-01
38										Mean-R .40E-01
39										Mean-R .37E-01
40		.14(17567)								Mean-R .44E-01
41	-.17(17514)		-.11(17557)	-.10(17517)-.14(17554)-.13(16941)		-.15(16285)	-.13(17600)	-.10(16994)	-.13(17343)	Mean-R .74E-01
42	.28(17514)	.15(17727)	.11(16511).13(17726)	.12(17250).15(17557)	.16(17517).19(17554).20(16941)	.13(17689).21(16285)	.18(17600)	.17(16994)	.18(17343)	Mean-R .11E+00
43	-.10(17471)					-.10(16250)		-.10(16953)		Mean-R .53E-01
44										Mean-R .30E-01
45		.14(17539)								Mean-R .22E-01
46	-.11(17475)	.10(17648)	-.16(17687)-.22(17685)		-.12(17487)-.10(17518)	-.16(17012)	-.14(17560)		-.13(17304)	Mean-R .79E-01
47	-.18(17475)		-.12(17687)	-.10(17220)-.13(17517)	-.14(17515)-.17(16903)	-.12(17012)-.17(16247)	-.16(17560)	-.12(16954)	-.16(17304)	Mean-R .78E-01
48	.14(17475)			.11(17516).13(16903)	.11(17012).13(16247)	.12(17560)	.10(16954)	.12(17304)	Mean-R .66E-01

No.	Values	Mean-R
49		.33E-01
50		.27E-01
51		.29E-01
52		.20E-01
53		.20E-01
54		.51E-02
55		.17E-01
56		.28E-01
57	-.14(17255) -.17(17520) -.12(17055) -.10(17559) -.11(16943) -.13(16288) -.11(17603) -.10(16995) -.11(17348)	.23E-01 .70E-01
58	-.12(17046) -.13(16481) -.12(15838) -.14(17123) -.11(16540) -.10(16877)	.54E-01
59	-.13(17519)	.17E-01

717

VIII. FIRST SCREEN CORRELATIONS
   INDICES WITH NCPP VARIABLES LISTED BELOW

NCPP VARIABLE 1 = VISUAL ACUITY WITHOUT GLASSES LEFT EYE
NCPP VARIABLE 2 = VISUAL ACUITY WITHOUT GLASSES RIGHT EYE
NCPP VARIABLE 3 = MUSCLE BALANCE: W/O GLASSES—YES ON TABLE
NCPP VARIABLE 4 = MUSCLE BALANCE: W/O GLASSES—OFF TABLE, NO PICTURE
NCPP VARIABLE 5 = MUSCLE BALANCE: W/O GLASSES—NOT SEEN OR OFF TABLE
NCPP VARIABLE 6 = BENDER GESTALT TEST: TOTAL SCORE
NCPP VARIABLE 7 = WECHSLER VERBAL: INFORMATION SCALED SCORE
NCPP VARIABLE 8 = WECHSLER VERBAL: COMPREHENSIVE SCALED SCORE
NCPP VARIABLE 9 = WECHSLER VERBAL: VOCABULARY SCALED SCORE
NCPP VARIABLE 10 = WECHSLER VERBAL: DIGIT SPAN SCALED SCORE
NCPP VARIABLE 11 = WECHSLER PERFORM: PICT ARRANGEMENT SCALED SCORE
NCPP VARIABLE 12 = WECHSLER PERFORM: BLOCK DESIGN SCALED SCORE
NCPP VARIABLE 13 = WECHSLER PERFORM: CODING SCALED SCORE
NCPP VARIABLE 14 = WECHSLER PRORATED: VERBAL IQ
NCPP VARIABLE 15 = WECHSLER PRORATED: PERFORMANCE IQ
NCPP VARIABLE 16 = WECHSLER PRORATED: FULL SCALE IQ
NCPP VARIABLE 17 = WECHSLER PRORATED: ADEQUACY OF EXAM
NCPP VARIABLE 18 = AUDITORY VOCAL ASSOC TEST: RAW SCORE
NCPP VARIABLE 19 = AUDITORY VOCAL ASSOCIATION ADEQUACY OF EXAM
NCPP VARIABLE 20 = GOODENOUGH-HARRIS DRAWING TEST: RAW SCORE
NCPP VARIABLE 21 = TACTILE FINGER TEST: TOTAL
NCPP VARIABLE 22 = WRAT: CURRENT GRADE IN MONTHS
NCPP VARIABLE 23 = WRAT: CURRENT GRADE NON-GRADED, SPECIAL CLASS
NCPP VARIABLE 24 = WRAT: CURRENT GRADE: DOES NOT ATTEND SCHOOL
NCPP VARIABLE 25 = WRAT: REPEATING GRADE
NCPP VARIABLE 26 = WRAT: REPEATING GRADE—NEVER ATTENDED SCHOOL
NCPP VARIABLE 27 = WRAT: SPECIAL SPEECH CLASS
NCPP VARIABLE 28 = WRAT: SPELLING RAW SCORE
NCPP VARIABLE 29 = WRAT: READING RAW SCORE
NCPP VARIABLE 30 = WRAT: MATH RAW SCORE
NCPP VARIABLE 31 = WRAT: ADEQUACY OF EXAM   (7YR PSYCH)
NCPP VARIABLE 32 = BEHAV: SEP FROM MOTHER—NO CONCERN   (7YR PSYCH)
NCPP VARIABLE 33 = BEHAV: SEP FROM MOTHER—LITTLE CONCERN   (7YR PSYCH)
NCPP VARIABLE 34 = BEHAV: SEP FROM MOTHER—APPROP RETICENCE   (7YR PSYCH)
NCPP VARIABLE 35 = BEHAV: SEP FROM MOTHER—MORE THAN USUAL CONC   (7YR PSYCH)
NCPP VARIABLE 36 = BEHAV: SEP FROM MOTHER—VERY UPSET   (7YR PSYCH)
NCPP VARIABLE 37 = BEHAV: FEARFULNESS—NONE   (7YR PSYCH)
NCPP VARIABLE 38 = BEHAV: FEARFULNESS—VERY LITTLE   (7YR PSYCH)
NCPP VARIABLE 39 = BEHAV: FEARFULNESS—NORMAL   (7YR PSYCH)
NCPP VARIABLE 40 = BEHAV: FEARFULNESS—INHIBITED   (7YR PSYCH)
NCPP VARIABLE 41 = BEHAV: FEARFULNESS—VERY FEARFUL   (7YR PSYCH)
NCPP VARIABLE 42 = BEHAV: RAPPORT W EXAMINER: EXCEPTIONLY SHY   (7YR PSYCH)
NCPP VARIABLE 43 = BEHAV: RAPPORT W EXAMINER—SHY   (7YR PSYCH)
NCPP VARIABLE 44 = BEHAV: RAPPORT W EXAMINER—INIT SHY, AT EASE   (7YR PSYCH)
NCPP VARIABLE 45 = BEHAV: RAPPORT W EXAMINER—FRIENDLY   (7YR PSYCH)
NCPP VARIABLE 46 = BEHAV: RAPPORT W EXAMINER—EXT FRIENDLY   (7YR PSYCH)
NCPP VARIABLE 47 = BEHAV: SELF-CONFIDENCE—LACKING, EXT SELF CRIT   (7YR PSYCH)
NCPP VARIABLE 48 = BEHAV: SELF-CONFIDENCE—DISTRUST OWN ABILITY   (7YR PSYCH)
NCPP VARIABLE 49 = BEHAV: SELF-CONFIDENCE—ADEQUATE
NCPP VARIABLE 50 = BEHAV: SELF-CONFIDENCE—MORE THAN USUAL   (7YR PSYCH)
NCPP VARIABLE 51 = BEHAV: SELF-CONFIDENCE—VERY   (7YR PSYCH)
NCPP VARIABLE 52 = BEHAV: SELF-CONFIDENCE—VARIABLE   (7YR PSYCH)
NCPP VARIABLE 53 = BEHAV: EMOT REACTIVITY—EXT FLAT   (7YR PSYCH)
NCPP VARIABLE 54 = BEHAV: EMOT REACTIVITY—SOMEWHAT FLAT   (7YR PSYCH)
NCPP VARIABLE 55 = BEHAV: EMOT REACTIVITY—NORMAL   (7YR PSYCH)
NCPP VARIABLE 56 = BEHAV: EMOT REACTIVITY—MORE VARIABLE THN AVRG   (7YR PSYCH)
NCPP VARIABLE 57 = BEHAV: EMOT REACTIVITY—EXT INSTABILITY   (7YR PSYCH)
NCPP VARIABLE 58 = BEHAV: DEG OF COOPERATION—EXT NEGATIVISM   (7YR PSYCH)
NCPP VARIABLE 59 = BEHAV: DEG OF COOPERATION—RESISTIVE   (7YR PSYCH)
NCPP VARIABLE 60 = BEHAV: DEG OF COOPERATION—COOPERATIVE   (7YR PSYCH)
NCPP VARIABLE 61 = BEHAV: DEG OF COOPERATION—ACCEPTS DIR EASILY   (7YR PSYCH)
NCPP VARIABLE 62 = BEHAV: DEG OF COOPERATION—EXT SUGGESTIBLE   (7YR PSYCH)
NCPP VARIABLE 63 = BEHAV: LEVEL OF FRUSTRA TOL—WITHDR COMPLETE   (7YR PSYCH)

718

NCPP VARIABLE 64 = BEHAV: LEVEL OF FRUSTRA TOL—OCCAS WITHDR   (7YR PSYCH)
NCPP VARIABLE 65 = BEHAV: LEVEL OF FRUSTRA TOL—ATTEMPTS TO COPE   (7YR PSYCH)
NCPP VARIABLE 66 = BEHAV: LEVEL OF FRUSTRA TOL—QUITE UPSET   (7YR PSYCH)
NCPP VARIABLE 67 = BEHAV: LEVEL OF FRUSTRA TOL—EXT ACTING—OUT BEHAV   (7YR PSYCH)
NCPP VARIABLE 68 = BEHAV: LEVEL OF FRUSTRA TOL—VARIABLE   (7YR PSYCH)
NCPP VARIABLE 69 = BEHAV: DEG OF DEPEND—VERY SELF RELIANT   (7YR PSYCH)
NCPP VARIABLE 70 = BEHAV: DEG OF DEPEND—RARELY NEEDS REASSURANCE   (7YR PSYCH)
NCPP VARIABLE 71 = BEHAV: DEG OF DEPEND—APPROPRIATE DEPENDENCY   (7YR PSYCH)
NCPP VARIABLE 72 = BEHAV: DEG OF DEPEND—DEMANDS MORE THAN AV ATTN   (7YR PSYCH)
NCPP VARIABLE 73 = BEHAV: DEG OF DEPEND—CONSTANTLY NEEDS ATTN   (7YR PSYCH)
NCPP VARIABLE 74 = BEHAV: DUR ATT SPAN—VERY BRIEF   (7YR PSYCH)
NCPP VARIABLE 75 = BEHAV: DUR ATT SPAN—SHORT   (7YR PSYCH)
NCPP VARIABLE 76 = BEHAV: DUR ATT SPAN—ADEQUATE   (7YR PSYCH)
NCPP VARIABLE 77 = BEHAV: DUR ATT SPAN—ABOVE AVERAGE   (7YR PSYCH)
NCPP VARIABLE 78 = BEHAV: DUR ATT SPAN—HIGH PERSEVERATIVE   (7YR PSYCH)
NCPP VARIABLE 79 = BEHAV: DUR ATT SPAN—VARIABLE   (7YR PSYCH)
NCPP VARIABLE 80 = BEHAV: GOAL ORIENT—NO EFFORT   (7YR PSYCH)
NCPP VARIABLE 81 = BEHAV: GOAL ORIENT—BRIEF ATTEMPT   (7YR PSYCH)
NCPP VARIABLE 82 = BEHAV: GOAL ORIENT—ABLE KEEP GOAL IN MIND   (7YR PSYCH)
NCPP VARIABLE 83 = BEHAV: GOAL ORIENT—KEEP GOAL AND QUEST IN MIND   (7YR PSYCH)
NCPP VARIABLE 84 = BEHAV: GOAL ORIENT—COMPULSIVE ABSORPTION   (7YR PSYCH)
NCPP VARIABLE 85 = BEHAV: GOAL ORIENT—VARIABLE   (7YR PSYCH)
NCPP VARIABLE 86 = BEHAV: LEVEL ACTIVITY—EXTREME INACTIVITY   (7YR PSYCH)
NCPP VARIABLE 87 = BEHAV: LEVEL ACTIVITY—LITTLE ACTIVITY   (7YR PSYCH)
NCPP VARIABLE 88 = BEHAV: LEVEL ACTIVITY—NORMAL AMT ACTIVITY   (7YR PSYCH)
NCPP VARIABLE 89 = BEHAV: LEVEL ACTIVITY—UNUSUAL AMT ACTIVITY   (7YR PSYCH)
NCPP VARIABLE 90 = BEHAV: LEVEL ACTIVITY—EXTREME OVERACTIVITY   (7YR PSYCH)
NCPP VARIABLE 91 = BEHAV: NATURE ACTIVITY—EXT INACT. PASSIVITY   (7YR PSYCH)
NCPP VARIABLE 92 = BEHAV: NATURE ACTIVITY—LITTLE ACTIVITY   (7YR PSYCH)
NCPP VARIABLE 93 = BEHAV: NATURE ACTIVITY—NORMAL AMOUNT   (7YR PSYCH)
NCPP VARIABLE 94 = BEHAV: NATURE ACTIVITY—UNUSUAL AMOUNT   (7YR PSYCH)
NCPP VARIABLE 95 = BEHAV: NATURE ACTIVITY—EXT OVERACTIVITY   (7YR PSYCH)
NCPP VARIABLE 96 = BEHAV: NATURE ACTIVITY—VARIABLE   (7YR PSYCH)

Row	1	2	3	4	5	6	7	8	9	Mean-R
1										.38E-01
2	-.11(16478)									.40E-01
3										.36E-01
4										.33E-01
5	.57(16478) .10(18791)		.23(18737) .51(18727)	.17(18574) .45(17595)	.18(18588)		.30(13769) .52(18607)	.17(18138)		.16E+00
6	-.47(18937)	-.25(19150) -.13(19145)	-.14(15903) -.13(19145)	-.16(16636) -.26(18975) -.17(17924)	-.22(16889) -.28(18977) -.48(18332)	-.14(16449) -.23(19108) -.50(17605)	-.20(19014) -.47(18840)	-.35(18750)	-.15(17255)	.18E+00
7	.11(14775) .57(18919)	.25(19127)	.17(15924) .15(19120)	.23(16654) .37(18959) .17(17915)	.26(16888) .41(18963) .57(18326)	.20(16456) .28(19088) .58(17595)	.12(14137) .26(18989)	.49(18839)	.41(18737)	.22E+00
8	.36(18911)	.17(19119)	.11(15916)	.13(16646) .27(18951) .10(17907)	.21(16879) .28(18955) .33(18318)	.12(16448) .15(19079) .34(17588)	.19(18980)	.23(18832)	.28(18730)	.14E+00
9	.64(18897) -.13(19152)	.32(19105)	.19(15906) .16(19098)	.19(16631) .46(18937) .19(17893)	.29(16862) .45(18941) .63(18304)	.15(16433) .25(19065) .62(17575)	.35(18966)	.45(18821)	.47(18717)	.24E+00
10	.50(18910)	.25(19118)	.17(15917) .16(19111)	.23(16644) .27(18950) .17(17905)	.23(16875) .46(18954) .51(18317)	.19(16445) .53(19078) .58(17586)	.16(14132) .19(18979)	.51(18833)	.35(18728)	.22E+00
11	.56(18931) -.11(19190)	.26(19142)	.15(15925) .13(19136)	.16(16657) .38(18971) .19(17923)	.24(16902) .38(18973) .58(18334)	.13(16465) .21(19100) .57(17602)	.28(19004)	.46(18844)	.41(18747)	.21E+00
12	.46(18929)	.23(19140)	.13(15924) .11(19134)	.12(16654) .29(18969) .19(17921)	.21(16900) .29(18971) .47(18332)	.10(16464) .20(19098) .48(17600)	.28(19002)	.40(18844)	.33(18746)	.17E+00

	C1	C2	C3	C4	C5	C6	C7	C8	C9	C10	Mean-R
13	.19(18906)		.14(19116)		.11(16638) / .11(18846)	.11(16883) / .14(18949) / .20(18310)	.22(17580)		.25(18823)	.15(18723)	.87E-01
14	.35(18916)	.50(16933)	.15(19124)	.11(15919) / .27(19117) / .42(19108)	.23(16650) / .40(18956) / .53(17912)	.16(16882) / .43(18960) / .39(18323)	.18(19084) / .23(17593)	.32(14134) / .61(18985)	.47(18837)	.25(18735)	.24E+00
15	.31(18911)	.43(16931)	.15(19121)	.27(19115) / .35(19104)	.17(16641) / .32(18951) / .47(17905)	.13(16885) / .32(18955) / .37(18316)	.10(19080) / .21(17586)	.26(14128) / .45(18983)	.45(18829)	.23(18728)	.20E+00
16	.43(18947)	.49(16963)	.22(19178)	.11(15919) / .32(19175) / .34(19144)	.23(16668) / .40(18997) / .50(17923)	.18(16915) / .49(18989) / .50(18355)	.21(19132) / .31(17602)	.29(14134) / .51(19036)	.54(18846)	.32(18763)	.25E+00
17	-.10(18893)	.10(19260)		.15(19229) / .36(19191)	.13(19041) / .41(17960)		-.18(17634)	.44(19086)	.14(18874)		.14E+00
18	.70(18863)	.10(19004) / -.16(19118)	.40(19077)	.23(15878) / .22(19069)	.25(16614) / .46(18906) / .17(17850)	.37(16853) / .48(18907) / .68(18270)	.22(16416) / .31(19040) / .71(17523)	.30(18938)	.53(18791)	.55(18676)	.27E+00
19	-.11(18956)	.46(16949)		.34(19150)	.37(17933)	.14(18997)	-.18(17606)	.23(14124) / .36(19038)	.17(18869)	-.11(18767)	.15E+00
20	.36(18917)		.21(19130)	.14(15896)	.16(16628) / .15(18958) / .11(17905)	.16(16878) / .24(18857) / .35(18317)	.14(16440) / .22(19090) / .39(17583)		.38(18861)	.26(18733)	.18E+00
21	.17(18921)	.23(16907)	.14(19133)	.18(19130) / .16(19116)	.16(16616) / .13(18958) / .24(17899)	.19(18961) / .20(18322)	.13(17578)	.19(14104) / .23(18994)	.27(18872)	.14(18736)	.12E+00
22	.12(18886)	-.12(16867)				.12(18294)	.12(19053) / .16(17558)		.27(18827)		.68E-01
23			-.13(19208)	-.19(19207)			-.13(16489)				.60E-01
24			-.12(19208)	-.15(19207)			-.11(16489)				.56E-01

Row 25: −.21(18942) −.12(19166) −.10(15892) −.10(16634) / −.11(18987) −.16(18983) / −.23(18344) −.11(16451) / −.13(19122) / −.26(17597) −.29(18870) −.17(18757) Mean-R .10E+00

Row 26: −.12(14779) / −.13(18974) .64(16971) / .11(19240) −.13(19206) .49(19170) .14(19020) / .50(17940) .15(19014) −.12(16488) / −.11(19160) / −.22(17615) .28(14128) / .51(19063) .15(18890) −.10(18783) Mean-R .17E+00

Row 27: .64(16934) / .10(19208) .24(19161) / .49(19140) .11(18988) / .46(17916) .15(18984) .31(14111) / .40(19027) −.17(17598) .14(18871) Mean-R .16E+00

Row 28: .56(18925) .31(19137) .18(15883) / .19(19133) .25(16620) / .30(18965) / .22(17902) .22(16868) / .39(18965) / .66(18325) .16(16429) / .32(19098) / .64(17579) .14(14103) / .24(19001) .84(18893) .41(18739) Mean-R .24E+00

Row 29: .59(18936) / −.11(19191) .32(19146) .19(15889) / .17(19142) .24(16626) / .30(18975) / .17(17915) .21(16871) / .38(18976) / .70(18335) .17(16432) / .34(19108) / .70(17591) .11(14109) / .21(19009) .85(18893) .43(18749) Mean-R .24E+00

Row 30: .11(14747) .58(18932) / −.11(19187) .33(19142) .18(15892) / .22(19137) .23(16629) / .29(18973) / .14(17912) .26(16871) / .38(18973) / .60(18333) .20(16433) / .33(19104) / .66(17590) .10(14111) / .16(19006) .67(18889) .44(18745) Mean-R .24E+00

Row 31: −.31(16952) −.23(19179) / −.26(19155) −.17(19004) / −.30(17933) −.14(19001) −.22(14125) / −.36(19043) −.20(18893) Mean-R .11E+00

Row 32: .25(12866) .17(14255) .19(13346) .13(10927) / .22(14205) Mean-R .72E-01

Row 33: Mean-R .14E-01

Row 34: Mean-R .28E-01

Row 35: Mean-R .38E-01

Row 36: .11(12866) Mean-R .31E-01

#									
37		.31(16962)	.22(19159)	.23(17929)		-.11(17604)	.16(14117) .22(19052)		Mean-R .82E-01
38									Mean-R .24E-01
39									Mean-R .31E-01
40	-.12(18962)				-.11(19003)			-.12(18771)	Mean-R .41E-01
41									Mean-R .24E-01
42	-.13(18952)	.20(16945)	.13(19148)	.13(17921)		-.14(17596)	.12(14109) .10(19041)	-.13(18761)	Mean-R .64E-01
43	-.14(18952)	-.12(18993) -.12(18352)	-.12(18999)		-.11(17596)	-.11(17596)		-.13(18761)	Mean-R .51E-01
44									Mean-R .26E-01
45	.12(18952)				.10(18352)	.11(17596)			Mean-R .39E-01
46									Mean-R .88E-02
47		.26(16935)	.16(19115)	.17(17897)		-.11(17576)	.12(14111) .18(19004)		Mean-R .65E-01
48	-.16(18923)		-.11(18966)		-.14(18966) -.15(18324)	-.15(17576)		-.13(18735)	Mean-R .63E-01

No.	Values	Mean-R
49	.12(18923) .10(18324) .13(17576)	.46E-01
50	.10(18923) .11(18324)	.35E-01
51		.87E-02
52	.15(16935)	.30E-01
53	.25(16961) .18(19158) .19(17927) -.11(18963) .14(14117) .16(19052) -.11(18772)	.74E-01
54	-.17(18963) -.13(19009) -.14(19002) -.16(18363) -.14(17604) -.15(18878) -.17(18772)	.72E-01
55	.12(19195) .21(18963) .10(16655) .12(19009) .10(16915) .15(19002) .20(18363) .11(16480) .11(19148) .22(17604) .17(18878) .20(18772)	.86E-01
56		.30E-01
57		.27E-01
58	.39(16957) .32(19153) .31(17922) .21(14114) .34(19047) .10(18872)	.11E+00
59	-.10(18956) -.10(18355) -.17(17597)	.47E-01
60		.41E-01

724

No.						Mean-R
61						.99E-02
62	.16(16957)			.12(19047)		.44E-01
63	.28(16957)	.16(19147)	.19(17922)	-.12(17597)	.15(14116) .15(19037)	.73E-01
64	-.17(18950)		-.12(18995)	-.14(18990) -.16(18349)	-.16(17597)	-.15(18873) -.14(18760)	.68E-01
65	.13(18950)		.11(18995)	.14(18990) .17(18343)	.10(19134) .19(17597)	.14(18873)	.16(18760)	.71E-01
66						.63E-02
67						.20E-01
68						.24E-01
69	.52(16955) .10(19212)	.17(19178) .35(19144)	.12(18994) .38(17915)	.12(18990)	-.16(17593)	.23(14114) .40(19036)	.13(18869)	.13E+00
70						.30E-01
71	.11(18950)			.11(18349)	.11(17593)	.11(18760)	.57E-01
72	-.14(18950)			-.13(18990) -.14(18349)	-.14(17593)	-.15(18869) -.13(18760)	.67E-01

725

| 73 | | -.12(18850) | | -.11(19178) | | -.10(18990) -.11(18349) | | -.10(18869) -.11(18760) | Mean-R .61E-01 |

73 -.12(18850) -.11(19178) -.10(18990) / -.11(18349) -.10(18869) / -.11(18760) Mean-R .61E-01

74 -.16(18954) .23(16953) -.14(19184) .18(19149) -.11(16909) / -.12(18354) .16(17920) -.14(16474) / -.12(19137) / -.20(17597) .15(19040) -.14(18765) Mean-R .96E-01

75 -.18(18954) -.11(16652) / -.10(18899) -.15(18994) / -.18(18354) -.12(19137) / -.20(17597) -.20(18875) / -.13(18765) Mean-R .82E-01

76 .19(18954) .11(19184) .10(16652) / .10(18899) .11(16909) / .14(18994) / .18(18354) .10(16474) / .13(19137) / .22(17597) .19(18875) / .15(18765) Mean-R .84E-01

77 Mean-R .64E-02

78 Mean-R .21E-01

79 Mean-R .14E-01

80 -.11(18954) .41(16953) / -.10(19186) .32(19149) / .34(17921) .24(14116) / .33(19043) -.19(17597) Mean-R .17E+00

81 -.24(18954) -.13(19186) -.12(19185) / -.14(19001) -.20(18964) / -.24(18358) -.16(19140) / -.26(17597) -.26(18876) / -.18(18765) Mean-R .11E+00

82 .15(18954) .10(18994) / .13(18353) .11(19140) / .17(17597) .13(18876) / .12(18765) Mean-R .67E-01

83 .13(18954) .10(18994) / .14(18353) .14(17597) .14(18876) Mean-R .51E-01

84 Mean-R .44E-02

85										Mean-R .13E-01
86	.37(16966)	-.10(18968)	.28(19163)			.20(14123) .29(19056)				Mean-R .10E+00
87		-.11(18968)	.27(17934)		-.16(17609)			-.11(18778)		Mean-R .46E-01
88		.15(18968)		.11(19008) .14(18367)	.16(17609)		.14(18884)	.14(18778)		Mean-R .78E-01
89							-.11(18884)			Mean-R .37E-01
90										Mean-R .39E-01
91	.42(16956)	-.12(18959)	.30(19156)	.33(17927)	-.11(16474) -.18(17604)	.23(14119) .31(19049)		-.10(18771)		Mean-R .39E-01
92		-.17(18959)		-.11(19006)	-.15(18999) -.15(18358)	-.16(17604)		-.14(18879)	-.15(18771)	Mean-R .70E-01
93		.21(18959)	.13(19191)	.10(19006)	.11(16910) .15(18999) .19(18358)	.11(16474) .13(19144) .22(17604)		.17(18879)	.17(18771)	Mean-R .87E-01
94										Mean-R .39E-01
95										Mean-R .20E-01
96	.74(16950)	-.10(14762)	.29(19182) .54(19151)	.14(19000) .55(17921)	.22(18993)	-.19(17594)	.31(14112) .57(19043)	.16(18873)		Mean-R .18E+00

727

IX. FIRST SCREEN CORRELATIONS
   INDICES WITH NCPP VARIABLES LISTED BELOW

NCPP VARIABLE 1 = BEHAV: NATURE OF COMM—LITTLE OR NONE   (7YR PSYCH)
NCPP VARIABLE 2 = BEHAV: NATURE OF COMM—ANSWERING DIRECTED QUESTIONS   (7YR PSYCH)
NCPP VARIABLE 3 = BEHAV: NATURE OF COMM—READILY ANSWERS QUESTIONS   (7YR PSYCH)
NCPP VARIABLE 4 = BEHAV: NATURE OF COMM—ANSWERS FREELY   (7YR PSYCH)
NCPP VARIABLE 5 = BEHAV: NATURE OF COMM—DIFF TO FOLLOW CHILD THINKING   (7YR PSYCH)
NCPP VARIABLE 6 = BEHAV: ASSERTIVENESS—EXTREMELY ASSERTIVE, WILLFUL   (7YR PSYCH)
NCPP VARIABLE 7 = BEHAV: ASSERTIVENESS—QUITE FORCEFUL   (7YR PSYCH)
NCPP VARIABLE 8 = BEHAV: ASSERTIVENESS—SELF-ASSERTIVE, ACCEPTS SIT   (7YR PSYCH)
NCPP VARIABLE 9 = BEHAV: ASSERTIVENESS—PASSIVE ACCEPTANCE   (7YR PSYCH)
NCPP VARIABLE 10 = BEHAV: ASSERTIVENESS—EXTREME PASSIVITY   (7YR PSYCH)
NCPP VARIABLE 11 = BEHAV: HOSTILITY—VERY HOSTILE   (7YR PSYCH)
NCPP VARIABLE 12 = BEHAV: HOSTILITY—UNUSUAL AMOUNT OF HOSTILITY   (7YR PSYCH)
NCPP VARIABLE 13 = BEHAV: HOSTILITY—NO UNUSUAL AMOUNT   (7YR PSYCH)
NCPP VARIABLE 14 = BEHAV: HOSTILITY—VERY AGREEABLE   (7YR PSYCH)
NCPP VARIABLE 15 = DEVIANT BEHAVIOUR: EXCESSIVE THUMB SUCKING   (7YR PSYCH)
NCPP VARIABLE 16 = DEVIANT BEHAVIOUR: EXCESSIVE NAIL BITING   (7YR PSYCH)
NCPP VARIABLE 17 = DEVIANT BEHAVIOUR: UNUSUAL, MEANINGLESS HAND MOTION   (7YR PSYCH)
NCPP VARIABLE 18 = DEVIANT BEHAV: MEANINGLESS SMILING AND LAUGHING   (7YR PSYCH)
NCPP VARIABLE 19 = DEVIANT BEHAV: CRYING   (7YR PSYCH)
NCPP VARIABLE 20 = DEVIANT BEHAV: ECHOLALIA   (7YR PSYCH)
NCPP VARIABLE 21 = DEVIANT BEHAV—OTHER OBVIOUS SPEECH DIFFICULTIES   (7YR PSYCH)
NCPP VARIABLE 22 = HANDEDNESS   (7YR PSYCH)
NCPP VARIABLE 23 = 7 YR NON-NEUROLOGICAL ABNORMALITIES   (7YR PSYCH)
NCPP VARIABLE 24 = CHILD LIVES WITH—MA AND PA, PA AND STPMA, MA AND STPPA   (FHH-9)
NCPP VARIABLE 25 = CHILD LIVES WITH—MOTHER ONLY   (FHH-9)
NCPP VARIABLE 26 = CHILD LIVES WITH—FATHER ONLY   (FHH-9)
NCPP VARIABLE 27 = CHILD LIVES WITH—OTHER RELATIVES   (FHH-9)
NCPP VARIABLE 28 = CHILD LIVES WITH—FOSTER HOME   (FHH-9)
NCPP VARIABLE 29 = CHILD LIVES WITH—ADOPTIVE PARENTS   (FHH-9)
NCPP VARIABLE 30 = CHILD LIVES WITH—OTHER   (FHH-9)
NCPP VARIABLE 31 = MOTHER MARITAL STATUS—SINGLE   (FHH-9)
NCPP VARIABLE 32 = MOTHER MARITAL STATUS—MARRIED OR COMMON LAW   (FHH-9)
NCPP VARIABLE 33 = MOTHERS MARITAL STATUS—WIDOWED, SEPARATED, DIVORCED   (FHH-9)
NCPP VARIABLE 34 = MOVES DURING LAST 7 YEARS   (FHH-9)
NCPP VARIABLE 35 = HOUSING DENSITY   (FHH-9)
NCPP VARIABLE 36 = PRESENCE OF HUSBAND WHO IS FOB IN HOUSEHOLD   (FHH-9)
NCPP VARIABLE 37 = PRESENCE OF FOB WHO IS NOT HUSBAND IN HOUSEHOLD   (FHH-9)
NCPP VARIABLE 38 = PRESENCE OF HUSBAND WHO IS NOT FOB IN HOUSEHOLD   (FHH-9)
NCPP VARIABLE 39 = PRESENCE OF NO HUSBAND OR FOB IN HOUSEHOLD   (FHH-9)
NCPP VARIABLE 40 = MOTHERS SCHOOLING SINCE CHILD BORN   (FHH-9)
NCPP VARIABLE 41 = TOTAL MONTHS MOTHER EMPLOYED   (FHH-9)
NCPP VARIABLE 42 = OCCUPATION OF MOTHER—NO OCCUPATION EXCEPT WELFARE   (FHH-9)
NCPP VARIABLE 43 = OCCUPATION OF MOTHER—PROFESSIONAL AND TECHNICAL   (FHH-9)
NCPP VARIABLE 44 = OCCUPATION OF MOTHER—PROPRIETOR, MANAGER, ARMED FORCES   (FHH-9)
NCPP VARIABLE 45 = OCCUPATION OF MOTHER—CLERICAL AND KINDRED WORKERS   (FHH-9)
NCPP VARIABLE 46 = OCCUPATION OF MOTHER—SALES WORKERS   (FHH-9)
NCPP VARIABLE 47 = OCCUPATION OF MOTHER—CRAFTSMEN, FOREMEN, KINDRED WORK   (FHH-9)
NCPP VARIABLE 48 = OCCUPATION OF MOTHER—OPERATORS AND KINDRED WORKERS   (FHH-9)
NCPP VARIABLE 49 = OCCUPATION OF MOTHER—PRIVATE HOUSEHOLD WORKERS   (FHH-9)
NCPP VARIABLE 50 = OCCUPATION OF MOTHER—SERVICE WORK (NO PRIVATE HOUSEHOLD)   (FHH-9)
NCPP VARIABLE 51 = OCCUPATION OF MOTHER—LABORERS, FARMERS   (FHH-9)
NCPP VARIABLE 52 = TOTAL INCOME: PRIOR 3 MONTHS   (FHH-9)
NCPP VARIABLE 53 = NUMBER OF PERSONS CARED FOR   (FHH-9)
NCPP VARIABLE 54 = CHILDS SIBLINGS: FETAL DEATH UNDER 20 WEEKS   (FHH-9)
NCPP VARIABLE 55 = CHILDS SIBLINGS: FETAL DEATH 20 WEEKS AND OVER   (FHH-9)
NCPP VARIABLE 56 = CHILDS SIBLINGS: MALE LIVEBORN   (FHH-9)
NCPP VARIABLE 57 = CHILDS SIBLINGS: FEMALE LIVEBORN   (FHH-9)
NCPP VARIABLE 58 = CHILDS SIBLINGS: PREMATURES   (FHH-9)
NCPP VARIABLE 59 = CHILDS SIBLINGS: DEAD 27 DAYS OR YOUNGER   (FHH-9)
NCPP VARIABLE 60 = CHILDS SIBLINGS: DEAD 28 DAYS OR OLDER   (FHH-9)
NCPP VARIABLE 61 = CHILDS SIBLINGS: RH CONDITION   (FHH-9)
NCPP VARIABLE 62 = CHILDS SIBLINGS: CONGENITAL MALFORMATION   (FHH-9)
NCPP VARIABLE 63 = CHILDS SIBLINGS: CONVULSIONS   (FHH-9)

NCPP VARIABLE 64 = CHILDS SIBLINGS: MOTOR DEFICIT
NCPP VARIABLE 65 = CHILDS SIBLINGS: SENSORY DEFECT (FHH-9)
NCPP VARIABLE 66 = CHILDS SIBLINGS: RETARDATION (FHH-9)
NCPP VARIABLE 67 = SINCE BIRTH: RH INCOMPATIBILITY, FETAL DEATH (FHH-9)
NCPP VARIABLE 68 = SINCE BIRTH: RH INCOMPATIBILITY, LIVEBORN, NO TRANSFUS (FHH-9)
NCPP VARIABLE 69 = SINCE BIRTH: RH INCOMPATIBILITY, LIVEBORN, TRANSFUSION (FHH-9)
NCPP VARIABLE 70 = SINCE BIRTH: RH INCOMPATIBILITY, JAUNDICE, TRANSFUS (FHH-9)
NCPP VARIABLE 71 = SINCE BIRTH: CLEFT LIP OR PALATE (FHH-9)
NCPP VARIABLE 72 = SINCE BIRTH: CLUB FOOT (FHH-9)
NCPP VARIABLE 73 = SINCE BIRTH: FINGERS OR TOES MALFORMED (FHH-9)
NCPP VARIABLE 74 = SINCE BIRTH: HEART MALFORMATION (FHH-9)
NCPP VARIABLE 75 = SINCE BIRTH: HEAD OR SPINE MALFORMATION (FHH-9)
NCPP VARIABLE 76 = SINCE BIRTH: NUMBER OF CHILD DEATHS (FHH-9)
NCPP VARIABLE 77 = SINCE BIRTH: PHYSICAL RETARDATION (FHH-9)
NCPP VARIABLE 78 = SINCE BIRTH: MENTAL RETARDATION (FHH-9)
NCPP VARIABLE 79 = SINCE BIRTH: SEVERE BEHAVIOURAL PROBLEM (FHH-9)
NCPP VARIABLE 80 = SEIZURES, CONVULSIONS, EPILEPSY—MOTHER OF CHILD (FHH-9)
NCPP VARIABLE 81 = SEIZURES, CONVULSIONS, EPILEPSY—FATHER OF CHILD (FHH-9)
NCPP VARIABLE 82 = SEIZURES, CONVULSIONS, EPILEPSY—STUDY CHILD (FHH-9)
NCPP VARIABLE 83 = SEIZURES, CONVULSIONS, EPILEPSY—SUBSEQ TO STUDY CHILD (FHH-9)
NCPP VARIABLE 84 = SEIZURES, CONVULSIONS, EPILEPSY—PRIOR TO STUDY CHILD (FHH-9)
NCPP VARIABLE 85 = SEIZURES, CONVULSIONS, EPILEPSY—OTHER RELAT OF MOTHER (FHH-9)
NCPP VARIABLE 86 = SEIZURES, CONVULSIONS, EPILEPSY—COMBO MOTHERS RELATION (FHH-9)
NCPP VARIABLE 87 = MOTOR DEFECT, INJURY—MOTHER OF CHILD (FHH-9)
NCPP VARIABLE 88 = MOTOR DEFECT, INJURY—FATHER OF CHILD (FHH-9)
NCPP VARIABLE 89 = MOTOR DEFECT, INJURY—CHILDREN PRIOR TO STUDY CHILD (FHH-9)
NCPP VARIABLE 90 = MOTOR DEFECT, INJURY—OTHER RELATIVES OF MOTHER (FHH-9)
NCPP VARIABLE 91 = MOTOR DECT, INFEC DISEASE—SIBS SUBSEQ TO STUDY CHILD (FHH-9)
NCPP VARIABLE 92 = MOTOR DECT, INFEC DISEASE—SIBS OTHER RELAT OF MOTHER (FHH-9)
NCPP VARIABLE 93 = SENSORY DEFECT, BLINDNESS—MOTHER OF CHILD (FHH-9)
NCPP VARIABLE 94 = SENSORY DEFECT, BLINDNESS—FATHER OF CHILD (FHH-9)
NCPP VARIABLE 95 = SENSORY DEFECT, BLINDNESS—STUDY CHILD (FHH-9)
NCPP VARIABLE 96 = SENSORY DEFECT, BLINDNESS—CHILD SUBSEQ TO STUDY CHILD (FHH-9)
NCPP VARIABLE 97 = SENSORY DEFECT, BLINDNESS—CHILD PRIOR TO STUDY CHILD (FHH-9)
NCPP VARIABLE 98 = SENSORY DEFECT, BLINDNESS—OTHER RELATIVES OF MOTHER (FHH-9)

729

#									Mean-R
1	-.13(18958)	.11(19220)	-.15(19186)	-.11(19185) .19(19151)	.23(17920)	-.18(17606)	.21(19042)	-.15(18765)	.99E-01
2	-.23(18958)	-.11(19186)	-.18(18999)	-.17(18896) -.22(18355)	-.20(17606)	-.12(19042)	-.16(18874) -.21(18765)		.86E-01
3	.21(18958)	.11(19186)	.12(18999)	.10(16905) .14(18996) .19(18355)	.10(16478) .20(17606)	.14(18874)	.21(18765)		.82E-01
4									.26E-01
5									.45E-01
6	.46(16951)	.21(19134)	.24(17905)	.10(18981)	-.20(17591)	.17(14113) .27(19025)			.98E-01
7									.36E-01
8	.21(18943)	.12(19170)	.13(18985)	.14(18981) .21(18342)	.22(17591)	.16(18862)	.20(18751)		.85E-01
9	-.19(18943)	-.11(19170)	-.15(18985)	-.14(18981) -.19(18342)	-.17(17590)	-.10(19025)	-.15(18862)	-.17(18751)	.78E-01
10									.27E-01
11	.59(16955) -.11(19102) .10(19207)	.41(19138)	.18(18987) .43(17910)	.14(18985)		.29(14116) .50(19028)	.11(18867)		.15E+00
12									.26E-01

| 13 | -.15(16955) | | | | | Mean-R | .38E-01 |

14 — Mean-R .96E-02

15 — Mean-R .34E-01

16 — Mean-R .15E-01

17 — Mean-R .27E-01

18 — Mean-R .36E-01

19 — Mean-R .25E-01

20 — -.11(14779) .47(16971) -.11(19132) .10(19233) -.13(19203) -.11(16923) -.14(16493) -.11(19155) -.26(17616) .20(14121) .35(19059) -.14(18780) Mean-R .13E+00

21 — -.20(18972) -.38(19202) -.19(15918) -.24(19201) -.26(16662) -.15(16923) -.13(19010) -.20(18370) -.21(16493) -.12(19154) -.21(17615) -.20(18862) -.24(18779) Mean-R .12E+00

22 — Mean-R .16E-01

23 — Mean-R .39E-01

24 — .22(18954) .11(19182) .10(18988) .10(16867) .24(18347) .25(17578) .20(18447) .15(18757) Mean-R .75E-01

#											Mean-R	
25	−.19(18954)				−.12(18988)	−.21(18347)	−.19(17578)	−.10(19036)	−.18(18447)	−.13(18757)	Mean-R	.68E-01
26											Mean-R	.82E-02
27											Mean-R	.25E-01
28											Mean-R	.27E-01
29											Mean-R	.10E-01
30											Mean-R	.76E-02
31	−.12(18050)					−.13(17469)	−.13(16745)				Mean-R	.40E-01
32	.21(18050)		.11(18270)		.10(18084)	.23(17469)	.24(16745)		.19(17576)	.15(17866)	Mean-R	.71E-01
33	−.18(18050)			.11(18218)	.10(17072)	−.17(17469)	−.24(16745)		−.13(17576)	−.13(17866)	Mean-R	.76E-01
34		.16(16012)					−.13(16699)	.13(18073)			Mean-R	.47E-01
35	−.35(18043)		−.21(18263)	−.12(15062)	−.27(18077) −.12(17066)	−.10(16006) −.21(18080) −.36(17463)	−.33(16739)	−.20(18120)	−.26(17569)	−.25(17859)	Mean-R	.13E+00
36	.22(18050)		.10(18270)		.11(18084)	.24(17469)	.25(16745)		.21(17576)	.15(17866)	Mean-R	.76E-01

No.	Values	Mean-R
37	.19(16050)	Mean-R .26E-01
38		Mean-R .22E-01
39	-.21(18050) .18(16050) -.11(18270) -.10(16008) -.22(17469) -.28(16745) -.16(17576) -.16(17866)	Mean-R .79E-01
40	.20(15937) .14(17989)	Mean-R .51E-01
41	.13(18080) .15(16939)	Mean-R .30E-01
42	-.10(17877) -.11(17303) -.11(16579) -.10(17415)	Mean-R .40E-01
43	.18(17877) .14(17912) .13(17914) .21(17303) .19(16579) .11(17954) .17(17415) .14(17697)	Mean-R .76E-01
44		Mean-R .13E-01
45	.12(17877) .12(17303) .12(16579)	Mean-R .40E-01
46		Mean-R .20E-01
47		Mean-R .20E-01
48	-.11(17303) -.11(16579)	Mean-R .34E-01

733

Row	Values	Mean-R
49	-.17(17877); -.12(18096); -.12(17912); -.17(17303); -.16(16579); -.12(17415); -.12(17697)	.59E-01
50	.44(15912); -.11(18034); -.16(17877); .29(18044); .31(16904); -.15(17303); -.28(16579); .20(13273); .34(17954); -.14(17697)	.13E+00
51	.85(15912); -.16(18034); .14(18112); -.12(13851); .13(18038); -.10(17877); .15(18096); .54(18044); .29(17912); .61(16904); .20(17914); -.15(17303); -.30(16579); .38(13273); .73(17954); .10(15358); .13(17415); -.12(17697)	.21E+00
52	.36(17689); .20(17905); .20(17723); .15(15757); .19(17726); .39(17123); .15(17864); .40(16410); .31(17229); .25(17507)	.13E+00
53	-.18(18035); -.14(18254); -.10(15051); -.15(18068); -.12(18071); -.20(17454); -.12(18111); -.16(16731); -.16(17562); -.15(17851)	.76E-01
54		.16E-01
55	.21(15867); .11(17886); .14(17796); -.13(16437)	.53E-01
56	-.17(17708); -.15(17928); -.11(14879); -.13(15567); -.11(17745); -.21(17142); -.18(16424); -.23(17251); -.14(17527)	.84E-01
57	-.16(17709); -.17(17743); -.11(17746); -.16(17144); -.14(16424); -.15(17786); -.11(17250); -.12(17528)	.61E-01
58	-.17(17737); -.11(17957); -.12(17771); -.10(17774); -.18(17169); -.18(16452); -.10(17814); -.16(17278); -.13(17556)	.69E-01
59		.17E-01
60		.31E-01

		Mean-R
61		.12E-01
62		.12E-01
63		.17E-01
64	-.12(15365)	.21E-01
65	-.13(15509) -.13(17862) -.11(17860)	.57E-01
66	-.21(17191) -.14(17469) -.12(15368) -.14(15760) -.13(15513) -.11(17865) -.12(17863) -.16(17646) -.10(17824) -.13(17682) -.18(16372) -.18(17083)	.86E-01
67		.18E-01
68		.11E-01
69		.11E-01
70		.16E-01
71		.19E-01
72		.14E-01

73				Mean-R	.64E-02
74				Mean-R	.90E-02
75				Mean-R	.19E-01
76				Mean-R	.14E-01
77				Mean-R	.21E-01
78	-.15(17491)	-.15(17702)	-.16(17700)	-.12(15170)	-.14(15398)	-.14(15027)
				-.12(17527)		
79				-.15(16938)	-.14(16236)	-.15(17040) -.14(17324) Mean-R .83E-01
80				Mean-R	.35E-01
81				Mean-R	.74E-02
82				Mean-R	.74E-02
83				Mean-R	.13E-01
84				Mean-R	.51E-02
				Mean-R	.75E-02

85	Mean-R	.10E-01
86	Mean-R	.12E-01
87	Mean-R	.21E-01
88	Mean-R	.47E-02
89	Mean-R	.86E-02
90	Mean-R	.75E-02
91	Mean-R	.54E-02
92	Mean-R	.63E-02
93	Mean-R	.12E-01
94	Mean-R	.44E-02
95	Mean-R	.82E-02
96	Mean-R	.55E-02

97   Mean-R   .15E-01

98   Mean-R   .79E-02

X. FIRST SCREEN CORRELATIONS
   INDICES WITH NCPP VARIABLES LISTED BELOW

NCPP VARIABLE 1 = SENSORY DEFECT, DEAFNESS: MOTHER OF CHILD   (FHH-9)
NCPP VARIABLE 2 = SENSORY DEFECT, DEAFNESS: STUDY CHILD   (FHH-9)
NCPP VARIABLE 3 = SENSORY DEFECT, DEAFNESS: CHILD SUBSQ TO STUDY CHILD   (FHH-9)
NCPP VARIABLE 4 = SENSORY DEFECT, DEAFNESS: CHILD PRIOR TO STUDY CHILD   (FHH-9)
NCPP VARIABLE 5 = SENSORY DEFECT, DEAFNESS: OTHER RELATIVES OF MOTHER   (FHH-9)
NCPP VARIABLE 6 = SENSORY DEFECT, TROUBLE SPEAKING: MOTHER OF CHILD   (FHH-9)
NCPP VARIABLE 7 = SENSORY DEFECT, TROUBLE SPEAKING: STUDY CHILD   (FHH-9)
NCPP VARIABLE 8 = SENSORY DEFECT, TROUBLE SPEAKING: SIB SUBSQ TO STDY CH   (FHH-9)
NCPP VARIABLE 9 = SENSORY DEFECT, TROUBLE SPEAKING: SIB PRIOR TO STDY CH   (FHH-9)
NCPP VARIABLE 10 = SENSORY DEFECT, TROUBLE SPEAKING: OTHER REL OF MOTHER   (FHH-9)
NCPP VARIABLE 11 = SENSORY DEFECT, TROUBLE SPEAKING: COMBINATN OF RELS MTH   (FHH-9)
NCPP VARIABLE 12 = SUGAR DIABETES: MOTHER OF CHILD   (FHH-9)
NCPP VARIABLE 13 = SUGAR DIABETES: FATHER OF CHILD   (FHH-9)
NCPP VARIABLE 14 = SUGAR DIABETES: CHILDREN PRIOR TO STUDY CHILD   (FHH-9)
NCPP VARIABLE 15 = SUGAR DIABETES: OTHER RELATIVES OF MOTHER   (FHH-9)
NCPP VARIABLE 16 = SUGAR DIABETES: COMBINATION OF RELATIVES OF MTH   (FHH-9)
NCPP VARIABLE 17 = NERV PROB NEEDING HOSP/THERAPY: MOTHER OF CHILD   (FHH-9)
NCPP VARIABLE 18 = NERV PROB NEEDING HOSP/THERAPY: FATHER OF CHILD   (FHH-9)
NCPP VARIABLE 19 = NERV PROB NEEDING HOSP/THERAPY: STUDY CHILD   (FHH-9)
NCPP VARIABLE 20 = NERV PROB NEEDING HOSP/THERAPY: SIBS SUBSQ TO STUDY CH   (FHH-9)
NCPP VARIABLE 21 = NERV PROB NEEDING HOSP/THERAPY: SIBS PRIOR TO STUDY CH   (FHH-9)
NCPP VARIABLE 22 = NERV PROB NEEDING HOSP/THERAPY: OTHER REL OF MOTHER   (FHH-9)
NCPP VARIABLE 23 = NERV PROB NEEDING HOSP/THERAPY: COMBINATN RELS OF MTH   (FHH-9)
NCPP VARIABLE 24 = EARS: SHAPE, SIZE, POSITION (7 YEARS)
NCPP VARIABLE 25 = EARS: OTOSCOPIC EXAMINATION (7 YEARS)

1   Mean-R .86E-02

2   .29(18092)   -.12(17947)   -.12(18074)   -.19(18025)   Mean-R .53E-01

3   Mean-R .67E-02

4   Mean-R .57E-02

5   Mean-R .89E-02

6   Mean-R .14E-01

7   -.18(18023)   -.12(14865)   -.15(15552)   -.19(15397)   -.21(18019)   Mean-R .72E-01

8   Mean-R .85E-02

9   Mean-R .11E-01

10   Mean-R .95E-02

11   Mean-R .24E-01

12   Mean-R .13E-01

13	Mean-R	.87E-02
14	Mean-R	.60E-02
15	Mean-R	.18E-01
16	Mean-R	.87E-02
17	Mean-R	.82E-02
18	Mean-R	.74E-02
19	Mean-R	.89E-02
20	Mean-R	.73E-02
21	Mean-R	.59E-02
22	Mean-R	.14E-01
23	Mean-R	.11E-01
24	Mean-R	.30E-01

741

25

.12(18112) −.13(17966)

Mean-R   .29E-01

SLH VARIABLE 1 = IDENTIFICATION OF FAMILIAR OBJECTS (3YR)
SLH VARIABLE 2 = UNDERSTANDING ACTION WORDS (3YR)
SLH VARIABLE 3 = UNDERSTANDING SPACE RELATIONS (3YR)
SLH VARIABLE 4 = NAMING OBJECTS (3YR)
SLH VARIABLE 5 = SENTENCE LENGTH (3YR)
SLH VARIABLE 6 = SENTENCE STRUCTURE (3YR)
SLH VARIABLE 7 = RELEVANCE (3YR)
SLH VARIABLE 8 = WORD ORDER (3YR)
SLH VARIABLE 9 = USE OF PRONOUNS (3YR)
SLH VARIABLE 10 = VERBAL EXPRESSION: SUMMARY ITEM SCORE (3YR)
SLH VARIABLE 11 = AUDITORY MEMORY: 2 DIGITS (3YR)
SLH VARIABLE 12 = AUDITORY MEMORY: 3 DIGITS (3YR)
SLH VARIABLE 13 = AUDITORY MEMORY: 2 SYLLABLES (3YR)
SLH VARIABLE 14 = AUDITORY MEMORY: 3 SYLLABLES (3YR)
SLH VARIABLE 15 = SPONDAIC WORD TEST: SUM TOTAL SCORE (3YR)
SLH VARIABLE 16 = PURE-TONE: SUM SCORE, RIGHT EAR (3YR)
SLH VARIABLE 17 = PURE-TONE: SUM SCORE, LEFT EAR (3YR)
SLH VARIABLE 18 = SPEECH MECHANISM: LIPS RETRACTION (3YR)
SLH VARIABLE 19 = SPEECH MECHANISM: LIPS PROTRUSION (3YR)
SLH VARIABLE 20 = SPEECH MECHANISM: TONGUE MID-LINE PROTRUSION (3YR)
SLH VARIABLE 21 = SPEECH MECHANISM: TONGUE LATERAL PROTRUSION (3YR)
SLH VARIABLE 22 = SPEECH MECHANISM: TONGUE ELEVATION (3YR)
SLH VARIABLE 23 = SPEECH MECHANISM: SOFT PALATE ELEVATION (3YR)
SLH VARIABLE 24 = DIADOCHOKINESIS: LIPS (3YR)
SLH VARIABLE 25 = DIADOCHOKINESIS: TONGUE (3YR)
SLH VARIABLE 26 = SPEECH PRODUCTION: VOICE PITCH (3YR)
SLH VARIABLE 27 = SPEECH PRODUCTION: VOICE LOUDNESS (3YR)
SLH VARIABLE 28 = SPEECH PRODUCTION: VOICE QUALITY (3YR)
SLH VARIABLE 29 = ARTICULATION: INITIAL CONSONANTS (3YR)
SLH VARIABLE 30 = ARTICULATION: FINAL CONSONANTS (3YR)
SLH VARIABLE 31 = ARTICULATION: VOWELS AND DIPHTHONGS (3YR)
SLH VARIABLE 32 = INTELLIGIBILITY OF SPEECH (3YR)
SLH VARIABLE 33 = DYSFLUENT EVENTS (3YR)
SLH VARIABLE 34 = STRUGGLE BEHAVIOR (3YR)
SLH VARIABLE 35 = AIR CONDUCTION: RIGHT EAR, 500 CPS (8YR)
SLH VARIABLE 36 = AIR CONDUCTION: RIGHT EAR, 1000 CPS (8YR)
SLH VARIABLE 37 = AIR CONDUCTION: RIGHT EAR, 2000 CPS (8YR)
SLH VARIABLE 38 = AIR CONDUCTION: LEFT EAR, 500 CPS (8YR)
SLH VARIABLE 39 = AIR CONDUCTION: LEFT EAR, 1000 CPS (8YR)
SLH VARIABLE 40 = AIR CONDUCTION: LEFT EAR, 2000 CPS (8YR)
SLH VARIABLE 41 = ABN AUDITORY ADAPT: RIGHT EAR, 4000 CPS (8YR)
SLH VARIABLE 42 = ABN AUDITORY ADAPT: RIGHT EAR, 500 CPS (8YR)
SLH VARIABLE 43 = ABN AUDITORY ADAPT: LEFT EAR, 4000 CPS (8YR)
SLH VARIABLE 44 = ABN AUDITORY ADAPT: LEFT EAR, 500 CPS (8YR)
SLH VARIABLE 45 = BONE CONDUCTION: RIGHT EAR, 500 CPS (8YR)
SLH VARIABLE 46 = BONE CONDUCTION: RIGHT EAR, 1000 CPS (8YR)
SLH VARIABLE 47 = BONE CONDUCTION: RIGHT EAR, 2000 CPS (8YR)
SLH VARIABLE 48 = BONE CONDUCTION: LEFT EAR, 500 CPS (8YR)
SLH VARIABLE 49 = BONE CONDUCTION: LEFT EAR, 1000 CPS (8YR)
SLH VARIABLE 50 = BONE CONDUCTION: LEFT EAR, 2000 CPS (8YR)
SLH VARIABLE 51 = DISCRIMINATION PERCENT: RIGHT EAR (8YR)
SLH VARIABLE 52 = DISCRIMINATION PERCENT: LEFT EAR (8YR)
SLH VARIABLE 53 = DIGITS: TOTAL PASS SCORE (8YR)
SLH VARIABLE 54 = SYLLABLES: TOTAL PASS SCORE (8YR)
SLH VARIABLE 55 = WORD IDENTIFICATION: RAW SCORE (8YR)
SLH VARIABLE 56 = ORIENTATION: TOTAL SCORE (8YR)
SLH VARIABLE 57 = UNDERSTANDING A STORY: RAW SCORE (8YR)
SLH VARIABLE 58 = ORAL READING: TOTAL PASSAGE SCORE (8YR)
SLH VARIABLE 59 = SILENT READING: TOTAL SCORE (8YR)
SLH VARIABLE 60 = MORPHOLOGY: RAW SCORE (8YR)
SLH VARIABLE 61 = CONNECTED DISCOURSE: OVERALL EVALUATION (8YR)
SLH VARIABLE 62 = WRITING FROM DICTATION: TOTAL SCORE (8YR)
SLH VARIABLE 63 = SPEECH MECHANISM: LIPS RETRACTION (8YR)

SLH VARIABLE 64 = SPEECH MECHANISM: LIPS PROTRUSION   (8YR)
SLH VARIABLE 65 = SPEECH MECHANISM: TONGUE MID-LINE PROTRUSION   (8YR)
SLH VARIABLE 66 = SPEECH MECHANISM: TONGUE LATERAL PROTRUSION   (8YR)
SLH VARIABLE 67 = SPEECH MECHANISM: TONGUE ELEVATION   (8YR)
SLH VARIABLE 68 = SPEECH MECHANISM: SOFT PALATE FUNCTION   (8YR)
SLH VARIABLE 69 = SPEECH PRODUCTION: RATE OF SPEECH SOUNDS   (8YR)
SLH VARIABLE 70 = SPEECH PRODUCTION: DYSFLUENT EVENTS   (8YR)
SLH VARIABLE 71 = SPEECH PRODUCTION: STRUGGLE BEHAVIOR   (8YR)
SLH VARIABLE 72 = SPEECH PRODUCTION: VOICE PITCH   (8YR)
SLH VARIABLE 73 = SPEECH PRODUCTION: VOICE LOUDNESS   (8YR)
SLH VARIABLE 74 = SPEECH PRODUCTION: VOICE QUALITY, PHONATION   (8YR)
SLH VARIABLE 75 = SPEECH PRODUCTION: VOICE QUALITY, RESONANCE   (8YR)
SLH VARIABLE 76 = INTELLIGIBILITY   (8YR)
SLH VARIABLE 77 = ARTICULATION: SCORE   (8YR)

1	.08(16400) .04(11971) .18(11897)	.04(18687) .04(11961) -.08(11966)	-.00(18320) .15(12011) .04(11892)	.11(17652) .12(12008) .03(11929)	.18(18362) .12(11876) .06(11305)	.56(18869) .13(11902) .18(11518)	.21(18178) .09(11983) .19(11111)	.10(15713) .20(11900)	.06(18098) .15(11513)	.04(11981) .19(11787)
2	.12(16383) .05(11824) .20(11753)	.02(18566) .03(11810) -.08(11818)	-.01(18210) .15(11862) .05(11748)	.14(17622) .13(11857) .02(11784)	.23(18256) .14(11731) .08(11173)	.68(18869) .15(11758) .19(11380)	.23(18073) .11(11836) .2?(10978)	.13(15702) .20(11752)	.10(18018) .16(11380)	.03(11834) .20(11646)
3	.09(16380) .01(11843) .32(11776)	.02(18592) .04(11829) -.08(11837)	-.02(18235) .19(11881) .03(11767)	.17(17630) .11(11877) .04(11803)	.26(18280) .22(11750) .10(11193)	.88(18869) .23(11779) .30(11397)	.22(18094) .13(11856) .31(10997)	.15(15706) .31(11770)	.07(18036) .21(11398)	.04(11854) .29(11671)
4	.13(16422) .04(11825) .23(11755)	.05(18652) .04(11816) -.07(11823)	-.02(18309) .18(11864) .05(11752)	.19(17673) .15(11862) .04(11788)	.29(18351) .13(11736) .08(11177)	.35(18630) .20(11763) .22(11384)	.31(18205) .17(11841) .25(10990)	.18(15738) .18(11756)	.08(18041) .22(11384)	.06(11837) .20(11657)
5	.14(16063) .02(11485) .23(11419)	.03(18282) .02(11480) -.04(11481)	-.05(18034) .17(11523) .04(11415)	.25(17253) .15(11520) .03(11449)	.36(18120) .13(11393) .08(10864)	.23(18064) .20(11424) .23(11047)	.78(18368) .17(11499) .25(10678)	.18(15445) .17(11415)	.08(17604) .21(11057)	.03(11499) .18(11329)
6	.14(16048) .04(11467) .16(11400)	.05(18256) .02(11462) -.03(11463)	-.03(18011) .15(11505) .05(11398)	.20(17235) .16(11502) .03(11431)	.36(18099) .07(11375) .05(10847)	.22(18037) .15(11406) .17(11028)	.84(18368) .16(11481) .18(10661)	.18(15438) .10(11397)	.11(17583) .18(11040)	.03(11481) .14(11310)
7	.11(16055) .04(11473) .18(11406)	.03(18267) .05(11468) -.07(11469)	-.02(18020) .18(11511) .05(11403)	.17(17242) .18(11508) .05(11437)	.29(18107) .10(11381) .07(10852)	.28(18049) .14(11412) .17(11033)	.72(18368) .12(11487) .18(10666)	.15(15442) .15(11403)	.11(17589) .14(11044)	.06(11487) .15(11317)
8	.12(16052) .06(11474) .15(11407)	.03(18260) .03(11469) -.06(11470)	-.02(18016) .19(11512) .04(11404)	.18(17239) .19(11509) .04(11438)	.29(18105) .07(11382) .06(10853)	.20(18041) .13(11413) .15(11034)	.82(18368) .14(11488) .16(10666)	.14(15439) .11(11404)	.10(17587) .14(11045)	.04(11488) .13(11317)
9	.12(16030) .04(11454) .16(11387)	.05(18236) .03(11448) -.04(11448)	-.02(17993) .18(11491) .05(11383)	.20(17217) .16(11488) .03(11417)	.34(18081) .07(11360) .06(10834)	.21(18017) .14(11392) .16(11015)	.81(18368) .15(11466) .17(10649)	.18(15418) .11(11382)	.10(17562) .17(11026)	.04(11467) .16(11297)
10	.17(16370) .04(11805) .22(11736)	.04(18684) .04(11799) -.05(11803)	-.05(18353) .22(11844) .06(11733)	.26(17615) .20(11842) .04(11769)	.42(18414) .10(11713) .07(11161)	.29(18543) .19(11743) .23(11359)	.89(18366) .19(11821) .25(10970)	.23(15689) .15(11735)	.12(17988) .23(11361)	.04(11820) .20(11639)
11	.11(15764) .01(10605) .10(10550)	.01(16928) .04(10601) -.01(10604)	-.01(16687) .07(10642) .03(10548)	.13(16825) .08(10634) .00(10576)	.17(16750) .05(10523) .03(10041)	.16(16849) .12(10563) .11(10221)	.17(16548) .13(10619) .13(9867)	.53(15761) .07(10536)	.05(16665) .13(10234)	.02(10616) .12(10475)
12	.14(15524) .03(10340) .14(10291)	.02(16584) .02(10335) -.00(10338)	-.02(16352) .05(10375) .04(10284)	.12(16508) .09(10367) .01(10311)	.22(16424) .05(10260) .05(9786)	.18(16507) .17(10304) .15(9963)	.21(16217) .25(10353) .19(9622)	.67(15761) .09(10273)	.07(16348) .19(9978)	.03(10350) .16(10217)

13	.11(15391)	.00(16649)	-.02(16409)	.12(16566)	.15(16479)	.13(16570)	.16(16265)	.57(15761)	.04(16405)	.03(10423)
	.04(15412)	.02(10407)	.08(10449)	.11(10441)	.05(10334)	.11(10375)	.12(10428)	.07(10347)	.12(10054)	.11(10288)
	.11(10362)	-.01(10412)	.04(10358)	.01(10385)	.04(9860)	.11(10041)	.13(9694)			
14	.15(15370)	.02(16332)	-.01(16099)	.12(16269)	.21(16172)	.17(16265)	.20(15967)	.76(15761)	.08(16113)	.03(10183)
	.04(10176)	.02(10168)	.05(10209)	.08(10201)	.04(10096)	.17(10138)	.25(10189)	.06(10109)	.17(9818)	.12(10051)
	.12(10124)	-.01(10173)	.05(10121)	.02(10148)	.06(9639)	.13(9806)	.17(9476)			
15	.12(15699)	.02(17318)	-.02(17055)	.15(16817)	.20(17117)	.23(17315)	.23(16932)	.18(15495)	.29(17241)	.03(10898)
	.05(10885)	.01(10873)	.13(10921)	.13(10916)	.07(10801)	.12(10834)	.11(10900)	.11(10818)	.13(10510)	.13(10748)
	.14(10829)	-.10(10888)	.10(10829)	.06(10860)	.07(10320)	.13(10500)	.17(10139)			
16	.06(15231)	.01(16823)	-.00(16526)	.07(16214)	.09(16584)	.08(16773)	.12(16410)	.04(14693)	.85(17034)	.03(10595)
	.03(10585)	.02(10577)	.08(10619)	.09(10616)	.03(10500)	.04(10523)	.05(10597)	.05(10521)	.03(10211)	.04(10435)
	.05(10521)	-.15(10595)	.09(10539)	.06(10570)	.04(10023)	.04(10174)	.06(9850)			
17	.06(15212)	.01(16792)	-.01(16496)	.07(16191)	.09(16550)	.08(16740)	.13(16380)	.04(14678)	.88(16992)	.04(10576)
	.05(10565)	.03(10557)	.06(10600)	.08(10597)	.02(10481)	.03(10504)	.04(10578)	.04(10502)	.02(10191)	.03(10416)
	.04(10502)	-.13(10576)	.08(10520)	.06(10551)	.03(10005)	.03(10155)	.04(9833)			
18	.17(16428)	.01(17569)	-.00(17275)	.04(17086)	.07(17314)	.08(17506)	.07(17104)	.04(15386)	.02(17229)	.02(11108)
	-.00(11099)	.00(11092)	.07(11135)	.04(11128)	.01(11009)	.03(11043)	.03(11112)	.03(11027)	.04(10702)	.06(10950)
	.05(11034)	-.00(11096)	.00(11031)	.00(11066)	.03(10495)	.05(10689)	.05(10310)			
19	.11(16326)	.03(17507)	.00(17217)	.08(17026)	.08(17249)	.09(17448)	.04(17034)	.07(15339)	.05(17158)	.01(11037)
	.00(11026)	.00(11019)	.05(11061)	.04(11055)	.02(10939)	.05(10968)	.04(11036)	.03(10956)	.05(10629)	.07(10880)
	.06(10961)	-.00(11024)	.02(10962)	.02(10996)	.01(10433)	.04(10626)	.05(10251)			
20	.06(16321)	.01(17584)	.00(17290)	.04(17085)	.05(17327)	.07(17528)	.04(17113)	.01(15349)	.03(17217)	.10(11128)
	.00(11118)	.03(11111)	.04(11151)	.04(11147)	.02(11027)	.01(11056)	.00(11128)	.03(11047)	.03(10709)	.04(10968)
	.03(11050)	.00(11115)	.02(11051)	.02(11084)	.04(10517)	.03(10701)	.03(10337)			
21	.07(15827)	.02(16909)	.01(16628)	.13(16478)	.12(16670)	.15(16848)	.05(16478)	.03(14872)	.02(16588)	.09(10668)
	.01(10656)	.02(10652)	.14(10690)	.04(10687)	.13(10573)	.12(10602)	.03(10669)	.17(10591)	.10(10263)	.17(10516)
	.19(10596)	-.04(10655)	.01(10597)	.01(10626)	.09(10093)	.16(10261)	.16(9914)			
22	.06(15499)	.01(16485)	.03(16221)	.12(16091)	.11(16246)	.14(16424)	.01(16055)	.03(14526)	-.01(16179)	.08(10324)
	-.02(10316)	.03(10308)	.09(10350)	.00(10342)	.05(10238)	.07(10266)	.01(10326)	.08(10253)	.03(9934)	.11(10176)
	.13(10256)	-.05(10319)	.00(10265)	.02(10296)	.06(9766)	.07(9935)	.08(9594)			
23	.06(15668)	.12(16393)	-.01(16146)	.02(16122)	.07(16179)	.03(16315)	.06(15976)	.03(14723)	.05(16120)	.01(10337)
	.03(10332)	-.02(10329)	.01(10364)	.01(10356)	-.02(10245)	.01(10278)	.02(10339)	-.02(10263)	.02(9956)	.01(10194)
	.00(10270)	.01(10331)	.03(10275)	-.00(10305)	-.01(9775)	.00(9949)	.00(9607)			
24	.84(16347)	.02(16625)	-.01(16388)	.09(16418)	.14(16424)	.10(16538)	.16(16224)	.14(14988)	.07(16342)	.03(10470)
	.01(10465)	.01(10459)	.04(10497)	.04(10490)	.01(10385)	.07(10415)	.10(10472)	.03(10400)	.08(10094)	.03(10334)
	.06(10405)	-.01(10464)	.03(10406)	.01(10439)	.02(9915)	.05(10089)	.07(9750)			

25	.96(16278) .02(10367) .05(10308)	.04(16431) .01(10361) -.02(10366)	-.01(16200) .04(10398) .03(10309)	.08(16235) .06(10391) .01(10341)	.14(16238) .01(10289) .02(9823)	**.10(16348)** **.06(10318)** .05(9991)	.14(16037) .08(10375) .06(9659)	.14(14858) .03(10304)	.09(16161) .07(9997)	.03(10371) .03(10234)
26	.05(16392) .02(11779) .04(11711)	.06(18878) .01(11773) -.03(11774)	.01(18448) .04(11819) .03(11705)	.04(17649) .04(11815) .01(11741)	.10(18477) .02(11687) .01(11131)	.09(18463) .03(11717) .04(11327)	.08(18195) .03(11796) .04(10939)	.04(15705) .04(11709)	.06(17989) .04(11331)	.02(11791) .05(11613)
27	.10(16409) .02(11789) .09(11721)	.03(18892) .01(11783) -.03(11784)	-.01(18465) .07(11829) .03(11714)	.08(17666) .05(11825) .00(11750)	.19(18494) .05(11697) .03(11140)	.09(18481) .07(11727) .09(11337)	.16(18213) .06(11806) .09(10949)	.06(15718) .08(11719)	.07(18006) .09(11341)	.03(11801) .09(11623)
28	.03(16307) .01(11708) .12(11643)	.33(18782) .01(11705) -.06(11705)	.00(18358) .09(11748) .02(11637)	.09(17560) .04(11744) .01(11673)	.15(18382) .08(11617) .05(11066)	.11(18362) .05(11648) .12(11262)	.02(18097) .01(11725) .12(10879)	-.00(15625) .12(11639)	.04(17896) .09(11265)	.00(11719) .12(11546)
29	.12(16227) .01(11169) .29(11113)	.05(17683) .04(11160) -.08(11171)	.00(17423) .32(11207) .04(11109)	.87(17741) .16(11199) .04(11142)	.51(17471) .16(11084) .13(10576)	.21(17584) .21(11121) .27(10773)	.25(17211) .14(11183) .30(10403)	.12(15671) .24(11098)	.06(17326) .22(10776)	.05(11176) .27(11034)
30	.13(16220) -.01(11160) .45(11104)	.05(17667) .06(11151) -.11(11162)	.00(17407) .37(11198) .03(11100)	.52(17737) .16(11190) .06(11133)	.48(17455) .28(11076) .18(10568)	.32(17568) .28(11112) .42(10765)	.25(17196) .15(11174) .44(10396)	.14(15667) .42(11090)	.04(17315) .29(10768)	.06(11167) .39(11025)
31	.12(16219) .02(11159) .13(11103)	.03(17667) .05(11150) -.02(11161)	-.00(17408) .19(11197) .03(11099)	.59(17741) .17(11189) .01(11132)	.35(17457) .06(11075) .05(10567)	.16(17569) .13(11111) .13(10765)	.24(17197) .14(11173) .15(10395)	.18(15668) .09(11089)	.06(17316) .12(10767)	.04(11166) .13(11024)
32	.20(16260) .06(11669) .23(11596)	.08(18555) .05(11661) -.09(11665)	.00(18277) .29(11706) .07(11595)	**.50(17486)** .25(11704) .05(11631)	.83(18557) .11(11576) .09(11018)	.32(18290) .20(11600) .24(11218)	.52(18147) .21(11682) .26(10831)	.22(15596) .17(11598)	.12(17824) .25(11216)	.07(11680) .23(11500)
33	-.00(16327) -.01(11642) -.04(11578)	-.00(18638) .06(11636) -.00(11639)	.98(18518) .01(11680) .00(11573)	-.00(17575) -.01(11673) -.02(11658)	.01(18418) -.05(11553) -.01(11019)	-.02(18303) -.04(11586) -.05(11208)	-.04(18138) -.02(11657) -.05(10835)	-.01(15661) -.08(11571)	-.01(17873) -.04(11213)	.01(11650) -.01(11487)
34	.00(16288) -.00(11602) -.00(11539)	-.01(18593) .04(11596) -.01(11599)	.54(18518) .01(11640) -.00(11535)	.00(17530) .00(11633) -.01(11569)	.02(18373) -.02(11524) -.01(10985)	-.00(18257) -.01(11546) -.01(11179)	.00(18097) .01(11617) -.01(10810)	-.00(15621) -.01(11542)	.00(17827) -.00(11181)	-.01(11610) .00(11449)
35	.03(10391) .05(19697) .10(19534)	.02(11852) .00(19693) -.73(19870)	.01(11574) .13(19763) .47(19706)	.06(11212) .12(19756) .31(19798)	.07(11647) .07(19576) .19(18498)	.08(11805) .07(19574) .08(18885)	.05(11492) .03(19722) .11(18159)	-.01(9774) .11(19618)	.09(11424) .05(18827)	.03(19706) .11(19338)
36	.01(10390) .04(19698) .14(19534)	.01(11850) .00(19695) -.77(19870)	.00(11572) .15(19765) .47(19706)	.06(11210) .14(19758) .32(19798)	.05(11646) .10(19576) .22(18498)	.09(11646) .09(19575) .14(18885)	.05(11492) .04(19723) .17(18159)	-.00(9772) .16(19618)	.10(11422) .09(18829)	.03(19708) .14(19338)

#										
37	.01(10391) .04(19698) .16(19534)	.02(11849) .02(19694) -.73(19870)	-.02(11571) .16(19765) .37(19705)	.05(11211) .15(19757) .33(19798)	.05(11645) .11(19576) .24(18498)	.09(11805) .10(19575) .16(18885)	.06(11492) .06(19723) .20(18159)	.01(9773) .18(19617)	.07(11422) .12(18829)	.02(19708) .14(19338)
38	.02(10390) .06(19695) .09(19531)	.03(11847) .01(19689) -.74(19870)	.01(11569) .12(19762) .48(19706)	.04(11210) .13(19753) .29(19798)	.05(11643) .05(19573) .19(18498)	.06(11802) .06(19571) .08(18882)	.05(11489) .03(19719) .11(18159)	-.01(9773) .09(19615)	.08(11422) .05(18826)	.04(19704) .11(19335)
39	.01(10392) .05(19707) .14(19542)	.02(11853) .01(19702) -.78(19870)	-.01(11574) .15(19774) .49(19706)	.04(11212) .14(19766) .31(19798)	.06(11648) .09(19586) .22(18498)	.09(11807) .09(19583) .13(18893)	.07(11493) .05(19732) .16(18159)	-.01(9774) .14(19628)	.10(11424) .09(18832)	.03(19716) .14(19343)
40	.02(10392) .04(19704) .17(19639)	.02(11851) .03(19699) -.74(19869)	-.01(11573) .17(19771) .37(19705)	.05(11211) .16(19783) .31(19797)	.05(11646) .12(19583) .24(18498)	.10(11805) .11(19580) .18(18890)	.05(11492) .07(19729) .22(18159)	-.01(9774) .19(19625)	.07(11423) .13(18830)	.02(19713) .15(19341)
41	.02(10198) .02(19354) .05(19208)	-.01(11620) .02(19347) -.06(19324)	-.01(11358) .04(19417) .03(19198)	-.00(11000) .02(19408) .01(19264)	-.00(11423) .03(19247) .15(18497)	-.02(11571) .04(19265) .04(18571)	.02(11266) .02(19396) .06(18157)	.01(9591) .05(19278)	.01(11206) .02(18524)	.02(19358) .05(19021)
42	-.06(270) .07(556) .10(557)	-.03(311) .05(555) .01(553)	-.02(301) .09(557) -.02(539)	-.06(294) .07(557) .02(546)	-.01(305) .07(549) .08(452)	.04(312) .10(**549**) .08(520)	.12(294) .11(554) .07(447)	.03(251) .06(550)	.04(300) .05(523)	.04(557) .06(545)
43	.01(10228) .02(19400) .04(19253)	.01(11655) .03(19391) -.07(19368)	.00(11389) .03(19461) .04(19241)	.01(11036) .02(19453) .02(19307)	.01(11458) .02(19293) .13(18496)	-.01(11603) .03(19309) .04(18614)	.03(11297) .01(19440) .06(18156)	.01(9625) .05(19324)	.01(11236) .02(18565)	.02(19402) .04(19068)
44	-.07(222) -.00(445) .13(440)	-.04(253) .05(443) -.07(443)	.05(247) .12(445) -.04(428)	-.02(235) .09(446) .08(438)	.00(246) .11(440) .14(359)	-.02(255) .13(439) .13(421)	.01(233) .06(445) .12(356)	-.04(210) .12(442)	.02(249) .05(419)	.07(445) .13(430)
45	.02(776) .05(1474) .09(1465)	.03(942) -.01(1482) -.37(1487)	-.03(903) .12(1487) -.16(1451)	-.01(866) .20(1487) .34(1466)	.06(917) .09(1472) .31(1309)	.07(949) .05(1461) .08(1417)	.12(897) .04(1485) .05(1311)	-.01(735) .15(1481)	.15(883) .02(1422)	.06(1486) .14(1444)
46	.05(773) .08(1468) .11(1461)	-.00(936) -.01(1477) -.47(1482)	-.06(898) .18(1482) -.09(1448)	.00(863) .21(1482) .37(1462)	.06(912) .08(1467) .33(1307)	.11(944) .08(1457) .12(1411)	.21(892) .09(1479) .10(1308)	.06(733) .18(1475)	.17(878) .08(1416)	.03(1481) .14(1440)
47	-.00(769) .11(1463) .12(1455)	.03(931) -.11(1471) -.53(1475)	-.03(895) .17(1475) .00(1445)	.02(860) .21(1476) .42(1458)	.09(909) .12(1461) .37(1307)	.11(940) .10(1451) .12(1405)	.19(887) .08(1474) .13(1304)	.06(728) .21(1470)	.17(875) .09(1411)	.01(1475) .13(1434)
48	.01(817) .05(1526) .12(1518)	.05(980) .01(1532) -.38(1538)	-.02(938) .16(1542) -.17(1501)	.02(900) .20(1539) .35(1516)	.05(959) .10(1525) .32(1353)	.13(974) .05(1517) .09(1464)	.14(940) .04(1540) .07(1353)	-.00(758) .17(1535)	.10(919) .05(1480)	.04(1539) .13(1492)

	-.02(814)	-.02(974)	.01(934)	-.01(898)	.05(954)	.13(969)	.20(936)	.03(755)	.13(915)	.02(1532)
49	-.02(814) .05(1520) .11(1513)	-.02(974) .03(1525) -.45(1532)	.01(934) .18(1535) -.11(1499)	-.01(898) .19(1532) .38(1509)	.05(954) .10(1518) .34(1352)	.13(969) .08(1512) .12(1459)	.20(936) .07(1532) .11(1348)	.03(755) .18(1527)	.13(915) .07(1474)	.02(1532) .10(1488)
50	-.08(808) .05(1513) .13(1509)	-.01(968) .03(1519) -.49(1524)	-.00(931) .16(1529) -.04(1488)	-.01(894) .19(1527) .40(1500)	.09(951) .13(1513) .39(1346)	.11(964) .11(1508) .15(1454)	.14(930) .09(1528) .16(1343)	-.01(751) .17(1522)	.12(911) .12(1469)	-.02(1526) .13(1485)
51	.06(10270) .07(19369) .32(19228)	.01(11697) .07(19361) -.10(19332)	-.02(11429) .29(19432) .06(19231)	.18(11082) .20(19422) .11(19282)	.13(11499) .22(19264) .18(18498)	.17(11649) .23(19294) .30(18596)	.10(11343) .13(19419) .34(18159)	.05(9668) .32(19291)	.01(11284) .25(18537)	.06(19372) .25(19042)
52	.06(10268) .08(19368) .32(19227)	.01(11694) .07(19360) -.11(19332)	-.03(11426) .29(19432) .05(19229)	.17(11080) .20(19422) .11(19280)	.13(11496) .22(19263) .17(18498)	.18(11647) .23(19292) .30(18594)	.09(11341) .14(19418) .33(18159)	.04(9664) .31(19291)	.01(11281) .24(18536)	1.07(19371) .24(19041)
53	.09(10370) .04(19745) .33(19581)	.02(11831) .04(19745) -.06(19614)	-.02(11554) .18(19815) .03(19476)	.14(11192) .17(19811) .02(19545)	.22(11628) .17(19628) .14(18493)	.15(11779) .55(19650) .34(18935)	.20(11471) 1.00(19808) .47(18159)	.23(9757) .24(19668)	.04(11401) .36(18867)	.05(19755) .23(19382)
54	.07(10371) .04(19746) .24(19584)	.00(11833) .04(19745) -.06(19616)	-.00(11557) .17(19814) .03(19478)	.13(11195) .14(19811) .02(19547)	.17(11631) .14(19630) .11(18496)	.09(11783) .57(19650) .24(18937)	.13(11474) .46(19806) .35(18159)	.15(9760) .18(19670)	.02(11404) .23(18870)	1.04(19754) .18(19385)
55	.05(10370) .02(19758) .68(19596)	.02(11829) .07(19757) -.17(19633)	-.07(11550) .37(19827) .02(19492)	.20(11188) .25(19824) .05(19565)	.20(11624) .60(19658) .26(18486)	.34(11780) .50(19637) .71(18958)	.17(11470) .24(19786) .71(18159)	.09(9756) 1.00(19708)	.01(11400) .49(18878)	.07(19769) .53(19393)
56	.06(10375) .02(19759) .82(19608)	.02(11833) .07(19759) -.12(19635)	-.04(11556) .33(19829) .03(19494)	.20(11197) .22(19824) .04(19566)	.22(11632) .42(19652) .66(18498)	.26(11787) .47(19645) .67(18953)	.19(11474) .30(19793) .80(18159)	.13(9762) .56(19693)	.03(11407) .62(18887)	1.07(19767) .47(19399)
57	.01(10372) -.01(19754) .44(19602)	.01(11828) .04(19750) -.07(19628)	-.04(11553) .19(19823) -.00(19489)	.10(11196) .12(19816) .03(19560)	.09(11627) .98(19658) .13(18495)	.17(11782) .75(19650) .61(18958)	.09(11469) .13(19786) .50(18159)	.04(9760) .43(19683)	.01(11403) .27(18883)	.05(19763) .35(19401)
58	.08(10371) .02(19753) .61(19591)	.03(11829) .08(19753) -.11(19624)	-.03(11551) .32(19821) .03(19485)	.17(11191) .20(19821) .03(19556)	.25(11624) .32(19639) .28(18482)	.23(11782) .41(19631) .80(18958)	.20(11470) .34(19780) .77(18159)	.15(9756) .47(19684)	.02(11399) .91(18890)	1.05(19766) .45(19390)
59	.07(10344) .02(19708) .62(19547)	.02(11802) .05(19706) -.12(19579)	-.04(11524) .30(19775) .03(19441)	.18(11168) .18(19774) .03(19512)	.24(11599) .36(19589) .27(18439)	.24(11754) .42(19589) .86(18958)	.20(11444) .31(19730) .72(18111)	.14(9733) .50(19630)	.02(11376) .75(18840)	.06(19719) .45(19349)
60	.05(10367) .01(19750) .85(19608)	.00(11824) .09(19742) -.17(19616)	-.04(11548) .46(19815) .03(19476)	.26(11191) .28(19806) .05(19548)	.25(11621) .51(19629) .30(18481)	.34(11776) .52(19636) .80(18958)	.20(11467) .29(19772) .82(18159)	.10(9758) .70(19665)	.01(11396) .60(18880)	1.08(19756) .65(19407)

#	C1	C2	C3	C4	C5	C6	C7	C8	C9	C10
61	05(10344) 03(19686) 72(19608)	-00(11795) 03(19681) -10(19558)	-02(11519) 22(19756) 04(19420)	14(11165) 20(19744) 04(19492)	17(11594) 37(19573) 16(18434)	21(11747) 68(19650) 45(18897)	17(11440) 21(19714) 45(18145)	11(9740) 38(19606)	05(11368) 34(18835)	06(19696) 60(19400)
62	09(10362) 04(19736) 57(19584)	02(11818) 08(19728) -11(19603)	-03(11541) 38(19800) 04(19463)	18(11184) 29(19792) 04(19536)	25(11615) 29(19613) 25(18470)	23(11772) 39(19623) 66(18933)	23(11462) 32(19752) 78(18159)	16(9749) 40(19651)	04(11391) 86(18893)	1.07(19743) 43(19383)
63	02(10372) 06(19771) 06(19592)	01(11831) 03(19760) -01(19628)	-01(11552) 10(19833) 01(19485)	02(11191) 10(19825) 01(19558)	03(11624) 04(19632) 11(18498)	02(11785) 05(19636) 05(18945)	04(11477) 02(19779) 05(18151)	01(9756) 04(19671)	04(11401) 04(18879)	1.24(19801) 09(19398)
64	04(10371) 05(19766) 05(19587)	-01(11829) 04(19756) -00(19623)	01(11551) 06(19829) 01(19480)	01(11190) 05(19821) -00(19553)	03(11622) 03(19627) 09(18497)	00(11783) 05(19631) 04(18940)	02(11475) 03(19774) 03(18146)	03(9756) 03(19666)	02(11400) 03(18875)	1.21(19800) 04(19394)
65	00(10375) 02(19776) 02(19595)	01(11834) 02(19765) -01(19631)	01(11554) 04(19838) 01(19488)	-00(11195) 06(19833) -00(19561)	01(11626) 02(19636) 10(18498)	02(11789) 02(19638) 01(18947)	01(11479) 02(19785) 01(18151)	00(9759) 01(19678)	00(11405) 00(18882)	34(19801) 03(19398)
66	01(10371) 02(19771) 06(19588)	02(11829) 04(19756) -02(19624)	-01(11550) 11(19831) 02(19481)	03(11190) 12(19822) 01(19554)	02(11621) 04(19628) 14(18497)	03(11784) 06(19631) 06(18941)	03(11474) 05(19776) 05(18146)	01(9755) 07(19669)	01(11400) 04(18879)	44(19800) 07(19394)
67	04(10359) 03(19734) 07(19551)	00(11814) 04(19721) -02(19589)	00(11534) 09(19795) 02(19446)	06(11175) 10(19787) 00(19519)	04(11605) 04(19591) 16(18498)	05(11767) 05(19594) 05(18907)	04(11459) 04(19740) 05(18113)	05(9742) 06(19633)	02(11385) 04(18843)	96(19801) 08(19358)
68	04(10350) 59(19787) 01(19545)	00(11802) 02(19711) -02(19580)	-02(11525) 04(19785) 03(19440)	-01(11167) 06(19776) 02(19512)	01(11598) 00(19585) 01(18460)	03(11757) 02(19587) 01(18902)	04(11449) 03(19731) 01(18113)	01(9736) 01(19624)	01(11375) 01(18836)	03(19739) 00(19350)
69	06(10368) 07(19742) 09(19570)	01(11820) 30(19762) -04(19605)	01(11543) 16(19807) 02(19463)	06(11185) 26(19805) 02(19536)	07(11616) 06(19612) 03(18467)	06(11766) 09(19614) 10(18924)	10(11461) 08(19757) 09(18131)	03(9750) 08(19652)	03(11390) 09(18860)	07(19749) 13(19377)
70	-00(10377) 03(19769) 08(19590)	00(11835) 94(19786) -02(19627)	05(11556) 11(19830) -01(19485)	03(11193) 11(19833) 00(19558)	03(11629) 05(19634) 05(18486)	04(11784) 05(19632) 09(18944)	03(11477) 02(19783) 09(18148)	03(9757) 07(19678)	03(11403) 08(18878)	05(19774) 07(19394)
71	00(10375) 03(19762) 03(19583)	00(11831) 70(19786) -01(19620)	03(11553) 05(19823) -00(19478)	02(11191) 07(19826) -01(19551)	01(11626) 02(19628) 01(18480)	03(11780) 02(19625) 03(18939)	02(11475) 02(19776) 02(18143)	02(9755) 02(19672)	02(11400) 03(18872)	04(19768) 03(19387)
72	02(10364) 06(19757) 03(19570)	-00(11823) 01(19750) -06(19608)	-00(11543) 07(19814) 03(19469)	05(11180) 12(19816) 03(19539)	05(11616) 00(19619) 04(18468)	03(11773) 02(19615) 02(18929)	07(11466) 03(19764) 03(18131)	02(9746) 02(19663)	01(11389) 03(18858)	05(19757) 07(19376)

73	−.00(10366)	−.00(11820)	−.00(11543)	.02(11615)	.01(11768)	.02(11464)	.02(9753)	.01(11388)	.05(19753)
	.04(19756)	.02(19747)	.06(19810)	.03(19616)	.05(19616)	.02(19762)	.04(19659)	.05(18861)	.11(19379)
	.06(19571)	−.04(19608)	.03(19469)	.03(18470)	.06(18931)	.05(18134)			
74	.02(10333)	−.01(11784)	.00(11506)	.03(11580)	−.01(11734)	.03(11429)	.03(9720)	−.00(11355)	.05(19696)
	.08(19700)	.03(19691)	.11(19754)	.03(19559)	.06(19554)	.05(19703)	.07(19601)	.11(18800)	.07(19315)
	.09(19508)	−.05(19547)	.04(19409)	.07(18411)	.09(18873)	.11(18072)			
75	.04(10356)	.01(11812)	.01(11535)	.03(11605)	.00(11762)	.03(11456)	.04(9737)	.04(11381)	.02(19741)
	.38(19748)	.02(19736)	.06(19799)	−.03(19603)	.01(19600)	.03(19748)	−.04(19647)	.01(18844)	−.01(19361)
	−.01(19555)	−.09(19594)	.11(19455)	.02(18457)	−.01(18913)	−.00(18118)			
76	.08(10374)	.01(11835)	−.01(11553)	.19(11626)	.16(11788)	.21(11480)	.11(9754)	.05(11404)	.13(19777)
	.13(19768)	.14(19768)	.52(19828)	.15(19631)	.21(19628)	.16(19781)	.23(19676)	.24(18874)	.40(19407)
	.28(19585)	−.15(19623)	.06(19482)	.11(18483)	.33(18958)	.27(18143)			
77	.07(10375)	.03(11833)	.01(11556)	.27(11627)	.22(11785)	.22(11475)	.07(9760)	.03(11403)	.12(19778)
	.09(19767)	.12(19761)	1.00(19853)	.25(19637)	.28(19639)	.18(19783)	.37(19677)	.36(18881)	.48(19407)
	.42(19595)	−.17(19630)	.06(19489)	.19(18491)	.44(18948)	.44(18152)			

Multiple Regression Statistics

Response Variable: 3YR Speech Mechanism

	Beta-Coefficients of Independent Predictors				
	At-Birth NCPP's	At-Birth NCPP's 8-Month NCPP's	At-Birth NCPP's 8-Month NCPP's 4YR IQ	3YR Indexes	3YR Indexes At-Birth NCPP's
Multiple R	.106	.109			
R Square	.0112	.0118			
3YR Speech Mechanism					
3YR Hypernasality					
3YR Fluency					
3YR Articulation					
3YR Intelligibility					
3YR Language Comprehension					
3YR Sentence Complexity					
3YR Auditory Memory					
3YR Hearing Screen					
Birthweight	.0322	.0259			
Gestation Age	−.00431	−.00817			
Education of Gravida	.0229	.00227			
Per Capita Income	.0450	.0420			
Education of F.O.B.	.0181	.0175			
Occupation of F.O.B.	.0240	.0240			
8-Month Mental Score		.0130			
8-Month Motor Score		.0173			
4YR IQ					
Race-Sex Marker I	−.0920	−.0897			
Race-Sex Marker II	−.0244	−.0238			
Race-Sex Marker III	.0154	.0154			

754

Response Variable: 3YR Hypernasality

	Beta-Coefficients of Independent Predictors				
	At-Birth NCPP's	At-Birth NCPP's 8-Month NCPP's	At-Birth NCPP's 8-Month NCPP's 4YR IQ	3YR Indexes	3YR Indexes At-Birth NCPP's
Multiple R	.0501	.0526			
R Square	.00251	.00277			
3YR Speech Mechanism					
3YR Hypernasality					
3YR Fluency					
3YR Articulation					
3YR Intelligibility					
3YR Language Comprehension					
3YR Sentence Complexity					
3YR Auditory Memory					
3YR Hearing Screen					
Birthweight	.0148	.0113			
Gestation Age	−.00282	−.00496			
Education of Gravida	.0207	.0205			
Per Capita Income	.00338	.00176			
Education of F.O.B.	.00309	.00242			
Occupation of F.O.B.	.0231	.0203			
8-Month Mental Score		−.00302			
8-Month Motor Score		.0184			
4YR IQ					
Race-Sex Marker I	−.0253	−.0236			
Race-Sex Marker II	−.0309	−.0305			
Race-Sex Marker III	.00919	.00910			

Response Variable: 3YR Fluency

	Beta-Coefficients of Independent Predictors				
	At-Birth NCPP's	At-Birth NCPP's 8-Month NCPP's	At-Birth NCPP's 8-Month NCPP's 4YR IQ	3YR Indexes	3YR Indexes At-Birth NCPP's
Multiple R	.0869	.0890			
R Square	.00756	.00793			
3YR Speech Mechanism					
3YR Hypernasality					
3YR Fluency					
3YR Articulation					
3YR Intelligibility					
3YR Language Comprehension					
3YR Sentence Complexity					
3YR Auditory Memory					
3YR Hearing Screen					
Birthweight	−.00237	−.00622			
Gestation Age	.00594	.00354			
Education of Gravida	−.0107	−.0109			
Per Capita Income	−.0421	−.0440			
Education of F.O.B.	−.0151	−.0152			
Occupation of F.O.B.	−.0355	−.0355			
8-Month Mental Score		.0194			
8-Month Motor Score		.00109			
4YR IQ					
Race-Sex Marker I	−.0331	−.0321			
Race-Sex Marker II	.0386	.0388			
Race-Sex Marker III	−.0147	−.0146			

756

Response Variable: 3YR Articulation

	Beta-Coefficients of Independent Predictors				
	At-Birth NCPP's	At-Birth NCPP's 8-Month NCPP's	At-Birth NCPP's 8-Month NCPP's 4YR IQ	3YR Indexes	3YR Indexes At-Birth NCPP's
Multiple R	.181	.200			
R Square	.0329	.0399			
3YR Speech Mechanism					
3YR Hypernasality					
3YR Fluency					
3YR Articulation					
3YR Intelligibility					
3YR Language Comprehension					
3YR Sentence Complexity					
3YR Auditory Memory					
3YR Hearing Screen					
Birthweight	.0327	.0126			
Gestation Age	.0123	−.000153			
Education of Gravida	.0426	.0418			
Per Capita Income	.0729	.0633			
Education of F.O.B.	.0578	.0562			
Occupation of F.O.B.	.0140	.0139			
8-Month Mental Score		.0531			
8-Month Motor Score		.0459			
4YR IQ					
Race-Sex Marker I	−.0677	−.0607			
Race-Sex Marker I!	.0477	.0494			
Race-Sex Marker III	−.0777	−.0775			

757

Response Variable: 3YR Intelligibility

	Beta-Coefficients of Independent Predictors				
	At-Birth NCPP's	At-Birth NCPP's 8-Month NCPP's	At-Birth NCPP's 8-Month NCPP's 4YR IQ	3YR Indexes	3YR Indexes At-Birth NCPP's
Multiple R	.230	.250			
R Square	.0531	.0626			
3YR Speech Mechanism					
3YR Hypernasality					
3YR Fluency					
3YR Articulation					
3YR Intelligibility					
3YR Language Comprehension					
3YR Sentence Complexity					
3YR Auditory Memory					
3YR Hearing Screen					
Birthweight	.0483	.0242			
Gestation Age	.0129	−.00189			
Education of Gravida	.0628	.0619			
Per Capita Income	.0531	.0417			
Education of F.O.B.	.0813	.0784			
Occupation of F.O.B.	.0330	.0328			
8-Month Mental Score		.0336			
8-Month Motor Score		.0803			
4YR IQ					
Race-Sex Marker I	−.152	−.142			
Race-Sex Marker II	.0648	.0673			
Race-Sex Marker III	−.0683	.0684			

758

Response Variable: 3YR Language Comprehension

	Beta-Coefficients of Independent Predictors				
	At-Birth NCPP's	At-Birth NCPP's 8-Month NCPP's	At-Birth NCPP's 8-Month NCPP's 4YR IQ	3YR Indexes	3YR Indexes At-Birth NCPP's
Multiple R	.253	.276			
R Square	.0638	.0761			
3YR Speech Mechanism					
3YR Hypernasality					
3YR Fluency					
3YR Articulation					
3YR Intelligibility					
3YR Language Comprehension					
3YR Sentence Complexity					
3YR Auditory Memory					
3YR Hearing Screen					
Birthweight	.0714	.0442			
Gestation Age	−.00515	−.0219			
Education of Gravida	.0675	.0665			
Per Capita Income	.0119	−.00101			
Education of F.O.B.	.0397	.0364			
Occupation of F.O.B.	.0490	.0488			
8-Month Mental Score		.0371			
8-Month Motor Score		.0916			
4YR IQ					
Race-Sex Marker I	.0594	.0702			
Race-Sex Marker II	.133	.135			
Race-Sex Marker III	−.156	−.157			

759

Response Variable: 3YR Sentence Complexity

	Beta-Coefficients of Independent Predictors				
	At-Birth NCPP's	At-Birth NCPP's 8-Month NCPP's	At-Birth NCPP's 8-Month NCPP's 4YR IQ	3YR Indexes	3YR Indexes At-Birth NCPP's
Multiple R	.157	.2116			
R Square	.0245	.0448			
3YR Speech Mechanism					
3YR Hypernasality					
3YR Fluency					
3YR Articulation					
3YR Intelligibility					
3YR Language Comprehension					
3YR Sentence Complexity					
3YR Auditory Memory					
3YR Hearing Screen					
Birthweight	.0551	.0207			
Gestation Age	−.00969	−.0310			
Education of Gravida	.0238	.0225			
Per Capita Income	.0237	.00718			
Education of F.O.B.	.0741	.0712			
Occupation of F.O.B.	.0314	.0312			
8-Month Mental Score		.0861			
8-Month Motor Score		.0829			
4YR IQ					
Race-Sex Marker I	−.125	−.113			
Race-Sex Marker II	.0327	.0358			
Race-Sex Marker III	−.0177	−.0175			

Response Variable: 3YR Auditory Memory

	Beta-Coefficients of Independent Predictors				
	At-Birth NCPP's	At-Birth NCPP's 8-Month NCPP's	At-Birth NCPP's 8-Month NCPP's 4YR IQ	3YR Indexes	3YR Indexes At-Birth NCPP's
Multiple R	.144	.151			
R Square	.0208	.023			
3YR Speech Mechanism					
3YR Hypernasality					
3YR Fluency					
3YR Articulation					
3YR Intelligibility					
3YR Language Comprehension					
3YR Sentence Complexity					
3YR Auditory Memory					
3YR Hearing Screen					
Birthweight	.0310	.0219			
Gestation Age	.00264	−.00284			
Education of Gravida	.0178	.0175			
Per Capita Income	.0611	.0570			
Education of F.O.B.	.0576	.0555			
Occupation of F.O.B.	.0421	.0419			
8-Month Mental Score		−.0187			
8-Month Motor Score		.0567			
4YR IQ					
Race-Sex Marker I	−.100	−.0956			
Race-Sex Marker II	−.0774	−.0761			
Race-Sex Marker III	.0717	.0714			

Response Variable: 3YR Hearing Screen

	Beta-Coefficients of Independent Predictors				
	At-Birth NCPP's	At-Birth NCPP's 8-Month NCPP's	At-Birth NCPP's 8-Month NCPP's 4YR IQ	3YR Indexes	3YR Indexes At-Birth NCPP's
Multiple R	.0688	.0731			
R Square	.00473	.00534			
3YR Speech Mechanism					
3YR Hypernasality					
3YR Fluency					
3YR Articulation					
3YR Intelligibility					
3YR Language Comprehension					
3YR Sentence Complexity					
3YR Auditory Memory					
3YR Hearing Screen					
Birthweight	.0212	.0166			
Gestation Age	−.00342	−.00632			
Education of Gravida	.000669	.000454			
Per Capita Income	−.00453	−.00683			
Education of F.O.B.	.0127	.0128			
Occupation of F.O.B.	.0211	.0211			
8-Month Mental Score		.0265			
8-Month Motor Score		−.00137			
4YR IQ					
Race-Sex Marker I	−.0433	−.0422			
Race-Sex Marker II	−.0589	−.0586			
Race-Sex Marker III	.0425	.0427			

Response Variable: 8YR Speech Mechanism

	Beta-Coefficients of Independent Predictors				
	At-Birth NCPP's	At-Birth NCPP's 8-Month NCPP's	At-Birth NCPP's 8-Month NCPP's 4YR IQ	3YR Indexes	3YR Indexes At-Birth NCPP's
Multiple R	.075	.091	.106	.089	.115
R Square	.006	.008	.011	.008	.013
3YR Speech Mechanism				.0220	.0246
3YR Hypernasality				−.00198	−.00171
3YR Fluency				.00580	.00548
3YR Articulation				.0452	.0411
3YR Intelligibility				−.00399	−.00516
3YR Language Comprehension				.0297	.0145
3YR Sentence Complexity				.0127	.0132
3YR Auditory Memory				.0354	.0400
3YR Hearing Screen				.0160	.0185
Birthweight	.00773	−.00492	−.00841		.0175
Gestation Age	.0272	.0197	.0203		.0163
Education of Gravida	.0292	.0289	.0194		.0238
Per Capita Income	−.0187	−.0241	−.0298		−.0327
Education of F.O.B.	.0202	.0176	.0101		.0117
Occupation of F.O.B.	−.00615	−.00489	−.00952		−.0230
8-Month Mental Score		.0300	.0230		
8-Month Motor Score		.0313	.0249		
4YR IQ			.0653		
Race-Sex Marker I	−.0125	−.00799	−.0158		.0171
Race-Sex Marker II	.0461	.0476	.0298		.0557
Race-Sex Marker III	−.0534	−.0537	−.0380		−.0702

Response Variable: 8YR Palatal Function and Hypernasality

	Beta-Coefficients of Independent Predictors				
	At-Birth NCPP's	At-Birth NCPP's 8-Month NCPP's	At-Birth NCPP's 8-Month NCPP's 4YR IQ	3YR Indexes	3YR Indexes At-Birth NCPP's
Multiple R	.050	.075	.086	.061	.086
R Square	.003	.006	.007	.004	.007
3YR Speech Mechanism				.000656	−.00397
3YR Hypernasality				.0169	.0159
3YR Fluency				.00334	.00263
3YR Articulation				.00449	.00571
3YR Intelligibility				.00839	.00129
3YR Language Comprehension				.00987	.0209
3YR Sentence Complexity				.0337	.0309
3YR Auditory Memory				.0178	.0125
3YR Hearing Screen				.0176	.0154
Birthweight	.0148	.0216	.0188		.0135
Gestation Age	−.00282	−.00854	−.00799		.00265
Education of Gravida	.0207	.0243	.0167		.0141
Per Capita Income	.00338	.0192	.0146		.0101
Education of F.O.B.	.00309	.0132	.00713		.0113
Occupation of F.O.B.	.0231	.00328	−.000440		.0104
8-Month Mental Score		.0129	.00725		
8-Month Motor Score		.00661	.00145		
4YR IQ			.0525		
Race-Sex Marker I	−.0253	−.0614	−.0677		−.0468
Race-Sex Marker II	−.0309	−.0416	−.0559		.00129
Race-Sex Marker III	.00919	.0401	.0527		.0350

Response Variable: 8YR Fluency

	Beta-Coefficients of Independent Predictors				
	At-Birth NCPP's	At-Birth NCPP's 8-Month NCPP's	At-Birth NCPP's 8-Month NCPP's 4YR IQ	3YR Indexes	3YR Indexes At-Birth NCPP's
Multiple R	.087	.103	.114	.084	.133
R Square	.008	.011	.013	.007	.018
3YR Speech Mechanism				−.00749	−.00406
3YR Hypernasality				.00245	.00308
3YR Fluency				.0508	.0532
3YR Articulation				.0272	.0182
3YR Intelligibility				.00222	−.000397
3YR Language Comprehension				.0336	.0102
3YR Sentence Complexity				.0141	.0142
3YR Auditory Memory				.0152	.0189
3YR Hearing Screen				.0270	.0324
Birthweight	−.00237	−.0159	−.0192		−.00417
Gestation Age	.00594	.000262	.000879		−.00123
Education of Gravida	−.0107	.00143	−.00725		−.00546
Per Capita Income	−.0421	−.00227	−.00749		−.00195
Education of F.O.B.	−.0151	.0254	.0186		.0316
Occupation of F.O.B.	−.0355	−.00482	−.00904		−.0115
8-Month Mental Score	.0246	.0246	.0182		
8-Month Motor Score		.0239	.0181		
4YR IQ			.0596		
Race-Sex Marker I	−.0331	.0192	.0120		.0299
Race-Sex Marker II	.0386	.0753	.0590		.0813
Race-Sex Marker III	−.0147	−.0936	−.0792		−.116

Response Variable: 8YR Articulation

	Beta-Coefficients of Independent Predictors				
	At-Birth NCPP's	At-Birth NCPP's 8-Month NCPP's	At-Birth NCPP's 8-Month NCPP's 4YR IQ	3YR Indexes	3YR Indexes At-Birth NCPP's
Multiple R	.321	.344	.397	.373	.447
R Square	.103	.119	.158	.139	.200
3YR Speech Mechanism				.00509	.0137
3YR Hypernasality				−.00145	−.000909
3YR Fluency				.0191	.0303
3YR Articulation				.219	.195
3YR Intelligibility				.0871	.0801
3YR Language Comprehension				.130	.0657
3YR Sentence Complexity				.0921	.0926
3YR Auditory Memory				−.0242	−.0201
3YR Hearing Screen				−.0139	.00107
Birthweight	.0366	.00643	−.00643		.0164
Gestation Age	.0207	.00277	.00527		.0245
Education of Gravida	.0810	.0802	.0452		.0584
Per Capita Income	.0750	.0623	.0412		.0304
Education of F.O.B.	.0626	.0569	.0292		.0663
Occupation of F.O.B.	−.0139	−.0108	−.0278		−.0417
8-Month Mental Score		.0825	.0567		
8-Month Motor Score		.0648	.0412		
4YR IQ			.241		
Race-Sex Marker I	.0512	.0615	.0326		.0834
Race-Sex Marker II	.192	.195	.130		.153
Race-Sex Marker III	−.229	−.230	−.172		−.212

Response Variable: 8YR Intelligibility

	Beta-Coefficients of Independent Predictors				
	At-Birth NCPP's	At-Birth NCPP's 8-Month NCPP's	At-Birth NCPP's 8-Month NCPP's 4YR IQ	3YR Indexes	3YR Indexes At-Birth NCPP's
Multiple R	.154	.198	.245	.277	.293
R Square	.024	.039	.060	.077	.086
3YR Speech Mechanism				.0281	.0295
3YR Hypernasality				−.0104	−.0107
3YR Fluency				.00101	.00439
3YR Articulation				.126	.117
3YR Intelligibility				.0341	.0275
3YR Language Comprehension				.0711	.0507
3YR Sentence Complexity				.122	.122
3YR Auditory Memory				.0454	.0453
3YR Hearing Screen				.0188	.0235
Birthweight	.0294	−.00102	−.0104		.00925
Gestation Age	.0169	−.00120	.000619		.0219
Education of Gravida	.0605	.0597	.0341		.0364
Per Capita Income	.0292	.0164	.000977		.00397
Education of F.O.B.	.0358	.0299	.00961		.0329
Occupation of F.O.B.	.00797	.0111	−.00134		−.0162
8-Month Mental Score		.0806	.0617		
8-Month Motor Score		.0680	.0507		
4YR IQ			.176		
Race-Sex Marker I	−.0225	−.0120	−.0332		.0125
Race-Sex Marker II	.0626	.0661	.0181		.0398
Race-Sex Marker III	−.0885	−.0891	−.0467		−.0772

767

Response Variable: 8YR Language Comprehension

	Beta-Coefficients of Independent Predictors				
	At-Birth NCPP's	At-Birth NCPP's 8-Month NCPP's	At-Birth NCPP's 8-Month NCPP's 4YR IQ	3YR Indexes	3YR Indexes At-Birth NCPP's
Multiple R	.422	.432	.511	.252	.461
R Square	.178	.186	.261	.063	.212
3YR Speech Mechanism				−.0290	−.0108
3YR Hypernasality				.000116	−.00135
3YR Fluency				−.0430	−.0129
3YR Articulation				.0803	.0501
3YR Intelligibility				.0172	.0255
3YR Language Comprehension				.199	.102
3YR Sentence Complexity				.0338	.0377
3YR Auditory Memory				−.00206	−.00952
3YR Hearing Screen				−.0160	.00264
Birthweight	.0352	.0126	−.00529		.0145
Gestation Age	.00106	−.0124	−.00894		.00869
Education of Gravida	.101	.100	.0518		.0816
Per Capita Income	.0910	.0813	.0521		.0693
Education of F.O.B.	.113	.109	.0701		.111
Occupation of F.O.B.	.0329	.0351	.0115		.0400
8-Month Mental Score		.0534	.0175		
8-Month Motor Score		.0564	.0236		
4YR IQ			.334		
Race-Sex Marker I	.229	.238	.197		.233
Race-Sex Marker II	.0756	.0784	−.0127		.0593
Race-Sex Marker III	−.100	−.101	−.0201		−.0822

768

Response Variable: 8YR Auditory Memory

	Beta-Coefficients of Independent Predictors				
	At-Birth NCPP's	At-Birth NCPP's 8-Month NCPP's	At-Birth NCPP's 8-Month NCPP's 4YR IQ	3YR Indexes	3YR Indexes At-Birth NCPP's
Multiple R	.330	.347	.494	.324	.411
R Square	.109	.121	.244	.105	.169
3YR Speech Mechanism				−.00538	.0000980
3YR Hypernasality				−.0120	−.0142
3YR Fluency				−.0255	−.00722
3YR Articulation				.0873	.0678
3YR Intelligibility				.0842	.0746
3YR Language Comprehension				.158	.104
3YR Sentence Complexity				.0713	.0674
3YR Auditory Memory				.0977	.0858
3YR Hearing Screen				−.00727	.00340
Birthweight	.0566	.0312	.00836		.0311
Gestation Age	.00694	−.00832	−.00389		.0151
Education of Gravida	.113	.113	.0504		.0839
Per Capita Income	.0668	.0563	.0188		.0369
Education of F.O.B.	.114	.110	.0608		.113
Occupation of F.O.B.	.0529	.0558	.0255		.0467
8-Month Mental Score		.0867	.0407		
8-Month Motor Score		.0395	−.00256		
4YR IQ			.428		
Race-Sex Marker I	.0554	.0635	.0121		.0513
Race-Sex Marker II	.0638	.0662	−.0506		.0165
Race-Sex Marker III	−.0688	−.0690	.0343		−.0166

Response Variable: 8YR Digits

	Beta-Coefficients of Independent Predictors				
	At-Birth NCPP's	At-Birth NCPP's 8-Month NCPP's	At-Birth NCPP's 8-Month NCPP's 4YR IQ	3YR Indexes	3YR Indexes At-Birth NCPP's
Multiple R	.213	.226	.336	.304	.342
R Square	.045	.051	.113	.093	.117
3YR Speech Mechanism				.0184	.0132
3YR Hypernasality				−.000774	−.00341
3YR Fluency				−.0108	−.00494
3YR Articulation				.0291	.0209
3YR Intelligibility				.112	.0926
3YR Language Comprehension				.0501	.0378
3YR Sentence Complexity				.0817	.0733
3YR Auditory Memory				.169	.158
3YR Hearing Screen				−.00276	−.0000360
Birthweight	.0676	.0528	.0366		.0505
Gestation Age	−.00567	−.0147	−.0115		−.00181
Education of Gravida	.0874	.0871	.0428		.0657
Per Capita Income	.0277	.0220	−.00459		.0121
Education of F.O.B.	.0542	.0526	.0176		.0525
Occupation of F.O.B.	.0725	.0746	.0531		.0666
8-Month Mental Score		.0781	.0455		
8-Month Motor Score		−.00171	−.0316		
4YR IQ			.304		
Race-Sex Marker I	−.0690	−.0652	−.102		−.0903
Race-Sex Marker II	.0423	.0431	−.0399		−.0102
Race-Sex Marker III	−.0433	−.0431	.0302		.0137

Response Variable: 8YR Word Identification

	Beta-Coefficients of Independent Predictors				
	At-Birth NCPP's	At-Birth NCPP's 8-Month NCPP's	At-Birth NCPP's 8-Month NCPP's 4YR IQ	3YR Indexes	3YR Indexes At-Birth NCPP's
Multiple R	.653	.662	.753	.370	.693
R Square	.426	.438	.567	.137	.480
3YR Speech Mechanism				−.0165	.0122
3YR Hypernasality				−.00261	−.00435
3YR Fluency				−.0670	−.0218
3YR Articulation				.116	.0688
3YR Intelligibility				.0391	.0543
3YR Language Comprehension				.289	.136
3YR Sentence Complexity				.0384	.0455
3YR Auditory Memory				−.000651	−.00832
3YR Hearing Screen				−.0305	−.000880
Birthweight	.0638	.0368	.0134		.0448
Gestation Age	.0104	−.00568	−.00115		.00969
Education of Gravida	.152	.152	.0878		.119
Per Capita Income	.129	.117	.0790		.114
Education of F.O.B.	.137	.132	.0812		.127
Occupation of F.O.B.	.0697	.0724	.0414		.0647
8-Month Mental Score		.0679	.0209		
8-Month Motor Score		.0637	.0206		
4YR IQ			.438		
Race-Sex Marker I	.358	.367	.315		.360
Race-Sex Marker II	.159	.162	.0429		.125
Race-Sex Marker III	−.180	−.181	−.0753		−.156

Response Variable: Written Communication

	Beta-Coefficients of Independent Predictors				
	At-Birth NCPP's	At-Birth NCPP's 8-Month NCPP's	At-Birth NCPP's 8-Month NCPP's 4YR IQ	3YR Indexes	3YR Indexes At-Birth NCPP's
Multiple R	.519	.526	.614	.349	.564
R Square	.269	.276	.376	.122	.318
3YR Speech Mechanism				.0124	.0117
3YR Hypernasality				−.00897	−.0119
3YR Fluency				−.0316	−.00720
3YR Articulation				.0579	.0162
3YR Intelligibility				.144	.103
3YR Language Comprehension				.139	.0537
3YR Sentence Complexity				.0874	.0735
3YR Auditory Memory				.0902	.0726
3YR Hearing Screen				−.0237	−.0000734
Birthweight	.0767	.0575	.0369		.0588
Gestation Age	−.00814	−.0197	−.0157		.000544
Education of Gravida	.153	.152	.0960		.139
Per Capita Income	.162	.154	.120		.138
Education of F.O.B.	.126	.123	.0787		.136
Occupation of F.O.B.	.0754	.0777	.0504		.0750
8-Month Mental Score		.0706	.0292		
8-Month Motor Score		.0253	−.0127		
4YR IQ			.386		
Race-Sex Marker I	−.0434	−.0374	−.0838		−.0787
Race-Sex Marker II	.226	.228	.122		.162
Race-Sex Marker III	−.246	−.246	−.153		−.190

Response Variable: 8YR Language Production

	Beta-Coefficients of Independent Predictors				
	At-Birth NCPP's	At-Birth NCPP's 8-Month NCPP's	At-Birth NCPP's 8-Month NCPP's 4YR IQ	3YR Indexes	3YR Indexes At-Birth NCPP's
Multiple R	.427	.438	.520	.387	.539
R Square	.183	.192	.270	.149	.291
3YR Speech Mechanism				−.0106	.00279
3YR Hypernasality				.0103	.00976
3YR Fluency				−.00175	.0235
3YR Articulation				.150	.115
3YR Intelligibility				.0592	.0508
3YR Language Comprehension				.249	.150
3YR Sentence Complexity				.0509	.0495
3YR Auditory Memory				.0589	.0545
3YR Hearing Screen				−.0338	−.0113
Birthweight	.0534	.0299	.0116		.0233
Gestation Age	.0143	.000525	.00407		.0172
Education of Gravida	.118	.117	.0677		.0944
Per Capita Income	.0840	.0737	.0437		.0788
Education of F.O.B.	.121	.115	.0758		.113
Occupation of F.O.B.	.0461	.0481	.0239		.0191
8-Month Mental Score		.0299	−.00682		
8-Month Motor Score		.0809	.0473		
4YR IQ			.342		
Race-Sex Marker I	.0876	.0968	.0558		.122
Race-Sex Marker II	.188	.191	.0982		.169
Race-Sex Marker III	−.189	−.190	−.107		−.179

Response Variable: 8YR Concept Development

	Beta-Coefficients of Independent Predictors				
	At-Birth NCPP's	At-Birth NCPP's 8-Month NCPP's	At-Birth NCPP's 8-Month NCPP's 4YR IQ	3YR Indexes	3YR Indexes At-Birth NCPP's
Multiple R	.550	.564	.692	.409	.611
R Square	.303	.318	.479	.168	.374
3YR Speech Mechanism				−.00949	.00674
3YR Hypernasality				−.0218	−.0234
3YR Fluency				−.0293	.00311
3YR Articulation				.139	.0969
3YR Intelligibility				.0824	.0745
3YR Language Comprehension				.258	.139
3YR Sentence Complexity				.0734	.0721
3YR Auditory Memory				.0422	.0344
3YR Hearing Screen				−.0150	.0112
Birthweight	.0719	.0431	.0170		.0369
Gestation Age	.0102	−.00713	−.00205		.0154
Education of Gravida	.147	.146	.0746		.116
Per Capita Income	.123	.112	.0687		.0983
Education of F.O.B.	.121	.117	.0602		.116
Occupation of F.O.B.	.0746	.0779	.0432		.0599
8-Month Mental Score		.0978	.0452		
8-Month Motor Score		.0452	−.00295		
4YR IQ			.490		
Race-Sex Marker I	.157	.166	.107		.159
Race-Sex Marker II	.225	.228	.0941		.173
Race-Sex Marker III	−.231	−.232	−.113		−.186

774

Response Variable: 8YR Hearing Severity

	Beta-Coefficients of Independent Predictors				
	At-Birth NCPP's	At-Birth NCPP's 8-Month NCPP's	At-Birth NCPP's 8-Month NCPP's 4YR IQ	3YR Indexes	3YR Indexes At-Birth NCPP's
Multiple R	.114	.123	.142	.143	.166
R Square	.013	.015	.020	.020	.027
3YR Speech Mechanism				−.00418	−.00510
3YR Hypernasality				−.0203	−.0207
3YR Fluency				.00164	−.00171
3YR Articulation				−.0312	−.0240
3YR Intelligibility				−.0235	−.0182
3YR Language Comprehension				−.0783	−.0598
3YR Sentence Complexity				−.0160	−.0132
3YR Auditory Memory				.0324	.0332
3YR Hearing Screen				−.0794	−.0836
Birthweight	−.0434	−.0327	−.0280		−.0418
Gestation Age	.0142	.0206	.0197		.00756
Education of Gravida	−.0325	−.0322	−.0194		−.0180
Per Capita Income	−.0232	−.0189	−.0112		−.0192
Education of F.O.B.	−.0175	−.0157	−.00557		−.0386
Occupation of F.O.B.	.000269	−.000952	.00527		.0165
8-Month Mental Score		−.0367	−.0273		
8-Month Motor Score		−.0162	−.00752		
4YR IQ			−.0878		
Race-Sex Marker I	−.00552	−.00890	.00165		.0130
Race-Sex Marker II	−.0741	−.0752	−.0512		−.0467
Race-Sex Marker III	.0578	.0578	.0367		.0347

Response Variable: 8YR Total Conductive Loss

	Beta-Coefficients of Independent Predictors				
	At-Birth NCPP's	At-Birth NCPP's 8-Month NCPP's	At-Birth NCPP's 8-Month NCPP's 4YR IQ	3YR Indexes	3YR Indexes At-Birth NCPP's
Multiple R	.075	.0767	.0909	.098	.122
R Square	.006	.00588	.00826	.010	.015
3YR Speech Mechanism				.0126	.00754
3YR Hypernasality				.00961	.00953
3YR Fluency				−.00181	−.00276
3YR Articulation				−.00301	−.00167
3YR Intelligibility				.0292	.0211
3YR Language Comprehension				.0273	.0378
3YR Sentence Complexity				.0265	.0215
3YR Auditory Memory				.0122	.00632
3YR Hearing Screen				.0573	.0552
Birthweight	.0374	.0335	.0303		.0381
Gestation Age	−.0143	−.0166	−.0160		−.00969
Education of Gravida	−.00639	−.00649	−.0151		−.00758
Per Capita Income	.0244	.0228	.0176		.0184
Education of F.O.B.	.0271	.0263	.0195		.0359
Occupation of F.O.B.	.00787	.00827	.00406		.00502
8-Month Mental Score		.0103	.00394		
8-Month Motor Score		.00859	.00274		
4YR IQ			.0595		
Race-Sex Marker I	−.0760	−.0746	−.0818		−.0720
Race-Sex Marker II	−.0257	−.0253	−.0415		−.0365
Race-Sex Marker III	.0412	.0411	.0554		.0528

776

Response Variable: 8YR Total Sensorineural Loss

	Beta-Coefficients of Independent Predictors				
	At-Birth NCPP's	At-Birth NCPP's 8-Month NCPP's	At-Birth NCPP's 8-Month NCPP's 4YR IQ	3YR Indexes	3YR Indexes At-Birth NCPP's
Multiple R	.035	.0442	.0564	.076	.082
R Square	.001	.00196	.00319	.006	.007
3YR Speech Mechanism				−.0101	−.0111
3YR Hypernasality				−.00398	−.00353
3YR Fluency				−.0137	−.0134
3YR Articulation				.00558	.00532
3YR Intelligibility				.0263	.0245
3YR Language Comprehension				.0198	.0202
3YR Sentence Complexity				.0290	.0275
3YR Auditory Memory				−.0117	−.0134
3YR Hearing Screen				.0430	.0431
Birthweight	.0232	.0165	.0142		.0190
Gestation Age	−.00391	−.00789	−.00745		.00483
Education of Gravida	−.00298	−.00315	−.00937		−.00456
Per Capita Income	.0171	.0142	.0105		.0151
Education of F.O.B.	.0134	.0121	.00716		.0134
Occupation of F.O.B.	.00501	.00567	.00264		−.00583
8-Month Mental Score		.0159	.0113		
8-Month Motor Score		.0166	.0124		
4YR IQ			.0427		
Race-Sex Marker I	−.0285	−.0261	−.0312		−.0201
Race-Sex Marker II	−.00583	−.00502	−.0167		−.00545
Race-Sex Marker III	.0153	.0151	.0254		.0224

Response Variable: Neurological Involvement

	Beta-Coefficients of Independent Predictors				
	At-Birth NCPP's	At-Birth NCPP's 8-Month NCPP's	At-Birth NCPP's 8-Month NCPP's 4YR IQ	3YR Indexes	3YR Indexes At-Birth NCPP's
Multiple R	.253	.259	.297	.155	.265
R Square	.064	.0671	.0881	.024	.070
3YR Speech Mechanism				.00437	.0108
3YR Hypernasality				.00212	.000802
3YR Fluency				−.00986	.00386
3YR Articulation				.0751	.0555
3YR Intelligibility				.0400	.0320
3YR Language Comprehension				.0690	.0140
3YR Sentence Complexity				.0185	.0166
3YR Auditory Memory				.0190	.0161
3YR Hearing Screen				.00705	.0197
Birthweight	.0266	.0131	.00372		.0107
Gestation Age	.00521	−.00273	−.000904		.00708
Education of Gravida	.0794	.0791	.0534		.0744
Per Capita Income	.0458	.0401	.0246		.0268
Education of F.O.B.	.0418	.0390	.0187		.0374
Occupation of F.O.B.	.0527	.0540	.0415		.0467
8-Month Mental Score		.0279	.00901		
8-Month Motor Score		.0366	.0192		
4YR IQ			.176		
Race-Sex Marker I	.0397	.0446	.0234		.0414
Race-Sex Marker II	.127	.128	.0803		.112
Race-Sex Marker III	−.113	−.113	−.0705		−.105

Response Variable: Communicative Effectiveness

	Beta-Coefficients of Independent Predictors				
	At-Birth NCPP's	At-Birth NCPP's 8-Month NCPP's	At-Birth NCPP's 8-Month NCPP's 4YR IQ	3YR Indexes	3YR Indexes At-Birth NCPP's
Multiple R	.612	.620	.724	.395	.660
R Square	.374	.385	.524	.156	.436
3YR Speech Mechanism				−.00895	.00647
3YR Hypernasality				−.00513	−.00738
3YR Fluency				−.0426	−.00573
3YR Articulation				.117	.0664
3YR Intelligibility				.102	.0846
3YR Language Comprehension				.230	.0960
3YR Sentence Complexity				.0817	.0772
3YR Auditory Memory				.0520	.0405
3YR Hearing Screen				−.0308	.0000348
Birthweight	.0651	.0406	.0163		.0404
Gestation Age	−.00471	−.0194	−.0147		.00614
Education of Gravida	.162	.162	.0955		.140
Per Capita Income	.155	.145	.105		.129
Education of F.O.B.	.140	.135	.0829		.141
Occupation of F.O.B.	.0810	.0836	.0514		.0791
8-Month Mental Score		.0715	.0227		
8-Month Motor Score		.0489	.00426		
4YR IQ			.454		
Race-Sex Marker I	.144	.153	.0981		.134
Race-Sex Marker II	.262	.264	.140		.209
Race-Sex Marker III	−.277	−.277	−.167		−.232

Response Variable: Auditory Processing

	Beta-Coefficients of Independent Predictors				
	At-Birth NCPP's	At-Birth NCPP's 8-Month NCPP's	At-Birth NCPP's 8-Month NCPP's 4YR IQ	3YR Indexes	3YR Indexes At-Birth NCPP's
Multiple R	.591	.601	.727	.427	.651
R Square	.349	.361	.528	.182	.424
3YR Speech Mechanism				.00167	.0145
3YR Hypernasality				−.0103	−.0132
3YR Fluency				−.0395	−.00513
3YR Articulation				.128	.0809
3YR Intelligibility				.111	.0928
3YR Language Comprehension				.235	.112
3YR Sentence Complexity				.0804	.0755
3YR Auditory Memory				.0833	.0705
3YR Hearing Screen				−.0244	.00327
Birthweight	.0817	.0558	.0292		.0511
Gestation Age	.00276	−.0128	−.00763		.00927
Education of Gravida	.167	.166	.0940		.146
Per Capita Income	.146	.135	.0914		.116
Education of F.O.B.	.139	.0402	.0774		.133
Occupation of F.O.B.	.0856	.0885	.0533		.0807
8-Month Mental Score		.0884	.0349		
8-Month Motor Score		.0402	−.00872		
4YR IQ			.498		
Race-Sex Marker I	.129	.138	.0779		.118
Race-Sex Marker II	.226	.229	.0927		.167
Race-Sex Marker III	−.264	−.264	−.144		−.211

Physical, Medical, and Behavioral Characteristics of the Samples

A. Method of Delivery.
B. Blood Type of Children.
C. Apgar Scores at One Minute.
D. Apgar Scores at Five Minutes.
E. Maximum Serum Bilirubin (mgm%).
F. Weight of Children from Birth to Seven Years of Age.
G. Mean Birthweight by Gestational Age (weeks).
H. Height of Children from Birth to Seven Years of Age.
I. Head Circumference of Children from Birth to Seven Years of Age.
J. Bayley Mental Scores at Age Eight Months.
K. Bayley Motor Scores at Age Eight Months.
L. Neonatal Neurological Abnormalities.
M. Neurological Abnormalities at One Year of Age.
N. Neurological Abnormalities at Seven Years of Age.
O. Nonneurological Abnormalities at Seven Years of Age.
P. WISC Full-Scale IQ at Seven Years of Age.
Q. Distribution of Multiple Births.

A. Method of Delivery

Method of Delivery	Male	Female	White	Black	0.0-1.9	2.0-3.9	4.0-5.9	6.0-7.9	8.0-9.5
3YR									
Vertex	93	92	92	93	92	92	93	92	93
Breech	3	3	3	3	3	3	3	3	3
C/S	5	5	5	5	5	5	4	5	4
Missing Data	.23	.20	.08	.32	.51	.26	.17	.09	.10
3YR/8YR									
Vertex	93	92	92	93	92	92	93	92	93
Breech	3	3	3	3	3	3	3	3	3
C/S	5	4	4	5	5	5	4	5	4
Missing Data	.22	.20	.09	.32	.43	.32	.17	.05	.06
8YR									
Vertex	93	92	92	92	91	92	93	92	93
Breech	3	3	3	3	3	3	3	3	3
C/S	5	5	5	5	6	5	4	5	4
Missing Data	.24	.19	.10	.33	.43	.35	.18	.07	.04
Non SLH									
Vertex	93	92	92	92	92	92	92	92	94
Breech	2	3	3	2	3	3	3	3	2
C/S	5	5	5	5	5	5	5	5	4
Missing Data	.22	.18	.15	.31	.35	.15	.14	.27	.27

B. Blood Type of Children

Blood Type of Children		Male	Female	White	Black	0.0-1.9	2.0-3.9	4.0-5.9	6.0-7.9	8.0-9.5
3YR	O	47	46	45	48	46	48	48	46	44
	A	31	33	40	26	28	30	31	35	38
	B	17	17	11	22	22	19	17	14	13
	AB	4	4	4	4	4	4	4	5	4
	Missing Data	3.9	3.7	2.7	4.6	4.8	4.1	4.4	2.7	1.6
3YR/8YR	O	46	46	44	48	46	47	47	45	44
	A	32	33	41	25	28	31	32	36	39
	B	17	17	11	23	23	19	17	14	13
	AB	4	4	4	4	3	4	4	5	4
	Missing Data	4.1	4.3	2.7	5.5	5.6	5.0	4.8	2.6	1.8
8YR	O	47	47	46	48	46	47	48	47	46
	A	32	33	39	25	28	30	32	35	37
	B	16	17	11	22	22	19	17	14	13
	AB	4	4	4	4	4	4	4	4	4
	Missing Data	4.0	4.1	2.8	5.3	5.6	4.7	4.3	3.0	2.1
Non SLH	O	46	47	45	50	46	47	47	46	46
	A	35	35	40	25	30	33	33	38	39
	B	15	15	11	21	21	17	15	12	12
	AB	4	4	4	4	4	3	4	3	4
	Missing Data	3.3	3.6	3.0	4.4	4.6	4.3	3.3	3.0	2.7

782

C. Apgar Scores at One Minute

Apgar Scores at One Minute	Male	Female	White	Black	0.0-1.9	2.0-3.9	4.0-5.9	6.0-7.9	8.0-9.5
3YR									
Mean	7.8	7.9	7.6	8.0	8.0	8.0	7.9	7.7	7.7
SD	2.0	1.8	1.8	1.9	2.0	1.9	1.9	1.9	1.7
Missing Data	7.8	8.3	6.9	8.9	8.9	9.1	8.4	7.2	4.3
3YR/8YR									
Mean	7.8	7.9	7.6	8.0	7.9	7.9	7.8	7.7	7.7
SD	1.9	1.8	1.8	1.9	2.1	1.9	1.9	1.8	1.6
Missing Data	8.1	9.3	6.2	11	9.7	11	9.1	6.9	3.7
8YR									
Mean	7.7	7.9	7.7	7.9	7.9	7.9	7.8	7.7	7.8
SD	1.9	1.8	1.8	1.9	2.1	1.9	1.9	1.8	1.7
Missing Data	7.8	9.0	5.3	12	10	11	8.9	5.5	3.5
Non SLH									
Mean	7.7	7.7	7.6	7.8	7.8	7.8	7.7	7.6	7.7
SD	2.0	1.9	1.9	2.0	2.0	2.0	2.0	1.9	1.9
Missing Data	6.2	5.9	4.4	9.4	9.0	9.2	6.5	3.9	2.7

D. Apgar Scores at Five Minutes

Apgar Scores at Five Minutes	Male	Female	White	Black	0.0-1.9	2.0-3.9	4.0-5.9	6.0-7.9	8.0-9.5
3YR									
Mean	9.0	9.1	8.9	9.2	9.2	9.1	9.0	8.9	8.9
SD	1.2	1.1	1.0	1.3	1.3	1.2	1.2	1.1	.85
Missing Data	6.0	6.4	4.9	7.2	6.7	7.2	6.7	5.2	2.3
3YR/8YR									
Mean	9.0	9.0	8.9	9.1	9.1	9.1	9.0	8.9	8.9
SD	1.2	1.1	1.0	1.3	1.3	1.3	1.2	1.1	.80
Missing Data	5.7	6.3	4.0	7.8	6.7	7.6	6.5	4.4	2.0
8YR									
Mean	8.9	9.0	8.9	9.1	9.1	9.0	8.9	8.9	8.9
SD	1.2	1.1	.95	1.3	1.3	1.2	1.1	1.0	.79
Missing Data	5.3	5.9	3.6	7.7	6.9	7.9	5.8	3.6	2.2
Non SLH									
Mean	8.9	8.9	8.9	9.0	9.0	9.0	8.9	8.8	8.9
SD	1.2	1.1	1.0	1.3	1.3	1.3	1.1	1.1	.87
Missing Data	4.9	5.1	4.2	6.6	5.9	7.6	5.1	3.4	3.2

E. Maximum Serum Bilirubin (mgm/%)

Maximum Serum Bilirubin (mgm/%)	Male	Female	White	Black	0.0-1.9	2.0-3.9	4.0-5.9	6.0-7.9	8.0-9.5
3YR									
10 or Less	87	90	88	90	89	89	89	88	88
11-15	9	7	9	8	8	8	8	8	8
16-20	3	2	3	2	2	2	2	3	3
21 or More	1	1	1	1	1	1	1	1	1
Missing Data	4.7	4.1	3.5	5.1	4.6	4.5	5.1	4.4	1.9
3YR/8YR									
10 or Less	87	90	88	89	89	88	88	89	88
11-15	9	8	9	8	8	9	9	8	8
16-20	3	2	3	2	2	2	2	2	3
21 or More	1	1	1	1	1	1	1	1	1
Missing Data	4.6	4.1	3.4	5.2	5.1	4.7	5.0	3.9	2.0
8YR									
10 or Less	87	90	89	89	89	88	88	90	89
11-15	9	7	8	9	8	9	8	7	7
16-20	3	2	3	2	2	3	2	2	3
21 or More	1	1	1	1	1	1	1	1	1
Missing Data	4.4	4.3	3.3	5.5	5.5	4.6	4.8	4.0	2.4
Non SLH									
10 or Less	87	90	88	89	90	88	88	90	90
11-15	9	7	8	8	7	9	9	7	7
16-20	3	2	3	2	2	3	2	3	3
21 or More	1	1	1	0	1	1	1	1	1
Missing Data	4.0	3.7	3.2	5.2	5.1	4.8	3.9	3.3	2.8

F. Weight of Children from Birth to Seven Years of Age

3YR **Weight of Children from Birth to Seven Years of Age**	Male	Female	White	Black	0.0-1.9	2.0-3.9	4.0-5.9	6.0-7.9	8.0-9.5
Birth (gms)									
Mean	3,213	3,096	3,290	3,053	3,056	3,109	3,146	3,233	3,304
SD	543	527	526	525	540	536	546	528	496
Missing Data	.10	.10	.07	.12	.15	.10	.12	.06	.05
Four Months (gms)									
Mean	6,539	6,043	6,494	6,145	6,014	6,154	6,286	6,508	6,690
SD	947	848	912	920	919	926	922	892	863
Missing Data	5.7	5.6	6.8	4.8	6.9	6.3	5.8	4.6	3.6
Eight Months (gms)									
Mean	8,778	8,170	8,671	8,323	8,207	8,329	8,483	8,683	8,747
SD	1,204	1,059	1,154	1,168	1,099	1,214	1,181	1,125	1,079
Missing Data	56	56	54	57	57	58	58	57	36
1YR (kg)									
Mean	10	9.5	10	9.6	9.5	9.7	9.8	10	10
SD	1.3	1.2	1.3	1.3	1.2	1.3	1.3	1.3	1.2
Missing Data	2.8	3.0	3.6	2.4	3.2	3.1	2.8	2.3	3.5
3YR (kg)									
Mean	15	14	14	14	14	14	14	15	15
SD	1.9	1.8	1.8	1.9	1.7	1.8	2.0	1.9	1.7
Missing Data	22	21	25	19	18	21	24	27	14
4YR (kg)									
Mean	17	16	17	16	16	16	16	17	17
SD	2.1	2.2	2.2	2.2	2.1	2.2	2.2	2.2	2.1
Missing Data	14	14	14	13	13	15	14	14	10
7YR (kg)									
Mean	24	23	24	24	23	23	24	24	24
SD	3.9	4.3	4.0	4.2	3.8	4.2	4.3	4.1	3.9
Missing Data	11	12	8.4	13	11	12	12	10	8.3

3YR/8YR
Weight of Children
from Birth to
Seven Years of Age

	Male	Female	White	Black	0.0-1.9	2.0-3.9	4.0-5.9	6.0-7.9	8.0-9.5
Birth (gms)									
Mean	3,224	3,102	3,295	3,048	3,057	3,109	3,152	3,238	3,312
SD	542	528	525	524	537	537	544	534	495
Missing Data	.09	.10	.05	.14	.17	.12	.06	.09	.06
Four Months (gms)									
Mean	6,563	6,068	6,518	6,148	6,017	6,154	6,304	6,541	6,697
SD	935	848	902	915	910	921	913	897	838
Missing Data	5.2	5.3	6.0	4.6	6.5	5.8	5.4	4.6	3.2
Eight Months (gms)									
Mean	8,830	8,191	8,688	8,323	8,230	8,312	8,509	8,705	8,741
SD	1,131	1,093	1,170	1,111	1,186	1,102	1,223	1,126	1,088
Missing Data	60	61	55	66	68	67	64	57	35
1YR (kg)									
Mean	10	9.5	10	9.6	9.5	9.7	9.8	10	10
SD	1.2	1.2	1.2	1.3	1.2	1.3	1.3	1.3	1.1
Missing Data	2.1	2.5	2.6	2.1	2.7	2.5	2.2	1.7	2.7
3YR (kg)									
Mean	15	14	14	14	14	14	14	14	15
SD	1.9	1.8	1.8	1.9	1.6	1.8	2.0	1.9	1.6
Missing Data	25	24	25	25	23	26	27	29	12
4YR (kg)									
Mean	17	16	17	16	16	16	16	17	17
SD	2.1	2.2	2.1	2.2	2.0	2.2	2.2	2.2	2.0
Missing Data	12	12	11	13	12	14	13	11	6.9
7YR (kg)									
Mean	24	23	24	24	23	23	24	24	24
SD	3.9	4.1	3.9	4.1	3.6	4.0	4.1	4.0	3.9
Missing Data	3.3	3.9	1.2	5.8	5.5	4.8	3.6	1.6	1.9

F. Weight of Children from Birth to Seven Years of Age (continued)

8YR **Weight of Children from Birth to Seven Years of Age**	Male	Female	White	Black	0.0-1.9	2.0-3.9	4.0-5.9	6.0-7.9	8.0-9.5
Birth (gms)									
Mean	3,233	3,112	3,291	3,053	3,054	3,108	3,164	3,246	3,317
SD	546	528	524	530	538	543	546	529	493
Missing Data	.07	.13	.06	.14	.12	.13	.07	.10	.09
Four Months (gms)									
Mean	6,549	6,063	6,462	6,153	6,010	6,159	6,298	6,473	6,617
SD	916	833	874	916	921	921	891	867	839
Missing Data	6.7	6.8	7.2	6.3	8.2	8.0	7.1	5.1	4.6
Eight Months (gms)									
Mean	8,862	8,235	8,679	8,309	8,252	8,347	8,532	8,702	8,725
SD	1,123	1,075	1,139	1,118	1,174	1,141	1,182	1,105	1,069
Missing Data	64	64	55	73	72	72	68	56	39
1YR (kg)									
Mean	10	9.5	10	9.7	9.5	9.7	9.8	10	10
SD	1.3	1.2	1.3	1.3	1.3	1.3	1.3	1.3	1.2
Missing Data	5.5	5.9	6.6	4.8	6.0	5.7	5.6	5.3	6.4
3YR (kg)									
Mean	15	14	14	14	14	14	14	14	15
SD	1.9	1.8	1.8	1.9	1.6	1.8	2.0	1.9	1.6
Missing Data	51	52	55	48	42	47	56	62	40
4YR (kg)									
Mean	17	16	17	16	16	16	16	17	17
SD	2.1	2.2	2.1	2.2	2.1	2.2	2.2	2.2	2.0
Missing Data	19	20	19	21	21	21	20	19	16
7YR (kg)									
Mean	24	23	24	24	23	24	24	24	24
SD	4.0	4.3	4.0	4.3	3.9	4.2	4.3	4.2	3.8
Missing Data	3.3	3.6	1.8	5.1	5.3	4.6	3.2	2.2	2.1

F. Weight of Children from Birth to Seven Years of Age (continued)

Non SLH Weight of Children from Birth to Seven Years of Age	Male	Female	White	Black	0.0-1.9	2.0-3.9	4.0-5.9	6.0-7.9	8.0-9.5
Birth (gms)									
Mean	3,279	3,122	3,279	3,055	3,067	3,133	3,179	3,265	3,319
SD	547	533	533	540	547	550	550	541	498
Missing Data	.09	.18	.09	.21	.35	.11	.20	.07	.07
Four Months (gms)									
Mean	6,597	6,062	6,434	6,141	5,982	6,204	6,318	6,457	6,459
SD	908	848	898	930	998	924	928	898	845
Missing Data	24	23	22	25	31	30	24	18	17
Eight Months (gms)									
Mean	8,872	8,264	8,697	8,365	8,336	8,465	8,509	8,641	8,806
SD	1,130	1,095	1,110	1,204	1,141	1,160	1,226	1,154	984
Missing Data	78	78	78	77	79	79	81	78	68
1YR (kg)									
Mean	10	9.6	10	9.6	9.5	9.8	9.9	10	10
SD	1.3	1.2	1.3	1.3	1.5	1.3	1.3	1.3	1.2
Missing Data	33	33	33	32	39	38	32	29	33
3YR (kg)									
Mean	16	13	17	14	12	15	15	17	16
SD	3.7	3.7	5.2	2.6	2.1	6.0	2.8	1.5	.14
Missing Data	99	99	99	99	99	99	99	99	99
4YR (kg)									
Mean	17	16	17	17	16	17	17	17	17
SD	2.2	2.4	2.3	2.4	2.9	2.4	2.4	2.3	2.2
Missing Data	69	69	68	71	75	74	66	65	73
7YR (kg)									
Mean	24	24	24	24	23	24	24	24	24
SD	4.0	4.4	4.2	4.2	4.2	4.3	4.3	4.2	3.8
Missing Data	56	56	52	64	66	65	54	50	55

G. Mean Birthweight by Gestational Age (weeks)

Mean Birthweight by Gestational Age	White Male	White Female	Black Male	Black Female
3YR				
21-25	3,134	2,983	2,679	2,586
26-30	2,775	2,567	2,447	2,452
31-35	2,678	2,574	2,742	2,578
36-40	3,250	3,141	3,106	2,996
41-45	3,550	3,395	3,315	3,205
46-50	3,540	3,403	3,207	3,122
3YR/8YR				
21-25	2,990	2,983	2,873	2,706
26-30	2,706	2,684	2,469	2,389
31-35	2,670	2,519	2,719	2,599
36-40	3,258	3,148	3,135	2,988
41-45	3,563	3,388	3,319	3,188
46-50	3,519	3,375	3,168	3,120
8YR				
21-25	3,036	2,983	2,606	2,741
26-30	2,498	2,591	2,427	2,463
31-35	2,614	2,584	2,727	2,608
36-40	3,263	3,146	3,114	2,991
41-45	3,554	3,399	3,328	3,191
46-50	3,528	3,458	3,236	3,102

H. Height of Children from Birth to Seven Years of Age

3YR Height of Children from Birth to Seven Years of Age (cms)	Male	Female	White	Black	0.0-1.9	2.0-3.9	4.0-5.9	6.0-7.9	8.0-9.5
Birth									
Mean	50	49	50	49	49	49	50	50	50
SD	2.7	2.7	2.6	2.8	2.8	2.7	2.8	2.6	2.5
Missing Data	1.5	1.4	1.5	1.4	1.9	1.6	1.3	1.4	1.1
Four Months									
Mean	63	61	63	61	61	61	62	63	63
SD	3.3	3.1	3.2	3.3	3.2	3.3	3.3	3.2	2.9
Missing Data	5.6	5.3	6.4	4.8	6.8	6.2	5.6	4.3	3.2
Eight Months									
Mean	70	68	70	69	68	69	69	70	70
SD	3.3	3.3	3.3	3.3	3.8	3.1	3.7	3.0	3.2
Missing Data	56	56	54	57	57	58	58	57	37
1YR									
Mean	75	74	75	74	74	74	74	75	75
SD	3.4	3.4	3.4	3.5	3.5	3.5	3.4	3.4	3.0
Missing Data	3.4	3.3	4.0	2.9	3.7	3.5	3.6	2.6	3.4
3YR									
Mean	95	94	95	94	94	94	94	95	96
SD	12	5.6	13	5.0	5.3	13	6.4	6.0	4.1
Missing Data	23	22	26	20	18	21	25	28	15
4YR									
Mean	102	101	102	102	101	101	101	102	103
SD	5.3	5.3	5.2	5.3	4.5	5.2	5.7	5.5	4.3
Missing Data	14	14	14	13	13	15	14	14	10
7YR									
Mean	122	121	121	122	122	122	122	122	122
SD	5.6	5.7	5.5	5.7	5.6	5.6	5.7	5.7	5.6
Missing Data	11	12	8.4	13	11	12	12	10	8.3

3YR/8YR
Height of Children
from Birth to Seven

Years of Age (cms)	Male	Female	White	Black	0.0-1.9	2.0-3.9	4.0-5.9	6.0-7.9	8.0-9.5
Birth									
Mean	50	50	50	50	50	50	50	50	50
SD	2.7	2.7	2.6	2.8	2.8	2.7	2.8	2.6	2.5
Missing Data	1.5	1.4	1.5	1.4	1.9	1.9	1.2	.93	1.1
Four Months									
Mean	63	61	63	61	61	61	62	63	63
SD	3.3	3.2	3.2	3.3	3.3	3.3	3.4	3.2	2.9
Missing Data	5.0	5.1	5.7	4.5	6.5	5.7	5.3	4.4	2.7
Eight Months									
Mean	70	68	70	69	68	69	69	70	70
SD	3.0	3.3	3.2	3.1	3.1	3.1	3.4	2.9	3.2
Missing Data	60	61	55	66	68	67	64	57	35
1YR									
Mean	75	74	75	74	74	74	75	75	75
SD	3.4	3.3	3.3	3.5	3.5	3.5	3.4	3.3	3.0
Missing Data	2.6	2.8	2.9	2.5	3.3	2.9	3.0	1.8	2.5
3YR									
Mean	95	94	95	94	94	94	94	95	96
SD	14	6.3	15	4.7	3.7	17	6.6	5.7	4.1
Missing Data	26	25	25	25	23	26	28	30	13
4YR									
Mean	102	101	102	101	101	101	101	102	103
SD	5.2	5.1	5.0	5.2	4.6	4.6	6.1	5.0	4.3
Missing Data	12	12	11	13	12	14	13	11	6.7
7YR									
Mean	122	122	121	123	122	122	122	122	122
SD	5.5	5.6	5.4	5.6	5.4	5.5	5.7	5.7	5.5
Missing Data	3.4	4.0	1.2	5.8	5.5	4.9	3.7	1.7	1.9

791

8YR
Height of Children from Birth to Seven Years of Age (cms)

	Male	Female	White	Black	0.0-1.9	2.0-3.9	4.0-5.9	6.0-7.9	8.0-9.5
Birth									
Mean	50	50	50	49	49	50	50	50	50
SD	2.8	2.7	2.7	2.8	2.8	2.8	2.8	2.8	2.5
Missing Data	1.5	1.5	1.6	1.5	1.8	2.0	1.2	1.1	1.7
Four Months									
Mean	63	61	63	62	61	62	62	63	63
SD	3.3	3.2	3.2	3.3	3.3	3.3	3.3	3.2	2.9
Missing Data	6.8	6.8	6.9	6.7	8.3	8.4	7.0	5.0	4.3
Eight Months									
Mean	70	69	70	69	68	69	69	70	70
SD	3.1	3.3	3.3	3.2	3.3	3.1	3.5	3.4	3.0
Missing Data	64	64	55	73	73	72	68	56	40
1YR									
Mean	75	74	75	74	74	74	74	75	75
SD	3.4	3.4	3.3	3.6	3.6	3.6	3.5	3.3	3.1
Missing Data	6.1	6.3	7.0	5.4	6.6	6.4	6.2	5.7	6.4
3YR									
Mean	95	94	95	94	94	94	94	95	96
SD	14	6.2	15	5.0	3.8	17	6.5	5.7	4.1
Missing Data	52	52	56	48	42	48	56	62	41
4YR									
Mean	102	101	101	102	101	101	101	101	102
SD	5.4	5.2	5.3	5.3	4.6	4.9	6.0	5.4	4.7
Missing Data	19	20	19	20	21	21	20	19	16
7YR									
Mean	122	121	121	123	122	122	122	121	122
SD	5.7	5.7	5.5	5.7	5.6	5.6	5.8	5.8	5.6
Missing Data	3.4	3.7	1.8	5.2	5.4	4.7	3.3	2.2	2.0

H. Height of Children from Birth to Seven Years of Age (continued)

Non SLH Height of Children from Birth to Seven Years of Age (cms)	Male	Female	White	Black	0.0-1.9	2.0-3.9	4.0-5.9	6.0-7.9	8.0-9.5
Birth									
Mean	51	50	50	49	49	50	50	50	51
SD	2.9	2.8	2.8	2.9	3.1	2.8	2.9	2.9	2.7
Missing Data	2.1	2.5	2.3	2.3	2.3	2.3	2.0	2.2	2.9
Four Months									
Mean	63	62	63	62	62	62	63	63	63
SD	3.5	3.4	3.5	3.4	3.5	3.5	3.5	3.6	3.3
Missing Data	24	23	22	25	31	30	24	18	17
Eight Months									
Mean	71	69	70	70	70	70	70	70	70
SD	3.8	4.3	4.4	3.7	3.9	3.7	4.2	4.2	4.6
Missing Data	78	78	78	77	79	79	81	78	68
1YR									
Mean	75	74	75	74	73	74	74	75	75
SD	3.4	3.5	3.4	3.8	3.9	3.7	3.5	3.4	3.5
Missing Data	33	33	34	32	40	38	32	39	33
3YR									
Mean	97	89	96	93	87	95	95	99	102
SD	6.8	8.6	9.1	7.7	2.7	11	6.1	5.5	1.4
Missing Data	99	99	99	99	99	99	99	99	99
4YR									
Mean	101	100	100	102	101	101	101	100	100
SD	6.5	22	19	6.5	4.8	6.1	25	6.5	6.6
Missing Data	69	69	68	71	75	74	66	65	73
7YR									
Mean	121	121	120	123	121	121	121	121	121
SD	5.7	5.8	5.6	5.8	6.4	5.9	5.8	5.7	5.7
Missing Data	56	56	52	64	66	65	54	50	54

I. Head Circumference of Children from Birth to Seven Years of Age

3YR Head Circumference (cms)	Male	Female	White	Black	0.0-1.9	2.0-3.9	4.0-5.9	6.0-7.9	8.0-9.5
Birth									
Mean	34	33	34	33	33	34	34	34	34
SD	1.6	1.6	1.5	1.7	1.7	1.6	1.6	1.5	1.4
Missing Data	1.1	1.0	1.2	1.0	1.5	1.1	1.0	1.1	.74
Four Months									
Mean	41	40	41	41	40	41	41	41	41
SD	1.5	1.4	1.5	1.6	1.6	1.6	1.5	1.5	1.4
Missing Data	5.1	4.8	6.0	4.1	6.5	5.6	5.0	3.9	2.9
Eight Months									
Mean	45	43	44	44	44	44	44	44	44
SD	1.7	1.8	2.0	1.6	1.7	1.7	1.9	2.1	1.6
Missing Data	56	56	55	57	57	58	59	57	37
1YR									
Mean	46	45	46	46	46	46	46	46	46
SD	1.5	1.5	1.6	1.6	1.6	1.6	1.6	1.6	1.5
Missing Data	2.5	2.6	3.1	2.1	2.7	2.7	2.6	1.8	2.8
3YR									
Mean	50	49	49	49	49	49	49	50	50
SD	1.9	2.0	2.3	1.8	2.0	2.0	1.9	1.8	2.4
Missing Data	23	22	26	19	18	21	24	28	15
4YR									
Mean	50	50	50	50	50	50	50	50	50
SD	1.9	1.7	1.9	1.7	1.6	1.8	1.9	1.8	1.9
Missing Data	14	14	15	14	13	15	15	14	11
7YR									
Mean	52	51	51	51	51	51	51	52	52
SD	1.6	1.5	1.6	1.6	1.6	1.6	1.6	1.6	1.5
Missing Data	11	12	8.5	13	11	12	12	10	8.5

I. Head Circumference of Children from Birth to Seven Years of Age (continued)

3YR/8YR Head Circumference (cms)	Male	Female	White	Black	0.0-1.9	2.0-3.9	4.0-5.9	6.0-7.9	8.0-9.5
Birth									
Mean	34	33	34	34	34	34	34	34	34
SD	1.6	1.5	1.5	1.6	1.6	1.6	1.6	1.5	1.4
Missing Data	1.1	1.1	1.2	1.0	1.5	1.4	1.0	.70	.84
Four Months									
Mean	41	40	41	41	40	41	41	41	41
SD	1.5	1.4	1.5	1.6	1.5	1.6	1.5	1.5	1.4
Missing Data	4.4	4.5	5.4	3.7	6.0	5.0	4.6	3.9	2.3
Eight Months									
Mean	45	43	44	44	44	44	44	44	44
SD	1.7	1.9	2.0	1.7	1.9	1.6	2.0	2.2	1.6
Missing Data	61	61	55	66	68	67	65	57	36
1YR									
Mean	46	45	46	46	46	46	46	46	46
SD	1.5	1.5	1.6	1.6	1.5	1.6	1.6	1.5	1.5
Missing Data	1.8	2.0	2.2	1.7	2.2	2.1	2.0	1.1	2.1
3YR									
Mean	50	49	49	49	49	49	49	50	50
SD	2.0	2.0	2.2	1.8	2.2	2.0	1.8	1.8	2.3
Missing Data	25	25	26	25	23	26	28	30	13
4YR									
Mean	50	50	50	50	50	50	50	50	50
SD	1.9	1.6	1.7	1.8	1.6	1.9	1.7	1.6	2.0
Missing Data	12	12	12	13	13	14	13	12	7.8
7YR									
Mean	52	51	52	51	51	51	51	52	52
SD	1.6	1.5	1.6	1.6	1.6	1.6	1.5	1.6	1.5
Missing Data	3.5	4.1	1.3	6.0	5.7	5.0	3.8	1.7	2.3

I. Head Circumference of Children from Birth to Seven Years of Age (continued)

8YR Head Circumference (cms)	Male	Female	White	Black	0.0-1.9	2.0-3.9	4.0-5.9	6.0-7.9	8.0-9.5
Birth									
Mean	34	33	34	33	34	34	34	34	34
SD	1.6	1.5	1.5	1.7	1.7	1.6	1.6	1.5	1.4
Missing Data	1.2	1.2	1.3	1.1	1.5	1.6	1.0	.70	1.5
Four Months									
Mean	41	40	41	41	40	40	41	41	41
SD	1.5	1.4	1.5	1.6	1.6	1.6	1.5	1.5	1.4
Missing Data	6.0	6.0	6.5	5.5	7.6	7.2	6.3	4.3	4.0
Eight Months									
Mean	45	44	44	44	44	44	44	44	44
SD	1.9	1.9	2.0	1.9	1.9	1.6	2.2	2.1	1.8
Missing Data	64	64	56	73	73	72	68	57	40
1YR									
Mean	46	45	46	46	46	46	46	46	46
SD	1.5	1.5	1.5	1.6	1.6	1.6	1.5	1.5	1.5
Missing Data	5.0	5.3	6.0	4.4	5.1	5.3	5.0	4.9	6.0
3YR									
Mean	50	49	49	49	49	49	49	50	50
SD	2.0	2.0	2.2	1.8	2.2	2.0	1.8	1.8	2.3
Missing Data	51	52	56	48	42	48	56	62	41
4YR									
Mean	50	50	50	50	50	50	50	50	50
SD	1.9	1.7	1.8	1.9	1.6	1.9	1.8	1.6	1.9
Missing Data	20	20	19	21	21	21	20	19	17
7YR									
Mean	52	51	52	51	51	51	51	52	52
SD	1.5	1.5	1.6	1.6	1.6	1.6	1.5	1.6	1.5
Missing Data	3.4	3.7	1.9	5.3	5.3	4.7	3.3	2.3	2.5

I. Head Circumference of Children from Birth to Seven Years of Age (continued)

Non SLH Head Circumference (cms)	Male	Female	White	Black	0.0-1.9	2.0-3.9	4.0-5.9	6.0-7.9	8.0-9.5
Birth									
Mean	34	33	34	33	33	34	34	34	34
SD	1.6	1.6	1.5	1.7	1.7	1.7	1.6	1.6	1.5
Missing Data	1.7	2.2	1.9	2.1	2.3	2.2	1.8	1.7	2.2
Four Months									
Mean	41	40	41	40	40	40	41	41	41
SD	1.5	1.5	1.5	1.7	1.6	1.7	1.6	1.6	1.4
Missing Data	23	23	22	25	31	29	24	18	17
Eight Months									
Mean	45	44	45	44	44	44	44	44	45
SD	1.9	2.3	2.3	1.9	3.0	1.7	2.3	2.0	2.3
Missing Data	78	78	78	77	80	79	81	78	68
1YR									
Mean	46	45	46	46	45	46	46	46	46
SD	1.5	1.5	1.6	1.6	1.6	1.6	1.6	1.5	1.5
Missing Data	33	33	33	32	39	38	31	29	33
3YR									
Mean	50	47	50	48	48	49	49	51	50
SD	1.4	2.2	2.2	1.8	2.3	2.0	1.5	1.2	1.4
Missing Data	99	99	99	99	99	99	99	99	99
4YR									
Mean	50	50	50	50	49	50	50	50	51
SD	1.6	1.7	1.7	1.6	1.9	1.8	1.6	1.6	1.6
Missing Data	69	69	68	71	75	75	66	65	73
7YR									
Mean	52	51	51	51	51	51	51	52	52
SD	1.6	1.5	1.6	1.7	1.7	1.6	1.6	1.6	1.6
Missing Data	56	56	52	64	66	65	54	50	55

797

J. Bayley Mental Scores at Age Eight Months

Bayley Mental Scores	Male	Female	White	Black	0.0-1.9	2.0-3.9	4.0-5.9	6.0-7.9	8.0-9.5
3YR									
Mean	79	79	80	80	78	79	79	80	80
SD	6.0	5.8	5.2	6.4	6.7	6.0	6.0	5.6	4.7
Missing Data	6.0	6.1	6.0	6.1	8.1	7.0	6.0	4.7	3.3
3YR/8YR									
Mean	79	79	80	79	78	79	79	80	80
SD	5.5	5.6	4.8	6.1	6.3	5.7	5.5	5.7	4.3
Missing Data	5.5	5.8	4.7	6.4	9.5	6.8	5.5	3.7	2.7
8YR									
Mean	79	80	80	79	78	79	80	80	80
SD	5.6	5.5	4.8	6.2	6.3	5.9	5.5	5.3	4.6
Missing Data	8.0	8.3	7.0	9.4	12	10	8.2	5.4	5.3
Non SLH									
Mean	80	80	80	79	78	79	80	80	80
SD	7.4	6.8	6.9	7.5	9.5	7.4	7.2	6.6	6.5
Missing Data	30	30	28	34	40	38	30	24	26

K. Bayley Motor Scores at Age Eight Months

Bayley Motor Scores	Male	Female	White	Black	0.0-1.9	2.0-3.9	4.0-5.9	6.0-7.9	8.0-9.5
3YR									
Mean	33	33	33	33	33	33	33	34	34
SD	4.8	4.5	4.7	4.6	5.0	4.6	4.7	4.5	4.4
Missing Data	5.9	6.2	6.0	6.1	7.9	7.0	6.1	4.7	3.2
3YR/8YR									
Mean	33	33	33	33	33	33	33	33	34
SD	4.7	4.4	4.6	4.6	4.8	4.6	4.6	4.5	4.3
Missing Data	5.5	5.8	4.8	6.4	9.2	6.9	5.6	3.7	2.7
8YR									
Mean	33	33	33	33	33	33	33	33	34
SD	4.7	4.5	4.6	4.6	4.9	4.7	4.6	4.5	4.3
Missing Data	8.0	8.3	7.0	9.4	12	10	8.2	5.4	5.3
Non SLH									
Mean	33	33	33	34	33	33	33	34	34
SD	5.2	4.9	5.1	5.0	5.6	5.2	5.1	4.9	4.7
Missing Data	30	30	28	34	40	38	30	24	26

L. Neonatal Neurological Abnormalities

Neonatal Neurological Abnormalities (%)	Male	Female	White	Black	0.0-1.9	2.0-3.9	4.0-5.9	6.0-7.9	8.0-9.5
3YR									
Normal	91	93	92	91	93	91	91	91	94
Suspect	8	7	7	8	7	8	8	8	5
Abnormal	1	1	1	1	1	1	1	1	1
Missing Data	6.9	5.8	5.6	6.9	6.6	6.3	7.4	6.2	3.5
3YR/8YR									
Normal	91	93	92	92	94	92	91	91	94
Suspect	8	7	7	7	5	7	8	8	5
Abnormal	1	1	1	1	1	1	1	1	1
Missing Data	7.1	6.2	5.8	7.5	6.1	7.2	8.2	5.8	3.4
8YR									
Normal	92	94	93	93	93	93	93	93	93
Suspect	7	6	6	7	6	6	7	7	5
Abnormal	1	1	1	1	1	1	1	1	1
Missing Data	6.7	6.1	5.3	7.4	6.7	7.1	7.3	5.2	3.9
Non SLH									
Normal	94	95	94	95	94	96	95	94	94
Suspect	5	4	5	4	5	4	5	6	5
Abnormal	1	1	1	1	1	0	1	1	1
Missing Data	7.4	6.0	6.8	6.7	5.9	6.7	7.0	7.2	5.6

M. Neurological Abnormalities at One Year of Age

Neurological Abnormalities at 1YR (%)	Male	Female	White	Black	0.0-1.9	2.0-3.9	4.0-5.9	6.0-7.9	8.0-9.5
3YR									
None	90	92	91	90	90	90	91	91	94
Suspicious	8	7	7	8	9	8	8	7	5
Abnormal	2	2	2	2	2	2	2	2	2
Missing Data	2.2	2.2	2.8	1.7	2.3	2.2	2.2	1.7	2.7
3YR/8YR									
None	91	93	92	92	91	91	92	92	94
Suspicious	8	6	6	7	7	8	7	6	5
Abnormal	2	1	2	1	1	1	2	2	1
Missing Data	1.5	1.6	1.9	1.3	1.6	1.8	1.6	1.0	1.9
8YR									
None	91	93	92	92	90	91	92	92	94
Suspicious	7	6	7	7	8	7	6	6	5
Abnormal	2	1	1	1	2	2	2	1	1
Missing Data	4.6	4.8	5.6	3.7	4.5	4.7	4.5	4.6	5.6
Non SLH									
None	91	90	90	91	88	89	90	91	92
Suspicious	7	8	8	7	9	8	8	7	7
Abnormal	2	2	2	3	4	2	2	2	1
Missing Data	32	32	33	31	39	37	31	28	32

N. Neurological Abnormalities at Seven Years of Age

Neurological Abnormalities at 7YR (%)	Male	Female	White	Black	0.0-1.9	2.0-3.9	4.0-5.9	6.0-7.9	8.0-9.5
3YR									
None	79	86	83	82	78	81	83	84	87
Suspicious	16	11	13	14	17	15	13	13	9
Definite	5	3	4	4	4	4	4	4	4
Missing Data	11	12	8.4	13	11	12	12	10	8.3
3YR/8YR									
None	80	87	83	84	81	82	84	84	87
Suspicious	15	10	13	12	15	14	12	12	9
Definite	4	3	4	3	5	4	4	3	4
Missing Data	3.5	3.9	1.2	5.9	6.0	4.9	3.6	1.5	2.0
8YR									
None	82	88	85	85	81	83	85	87	88
Suspicious	14	9	11	12	14	13	11	10	8
Definite	5	3	4	4	5	4	4	3	3
Missing Data	3.3	3.5	1.7	5.1	5.4	4.6	3.1	2.0	2.1
Non SLH									
None	85	89	87	84	81	85	85	88	91
Suspicious	10	7	8	10	13	10	9	7	7
Definite	5	4	4	6	6	5	6	4	2
Missing Data	56	56	52	64	66	65	53	49	54

O. Non-Neurological Abnormalities at Seven Years of Age

Non-Neurological Abnormalities at 7YR (%)	Male	Female	White	Black	0.0-1.9	2.0-3.9	4.0-5.9	6.0-7.9	8.0-9.5
3YR									
None	66	70	64	71	70	68	68	66	68
Minor	32	28	34	27	28	30	30	32	30
Definite	2	2	2	2	2	2	2	2	1
Missing Data	13	14	11	15	13	14	14	12	9.7
3YR/8YR									
None	65	70	62	72	71	67	67	65	68
Minor	33	28	36	26	27	31	31	33	30
Definite	2	2	2	2	2	2	2	2	1
Missing Data	5.5	5.2	3.7	6.8	6.5	6.7	5.6	3.6	3.0
8YR									
None	67	71	65	73	70	69	69	68	70
Minor	31	27	33	25	28	29	29	30	29
Definite	2	2	2	2	2	2	2	2	2
Missing Data	5.2	5.0	3.9	6.3	6.9	6.5	4.9	4.0	2.9
Non SLH									
None	73	77	75	74	71	73	75	75	77
Minor	25	22	23	25	27	25	23	23	21
Definite	2	2	2	2	2	2	2	2	2
Missing Data	57	57	53	64	68	66	54	50	55

P. WISC Full-Scale IQ at Seven Years of Age

WISC Full-Scale IQ at 7YR	Male	Female	White	Black	0.0-1.9	2.0-3.9	4.0-5.9	6.0-7.9	8.0-9.5
3YR									
Mean	95	95	102	90	87	90	94	101	110
SD	15	14	14	13	13	13	13	14	13
Missing Data	10	11	9.0	12	10	10	11	11	8.5
3YR/8YR									
Mean	96	96	102	91	89	91	95	102	111
SD	15	14	14	13	13	13	13	14	13
Missing Data	3.1	3.3	2.1	4.1	5.4	3.5	3.0	2.2	2.3
8YR									
Mean	97	97	103	91	88	92	96	103	111
SD	15	14	14	13	13	13	13	13	13
Missing Data	3.4	3.5	2.6	4.4	5.3	4.0	3.1	2.6	3.1
Non SLH									
Mean	102	101	105	92	87	94	100	105	112
SD	16	15	14	15	16	15	14	14	15
Missing Data	56	56	52	64	66	65	54	50	54

Q. Distribution of Multiple Births

			Number of Children
ALL 3YR	Singletons	19,487	19,487
	Twins (# pairs)	171 ⎰ # white = 65 ⎱ # black = 106	342
	Triplets (# sets)	3 ⎰ BF, BF, BM ⎱ WF, WF, WF ⎱ WF, WF, WF	9
	Incomplete*	47	47
			19,885
3YR/8YR	Singletons	12,209	12,209
	Twins (# pairs)	108 ⎰ # white = 48 ⎱ # black = 60	216
	Triplets (# sets)	0	0
	Incompletes*	39	39
			12,464
ALL 8YR	Singletons	19,719	19,719
	Twins (# pairs)	185 ⎰ # white = 83 ⎱ # black = 102	370
	Triplets (# sets)	0	0
	Incompletes*	45	45
			20,134

*e.g., only one of a pair of twins, one or two of a set of triplets took the SLH test battery.

Distributions of Discrimination Scores, Expected and Observed, as Related to Selected SLH Variables. Comparison between 8YR Hearing Loss Variables and Other NCPP Variables Showing Correlations and Differences between Expected and Observed Frequencies of Occurrence.

In Sections A through J, Discrimination Scores are divided into three ranges; more than five errors, four or five errors and less than four errors. Scores on the second variables have been grouped as shown along the left margins. For each interval there are three rows. The first shows the difference between the number of children expected and observed; the second the number observed; and the third the number expected. Each of these numbers represents numbers of children per thousand.

The expected row represents the number of children per thousand that would be expected to score in the indicated range if the two variables are independent; that is, these numbers are computed from the marginal totals of the table. For example, for White Males on Oral Reading, only two children per thousand would be expected to score between 0 and two *and* to make five or more errors on Discrimination if the variables were unrelated. Instead, five children per thousand were counted in this category.

Sections K through Q deal each with one of the 8YR Hearing Loss categories with which selected NCPP variables were compared. The rows under the selected variables give actual numbers of observed cases, the number of cases expected from the entire sample, and the differences between these numbers.

A. Joint Distributions of Better Ear Discrimination and Word Identification Scores by Sex, Race and Total.

B. Joint Distributions of Better Ear Discrimination and Word Identification Scores by SEI.

C. Joint Distributions of Better Ear Discrimination and Written Communication Scores by Sex, Race and Total.

D. Joint Distributions of Better Ear Discrimination and Written Communication Scores by SEI.

E. Joint Distributions of Better Ear Discrimination and Articulation Scores by Sex, Race and Total.

F. Joint Distributions of Better Ear Discrimination and Articulation Scores by SEI.

G. Joint Distributions of Better Ear Discrimination and Oral Reading Scores by Sex, Race and Total.

H. Joint Distributions of Better Ear Discrimination and Oral Reading Scores by SEI.

I. Joint Distributions of Better and Poorer Ear Discrimination and Digit Scores by Race and Sex.

J. Joint Distributions of Better and Poorer Ear Discrimination and Digit Scores by SEI

K. Relation between Monaural Sensorineural Acuity and Selected Variables.

L. Relation between Binaural Sensorineural Severity and Selected Variables.

M. Relation between Binaural Sensorineural Acuity and Selected Variables.

N. Relation between Binaural Conductive Severity and Selected Variables.

O. Relation between Binaural Conductive Acuity and Selected Variables.

P. Relation between Binaural Heterogeneous Severity and Selected Variables.

Q. Relation between Binaural Heterogeneous Acuity and Selected Variables.

A. Joint Distributions of Better-Ear Discrimination and Word Identification Scores by Sex, Race and Total

Word Identification Score	*	White Male N = 3,663			White Female N = 3,902			Black Male N = 3,531			Black Female N = 3,814			Total N = 14,910		
		>5	4-5	<4	>5	4-5	<4	>5	4-5	<4	>5	4-5	<4	>5	4-5	<4
≤51	**	+1	+1	0	+2	+2	−5	+10	+17	−27	+18	+21	−38	+10	+16	−25
	***	1	1	8	3	3	21	19	39	76	36	60	161	15	26	67
	****	0	0	8	1	1	26	9	22	103	18	39	199	5	10	92
52-55		+1	0	−1	+1	+1	−2	+7	+10	−16	0	+5	−6	+4	+7	−12
		1	1	12	2	2	28	17	34	99	12	30	120	8	16	64
		0	1	13	1	1	30	10	24	115	12	25	126	4	9	76
56-58		0	+3	−3	+1	+3	−3	0	+6	−5	−5	+2	+3	+1	+7	−8
		1	4	.23	2	5	57	12	35	134	8	30	146	6	18	89
		1	1	26	1	2	60	12	29	139	13	28	143	5	11	97
59-60		+1	0	−1	0	+1	−2	0	−2	+3	−2	−2	+3	0	+1	−2
		2	2	37	2	4	69	8	17	96	6	15	88	4	10	73
		1	2	38	2	3	71	8	19	93	8	17	85	4	9	75
61-63		+2	+3	−4	+1	0	−2	−4	−7	+11	−4	−10	+14	−1	−3	+4
		4	7	97	4	5	111	6	17	127	5	8	107	5	9	110
		2	4	101	3	5	113	10	24	116	9	18	93	6	12	106
64-65		−1	−2	+2	0	0	0	−2	−6	+9	−2	−4	+7	−2	−4	+5
		1	2	84	2	4	89	3	6	66	2	4	50	2	4	72
		2	4	82	2	4	89	5	12	57	4	8	43	4	8	67
66-68		+1	−1	+1	+1	−1	0	−5	−7	+11	−3	−5	+7	−3	−6	+9
		4	5	138	4	5	149	1	7	76	1	3	48	2	5	103
		3	6	137	3	6	149	6	14	65	4	8	41	5	11	94
69-71		+1	−1	0	−2	−3	+5	−3	−6	+8	−2	−3	+5	−3	−6	+10
		4	6	153	2	4	170	1	3	49	0	2	31	2	4	102
		3	7	153	4	7	165	4	9	41	2	5	26	5	10	92
72-74		−2	+1	+1	−1	−2	+4	−2	−3	+6	−1	−3	+3	−3	−5	+8
		1	7	139	1	3	115	0	2	32	0	0	16	1	3	76
		3	6	138	2	5	111	2	5	26	1	3	13	4	8	68
75+		−3	−5	+9	−2	−3	+5	0	−2	+3	−1	−1	+2	−4	−8	+12
		2	5	249	1	2	131	1	1	19	0	0	9	1	2	102
		5	10	240	3	5	126	1	3	16	1	1	7	5	10	90

*Number of discrimination errors.
**Difference between expected and observed cases per 1,000 SS.
***Observed cases per 1,000 SS.
****Expected cases per 1,000 SS.

B. Joint Distributions of Better-Ear Discrimination and Word Identification Scores by SEI

Word Identification Score	*	SEI I N = 1,132			SEI II N = 4,269			SEI III N = 4,502			SEI IV N = 3,162			SEI V N = 1,845		
		>5	4-5	<4	>5	4-5	<4	>5	4-5	<4	>5	4-5	<4	>5	4-5	<4
≤51	**	+19	+17	−38	+13	+19	−32	+7	+13	−20	+2	+5	−8	0	+2	−2
	***	42	62	148	26	44	109	11	22	62	3	7	24	0	2	2
	****	23	45	186	13	25	141	4	9	82	1	2	32	0	0	4
52-55		+1	+4	−4	+3	+6	−9	+3	+8	−10	+2	+3	−5	0	+1	−1
		18	37	133	13	25	96	7	17	66	3	5	30	0	1	5
		17	33	137	10	19	105	4	9	76	1	2	35	0	0	6
56-58		−6	+8	−2	−2	+6	−4	0	+6	−5	+1	+4	−4	+1	0	−1
		10	39	128	11	30	131	5	18	98	2	7	53	1	0	11
		16	31	130	13	24	135	5	12	103	1	3	57	0	0	12
59-60		0	−3	+3	−1	−1	+2	+1	0	0	+1	+2	−3	0	0	0
		9	16	81	7	15	89	5	10	91	2	5	53	0	1	16
		9	19	78	8	16	87	4	10	91	1	3	56	0	1	16
61-63		−5	−7	+12	−2	−8	+10	0	−4	+5	0	+2	−1	+1	+1	−2
		4	12	90	8	12	121	6	10	129	2	8	114	1	3	47
		9	19	78	10	20	111	6	14	124	2	6	115	0	2	49
64-65		−2	−6	+9	−3	−4	+7	−2	−3	+5	0	−2	+2	+1	−1	0
		3	3	46	2	5	58	2	6	87	2	3	87	1	1	59
		5	9	37	5	9	51	4	9	82	2	5	85	0	2	59
66-68		−2	−6	+8	−3	−7	+9	−2	−6	+9	−1	−2	+3	0	0	0
		3	4	49	3	5	74	3	5	110	2	6	142	1	4	119
		5	10	41	6	12	65	5	11	101	3	8	139	1	4	119
69-71		−1	−3	+4	−3	−5	+8	−2	−6	+7	−2	−4	+6	+1	+1	−1
		2	2	27	1	3	53	2	4	98	1	4	153	2	7	179
		3	5	23	4	8	45	4	10	91	3	8	147	1	6	180
72-74		−2	−2	+4	−2	−4	+6	−2	−3	+5	−1	−2	+3	−1	+1	0
		0	1	16	0	1	32	1	3	63	1	4	120	0	7	170
		2	3	12	2	5	26	3	6	58	2	6	117	1	6	170
75+		−1	−2	+4	−1	−3	+3	−2	−4	+6	−2	−6	+8	−1	−4	+6
		0	1	16	1	0	22	1	2	59	1	2	157	1	8	352
		1	3	12	2	3	19	3	6	53	3	8	149	2	12	346

*Number of discrimination errors.
**Difference between expected and observed cases per 1,000 SS.
***Observed cases per 1,000 SS.
****Expected cases per 1,000 SS.

C. Joint Distributions of Better-Ear Discrimination and Written Communication Scores by Sex, Race and Total

Written Communi-cation Score	*	White Male N = 3,553			White Female N = 3,811			Black Male N = 3,424			Black Female N = 3,683			Total N = 14,471		
		>5	4-5	<4	>5	4-5	<4	>5	4-5	<4	>5	4-5	<4	>5	4-5	<4
	**	+3	+5	−7	+1	+4	−5	+8	+11	−20	+6	+6	−12	+6	+8	−14
C-135	***	5	8	72	2	6	33	21	43	132	12	19	56	10	18	72
	****	2	3	79	1	2	38	13	32	152	6	13	68	4	10	86
		−1	0	0	+2	+2	−4	+4	+4	−8	+3	+3	−5	+2	+5	−7
136-161		1	4	82	3	4	41	16	32	129	10	19	78	7	15	81
		2	4	82	1	2	45	12	28	137	7	16	83	5	10	88
		0	+2	−2	0	+2	−1	−2	+1	+1	+2	+5	−8	+1	+3	−5
162-180		2	5	73	1	4	55	7	23	107	10	23	84	5	13	79
		2	3	75	1	2	56	9	22	106	8	18	92	4	10	84
		+1	0	0	+1	0	−2	0	0	+1	0	−1	+1	+1	+1	−3
181-196		3	4	86	2	3	60	8	20	98	9	19	100	5	11	85
		2	4	86	1	3	62	8	20	97	9	20	99	4	10	88
		+1	−1	0	+2	−1	−1	−3	−2	+5	0	+2	−2	+1	0	−1
197-210		3	3	84	4	2	72	4	14	81	9	21	95	5	10	83
		2	4	84	2	3	73	7	16	76	9	19	97	4	10	84
		−1	0	0	0	−1	+1	−3	−2	+5	−1	+1	−1	0	−1	+1
211-223		1	4	93	2	3	85	3	12	74	7	19	89	4	9	86
		2	4	93	2	4	84	6	14	69	8	18	90	4	10	85
		0	−2	+3	−1	−1	+1	−1	−5	+6	−1	−4	+5	−2	−3	+5
224-237		2	3	114	1	4	111	3	6	58	7	13	92	3	7	94
		2	5	111	2	5	110	4	11	52	8	17	87	5	10	89
		+1	−1	+1	−1	−2	+2	−1	−3	+5	−2	−4	+8	−1	−3	+6
238-253		3	4	106	2	3	121	2	5	44	4	10	81	3	6	89
		2	5	105	3	5	119	3	8	39	6	14	73	4	9	83
		−1	−2	+4	−2	−2	+4	0	−1	+1	−4	−4	+8	−2	−5	+8
254-275		1	3	119	2	4	161	2	4	27	1	7	63	2	5	94
		2	5	115	4	6	157	2	5	26	5	11	55	4	10	86
		−1	0	+2	−2	−4	+6	−2	−3	+5	−2	−4	+6	−3	−7	+10
276-383		1	5	111	2	4	200	0	1	23	1	2	39	1	3	95
		2	5	109	4	8	194	2	4	18	3	6	33	4	10	85

*Number of discrimination errors.
**Difference between expected and observed cases per 1,000 SS.
***Observed cases per 1,000 SS.
****Expected cases per 1,000 SS.

807

D. Joint Distributions of Better-Ear Discrimination and Written Communication Scores by SEI

Written Communication Score	*	SEI I N = 1,088			SEI II N = 4,122			SEI III N = 4,377			SEI IV N = 3,090			SEI V N = 1,794		
		>5	4-5	<4	>5	4-5	<4	>5	4-5	<4	>5	4-5	<4	>5	4-5	<4
0-135	**	+5	+7	-12	+6	+6	-12	+4	+9	-13	+2	+5	-7	0	+1	-1
	***	23	43	138	17	29	113	8	18	73	3	7	29	0	1	9
	****	18	36	150	11	23	125	4	9	86	1	2	36	0	0	10
136-161		+3	+3	-6	+2	+1	-4	+2	+3	-6	+1	+4	-5	0	+1	-1
		19	35	128	12	21	108	7	14	93	2	7	50	0	2	17
		16	32	134	10	20	112	5	11	99	1	3	55	0	1	18
162-180		+1	+6	-6	0	+3	-3	0	+2	-1	+1	+3	-4	0	+2	-3
		12	27	84	10	22	104	4	11	85	2	7	66	0	3	28
		11	21	90	10	19	107	4	9	86	1	4	70	0	1	31
181-196		-2	-1	+3	0	0	-1	0	+2	-2	+1	-1	+1	0	0	0
		8	19	85	9	18	100	5	13	98	2	3	72	0	2	45
		10	20	82	9	18	101	5	11	100	1	4	71	0	2	45
197-210		-1	-4	+4	0	-2	+2	+1	0	-1	+1	0	-2	+1	+1	-2
		11	19	99	7	13	84	5	10	89	3	5	84	1	3	52
		12	23	95	7	15	82	4	10	90	2	5	86	0	2	54
211-223		0	-3	+3	-2	+2	+1	0	-1	+1	-1	+1	0	0	0	0
		7	11	63	5	16	81	4	8	87	1	6	98	1	3	87
		7	14	60	7	14	80	4	9	86	2	5	98	1	3	87
224-237		-1	-1	+2	-2	-4	+6	-1	-2	+3	-1	-3	+4	0	-1	+2
		6	12	56	4	8	72	4	8	98	1	3	122	1	3	114
		7	13	54	6	12	66	5	10	95	2	6	118	1	4	112
238-253		-1	-3	+3	-2	-2	+3	-1	-5	+5	-1	-3	+4	0	0	-1
		3	6	40	3	8	57	3	5	92	1	3	121	1	5	128
		4	9	37	5	10	54	4	10	87	2	6	117	1	5	129
254-275		-2	-2	+5	-1	-3	+5	-3	-4	+7	-2	-1	+2	0	-3	+3
		1	3	26	3	4	43	1	5	86	1	6	140	1	4	194
		3	5	21	4	7	38	4	9	79	3	7	138	1	7	191
276-383		-2	-3	+5	-1	-2	+4	-2	-3	+5	-2	-5	+6	0	-2	+2
		0	0	17	1	2	26	1	3	62	1	3	151	2	8	285
		2	3	12	2	4	22	3	6	57	3	8	145	2	10	283

*Number of discrimination errors.
**Difference between expected and observed cases per 1,000 SS.
***Observed cases per 1,000 SS.
****Expected cases per 1,000 SS.

E. Joint Distributions of Better-Ear Discrimination and Articulation Scores by Sex, Race and Total

Articulation Score	*	White Male N = 3,664 >5	4-5	<4	White Female N = 3,907 >5	4-5	<4	Black Male N = 3,530 >5	4-5	<4	Black Female N = 3,812 >5	4-5	<4	Total N = 14,913 >5	4-5	<4
	**	+4	−1	−2	+1	+2	−3	+16	+19	−36	+9	+11	−21	+8	+9	−17
0-40	***	6	4	108	2	5	61	28	47	97	15	25	50	13	20	78
	****	2	5	110	1	3	64	12	28	133	6	14	71	5	11	95
		−3	+1	+1	−1	−2	+3	−16	−19	+36	−9	−11	+20	−8	−9	+16
41-50		15	37	831	19	34	878	39	114	674	56	128	725	32	78	779
		18	36	830	20	36	875	55	133	638	65	139	705	40	87	763
		+2	−1	−2	+1	+2	−3	+11	+9	−19	+4	+6	−9	+5	+5	−9
0-35		3	1	36	1	3	18	17	24	53	7	12	23	7	10	32
		1	2	38	0	1	21	6	15	72	3	6	32	2	5	41
		−2	+1	+2	−1	−2	+4	−10	−8	+19	−3	−6	+9	−5	−5	+9
36-50		17	40	903	20	36	922	51	138	718	65	141	753	38	88	826
		19	39	901	21	38	918	61	146	699	68	147	744	43	93	817

*Number of discrimination errors.
**Difference between expected and observed cases per 1,000 SS.
***Observed cases per 1,000 SS.
****Expected cases per 1,000 SS.

F. Joint Distributions of Better-Ear Discrimination and Articulation Scores by SEI

Articulation Score	*	SEI I N = 1,134 >5	4-5	<4	SEI II N = 4,269 >5	4-5	<4	SEI III N = 4,500 >5	4-5	<4	SEI IV N = 3,163 >5	4-5	<4	SEI V N = 1,847 >5	4-5	<4
	**	+15	+18	−32	+11	+13	−24	+8	+8	−15	+2	+2	−5	0	+1	−1
0-40	***	29	46	86	21	32	81	12	18	76	4	7	78	0	4	76
	****	14	28	118	10	19	105	4	10	91	2	5	83	0	3	77
		−15	−17	+32	−11	−13	+25	−7	−8	+15	−2	−2	+5	0	−1	+1
41-50		60	131	649	52	109	706	31	78	786	13	44	854	5	30	884
		75	148	617	63	122	681	38	86	771	15	46	849	5	31	883
		+6	+12	−19	+8	+6	−13	+4	+4	−8	+1	+1	−3	0	+1	−1
0-35		13	27	42	13	15	39	6	9	33	2	3	25	0	2	18
		7	15	61	5	9	52	2	5	41	1	2	28	0	1	19
		−6	−12	+18	−8	−6	+13	−4	−4	+8	−1	−1	+3	0	−1	+1
36-50		76	149	692	60	126	747	37	87	829	15	48	907	5	32	943
		82	161	674	68	132	734	41	91	821	16	49	904	5	33	942

*Number of discrimination errors.
**Difference between expected and observed cases per 1,000 SS.
***Observed cases per 1,000 SS.
****Expected cases per 1,000 SS.

G. Joint Distributions of Better-Ear Discrimination and Oral Reading Scores by Sex, Race and Total

Oral Reading Score	*	White Male N = 3,661			White Female N = 3,906			Black Male N = 3,531			Black Female N = 3,814			Total N = 14,912		
		>5	4-5	<4	>5	4-5	<4	>5	4-5	<4	>5	4-5	<4	>5	4-5	<4
0-2	**	+3	+5	−7	0	+4	−5	+7	+14	−20	+4	+3	−8	+5	+9	−13
	***	5	8	68	1	6	32	19	44	123	10	16	56	9	18	69
	****	2	3	75	1	2	37	12	30	143	6	13	64	4	9	82
3-7		0	0	0	+1	+1	−2	+4	+2	−6	+4	+3	−6	+3	+5	−8
		2	3	74	2	3	39	18	35	153	11	19	75	8	15	84
		2	3	74	1	2	41	14	33	159	7	16	81	5	10	92
8-10		−1	+2	−1	+2	+2	−3	0	+2	−3	+3	+2	−7	+2	+4	−7
		1	5	79	3	4	54	11	28	120	13	23	98	7	15	87
		2	3	80	1	2	57	11	26	123	10	21	105	5	11	94
11-13		−1	−1	+1	+1	+2	−13	−3	−1	+5	+1	+1	−4	0	+2	−2
		1	3	86	2	4	52	4	16	88	10	20	91	4	11	79
		2	4	85	1	2	65	7	17	83	9	19	95	4	9	81
14-16		0	+2	−2	−1	−1	+1	−1	−2	+3	−2	+4	−1	0	0	−1
		2	5	80	1	2	66	5	12	70	6	20	82	4	9	74
		2	3	82	2	3	65	6	14	67	8	16	83	4	9	75
17-20		+1	−1	+1	+1	+1	−1	−2	−3	+6	−1	−2	+2	0	−1	+1
		4	4	121	3	5	102	4	12	80	8	18	101	5	10	101
		3	5	120	2	4	103	6	15	74	9	20	99	5	11	100
21-23		0	−2	+2	0	−1	+1	−2	−1	+2	0	0	+1	−1	−2	+3
		2	2	101	2	3	101	2	8	45	6	14	73	3	7	80
		2	4	99	2	4	100	4	9	43	6	14	72	4	9	77
24-27		−1	−1	+3	0	−1	+1	−1	−3	+5	−4	−2	+6	−3	−3	+6
		1	4	118	3	5	136	2	5	45	3	14	86	2	7	97
		2	5	115	3	6	135	3	8	40	7	16	80	5	10	91
28-32		−1	0	+2	−2	−2	+4	−1	−3	+6	−3	−6	+9	−2	−5	+9
		1	4	102	2	4	154	1	2	32	3	6	70	2	4	91
		2	4	100	4	6	150	2	5	26	6	12	61	4	9	82
33-54		−1	−2	+4	−3	−4	+7	0	−2	+2	−3	−5	+7	−3	−7	+10
		1	3	112	2	4	204	1	1	15	0	2	43	1	3	95
		2	5	108	5	8	197	1	3	13	3	7	36	4	10	85

*Number of discrimination errors.
**Difference between expected and observed cases per 1,000 SS.
***Observed cases per 1,000 SS.
****Expected cases per 1,000 SS.

H. Joint Distributions of Better-Ear Discrimination and Oral Reading Scores by SEI

Oral Reading Score	*	SEI I N = 1,133			SEI II N = 4,268			SEI III N = 4,504			SEI IV N = 3,162			SEI V N = 1,845		
		>5	4-5	<4	>5	4-5	<4	>5	4-5	<4	>5	4-5	<4	>5	4-5	<4
0-2	**	+2	+10	−12	+4	+7	−11	+4	+6	−10	+2	+6	−8	0	+2	−2
	***	18	41	117	15	28	105	8	16	76	3	8	29	0	2	6
	****	16	31	129	11	21	116	4	10	86	1	2	37	0	0	8
3-7		+4	+6	−10	+2	+2	−5	+2	+3	−4	+3	+1	−4	0	0	0
		22	41	136	13	23	110	7	14	95	4	4	48	0	1	23
		18	35	146	11	21	115	5	11	99	1	3	52	0	1	23
8-10		+2	0	−1	+2	+2	−4	+1	+3	−5	+1	+3	−4	0	+2	−2
		15	25	102	13	24	117	6	14	94	2	7	67	0	3	25
		13	25	103	11	22	121	5	11	99	1	4	71	0	1	27
11-13		−1	−8	+9	−1	+2	−1	0	+3	−2	0	0	+1	0	+1	−2
		10	15	103	7	17	84	4	12	83	1	4	79	0	3	44
		11	23	94	8	15	85	4	9	85	1	4	78	0	2	46
14-16		−3	0	+2	−1	−1	+2	0	+1	−2	−1	+1	0	+1	+3	−4
		4	15	64	6	13	81	4	10	76	1	5	83	1	5	46
		7	15	62	7	14	79	4	9	78	2	4	83	0	2	50
17-20		+3	0	−2	−2	−2	+4	0	−2	+3	0	−2	+1	+1	0	0
		11	16	66	7	14	96	5	10	110	2	4	111	1	3	96
		8	16	68	9	16	92	5	12	107	2	6	110	0	3	96
21-23		−1	+1	0	0	−3	+2	0	−1	+1	−1	−2	+3	−1	−1	+1
		4	12	46	6	8	62	4	8	84	1	3	100	0	3	101
		5	11	46	6	11	60	4	9	83	2	5	97	1	4	100
24-27		−2	−4	+7	−2	−1	+3	−2	−3	+5	−2	0	+2	0	−1	+1
		4	8	55	3	8	56	3	7	98	0	7	128	1	5	163
		6	12	48	5	9	53	5	10	93	2	7	126	1	6	162
28-32		0	−2	+2	−2	−3	+5	−3	−5	+8	0	−2	+3	0	−2	+3
		3	4	27	2	4	47	1	3	80	2	5	135	1	4	183
		3	6	25	4	7	42	4	8	72	2	7	132	1	6	180
33-54		−2	−3	+5	−1	−3	+5	−2	−4	+7	−1	−5	+6	0	−3	+3
		0	0	18	1	2	30	1	3	66	2	3	151	1	7	272
		2	3	13	2	5	25	3	7	59	3	8	145	1	10	269

*Number of discrimination errors.
**Difference between expected and observed cases per 1,000 SS.
***Observed cases per 1,000 SS.
****Expected cases per 1,000 SS.

I. Joint Distributions of Better and Poorer-Ear Discrimination and Digit Scores by Race and Sex

Digit Score	*	White Male N = 3,664			White Female N = 3,908			Black Male N = 3,532			Black Female N = 3,817		
		>5	4-5	<4	>5	4-5	<4	>5	4-5	<4	>5	4-5	<4
Better Ear:													
≤4	**	+2	+4	−6	+1	+5	−5	+4	+4	−8	+6	+1	−7
	***	4	9	101	3	8	68	12	23	83	12	15	64
	****	2	5	107	2	3	73	8	19	91	6	14	71
≥4.5		−1	−4	+6	0	−5	+6	−4	−4	+7	−6	−1	+7
		16	32	838	19	31	872	55	138	688	59	138	712
		17	36	832	19	36	866	59	142	681	65	139	705
Poorer Ear:													
≤4		+1	+2	−3	0	+2	−1	+1	+4	−5	+2	+4	−7
		2	4	108	1	3	75	4	13	101	4	11	76
		1	2	111	1	1	76	3	9	106	2	7	83
≥4.5		−1	−2	+3	0	−1	+1	−1	−4	+5	−2	−4	+7
		7	16	863	7	16	899	19	63	800	16	61	832
		8	18	860	7	17	898	20	67	795	18	65	825

*Number of discrimination errors.
**Difference between expected and observed cases per 1,000 SS.
***Observed cases per 1,000 SS.
****Expected cases per 1,000 SS.

J. Joint Distributions of Better and Poorer-Ear Discrimination and Digit Scores
   by SEI

Digit Score	*	SEI I N = 1,134 >5	4-5	<4	SEI II N = 4,271 >5	4-5	<4	SEI III N = 4,506 >5	4-5	<4	SEI IV N = 3,164 >5	4-5	<4	SEI V N = 1,846 >5	4-5	<4
						Better Ear:										
≤4	**	+2	+4	−7	+5	+2	−6	+3	+4	−6	+1	+2	−3	0	+2	−3
	***	15	29	97	14	19	91	7	14	85	2	6	64	0	4	49
	****	13	25	104	9	17	97	4	10	91	1	4	67	0	2	52
≥4.5		−2	−4	+7	−5	−1	+6	−2	−4	+6	−1	−2	+3	0	−2	+3
		74	147	638	59	122	695	36	82	777	15	45	869	5	30	911
		76	151	631	64	123	689	38	86	771	16	47	866	5	32	908
						Poorer Ear:										
≤4		+1	0	−2	+3	+2	−5	+1	+4	−5	−1	+1	−1	0	+1	−1
		4	12	124	6	11	107	2	9	94	0	3	69	0	2	51
		3	12	126	3	9	112	1	5	99	1	2	70	0	1	52
≥4.5		−2	0	+2	−3	−2	+5	−1	−4	+5	+1	−1	−4	0	−1	+1
		19	71	769	19	60	797	10	35	850	7	18	904	7	14	926
		21	71	767	22	62	792	11	39	845	6	19	908	7	15	925

*Number of discrimination errors.
**Difference between expected and observed cases per 1,000 SS.
***Observed cases per 1,000 SS.
****Expected cases per 1,000 SS.

K. Monaural Sensorineural Acuity

Brief Attention Span (4YR)   r = .26   N = 71

	No	Yes
Observed	67	4
Expected	69	2
	*−2	+2

*Difference between observed and expected.

L. Binaural Sensorineural Severity

Infectious Diseases during Pregnancy   r = .28   N = 95

	0	1	2	3
Observed	76	15	3	1
Expected	77	16	1	0
	*−1	−1	+2	+1

Deafness Judgment (1YR)   r = .65   N = 87

	No	Yes
Observed	69	18
Expected	87	0
	*−18	+18

Trouble Speaking (through 7YRS)   r = .29   N = 89

	No	Yes
Observed	79	10
Expected	88	1
	*−9	+9

Wechsler Verbal IQ (7YR)   r = −.35   N = 89

	45−	56−	66−	76−	86−	96−	106−	116−	126−
Observed	1	7	10	17	24	20	10	0	0
Expected	0	1	5	13	26	23	13	1	0
	*+1	+6	+5	+4	−2	−3	−3	−1	0

Auditory Vocal Association (7YR)   r = −.43   N = 89

	0-1	2-3	4-5	6-7	8-9	10-11	12-13	14-15	16-17	18-19	20-21	22-23	24-25
Observed	1	2	2	2	6	3	6	14	13	13	21	6	0
Expected	0	0	0	1	1	2	5	8	14	22	21	11	3
	*+1	+2	+2	+1	+5	+1	+1	+6	−1	−7	0	−5	−3

*Difference between observed and expected.

L. Binaural Sensorineural Severity (continued)

Eight-Month Mental Score   r = −.30   N = 94

	47-52	53-55	56-58	59-61	62-64	65-67	68-70	71-73	74-76	77-79	80-82	83-85	86-88	89-
Observed	1	1	0	3	0	0	2	5	14	25	26	11	4	2
Expected	0	0	0	0	0	1	1	3	11	26	29	15	5	1
	*+1	+1	0	+3	0	−1	+1	+2	+3	−1	−3	−4	−1	+1

Response to Rattle (Bayley)   r = .24   N = 94

	Pass	Fail
Observed	93	1
Expected	93	1
	* 0	0

Social-Emotional Development (8 months)   r = .21   N = 91

	Advanced	Normal	Suspect	Abnormal
Observed	1	80	9	1
Expected	2	81	7	0
	*−1	−1	+2	+1

Communication Nonverbal (4YR)   r = .57   N = 90

	No	Yes
Observed	79	11
Expected	89	1
	*−10	+10

Wechsler Vocabulary Score (7YR)   r = −.35   N = 89

	0	1	2	3	4	5	6	7	8	9	10	11	12	13	14	15	16
Observed	1	1	1	1	8	12	9	10	8	8	11	8	6	3	1	1	0
Expected	0	0	0	1	3	7	9	7	12	1	11	10	7	5	3	2	1
	*+1	+1	+1	0	+5	+5	0	+3	−4	+7	0	−2	−1	−2	−2	−1	−1

*Difference between observed and expected.

L. Binaural Sensorineural Severity (continued)
Indexes

8YR Articulation

	0-5	6-10	11-15	16-20	21-25	26-30	31-35	36-40	41-46	46-
Observed	3	3	0	5	7	4	12	6	15	43
Expected	0	0	0	0	1	1	3	7	18	67
	*+3	+3	0	+5	+6	+3	+9	−1	−3	−24

r = −.66   N = 98

8YR Intelligibility

	Unintelligible	Considerable Difficulty	Some Difficulty	No Difficulty
Observed	5	9	13	72
Expected	0	1	4	94
	*+5	+8	+9	−22

r = −.66   N = 99

8YR Language Comprehension

	0-20	21-40	41-60	61-80	81-100	101-120	121-140	141-160	161-180	181-200	201-220	221-
Observed	1	4	5	5	6	11	6	23	12	9	9	1
Expected	0	0	2	3	7	10	11	19	10	15	8	6
	*+1	+4	+3	+2	−1	+1	−5	+4	+2	−6	+1	−5

r = −.26   N = 92

8YR Word Identification

	5-	10-	15-	20-	25-	30-	35-	40-	45-	50-	55-	60-	65-	70-	75-	80-	85-
Observed	1	2	1	2	1	2	2	5	9	13	17	19	8	12	2	2	0
Expected	0	0	0	0	0	0	1	2	6	9	19	20	18	14	7	2	1
	*+1	+2	+1	+2	+1	+2	+1	+3	+3	+4	−2	−1	−10	−2	−5	0	−1

r = −.52   N = 98

8YR Concept Development

	1-5	6-10	11-15	16-20	21-25	26-30	31-35	36-40	41-45	46-50	51-55	56-60	61-
Observed	3	1	3	5	3	10	15	10	21	8	10	3	0
Expected	0	0	1	2	3	6	10	14	16	16	13	7	2
	*+3	+1	+2	+3	0	+4	+5	−4	+5	−8	−3	−4	−2

r = −.34   N = 92

*Difference between observed and expected.

M. Binaural Sensorineural Acuity

Infectious Diseases during Pregnancy

r = .27   N = 101

Number	0	1	2	3
Observed	81	16	3	1
Expected	82	17	1	0
	*−1	−1	+2	−1

Judgment of Deafness (1YR)

r = .59   N = 93

	No	Yes
Observed	75	18
Expected	93	0
	*−18	+18

Trouble Speaking (through 7YRS)

r = .32   N = 95

	No	Yes
Observed	85	10
Expected	94	1
	*−9	+9

Eight-Month Mental Score

r = −.30   N = 99

	47-49	53-55	59-61	65-67	68-70	71-73	74-76	77-79	80-82	83-85	86-88	89-91
Observed	1	1	3	0	2	6	15	26	27	12	4	2
Expected	0	0	0	1	1	3	11	28	31	16	5	1
	*+1	+1	+3	−1	+1	+3	+4	−2	−4	−4	−1	+1

Response to Rattle (Bayley)

r = .28   N = 96

	Pass	Fail
Observed	98	1
Expected	98	1
	* 0	0

Social-Emotional Development (8 months)

r = .27   N = 94

	Advanced	Normal	Suspect	Abnormal
Observed	1	85	9	1
Expected	2	86	7	0
	*−1	−1	+2	+1

*Difference between observed and expected.

M. Binaural Sensorineural Acuity (continued)

Communication Nonverbal (4YR) r = .59   N = 94

	No	Yes
Observed	83	11
Expected	93	1
	*−10	+10

Wechsler Vocabulary (7YR) r = −.43   N = 94

	0	1	2	3	4	5	6	7	8	9	10	11	12	13	14	15
Observed	1	1	1	1	8	13	10	10	11	8	11	8	6	2	1	2
Expected	0	0	1	1	3	7	10	8	13	9	12	10	8	5	3	8
	*+1	+1	0	0	+5	+6	0	+2	−2	−1	−1	−2	−2	−3	−2	−6

Wechsler Verbal IQ (7YR) r = −.45   N = 94

	45-55	56-65	66-75	76-85	86-95	96-105	106-115	116-125	126-
Observed	1	7	10	17	27	22	9	1	0
Expected	0	1	6	14	28	24	14	6	1
	*+1	+6	+4	+3	−1	−2	−5	−5	−1

Auditory-Vocal Association (ITPA)(7YR) r = −.55   N = 94

	0-1	2-3	4-5	6-7	8-9	10-11	12-13	14-15	16-17	18-19	20-21	22-23	24-25
Observed	1	2	2	2	6	3	6	15	13	15	21	8	0
Expected	0	0	0	1	1	3	5	9	16	23	22	11	3
	*+1	+2	+2	+1	+5	0	+1	+6	−3	−8	−1	−3	−3

Indexes

8YR Articulation r = −.59   N = 104

	0-5	6-10	11-15	16-20	21-25	26-30	31-35	36-40	41-45	46-
Observed	3	3	0	5	7	5	12	7	17	45
Expected	0	0	0	0	1	2	3	7	19	71
	*+3	+3	0	+5	+6	+3	+9	0	−2	−26

8YR Intelligibility r = −.77   N = 105

	Unintelligible	Considerable Difficulty	Some Difficulty	No Difficulty
Observed	5	9	13	78
Expected	0	1	5	99
	*+5	+8	+8	−21

*Difference between observed and expected.

M. Binaural Sensorineural Acuity (continued)
Indexes

8YR Language Comprehension   r = −.37   N = 98

	0-20	21-40	41-60	61-80	81-100	101-120	121-140	141-160	161-180	181-200	201-220	221-
Observed	1	5	6	5	6	11	6	23	15	10	9	1
Expected	0	0	2	3	7	11	12	20	11	16	8	7
*	+1	+5	+4	+2	−1	0	−6	+3	+4	−6	+1	+6

8YR Auditory Memory   r = −.28   N = 92

	0-20	21-40	41-60	61-80	81-100	101-120	121-140	141-160	161-180	181-	201-	221-	241-
Observed	1	1	2	7	5	4	14	12	20	10	11	4	1
Expected	0	0	0	1	3	5	11	15	17	17	13	6	2
*	+1	+1	+2	+6	+2	−1	+3	−3	+3	−7	−2	−2	−1

8YR Word Identification   r = −.58   N = 104

	5-9	10-14	15-19	20-24	25-29	30-34	35-39	40-44	45-49	50-	55-	60-	65-	70-	75-	80-
Observed	1	2	1	2	1	2	3	5	10	13	20	19	8	12	3	2
Expected	0	0	0	0	0	0	1	3	6	10	20	21	19	15	7	2
*	+1	+2	+1	+2	+1	+2	+2	+2	+4	+3	0	−2	−11	−3	−4	0

8YR Concept Development   r = −.44   N = 98

	1-5	6-10	11-15	16-20	21-25	26-30	31-35	36-40	41-45	46-50	51-	56-	61-
Observed	3	2	4	5	3	0	18	10	20	8	12	3	0
Expected	0	0	1	2	4	7	11	15	17	18	14	7	2
*	+3	+2	+3	+3	−1	−7	+7	−5	+3	−8	−2	−4	−2

*Difference between observed and expected.

N. Binaural Conductive Severity

Direct Coombs Test   r = −.30   N = 163

	Positive	Negative
Observed	7	156
Expected	4	159
	*+3	−3

Maximum Serum Bilirubin   r = .21   N = 163

	0-4	5-9	10-14	15-24	25-
Observed	75	70	13	4	1
Expected	66	74	16	5	2
	*+9	−4	−3	−1	−1

Ear Conditions at 12 Months   r = .25   N = 168

	0	1	2
Observed	158	8	2
Expected	162	5	0
	*−4	+3	+2

Syndromes at 12 Months   r = .33   N = 168

	0	1	2
Observed	161	6	1
Expected	163	4	0
	*−2	+2	+1

Acute Toxemia   r = .33   N = 98

	0	1	2	3
Observed	68	8	16	6
Expected	71	6	20	2
	*−3	+2	−4	+4

Deafness Judgment (1YR)   r = .31   N = 155

	No	Yes
Observed	152	3
Expected	154	1
	*−2	+2

*Difference between observed and expected.

820

Trouble Speaking (through 7YRS)   r = .27   N = 157

	No	Yes
Observed	154	3
Expected	155	2
	*−1	+1

Enjoys Sound Production (Bayley)   r = .30   N = 159

	Pass	Fail
Observed	152	7
Expected	150	9
	*+2	−2

Social-Emotional Development (8 Months)   r = .31   N = 151

	Advanced	Normal	Suspect	Abnormal
Observed	3	132	13	3
Expected	3	135	12	1
	* 0	−3	−1	+2

Communication Nonverbal (4YR)   r = .28   N = 152

	No	Yes
Observed	148	4
Expected	150	2
	*−2	+2

Wechsler Vocabulary Score (7YR)   r = −.23   N = 165

	2	3	4	5	6	7	8	9	10	11	12	13	14	15	16	17
Observed	1	2	6	12	17	14	22	19	24	19	14	9	6	0	0	0
Expected	1	2	5	13	17	14	22	17	22	18	14	9	5	3	1	1
	* 0	0	+1	−1	0	0	0	+2	+2	+1	0	0	+1	−3	−1	−1

*Difference between observed and expected.

N. Binaural Conductive Severity (continued)
Indexes

8YR Articulation
r = −.25   N = 169

	0-5	6-10	11-15	16-20	21-25	26-30	31-35	36-40	41-45	46-
Observed	2	0	1	1	3	4	7	18	23	110
Expected	0	0	0	1	1	2	6	12	30	115
	*+2	0	+1	0	+2	+2	+1	+6	−7	+5

8YR Language Comprehension
r = −.29   N = 169

	0-20	41-60	61-80	81-100	101-120	121-140	141-160	161-180	181-200	201-220	221-240	241-
Observed	1	5	4	11	22	17	34	19	26	20	9	1
Expected	0	4	5	13	19	20	34	19	28	15	11	0
	*+1	+1	−1	−2	+3	+3	0	0	−2	+5	+2	+1

8YR Word Identification
r = −.41   N = 169

	0-4	35-39	40-44	45-49	50-54	55-59	60-64	65-69	70-74	75-79	80-84	85-89	90-
Observed	1	1	2	12	18	30	36	31	26	7	4	0	1
Expected	0	1	4	10	16	32	35	31	24	11	3	1	1
	*+1	0.	−2	+2	+2	−2	+1	0	+2	−4	+1	−1	0

*Difference between observed and expected.

O. Binaural Conductive Acuity

Direct Coombs Test
r = −.23 N = 175

	Positive	Negative
Observed	7	168
Expected	5	169
	*+2	−1

Maximum Serum Bilirubin
r = .21 N = 176

	0-4	5-9	10-14	15-19	20-24	25-
Observed	85	72	15	3	0	1
Expected	70	80	17	5	2	0
	*+15	−8	−2	−2	−2	+1

Ear Conditions at 12 Months
r = .27 N = 180

	0	1	2
Observed	169	9	2
Expected	173	5	0
	*−4	−4	+2

Syndromes at 12 Months
r = .29 N = 180

	0	1	2
Observed	173	6	1
Expected	175	4	1
	*−2	+2	0

Acute Toxemia
r = .32 N = 106

	0	1	2	3
Observed	72	9	19	6
Expected	74	7	21	3
	*−2	+2	−2	+3

Deafness Judgment (1YR)
r = .29 N = 166

	No	Yes
Observed	164	3
Expected	165	1
	*−1	+2

*Difference between observed and expected.

O. Binaural Conductive Acuity (continued)

Trouble Speaking (through 7YRS) r = .27 N = 169

	No	Yes
Observed	165	4
Expected	166	2
	*−1	+2

Enjoys Sound Production (8 Months) r = .33 N = 172

	Pass	Fail
Observed	164	8
Expected	162	10
	*+2	−2

Social-Emotional Development (8 Months) r = .39 N = 163

	Advanced	Normal	Suspect	Abnormal
Observed	4	143	13	3
Expected	3	145	13	0
	*+1	−2	0	+3

Communication Nonverbal (4YR) r = .28 N = 166

	No	Yes
Observed	162	4
Expected	164	2
	*−2	+2

Indexes

8YR Language Comprehension r = −.33 N = 182

	0-20	21-40	41-60	61-80	81-100	101-120	121-140	141-160	161-180	181-200	201-220	221-	241-
Observed	1	1	5	4	13	22	15	36	20	28	25	11	1
Expected	0	0	4	6	14	21	21	37	20	30	16	12	1
	*+1	+1	+1	−2	−1	+1	−6	−1	0	−2	+9	−1	0

8YR Word Identification r = −.43 N = 182

	0-4	30-34	35-39	40-44	45-49	50-54	55-59	60-64	65-69	70-74	75-79	80-84	85-89	90-
Observed	1	1	2	2	11	19	36	37	34	25	8	4	1	1
Expected	0	0	1	5	11	17	35	37	33	25	12	3	1	1
	*+1	+1	+1	−3	0	+2	+1	0	+1	0	−4	+1	0	0

*Difference between observed and expected.

P. Binaural Heterogeneous Severity

8-Month Mental Score r = −.22 N = 46

	41-43	68-70	71-73	74-76	77-79	80-82	83-85	86-88	89-91
Observed	1	2	1	4	19	12	6	0	1
Expected	0	1	1	5	13	14	7	2	1
	*+1	−1	0	+1	+6	−2	−1	−2	0

Auditory-Vocal Association (ITPA)(7YR) r = −.23 N = 51

	8-9	10-11	12-13	14-15	16-17	18-19	20-21	22-23	24-25
Observed	1	2	2	13	10	11	9	2	1
Expected	1	1	3	5	8	12	12	6	2
	* 0	+1	−1	+8	+2	−1	−3	−4	−1

Indexes

8YR Language Comprehension r = −.23 N = 52

	21-40	41-60	61-80	81-100	101-120	121-140	141-160	161-180	181-200	201-220	221-
Observed	1	3	2	1	10	7	11	9	4	3	1
Expected	0	1	2	4	6	6	11	6	9	5	3
	*+1	−2	0	−3	+4	+1	0	+3	−5	−2	−2

8YR Auditory Memory r = −.29 N = 51

	21-40	61-80	81-100	101-120	121-140	141-160	161-180	181-200	201-220	221-240	241-
Observed	2	2	1	5	10	8	9	6	4	2	2
Expected	0	1	1	3	6	8	10	9	7	4	1
	*+2	+1	0	+2	+4	0	−1	−3	−3	−2	+1

8YR Word Identification r = −.24 N = 52

	30-34	40-44	45-49	50-54	55-59	60-64	65-69	70-74	75-79	80-84	85-89
Observed	1	2	4	6	14	10	9	5	0	0	1
Expected	0	1	3	5	10	11	9	7	3	1	0
	*+1	+1	+1	+1	+4	−1	0	−2	−3	−1	+1

*Difference between observed and expected.

P. Binaural Heterogeneous Severity (continued)
Indexes

8YR Written Communication   r = −.27   N = 51

	0-89	90-119	120-149	150-179	180-209	210-239	240-269	270-299	300-
Observed	0	7	12	6	6	11	5	4	0
Expected	1	3	5	7	10	11	8	4	1
	*−1	+4	−7	−1	−4	0	−3	0	−1

8YR Concept Development   r = −.20   N = 50

	6-10	16-20	21-25	26-30	31-35	36-40	41-45	46-50	51-55	56-60	61-65
Observed	1	2	1	7	11	8	6	10	3	1	0
Expected	1	1	2	3	6	8	9	9	7	4	1
	* 0	+1	−1	+4	+5	0	−3	−1	+4	−3	−1

*Difference between observed and expected.

Q. Binaural Heterogeneous Acuity

Response to Direction (4YR)   r = −.27   N = 44

	No	Yes
Observed	19	25
Expected	13	31
	*+6	−6

Indexes

8YR Articulation   r = −.32   N = 51

	11-15	16-20	21-25	26-30	31-35	36-40	41-45	46-50
Observed	2	2	1	1	4	4	11	26
Expected	0	0	0	1	2	4	9	35
	*+2	+2	+1	0	+2	0	+2	−9

8YR Auditory Memory   r = −.31   N = 51

	21-40	61-80	81-100	101-120	121-140	141-160	161-180	181-200	201-220	221-240	241-260
Observed	2	2	1	4	10	9	11	5	3	2	2
Expected	0	1	2	3	6	8	10	9	7	4	1
	*+2	+1	−1	+1	+4	+1	+1	−4	−4	−2	+1

8YR Concept Development   r = −.34   N = 50

	6-10	16-20	21-25	26-30	31-35	36-40	41-45	46-50	51-55	56-60	61-65
Observed	1	2	1	7	10	9	6	11	3	0	0
Expected	1	1	2	3	6	8	9	9	7	4	1
	* 0	+1	−1	+4	+4	+1	−3	+2	−4	−4	−1

*Difference between observed and expected.

APPENDIX **11**

Listing of Speech, Language, and Hearing Examiners

Boston Lying-In Hospital, Boston, Massachusetts

Bashir, A.
Bostwick, R.
Cohen, L.
Finlayson, B.
Goodman, L.
Jones, L.
Levine, H.
London, S.

Looney, P.
Mathias, D.
Musher, K.
Ourth, S.
Pinskey, R.
Port, K.
Rothfarb, H.
Schwimmer, A.

Strominger, A.
Sweitzer, R.
Topp, S.
Wallace, K.
Wildstein, N.
Zelder, I.

Pennsylvania Hospital, Philadelphia, Pennsylvania

Brodkey, E.
Brown, T.
Dupuis, P.
Findlay, R.
Franklin, J.
Gaskins, L.
Gill, L.
Goldsmith, L.

Levin, S.
Levy, J.
Levy, M.
Lobron, B.
London, J.
Marlow, W.
McCrary, E.
Mucchino, E.

Schmerling, S.
Sharp, D.
Shor, B.
Silver, G.
Spickard, E.
Vergara, C.
Wesley, L.
Winchester, R.

Medical College of Virginia, Richmond, Virginia

Alexander, J.
Beale, M.
Choate, M.
Gaskill, M.
Gondos, M.

Gonzalez, J.
Grove, E.
Hedelt, F.
McPherson, C.
Pierce, J.

Polon, M.
Richardson, C.
Seay, H.

Johns Hopkins Hospital, Baltimore, Maryland

Block, L.
Brinker, C.
Brown, L.
Case, I.
Clark, S.
Epstein, G.
Gross, S.
Hoffman, C.

Hoffman, R.
Huffman, L.
Kolman, I.
Kolman, S.
Kowal, K.
Kreuz, S.
Martini, R.
Masland, M.

Moorhead, B.
Posner, E.
Rose, N.
Schuman, M.
Shaw, S.
Willig, S.
Winston, S.

Columbia-Presbyterian Medical Center, New York, New York

Becker, M.
Frost, A.
Goldstein, E.
Goldstein, S.
Grant, P.
Grantham, R.

Haroldson, O.
Hubletz, S.
Klein, M.
Lewis, B.
Metzel, M.
Schuman, M.

Snyder, M.
Stein, S.
Stern, M.
Tauber, R.

828

New York Medical College, New York, New York

Fuchs, P.	Pinkernell, M.	Weiner, L.
Howells, K.	Shuster, L.	Young, S.
Jeklicka, C.	Urban, G.	

University of Minnesota Hospital, Minneapolis, Minnesota

Becker, M.	Grong, L.	Park, M.
Becklund, C.	Gross, G.	Schmechel, J.
Dorley, J.	Gunderson, D.	Sjodin, A.
Edmonds, J.	Johnson, M.	Statland, A.
Etten, H.	Kimmel, R.	Stensland, D.
Frerker, V.	LaBenz, E.	Waterman, K.
Fulton, H.	McClellan, E.	Wiest, K.

University of Oregon Medical School, Portland, Oregon

Chaney, T.	Meek, M.	Nelson, D.
Fay, W.	Moffit, P.	Venturo, P.
Kaji, A.	Murray, R.	

University of Tennessee College of Medicine, Memphis, Tennessee

Baskin, V.	Dunlap, A.	Sewell, A.
Boone, J.	Durand, L.	Southall, J.
Daniels, A.	Lindsay, A.	Thompson, M.
Diament, A.	McCrary, E.	

Providence Lying-In Hospital, Providence, Rhode Island

Baker, C.	Hallett, S.	Portnoy, J.
Bauer, C.	Jizmagian, C.	Regan, B.
Baumstark, S.	Kishimoto, B.	Simner, P.
Bobola, S.	Lang, M.	Sype, S.
Dahill, C.	Liberman, E.	Villa, C.
Finck, S.	Nezelek, K.	

Charity Hospital, New Orleans, Louisiana

Arnold, A.	Jones, L.	Sprouse, B.
Ellender, E.	Langhart, M.	Steiner, C.
Farr, L.	Rich, R.	
Greve, R.	Robichaux, G.	

Children's Hospital, Buffalo, New York

Alexander, C.	Goupil, M.	Knight, E.
Armstrong, E.	Grantham, R.	Purdy, R.
Battle, D.	Kaiser, P.	Robinson, N.

Index

Anticonvulsants, nonbarbiturate, in pregnancy, and hearing loss risk, 155
Antidepressants in pregnancy, and hearing loss risk, 155
Antihypertension agents in pregnancy, and hearing loss, 155
Apgar score group, and the premature sample, 143
Apgar scores, 140, 178, 180
  five-minute, 256
  premature children, in, 149
  3-year and 8-year SLH preformance, and, 364
  variable, as a, 87
Aphasia, Minnesota Test for Differential Diagnosis of, 16
Apnea, and 3-year and 8-year SLH performance, 366
Appendages, auricular, 138, 139
Applebee, A. N., 351
Apraxia, developmental, 228
Arndt, W. B., 228
Articulation, 69, 149, 242, 251
  auditory memory, and, 195
  Bayley Scales, and the, 389
  complexly interrelated skills involved in, 228
  consonants measures, and, 240
  correlated with language measures, 240
  correlations and conditional probabilities, 242, 400
  diphthongs, of, 24
  education of parents, and, 254
  8-year SLH examination, and the, 15, 132, 233, 240, 256, 260, 261, 367
    mean scores, in, 260
  failure not predicted by hearing tests, 252
  Index, 133
  intelligibility measures, and, 264
  Language Comprehension correlations, and, 282
  measures of, 240
  Morphology, relationship with, 240
  normative study of, 24
  prematurity, and, 406
  scoring administration in examinations, 29
  social variable and development of, 406
  special study, in, 256
  Speech Mechanism study, in, 206, 208
  Speech Production, and, 29
  Speech Production variables, and, 241, 242
  Spondaic Word Test, and the, 86
  Templin-Darley Test of, 15, 36, 232
  testing for, 24, 228, 232
  3-year examination of, 233
  3-year index of, 264
  vowel and diphthong, of, 24
  Written Communication study, and the, 352
Asphyxia, prenatal, 2
Asymmetry, auricular, 138

Ataxia, 225
Attention Span, Very Brief, 180
Audiometry
  audiograms in British study, 22
  8-year SLH examination, in the, 14
  pure-tone air conduction, 32
  techniques, play, 79
  zero setting and average hearing sensitivity, and, 93
Adaptation, auditory
  abnormal, 101, 146
    See also Tone Decay
  test procedure in, 101
  test-retest coefficient, 111
Auditory comprehension
  See Comprehension, Auditory
Auditory Memory
  See Memory, Auditory
Auditory Processing
  See Processing, Auditory
Auditory screening
  See Screening, auditory
Auditory-Vocal Association Test of the ITPA, 4, 25, 34, 132, 180, 232, 267, 292, 345, 394, 408

Bagur, J. S., 384
Baratz, J. C., 325
Bayley, N., 7, 132, 356, 390, 392, 406
Bayley bell localizing task, the, 252
Bayley Mental and Motor Development scores, 7, 212, 214, 230, 251, 291, 295, 297, 300, 302, 304, 326, 342, 387, 388, 389, 408
  bell, turns head to sound of, 389
  rattle, turns head to sound of, 389
  Child's response to sound, and the, 210
  cross-tabulated with indices, 387
  dichotomized, 387
  8-month, 148, 180, 251, 304
    variables, as, 70
  Intelligibility, and, 387
  items from the, 389–390
  regression analyses, and, 70
  variables, as, 295
  vocalization items, and, 390
Bayley Scales of Infant Development, the, 3, 7
Behavior
  behavior syndromes, 1
  behavioral observations in SLH examinations, 30
  language, assessment of, 256, 316, 319
  peculiarities of behavior noted in 8-year examination, 36
  SLH, prediction of, 71
  struggle behavior, 241, 264
  unusual, during testing, 30
Belmont, J. M., 195
Bender Gestalt Test, 4, 299, 345, 408
  correlations with indices, 395
  cross-tabulations with indices, 396
  described, 395

Benton, A. L., 33
Benton Laterality Test, the, 33
Berendes, H., 8
Bias toward standard English in tests, 188
Bierman, J. M., 293
Bierne, Harry, 16
Bilirubin level, 180
    cognitive impairment, and 367
    determination of, 3
    maximum total, as a variable, 132
    sensorineural hearing loss, and, 367
    3-year and 8-year SLH indices, and, 366, 367
    Written Communication Index, and the, 345
Binaural hearing loss, 83, 120
    conductive, 120
    sensorineural, predicted at age 3, 121
Binaural Sensorineural Index, 148
Biological variables, 197
Birch, H. G., 195
Birth conditions, unusual, and speech mechanism, 225
Birth defects and drug exposure during pregnancy, and hearing loss, 151
Birth, SEI data at, 379
Birthweight of child, 50, 214, 225, 254, 256, 326, 346
    articulation deficits, and, 263
    hearing level of poorer ear, and, 149
    hearing loss, and, 142
    Language Indices, and, 319
    sensorineural loss incidence with low birthweight, 143
    speech production, and, 256
    variable, as a, 70, 132, 293
    Written Communication, and, 346
Black English, 331
    Connected Discourse, and, 325
    Language Comprehension, and, 325
    Language differences in, 325
    Morphology, and, 325
    test selection, and, 325
Blacks, distribution in study samples, 45
Blindness, 21
Blood pressure, high, 359
Blood sampling in Collaborative study, 3
Blood typing in Collaborative study, 3
Bloom, L., 285, 320, 385
Boen, J., 17, 57
Boggs, T., 366
Bone Conduction
    air conduction hearing tests, and, correlation between, 101
    audiometry, measurement of, 32
    coefficients for, 115, 118
    hearing test at 8-years, 97
Bonham, D. G., 21
Bordley, J. E., 24, 252, 389
Boston Children's Medical Center, 2
Boston Lying-In Hospital, the, 2, 16, 38

problems of screening procedure used at, 65
Boston University School of Medicine, 151
Branchial cleft anomaly, 129
Brief attention span as a variable, 132
Broman, S. H., 19, 23, 53, 58, 356, 367, 387, 388
Brown, R. A., 285, 320
Brown University, 2
British Perinatal Mortality and National Child Development Study, 19, 21, 385
    audiograms in, 22
    cerebral palsy in, 23
    confounding variables in, 22
    congenital malformations in, 22
    educational assessment in follow-up in, 21
    family size factors in, 23
    family variables in, 22
    gestation length findings in, 23
    intelligibility of speech in, 22
    medical examination in follow-up in, 21
    mongolism in, 23
    parental interview in follow-up in, 21
    social class of parents in, 23
    speech evaluation in, 22
    speech intelligibililty rated in, 22
    speech performance differential by sex in, 22
    speech therapy in, 22
Buffalo, Children's Hospital, 40
Buffalo, University Medical School, 16
Bush, E. S., 195
Butler, N., 19, 21, 351, 385
Butterfield, E. C., 195

Cameron, J., 390
Canter, G. J., 228
Carhart, R., 84
Census, U.S. Bureau of, 43, 379
Cerebral palsy
    See Palsy, cerebral
Child development study, British, 21
Childbearing, the best age for, 356
Children
    adopted, 220
        8-year speech mechanism index, and, 220
        hearing measurement of, 144
        hearing sensitivity of, 149
        socioeconomic status, and, 187
        auditory memory study, in, 187
    development of skills at age eight, 13
    foster, hearing measurement of, 144
    hearing test differences between Black and White children, 80
Children's Hospital of Buffalo, 40
Cigarette smoking in pregnancy, 87, 131, 178, 180, 345, 407
    hearing loss, and, 161
    variable, as a, 87, 131
    Written Communication, and, 345

833

deHirsch, Katrina, 14, 316, 319, 327, 351
Delivery of child
    forceps, with
        3-year and 8-year SLH indices, and, 364
        Written Communication, and, 345
    method of, and 3-year and 8-year SLH indices correlations, 364
    vertex, and 3-year and 8-year SLH indices, and, 364
Demographic characteristics in study samples, 42, 43, 45, 47
Denhoff, E., 351
Descriptive statistics
    See Statistics, descriptive
Detroit Test of Learning Aptitude, the, 33
Deutschberger, J., 356, 368
Diabetes, 3-year and 8-year indices correlated with, 359
Diadochokinesis, 62
    lip, 68, 200
    Mase on, 228
    oral, 199
    scoring for, 29
    spastic and dysarthric subjects, in, 228
    3-year-old children, and, 225
    tongue, 68, 203
Dicarlo, L. M., 389
Dictation, Writing from, 34–35, 282
    measurement of, 35
    tests of, 15
Digits, 69
    auditory memory for, 30
    correlated with Written Communication, 333
    correlated with SLH indices, 174–175
    digit span and verbal abilities, 9
    digits memory in 8-year SLH examination, 15
    8-year
        auditory memory study, in, 184, 186–187
        recoding of, in auditory memory study, 174
        SLH measures compared with, 133, 367
    recall of, 9
Diphthongs
    articulation measures, and, 24, 242
    3-year, 242
Diplegia, spastic, 225
Directions, responds to, as a variable, 132
Discourse, Connected
    See Connected Discourse
Discrimination for monosyllabic word list, testing for, 32
Discrimination Test of hearing for speech, 146
Disorder, neurological, speech and hearing manifestations of, 6
Distributions for hearing loss sample and total sample, discrepancies between, 132
Doerfler, Leo, 14, 16, 25, 79, 93, 101
Douglas, J. W. B., 351

Downs, M. P., 389
Down syndrome, 211, 217, 319
Drage, J. S., 364, 366–367
Drawings used in language evaluation, 28
Drillien, C. M., 319, 326
Drorbaugh, J. E., 65
Drug exposure during pregnancy
    crude relative risk, and, 152
    hearing loss, and, 151, 407
    list of those studied for hearing loss effects, 155
    race differences and hearing loss measures, and, 152
    sensorineural hearing loss, and, 151
    standardized relative risk for hearing loss, and, 152
Drug information, coded, in drug exposure in pregnancy study, 151
Dunn, L. M., 25, 233, 267, 292, 297, 306, 384
Durrell, D. D., 34, 173, 233, 282, 330, 331
Durrell-Sullivan Reading Capacity and Achievement Tests, 34, 233
Dysfluency, 407
    dysfluent events, assessments of, 30, 241
    8-year examination, in, 35
Dysfunction in speech
    early indicators of, 211
    early observations portending, 227
Dyskinesia, 225

Eagles, Eldon, 17, 25, 79, 80, 93, 101, 136
Ear conditions, abnormal
    conductive loss examined in, 138
    deformities, 129
    descriptive statistics, and, 140
    draining ears, 138
    fluency, and, 140
    hearing loss, indicating, 147
    hearing loss severity, and, 139
    intelligibility, and, 140
    list of, 138
    low-set, 129
    microtia, 138, 140
    noticed at pediatric examination, 130
    otoscopic, as a variable, 131
    perforated eardrum, 129
    race and incidence of, 140
    results of tests, and the, 139
    sample of children with, study of, 138
    sensorineural loss examined in, 139
    sex incidence of, 140
    SLH indices, and, 138, 140
    small external canal group having poorest hearing, 139
    socioeconomic index incidence, and, 140
    special study of sample of children with, 148
    speech and language indices, and, 138
    12 months, at, as a variable, 132

Hearing (*Continued*)
    sensitivity of hearing, and, 140
    severity and abnormal conditions of the
        ear, 138
    severity, 8-year, 67
    SLH indices, and, 132
    Socioeconomic Index, and, 320
    speech mechanism, and, 225
    streptomycin, and, 161
    stutterers, in, 142
    sulfa drugs, and, 161
    sympathomimetic drugs, and, 161
    3-year screening test failures, and, 87
    twins, greater in, 142
lower testing level, and the, 78
masking in tests of, 26, 32, 97
measurement of pure-tone air conduction,
    32
middle-ear problems, and, 84
monaural losses in, 82
normal, 117
otitis media, and, 80
pediatric examination at 12 months, at, 130
Pittsburgh study, 93
poorer, 83, 97, 120
prediction of status at later age, 121
Pure-Tone, Written Communication corre-
    lated with, 333
race and loss probabilities, 121
rapid learning effects, tests and, 92
seasonal effects on data from hearing tests,
    136
Screen hearing, 69
sensitivity
    Pure-Tone Screen, measured by, 84
    statistical distribution of, 89
sensorineural losses, and, 118, 139
severity, 356
    3-year, 401
sex differences in tests of speech discrimi-
    nation, 111, 115
socioeconomic levels, and, 83, 101, 402
Speech Discrimination Test, 33, 111, 146
    8-year-old children, in, 111
    measures for, 133
    performance comparisons, 136
    pure-tone test measures, and, 111
    PBK lists used in, 33, 133
    race differences in tests, 111, 115
    socioeconomic index and results in, 111,
        115
speech reception threshold, the, 111
speech recorded for testing of, 9
Spondaic Word Test, and the, 83
spondee screening test of, 9
statistical distribution of sensitivity of, 89
study at Johns Hopkins Hospital, 24
subtest, procedures for, 29
3-year Index and SLH variables, 87
3-year tests of, 78, 145

correlations and conditional probabilities,
    401
    Hearing Screen, in, 87
thresholds of pure-tone air conduction,
    testing for, 32
test performances by race, 83–84
testing at Wisconsin State Fair, 92
total conductive loss categorization, 121
total sensorineural loss categorization, 121
twins', 142
variables, and, 87
voice pitch, and, 118
word lists used in testing, 78
Hedgecock, L. D., 9
Height, 4-year measurement, 368
Height of mother
    See Mother's height
Heinonen, O. P., 151, 152
Heltman, H. J., 228
Hematuria, 407
Hemiparesis, 225
Hemoglobin count, 180
Herrick, V. E., 316
Hertzig, M. E., 195
Hirst, Katherine, 57
Hobson, S., 195
Hogarty, P. S., 390
Housing density
    See Overcrowding
Hydrocephalus, 23
Hyman, C. B., 367
Hyperactivity, observation during testing, 30
Hyperemesis gravidarum, 161, 407
Hypernasality, 69, 175, 200, 203–204, 206,
    208, 212, 214, 216, 220, 228
    3-year
        correlations and conditional probabilities,
            400
        poor predictor of 8-year speech mecha-
            nism, 229
Hypertension, 359, 407
    hearing loss, and, 161
Hypertensive disease of gravida, chronic, as a
    variable, 132
Hypoactivity, observation during testing, 30
Huffman, E., 228
Hull, F. M., 19, 26
Hunt, B. C., 331
Hunter College, 7
Hurlburt, N., 390
Husband or father present in home, as a vari-
    able, 132
Husband's education, as a variable, 132

Identification of Familiar Objects, 266, 290
Illinois Test of Psycholinguistic Abilities, 9, 25,
    34, 232–233, 267
Income
    family
        study samples, and, 45

845